JEWISH HISTORY

Note from the Editors

WE would like to acknowledge the valuable contribution made to this volume by a number of collaborators and friends.

Seven of the essays were translated from Hebrew as follows: Morris Hoffman translated the essays by Avraham Grossman, Rachel Elior and Anita Shapira; Zvi Rosenwasser translated the essays by Joseph Shatzmiller and Chone Shmeruk; Connie Wilsack translated the essay by Moshe Mishkinsky, and Ami Raz translated the essay by Ran Aaronsohn and Yehoshua Ben Arieh.

We are especially grateful to our publishers, Peter and Martine Halban, who have been closely involved with the book at every stage of its production, and whose commitment to it remained unshaken, even when the enterprise proved to be much bigger and more complex than any of us had anticipated.

For technical and editorial assistance, thanks are due to Didi Kerler, Anna Zarenko, Betty Palmer, Jennifer Baines, and especially Judy Gough.

Miriam Abramsky's affection, support and proverbial good sense were invaluable from the very beginning of the project.

Although the publication of a *Festschrift* is an occasion for celebration, in this case it is tinged with sadness at the death of one of the most distinguished contributors to the volume—Arnaldo Momigliano, a member of our International Advisory Board whose contribution is the last full-length essay he wrote, on a subject which had intrigued him, and was close to his heart from the very beginning of his long and fruitful career. יהי זכרו ברוך

Ada Rapoport-Albert
Steven J. Zipperstein
August 1988

xi

Foreword

THE sheer variety of the contributions to this volume is, itself, ample evidence of (and a tribute to) the breadth of Chimen Abramsky's interests and learning. Fortunate indeed is the scholar whose field of enquiry is intimately bound up with his own roots, with the world in which he was born and bred, a society the traditions and culture of which have shaped his mind and outlook so deeply that he is able to understand it and interpret it with the inner eye of a participant, not of an outside observer, however intuitive and sympathetic. This is what has given the entire work of Professor Abramsky (to give him his proper title), apart from its meticulous scholarship, an authority and a degree of imaginative insight all too rare in the field of historical reconstruction, not least in that of Jewish studies. What German pietism gave Herder—a natural sense of the changing forms of life and of values of his own in relation to other cultures—his traditional upbringing gave Chimen Abramsky. Historian, critic, publicist, bibliophile, bibliographer, widely respected expert on books and manuscripts in the field of Judaica—all this, combined with his deep concern with the central social and political issues of our time, have made him a unique figure in the republic of letters. Possessed of apparently inexhaustible curiosity, vitality and tenacity, he has shared the fruits of his labours most generously with researchers in many fields. I am glad to be given this opportunity of saluting my old friend, and wish him many years of happy and productive life.

Isaiah Berlin
All Souls College
Oxford

23. The Bund in Polish Political Life, 1935–1939   547
   Antony Polonsky

8 PALESTINE AND THE JEWISH NATIONAL MOVEMENT

24. The Establishment of the Jewish Settlement in Eretz Israel and   581
   the Gaster Papers
   Ran Aaronsohn and Yehoshua Ben Arieh

25. Reflections on the Growth of the Jewish National Home, 1880–1948   595
   Jehuda Reinharz

26. Patterns of Communal Conflict in Palestine   611
   Bernard Wasserstein

27. The Dynamics of Zionist Leftist Trends   629
   Anita Shapira

28. Diplomacy in the Jewish Interest   683
   David Vital

Notes on Contributors   697

10. Jewish Historiography in the United States and Britain   199
    Lloyd P. Gartner

4 PERCEPTIONS OF JEWS IN THE WIDER SOCIETY

11. The Romans and the Maccabees   231
    Arnaldo Momigliano

12. English Charity and Jewish Qualms: The Rescue of the   245
    Ashkenazi Community of Seventeenth-Century Jerusalem
    David Katz

13. Gregorio Leti (1631–1701) and the Dutch Sephardi Elite at the   267
    Close of the Seventeenth Century
    Jonathan Israel

14. A Historiographical Oversight: The Austrian Consul-General   285
    and the Damascus Blood Libel (with the Laurin–Rothschild
    Correspondence, 1840)
    Jonathan Frankel

15. Did the Russian Jacobins (Blanquists) Have a Special Attitude   319
    Towards the Jews?
    Moshe Mishkinsky

5 LINGUISTIC TRANSMUTATIONS

16. A Mediaeval Latin–German Magical Text in Hebrew   345
    Characters
    Raphael Loewe

17. Pierre Leroux and the Book of Job   369
    Anita Haimon-Weitzman

18. 'Prinzessin Sabbat' by H. Heine in a Yiddish Translation by   379
    H.N. Bialik
    Chone Shmeruk

6 HASIDISM

19. Between *Yesh* and *Ayin*: The Doctrine of the Zaddik in the   393
    Works of Jacob Isaac, the Seer of Lublin
    Rachel Elior

20. Self-sacrifice of the Zaddik in the Teachings of R. Dov Ber,   457
    the *Mitteler Rebbe*
    Naftali Loewenthal

21. On Women in Hasidism: S.A. Horodecky and The Maid   495
    of Ludmir Tradition
    Ada Rapoport-Albert

7 JEWISH SOCIALISM

22. Rosa Luxemburg, Leo Jogiches and the Jewish Labour   529
    Movement, 1893–1903
    Robert S. Wistrich

Contents

Foreword   ix
Isaiah Berlin

Note from the Editors   xi
Ada Rapoport-Albert and Steven J. Zipperstein

1 THE MEDIAEVAL JEWISH COMMUNITY

  1. The Historical Background to the Ordinances on Family Affairs   3
     Attributed to Rabbenu Gershom Me'or ha-Golah ('The Light
     of the Exile')
     Avraham Grossman

  2. Sexual Behaviour in Mediaeval Hispano–Jewish Society   25
     Yom Tov Assis

  3. Rabbi Isaac Ha-Cohen of Manosque and His Son Rabbi Peretz: 61
     The Rabbinate and its Professionalization in the Fourteenth Century
     Joseph Shatzmiller

2 JEWISH CULTURE AND EDUCATION

  4. Transforming the Heder: Maskilic Politics in Imperial Russia   87
     Steven J. Zipperstein

  5. Anglicization and the Education of Jewish Immigrant Children   111
     in the East End of London
     Suzanne Kirsch Greenberg

  6. A Hebrew Island in the British Isles: *Hayehoody* and its Editor   127
     I. Suwalski (1897–1913)
     Risa Domb

3 HISTORIOGRAPHICAL ISSUES

  7. The Expulsion from Spain and Jewish Historiography   141
     Eleazar Gutwirth

  8. The Quest for Philo in Sixteenth-Century Jewish   163
     Historiography
     Joanna Weinberg

  9. Yiddish Song as Historical Source Material: Plague in the   189
     Judenstadt of Prague in 1713
     Chava Turniansky

FIRST PUBLISHED IN GREAT BRITAIN BY
PETER HALBAN PUBLISHERS LTD
42 South Molton Street
London w1y 1hb
1988

British Library Cataloguing in Publication Data
Jewish history: essays in honour of Chimen Abramsky.
1. Jews to 1986
I. Zipperstein, Steven J. II. Rapoport-Albert, Ada
III. Abramsky, Chimen
909´.04924

ISBN 1-87001-519-3

Typeset at Oxford University Computing Service

Printed in Great Britain by
WBC Print Ltd, Bristol

JEWISH HISTORY

Essays in Honour of
Chimen Abramsky

———————————

Edited by
Ada Rapoport-Albert and
Steven J. Zipperstein

Foreword by
Isaiah Berlin

PETER HALBAN
———
LONDON

I

THE MEDIAEVAL JEWISH COMMUNITY

The Historical Background to the Ordinances on Family Affairs Attributed to Rabbenu Gershom Me'or ha-Golah ('The Light of the Exile')

Avraham Grossman

THE question of the ordinances (*takkanot*) attributed to Rabbenu Gershom Me'or ha-Golah (d. Mainz 1028) is one of the most complicated of those which confront us in the study of the internal organization of Jewry in mediaeval Europe. On the one hand, the subject is of great importance for the investigation of the organizational frameworks and methods of operation which were typical of the first Jewish settlements in Europe, and for the study of the character of Jewish society at that time. On the other hand, the literary condition of the sources—dating from the thirteenth century onwards—which include the collections of Rabbenu Gershom's ordinances is such as to render their study extremely difficult. It is not surprising, therefore, that these ordinances have been accorded such extensive treatment in the historiographical literature in the past, and that they continue to constitute one of the burning questions in the field of current research.[1]

The main problem that scholars working on this subject have set themselves has been that of dating the ordinances, and opinions on this could scarcely have been more divided; some accepted the attribution of most of the ordinances to Rabbenu Gershom, others were prepared to date them as late as the thirteenth century. Today this question is much nearer a solution.[2] The attempt of some scholars to adopt a late date for these ordinances, assigning them to the end of the twelfth or even the beginning of the thirteenth century, has been shown to be ill-founded. Even if the personal authorship of Rabbenu Gershom is still in doubt, it is clear that a large proportion of them were already in operation in the eleventh century.[3]

The present paper is devoted to a consideration of some of these ordinances which concern family affairs and which were of great importance in shaping the character of Jewish society in Germany and France—and, to a certain extent, in the rest of Europe—from the eleventh century onwards.

3

We will concentrate mainly on the question which deserves precedence from the historical point of view: what was the historical background to the enactment of these ordinances, and how do they fit into the structure of Jewish society of that period in Germany and northern France? We will first consider the prohibition on polygamy, which is the most famous of the ordinances attributed to Rabbenu Gershom. The extensive discussion of this ordinance in the literature has been devoted chiefly to the question of whether Rabbenu Gershom was its author: did he really enact it himself, or at least take part in drawing it up? Or was this ordinance of a later date and incorrectly attributed to him out of a desire to invest it with the authority of a great name? For, from the end of the eleventh century onwards, his fame exceeded that of any other sage in Germany or France and he was credited with a unique degree of authority—as even Rashi attests.[4]

The state of the sources is such that we cannot yet give a definite answer to this question. At the same time, it is clear that the attempt of some scholars to date this ordinance as late as the end of the twelfth, or possibly even the beginning of the thirteenth century, is mistaken. Three main factors contributed to the tendency to deny that Rabbenu Gershom was its author and to assume that it was of later origin: the fact that he himself did not mention it at all, even when he was asked about the right of a man to marry a second wife in a case where, after ten years of marriage, the first wife had not borne a child; the fact that eleventh-century sages in Germany made no reference to any such ordinance in their discussions; and the fact that the Maharam of Padua, who lived in the sixteenth century, quoted *Nimukei Yosef* as saying that a sage by the name of Rabbi Samson had enacted it.[5]

But these facts prove nothing. Obviously Rabbenu Gershom—or the communities of his time—did not intend this ordinance to operate 'where a *mitzvah* applied', i.e. where, from a halakhic point of view, a man had not fulfilled the biblical commandment to be fruitful and multiply, since his first wife had not borne a child; according to Talmudic tradition it was his duty to marry a second wife after ten years of childless marriage. In such a case it was unnecessary to mention the ordinance—assuming it was in existence—either in the *responsum* of Rabbenu Gershom or in that of R. Solomon ben Samson. It is true that, as will be pointed out below, later generations contented themselves with the question whether Rabbenu Gershom had really intended a general ban. But the straightforward interpretation of the facts is that the ordinance did not operate in 'cases where a *mitzvah* applied'.[6] In any event, how can we be sure that the question of marriage to a second wife, mentioned above, was not put to Rabbenu Gershom before the enactment of the ordinance?

4

As for the question of reliance on the attribution of the ordinance to 'R. Samson' by the Maharam of Padua, it is very doubtful whether we can accept as authoritative the statement of a sage who lived so much later and was basing himself on another work of relatively late date (fifteenth century), especially when it is very likely that an error had occurred in the version he had before him—a point already made by S. Eidelberg.[7] At all events, it is quite clear that it is impossible to bring the date of the ordinance forward to the period of R. Samson of Sens (end of the twelfth and beginning of the thirteenth century), because, as will be shown below, it was explicitly attributed to Rabbenu Gershom some two generations earlier by a sage of the first rank.

The attempt to deny Rabbenu Gershom's authorship of this ordinance on the ground that R. Eliezer ben Nathan, the greatest of the sages of Mainz in the middle of the twelfth century, describes it as 'an ordinance of the communities' without quoting it in the name of Rabbenu Gershom is similarly unconvincing. At first sight this argument appears to have some substance, for if Rabbenu Gershom did introduce this ordinance, why should it not be quoted in his name by an outstanding sage who lived and worked in the same place four generations later? But it must be realized that even those ordinances which were enacted by Rabbenu Gershom were not drawn up by him alone. He enacted them together with the Beth Din (rabbinical court) of Mainz, and they were intended in the first place for the community of Mainz or neighbouring communities which were prepared to accept them. It was agreement and acceptance which gave them the force of law. In the absence of this readiness to accept them, these ordinances would have been binding only on the members of the Mainz community. Moreover, it may well be that sages would quote this and other similar ordinances as being 'ordinances of the communities' out of a desire to emphasize their binding force for many communities. This attribution would be preferable from many points of view to an attribution to a single person, even if he were an extremely eminent Torah scholar. Later, when Rabbenu Gershom had become so charismatic a figure, they preferred to ascribe the ordinances to him.

The earliest source in which the ordinance is expressly attributed to Rabbenu Gershom dates from the middle of the twelfth century. The attestation in question is that of R. Eliezer ben Joel Halevi, and relates to an incident of his own time in which litigants described this ordinance without elaboration—treating it as a matter of common knowledge—as having been enacted by Rabbenu Gershom.[8] We may infer from this that the tradition quoted was even older. The people concerned were expressly stated to be elderly. This adds even more strength to their testimony as to the existence of a tradition; their knowledge must go back to the beginning of the twelfth century at latest, and perhaps even earlier. Since we have not traced any attempt by any of the sages of Germany or France from the twelfth century onwards to contradict this attribution of the ordinance to Rabbenu Gershom, there are grounds for assuming the tradition to be based on fact. This assumption applies particularly to the first *Hasidim* (twelfth–thirteenth centuries) in Germany. Their leaders were among the descendants of the distinguished families which were active in Mainz in the eleventh century, they had splendid traditions going back to that period, and the fact that they, too, accept this attribution strengthens the tradition. Clearly, however, that is not enough to furnish definite proof. And, as stated above, even if Rabbenu Gershom had a hand in the enactment of the ordinance, he should not be seen as solely responsible for it but as having taken an active part in its enactment and in securing its acceptance by the communities of Germany—perhaps also by the contemporary communities of northern France. It is also possible that it was accepted in the first place by the people of Mainz, and gradually by other communities.

The scholars involved in the discussion as to the date of the ordinance have made no attempt to examine the historical state of affairs revealed in the source material left behind by the eleventh-century sages of Germany. These sources are relatively numerous and very varied—halakhic decisions, exegesis, descriptions of Jewish customs (*minhagim* books), religious poetry, and chronicles, including the *Memorbuecher* containing the names of those who lost their lives in the First Crusade in 1096. In none of these sources have we found evidence of a single example of a marriage to a second wife during the lifetime of the first, except in the special case 'where a *mitzvah* applied', i.e., where the first wife had been childless for more than ten years.[9] This shows that marriage to two wives was already unknown in Germany in the eleventh century. In the consideration of this question special weight must be attached to the absence of information, or even indirect references, in regard to polygamy in the chronicles of 1096, and especially in the lists of martyrs which have come down to us in the *Memorbuecher* relating to the massacres of that time. They do not contain even one indication of any family in which there was more than one wife.

From all the foregoing it may be concluded that monogamy was indeed accepted as the rule among Jews in Germany in the second half of the eleventh century. Certainly this fact alone is not enough to show that Rabbenu Gershom was the man who enacted this ordinance, but it seems not unreasonable to assume that it was accepted in his time or in the following generation. If we take into account that in many sources, from the middle of the twelfth century onwards and including distinguished scholars in Germany and France, this ordinance is attributed to Rabbenu Gershom himself, and that the pupils of Rashi—himself a pupil of R. Jacob ben Yakar, who was a favourite pupil of Rabbenu Gershom—called Rabbenu Gershom 'the great luminary who enacts ordinances for the whole of the Exile', we can see that there may indeed be substance in the tradition which tends to ascribe an important part in the enactment of this ordinance to Rabbenu Gershom, even though, as yet, the point cannot be conclusively proved.

The question to which, from a historical point of view, it would be proper to give precedence is: what historical motive prompted this ordinance forbidding polygamy? An examination of the origin of communal ordinances in the early Middle Ages shows that only actual cases of vital importance led sages and heads of communities to depart from a long-established rule—hallowed, for them, by antiquity—and to establish a new practice binding upon the members of their communities.[10] It is clear from what we have already said that polygamy was a most unusual phenomenon among Jewish communities in Germany during the period we are considering. Why, then, did they find it necessary to enact such an ordinance?

The problem has, indeed, troubled the scholars who have considered it. Five principal solutions have been suggested. The opinion of Eppenstein is that at the beginning of the eleventh century and earlier migrants to Germany from oriental countries already had two wives, as was sometimes the practice among Jewish families in Muslim lands. The ordinance would have been directed against them. But this explanation—as N. Z. Roth has shown—is improbable. It is inconceivable that these men, who had had two wives for many years and had established a family and reared children, would have been compelled by Rabbenu Gershom to part from one of their wives and break up the family unit. On the other hand, it is unlikely that he was concerned to prevent such marriages between women of the established communities and the newcomers: it is hard to imagine that the daughters of the Jews in Germany would agree to marry the new immigrants if they did not consent to adopt the local custom of monogamy. We would be obliged to offer the explanation that Rabbenu Gershom's intention was to prevent such marriages within the newcomers' families. But in fact our information on migration to Germany at that time does not indicate any substantial movement from Islamic countries.[11]

Roth himself is of the opinion[12] that there was a minority among the Jews of Germany themselves who followed the practice of polygamy, which was why there was a vital need for the ordinance. We are not in a position to contradict this hypothesis, even though it, too, is somewhat doubtful. It is not supported by the sources (though the sources earlier than Rabbenu Gershom and those contemporary with him are not particularly plentiful or varied). Roth seeks to draw an inference from the accusation said to ahve been made by Maimonides that the Jews of France, for the most part, were in the habit of taking more than one wife and wasted their time in the company of their wives.[13] However, this proof is no proof at all, for the allegation quoted is almost certainly of later date and attributed to Maimonides to give it greater importance. In any event, it is not to be supposed that polygamy was accepted and common among Jews *in Germany* in the twelfth century. Even if the accusation in question was penned by Maimonides, it should be taken as applying—and that only partly—to the communities of Provence and not to those of Germany and northern France.[14] If polygamy was a common occurrence in Jewish society in Germany in the generations which preceded Rabbenu Gershom, it is surprising that we have found no trace of it in Christian polemical literature directed against Judaism and the Jews. This extensive literature contains many accusations, varied—and sometimes fantstic—in regard to the Jews of Germany and France from the time of Agobard of Lyons onwards, but no reference to bigamy.

In the opinion of Baron it was another factor, similar to the one we have just discussed, which led to the ordinance forbidding polygamy:

> With the increase of Eastern Jewish immigration into Western lands and the spread of Eastern literary sources clearly showing the permissibility of plural marriages, some individuals may have begun clamoring for their reintroduction into the Western communities as well. This demand now appeared more feasible as segregation between Jews and Christians grew tighter and Jewish leaders were given even greater leeway in the management of Jewish affairs. Gershom and his associates may well have been prompted by such demands to reinforce the existing Western order and to threaten banishment of all would-be bigamists . . . this situation can merely be conjectured.[15]

Although Baron did hedge his remarks by this declaration that they only represented a hypothesis, it is very possible that they have a foundation in fact. It is the case that at the beginning of the eleventh century works on *halakhah* and various halakhic traditions reached Germany and France from Babylonia and had a strong influence on Jewish culture in those two countries at that time. Sources newly available through publication in the last few years throw light on the extensive scope of this phenomenon and show how powerful it was.

There were even some heads of communities in this part of the world who themselves travelled to Eastern countries and spent fairly long periods there, especially in the academy of Rav Hai in Pumpeditha.[16]

Falk's opinion was that the main factor underlying the ordinance was the influence of conditions in the Jews' Christian surroundings:

> The campaign against polygamy, which among the Christian population came to a conclusion some 150 years before the time of Gershom, and the campaign against concubinage which took place in his own day, doubtless aroused considerable argument between the clergy, civil authorities, and the population at large. The Jewish townsfolk, who did not always dwell apart in special quarters, must surely have learnt of the problem and come to understand certain cases of friction within their own families that they had never previously considered.
>
> Meanwhile, the position of woman in Jewry changed for the better; she had come to win greater respect, and people now thought it unjust that she should have to share her privileges with a co-wife. The demands of the Jewish woman, which at long last moved the communities to deliberate this vexing problem, had already been mentioned in the *responsum* of Gershom. Though at that time woman's claim had not yet won rabbinical support, it seems at any rate that her case could not remain ignored for ever, and thus at long last a general regulation was laid down.[17]

It is hard not to agree with this assumption that the tendency to prevent any possibility of taking a second wife (otherwise than where required by the *halakhah*) and to enact communal ordinances for this purpose must have been influenced to some extent by the Christian environment in which the Jews lived and worked. We know from various sources how great was the influence of the Gentile environment, both in Christian Europe and in Muslim countries, on the structure of the Jewish family. A work as early as *Sefer Hasidim* states with some emphasis, in discussing the nature of the Jewish family, that 'in every town the custom of the Jews is the same as the custom of the Gentiles'.[18] All the same, it is difficult to regard this alone as providing the main motive for the enactment of the ordinance, since in practice, as we have said, polygamy did not occur among Jews in Germany. Consequently, there was no occasion for Christian polemicists to condemn the Jews for it, while, on the other had, the Jews themselves had no reason to feel inferior on account of their practice in this respect. Further, in the absence of any actual case of polygamy among them in that part of the world, the Jews would simply regard themselves as following the same practice as their neighbours. The existence of a formal distinction, in that the prohibition of polygamy was embodied in Christian but not in Jewish law, should not have had any effect if the

9

actual mode of life was the same in both societies.

Recently M. A. Friedman has put forward a new suggestion to explain the motive for this ordinance:

> The question still needs to be considered whether we should not recognize, in the enactment of the ordinance against polygamy— precisely in Germany—not only the influence of the monogamous Christian environment, which is the explanation customarily offered for it, but also the monogamous tradition of Eretz Israel . . . Perhaps there were popular or family traditions in Germany corresponding to the Palestinian school of thought of R. Ammi. If such traditions had been preserved, they could have prepared the ground for the ordinance even though they were not acceptable to those who taught the *halakhah*.[19]

This is an interesting suggestion, for we know that nowhere else in Jewish society of that period were family traditions as strong and influential as among the Jewish communities in Germany.[20] Nevertheless, the hypothesis seems doubtful to me. Firstly—as Friedman himself has already pointed out—Rabbenu Gershom determined the *halakhah* explicitly against the opinion of the Palestinian Amora, Rabbi Ammi, who opposed polygamy, and in accordance with the view of the Babylonian Amora, Rava, who permitted it.[21] Consequently, we should have to conclude that the ordinance was not the work of Rabbenu Gershom and that he played no part in its acceptance. Moreover, we know that the families of superior lineage in eleventh-century Germany jealously guarded their family traditions and refused to abandon them even if it became clear that they were contrary to Talmudic *halakhah*. Because of this, differences in customs and family traditions were more widespread at this time among the Jews of Germany than anywhere else in the Diaspora, and this is one of the interesting basic characteristics of the early Jewish settlements in mediaeval Germany.[22] If monogamy were indeed a family tradition at all, whether of one family or of a number of families—and we have no evidence of this—it must have remained theirs alone, as happened with other matters, and would not have become a statute binding upon the whole of Jewish society. What is more, among those who held polygamy to be permissible from a fundamental halakhic point of view (in the absence of any communal ordinance springing from actual local conditions) was, as we have said, the greatest of the Jewish sages in Germany at that time—Rabbenu Gershom, a member of the family of Machir, one of the oldest and most distinguished families in mediaeval Germany.

It is difficult not to agree with the opinion of Falk and others who think that conditions in Christian society had some influence—at least in preparing the ground—on the enactment of the ordinance we are considering and on the readiness of many different communities to accept it. It is also probable that there is some truth in the opinion, mentioned earlier, which seeks to connect the need for this ordinance with an increase in the influence of the Babylonian tradition on German Jewry, although, as stated, that alone does not afford a sufficient explanation. It seems to me that to these factors must be added another which was of importance in leading to the enactment of the ordinance: the long absences of many members of the German communities in distant countries because of the international trade in which they played an active part. We now have much more evidence of this, as a result of the correct identification of many anonymous sources in the literature of *responsa* as the product of German-Jewish sages of that period. Only now, when we have before us a fuller and more comprehensive picture of many traders frequently journeying to distant parts, and often away from home, can we assess the full significance of the phenomenon and its effect on the family unit. This applies particularly to the *responsa* of Rabbenu Gershom and his pupil R. Judah Hakohen, who was active in Mainz in the second quarter of the eleventh century.[23]

The merchants spent time in many countries, among them Provence, Spain, North Africa and other Muslim lands. Their stay in these remote places often lasted a number of years, and various attestations of this are preserved in the *responsa* literature. This is also the explanation of the remarkable phenomenon that technical commercial terms of Arabic origin current in Islamic lands penetrated the language of the Jews of Germany in the eleventh century.[24] In order to render more tangible the problem posed for the structure of the family unit by the economic facts of life and the long absences they entailed, it is worth quoting the ordinance of Rabbenu Jacob Tam against the prolonged absence of husbands from their families:

1. We have decreed . . . that no one shall be permitted to leave his wife for more than eighteen months without permission of the Court of the nearest city, unless he receive the consent of his wife in the presence of proper witnesses.
2. We have permitted the absence of eighteen months only to such as leave out of necessity to earn and provided the husband is at peace with his wife.
3. No one may remain away from his wife against her will unless the Court of Seven Elders before whom the matter is taken permit the continuance of his stay . . .
4. When the husband returns from his journey he must remain at home for no less than six months before undertaking a second journey.
5. But in no case may one forsake his wife as the result of a quarrel or

with bitter feelings, but only with the consent of the Court in the manner described . . .

7. We have decreed that no one shall evade the law and leave unless he is sincerely attached to his wife . . .[25]

This whole ordinance, with its many details, demonstrates the seriousness of the problem and the fact that there were husbands who exploited the opportunity to stay away from home for long periods because of quarrels within the family. The authorization of absences of no more than eighteen months shows that, in practice, the time spent in distant places was longer. To judge from what we find in some of the versions, this was an older ordinance, re-enacted by Rabbenu Tam in the twelfth century with added emphasis on the severity of the penalty.

We are dealing with the middle of the twelfth century. This was after the peak of Jewish activity in international trade and during the period of its decline,[26] and therefore we can draw conclusions from it *a fortiori* as to the gravity of the problem—from the point of view of family life—in the eleventh century and, to all appearances, even earlier. It would not be in the least surprising if the Jewish merchants sometimes married a second wife while they were so far from home for such a long time. This development would have been assisted not only by the realities of life but also by ancient and authoritative sources in the Babylonian Talmud. The Talmud tells of great sages who used to take other wives when they were away from home. It is told, for example, of two of the greatest of the Amoraim: 'Rav, when he chanced to come to Darshish, used to proclaim: "Who will be my wife for a day?" Rav Nahman, when to chanced to come to Shekhanziv, used to proclaim: "Who will be my wife for a day?"', which is to say, for the duration of their stay in the locality.[27] If these two great Amoraim followed this practice when what was in question was an absence for a short period within Babylonia itself, why should not Jews from Germany grant themselves licence to follow it when they were spending years in Muslim countries? It need hardly be said that the fact that, in Islamic countries, the Muslims—and some of the Jews, too—practised polygamy would have provided an encouragement to act similarly. And we do have evidence, in the literature of the period, of 'foreign' men who came from distant places to local communities, married local women and lived in wedlock with them for a time, and then returned home and divorced their new wives, or left them for a lengthy period until they came back on another trading expedition. Thus, for example, R. Isaac Alfasi—who lived and was active in North Africa and Spain in the eleventh century—was asked: 'Reuben married a woman and lived with her, and then left her, so making her an *agunah* [i.e., a woman deserted but not divorced] and married another woman in another country . . . '; 'Reuben departed from his locality and left his wife . . . and there he married another woman . . . '; and it is instructive to note the threat of a husband to his wife that if she does not do as he wishes he will go to another country and marry another woman there.[28] The references are to Jews living in Muslim lands—and sometimes the desertion is a move from one region to another within Spain—but it is reasonable to suppose that Jews coming to Muslim countries from Christian Europe would behave in the same way.

An ordinance by Maimonides in the twelfth century testifies to the seriousness of the phenomenon of desertion of wives by 'foreign' men—men who came from elsewhere—and of marriage to a second wife in a different country:

> Maimonides, of blessed memory, enacted an ordinance to regulate the position of the daughters of Israel, that we should not give a woman in marriage to a stranger [nokhri, here a Jew from abroad who was not a member of the community] anywhere in Egypt until he brings proof that he is unmarried or swears an oath on the Pentateuch to that effect. And if he has a wife, let him write her a bill of divorce, and then we may permit him to marry in this country. And as for any stranger who marries a woman here and wishes to leave for another country, we will not allow him to go even if his wife has given her consent, until he writes and delivers to her a conditional bill of divorce, to come into effect at such time as may be agreed between them, being a year or two years or three years, but not longer.[29]

Particular interest attaches to the second part of this ordinance, namely that which prohibited the 'foreign' Jew from leaving Egypt unless he wrote his wife a bill of divorce. Only the harsh reality of cases in which wives were left for lengthy periods can explain so drastic an ordinance, which would bear very hard on Jews engaged in commerce, since in practice they were not allowed to leave their locality without depositing a bill of divorce; and this at a time when Jews from Egypt still often travelled to other places for the sake of their livelihood.[30] Since economic and social conditions in neighbouring countries where there were Jewish communities were similar to those in Egypt, even before the time of Maimonides, it is hard to imagine that the same phenomenon was not experienced in other places than Egypt and in earlier periods.

Our hypothesis as to the connection between the prolonged absences of Jewish merchants from Germany and Rabbenu Gershom's ordinance is not disproved by the fact that we have found no evidence in German-Jewish literature of merchants who married bigamously while abroad. The literature we have from the time of Rabbenu Gershom and earlier consists mostly of *responsa* and liturgical poetry. It is scarcely to be supposed that any halakhic doubt was aroused in Germany itself by the fact that a husband had married a second wife in some far-off place. This wife did not come back with him. Often the husband had parted from her even before the time of his return to Germany, and there was no halakhic aspect of the case that would have exercised the minds of the sages. The natural place where such doubts would have arisen was precisely in the countries where the second wife had been married, and where she suddenly found herself in fear of being deserted, or involved in divorce procedure—often without having had any previous suspicion that the man in question had a wife and family somewhere else. All this emerges clearly from the halakhic literature of the sages in Islamic countries from the tenth to the twelfth centuries and from the ordinance by Maimonides quoted above.

The action against polygamy by the Jewish sages of Germany in the eleventh century cannot be considered in isolation from the socio-economic structure of the Jewish communities in Germany at that time. Two factors were of outstanding importance for the subject of our consideration: the large number of rich merchants of good family who formed the original nucleus of the local communities in the ninth and tenth centuries, and around whom other people gathered, according a clear pattern of seniority in the leadership of the community to these distinguished families;[31] and the relatively high status of the Jewish woman in these communities, a status which was better and more firmly based than in any other part of the contemporary Jewish world. This superior status was evinced in various forms, for example, in the amount of dowry which these young women brought their husbands; the high level of compensation which husbands bound themselves by their marriage contracts to secure to their wives in the event of death or divorce; and the honourable position of the woman in the conduct of domestic and business affairs. Generally the women were in charge of all these affairs during the long absences of their husbands. In spite of the rules of modesty formally imposed on women by the *halakhah*, many of them went out to conduct negotiations with feudal princes and with other Jewish and Gentile merchants. The attitude of Jewish society to its womenfolk as a class was good, and they were held in respect in their communities. Clear evidence of this is to be found, for example, in the chronicles which describe the massacres of the communities of Mainz and Worms in the Crusade of 1096.[32]

In social conditions such as these, wealthy parents would naturally concern themselves for the honour of their daughters and for the rich dowries which brides brought with them, and would act in various ways, including the use of communal ordinances, to prevent any possibility that their daughters' husbands might take a second wife while still married to the first, even though this was a rare and unlikely occurrence. Society as a whole was all the more ready to accept such ordinances in view of the general attitude to women.

It is no coincidence that the other Jewish centre in which an attempt was made to prohibit husbands from taking an additional wife—though without enacting a communal ordinance of general effect—was Egypt, where there were many rich Jewish merchants. Concern for their daughters and for their large dowries motivated them in this centre, too.[33]

These factors taken together—marriage to a second wife while far from home, and the solid status of women—underlay another ordinance attributed to Rabbenu Gershom, namely the prohibition on divorcing a woman against her will.[34] In practice, a husband away from home could circumvent the first-mentioned ordinance—which exposed him to the risk of excommunication by the whole community when he returned, or when his secret was discovered by fellow-merchants similarly visiting the countries of southern Europe or Islam: he could send his first wife a bill of divorce. It is possible that this occurred more often when the couple were still childless.[35] Given the strong position of the woman in society, it was only natural, once the first ordinance had been enacted, to complement it by the further ordinance forbidding divorce against her will, whether or not the husband was away from home. Of course, in this case too, the motive for the ordinance is indissolubly linked with the socio-economic conditions already referred to, which brought about a general improvement in the status of women in Jewish society in Germany.

The same conditions—journeys abroad and long absences from home—appear to underlie a third ordinance attributed to Rabbenu Gershom: the imposition of a ban on reading another man's letter without his consent. It need hardly be said that, once again, we cannot be sure that the ordinance was really the work of Rabbenu Gershom, but it fits in well with the historical circumstances of the time.[36] At first sight, this ordinance looks quite trivial compared with the others with which Rabbenu Gershom is credited: it seems to be concerned with a purely ethical point. But in practice, it was of great importance, in view of the economic circumstances of contemporary German Jewry. The merchants, while away from home, sent letters to their wives and their partners by the hands of companions returning to Germany. In these letters they gave details of their business affairs (export and import), of goods they were seeking to buy in the hope of marketing them, of decisions not to buy merchandise which was no longer urgently needed, or economic links they had succeeded in establishing, or were planning to establish, with local Jews, and so on.[37] Naturally this information was confidential in character, for there was constant competition between these Jewish merchants for potential markets. Only the sacramental force carried by the ban could have overcome, or at least restrained, the great temptation to read these personal letters.

Together with the three ordinances already discussed, another is ascribed to Rabbenu Gershom: the ban on cancelling a betrothal. It is described in the collection of Rabbenu Gershom's as as 'a ban by ordinance of the communities concerning betrothal' (*herem takkanat ha-kehillot mi-shiddukhin*).[38] Since it is defined in this vague way, unlike the preceding ordinances attributed to Rabbenu Gershom, it seems evident that it was not attributed to him personally in earlier times. In other centres of Jewry, too, in Muslim countries and Europe, sanctions were imposed for breach of promise by one of the parties to a betrothal agreement; but these were monetary sanctions, usually a fine of an amount stipulated in the agreement. Rav Saadia Gaon (first half of the tenth century, in Babylonia) laid it down explicitly that each of the parties to a betrothal agreement must be regarded by the families as entitled to withdraw from it. That was also the opinion of R. Joseph ibn Abitur, one of the great sages of Spain in the eleventh century.[39] Only in Germany was withdrawal from the agreement treated as a most serious matter, meriting the imposition of a *herem*—a ban involving excommunication, the maximum available penalty, with all the force of a religious injunction—against anyone who sought to retract. It emerges from the sources that, in practice, the ban was usually directed against the bridegroom and his family, there being more fear that they would breach the agreement than that the bride and her family would do so.

When did this 'ordinance of the communities' become accepted in Germany and what was the historical motive for its enactment? An important contribution to the consideration of this question was made by Z. Falk. In his opinion, the ordinance is of late origin, dating from the end of the twelfth century and the beginning of the thirteenth century, and the main motive for its introduction was the extremely strict view of breach of promise taken by the Christian Church and the Germanic tribes.[40] He asserted that it was as a result of conditions in their Christian environment that Jewish society gradually adopted a similar point of view, going so far as to compel a man to marry a girl against his will, even if it were clear that he would divorce her immediately after the wedding. In reaching this conclusion Falk relied on various sources which, in his opinion, supported the hypothesis that the ordinance was not current in the eleventh century or the beginning of the twelfth century. He attached considerable weight to the fact that his ban is not mentioned by various scholars, including Rashi, even though one would have thought it appropriate for them to do so when they were dealing with questions connected with the cancellation of betrothals.

This conclusion, which argues a late date for the ordinance, has now been placed in considerable doubt, and it is clear that at least some of the communities in Germany and France were already following the practice in question in the eleventh century. The evidence for this is contained in a source preserved in manuscript, in which it is related that R. Isaac ben R. Judah—one of the teachers of Rashi, and head of the academy at Mainz from 1064 onwards—took part in the enforcement of a ban of this kind on a man who refused to accept the decree of the leaders of his community and marry his fiancée:

> Now it happened that a man in Avallon who had betrothed [*kiddesh*] a maiden wished to go back on his undertaking. And he swore impetuously that if a decree were issued against him, he would not accept it. And the members of his community issued a decree against him (*gazeru alav*), and the inhabitants of Meyoaynina agreed with them, and he married her. And our master R. Isaac ben R. Judah agreed with them too, and he influenced the community to accept the ban.[41]

Two parallels to this source, also preserved in manuscript, confirm that the incident occurred in Avallon, in Burgundy.[42] It is not surprising that the members of the Mainz community and the head of their academy took an active part in the enforcement of the decree. The Mainz academy was looked upon as the senior spiritual institution in the region, and even the Jews of northern France regarded themselves as subordinate to it.

The source quoted above does not remove all doubt. It is clear from it that at the time (the third quarter of the eleventh century) the cancellation of a betrothal was already regarded, both in Mainz and in Avallon, as a most serious matter, and one which should not be allowed to occur. Since, as we have said, the community of Mainz was the senior community in the region, with scholars whose leadership had great influence over the spiritual character of Jewry in Germany and northern France, we may assume with a good deal of confidence that their opinion on this subject was accepted by other communities, too. It is also evident that the resistance offered was so strong that the authorities were prepared to excommunicate the bridegroom who cancelled the betrothal and that they ignored the oath he had sworn to reject their decree, in spite of the extremely serious attitude to the breaking of an oath which was current among Jews at that time. This oath was regarded from a halakhic point of view as *shevuat shav'*, a vain oath, i.e., one which was invalid in the first place, because the duty to obey the ordinances of the community was considered to be one enjoined by the Torah. According to the *halakhah*, an oath to treat as null a commandment of the Torah was itself null and void. At the same time, it appears that the ban had not yet been applied generally by the communities, for had it been of general application there would have been no need to impose a specific ban in this case. However, this cannot be said with complete assurance. The fact that the man in question was afraid from the outset that a decree (*gezerah*) requiring him to marry his bride might be issued against him under threat of excommunication (for that was the accepted meaning of the term *gezerah* at that time) is an indication that this was a familiar practice in that community. It seems likely that there was a general prohibition on the breach of a betrothal, but that each community examined the legal force of the act of betrothal, looking to see whether the conditions in the agreement (*tenaim*) between the two sides had in fact been fulfilled. Only then would they impose a ban on the party wishing to withdraw.

As for the presumed motive for the enactment of the ordinance: it is hard to see, in the factor named by Falk—the influence of the Christian environment—the sole, or even a principal, cause. Rashi, in one of his *responsa*, states that the practice which had been accepted in Germany since the earliest times was to deposit a pledge that would serve as an insurance against breach of the betrothal agreement ('to the intent that the party retracting should forfeit his pledge, as has become the custom in most places');[43] the purpose of instituting this practice was 'in order not to put the daughters of Israel to shame'. The ordinance was insufficient to prevent the cancellation of betrothals entirely. Since betrothals of small children and marriages between minors were common practice at certain times during this period,[44] it was reasonable to fear that by the time the children had grown up, one or other of the parties would wish to withdraw from the agreement—whether for economic, social or personal reasons. Because of this the ordinance forbidding breach of betrothals and requiring the prospective bridegroom to marry his betrothed in every case was introduced. At that time, the communities of Germany and northern France attached extremely great importance, as a rule, to a person's family connections. The fear was that the cancellation of a betrothal might be interpreted as due to information having reached one of the parties that there was some blemish on the reputation of the other family. As the Jewish communities in Germany and France were mostly small at the time, it was reasonable to expect that the ending of a betrothal would quickly become public knowledge and give rise to various rumours and

18

tittle-tattle as to the supposed motive for the cancellation. This could place extreme difficulties in the way of any future marriage of members of the family with whom the betrothal had been broken off, even if the real reason was entirely different from the rumoured one. It was especially feared that the cancellation might be interpreted as stemming from the discovery that the family was tainted by the conversion of one of its members to Christianity: there are various attestations to this in the sources. We have found extremely great sensitivity to this point in another ordinance which was enacted by Rabbenu Gershom according to no less a person than Rashi, who, as we have said, lived and worked only two generations after him. The ordinance prescribed that anyone who mentioned that a member of any family had been 'immersed in the water of apostasy' should be excommunicated. And indeed, in a quarrel which broke out between two families in one of the communities of Champagne, one of the disputants mentioned that there was an apostate in the other family, and scholars were greatly exercised as to whether there was any way in which his excommunication could be avoided.[45]

CONCLUSION

The ordinances on family matters which are attributed to Rabbenu Gershom owe their origin to three factors: the socio-economic structure of Jewish communities in Germany in the eleventh century (the principal factor); the relatively good status of women in society; and, to a certain extent, greater sensitivity towards injustice to the individual living in these communities.[46] These ordinances had the effect of improving still further the status of women and strengthening the foundations of the family unit. On the other hand, they could sometimes cause hardship and create misery. Thus, for example, it is reasonable to assume that a family created against the will of one of the parties, as happened in Avallon, where the bridegroom was forced to marry, would be a family ruined from the outset. We may suppose that it would quickly break up, with the husband divorcing his wife immediately after the wedding, a step which the ordinance was powerless to prevent. Nevertheless, these ordinances were able to enhance the position of the Jewish woman in Germany in the eleventh century and even later, giving them a status that was better than in most Jewish centres of the period.

Avraham Grossman

Notes

1 The following are some of the principal studies dealing with this subject: F. Rosenthal, *Einiges über die Takanot des Rabbenu Gershom der Leuchte des Exils, Jubelschrift* . . . I (Berlin, 1890); L. Finkelstein, *Jewish Self-Government in the Middle Ages* (2nd edn, New York, 1964), pp. 6–35, 111–47; F. Baer, *MGWJ*, vol. 71 (1927), pp. 392–7; vol. 74 (1930), pp. 31–4; Z. Falk, *Jewish Matrimonial Law in the Middle Ages* (Oxford, 1966); A. Grossman, *Hakhmei Ashkenaz ha-Rishonim* (Jerusalem, 1981), pp. 132–49; S. Z. Havlin, 'Takkanot Rabbenu Gershom Me'or ha-Golah be-Inyeney Ishut bi-Tehumey Sefarad u-Provence', *Shenaton ha-Mishpat ha-Ivri*, vol. 2 (1975), pp. 200–57. Other studies are mentioned in the notes below. There is a detailed bibliographical note in Falk, op. cit., p. 1, n. 1, and in Grossman, op. cit., pp. 133–9.

2 The reference is to a collection of Rabbenu Gershom's ordinances, numbering eleven in addition to those relating to family matters. All these were ascribed to Rabbenu Gershom in sources dating from the thirteenth century onwards. The main sources, together with variant readings, were reproduced by Finkelstein (note 1 above), pp. 118–27, 139–41. No reference is intended here to attempts made in scholarly research to ascribe dozens of later ordinances also to Rabbenu Gershom. See, e.g., the discussion of Schepansky's opinion in Grossman (note 1 above), p. 139 and n. 118.

3 See Grossman (note 1 above), pp. 140–4. As will appear from the discussion in the present paper, one cannot yet speak of a complete and definite solution.

4 The status of Rabbenu Gershom, and his great reputation in the school of Rashi and among the scholars of Germany and France as a whole, are described in detail in Grossman (note 1 above), pp. 107–13.

5 On these arguments, see Falk (note 1 above), pp. 13–19; P. Tishby, *Tarbiz*, vol. 34 (1965), pp. 49–55.

6 Various examples of the grant of authorization where a *mitzvah* applied are quoted by S. Eidelberg from works by the scholars of Germany: *Tarbiz*, vol. 34 (1965), pp. 287–9.

7 *Ibid.*

8 'When I was a young man I saw that Mistress Origyah, who was old when her husband died . . . and the two brothers of her late husband were R. Hillel and R. Ephraim, and they appeared before our rabbis in the council of the communities . . . and they wished to marry their brother's widow [in obedience to Deut. 25:5–6] although they already had wives . . . and they said the ordinance of Rabbenu Gershom Me'or ha-Golah did not operate where it would prevent the performance of a *mitzvah*'; Avigdor (Victor) Aptowitzer, *Mavo la-Ravyah* (Jerusalem, 1938), p. 203. See Aptowitzer's discussion of the time when this occurred, *ibid.*, n. 3, and the remakers of Y. Ta-Shema in *Tarbiz*, vol. 35 (1966), p. 193.

9 The single exception is found in a *responsum* of Rashi. See *Teshuvot Rashi*, ed. Elfenbein (New York, 1943), p. 97. But it is expressly stated there that the wife in question had been married for ten years and had borne no children, and that her husband married a second wife according to the *halakhah* laid down in the Talmud.

10 For a detailed discussion of the significance of rabbinical ordinances and community ordinances, their great importance, manner of enactment and development, see M. Elon, *Ha-Mishpat ha-Ivri*, vol. 2 (Jerusalem, 1973), pp. 391 ff.

11 *MGWJ* (1919), p. 79.

12 See *Mekharim be-Hokhmat Yisrael le-Zikhro shel Y. M. Guttman* (Budapest, 1946), pp. 114–36, where Roth contributed an important study of the history of monogamy among the Jews from biblical times to the Middle Ages. His discussion of Rabbenu Gershom's ordinance is on pp. 119–25.

13 *ibid.*, p. 124.

14 For the literature dealing with this point, and a discussion of it, see Tishby (note 5 above).

15 S. Baron, *A Social and Religious History of the Jews*, vol. 6 (Philadelphia, 1958), p. 137.

16 In recent years some important sources have been discovered which testify that this was occurring. It need hardly be said how vital this is for the history of Jewish culture and the study of the ties between the various European centres and the centres of Torah in Babylonia and Eretz Israel. These sources have been published in several places, and this is not the occasion to enumerate them in detail. I shall confine myself to the observation that all the great Jewish scholars who were active in north Italy in the first half of the eleventh century are mentioned as having studied with Rav Hai Gaon in Babylonia (Bodleian MS. 1101, p. 184a). R. Elijah ben R. Menahem, one of the founders of the Torah centre in northern France, was another who spent a fairly long time in the academy of Rav Hai, and he also visited Eretz Israel a number of times. The evidence is supplied in my article 'Elijah ben Menahem's Pilgrimage', *Tarbiz*, vol. 56 (1987), pp. 273–8.

17 Falk (note 1 above), pp. 25–6.

18 *Sefer Hasidim*, ed. Wistinetzki (Berlin, 1891), s. 1301.

19 M. A. Friedman, *Ribbui Nashim be-Yisrael* (Tel Aviv, 1986), p. 20.

20 Grossman (note 1 above), pp. 400–11.

21 S. Eidelberg, *Teshuvot Rabbenu Gershom Me'or ha-Golah* (New York, 1956), pp. 113–14. A discussion of the opinions of R. Ammi and Rava, and of the Babylonian and Palestinian traditions with regard to polygamy, is contained in Friedman (note 19 above), pp. 7 ff.

22 The first book to describe the various customs of the scholars and families in Germany, written in the second half of the eleventh century, was *Maaseh ha-Geonim*, ed. A. Epstein (Berlin, 1910). I dealt with this work and its importance in my book (note 1 above), pp. 361 ff.

23 Many of the *responsa* of these two scholars which describe the journeys of the merchants are quoted and discussed in detail by I. A. Agus in his books *Urban Civilization in Pre-Crusade Europe*, 2 vols. (New York, 1965) and *The Heroic Age of Franco-German Jewry* (New York, 1969). However, his analyses and conclusions should be treated with caution. R. Judah Hakohen and his *responsa* are considered in Grossman (note 1 above), pp. 175–210.

24 I commented on some expressions of this kind in my book (note 1 above), p. 56; but no full and detailed study on this subject has yet been undertaken.

25 See Finkelstein (note 1 above), p. 168, where variant readings are given and the significance of the ordinance considered.

26 See R. S. Lopez and I. W. Raymond, *Medieval Trade in the Mediterranean World* (New York, 1955), pp. 29–32; C. Roth, *The World History of the Jewish People, The Dark Ages* (Tel Aviv, 1966), pp. 13–48.

27 Babylonian Talmud, *Yoma*, 18b, and the parallel passage in *Yevamot* 37b.

28 The sources are contained in the *responsa* of R. Isaac Alfasi, ed. Leiter (New York, 1954), ss. 28, 67, 185.

29 *Responsa* of Maimonides, ed. Blau, vol. 2 (Jerusalem, 1960), s. 347, p. 624.

30 Many sources testifying to this are contained in S. D. Goiten, *Letters of Medieval Jewish Traders* (Princeton, 1973).

31 I discussed this in detail in 'Hagirat Yehudim el Germanyah ve-Hityashvutam bah ba-Me'ot 9-11', in *Hagirah ve-Hityashvut*, ed. A. Shinan (Jerusalem, 1982), pp. 109–28.

32 The women are described in these chronicles as having encouraged the men to fight and as having played an extremely active part in the groups who martyred themselves

for the sanctification of the Divine Name. They were distinguished in the chronicles by epithets the like of which, in general, it is hard to find applied to women in mediaeval Jewish literature—'saintly', 'esteemed', 'holy'. See, e.g., the chronicle of R. Solomon ben Samson, *Sefer Gezerot Ashkenaz ve-Tsarefat*, ed. A. M. Habermann (Jerusalem, 1971), pp. 24–60. (English translation in S. Eidelberg, *The Jews and the Crusaders*, Madison, 1977, pp. 21–72.) See also Grossman, 'Yihus Mishpaha u-Mekomo ba-Hevra ha-Yehudit be-Ashkenaz ha-Kedumah', *J. Katz Jubilee Volume* (Jerusalem, 1980), pp. 9–23.

33 On dowries and the marriage contract in Germany in the eleventh century, see Agus, *The Heroic Age* (Note 23 above), pp. 203–77; on the condition imposed in Egypt, see Friedman (note 19 above), pp. 55–82.

34 See Finkelstein (note 25 above); Falk (note 1 above), pp. 113–43 (including p. 113, n. 1). Here, too, the first scholar to mention this ordinance, which he does without elaboration (together with the ordinance which forbade marriage to a second wife), is R. Eliezer ben Nathan. See the discussion by Falk, op. cit., p. 117, and by Eidelberg (note 21 above), pp. 19–20.

35 From the allusions in the *responsa* literature and elsewhere, it is apparent that divorce was fairly common in German-Jewish society at that time. For the more frequent and surprisingly widespread resort to divorce at a later time, see Y. Yuval, 'Takkanot neged Ribbuy Gerushin be-Germanyah ba-Meah ha-Tet-Vav', *Zion*, vol. 48 (1983), pp. 177–215.

36 Finkelstein (note 1 above), pp. 31, 189–201. In his discussion (p. 31) of the purpose of this ban and its ordinance, Finkelstein rightly points to its ethical aspect.

37 Many examples of such partnerships are mentioned in the *responsa* of R. Judah Hakohen (note 23 above). There are scores of other descriptions of similar situations among the *responsa* of the Babylonian Geonim. A large number of these are assembled in *Teshuvot Geonim, Sha'arey Zedek*, Part 4. We will content ourselves with three short quotations, purely for the purpose of illustration: 'And as for the question you asked me: Reuben has a partner overseas, and Simeon says to Reuben: Write to your partner for me and ask him to buy such and such an article for me and send it to me together with what he sends you' (*Sha'arey Zedek*, p. 40b, s. 24); 'Simeon who came to Africa and went into partnership with Benjamin. Each contributed a hundred dinars, and Simeon went overseas on that business, travelling from place to place and from country to country' (*Hemdah Genuzah*, s. 49); 'Reuben, Simeon and Levi went into partnership and bought some merchandise and jointly pledged their property and took their merchandise to Babylonia and found that merchandise like theirs was cheap there, and they were desolated over their purchase and returned to their homes' (the question was addressed to Rav Saadia Gaon) (*Sha'arey Zedek*, Part 4, ch. (*sha'ar*) 8, s. 11).

38 Finkelstein (note 1 above), pp. 140–1.

39 Rav Saadia Gaon, *Sha'arey Zedek*, Part 3, ch. 6, s. 12 ('that if he wished to withdraw from the marriage arrangement he could do so'). *Teshuvot Geonei Mizrah u-Maarav*, s. 195, contains the following statement: '. . . that in this generation neither disgrace nor discredit is involved. For it is the way of the world that a number of men may seek the hand of the daughters of Israel in marriage, but our daughters marry only those whom it is their destiny to marry; because the bringing together of marriage partners is decided nowhere but in Heaven.' Müller, in his comments in this volume, attributed this *responsum* to R. Meshullam ben Kalonymos (Italy, end of tenth century), or to Rabbenu Gershom. But its style, and especially its position in the manuscript from which Müller copied it (Montefiore 98, in a section consisting of *responsa* from the early sages of Spain), show that the source of the *responsum* was Spain. Some peculiar turns of phrase, and the style generally, match very closely those of R. Joseph ibn Abitur.

40 Falk (note 1 above), pp. 98–112. On the strict attitude to betrothals in German society, see G. H. Goyce, *Christian Marriage* (London, 1948), p. 85.

41 Jewish Theological Seminary, New York, MS. Rabb. 1077. I published this document for the first time in *Shenaton ha-Mishpat ha-Ivri*, vol. 2 (1975), p. 188. 'The inhabitants of Meyoaynina' (an approximate transliteration) = 'of Alemania', i.e. of Germany, as is explained in another manuscript and as I pointed out in my comments on this document.

42 On this community, see H. Gross, *Gallia Judaica*, 2nd edn (Amsterdam, 1969), p. 17.

43 *Teshuvot Hakhmei Tsarefat ve-Lothair*, ed. Müller (Vienna, 1881), s. 27. This custom of giving pledges was traditional in other Jewish centres, too, and is of ancient origin. See the remarks of S. Assaf on this, *Mekorot u-Mehkarim* (Jerusalem, 1946), p. 64.

44 See I. A. Agus, *The Heroic Age* (note 23 above), pp. 277–84. The age at which marriages took place in Jewish society in the ninth to the twelfth centuries is the subject of a detailed study of mine which will be published in the near future.

45 *Teshuvot Rashi* (note 9 above), s. 70, pp. 82–7. This source is very important for the study of the whole question of the ordinance attributed to Rabbenu Gershom. In it, Rashi accepted the tradition that Rabbenu Gershom enacted an ordinance against raking up the past of those who had undergone forced conversion, but he did not know the exact text of the ordinance and the ban (pp. 82–3). This is surprising. Rashi spent some years in Mainz only one generation after the death of Rabbenu Gershom. How is it that he did not take a copy of the text of Rabbenu Gershom's ordinances and bring it back with him when he returned to Troyes, in France?—especially in the light of the fact that he held Rabbenu Gershom in exceedingly high esteem and regarded him (as he expressly stated in this *responsum*) as the greatest man of his generation, saying: 'There is no other like him.' Surely he could have foreseen the possibility that these ordinances would be of great importance in the administration of the affairs of his own community too? My colleague Professor Ta-Shema thinks we may deduce from this that Rabbenu Gershom did not commit his ordinances to writing. It is very possible that there is a different explanation—that Rabbenu Gershom did not concentrate his ordinances into a corpus of enactments, nor were they all enacted at one time or at one assembly of communities, but they were promulgated at various times, when cases which came before Rabbenu Gershom's court showed them to be necessary. Consequently, not all the ordinances would have received the same degree of publicity and some would have been more widely distributed than others. At all events, only two generations after his death he was already seen, in France too, as a central figure whose ordinances exerted a strong influence even in centres outside Germany, even though there was already no exact version extant of all those ordinances.

46 See, e.g., the evidence adduced in my article 'Reshiyyotav vi-Yesodotav shel Minhag Ikkuv ha-Tefillah', in *Milet*, vol. 1 (Tel Aviv, 1983), pp. 199–219.

Sexual Behaviour in Mediaeval
Hispano-Jewish Society

Yom Tov Assis

RELATIONS between men and women occupy, quite naturally, an important part in the life of any society. That such relations vividly reflected on socio-economic, religious and political conditions and attitudes is so obvious that it hardly needs to be substantiated. Yet scarcely any sphere of life has been so subjected to censorship and distortion as has sexual behaviour, particularly in the Christian and Muslim worlds in which the bulk of mediaeval Jewry lived.

Our knowledge of this subject is, not surprisingly, impaired by lack of documentation: such relations tended to remain, as their intimacy required, hidden from outsiders. In addition, the written records related to the topic, whether judicial, literary, ethical or legal, are often deficient and do not lend themselves to balanced historical analysis.

The judicial records report only a small proportion of the total number of crimes and transgressions, leaving unknown to posterity numerous instances of deviant and illicit sexual conduct. The fear and shame of the victims frequently caused this silence. There is also reason to believe that the extant records contain many false accusations levelled by rivals, disappointed lovers or other enemies. Ethical works, critical of sexual laxity, sometimes present a realistic picture; others tend to idealize. Literary sources tend to reflect the lives of the upper classes and ignore the majority of the population. In this area more than others, we confront a vast silent population which could neither read nor write. One other problem is that legal records, which shed light on many obscure aspects of family and sexual life, suffer from a tendency to incorporate automatically old laws which no longer necessarily mirror prevalent conditions.

Standards of sexual behaviour in mediaeval Christian and Muslim Europe were shaped by Christianity and Islam. Such standards should not be confused with actual practice, since in both civilizations there existed a gap between reality and theory: nevertheless, religious norms constituted a crucial factor in daily life.

The condemnation of physical pleasure and the insistence on the procreative function of marriage in Christianity go back to its early formative period (although this was not a natural development of any trend emanating from the Bible). Chastity and virginity were praised while sexual attraction was ignored or suppressed.[1] From the twelfth century onwards, confessors were instructed to ask a series of questions to find out whether husbands had excessive passion towards their wives; and if they did, they were automatically suspected of unnatural conjugal relations.[2]

One can infer from the frequent condemnations and prohibitions that the gap between theory and practice in the mediaeval Christian world was wide. The repeated bans on all contraception certainly point in this direction.[3] Clerics, who were supposed to set an example to the masses and supervise their conduct, were themselves by no means innocent of behaviour which was considered immoral.[4] Concubinage in mediaeval Christian Europe, forbidden by the Church, was widespread among churchmen, who continued to practise it until the sixteenth century when it began to decline.[5]

In Spain, the Councils and the Cortes severely and repeatedly censured the lax morals of clerics. Innocent IV withdrew the papal sanctions against clerics who kept concubines in 1251 because of their great number. The Cortes of Castile complained in 1351 about this state of affairs. In 1359 the Bishop of Tortosa forbade churchmen to bequeath their posts to their 'natural' sons. In 1380 the Cortes decided that such children had no right to inherit and that the concubines should wear a distinctive sign so that they could not pose as wives. From the debates in the Cortes of Braga in 1401, we learn that many young women preferred to live with churchmen since they could buy them fine clothes. Worse still, some clerics had Muslim or Jewish concubines. The kings of Castile and Aragon did little to combat the situation and did not even refrain from favouring churchmen who kept women. Such clerics behaved in keeping with the standards of their society: a churchman in bed with his concubine as depicted in one of Alfonso X's *Cántigas* appear quite natural in thirteenth-century Castile.[6]

Sexual morality in mediaeval Western Europe was certainly very low, if we judge it by the standards set by canon and secular laws or by social and religious norms laid down in the ethical literature of the period. Sexual crimes were committed frequently. Rape was extremely widespread; until the sixteenth century mass rape in public was witnessed in many European cities. In numerous places this was an accepted practice. In mediaeval Dijon it is estimated that some fifty per cent of the inhabitants participated at one time or another in public rape. In fact, the need for prostitutes in many parts of Europe arose as a result of the need to protect wives and daughters from single young rapists. Thus brothels were established in France with public funds. In the fifteenth century many towns in the valley of the Rhône and Saône had municipal 'public houses'. The fees were reasonable, so that every wage-earning man could afford the visit.[7]

If religion in Christian Europe did not substantially restrict sexual behaviour, even greater laxity and permissiveness characterized Muslim society. This is confirmed by recent research which is still in its pioneering stages. What is clear is that despite the legality of polygamous marriage, concubinage, extra-marital liaisons and homosexual relations were widespread.[8] The upper classes in Moorish Spain, in particular, led an extremely permissive life, notwithstanding criticism from pietists and ascetics. Even the puritan waves of conquerors from North Africa, the Almoravids and the Almohads, were unable to do away with the Muslim élite's taste for dancing, music, wine, women and young men. Homosexuality—widespread and practised openly in all classes of society—was professionalized in several Andalusian cities. Female prostitutes were not uncommon. They often chose to work in special houses, *khans*, or *dar al kharadj*. Needless to say, there was little difficulty in finding wine everywhere in Andalusia, despite the Islamic prohibition of alcoholic drinks. Music, dancing and singing accompanied most types of social gatherings.[9]

The Jews of Spain were exposed to influences from both Christian and Muslim societies. On both sides of the ever-changing border in the Iberian peninsula, they were more deeply involved in the social, economic, cultural and political life of the land than was any other mediaeval Jewish community. Iberian Jewry, at a crossroads between the Jews of Ashkenaz or Franco-Germany, and the Jews of Islam, served not only as a bridge and channel between the two for reciprocal influences but also as a meeting point, where divergent concepts and approaches to life intermittently clashed and fused: despite its integration, Hispano-Jewish society remained, at the same time, part of the mediaeval Jewish world. Torn between extreme and contradictory trends, it found itself characterized by sexual laxity to an extent unknown elsewhere in mediaeval Jewry.[10]

COURTSHIP AND LOVE

The Hebrew poetry of Spain introduces us to a society where holy and profane merge into an indivisible and harmonious whole, where the borders between them essentially disappear. The lofty and base go hand in hand without many scruples. The hand that wrote 'Singing God's Praise' is the same hand that wrote 'The Apple'. Judah Halevi joined all the morning stars in singing to God—sang with no less passion to the lady who captured him with her charms.[11]

That the worldly love poems of Spanish Jews are nothing more than fanciful literary exercises is implicit in the idealized accounts of the Jews' high moral standards and self-restraint which can be found in mediaeval Jewish texts. R. Solomon ibn Adret's 'praise to God for the purity of the generations in these regions, where Jewish girls are modest and do not break the fence by choosing their own husbands without their fathers' consent' is a sweeping generalization incompatible with the general atmosphere prevailing in Judaeo-Spanish society.[12] Moreover, a number of scholars of our own time have been unable to entertain the thought that Jewish life in mediaeval Spain might have been anything but morally impeccable. Any discrepancy between the sources and their own idealized vision of Jewish family life has been resolved either by interpreting it away or by discarding the 'inconvenient' sources.[13]

In fact the Hebrew poetry of thirteenth century Castile, above all the poems of Todros ben Judah Halevi, depict illicit sexual relations among Jews of the upper classes. In beautiful Hebrew verse, the poet reminds his patron, the Jewish statesman Don Çag de la Maleha, how they each danced in the arms of lovely young women.[14] Men in these circles conducted intensive amorous correspondences with women, most of them probably non-Jews.[15] Todros himself informs us that, in his youth, he pursued indiscriminately women of all types. As he grew older,however, he became more selective, respectable and moderate in his flirtations. He refrained, so he confesses, from any physical contact and was content to hear the voice and admire the beauty of his beloved. He now preferred Platonic love to physical pleasure, and the sarcastic remarks of his friends did not deter him from pursuing pure love.[16] We have reason to believe that at the time of writing Todros was in the midst of one of his penitential moods which never lasted long. Such periodical spells of remorse were not uncommon in the Jewish community and often followed in the wake of the deterioration of relations between king and Jewish courtiers.

Among the penitents we find Samuel ben Josef Alnaqave who promised never to look at women again.[17] In fact, the community had issued a ban on laxity in sexual behaviour. The downfall of many aristocrats encouraged rabbis, long critical of their free conduct with the opposite sex, to preach repentance. In one of his sermons, R. Todros ben Josef Halevi Abulafia, the poet's namesake, insisted that the destiny of Jewry depended on its daily conduct. The preacher admonished his audience to abandon their bad habits, specifically, those Jews who had made it their custom to gather in the streets on Sabbaths and festivals, leering at the women and making passes at them.[18]

Jewish women were often harassed and maltreated. Excluded from active participation in social life, they lacked men's experience in intrigue. Consequently, many cases of women who had fallen victims to unscrupulous men were tried in both the Jewish and the Gentile courts. These cases undoubtedly represent only a small proportion of the occurrences of abuse.

The most frequent cases involved the use of fraudulent means to force young women into marriage. It was sometimes enough for a man to spread the rumour that a certain woman had been wedded or betrothed to him, in order to prevent her from marrying anyone else. Two false witnesses, a forged marriage contract or both were more than sufficient to complicate a girl's life and obstruct (at least temporarily) her plans to marry the man of her choice. Until the matter was settled, she was considered legally unfit for marriage. Rabbinic authorities reacted angrily to such an abuse of Jewish law and to the suffering of these young women.[19] Even the king was involved at times in cases of men who tried to stop the marriages of Jewish women by falsely claiming to be their husbands.[20]

Fraudulent marriages sometimes involved ingenious and impertinent actions. A woman who entrusted a man with a ring to be taken for repair was asked subsequently to let him try it on her finger. When she innocently allowed him to do so, he pronounced the Jewish marriage formula in front of witnesses.[21] Violent men acted more bluntly and simply used force. An influential and unscrupulous man whose passion for a certain woman—a defenceless indigent orphan—could not be satisfied through seduction, did not hesitate to force her to marry him. He bribed local authorities without fearing the community's sanction.[22]

As in other mediaeval Jewish communities, it was the norm for the girl to be guided in her choice of a husband by her father or, in his absence, by her mother and older brothers and uncles. We have already referred to Adret's observation that in this matter no Jewish girl would defy her father. In another *responsum* Adret sounds less sure and admits that a small minority of young women would insist on the freedom to choose their partners, refusing to abide by arrangements made between their parents or other close relatives. Adret acknowledged the girl's legitimate right to do this once she reached adulthood.[23] While still a minor, however, her father was free to marry her off to whomever he wished.[24] As for a childless widow who refused to marry her brother-in-law on the grounds of personal dislike, Adret declares that she should be compelled to marry.[25]

It seems that in some parts of Spain, once both sides had agreed on a marriage, the rules regulating the relations between the couples were greatly relaxed. Some sources inform us that even prior to marriage they were free to spend much of their time alone together both day and night. In such circumstances, pre-marital sexual relations were by no means unknown.[26]

HUSBANDS AND WIVES

Jewish family life in mediaeval Spain combined features drawn from both the Christian and the Muslim environment. Certain contradictory trends derived from both civilizations can be clearly seen and were partly responsible for a variety of problems characteristic of the Judaeo-Spanish family.

Monogamy was one of these. While the Jewish communities north of the Pyrenees affirmed monogamy, among the Jews of Islam polygyny was widely practised. Spanish Jews wavered between the two trends. which coexisted with various clashes until the expulsion.[27] Jews in the Christian kingdoms of Spain continued to marry second wives as was practised under Muslim rule, and the *Reconquista* did not eradicate such behaviour. Bigamy persisted among Jews, despite all rabbinic efforts to ban it and despite its prohibition by the Spanish authorities. All applications by Jews to the Crown to permit them a second wife were based on the permissibility of this practice in Jewish law as prevailing in Muslim lands.[28]

Obviously, the rabbinic authorities in Spain, like their counterparts elsewhere, stressed unanimously the need for the proper and dignified treatment of wives.[29] Such emphasis, however, raises doubts as to whether or not this was generally practised. A close examination of the sources reveals that, alongside general observations applicable to any other mediaeval community, they contain some remarks which refer to conditions peculiar to Iberian Jewry.

The sources emanating from the Muslim period and region often refer to the wife's status in connection with the prevalence of bigamy. With regard to the almost inevitable neglect suffered by one of the wives, usually the first, Alfasi adopts a realistic attitude. While admitting that invariably one of the wives would be favoured, he insists that the marital rights (that is, the sexual needs) of the less fortunate wife must not be neglected.[30] There arose also the problem of maintaining two homes, when one of the wives refused to dwell under the same roof as her rival.[31] Here again, the sensitive issue was the financial implications of such a split but also the husband's sexual obligations towards the neglected wife. Even though, in most cases, the husband chose one of his two homes as his permanent abode (whether by preference or by force of circumstances), he had to visit his other wife, if only 'to fulfil his duty as a husband'. Even in those cases where no bigamous household was involved, if husband and wife lived separately during the week they were obliged to eat together on the Sabbath and spend the night together.[32]

Spanish rabbis frequently encouraged considerate behaviour which might contribute to love between husband and wife. Adret, among other rabbis, forbade husbands to force their wives to engage in activities which were not generally considered fit for women, or which they might not have been expected to carry out in their parents' home. He was emphatic, though, that a wife should prepare her husband's bed since this could contribute toward nurturing their love.[33]

From Adret's *responsum* we learn that it was sometimes the extreme youth of wives that was said to be responsible for their inability to perform even the simplest domestic tasks. Iberian Jews had for many years married their women at a very tender age, so much so that the practice aroused protests from the rabbinic authorities, particularly where a second wife was younger than her husband's children by his first wife.[34]

It was men's sexual desires which constituted, quite typically, the basis for such relationships, but this sometimes proved a tenuous foundation. At times, a wife married off while a minor to a man who was probably more than double her age developed a dislike for her husband. A woman who was asked, a few months after her marriage, why she refused to live with her husband, claimed that she hated him because he was too old.[35]

The chances that the young wife of a much older man would become a widow at a young age were very real. A beautiful young widow, who had promised her dying husband that she would not remarry until their son and daughter had attained their majority, became the subject of learned correspondence between Adret, R. Yom Tov Alsabili and R. Dan Ashkenazi. The latter refers to the distress of the young woman who could not marry, and especially to the sexual dangers she faced: since she had already experienced the pleasures of sexual intercourse, it was argued, she might be easily tempted now to engage in intercourse outside marriage.[36]

There were also young men who married wealthy older women. In one such case a certain young man had married an older woman who could no longer bear him children. He had to promise not to marry a second time while she was still alive, and he signed a document pledging the payment of 25,000 gold pieces in the event of a divorce. After five years of marriage he found himself trapped, penniless and childless, since his wife gave him no money and secretly transferred her wealth to her son from a previous marriage. In his request to be allowed to marry a second wife who would bear him children, he admitted that he had married for money, in order to help his unmarried sisters.[37]

Peaceful marital life in general, and harmonious sexual relations in particular, scarcely feature in our sources, since the extant records mostly represent problematic cases of discord. This should be kept in mind in any discussion of sexual life as it was debated in the Jewish courts of law and evaluated by rabbinic authorities.

Rabbis were forced to confront problems of the most intimate nature. Should the newly wed, for example, continue to have intercourse during the seven days following the nuptial night or should this be precluded by the show of virginal blood?[38] Jewish law prohibits contact between husband and wife during the wife's menstruation, but local custom and superstition in certain regions sometimes went even further than the halakhic requirements, causing disruption in domestic life.[39] As sexual relations could only be resumed after the ritual immersion of the wife in the *mikva*, this condition was often used (or abused) by the wife who preferred to prolong the abstention period beyond its normal limits, in disregard for her husband's inclination. In one case, a desperate husband swore that if his wife did not immerse herself on that very night, as she was required to do by the *halakha* (Jewish law), he would never have sexual intercourse with her again and would seek a divorce.[40] On another occasion the wife refrained from intercourse in order to avoid pregnancy, but delayed immersion was often due simply to the woman's lack of enthusiasm about her conjugal life. Some wives expressed their distate for their husbands more bluntly, and sexual abstinence was not always intended to be temporary. R. Nissim Gerondi was asked to give his opinion of a woman who refused to have intercourse with her husband, claiming that she could not bear to be with him in bed.[41] On the other hand, the same rabbi was consulted about the case of a man who, having failed to seduce a poor orphan girl, began to press her to marry him and eventually managed to satisfy his sexual desire.[42] Cases of coercion in marital relations were no less common among Spanish Jews than they were in every other community.[43]

Rabbinic sources reveal the sexual tastes and practices of Iberian Jews. A wife who wanted to drink a syrup that would help her conceive was prevented from doing so by her husband who claimed that pregnancy would spoil her beautiful figure. His objection was overruled by Adret who referred to the Jewish obligation to procreate.[44] Another woman objected to her husband's use of masturbation in their lovemaking, a practice which she found painful. She claimed that he did this because he was impotent. The angry husband threw her out of the house, brought in a Jewish mistress, and felt triumphant when she bore him a daughter.[45]

Childless couples frequently blamed each other for their condition. The husband enjoyed a legal advantage in that he could more easily prove his virility as well as his fertility to put an end to the recriminations. After twenty years of a barren marriage, one husband divorced his wife and married another who soon conceived. Having proved his point, he remarried his first wife and fixed his permanent home with her.[46] Under biblical law, this course of action was not open to a wife who found herself in a comparable situation.

The *halakhah* forbids the husband to deprive his wife of her sexual marital rights. In a society which allowed men to satisfy their sexual needs with second wives or even with concubines, many wives could be easily ignored or neglected. Such husbands might be reprimanded or ultimately sued for divorce if they persisted.[47] If, in anger, a husband swore that he would withhold sexual rights from his wife even for a short period, his oath would be considered illegal and unbinding.[48]

We are struck at times by the laxity in the sexual conduct of some Jewish couples. This does not refer to adultery (on which see below), but to what one may call the generally permissive attitudes of some marriage partners. A noteworthy example was the case of a husband who suspected that his wife was having an affair with his brother. He invited his brother to sleep in his own bedroom. One morning he contrived to leave the room early. When he returned, he surprised his brother and his wife under the same blanket.[49] That such casual sleeping arrangements between members of what appears to have been a poor Jewish family should have been possible in twelfth-century Muslim Spain is illuminating, and it suggests that Hispano-Jewish society under the Christians was much influenced by earlier standards set by the Moors.

The permissiveness and daring in the sexual life of married couples in Christian Spain may be best illustrated by Judaeo-Catalan poems composed most probably in the fourteenth century in northern Catalonia or in Roussillon (politically, linguistically and culturally part of Catalonia). These wedding-poems contain much direct and daring advice to the bride and bridegroom for their mutual sexual satisfaction. The bride is advised on how to ensure that her husband remains attracted to her and to no other woman. The most explicit, indeed almost pornographic, is the one called 'A Beautiful Poem' (*Piyyut Naeh*), introduced by the Hebrew words 'A poem on the occasion of the bridegroom's copulation with his bride'. It relates, somewhat satirically, various problems that an old husband and his much younger wife might encounter in bed. The poem contains many biblical and

Talmudic references, some of them parodied with admirable expertise and designed to arouse sexual passion. Such poems had their (milder) parallels elsewhere outside Spain but, while they were undoubtedly influenced by the style of troubadour poetry, they reflected local conditions.[50]

At the other end of the spectrum, wife-beating was widespread among Spanish Jews. This must be seen as part of the general trend of violence in Hispano-Jewish society.[51] The husband in the Jewish family in Spain, whether under Islam or Christianity, generally behaved as the undisputed master of the house, despite the Jewish norm that the mistress of the house should be honoured. R. Judah, son of R. Asher, writing in fourteenth-century Toledo, stated that 'it is well known that the wife fears her husband and that the husband rules in his home while she (i.e. the wife) does not contradict him'.[52]

We must distinguish between the occasional and the habitual use of force. A husband who beat his wife in a moment of anger during a heated row and later apologized rarely appeared in court.[53] Far more dangerous was the husband who regularly beat his wife. Such violent men often denied the accusations when they were brought before the Jewish courts, and they were rarely willing to promise that they would not beat their wives again.[54] The poor wife often had no choice but to seek refuge in her father's house.[55] The beaten and fugitive wife found the rabbis to be her allies: they usually gave little credence to the husband's counter-accusations.[56] They would refuse, for instance, to declare 'rebellious' a wife who, by refusing to dwell under the same roof with her violent husband, would forfeit her marriage rights.[57]

If wives left home to avoid being beaten, husbands would abandon their wives for other reasons. In Muslim Spain, where many Jews engaged in commerce, wives were often left alone at home for long periods while their husbands travelled on business. These abandoned wives were consequently sometimes unaware that their husbands had found themselves other women whom they either married or kept as concubines. At times the wives were abandoned without adequate financial provisions.[58] Worst of all, they remained married to absentee husbands. To procure a bill of divorce was extremely complicated: some husbands claimed that they wished to remain married to both wives, dividing their time between the two.[59]

The misfortune of an abandoned wife was evident to all, and some husbands threatened to desert their wives if they did not comply with their wishes.[60] The rabbis were aware of the consequent tragedies. Alfasi stated categorically that men who could earn their livelihood in their home towns should not travel elsewhere to do business without their wives' consent, and certainly must not go away and marry a second wife.[61] In Christian Spain, such problems became less frequent. Some husbands still deserted their wives and children;[62] others abandoned their families because their wives had refused to follow them.[63]

The Jewish court of law was a last, often efficient, resort for the maltreated wife. The halakhic authorities of every generation and region demanded that all precautions be taken so that 'the daughters of Israel should not be treated casually'.[64] The litigant wife was usually supported by her family, above all by her father. When the court seemed incapable of solving the problem, or when the problem was not restricted to marital affairs, the wife and her parents turned for assistance to the king's court.[65]

A few illustrative cases involving divorce are perhaps necessary to complete our account of marital relations. Let us first examine the cases in which the woman sued.

A frequent cause for a wife's request for divorce was simply that she could no longer bear her husband. Often the wife did not hide her distaste. In such cases, it was implied that normal sexual relations had ceased long before the couple's appearance in court. It is not, therefore, surprising that the husband was occasionally the plaintiff. According to Jewish law, a wife who refused to go to bed with her husband could be considered 'rebellious' and would forfeit some of her financial rights incorporated in the ketubah (marriage contract). Adret ruled on several cases such as these.[66] One of the problems faced by Adret and his colleagues was to decide whether the wife whose divorce case was based on her distaste for her husband and her refusal to have sexual intercourse with him, had set her eyes on another man. Such cases were very complex.[67] The Jewish courts were reluctant to facilitate such conduct on the part of a married woman.

R. Asher ben Yehiel had to decide in a divorce case where a wife was claiming that her husband was impotent. The husband retorted indignantly that not only did he possess full virility but that it was his wife who was barren.[68] Wives who had been forced into marriage had a particularly sympathetic hearing when they applied for divorce.[69]

The dayyanim were also sympathetic to wives who wished to be divorced from husbands who indulged in gambling. The problem of gambling was quite widespread in various parts of Spain, and measures taken by Christian and Jewish authorities alike proved ineffective. From a query addressed to R. Yom Tov Alsabili, it is clear that it was a serious factor in the deterioration of relations between husbands and wives. Many women turned to court to obtain a divorce from husbands who had lost most of their money in dice games. Should the court force such husbands to divorce? The Jewish authorities could not remain idle, 'since the daughters of Israel must not be abandoned as the captives of their husbands'.[70]

Wives' families sometimes resorted to unconventional means in obtaining the husbands' 'consent' to divorce. In one case two Gentile gangs were hired to terrorize the husband, who was beaten and attacked with a knife.[71]

Far fewer divorce cases initiated by husbands have come to our attention, since Jewish law enables men to divorce their wives by way of a simple procedure. The few cases that appear in the sources must have resulted from actions taken by husbands who wished to avoid the financial payment stipulated by the *ketubah*. In one such case, a husband used various methods, instigating, for instance, constant quarrels with his wife, spreading false rumours about her, and so on.[72] Another man who was in love with a woman and wished to divorce his wife, raised every possible accusation against her, including theft, the claim that she had 'blemishes', that she indulged in unnecessary conversations with a non-Jew and finally that she had committed adultery.[73]

CONCUBINES

In some parts of the Muslim world, Jews kept concubines, as did their Muslim neighbours. The custom was widely and most strongly condemned by spiritual leaders but never in mediaeval times was it completely eradicated.[74] In Spain it was quite common for Jews married to only one wife to keep concubines. This was true of both Muslim Spain and the Christian kingdoms of Castile and Aragon well into the thirteenth and fourteenth centuries. Had they kept only Jewish concubines, it might be concluded that this was largely an attempt to avoid the difficulties, and particularly the financial commitment, of a second marriage; but the fact that Jews kept Gentile concubines as well indicates that the phenomenon must be explained as part of the general sexual permissiveness of mediaeval Spain. There is little doubt that Jews, deeply involved as they were in the social, cultural and political life of the country, followed the fashions current in the wider society. Although this was most characteristic of the upper classes, the path was paved also for poorer Jews, who favoured such arrangements especially since concubines were cheaper to maintain than wives.

It is important to understand fully the workings of the institution of concubinage in the mediaeval Hispano-Jewish community. A concubine in this context would be a Gentile woman who entered into a permanent (or at least stable) relationship with a Jewish man and is known to 'belong' to him. This relationship implied, first and foremost, sexual relations. Unlike the clandestine sexual relations which Jews might have had with either Christian or Muslim women (risking, of course, the penalties prescribed by law), a concubine was usually, though not necessarily, a woman publicly known to be living with a man who was not her husband. Neither in the Muslim south nor in the Christian north could a woman who was a member of the ruling denomination be the concubine of a Jew. On either side of the border, the penalty would be extremely severe, even death.

The sources at our disposal do not refer to Muslim Spain. In Christian Spain, however, almost all the cases known are of Muslim concubines. For a Jew under Christian rule to maintain a Muslim concubine was neither an offence to Christian pride, nor strictly illegal by Christian law. (Complications did arise when Muslim concubines chose to convert to Judaism.) Many, though by no means all, were either slaves or nearly so, the product of Jewish involvement in the slave trade.[75]

In thirteenth-century Spain, and particularly in Castile, the number of Jews who kept Muslim concubines rose to an extent that considerably alarmed the rabbis. Spanish Jews were internationally known for their licence in this matter. R. Moses of Coucy, who visited Spain in 1236, was shocked and disgusted by what he saw. He wrote: 'You have thus learned that he who has sexual intercourse with a Gentile woman is considered as if he were married to idolatry . . . I have dwelt at length on this matter in my sermons delivered in the "exile of Jerusalem that is in Spain",[76] as a result of which they left their numerous Gentile women in the year (4)996 . . .'.[77] These were not the words of an unduly zealous orator, as we shall see later. The renewed *Reconquista* during the thirteenth century, in Castile under Fernando III and in the Crown of Aragon under Jaime I, added to both kingdoms a vast Muslim population which provided a large market of male and female slaves. Among the conquered and vanquished population there were now many women available for Christians (and also for Jews). Generally, the Muslim concubine was a luxury item that only the wealthy could afford.

The status of the Muslim concubine in Spain varied. In one category was the servant girl who had sexual relations with her master, and her status was the lowest. She was often bought for the purpose of satisfying sexual needs alone.[78] Typically, the Jewish master would be a married man, which is why he had to resort to the services of a Muslim concubine; in such cases the men preferred this arrangement to the expense of contracting a second marriage and was apparently less objectionable to the wife. Offspring frequently resulted from these relations and their status was problematic.[79] Sometimes Muslim concubines (though not necessarily servants) cohabited openly with

Jewish widowers who would not, of course, marry them.[80]

In the second half of the thirteenth century many members of the high society of Castilian Jewry kept Muslim servants as their mistresses. One of the élite of the Toledo community in Todros Halevi's times had a beautiful Muslim concubine with whom the poet himself had an affair which shocked the community.[81] In addition, Todros maintained intermittent relations with Muslim mistresses.[82]

In the Crown of Aragon, too, we have evidence that some Jews kept Muslim concubines, although this was less widespread than in Castile. From the correspondence between Nahmanides and R. Jonah Gerondi on the question of concubines, we may infer that Muslim concubines were not uncommon.[83] Latin documents from Aragonese and Catalan archives also show that the practice was prevalent among the Jews in north eastern Spain. Aragonese Jews engaged in the traffic of Muslim slaves, particularly female slaves,[84] so the opportunities for acquiring Muslim concubines were abundant. In 1285, Abraham de Torre, a Jew from Figueras, was accused, among other things, of having strangled two new-born babies born to him by a Muslim, while at the same time he kept a Muslim concubine at home, by whom he had several other children.[85]

As might be expected, the Spanish rabbis reacted to this type of misconduct with strong disapproval. The keeping of Muslim concubines was by no means the only practice which, they believed, had to be eradicated, but they regarded it as the most serious danger whose consequences could be devastating. The children born to a Jewish father, and a Muslim mother, if brought up by the father would present the Jewish communities with a grave social and halakhic problem.

The rabbis were also enraged by the abuse of lawful Jewish wives whose dignity and status were so blatantly undermined. Adret complains of the husband who rejected his loving lawful wife to associate with 'a hateful one'.[86]

In Castile there was even more cause for alarm. Some of the most influential communal leaders were guilty of similar offences, and their critics needed more than sheer piety and courage to wage a war against men who enjoyed considerable political and economic power. An opportunity arose in the late 1270s, when the political fortunes of the élite changed almost overnight. The internal struggle that split the royal family of Alfonso resulted in the elimination of several important Jewish figures involved in the politics of the country. The tragic downfall of Don Çag de la Maleha and many other Jewish tax collectors was seen by those who had been critical of the Jewish courtiers as a divine omen, a sign of God's displeasure with their poor standards of sexual morality.[87]

Many former courtiers were imprisoned and tortured. The poet Todros Halevi, not the only one to re-evaluate his past conduct in his prison cell, he expressed his repentance vividly in a poem sent from prison to his namesake Rabbi Todros Halevi who had been consistently preaching against immorality.[88]

The spirit of repentance and moral reform literally permeated the Jewish community of Toledo where, in 1281, a formal ban was issued against sexual immorality and in particular against those Jews who kept Muslim concubines.[89] Yet many of the penitents soon broke their vows to abandon Gentile mistresses.[90] Following their failure to abide by their promises, the spiritual leaders of Toledo consulted R. Solomon ibn Adret, who took a moderate and realistic stance, much more moderate than that of his zealous colleagues in Castile.[91]

The Toledo reformers demanded that the ban be fully obeyed and that all concubines, above all Gentile ones, be sent away. Those Jews who did not abide by the ban were threated by Rabbi Todros ben Yosef Halevi Abulafia with severe punishments. 'Because of our sins,' he said, 'so many children were born to Jews by servants.' He concluded that, 'it is not worthy of Israel, a holy nation, to render impure their seed in the womb of foreigners and to beget idolatrous (i.e. non-Jewish) children . . . '.[92] R. Moses de Leon wrote in 1292 against those who claimed that Muslim women were not idolaters; quite incorrectly, he argued, they based their claim on Islam's belief in one God, its practice of circumcision and abstinence from certain types of food.[93]

In order to regularize their childrens' status, some Jews converted their Muslim women to Judaism. Often the conversion took place after the Muslim concubine had become pregnant but before childbirth.[94] In other cases, Jews married converted concubines but gave them no *ketubah*. This was viewed as completely unacceptable by the Castilian rabbinic reformers who turned to Adret for support.[95] Yet even after conversion, the status of the child was not always clear-cut. Cecrim Abraham of Huesca, who converted his Muslim concubine around 1286, was unable to determine to the satisfaction of the rabbinic authorities the religious status of his offspring.[96]

With this background in mind, we can better understand the sometimes surprisingly tolerant attitude of some of the rabbinic authorities towards concubinage in mediaeval Spain. Their reluctant acceptance of the institution as legal must be seen as the product of sober realism and a pragmatic approach. In the view of Nahmanides, for instance, a prohibition on concubinage would have driven many men into Gentile arms and to ever more dangerous illicit sexual activities and promiscuity. Nahmanides preferred the men to be attached to no more than one woman at a time each, and to acknowledge them publicly as their concubines rather than resorting to indiscriminate relations with a number of women.[97]

In the middle of the fourteenth century, R. Nissim Gerondi was still holding similar views. In one case he defended a decision by claiming that 'she is living with him legally, raising his son while he is treating her as his concubine'.[98] He, like Nahmanides, recognized the legality of the practice of concubinage. In another case, having lived together for several years and raised a child, a man and his concubine separated at his instigation. The woman soon announced that she wished to marry the man. The question arose whether she had to wait for the prescribed three months. R. Isaac ben Sheshet Perfet wrote in a *responsum* that 'a concubine who lives with her lover is like a woman living with her husband'.[99]

Casual sexual relationships sometimes turned into lasting ones.[100] In some cases the men claimed that sexual intercourse constituted an act of betrothal.[101] Maids and their masters could enter into permanent relationships in this way. When Adret, for example, heard of a man who seduced his Jewish maid and married her as soon as he realized that she was pregnant, he angrily pronounced the matter 'an ugly affair' in which a Jewish girl was treated as a harlot.[102] Another married man who had left his maid pregnant supported her after the birth of the child but would not help pay for the baby's circumcision.[103] In 1318, Astrug Avincendut of Lérida was accused of cohabitation contrary to the *çuna* with a Jewess who bore him a daughter.[104]

Sometimes an adult son rather than the father of the family would seduce the Gentile maid. The problem would arise when the girl became pregnant and the family refused to accept her as a daughter-in-law. On one such occasion, the son acquired and furnished a house for the maid and continued his relations with her as his concubine.[105]

Finally, some Jewish women served as *barraganas* or concubines for Christians.[106]

The institution of concubinage among the Jews of Spain highlights some characteristic features of Jewish society. First and foremost, it reflects the influence of the Christian and especially the Muslim background. Secondly, it is closely connected with the social stratification of the Jews.[107] In most cases the Jewish men who kept concubines belonged to the wealthy classes while the Jewish concubines came from poor families. Many poor women preferred the status of a rich man's concubine to that of a poor Jew's wife. Lastly, the reluctant toleration of concubinage by the leading rabbis of Spain must be seen as part of their endeavour to contain and control sexual relations in general and especially between Jews and Gentile women.

PREMARITAL AND EXTRA-MARITAL SEX

According to Jewish law, sexual relations between mutually consenting unmarried Jews (or even if the man involved is married) are not punishable although they are condemned by the halakhists on moral grounds. R. Jonah Gerondi was the most outspoken opponent of such relations during this period, claiming that they fell into the category of 'making one's daughter a harlot', prohibited in the Pentateuch.[108] For him such behaviour was symptomatic of the moral degeneration of his contemporaries. Free sexual intercourse, he insisted, would inevitably lead to still more serious transgressions.

Yet such relations were prevalent in his milieu, as is attested by numerous Hebrew sources. In some cases both parties involved were single.[109] The problem became much more serious when the men were married. In some cases, married men abused Jewish domestic servants, occasionally impregnating them.The identity of these men was not always certain, since it could be contended or suspected that the girls had had intercourse with several men.[110] In some cases allegations of seduction were brought before the Gentile courts.[111] R. Isaac bar Sheshet Perfet was asked to give his opinion of a single woman who sued two other women for spreading the rumour that she was pregnant. The two women finally broke down in court and accused one another of fabricating the allegation. Asked to explain her unusual fatness (she was in fact five months pregnant) the woman attributed it to illness. In the end, she received a signed document clearing her name. Four months later she delivered a child to the astonishment of all. She now claimed that a different Jew was the father of the child. The bewildered court reopened the case. The accused man asserted that he knew the real father but that he himself was not responsible. [112]

Much more complicated were cases involving sexual relations between Jews and Gentiles. Such relations were prohibited to both sides, on legal as well as moral grounds. In his famous epistle to his son, Nahmanides warned him not to engage in sexual relations with non-Jewish women.[113] However, it was common practice among Spanish-Jewish courtiers, as is evidenced by the famous 1281 sermon of R. Todros Halevi Abulafia, who compared sexual relations with non-Jewish women to idol-worship.[114] The *Zohar* too expressed its distaste for such sexual indulgence.[115]

No less intense was the opposition to such liaisons on the Christian side. Legislation on this subject was more binding and definitive than were the Jewish communal ordinances, since it applied to both Jews and Gentiles. In the Crown of Aragon, Christian women were forbidden to sleep in the houses of Jews. Ecclesiastical influence is apparent in many of these legislations and rulings.[116] Death by burning was prescribed for both Jewish and Christian offenders.[117] Such restrictions were probably welcomed by the spiritual leadership of Aragonese Jewry, and some charters obtained by Jewish communities at their particular request included prohibitions on sexual relations between Jews and Christians. In a charter granted to the community of Catalayud in 1277, Pedro III (II of Catalonia) set a fine of 300 *maravedis* on any Christian found in bed with a Jewess in the presence of witnesses. The community was authorized to arrest him and hand him over to the authorities.[118] In regions where the Muslim population was large, royal decrees prohibited sexual relations between Saracen women and Jewish or Christian men.[119] Both Jews and Muslims were usually put to death if found in bed with Christian women. The Castilian *Las Siete Partidas* prescribed the death penalty for the cohabitation of Jews with Christian women.[120]

Life, though, took its course, and the relations between Jews and Christians none the less could develop in ways inconsistent with the laws and ordinances promulgated by the various authorities. In Castile, as the poetry of Todros Halevi reveals, Jews and Gentiles enjoyed unrestrained sexual relations despite legal restrictions which seem to have been ineffective. In Todros' circles Muslim women were readily available, as has been noted, and Todros himself had an affair with a Muslim woman who was the concubine of an important Jewish figure.[121] His poetry, particularly that dating from the period of his repentance, reveals how active he had been in his amorous relations with Gentile women, mostly Muslim servants.[122] The ban of 1281 included a strict warning against sexual relations with non-Jews;[123] from Todros' poems we are left in no doubt as to the extent of such relations. The 'sin of the Gentile woman' was widespread among the wealthy and is mentioned time and again as the reason for the downfall of the community.[124] The campaign against sexual corruption was led by the rabbis, who saw it as a primary cause of assimilation leading to a host of other transgressions. They viewed with horror the freedom of some Jews with Muslim women.[125] Although they were powerless to deal with them in the rabbinical courts, they gave a free hand to zealots who would attack the culprits if they could catch them *in flagrante delicto*.[126]

Nevertheless, in the Crown of Aragon we have much archival evidence demonstrating that sexual relations between Jews and Christians (as well as Muslims) were prevalent and the source of substantial revenue for the Crown. Many prosecutions against Jews accused of intercourse with Christian women were dismissed for lack of conclusive evidence. In a few cases of this type the royal authorities confirmed acquittals. Roven, son of Vidal of Gerona (in 1285), and Vidal Malet, a prominent member of the Barcelona community (in 1309), were among the lucky ones who were acquitted.[127] Occasionally, the king would pardon the accused on the grounds of insufficient evidence, even when the Jewish males were suspected of impregnating Christian women.[128] Absence of evidence was usually given as the reason for a royal pardon[129] which in fact would simply confirm a decision already taken by an official of the king.[130] Yet royal pardons could cost a great deal. Çulema Abinculana of Valencia, for instance, was caught with a Christian woman in his brother's shop. The lovers confessed, and Çulema had to pay 5000 *sous reals*.[131] Sexual relations with a Christian woman cost Jucef Avenhalahu of Jaca 6000 *sueldos*, with various other sexual crimes being taken into consideration as well.[132] Açach Avenecara of Tortosa was similarly fined.[133] Others were found innocent but none the less were required to pay. Belshom, son of Momet, from Besalú, against whom no evidence was found, nevertheless paid 3000 Barcelonese *sous*,[134] while Abraham, the son of Solomon Adret, was required to pay 500 Barcelonese *sous*,[135] as was Bargell, son of Açach Almozni, from Jaca, for having been falsely accused of sexual intercourse with many Christian women.[136] Astrug Caravida of Barcelona was similarly acquitted for lack of evidence, but he had to pay 900 *sous* for his royal pardon.[137]

There is also evidence of legal proceedings initiated by the royal authorities against Jews accused of carnal relations with Christians. In 1283, the Infante, Alfonso, ordered proceedings against Jews in Gerona, Barcelona and Villafranca, who were suspected of having had relations with Christian women.[138] Some time later a Jew from Saragossa was prosecuted along the same lines by the local *zalmedina* and the *alcayde*.[139] In 1290, Alfonso IV ordered the *baile* of Lérida to prosecute Abrahim Abenafio, also suspected of relations with a Christian woman.[140]

We are not in a position to determine in each case whether the accused was innocent or guilty—more often than not we possess no details of the actual process. When such details are available, we are occasionally able to reconstruct the circumstances. In 1286, Jahuda Avenbruch, from Lérida, complained to the king of Aragon that while he was in Albesen, some local inhabitants broke into the house where he was staying and brought with them a Christian woman in order falsely to accuse him of having sex with her. The case illustrates the difficulties involved in assessing the truth. It seems strange that local inhabitants should have used a Christian accomplice in this way, implicating her in a serious crime. On the other hand, Jahuda's claim that he was robbed (and the fact that the Count of Urgel used the occasion to extort form him 5000 Jaca *sueldos*) appears to substantiate his claim. So does the fact that the king subsequently ordered that the Jews of the *collecta* of Lérida be protected.[141]

Legal proceedings against Jews accused of sex with Christian women often implicated other family members, occasionally forcing the king to intervene. Family assets would be confiscated and relatives arrested,[142] and suspected or accused Jews were therefore fought over by various authorities, each claiming the right of jurisdiction over them.[143]

In nearly all the cases discussed above, a royal pardon was granted upon the payment of a certain sum, despite the fact that the penalty for sexual intercourse with Christians was death. Indeed, in the Crown of Aragon we know of only one case in which the death penalty was imposed on both the Jew and the Christian found guilty of sexual relations, and this case, in 1381, involved a nun.[144] (Sexual intercourse between Jews and Muslims in the territories of the Crown of Aragon was, unfortunately, undocumented.)[145] The royal pardon granted to so many Jews did not necessarily imply that the accusations were false: the Jew paid whether found guilty or innocent, and whether proof was considered sufficient or not. This is an interesting example of the discrepancy between legislative ideals and the realities of life: the kings of Aragon refrained from putting into effect the capital punishment which was prescribed for such sexual transgressions. because pardons were financially rewarding, and the law clearly did not act as an effective deterrent. Many Jews, unrestrained by either moral or religious considerations, continued to have sex with Gentile women. It is obvious that only a fraction of these cases was brought before the judiciary, and that enough Jews were willing to take the risk. The heavy payments exacted from those who were caught or accused would suggest that many of the transgressors were rich.

PROSTITUTION

Although available sources on the involvement of Spanish Jewesses in prostitution are few in number, they do give a good idea of the prevalence of Jewish prostitution. As we have already seen, Jews had ample opportunity to satisfy their sexual desires with either Muslim or Christian women, and there is evidence that some Jews availed themselves of the services of both Christian and Muslim prostitutes. In one of his poems, Todros Halevi did not hesitate to describe the advantages of Muslim over Christian prostitutes.[146]

There can be no doubt that there were Jewish prostitutes in Aragon and Castile. In 1283 the famous Muça de Portella complained to the *Infante* that Jewish courtesans had set up a brothel in a building near his house in Saragossa. From the same source we learn that the Jewish prostitutes did not usually reside within the Jewish quarter: the *Infante* accordingly ordered the communal leaders, the *adenantados*, to expel all prostitutes from the *judería*. In Barcelona, Jewish prostitutes were permitted to operate in Castel Nou, adjacent to the Call, as we learn from a source dating from the fourteenth century.[147]

In fourteenth-century Castile, the community was divided over the issue of Jewish prostitutes. One party was eager to eradicate prostitution from the town and expel courtesans, whom they considered the cause of immorality and sin. The other party was in favour of letting them remain, so that Jews would not need to resort to Gentile prostitutes and 'mix the holy seed in Gentile women'.[148] This second group assumed, then, that Jews needed (or would inevitably seek) the services of public women. Their opponents were the reformers who were shocked to see Jewish girls turning to prostitution. The very idea horrified rabbinic leaders,[149] not least because the existence of Jewish prostitutes implied the involvement of other Jews serving as agents and intermediaries between the girls and their customers. Some Jews performed the same function for Christian prostitutes and their clients. Jahuda Aladef from Valencia was in 1304 acccused of pimping for Christians and was expelled from the *judería*.[150]

The most vivid and significant evidence of Jewish prostitution comes from the pen of R. Isaac 'Arama, one generation before the Expulsion. Having served as a preacher in several Spanish communities, he was in a good position to describe the conditions prevailing in various regions. He confessed that he was often troubled by the presence of Jewish prostitutes who were treated leniently in the Jewish courts. Some communities had even arranged for general pardons, while others compensated accused prostitutes out of public funds, arguing that such women saved men from sinning with married women. (Adultery was by far the more serious crime from the Jewish legal point of view.) R. Isaac 'Arama informs us that he frequently debated the matter with Jewish communal leaders, explaining to them that a grave sin, if committed privately by an individual without the knowledge or blessing of the public, remained punishable by Heaven, while a lesser sin if committed with the connivance of the public, was an abomination and a crime for which the entire community was responsible. R. Isaac Arama concluded that in order that no aspect of the Torah should be transgressed with the tacit consent of the public, transgressors should be cut, burned and stoned.[151]

ADULTERY

Fears for the safety of their daughters and (especially) their wives led some Jews to advocate the legalization of prostitution in Jewish communities. Such fears were not unfounded. Sexual laxity among Spanish Jews resulted in some cases of adultery in the technical Jewish legal sense (that is, illicit sexual relations with married women). The sources indicate that adultery in Hispano-Jewish society was more frequent than elsewhere in the mediaeval Jewish world.

Hebrew sources make it clear that in some circles men and women did not adhere to the rule forbidding them to be alone with one another. The relaxation of such restrictions could be (and sometimes was) the first step leading to adultery. Suspicions of tête-à-tête encounters between married men and women were often substantiated in this rather lax milieu.[152]

Some men were not deterred by the fact that the women they pursued were married. Complaints by married women of harassment were frequently heard in the courts of law. For instance, late in the fourteenth century, Aljohar, wife of R. Ya'akov ben Josef complained before the Beth Din of Alcira that Yishaq Cohen had been pestering her with his declarations of love. He would die, he said, if she did not give in to him, and he begged her for at least one kiss. On false pretences he invited her to come to his house. She told the court that he had had affairs with married women and had been warned six years previously by the *berurim* (judges) about his flirtation with R. Samuel Peniel's wife. When asked by the *berurim* why she had not turned to the Beth Din earlier, she said she wanted to spare her husband embarrassment.[153]

Men suspected of committing adultery with married women were sometimes brought to court on the basis of such rumours. The suspect's confession would automatically implicate the woman.[154] The implications were, of course, quite serious. If, for example, the husband of a woman suspected of adultery had died and the suspected man wished to marry her, grave legal complications arose, since a couple guilty of such relations is not permitted to marry under Jewish law.[155]

Women suspected of adulterous relations were often brought to trial by their husbands.[156] The *responsa* literature offers extraordinary details relating to such accusations. In one case, brought to Adret's attention, a young husband claimed that he had seen his wife walking towards a young man and then heard from behind a wall voices and heavy breathing which proved to him the two were engaging in sex. On another night, when his wife was late to bed, he had earlier overheard the sound of breathing which suggested to him that someone was having sexual intercourse with his wife in his own house. He said he often rebuked her for her conduct, but to no avail. He confessed that although he loved her, she would not change her ways, and would only have sex with him unwillingly.[157] In another case the husband claimed that one night, as he came to bed holding a candle, he found his wife there with a naked Gentile man hiding under the bed. There followed a violent struggle between the two men. The intruder disappeared leaving behind his trousers and a shirt which the woman, who was a dressmaker, claimed she had been given for repairs. The husband later admitted that the man might have been a burglar or a rapist. The couple resumed their normal life until they moved to Lérida where the *berurim*, engaged in religious and moral reforms, asked the husband to confess whether he had ever suspected his wife of adultery in which case she would be forbidden to him by Jewish law. After changing his versions several times, he finally declared that he had never doubted her.[158]

Complaints about the immoral conduct of married women were so numerous that they cannot all be ascribed to the jealousy of husbands. At times the allegations were simply too easily verifiable.[159] The misbehaviour of a married woman who lived with her husband in the house of one of her relatives in Villafranca was another case brought to the attention of Adret. The landlord was well known for his violence and sexual immorality. He attempted several times to initiate an affair with his relative, but when this failed he accused her of adulterous relations with others; the husband warned his wife to stay away from the man. A month later he noticed that his wife was looking for every pretext to be in the company of her relative. His admonishments were to no avail. He found her in her relative's room making his bed, something which she had never done in her own home, always offering excuses which the husband could not verify without showing that he suspected her of immoral conduct. When at last he sought legal advice in another town, and the rabbis allowed him to remain with his wife, he was very happy and eager to return. On the way back he met a group of travellers who told him that as soon as he had left the town, his wife moved in with her relative for eight days and nights. They were alone in the house except for his young children and a Gentile maid. The wife subsequently claimed she had gone to look after the small children. The desperate husband abandoned her for two years, during which time she had several scandalous affairs with various men, some of them married. Finally she was suspected of being pregnant. The husband did not have conclusive evidence of this, and asked Adret whether or not he could divorce her against her will in the lack of such evidence.[160]

The records at our disposal indicate that the incidence of adultery was high.[161] Isaac Xaprut and Abraham Camis from Valencia both lived with married women and had to pay large sums of money to obtain a royal pardon.[162] A man who was surprised in bed by his partner's husband, admitted publicly that he had had sexual relations with the woman on numerous occasions.[163] Another Jew from Seville took up with a married woman, and they posed as a married couple.[164] Some thoroughly unprincipled men lived openly with married women of their fancy, fearing neither the reactions of the abandoned husbands nor the condemnation of the Jewish community. Such was Moshe Vidal from Murviedro, who maintained an adulterous relation with a married woman and, when warned, expressed his contempt for the Mosaic law which, he said, he transgressed quite knowingly.[165]

The most tragic aspect of adultery in Jewish law is the status of the offspring: the *mamzer* in Jewish law is not the bastard of Christian society who is simply the illegitimate child of an unmarried couple. *Mamzerim* encountered halakhic complications when they wished to marry, and their rights as heirs were frequently contested.[166] Adultery in Jewish law is far more specific than the equivalent Christian concept: sex outside marriage counts as adulterous only when the woman involved is already married.[167] Adultery, included in the general category of 'incest', was one of the three major transgressions which Jews were required to die rather than commit; the fact that it occurred among Spanish Jews with such frequency reflected widespread sexual laxity.

ILLEGAL MARRIAGES AND INCESTUOUS RELATIONS

In general, marriages forbidden by Jewish law fall into two categories, very different in degrees of gravity. There are those which are forbidden *a principio* but, once contracted, are considered valid, while others are never held valid and such marriages if contracted are automatically null.

The marriage of a *Cohen* (a man descended from the priestly tribe) to either a divorcée or a convert belongs to the former type. Despite its illegality, the marriage, once contracted, is considered valid, and all that the Jewish authorities can do is to press for a divorce. The children born of such a union are not considered *Cohanim*. Spanish rabbis debated the various means by which they could register their displeasure with the rebellious family. The father, for instance, would not be called up to the reading of the Law as a *Cohen*, even though he was technically still considered a *Cohen*.[168] On the other hand, in Castile, up until the Expulsion, some communities found the means of abrogating legally contracted marriages, in order to allow abandoned wives (*agunot*) to remarry lawfully.[169]

In the second category we have the most serious sexual crime according to Jewish law—incestuous relations between close relatives. These relations are neither sanctioned nor tolerated under any circumstances.

We have already discussed a case involving the possibly incestuous relations between a Jew and his sister-in-law.[170] In another instance, Adret questioned a young *Cohen* who was suspected of incest on the basis of the testimony of a woman. The accused fled but later confessed his crime before a rabbi.[171] In 1310, King Jaime II granted amnesty in return for a very heavy fine to Açach Avenecara, from Tortosa, who was accused of various crimes, including illicit relations with his daughter-in-law.[172]

RAPE

In a commmunity where physical violence and sexual permissiveness were widespread, rape naturally occurred. Significantly, the sources dealing with Jewish rapists are all Latin archival records: the Hebrew sources are totally silent on this issue. This is due to the nature of the crime and to the fact that the Crown usually reserved to itself the right to prosecute rapists.

When, in 1279, Jucef Contatxich from Calatayud was brought to trial for raping a local Jewess whom he had removed from her home by force, he claimed that he had been deprived of his right to see the witnesses taking the oath and a copy of the investigation. King Pedro III ordered the judge to proceed in accordance with the law, and to check the complaints of the accused.[173] In 1293, Astrug Caravida, from Villafranca, was prosecuted for various crimes, of which one was the rape of Bonafilia, the daughter of Druda.[174] Jucef Xaprut, from Valencia, was accused in 1302 of having raped and injured a married woman. He was required to pay an indemnity to the king and his case was dropped.[175] The same man was prosecuted for many other crimes, including a sexual assault on a young Jewess. Jaime II decided to deal with him mercifully and he was required to pay 2000 *sous reals*.[176] Abraham Camis, another Jew from Valencia, was prosecuted for a number of crimes, including the attempted rape of a Jewess in the city's public bath.[177] There is reason to suspect that political and financial interests often lay behind the charges, and the trials were usually interrupted after the payment of a handsome fine. It is not surprising, therefore, that many Jews were unhappy with the methods employed by the royal courts and there was widespread disapproval of Jews who referred to the Christian courts cases of rape involving fellow-Jews.[178]

The absence of sources should not mislead us into thinking that the Jewish judiciary was not organized to deal with rapists. We have sufficient evidence to show that the Jewish courts of law had their own procedure and penalties for Jewish rapists, and these were more stringent than the methods used by Christian courts: torture and other forms of corporal punishment were used. In 1281, Pedro III instructed his *baile* and *zalmedina* in Huesca to check whether in the case of Assach Alcutavi, who had raped Gemila, they had been consulted by the *adelantados* of the community. If the penalty prescribed by Jewish law was more severe than the *fuero*, they should, he said, apply the penalty according to Jewish law.[179]

HOMOSEXUALS

Homosexuality was very widespread in Muslim Spain and by no means rare in the Christian north.[180] Arabic poetry of the period is sufficient to give some idea of the extent of homosexual practice in Andalusia. However, homosexual life knew no political or religious boundaries, and involved Muslims, Christians and Jews.

In a *responsum* from Spain we read about a cantor (*hazan*), who was a *Cohen* and who maintained illicit sexual relations with non-Jewish prostitutes, with Jewish women and also with a boy. He was eventually removed from office.[181] The Hebrew poetry of Muslim Spain is our standard source on homosexuality among the Jews. Some of the poems by well-known Hebrew poets from the Muslim period contain clear references to love between males, often with young boys.[182]

On homosexual relations in Castile we learn from Todros' poetry. In a poem he dedicates to R. Shlomo ben Abudarham, he makes clear reference to the advantages of young men over women.[183] In the Crown of Aragon homosexuals, or those accused of homosexual relations, were tried and often pardoned for a sum of money. Alaçar, grandson of Vives de Limoux from Lérida, was thus pardoned by the king in 1263. It was reported that two Jews had falsely accused him of homosexual relations;[184] two days later the king issued an order to all his officials and subjects, to consider all testimonies against Alaçar null and void, but apparently, David Avendayan and others did not give up their attempts to incriminate Alaçar.[185] In 1274, Vives, son of Jucef Abenvives, *baile* of Affandech and Marines, was accused of corruption and sodomy by a group of Jews and a Saracen. In 1328 three Jews of Alagón were released at the order of Alfonso IV, after having been accused of sodomy, and in 1374 a Jew was burned to death for his homosexual liaisons.[186] There is evidence that while young boys were often the object of adult male desire, there were also youngsters who engaged in sexual relations among themselves. In one of Adret's *responsa* we are told of two youngsters, eleven and twelve years old, who were accused by some twenty Gentile witnesses of having had sexual relations with one another.[187]

The evidence presented shows how deeply the Jews of Spain were influenced by their larger milieu. Jews, Christians and Muslims responded differently to various situations as a result of their distinct cultural and religious traditions, but they all shared a wide range of common sensibilities, including sexual mores, which were governed by their social and economic status. Despite the fact that family affairs and sexual relations could be an area almost entirely controlled by Jewish law and traditions, sexual behaviour among the Jews was much influenced by the standards which prevailed in the society at large. Virtually all sexual practices found among Spanish Jews have their parallels in non-Jewish society.[188]

Sexual laxity was prevalent among Jews of all classes.[189] It is, however, undeniable that it was particularly widespread among members of the upper social stratum, just as it was among their non-Jewish counterparts. Jewish translators, diplomats, financiers and others in the royal service[190] found it extremely difficult to observe the precepts of Judaism. Nahmanides' famous letter to his son who was stationed at the Castilian court,[191] and R. Menahem ben Aharon ben Zerah's desire to write a compendium of Jewish law for Jewish courtiers[192] are only two of many other indications that, from the Jewish point of view, courtly life, away from the Jewish community and in the midst of a rarefied non-Jewish milieu, was extremely risky. Prolonged stays at court led to the gradual neglect of religious observance,[193] and it was the élite of Jewish society that was most exposed to this risk.[194] Sexual laxity was one step along the way. In these ways Jewish society in the Iberian peninsula anticipated some of the problems and challenges that would later characterize modern Jewish life.

Notes

Abbreviations

ACA	Archivo de la Corona de Aragón, Barcelona
Adret I	R. Shlomo ibn Adret, *Sheelot u-Teshuvot*, vol. I (Bologna, 1539)
II, III	*ibid.*, vols. II, & III (Leghorn, 1657, 1778)
IV	*ibid.*, vol. IV (Vilna, 1881)
V	*ibid.*, vol. V (Leghorn, 1825)
VI, VII	*ibid.*, vol. VI & VII (Warsaw, 1868)
VIII	*Teshuvot R. Shlomo ibn Adret ha-meyuhasot Le R. Moshe ben Nahman (Warsaw, 1883). (Adret's responsa* attributed to Nahmanides.)
Al Asabili	R. Yom Tov ben Abraham Al Asabili, *Sheelot u-Teshuvot*, ed. Y. Kapah (Jerusalem, 1959)
Alfasi	R. Isaac Alfasi, *Sefer Sheelot u-Teshuvot* (Leghorn, 1781)
Asher	R. Asher ben Yehiel, *Sheelot u-Teshuvot* (Venice, 1607)
Baer II	F. Baer, *Die Juden im christlichen Spanien*, II, *Kastilien, Inquisitionsakten* (Berlin, 1936)
CR	Cartas Reales
f	folio
Ibn Megash	R. Josef ha-Levi ibn Megash, *Sefer Sheelot u-Teshuvot* (Salonica, 1791)
Jacobs	J. Jacobs, *An Inquiry into the Sources of the History of the Jews in Spain* (London, 1894) (follows no. of document)
Gerondi	R. Nissim b. Reuben Gerondi, *Sheelot u-Teshuvot*, ed. L.A. Feldman (Jerusalem, 1984)
Perfet	R. Isaac ben Sheshet Perfet, *Sefer Sheelot u-Teshuvot* (Lvov, 1805)
R	Registro
Régné	J. Régné, *History of the Jews in Aragon, Regesta and Documents 1211-1327*, ed. Yom Tov Assis (Jerusalem, 1978) (re-edition of Régné's *Catalogue* in *REJ* 1910–1925) (follows no. of document)
Zikhron Yehuda	R. Yehuda ben Asher, *Zikhron Yehuda* (Berlin, 1846)

1 This tendency drew its inspiration from Matthew 19:12; 24:19; Luke 21:23.

2 J. L. Flandrin, *Le sexe et l'occident. Evolution des attitudes et des comportements* (Paris, 1981), p. 106.

3 See *ibid.*, 'Contraception, mariage et relations amoureuses dans l'occident chrétien', *Annales d'Economies Sociétés et Civilisations* (= E.S.C.) vol. 24 (1969) pp. 1370–90. Until the eleventh century the popular mode of contraception (*coitus interruptus*) drew very little attention. The tendency was to punish the scandalous results of illicit relations rather than the actual prohibited act. See H. Bergues, *La prévention des naissances dans la famille* (1960), p. 209 and Flandrin, *Le sexe* . . . (note 2 above), p. 114. From the twelfth century onwards the Church's legislation against contraception became more frequent and is to be found in the *Decretum* of Gratian, the *Sentences* of Peter Limbard, the *Decretals* of Raymundus de Penyaforte, the *Commentaries on the Sentences* and the *Summa Theologiae* of Thomas Aquinas. The subject is fully treated in J. T. Noonan, *Contraception, History of its Treatment by the Catholic Theologians and Canonists* (Cambridge, Mass, 1966).

4 The sources referring to punishments prescribed for sexual transgressions by clerics cannot be pure fiction. See J. p. Migne, *Patrologia Latina*, vol. 99, cols. 1971–2.

5 J. L. Flandrin, *Familles, parenté, maison, sexualité dans l'ancienne société* (Paris, 1976), pp. 176–8. The prohibition on keeping a concubine had very little effect in reality,

and the number of 'bastards' in the Middle Ages was very high. Despite various limitations imposed on them in several regions, some reached high positions. The most obvious example is, of course, William the Conqueror.

6 For a description of clerical behaviour see J. F. O'Callaghan, *A History of Medieval Spain* (Ithaca and London, 1975), p. 631 and J. N. Hillgarth, *The Spanish Kingdoms 1250–1516*, vol. I (Oxford 1976), pp. 111–13 and the sources quoted there.

7 Flandrin, (note 2 above), pp. 283–4; *ibid.*, (note 5 above), p. 184; J. Rossiand, 'Prostitution, jeunesse et société dans les villes du Sud-Est au XVe siècle', *Annales E.S.C.*, vol. 31 (1976) pp. 289–325.

8 G. H. Bousquet, *L'Ethique sexuelle de l'Islam* (Paris, 1966) (a new edition of *La Morale de l'Islam et son éthique sexuelle*); A. Bouhdiba, *La Sexualité en Islam* (Paris, 1975); M. Berge, *Les Arabes* (Paris, 1978), pp. 526–39.

9 E. Lévi Provençal, *Histoire de l'Espagne musulmane*, vol. 3 (Paris, 1953), pp. 444–51. Republished in Spanish in R. Menendez Pidal (ed.), *Historia de España*, vol. 5, *España musulmana* (Madrid, 1957), pp. 288–92.

10 In general see I. Abrahams, *Jewish Life in the Middle Ages* (3rd edn, New York, 1975), pp. 86–92, 113–23, 163–210, L. M. Epstein, *Sex Laws and Customs in Judaism* (New York, 1967); for Ashkenazi Jewry see J. Katz, 'Marriage and Sexual Life among the Jews at the Close of the Middle Ages', (Hebrew), *Zion*, vol. 10 (1945), pp. 21–54; for the Jews under Islam see S. D. Goitein, *A Mediterranean Society*, vol. 3. *The Family* (Berkeley–Los Angeles–London, 1978), pp. 142–79, 189–212. On relations of Jews with their slaves or servants in Muslim lands see M. A. Friedman, *Jewish Polygyny in the Middle Ages* (Hebrew) (Jerusalem, 1986), pp. 291–339.

11 An English translation of Judah Halevi's two songs is to be found in D. Goldstein, *Hebrew Poems from Spain* (London, 1965), pp. 99, 119.

12 Adret I, 1219. The *responsum* sent to the community of Saragossa deals with the annulment of a young woman's marriage on grounds of minority. Her father had previously claimed that she had attained her majority.

13 See, for example, Abrahams (note 10 above), pp. 86–7, 164–5; A. Neuman, *The Jews in Spain*, vol. 2 (Philadelphia, 1944), pp. 8–11. On Neuman's attempt to dismiss R. Moses of Coucy's remarks about the relations between Spanish Jews and Gentile women, see note 77 below. For an attempt to excuse Zabara's anti-feminine remarks see I. Abrahams, 'Joseph Zabara and his "Book of Delight"', *JQR*, vol. 6 (1894), pp. 505–6.

14 Poem no. 390, verse 82. The references are to the *Diwan of Todros son of Yehuda Abu-l-Afiah Gan Hammeshalim we-hahidoth*, ed. D. Yellin, 2 parts, 3 vols (Jerusalem, 1932, 1934, 1936). The edition was prepared from the autograph copy of Saul Joseph which was reproduced by M. Gaster under the same title (= *The Garden of Apologues and Saws*, London, 1926). Yellin changed the sequence of the poems. For a full historical treatment of Todros' poems see Y. Baer, 'Todros ben Judah Halevi and his Time' (Hebrew), *Zion*, vol. 2 (1937), pp. 19–55 and *ibid.*, *A History of the Jews in Christian Spain*, vol. I (Philadelphia 1966), pp. 236–42.

15 Poem no. 433, ll. 71, 74–6

16 Poems no. 714, ll. 15–24; no. 715, ll. 8, 30–1.

17 Poem no. 595. Written during a spell of harsh royal measures against the Jews, the poem, which is preceded by an introduction found in Yellin's notes to it, supplies detailed descriptions of the spirit of repentance that swept through the Jewish community of Toledo in 1280.

18 *Zikhron Yehuda*, no. 91

19 Adret, I, 1209. For further examples of fraudulent marriages and false claims see Adret, I, 706, 774, 1210; VII, 221.

20 ACA, R13, f 157 (= Régné 250). Surprisingly, Jaime I pardoned the imposter

Jahuda Albala who claimed that he only pretended to have married Mira, the daughter of Jucef Almuli, from Valencia, in order to prevent her marriage to someone else, not to make any spurious allegations against her.

21 Adret, VII, 58

22 Gerondi, 62

23 Adret, III, 211 and see note 12 above.

24 Adret, IV, 174

25 Adret, VII, 421. The halakhic difficulties grew when the brother-in-law wanted to marry someone else; see Adret, VIII, 123.

26 Adret, VIII, 135, for the case of a Jew in Navarre who was fined for having relations with a woman prior to the marriage ceremony in synagogue: see Archivo General de Navarra, Caja 8, no. 22.

27 On polygamy among Jews in general see Friedman, (note 10 above); on Spain see Y. Assis, 'The "Ordinance of Rabbenu Gershom" and Polygamous Marriages in Spain' (Hebrew), *Zion*, vol. 46 (1981), pp. 251–77 (Hebrew); Baer, *A History* (note 14 above), vol. 1, pp. 254–6; S. Z. Havlin, 'The Takkanot of Rabbenu Gershon Me'or ha-Golah on Family Law in Spain and Provence (in the Light of Manuscripts of *Responsa* of RASHBA and R. Isaac de-Molina)' (Hebrew), *Shenaton ha-Mishpat ha-Ivri*, vol. 2 (1975), pp. 200–57.

28 For requests to the king to permit bigamous marriages see Assis (note 27 above) and ACA, Caja 134, No. 211. The following Hebrew sources belonging to the latter part of the fourteenth century are worth noting: Perfet, 91, 107, 145, 179, 208, 509.

29 For sources see Abrahams (note 10 above), pp. 87–8.

30 Alfasi, 151

31 Alfasi, 282

32 Adret, VIII, 104

33 Adret, IV, 169

34 Ibn Megash, 139

35 Adret, I, 572

36 Al-Asabili, 43. For reasons which are not pertinent to our subject, the three rabbis agreed that the woman's oath could be declared null. On the sexual experiences of old husbands and young wives in a Catalan satirical wedding-poem, see note 50 below.

37 Asher, VIII, 8

38 Adret, II, 244

39 Alfasi, 129

40 Adret, I, 854

41 Gerondi, 13

42 Gerondi, 62

43 On this subject in general see N. Rakover, 'Coercive Marital Relations between a Man and his Wife' (Hebrew), *Shenaton ha-Mishpat ha-Ivri*, vols. 6–7 (1979–80), pp. 295–317.

44 Adret, IV, 122

45 Adret, I, 628

46 Asher, VIII, 7. For the biblical prohibition on remarrying one's divorced wife after she had been married to someone else, see *Deuteronomy* 24:1–4.

47 Alfasi, 151

48 See, for example, Adret, VIII, 270.

49 Alfasi, 73

50 M. Lazar, 'Catalan–Provençal Wedding Songs (14th–15th centuries)' (Hebrew), in *Hayyim (Jefim) Schirman Jubilee Volume* (Jerusalem, 1970), pp. 159–77.

51 On this subject see Y. Assis, 'Crime and Violence among the Jews of Spain (13th–

14th centuries)' (Hebrew), in *Zion Jubilee Volume*, vol. 50 (1986), pp. 221–40.

52 *Zikhron Yehuda*, 78 (f. 27 recto)
53 If he was brought to court, this was because he was accused of more than just beating. See, for example, Alfasi, 176.
54 Adret, V, 264
55 Adret, VII, 477
56 Adret, VIII, 102
57 Adret, IV, 113
58 Alfasi, 28, 185
59 Alfasi, 28, 120
60 Ibn Megash, 122; Alfasi, 67
61 Alfasi, 120
62 Adret, VIII, 146
63 Adret, V, 204; VIII, 267
64 Gerondi, 43
65 ACA, CR, Jaime II, Caja 134, no. 198
66 Adret, VI, 73; VIII, 134, 138
67 Adret, VI, 72
68 Asher, XLIII, l; LXIII, 2
69 See note 64 above.
70 Al-Asabili, 122. Cf. also 146. I treat the subject of Jewish gamblers in Spain in a forthcoming paper.
71 Adret, I, 573
72 Adret, VIII, 133
73 Adret, I, 1237. See also note 72 above.
74 See S. D. Goitein, 'Slaves and Slavegirls in the Cairo Geniza Records', *Arabica*, vol. 9 (1962), pp. 1–20; S. Stober, 'On Two Questions Posed to R. Abraham b. Maimonides (concerning Servant-Concubines)' (Hebrew), *Shenaton ha-Mishpat ha-Ivri*, vols. 6–7 (1979–80), pp. 339–403; see also the literature cited above, note 10.
75 I am currently preparing a study of the 'Jewish Slave Trade in Medieval Spain' which I hope to publish in the near future.
76 This is a quotation from Obadiah, verse 20, associated with the Jews of Spain since a very early age. The word for Spain in the Biblical verse is *Sefarad*. See S. Krauss, 'The Names Ashkenaz and Sefarad' (Hebrew), *Tarbiz*, vol. 3 (1932), pp. 423–35.
77 R. Moses of Coucy, *Sefer Mitsvot ha-Gadol* (= *The Major Book of Commandments*), Prohibition (i.e. Negative Commandment) 112, no. 3 at the end.
78 '. . . Reuven married a wife . . . then his passion overcame him and he bought a servant who conceived by him without being wedded to him . . . After the delivery, he did not separate from her . . . ' Ms. Oxford 2550, Gittin no. 71, p. 211 = Adret, I, 1205; Havlin (note 27 above), pp. 237–8, *responsum* no. V.
79 'He who has a servant who bore him a son whom he treats as his child . . . this son shall inherit him, although he cannot marry a Jewish woman until he brings proof that his mother had been emancipated . . . ' Adret, I, 1183.
80 Adret, I, 26
81 *Diwan of Todros* (see note 14 above), poem no. 433
82 *ibid.*, Poem 542
83 Adret, VIII, 284
84 See, for example, Y. Assis, *The Jews of Santa Coloma de Queralt* (Jerusalem, 1988), documents XI, XIX. Régné 46, 101, 177, 433, 562, 620, 687 = XI, 792, 1097, 1401, 1479 = XX, 1617, 1918, 1996, 2516, 2528, 2892, 2919, 3246, XVI; S. Assaf, 'Slavery and the Slave-Trade among the Jews during the Middle Ages' (Hebrew), *Zion*, vol. 4 (1939), pp. 106 ff.

85   ACA, R62, f 136verso-137 (= Régné 1316 = XV)
86   See note 78 above
87   On these events see Baer (note 14 above), vol. 1, pp. 129 ff.
88   *Diwan of Todros* (see note 14 above), poem no. 422
89   *ibid.*, poem no. 595
90   *ibid.*, poems nos. 540–3
91   Adret, V, 238–43
92   See note 18 above. On R. Todros Abulafia being the author of this source see Baer,
      'Todros' (note 14 above), p. 40, n. 51. See also the passages quoted from the *Zohar*
      and the *Ra'aya Mehemna*, *ibid.*, p. 43.
93   R. Moses de Leon in his *The Holy of Holies* (*Kodesh ha-Kodashim*), quoted by Baer,
      'Todros' (note 14 above), p. 44.
94   Adret, I, 1205
95   Adret, V, 242
96   ACA, R 67, f 1 (= Régné 1543)
97   See note 83 above. On R. Jonah Gerondi's opposition to concubinage see his *Shaare
      Teshuva* (= *Gates of Repentance*), ch. 43, 94, 131–3.
98   Gerondi, 68
99   Perfet, 217. From the statement in another *responsum* that a man was treating a
      married woman 'as if she were his wife or concubine' it is clear that concubinage
      was well established at the end of the fourteenth century. See Perfet, 351.
100 Asher, XVII, 7; XXXII, 1; XXXV, 2, 10; Gerondi, 42. However, the opposite could
      also occur, when a man would leave his long-standing concubine who had borne
      him a child and decide to marry someone else. See Asher, XVII, 7.
101 Asher, XLIV, 8
102 Adret, IV, 314
103 Adret, I, 610
104 ACA, R 216, f 55verso (= Régné 3091)
105 Gerondi, 68
106 Baer, II, no. 163
107 On the structure of Jewish society in Spain see Y. Assis, 'Social Unrest and Class
      Struggle in Hispano-Jewish Society before the Expulsion' (Hebrew), in J. Dan (ed.),
      History and Culture, (Jerusalem, 1987), pp. 121–45.
108 R. Jonah Gerondi, *Sha'are Teshuva*, part III, ch. 94. He relied on Leviticus 19:29: 'Do
      not degrade your daughter, making her a harlot, lest the land fall into harlotry and
      the land be filled with depravity', and on the *Babylonian Talmud*, *Sanhedrin*, 76a (for
      an English translation see *The Soncino Talmud*, *Seder Nezikin* , vol. 3 (London, 1935),
      p. 516).
109 Adret, VII, 55. The *responsum* which Perfet sent to the rabbi of Huesca, R. Isaac
      Attinsi, seems to confirm this. The question was whether the prohibition on sexual
      relations with a menstruating woman applied also to a single woman. See Perfet,
      425.
110 Adret, I, 610
111 For the case of Astrug Avincendut, who in 1318 tried to seduce his friend's daughter
      who had been entrusted to him, see ACA, R 216, f 55verso (= Régné 3091)
112 Perfet, 41
113 '... whoever goes astray with Gentile women desecrates the covenant of Abraham .
      . . ' H. D. Chavel, *Kitvei Rabenu Moshe ben Nahman*, vol. I (Jerusalem, 1964)
      (= 5724), p. 370.
114 *Zikhron Yehuda*, 91
115 *The Zohar*, Exodus, III, 2, 3a and b, and see *Zikhron Yehuda*, 92
116 See for example, E.C. Girbal, *Los judíos en Gerona* (Gerona, 1870), p. 65: 'Mandantes

vobis vicariis, baiulis et judicibus ea districcione qua possumus ut hoc statutum et illud quod fecimus de Christianis mulieribus Judeis non cohabitandis . . . ' (1229).

117 In April 1394, the following decree was proclaimed in Valencia by Juan I: 'si algun dels dits Juheus sera atrobat amb fembra crestiana en loch sospitos per haver copla carnal ab ella, que sien abdost cremats sens tota merce.' Sanpere y Miguel, *Las costumbres catalanas en tiempo de Juan I* (Barcelona 1878), p. 279.

118 ACA, R39, f 155 recto-verso (= Régné 674 and Document X)

119 In 1283 such a decree was issued for the Saracens of Játiva. See ACA, R 61, f 101verso (= Régné 1045 = J.E. Martínez Ferrando, *Catálogo de la documentación relativa al antiguo reino de Valencia*, vol. 2, Madrid, 1934, no. 1726).

120 *Las Siete Partidas* VII, 24, 9, published in Baer II, no. 63, p. 48.

121 *Diwan of Todros* (see note 14 above), poem no. 433

122 ibid., poems nos 715, 422

123 ibid., poem no. 595

124 ibid., poem no. 602

125 *Zikhron Yehuda*, 91

126 ibid., 63

127 For the acquittal of Roven of sexual relations with many Christian women, see ACA, R 62, f 128verso (= Régné 1289); Vidal Malet was accused together with Escapat Açach, the secretary of the community, of having had relations with many Christian women, ACA, R 206, f 32 (= Régné 2898, 2899).

128 ACA, R 12, f 93 (= Jacobs 236 = Régné 200)

129 ACA, R12, f 96verso (= Jacobs 239 = F. Bofarull y Sans, *Los judíos en el territorio de Barcelona*, Barcelona, 1911, XXXII = Régné 206); ACA, R20 f 302 (= Jacobs 603 = Régné 646).

130 ACA, R20, f 226 (= Régné 619)

131 ACA, R12, f 24 (= Régné 189 = Martínez Ferrando, *Catalogo* . . . , I, 453)

132 ACA, R 203. f 150verso-151 (= Régné 2855)

133 ACA, R 207, f 154 (= Régné 2915)

134 ACA, R37, f 38verso (= Régné 510)

135 ACA, R 21, f 31recto-verso (= Jacobs 632 = Régné 515). It is noteworthy that the person involved was the namesake of the son of the famous R. Solomon, son of Abraham ibn Adret.

136 ACA, R 199, f 102, 126 (= Régné 2788; 2795)

137 ACA, R203, f 201 (= Régné 2861)

138 ACA, R 60, f 42verso (= Régné 1029)

139 ACA, R 61, f 162 (= Régné 1074)

140 ACA, R 81, f 39verso (= Régné 2065)

141 ACA, R 70, f 23 (= Régné 1693 = XXI, pp. 439–40)

142 See, for example, ACA, R88, f 207 (= Régné 2517)

143 ACA, R 89, f 124verso (= Régné 2588)

144 J. Villanueva, *Viage Literaio a las iglesias de España* (Madrid, 1803–52), vol. 21, p. 219; A. Morel-Fatio, 'Notes et documents pour servir à l'histoire des Juifs des Baléares sous la domination aragonaise du XIIIe au XVe siècle', *REJ*, vol. 4 (1882), no. 22, p. 37.

145 The case of Abraham de Torre, from Figueras, accused with his son of numerous crimes and atrocities, was quite exceptional. He was the man said to have suffocated two babies born to him by a Muslim woman. See note 85 above.

146 *Diwan* (see note 14 above), poem no. 721

147 For the prostitutes in Saragossa, see ACA R 61, f 134 (= Régné 1053); for the establishment of Jewish prostitutes in Castel Nou see ACA, R 953, f 64verso. The latter source was brought to my attention by Mr J. Riera whom I should like to thank.

148 *Zikhron Yehuda*, 17
149 See, for example, Adret, I, 1210
150 ACA, R 202, f 204 (= Régné 2832)
151 R. Isaac 'Arama, *Sefer Akedat Yitshak* (= *The Book of the Sacrifice of Isaac*) (Pressburg, 1849), 'Genesis', ch. 20, p. 145
152 Alfasi, 136; Adret, V, 241
153 Perfet, 265
154 Adret, I, 596; VII, 222
155 Adret, I, 1177
156 Adret, I, 557
157 Adret, I, 832
158 Adret, I, 1187
159 Adret, I, 557; 1250
160 Havlin (note 27 above), pp. 219–33. The *responsum* without the details of the question is to be found in Adret, I, 557. I see no reason to accept Havlin's suggestion that the question was sent to Adret from Villefranche-de-Conflent in southern France (to be precise, Roussillon). It could have been sent from Villafranca del Panadés, or Villafranca de Ampurias. While they were under Aragonese (or Majorcan) rule, they were each known as Villafranca.
161 In Castile the situation was essentially the same. There were women who committed adultery while their husbands were away. One woman did not deny that she had become pregnant as a result of such an adulterous liaison. See *Zikhron Yehuda*, 80 (f. 29verso); 88.
162 ACA, R 199, f 34verso (= Régné 2770); ACA, R 268verso–269 (= Régné 3084)
163 Adret, I, 1249
164 Adret, V, 240
165 Perfet, 351
166 Adret, II, 219
167 See note 150 above and also ACA, R202 f 212 (= Régné 2835)
168 Adret, VII, 21
169 Y. M. Toledano, 'Conditional Marriage and the Abrogation of Marriage' (Hebrew), in *Otsar ha-Hayyim*. vol. 6, ed. H. Y. Ehrenreich, 1930, pp. 211–14.
170 See note 49 above.
171 Adret, V, 239
172 ACA, R 207, f 154 (= Régné 2915)
173 ACA, R 42, f 144 (= Régné 744)
174 ACA, Procesos de Audiencia, 501/2
175 ACA, R 199, f 34verso (= Régné 2770)
176 See note 154 above.
177 ACA, R 215, f 268–9 (= Régné 3084)
178 See Y. Assis, 'The Jews of Spain in Christian Courts of Law' (Hebrew), *H. H. Ben Sasson Memorial Volume* (in press). For an extreme case of a Jew who had denounced a fellow-Jew to the Christian court, and for good reasons, but who was subsequently harassed by members of his own community in Teruel, see, ACA, R89, f 48 (= Régné 2558).
179 ACA, R 49, f 95 (= Régné 866)
180 For mediaeval Christian Europe see J. Boswell, *Christianity, Social Tolerance and Homosexuality: Gay People in Western Europe from the Beginning of the Christian Era to the Fourteenth Century* (Chicago, 1980).
181 *Teshuvot Geonei Mizrah u-Ma'arav* (= *The Responsa of the Scholars from the East and the West*), ed. J. Müller (Berlin, 1888), no. 171
182 The subject is treated by N. Roth, '"Deal gently with the young man": Love of

Boys in Medieval Hebrew Poetry of Spain', *Speculum*, vol. 57 (1982), pp. 20–51. Roth quotes passages from the poetry of Yishak ben Mar-Saul, Yosef ibn Saddiq and Samuel ibn Nagrela. On the latter see also J. Ratzaby, 'The Love Poetry of R. Shmuel Hanagid' (Hebrew), *Tarbiz*, vol. 39 (1969), pp. 137–69. See the poem 'Bekhi Tisu' (= The Dirty Old Man) of Isaac ibn Ezra, which speaks of homosexual relations between an old man and his boyfriend. An English translation of the poem is to be found in *The Penguin Book of Hebrew Verse*, ed. T. Carmi (London, 1981), p. 356.

183 *Diwan* (note 14 above), no. 584

184 ACA, R 12, f 91 (= Jacobs 234 = Régné 201)

185 ACA R 12, f 93verso (= Jacobs 237 = Régné 203)

186 For Vives, son of Jucef Abenvives, see ACA, R 19, f 156 (= Jacobs 558 = Régné 610 = Martínez Ferrando, *Catálogo . . .* I, no. 1721); for the order pardoning the three Jews of Alagón, see ACA, CR, Alfonso IV, *Caja* 2, No. 155; for the burning of a homosexual in the fourteenth century, see ACA, Real Patrimonio, R1682, f 83verso. I would like to thank Mr J. Riera for drawing my attention to this last source.

187 Adret, V, 176

188 On sexual practice in Spain see E. Amegua, *La erótica española en sus comienzos* (Barcelona, 1974); J. Latorre, *Los españoles y el vi mandamiento* (Madrid, 1969); L. Cantero, *Los españoles y los ritos sexuales* (Barcelona, 1923).

189 On the structure of Jewish society in Spain see Assis (note 107 above).

190 An extensive bibliography is available on Jews in the service of the Spanish kings. See D. Romano, *Judíos al servicio de Pedro el Grande de Aragón (1276–1285)* (Barcelona, 1983); Y. Assis, 'Jewish Diplomats from the Crown of Aragón in Muslim Lands (1213–1327) (Hebrew), *Sefunot*, vol. 3 (18) (1985), pp. 11–34, and the bibliography cited there.

191 See note 113 above.

192 Menahem ben Zerah, *Tsedah Laderekh* (= *Provisions for the Journey*) (Sabionetta, 1567?), introduction, p. 7.

193 Baer, *A History* (note 14 above), vol. 1, pp. 236–81; vol. 2, pp. 253 ff.

194 On the upper classes see H. Beinart, 'The Image of Jewish Courtiers in Christian Spain' (Hebrew), *Elites and Leading Groups* (Jerusalem, 1966), pp. 55–71.

Rabbi Isaac Ha-Cohen of Manosque and His Son Rabbi Peretz: The Rabbinate and its Professionalization in the Fourteenth Century

Joseph Shatzmiller

I

In 1937, Professor Simha Assaf published four letters by the Ran, Rabbi Nissim Gerondi (*c.* 1310–1375), two of which are of immense importance for the study of the history of the rabbinate in the Middle Ages.[1] In these letters the Ran presented to the communities of Catalonia and Aragon one of the great personalities of that generation, Rabbi Peretz Ha-Cohen, and he urged them to contribute their share to his salary together with the community of Barcelona. On reading these two letters it becomes apparent that, while he was still in Marseilles, the Rabbi Peretz Ha-Cohen had contacted the Ran and asked him to find work for him in Spain. In response to the Ran's letters, the Barcelona community agreed to engage R. Peretz as its rabbi and even fixed for him, for a period of five years, an annual salary of one thousand 'silver' which, as I suspect, is a reference to one thousand *croats* (= *denarius argenti*), equivalent to fifty pounds.* After one year in Barcelona, the Rabbi realized that this was not enough to maintain his family, and as at that time he was offered a rabbinical position in Toledo on better financial terms, he considered leaving Barcelona and perhaps even decided privately in favour of such a move. The Ran who reports all this in his letters was quick to intervene. He invited the Rabbi to a meeting in the small town of San Celoni, half-way between Gerona and Barcelona, and there, with the help of a notable by the name of Don Crescas Solomon, he tried to dissuade R. Peretz from carrying out his plan of moving to Toledo. Crescas Solomon and his community were willing to increase the Rabbi's salary by a certain amount, but this did not satisfy him fully. It occurred to the Ran that it might be

---

* The translation of *Libra*, used all over the mediaeval west to designate 20 shillings (*solidi*) or 240 denarii. *Librae* and *solidi* did not exist as coins; they were units of calculation.

possible to rally the support of other communities in the region which were also benefiting from Rabbi Peretz's presence in Barcelona: 'for through the welfare of the city, they will fare well', (*bi-shelom ha-ir shalom yihyeh lahem*), as he put it. To this end he wrote the two letters which have been preserved in a unique manuscript, at one time kept in the community library of Prague, now existing in photocopy in the Schocken Library in Jerusalem.

The value of these documents for the study of the history of the rabbinate as a profession, capable of generating an income, would seem obvious. But before we approach this question, it is important to establish Rabbi Peretz's identity, his origins and the positions he occupied before coming to Barcelona. Assaf, in the preface to his edition of the letters, provided the answers to some of these questions. First, he noticed that the rabbi in question was the teacher of the famous Ribash, Rabbi Isaac ben Sheshet (1326–1408) who mentioned him in his own writings as 'my teacher and rabbi, the great Rabbi Peretz Ha-Cohen of blessed memory' and again as 'my teacher and rabbi, Rabbi Peretz Ha-Cohen'. The Ran, too, was a particular teacher of the Ribash, who refers elsewhere to 'my teachers, Rabbi Peretz Ha-Cohen, of blessed memory and Rabbi Nissim . . . '. Assaf was able also to relate to these items of information a document published by Fritz Baer, dating from the beginning of 1357.[2] From this document we learn that even the King of Aragon knew of the collaboration between these two great rabbis, *Magister* Nissim and Rabbi Peretz, referred to in this document as Pinoperiç. Regarding Rabbi Peretz' Provençal origin, Assaf was able to cite a contemporary witness, Rabbi Isaac de Lates, who in 1372, in his *Gates of Zion*, wrote as follows on Rabbi Peretz, his brother and their father R. Isaac Ha-Cohen:

> And also the great rabbi, R. Isaac Ha-Cohen, taught Torah and produced many disciples and students. He interpreted the law orally, and through his sons, the great R. Peretz Ha-Cohen and our master R. Meshulam Ha-Cohen, he left behind him eternal blessing and life. Rabbi R. Peretz wrote a commentary on the Talmud and made halakhic decisions based on sound and highly esteemed interpretations. He wrote prolifically, but his works have not yet become known in the world.[3]

Indeed, writings ascribed to R. Peretz are to be found in collections of manuscripts and early printed works such as the *Commentary on the Kaddish*, which still await scholarly attention.[4] R. Yehudah Ha-Cohen Blau recently published in New York 'The Novelae of R. Peretz, son of Isaac Ha-Cohen of Barcelona, on the tractate Nazir', novelae in which R. Peretz first cites his father's commentaries as he had heard them, and then adds his own glosses.[5] In his important preface Blau managed to identify the father of Rabbi Peretz as Rabbi Isaac, son of Rabbi Yehudah Ha-Cohen of Manosque. Three of R. Isaac's *responsa* have been published: one appeared in a collection of Provençal *responsa* which R. Isaac ben Immanuel de Lates included in his own *responsa*, and the other two appeared in the *Responsa of the Sages of Provence* which A. Sofer (Schreiber) published some years ago in Jerusalem.[6]

Scholars of rabbinic literature have not so far provided us with precise bibliographical details or any characterization of the exegetical work of either the father or the son; nor have they evaluated their contribution to rabbinic thought. Systematic research in the royal Aragonese archives in Barcelona should bring to light new documents relating to the life of R. Peretz and his activities, documents such as the one discovered by Baer. In the Provençal archives appertaining to the town of Manosque and its surroundings there are a number of items relating to the life of the father, R. Isaac Ha-Cohen; one of these documents refers to R. Peretz Ha-Cohen himself. I hope the material I have uncovered in these archives will arouse the interest of my friend Chimen Abramsky and that he will expand and enlarge on it as he has always done in the past.

II

Isaac Ha-Cohen ben Yehuda Ha-Cohen 'the Frenchman' (*tsarfati*) is a figure from the first quarter of the fourteenth century, an age of flourishing creativity unrivalled in the history of the Jews of Provence. The Latin documents from Manosque, which are usually dated, shed much light on his life in this city during the decade of 1306–16 and even a little earlier. We do not know the dates of his birth and death, and likewise his 'French' origin is obscure, as is the question of his last town of residence. If it was Manosque, it is difficult to explain why the town records stop referring to him after 1316.[7] We know for certain that Isaac Ha-Cohen was still active at the beginning of 1326. At this time he was called upon to arbitrate in a dispute which occurred in the town of Forcalquier, near Manosque, between a Jew named Tobias and his sister 'Mrs Zeviah'.[8] An arbitration bill between the two claimants was issued and signed in Forcalquier 'on Wednesday, the 25th of the month of Tevet, in the year 5086 (1326)', and Rabbi Isaac was still dealing with this case some time later.

The town of Manosque in Upper Provence, on the banks of the River Durance, was not distinguished during this period as an economic, administrative or cultural centre of any particular importance. For Kalonymos ben Kalonymos (1286–after 1328), a young inhabitant of the town of Arles, the metropolis lying on the banks of the River Rhône, Manosque was a boring and unattractive town: 'The town is situated in a dead end and visitors come by only once in a blue moon' (literally. 'once in a Jubilee'), he says hyperbolically, in order to explain why he refused to settle there even for a short while: 'this would trap me in a net of agony and I would die'.[9]

In many respects, Manosque represents an average mediaeval town of the beginning of the fourteenth century, an important centre for the surrounding villages but remote from the bustle of the large international commercial cities such as Marseilles and Montpellier. It has attracted the attention of scholars on account of the wealth of Latin documents which are preserved there. These are among the most important collections of records in France.

Alongside the notarial registers, the earliest of which date back to the 1250s, there is an impressive series, equally old, of municipal court registers, which include inquests and sentences passed in criminal as well as civil cases. The Jews are mentioned in all of these, far more frequently than may be expected from their numerical strength in the population of the town (there were 200 Jews among the 3500 inhabitants), reflecting their prominence in the economy of the town, particularly in moneylending.[10] Regarding some members of the Jewish community, tens and even hundreds of items of information have been preserved. R. Isaac Ha-Cohen , who does not appear to have been an important moneylender, is one of those mentioned on numerous occasions. If we add to these records, especially those dealing with cases of litigation against him, the Hebrew material relating to R. Isaac, which is considerable, a rich and colourful picture emerges, which may well afford the best reconstruction of any rabbinic career of this period.

Until the year 1300, perhaps even later, no information about Isaac Ha-Cohen or his family appears in these documents. Since the archives contain an abundance of documents from the last quarter of the thirteenth century, including four comprehensive lists of the Jews of Manosque (from the years 1286 and 1296),[11] it can be assumed that he did not live in the town during this period. From his nickname 'the Frenchman' one might conclude that he was one of the Jews expelled from France in the summer of 1306, but this was not the case. Kalonymos ben Kalonymos reports on his meeting with the rabbi 'a year and a half ago' in his own town of Arles. At this meeting R. Isaac had proposed that Kalonymos should come to Manosque to study with him. The meeting took place near the time of, but before, the expulsion from France, as I have argued in the preface to the 'The Scroll of the Minor Apology'.[12] Indeed, the first clear indication that Isaac was living in Manosque is from the year 1303. He was mentioned in this as in all the other Latin documents as *Magister Isaac de Talardo*, after the name of the town Talard in the northernmost part of Provence, bordering on the Dauphiné. The late Professor Gerard E. Weil, in a study of the Jews of Talard in the beginning of the fourteenth century, noticed that the town—like Manosque—was under the rule of the Order of St John of Jerusalem, a fact which must have made it easier for Isaac and his family to move to the south.[13]

In Manosque, Isaac lived within his family, which included not only the immediate members of his household but also at least a brother and a sister. The sources do not enable us to decipher the structure of this clan, especially since it is quite possible that other members of the community may have belonged to it as well, without this being indicated by their names. With certainty, then, we can identify his brother David, who is similarly called *Magister*, pointing to his membership of the scholarly class, and his sister Blanca. A son by the name of Amideus is also mentioned in the documents, but we do not know whether this was one of the two brothers Peretz and Meshulam, mentioned by the author of the *Gates of Zion*, or whether this book refers to two additional sons. The archives contain evidence of two other Jews known by the name of the town Talard, Bonus Amicus and David ben Moshe.[14] Both may have belonged to the Rabbi's family.

Was Isaac a 'professional' rabbi? His son Peretz, in Barcelona in the middle of the fourteenth century, can be labelled a professional rabbi since he had a pecuniary agreement with the community whereby his livelihood was provided out of public funds. In the case of R. Isaac no information exists regarding any such agreement. From the facts that the notarial registers mention his moneylending activities only very infrequently, and that the sums he lent are fairly modest,[15] one might have drawn the conclusion that moneylending was only his occupational sideline, but it is not impossible that the records of those notaries with whom he used to register his transactions are simply no longer extant. On the other hand, he may have spent most of his life in poverty, unlike that other eminent rabbinic authority of his time, Aaron Ha-Hedri (de Camera) of Marseilles.[16] It is noteworthy that some of his money-lending transactions were carried out by other people on his behalf.[17] This suggests that he may have been engaged in other matters.

Indeed, our documents show clearly how, in his capacity of rabbi, his involvement in the daily affairs of the community was intense and time-consuming. The notaries refer to him either '*Magister*' or as '*Herbinus*', or '*Erbi*', which must be how they heard the word 'rabbi'.[18] He was entitled to be called '*Magister*' not because he was a physician (he is never referred to as *'medicus'* of *'physicus'*) but as a 'master of the law'—*Magister in Lege*. In most cases he was called *'Magister* Isaac' although occasionally a speaker would refer to him simply as *'Magister'*; clearly, among the Jews of Manosque, everybody must have known who the *Magister* was.[19]

It is virtually certain that *Magister* is simply the translation of the title rabbi or rav. One is led to this conclusion not only by the context in which the title appears; there is textual proof that the terms were equivalent. In 1357 in Spain, for example, a Latin document speaks of handing over a house to him 'who becomes the *Magister* or rabbi of the community *(Aljama)'*.[20] The Jews of England in the thirteenth century also translated the Latin *Magister* as 'rabbi' or 'rav'. As a result, Christian *Magisteri*, among them members of the clergy, were granted the title 'rav' in some Anglo-Jewish Hebrew deeds. This occurred, for example, in the cases of *'rav* Alan of Stockwell', *'rav* John Priest de Verdun' or *'rav* Hugh of London, Archdeacon of Colchester'.[21]

As a *Magister* among the Jews, Isaac owed his authority to his talmudic erudition. He maintained a large talmudic academy in Manosque and, according to Kalonymos b. Kalonymos,[22] he was one of the few who kept such an institution in Provence at the beginning of the fourteenth century. As was the case with other scholars, his duties were not confined to the teaching of rabbinics, but embraced also the application of rabbinic law in everyday life. It is only natural that we should find him featured in the Latin documents as an adjudicator among his congregants in civil cases, and as an arbitrator in family affairs—marriage, inheritance and the appointment of guardians for orphans. In the register of the Manosque notary, Petrus Gibosi, a dossier of fourteen documents has been preserved concerning a case of arbitration in family affairs which Rabbi Isaac and his bench conducted in early January 1305.[23] Rabbi Isaac's colleagues in this case were Bonusnomen—one of the elderly dignitaries of the community—and Abraham of Forcalquier, who was replaced on two occasions, with the consent of both sides, by Bonvayletus of Reillanne—perhaps the 'Yedidya of Rellania' who appears once in the *Responsa of the Sages of Provence*.[24] From the general legal standpoint, Isaac and his colleagues do not figure in these Latin texts as a court of law or as judges but as *arbitratores compromitores*, 'friends of the litigating parties', whose aim it is to suggest an *amicabile* compromise. Isaac and his colleagues published the details of their arbitration in several Hebrew writs which have not been preserved; the interested parties, various members of a family originating from Pernes in Comtat Venaissin, decided to register the outcome of the arbitration with the Manosque notary Petrus Gibosi, so that they would hold 'Christian' writs in case a non-Jewish court should ever be called upon to adjudicate in their affairs. This was fairly common practice in the region.

As stated above, the family in whose dispute Isaac and his colleagues had been asked to arbitrate in January 1305 were not for the most part residents of the town. With regard to one of them, Amideus, we hear that he did business 'on the other side of the River Rhône, in the town of Nîmes', at a considerable distance from Manosque; as noted above, his father lived in Pernes. On the other hand, Amideus' brother, Bonsenior lived in Manosque, and it was he, together with another brother, Jacob—a resident of Apt near Manosque—who invited Isaac to undertake the arbitration and the set of ramified agreements which resulted from it.

The particulars of this arbitration are of some interest, since they offer an insight into the nature and complexities of the cases brought before a *Magister* at the time. From the dossier it emerges that Amideus, Bonsenior and Jacob, together with a fourth brother by the name of Leo (who apparently was not present at the arbitration in Manosque) were all the sons of a Jew by the name of Benedictus of Pernes and his wife Agnes. It appears that Amideus had died some time before the arbitration took place, leaving five children and a widow, Sarah. The head of the family, Benedictus, father of the aforementioned four sons, also died near that time. All the family affairs required some re-organization. Sarah, who had already been made legal guardian of her five children, was required to give one of them, Salves, his share of his father's inheritance, since he was over fourteen years old and had become the legal charge of his uncle. The brothers Jacob and Bonsenior were required to return the *ketubah* (marriage contract) to their mother Agnes and to secure her livelihood in the future. The rabbinical court, for its part, was commissioned not only to divide the inheritance but also to take charge of arranging the marriages of Amideus' three young orphaned daughers. One daughter, Astes, had been betrothed by her father before his death to a young man by the name of David, son of Moshe Cohen. He had even fixed her dowry and deposited appropriate sureties. The rabbinical court was now asked to confirm this agreement. On the same occasion arrangements were made for the marriage of Amideus' son Sija to Sareta, daughter of Isaac de Pugeto, and the *tenaim* ('conditiones') were fixed with regard to the dowry as well as to the provision of livelihood, accommodation and clothing for the young couple. The case of another daughter, Comtessa, was not brought up at all, probably because she was still a minor, but regarding the third daughter, Bonhore, who was also a minor, it was agreed that she should be married 'in six years' time' to one of the two sons of a Jew by the name of Aquinetus de Pugeto: 'whichever one of them Aquinetus de

Pugeto and Bonahora, daughter of the late Amideus, would prefer'.[25]

Traces of Rabbi Isaac's activities as a *dayan* and arbitrator can also be found here and there in the registers of the general court of Manosque. At the end of 1307 this court had to consider the case of Astrug, son of the above-mentioned Bonusnomen, versus another member of the community, a certain Botinus. The cause of the litigation was a small sum of ten *solidi*, amounting to half a pound.[26] On 13 December in the same year the clerk of the court wrote, in closing the file, that 'the two parties have compromised regarding this and all other matters, in the presence of the *Magister* Isaac de Talardo and in the presence of Joseph'. Some eight years later, Isaac was involved in a similar arbitration, concerning a much larger sum:[27] Bonafos, son of the aforementioned Joseph, and Regina, daughter of Astrug the Jeweller, were disputing over the sum of 150 pounds. On the bench alongside Isaac sat one Moses who was not a resident of the town. A third indication of Rabbi Isaac's activities comes from the arbitration of 1326 which finds Rabbi Isaac in Forcalquier, exercising his authority fully: he invalidates an agreement in which the two parties had pledged in advance to accept irrevocably the arbitration of a dignitary by the name of Shimshon, son of the 'noble R. Benjamin', when one of the parties nevertheless felt disadvantaged by this agreement.[28] All these instances must represent, however, no more than faint echoes of R. Issac's activities as a judge and mediator.

The non-Jewish authorities of Manosque were fully aware that Isaac embodied the highest public and religious authority among the Jews of the town. To be sure, in an incriminating statement issued against him in 1310, they spoke about R. Isaac angrily and even mockingly, as of a man who fancied himself to be in possession of juridical power and who assumed the right of authority that belonged to the true masters of the town, imagining that he was the priest of the Jews; yet neither they nor the other residents of Manosque could ignore his authority, and on other occasions they acknowledged it respectfully.[29] Thus, in August 1312 a financial dispute arose between Jacob Padre, a Jew, and Guillmus Jantivayre, a Gentile resident of the town. Jantivayre did not have records to prove his claim, and he demanded that the judge should compel the Jew to take an oath in the synagogue 'according to the custom of the Jews', and to listen to the series of bans and curses which formed a part of this solemn oath-taking ceremony. The Christian citizen stressed that *Magister* Isaac of Talardo must officiate at this ceremony.[30] Five years earlier, in 1307, the authorities had given their official stamp of recognition to the Rabbi's special status: the Jewish community of Manosque, undergoing some sort of crisis at the time, perhaps as a result of an influx of refugees from France, encountered great difficulties in collecting taxes. In a special writ issued by the authorities of Manosque, it was stated that two members of the community would be authorized to levy taxes on their co-religionists and to enforce payment, and that both would be empowered to decide in disputed cases. If they so wished, said the authorities, the two would be free to consult with other Jews, it being clearly understood that they were at liberty to make decisions as they saw fit.[31] One of the two nominated was Joseph of Alesto, a rich moneylender and member of a family long established in the town. The other was *Magister* Isaac Cohen.

Other documents shed light on dramatic moments in his life, and show him exercising his power and authority. In a *responsum* of the Rashba (R. Solomon ben Adret), no. 460, he is pictured standing at his academy, 'in front of his group [of students]', 'twenty-two in number', a Torah scroll in his hand, placing one of his former pupils under ban:. 'On behalf of God and on all your behalfs I ban, excommunicate and anathematize that man . . . even though he is one of my pupils'. The text continues: 'And they all responded with Amen and said: it is truly so, our Rabbi, we agree with you, and let the man who spread the rumour be anathematized'. Another scene from R. Isaac's life, in 1310, is similarly connected with the ban of excommunication, which had been placed in this case on Leonetus, a certain member of the Manosque congregation.[32] Isaac Dolobrega, another inhabitant of the town, hurried to find out whether R. Isaac had indeed forbidden his congregants to attend the circumcision ceremony of the son of the excommunicated Leonetus. He did this at the request of a group of Jews who had gathered in the synagogue, hesitating whether or not to attend the ceremony. 'Magister', Dolobrega addressed the Rabbi: 'are you preventing others from attending the circumcision of this child?' Another Jew, Bonusnomen, addressed the Rabbi respectfully, using the plural form of address:[33] 'Magister, are you forbidding the rest of the Jews to attend the circumcision of Leonetus's son, an act which contravenes the Torah?' The Rabbi replied: 'Not at all. It is my wish and my command that they should go and do what has been prescribed in the Torah.'

In the writings of his contemporaries, the name of R. Isaac is mentioned with the utmost respect and awe. David of Estella and Joseph Samuel ben Abraham refer to him as 'the honourable, holy man of God' at the beginning of 1305.[34] 'Great Prince of Israel, divinely endowed with reverence and wisdom beyond the limitations of human understanding, and the humblest of all men', write the sages of Arles during the same period.[35] Others also emphasize his unique personality, stressing his 'exceeding modesty' and describing him as 'the humblest of men'.[36] This may have been a response to his own habit of signing his letters as 'the lowly Isaac'. At the end of his life, when he became 'exceedingly old' (*hiflig be-seivah*), another prominent scholar, Isaac ben Mordechai Kimchi (*Petit de Nyons*), referred to him in terms which go beyond the stereotypes and literary conventions of traditional rabbinic correspondence:[37]

> It is widely acknowledged that he is the crown and insignia of our time, the bowl of the capital to those who dwell among the plantations [the Jews] and a hedge around the garden. Behold, his fame has been spreading for some years now in most parts of this region and we, all of us, must not detract from the honour due to him even by the breadth of a hair. Even if he should declare the clean unclean and the unclean clean, it is our duty to be kind to him and to find mitigating circumstances for his actions to the best of our ability.

Kimchi testifies that he conducted himself in this manner even when he was convinced that the Rabbi was wrong. It is no wonder, therefore, that the small community of Reillanne, in the vicinity of Manosque, decided in 1313 to empower Isaac Ha-Cohen to act as interpreter of its statutes in the event of a dispute.[38]

III

If we were dependent only on such expressions of admiration and affection for the Rabbi of Manosque, we would not obtain an accurate picture of his life and his position in the world of French Jewry during this period. In reality, R. Isaac Ha-Cohen was not universally admired and obeyed. There were those who wished him ill, questioned his decisions and even entangled him in legal battles with the authorities. Sometimes his difficulties were caused by simple, uneducated people, and at other times they were caused by his pupils and friends.

Indirectly, we learn of his dispute, near the end of his life, with R. Levi ben Gershom (1288–1342) (Gersonides).[39] This emerges from a letter of Isaac ben Mordechai Kimhi. Gersonides, the famous philosopher who was known in his day as an important mathematician and astrologer, and who had connections in this capacity with the papal court in Avignon, tried his hand also at matrimonial law. At a date unknown to us, probably in the 1320s or 1330s, he involved himself in the problems of a woman who had received a questionable *get* (bill of divorce) and who was about to remarry. In connection with this case he found himself in confrontation with Isaac Ha-Cohen in Manosque. Isaac ben Mordechai Kimhi, who knew of two letters which Gersonides had written with regard to the case (they are not in our possession today), found in one of them personal insults directed at the Rabbi of Manosque. 'You have gone too far in your second letter with your insinuations against the great Rabbi, may God protect and guard him', Kimhi scolded Gersonides. He stated his own opinion that 'we must treat him respectfully', and sided with R. Isaac on the point of law in question. In the closing lines of his letter Isaac ben Mordechai makes an incidental allusion to Gersonides' standing at the papal court and to the benefits that could accrue from it to all Jews: 'May the Lord of peace augment your learning and magnify your success and extend his grace to you, and may you find favour in the eyes of the great king, so that we would all benefit from this', he writes.[40]

The records of the municipal court in Manosque for the year 1310 contain an abundance of information regarding the breakdown of relations between R. Isaac Ha-Cohen and individual members of his community. I have dealt with these records in my French book on the community of Manosque, and it is sufficient here to go over the main points.[41]

Isaac came into conflict with two rivals during that year. One was Jacob ben Joseph and the other Leonetus, son of Bonafos. We do not know much about either of them, except that they were brothers, sons of one mother, and that they were related somehow to the family of the influential Joseph of Alesto. It is particularly unfortunate that the reasons for the Rabbi's wrath against them remain unknown: the records mention the dispute for the first time at the stage by which the brothers had already been placed under the rabbinical ban. It appears that Jacob had taken *Magister* Isaac, as well as the heirs of Joseph of Alesto, to the court of the Bishop of Sisteron. This enraged the Manosque authorities, who guarded zealously their own jurisdiction and the income that they derived from it. They in turn took Jacob to court, and thus the floodgates were opened and the waters of strife gushed forth. On the very same day (22 June) extensive and detailed investigation proceedings were set in motion, no doubt through Jacob's initiative, against the *Magister* himself.

On this occasion the issue was the death of a new-born child through a haemorrhage suffered at his circumcision, and the question of Isaac's responsibility, however indirect, for this fatal misadventure. It becomes clear that the circumcision took place at a time when the child's father, the above-mentioned Leonetus, was under the ban. While it was the usual practice in Manosque during those years for the professional doctor Bonafos to carry out this operation, he had refused to perform it on this occasion (according to the testimony of the first witness in court, Jacob ben Joseph) as a result of the conflict between the two men and the Rabbi. 'Because an exchange of unacceptable words between them and the *Magister* has taken place',[42] noted the clerk of the court. Another member of the community, Vitalis the Tailor, was told that the *Magister* and his supporters would not attend the ceremony 'unless the *Magister* is first treated with the respect which is due to him'. The court set out to establish, therefore, whether in fact such a prohibition on attending the circumcision ceremony had been issued by R. Isaac. As we saw above, some of the witnesses denied this accusation and, indeed, the *Magister* was found not guilty of the charge. Be this as it may, the circumcision was carried out by a Jew named Mosse Anglicus, whose lack of expertise (as the writ of indictment stresses) had caused the fatal haemorrhage. One can only imagine the anguish of the child's family over the tragic accident. Some time later, when it was announced in the synagogue on the Sabbath that Jacob had been placed under the ban, he could not control himself and said: 'it would have been more correct to excommunicate the *Magister* for having caused the death of a child'.[43]

As soon as the findings in this case were concluded, another investigation was opened into related events. The Rabbi was accused of having infringed the prerogative of the authorities by taking upon himself the power to impose a ban on Jacob. And indeed, in southern France during those years, the Jews did not possess the power of imposing the ban but were expected to seek permission from the authorities in each case.[44] R. Isaac was well aware of this restriction of his power and he prepared his defence accordingly. He did not argue, as did another rabbi in Manosque twenty years earlier,[45] that in his capacity of talmudic scholar he had the right to excommunicate anyone who disparaged his dignity. Instead, he denied the facts altogether and argued that Jacob had been excommunicated by another *Magister*. His argument was accepted by the court.

The *responsum* of R. Solomon ben Adreth, no. 460, similarly touch on R. Isaac and the tribulations to which he was subjected in the course of his life. The Hebrew text in our possession speaks cryptically of 'a certain student who had studied with one rabbi most of his days, but then went on to another rabbi and made in front of him statements amounting to slander, defamation and a tainting blemish on his previous rabbi, statements which could sully that Rabbi's reputation and his descendants' for generations'. There can be no doubt that the offended rabbi was none other than R. Isaac Ha-Cohen. This is suggested not only by the fact that this particular *responsum* was sent to 'Manuasca', but also mainly because the early fourteenth-century Provençal *responsa* copied out by Isaac ben Immanuel of Lates in the sixteenth century include three which identify the denigrated rabbi as

Isaac.[46] Unfortunately, neither of these sources reveals the name of the student or the nature of the 'blemish for generations' which he had cast on his rabbi, but we do know the approximate date of these events, which occurred some time before 'the second month of Adar, on the seventh day, in the year 5065', the day on which a number of sages from the town of Arles addressed themselves to this issue.[47] Rabbi Isaac stood 'trembling all over' and excommunicated his pupil. But this was not the end of the affair. The rabbi in front of whom the calumny and the slanderous statements had been made, released the student from his ban. In support of his action he cited a French ordinance whereby 'no sage should use the power of excommunication to protect his own honour'. The least we can learn from this is that Isaac had adversaries who were prepared to go to great lengths to besmirch him. Equally interesting is the fact that a rabbi could be found, French by all indications, who was prepared to oppose him openly.

'He is French and charming'(*Tsarfati hu, ve-ish hamudot*), says Kalonymos ben Kalonymos about R. Isaac in the 'Scroll of the Minor Apology'. In Provence, in the context of considerable hostility towards the French generally and even towards the Jews of France, this pronouncement could well be taken to mean: 'He is French *but* charming'.[48] Isaac himself in one of his *responsa* describes himself as French, and in this respect a stranger to his new Jewish environment.[49] It appears, however, that his relations with the rabbis of France were always strained, and it was to the rabbis of Provence, his new homeland, that he turned for support and encouragement. So, for instance, in the case of the French ordinance whereby 'no sage should use the power of excommunication to protect his own honour'. The rabbis of Provence supported R. Isaac and declared that 'even if an ordinance was issued by some communities, this ordinance could not invalidate an excommunication which had already been declared, the more so in such regions in which the ordinance remained unknown, and in the cases of individuals who were not aware of it'.[50] It was, concluded the Provençal scholars, up to the student who had slandered R. Isaac to come before him 'in submission, so that he would repeal the ban'. No wonder, then, that in another major clash between R. Isaac and one of the most eminent rabbis of the time, his opponent should have taken the matter to the rabbis of France, whereas R. Isaac, for his part, preferred to abide by the ruling of the 'two sages of the land' or, as he says more precisely, 'two of the sages of Provence'.

Isaac's opponent in this second confrontation was a rabbi by the name of Baruch who appears to have been resident in the town of Digne, not far from Manosque. No information about him has survived, but he was regarded as one of the greatest rabbinic authorities of his time: 'His wisdom and piety were widely known, and the greatness of our teacher, Rabbi Baruch, was apparent to all and celebrated even in the most remote regions', wrote the sages of Avignon who were drawn into the dispute. In the opinion of another rabbi, Yekutiel bar Shmuel, who became similarly involved, 'his virtues and learning are unlimited, and he comes close to being credited with the gift of prophecy'.[51] From some of the expressions used by R. Isaac in connection with this affair, it appears that the relationship between the two adversaries was that of student and teacher, with Isaac in the role of the student, although by the time of the controversy between them they had become equal in status. Once again, humiliation and insults gave rise to the conflict which was recorded and has been preserved in R. Isaac's version only. In this version rabbi Baruch is presented as the aggressor, who in the course of the quarrel called Isaac 'a fool, a wicked man, an ignoramus and an obdurate sinner'. Isaac who, if we follow his own account, did not lose his composure, appears to have hinted in his reply at what he considered to be his opponent's vices of indolence and idleness: 'Even if I am an ignoramus, this is not due to any indolence on my part or the neglect of assiduous study at places of learning; for I have not wasted my time.' In reply to the charge of obduracy R. Isaac says: 'if I am obdurate, you are obdurate as well'. Because of the importance of the protagonists and the gravity of the insults exchanged, contemporaries attached to the incident perhaps greater importance than we would today. Baruch, when he called on the rabbis of France, was well aware of what he was doing. They sided with him and put the Rabbi of Manosque under the ban. Isaac, for his part, deemed it right to make a written statement in which he formulated with great precision his proposal for ending the conflict and his reaction to the ban. This statement is unique in the rabbinic literature of that time. It reads as follows:[52]

> I, the undersigned, hereby declare to all who read this letter that I am still willing to abide by the decision of the two sages from Provence and make amends for such offence as I may have committed against the rabbi R. Baruch. I have said as much on numerous occasions, and my undertaking has remained firm, even though in my opinion I have not committed any offence against him. I have held myself bound by this undertaking since the day of his departure from Digne to France, and I was willing to fulfil it at any moment, as I told him in the presence of the entire community prior to his departure. I would like, therefore, to declare now that I cannot believe any of the sages in France to have accused or censured me [on this score]. However, if any one of them should have done so in error, Heaven forbid, if he has made improper remarks about me, God forbid, or if he has censured, accused or

pronounced the ban against me, I hereby refute him and moreover declare that his censure, accusation or ban apply to none other than himself. In order that my statement should be accepted as valid, and in order to spare myself [further distress], I have written this down for all to see, and have signed it below.

As in the case of the famous ordinance of Barcelona concerning the study of philosophy (which was issued a few months after the events described above), a whole series of bans and counter-bans followed.[53] The rabbis of France excommunicated Issac and he retaliated. Baruch responded by placing an additional ban on R. Isaac because 'he repudiated the authority of the sages', and Isaac retaliated again by pronouncing yet another ban on R. Baruch. Isaac, who knew that he could not expect sympathy from the rabbis of France, now turned to his colleagues in southern France, and they—judging by the records in our possession today— did not hesitate to side with him.

Undoubtedly, these incidents bear witness to the stormy and tense career of the rabbi of Manosque. How typical was this career, and how representative of the position of the rabbinate during this period? Was his an exceptional case, conditioned by the peculiar character and temperament of Isaac Ha-Cohen? It is difficult to answer this question conclusively, as we do not possess a comparable collection of documents regarding any other town or rabbi. Nevertheless, we should not pin the blame for his apparent contentiousness on Isaac Ha-Cohen's character exclusively. We have seen that he was by no means the only one to take up arms, and that in every case he was confronted not only by pugnacious opponents who initiated hostilities against him, but also by indirect adversaries who were prepared to impose and repeal the ban from a distance. When it comes to a propensity to contentiousness, he was certainly not alone. As for his frequent resort to the ban, we would have been better qualified to judge it if we knew how widely and frequently this sanction was used elsewhere.

As it happens, a register has survived of Christian excommunications from the diocese of Riez in upper Provence during the same period. It testifies to frequent, and sometimes repetitive and parallel impositions of the ban of excommunication in the diocese.[54] As early as the end of the thirteenth century, Joinville, the biographer of King Louis IX, testifies that in the society of his time excommunications were not taken particularly seriously, probably because of their excessive frequency.[55] It is not at all unlikely that among the Jewish communities of the same period similar patterns of conduct evolved, as was the case in other spheres of life, where the Jews came to adopt the norms prevailing in the surrounding society. What appears to us today exaggerated and extreme would have seemed to contemporaries a normal part of everyday life. The fact is that R. Isaac Ha-Cohen, in spite of all these controversies and bans of excommunication, continued to hold rabbinical office in this region for twenty years or more, and inspired expressions of admiration from the Jews of his adopted land, such as were rarely equalled in the literature of the time.

IV

After 1316, Isaac disappears from the Manosque records together with all members of the 'de Talardo' tribe. However visible he is in the sources up to that year, from then on he is never mentioned. It may be assumed with virtual certainty that both he and his relatives left the town at that point. During the ensuing two decades, the non-Jewish court of the town was considering several cases of scandal surrounding the local synagogue, and *Magister* Isaac would have given evidence before this court had he still lived in Manosque at that time. Most pertinently, on the Day of Atonement of 1338, a serious quarrel broke out in the synagogue on the question of the proper manner of conducting the service. The local rabbi was called to avert the crisis, but his name was '*Magister* Vitalis', not Isaac Cohen.[56] In a document dating from 1323 (or 1324), we hear that the de Talardo family had moved out of town and left behind them an empty and derelict house. The owners, Aquinetus and Dayot, sons of Bonus Amicus de Talardo, did not appear in court themselves, but sent Abraham de Rellania, a resident of Forcalquier to represent them.[57] As for the whereabouts of R. Isaac and his relatives, two pieces of evidence, already considered above, suggest that after 1316 they settled in the neighbouring town of Forcalquier or somewhere else nearby. These were, first, the case of R. Isaac's arbitration in the *castrum* of Forcalquier in 1326 and, secondly, the appearance of Abraham de Relliana (of Forcalquier) in the court of Manosque two or three years earlier, to represent the de Talardo brothers. There exists a third piece of evidence which is of particular interest in that it introduces us to a certain R. Peretz Ha-Cohen who is almost without a doubt one and the same as R. Peretz, son of R. Isaac Ha-Cohen. This is a brief note in Hebrew and Provençal, entered on 6 May 1331 in the register of a certain cloth merchant in Forcalquier, Ugo Teralh.[58] Ugo, who was a notary as well as a cloth merchant, kept in his shop a neat register in the Provençal language, in which he entered all sums owed to him by his customers for merchandise purchased at the shop. He would ask his Jewish customers to write a sentence or two in Hebrew, stating their obligation to him, and he himself would note immediately afterwards the essentials of the transaction in Provençal.

Paragraph 77 in the register (following the enumeration of Paul Meyer, who published the document) touches on our subject. The Hebrew entry runs as follows: 'I, Nehemiah, owe Ugo Teralh for half a *canna* of "blue [of Carcassonne]" and for a pair of trousers of white *camelin*, 30 white *solidi*, the white [solidus amounting to] 13 *denarii*. Of these, our master rabbi Peretz owes 7 solidi [which] I have paid.'[59] The technical details of this entry are of secondary importance for us here, but they should be clarified nevertheless: *canna* is a length measurement; the *denarius* is indicated by the Hebrew term *pashut*, while the Hebrew *dinar* equals a *solidus*. This, however, is not the ordinary *solidus* but one of which thirteen dinarii (there were twelve *dinarii* in the *solidus*) equalled in value the French *denarii* coined in Tours. In addition we learn what types of cloth were purchased, and that the Hebrew term *bate shokayim* indicated the Provençal *chausas*—trousers. The Provençal text further informs us that Nehemiah's non-Jewish name was Creyson. As regards Rabbi Peretz, his non-Hebrew name may well have been recorded but Meyer did not manage to decipher it. Directly after it appear the words *Lo Maystre*, which indicate that Ugo was aware of Peretz's rabbinic position.

Nothing in this note explains why Nehemiah-Creyson should have acted on behalf of the Rabbi on this occasion, just as the document from 1323 which was cited above could provide no clue as to why Abraham of Relliana had to represent the de Talardo brothers in the Manosque court. But the two names Nehemiah and Abraham, and the association between them as representing, on two separate occasions, the interests of Rabbi Peretz and the de Talardos respectively, help establish the identity of 'our master Rabbi Peretz' mentioned in Ugo Teralh's Forcalquier register in May 1331. A certain 'Abraham bar Nehemiah' is the addressee, in Forcalquier, of a *responsum* by R. Nissim Girondi (nos. 7 and 7b in Feldman's new edition).[60] The *responsum* is unfortunately undated, but it suggests that the Ran had some connection with Forcalquier through an individual whose name happens to coincide with those of both Abraham of Relliana and Nehemiah-Creyson who were both residents of Forcalquier. Since the Jewish community of Forcalquier was very small (a list dating from 1299 or 1300 enumerates only eleven Jewish taxpayers),[61] it is almost certain that the Abraham bar Nehemiah addressed by the Ran was related to both Abraham of Relliana and Nehemiah-Creyson and may even be identified with the former. All these connections with Forcalquier, linking R. Isaac Ha-Cohen and his sons, the Ran and R. Peretz Ha-Cohen point with virtual certainty to the identity of *Maystre*

Peretz Ha-Cohen, mentioned in Ugo Teralh's register with R. Peretz Ha-Cohen, son of Isaac Ha-Cohen, who was engaged as Rabbi of Barcelona at the instigation of the Ran. In 1331, therefore, he was still living in Upper Provence, in Forcalquier or its vicinity.

V

Let us now return to the two letters by the Ran with which we opened the present discussion, and to the question of R. Peretz's salary in Barcelona. At that time, in the middle of the fourteenth century, R. Peretz was by no means unique in reaching a pecuniary arrangement with the community he was to serve. A similar situation arose in 1338 in the town of Teruel in Aragon:[62] more than a year earlier, Samuel Abenposat had agreed to serve as *Rabinus*, acting as a teacher for boys and a preacher for the community, for an annual salary of 350 *solidi* (17.5 pounds). For some reason he remained in office for a further four months. In a writ which he submitted to the authorities in 1338, he itemized his conditions of employment and worked out that the community still owed him the sum of 116 *solidi* and 8 *dinarii* for his additional four months of service. He requested that the authorities should compel the community to pay him not only his yearly salary plus the additional fee for the extra four months, but also the sum of 100 *solidi* for legal costs and other expenses incurred in enforcing the payment of these debts. The community of Valencia was similarly bound to its rabbi by contract. A crown document dating from 1371[63] concerns the relationship between the elders of the community and the Rabbi Joseph Abenuva. Although it reveals nothing of any detailed pecuniary agreement between them, the document indicates clearly that Joseph had been elected by the leaders of the community to serve in the capacity of *Rabinus et Capellanus* in Valencia, and that an agreement was drawn up in Hebrew which was to regulate the relations between the parties. The authorities declare their intention to see to it that the parties abide by the letter and spirit of this agreement.

The most important example of financial arrangements between a rabbi and his community, comparable to the agreement between R. Peretz and the community of Barcelona, is the contract, in fact a series of contracts, between the community of Toledo and R. Judah ben Asher (1270–1349)—the most famous rabbinic authority of his day. From his well-known testament[64] it appears that in the decade to 1340 his annual salary amounted to 1500 'gold pieces' (*zehuvim* = maravedi), and that this sum was doubled in 1341 and fixed at 3000. In 1358, according to the findings of K. H. Schäfer,[65] *maravedi* in Castile were equivalent to one florin and approximately two-thirds of a pound. Judah's annual salary was, therefore, set at what amounted to sixty florins and later raised to 120, this being equivalent to forty pounds rising to eighty approximately. In addition, his wife was to receive a pension of 1000 *maravedi* per annum for a period of ten years in the event of his death, and special provisions were made for the maintenance of his sons, on condition that they continue what had become a family tradition of serving the community in rabbinic office. Rabbi Peretz in Barcelona, with his salary of 1000 'silver' croats per annum (50 pounds), would have considered himself underpaid by comparison. Judah ben Asher reports that the community was willing to raise his salary because they had 'heard that it was my intention to seek a resting-place elsewhere', and also because 'it became known to the heads of the community that I was planning to emigrate to Seville'. It appears that R. Peretz similarly used this kind of pressure on the community by threatening to leave: 'It had occurred to him that he should wander afar,' says the Ran in his letter, 'and the elders of the community in Toledo have sent for him, so that his light should shine upon them.' And he adds: 'they will furnish him liberally with pieces of silver', to stress the fact that he was being offered better pay than he had been getting in Barcelona.

When did this proposal from Toledo reach R. Peretz? It is important to clarify this point in order to date the Ran's letters and R. Peretz's move to Catalonia. Since the basic data are missing, we may accept Assaf's suggestion of 1349, the year of Judah ben Asher's death. Rabbi Peretz was, therefore, intended to fill his vacant position in Toledo. This date may explain also the atmosphere of gloom and desolation which characterizes the opening lines of each of the Ran's letters; they may echo the havoc wrought by the plague which occurred in 1348. This emerges from sentences such as 'the ends of the earth are filled with bitterness, [as if] suckling the poison of creatures that crawl in the dust' (cf. *Deut.* 32:24), and 'then was the Lord jealous for his land; He ran and returned from the heat of [His] great anger. He took pity on his people whom He had made drink a cup of trembling'. But all this is very uncertain. We can, however, say with certainty that R. Peretz was in Barcelona in 1357 at the latest (according to the document published by Baer), and that he died twelve years later, as Herschman has established on the basis of the *responsa* of R. Issac ben Sheshet, the Ribash.[66] It is possible, as Leon A. Feldman has suggested, that the earliest indication of his presence in Spain should be set as far back as 1352.[67] What did he do during the years prior to this date, and when precisely did he move from Forcalquier to Marseilles (for it was from Marseilles that he wrote to the Ran)? The answers to these questions may well lie buried in the archives of the region, awaiting discovery.

Notes

1 S. Assaf, 'Four letters by R. Nissim Gerondi' (Hebrew). The article was first published in *Horev*, vol. 3 (1937), pp. 93–100. It is reproduced in his collection *Sources and Studies in Jewish History* (Hebrew) (Jerusalem, 1946), pp. 173–81. The letters were recently re-published, following a thorough examination of the manuscript, by A. L. Feldman in his new edition of the *Responsa of R. Nissim Gerondi* (Hebrew) (Jerusalem, 1984), pp. 417–20.

2 F. Baer, *Die Juden im christlichen Spanien*, vol. 1 (Berlin, 1929), pp. 366–67. On Rabbi Peretz's role as teacher of R. Isaac ben Sheshet, see A. Herschman, *R. Isaac ben Sheshet (Ribash), his Life and his Epoch* (Hebrew) (Jerusalem, 1957), p. 12.

3 S. Buber (ed.), *Schaare Zion . . . von Rabbi Issac de Lattes* (Hebrew) (Jaroslau, 1885), p. 47.

4 See H. Michal, *Or ha-Hayyim* (Hebrew) (Jerusalem, 1965), pp. 570, 1168; A. Freimann: *Union Catalogue of Hebrew Manuscripts and their Location*, 2 vols (New York, 1964, 1973), *sv*. I would like to thank Professor Moshe Idel of the Hebrew University for pointing out to me that our R. Peretz was not the author of the kabbalistic treatise *Maarekhet ha-Elohut*. See G. Scholem, 'Le-Ba'ayat Sefer *Maarekhet ha-Elohut* u-Mefarshav', *Kiryat Sefer*, vol. 21 (1945), pp. 284–95.

5 M. Y. Blau (ed.), *Commentary of the Ancients on the Tractate 'Nazir'* (Hebrew) (New York, 1977).

6 M. Z. Friedländer (ed.), *Responsa . . . of R. Isaac b. Immanuel de Lates* (Hebrew) (Vienna, 1860), pp. 51–3, where the signature reads: 'I, the humble (*he-Aluv*) Isaac ben Judah Ha-Cohen'; A. Schreiber, *Responsa of the Sages of Provence* (Hebrew) (Jerusalem, 1967) pp. 243–9; 321–2, with the same signature.

7 These Latin documents are located in the departmental archives of the Bouches-du-Rhône in Marseilles and of the Basses-Alpes in Digne. For the latest document concerning R. Isaac, see Fonds Meyer 10 (Digne) 35 recto, dating from 10 October 1316.

8 Schreiber (note 6 above), pp. 321–3. The deed was copied in Forcalquier some weeks later, the exact date being 'the 28th of Adar, in the year 5086'.

9 See J. Shatzmiller (ed.), 'The Scroll of the Minor Apology of R.Kalonymos ben Kalonymos' (Hebrew), *Sefunot*, vol. 10, (1966), pp. 9–52, especially p. 38.

10 J. Shatzmiller, *Recherches sur la communauté juive de Manosque au moyen âge* (Paris, 1973), pp. 149–64. For the four lists of the Jews of the city see pp. 165–80 and also pp. 7–8, 67–8.

11 *ibid.*, pp. 149–64. See, however, n. 14 where mention is made of a certain '*Benlivena filius magistri Isaac*'.

12 See note 9 above.

13 G. E. Weil, 'Tallard et Espinasses, Venterol, Pellentier, Vitrolles et Esparron. Corrections et additions à la *Gallia Judaica* d'Henri Gross', *Provence Historique* vol. 32 (1982), pp. 437–46.

14 For '*Amideus filius Isaac de Talardo*', see Fonds Meyer 6, f 143recto; for '*David filius Mosse Cohen judeus de Talardo*', see Fonds Meyer 2, f 137recto (both in the Archives in Digne). A certain '*Benlivena filius magistri Isaac*' appears, however, in 1292 (Marseilles Archive, 56H954, f 88verso). If further research reveals that this is a reference to Isaac de Talardo, the chronology of the family's establishment in

Manosque will have to be reconsidered.

15 All in all, I was able to identify 19 loans made by him or on his behalf. The sums of money involved are generally very modest, between 30 and 50 shillings. Exceptional is a loan of 6 pounds and 15 *solidi* recorded in Fonds Meyer 8, f 5recto. This is not a negligible sum, to be sure, but it is not a breathtaking one either.

16 Kalonymos reports on Aaron Ha-Hedri (de Camera) whose 'wealth and property were increased by God, in His great favour', with the effect that he could no longer look after his students. See note 9 above p. 37.

17 Examples are to be found in the notarial registers in the Archives of Digne, Fonds Meyer 5, f 7recto and Fonds Meyer 10, f 35verso, where *Isaac filius Leonis de Aurayca* acts in his name.

18 For *Herbinus* see Marseilles Archive, 56H964 ff, 17recto–20verso, where *frater Herbini* or *de mandato Herbini* appear several times. For *Erbi*, see note 30 below.

19 See note 61 below.

20 A. Rubio y Lluch, *Documents per l'historia de la cultura catalana mizeval.* vol. 2 (Barcelona, 1926), p. 123. See also Baer (note 2 above), p. 129, *et passim* (s.v. *Rabiner*, p. 1166).

21 See I. Abrahams, H. P. Stokes and H. Loewe, *Starrs and Jewish charters preserved in the British Museum*, vol 1 (Cambridge, 1930), p. 75 (for Alan of Stockwell), p. 85 (for Hugh of London). See also the discussion in vol.2 (Cambridge, 1932), pp. 219–21, 234. For John of Verdun, see M. D. Davies, *Hebrew deeds of English Jews before 1240* (London, 1888), pp. 327, 325.

22 Kalonymos (note 9 above) informs us of no more than ten cities in Provence and Languedoc where he might have considered establishing himself for the sake of pursuing his studies. Manosque, as far as I can see, is the only town for which we have the exact number of students in the Jewish academy (*yeshivah*)—22. See M. Breuer, 'Towards an investigation of the typology of Western *yeshivot* in the Middle Ages' (Hebrew), in *Studies in the History of Jewish Society* (. . .presented to Professor Jacob Katz . . .) (Jerusalem, 1980), pp. 45–55, in particular p. 49.

23 The 'dossier' is to be found in ff 137recto—140recto of Fonds Meyer 2 (Digne). In order not to overburden these notes, in what follows I shall not indicate the exact folio references.

24 See Schreiber, (note 6 above), p. 322, where Rabbi Isaac establishes that Samson of Forcalquier and Yedidya of Rellania will re-examine the case. Schreiber read 'Yedidya of Nelana', but such a place does not exist. Bonvayletus appears at the head of the list of four Jewish taxpayers in Reilanne (in 1299 or 1300: see note 61 below) and is the major contributor. Notably, our Hebrew text calls him *ha-Naale* (the eminent) which is an honorific title denoting wealth, similar to the title *ha-Nadiv* (the generous).

25 Fonds Meyer, 2 f 139recto: 'de matrimonio contrahendo inter Abramonum seu Bonfilonum quem magis placuerit Aquineto de Puieto et Bonahora filia quondam dicti Amidei . . .'.

26 56H912, ff 22recto–23recto (Marseilles): 'Anno quo supra die xiii december, dicte partes compromisunt de ipsa questione et de aliis in magistrum Isacum de Talardo et Jocepum.'

27 Fonds Borel 2, f 4recto (Digne). This act is dated 16 June 1316 or 1315.

28 See note 8 above.

29 See Shatzmiller (note 10 above), p. 51 where references to these documents may be found.

30 56H965, f 34verso, 25 August 1312 (Marseilles): 'Petens et requirens . . . dominum judicem dicte curie ut magister Ysaac dictum 'Erbi' compellere debeat more et lege ebrayca ut excommunicationem seu maledictionem pronuntiare debent in scolis

judeorum contra dictum Jacob si culpabilis in predictis fuit et ipsum Jacob compellere ad predictam excommunicationem seu maledictionem audientiam. Et hoc petiit fieri ut veritas non valeat occultari.'

31 56H885, f 13recto 19 May 1307 (Marseilles): 'judex curie Hospitalis . . . posuit et constituit . . . Jaucepum judeum de Alesto et magistrum Isacum Cohen qui habeant potestatem faciendi taliis quoerquandi et exigendi et dubia solvendi que in taliis predictis orientur. Qui predicti judei possint habere consilium ab aliis judeis si habere voluerint super dictis questionibus et taliis tallandis determinandis . . . '

32 See the text in Shatzmiller (note 10 above), pp. 47–8.

33 *ibid.*, p. 48. The Rabbi answered: 'non facio ymo volo et precipio ut eant et faciant prout traditor a lege'.

34 Friedländer (note 6 above), p. 42.

35 *ibid.*, p. 44

36 *ibid.*, p. 34

37 I. Levi, 'Un receuil des consultations inedites de rabbins de la France meridionale', *R.E.J.*, vol. 44 (1902), pp. 73–86, especially pp. 82–6. See Isaac of Nyons' testimony, p. 83: 'And we have always dealt with him in this way, as you know from the treatise you saw in our academy, where we refrained from dishonouring him . . . We have also overlooked all that was included in his letter against us, things that he neither saw nor heard and yet attributed to us, things that are foreign to us. In spite of all this, we kept silent.'

38 S. Schwartzfuchs, 'An Ordinance from 1313' (Hebrew), in *Bar Ilan*, vols 4–5 (1967), pp. 209–10, and my suggestions in 'Provençale ordinances of 1313' (Hebrew), in *Kiryat Sefer*, vol. 50 (1975), pp. 663–7.

39 The most recent discussion of Gersonides' life and works is to be found in C. Touati, *La pensée philosophique et théologique de Gersonide* (Paris, 1973), pp. 33–82.

40 See note 37 above.

41 Shatzmiller (note 10 above), pp. 43–54.

42 56H963 f 31recto (Marseilles): 'Ipse requisivit dictum Fossonum ut circumcideret dictum infantem qui respondendo dixit ei quod non faceret quia ipse Jacob verba inordinata habuerat cum magistro.'

43 *ibid.*, f 32recto: dictus Jacob dixit 'melius deberet excommunicari magister qui causam dedit et fecit ut mortuus est unus infans.'

44 See J. Shatzmiller, 'L'Excommunication, la communauté juive et les authorités temporelles au moyen âge' in M. Yardeni, *Les juifs dans l'histoire de France* (Leiden, 1980), pp. 39–63.

45 Shatzmiller, (note 10 above), pp. 40–2

46 Friedländer (note 6 above), pp. 42–5

47 *ibid.*, p. 45

48 S. Schwartzfuchs, 'L'opposition Tsarfat Provence: la formation du Judaism du nord de la France', in *Hommages a Georges Vajda: Etudes d'histoire et de la pensée juives* (Louvain, 1980), pp. 135–150; and, more recently, N. Coulet, 'Frontiers incertaines: les juifs de Provence au moyen âge', *Provence Historique* 35 (1985), pp. 371–6.

49 Schreiber (note 6 above), pp. 239–43

50 Friedländer (note 6 above), p. 43

51 *ibid.*, p. 34

52 *ibid.*, p. 38

53 See J. Saracheck, *Faith and Reason, the Conflict over the Rationalism of Maimonides* (New York, 1970), pp. 229–50; C. Touati: 'La controverse de 1303–1306 autour des études philosophiques et scientifiques', *R.E.J.*, vol. 127 (1968), pp. 21–37.

54 R. Collier, 'Excommunication à Mousitiers-Saint-Marie (Basses Alpes) au début du XIVe siécle', in *Bulletin philologique et historique (jusqu'en 1610) du Comité des travaux*

historiques et scientifiques, année 1962 (Paris, 1965), pp. 565–7.

55 M. R. B. Shaw (trans.), *Joinville and Villehardouin; Chronicles of the Crusades* (Harmondsworth, 1963), pp. 177–8.

56 See J. Shatzmiller, '*Tumultus et Rumor in Sinagoga*: An Aspect of Social Life of Provençal Jews in the Middle Ages', *A.J.S. Review*, vol. 2 (1977), pp. 227–55, especially p. 250: 'Abraham de Baherias . . . ivit ad magistrum Vitalem qui est quasi dominus et magister eorum et dixit ei: 'Domine, quare sustinetis vos quod iste . . . dicat misterium in tali festo . . . '.

57 The document in the Archives of the Bouches-du-Rhône in Marseilles, 56H924, ff 118recto–120verso.

58 P. Meyer, *Le livre journal de maître Ugo Teralh, notaire et drapier à Forcalquier (1330–1332)* (Paris, 1898), p. 22.

59 The Provençal note, written by Ugo Teralh, reads as follows: 'Deu Creyson, juyeus, xxx s. contant, tornes d'argent am o redon per xiiid. per miaga canna d'arangelat et per miaga canna de blau de Carcasons et per unas chausas de camelin blanc. Pagar a la fiera et den en [. . .] lo maystre vii s. e a n'i escritz de sa man: e pres o lo viii jor de may m.ccc.xxxi.'

60 See Feldman (note 1 above), pp. 52–4. Feldman noticed that the transcription of the city's name in the Hebrew manuscripts is 'Folcalquier' (spelt with an 'l' rather than 'r'). For similar transcriptions see Schreiber, pp. 321–3.

61 For this document, see Archives des Bouches-du-Rhône, B1884, ff 24verso–25recto.

62 Rubio y Lluch (note 20 above), pp. 58–9

63 Archivo de la Corona d'Aragon, Reg. 1580 f 68recto. I thank H.J. Riera y Sans for letting me have a microfilm reproduction of this document.

64 References are to Judah's autobiographical 'ethical will' as published in Israel Abraham's *Hebrew Ethical Wills*, vol. 2 (Philadelphia, 1976), pp. 163–200, in particular pp. 180–3. Judah employs the term *zehuvim* to designate the type of currency in which he was paid. Abrahams translates this literally 'pieces of gold'. In my opinion *maravedi* are meant. A Hebrew document from Barcelona dated 1108 has '14 and a half big *zehuvim* murabita' and the Latin text which follows it has 'XIII morabitanos de auro'. See M. Schwab and J. Myrety Sance, 'Nouveaux documents des juifs Barcelonnais au XIIe siècle', *Boletin de la Real Academia de la Historia*, vol. 69 (1916), pp. 563–83, especially p. 577.

65 See K. H. Schäfer, *Die Ausgaben der apostolischen kammer unter Johann XXII, nebst der Jahresbilanzeen von 1316–1378* (Paderborn, 1911), p. 83.

66 See A. Herschman, *Rabbi Isaac bar Sheshet (ha-Ribash): his life and his Times* (Hebrew) (Jerusalem, 1957) pp. 159–60.

67 In the introduction to his edition of the *Responsa of R. Nissim Gerondi* (note 1 above), p. 33.

2

JEWISH CULTURE AND EDUCATION

Transforming the Heder:
Maskilic Politics in Imperial Russia

Steven J. Zipperstein

HEDERS, the privately-run elementary schools that dominated East European Jewish educational life into the 1920s, were among the most visible and perhaps the most influential bulwarks (so said admirers and detractors alike) of traditional Jewish society. Here, in classes of some ten or twenty students held typically in the homes of teachers, boys between the ages of four and twelve were drilled in basic biblical, liturgical and rabbinic texts. They provided students with the ability to read and comprehend the most widely used sacred literature; even most of their critics acknowledged that they succeeded in this respect. But the heder's curriculum, they maintained, was otherwise lamentable, its teachers hopelessly ill-prepared, its goals retrogressive and its general impact on Jewish society shocking. Such boors and rogues ran heders, claimed Isaac Baer Levinsohn, the leading figure of the nineteenth-century Russian Jewish enlightenment movement, that it would be impossible to find elsewhere Jews of comparable venality. 'Classrooms filled with death', is how Levinsohn referred to the schools.[1]

Levinsohn's movement, the *Haskalah*, defined its agenda largely in pedagogical terms. Jewry must, the *Haskalah* argued, be re-educated (quite literally) in order to make way for its integration into a multi-national, tolerant Russia. Once Jews were reared on the study of systematic grammar (Hebraic and that of the vernacular), introduced to a curriculum that included secular and Jewish studies and which aimed at making them into both responsible citizens and faithful Jews, they would be ready to embrace emancipation. Education was the key to the Russian *Haskalah*'s campaign and the *melamed*, or heder teacher, was considered among its outstanding foes.[2]

When Russian *Maskilim* established their first officially-recognized organization, the Society for the Promotion of Enlightenment Among the Jews of Russia (*Obshchestvo dlia rasprostraneniia prosveshcheniia mezhdu evreiiami v Rossii*, referred to below as OPE), whose charter was approved in 1863, Jews and Russian officials alike assumed that it

87

would count among its primary goals the eradication, or at least the diminution, of the heder and its influence. But OPE did not. Though prodded on this score by many of its members, and despite the fact that the organization's leadership readily acknowledged that heder reform was one of the most important tasks facing those interested in transforming East European Jewry, it was a decade before OPE set up in 1874 its first fund to support such educational change. Before then it neglected heders, a surprising stance in view of the tenets of the *Haskalah* movement that had inspired it.

This study attempts to explain why and, *inter alia*, to examine how the actions of Russian maskilic leaders in the 1860s and early 1870s were shaped and constrained by influences outside the realm of maskilic ideology and its imperatives. It is the nexus between *Haskalah* thought and policy that will concern us, the shaping of the Jewish educational agenda at a time when commitments of Russian *Maskilim* were first institutionalized during Russia's great reforms. In principle, no *maskil* would have disputed the need for heder reform; in practice, the issue was hotly contested, in fact it was considered so sensitive that OPE leaders refused to explain fully why they took the position they did. A reconstruction of the debate within OPE over heder reform helps illuminate how the same pressures could be understood in thoroughly different (yet entirely credible) ways by *Maskilim* with different social and cultural agendas.

In the absence of relevant archival material, the student of OPE must rely on two major published sources: Leon Rosenthal's two-volume documentary history *Toledot hevrat marbei haskalah be-yisrael be-eretz rusiah* (St Petersburg, 1885–90), an approximately 450-page Hebrew-language collection of organizational transcripts and correspondence; and I. M. (Elias) Tcherikover's *Istoriia obshchestva dlia rasprostraneniia prosveshcheniia mezhdu evreiiami v Rossii* (St Petersburg, 1913), a copiously documented analytical history of the society. Both authors had access to OPE's archives; both were closely associated with the group; Rosenthal was its treasurer from its founding until his death in 1887 (the second volume of his work was published posthumously) and Tcherikover was secretary of OPE at the time that he wrote his study. Neither probed systematically OPE's attitude towards heder reform, but the documents they cite provide a sufficiently detailed indication as to why Russia's first major maskilic organization eschewed in its first decade the *Haskalah*'s central pedagogical goal.

I

Indifference to heders and their reform was by no means the reason for this policy. Quoted in full by Tcherikover was the draft of a charter prepared at the initiative of the group's founding chairman, the financier Yuzel Ginzburg, and completed in early 1860, nearly four years before OPE's establishment. This prospective charter, entitled *Obshchestvo dlia rasprostraneniia russkago iazyka i sovremennago obrazovania mezhdu evreiiami v Rossii* (Society for the promotion of the Russian language and contemporary education among the Jews of Russia), defined the group's goals as concerned primarily with Jewish elementary education and, broadly speaking, heder reform. Other items were included in its agenda—subsidies for 'modern' Jewish publications and help for Jewish university students (items later given priority in OPE)—but it was the alteration of the elementary-school Judaic curriculum that dominated.[3]

The first clause called for the mobilization of young teachers ('equipped with good knowledge of both the spirit and needs' of the Jews) who would help to introduce Russian and other secular subjects into Jewry's communally funded elementary-level Talmud Torahs and the bastions of Talmud learning, the *yeshivahs*. The society should organize, it continued, basic literacy classes designed for the children of Jewish artisans and other manual labourers that would teach Russian, mathematics and Bible. Privately-run boarding or day schools should also be set up with the group's help for children whose parents could pay for their education in schools that taught a mixed curriculum of Jewish and secular studies.[4] In September 1860, Osip Rabinovich wrote about the need for such a society in the pages of his newspaper *Razsvet*, and he too affirmed that it should devote itself mainly to elementary school reform.[5] The group's leading figures then concurred: as Leon Rosenthal, one of its founders, stated, characterizing its goals at this stage: 'The salvation of Israel is depending upon three things,' paraphrasing a standard Judaic maxim, 'good education, the spread of the vernacular, and support for Jewish writers', in this order.[6] In 1863 the Minister of the Interior, p. A. Valuev, wrote in a memorandum that the control of Jewish education by the *melameds* (a preoccupation, as we shall see, of those Russian officials concerned with Jewish educational affairs) would soon be challenged by a Jewish society devoted to undermining them and their prominence.[7]

In fact, OPE's leaders had a year earlier abandoned this position and readjusted their priorities, now relegating heder reform to the lowest possible level of importance. In the next draft, written in late 1862 or early 1863, and quite similar in content to the final charter adopted by

OPE, all mention of heder education was deleted. Even the word 'education' was dropped from the group's title and the less specific 'enlightenment' substituted in its place. Emphasized now was financial support for Jewish secondary and university students, assistance for teachers and the publication of books. Only in the fifth clause was help for Jewish schools affirmed and without specific mention of elementary education. The final draft dropped even this.[8]

Writing some fifteen years later, Rosenthal recalled that he and OPE's other leaders had made some changes to the original proposal but essentially it remained the same: 'We agreed to several changes but did not abandon our [essential] goals.' And, he added: 'We reached these [new] conclusions after considerable written and oral negotiations.'[9]

Pressure, said Rosenthal, had come from various Jewish 'sects' either entirely opposed to change in the traditional curriculum or, alternatively, so radical that they resisted any moderation when attacking traditional Jewish mores. Rosenthal also observed that the government too had objections to the first draft and neither liked the fact that OPE had committed itself to establishing branches wherever there was sufficient interest nor approved of its original and quite nominal membership fees. In short, it objected to the prospect of a popular or 'mass' organization and insisted that the group restrict itself accordingly. What remains curious, though, is why Rosenthal and his entourage felt the need to yield in the wake of the objections of Jewish interest groups whose criticisms were predictable and easily manipulated by powerful figures such as Ginzburg and Rosenthal? More puzzling is why heder reform was dropped from the agenda if the government had objected only to OPE's organizational structure but raised no substantive criticisms of its goals? Had traditionalists objected strenuously to heder reform? If, so, why did Ginzburg capitulate? And if it was the government that demurred, why was this not mentioned by Rosenthal?

Rosenthal, in any event, minimized the differences between the various drafts. Tcherikover did not, but the explanation he offered for the changes in OPE's new charters (which he called 'considerably more modest and practical')[10] is contradicted by documents he cites elsewhere in his book: he contends that such change was due to the fact that Ginzburg and his circle were unable to appreciate properly the needs of the Jewish masses whose problems they addressed from afar, living as they did outside the Pale of Settlement and insulated by wealth and privilege.[11] Yet contrary to Tcherikover's conclusions, based as they are in this case on a rather rigid socialist reading of Jewish history, the importance of heder reform was by no means unknown to OPE's leaders who had stressed precisely this plank in the group's original charter. Moreover, within a few years of OPE's establishment, Ginzburg had his associates draw up still another document; the date of its completion is unclear as it was never submitted to the authorities. It called for the creation of a new and separate group devoted exclusively to Jewish elementary school reform. (In fact, Tcherikover first discovered and published this document.)[12] Other explanations must be offered, then, not the cultural insularity of OPE's undoubtedly conservative élite, to explain the decision to downplay heder reform which it had only a few years earlier placed at the top of the Jewish communal agenda.

The leading advocates of heder reform within OPE (and the issue continued to haunt the group's leadership for years) were, in fact, little more embedded in the socio-economic and cultural realities of Russian Jewry than were their opponents. The most important were members of OPE's Odessa branch, its leading figures doctors, journalists and other free professionals who were, while by no means as economically comfortable as were the leaders of the St Petersburg OPE, still set apart from the bulk of the Pale's Jews by their (albeit tenuous) bourgeois life-styles and their left-liberal positivist commitments. Others highly critical of OPE's orientation included government rabbis, a group widely known and distrusted for its reputedly maskilic orientation and disliked, or at least widely patronized, by *folk* and rabbinic intelligentsia alike. Such figures can hardly be said to have maintained a much more intimate connection to the masses than OPE's decorously pious, moderate maskilic leaders.

The first OPE member to raise objections publicly was Dr Iosif Bertensohn, a Nikolaev-born physician who had recently returned from abroad to take up a post in the medical department of the Ministry of the Interior. A prolific, later quite distinguished, heart specialist, he devoted much of his subsequent career to publicizing the views on sanitation of the seminal Russian medical figure Nicholas Pirogov. Pirogov's views on medical and educational topics continued to influence him throughout his life and Bertensohn, who later converted to Lutheranism, drew primarily on Russian and German educational precedents in his exposition on heders. His recommendations, wrote Tcherikover, were the products of his larger perspective on the function of primary education in modern society, rather than an intimate or recent acquaintance with Jewish conditions.[13]

Arguing at length at OPE's first public meeting in December 1863, Bertensohn affirmed that it was essential, contrary to OPE's stated goals, to introduce into the Jewish school curriculum a new pedagogical system based on 'rational foundations' which would replace the dismal, anarchic conditions so widespread in the Pale. Such renovated primary schools would help establish a solid basis—the 'first foundation stones' in Bertensohn's words—for Jewry's social transformation. Education was the essential tool for such regeneration.[14]

Ginzburg's reply as chairman was curt. The function of OPE, he explained, was the support of Jewish university students and the publication of Jewish books. These were its stated and exclusive goals, and he left the clear impression that if the society embraced Bertensohn's agenda it would mean that it had abruptly abandoned them. Why primary education reform, its *raison d'être* only a few years earlier, was now unacceptable, he did not say.[15]

Two other proposals, submitted by government rabbis in 1868 and 1873 respectively, elicited much fuller responses. In both cases the petitioners put themselves forward as candidates for OPE subsidies for the operation of reformed heders and other schools for basic education in smaller, culturally insulated Jewish communities. In the first one, a Rabbi Bronstein of the town of Luibar in the Volhynia province (its Jewish population in 1847 was 3770) proposed that government rabbis in towns like his should be allocated sixty roubles annually by OPE for two years at a time to help them set up schools for Russian-language instruction: 'reading heders supplied with Russian books' is how the rabbi described them.[16]

Marcus Gurovich, a 'learned Jew' in the New Russia governor-general's office, was asked by OPE for his opinion (he had reported on small south Russian-Jewish communities in a detailed study completed in the late 1850s) and he recommended its rejection. Any proposal, he wrote, that addressed the inadequacies of traditional Jewish education was of some value, but this one was simply impracticable. It was, above all, too expensive. If only a small proportion of the towns that needed such schools were provided with funding—say if 100 were included, speculated Gurovich—OPE would have to allocate some 14,300 roubles. And who could ensure, he asked, that these schools would be better attended than the government school system set up in the 1840s and 1850s and with a rather dismal response? Even the government schools in Kishinev, a city with 30,000 Jews, attracted no more than fifty-six pupils.[17]

Is there, he asked rhetorically, a large enough cadre of russified government rabbis to run the schools? And even the best of such rabbis had to face re-election in their communities every three years, something far from certain particularly for those *Maskilim* who served rather benighted communities (precisely the sort of communities targeted by Bronstein). Moreover, if sixty roubles were given to rabbis, who would pay the teachers' salaries? (An average annual salary would run to 400 roubles, Gurovich estimated.) If a community could afford to pay such salaries, was an additional sixty roubles really necessary? The inefficient and corrupt *korobka* tax, in place in most Jewish communities, would in any event, he predicted, simply absorb the funds without putting them to proper use. If Bronstein wished to distribute maskilic books (in the same petition he had proposed the creation of maskilic libraries) he and other like-minded men could buy or distribute them themselves. They might also tutor local youths; more ambitious plans must for the present be set aside.[18]

He called Bronstein's schools 'Sunday schools', although Bronstein had never used the term; and when the government in June 1869 supported Gurovich's rejection by informing OPE that the proposal, which the group had also submitted for assessment to the Ministry of Education, if implemented, would contravene OPE's charter, it characterized them in the same way: 'It is neither within the scope of [OPE's] brief to open Sunday schools for beginning students nor schools for basic literacy.'[19] Rabbis such as Bronstein might, if they wished, submit applications individually to the authorities, but OPE could not as an educational body initiate such efforts. Once again, OPE's attitude towards heder reform was linked directly to official constraints; here we have confirmation that the government (and not only the over-cautious St Petersburg magnates) felt strongly about the issue. Why, was still not explained.

In the other case, several government rabbis in 1873 published articles in the Orthodox Hebrew-language newspaper *Ha-Lebanon* calling on OPE to promote heder reform. OPE responded in a lengthy rejoinder written probably by Rosenthal. The rabbis' proposals had argued that OPE must supervise with their help the re-education of the masses to persuade them that 'enlightenment' and 'education' were not incompatible with the observance of Judaism.[20] Such activity, OPE answered, fell outside its province: it could not challenge Jewish religious practices and if it was perceived as doing so it could be challenged by the government as acting as a religious rather than educational body: it was in its origins, and by virtue of the charter granted to it by the government which neither permitted it to move 'to the right nor left', an enlightenment organization; this constituted the very cornerstone, in Rosenthal's words, of his group. Particularly in view of the acute sensitivity that Russian Jews felt about religious reform of any kind, OPE must, the document affirmed, distance itself from such activity. OPE must not interfere in the struggle between a maskilic and non-maskilic Judaism, at least not in the direct and potentially confrontational way promoted by the government rabbis. They themselves could set up model heders in their communities, but the society would do no more than lend moral support to this minimalist agenda. Heder reform, OPE affirmed once again, was important but could not be addressed by the group, if only because of the restrictive nature of its charter.[21]

Yet, without changing its charter, OPE reversed itself the next year and set up an (albeit rather modest) fund to support new and progressive heders.[22] It never explained why it had resisted such policies for so long in the face of both formal protests by Bertensohn, Bronstein, *et al.* and the many other calls for heder reform raised in its correspondence and meetings. When, for instance, Jewish public opinion on the government school system was canvassed by OPE in 1866 (the system was planned for closure by the authorities, but managed to remain intact for several more years) many letters spoke of heders and their deleterious impact. They complained of the ignorance of *melameds*, and some even recommended that they be punished (and their children redeemed) by forcing the children to attend government schools. *Melameds* were so ignorant, claimed Rabbi Minor of Minsk, later Moscow (a rare example of a distinguished and widely respected government rabbi), that they typically did not even know Hebrew properly.[23] OPE did subsequently initiate a few, rather tepid projects addressing these issues: it funded model heders in Jewish agricultural settlements in New Russia and, elsewhere, started one or two Talmud Torahs designed along modern lines.[24] Beyond this nothing was attempted or—judging from the published transcripts, at least—contemplated by the St Petersburg OPE leadership before its turnabout in 1874.

II

It was the Odessa branch of OPE, set up in 1867, the only branch outside St Petersburg in this period (a second branch, in Riga, was established in 1898) that was the most consistent and vigorous proponent of heder reform. That the leaders of St Petersburg and Odessa OPE clashed was, as we shall see, probably inevitable; that heder reform should emerge as central in the cluster of issues that distinguished the society's socially radical Odessa from conservative St Petersburg *Maskilim* is nonetheless striking.

The leaders of the groups were very different. At the helm of the St Petersburg OPE were bankers and financiers dominated by the fabulously wealthy Ginzburgs, whose banking empire was the product of astute investments in liquor and tax-farming in the first half of the century. Close to Ginzburg was Leon Rosenthal, the bookish and formidable Hebraist and financier, son of a wealthy Vilna Jew, who substantially augmented the family fortune when he moved to the capital. Other magnates, Odessa's Brodsky, for instance, were on OPE's board but took a much less active role. Well-known *Maskilim* were also represented, including Rabbis Minor and Neumann, the writers and editors Slonimski, Fuenn, Tsederbaum, and Osip Rabinovich, who soon transferred his allegiance to the Odessa branch. By all accounts, it was Ginzburg (along with Rosenthal) who controlled the agenda. The Ginzburgs provided OPE with 2000 roubles annually, which amounted to some 28 per cent of its annual income between 1872 and 1884; in the same period Leon Rosenthal's donations added up to another 10 per cent of the budget. Membership fees accounted for less than 30 per cent.[25]

The Odessa OPE's first leader was Shimon Aryeh Schwabacher, the city's German-born government rabbi who, along with Brodsky, had been urged by the St Petersburg leaders to start the branch if only because the New Russia University would attract many Jews in need of subsidies. Both Schwabacher and Brodsky were pushed aside—the first more quickly and decisively than the second but both within three years of the branch's opening—by the doctors, journalists, un- or underemployed lawyers and other free professionals who took charge. Its first committee included three doctors, one notary (*Razsvet*'s editor Osip Rabinovich), two freelance journalists. Brodsky, its chairman, was the only exception until he resigned his post in 1870 and was replaced by the physician Emmanuel Soloveichik, in fact the dominant figure in the branch since it opened. The four new committee members selected the year Soloveichik became chairman were all professional men and when Soloveichik died in 1875, Menashe Morgulis, a lawyer by training, replaced him.[26]

They had little money (the branch was always short of funds and St Petersburg was unwilling to augment these), they worked closely on various interlinked projects (the same people ran *Razsvet*, *Sion'* and *Den'*, the local artisanry school *Trud* and other innovative schemes) and, in contrast to those intellectuals associated with the St Petersburg OPE, they were university-educated; the *Maskilim* associated with the capital's society were self-taught Hebrew scholars of a more traditional, less acculturated mould. Odessa's men were also political liberals, western-izers in the standard Russian meaning of the term. Ginzburg and Rosenthal also looked to the West for political inspiration but, while they saw figures like England's stolid and conservative Jewish leader Moses Montefiore as exemplifying the best of western Jewish values, the Odessa OPE looked to a radical-liberal such as Germany's Gabriel Riesser, whose biography was recounted in their newspapers and whose democratic principles more closely meshed with those extolled by the university-trained Russian liberals. Both groups linked their work for Jewry's cultural improvement with its eventual emancipation, but their beliefs as to what such emancipation entailed differed substantially. In Odessa it was linked to bourgeois democracy and a willingness to confront the state bureaucracy as inspired, above all, by the dignified example of Pirogov, whose tenure in Odessa as head of the local educational district (1856–8) had a decisive impact on the russified intelligentsia now at the helm of the city's OPE. Hence the integrationist visions of these two leadership cadres differed, as did their assumptions as to what constituted a properly 'civilized' human being; this was a topic of extensive theoretical debate in the group during OPE's first years.[27]

When it started, the Odessa OPE saw itself as the Jewish clearing-house for russification, as a cultural centre which would facilitate the translation of the Bible, the Jewish prayers, basic Judaica primers, rendering the most essential works of Jewish literature into the vernacular that would soon, it felt, constitute the *lingua franca* of East European Jewry. The branch soon ran afoul of the government in its efforts to publish a translation of the Bible (a modern Russian translation had still not appeared); the St Petersburg OPE leadership urged it not to pursue its prayer book translation because, it said, nothing would grate more on the sensibilities of Jewish traditionalists. It urged more 'neutral', less provocative activities.[28] Yet it was not pleased when pedagogical reform, especially of primary schools, took the limelight.

Among the branch's first successful projects was the publication in 1869 of a primer on Judaism for elementary classroom use written by the local pedagogue Isaac Warshawsky. More directly relevant to heders was OPE's sponsorship of Bronstein's application; indeed, even in its first year Odessa OPE considered actively involving itself either in setting up new locally-based Jewish primary schools or in reforming those existing ones most amenable to change. Pressed by several of Odessa's more progressive *melameds* to provide their schools with financial help, the branch decided to embark on a systematic study of all the city's heders which was published in *Den'* in 1870; it found only a small number of the schools to be impressive by modern standards, but that many more were sufficiently susceptible to modernization to be won over.[29] The branch closed the next year (in the wake of the 1871 Odessa pogrom that left its leadership disillusioned with the efficacy of maskilic cultural politics), but when it reopened in 1878 it characterized its major focus now, as in the past, as the introduction of 'model heders' into New Russia. Its new chairman, Morgulis, said that he hoped to continue in the same general direction. Four years earlier, in 1874, when the prospect of reactivating the branch was floated in St Petersburg, the project that Odessa leaders proposed was the creation of a local Jewish teacher's seminary with affiliated and modernized heders. When the Odessa OPE finally reopened the issue of the creation of such heders, this time a network in the poorer sections of the city, was at the top of its agenda.[30]

None of these projects materialized in the 1860s or 1870s, mainly for financial reasons. The branch ran on a budget of 1225 roubles in 1868, about one-seventh of that of the St Petersburg OPE. Its financial situation, rather than improving, deteriorated.[31] Unrealized though these projects were, the fact that they were promoted with such vigour and consistency was indicative of the Odessa OPE's willingness to break ranks with the society's leadership and its priorities.

This opposition was surprising if only because Odessa was, by any standards, an ideal spot for the support of high school and university students; this was the reason why the branch was started in the first place on the initiative of the St Petersburg leadership. Since the mid-1820s Russian education had captured an important role in local Jewish cultural life, and the city, with its many superb schools, first-rate gymnasiums and the New Russia University (established in 1865), attracted large numbers of Jewish students eager to pursue a secular education. In 1863, 252 of the 990 Jews in the empire's gymnasiums were enrolled in Odessa; the same year another 286 Jews attended the district's other secondary schools, amounting to 11.7 per cent of their total enrolment. A higher proportion of local Jews attended gymnasiums and universities here than anywhere else in the empire, outside the capitals. Many of these students were poor and in need of aid: in 1878 an Odessa school inspector informed Odessa OPE that a 'large' number of Jewish students were too poor to pay gymnasium tuition and would be expelled. The list was so long that the society asked that the names be ranked according to academic promise.[32] Before the branch closed in 1871 it declared itself opposed on principle to such assistance, but while it later moderated this position it still continued to commit itself primarily to the promotion of basic Russian literacy and elementary education.

This emphasis reflected the impact that populism (as a cultural, not necessarily as a political force) had on the Odessa OPE's young, russified, university-trained leadership and constituency. It persuaded them of the obligations incumbent upon the culturally privileged and provided them with an alternative model of what Russian Jewry should look like, very different from that shared by Ginzburg and his entourage. It was this impact, certainly more so than the geographical proximity of the Jewish *folk*, that helped shape Odessa's priorities on this score. Hence the 'Russian masses' were described repeatedly as the object of Jewish *sblizhenie* (rapprochement) by the Odessa branch: the term 'masses' does not once appear in the transcripts of the St Petersburg meetings until June 1872 and then only in reference to Jews, not Russians.[33] The Odessa branch's view of the sort of society into which Jews would fit was much more egalitarian, and this probably helped determine its cultural and educational priorities.

Indicative in this respect was the proposal of Ilya Orshansky of Ekaterinoslav, made in 1865, to the St Petersburg OPE, in which he urged that the society fund the collation and publication of letters written by anonymous, simple East European Jews. (Orshansky, later one of Russian Jewry's leading historians, was active in the Odessa branch once it opened and, in 1870, was elected a member of its committee.) Influenced perhaps by the publication in 1861 of Moisei Berlin's *Ocherk etnografii evreiskago naseleniia v Rossii* (Ethnographic sketch of the Jewish population of Russia), an impressive, pioneering work which attempted to examine systematically Jewish folk and religious customs, Orshansky suggested, as summarized in OPE's transcripts, that the group

> publish letters written by the masses of Russian Jews. All those acquainted with the historical work of Jewish scholarship know that it is overwhelmingly preoccupied with the biographies of our scholars and with studies of their works . . . but contains little information about the lives of simple Jews. We have hardly any [written] source to illuminate this history.[34]

He called the book that would emerge a 'memorial' to the activities of the masses of Jews and he expected it to serve as a crucial source book for future historians of Russian Jewry.

We can do no more than speculate on the extent to which populist inclinations had an impact on the educational or cultural priorities supported by Orshansky and his Odessa colleagues; a connection between the two seems likely. The most important keys to our mystery are to be found elsewhere, though. The reasons why heder reform, a seemingly innocuous issue, became the subject of such intense debate, are clear from a review of OPE's transcripts—reticent and heavily edited though they are in parts. They show that the issue's prominence was neither surprising nor probably even avoidable.

III

First, as the transcripts indicate, OPE was simply loath to do anything that would be interpreted as persecuting *melameds*. Severe treatment had been meted out to them by the government for several decades (the most oppressive predating OPE's establishment) and many Russian Jews continued to fear the introduction of new restrictions. OPE wished to avoid any hint of coercion on this score: it is in this light that its response to the 1873 proposal by government rabbis should be seen. They had urged OPE to involve itself actively in persuading religious Jews that heders were Judaically acceptable. OPE had replied that it refused to do anything that might give the impression that it wished to impose new religious values on traditional Jews. It was coercion that was responsible, it claimed, for alienating East European Jews from cultural change and OPE would have nothing to do with such methods. Jews, OPE insisted in its reply, had not in the past rejected *Haskalah* in itself, only the methods sometimes used to promote it.[35] OPE, particularly in view of its (unwitting but inevitable) function as Jewry's central address for *shtadlanut*, or intercession, would do nothing to give the impression that it condoned forcing traditional Jews either to change their schools or to reject their teachers.[36]

The first restriction on *melameds* dated back to 1844, when heders were told to teach German and Russian and when prospective *melameds* were first required to pass official examinations. *Melameds* managed to resist such obligations, however, as they did attempts to make them register with the authorities: a total of 2197 *melameds* were counted in 1849, 10,000 less than were known to teach two years earlier. Official harassment increased in the 1850s. Certain subjects and religious texts (including some talmudic tractates) were declared officially unacceptable; school inspectors would periodically visit heders and threaten them with closure. Teachers and students alike were informed that they would be examined by the state for subjects rarely taught (or teachable) within the context of traditional heders. In 1859 such harassment stopped, but the government now warned *melameds* that by 1875 it would expect them to hold certificates from either gymnasiums or government Jewish schools. Such policies had left a bad taste in the mouths of traditional as well as maskilic Jewry and OPE leaders were hesitant to do anything that would suggest that heders were once again the objects of official or semi-official scrutiny, let alone persecution. *Maskilim* had played a highly visible role in government-sponsored heder reform, serving as examiners of *melameds*, as inspectors of heders and in other supervisorial capacities.[37] The belief of Valuev, Minister of the Interior, that OPE would take over where the government had left things in 1859 and continue to challenge the hegemony of the *melamed* is indicative; OPE refused to play this role.

Second, if Jewish schools were to be the subject of special scrutiny by OPE in the 1860s, it is not surprising that these were not heders but the government school system designed for Jews and intended for closure soon after OPE was established. In a report prepared by p. Postels on the basis of his inspection of government schools in 1864, it was recommended that the *korobka* tax supporting the schools be abolished, that all but their first grades be closed, and the Judaic component of these reduced to a minimum. The report generated much debate within OPE, which served in this instance (and by no means in this case alone) as both a sounding-board for Jewish educational opinion and as an agency for *shtadlanut*, spearheaded as it was by Russian Jewry's leading figures.[38]

Few Jews canvassed agreed with Postels' conclusions (Osip Rabinovich was, on this occasion as in so many others, an exception) and, based on these responses, OPE proposed an alternative course to the government. The system should continue, OPE argued, as should the *korobka* tax, but much greater emphasis should be placed on the students' technical expertise as artisans and craftsmen. The present two-tier system should be augmented by a third; only Jews should be appointed principals of the schools (Christians, often converted Jews, now served in this capacity); and tuition fees should be introduced because Jewish parents would value schools only if they paid fees.[39] OPE's (successful) intervention occupied much of its attention in its first few years and it was only in 1874 that most of the government schools were closed and the two rabbinical schools which stood at the system's apex were transformed into teachers' seminaries.

Third, heder reform was shunted aside because Ginzburg himself was intensely interested in the support of secondary and university students, an interest that had predated the establishment of OPE. As he wrote to a group of twenty very poor Jews, in attendance at Kharkov University, in 1863, OPE was to be started 'primarily for the reason' of supporting students like themselves. He assured them of his own longstanding interest and that their request for funding would be honoured. Three-eighths of OPE's 8000-rouble budget for 1866 was allocated to help secondary and university students, by far the largest single item, and this remained constant. Ginzburg's own priorities meshed nicely with those of the Russian educational establishment, which had since the eighteenth century built from the top down, with higher educational establishments allocated generous sums long before comparable ones were given to either primary or secondary schools.[40]

Fourth, the prospect of reforming all heders, the schools responsible for the education of nearly every school-age Jewish boy in the Pale and Poland, was seen by OPE as simply too vast, complicated, even intractable. OPE's repeated assertions that only small, localized efforts at reform were practical must be seen in this light, a minimalism that reflected the overridingly sceptical attitude of the Russian educational authorities towards the prospect of thorough or rapid change. When compared with the hundreds of thousands of children enrolled in heders in every obscure corner of the Pale, Jewish university or gymnasium students (2,045 Jews attended Russian universities in 1870) constituted a relatively compact, modernized and keenly receptive constituency.[41] And by no means was OPE, even if it devoted all its energy to heder reform, assured of the sort of visible success that it enjoyed when subsidizing the education of motivated older students. Educational change, particularly at primary school level, is, as Lawrence Stone has observed within the context of his study of English literacy, extraordinarily difficult, if only because it requires the retraining of an entire generation of teachers before a discernible impact is felt by pupils:

> Except for education in the home, which is temporary, geographically and socially a restricted phenomenon, all education is concerned with the establishment of formal institutions, which once set up are exceedingly difficult to alter. Moreover . . . educational improvement is dependent upon the training of more and better teachers and is therefore inevitably a very sluggish process, with policy decisions only producing concrete results ten or fifteen years later.[42]

OPE's decision to avoid this sphere can be seen as reflecting its unwillingness to wait so long before it made its mark on Russian Jewish life; heder reform, an issue of seminal importance, was also, from its perspective, one that must remain in abeyance as the Society grew in prestige, wealth and influence. Its first successes were unlikely to be scored in this elusive, complex arena, one that seemed all the more elusive in view of the belief that Russian illiteracy was itself essentially intractable, or at least a problem that would be unlikely to be solved for the foreseeable future. A minimalist rhetoric was readily at hand and it served to reinforce and substantiate OPE's cautious stance.

There is a fifth and final reason, however, one that proved much more decisive in shaping OPE's policy in respect to heders and in ensuring that it remained unchanged for more than a decade. None of the reasons listed above, influential as they were, can really claim to have done this: the fact that heder reform before 1862 and later (in 1874) emerged as an important plank in OPE's agenda argues against the likelihood that either an implacable unwillingness to battle *melameds*, tackle the irksome realm of Jewish primary education, or detract from the importance of higher education were of paramount significance. As far as the debate over government schools is concerned, the issue first surfaced in 1865 with word of Postels' impending report: why did OPE drop heder reform from its charter nearly three years earlier? Without doubt the debate over the future of the Jewish government school system, along with the other factors reviewed above, had their impact on OPE's policy, but they do not explain how it originated or, in truth, why it was sustained for so long. What had occurred in 1862 to persuade OPE's leaders to change significantly the direction of their group? Why were they convinced in 1874 that heder reform was now a goal that they should finally pursue?

This decision was, in fact, a by-product of the impact on OPE of Russia's Sunday school movement, a factor never acknowledged by OPE's leaders but evident from the available primary sources.[43] The first draft of OPE's charter was designed overwhelmingly along the lines of the Sunday schools, the popular education movement that appeared on the Russian cultural scene in 1859 in the wake of the Crimean débâcle and which, by the end of 1860, led to the formation in St Petersburg alone of twenty-three schools for workers and artisans; a total of 274 such schools existed by the same time in cities throughout European Russia. The schools were under the intellectual sway of Pirogov (the first were started in Kiev where he became education curator after he left Odessa in 1858) as well as the liberal educator and historian Platon V. Pavlov; they called, in Pavlov's words, for 'la révolution par école', a goal that the government uncharacteristically allowed them to pursue without undue interference, at least during their first year or two.[44]

Topics taught in the schools consisted of Russian, mathematics and religion; from the perspective of the government the last subject was crucial in line with its patriarchal view of the schools as bodies that would instil a heightened respect for authority in the potentially recalcitrant labouring classes. The Ministry of the Interior was from the outset sceptical of their usefulness (and especially of the young men and women who devoted themselves to working-class literacy) but the Ministry of Education proved a steadfast supporter. By 1862, hundreds of such schools remained in existence with many located in centres of Jewish life, including Zhitomir, Vilna, Kherson, Ekaterinoslav, Kishinev, Riga and Odessa.[45] The network came to a sudden end in June 1862 as part of the official reaction that followed the mysterious May fires in St Petersburg which were attributed to revolutionaries. At the same time it was discovered that a handful of Sunday school teachers were engaged in revolutionary propaganda which led to the system's abrupt closure, now declared illegal outside the Baltic area. Sunday schools, only recently officially supported, were now under a dark cloud and their leading figures were suspected of disloyalty. Pavlov, whose remarks at a speech a few months earlier were deemed suspicious, was already in provincial exile before the announcement of the schools' discontinuance.[46]

At the time that Ginzburg approved the earliest draft of OPE's charter the Sunday school movement was just getting under way. The document called for young people to teach their skills to otherwise illiterate Jews (illiterate in Russian, that is) and its emphasis on the organization of special courses for the labouring classes, even its curriculum which stressed Russian, mathematics and Bible—all these were modelled directly on the government-sanctioned Sunday schools.[47] This was in early 1860. The group's subsequent and abrupt turnabout, which Rosenthal admitted was due, at least in part, to government pressure, dated from the same time that the Sunday school movement was forcibly closed. OPE's revised charter vividly reflected this change by deleting all reference, however indirect, to the goals that it had in common with the now discredited system.

Yet Sunday schools remained a preoccupation for OPE. Gurovich characterized the schools proposed by Bronstein (a system that he disliked) as 'Sunday schools'; so did the spokesman from the Ministry of Education who contended that they were not only impracticable but also potentially illegal. For the St Petersburg leaders, aware that their ability to navigate successfully in the treacherous waters of Russian-Jewish diplomacy was predicated on their ability to avoid anything vaguely contentious, let alone seditious, their decision to disassociate themselves from the Sunday schools was self-evident and, arguably, even correct. That they ensured that OPE avoid any association with efforts aimed at the improvement of basic literacy may have been due to government pressure; or they may have done this on their own initiative. Perhaps, as the letter sent by the Ministry of Education in response to Bronstein's application indicates, this was a product of both external pressure and organizational prudence.

Odessa, however, reacted very differently. Sunday schools had struck deep roots here and, in any event, local OPE leaders typically reacted to government restrictions (particularly those aimed at public work that they considered important) in neither as cautious nor as accommodating ways as did their counterparts in the capital. Pirogov, the godfather of the Sunday school movement, had made a profound impact on the city's Jewish intellectuals and his spirited support of the local modernized Talmud Torah (he stated in the *Odesskii vestnik* that it constituted a model for Russian emulation) helped introduce them to the system's principles in a way that would leave them particularly receptive and loyal. The democratic ideals espoused by Pirogov in a two-volume collection of his educational essays published in 1862, which saw elementary schools as the foundations for a more egalitarian Russia, further solidified his impact on Odessa's russified intelligentsia.

Such influence was already evident in Osip Rabinovich's *Razsvet* (1860–1) which described Sunday schools extensively and with great sympathy. On its front page on 13 January 1861, for instance, it announced that one local Jewish school had opened only three weeks earlier with a mere 15 students and now had 120. Odessa's wealthiest Jews now contributed to the cause, the newspaper announced, including Efrusi (twenty-five roubles) and Brodsky (ten roubles).[48]

That Brodsky would have disassociated himself from such work two years later is indisputable; Rabinovich's circle would not. For them Sunday schools remained symbols of decent, practical cultural work. They continued to speak of its devotees in most admiring terms. An example of this is the Odessa OPE's reaction to the application in 1870 for a subsidy by a local gymnasium graduate now bound for medical studies in St Petersburg. He was described as the son of poor parents, educated in the local, rather decrepit Talmud Torah (before its improvement under Pirogov's tutelage) and in a local Jewish government school. He had managed to obtain, despite this unfortunate background, a secondary school diploma. There was a considerable opposition to the application, however, because the Odessa OPE had, as mentioned above, established as a matter of principle that it would not provide such subsidies. This case, argued the boy's advocates, was an exception since, in addition to his other qualifications, he had actively promoted Jewish enlightenment and was in the past 'without pay . . . a Sunday school teacher'. In the end, the application was sent to the municipal authorities who were asked to help him with the use of *korobka* funds.[49] The fact that his record as a Sunday school teacher had apparently nearly swayed his opponents (and served as a major argument for his supporters) is none the less telling.

Heder reform may have seemed on the surface a rather improbable focal point for activists of the Odessa OPE's ilk. Their willingness to combine broad, ambitious, even radical projects (from the vantage point of religious Jews) in their agenda with others aimed at reforming local heders is, at first glance, surprising, even discordant. Yet heder reform assumed for them a symbolic importance in the wake of the closing of the Sunday school movement which made this issue all the more compelling and attractive for the Odessa OPE and (for many of the same reasons) awkward for St Petersburg. Both responded to pressures of the larger milieu. Their reading of such pressures was entirely at odds, reflecting much deeper differences in their respective cultural and political outlook.

The creation by the government of a network of new urban elementary schools in May 1872 designed to provide talented but poor children with access to higher education served to signal OPE that it no longer needed to avoid, as it had for so long, Jewish elementary school reform. Once the Jewish government schools were all but closed down the next year, and the 1874 military reforms announced, which introduced universal conscription but reduced substantially the conscription period for those with a higher education, OPE was compelled to take a new look at the whole realm of primary as well as secondary education for Jews. With the closure of the government schools, greater integration of Jews into general schools was necessary; now that the new conscription laws, which relaxed the opposition of many Orthodox Jews to secular education, had their impact, many Jewish parents began to insist that their own schools prepare children better to qualify for entrance into Russian ones. *Maskilim* had long urged the reform of heders so that they could prepare pupils to enter government schools; there had been little response, mostly because parents were indifferent to the government school system and had little interest in their children attending it. Now that large numbers of parents were (quite suddenly and keenly) interested in ensuring that their children enter Russian elementary and secondary schools, they began to push for a more integrated curriculum so that secular and Jewish subjects alike were taught.[50] The impact of these changes was quickly felt in Odessa's heders: the Odessa OPE's investigation of 1870 found them to be rather miserable, on the whole. By the mid-1870s the major thrust in local Jewish educational life was to introduce (at least some modicum of) secular study into even the most traditional heders: even *Hasidim* here, said one impressed visitor in 1876, 'learn Torah and also study mathematics'.[51]

By 1874, when OPE, still quite cautiously, reaffirmed its interest in heder reform by setting up a fund to support such work, the atmosphere was immeasurably more conducive. A year earlier Ginzburg had suggested (but did not press hard for) the formation of an OPE subcommittee that would consider proposals for heder reform. Ten years later, in 1884, OPE would assert that such reform was at the centre of its agenda.[52] No longer constrained by the ghost of the Sunday school movement, OPE felt able to put forward a policy that maskilic conservatives and liberals alike recognized to be crucial. OPE now confirmed its commitment to this, one of the *Haskalah*'s chief cultural concerns.

While the vision and moral courage of Odessa OPE's leaders was compelling and admirable, Ginzburg's caution in respect to heder reform in the 1860s—doubling as he did as leader of OPE and, in effect, of Russian Jewry as a whole—was, probably, the only conceivable tactic for his group. Ginzburg, along with Russia's other *shtadlans*, was eventually savaged in the late nineteenth and early twentieth centuries by the Jewish nationalist movement, particularly its more democratic, less Herzlian school, which posed the alternative of mass mobilization to that of quiet diplomacy which was now judged as inevitably obsequious and élitist.[53] Zionists (and other post-liberal Jewish ideologues) constituted themselves an alternative leadership, vying for influence, even hegemony, over Russian and world Jewry. Their analysis of *shtadlanut*, and this includes also Tcherikover's academically rigorous history of OPE, must be read with this in mind. Yet the discreet, and undoubtedly élitist, stance of Ginzburg and Rosenthal constituted in the 1860s—and probably well into the 1890s, for Jews at least—the only conceivable course for minority politics in imperial Russia. Until the appearance of non-Jewish allies, a Jewish press with a sizeable readership and reasonably viable financial structure, and some semblance of a political arena outside that of the Tsarist ministries and their provincial representatives, Jewish politics had little recourse but to pursue quiet interventionism, to rely on persuasion rather than on more 'modern' political strategies.[54]

This stance was not synonymous, as some Zionist or Bundist critics would later have it, with passivity: Ginzburg, after all, often pressed the government well beyond the point it preferred to go. He managed to circumvent government restrictions that he felt were unfair; at times he pushed officials with such persistence that the government warned him sternly to cease.[55] At the same time, he and his colleagues were aware that if they were to take seriously their responsibility as Jewry's leaders, they had to maintain a constructive relationship with the government, balancing the need to defend and transform Jewry, the pursuit of short- and long-term goals. *Shtadlanut*, and not the morally attractive but impracticable politics of Emmanuel Soloveichik and his populist, democratic Odessa colleagues, dominated Jewry's only empire-wide organization in mid-nineteenth century Russia. No other organizational scenario was then conceivable; no other leaders could as effectively represent Jews' needs. Otherwise admirable, but temporarily contentious concerns (such as elementary school reform in the 1860s) were, quite reasonably, held in abeyance by a leadership that prided itself on its patience, its willingness to compromise, to withstand temporary adversity, to achieve by dint of quiet persuasion what others could only dream of achieving by less dignified and discreet means.

Notes

1 Levinsohn is quoted in Dov Baer (Bernard) Natanson, *Sefer ha-zikhronot, divrei yemei Ribal* (Warsaw, 1889), p. 13. The best study of East European heders is *Sovremennyi kheder* (St Petersburg, 1912), commissioned by the Society for the Promotion of Enlightenment Among the Jews of Russia. Also see Kh. S. Kazhdan, *Fun heder un shkoles biz Zisho* (Mexico City, 1956); Eliezer Meir Lipschütz, *Ketavim*, vol. 1 (Jerusalem, 1947), pp. 307–80; Y. Shtern, *Kheder un beis medresh* (New York, 1950); G. Vol'tke, 'Kheder i melamed (v Rossii i Tsarstve Pol'skom)' *Evreiskaia entsiklopediia*, vol. 15, cols. 590–6; D. Patterson, *The Hebrew Novel in Czarist Russia* (Edinburgh, 1964), pp. 168–81. A discussion of official policy toward Polish heders may be found in M. J. Ochs, 'St Petersburg and the Jews of Russian Poland, 1862–1905' (unpublished Ph.D. thesis, Harvard University, 1986), pp. 149–73. Maskilic denunciations of the heder gave way in the late nineteenth century to much less critical, even laudatory assessments, especially in Jewish nationalist circles. See, for instance, M. Lilienblum, *Kol kitveh*, vol. 3 (Cracow, 1913), pp. 38–9.

2 On the political ramifications of *Haskalah* ideology see E. Lederhendler, 'From Autonomy to Autoemancipation: Historical Continuity, Political Development and the Preconditions for the Emergence of National Jewish Politics in Nineteenth-Century Russia' (unpublished Ph.D. thesis, Jewish Theological Seminary of America, 1986). I am indebted to Dr Lederhendler for showing me his work which provides numerous insights into East European Jewish political life.

3 I. M. Tcherikover, *Istoriia obshchestva dlia rasprostraneniia prosveshcheniia mezhdu evreiiami v Rossii* (St Petersburg, 1913), pp. 39–40

4 *ibid.*, p. 40

5 *Razsvet*, no. 19 (30 September 1860), pp. 299–301.

6 Y. (Leon) Rosenthal, *Toledot hevrat marbei haskalah be-yisrael be-eretz rusiah*, 2 vols (St Petersburg, 1885–90), vol. 1, p. viii.

7 Tcherikover (note 3 above), p. 43

8 *ibid.*, pp. 41, 43–4.

9 Rosenthal (note 6 above), vol. 1, pp. viii–ix

10 Tcherikover (note 3 above), p. 41

11 *ibid.*, pp. 169–70

12 *ibid.*, pp. 200–1

13 *ibid.*, pp. 59–61; 'Bertensohn, Iosif Vasil'evich', *Evreiskaia entsiklopediia*, vol. 4, vols 330–1.

14 Tcherikover (note 3 above), p. 61; Rosenthal (note 6 above), vol. 1, p. 1.

15 *ibid.*

16 Rosenthal (note 6 above), vol. 2, p. 145

17 *ibid.*, pp. 145–7

18 *ibid.*

19 *ibid.*, vol. 1, pp. 62–3

20 *ibid.*, p. 97

21 *ibid.*, p. 98

22 Tcherikover (note 3 above), p. 206

23 Rosenthal (note 6 above), vol. 2, pp. 69–70, 72–3, 77, 89, 95

24 Tcherikover (note 3 above), pp. 198, 205; Rosenthal (note 6 above), vol. 2, p. 81

25 See G. B. Sliozberg, *Baron G. O. Guenzburg* (Paris, 1933); Ben-Zion Katz, *Zikhronot* (Tel Aviv, 1963), pp. 68–73, 98–104; S. L. Tsitron, *Shtadlonim* (Warsaw, 1926), pp. 324–76. For a discussion of this élite in a later period in imperial Russian history see S. J. Zipperstein, 'The Politics of Relief: The Transformation of Russian Jewish

Communal Life during the First World War', *Studies in Contemporary Jewry*, vol. 4 (Oxford, 1988).

26 On the Odessa branch see Tcherikover (note 3 above), pp. 238–54; Rosenthal, (note 6 above), vol. 2, pp. 129–60. On the socio-economic standing of free professionals in Tsarist Russia see N. Frieden, *Physicians and the State: The Development of the Russian Medical Profession, 1856–1896* (Princeton, 1974), pp. 16–17.

27 See S. J. Zipperstein, *The Jews of Odessa: A Cultural History, 1794–1881* (Stanford, 1985), pp. 70–113; financial information on the Odessa OPE is mentioned in Tcherikover, *Istoriia*, p. 244: on the debate over the character of a 'civilized' Jew, see Rosenthal, *Toledot*, 2, esp. pp. 14–15. For a detailed study of the socio-political values of OPE's leadership in both St Petersburg and Odessa see S. J. Zipperstein, 'Jewish Acculturation and Its Limits in Imperial Russia: The Society for the Promotion of Enlightenment Among Jews, 1863–1881', *Assimilation and Community in European Jewry, 1815–1881*, J. Frankel and S. J. Zipperstein (eds.), (Cambridge, forthcoming).

28 Rosenthal (note 6 above), vol. 2, pp. 132–3; Tcherikover (note 3 above), pp. 241, 244. Also see the earliest application put before OPE for a Russian-language translation of prayers, by Ilya Orshansky in February 1864: Rosenthal, op. cit., vol. 1, p. 2.

29 Tcherikover (note 3 above), p. 244. On Odessa OPE's investigation of local heders, see Rosenthal (note 6 above), vol. 2, pp. 151–3. The report was published in *Den'*, nos. 41–2 (1870), pp. 664–6, 679–80.

30 Rosenthal (note 6 above), vol. 2, pp. 108, 148; Tcherikover (note 3 above), pp. 291–4. On the re-establishment of the Odessa branch, see Rosenthal, op. cit., p. 155.

31 Zipperstein (note 27 above), pp. 129–30; Tcherikover, (note 3 above), p. 244. For information of OPE's budget see Rosenthal (note 6 above), vol. 1, p. 28, and Lederhendler (note 2 above), p. 319.

32 Rosenthal (note 6 above), vol. 2, p. 158. On the education of Jews in Odessa, see Zipperstein (note 27 above), pp. 44–55, 129–34.

33 Tcherikover (note 3 above), pp. 203–4, 239, 243

34 Rosenthal (note 6 above), vol. 1, p. 114. On populism as a cultural force see R. Wortman, *The Crisis of Russian Populism* (Cambridge, 1967).

35 Rosenthal (note 6 above), vol. 1, p. 98.

36 S. Pozner, 'Melamed i zakon—Istoricheskii ocherk', *Knizhki Voskhoda* (Sept.–Dec. 1903); for a succinct summary of governmental policy towards heders see Tzvi Scharfstein, *Toledot ha-hinukh be-yisrael ba-dorot ha-aharonim*, vol. 1 (New York, 1945), pp. 298–305.

37 *ibid.*

38 See Tcherikover (note 3 above), pp. 171–2. On the protracted discussion within OPE about the fate of Jewish government schools, see Rosenthal (note 6 above), vol. 2, pp. 63–99 and Tcherikover, op. cit., pp. 170–90. On OPE's role as the central address for Jewish petitioners and intercession, Lederhendler (note 2 above) writes, p. 321: 'The OPE seemed ill-at-ease with the idea of fulfilling a broader function as a chief bureau for *shtadlanut*, yet this is precisely the way in which it was perceived.'

39 Rosenthal (note 6 above), vol. 2, pp. 88–99

40 Tcherikover (note 3 above), pp. 132, 147; Rosenthal (note 6 above), vol. 1, p. 28; 'Ginzburg, Evzel' Gavriilovich, Baron',*Evreiskaia entsiklopediia*, vol. 6, esp. col. 534.

41 Rosenthal (note 6 above), vol. 2, p. 84; Zipperstein (note 27 above), p. 129.

42 L. Stone, 'Literacy and Education in England, 1640–1900', *Past and Present*, no. 42 (1969), p. 70.

43 The best recent discussion is R. E. Zelnik, 'The Sunday-School Movement in Russia, 1859–1862', *Journal of Modern History*, no. 2 (June, 1965), pp. 151–70. Also see M. K. Lemke, *Ocherki osvoboditel'nago dvizheniia "shestidesiatykh godov"* (St Petersburg, 1908), pp. 401–38.

44 Zelnik (note 43 above), pp. 151–4; Lemke (note 43 above), p. 416.
45 *ibid.*
46 Zelnik (note 43 above), pp. 154–60
47 Tcherikover (note 3 above), p. 40
48 *Razsvet*, no. 34 (13 January 1861)
49 Rosenthal (note 6 above), vol. 2, p. 152
50 On the new urban schools see A. Sinel, *The Classroom and the Chancellery: State Educational Reform in Russia Under Count Dmitri Tolstoi* (Cambridge, Mass., 1973), pp. 215–30; Zipperstein (note 27 above), pp. 129–33.
51 *ibid.*, Zipperstein, p. 129
52 Rosenthal (note 6 above), vol. 1, pp. 101–2, 188
53 See J. Frankel, *Prophecy and Politics: Socialism, Nationalism and the Russian Jews, 1867–1917* (Cambridge, 1981), pp. 49–132.
54 For a discussion of this theme, see Lederhendler (note 2 above), pp. 149–261.
55 Tcherikover (note 3 above), pp. 220, 241; Lederhendler (note 2 above), pp. 324–7.

Anglicization and the Education of Jewish Immigrant Children in the East End of London

Suzanne Kirsch Greenberg

BETWEEN 1881 and 1914 well over two million Eastern European Jews left their homes and began the long and arduous journey in search of a better life in the West. Great Britain was second only to the United States in the number of Eastern European Jewish immigrants who sought new lives on her shores: the population of Jews in England grew from 60,000 in the middle of the nineteenth century to more than three times that number by the eve of the First World War. London Jewry alone gained 2000–5000 Jewish immigrants a year between 1881 and 1905, when passage of the Aliens Act caused a steady decline in the numbers seeking entry to Great Britain.[1] Like other immigrants before them, these refugees gravitated to the East End of London and particularly to the borough of Stepney, which became the centre of a swelling Jewish working-class population.

For immigrants, this period represented the transition from the relatively restrictive milieu of Eastern Europe to the freer society of the West. The years between 1881 and 1905 witnessed intense upheaval, change and growth both for the Russian, Polish and Romanian Jews who made their way to London and the English Jewish community obligated to receive them. The institutional and ideological character of a redefined Jewish community emerged—a synthesis of established Anglo-Jewry and the new immigrants, indelibly imprinted by the rich diversity of culture, religion and politics which these refugees brought to their new homes in London's East End.

An examination of the educational arrangements for immigrant children provides an excellent lens through which to view the interior drama of the Jewish experience during this period. The educational goals of both the old and new communities incorporated not only current beliefs but also future aspirations for these children and for the character of the Jewish community as a whole. Immigrants and native Jews alike viewed the educational process as a means to reinforce and

111

perpetuate their own particular vision of Jewish life. For Anglo-Jewry that vision was a unified, anglicized Jewish community which relied on an English secular and religious education to transform Yiddish-speaking, 'uncivilized' immigrant children into English Jews. While the immigrant community had a separate and often conflicting vision, especially with respect to religious education, the purpose of this study is to examine the anglicization process in terms of how the state-supported educational system accommodated these children, often with the consent and support of Anglo-Jewry.

Late nineteenth-century educational reform, which paved the way for universal, free and compulsory primary schooling, may have been the most potent force in this process of anglicization. Therefore the educational experience of this immigrant minority illuminates not only the process of acculturation for a particular community, but also by extension furnishes us with a valuable perspective on the development of popular education and educational reform in Victorian England.

By the beginning of the 1880s a national system of primary schools had been established with the explicit goal of educating the working classes. The working poor of Great Britain were, in their own way, the 'immigrants' of a class-differentiated society; their language and customs were alien, and reformers viewed the schools as social agencies for transforming the younger generation into disciplined, productive and morally responsible members of the lower classes.[2] Like their Gentile contemporaries, English Jews subscribed to the Victorian belief that the purpose of the state-directed educational process was to control and civilize the labouring poor and in particular their immigrant brethren. As the editor of the *Jewish Chronicle* argued:

> Above all, the most hopeful method is to act on the young of our foreign Jews by means of a thoroughly English education. Their parents, when they arrive here, have their characters fully formed and incapable of undergoing the radical change that is necessary to transform them into Englishmen. But the young mind is plastic; we can develop it in any direction we require. We can place a young Pole in the Jews' Free School with the assurance that at the end of his training he will be turned out a young Englishman . . . This has been recognized by our philanthropists as the most direct method of acting upon the adult foreigners who form so large a portion of its community and upon whose conduct its reputation so largely depends.[3]

This process of anglicization depended upon the agreement of the immigrant community, but at what cost was integration into a Christian English culture achieved? Immigrant children entered an educational environment in which the separation of church and state was extremely blurred. In fact, many reformers, both Jewish and Christian, viewed religious instruction in primary schools as an essential ingredient in the creation of a competent and civilized working-class electorate. After 1870, the central issue was not whether religion would be taught in the schools, but rather how to incorporate religion most adroitly into the school day. How could Jewish immigrant children come to terms with an educational ideology intrinsically bound to Christian observance? Or conversely, how would that ideology accommodate differences in religious orientation? In the 1890s, the debate surrounding the right to teach denominational Christian doctrine in the schools obliged the Jewish community to grapple with these questions, as well as to confront the consequences of anglicization.

The course of public education for the poor relied on the ideological compromises incorporated into the 1870 Education Act, which established the first national system of non-denominational primary schools. Steering an uneasy course between those who advocated secular education and an end to voluntary or denominational schools, and others who promoted the prevailing and predominantly Christian, semi-private denominational system, the 1870 Act provided for a public system of universal but not free or compulsory education. The Act divided the nation into school districts which were to provide each child between the ages of five and thirteen with a place in an elementary school. Church-affiliated voluntary schools could continue to function if they met the conditions of the Act, but if the voluntary system could not provide an adequate number of places, a School Board, charged with building non-denominational Board Schools, was to be elected by all rate-payers (including women) in the district. Both Board and voluntary schools received government grants, but the Board Schools had the added advantage of being able to draw upon the rates, and were therefore more financially secure. Education was free only for the very poor; all other children paid a weekly fee not to exceed ninepence. School Boards alone had the power to make attendance compulsory between the ages of five and thirteen, with a partial or total exemption for children between the ages of ten and thirteen who had been certified by an inspector to have reached the specified standard.[4] The next twenty years saw greater commitment on the part of the state to control the direction of primary schooling. By the end of the 1880s attendance became compulsory without exception, and the 1891 Education Act at last abolished the payment of school fees.

The 1870 Education Act had far-reaching consequences for the Jewish community, particularly Section 14(2) which mandated that in Board Schools 'no catechism or religious formulary which is distinctive to any particular denomination shall be taught in the school'. Voluntary schools could remain denominational, but Section 7 of the Act decreed compulsory acceptance by both Board and voluntary schools of the 'time-table conscience clause' in order to receive government funds. To comply with this rule, any religious instruction must come immediately before or after secular instruction in a given session, allowing a pupil to absent himself on grounds of conscience without interrupting his secular studies. Neither provision guaranteed that a child would attend a state school free of religious indoctrination, as it was not the intention of the Act to remove religion entirely from the schools.

Any teacher, headmaster or headmistress could teach religion if such instruction was not part of any particular creed, 'religious catechism or religious formulary' and as long as such instruction conformed to the provisions of the 'time-table conscience clause'. Even so, the 1870 Act removed religion from a pivotal position in the new schools. It was no longer possible to provide an integrated curriculum; religious instruction had to be separated from the secular course of study, and the government allocated funds based only on an inspector's examination of a pupil's performance in the secular subjects. Although religion remained an ideological component of primary education, the state, in essence, removed itself from the Christian sectarian debate surrounding the implementation of any specific religious dogma in what it hoped would be neutral Board Schools.

Many supporters of the 1870 Education Act expected that school boards would proliferate throughout England and Wales and eventually replace voluntary schools. However, during the six-month period of grace after the passage of the Act, both Nonconformist and Anglican churches engaged in campaigns to build additional schools and thereby circumvent the need for School Boards. The number of Protestant voluntary schools reached its peak at the end of the 1870s and then began to decline, perhaps because Board Schools could meet religious needs less expensively. Not trusting the religious intentions of these predominantly Protestant Board Schools, Roman Catholics elected, instead, to educate their children in their own schools. Thus, Roman Catholic schools more than doubled in number, from 400 in 1871 to 1000 at the end of the 1890s.[5]

Thus, after the passage of the 1870 Education Act the Christian denominational school system entered a period of rapid expansion. Why, then, did the number of Jewish denominational schools in London remain static when, especially after 1881, the population of Jewish schoolchildren in the East End rose dramatically owing to the influx of Jewish immigrants from Eastern Europe? Most Jewish schools had been established in the early and mid-nineteenth century, when elementary education for the poor relied upon support from religious groupings. Without these Jewish schools many Jewish families would have been compelled to send their children to Christian denominational schools, and the Jewish community felt itself obliged to provide separate schools in order to protect Jewish children from Christian indoctrination. But when the 1870 Education Act promised 'conscience free' elementary education supported by the rates, the Jewish community was unwilling to add the construction and maintenance of new Jewish schools to its financial burden. 'Why, it is contended,' asked the *Jewish Chronicle*, 'should Jews continue to tax themselves with the cost of special secular instruction for their poor when the machinery which they are compelled by the state to assist in maintaining is available for the purpose?'[6] Unlike many Anglicans, Nonconformists and Catholics, who viewed primary schools as institutions for propagating and disseminating their own specific religious dogmas, Anglo-Jewry, at least initially, welcomed the new Board Schools because of their avowed religious neutrality. Since the Act stipulated that all children must be provided a place in an elementary school which was non-denominational as well as 'conscience free', English Jewry could confidently lay responsibility for educating the growing number of Jewish immigrant children in the East End on the London School Board.

The first Board School erected in the 1870s by the London School Board was the Old Castle Street School, nearly adjacent to the Jews' Free School, the largest Jewish denominational school in the East End. With a pupil capacity of 1000, Old Castle Street was built to educate Jewish immigrant children whom the Jews' Free School could not accommodate. However, much to the surprise and consternation of the London School Board, when this brand new, modern school opened its doors, only 70 pupils enrolled. Many parents in the neighbourhood kept their children at home because they feared that Board Schools appointed Christian teachers whose avowed goal was to convert Jewish children. The Board sought the advice of Moses Angel, the renowned headmaster of the JFS. Jewish immigrants, according to Angel, were deeply suspicious of schools run by Christians whom they believed were likely to teach even the Hebrew Scriptures as a Christian text. If the Board wanted Jewish children to attend the school, Angel recommended that all references to Christianity be removed.

In co-operation with the Jewish community the Board made the Old Castle Street Board School, in essence, a Jewish school, designating Abraham Levy as headmaster and appointing a predominantly Jewish teaching staff.[7] Hebrew became a special approved subject under the Education Code, the school observed Jewish holidays and during the winter classes were dismissed at 2 p.m. on Fridays so that pupils could prepare for the Sabbath.[8] By 1883, both the Jewish community and the London School Board considered the Old Castle Street School to be an enormous success. After these administrative changes Jewish immigrant children flocked to the school, and the roll climbed to just under 1500, 95 per cent of which was Jewish.[9] In effect, the Board set aside schools with a high proportion of Jewish pupils as Jewish schools within the state system. Using the Old Castle Street School as a model, it viewed this policy as the most efficient means of accommodating the rising number of immigrant children, in fact the only way of persuading many immigrants to send their children to Board Schools.[10] Still, the relationship between the London School Board and the Jewish community was not always an amicable one, particularly when special advantage for Jewish children resulted in a reassessment of Jewish Board Schools.

At the beginning of 1893, Athelstan Riley, a prominent and highly vocal Anglican member of the London School Board, resurrected the divisive sectarian debate which had surrounded the birth of the first national Education Act in 1870. According to Riley and his supporters, the Board should amend the Education Code for London and adopt a more definite and specific policy with regard to the teaching of religion in Board Schools. It was not sufficient, they claimed, to require non-denominational Bible reading and religious instruction fitted to the capacity of the child. They decried current religious education as too general and empty of moral and religious content. Instead, they demanded that the Board make compulsory the teaching of the Holy Trinity and the divinity of Jesus Christ.

To add legitimacy to his campaign, Riley argued that for many years Jews had enjoyed the privilege of teaching their own religion in Jewish Board Schools. These state-supported schools, Riley claimed, observed Jewish and not Christian holidays, and the Board appointed Jewish teachers who gave Jewish religious instruction during normal school hours, contrary to the provisions of the 1870 Education Act. He concluded:

> At the present moment, whilst the School Board for London hesitates to guarantee to Christian parents, who are compelled to send their children to Board Schools, that those children shall be taught that Christ is God, and shall not be placed under an infidel teacher to receive instruction, it is at the same time *paying Jewish teachers out of the rates to* teach Jewish children that Christ is not God. That to my mind is a monstrous injustice.[11]

These proposals created an instant furore, not only within the Jewish community but also among Christian non-Trinitarians who had fought

and struggled in 1870 for the adoption of a non-sectarian Education
Act. Publicly reflecting the views of many in the Jewish community,
Chief Rabbi Hermann Adler and Sir John Simon registered their
disapproval of Riley's views by signing the Revd Dr Martineau's
'Memorial' to the London School Board protesting against the
intrusion of purely Christian education in Board Schools.[12] Others,
perceiving the threat to community privilege and to the educational
welfare of immigrant children in the East End, tried to accommodate
and pacify the Riley faction. Sir Philip Magnus and Claude Montefiore, representing this latter faction of Anglo-Jewry, responded with a
letter to *The Times*. As past members of the London School Board,
they objected to any Jewish interference in Board affairs. Jews, they
claimed, always had recourse to the 'conscience clause' if religious
instruction was Christian, and Jews were also in the privileged position
of having special advantages in Board Schools populated predominantly by Jewish children. On the other hand, in schools in which the
vast majority of pupils was Christian, the content of religious
instruction should be a matter determined by Christians and not Jews.
'We regret, therefore,' they admonished, 'that the Jewish community,
as a community, has expressed any opinion on the proposed alterations.'[13]

For most Jews, Riley's aggressive efforts to amend the Education
Code were not simply a threat to their special treatment by the London
School Board. Coupled with the growing clamour for restrictions on
immigration, these proposals further to Christianize state primary
education forced Jews to examine their position in English society. In
addition, the role of the Board Schools as the anglicizers of the
immigrant young became suspect, when it seemed that part of
becoming English would mean discarding Judaism in favour of the state
religion as taught in these schools.

For Riley and other Anglicans on the London School Board the
issue of supposed Jewish privilege in Board Schools, which had begun
as a minor part of the argument in favour of specifically Christian
religious teaching, now assumed a major position in the debate. Riley
again charged that East End Jewish Board Schools contravened the
Education Act by the appointment of Jewish teachers, by the observance of Jewish holidays and by teaching the Old Testament and the
Chief Rabbi's Code during school hours. The last accusation was the
most damning, if true, because it meant that the rates which supported
London Board Schools were also supporting the teaching of a specific
creed, a right which Riley demanded for Christians as well. Jewish
leaders denied the charge, insisting that all denominational religious
education took place in classes held after school. Riley countered that

'the Chief Rabbi's Syllabus is used by the teachers, i.e., when acting on behalf of the School Board, as well as when acting on behalf of the Jewish Association'.[14]

Finally, the London School Board realized it must take a position on this conflict. At a meeting on 10 November, 1893, after much preliminary discussion, Sir Cameron Gull moved that

> in the opinion of the Board, having regard to the special circumstances of the case, especially with reference to the difficulty of securing the attendance of Jewish children under other conditions, and to the manner in which the present custom had grown up, and seeing that the present practice is working well, and gives rise to no objections from other parents of other children in the schools, the members are not prepared to take any further action in the matter.[15]

The motion was seconded by the Revd Charles Ridgeway and supported, understandably, by Athelstan Riley, who then took the opportunity to point out to the Board the injustices done to Christians who lacked the privileges given to Jews. If Riley had voted against the motion, he would, in effect, have been voting against a policy which he wanted not only affirmed but extended throughout the jurisdiction of the Board.

'The time seems to be fast approaching,' proclaimed a 'correspondent' to the *Jewish Chronicle*, 'when the Jewish community will be called upon to declare what its policy is in regard to the question of religious education in Board Schools. Till now we have been living in a sort of Fool's Paradise. . . . We have enjoyed privileges which have been denied to other communities, and of which we ourselves scarcely seemed to be aware. But these halcyon days of fancied security are over.'[16] According to this writer, the problem was not Mr Riley but the interpretation given to denominational religion in schools. In other words, was it legitimate to teach denominational religion alone, without any specific creed or formulary, or was denomination instruction in Board Schools prohibited altogether?

Debate on this issue and on the fate of Jewish Board Schools resumed when the London School Board met again in November and in late December. Finally, on 25 January 1894, Riley and his supporters won the day. The Board voted that the word 'Christian' would be inserted in Article 81 of the Education Code, thus negating the 'compromise' of the 1870 Education Act; the teaching of Christianity, not simply 'religion and morality', became compulsory in Board Schools. Jewish Board Schools had the legal right to appeal under Clause 2 of the amended Article 81 which stated that 'in regard to any particular school, the Board shall consider and determine upon any application by managers or ratepayers of the district who may show special cause for exception of the school from the adoption of this resolution in whole or in part'.[17] However, the only recourse of Jewish children in other Board Schools was to claim the 'conscience clause' in order to avoid Christian religious instruction. In effect, Jewish teachers could only be assigned to Jewish Board Schools, since they would not have the proper qualifications to instruct pupils in Christianity.

'We stand between two fires,' the *Jewish Chronicle* warned its readers:

> If we express ourselves satisfied with the original compromise, it may be urged against us that having secured special privileges for ourselves, we are indifferent to the religious interests of others. On the other hand, should we favour the introduction of specifically Christian teaching, we may be making a rod for our own backs, the more so as our so-called privileges are not absolutely guaranteed.[18]

In order to protect these 'so-called privileges', that is, to safeguard the system of Jewish Board Schools, Jewish leaders informed the London School Board that they had instructed Jewish teachers 'to avoid teaching Jewish doctrines or observances during the school hours and to limit the religious instruction in those hours to Bible only—of course, the Hebrew Scriptures'.[19]

In March 1894 another Board decision which had possible consequences for Jewish pupils and teachers forced the Jewish community to take a stand. By a narrow margin, the Board approved a circular to be sent to all teachers instructing them to include the doctrine of the Trinity in daily religion classes. To the consternation of Claude Montefiore, who criticized the *Jewish Chronicle* for abandoning 'its attitude of judicial impartiality on the religious question', the newspaper came out strongly against the circular, describing it as a 'declaration of war against utilitarianism', and adding, 'we Jews are *par excellence* Unitarians—monotheists to the backbone, by inheritance, by tradition and by conviction'.[20]

In addition, the circular increased the danger that school managers would next employ religious tests in appointing teachers and thus discriminate not only against Jewish candidates but also against anyone not sharing the Christian religious affiliating of particular school managers. The vast majority of London teachers joined the *Jewish Chronicle* in its protest. While the London School Board did not revoke the circular, Canon Bristow withdrew his resolution to add it to the Education Code. The opposition to the circular diminished its power; instead of approved policy it became only an instruction and suggestion to school managers, 'a mere pious aspiration of the Board's majority'.[21]

It soon became evident that this continued furore regarding the status of religion in Board Schools, and particularly the status of the Jewish religion in these schools, had caused additional scrutiny of the relationship between the Board and the Jewish community. In October 1894, a month before the election for the London School Board, the *Jewish Chronicle* reported that 'a motion calculated, under existing circumstances to deal a blow at Jewish interests, was brought forward by the Hon. E. Lyulph Stanley'.[22] Stanley proposed that henceforward the Jewish Association for the Diffusion of Religious Knowledge (an Anglo-Jewish organization dedicated to providing after-school religion classes for immigrant children) must pay rent for the use of Board Schools on Sundays for the purposes of religious instruction. With an election imminent, the time was not appropriate for antagonizing any section of the electorate, so the motion failed; but the issue was far from dead.

Many Anglo-Jewish leaders as well as the *Jewish Chronicle* advised the Jewish community to remain aloof from the London School Board controversy, at least in public. The Board election, however, offered individual voters the opportunity to elect candidates sympathetic to Jewish Board Schools and thereby anonymously protect Jewish interests. But how were Jewish interests best served? Even the *Jewish Chronicle*, although clearly favouring one side, avoided an overt endorsement of its preferred candidates. 'Jews must vote for freedom of conscience,' argued one correspondent, 'either for the enlightened Churchmen prepared to support the policy of the last twenty-three years, or the Nonconformist, who, true to his traditions, is not fighting, not for us alone, but for the whole country, the Battle of Religious Liberty.'[23]

Moses Angel, headmaster of the Jews' Free School, unhesitatingly supported Riley and his 'moderates', also known as the Church Party. For Angel the Progressives (Nonconformists) were synonymous with secular education, and therefore, he argued, 'To help place Progressives on the School Board is to aid in cutting away the ground on which Jewish schools stand, and to destroy the foundations on which all teaching is reared.'[24] Like many orthodox Jews, Angel believed there could be no real separation of education and religion. He felt more comfortable with the Church Party, confident that its members would promote Christianity for Christians in Christian schools and Judaism for Jews in Jewish schools. More important was his conviction, shared by many in the Jewish community, that the Progressives' advocacy of non-sectarian schools meant, in reality, non-sectarian Christian Board Schools and an end to denominational schools.

When the returns were in, it was clear that Jews and Gentiles alike had supported the Moderates. Attempting to regain his seat on the Board, Claude Montefiore claimed to represent Jewish interest as an 'independent' neutral on the matter of the circular, but he nevertheless met defeat. The *Jewish Chronicle* reported that Montefiore lost the election because the Church Party backed out of an agreement to support him and 'at the last minute threw him over'.[25] The *Daily News*, however, blamed Montefiore's defeat on his neutrality, arguing that had he come out against the circular and united with the Progressives, he might have won, along with the only successful Progressive, Miss Davenport-Hill (a popular incumbent).[26] With no Jewish member on a Board heavily weighted towards the Church Party, the future of Jewish Board Schools seemed by no means certain.

However, contrary to dire predictions, Jewish Board Schools continued to be a permanent fixture of the immigrant East End. Apparently satisfied with the removal of specific religious instruction from the secular school day, the Board abandoned any attempt to impose the teaching of the New Testament instead of the Hebrew Scriptures. There remained, however, the question of Jewish teachers for Jewish pupils and the free use of Board Schools for out-of-hours religious instruction. Riley again criticized the appointment of Jewish teachers to teach Jewish children as contrary to the law, especially since the same privilege was not extended to Christians. He did not succeed in changing the majority views of the Board, who accepted the premise that immigrant children needed teachers of the same 'race' who spoke their language.[27] The Board, with agreement of Moderates and Progressives alike, did vote to charge rent for school use by the Jewish Association for the Diffusion of Religious Knowledge.[28] Although the debate surrounding Riley's proposals did not result in a negative appraisal of Jewish Board Schools, the Board was no longer willing to subsidize Jewish religious instruction by providing rent-free facilities. The Board placed the financial responsibility for the maintenance of religious education firmly on the shoulders of the Jewish community.

The 1894 election had settled the 'religious question'. Both in the 1897 and 1900 elections, candidates concentrated on the less divisive economic issue of funding for Board schools, and there seemed to be little difference between Moderates and Progressives on this subject. In the 1900 election two Jews, one a Moderate and one a Progressive, ran for seats on the Board, but neither won. The Jewish community found little to criticize about the new Board and had come to terms with the fact that rent-free space for after-school religion classes was a benefit of the past.

Not only did the Board continue to maintain its twelve existing Jewish schools; owing to the increase in the immigrant population, it added four more schools in the East End. In 1901, at the opening of two of these new buildings, one in Christian Road and the other in Commercial Road, E. Lyulph Stanley, Vice-Chairman of the London School Board, confirmed the Board's policy towards its Jewish clients. 'The London School Board,' Stanley told his audience, 'hopes to make all the children good English subjects, at the same time respecting the conscientious scruples of the parents of whatever nationality they might be.'[29] The London School Board and Anglo-Jewry shared the same goals for the children of Jewish immigrants. As for the immigrants themselves, their readiness to educate their children in state schools, whether Board or denominational, demonstrated their commitment to the anglicization process.

Despite the Board's sensitivity to Jewish needs and the provision of additional Jewish Board schools, by 1900 an estimated 2000 Jewish children in the East End attended Christian denominational schools, joining in Christian prayers during religion classes.[30] Most immigrant parents forced to send their children to these schools were either ignorant of or apathetic to the use of the 'conscience clause'. Unlike the immigrants who refused to send their children to the newly opened Old Castle Street Board School, these newer refugees either did not understand or were not concerned that their children were exposed to Christian dogma.

It was not only Jewish pupils at Church schools who caused concern. In 1895, the Chief Rabbi reported that many children at Board Schools attended Christian religious instruction. Both the Federation of Synagogues (founded by immigrants) and Lord Samuel Montagu, a prominent Anglo-Jewish leader, attempted to find some way to remove these children from exposure to Christian teachings. The *Jewish Chronicle* reported that Montagu 'dwelt at length upon the importance of the prevention of the perversion of the infantile minds'. On Montagu's motion the Federation unanimously resolved that a circular in Yiddish and in English explaining the 'conscience clause' should be distributed to East End Jewish families. Along with this circular, the Federation supplied a copy of a letter which parents could give to the headmaster requesting that under the clause their child be excused from Christian instruction.[31] At a Federation meeting held six years later to discuss the same problem, the unhappy consensus was that the circular and accompanying letter had been largely ineffective.[32]

Next the Federation appealed to the London School Board, complaining that Jewish children continued to attend Christian religion classes and that despite efforts by the Federation most of the parents of these children were unaware of their rights. In reply, the Board announced its decision 'to request the Board Inspector in each of the cases mentioned to visit the School, and see that suitable arrangements are made to enable those children whose parents have claimed the benefit of the Conscience Clause to take advantage of it with the least possible inconvenience, and to report their action to the School Managements Committee'.[33] This policy clearly did not address the root of the problem, since the vast majority of parents did not claim the 'conscience clause' at all, and the Board was very specific in stating that nothing could be done unless the parents themselves initiated action.

Writing to the *Jewish Chronicle*, Morris Harris, a prominent member of the Jewish Religious Education Board (formerly the Jewish Association for the Diffusion of Religious Knowledge), argued that the 'conscience clause' had been a failure. According to Harris, in all but Jewish Board Schools, 'it has become the rule for Jewish children of all ages to wait in their classes after the roll is called and listen, if they do not even join in the distinctive Christian prayers. . . . Their parents either cannot, or will not, or do not, for various reasons, send in the necessary written notice to the Head Teacher.' Even in classes in which teachers announced the Jewish children could wait outside during prayers, few did so. The Jewish Religious Education Board listed in Stepney alone 4508 Jewish children who attended non-Jewish Board Schools and 1153 in Christian denominational schools for whom only Christian religious instruction was available. Harris proposed a very simple solution: 'that a declaration to the teacher by the parent or person who brings the child to the school, that the child is of a religion other than that taught in the school shall oblige the Head Teacher to exempt that child from the religious worship or teaching of that school'.[34] By this means, responsibility for appropriate action rested with the school and not with the parent or child.

The proposed extension of the 1902 Education Act to London galvanized not only Morris Harris, but also other concerned representatives of the Jewish community, to lobby for the inclusion in the Act of safeguards for Jewish children in non-Jewish schools. But none of these proposals succeeded in gaining the necessary support, and the 1903 Education Act for London mirrored the 1902 Act for England and Wales, including a section almost identical to the 'conscience clause' of the 1870 Education Act. Parliament would continue to rely on the 'conscience clause', initiated by parents, to guard against religious indoctrination.

It was the responsibility of immigrant parents to demand their rights under the 'conscience clause', and the fact that most parents did not take advantage of this privilege remained a problem that the state educational system could not remedy. One solution on which school authorities and the Jewish community agreed was to decrease the number of Jewish immigrant children attending non-Jewish Board Schools by increasing the number of Jewish Board Schools. However, by 1905, the sixteen Jewish Board Schools (or Provided Schools as they were called after the 1902–3 Education Act) and two Jewish denominational schools could acccommodate the majority but certainly not all of the approximately 25,000 school-age Jewish children in the East End.[35] Any another solution depended solely on the resources of the Jewish community. As early as 1888, the Jewish Association for the Diffusion of Religious Knowledge had instituted a policy of renting space after school hours in a few non-Jewish Board Schools in order to provide religious instruction for the many children who were unable to attend Jewish schools.[36] If immigrant parents failed to claim the 'conscience clause' for their children in Christian schools, this policy, while not strikingly successful, offered one way of counteracting exposure to Christian religious instruction.

As the debate on Christianity in Board Schools so cogently illustrated, for the Jewish community the price of anglicization was too dear if bought with the loss of Jewish religious identity. But Anglo-Jewry was unwilling to support the separatism which an expanded Jewish denominational school system would create; therefore, a certain degree of accommodation to the majority culture was necessary. Perhaps more important, to a great extent the state educational bureaucracy, and more precisely the London School Board, legitimized the religious requirements of its Jewish clientele. An educational ideology which developed as a means of ensuring and protecting competing Christian sects in a Christian state proved to be flexible enough to extend to non-Christians as well.

While only marginally successful in moulding the adult immigrant community in their own image, time was on the side of Anglo-Jewry. The desire to adapt to a new environment was a powerful incentive to discard the trappings of Eastern European Jewish life. But it was the children of these immigrants on whom expectations for an anglicized immigrant community depended. Primary schools served as the institutional means to achieve this goal, an investment in the transformation of the immigrant young. 'In the children above all,' argued the *Jewish Chronicle*, 'must be centred our best and greatest hopes. . . . They will drag down, submerge and disgrace our community if we leave them in their present state of neglect; they will adorn and do honour to our community if we elevate them and render them good Jews and civilized, self-reliant Englishmen.'[37] To produce 'good Jews and civilzed, self-reliant Englishmen'—this was the definition of anglicization, the ambition of Anglo-Jewry and the task of English public education.

Notes

1 L. Gartner, 'Notes on the Statistics of Jewish Immigration to England'. *Jewish Social Studies*, vol. 22 (1960), pp. 97–102. Gartner provides an excellent analysis of the problems associated with using census and Board of Trade reports to determine the number of Jewish immigrants who settled in England. Although the census enumerated aliens only by their nationalities, according to Gartner, both Jews and non-Jews clearly recognized that almost all Russians, Poles and Rumanians were Jewish, 'with the exception of perhaps 1000 to 1500 Christians who came to work in Scottish collieries and in sugar refineries near Liverpool, probably as strikebreakers' (p. 99); V. D. Lipman, *Social History of the Jews in England 1850–1950* (London, 1954), p. 94. Lipman relies on Jewish community collections of marriage and burial statistics, perhaps not as reliable a method of determining the number of Jewish immigrants. For further data on the number and origin of Jewish immigrants in England, see L. Gartner, *The Jewish Immigrant in England, 1870–1914* (Detroit, 1960); H. Pollins, *Economic History of the Jews of England* (London, 1982).

2 Although none of the following historians has investigated the impact on minorities of the extension of popular education, each has contributed to an understanding of the creation and operation of a system of popular education in Victorian England. For an analysis of London Board Schools, see D. R. Rubenstein, *School Attendance in London, 1870–1904: A Social History* (New York, 1969). For more general surveys of the development of universal schooling for the newly enfranchised working poor, see: J. Lawson and H. Silver, *A Social History of Education in England* (London, 1973); G. A. N. Lowndes, *The Silent Social Revolution* (London, 1969); E. Midwinter, *Nineteenth Century Education* (London, 1970); R. J. W. Selleck, *The New Education, 1870–1914* (London, 1968); H. Silver, *The Concept of Popular Education* (London, 1965); D. Wardle, *English Popular Education* (London, 1970).

3 *Jewish Chronicle*, 12 August 1881.

4 J. W. Adamson, *English Education, 1789–1902* (Cambridge, 1964); Lawson and Silver (note 2 above), pp. 314–24.

5 Lawson and Silver, p. 321.

6 *Jewish Chronicle*, 4 May 1883.

7 Abraham Levy began his career as a pupil teacher at the Jews' Free School. The headmaster, Moses Angel, encouraged him to become head of the boys' department at the Old Castle Street Board School, and 'In those days, for a Jewish child to attend a Board School was regarded as a first step on the road to conversion.' Levy then assumed responsibility for the girls' department as well, at a time when coeducational Board Schools were very unusual. After a long career, Levy retired in November 1899, leaving a school which had always received the maximum in government grants and which educated well over 1500 immigrant children a year, a model for all Jewish Board Schools in the East End. 'Twenty-five Years Headmaster at the Old Castle Street Board School', *Jewish Chronicle*, 10 November 1899.

8 p. L. S. Quinn, 'The Jewish Schooling Systems of London, 1656–1956' (Ph.D. thesis, University of London, 1958), pp. 515–20; Gartner, *The Jewish Immigrant* (note 1 above), p. 227.

9 *Jewish Chronicle*, 3 August 1883.

10 C. Jones, *Immigration and Social Policy in Britain* (London, 1977), pp. 105–7: 'It can be argued that the Anglo-Jewish community had merely shifted its ground in this case from direct to indirect social intervention. As pillars of the rate-paying establishment in London and as sources of both educational and political power, English Jews did not need, it would seem, to expand their voluntary schools provision in order to

insure an effective and suitable education service for the children of Jewish immigrants.'

11 'Notes of the Week', *Jewish Chronicle*, 25 August 1893. Reprinted from the *Christian Commonwealth*, 17 August 1893.

12 'Notes of the Week', *Jewish Chronicle*, 21 April 1893.

13 *Jewish Chronicle*, 5 May 1893. Reprinted from *The Times*, 3 May 1893.

14 *Jewish Chronicle*, 8 September 1893.

15 'Last Meeting of the London School Board', *Jewish Chronicle*, 10 November 1893.

16 'Denominational Education', *Jewish Chronicle*, 24 November 1893.

17 *Jewish Chronicle*, 2 February 1894.

18 *ibid.*

19 'Jewish Teaching in Board Schools', *Jewish Chronicle*, 16 February 1894.

20 *Jewish Chronicle*, 30 March 1894; 'The Struggle for Religious Liberty', *Jewish Chronicle*, 23 March 1894.

21 *Jewish Chronicle*, 13 April 1894; *Jewish Chronicle*, 20 April 1894.

22 'Jewish Instruction in Board Schols', *Jewish Chronicle*, 5 October 1894.

23 'The Jews in the Next School Board Election', *Jewish Chronicle*, 9 February 1894.

24 *Jewish Chronicle*, 16 November 1894.

25 *Jewish Chronicle*, 30 November 1894.

26 *ibid.* Miss Davenport-Hill was a manager of a group of East End Board Schools. 'Miss Davenport-Hill', reported the *Jewish Chronicle*, 'has been for many years one of the most active and intelligent members of the London School Board. Her influence has always been used in obtaining all reasonable privileges for the Jews, and it is no secret at all that it was mainly at her suggestion that the Board appointed a Jewish Head Mistress at Gravel Lane and Jewish Head Master at Church Row.' From 'The Jews and the Next School Board Election', *Jewish Chronicle*, 16 February 1894.

27 *Jewish Chronicle*, 25 October 1895.

28 *Jewish Chronicle*, 26 July 1895.

29 'Jews and Board Schools', *Jewish Chronicle*, 11 october 1901.

30 'Notes of the Week' *Jewish Chronicle*, 7 December 1900.

31 'Federation of Synagogues', *Jewish Chronicle*, 7 June 1895.

32 'Federation of Synagogues', *Jewish Chronicle*, 15 February 1901.

33 'Federation of Synagogues', *Jewish Chronicle*, 12 July 1901.

34 *Jewish Chronicle*, 3 April 1903.

35 In 1901 the *Jewish Year Book* estimated that there were 21,298 Jewish children attending Board and voluntary schools in the East End. That may be a conservative estimate, and certainly by 1905 the number was probably greater than 25,000.

36 *Annual Report for the Jewish Association for the Diffusion of Religious Knowledge*, 1890, p. 15.

37 *Jewish Chronicle*, 3 February 1893.

A Hebrew Island in the British Isles:
Hayehoody and its Editor I. Suwalski (1897–1913)

Risa Domb

THE weekly *Hayehoody*[1] was the only Hebrew journal published in England for seventeen years without interruption. Its relatively long duration is curious, considering the fact that Anglo-Jewry never excelled in the Jewish-Hebrew cultural sense, even though a continuous Jewish presence in England, excluding the pre-expulsion mediaeval period, can be traced back some five hundred years.

It is reasonable that the Jewish population of England, always small in relation to the Jewish populations of other communities of the Diaspora, should have made a correspondingly minor contribution to the development of Jewish culture. Furthermore, since the seventeenth century, the Jews of England have enjoyed the full freedom of choice of both residence and occupation, and since the second half of the nineteenth century, freedom of political activity as well. These factors facilitated the integration of the Jews, so that their ethnic and national identity, of which the Hebrew language has always formed an important ingredient, gradually weakened.

Against this background, the apparent success of *Hayehoody* is intriguing. A closer examination of its contents, and of the circumstances in which it was published, may offer a fresh insight into the state of Jewish culture in England at the turn of the century.

Periodicals had played an important role in the development of European literature generally, and of Yiddish and Hebrew literature in particular. In his important study of Hebrew fiction between 1880 and 1970, Gershon Shaked notes: 'Literary periodicals often serve as a meeting place for writers from different countries and continents, whose love for one particular culture has brought them together.'[2] We know, of course, that the geographical distribution of Hebrew periodicals in Europe was often prescribed by historical, political and economic rather than purely literary circumstances. On the whole, these periodicals need not reflect the specific conditions of their countries of publication. The Hebrew periodical *Ha-Olam*, for example, began publication in Cologne (in 1907, under the editorship of Nahum Sokolow), then moved to England (between 1919 and 1921, under the editorship of of A. D. Idelsohn), and from there on to Berlin (under the editorship of Moses Kleinman); it returned to London in 1924 and finally moved to Eretz Israel in 1936. The fact that *Ha-Olam* was being published in England for a while was almost arbitrary; the journal hardly related to its immediate surroundings. Another Hebrew period-ical, *Ha-Meorer*, which was published in London in 1906–7 under the editorship of Joseph Hayyim Brenner, similarly failed to reflect the environment in which it was being published. This may be illustrated by the fact that of all the publicity notices which appeared in the first volume of *Ha-Meorer*, only one suggested that the journal was being published in London (this was the notice placed by a certain Benjamin Gaard, offering his services as translator and an expert in Russian law). Moreover, the number of British writers who contributed to *Ha-Meorer* was very small.[3]

During the first phase of *Ha-Olam* in London, a circle of Hebrew writers had come to realize that a literary platform was needed 'to reflect the nature of the country which has taken upon itself the management of the mandate and the establishment of a [Jewish] national home in Eretz Israel'. In 1927 they launched the periodical *Iyyim* of which only one volume was ever published (under the editorship of Asher Beilin, S. Goldenberg and Shamai Pinsky). The literary section contained both prose and poetry which represented the specifically English setting and the reactions to it of newly arrived Jewish immigrants.

The Hebrew weekly *Hayehoody*, and its editor Isaac Suwalski, would appear to have anticipated by three whole decades the need to provide a literary outlet for Anglo-Jewry.

Isaac Suwalski was born in Poland in 1863 and died in London in 1913.[4] He studied at the *yeshivah* of Volozhin where he was a pupil of R. Hayyim Soloveichick. He began to publish in *Ha-Levanon* in 1879, and later contributed regularly to *Ha-Zefirah*, *Ha-Melits* and *He-Asif*. He wrote mainly on Jewish literature and its history, and published in addition a volume entitled *The Life of the Jew According to the Talmud* (Warsaw, 1889), as well as founding in Warsaw the periodical *Keneset ha-Gedolah* (1890–1).[5] Throughout his life he belonged to the religious camp, and in his later years to the religious Zionist movement. He arrived in London in 1896–7, and there, for seventeen years, he both edited and published *Hayehoody*.

How did one man, apparently single-handedly, manage to publish a Hebrew weekly in England for so long?

An insight into the difficulties which this entailed is provided by

A. L. Bisco (ביסקא, 1859–1929), writing in the penultimate issue of *Hayehoody* (22 May 1913): 'Three qualities are required of the publisher of a Hebrew journal in London: wisdom, experience and self-sacrifice. The late Suwalski possessed all three.' In an earlier issue, while Suwalski was already suffering from what turned out to be his fatal illness, Bisco compared the problems confronting the editors of the two London-based Hebrew journals, *Ha-Meorer* and *Hayehoody*:

> J. H. Brenner has become one of the better known [Hebrew] writers, and with the self-assurance which comes through recognition, he now writes critically and authoritatively on many issues. However, during his early days in London he was more humble. He nearly died of starvation, yet when I advised him to write something for *Ha-Dor* and earn some money, he was afraid of Frischmann who valued form more than content. Still, before long Brenner had launched his *Ha-Meorer*, and among the contributors were not only Fichmann and Berdyczewski but even Frischmann himself. In spite of this, the days of *Ha-Meorer* or the days of Brenner in London were numbered. He could not continue to dissipate his energy by working as typesetter, administrator and distributor of *Ha-Meorer* all in one . . .
>
> I have mentioned this period of Brenner's life because it is relevant to our problem. The editor of *Hayehoody* is not only the typesetter of his journal, but he is also the proofreader, administrator and distributor, on top of which he has a wife and two children. Brenner, who was a bachelor, could not endure this life for as long as two years, while the editor of *Hayehoody*, who has a family to support, labours hard at it in body and in soul . . . Here in England, if *Hayehoody* should die, there will not be another Jew to resurrect it, and then we shall have nothing in this country. The few subscribers to *Hayehoody* will read the Yiddish papers or else not read at all, and in the end, our national language will be totally forgotten here'.

The extract quoted above shows that Suwalski was working under considerable emotional as well as—and not surprisingly—financial strain. It seems that initially he must have financed the publication of the weekly out of his own pocket. This is borne out by his statement in the first issue of the second year of publication (27 October 1898): 'The *Hayehoody* is my own property and it is wholly mine; no one may interfere with my affairs. I am acquainted with the principles of editorial work, and I give freedom of expression to everyone.' However, by the beginning of the eighth year of publication (9 June 1904), the editor announced that the journal was self-supporting and did not require any financial sponsorship. It was apparently run on a purely commercial basis.

It is extremely difficult to identify the reading public of *Hayehoody*. A clue appears in the issue of 27 October 1898, where the editor remarks bitterly that 'the readership from among the Christian clergy is probably larger than from among their Jewish counterparts'. He goes on to complain that his brethren in England are influenced by the non-Jewish culture surrounding them. Withholding their support from his journal, they alienate themselves from their own people and language. Indeed, it has been noted that 'the most paradoxical aspect of the situation was that the Jewish immigrants had no access to a Hebrew or even a Yiddish paper except in the library of the [Christian] mission'.[6] However, in the issue of 9 June 1904 the editor states that 'ninety-nine of the readers of *Hayehoody* take at least one other Yiddish or English daily, and this is the reason for concentrating [in *Hayehoody*] on news concerning Jews alone'. Were there in fact only 99 readers of *Hayehoody* in England, or did he mean to say 99 per cent? A further clue as to the identity of the readers emerges from the editor's repeated pleas which are directed at Hebrew language teachers, mostly members of 'The Society of Hebrew Speakers'. This society helped establish the periodical *Ha-Meorer*, as is evident from the first issue which appeared in 1906. The same Hebrew language teachers must have formed a significant proportion of the readership of *Hayehoody*. Most of the advertisements were clearly aimed at a religious readership; they advertised kosher meat, kosher bakeries and halls suitable for Jewish public functions. The nature of the readership of *Hayehoody* may be deduced also from the cost of the annual subscription to the journal in the various countries in which it was distributed, including [South] Africa (ten shillings), America (two dollars), France and Turkey (ten francs), Austria (five florins), Germany (eight marks) and Russia (four roubles). The cost of a subscription in England was eight shillings.

The list of countries in which *Hayehoody* was distributed remained unchanged from its earliest publication in the first issue of the journal. The annual subscription fee also remained unchanged (except for Russia, where it rose from four to five roubles). The editorial address in London changed several times during the years of publication, the Warsaw address was the same as that of *Ha-Zefirah*, while in St Petersburg it shared the address of *Ha-Melits*. It would be interesting to examine the relationship between these two journals and *Hayehoody*.

The name of the journal is printed in Hebrew characters and in English translation (*The Jew*) and transliteration—*Hayehoody*. Below this title appears the following statement in Hebrew: 'This is a periodical which deals with all matters concerning Jews and Judaism in all countries.' It is interesting to note that the English version of this statement is somewhat different and mentions 'Hebrew literature and matters of Jewish interest'. In neither version are the aims of the journal defined with any precision. The first issue of *Hayehoody*, published on

28 October 1897, opens with a manifesto in which the editor declares:

> The journal is open to everyone, so long as what they have to say is worthy of being heard . . . We shall supervise only the technical layout of the articles, improve the style and translate from other languages if the author's Hebrew is not good enough . . . The responsibility for the contents is the author's, not my own . . . I shall publish the following: 1) Literary materials . . . to strengthen our impoverished literature in this country. 2) News and current affairs of the Jewish world. 3) Scientific articles—only specialists will contribute here. 4) Feuilletons—to entertain the readers. 5) Stories and sketches—this section will be devoted totally to [pieces written originally in] Hebrew, and should reflect the lives of our people both in the present and in the past. 6) Book reviews and literary criticism—this hardly exists in our literature . . . We shall not concern ourselves with the personalities of the authors but only with the books themselves.

Section 7 contained obituaries of well known people. The journal maintained these seven sections throughout the years of its existence, even when it grew from eight pages to sixteen. It should also be noted that it contained virtually no printing or other errors.

A close examination of the literary material published in *Hayehoody* over a sample period of six months may serve to highlight the representative features of the journal. The period chosen for the purpose of the present study is from April to September 1904, marking the mid-point of the periodical's life. The year 1904 was marked also by two significant events in the Jewish world, Herzl's death and the arrival of J. H. Brenner in London. Herzl featured as a central topic in all the articles on current affairs after the announcement of his death in the issue of 7 July. In the literary section his death inspired a story entitled 'Without Him' by Yeshayahu Vasilevsky. (The same Vasilevsky was the author of a Hebrew play entitled *Hannah and her Seven Sons* which was much praised in an earlier issue of *Hayehoody*, 14 April 1904, and which was presented as 'a sign of the revival of the Hebrew language, regarded by most people as long dead'.) In the same issue Alfred Austin, the English poet laureate, published an obituary of Herzl which appeared in Hebrew translation.

According to Y. Bakon, this period of Brenner's life is insufficiently and unreliably documented.[7] It is interesting to look at such Hebrew-Jewish cultural activities as were taking place in London at the time of Brenner's arrival insofar as these are reflected in *Hayehoody*—a journal to which Brenner himself later contributed. Bakon suggests that it was in *Hayehoody* (of 6 April 1905) that Brenner published his first literary review.[8] It was, however, only after his London period that Brenner became a leading figure in Jewish literary and intellectual life, and his influence on his generation was unequalled.

Brenner, like many other uprooted Jews at that time, had come to London quite by chance, as he says in his letter to C. N. Bialik: 'I wanted to go to New York, but I have no money. I therefore decided to go to Bern in Switzerland, but I have no permit to go there from here. I have to go to London. There is no other place. I have bought a ticket, and all I have left is two marks.'[9] From his letters of that period in London it emerges that Brenner was often on the verge of starvation, and in October 1904 he was compelled to leave his lodgings and to give the name *Ha-Degel* (*Hayehoody*) as his postal address. During this low point in Brenner's life he was sustained by his obsessive commitment to the Hebrew language. As A. Zemach has remarked: 'His adherence to the language expresses an adherence to a whole world, for a whole world is enfolded in the language. Anyone to whom writing in Hebrew is vital would require the bare minimum to keep alive his soul: a small number of readers or some means of communication.'[10] This was an obsession which Brenner clearly shared with the editor of *Hayehoody*, Suwalski.

The articles on current affairs were written by 'special correspondents' and were more often than not translations into Hebrew from various European languages. The editor was clearly interested in specifically Jewish affairs, and *Hayehoody* can, therefore, supply valuable information on Jewish life, especially Anglo-Jewish life, and cultural activities at the turn of the century. In his regular editorial column, often stretching over two whole pages, Suwalski repeatedly discussed on particular topic which concerned the Anglo-Jewish community directly: this was the Aliens' Immigration Act. The influx of Jewish immigrants to England in 1904 created resentment in the native population which demanded restriction of immigration. Although attempts were made to distinguish between the new immigrants and the established Jewish community, the editor of *Hayehoody* presented the public discussion of this issue as anti-Semitic, illustrating his view with a report on the harassment of thirty-two Jewish families in Ireland (9 June 1904). In the issue of 12 May 1904 he called for the naturalization of all British Jews, to increase the number of Jewish voters and so have an effect on Parliament. 'The time is ripe', he proclaimed, 'for us to open our eyes and see how little we are respected.'

Another topic of Anglo-Jewish interest in this section during the sample period was the death of the prominent Zionist (and probable model for George Eliot's Daniel Deronda) Albert Edward Williamson Goldsmid. Goldsmid's dedication to the Hebrew language was singled out: 'He believed that there could be no national revival for Israel without the revival of Israel's language. He made it his habit to use only Hebrew words for all domestic objects in his home' (28 April 1904).

The journal usually carried numerous announcements of Hebrew classes, especially classes where Hebrew was taught by the 'natural' method, without resort to another language. This must have reflected the editor's keen interest in the Hebrew language and its modern revival.

Zangwill's literary activity is reported, but his 'territorial' Zionism is treated ambiguously.

By contrast with this concern with Anglo-Jewish affairs, the literary section of *Hayehoody* hardly related to its immediate English surroundings. It consisted of some two out of the sixteen pages of the journal (five or six pages were given to announcements and advertisements, the rest to current affairs). The section contained prose, not poetry, and all the pieces published attempted to give artistic expression to topical Jewish problems. This selectivity of subject-matter appears to have been an editorial policy, and it may account for the general mediocrity and even poverty of literary standards which prevailed throughout this section of *Hayehoody*.

During the six months chosen as a sample, April—September 1904, forty-six writers contributed to the literary section of *Hayehoody*. I have divided them into three groups: writers residing in England, those living abroad, and those who have not been identified.

The number of writers who are known to have been resident in England (excluding Suwalksi) is disappointingly small and consists of five. These are: 1) Zevi Hirsch Gelber (1847–1930), publishing a sharp satire directed against the modern Hebrew printers who fail to supply new illustrations for the Passover *Haggadah*;[11] 2) the orientalist Benzion Halper (who subsequently moved to Philadelphia where he became editor of the Jewish Publication Society in 1916); he contributed a short story, written in flowery Maskilic Hebrew, about a poor orphan catching his step-mother in the act of adultery, and depicting Jewish life in the impoverished shtetl from the perspective of the child; 3) Isaiah Raffalovich (1870–1956),[12] who published a humorous Chinese folk-tale; 4) M. Schechter who reported on his travels by train through Europe, and also on his meeting with a poor Jew who, he thought, would be better off in Eretz Israel than in the Diaspora where he chose to lead a miserable life. Schechter also contributed a sketch entitled 'She', which tells the story of a young girl who, having been betrayed by her first lover, punishes all the men she meets subsequently, and a short story entitled 'Judith of Bialopol (of the year 1675)' which was published in several instalments;[13] 5) Leon S.

Kreditor—a Hebrew teacher and active Zionist—who published three short stories featuring the problems of immigration to England and allowing the difficulties experienced by the immigrants to emerge from the dialogues between the protagonists. In contrast to all the other writers listed above, Kreditor paid close attention to the details of the new English environment encountered by the immigrants.[14]

The contributions from abroad may be divided into two categories, fiction and literary criticism. In the first category we find: 1) a sensitive short story by Yakir Warshavsky (1885–1942), told in the first person and describing the experiences of a young couple on a deeply melancholy journey; 2) an overtly didactic short story by 'Y. D. Freier',[15] following the career of a poor Jew who becomes rich through the practice of flattery; 3) a short story entitled 'Dreams' by Pesakh Kaplan (1870–1943), describing the gloomy thoughts of a Jew forced to serve in the Russian army; 4) a short story entitled 'The Conversation' by Reuben Brainin,[16] in which a son explains his reasons for rejecting his father's humble way of life.

All these stories reflect the problems of Jewish existence in Europe, and are critical of Jewish passivity. On the whole their didactic intent is as blatant as their aesthetic merit is poor.

The literary–critical articles all focus on the Hebrew periodical press. Yehoshua Mezah (1834–1917), using the pseudonym 'Prince of the Sea' (*Sar shel YaM, YaM* standing for his initials), deals with a particular periodical in one of his four imaginary conversations between 'an ordinary man' and an angel during a tour of various impoverished Jewish communities in Europe. The death of K. Z. Wissotzky (who sponsored the important Hebrew periodical *Ha-Shiloah*) leads to a discussion in which the 'ordinary man' argues that the deceased had done much for the benefit of his people, while the angel argues more convincingly that 'the world of literature was short of nothing prior to the establishment of *Ha-Shiloah* . . . Now that it has been established, what good does it bring to the widows, the orphans and the poor?'

Yakir Warshavsky (see above) welcomes the demise of *Ha-Melits* and *Ha-Zeman*, both of which he considers to be absolutely superfluous. Yizhak Gruenbaum (1879–1970) who was among the editors of *Ha-Olam* and *Ha-Zefirah*, criticizes the monthly *Kiryat Sefer* for publishing, instead of literary criticism, nothing more than book lists and prices. Yehezkel Levitt (1879–1945) reports from New York on his sad visit to the impoverished Moshe ha-Cohen Reicherson (1827–1903), the much admired Hebrew author and grammarian who had emigrated from Vilna to New York in 1890. Levitt reproaches all Western Jews for alienating themselves from their Russian brethren.

All the literary–critical articles published in *Hayehoody* during the

Hayehoody and its Editor I. Suwalski

Notes

1 For distribution in Russia, *Hayehoody* was re-named *Ha-Degel*. See G. Kressel, *Lexicon of Hebrew Literature* (Hebrew) (2 vols) (Merhaviah, 1967), vol. 2, p. 477.

2 G. Shaked, *Hebrew Narrative Fiction*, 2 vols (Hebrew), vol. 1 (Tel Aviv, 1978), p. 35.

3 See H. Matras, *Ha-Meorer—A Journal and its Editing* (Hebrew) (Jerusalem, 1983), Appendix A.

4 However, according to N. M. Gelber in an article published in the last issue of *Hayehoody*, he was 53, not 50 when he died.

5 See Kressel (note 1 above), vol. 2, p. 477.

6 Y. Bakon, *The Young Brenner* (Hebrew), 2 vols (Tel Aviv, 1975), vol. 1, p. 126.

7 *ibid.*, p. 12.

8 *ibid.*, vol. 2, pp. 467–8.

9 J. H. Brenner, *Collected Works* (Hebrew), vol. 2 (Tel Aviv, 1961), p. 230.

10 A. Zemach, *A Movement at the Spot* (Hebrew) (Tel Aviv, 1984), p. 220.

11 His contributions to *Hayehoody* are overlooked by Kressel. See Kressel (note 1 above), vol. 1, p. 483.

12 He was the author of an English–Hebrew dictionary published in London in 1926. See *ibid.*, vol. 2, p. 873.

13 The story is presented as 'a translation' by the author without any indication of the original language or, indeed, whether or not Schechter was its original author.

14 As I discovered in a recent conversation with Miriam Abramsky, the same Leon Kreditor was her Hebrew teacher during the 1930s. He was an old family friend and a frequent visitor to the Shapiro Vallentine family bookshop. He taught at the Reverend Goldblum Talmud Torah in London, and his daughter Dora married the Labour politician Hugh Gaitskell.

15 This is the pseudonym of Henech Kazakewich. See Z. Rejzen, *Lexicon fun Yiddisher literatur presse un philologie*, 4 vols (Vilna, 1929), vol. 3, pp. 412–13.

16 The editor of both *Ha-Melits* and *Ha-Toren* who was to quarrel with Bialik in 1926 over Bialik's advocacy of Jewish settlement in Russia.

17 See 'Ha-Genre ha-Eretz Israeli va-Avizarayhu', in Brenner (note 9 above), pp. 268–70.

No. 1.   שנה ראשונה.   גליון א.

28 October 1897, London.   ב' מרחשון, תרנ"ח לונדן.

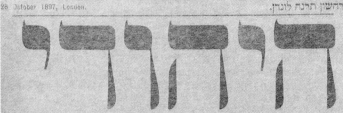

היהודי

The JEW.

מביע עמו בכל עניני היהודים והיהדות בכל הארצות.

יוצא לאור אחת בשבוע בכל יום חמישי מאת

יצחק סובאלסקי.

בית המערכת: לונדן, 40 בערנער סט. מאמ. רייד איסט.

Office 40 Berner St., Commercial Road, London E.

בית הספר תורת חיים

40 Berner St. Com. Road E.

חאבננט יעסט פאר קינדער
ווענזכע אזוי אלס די מעהרע
חל בית הספר תורת הנל, הקודש
כיום תהלה, בי נינדערטהנלדזם,
כאשר יעשון ובה הכבלי,
חייתים הרבנים הגאונים
ושעתנורנק ברננ את
החכמיהם יראו פעל
י. ה. כהן לאמק

בית המערכת

תקבל עלויותהיות הנשמעיי
ואים הנבנים, בכל כבד
וראשת, מצייב שאות היהודים
מרחוב היהודים. ורחבינ, כם כבדיבינ,
אלטמאם, לונד לונדן. אין, פארין, קול מעיר
שעניץ שתהינ בי רבם. הוות קשת, מודעות,
אלה נבניא: שענ, חבנא, מודעות.

ללבוי יבו הנבל

טוב.

טוב, יוסף חיים בחן לאסק הוא סוכן ראשי לקבל העוסקים בעד "היהודי".
ורקבל מיותנ, ירו כורי וכל מה שעשה עשי.

ימי השבוע

שנן תקונם.	סדן ישראל.	
28	ב'	ח'
29	ג'	ו' שקהת"א 4
30	ד'	ש"ק נח ובר"כבן בהר"ב, עחר"ב, 18 33.
31	ה'	א'
נאנו 1	ו'	ב' תענית ב' קמא
2	ז'	ג'
8	ח'	ד'

תכן הענינים

מאמרתנו. לשען ציון. מכתבי מופרים גלאווני
וראשת, מציית שאות היהודים במצרים באינגליא.
מרחוב היהודים. ורחבינ, כם כבדיבינ,
אלטמאם, לונד לונדן. אין, פארין, קול מעיר
שעניץ שתהינ בי רבם. הוות קשת, מודעות.
אלה נבניא: שענ, חבנא, מודעות.
יבו הגדול

מאמרתנו

לא חשול אננו לקהקראים עברית,
ולא זה אנכי לאונו תעוסקם בםמרות ישראל,
ולא בזנום חדשום אבוא בבריה ההפרות, כי
במשך רמי ענכדתי הרבום בכמבתי: עתום
לבניי ובמכספים שנים קניתי לי ובת
אזרה קר בי לא נאוהו התיום ל' הם אוסו.
גן, כי הקלה הקרוא, עברית, כל הקהל
התשיא רק בנמצו עתים עברים יהוד פני
שני ל' ב' מ"צ. ויר"ע לחויר' את על עשול
בםפרותינו אלה הקדשתי מברי ימי וענותי.
הני את הבקקים חובם כהעוסן היהודות.

לא נרפא שבר העם ענ נקלה לאמר : שלום
שלום בשעת שבוחלת החולה אנושה, ומהלתו
מסוכנ, ויכולה לחצעצדהו לבאר שרת, לא
נשרד שריך ים יום וערבים באונו העם לישנו
שנד שוקתה בשעה שבכלו כוענ כוני בזאם,
חרים ובנו יוענ.
חאבת, נבת קניה הכוהבת הואת
מבילה לא יוהב מן שלושה אותיות, זמת קשה
לאמם לבנו אשריה על פנה, כמה מפות
של מרה תלויות בה, וכבת קועות של
שרגים תלוות לת מאחריה. כי מצע ורדעים
אנחנו בי בצואנו לנתח רבויים שובשים
בעלי שותלתנו, ואף אם נא נאמר לנחות לם
מפת בהקופינו רק כקעה זו, המצפשם
תענומיש החמימום ובצבלה הנצשום יום
יום, פאמכינו לתנות רק פחת קטן
במדרלזים של מר של בכת"–איפל של קהלותינו,
בנצהתורק להנום את ית, ולאחרי מכב
עין לא יקום
קול, שאנו, ותנזד, האחוזים ויאשרו לחקרי בני
צהירות, מכהו או מפת קתם, וכב לרבינוני
אלח לבב גדלום לישמוז מדינו קיל רצע
גדול, לא קל קל ונע קנוא ומשבבחי ואנדינו
יסח חדשת, הוצניאה נא את הטורינך אלינו
והלאם, בי אם קול קול ענות מחתה ומצרה, קול
מצק ובגנם וגהרה בעלי מובות שכוללנים
את שרת ישראל ובהרוחמום לישמוה. קול
רועה, הרועם. את עצמם ואת הצאן לא
יודעי. קול ומבינ שלוקחו את הקרב בישה
מבב. מ"ק הטמאור סדר א'.

"וחבו אנםא כי ישמתו לקראת התשורה
בחורתם כי אומר אנני דבריאם ביראה חדשה
ולך עברו, תנצם ישראל, נזור אלהים והיא
מב"צ בשמה קודש בארין, תלאוכית זו
הקריאים בכר בתנוני יראי פעל בשרה
ישראל בכר נעשני בבמכה פחות מלל
בישראל, ודומתי ברות והשקפתי עז התשוה
כבר נעול כספר במפרי שמבב היול, לא
אתחבר בוני חטידים, ולא אתהם עם תבוגם ם,
לא ארשע אתראענם ולא אתאל עם נגתולום
רק האמת מוהסר של הקב"ה תחי כי
לרעלינו. אם עמם רש, ונר מטאם נראה
במדרנה נחמה על התוטן, וערם ל כאושר
כולני לתנור לבעלי טובתינו בצשב, אם
שלימם על טלמות שמם, ותיים שר הפקר
נ"את באדן, מ אל הבנג שוב לתנה לבנה
חרבם בבתו תיי פניטום, ולא. יחית פישה
הני את הבקקים חובם כהעוסן היהודות.

3

HISTORIOGRAPHICAL ISSUES

The Expulsion from Spain and Jewish Historiography

Eleazar Gutwirth

IT is by now a critical commonplace that the series of expulsions from the Iberian peninsula, beginning with the Edict of Expulsion of 1492, had a decisive effect on the subsequent writing of Jewish history. This is a view which had been put forward with some force by Baer, Ben Sasson, Neuman and others.[1]

This apparent 'sudden rise of Jewish historiography'[2] seems all the more remarkable in view of another commonly held opinion, namely that mediaeval Jews had lost interest in history. Indeed Steinschneider maintained that

> Entwickelnde Geschichte verträgt sich mit der Evolutionstheorie, mit Optimismus . . . Sinn und Interesse fur entwickelnde Geschichte überhaupt gehen in der Regel von der Vaterlandsliebe aus, wie der Imperialismus. Ein kaum Geduldeter . . . hat nur eine Leidensgeschichte . . .[3]

With such authority behind him, Neuman could afford to elaborate; for him it was 'as if a surgeon had cut the historic nerve in the national brain'. After the trauma of expulsion, for historians such as Neuman, Jewish historians 'probed for the key of the riddle of Jewish existence in the inner recesses of Jewish experience. Anxiously they scanned the dim outlines of the past, the better to understand the course of the future. Thus it was deep concern with Jewish fate that led to the revival of interest in Jewish history.'[4]

The *Shevet Yehudah* is only one of a number of works which have been perceived as typifying this 'sudden rise of Jewish historiography' following the Expulsion. Indeed, few historians have disagreed with Baer's contention that the main purpose of the book is to account for the expulsion of the Jews from Spain.[5]

While exile is certainly one of the themes in the *Shevet Yehudah*, it would be difficult to see this motif as in any way exclusive to this work or sufficient for apprehending its specificity. On the contrary, research on the mentality of Jews and conversos has shown how widespread the theme of exile became during the sixteenth century. This might lead one to point to the differences between the *Shevet Yehudah* and various chronicles, historiographical fragments and personal accounts of the Expulsion, in order to emphasize its moralist, polemical and imaginative response to expulsion. It could be argued that Jewish historiography of the post-Expulsion period in general (and the *Shevet Yehudah* in particular) is but a branch of the wider literary phenomenon of sixteenth-century 'exile literature' which appealed to both Jews and conversos. Indeed, such a genre has been recognized by a number of modern scholars who study the literary output and production of the printing presses of the sixteenth century. McPheeters,[6] for example, has noted the particular emphasis on exile in the Hebrew poem in honour of the Hebrew translation of the *Celestina*. Joseph Tsarfati compares the anguished moans of the thwarted lovers to those of the 'poor exiles', and then the poet expatiates in a description of exile. Nora Weinerth, in her analysis of Torres Naharros' *Diálogo del Nascimiento*, suggests that behind the conventional lament of Petrispano, at the beginning of the play (when he arrives from Jerusalem) there may lurk the converso's experience of exile and persecution.[7] MacKay has tried to present the *Lozana Andaluza* as a type of exile literature in the understanding of which the phenomenon of Andalusian conversas is particularly useful.[8] For Constance Rose[9] the rediscovery of and vogue for the Byzantine novel may be interpreted as 'a means of depicting enforced exile with its attendant endless wandering and travail. The growth of the pastoral expressed the desire for a tranquil land immune from the mutability of fortune.' If we are correct in our classification, then Alonso Núñez Reinoso's *La Historia de los amores de Clareo y Florisea y de los trabajos de la sin ventura Isea* is as concerned with exile as the Damascus sermons of Rabbi Joseph ben Meir Garson.[10] It is within this genre of creative, imaginative responses to exile that one may class the *Shevet Yehudah*.

Although the topic of exile in the *Shevet Yehudah* is diffuse, much of the scholarship on the subject has concentrated on this topic to the virtual exclusion of all the book's other concerns. It has, perhaps paradoxically, tended to emphasize the break with Spanish and Hispano-Jewish culture of the period of the Expulsion and that immediately preceding it. One may notice a tendency, albeit mixed, to divorce the book from the other aspects of its fifteenth- and early sixteenth-century background. Like the protagonist of A. Lesin's poem, who invites the putative author of the '*seferl*' (i.e. the *Shevet Yehudah*) to join the other '*ushpizim*' in the *sukkah*, much of the scholarship has selected for treatment those concerns which belong to non-specific Jewish thought, and tried to relate them to non-Hispanic traditions.

Even Baer, who contributed so much to placing the ideas of the *Shevet Yehudah* within a specifically peninsular context (notably through his discovery of the Bachiller de la Torre and Guevara as sources), was of the opinion that, in the final analysis, these aspects were not decisive in the understanding of the book. Such attempts as have been made to highlight the Hispanic character of the work have been generally ignored or found debatable.[12]

The initial facts to bear in mind are that the *Shevet Yehudah* is a text published in the 1550s,[13] that it was thought adequate for a Hebrew reading public of that period; and that within that public it appealed to a subsection, the exiles from Spain, who understood the numerous *leazim* which occur in the book. An emphasis on Hispanic antecedents is therefore not out of place, even if non-Hispanic analogues are available. The attention to the non-Jewish context hardly needs an apology, nor is it new. Baer's constant awareness of the historiographic standards of the Gentile population or Shatzmiller's comparisons with non-Jewish historiographic practice[14] provide sufficient justification for seeing this example of post-Expulsion Jewish historiography in its synchronic context. Nor should one ignore the fact that the mediaeval notion of the function of history, to delight and instruct, typical of which is the *confabulator*,[15] was still alive in fifteenth-century Spain. Chronicles were still being written as *exempla* and events recorded because they had been found 'fit for remembrance'. This 'fitness for remembrance' was determined by theological, literary and political reasons rather than a desire to reconstruct the past 'as it really was'.[16] Obviously, not a Jewish distaste for history but the mediaeval notions of history are behind this apparent lack of concern for the past *wie es eigentlich gewesen*. It is hardly necessary to repeat what is well known about the typological and analogical tendencies of mediaeval European historiography in general— schematism or the use of history to justify the transmission of authority.[17] Recent research has emphasized the accuracy of this picture for Castilian historiography as well. Deyermond has pointed to the importance of the mediaeval model of fall and redemption in the writing of the passages on the death and rebirth of Visigothic Spain in the *Estoria de España*.[18] Burke has underscored the typological and figural interpretation of character and situation in mediaeval Spanish works, and argued that, in the mediaeval perception, the difference between a literary work and a historical one would have been slight indeed.[19]

In any case, the notion of history as literature was equally operative in sixteenth-century Jewish historiography, where chronicles articulate time and again the desire to delight.[20] It is therefore valid to concentrate on the themes which express the edifying and polemic purpose of the book.

The attraction of the *Shevet Yehudah* surely lies in the richness and ambiguity of its motifs. Of these motifs it is possible to select those which are prominent in late mediaeval and/or early sixteenth-century Hispanic sources (Jewish and Christian), and particularly those which appear in the thought and writings of the conversos.[21] The *Libro Aureo*, a source of the *Shevet Yehudah* could be one of the convenient foci of the reconstruction of the way in which the book was read by its early public.[22] The criticisms of courtly life, strife, lack of *mesura*, cupidity and worldliness are examples of general motifs which may be understood in terms of their Hispanic and converso currency. More generally recognized will be the relevance of issues such as the activities of the Inquisition.

CONTEMPT OF COURT LIFE

'Contempt of court life and praise of the country' is familiar to readers of one of the sources of the *Shevet Yehudah*, Antonio de Guevara, as a major theme in his writings. Even before the *Menosprecio de corte y alabanza de aldea* appeared, the theme was quite central to the book which the author of the *Shevet Yehudah* used as a source, the *Libro Aureo*.[23]

Whether or not the Marqués de Santillana's *Comedieta de Ponza* is really the first Spanish occurrence of the Horatian *beatus ille*, as maintained by Menéndez y Pelayo, Spanish Jews had an internal, thematically cognate tradition. Don Meir Alguadex's introduction to his translation of the *Nichomachean Ethics* lists (as a variation on *captatio benevolentiae*) the problems of translating any work. Among these he includes the lack of tranquillity which is his lot as servant of the king.[24] It is perhaps possible to see an example of this motif in the *'Iggeret Purim* of Shlomo Halevi. He compares the court to a prison and complains that he has been separated from his friends, and could not rejoice in Purim as is fit.[25]

Solomon Bonafed writes a consolatory poem to Envidal Bonsenyor of Solsona who has lost all his possessions. He sets up an opposition between town and country which is thematically reminiscent of the *beatus ille*. In it he criticizes the town and its artisans and contrasts them with an idyllic vision of country roads, flowers, birds and the other accoutrements of such poetic descriptions.[26] Moses Arragel's letters to the Master of the Order of Calatrava prior to his acceptance of the task of translating the Bible, *c.* 1422, similarly enlarge on the topic. He bemoans the strains of life at court and lists them.[27] This tradition may have added a certain literary legitimacy to the development of the theme in the *Shevet Yehudah*.

The courtly code demanded moderation in speech and action and a correspondence between situation and manners which was known at times as *mesura*, a demand expressed by, among others, Guevara in the *Libro Aureo*.[28]

It is to this decorum that certain criticisms of Jewish behaviour voiced in the *Shevet Yehudah* are appealing. Hence the description of Jews who yell at each other at Tortosa, or the advice to Jewish envoys at court not to address the Christian rulers as they do their own leaders and scholars.[29]

It would seem that a corresponding irony is intended in certain 'vignettes' of the 'court of Alfonso' in which the rules of decorum are transgressed again and again. The ideal courtier simply does not reply to a question by his king with the utterance: 'that is as much a question as why has God not made the ass a philosopher and the mule a prophet or why has He not given the ant the light He gave to the sun' (p. 35, ll. 16ff). No great critical acumen is needed to realize that the irony here is directed against the atmosphere prevailing in the Christian courts, and that this irony is not compatible with the opinion held by historians such as Loeb, that the *Shevet Yehudah* had an unequivocally sympathetic attitude to Christian kings and aristocrats.[30] Examples could be multiplied. The king answers: 'I did not ask what the idiots say.' He says to Tomás: 'Were you someone else, I would have thought that you had eaten a cat's brain' (p. 40, l. 4). They cast slurs on each other's *'limpieza de sangre'* (e.g. p. 34), and the king and courtiers are portrayed as being constantly engaged in farcical and venomous bickering, rarely relieved by any subtlety. This portrayal may contribute greatly to the reader's amusement, but it does not enhance the royal image in the *Shevet Yehudah*.

A classic case of contempt of court life in the *Shevet Yehudah* is the story of the *'salvaje'* Don Enrique de Mendoza,[31] who is brought to court and refuses to sit at the king's table. To explain this refusal he engages in an enlargement of the theme, criticizing the immorality of the imaginary Christian Spanish court which is portrayed in the *Shevet Yehudah* by means of a series of rhetorical questions (p. 160):

Even if you gave me your palace full of silver, I would still not sit at your table. Where is the desire to be found for seeking food which nature finds hard to digest, if not at the table of kings? Where else the seeking of clothes from the ends of the earth, the pursuit of the furs of beasts? Where the lust for women who wear garments of variegated colours and dance before you while Satan dances within you? Where else do princes play music in praise, not of the Lord but of the bosoms of women, to excite desire? why do you seek that which is fit for the horse and the ass but is most unseemly in a man?

The *Shevet Yehudah*'s irony gains depth from its ambiguity. The house of Mendoza, a relatively new but extremely powerful dynasty of noblemen, was renowned for its pursuit of fame and wealth as well as for its poetry in praise of women. What could be more ironic than to present a member of this house as a hermit, a *salvaje* who condemns the refinements of life at court? And yet it was a member of this family, Fray Iñigo de Mendoza (also related to the Rabbi of Burgos, Shlomo Halevi), who attacked these elements of courtly life in his circumcision poem.[32] More generalized is the criticism of inner strife and the notion of strife as a cause of decline.

STRIFE

The theme of inner strife as a cause of decline recurs throughout the *Shevet Yehudah* (see e.g., p. 128, ll. 4–7). Various antecedents of this theme have been suggested. Baer pointed to Petrarch and other Italian writers on political thought who followed him, and the theme is best known from a number of popular passages in the Talmud and Josephus. Rubinstein's analysis of fourteenth-century Italian, and particularly commune, political thought may add to this rich array of precedents.[33] But Hispano-Jewish thinkers of the late Middle Ages— surely a more relevant context—could also be adduced. Profayt Duran, using a narrative framework which appears in various mediaeval sources (e.g. the *Gesta Romanorum*), listed strife among the causes of decline in a letter which he composed following the events of 1391 and in which he attempts to explain the decline of Spanish Jewry: 'An old philosopher was asked for the reasons for the destruction of his country and he answered that these were three . . . the second one was that the leaders hated each other bitterly.'[34] In his collection of homilies the *Nahar Pishon*, Isaac Aboab similarly inveighed against inner strife.

> The verse in the pericope 'if you walk in my statutes' [Lev. 26:3ff] says: 'and you shall eat your bread to the full'; and the verse also says: 'and dwell in your land safely'. As has already been said in the Tractate *Hagiga* [9b], 'Poverty suits the Jews as a red trapping suits a white horse.' And here the Bible promises us great wealth. For when the Jews are rich, strife is present amongst them (*ha-mahloket benehem*), as each one lords it over his fellow. That is why Scripture says that even though the Jews will be very wealthy, they will 'dwell . . . safely'.[35]

Conversos of the late fifteenth century and onwards were particularly receptive to the passages in Petrarch's *De Remediis* which dealt with the universality of strife. Gilman has emphasized that conversos such as the author of the *Celestina* (1499), Villalobos or Guzmán, understood the state of the world as a state of perpetual strife and portrayed the natural world as a battleground:

> The remark of Villalobos . . . that 'we are subject to wars and tumults and dissensions' reminds us of the section of the *De Remediis* which Rojas translated in the Prologue as a gloss to Heraclitus' 'all things come to pass through the compulsion of strife.' The introduction to the second part of the *De Remediis* is an astonishing compilation of anecdotes depicting the natural world as battleground. Animals, insects, birds, fish and even the four elements are engaged in constant strife . . . But worst of all is the world of men . . . Many of the conversos who lived through the riots of the 1470s and the first years of the Inquisition . . . [Like Petrarch they] . . . experienced history as a complex and senseless warfare of individuals and groups, a warfare in which they were helplessly involved. The major battle was of course the one waged by the Old Christians against the conversos . . . But . . . it is a sociological commonplace that minority groups tend to develop internal patterns of discrimination resembling those imposed on them . . .[36]

WEALTH

The condemnation of cupidity is one of the great themes of late mediaeval European literature. A long list of Hispano-Jewish thinkers, especially those writing paroenetic treatises and collections of homilies, could be cited to provide antecedents to the condemnation of the Jewish pursuit of wealth in the *Shevet Yehudah*. Late mediaeval Hebrew poetry of the period, not infrequently moralistic in tone, parallels this concern with cupidity. In this connection Da Piera can be cited along with Alami, Joel ibn Shoaib, Arama and others. That there is such a critical concern with cupidity in the *Shevet Yehudah* hardly needs to be demonstrated. 'The Jews are greedy' (*baalei hemdah*) (p. 32) is only one of many, apparently unanswered, accusations of this type. Indeed, one can feel Baer's indignation in his article on the *Shevet Yehudah* at the presence of such 'anti-Semitic' comments in the book. But there is a corresponding condemnation of Christian courtly greed in the *Shevet Yehudah*, which emulates the tone of similar attacks on the greed of Christian courtiers in the *Libro Aureo*.[37] One example among many is a short exchange between the king and Tomás (ch. 7, p. 33). The king says to Tomás: 'You have come and enlightened me. May you receive a great reward from the Lord in the next world.' Tomás says: 'I wish I could receive it from you in this world' (see also pp. 50, 61, 76 and ch. 39).

LINEAGE

The particular importance of lineage in the *Shevet Yehudah* may be seen as a continuation of the ideas of the Arabiyya absorbed and transmitted by Halevi and Moses ibn Ezra.[38] But when the *Shevet Yehudah* is examined against its fifteenth-century Hispano-Jewish background and antecedents, the often observed preoccupation with lineage seems far from unique or striking. Such a concern was endemic in Spanish society generally. The conversions of 1391 had created a new group of Christians who were never regarded as equal to the Old Christians. From 1392 onwards there is a continuous flow of evidence that the New Christians were categorized as conversos. To this sometimes underrated feature of Spanish mentality should be added the later and well-known discussions and statutes of the purity of blood. The Gothic revival in Spain may also be taken into consideration from the reign of the Catholic monarchs onwards. Jews were not immune to the intense preoccupation with lineage of the society which surrounded them. While these ideas were not institutionalized by the Jews in the same way, evidence of their presence is not lacking. There are documents produced by communal 'chancelleries' to attest to the *kashrut* of an individual's family. The phrase '*taharat ha-dam*', purity of blood, occurs during the 1480s in a Sabbath homily. Such extreme formulations of ideas which are admittedly commonplaces of Christian as well as Muslim political and social thought tend to weaken the notion of a peculiar concern with lineage.[39]

STYLE AND NOVELTY

That the *Shevet Yehudah* has a startlingly different prose style is obvious to any reader who comes to the book after reading the works of other Hispano-Jewish chroniclers. The one feature which has been especially noticed is the use of dialogue.[40] Here again there may be a Spanish context which recent research could help to clarify. Dialogue in the *Shevet Yehudah*, with its careful characterization of the interlocutors, its ironic humour and its conscious efforts to minimize technicalities, differs considerably from the mediaeval dialogues available in Hebrew, such as the *Kuzari* or the *Uncle and Nephew*.[41] More than any other mediaeval dialogue or polemic, the dialogue found in the *Shevet Yehudah* is an attempt to mimic in Hebrew a Spanish Christian mentality and its image of the Jew. Indeed, the historic background of this feature of the book is that early sixteenth-century vogue for dialogue in which Spanish works figure so prominently. The 'dialogue structure' has been recognized as ultimately responding to a dialectic, anti-dogmatic tendency. It has been suggested that this structure became the characteristic literary genre of humanism and expressed its pluralist vision. This explanation of the dialogue form has been as helpful in understanding Leone Ebreo's *Dialoghi* as it has in the case of the dialogues of Juan de Valdés.[42] Ferreras' recent survey and analysis of approximately 100 sixteenth-century Spanish dialogues by some 79 authors puts on a solid basis the impression that this was an important literary form in Spain:

> La floraison de *Dialogues* coincide avec le règne de Charles Quint . . . l'impact d'Erasme est évident. Mais c'est parce que, ainsi que l'a démontré M. Bataillon, l'élite de la péninsule était prête spirituellement à accueillir la leçon de l'auteur de l'*Enchiridion*. Et si les espagnols adoptent le moule littérarie du *Dialogue* avec un tel enthousiasme, et y versent tant de choses, à première vue disparates, c'est qu'ils ont eux-mêmes beaucoup á dire: *le Dialogue connait en Espagne une fortune qui déborde très largement le modèle érasmien.*[43] [my emphasis EG]

The concern with eloquence and rhetoric in the *Shevet Yehudah* has been widely recognized. Its context, however, has not been adequately established. The influence of Judah Messer Leon's *Nofet Tsufim* on the *Shevet Yehudah* has not been demonstrated conclusively. Reminiscences of classical rhetoric in the *Shevet Yehudah* need not be attributed to direct contact with Latin rhetorical manuals or prose works. On the other hand, one of the more widely attested tendencies of fifteenth-century Castilian prose is to attempt to create a Latinate romance prose, a literary enterprise in which conversos were particularly prominent. Alonso de Cartagena, Juan de Lucena, Hernando del Pulgar are some of the protagonists of the Latinization of Castilian which has at times been thought rather extreme. M. Morreale has noticed, for example, the use of the apostrophe in Lucena. The typical exordium of the *Shevet Yehudah* seems to betray some influence of a device which at times increases the pathos and, at times, simply conveys an idea of elevated or courtly speech patterns. See, for example, Chapter 40, p. 34:

> Noble sons of Israel! Nobles of Judah who
> have power and fame in their houses and walls!

or p. 80:

> Oh chosen people! Sons of Abraham! Disciples of Moses!
> Inhabitants of Jerusalem! Dwelling place of the divine presence!
> Joy of the earth!

or again on p. 82

> Oh faithful city, Jerusalem! Oh dwelling place of the divine presence!
> Oh glory of Palestine! Oh joy of the angels above!

Series of balanced rhetorical questions are employed:

Who brought Antonius and Sosius?
And who brought Emperor Nero? (p. 82)

Or:

Where are the intelligent ones in times like these?
Where are the strong arms
Helped by purity of heart
Shooting a thousand arrows without missing one? (p. 81)

One of the glaring features of the *Shevet Yehudah* is the unusually frequent and deceptive use of standard Spanish names for apparently historical but evidently fictitious characters. This device was so successful that as late as the nineteenth century there were still historians who tried to identify 'King Alfonso', for example. To explain this feature in terms of hypothetical authorial intentions to erect 'memorials' or 'monuments' to fifteenth-century Spanish personalities is hardly satisfying. Basic rhetorical strategies are more in keeping with the general stylistic trend of the book.

In the rhetorical tradition studied by Lausberg,[44] among the types of mimesis, verisimilitude was an aspect of universality. An important means of achieving verisimilitude is the use of names. In tragedy especially, the use of historical names has the effect of giving an increased appearance of truth to the action. The poet may take one or two names from historical tradition and invent the action or plot. This is the general basis in poetics of such mediaeval genres as the pseudohistorical *Chanson de Geste* or the historical novel. In the *Chanson de Roland*, for example, the virtues of *fortitudo* and *sapientia* are clothed in historical garb by attributing them to historical personalities. More closely related to the *Shevet Yehudah* is the use of names in its source, the *Libro Aureo*. As M. R. Lida de Malkiel has observed,[45] Guevara's use of names is a function of the recreation of a fictional 'classical' atmosphere. The use of Roman names in the *Libro Aureo* increases the classical atmosphere just as the use of Spanish names in the *Shevet Yehudah* gives verisimilitude to claims of historicity and use of Spanish chronicles.

The use of orations or speeches was another mode of the *narratio verosimilis* which had been used by historians (e.g. the converso Pulgar) and is particularly noticeable in Guevara's *œuvre*. In the *Shevet Yehudah* the use of this device is particularly noticeable because it contrasts with the style of the mediaeval Spanish Jewish chronicles (e.g. Ibn Dawd, Joseph ibn Saddiq) or chronicles written by exiles schooled in Spain (Abraham ben Solomon, Abraham Zacuto). One may point to the speech of the ambassador from Judaea taken from the *Libro Aureo* (see below). Other occasions serve as excuses for such speeches as well. An example would be the speech of Josephus before the walls of Jerusalem (pp. 80–2).

CONVERSO HUMOUR AND POLEMICS

The mordant criticism of Christian typological exegesis can similarly be traced to fifteenth-century Hispano-Jewish sources. In the disputation (p. 87) between a Jew and a Christian before King Don Alfonso of Portugal, the Jew argues that if Psalm 22 can be interpreted typologically to prefigure the passion of Jesus, then Lamentations 3 and Psalm 22 prefigure the story of the Jewish disputant who, angry at his chicken, hit it, skinned it, took it into a dark room and then cooked it. The point that the biblical verses should not be understood outside their own context was crucial in mediaeval polemics and had been developed with particular clarity and force by the predecessors of the *Shevet Yehudah* in fifteenth-century Spain, as, for example, in the writings of Profayt Duran, Simeon ben Zemah Duran and Hayim ibn Musa.[46] As elsewhere in the book, the differences between the fifteenth-century treatment of themes and their presentation in the *Shevet Yehudah* is extremely telling. Technical terms and Bible citations are kept to a minimum. Humour and irreverence are predominant and give the narrative the popular tone which is reminiscent of the religious scepticism expressed verbally by fifteenth-century conversos and recorded in a number of Inquisition testimonies.[47]

TEMPLE RITUAL AND PAGEANTRY

In Chapter 64 the king claims that his interest in the Temple derives from his wish to build a church. After a lengthy description of matters relating to the Temple, the chapter concludes with one of the few comments attributed explicitly to Solomon ibn Verga (p. 141):

> And I, the poor Solomon ben Verga, was sent by the communities of Spain to collect ransom for the [Jewish] prisoners of Malaga. And there [in Spain], at the court of the king, the Gentiles tried to act out the Passover sacrifice and actually built an altar and had lines of priests with silver instruments and singers of songs of praise, and the people and the court officials marvelled exceedingly. And the king said: the Jews who had witnessed such things and lost them, death is preferable for them than life.

The story has been dismissed as mere invention, but that only begs the question of the historical context of such an obviously intense preoccupation with pageantry in this section of the *Shevet Yehudah*. The recent interest in late mediaeval ritual and pageantry[48] has revealed its importance as an expression of a dominant ideology. Biblical history gives authority to the ritual re-enactment of the realities of power. The *Victorial*, for example, a chronicle of Pero Niño, was written by Gutierre Díez de Games in order to provide the knightly stratum with '*exemplos*'. The chronicle expatiates on the Jewish welcome of Alexander:

> From there he went to Judaea and conquered it. And from there he went to Jerusalem. The Jews were greatly afraid. They came out in a great procession to welcome him with their bishop in his robes and the Law in his hands. And Alexander dismounted from his horse and knelt before the bishop, and worshipped the Law because of a vision he had had.[49]

The inclusion of the story in this fifteenth-century chronicle, the use of the term 'bishop', the selection of such elements as would validate mediaeval ritual symbolism, all reinforce the view that ancient Israelite history was not a random object of interest in fifteenth-century Spain. More relevant is the role of the Jews in the festivities for the Catholic monarchs at Saragossa in 1481. The elaborate Jewish ceremonies of the reception of the monarchs are described by Bernáldez because 'they were very appropriate and [based on] the number twelve.'

> In Saragossa the Jews and their chapter [i.e. the *aljama* authorities] presented them with [a gift] based on the number twelve in a very singular order. This was as follows: twelve calves, twelve sheep, all adorned. They were followed by the most singular silverware borne by twelve Jews carrying plates. One of them carried on his plate a rich cup full of 'castellano' coins (of gold) and another one carried a silver jug on a plate.

The episode attests to both the Spanish concern with ritual and pageantry (shared with the rest of Europe) and to active Jewish participation in it (amply demonstrated in this or earlier examples such as the Jewish participation in the festivities for the coronation of Ferdinand of Antequera). In short, not only the general mentality of the period but also the precise description of the Jewish role in the pageantry and its very nature during the reign of the Catholic monarchs reinforce the feeling that the casual dismissal of the story as fictitious overlooks its value as a clue to the Hispanic cultural milieu of the book.

THE AMBASSADOR FROM JUDAEA

The speech of the Jewish ambassador to the Roman Senate in the *Shevet Yehudah* has attracted attention as a lead to the sources and date of composition of the work, rather than as an integral part of the text that has stood before the readers since the 1550s. Gilman's analysis of the 'Villano del Danubio' episode in the *Relox*[50] has underlined the contemporary implications of the villein's speech to the Roman Senate. The accusations of injustice refer to the activities of the Inquisitor Lucero, and the whole speech is an attack on 'the horrible inhumanity of the Inquisition'. Redondo doubts whether Lucero is the intended target.[51] In any case, the essential arguments of the 'Villano del Danubio's' speech are set forth in the tenth letter of the second book of the *Libro Aureo*. This letter, according to Redondo,[52] may be related to the period of Fray García de Loaysa's activities (February 1522 to the end of 1523) with its concomitant increase in inquisitorial repression. The consensus is clear: whoever the personal target may be, the general tenor of the letter ascribed to an ambassador from Judaea, with its allusions to injustice, fire and 'other things which I have to tell you in secret', is allusive to inquisitorial activity.

The implications for the reader of the *Shevet Yehudah* are obvious. The selection of this particular letter for inclusion (according to Baer, the first such translation into Hebrew of a belletristic prose work from a European modern language) is neither coincidental nor simply designed to show the cleverness of the Jews. It is part and parcel of a general interest in converso issues in the *Shevet Yehudah*, and should be classed with stories such as that of Judah ibn Verga in Chapter 62, and others which show obvious interest in the Inquisition as a converso issue.[53] The Spanish exiles were by no means isolated from Spain; on the contrary, there is every probability that they understood the implications of the letter as well as did the peninsular readers of Guevara.[54]

CONVERSOS AND THE KING'S SLUMBERS

The story included in Chapter 16 of the *Shevet Yehudah* appears also among the testimonies given in Segovia on 27 June 1489 by Maestre Alonso Henríquez and ratified before the inquisitors from the monastery of Santa Cruz. His testimony is directed against Diego Arias Dávila.[55] He testified that he visited the '*maestrescuela*' (i.e. the cathedral canon in charge of teaching at the cathedral school) and told him how he was afraid of everyone in Segovia, including the *maestrescuela* himself. The *maestrescuela* replied by telling him a story which he had heard from another converso, the *contador mayor* of Enrique IV, Diego Arias. Diego Arias had informed him of a conversation he had with Enrique IV. The King said that he wished to destroy the conversos. The *maestrescuela* answered: 'Sir, fear not, for the Lord will not allow this to pass because it is written, "*Esse non dormitavit nec dormiet qui custodit Hisrael*", and we are Hisrael, sons of Habrahan, and these are idolatrous

Gentiles and no one has ever attacked this nation without coming to a bitter end.' Diego Arias answered:

> You speak the truth. I hope so and I believe it to be the case. You have comforted me greatly. Now I wish to tell you what happened to a certain king. He had a Jew who was exceedingly close to him. Members of the king's household were envious of the Jew and his intimacy (*pribanza*) with the king. In order to disrupt it, seeing that the Jew lived near the palace, they created a commotion by the Jew's house and contrived to have a man killed. Once he was dead, they threw the man into the Jew's house, thus giving the impression that he had been killed by the servants of the Jew. They acted thus in order to win the favour of the king who, they hoped, would punish the Jew for having caused the death of a Christian. While these events were taking place, the king was not asleep but he had seen everything, including the manner in which they threw the corpse inside, and he heard the noise made by his men. He ordered the Jew to be summoned and asked him why he had done the deed, dissembling that he had not seen anything. The said Jew swore that he had not committed the deed and that he was hoping for a miracle and trusting God who never slept. The king said: 'In truth, I am in God's place, and I never sleep either. I saw what transpired. Have no fear . . .' And thus both lost their fear.

The value of this document need hardly be emphasized. It grants the mediaevalist the rare opportunity of dealing with the type of data usually reserved for field-workers in contemporary oral transmission. The document gives us a glimpse of the mediaeval transmission of folklore—the circumstances in which it was handed on, information on the story-tellers, the purpose of the story and the way in which it was understood by the listeners. The implications for the study of the *Shevet Yehudah* are noteworthy. The presence of the same story in both Chapter 16 of the book and in the Inquisition file of 1489 shows that, whatever the merits of comparing the *Shevet Yehudah* with the later version of the story in the *Mayse Bukh* (which could not have been completed before 1581), it is quite clear that the shift of *Shomer Yisrael*—the keeper of Israel who 'shall neither slumber nor sleep' (Ps. 121:4)—from God to the king does not represent an exegetical twist exclusive to the *Shevet Yehudah*. The attribution of the verse to the king is already present in a story which circulated in Enrique IV's reign before 1466. The story, of course, was not told to enhance the royal image but to derive comfort from and assuage fear through faith in God (whoever his emissaries) in times of stress. The story, as far as the present available documentation shows, is a converso story, in the sense that it is originally documented as circulating in converso circles. They saw themselves as the true Israel, of whom God is a guardian.

As for the king, the story is accompanied by a remark to the effect that those who try to destroy the Jews come to a bitter end. The perpetrators of the murder are not commoners but members of the royal household ('*los de su casa*', '*el clamor de todos los suyos*'). In the *Shevet Yehudah* the last element is not formulated in identical terms. Rather it is 'one of the king's councillors' who 'spoke evil against the Jews' in the matter of the libel. The actual perpetrators of the crime are described as follows: 'moreover, they were bearing swords'. It need hardly be pointed out that it was not the peasants who were sword-bearers in mediaeval Spain. The criminals were known to the palace guards: '[the king's men] recognized two of the people carrying the corpse'.

The *Shevet Yehudah*, then, draws on the issues and ideas which belonged to the converso mentality from the fifteenth century onwards. But the sixteenth *shemad*, or chapter, is also an example of the adaptation of an oral narrative framework to particular circumstances and a particular medium which is in some ways comparable to a reverse oicotypification. While the Segovian conversos spoke of a particular Jewish courtier and the royal household's envy of him, the *Shevet Yehudah* story is generalized and applied to all the Jews. The situation of Jews or conversos in the king's service is replaced by a more general Jewish milieu. The king's ruse, so necessary to hold up the plot and increase the tension, is similar in both. But in the oral converso version it is used to bring out the hope of the Jew, a hope which proves well-founded. In the *Shevet Yehudah* it is used to develop debate, polemic and dialogue with characteristic '*agudeza*' and an apparent critique of mediaeval exegesis. This takes the form of a series of subclauses, gradually increasing in length;[56] and it is apparently the first documented incidence of the story.[57]

CONCLUSION

The course of *Shevet Yehudah* research is not entirely surprising. In the nineteenth century its main importance consisted in furnishing information about the subjects it treated. It was considered a primary source. Later, classical methods of source analysis were applied to it by Baer and others. The *Quellenforschung* of subsequent scholars such as Y. D. Abramsky, Braun, Pries-Horev and Schohat served to demonstrate that the *Shevet Yehudah* could not furnish significant data about the events it treated and that the focus of research had to shift to an analysis of the book as a creative, imaginative work. The discoveries of Benayahu may be interpreted as showing that a Hispanic rather than an Italian focus is called for. In any case, this is not the type of text which historians of fifteenth-century Hebrew historiography are used to dealing with. To explain its elusive singularity has been a major challenge. One tendency has been to present the book as a response to another disruptive event: the expulsion, it seemed, would explain its use of non-Jewish sources and its apparently novel historiographic stand. What has been attempted here is not to deny that the theme of exile is present in the book. Throughout the paper it has been argued that if the *Shevet Yehudah* seems novel, it is so in relation to the particular genre of Jewish mediaeval chronicles, with which it has only partial affinities. Part of the novelty lies, no doubt, in stylistic strategies which the present paper has only begun to uncover. But one has to come to grips with the proximity of the book to fifteenth- and sixteenth-century Hispanic (Jewish, converso and Christian) non-historiographic sources, in order to place it in the context to which it belongs. This is the context of moralizing, polemical writings, but also the context of a literature that seeks to delight.

Notes

1 Y. Baer, 'New notes on *Shevet Yehudah*' (Hebrew), *Tarbiz*, vol. 6 (1935), pp. 159–79, reprinted in id., *Studies in the History of the Jewish People* (Hebrew) (Jerusalem, 1985), vol. 2, pp. 417–44; A. A. Neuman, *Landmarks and Goals* (Philadelphia, 1974), pp. 82–104; C. Roth, 'Historiography', *Encyclopaedia Judaica* (Jerusalem, 1972); H. H. Ben Sasson, 'Le-Megamot ha-khronografiya ha-yehudit shel yemei ha-benayim u baayoteha', *Historionim ve-Askolot historiot* (Jerusalem, 1962), reprinted in *Retsef u-Temura* (Tel Aviv, 1984), pp. 379–401; L. Kochan, *The Jew and his History* (Chico, California, 1985); Y. H. Yerushalmi, 'Clio and the Jews', *PAAJR*, vols. 46–7 (1980), 613ff.

2 To be sure, recent research has tried to qualify the emphasis on discontinuity in Sephardi Jewry after the Expulsions in general (kabbalistic thought, talmudic methodology, economic activity) and in the special branch of history writing in particular. For a critique of the 'sudden rise' theory see, e.g., M. Breuer, 'Modernism and traditionalism in sixteenth-century Jewish historiography: A study of David Ganz' *Tzemach David*' in *Jewish Thought in the Sixteenth Century*, ed. B. D. Cooperman (Cambridge, 1983), pp. 308–25. For continuities in linguistic usage, folklore, liturgy and the structures of economic activity, see E. Gutwirth, 'Fragmentos de Siddurim españoles de la Genizah', *Sefarad*, vol. 40, fasc. 3 (1980), pp. 389–401; id., 'A Judaeo-Spanish letter from the Genizah', in I. Benabu and J. Sermoneta (eds.), *Judeo-Romance Languages* (Jerusalem, 1985), pp. 127–38; id., 'The family in Judeo-Spanish Genizah letters (xvi–xviii c.)', *Vierteljahrschrift für Sozial- und Wirtschaftsgeschichte*, vol. 73, pt. 2 (1986), pp. 210–15; id., 'Fragments of a Judaeo-Spanish ballad manuscript' from the Genizah' (Hebrew), *Jerusalem Studies in Folklore*, vols. 5–6 (1984), pp. 71–83; id., 'Adiciones manuscritas a una paráfrasis caldaica', *El Olivo*, vol. 9, no. 22 (Jul.–Dec. 1985), pp. 235–241; id., 'On the hispanicity of Sephardi Jewry', *Revue des Etudes Juives*, vol. 145, fasc. 3–4 (1986), pp. 347–57.

3 M. Steinschneider, *Die Geschichtsliteratur der Juden in Druckwerken und Handschriften* (Frankfurt a. Main, 1905), p. vii.

4 Neuman (note 1 above), pp. 84–8.

5 Baer: 'The book is mainly trying to discuss the causes of the expulsion', introduction to *Shevet Yehudah*, ed. Shochat (Jerusalem, 1946–7), p. 7. All references are to this edition. Despite the lack of biblical references and misprints (see the review by Judah Pries-Horev, *Kiryat Sefer*, vol. 24, nos 3–4 (1947–8), pp. 173–8), there is no better edition. See also Baer's *Galut* (Berlin, 1936), pp. 64ff; I. Loeb, 'Le folklore juif dans la chronique du Schebet Iehuda d'ibn Verga', *REJ*, vol. 24, no. 97 (1892), pp. 1–29. See also the stimulating essays by Y. H. Yerushalmi, *The Lisbon Massacre of 1506 and the Royal Image in the Shevet Judah* (Cincinnati, 1976), and *Zakhor* (Seattle, 1982).

6 'Una traducción hebrea de La Celestina en el s. xvi', *Estudios Humanísticos sobre La Celestina* (Potomac, 1985), pp. 34–49, 40–1; U. Cassuto, 'Some poems of Joseph Tsárfati' (Hebrew), *Occident and Orient Studies . . . M. Gaster* (London, 1936), pp. 58–63.

7 N. Weinerth, 'Bartolome de Torres Naharro's *Diálogo del Nascimiento*: A converso Christmas Play', *Revista de Estudios Hispánicos (Homenaje . . . Gilman)*, vol. 9 (Puerto Rico, 1982), pp. 249–54, 251.

8 Paper presented at the *Colloquium Hierosolymitanum, Litterae Judaeorum in terra hispanica* (forthcoming).

9 C. Rose, *Antonio Nuñez Reinoso* (New Jersey, 1971), pp. 152ff.

10 On the theme of exile in his sermons, see M. Benayahu, 'Drushav shel Rabi Yosef ben Meir Gershon: makor nekhbad le-toledot gerush sefarad u-tefutsot ha-megorashim ba-mamlakha ha-turkit', *Michael*, vol. 7 (1982), pp. 42–205.

11 The Yiddish poem 'Mitn Sheyvet Yehude in Suke' was published in *Die Zuqunft* (1938), p. 485 and is mentioned here as a striking but by no means unique example of a tendency to blur historical distinctions. Much of the fiction generated by the *Shevet Yehudah* exhibits this tendency. See, for example, the modernist trilogy of Z. Barmeir, 'Dialogues by Verga' (Hebrew), *Gazit*, vol. 16, nos. 11–12 (1959), pp. 4–9.

12 See e.g. J. D. Abramsky's thesis of a Solomon ibn Verga stratum which is characterized by Spanish 'haughtiness': J. D. Abramsky, *On the nature and content of the Shevet Yehudah* (Hebrew) (Jerusalem, 1942); cf. J. D. Abramsky, in *Gesher*, vol. 9 (1963), pp. 146–52. For the debate generated by Yerushalmi's theory of the royal image, see I. Tishby, *Messianism in the time of the Expulsion from Spain and Portugal* (Hebrew) (Jerusalem, 1985), pp. 59, 172, p. 20 n. 29; Y. Hacker, 'New Chronicles of the Expulsion of the Jews from Spain, its causes and effects' (Hebrew), *Zion*, vol. 43 (1979), pp. 211–13; M. Kohn, *Jewish Historiography and Jewish self-understanding in the period of the Renaissance and Reformation* (Ph.D. thesis, UCLA, 1978).

13 See M. Benayahu, 'A source on the Spanish and Portugues exiles and their emigration to Salonika' (Hebrew), *Sefunot*, vol. 9 (1971–5), pp. 249–56

14 J. Shatzmiller, 'Khronografiya provensalit be-kundreso he-avud shel Shem Tov Sanzolo', *Proceedings of the American Academy of Jewish Research*, vol. 52 (1985), pp. 43–61.

15 The *Tanquinum sanitatis*, a mediaeval manual translated from the Arabic of Ibn Butlan (eleventh-century Baghdad) for Charles d'Anjou in 1296 contains a description of the *confabulator* who 'should be proper in manner and courtesy', be able to stay awake, be a good judge of discourse '*not only of histories of great princes* but also delightful stories that provoke laughter . . .' Both serious historical narrative and humorous stories qualify as *confabulatio*. See G. Olson, *Literature as Recreation in the Later Middle Ages* (Ithaca, 1986), pp. 78ff.

16 E. Gutwirth, 'Jews in Castilian Chronicles', *JQR*, vol. 74, no. 4 (1984), pp. 379–96, 385

17 A recent book which touches on the subject is A. Funkenstein, *Theology and the Scientific Imagination from the Middle Ages to the Eighteenth Century* (Princeton, 1985).

18 See A. Deyermond, 'The Death and Rebirth of Visigothic Spain', *Revista Canadiense de Estudios Hispánicos*, vol. 9 (1985), pp. 345–67. See also his 'Historia Universal e Ideología Nacional en Pablo de Santa María' in *Homenaje a Alvaro Galmés de Fuentes*, vol. 2 (Oviedo–Madrid, 1985), pp. 313–24.

19 James F. Burke, 'Alfonso X and the structuring of Spanish History', *Revista Canadiense de Estudios Hispánicos*, vol. 9 (1985), p. 464.

20 M. Benayahu, *Rabbi Eliyahu Capsali of Crete* (Tel Aviv, 1983), ch. 15.

21 The interest in converso matters is apparent throughout the book. It may be asserted that there are few chapters which do not contain some allusion to conversion or conversos. The phrase (p. 129) 'what is the use of throwing some water on the Jews and calling us Pedro and Pablo, if the Jews are steady in their religion like Akiva and Tarfon' is only one of a multitude of well-known examples. See also pp. 21, 22, 24, 52, 66, 69, 120, 71.

22 On the *Libro Aureo* see A. Redondo, *Antonio de Guevara et L'Espagne de son temps* (Geneva, 1976). I have used the edition of Foulche Delbosc in *Revue Hispanique*, vol. 76 (1929). See also E. Grey, *Guevara: A Forgotten Renaissance Author* (The Hague, 1973).

23 On this motif see Redondo (note 22 above), pp. 94, 402–5, 575, no. 304. In general see Huizinga, *The Waning of the Middle Ages. A study in the forms of life, thought and art in France and the Netherlands in the fourteenth and fifteenth centuries* (London, 1924). See also Isaza y Calderón, *El Retorno a la naturaleza. Los orígenes del tema y sus direcciones fundamentales en la literatura española* (Madrid, 1934); G. Agrait, *El Beatus Ille en la poesia lírica del Siglo de Oro* (Puerto Rico, 1971); he considers Guevara as the culmination of the criticism of the chivalrous life-style which had been steadily growing since the beginning of the fifteenth century; p. M. Smith, *The anti-courtier trend in sixteenth-century French literature* (Geneva, 1966). See also the remark of 'Versorius' (*Shevet Yehudah* p. 128): 'If I left the court it was because I saw that those who are younger than myself seek to lord it over us, and though the king sees this, he does not speak.'

24 See on this text, E. Gutwirth, 'Actitudes judías hacia los cristianos en la España del s.xv: Idearío de los traductores del latín en el siglo xv', *Proceedings Second Toledo Congress on the Three Cultures* (Toledo, 1985), pp. 189–96.

25 See the edition of M. Roest, 'Brief van Salomo ha-Lewi (later als Christen bisschop Paulus de Burgos) aan Meir Alguadez', *Israelitische Letterbode*, vol. 10 (1884–5), pp. 78–85. See also I. Abrahams, 'Paul of Burgos in London', *JQR*, vol. 12 (1900), pp. 255–63. See also Y. Baer, *A History of the Jews in Christian Spain* (Philadelphia, 1978), pp. 139–51 and the bibliography in the notes.

26 See the notes to E. Gutwirth, 'The world upside down in Hebrew', *Orientalia Suecana*, vol. 30 (1981), pp. 141–7.

27 See Paz y Melia (ed.), *Biblia (Antiguo Testamento) traducida del Hebreo al Castellano por rabi Mose Arragel de Guadalfajara y publicada por el duque de Berwick y de Alba* (Madrid, 1920–22), Introduction.

28 See Redondo (note 22 above), p. 388: '*el hazer de la mesura es primor de cortesanos*', or '*ninguno en verdad se puede llamar buen cortesano si no se prescia de ser limpio en las ropas que trae y de ser bien criado en las palabras que dize*'. See the title of the second of the *Siete Partidas*, which is concerned with '*qual debe ser el rey en sus palabras . . . las grandes voces sacanle de mesura*', or the *Setenario*, ed. K. Vanderford (Buenos Aires, 1945), p. 31: '*non muy rrezio nin muy bravo nin otro si muy fflaco mas en buen sson mesurado . . .*'. See C. Faulhaber, *Latin Rhetorical Theory in thirteenth and fourteenth century Castile* (Berkeley, 1972).

29 Another perspective on the passage in E. Gutwirth, 'Centralization in fifteenth-century Hispano-Jewish communities' (Hebrew), in M. A. Friedman and M. Gil (eds), *Te'uda*, vol. 4 (1986), pp. 231–46.

30 I. Loeb (note 5 above), p. 5.

31 Little work has been done on the use of *leazim* in the *Shevet Yehudah*. The term *salvaje* itself seems to be documented no earlier than the *Libro de Buen Amor*. There seems to be a relatively clear difference between the concept in the Middle Ages, where it had connotations of brute strength and ugliness (being in fact related to the '*ome mui feo*') and the Renaissance, when its use in literature is a function of the criticism of 'civilized' life as is the case here in the *Shevet Yehudah*. See, for example, S. D. Kirby, 'Juan Ruiz's *Serranas*—The Archpriest-Pilgrim and Medieval Wild Women', in J. S. Miletich (ed.), *Hispanic Studies in Honor of Alan D. Deyermond* (Madison, 1986), pp. 151–69. See also J. M. G. Tabanera, 'La conseja y el hombre salvaje en la tradicion popular de la Peninsula ibérica', *Homenaje a Julio Caro Baroja* (Madrid, 1978), pp. 471–510; id., *Teoría e Historia de la Etnología*, vol. 1 (Madrid, 1964), pp. 636ff. See also J. A. Madrigal, *El salvaje y la mitología el arte y la religión* (Miami, 1975) and id., 'El "ome mui feo"; primera aparición de la figura del salvaje en la iconografia española', *Studies in Honor of John E. Keller* (Newark, 1980), pp. 67–76. See, in general, R. Bernheimer, *Wild Men in the Middle Ages* (Cambridge, Mass., 1952). A possible iconographic example (in the codex of the *Cantigas de Sta. Maria*) is assumed by J. E. Keller and R. p. Kinkadein, *Iconography in Medieval Spanish Literature* (Lexington, Kentucky, 1984), p. 32.

32 See J. Rodríguez Puértolas, *Fray Iñigo de Mendoza y sus Coplas de Vita Christi* (Madrid, 1968). For similar criticisms in Guevara's work see Redondo (note 22 above), pp. 616–7.

33 N. Rubinstein, 'Marsilius of Padua and Italian Political thought of his time', in J. Hale (ed.), *Europe in the Late Middle Ages* (Evanston, Ill., 1965).

34 See J. Friedländer and J. Kohn (eds), *Maase Eford* (Wien, 1865), Appendix.

35 (Zolkiew, 1806), f. 12a.

36 See the section 'as if in contest or battle' in S. Gilman, *The Spain of Fernando de Rojas* (Princeton, 1972), pp. 176–7, 181–4.

37 See Redondo (note 22 above), pp. 618–21. For the Hispano-Jewish antecedents, see E. Gutwirth, 'Late medieval Fortuna of Maimonidean ideas on wealth', *Proceedings International Congress on Maimonides* (Cordoba, 1985) (in press). See also the 'additions' of the *Shevet Yehudah* to the story of David Alroy (taken from Benjamin of Tudela) which are clearly aimed at portraying the greed of the Gentile ruler.

38 See, e.g., N. Alony, 'The reaction of Moses ibn Ezra to Arabiyya', *Actes du xxixe Congrès International des Orientalistes* (Paris, 1975), Section 3, Etudes hébraïques, pp. 1–16; id., 'Views of reaction against Arabiyya in our mediaeval literature' (Hebrew), *Sefer Meir Wallenstein* (Jerusalem, 1979), pp. 134ff; id., 'The reaction of Moses ibn Ezra to Arabiyya', *Bulletin Institute of Jewish Studies*, vol. 3 (1975), pp. 19–40 (revised version of an article in *Tarbiz*, vol. 42 (1973), pp. 97–112.); id., 'The Kuzari of R. Yehuda ha-Levi in the light of the Shu'ubiyyá' (Hebrew), *Bitsaron*, vol. 65, no. 3 (1974), pp. 105–13.

39 On the Gothic myth see J. A. Maravall, *El concepto de España en la Edad Media* (Madrid, 1963), ch. 7, pt. 2, p. 301 and A. Van Beysterveldt, *Amadis Esplandian-Calisto* (Potomac, 1982), p. 67; E. Gutwirth, 'Lineage in xv c. hispano-Jewish thought', *Miscelánea de Estudios Arabes y Hebraicos*, vol. 34, fasc. 2 (1985), pp. 85–91. Muslim and Christian parallels to Joseph ibn Shem Tov's concern with the lineage of the ideal leader in his (MS) sermon on the Korah pericope are discussed in E. Gutwirth, 'El gobernador judio ideal: Acerca de un sermón inédito de Joseph ibn Shem Tov', *Proceedings Third Toledo Congress on the Three Cultures* (Toledo, 1988).

40 See especially the penetrating analysis of Y. Dan, *The Hebrew Story in the Middle Ages* (Jerusalem, 1974), pp. 188ff; id., 'The art of storytelling in the *Shevet Yehudah*' (Hebrew), *Molad*, vol. 4 (1972), pp. 671–89. The use of proverbs and letters deserves separate treatment.

41 See Berakhia ben Natronai Nakdan, *Dodi Ve-Nekhdi Now edited from MSS at Munich and Oxford with an English translation, introduction . . . by H. Gollancz* (London, 1920). The comparison is not random; the *Uncle and nephew* deals with questions similar to those found in ch. 7 of the *Shevet Yehudah*.

42 Cristina Barbolani, 'Los Diálogos de Juan de Valdés: reflexión o improvisación?', *Actas . . . Doce consideraciones sobre el mundo Italiano en tiempos de Alfonso y Juan Valdés* (coordinador F. Ramos Ortega) (Rome, 1979), pp. 135–54. A. Soria Olmedo, *Los Dialoghi d'Amore de León Hebreo. Aspectos literarios y culturales* (Granada, 1984) ch. 2; see also S. Gilman, 'Diálogo y estilo en La Celestina' *Nueva Revista de Filología Hispana*, vol. 7 (1953), pp. 461–9.

43 See J. Ferreras, *Les Dialogues espagnols du xvie siècle ou l'expression littérarie d'une nouvelle conscience* (Paris–Lille, 1985).

44 Heinrich Lausberg, *Hanbuch der literarischen Rhetorik*, vol. 1 (Munich, 1960), no. 1218 and n. 1 and 2, pp. 588ff.

45 M. R. Lida de Malkiel, *Hérodes, su persona, reinado y dinastía* (Madrid, 1977).

46 See E. Gutwirth, 'History and apologetics in fifteenth-century Hispano-Jewish thought', *Helmántica*, vol. 35, no 107 (1984), pp. 231–42.

47 I deal with the similarities between Jewish and converso humour in 'From Jewish to Converso Humour in fifteenth-century Spain' *Bulletin of Hispanic Studies* (in press). I have not been able to consult J. L. Saiz's thesis, *El Humor en la obra de Guevara* (University of British Columbia). On '*agudeza*' and humour in Guevara see Redondo (note 22 above), pp. 113ff.

48 A. MacKay, 'Ritual and propaganda in fifteenth-century Castile', *Past and Present*, no. 107 (1985), pp. 3–43. E. Lourie, 'Jewish participation in Royal Funerary rites: an early use of the Representatio in Aragon', *Journal of the Warbug and Courtauld Institutes*, vol. 45 (1982), pp. 192–4. Aspects of the question are studied in *Simboli e Simbologia nell'Alto Medioevo* (Spoleto, 1976). For fifteenth-century Spain see e.g. I. Beceiro Pita, 'La imagen del poder en las tomas de posesión bajomedievales castellanas', *Studia Historica*, vol. 2, no. 2, pp. 157–62. See also B. Palacios Martín, *La Coronación de los reyes de Aragón (1204–1410)* (Valencia, 1975).

49 E. Gutwirth, 'Jews in Castilian Chronicles', *JQR*, vol. 74, no. 4 (1984), pp. 379–96, 385. Of course, this is not the only place where the *Shevet Yehudah* expressed interest in ritual and pageantry: see also ch. 42.

50 S. Gillman, 'The sequel to *el Villano del Danubio*', *RHM*, vol. 31 (1965), pp. 174–84. In the *Shevet Yehudah*, of course, the story is connected to another concerned with judges. On the criticism of judges in Guevara see Redondo (note 22 above), p. 644.

51 Redondo (note 22 above), p. 646.

52 *ibid.* and n. 361, and ch. 9.

53 See note 21 above.

54 See Gutwirth (note 2 above).

55 This section is part of a lecture on 'Jews and Conversos at the court of Enrique IV' given in the spring term of 1983 to *Bamat ha-Hoker*, Rosenberg School of Jewish Studies, Tel Aviv University. On this Inquisition case and its file at Madrid see E. Gutwirth, 'Jewish Converso relations in xv c. Segovia', *Proceedings Eighth World Congress of Jewish Studies*, Section B (Jerusalem, 1982), pp. 49–53; id., 'Elementos etnicos e historicos en las relaciones judeo-conversas en Segovia', *Jews and Conversos*, ed. Y. Kaplan (Jerusalem, 1985), pp. 83–102; id., 'On the background to Cota's Epitalamio Burlesco', *Romanische Forschungen*, vol. 97, no. 1 (1985), pp. 1–14. The transcription of the file may now be found in C. Carrete Parrondo *Fontes Iudaeorum Regni Castella*, vol. 3 (Salamanca, 1986).

56 The story belongs, in a sense, to a larger motif of international folklore. It may be said to fit in with Stith Thompson's k2100–k2199: 'false accusations' and within this with

motif k2199: 'innocent persons accused of murder'. See Stith Thompson, *Motif Index of Folk Literature* (Copenhagen–Bloomington, 1955–8). Within this its main structure has been classified as a more particular Jewish oicotype. What is crucial is the use of the Bible verse as the main point. For a discussion on blood libels from the point of view of folklore see D. Noy 'Alilot Dam be-Sippurei Edot', *Mahanayim*, vol. 110 (1967), 32–51 and T. Alexander, 'The Judaeo-Spanish Legend about R. Kalonymos in Jerusalem' (Hebrew), *Jerusalem Studies in Folklore*, vol. 5–6 (1984), pp. 85–122.

57 The *Shevet Yehudah* contains allusions to and shows interest in fifteenth- and early sixteenth-century Hispano-Jewish matters at various levels. Some of the larger themes have been touched upon above, but it may be suggested that there are minor motifs or idiomatic usages which help to recreate the concerns of that particular milieu and period. An example of the research needed for developing this further might be the analysis of the particular fifteenth-century use of the term *mahoz* in the *Shevet Yehudah*. See D. Flusser, *Josippon* (Jerusalem, 1980), pp. 88–9, n. 264a. On pp. 41–3 the 'King' is made to say: 'you have spoken well, and it is like the thief who is a member of the household.' These are precisely the comments which Isabella is credited with upon hearing or reading the *Epitalamio Burlesco* of Rodrigo de Cota against the Jewish customs at a wedding of the Arias Davila family in the 1470s. See E. Gutwirth, 'On the background . . . ' (note 54 above). At various points the characters in the book use the phrase 'like old women who knit by moonlight', a phrase which appears in earlier Hebrew poetry. This particular choice in the *Shevet Yehudah* might recall its currency in fifteenth-century Spain e.g. in the title of the Marquis de Santillana's *Refranero*. See U. Cronan, 'Refranes que dizen las viejas tras el fuego', *Revue Hispanique*, vol. 25 (1911), pp. 114–19. The apparently unnecessary *leazim* like *salvaje* or *monstruos* might help to draw attention to concepts the contemporary currency of which is attested in the *Libro Aureo* for example. On the *salvaje* see note 31 above. On the period's fascination with monsters, see, e.g. Redondo (note 22 above), p. 479, where he refers to the famous monster of Ravenna, Hieronymus Bosch's paintings, the *Silva Palatina*, and the interest in Mandeville's *Voyages* as a source of information on monsters.

Parts of this study were read as lectures at Harvard University (Centre of Jewish Studies) and at my postgraduate seminar on Mediaeval Jewish Historiography. My thanks are due to my colleagues and students, and to Ada Rapoport-Albert and to Paul Julian Smith for useful comments.

The Quest for Philo in Sixteenth-Century Jewish Historiography*

Joanna Weinberg

IN the last decades of the sixteenth century, the writings of the Hellenistic Jew Philo of Alexandria became associated with various controversial issues. The patristic interpretation of Philo and his works was now called into question. Catholics who were unwilling to forgo their allegiance to patristic authority were compelled under storm by Protestants to provide historical evidence in support of their views. These scholarly debates, which continued into the seventeenth century, signalled the beginnings of a historical approach to the work of Philo Judaeus.[1]

The source of the Philonic problem was Eusebius. He had identified the 'Therapeutae' described by Philo in his *De vita contemplativa* as the first Christian monastic order; he had also detected reference to the Trinity in Philo's writings. These views of Eusebius were further corroborated by the traditions recorded by him that Philo had met Saint Peter in Rome[2] and that Saint Mark had made his first converts in Alexandria.[3] Eusebius's opinions were adopted by Jerome, who allocated Philo a place in his list of 'Ecclesiastical Writers'.[4] Indeed, Philo's works were included in the sixth- and seventh-century compilations of the early Church Fathers.[5] Implied in the reports of the Church Fathers was that Philo, if not a Christian, was at least a propounder of Christian truths. The legend, once propagated, became embellished in a variety of ways. Thus Photius could claim that Philo had converted to Christianity but later reverted to his own faith 'in disappointment and rage'.[6]

When the first translations and editions of Philo's works were printed in the middle of the sixteenth century, the editors made it clear that they also espoused the patristic view.[7] But this unquestioning

* This article is based on a chapter of my doctoral dissertation (London, 1982), which I wrote with the understanding and supportive guidance of Chimen Abramsky. I would like to thank him, and to acknowledge helpful comments by Alastair Hamilton, the late Arnaldo Momigliano and Ada Rapoport-Albert.

regard for patristic authority, as has already been indicated, was not to persist much longer. The extent to which the Philonic problem became a feature in late sixteenth-century Christian historiography is perhaps best demonstrated by the various pronouncements made by Joseph Justus Scaliger on the subject at different stages of his life. In 1583, Scaliger published the first edition of his *De emendatione temporum*. In Chapter 6 of the work he ridicules Eusebius for transforming Philo's Therapeutae into Christians.[8] This was not the end of the matter. By 1598 the question had become a bone of contention between Protestants and Catholics. In the 'prolegomena' to the third edition of the *De emendatione*, Scaliger inveighs against various scholars for their misinterpretation of Philo's description of the Essenes (the Judaean sect described in *Quod omnis probus liber* as akin to the Therapeutae and often mistaken for it) and the Therapeutae.[9] In particular, he directs his vitriolic pen against Baronius, who in Volume 1 of the *Annales* had attempted to challenge the 'Novatores' on the question of the sects. Recognizing the need to attack the reformers with their own tools, Baronius attempted to reconsider the issue historically. He argued that Philo's description of the Therapeutae as a sect of great numbers could only be understood with reference to converts to Christianity. The patristic view had to be upheld at all costs.[10] In the 'prolegomena', Scaliger treats this argument with total contempt. He scolds Baronius for confusing Judaism with Christianity, and thus obliterating all distinctions between the two religions.[11]

These debates continued late into the seventeenth century and vestiges of the arguments could still be heard at a later date. At the beginning of the eighteenth century, the English orientalist Humphrey Prideaux could exclaim: 'Our holy Christian profession is so far from having any of the documents or institutions of the Essenes in it that almost all that is peculiar in that sect is condemned by Christ and his Apostles.'[12]

It is generally held that these discussions inaugurated a new era in Philonic studies; such a claim is certainly valid as far as Christian historiography is concerned. But this assessment is only a partial one. Contrary to what Scaliger claimed,[13] the chronicler Abraham Zacuto was not the only Jew to refer to Philo.[14] During the sixteenth century, a few Italian Jews were eagerly perusing the recently-printed works of Philo Judaeus. Unlike their contemporary Christians, these Jews could not draw on their own traditions to assist them in their reading of Philo. Indeed, the rare (and usually indirect) references to Philo in Jewish literature are almost entirely to be found in Karaite writings.[15] The rediscovery of the Jew Philo had to proceed cautiously. Rabbinic silence on the subject could be interpreted as implied censure, while the widespread Christian approbation of Philo could not be ignored. Given the anomalous position of Philo—'one of the ancient enigmas' as Nachman Krochmal called him[16]—he could not be adopted by his co-religionists without due consideration. It is for this reason, I should like to suggest, that one of the first 'rediscoverers' of Philo, Azariah de' Rossi, decided to produce a critique of the Hellenistic Jew.

De' Rossi's appraisal of Philo was incorporated in his *Me'or 'Enayim* (the *Light of the Eyes*) which was printed in his native town of Mantua in 1573.[17] The critique raises some of the most crucial questions connected with Philo which continue to intrigue modern scholars. De' Rossi claimed that his discourse contained unknown material (*hiddush*).[18] What was truly original was the enterprise itself, the first comprehensive assessment of Philo to be undertaken by Jew or Christian.

De' Rossi's avowed purpose was to ascertain whether Philo, who had devoted the major part of his literary output to scriptural exegesis, could be claimed as a representative of his people. Some of de' Rossi's contemporaries (he explicitly refers to the Provenzali brothers)[19] had championed the cause of Philo, 'setting a golden crown on his head and regarding him as a noteworthy member of our people.'[20] De' Rossi was more circumspect in his approach. He coined a neutral Hebrew name for Philo, 'Yedidya the Alexandrian',[21] and divided his critique into equal sections of prosecution and defence.[22] He maintained this ambivalent attitude to his subject right to the end of his critique. As he writes in the conclusion:

> This was a man who, in my opinion, fell between two stools and about whom no decision can be reached . . . I will not pass an unconditional verdict on him and absolutely absolve or convict him. I shall not call him Rav or sage,[23] heretic or sceptic. My only name for him shall be Yedidya the Alexandrian.[24]

De' Rossi's constant oscillation between condemnation and defence of Philo is understandable. Partly, it could be viewed as a token gesture on his part to demonstrate his own orthodoxy, which may have seemed suspect to some contemporary rabbis. By refusing to approve those ideas of Philo which were at variance with rabbinic tradition, he would show his readers where his allegiances lay. But de' Rossi's ambivalence must also be understood as his response to the patristic interpretation of Philo with which he was familiar. (It should be remembered that he was writing before the Protestant–Catholic confrontation on the question of Philo had become so fraught.) There seems to be an underlying strand to his critique whereby de' Rossi is attempting to undermine the Christianizing process and to find the Jewish, or rather

Pharisaic, elements in Philo. According to de' Rossi, Philo was an Essene, ignorant of the Holy Tongue and Palestinian rabbinic *halakhah*. De' Rossi's emphatic description of Philo as a sectarian Jew of the second Temple period may be contrasted with the patristic statements mentioned above, in which Philo is portrayed as a writer recording Christian truths and praising Christian institutions. The editions which de' Rossi was using were furnished with the *testimonia* of the Church Fathers and editorial pronouncements of a similar nature. De' Rossi employs some of their general assessments of Philo for his intellectual profile of the philosopher. On no occasion, however, does he refer to the legends about Philo's meeting with Saint Peter, nor indeed to any of the explicitly Christian reports. His silence is telling. It may be argued that one of his main purposes in defining Philo's status in relation to the Jewish community was to counter the claims of those who associated Philo with the primitive Christian Church.

De' Rossi's critique is comprehensive in scope. In addition to the examination of Philo's association with the Jewish sectarians, Philo's theology and *halakhah* come under scrutiny. De' Rossi's interpretation of theology is shaped by his reading of the Christian Platonists such as Marsilio Ficino and Symphorien Champier of Lyons, who regarded Philo as one of those Platonists 'who had appropriated the mysteries of the Christians' and had used 'their divine light for interpreting the divine Plato'.[25] De' Rossi was also indebted to Augustinus Steuchus, a proficient biblical scholar who was appointed librarian of the Vatican library in 1543.[26] Steuchus' *Recognitio veteris testamenti* supplied de' Rossi with invaluable material, particularly for the section on Philo's knowledge (or rather ignorance) of Hebrew.[27] De' Rossi, in other words, was acquainted with the various different treatments of Philo and Philonic writings. Equipped with this knowledge and with his mastery of rabbinic literature, de' Rossi could proffer himself as an objective assessor of Yedidya the Alexandrian.

In 1949, Ralph Marcus wrote a synopsis of de' Rossi's four-chapter critique. Instead of presenting yet another general description, I shall single out certain passages in the critique which uphold my basic thesis. In addition, I shall provide detailed examination of de' Rossi's sources in order to ascertain the exact content of his discourse.

By 1570, the year in which de' Rossi began to write his *Me'or 'Enayim*, the main corpus of Philonic writings, genuine and spurious, had been published. The desire to make Philo's works accessible had already begun in the fifteenth century. Between 1479 and 1484, Lilius Tifernas, the teacher of Raphael Volaterranus, wrote a Latin translation of the main works of Philo from a manuscript brought to Italy by Bessarion.[28] His translation was never printed, but in 1554 the German scholar and renowned translator of Josephus, Sigismund Gelenius, published a new translation which was reprinted several times.[29] This was the translation that de' Rossi used.[30] He did not have enough competence in Greek to consult the *editio princeps* which Turnèbe published in 1552.[31] In addition to the genuine Philo, de' Rossi also consulted the *Liber antiquitatum biblicarum*, a work ascribed to Philo. Guillaume Budé had questioned the authenticity of the work;[32] de' Rossi, for reasons that will be explained below, chose to treat it as genuine.

In volume one of the *Centuries* of Magdeburg, Flavius Illyricus wrote a section on the Jewish heretical sects: the Pharisees, Sadducees and Essenes. His purpose was to identify the relation of these sects to the early Christian Church.[33] It is highly unlikely that de' Rossi would have had access to the work. Yet the excursus on the sects with which his critique begins has a similar objective: to define Philo's status in relation to the various Jewish groups of his time.

De' Rossi's excursus contains a discussion of one sect not usually known to the Christians—the Boethusians. Mention of this sect only occurs in rabbinic literature and usually in association with the Sadducees. According to de' Rossi, Boethusian was just another name for Essene. Philo, in his view, was an adherent of the Boethusian–Essene sect. De' Rossi reaches this conclusion by means of a comparison between Philo's interpretations of certain legal passages in Scripture and those of the Boethusians as recorded in the Talmud. Philo, for example, understands the expression 'eye for an eye' (Ex. 21:34) literally; in Tractate *Baba Kama* (83b), the Boethusians are accused of upholding a literal interpretation of the term. Clearly, this was a deviation from rabbinic tradition which explains the expression in terms of monetary compensation equivalent to the loss sustained.[34] As opposed to this kind of deviation from Pharisaic tradition, de' Rossi notes that the Boethusians are never accused of the sin attributed to the Sadducees of rejecting belief in the immortality of the soul and in the doctrine of reward and punishment in the afterlife. As C. D. Ginzburg briefly indicated, de' Rossi's arguments are not substantiated by the sources he himself cites.[35] In discussing the origins of the Sadducean sect, de' Rossi refers to Chapter 5 of *'Avot de' Rabbi Nathan* which comments on the saying of Antigonus of Sokho, 'Do not be like servants who serve their master in order to receive a reward.'[36] Zadok and Boethus, it is said, misinterpreting Antigonus's saying, deduced that there was no reward in the afterlife nor resurrection of the dead. They founded two heretical sects; Zadok became the leader of the Sadduceans, Boethus the leader of the Boethusians. De' Rossi chose to ignore this evidence because, as will be shown, it contradicted his theory that the Boethusians were a Greek sect.

In his brief sketch of the Essenes,[37] de' Rossi conflates the descriptions of Philo, Josephus[38] and Eusebius,[39] disregarding the various divergences between all these accounts. For example, he portrays the Essenes as a group of about 4000 adherents, coming mainly from Alexandria and living a communal life outside the cities. He does not acknowledge that Josephus makes no reference to Greek Jews in his description of the Essenes; he dismisses the fact that Philo distinguishes between the Essenes and the Therapeutae on the grounds that Josphus and Eusebius do not differentiate between the two.[40] He does not mention that the Therapeutae are not described as sharing their homes and clothing, as are the Essenes.

A reason for de' Rossi's apparently superficial reading of his sources may perhaps emerge from his main thesis. At the end of the first chapter of the critique,[41] he quotes a Talmudic passage in which a Boethusian uses the Greek word *kalos* in reply to a Pharisee.[42] On the basis of this one passage, de' Rossi concludes that the Boethusian was a Greek-speaking Jew,[43] or according to his own definition, an Essene, one of the 4000-member community described by Philo and Josephus. The detail about the communal housing of the Essenes is used by de' Rossi to explain the etymology of the word Boethusian: he suggests that it is a conflation of the words *bayit* (house), 'Because their homes were held in common', and the word Esse or Essene. (It is interesting to note that the name Boethusian is separated into two words in the *Tosefta* and in the first edition of the '*Arukh*.)[44]

The etymologies of the names of the sects were often discussed by Christian historians. Epiphanius's conjectural etymologies were frequently cited.[45] De' Rossi also quotes Epiphanius's statement that the Sadducees gave themselves that designation in order to indicate that their objectives were righteous (*Tsedek*).[46] Interestingly, de' Rossi does not quote the etymology suggested by Epiphanius and quoted by Baronius and others that the Essenes were really *Iessaei* (of the stock of Jesus).[47]

According to de' Rossi, therefore, Philo was a Jew of the second Temple period who wrote about the life of a Jewish schismatic group to which he himself belonged. De' Rossi's edition of Philo, as was stated above, contained various 'testimonia' about Philo. It included Jerome's statement that the Therapeutae were living in the manner that 'monks endeavour to live nowadays'.[48] De' Rossi, without explicitly saying so, suggests an alternative interpretation:

> They observed all the same regulations which Christian orders of monks of our own time maintain and which affect all aspects of the upkeep of their community. We could thus infer that these Christian orders

followed in their footsteps and took the Essene life-style as their model.[49]

In this unobtrusive aside, de' Rossi corrects some Christian assumptions. The origins of Christian monastic institutions were Jewish: Philo's Essenes were a Jewish, not a Christian, sect.

'Either Philo is like Plato or Plato is like Philo.' This Greek saying quoted by Jerome in his profile of Philo influenced all subsequent readers of Philo. In the preface to his Latin translation of Philo's works, Sigismund Gelenius quotes the proverb and then writes:

> I believe that it is rather Plato who is like Philo because he emulated Moses whose disciple Philo was. After all, it is agreed that Plato travelled to Egypt where he received instruction from both Jewish and Egyptian priestly scribes.[50]

This pronouncement of Gelenius offers us an insight into Renaissance Platonism rather than an elucidation of the Greek proverb. Gelenius clearly subscribes to the tradition of Christian apologetic theology known as the 'prisca theologia'. This 'ancient theology' was used by the Church Fathers (Augustine and Lactantius in particular) and was popular in the Renaissance. Inherent in the notion of 'prisca theologia' was the idea that Plato's philosophy contained perennial truths which were compatible with Christianity. Plato had not discovered these truths for himself. Ultimately deriving from Egypt, they had been transmitted through the medium of an uninterrupted line of 'ancient theologians' going back to Zoroaster or Hermes Trismegistus.[51] According to Gelenius, Philo had a distinct advantage over Plato in that, in his role as interpreter of the Mosaic law, he had a more direct link with the source of true theology.

De' Rossi was not a philosopher or theologian of any description; his approach to Philo was simply that of a historian. But he had a task to fulfil. He had to prove that the Platonic Philo (he quotes the Greek proverb) was a respectable theologian whose views were not incompatible with the teachings of Scripture and rabbinic tradition. The way was already paved for him by the Christian Platonists and especially by Marsilio Ficino, Symphorien Champier and Augustinus Steuchus.

In his discussion of Philo's theology, de' Rossi treats the standard subjects: the nature of the soul and its immortality, providence and free will, the unity and incorporeality of God and creation. De' Rossi was satisfied that Philo believed in the soul's immortality and in the doctrine of reward and punishment in the afterlife.[52] What did concern him was that Lactantius had claimed that Plato had not professed a belief in the eternal state of happiness of the virtuous soul. De' Rossi was intent, and not without justification, in proving Lactantius wrong. The Philonic Plato could not be suspected of this heretical view. De' Rossi's defence of Plato is partially reliant on Ficino, although he does not acknowledge his debt.

Plato discusses the subject of the respective fates of the virtuous and wicked souls in several of his dialogues. It is only in the *Apology* that the question of the immortality of the soul is left open. De' Rossi refers to the passage at the end of the *Phaedo* in which Plato describes the happiness of the virtuous souls 'in the Elysian fields which corresponds to our Garden of Eden'.[53] What is interesting is the use of the expression 'Elysian fields' which never occurs in any Platonic work, although the word 'field' is used by Plato to describe 'limbo'. De' Rossi appears to have borrowed the term from Ficino: in the 'argumentum' to the tenth book of the *Republic*, Ficino states that the 'Elysian fields' are located in the terrestrial paradise of the virtuous souls as described by Plato at the end of the *Phaedo*.[54]

De' Rossi's criticism of Lactantius is a good example of the syncretistic approach to Platonic philosophy. Plato and his interpreter Philo had a notion of the paradise of the virtuous souls, the pagan counterpart to the biblical Garden of Eden. De' Rossi refers to Ficino's translation of the Platonic dialogues in other parts of his *Me'or 'Enayim*. In this case, his failure to mention Ficino indicates his total immersion in the Christian interpretation of Platonism.

De' Rossi does not examine any aspect of Philo's theology systematically. The particular points he chooses to examine thus gain greater significance, revealing the underlying motive for his discourse. His discussion of Philo's concept of the 'logos' is almost entirely concerned with terminology. Philo's use of the terms 'first-born of God' and 'incorporeal light' hint at a notion of a corporeal God. De' Rossi's treatment of this sensitive issue is again grounded in Renaissance Platonism. A kabbalistic dimension is grafted on the Platonic, neo-Platonic and 'prisca theologia' ideas. Jewish Platonists such as Johanan Alemanno had also formulated general comparisons between Kabbalah and Platonism even though, as Idel has pointed out,[55] there is sometimes no real connection between the two.

Like his contemporaries, de' Rossi did not doubt the authenticity of the hermetic writings (which were forged in the fourth century AD). He accepted what Ficino and others told him: Hermes Trismegistus was an Egyptian priest, philosopher and king who lived in the time of Moses and was influenced by the teachings of the Torah.[56] Equipped with this knowledge, de' Rossi could then, like Ficino, proceed to detect the similarities between Scripture and the hermetic texts.

Both Philo and pseudo-Hermes used the term 'son of God' to

designate the emanating light. Similar vocabulary had been used in kabbalistic texts. It is to these that de' Rossi alludes when he writes:[57]

> In view of the statements of these two sages [i.e. Philo and Hermes], and provided it is indeed true that the kabbalists wrote the passage indicated *qaddisha abba* etc.[58] one has no reason to be surprised by the statements of a similar nature made by the sage Recanati[59] . . . The enlightened will correctly gauge the meaning of these passages.[60]

This passage is, at first sight, incomprehensible (that is probably why modern scholars have failed to comment on it). The *qaddisha abba* quotation is actually an allusion to a Christian interpretation of the *trishagion* 'Holy, holy, holy, is the Lord of Hosts . . . ' (Is. 6:3). The passage occurs in no extant Jewish kabbalistic text. It is cited in the *Zelus Christi* written in 1450 by Pedro della Caballeria,[61] and it is cited by Paulus de Heredia, one of the teachers of Pico della Mirandola. De Heredia's work *Epistola de secretis* (1487) contains various letters attributed to the Tanna Nehunya ben Hakkana and other references to known figures traditionally associated with the Kabbalah including Simeon bar Yohai, in whose name the *trishagion* passage is cited.[62] The *Epistola* was used by Pietro Galatino in his anti-Jewish tract of Christian Kabbalah entitled *De arcanis catholicae veritatis* (Orthone, 1518).[63] In book two of the *De arcanis*, Galatino claims that the trinitarian interpretation of Isaiah 6:3 is confirmed by 'Rabbi Symeon Iohai filius' and by Rabbi 'Jonathan Uzielis filius' in their commentaries to the verse in question. He writes:

> Nam Rabbi quidem Symeon sic hebraice ait . . . Id est sanctus hic est pater: sanctus hic est filius: sanctus hic est spiritus sanctus. Rabbi vero Ionathan ita caldaice inquit *qadish abba*, qadish bera, qadish ruha qadisha. Id est sanctus hic est pater, sanctus hic est filius, sanctus hic est spiritus sanctus.[64]

De' Rossi knew Galatino's work and he may well have been alluding to this passage.[65] Alternatively, he may have become acquainted with the trinitarian interpretation from his reading of the *Magen Abraham* of Abraham Farissol which was written in Ferrara in about 1514.[66] Farissol suggests that the *qadish abba* quotation and many other references to *aggadot* and the Zohar cited in Christian kabbalistic works were probably forged by certain converted Jews of Spanish origin.[67] Unlike Farissol, de' Rossi is prepared to give credence to the passage provided the concept of an incorporeal God is not undermined.

> This is valid as long as you do not overstep the limit in ascribing incorporeality. Realize that in every question the intellectual concept is divided in our perception, but unified in the Blessed Lord. It is merely a

matter of terminology whether it is called son or emanation or light or *sefira* or idea as Plato cleverly puts it.[68]

As Idel has pointed out,[69] this passage also betrays the mark of Ficino and Pico. The comparison between the terms *sefira* and 'idea' implies that the ideas are to be found in God himself and not only in the 'logos'.

As in many other passages in the *Me'or 'Enayim* in which he is conscious of proposing controversial and possibly also heretical views, he qualifies his whole discussion by expressing willingness to retract his opinion should scholars find it unacceptable. Yet his total absorption of the material pervades his discussion. He alludes to Champier's quotation of Augustine, in which Hermes is seen in his role of transmitter of the 'prisca theologia', as foreshadowing and predicting revelation.[70] His final word on the matter is provocative to say the least: 'Truly, the upright will deem them worthy of praise. For the more a person can transform something to the merit of his own religion, the more deserving is he of praise (*hare ze meshubah*).'[71] The use of the expression 'the more deserving is he of praise' is most surprising. To a Jewish reader this expression would immediately be associated with the Seder liturgy. In the *Haggada* it is expressly stated, 'The more he relates about the exodus from Egypt, the more deserving is he of praise (*hare ze meshubah*)'.

De' Rossi brings four serious charges against Philo: ignorance of Hebrew and Aramaic, belief in the eternity of matter, allegorization of the biblical stories and ignorance of the Oral Law.

De' Rossi was not the first nor indeed the last scholar to assess Philo's knowledge of Hebrew.[72] Steuchus's *Recognitio* supplied him with invaluable material for his study.[73] De' Rossi was ready to accept Steuchus's conclusions that Philo knew no Hebrew (or Aramaic): 'Observe how he was like a dreamer, acquiring his knowledge from hearsay because his only source of information was the Greek Septuagint translation.'[74]

Philo may have been alienated from the 'Hebraica veritas', but de' Rossi still attempts to prove that he was acquainted with some aspects of the Palestinian rabbinic tradition. This is evident from the contorted arguments he adduces in favour of the authenticity of the pseudo-Philonic work, the *Liber antiquitatum biblicarum*.[75] This work recounts biblical history from Adam to Saul. De' Rossi recognized that the work contained striking parallels to some of the rabbinic Midrashim. In his evaluation of the intrinsic importance of the work he writes:

> The righteous person will be overjoyed to observe that some of these passages are also mentioned by our rabbis in various Midrashim. Now an intelligent person might regard them as dubious stories and think to

himself, 'These fact and stories belong to a remote past. Who were their informants? What are these fantasies?' But on discovering that the same or similar accounts were written in a book like this (whether by Philo or another) written in the time of the second Temple, in a barbarous tongue, in another language, he would rightly check his tongue and bite back his words and say: 'There must be some basis to what they say'. We may take this as indication that these stories were transmitted to the people through the medium of the tradition and were related to us by our wise ancestors insofar as they were remembered by the older generations.[76]

According to de' Rossi, rabbinic traditions gain authority when corroborated by other works of antiquity. Here it should be noted that de' Rossi does not claim historical veracity for the stories of the *Biblical Antiquities* and Midrashim. He expresses his view quite explicitly in Chapters 14–18 of the *Me'or 'Enayim*: the *aggadot* are not historical documents nor are they intended to be regarded as such. The elaborations of biblical stories contained in the pseudo-Philonic work and in the rabbinic Midrashim are valuable only insofar as they reflect the religious teachings of the ancient sages.

In his 'prolegomenon' to James's edition of the *Liber antiquitatum biblicarum*, Feldman draws attention to de' Rossi's important contribution to the study of the work. He makes extensive use of the references to rabbinic literature which de' Rossi supplies (de' Rossi gives 24 examples of parallel passages).[77] Feldman also illustrates the weakness of de' Rossi's arguments on the question of the work's authenticity. First, de' Rossi argues that the *Liber antiquitatum* reverses the masoretic order of the ten commandments, placing the prohibition of adultery before that of murder. The same reversal is also found in Philo's *De decalogo*, *De legibus specialibus* and *Quis rerum divinarum heres*.[78] As Feldman points out, the *Liber antiquitatum* does follow the masoretic order of the ten commandments in the section about the prophet Micah.[79] The second argument is based on the translation of the Hebrew word *teva* (Ex. 2:3) in ' . . . and she took for him an ark (*teva*) of bulrushes'. The *Liber antiquitatum*, like the Septuagint, did not translate the word *teva*, but merely transcribed it into a Greek form, *thibis*.[80] Since, according to de' Rossi, Philo's Bible was the Septuagint and since both the Septuagint and the *Liber antiquitatum* retain the Hebrew form of the word, de' Rossi concludes that the work must have been written by Philo. As corroboration of his view, de' Rossi refers to Steuchus, who had expressed surprise at the retention of the Hebrew form of the word. But de' Rossi misread Steuchus. He actually refers to the genuine *De vita Mosis* (I.82), where Philo omits the word *teva* altogether and simply writes, 'and weeping they put the child by the banks of the river'.[81]

Steuchus deduces that Philo deviated from the Septuagint in the citation of this verse because he was unable to recognize the Graecized form of a Hebrew word. Steuchus's argument, signifying that Philo did not follow the Septuagint on this occasion, weakened de' Rossi's thesis. His proof relied on the supposition that a text which contained an anomalous word like *thibis* used in the Septuagint must have been written by Philo. For his third argument, de' Rossi points out that the *Liber antiquitatum* and Philo's *De gigantibus* both connect the 120-year age limit for man with that of Moses.[82] Feldman points out that the connection may easily be made by anyone recalling Genesis 6:3.[83]

Despite the obvious weakness in de' Rossi's arguments, there can be no question as to the originality of his contribution to the study of the *Liber antiquitatum*. Petrus Comestor and Nicholas of Cusa made occasional references to the work in their writings.[84] Sichardus, the editor of the first printed edition, indicated biblical references and variant readings in marginal glosses to the text. De' Rossi went futher and supplied the rabbinic parallels. Sixtus Senensis, author of the *Bibliotheca sancta* (Venice, 1566) detected certain Hebraisms in the text.[85] By virtue of his mastery of the rabbinic material, de' Rossi was able to establish the link between the pseudo-Philonic work and the *aggadot*. Philo and the question of the authorship were secondary issues in this fine display of scholarship.

From a reading of Philo's *De opificio mundi*, *Quod mundus sit incorruptibilis* and an extract from Philo cited by Ficino,[86] de' Rossi must admit that Philo believed in the eternity of matter. This was a serious charge, since 'all those who uphold the Torah . . . openly declare that the creation was absolutely and totally new and not preceded by any matter'. De' Rossi's presentation is full of ambiguity. In the course of the argument, he digresses to challenge Augustinus Steuchus's allegation that 'quidam Hebraei' (and he was not referring to Philo) also denied the notion of 'creatio ex nihilo'. De' Rossi's attack on Steuchus helps us to understand his stance on Philo.

According to de' Rossi, Steuchus claimed that Nahmanides had misconceived the true meaning of the expression *tohu wevohu* ('null and void') when he identified it with the Greek term *hyle*, or primordial matter. In his commentary to Genesis (1:2) Nahmanides had written: 'This matter which they call the *hyle* is *tohu* in the Holy Tongue . . . and the form with which the matter is clothed is called *bohu* in the Holy Tongue.' According to de' Rossi, Nahmanides posited a *hyle* created by the Creator from nothing; from the *hyle* He formed and made the specific works of creation. Following Ficino's explanation of the Platonic view of creation, de' Rossi explains the concept of precedence in this context as having no temporal meaning, since time itself was created at the creation. It merely refers to a precedence of order and number.

De' Rossi does not give a faithful presentation of Steuchus's views. He writes:

> The term primordial matter which certain Jews [*quidam Hebraei*] applied in reference to the thou [*tohu*] and bou [*Bohu*] such that the thou represents the totally deficient matter, while bou represents the matter requiring form and being ready to be its recipient is a Peripatetic rather than a Mosaic notion. Indeed, Jews have been corrupted into the same practices as ourselves. They have a predilection for contorting Holy Scripture into Aristotelian and Averroistic notions . . . The *hyle*, i.e. the primordial matter, is a philospher's invention which Moses never dreamt of . . .[87]

Steuchus does not identify the 'certain Jews' who adopt Aristotelian concepts. Nahmanides may not have been the philosopher whom he had in mind. Gersonides, for example, explicitly reduced the world to a formless substratum out of which all existence derived. In his commentary to Genesis he states: 'Our sages of blessed memory said that *tohu* is a point which encompasses the world—this is an allegory for matter.'[88]

Steuchus insisted that the ancient concept of Chaos and the Biblical *tohu* and *bohu* (*tohu va-vohu*) meant nothing:[89] 'Chaos et thou et bou et nihil idem sunt.' In other words, he negated the concept of the eternity of matter. (In his *De perenni philosophia*, he even claims that Aristotle conceived of a *creatio ex nihilo*.)[90] Nahmanides did not posit the eternity of matter, although he does seem to refer to an unformed matter created by God. Admittedly, he uses the Greek terms imprecisely, for which he was duly criticized by the Ritba (Yomtov ben Abraham of Sevilla) in his *Sefer Ha-Zikkaron*.[91] But insofar as he did apply Greek terminology to the *tohu* and *bohu*, Steuchus's criticisms of those who used Greek notions 'which Moses never dreamt of' are equally valid in Nahmanides's case.

De' Rossi's defence of Philo on the question of creation basically follows the lines established by Christian Platonists in their defence of Plato. De' Rossi quotes an oft-cited statement from a work attributed to Justin Martyr:[92] Plato did not promulgate his true religious convictions, but wrote in a deliberately ambiguous manner lest he suffer the same fate as his master Socrates. In other words, underlying Plato's confusing discussions of creation lay a belief in *creatio ex nihilo*. As further confirmation of this interpretation of the Platonic concept of creation, de' Rossi also cites the view of Leone Ebreo (Abravanel), author of the *Dialoghi d'amore*.[93] A Jewish Platonist's interpretation of Platonism was not out of place in a defence of the Jew Philo. According to Leone Ebreo, Plato held that matter or Chaos was created by God *ab eterno*, and the universe created from that matter at the beginning of time.[94] This view could easily be reconciled with the Mosaic account of the creation of the world.

The juxtaposition of Jewish and Christian versions of Platonism is de' Rossi's overall method of treating the topic. He provides a synthesis of Ficinian Platonism and mediaeval Jewish philosophy represented by Judah Halevi and Maimonides. De' Rossi's method of using Ficino's work is highly selective. He makes no effort to understand Ficino's philosophical system.[95] By means of Ficino's commentary to the *Timaeus*, he can establish that the Platonic, Philonic and Mosaic views of creation can be interpreted uniformly. The Platonic *hyle*, the Mosaic *tohu* and *bohu*, are given a temporal origin but precedence over the world, since it was by a process of the order of primordial matter that the world came into being.[96] Ficino does indeed say this; but what de' Rossi does not note is that the idea of a hierarchy of order is a key concept in Ficino's philosophical system.

De' Rossi also cites a passage from Judah Halevi's *Kuzari* which bears some similarity to Ficino's view.

> If an upholder of the Torah is bound to profess a belief in the primordial *hyle* and in the existence of many worlds prior to this one, it should not be accounted as a flaw in his belief. It is sufficient that he believes that this world was created at a specific moment in time and that Adam and Eve were the first human beings.[97]

One of Maimonides's rare references to Plato is also quoted regardless of the context of the passage.

> He who believes in the eternity of the universe according to the second of the theories expounded above, i.e. the Platonic view that the heavens both come into being and are destroyed, does not contravert the fundaments of the Torah, nor does it lead to a negation of miracles. Is is possible to interpret Scripture in accordance with this notion and many examples can be found in Scripture and writings which corroborate, and even testify to, the phenomenon.[98]

According to a superficial reading of the passage, Maimonides would seem to corroborate the Platonic–Philonic view of primordial matter as expounded by Ficino.

In his quest for statements upholding the orthodox view of creation, de' Rossi finds a passage from a lost work of Philo quoted by Eusebius and two further passages from Philo's published works.[99] Finally, however, de' Rossi has no alternative but to admit that 'the other passages give good reason to doubt that Philo did indeed believe in *creatio ex nihilo*'.

There were distinct advantages in interpreting Steuchus's 'certain Jews' as a reference to Nahmanides. By insisting on Nahmanides's orthodoxy,[100] de' Rossi brings out by contrast the uncertain position of Philo the Alexandrian. The Platonic Philo could not be regarded as a true representative of the Jewish people.

Some of the most heated debates among Jews during the Middle Ages concerned the allegorization of Scripture.[101] The controversies continued to de' Rossi's own time. In 1539, Yehiel Nissim da Pisa wrote his *Minhat Kenaot*, a polemic against Yedaiah Bedersi's philosophical allegorization of Scripture.[102] De' Rossi's castigation of Philo for his allegorization of the biblical stories must be seen against the background of these debates. When de' Rossi describes Philo 'as a thief, divesting the word of the Lord of its real meaning', the issue at stake is not simply the preservation of the literal meaning of the stories. This is demonstrated by the quotation from the *Zohar*: 'Woe to the man who says that the Torah is just a story-book . . . For the words of Torah belong to both the upper and lower worlds.'[103] The problem must therefore be reformulated; given that the literal meaning of Scripture is beyond dispute, whose interpretation may be regarded as authoritative? In the *Minhat Kenaot*, da Pisa stresses that the implicit meaning of Scripture was revealed to an élite, ensuring that the meaning of Scripture would not become distorted in the hands of the unlearned.[104] Similarly, de' Rossi accepts the guidance of the authority of tradition when he writes:

> The symbolism of Scripture must have somehow been transmitted to us by a sage 'who is better than a prophet'. Not just anyone who wishes to show off and devise his own explanation may interpret Scripture in this way. The divine Simeon bar Yohai opposed such practices. In the *Zohar* he comments on the verse, 'Do not make for yourself another Torah which you do not know and which you have not learnt from your teacher.'[105]

De' Rossi's attacks on Philo as an interpreter of Scripture not invested with the authority of tradition has more than its obvious implications. Taken to its logical conclusion, it implies that all those who used Philo's interpretations as reflecting the true meaning of Scripture were beguiled by an interpreter whose words were not sanctioned by authority. Philo's allegories were used and praised by the Christians: Origen, in particular, was influenced by Philo's allegorical interpretation of Scripture, and Sixtus Senensis praises Philo for his allegorical method.[106] In his *De arcanis*, Galatino speaks of both Josephus and Philo as reporting the Christian revelation in their interpretation of the Old Testament.[107] De' Rossi's dismissal of writers not invested with the requisite authority applied not only to Philo and other Jewish allegorists, but it must have also included those Christian writers who used Philo's interpretations of the Old Testament as confirmation of the Christian revelation.

Philo's interpretations of the legal parts of Scripture display neither familiarity with, nor recognition of, the traditional enactments of the Oral Law. De' Rossi regarded Philo's rejection of, or unfamiliarity with, the Oral Law as a most serious charge, 'weighty enough to sink him into bottomless waters'.[108] In arguing the point, de' Rossi cites 25 examples which demonstrate that Philo's literal interpretations of the Pentateuchal laws do not concur with rabbinic rulings.[109] The results of his enquiry corroborate his original thesis: Philo was affiliated to the Essene–Boethusian sect who were associated with the Sadducees for their rejection of some of the Pharisaic rulings. According to this definition, Philo could also be compared to the Karaites, who in their repudiation of Rabbanite authority were regarded by some mediaeval writers either as direct descendants of the Sadducees, or else as a revivalist Saducean sect.[110] De' Rossi found one case in which Karaite and Philonic interpretation of a biblical verse was identical.[111] This was particularly incriminating and quite distinct from the problems posed by Philo's allegorical method or by his concept of creation. Traditional Jewish writers had also used the allegorical method, and they too had propounded unorthodox views about creation, but only Karaites and other sectarian Jews had ignored the rulings of the Oral Law. Justification of Philo's interpretations of the legal parts of Scripture would be regarded as tantamount to a vindication of Karaism and rejection of the basis of rabbinic law.

De' Rossi does not attempt a systematic presentation of Philo's philosophy. His main concern is to place Philo in his historical setting. In detecting Philo's sectarian proclivities, de' Rossi was conscious of challenging some of his contemporary Jews 'who thirstily imbibe Philo's words'. From de' Rossi's own evidence we know that one such contemporary was David Provenzali who had written a defence of Philo. De' Rossi writes: 'It is indeed fitting that he should defend him since he was the first to promulgate the name of Philo among our people through his learned studies. He is justified in not giving an impression of introducing an alien among the holy.'[112] Provenzali, the first Jew to write about Philo according to de' Rossi, was ready to accept Philo. De' Rossi could not display the same openness. His reading of Christian views about Philo must surely have dictated the extreme caution with which he treats his subject. His conclusion that Philo was an Essene, or at least a fellow-traveller of the Essenes, may not stand up to modern scholarship. But the questions he raised about

Philo have not yet been definitively solved. Scholars have been unable to reach any consensus on any one of the problems, be it Philo's knowledge of Hebrew or his belief in *creatio ex nihilo*.[113] De' Rossi's views may not have been adopted by his co-religionists, but he certainly roused their interest in Philo. De' Rossi's friend and mentor Judah Moscato makes several references to Philo in his works,[114] but he modifies de' Rossi's designation for Philo and calls him 'Rabbi Yedidya'. Joseph (Yashar) del Medigo planned to publish his Hebrew translation of excerpts from Philo.[115] In his *Discorso* (Venice, 1638), Simone Luzzatto expresses the regret that Philo had not undertaken to educate the Jews rather than 'convert the Greeks'.[116] The writings of Philo could no longer be ignored by the Jews. Nevertheless, two hundred years were to elapse before another scholar, Nahman Krochmal, endeavoured to follow de' Rossi's initiative and attempt to decipher the 'ancient enigma'.

Notes

1 T. H. Billings, *The Platonism of Philo Judaeus* (Chicago, 1919), divides the history of Philonic interpretation into three distinct periods: 1) up to the middle of the sixteenth century, Philo is regarded as a Church Father; 2) to the middle of the seventeenth century, when enquiry is related to the doctrine of the Trinity; 3) from the publication of Fabricius's *De Platonismo Philonis* (1693), the period of untrammelled free investigation. On the controversies between Protestants and Catholics, see the survey of F. C. Conybeare, *Philo about the contemplative life* . . . (Oxford, 1895), pp. 318–26.

2 Eusebius, *Hist. Eccl.*, II.17.1

3 *ibid.*, II.16.1

4 Hieronymus, *De viris illustribus*, ch. 11: 'Philo Judaeus natione Alexandrinus de genere sacerdotum idcirco a nobis inter scriptores ecclesiasticos ponitur . . .'

5 For a list of the *testimonia* on Philo, see the standard edition of Philo, eds. L. Cohn and P. Wendland (Berlin, 1896), pp. lxxxxiv–cxiii. All references to Philo's works cited in this article are to Cohn and Wendland's edition.

6 Photius, *Biblioteca*, cod.105, ed. R. Henry (Paris, 1959), vol. 2, p.72. For a discussion of the legend, see J. Edgar Bruns, 'Philo Christianus. The debris of a legend', in *Harvard Theological Review*, vol. 66 (1973), pp. 141–5; he considers these legends as an example of the early Church's eagerness to appropriate distinguished figures from a non-Christian milieu.

7 See, e.g., Turnèbe's preface to his *ed. pr.* of the complete works of Philo (Paris, 1552); Gelenius's preface to his Latin translation of Philo (Basel, 1554); Lilius Tifernas's letter to Nicholas V (note 28 below) in *Analecta sacra spicilegio solesmensi parata*, ed. J. B. Pitra, vol. 2 (1884), p.333.

8 J. J. Scaliger, *De emendatione temporum* (Paris, 1583), lib, VI (Geneva, 1625), p.539: '. . . Sed Philo genere Iudaeus patria Alexandrinus eorum dumtaxat meminit quos ipse in patria sua viderat et norat. Tantum igitur abesset ut illi Therapeutae Christiani fuerint ut pernaciores hostes non habuerint veri Christiani quam eos qui pluribus cerimoniis Iudaicis addicti erant . . .'.

9 *ibid.*, (Leiden, 1592), (Geneva, 1629), 'prolegomena' p. xxii. He accuses these scholars of relying on Eusebius without actually reading Philo. ' . . . Atqui ex Eusebio hoc desumpserunt et eius authoritate contenti Philonem non consuluerunt quem si legissent nunquam tam ridiculae sententiae assensum accomodassent. Haec vero puerilia sunt.'

10 Baronius, *Annales ecclesiastici*, vol. 1 (Antwerp, 1597), p. 304, discusses Philo's relation to the Christians; pp. 633–6 examines whether Philo's Essenes were Christians: ' . . . Et unde rogo, tantopere post Evangelii praedicationem testante Philone, longe lateque per Orbem auctus est numerus Essenorum nisi quod iidem erant Christiani praedicatione apostolica ubique gentium propagati?'

11 Scaliger (note 9 above): 'Mirati sumus quomodo ille putavit in unum haec bene convenire posse, Iudaismum et Christianismum.' Scaliger also takes issue with Nicholas Serarius, who had written an entire work devoted to the sects: *Trihaeresium seu de celeberrimis sectis apud Iudaeos* . . . (Mainz, 1604). Scaliger's refutation *Elenchus Trihaeresii Nicolai Serarii* . . . (Franeker, 1605) includes an attack on the 'fanaticum et impudentissimum mendacium' that the Essenes were Christians. See A. Grafton, 'From *De die natali* to *De emendatione temporum*: The Origin and Setting of Scaliger's Chronology', *Journal of the Warburg and Courtauld Institutes*, vol. 48 (1958), p. 129.

12 H. Prideaux, *The old and new Testaments commented in the history of the Jews and neighbouring nations* . . . *to the time of Christ*, vol. 2, bk 5 (3rd edn, London, 1718), p. 284.

13 Scaliger, *Elenchus* (note 11 above), p. 175: 'Sed nullus Iudaeus scriptor praeter Abraham Zachuth, Essenorum meminit.'

14 A. Zacuto, *Sefer Yuhasin* (Constantinople, 1566), 148recto. 'A great Jewish sage called Philon the Jew, the priest, wrote a book on the soul in Greek.' Zacuto clearly had little knowledge of Philo.

15 There is a reference to 'Philo, friend of Joseph son of Gorion' in *The Chronicles of Jerahmeel* (11th century?), ed. M. Gaster (London, 1899), vol. 57 (reprint New York, 1971), p. 165. On Philo's influence on Karaism, see S. Poznanski, 'Philo dans la littérature judéo-arabe', in *R.E.J.*, vol. 50 (1905), pp. 10–31; B. Revel, 'The karaite *halakah* and its relation to Saduccean, Samaritan and Philonian *halakah*' (diss., 1931) in *Karaite Studies*, ed. p. Birnbaum (New York, 1971), pp. 1–88; W. Bacher, 'Qirqisani the Karaite and his work on the Jewish sect', in *Karaite Studies*, op. cit., pp. 259–82. For a more recent discussion of Karaite use of Philo, see B. Chiesa, 'Ya'qub al Qirqisani come fonte. storiografica', in *Ya'qub al Qirqisani on Jewish Sects and Christianity*, eds B. Chiesa and W. Lockwood (Frankfurt, 1984), pp. 11–49. He suggests (pp. 28–9) that al Qirqisani may have gained his knowledge from a reading of Mukammis, who was familiar with Christian tradition.

16 N. Krochmal, *More Nevukhei ha-Zeman*, ed. S. Rawidowicz, vol. 12 (London, 1961), pp. 165–87; '*hidot mine kedem*'; Krochmal also uses the term in reference to other hellenistic writings.

17 On de' Rossi, see S. Baron, *History and Jewish Historians* (Philadelphia, 1964), pp. 167–239; R. Bonfil, 'Some reflections on Azariah de Rossi's MEOR ENAYIM in the cultural milieu of Italian Renaissance Jewry' in *Jewish Thought in the Sixteenth Century*, ed. B. D. Cooperman (Cambridge, Mass., 1983), pp. 23–48; J. Weinberg, 'Azariah de' Rossi and LXX traditions' in *Italia*, vol. 5, nos 1–2 (1985), pp. 7–35; 'Azariah de' Rossi: Towards a reappraisal of the last years of his life' in *Annali della scuola normale superiore di Pisa*, vol. 8, no. 2 (1978), pp. 493–511.

18 *Me'or 'Enayim*, ch. 3, p. 90. (All references are to Cassel edn, Vilna 1864–6.)

19 Judah, David and Moses Provenzali were contemporaries of de' Rossi and fellow Mantuans. All three brothers, according to de' Rossi (pp. 145, 149), were enthusiastic readers of Philo.

20 Ch. 6, p. 129

21 He says (p. 90) that he coined the name in conformity to contemporary practice. Cf. the use of names Melanchthon (Schwarzerd), Hortusbonus (Casaubon).

22 The critique is contained in chs 3–6, ch. 3 on the sects, ch. 4 on the philosophical and theological ideas of Philo compatible with rabbinic tradition, ch. 5 on Philo's four main defects, ch. 6 a defence of Philo.

23 This is an allusion to *Baba Mezia* 86b about Samuel Yarhina, who was 'to be called sage, but not Rabbi'.

24 Ch. 6, p. 129

25 This is a reference to a passage from Champier of Lyon's *De triplici disciplina* quoted and discussed by D. P. Walker, *The Ancient Theology* (London, 1972), pp. 80–1. Ficino usually refers to Philo as 'Philo Iudaeus Platonicus'.

26 On Steuchus (1497/8–1548), see Th. Freudenberger, *Augustinus Steuchus aus Gubbio, Augustinerchorherr und päpstlicher Bibliothecar* (Münster, 1935). Apart from his philological work on the Bible versions, Steuchus is known for his exposition of the perennial philosophy, on which see C. B. Schmitt, introduction to *De perenni philosophia* (New York and London, 1972) (facsimile reprint of Lyons 1540 edition); 'Prisca theologica e philosophia perennis: due temi e la loro fortuna; (1970), pp. 211–36, and 'Perennial philosophy: From Agostino Steuco to Leibniz' (1966), pp. 505–32, in *Studies in Renaissance Philosophy and Science* (London, 1981) and D. P. Walker (note 25 above), *passim*. Steuchus's works are full of references to the 'prisca theologia' and de' Rossi was clearly influenced by his presentation of these ideas.

27 R. Marcus, 'A sixteenth-century Hebrew critique of Philo', in *H.U.C.A.*, vol. 21 (1948), pp. 29–61. M. E. Neylan wrote an M. Phil. thesis (Leeds, 1974) on de' Rossi and also describes his critique of Philo.

28 Lilius Tifernas was encouraged by Bessarion and Nicholas V to translate Philo. His translation is in the Vatican, Vat. lat. 180–5 (cf. Cohn's Prolegomena, note 5 above, vol. 1, lxxx).

29 Basel 1554; Lyons 1555, 1561, Antwerp 1614. On the translations and editions of Philo's works, see H. L. Goodhart and E. R. Goodenough, *The politics of Philo Judaeus . . . with a general bibliography of Philo* (New Haven, 1938).

30 De' Rossi used the Lyons edition printed by Joannes de Gabiano in 1555 (2 vols) and not the Paganus edition as Marcus claims.

31 Turnèbe's remained the standard edition until Mangey's of 1742.

32 Sichardus was the editor of the *ed. pr.* which was published in Basel, 1527. Sichardus refers to Budé's opinion in his preface (a2recto): 'Nisi in ea simus opinione ut credamus alterum quendam Philonem fuisse nonnullorum autorem quae deinde coepta sunt et istius nomine legi cui sententiae vir nostra aetate eruditissimus Gulielmus Budaeus palam subscribit . . . ' Sichardus himself thought the work very corrupt, but authentic. De' Rossi followed Budé in believing incorrectly that Philo's *Quaestiones et solutiones in Genesin* was spurious. He never refers to the claim of some Christian writers that Philo wrote the *Wisdom of Solomon*. he discusses the work in ch. 57 (p. 461) and suggests that it was originally written in Aramaic.

33 *Centuriae*, lib. I, cap. V (Basel, 1564): 'De haeresibus seu sectis Iudaeorum'. Illyricus quote Josephus and Pliny, but not Philo.

34 *De leg. spec.*, III, 181–2. (He quotes the passage in ch. 5, p. 117.)

35 C. D. Ginzburg, *The Essenes. Their history and doctrines* (1864) (London, 1955), pp. 60–2

36 '*Avot de' Rabbi Nathan*, ed. S. Schechter, rec. I, ch. 5, 13b. See J. Le Moyne's discussion of this passage in *Les Sadducéens* (Paris, 1974), pp. 113–17.

37 Ch. 3, pp. 94–6. He does not refer to Pliny's reference to the Essenes in *Historia Naturalis*, 5:17.

38 Philo, *Quod omnis probus liber*, 75–91, *De vita contemplativa*; Josephus, *Wars*, II.8.2–13,*Ant.*, 18.1.5.

39 Eusebius, *Praep. Ev.*, VIII, 12. De' Rossi used George of Trebizond's Latin translation which has different pagination (8, ch. 4).)

40 Ch. 3, p. 95 (revised text): 'According to Philo, these Essenes who were called 'holy', devoted themselves to the practical life. He spoke of them in ch. 36 [i.e. in *Quod omnis probus liber*]; but those who were devoted to the contemplative life were grouped under the one designation 'healers', i.e. healers of the soul . . . In any case, there is no reason to claim that this group did not belong to the Essene sect since both Josephus and Eusebius apply that which is said about the one group to the other.'

41 Ch. 3, p. 96.

42 *Shabb.* 108a

43 Le Moyne (note 36 above) refers to this argument (p. 340) and dismisses it as tenuous.

44 *Tosefta* to Sukka 3:1. See *Tosefta Ki-feshuta*, ed. S. Lieberman (New York, 1955), p. 870, for citation of other passages in which the two words *bet sen* occur. See also '*Arukh*, s.v. Boetsin.

45 All the Christian historians mentioned above devote a large part of their discussions to the derivations of the names of the sects.

46 Epiphanius, *Adversus Haereses*, I, tom. I, Haeres. XIV (P.G.41, col. 239): 'Qui nimirum sadducaeos a iustitia se nominant. Sedec enim iustitiam significat.' (It is quoted by de' Rossi, p. 92.)

47 *ibid.* I, tom. 2, Haeres. XXIX, col. 397. Epiphanius suggests that the name Iessaei may derive from the name of either Jesse or Jesus and thus signify that they were disciples of Jesus, of the stock of Jesse. He refers to Philo's *De Essaeis*.

48 Hieronymus (note 4 above): 'Ex quo apparet talem primum Christo credentium fuisse Ecclesiam quales nunc monachi esse nituntur et cupiunt.'

49 p. 94.

50 'Mihi Plato potius filonizein videtur id est Mosen aemulari cuius Plato fuit discipulus. Constat enim Platonem in Aegypto peregrinatum ibi audisse non magis Aegyptiorum quam Iudaeorum hierogrammateis.' '*Epistola nuncupatoria*' (2ᵛ) to Gelenius's Latin translation of the works of Philo (Lyons, 1555). (I have transliterated the Greek words.)

51 On the subject see Walker (note 25 above); Schmitt (note 26 above); F. Yates, *Giordano Bruno and the Hermetic Tradition* (London, 1964).

52 He refers to *De sacrificio Abelis* 5: 'When Abraham left mortal life he was gathered to the people of God and enjoyed eternal life like the angels who are the divine host and the unembodied souls whose lot is eternal happiness.'

53 Ch. 4, p. 99. Cf. Lactantius Firmianus, *Divinae institutiones*, 7:8 (*Corp. Script. Lat.* 19, pp. 608–9): 'Nam licet verum de animae immortalitate sentiret [Plato] tamen non ita de illa tamquam de summo bono disserebat.' Cf. *Phaedo* 114b–c: 'Those who have lived an exceptionally holy life . . . go up to a pure habitation and live on earth [i.e. the true earth—the earthly paradise].'

54 *Divini Platonis Opera Omnia* (Basel, 1561), 'Argumentum Marsilii Ficini in decimum dialogum de Iusto'; p. 687: 'Sint ergo eiusmodi prata sublimes quaedam aeris plagae contiguae sublimibus illis terrae plagis quas in Phaedone describit in paradisi terreni formam felices sub vere perpetuo habere cultores. Ibidem campos ponunt Elysios terrenos inquam, nam coelestes Elysios coelum habet octavum.'

55 M. Idel, 'The magical and Neoplatonic interpretation of the Kabbalah in the Renaissance', in Cooperman (ed.) (note 17 above), pp. 186–242 (p. 219).

56 On the hermetic texts, see Yates (note 51 above) and Walker (note 25 above). Isaac Casaubon detected the apocryphal nature of the hermetic texts in 1614. The majority of the syncretists in the sixteenth century considered Hermes to have been either a

contemporary of or younger than Moses. Ficino translated the *Asclepius* and *Pimander* into Latin in 1463 and there were several sixteenth-century editions of his translation. De' Rossi professes a desire to translate the *Asclepius* and *Pimander* into Hebrew and to provide an introduction and notes 'in order to distinguish between the holy and the profane'. (The reference to the 'profane' is probably an allusion to the magical and idolatrous parts of the *Hermetica* which Augustine denounces in *De civ. Dei*, 8.13–22.)

57 He points out the similarities between the first chapter of the *Pimander* and the biblical account of creation. Ficino in his translation (Lyons, 1549), pp. 379–80, draws the same parallel.

58 Ch. 4, p. 101

59 This expression does not appear in the standard Jewish kabbalistic texts.

59 M. Recanati, *Perush al ha-Torah*, 'ahare mot', 63 col. b (Jerusalem, 1961). I assume that de' Rossi is referring to the passage about the forbidden sexual unions where Recanati speaks about the *sefirot* in terms of family relationships.

60 Ch. 4, p. 101

61 This Midrash may have originally been of Jewish origin, but eradicated as a result of its Christian resonances. On the lost Midrashim, see S. Lieberman, *Shkiin* (2nd edn, Jerusalem 1970). Pedro della Caballeria (1415–61), *Zelus Christi contra Iudaeos, Saracenos et infideles* (Venice, 1592), f. 34. On della Caballeria, see G. Scholem, 'Débuts de la Kabbale chrétienne' (revised French translation of 'Zur Geschichte der Anfänge der christlische Kaballah' in *Essays to Leo Baeck*, London (1954), pp. 158–93) in *Kabbalistes chrétiens*, eds A. Faivre and F. Tristan (Paris, 1979), p. 31.

62 *Necuniae filii haccanae epistola de secretis* . . . (Florence, 1482). On Paulus de Heredia, see Scholem (note 61 above), pp. 31–6; F. Secret, *La Zôhar chez les Kabbalistes chrétiens* (Paris, 1964), p. 114.

63 Pietro Galatino (1460–1540). *Opus* . . . *de arcanis catholicae veritatis contra obstinatissimam Iudaeorum nostrae tempestatis perfidiam* (Othone, 1518). On Galatino, see A. Morisi, 'Galatino et la Kabbale chrétienne' in *Kabbalistes chrétiens* (note 61 above), pp. 213–41. Galatino's dialogue plagiarized Raymond Martini's *Pugio fidei* as well as the work of Paulus de Heredia.

64 Galatino (note 63 above), xxxirecto. Galatino claims that the passage was deleted by the Jews, but that he saw an original copy of the text when he was in the Kingdom of Naples at the time of the expulsion of the Jews from the kingdom.

65 Amatus Lusitanus (Joannes Roderighes), the Marrano doctor, describes a meeting with de' Rossi in a bookshop during which they discussed Galatino's work. See *Curationum medicinialium centuriae* (Basel, 1556), Cent. IV, curatio 42, p. 355.

66 Farissol refers to the passage in ch. 72 of the *Magen Abraham* (published by S. Loewinger, in *R.E.J.*, vol. 105 (1938), pp. 43–6.)

67 For a discussion of Farissol's *Magen Abraham*, see D. Ruderman, *The World of a Renaissance Jew: The Life and Thought of Abraham ben Mordechai Farissol* (Cincinnati, 1981), pp. 57–84. Leone Modena refers to de' Rossi's statement and also quotes the passage from Galatino in his *Magen weherev*, ed. S. Simonsohn (Jerusalem, 1966), p. 26.

68 Ch. 4, p. 101

69 Idel (note 55 above), p. 227

70 *Symphoriani Champerii de triplici disciplina* . . . (Lyons, 1508), hhiiiirecto-verso. On Champier, see Brian P. Copenhaver, *Symphorien Champier and the Reception of the Occultist Tradition in Renaissance France* (The Hague, 1978). See also Walker (note 25 above), ch. 3, who shows the differences between French and Italian attitudes to the 'prisca theologia'. The comparison between Kabbalah and hermetic wisdom is pronounced in Champier's work.

71 Ch. 4, p. 101.

72 Modern scholars are divided on this question: e.g. V. Nikiprowetzky, *Le commentaire de l'écriture chez Philo d'Alexandre* (Leiden, 1977), thought that Philo knew no Hebrew; H. Wolfson, on the other hand, *Philo* (1947) (Cambridge, Mass., 1968) argued that Philo did know Hebrew.

73 A. Steuchus, *Recognitio veteris testamenti* (Venice, 1529). De' Rossi compares Philo's scriptural quotations with the Septuagint and analyses Philo's etymologies for biblical names. He only uses Latin translations. Steuchus supplied variant readings of the Septuagint and quoted the original Greek sources with Latin translation. Many of the 25 examples of Philo's readings of Scripture which de' Rossi gives as proof of Philo's ignorance of the Hebrew are also to be found in Steuchus's work. De' Rossi also argues that Philo knew no Aramaic.

74 Ch. 5, p. 112.

75 G. Kisch published the Latin text with an introduction (Notre Dame, Indiana, 1949). M. R. James's English translation was reprinted with a 'prolegomenon' by L. H. Feldman (New York, 1971).

76 Ch. 4, p. 104

77 Feldman (note 75 above), xv, lxvii, lxxxi and *passim*: e.g. de' Rossi cites *L.A.B.* 7: that it did not rain in the land of Israel duirng the Flood, which statement is also found in Tractate *Zevahim* 113a and Midrash *Shir ha-Shirim Rabba* 1:15.

78 *L.A.B.* 11:10–11; Philo, *De decalogo* 121; *De leg. spec.* 3:8; *Quis heres* 173; Romans 13:9. In his notes to *L.A.B.* 11, 10–11 (xcv), Feldman points out that the same inversion occurs in the Hebrew Nash papyrus.

79 *L.A.B.* 44:6–7

80 *L.A.B.* 9:12: 'Et accepit infantem suum et fecit ei thibin de cortice arboris pini et posuit thibin in os fluminis.'

81 Steuchus (note 73 above), 104recto: 'Usi sint hoc loco LXX vocabulo Hebraico arcam exprimere volentes, neque ipsam vocem immutarunt. Arca enim hebraice thebat dicitur. At illi inusitato apud Graecos nomine, eodem modo appellarunt thibin . . . Quae vox nusquam apud alios authores reperitur atque hinc factum suspicor quod Philon Judaeus hebraicae linguae imperitus ut ex multis sit manifestum totam hanc rem de fiscella scirpea omisit . . . Ecce de arcula nulla sit mentio, credo quod ignoraret quod esset thibis.'

82 *De gig.* 55; *L.A.B.* 9:8

83 Feldman (note 75 above), xxiii. De' Rossi also adds another argument which weakens his case further. He points out that *L.A.B.* calculates 1656 years (it actually reads 1652) for the period from Adam to the Flood, which agrees with the Hebrew Scriptures but not the Septuagint, which counts 2252 years. De' Rossi argues that Philo dismissed the reading of the Septuagint in this case in favour of the correct Hebrew text.

84 Petrus Comestor, *Historia scholastica* (P.L. 198, 1088 col. d). On Nicholas of Cusa's use of pseudo-Philo, see P. Wilpert, Philon bei Nikolas von Kues', in *Orient im Mittelalter* (Berlin, 1962), pp. 69–79.

85 Sixtus Senesis, *Bibliotheca sancta* (Venice, 1566), p.455: 'Liber qui bibliothecarum antiquitatum praenotatur in quo per modum brevis historiae vetus omne testamentum perstringitur; sed phrasis eius ubique hebraismum redolens et narratio rebus apocryphis passim abundans, indicant opus aut huius non esse Philonis, aut si forte eius sit, non graeco sed hebraico sermone ab ipso fuisse conscriptum.'

86 *De opif. mundi*, 21; *Quod mundus*, 5; Ficino cites Philo in his 'compendium in Timaeum' cap.XII to his translation of the dialogue (note 54 above), p.708. Ficino claims that Philo's interpretation of Genesis assists understanding of Plato's views. For a modern discussion of Philo's use of the *Timaeus*, see D. Runia, *Philo of Alexandria and the Timaeus of Plato* (Leiden, 1986).

87 *Recognitio* (note 73 above), 10recto: 'Quod autem quidam hebraei thou et bou ad materiam primam referunt ut thou sit ipsa privatio materiae, bou desiderium eius et aptitudo ad formas, non tam est mosaicum quam peripateticum. Hebraei siquidem eadem qua et nos consuetudine corrupti sunt ut sacras literas ad placita Aristotelis atque Averrois voluerunt torquere . . . Hyle, enim, i. prima materia inventum philosophorum quam ne somniavit quidem Moses.' Steuchus repeats this opinion in his *Cosmopoeia* (Lyons, 1535), pp. 30–1.

88 Levi ben Gershon, *Comm.* to *Gen.* 1:2. (Gersonides denied the idea of the temporal origin of prime matter in his *Milhamot Adonadi*, 6.1.7.)

89 *Recognitio* (note 73 above), 9verso.

90 *De Per. phil.* (Lyons, 1540), 7,15, p. 364. Nevertheless, Steuchus's *Cosmopoeia* was denounced by Domingo de Soto in 1546 and the Venetian *Opera omnia* censured, his controversial views being those on the eternity of the empyrean heavens, the denial of a terrestrial paradise and the consequences of original sin. See Schmitt (note 26 above), p. 525.

91 *Sefer ha-Zikkaron*, ed. K. Kahane (Jerusalem, 1956), pp. 35–6.

92 Pseudo-Justin, *Cohortatio ad gentiles* 20 (P.G. 6, col. 276). See Walker (note 25 above), p. 14, who discusses the use of pseudo-Justin.

93 Leone Ebreo Abravanel's *Dialoghi d'amore* were first published in Rome in 1535 and then reprinted many times and translated into many languages. On Leone Ebreo's Platonism, see W. Melczer, 'Platonisme et Aristotélisme dans la pensée de Léon l'hébreu' in *Platon et Aristote à la Renaissance. XVIe colloque international de Tours* (Paris, 1976), pp. 293–306.

94 *Dialoghi*, ed. S. Caramella, vol. 2 (Bari, 1929), p. 109: 'perche essendo Iddio produttore di tutte le cose bisogna ancora che abbi prodotto la materia de la quale sono generate, ma si debbe intendere che essi significano che per essere stato il Chaos in compagnia di Dio ne la eternità, essere da Lui prodotto ab eterno e che Dio producesse tutte l'altre cose di esso Chaos di nouvo in principio di tempo (secondo l'oppinione platonica) e chiamanla compagna non ostante che sia produtta, per esser prodotto esso Chaos ab eterno e trovarsi sempre mai in compagnia di Dio.'

95 On Ficino, see P. O. Kirsteller, *The Philosophy of Marsilio Ficino* (New York, 1943).

96 Ficino, 'Compendium in Timaeum' (note 54 above), p. 708: 'Ex his omnibus colligere possumus materiam non esse ante mundum ullo temporis intervallo licet originem quadam et ordine non iactari inordinate ante ordinem sed erraturam fuisse procul ab ordine quantum in se est nisi statim desuper inordinata fuisset.'

97 *Kuzari* I, 67

98 *Guide* II, 15

99 Eusebius, *Praep. ev.* (P.G. 21, 7, cols 563–567). Philo, *Leg. All.* 1, 1; God is said to have created everything from nothing; *De vita Mosis* II, 266, the creation of the 'manna' is compared to the creation of the world from nothing.

100 In his *Comm.* to *Gen.* 2:1, Nahmanides also states: 'He produced a very fine element of no consistence from the complete and absolute nothing.' The concepts of *hyle* and 'form' were commonly used in connection with the *tohu* and *bohu* by kabbalists. According to G. Scholem, *Ursprung und anfänge der Kabbalah* (Berlin, 1962), pp. 374–81, the kabbalists of Gerona express the opinion of Averroes, according to which the forms in their origin are inherent in the *hyle*. *Bohu* is a product of the development of the *tohu* and is not a separate entity.

101 One of the fiercest debates over philosophical allegorization occurred in the fourteenth century, culminating in Solomon ben Adret's ban (1305) forbidding Jews of Aragon and other communities from studying philosophy or science before they have reached the age of 25. The ban was levelled against the Jews of Provence who, according to ben Adret, undermined the teachings of the Torah by treating all the

stories in the Bible not as fact, but as allegory. The primary source for the controversy is Don Astruc's *Minhat Kenaot* (Pressburg, 1833; reprint Jerusalem, 1968). On the debate, see A. S. Halkin, 'Yedaiah Bedersi's Apology' in *Jewish Medieval and Renaissance Studies*, ed. A. Altmann (Cambridge, Mass., 1967), pp. 127–50.

102 The first edition of the work was published by D. Kaufmann (Berlin, 1898).

103 *Zohar Lev.* 152a. This was also quoted by Isaac Arama in his *Hazut Kasha* (Pressburg, 1859), 7:54b. De' Rossi also refers to Arama's citation of the *Zohar* (ch. 5, p. 116).

104 *Minhat Kenaot* (note 101 above), pp. 12ff.

105 Ch. 5, p. 116

106 Sixtus Senensis (note 85 above): 'Fuit [i.e. Philo] . . . admirabilis in divinis scripturis exponendis quas triplici sensu iuxta LXX editionem praeclarissime explicavit, litterali scilicet morali et praecipue allegorico in quo quidem expositionis genere ita excelluit ut omnes pervetusti ecclesiae Doctores in deducendis mysticis allegoriis imitati sunt ipsum, tamquam sacrarum allegoriarum inventorem et artificem.'

107 Galatino (note 63 above), bk. I, 16 recto: 'Hi igitur viri tam excellentes Philo et Josephus qui et si graece scripserint Iudaei tamen ambo fuerunt paternarumque traditionum acerrimi emulatores nisi ea quae per prophetas de Messia praenunciata fuerant recte intellexissent neque de Christo tam bene opinati fuissent neque quae de ipso dixerunt tam veridice retulissent.'

108 Ch. 5, p. 117

109 For examples, see Marcus (note 27 above), pp. 50–1.

110 See, e.g., Maimonides to *'Avot* 1:3 (quoted by de' Rossi, p. 97) who states: 'In Egypt, they are called Karaites, whereas in the Talmud, they are named Sadducees and Boethusians.' Abraham ibn Daud, *Sefer ha-Kabbalah* (ed. G. D. Cohen, Philadelphia, 1967, p. 38), states: 'After the destruction of the Temple, the heretics dwindled to almost nothing until Anan [the reputed founder of the Karaite sect] appeared and strengthened their ranks.' The question of the link between Sadduceeism and Karaism was considered by Messer David Leon (1470/2–1560) in his *Magen David*. See S. Schechter, 'Notes sur Messer David Leon', in *R.E.J.*, vol. 24 (1892), pp. 118–38.

111 He says that during his stay in Venice, he found two mss of Karaite works: the *Keter Torah* by Aaron bar Eliyahu (1328?–69) and the *Ha-Mivhar*, by Aaron bar Joseph (1250–1320). Philo (*De spec. leg., II, 229*) had stated contrary to rabbinic ruling that a High Priest may only marry a wife of priestly lineage. The Karaites (see *Keter Torah* [Goslaw, 1866], 2,59a to Lev. 21:14 and *Ha-Mivhar* [Goslaw, 1835], 1, 39a) had made the same interpretation as Philo.

112 He writes this in his answer to Moses Provenzali's critique of his work which was incorporated into later printings of the text (p. 506).

113 For a review of the literature on Philo, see P. Borgen, 'Philo of Alexandria. A critical and synthetical survey of research since World War II' in *Aufstieg und Niedergang der Römischen Welt*, ed. W. Haase (Berlin, 1984), II, 21, 1, pp. 98–154.

114 See his sermons, *Nefuzot Jehudah* (Mantua, 1589), 2b, where he quotes Rabbi Yedidya on the Decalogue. He also refers to Philo in his commentary to the *Kuzari, Qol Jehudah* (*ed. pr.* Venice, 1594) *passim*. He also used the Gelenius Latin translation. He makes comparisons between Philo's thought and rabbinic ideas. On *Kuzari*, 2:20, e.g., he compares Philo's statement on the 'manna' which, like the world, was created from nothing (*De vita Mosis* II, 266) with a similar passage in *Shabb.* 87b.

115 Del Medigo writes in a letter to Zerah the Karaite that his translations had been

stolen. He stresses the importance of Philo for the Jews. See J. Mann, *Texts and Studies in Jewish History* (Cincinnati, 1931), vol. 2, p. 1228, n. 134.

116 Simone Luzzato, *Discorso circa il stato de gl'hebrei et in particolar dimoranti nell'inclita città di Venetia* (Venice, 1638), p. 78: ' . . . e s' egli havesse piu tosto applicato l'animo ad erudire gl'Hebrei ch'à convertire li Greci, forsi haverebbe raccolto maggior frutto dalle sue fatiche.' Luzzatto classes Philo as one of the 'theologi overo filosofanti' of his people. In reading this passage, one must bear in mind that Luzzatto was addressing himself to Gentiles, not to Jews.

Yiddish Song as Historical Source Material: Plague in the Judenstadt of Prague in 1713[*]

Chava Turniansky

BUBONIC plague struck Prague in the second half of 1713, during one of the only two outbreaks of the disease in the eighteenth century outside Turkey and its environs.[1] It appears to have started in 1707, spreading from Russia to Silesia, Prussia and Pomerania, and from there to Brunswick and Holstein, Denmark and Sweden. The Prussian plague is the theme of a Polish 'historical' song written in 1709,[2] while the devastation in Poland, Denmark and Sweden is mentioned in a Yiddish song of the same type describing a fire in Altona in 1711.[3] The plague reached Bohemia, Austria, Styria and south-east Bavaria in 1713.

At the time, Prague was among the largest Jewish communities of Europe. Some 11,500 Jews, about one-fourth of the city's population, crowded together in the 300 buildings along the narrow streets of the ghetto. Its density—a product of a very high fertility rate and considerable immigration—along with the appalling poverty of many and the very poor sanitary conditions[4] probably helped precipitate the disaster: the plague claimed some 3500 victims, one-third of the Jewish population of Prague.

However, no substantial record of this disaster is to be found in the contemporary Hebrew sources available to us.[5] Only a few sporadic details of the event are preserved in the *responsa* literature and in commemorative elegies. Most historians of Prague Jewry have ignored the event altogether; others mention it briefly, and only one deals with it at length, though indirectly, while discussing the relations between the University of Prague and the Jews, and relying on external documentation only.[6]

Historical research on Prague has, in general, paid little attention to this incident of the plague. A series of documents—mainly edicts restricting transit, travel and trade during the epidemic (showing, in

[*] This is the text of a paper presented at the International Conference of the Commission for the History of Historiography on 'Jewish Memory and its History', held at the University of Haifa, 4–7 January 1987.

fact, greater severity towards Jews than non-Jews)—was published in 1901 in a history of pestilence in the Kingdom of Bohemia in the sixteenth to the eighteenth centuries.[7] Only one rather short study, published in 1852, deals directly and in its entirety with the bubonic plague in Prague in 1713.[8] The author, Wilhelm Rudolph Weitenweber, a medical historian, based his work on various documents preserved in the minute books of the Faculty of Medicine of the University of Prague. His account deals mainly with the medical organization of the city authorities during the plague: the measures taken to ensure medical inspection and supervision as defined in special edicts, as well as specific regulations concerning the methods of quarantining the sick, administering drugs, operating pharmacies, sealing contaminated houses and burying the dead. Procedures for the appointment of doctors and chemists, the definition of their activities, details concerning their wages and other matters were recorded in the minutes of the meetings of the Faculty.

Although very little detail is provided by Weitenweber about conditions in the ghetto, the situation of the Jewish population is mentioned in such a way as to suggest that the devastation caused by the plague in the Judenstadt was particularly severe. This verifies the assertion made in the Faculty minutes that '*Inter Judaeos terribiliter grossator pestis*'. But most of the references to Jews concern the various negotiations between their representatives and the authorities for either laying down standard administrative procedures, or for approving or rejecting particular requests. Thus Weitenweber's study reveals only those aspects of the plague among the Jews that were recorded by the medical authorities, mostly medical details. Even so, the importance of his study in providing details of an event concerning Jews which went all but unrecorded in the Hebrew sources, is obvious. Were it not for the existence of other Jewish, if not Hebrew, contemporary texts which deal with the event, its importance would have been still greater. But, in fact, the Prague epidemic of 1713 is the sole concern of no less than three 'historical' songs in Yiddish. All three were printed at or close to the end of the epidemic, and at least one was reprinted subsequently.

The fact that three such songs about this particular epidemic have reached us, while not one has survived from the earlier incidence of the plague in Prague in 1680, claiming more than one-third of its Jewish population, supports our assumption that only very few of the 'historical' songs of this type have come down to us. Although all three songs concerning the plague in Prague in 1713 have been noted by the bibliographers,[9] and a copy of each survives in the Bodleian Library in Oxford,[10] no scholar has hitherto used them.

The longest of the three—109 four-line stanzas—was written by

Moshe ben Hayim Eisenstadt Katznellbogen, and printed, undated, in Amsterdam.[11] Its title is: '*Eyn nay kloglid benign Prostitser-kdoyshim-lid iber den groysn ershreklekhn ipesh velkher po kak Prag ongehoybn hot kof-khes tamuz tof ayin giml le-pak un regirt ad rosh-khoydesh teyves shono hazoys tof ayin dalet le-pak*'. That is: 'A new elegy to the tune of the song on the martyrs of Prostajev, about the great and dreadful plague that began here in the holy community of Prague on the twenty-second of July 1713 and prevailed until the twelfth of December of this year, 1713'. Two remarks concerning the title: the song about the martyrs of Prostits is a Yiddish 'historical' song, printed in 1684.[12] Although the title-page suggests two different tunes to which it may be sung (that of the 'Akeydah'—a liturgical poem on the sacrifice of Isaac, or that of the 'Brauneslid'—a German popular song), the fact that its name is given as the tune for a new song in 1713 indicates that it enjoyed great and long-lasting popularity. Secondly, *ipesh*—the common Yiddish term for 'plague', originates in the Hebrew word *ippush*—stench.

The title page of Eisenstadt's eight-leaved octavo-size booklet also lists its contents. The first component is the song itself, defined both as '*eyn oysfirlikhe un grundlikhe varhaftige ertseylung*'—'a detailed, thorough and truthful account' of the plague in Prague, and a great lamentation for the victims' souls. The second component is a set of 'cures' for the plague, which are said to have saved 'several hundred souls'. The last is a day-by-day roster of the number of victims. Similar cures can be found in contemporary Yiddish books of charms and cures, but the death-roll, listing daily the number of the deceased, makes this a particularly important document. It enables us to follow the development of the epidemic from beginning to end.

The other two songs have no such appendices. One, the '*Ipesh lid fun Prag*'[13] (Song of the pestilence of Prague) was written by Berl Katz of the well-known Gershoni family of printers.[14] Berl Katz worked for many years in the family's printing shop in Prague and it was there, at the epidemic's end, that he printed his song in a six-leaved octavo-size booklet. The song, comprising 76 four-line stanzas, was published with the financial help of a fellow-printer.

The third song—'*Far loyf den ipesh*' (Course of the pestilence)[15] was also printed in Prague, but *sine anno*. Although the anonymous author evidently tried to produce orderly four-line stanzas, the text we have is extremely corrupt; it includes verses and even complete stanzas which appear in Berl Katz's song as well. This may indicate that the songs were sung, or that parts of them circulated orally, before they were committed to print. The author was obviously a simple man, and it is only at the end of the song that it becomes obvious that he was a bereaved father who lost his only child, a daughter, during the plague.

Together, the three songs provide a rich and multi-faceted depiction of the progress of the epidemic, and of the various ways in which it affected both public and private life. Although the authors share a general theme, each follows his own path in terms of the details he incorporates and the way he shapes them—a product of his ability, taste, sensitivity and the images engraved in his memory. There can be no doubt that all three poets were in Prague at the time of the disaster. Two of them helped bury the dead. Thus, their writing reflects actual experience, what they heard on the spot, first-hand, along with their beliefs, attitudes and other reflections. The fact that each of the authors belonged to a different social stratum, which left its mark on their perceptions of reality, provides the reader with a complex perspective on both the event itself, and the impact it made on various sectors of the Jewish population. Moreover, the fact that the three songs were written and published near the time of the event may help authenticate the details they supply, and it certainly contributes to their freshness. These characteristics of the songs, as well as the scope and nature of their depictions and the variety of topics with which they deal in such rich detail, make them important historical documents. All three authors are concerned only with the Jewish community of Prague; none so much as hints at the fact that non-Jews, too, were affected by the plague. Quite the contrary: they present the event as exclusive to the Jewish community, confined within the borders of the city's Jewish quarter, with only two indications of life outside: the *shtadlanim*, who interceded with the authorities on behalf of the Jews, and the spot where the dead were buried. Their time-frame, too, begins on the day that the plague first appeared in the Judenstadt and ends on the day it essentially ended there (but not outside it)—a period of five months.

Apart from rather vague indications of stomach trouble and wounds, the songs offer no details of the symptoms of the disease. Although they do not describe the course of the epidemic in an orderly, chronological manner, they do help us trace its consecutive stages.

Until Thursday 20 July, when six people in one house fell ill all at once, there had been no indication of 'bad air'. Four of the sick died three days later, on Sunday, and the other two succumbed the following Tuesday. News of the fatal event terrified the public and triggered a flight from the ghetto, in keeping with the established principle that, when plague breaks out, *primum remedium—fuga*. It was indeed a mass escape: thousands of people collected their belongings and fled. These belonged mostly to the wealthy and powerful, including spiritual leaders, such as the head of the rabbinical court and Chief Rabbi. Their flight was a source of embitterment and anger for some of those who lacked the means to escape. At first, many refugees found shelter with country estate owners in the vicinity of Prague. As the epidemic worsened, the landlords withheld this privilege, denying refugees even one night's stay. Temporary residents of Prague, mainly students in the city's *yeshivot*, also joined the exodus and returned home. Flight from Prague, however, does not seem in all cases to have guaranteed escape from the disease.

The flight from the ghetto lasted about three weeks. On Monday 14 August twenty people died of plague, three times as many as the previous day's toll. The city authorities ordered the gates of the quarter shut, the guards were discharged, and the flight came to an end. Many people who had planned to leave were prevented from doing so. They still waited for a couple of days, with their belongings packed and loaded on carts, until they found their hopes finally frustrated. Reb Shmuel Tausk, the leader of the community, along with other leaders, had left the ghetto but remained in Prague, where they worked on the community's behalf throughout the epidemic, interceding with the authorities, seeing to the community's needs, and promoting its internal organization by co-operation with those *Kahal* members who had remained in the ghetto.

Inside the Jewish quarter, the plague struck everywhere and devastated every sector of the population, irrespective of sex, age or social status. However, its effects were worst for children and pregnant women. While it sometimes struck only one or several members of a family, it frequently killed entire families. A high proportion of the infected died, but a good many recovered. Some were stricken more than once, recovering on each occasion.

The small number of victims recorded at first encouraged the belief that this was only a limited outbreak. But it rapidly spread and the communal leadership—probably at the advice of the city authorities— put into effect a law according to which anyone displaying the first symptoms of the disease must be quarantined and moved to the *baydlekh*—huts or stands in the market-place or elsewhere in the open spaces within the ghetto. The belief that danger lurked both in the sick themselves and in their 'impure', 'contaminated' dwellings motivated people not only to flee the houses but to seal them up. As the plague intensified, the number of sealed houses grew, and the places of refuge became more and more crowded. The roster of patients swelled, reaching at times a hundred all at once; the *baydlekh* and the bath-house along with its courtyard could no longer hold them all.

Apart from the necessity of satisfying the needs of the growing throngs of patients, it was also necessary to care for others who, though healthy, were destitute. They constituted a large population, constantly augmented by new paupers who, now that the ghetto was closed, were left without any sources of livelihood. In this dire situation, tremendous efforts were made to care for the poor. Substantial sums of money were distributed among them every week, and large quantities of meat and poultry were cooked for the poor and sick daily on improvised bonfires in the streets. Notwithstanding all this, cases of starvation occurred.

The community purchased and installed some two hundred beds for the indigent sick, employed healers and nurses and bought medicines. However, even the considerable public funds deployed (and the additional donations) failed to meet the massive, ever-multiplying needs. Those responsible for the distribution of public funds faced grave dilemmas in selecting the groups of highest priority: whether these were the still healthy, the sick or the dead.

The problem of burial, terrible even in less catastrophic times, whenever the daily number of corpses buried in the ghetto's cemetery exceeded ten, grew worse as the roster increased. Shortly after the ghetto was closed, the city authorities forbade Jews to use their own cemetery, and ordered them to rely on grounds outside the ghetto, at the lazaret. The corpses were first brought to the ghetto's cemetery and from there taken—through the gate which was opened for this purpose only after dark—to the special burial plot. The community purchased several large carts but, even when put to full use, they could not keep up with the number of corpses. These piled high in the cemetery, numbering hundreds. The Yiddish songs provide horrifying descriptions of these scenes. Left for long periods under the sun, the corpses decomposed until they were unrecognizable. Their removal to the lazaret grounds was not the end of the story. The relatively small number of undertakers precluded a swift burial and the shocking scenes at the ghetto's cemetery recurred here. The burial society (*Hevra Kaddisha*), and the undertakers who assisted them worked relentlessly, with extreme dedication, while some community leaders gave a hand as well. Some of the ghetto's poor were persuaded to serve as grave-diggers with the promise of double pay.

The *Kahal* and the public made every effort to bury the dead according to Jewish law and custom. Some one hundred men worked day and night constructing coffins; when the supply of wood ran out, and all the dispensable rafters had been removed from the houses, the community leadership urged the public to sell its various items of furniture. Hundreds of women worked round the clock sewing shrouds, and when their output proved insufficient, the leadership asked for donations of white garments. The public responded willingly and generously—partly in the belief that this act of charity would spare their lives. Despite all the efforts, the ideal of observing all Jewish burial practices proved impossible to realize. The deceased were not escorted to their burial place and *Ha-tsur Tamim* was not always recited. There were problems in reciting Kaddish. Many did not know when their relatives died or where they were buried. Corpses could not always be cleansed as stipulated, and the dead were not buried beside their relatives (even when they had requested this in their wills) or at the plot which they had purchased. The cessation of burial in the ghetto's cemetery was considered a particular hardship, and the community leaders gained widespread approval when they obtained the authorities' permission to bury a few of the deceased there.

The leadership also made provisions to maintain law and order at a time when moral standards were most liable to slacken. Four men were appointed as a special court and placed in charge of twelve *yidishe bal-milkhomes*—Jewish policemen or armed guards. These guards were empowered to arrest and incarcerate persons who refused to submit to authority or who conspired to carry out criminal acts. Apart from these indirect references, the songs mention neither crime nor violence, except for the incidence of theft by nurses of the belongings of the sick.

The shortage of medical personnel, including midwives and wet-nurses, caused tremendous price inflation and demands for advance payment for services. Communal and individual resources were severely depleted owing to the disruption of economic life in the closed ghetto. Thus it was extremely difficult to pay for medical and other services. The pharmacies found demands hard to meet even at the inflated prices, and customers were forced to wait in long lines. Lemons and drinks made from tobacco were considered useful remedies. A poultice with a home-made ointment was recommended for sores. Special plague-songs were played in order to calm the sick and lull them to sleep.

Our songs also tell us of the distress of the healthy and their dread of becoming infected. In their desperate effort to avoid contagion, they used various preventive measures. Some of these had long been conventional, and others caught on in the wake of new rumours that proclaimed them reliable. Since the source of the epidemic was believed to be the 'bad air', people tried to avoid leaving home; when they found this unavoidable they covered their mouths and noses with sponges dipped in vinegar. Others held the opposite view; the best prevention was a walk along the river. In addition to the fear of 'impure' water, there was also the belief that one risked infection by direct as well as indirect contact with the sick. These notions posed a harsh dilemma for anyone whose relatives, friends or neighbours had contracted the disease. Such a person would have to choose between abandoning or expelling the victim in the hope of saving himself, or remaining at the victim's side at his own peril. Decisions naturally varied: some cruel and selfish (though understandable), others selfless.

It seems that it was not commonly believed that infection was risked by public interaction. People continued to meet and visit each other, mainly for the purpose of consoling the bereaved. They also continued to assemble in the synagogues for prayer (and not only on holidays), and even took part in large funerals. The approach of the High Holidays aroused the hope that God would hearken to their prayers and bring the epidemic to an end, but this did not occur. The month of the High Holidays, Tishrei, marked the very climax of the plague. The period between Rosh ha-Shana and Yom Kippur was particularly grievous: 120 deaths were registered on a single day—6 Tishrei. Nevertheless, the community assembled in the synagogues for the High Holiday services, and tried to observe as closely as possible all the laws and customs pertaining to the festivals. On Sukkot (the Feast of Tabernacles) for example, the service was halted during the recitation of the Hallel until the *etrog* and *lulav*, delayed en route, finally arrived. Even the bedridden refused to take their medicine before they knew for certain that these special ritual objects had arrived, permitting them to recite the required blessings.

The authorization to perform on the Sabbath and holidays all sorts of labour for the sick, the needy and the dead was, no doubt, given in perfect accordance with Jewish law, but this was a source of great distress. The recurrent mention of this issue in all three songs reflects the general feeling in the public that the essence of the tragedy was epitomized by this drastic change in the 'natural', conventional order of things.

The sight of sickness and death in the streets, the visible dwindling of the population and the ever-growing numbers of mourners in black, not only intensified the individual's fear for his own life, but also conjured the thought that, in the end, none would survive. It seems, however, that neither these reflections nor the massive presence of death could diminish the grief of the bereaved. They bitterly lamented the loss of their loved ones, never stopped speaking of them, and observed as strictly as possible all laws and customs pertaining to mourning.

All three songs indicate clearly that the plague was perceived as divine punishment for individual and collective sins. This belief did not lead to fatalistic attitudes or passive resignation. People took all possible action to save their lives—whether through repentance, prayer and charity—in the hope of arousing God's mercy, or in attempting to escape the ghetto or, at least, an 'infected' house, or else in getting hold of medicines.

Throughout, the three songs exude the concept of *zidduk ha-din* (justification of God's verdict) and perfect faith in the God of Israel. In different ways they express deep gratitude to the Almighty for having brought the epidemic to an end. Reading between the lines, however, one becomes aware of some note of protest and complaint. Here and there the authors of the songs seem to be replying to such critics, chiefly to those who questioned the link between sin and affliction. However, none of the songs as much as hints at a search for either the 'sinner' who may have 'caused' the plague or some other scapegoat. There is no indication whatsoever of any opposition—by either groups or individuals—to the city authorities and community leaders, their rulings and regulations. The songs report only one instance of collective protest: a group of pregnant women vehemently demanded assurance that virgin burial grounds would be found for them should the need arise. Their demand was met.

Only in one song is fierce anger or criticism expressed at the leaders and the wealthy who fled the ghetto when the plague broke out, abandoning their community in its hours of distress. Though the author of this song is the most scholarly of them all, it is he who seems to serve as a mouthpiece for the common folk. He shares the other two authors' praise of Reb Shmuel Tausk for his boundless dedication to the suffering community, but he does not join the others in praising ordinary individuals whose limitless selflessness in burying the dead the others describe in great detail. Instead, he records the names of important members of the community who died in the plague.

The general picture evoked by these songs, of worthy and positive organizational action on behalf of the public, taken in an atmosphere of willing collaboration, without any real clashes, may seem too harmonious to be credited; it indicates an adherence to literary conventions rather than factual reality. On the other hand, the fact that none of the songs records any detail that conflicts with the information provided by the others, may attest to their general credibility, although this does not guarantee that they supply the whole truth. The information contained in our songs must, therefore, be examined together with all available Jewish and non-Jewish documents and testimonies of the event. The result would make possible a comparison between this epidemic in an urban ghetto and similar events elsewhere.

However, even at this stage of the present study, there is no doubt that the three songs are of central importance for the history of the event they describe. The poetic accounts of three eye-witnesses offer us more than a description of daily life in a plague-stricken Jewish community. Although the songs were clearly written and printed for the benefit of the authors' contemporaries, in surviving they have become a historical source-material of primary importance.

Notes

1 A. Hirsch, *Handbook of Geographical and Historical Pathology*, vol. 1 (London, 1883), pp. 501–2; Weitenweber (note 8 below), p. 3, the sources listed at the bottom of the page.

2 See 'Mor w Prusach w roku 1709', *Karnawał dziadowski*, Pieśni wedrownych śpiewaków (XIX–XX w.), Wybor i opracowanie Stanisława Nyrkowskiego, Wstepem poprzedzifl Julian Krzyżanowski (Warsaw, 1973), pp. 42–5.

3 *Eyn nay lid fun der grose srefe be-kak Altneu bay Hamburg* (Halle, 1712); see M. Steinschneider, *Catalogus Librorum Hebraeorum in Bibliotheca Bodleiana*, Berolini 1852–1960, No. 3699; A. E. Cowley, *A Concise Catalogue of the Hebrew Printed Books in the Bodleian Library* (Oxford, 1929), p. 665.

4 See, for example, O. Placht, *Lidnatost a spolenčenská skladba českeho statu v 16–18 stolet* (Prague, 1957), pp. 310–11, and the bibliography; Jaroslav Prokeš, 'Der Antisemitismus der Behörden und das Prager Ghetto in nachweissbergischer Zeit', *Jahrbuch der Gesellschaft für Geschichte der Juden in der Čechoslovakischen Republik*, I (Prague 1929), pp. 202–3 and the notes on pp. 228–9; W. Brosche, 'Das Ghetto von Prag', *Die Juden in den böhmischen Ländern*, (Munich–Vienna, 1983), pp. 109, 117.

5 Two Hebrew prayers concerning the plague were written by R. David Oppenheim, the Chief Rabbi of Prague at the time, and printed in 1713: see Cowley (note 3 above), p. 153. They deal with the plague in the abstract, without supplying details.

6 See G. Kisch, *Die Prager Universität und die Juden 1348–1848*, (Mährisch-Ostrau, 1935), pp. 43–5. The relevant documents are quoted on pp. 140–3.

7 V. Schulz, *Přǐspěvky k dějinám moru v zemích českých z let 1531–1746* (Prague, 1901) [*Historický Archiv* vydava I. trida České Akademie Cisaře Františka Josefa pro vědy, slovesnost a uměni v Praze, Čislo 20], pp. 167, 170–2, 176, 189.

8 W. R. Weitenweber, *Mittheilungen über die Pest zu Prag in den Jahren 1713–1714, Ein Beitrag zu medicinischen Geschichte* (Prague, 1852). (I am most grateful to the Universitäts-Bibliothek in Vienna for allowing their copy to be sent to Jerusalem for my inspection.) Weitenweber's study is based on many of the documents quoted by G. Kisch (note 6 above).

9 See, for example, M. Steinschneider, *Die Geschichtsliteratur der Juden in Druckwerken und Handschriften* (Frankfurt a. Main, 1905), no. 219 (pp. 138–9); O. Muneles, *Bibliographical Survey of Jewish Prague* (Prague, 1952), p. 64, Nos. 227–9.

10 In the well-known collection of R. David Oppenheimer, who was Chief Rabbi of Prague at the time of the event.

11 See Cowley (note 3 above), p. 465 (opp. 8° 632), and Steinschneider, (note 3 above), p. 1800, no. 6458, 3. This is explicitly identified as the second printing. One leaf (the front page and the first ten strophes) of what appears to be the first edition was found in July 1986 in the synagogue-*genizah* of Veitshöchheim near Würzburg (I am very grateful to Dr. E. Timm and Dr. S. Zfatman for reporting this to me). The front page shows neither the date nor the place of publication, but 'Amsterdam characters' are indicated.

12 See Steinschneider (note 3 above), nos. 3692, 4712; Cowley, (note 3 above), p. 238.

13 See Steinschneider (note 3 above), no. 8143, on

14 *ibid.*, pp. 2969–70, on the Gershoni–Gersonides family.

15 *ibid*, p. 3967; Cowley (note 3 above), p. 528.

Jewish Historiography in the United States and Britain

Lloyd P. Gartner

JEWISH history, whose subject is an ancient and living people, was long withheld recognition as a field of teaching and research resembling other fields of history, and therefore a place in the university. Professional opportunities for the Jewish historian barely existed until recently, although American universities taught history from the 1880s and British universities a few decades earlier. This was also the state of affairs at Oxford and Cambridge in Britain, and at the German universities which exerted powerful influence upon their British and American counterparts during the nineteenth century and until the Nazi era.

The reason for the absence of Jewish history from universities and the historical profession may be found in Christian traditions much older than these countries. The American, British and German institutions shared a Christian heritage which essentially continued an ancient doctrine: the Jews had forfeited the spiritual heritage of biblical religion to Christianity. What remained to the Jews was merely 'rabbinic legalism', 'petrified rabbinism' of the Pharisees, devoid of true religious inspiration. The fate of the Jews in wandering, persecution and compulsory moneylending deserved pity, but the Jews themselves stood outside the field of attention. Enlightened men, including historians, could refer sympatheticaly to Jewish sufferings without taking the history or culture of the Jews seriously. The emancipation of European Jewry was not taken to mean the placing of their religion and culture on a plane of equality with that of the Christian countries who had granted them this emancipation.[1]

The history of the Jews had no foothold in British and American universities. Biblical and pre-Christian history were taught as *heilsgeschichte*, 'preparation for the Good News', rather than as the history of the Jewish people. Even when ancient Jewish history was secularized somewhat, thanks to biblical criticism and the general secularization of universities, the fundamental assumptions hardly changed. Secular and public universities for their part usually considered the history of the Jews to be Church history, a subject which they did not teach. One current of liberal opinion believed it would be kinder not to mention the Jews in universities, thereby facilitating their desirable social and cultural assimilation. Thus the ancient history of the Jews before the rise of Christianity was out of bounds to Jewish teachers and Jewish scholarship was ignored, while the history of the Jews afterwards was deemed negligible or ahistorical, not meriting attention.[2]

The Jews themselves cultivated their own history, generally at rabbinical seminaries, mainly Hebrew Union College (1875), the Jewish Theological Seminary (1886; refounded 1902), the Jewish Institute of Religion (1925; amalgamated in 1948 with Hebrew Union College), and to an extent at Jews' College (1855) in London. Jewish history as taught in those institutions, which generally maintained high scholarly standards in the twentieth century, was not apologetics. Nearly all the professors, however, treated Jewish history as the handmaid to the study of Jewish literature. They saw the Jewish past in purely spiritual terms and consequently stressed the biobibliographic study of the great cultural figures, leavened with the history of persecutions.

In England the fabled collections of the Bodleian and the British Museum served Jewish historians, but they were generally visitors from abroad. Little of the work on the Genizah material at Cambridge University was done by British Jewish historians. London University did have a professorship of Hebrew, endowed by one of its founders when University College opened its doors in 1828, but until recent years the incumbents were not historians. Adolf Neubauer (1831–1907) was Hebrew sub-librarian at the Bodleian, where he came after beginning his career abroad, and utilized that great collection to publish a long series of literary and historical texts.[3]

Jewish historians had little to hope for, but opportunities for Hebrew scholars did exist somewhat in departments of Semitics or in several new departments of modern Hebrew at universities. The work of many a scholar in Bible, Talmud, and mediaeval Hebrew literature has been of the first importance for Jewish historical research. The line between the study of Jewish history and of Jewish literature is not sharp and scholars can be found who worked on both sides, rather as the study of Greek and Latin has been combined with Greek and Roman history. Such a pioneer scholar in America as Henry Malter (1864–1925), for example, produced important work in Talmud and mediaeval philosophy and also wrote the standard *Saadia Gaon: His Life and Works* (Philadelphia, 1921 and later reprints).[4]

Even in the unpromising atmosphere that prevailed, two momentous university appointments were made, at Harvard University in 1925 and at Columbia University in 1930, both the outcome of generous endowments by Jewish donors. Harry A. Wolfson (1887–1974) was appointed Littauer Professor of Jewish Literature and Philosophy at Harvard,[5] and Salo W. Baron[6] (b. 1895) became Miller Professor of Jewish History, Literature and Institutions at Columbia. Wolfson's brilliant and voluminous life's work argued that Jewish philosophy was the essential component of mediaeval philosophy, whose basic premises had been laid down by Philo and dissolved by Spinoza. Wolfson came to America as a youth from a Lithuanian *yeshivah*, and Baron came in 1925 at the age of thirty from his native Galicia and Vienna, transferring five years later from the Jewish Institute of Religion to Columbia. During the first decades of their respective service Wolfson and Baron had few advanced students and intellectually were relatively solitary. Yet each established a 'beachhead' of Jewish studies within outstanding universities at the highest level of scholarly accomplishment.

Typically, the *American Historical Review*, the leading journal of history in the United States, before approximately 1960 reviewed books on Jewish history in very uneven fashion in its extensive and polylingual book review section. Many books that were noticed were the victims of ill-chosen critics who produced incompetent even when favourable reviews.[7]

The transition to a conception of the Jews as a people with a history comprehending millennia was slow to establish itself. Sociology provided a partial opening. As a result of the mass immigration of East European Jews to the United States, and then of refugees from Nazi Germany during the 1930s, an extensive literature was produced on contemporary Jewish social problems which treated the Jews as an ethnic group. Secular Jewish movements produced a similar effect. Before the Second World War there was only slight influence from East-European-Jewish historiography and its representative institution, the Yidisher Visenshaftlikher Institut (YIVO; now the YIVO Institute for Jewish Research in New York), then established in Vilna.[8]

A far-reaching influence operating indirectly on Jewish historiography was Zionist nationalism. This new, secular effort at Jewish redemption implied that earlier redemptory messianic movements and related mystical currents were to be taken much more seriously than heretofore by historians, as was the political and communal frame of Jewish life. The revival of Hebrew as the vernacular of a modern society meant that the study of Hebrew literature, as old as Jewish studies itself, turned more to popular and secular Hebrew writing. Conceived by Zionism as a national group seeking to normalize itself among the nations, the Jews came to be studied historically as such even when lacking some essential national attributes, above all a land.

The Jewish historians were immigrants to America. They had acquired their education and often their early professional experience abroad. As men who lived in the history of culture the change was peculiarly hard, even when their material circumstances were easier than those of the masses of Jewish immigrant artisans and small tradesmen who came at the same time. It remains an open question how much the American environment and the Jewish community influenced them and their work: by their own desire, probably little. One detects, and hears from former pupils of theirs who heard it orally from them, that the Jewish scholars, historians included, nourished resentful feelings towards the Jewish community whose traditions bade it honour and support scholars but which disregarded them and their work. The Jewish scholars kept company with the sympathetic few and stayed away from communal affairs. The same may be said for England. The exceptions were Solomon Schechter (1847–1915)[9] as head of the Jewish Theological Seminary, who did most of his scholarly work in rabbinics while at Cambridge University, the Judaeo-Arabist Israel Friedländer (1876–1920),[10] and Salo W. Baron. Until the Nazi period most scholars' connections were with Germany, the seat of modern Jewish studies, and rarely with American universities. Louis Ginzberg, at the Jewish Theological Seminary which stood a few streets away from Columbia, might have been 5000 miles distant according to his son, himself a Columbia professor.[11]

Two much smaller groups are to be found among the historians later on. A number of sojourners, principally Israelis, spent years in America before returning home, and a few others by conscious choice never quite unpacked in America. There is also a group of emigrants who were trained in the United States, began their professional career there, and later settled in Israel.

The most common social origin of Jewish historians is as children of rabbis and teachers, who grew up in an atmosphere of learning, or of parents who were also in the Jewish professions as teachers, scribes, writers, sextons, and ritual meat slaughterers. At least two were the children of bankers and Jewish communal leaders, while the rest seem to be offspring of professionals, clerks and small businessmen. No correlation is evident between parental occupation and field of interest in Jewish history, although it may be that sons of rabbis followed their fathers into *yeshivah* study—an intellectual regimen which might incline them towards textual concentration.

Dynasties have been quite common among rabbis, but among the historians cited here none is the child of an historian nor of a scholar in some other field of Jewish studies. Connections by marriage, however, are not unusual. In this socially significant respect Jewish historiography followed the pattern of university society rather than that of traditional and sometimes modern Jewish society.

Jewish history as a university subject actually began in 1930 with Professor Baron's appointment at Columbia and the gradual development of doctoral work under his direction. By his long tenure at a major university in the world's largest urban Jewish community, his devotion as a teacher and lecturer, and above all his prodigious productivity in almost every field and period of Jewish history, Salo W. Baron attained a primacy in the field in America during the 1930s which has continued into his high old age. No one appears ready to succeed this primacy, in part because the field has developed and branched out during the last half-century.

Some of the work of Louis Ginzberg (1873–1953), Professor of Talmud at the Jewish Theological Seminary from 1903 and recognized as the foremost Talmudist of his time, demonstrates what talmudic learning can contribute to Jewish history. In the first volume of his *Geonica*,[12] Ginzberg analyses the structure of Jewish autonomy in the Muslim world under the headship of the Exilarch and the frequently rival Babylonian academies. His 'The Significance of the *Halakhah* for Jewish History'[13] suggests an economic and social interpretation of the disputes between the juridical schools of Hillel and Shammai of the first century, and has had extensive influence on the interpretation of Second Commonwealth times. Like almost anything written about that era it touches on Christian beginnings. Ginzberg's successor Saul Lieberman (1898–1983),[14] who came to America in 1941 as an accomplished talmudic master, rarely wrote history, but his penetrating and erudite textual studies opened new perspectives on Jewish history during the talmudic era, notably its Greek bearings.

Louis Ginzberg's seminary colleague Alexander Marx (1878–1953)[15] was the greatest authority of his time on Hebrew books and manuscripts, and his writings deal mainly with literary sources which he discovered, as well as with *gelehrtengeschichte*. With the biblical philologist Max L. Margolis (1866–1932),[16] Marx wrote the widely used *History of the Jewish People* (1927), which expresses a modified conception of the *Wissenschaft des Judentum*'s view of Jewish history. Few compact general histories have ever been written from as close a knowledge of original sources as these two scholars commanded. Unlike Margolis' scholarly views, the biblical history within the book was very conservative. The account of the Muslim and Geonic period was novel, reflecting the achievements of Genizah studies. In 1927 the attitude to Jewish emancipation was still hopeful, and the future of Palestine was viewed optimistically. This well-written but densely factual work differs from its German intellectual forebears in placing the Jews, not the idea of Judaism, at its centre: a serious effort is made to write the history of the Jews as a people, although the emphasis remains on intellectual history.

While the Marx–Margolis manual long remained the leading general work, the foremost synthesis was that by Salo W. Baron, *A Social and Religious History of the Jews* in three volumes (New York, 1937). This was a fresh, original study which included a massive apparatus and excursuses, as was its author's wont. Professor Baron offered his fundamental view of the mutual influence of Jewish society and religion upon one another throughout millennia of Jewish history, which he moulded as a continuous development without sharp divides or abysses. The 'emancipation' of Jewish religion from a localized geographical area enabled Judaism to develop out of a people's history rather than from a material environment and its imperatives. Hence the Jews, and Judaism, survived in exile as a people. Baron's work combined intensive erudition with breadth of scope in its twelve large chapters. It said something new on practically every topic it touched in the text and perhaps more so in its excursuses. Five years later the author followed with *The Jewish Community: Its History and Structure to the American Revolution*, also in three volumes (Philadelphia, 1942), in which he traced the organized Jewish community from its origins in tribal existence and the ancient Land of Israel through Graeco-Roman and talmudic times, culminating in the autonomous deterritorialized communities of mediaeval Christian Europe. Baron treated synthetically such topics as taxes, officials, charity and the like, drawing on sources scattered across centuries and continents.

During the three decades which ended around 1940, the most innovative fields were Second Commonwealth and Genizah studies employing material from the vast mediaeval treasure trove in Fustat opened by Schechter. Apart from the remarkable literary finds, the most famous of which was the Hebrew original of Ben Sira (the Widsom of Ecclesiasticus in its Greek version), the Genizah yielded treasures of historical sources. Schechter published the documents of supposedly Zadokite sectaries, and they were subjected to lively debate which was renewed with the fresh discoveries of sectarian literature in the Judaean desert beginning in 1947. To Schechter's argument for Zadokite authorship, Ginzberg replied with the suggestion that this was a quasi-Pharisaic sect, in line with his general tendency to see Pharisaic Judaism as the vast mainstream of Second Commonwealth Judaism.[17] Historical texts from the Genizah were published in great abundance with a somewhat antiquarian tendency by Jacob Mann (1888–1940),[18] who came to Hebrew Union College in Cincinnati via Galicia and

England. It has been persuasively suggested that the best way to read Mann's work is by starting with his imposing textual appendices and then reading the history as a commentary on the texts. However, Mann was also alive to larger issues in historiography and could write chapters of synthesis and articles.

Ginzberg's view of the sectarians points to the fresh view of Jewish socio-religious history in Second Commonwealth times which became widespread between 1910 and 1940. The reinterpretation of the Pharisees refutes the ancient image of Judaism as taught in Christianity, at the centre of which is the hostile evaluation of the Pharisees. To evaluate the Pharisees is to evaluate rabbinic Judaism even of the present day. Jacob Z. Lauterbach (1873–1942), like Ginzberg an East European Talmudist and a rabbinical seminary professor, at Hebrew Union College, pursued the subject in widely influential studies, 'The Sadducees and Pharisees', 'A Significant Controversy Between the Sadducees and the Pharisees' (1927) and several others.[19] Ginzberg's 'The Religion of the Pharisee' originated as a lecture in 1920, but was not generally available before 1928.[20] They were followed by two Christian scholars, the English Unitarian R. Travers Herford (1860–1950), *The Pharisees* (1924), and the American George Foot Moore (1851–1931), *Judaism in the First Two Centuries of the Christian Era* (1930), both of whom avowedly accepted the Ginzberg–Lauterbach interpretation. The British scholar Adolph Büchler (1867–1939), Neubauer's nephew and a native of Hungary whose career had been mainly in Vienna until he came to London as principal of Jews' College in 1907, produced important studies on the rabbinic and priestly classes and their status, and on the social and religious history of the Jews in Roman Palestine.[21] A native of Britain, Israel Abrahams (1858–1925), was the author of *Studies in Pharisaism and the Gospels* (2 vols, Cambridge, 1918–25, reprinted in one vol., New York, 1967 with introduction by M. S. Enslin), which emphasized the roots of Christianity in Pharisaic Judaism.[22] A younger contemporary, Solomon Zeitlin (1886–1976), held rather similar views in his writings, which later turned to Hellenistic and sectarian dimensions.[23]

All in all, this scholarly school saw the Pharisees as the party of the people, whose Oral Law traditions adapted the written law of the Bible to the needs of the time. The Sadducees were regarded as biblical literalists of the upper lay and priestly classes, formalized in their faith and somewhat Hellenized. The Pharisees, who considered the oral no less than the written law to be divinely inspired and obligatory, revered the Sadducee-controlled Temple while making religious life autonomous of it. Moreover, this school, somewhat following Solomon Schechter's *Aspects of Rabbinic Theology* (1909) and the general thrust of

Jewish law itself, emphasized the ethical content of Jewish ritual and ceremonial. Ginzberg's conception of a socio-economic difference between the jurisprudence of the Hillelites and Shammaites was developed into an elaborate 'sociological interpretation' by his disciple Louis Finkelstein (b. 1895), in a 1929 article and then in *The Pharisees: The Sociological Background of their Faith* (2 vols., Philadelphia 1938; third rev. edn 1962) with apologetic overtones.[24]

These works were the culmination of a century's efforts by Jewish scholars to do justice to the religion and historic significance of the Pharisees. Pharisaism was regarded virtually as the common faith of all Jews in the Roman world. Here, however, significant dissent remained, centring on the interpretation of Philo and Alexandrian Judaism, of Jewish arts and tombstones, and of the place of Greek language and culture even in Palestine and among the rabbis. Saul Lieberman, the foremost Talmudist after Ginzberg, demonstrated the prevalence of Greek language, manners and customs within Palestinian Judaism and among the rabbis themselves without claiming, however, that these were more than outward cultural garb.[25] Elias Bickerman (1896–1981), the ancient historian of Russo-German-French background, argued for a much deeper Hellenistic influence on Judaism.[26] From his reading of Philo and elaborate analysis of *Jewish Symbols in the Greco-Roman Period* (13 vols, Princeton, 1953–68), Erwin R. Goodenough (1893–1965)[27] contended that Pharisaism was far from the common religion of Jews in the Graeco-Roman Diaspora, which was quite Hellenized.

After 1950, an unmistakeable reaction set in against Ginzbergian pan-Pharisaism. Much more attention was paid to apocalytpic, mystical and messianic currents. Morton Smith (b. 1915), like Goodenough not Jewish but trained at the Hebrew University in addition to divinity school, pursued a radical course of interpretation of Second Commonwealth Judaism and Christian origins.[28] Jacob Neusner (b. 1932), after writing a large *History of the Jews in Babylonia* (5 vols, Leiden, 1965–70), a significant contribution to a little-known area, pursued talmudic studies in a polemical spirit, emphasizing talmudic interest in cultic and ritual purity over moral and social aspects.[29]

Mediaeval Jewish history is another area of classic interest. Before the 1930s it meant the history of Spanish, Italian and Franco-German Jewry in Western Europe. The supposed close of the Babylonian Geonic period in 1038 transferred the centres of learning to western and southern Europe, but even without such exaggeration European Jewry was in the ascendant. Its history attracted attention on the part of Jewish historians in England. An early classic in the field was Israel Abrahams' *Jewish Life in the Middle Ages* (London, 1896; rev. edn by Cecil Roth, 1932; repr. 1961), delightfully written, perhaps slightly elegiac and sentimental, and based largely on rabbinic writings in Western Europe from the thirteenth to the eighteenth century. Eminent non-Jewish mediaevalists contributed to the field, including F. W. Maitland, Sir Hilary Jenkinson and H. G. Richardson, who wrote the already classic *The English Jewry under Angevin Kings* (London, 1960). James W. Parkes (1896–1981), writing under the impact of rampant European anti-Semitism, published two notable studies, *The Conflict of the Church and the Synagogue: A Study in the Origins of Antisemitism* (London, 1934; repr. Cleveland and New York, 1961)—the title indicates Parkes's argument that the Christian churches and doctrine are at the foundation of anti-Semitism—and its sequel, *The Jew in the Medieval Community* (London, 1938), which describes the consequences of these doctrines for the Jews in mediaeval Europe.[30] Slightly before Parkes, Solomon Grayzel (1899–1981) systematically investigated *The Church and the Jews in the XIIIth Century* (Philadelphia, 1933), publishing with valuable apparatus and introduction papal letters and conciliar decrees. He continued with shorter studies on this highly important subject. More inwardly oriented are three works by the British Louis I. Rabinowitz (1907–84), who emigrated to become Chief Rabbi of the Transvaal in 1945 and settled in Israel in 1961. They are *The Social Life of the Jews of Northern France in the XII–XIV Centuries* (London, 1938), *The Herem Hayyishub* (London, 1945), concerning the autonomous mediaeval Jewish community's power to accept or exclude newcomers, and an attempt to identify the 'Radanite' international traders, *Jewish Merchant Adventurers* (London, 1948).[31] Leadership in Jewish historiography in England from the 1930s was assumed by Cecil Roth (1899–1970), a Londoner who lived from his writing until his appointment, thanks to a private endowment, as Reader in Post-Biblical Jewish Studies at Oxford in 1939. He had started in Italian Renaissance studies and shifted to Italian Jewish history, then added an interest in *The History of the Marranos* (Philadelphia, 1932, repr. 1959) and expertise in *Jewish Art* (London, 1961; other edns), while all along acquiring special knowledge of rare books and manuscripts. In his last years he contributed to Qumran studies. Roth made major contributions to mediaeval and modern Anglo-Jewish history in a long series of books and article, headed by the standard *History of the Jews in England* (Oxford, 1939; 3rd edn, 1964). In addition he wrote books and articles, always in a vivacious, attractive style, and many of his works, above all his *Short History of the Jewish People* (London, 1936; many revisions and printings) sold well on both sides of the Atlantic and was extensively translated. Even more than Jewish historian, Cecil Roth was a complete man of Jewish letters.[32]

In the United States, Louis Finkelstein's *Jewish Self-Government in the*

Middle Ages (1925) dealt mainly with Jewish synods in the Middle Ages, and was stronger in textual than historical analysis. Guido Kisch (1889–1985), a German refugee sojourner, contributed a series of basic studies on the legal status of mediaeval German Jews.[33] Abraham A. Neuman (1890–1970) wrote *The Jews in Spain* (2 vols, 1942), the leading American study, dealing with thirteenth-century Spanish Jewry on the basis of F. (Y.) Baer's great collection of archival and other sources (*Die Juden im christlichen Spanien*, 2 vols, Berlin, 1929, 1937) and two major rabbinic respondents.[34]

However, the contribution made by Jewish historiography in America was to lie more to the eastern Mediterranean and Muslim lands. The pioneer was the short-lived Joshua Starr (1907–49),[35] whose *Jews in the Byzantine Empire* (1939) and *Romania: The Jewries of the Levant after the Fourth Crusade* (1948) virtually opened the field. A different sort of pioneering work of broad significance was undertaken by Joshua Trachtenberg (1904–59),[36] a congregational rabbi, in *The Devil and the Jews: The Medieval Conception of the Jew and Its Relation to Modern Antisemitism* (New Haven, 1943; repr. 1961). Published when genocidal anti-Semitism was raging unchecked, the work explores the folk and psychic as well as the theological roots of anti-Semitism. Trachtenberg's erudite psychohistory found few successors until years later, in Norman Cohn's *Warrant for Genocide: The Myth of the Jewish World-Conspiracy and the Protocol of the Elders of Zion* (New York, 1969), which argued that racist anti-Semitism is a secularized version of the mediaeval demonic conception of the Jew. Another book by Trachtenberg, *Jewish Magic and Superstition: A Study in Folk Religion* (New York, 1939; repr. 1961), deals with folklore from extensive Jewish literary sources. It too found few successors, except for the learned if pedestrian work in England of H. J. Zimmels, *Magicians Theologians and Doctors: Studies in Folk-medicine and Folk-lore as reflected in the Rabbinical Responsa (12th–19th Centuries)* (London, 1952).

At the close of the 1930s, when it was cut off from its European heartland, Jewish historiography in England and in America could list to its credit a number of significant and original works. Active scholars of high standing were on the scene, working in Jewish history and in overlapping fields of literature, including Bible and Talmud as well as philosophy. However, Jewish history hardly existed as a scholarly profession, and its intellectual attachment to general history was still tenuous.

Some scholars arrived from Germany during the 1930s but, surprisingly, their importance within American Jewish scholarship was less decisive than that of the refugee scholars and scientists of 'the intellectual migration', the great majority of whom were also Jews, within their respective fields. Jewish historians in America were able to help some of their German colleagues to settle in the United States during the 1930s. Thereafter, until the late 1950s, Jewish history in America worked in relative isolation. After the destruction of the Jews of Europe and their institutions (although many library holdings were later salvaged and redistributed), the Israeli focus of Jewish historiography, with conceptions and leaders of its own, moved to the centre of the scholarly stage. Extensive connections with the American group began only during the 1960s.

Some characteristics of Jewish historians educated in America began to be apparent during this period of isolation. As a rule they were trained more in history, particularly general history, than in textual study, and their linguistic scope, while seldom equalling that of the Europeans, usually surpassed that of other American historians. These may be the reasons why the questions which have interested Jewish historians in the United States do not as a rule arise from the study of texts but from the contemplation of a broad historic field. Increasingly, the Americans tended to take on problems deriving from general history and to write monographic works of survey and synthesis. As the field matured after about 1950 and became more autonomous of its European past and closer to American historiography, these characteristics became more noticeable. Discussion of Jewish history in its totality was avoided as an undertaking too vast for disciplined study. Like British and American historians in general, the Jewish historians wanted to keep their distance from what they regarded as speculation or ideology which might also impair the credentials of Jewish history as history. Ellis Rivkin (b. 1918) of Hebrew Union College, who moved from Italian Renaissance Jewish history mainly to that of the Second Commonwealth, braved this opposition, but his aggressive and daring works, such as *The Shaping of Jewish History: A Radical New Interpretation* (New York, 1971), found little acceptance. Distinctive fields were strongly preferred. Joshua Starr's Byzantine work was followed by that of an Israeli sojourner, Zvi Ankor (b. 1921), like Starr a Baron disciple, who wrote *Karaites in Byzantium: The Formative Years 900–1200* (New York, 1959). Spanish Jewry was comparatively neglected. However, another long-term sojourner, B. Netanyahu (b. 1910), raised the fundamental question of the Spanish Marranos' genuineness as crypto-Jews in a contentious book, *The Marranos of Spain: From the Late XIVth to the Early XVIth Century According to Contemporary Hebrew Sources* (rev. edn, New York, 1973). Some of this had been adumbrated in his earlier, important, *Don Isaac Abravanel: Statesman & Philosopher* (Philadelphia, 1953).

Besides the eastern Mediterranean area, the Muslim world to its east has extensively occupied Jewish historians in the United States. This derives somewhat from the prolonged prominence of Jews in Islamic studies since the era of Ignaz Golziher (1850–1912). One result for Jewish history has been the ready integration of Jewish and Muslim components in the historiography of the Jews under Islam. Distinguished scholars including Shlomo D. Goitein, Franz Rosenthal and Bernard Lewis have written on general Islamics and contributed to the history of the Jews under Islam. Such integration is little known for mediaeval and modern Jewish history in Christendom. Jacob Mann's pioneering was surpassed by the vast, polished work of Shlomo D. Goitein (1900–85), of German birth and education, who came to America in 1957 after many years in Israel.[37] No historian exploited the Genizah to better effect, and his great work *A Mediterranean Society: The Jewish Communities of the Arab World as Portrayed in the Documents of the Cairo Geniza* (4 vols to date; Berkeley and Los Angeles, 1967ff.) set the Jewries of Egypt and surrounding countries securely in the framework of Islamic society and polity. Walter J. Fischel (1902–73) went further afield, to study Iranian and Indian Jewry. An interesting example of integrating Jewish and Islamic studies is the literary and religious texts and history produced by the talmudic scholar of the Jewish Theological Seminary, Moses Zucker (1904–87), of Galician birth and Viennese training. His learned studies of the polemic and exegetic works of the Babylonian Geonim, especially R. Saadiah Gaon, are firmly linked with Muslim and Jewish sectarian disputes and polemics.[38] Raphael Mahler's attempt to interpret the Karaite schism in Marxian terms was generally rejected.[39] Moshe Perlmann (b. 1905), who arrived as a finished scholar via Russia, Palestine and England, has specialized in Muslim–Jewish poemics besides contributing to the quite different field of Russian-Jewish history.[40] A significant group of younger scholars, frequently pupils of Goitein, has taken up Jewish history under Islam, which was little studied until recently except in its literary aspect. While it flourished, the once classic field of mediaeval Jewry in western Europe has been somewhat overshadowed. Studies on the Jews of Norwich by the British V. D. Lipman (b. 1921) and of Perpignan by R. W. Emery (b. 1912),[41] on French Jewry and the Crusades by R. L. Chazan and on Rouen by N. Golb,[42] Jewish-Christian polemics by D. Berger, J. M. Rosenthal (1903–76),[43] and F. Talmage, who also wrote on Spanish Jewish culture,[44] and on German-Jewish religious life by I. G. Marcus[45] were the main exceptions. Two young scholars, K. R. Stow and Jeremy Cohen, proposed new perspectives on Church–Jewish relations. The British rabbinic scholar H. J. Zimmels, an immigrant from Germany, examined the two great divisions of the Jewish people from the early Middle

Ages mainly in religious and linguistic terms in his *Ashkenazim and Sephardim: Their Relations, Differences and Problems as Reflected in the Rabbinical Responsa* (London, 1958). Scholarly writing about mediaeval rabbis and their times on the basis of their published *responsa* has been a traditional historiographic genre. However, Isidore Twersky at Harvard set a high standard for the study of rabbinic culture during the Middle Ages, beginning with *Rabad of Posquieres* (Cambridge, Mass, 1962) and culminating in his comprehensive *Introduction to the Code of the Maimonides* (New Haven, 1980). Several other scholars trained by him have tilled the same field.[46]

By far the largest project of post-Second World War Jewish historiography in the United States or anywhere was Salo W. Baron's new edition of his *Social and Religious History of the Jews*. Originally intended to contain two volumes each for ancient, mediaeval and modern history with an extra one for apparatus, its first two volumes appeared in 1952. However, from that point the work became enlarged so that the two mediaeval volumes have become sixteen to date. The project now contains 5189 pages of text and 2419 pages of astonishingly learned and diverse notes, supplementary documentation, bibliography, and excurses employing at least a dozen languages. More volumes are on the way. This immense work penetrates the remotest and least noticed areas of Jewish history, combining scores of syntheses of individual topics with sage judgements on controversial problems, and is an inexhaustible mine of suggestion and information. Generally the analysis—of narrative there is little—is thematic rather than territorial, and the latter, when it appears, usually transcends national boundaries. Professor Baron's basic divisions follow general history, so that the titles of individual volumes employ such terms as Caliphate, Holy Roman Empire, Renaissance, Reformation, and Wars of Religion. On the other hand he divides the Middle Ages by Jewish criteria at 1200, and the Later Middle Ages extend to 1650. The shift of gravity from east to west and general cultural decline characterize the later period. The hugeness of the work has made it an omnipresent research tool for historians; but it also led to some loss of the sharpness of focus on its author's socio-religious conception which he set forth more concisely in the three volumes of the 1937 edition. Altogether, Baron's *History* is one of the most immense historical projects ever undertaken by one man alone. The work and its author hold the predominant position in Jewish historiography in America.

The writing of Jewish history since 1500 has been undertaken mainly since 1950. It lacks the guidance and constraints of the classic tradition exemplified by the mentors of the *Wissenschaft des Judentums* and their disciples, which emphasized biblical and rabbinic Judaism; a hallmark of modern times is the weakening of these traditions to the point of dissolution in some countries. None of the early scholars ventured eastward to Poland and Russia, although a few took up Renaissance Jewry in Italy. Early modern times, or the last phase of the Middle Ages in the view of some Jewish historians, remained neglected, with the exception of Volumes 15–18 of Baron's work covering 1500–1650. The dense and variegated life of Polish Jewry, numerically several times as large as the rest of European Jewry, encouraged the somewhat populist historiography which came out of Eastern Europe, emphasizing the material realities of Jewish life, its communal struggles, rich versus poor, and the social basis of cultural and religious life. This historical trend was rather long in documentation but shallow in conceptualization; and its homeland was annihilated during the destruction of European Jewry. A few of its exponents reached America in time. Jacob Shatzky (1893–1956),[47] the historian of Warsaw Jewry, settled in America in 1924. He wrote extensively in Yiddish on the communal and cultural history of Polish Jewry, besides several suggestive essays on large questions of interpreting Jewish history. Shatzky was very learned and wrote vividly, but was not always a careful scholar. The Marxist Zionist Raphael Mahler (1899–1978),[48] who sojourned in America between Poland and Israel from 1937 to 1950, dealt while in America with the social and religious conflict between *Hasidim* and Jewish enlighteners. Two Polish-Jewish historians who survived the Holocaust, Isaiah Trunk (1905–81)[49] and Philip Friedman (1902–61)[50] devoted themselves to its history after coming to the United States. Friedman was the founder of serious Holocaust historiography, while Trunk's *Judenrat: The Jewish Councils in Eastern Europe under Nazi Occupation* (New York, 1972) is the basic account of that ambivalent phenomenon of the years of annihilation. Among Americans only Abraham G. Duker (1907–87)[51] and Isaac Levitats (1907–84),[52] pupils of Baron, produced serious work on East-European-Jewish history, as did the immigrant B. D. Weinryb (1899–1983)[53] and C. Abramsky (b. 1915) in England. *Poland and Lithuania*, Volume 16 of Baron's *Social and Religious History* which appeared in 1979, is an original, comprehensive presentation. The revival of East-European-Jewish history has occurred recently, almost suddenly, among younger Jewish historians in the United States and Canada. Arcadius Kahan (1920–82), a native of Vilna who became a prominent economic historian, provided a stimulating example of modern techniques in his field as applied to East European Jewry.[54]

Modern Jewish historiography is beset by problems of definition and periodization. Does Jewish history turn modern on account of external events such as capitalism, the Enlightenment and the French Revolution which deeply affected the Jews? Or does modern Jewish history begin with some inner development such as Sabbataean messianism or the Jewish Enlightenment? The line between internal and external developments is somewhat artificial, since such a movement as the Jewish Enlightenment drew heavily upon its European counterpart. The role of capitalism and the Jewish role within capitalism as initiating modern Jewish history was once a matter of lively debate. A significant work on Jews and capitalism in Amsterdam was published by Baron's pupil H. I. Bloom (1899–1966).[55] Lately the subject has largely dropped from notice.

Classic issues of modern Jewish history, mainly the transition to modernity, emancipation, anti-Semitism, migration and Zionism, have usually been treated in the United States within a specific territorial and chronological framework and less as general problems of historiography, as is the practice in Israel. There are exceptions, however, beginning with the inexhaustible Salo W. Baron, who has written seminal essays on emancipation, capitalism and the Jewish Enlightenment, besides weighty studies on the 1848 revolutions and the Jews.[56] Isaac Barzilay (b. 1915) wrote numerous studies on Hebrew Enlightenment ideology.[57]

There has been very little American contribution to the study of mysticism, messianism and sectarianism, central concerns of Israeli historiography inspired especially by the celebrated studies of Gershom Scholem. Neither has the Hasidic movement of the late eighteenth and nineteenth centuries drawn much scientific attention in the United States except for the Yiddish scholars mentioned above, several studies by the religious philosopher Abraham J. Heschel (1907–72), originally written in Hebrew and Yiddish,[58] and Arthur Green's thorough and penetrating *Tormented Master: A Life of Rabbi Nahman of Bratslav* (Tuscaloosa, 1979). In England Louis Jacobs,[59] and particularly Joseph Weiss—a student of Scholem who arrived in England from Hungary via Israel—produced a number of original and influential studies of Hasidism.[60]

While anti-Semitism has been a comparatively minor affliction to the Jews in the United States and Britain, not to mention their physical remoteness from the Holocaust, Jewish historians there have shared in the sceptical reappraisal of Enlightenment and emancipation as the sources of Jewish freedom in the modern world. Arthur Hertzberg (b. 1921), in *The French Enlightenment and the Jews* (New York, 1968), is not only sceptical but has also claimed that the French Enlightenment, and Voltaire in particular, are the fountainhead of modern secular anti-Semitism. The issue is whether the animadversions of Voltaire, Diderot and others are central to their thinking or are mere passing expressions of ill-temper, residues of ancient prejudice of which they failed to free themselves. Hertzberg takes their remarks very seriously, and traces from them the line of intolerance towards Jewish separatism and distinctiveness to be found in the liberal secular West. Other Enlightenment scholars such as Peter Gay, Frank E. Manuel and Arthur M. Wilson preferred the milder approach.[61] Zosa Szajkowski (1911–78), in a series of densely factual studies, insisted on the Jacobin view of the French Revolution and the Jews. This hyper-prolific scholar of Polish and French background also dealt intensively with the Napoleonic period, Jewish migration, the First World War, American Jewry and the Holocaust. His work is notable largely for its masses of archival documentation.[62]

The finest work on the Jewish Enlightenment is Alexander Altmann's (1904–87) voluminous biography of its central figure, *Moses Mendelssohn* (Philadelphia, 1973), a calm, unhurried work which brings into full account the Jewish and German dimensions of that protean man. Professor Altmann, of German birth and education and a resident of England until he moved to the United States in the late 1950s, avoided anachronisms about German–Jewish relations and saw Mendelssohn as both successful Jewish scholar and enlightener and significant German philosopher and intellectual. It has been questioned whether Altmann did not exaggerate the harmony of Mendelssohn's fusion of cosmopolitan European culture with traditional Judaism. But there is no doubt of the magnitude of Altmann's achievement, which also included the republication and completion of the *Jubiläumsausgabe* of Mendelssohn's writings, begun in 1929 and stopped by the German government in 1938.[63] A necessary preface to Altmann's work is Chimen Abramsky's suggestive 'The Crisis of Authority Within European Jewry in the Eighteenth Century', appearing appropriately in *Studies . . . Presented to Alexander Altmann* (eds R. Loewe and S. Stein, Tuscaloosa, 1979). The logical continuation of Altmann's work is the brisk synthesis by Michael A. Meyer (b. 1937): *The Origins of the Modern Jew: Jewish Identity and European Culture in Germany, 1749–1824* (Detroit, 1967), which analyses persuasively the social and cultural predicament of Mendelssohn's successors, who were struggling to achieve a satisfying dual identity as Germans and Jews. Almost as counterpoint, Todd M. Endelman's recent study of English Jews during the same period, *The Jews of Georgian England 1714–1830: Tradition and Change in a Liberal Society* (Philadelphia, 1979), emphasizes the absence from England of the ideological issues and the accompanying intellectual vigour of German Jewry. Endelman finds instead that the transition to modernity in a liberalizing English society was undertaken by Jewish institutions, against a social reality of poverty and assimilation by Jews of the upper as well as the lower class.

At this point Jewish historiography is well into the post-Second World War era. Jewish history began to acquire university recognition not only for its intellectual merits but also for reasons lying deeper. The American university expanded its intellectual scope as the European–North American centrality diminished. Russian studies, Far Eastern and Islamic history assumed places of importance. American history continued to dominate historiography and the teaching of history, but shifted its bearings as immigrants, Blacks, Indians and ethnic minorities became the subject of historical research. If these trends reflect the 'arrival' of these groups in American life, and if the broadening of the scope of history as taught and written somewhat reflects the United States' world role, they also imply that the self-confidence of the Western Christian and Enlightenment tradition was badly shaken. Not only Jews regarded the systematic German Nazi murder of European Jewry as the most extreme expression of the impotence, or the guilt, of these traditions.

For their part, Jewish historians in the United States showed awareness of the philosophical and methodological aspects of their work mainly by the attention they gave to historiography and the history of historical thought. During the 1920s Professor Baron opened the subject in America with two studies on the Renaissance historian and philologist Azariah de' Rossi, followed by 'The Historic Outlook of Maimonides' in 1935, and by later studies of nineteenth-century masters like Steinschneider and Levi Herzfeld and programmatic discussions of mediaeval and American-Jewish history.[64] Probably the most important mediaeval study was Gerson D. Cohen's (b. 1924) study and edition of *The Book of Tradition (Sefer ha-Kabbalah) by Abraham ibn Daud* (Philadelphia, 1967), which sheds piercing light on the historical as well as the social and religious thought of three mediaeval centuries. Yosef H. Yerushalmi (b. 1932) accomplished as much for Marrano history and historical thought in his eloquent *From Spanish Court to Italian Ghetto: Isaac Cardoso: A Study in Seventeenth Century Marranism and Jewish Apologetics* (New York, 1971).[65] Other historians of the past have been scrutinized: the perennial Josephus (R. Marcus, S. J. D. Cohen, L. H. Feldman), Renaissance scholars, printers and geographers (A. A. Neuman, I. Sonne, M. A. Cohen, M. A. Shulvass) and Heinrich Graetz (I. Schorsch).[66] David B. Ruderman provided a comprehensive vista of the Jew within Italian Renaissance culture and society in *The World of a Renaissance Jew: The Life and Thought of Abraham ben Mordecai Farissol* (Cincinnati, 1981).

The re-evaluation of modern Jewish history obviously begins with

Germany, inevitably in the shadow of the Nazi catastrophe. The German refugee scholar and novelist Selma Stern-Taeubler (1890–1981) salvaged and finally published in full a vast accumulation of documents and studies *Der preussische Staat und die Juden* (4 parts in 7 vols, Berlin and Tübingen, 1925–75), realities which her *Court Jew* (Philadelphia, 1950) effectively described. Her *Josel of Rosheim: Commander of Jewry in the Holy Roman Empire of the German Nation* portrayed the sixteenth-century leader (Philadelphia, 1965: first published in German, 1959).[67] Jacob R. Marcus (b. 1896) wrote a significant study in the history of social welfare, *Communal Sick-Care in the German Ghetto* (Cincinnati, 1947). But these and similar meritorious studies were somewhat obscured by the literature on German Jewry after 1750. General as well as Jewish historians participated not simply in digging for the historic roots of Nazi anti-Semitism but intensely sharpened their perception of Jewish status in nineteenth-century Germany and of the underlying tenuousness of German Jewish life. Such a book as Fritz Stern (b. 1926), *Gold and Iron: Bismarck, Bleichröder, and the Founding of the German Empire* (New York, 1977), while not specifically Jewish history, is permeated with the Jewishness of Gerson von Bleichröder and the festering problem of the Jewish position in Bismarckian Germany. Dozens of studies published in the excellent series of *Year Books* of the Leo Baeck Institute of Jews from Germany (1956ff; 31 vols to date) not only explore this theme but also delve into the important social and intellectual history of modern German Jewry. A parallel is provided by the extensive critical examination by Colin Holmes *Anti-Semitism in British Society 1876–1939* (London, 1979). The literature on German anti-Semitism is vast, interdisciplinary and international, and too extensive to be cited. Whether this subject truly belongs to Jewish history, or is an external impact, was questioned then and since. But its actual impact may be seen in studies of German-Jewish historical themes by younger scholars: Ismar Schorsch (b. 1935), *Jewish Reactions to German Anti-Semitism* (New York, 1972), Stephen M. Poppel (b. 1943), *Zionism in Germany 1897–1933: The Shaping of Jewish Identity* (Philadelphia, 1977) and Jehuda Reinharz (b. 1944), *Fatherland or Promised Land: The Dilemma of the German Jew, 1893–1914* (Ann Arbor, 1975) and other studies by him on Zionism in Germany. The huge and constantly growing literature on Nazism inevitably pays considerable attention to Nazi anti-Semitism and its Jewish victims, and the horrific climax of the Holocaust has become, after considerable hesitation even in carrying on research about it, a prominent interest of Jewish historians. The quality of the work to date is variable. Most of the better American and British historiography on the subject has scrutinized diplomacy and rescue attempts more than the actual machinery of mass murder.[68]

The international theme of the great migration from Eastern Europe, which went around the world but mainly to the United States, is another broad interest. Jewish historians in America who have been active in this field include Paula E. Hyman (b. 1946), *From Dreyfus to Vichy: The Remaking of French Jewry, 1906–1939* (New York, 1979) and for England, Lloyd P. Gartner (b. 1927), *The Jewish Immigrant in England 1870–1914* (London and Detroit, 1960) besides other immigration and local history studies by the same author.[69] The Jews and socialist movements has dwindled as a subject for research, but Robert S. Wistrich has written a lengthy series of studies, headed by *Socialism and the Jews: The Dilemmas of Assimilation in Germany and Austria Hungary* (Rutherford, N.J., and London, 1982). A good example of broadened horizons with a territorial focus is provided by the American contribution to the historiography of the Jews in France. *The Sephardic Jews of Bordeaux* (Tuscaloosa, 1978) until 1815 constitute Frances Malino's subject, while Hertzberg's book, mentioned above, deals with the eighteenth century from another angle. The indefatigable Zosa Szajkowski published a remarkable annotated bibliography, *Franco-Judaica: An Analytical Bibliography of Books, Pamphlets, Decrees, Briefs and Other Printed Documents Pertaining to the Jews in France 1500–1788* (New York, 1962), and also treated the revolutionary period in scores of minutely detailed articles which were gathered in *The Jews and the French Revolutions of 1789, 1830 and 1848* (New York, 1970). His work also appears prominently in YIVO's valuable collection, *Yidn in Frankraykh* (ed. E. Tcherikower, 2 vols, New York, 1942). The history of the French-Jewish community structure established by Napoleon has been thoroughly studied by Phillis Cohen Albert, *The Modernization of French Jewry: Consistory and Community in the Nineteenth Century* (Hanover, New Hampshire, 1977). The Dreyfus affair, that watershed between the emancipation era and the twentieth century's realities, draws continuous attention, and Robert F. Byrnes took it up in *Antisemitism in Modern France, I: The Prologue to the Dreyfus Affair* (New Brunswick, N.J., 1950). He did not continue, but the English Stephen Wilson presented an immense cross-section entitled *Ideology and Experience: Antisemitism in France at the Time of the Dreyfus Affair* (London, 1982). Michael R. Marrus, a Canadian, examined French Jewry of that day in *The Politics of Assimilation: A Study of French Jewry at the Time of the Dreyfus Affair* (Oxford, 1971). Paula E. Hyman's study of Jewish immigration, mentioned above, appeared just after David H. Weinberg's *A Community on Trial: The Jews of Paris in the 1930s* (Chicago, 1977). The tragic sequel of these books' themes is impressively portrayed by Marrus and Robert O. Paxton, *Vichy France and the Jews* (New York, 1981). Szajkowski again presented a prodigious work of reference in *Analytical Franco-Jewish Gazetter 1939–1945* (New York, 1966). In these themes Jewish historiography in America has probably appeared at its best, by weaving together Jewish and general history.

It is natural for Jewish history in the United States to be concerned with American-Jewish history, and for English Jews to pay special attention to Anglo-Jewish history. The American Jewish Historical Society has existed from 1892,[70] and the Jewish Historical Society of England from 1893.[71] American-Jewish history was in fact the first field of Jewish history to be studied in the United States. For a long time it was cultivated in the spirit of Americans recounting the flight of the Puritans and other minorities from persecution to a new world, and of memorializing colonial and revolutionary heroes. The history of American Jewry was similarly written until the 1940s, largely about early American-Jewish refugees from the Inquisition, and patriotic Jewish contributions to their country's independence and its wars—all with heavy apologetic emphasis. Outside the mediaeval period, Anglo-Jewish history long concentrated, also somewhat apologetically, on the Resettlement of the 1650s and the nineteenth-century struggle for political emancipation. While this writing found considerable favour with the Jewish community, many Jewish historians, mindful also of the negligence with which the community treated them, were disdainful of American-Jewish history, which lacked literary monuments and intellectual eminence. The situation was slightly different with Anglo-Jewish history. Only during the 1950s did attitudes begin to change as better work was produced and the American-Jewish community appeared more significant in the historical perspective. A long line of books began to appear. The history of colonial American Jewry was treated magisterially by Jacob R. Marcus, who also founded and built up the excellent American Jewish Archives in Cincinnati.[72] Immigration from Germany in the mid-nineteenth century and especially from Eastern Europe several decades later, was one of the preoccupations. A long series of local histories was written, varying in quality from naïve compilations to sophisticated studies in the quantitative or the socio-communal mode. The Jewish labour movement, Zionism and Jewish politics drew considerable attention. On the other hand, it is curious that the religious and cultural history of American Jews has been relatively neglected.[73]

Jewish historians in England and the United States gradully established a working partnership with Israeli historians. Few American-Jewish works appeared in Hebrew translation, but various studies by Israeli historians have proved influential. Yitzhak F. Baer's *History of the Jews in Christian Spain* (2 vols, Philadelphia, 1961) has had respectful attention and frequent citation. The works of Gershom Scholem,

Sabbatai Sevi: The Mystical Messiah (Princeton, 1973), *Major Trends in Jewish Mysticism* (New York, 1941; 2nd edn, 1946; 3rd edn 1954), *The Messianic Idea in Judaism* (New York, 1971) and *On the Kabbalah and Its Symbolism* (New York, 1965) brought fame in broad intellectual spheres as well as profound professional respect to that scholar, who came to Jerusalem from Weimar Germany. Jacob Katz's influential works of sociologically oriented history have laid out avenues of analysis almost unknown before him, particularly in the analysis of Jewish 'traditional society' and its painful transition to modernity.[74] Other scholars' translated works have brought them less attention abroad than they received at home in Israel.

Israeli historical scholarship, with its somewhat inbred habits and tendency to analyse texts and concepts subtly and at length, as well as its deep methodological conservatism, was slow in taking to Jewish history as written in the United States and England. Nearly all the younger Americans and British have studied for some period in Israel and gone there for sabbaticals or research, or both. Inevitably, personal and professional connections grew, especially as a number of historians and other scholars in Jewish studies settled in Israel. We are likely to witness some degree of convergence in subjects and methods. Even on its own, however, Jewish historiography in the United States, after slow and rather painful beginnings, has successfully established its credentials as history. This has yet to happen at most British universities. Jewish historians have claimed a succession to the European masters of the nineteenth and early twentieth century.

The Jewish community for its part has recently shown striking interest in fostering Jewish history at American universities. During the last ten to fifteen years large endowments at some of the foremost private universities, such as Columbia, Stanford, Harvard and Yale, have opened or enlarged research and teaching in Jewish history. State and municipal universities, including Michigan, Florida, Indiana, California and New York have also appointed Jewish historians, in some cases with the aid of private funds. Thirty years ago even the most sanguine would not have imagined such an expansion. At an early stage it appeared to be in the nature of a Jewish response to the short-lived vogue for Black studies during the late 1960s, yet after they declined sharply Jewish history, including other Jewish studies as well, continued to grow on the campuses. A remarkable change has also occurred in American-Jewish attitudes to Jewish scholarship, if only in terms of the sums donated. It is even reported that major universities now believe that in order to arouse the benevolent disposition of potential Jewish benefactors it is a prerequisite to provide Jewish history in the curriculum, with suitable scholars to teach it.

What has brought about this development, which is unprecedented in regard to both Jewish interest and university recognition? At one level, it seems to be a symbol of the presence of Jews as Jews on American campuses, after many instances of discrimination and rejection. There is another level, one which is suggested by Professor Yosef H. Yerushalmi's influential recent work *Zakhor: Jewish History and Jewish Memory* (Seattle and London, 1982). This book begins by examining the communal and religious role of collective memory in the Jewish past. To remember mighty events such as the Exodus, the infamy of Amalek, and the destruction of the Temples is a religious obligation to which more memories were added with time. This burden of collective Jewish memory was not history, for that requires some critical distance and reserve, but wholehearted empathy with the past. The writing of history in its scholarly sense held little interest in traditional Judaism, since it was memory which was essential. Yerushalmi observes that traditional collective Jewish memory has faded. Moreover, historiography since the early nineteenth century, by contributing to the historicization of the Jewish past, has also helped to erode empathetic Jewish memory.

True as this may be, there yet exists in our day a palpable desire among Jews for collective memory. American and British Jews, aware of the tremendous events their people have undergone in the last century, find themselves with only faded remnants of once vivid memory. They remember deeply the exodus from Eastern Europe to the west of their grandparents and great-grandparents, a movement made still more poignant by another matter for collective memory, the annihilation of the Jews during the Holocaust in those countries of origin. Israel's founding and survival, also a matter of great meaning, is another new theme for memory. Contemporary Judaism, however, appears unable to transmute these experiences into the religious symbols and theology of memory. The quest for collective memory may therefore be fostered not in traditional religious terms but in those of secular history. This quest, based now on history, leads to universities and to Jewish historians within them. Perhaps this is the Jewish historian's hour.

For the Jewish historian, a person trained in the ways of critical scholarship and wary of stirring waves of group emotion, this is a problematic assignment. He may reject or at least sidestep it. Yet the creation or enhancement of collective memory has been undertaken by some of the greatest historians. Bancroft and Ranke, Michelet and Macaulay, functioned not only as scholars of history but also as men who aroused and expounded the memory of their respective nations. Graetz, slightly younger than these giants, performed a task not very different, but found German Jewry cautious when not embarrassed by his Jewish fervour. East European Jewry, however, took avidly to his great history. In more recent times Jewish historians have generally avoided the role of guides and mentors of historic memory; but Jewish historians, simply by being historians and doing their job with a modicum of literary skill, may well renew and enhance collective Jewish memory. Their researches, dispassionate and erudite as they may be, indirectly foster feelings of pride, interest and responsibility towards the Jews, alongside the overt purpose of imparting knowledge and critical understanding.

Yerushalmi has contended that past generations have been unable to bequeath Jewish collective memory to contemporary Jews. In the custody of Jewish historians, the new collective memory will differ from that of the past by being largely secular and critical, subject to professional and public debate and open to continued research and revision. Historians who accept this task may find that they are at long last bringing together what have long been apart—Jewish scholarship and the Jewish community. They will be no less historians for that.

Notes

This paper was originally a lecture in a symposium on Jewish historiography at the sixteenth International Congress of Historical Sciences held at Stuttgart, August 1985. It has been revised and amplified, and the data are up to date to the end of 1986.

Abbreviations

AHR	American Historical Review
AJYB	American Jewish Year Book
EJ	Encyclopedia Judaica (16 vols, Jerusalem, 1971)
HJH	Salo W. Baron, History and Jewish Historians (Philadelphia, 1964)
JSS	Jewish Social Studies
LBIYB	Leo Baeck Institute of Jews from Germany, Year Book
MJHSE	Miscellanies of the Jewish Historical Society of England
PAAJR	Proceedings of the American Academy for Jewish Research
TJHSE	Transactions of the Jewish Historical Society of England

1 See S. W. Baron's Hebrew lecture 'Halom she-hitgashem' (Tel Aviv, 1972), esp. pp. 20-6; I. Schorsch, Jewish Reactions to German Anti-Semitism, 1870–1914 (New York, 1972), pp. 168–77; ibid., 'The Religious Parameters of Wissenschaft-Jewish Academics at Prussian Universities', LBIYB, vol. 25 (1980), pp. 3–19; U. Tal, Christians and Jews in Germany: Religion, Politics and Ideology in the Second Reich, 1870–1914 (Ithaca and London, 1975), pp. 121–59; A. Jospe, 'The Study of Judaism in German Universities before 1933', LBIYB, vol. 27 (1982), pp. 295–319; for a pained negative evaluation of the level of Jewish learning at German universities see D. Kaufmann, 'Die Vertretung der jüdischen Wissenschaften an den Universitäten' and

'Paul de Lagarde's jüdische Gelehrsamkeit', *Gesammelte Schriften*, vol. 1 (Frankfurt a./Main, 1908), pp. 14–38, 207–57, esp. pp. 212–14.

2 There is no substantial study on the theme treated here. See *Jewish People Past and Present*, vol. 4 (New York, 1955), 'American Jewish Scholarship', by J. Trachtenberg, pp. 411–55, esp. pp. 411–13, 440–8; Baron, *HJH*, pp. 343, 454, quoting German Christian scholars; *EJ*, 'Hebraists, Christian', by R. Loewe.

3 On the Bodleian Library and Neubauer, *EJ*, s.v., including bibliography: E. N. Adler, 'A Bibliography of the Writings of Adolf Neubauer (1832–1907)', *Studies in Jewish Bibliography and Related Subjects in Memory of Abraham Solomon Freidus (1867–1923)* (New York, 1929), pp. 31–54; S. Schechter, 'The Hebrew Collection of the British Museum', *Studies in Judaism*, vol. 1 (Philadelphia, 1896; repr. 1938), pp. 252–69; S. Stein, *The Beginnings of Hebrew Studies at University College* (London, 1952).

4 *EJ*, s.v.; A. Marx, *Studies in Jewish History and Booklore* (New York, 1944), pp. 409–17, slightly updating *AJYB*, 1926, pp. 261–72.

5 L. W. Schwarz, *Wolfson of Harvard: Portrait of a Scholar* (Philadelphia, 1978); *ibid.*, 'A Bibliographical Essay', *Harry Austryn Wolfson Jubilee Volume*, 3 vols (Jerusalem, 1965), vol. 1, pp. 1–46; *PAAJR*, vols 41–2 (1973–4), pp. xxxvii–xliii; *EJ*, s.v.

6 Baron, *HJH*, Foreword by A. Hertzberg and L. A. Feldman; *EJ*, s.v.; J. M. Baron, 'A Bibliography of the Printed Writings of Salo Wittmayer Baron', *Salo Wittmayer Baron Jubilee Volume*, 3 vols. (Jerusalem, 1974), vol. 1, pp. 1–37.

7 Very few books of those mentioned here and published before 1945 were reviewed, and only one, by G. F. Moore, before 1930. On the other hand, reviewers before 1945 included S. W. Baron, A. Marx, G. Kisch and K. S. Pinson. For examples of poor reviewing, see *AHR*, vol. 42, p. 578; vol. 43, pp. 569–71; vol. 48, pp. 549–50; vol. 50, pp. 103–4; many more can be cited in later years as well.

8 *EJ*, s.v.; *Di Oysgabes fun Yidishn Visenshaftlikhn Institut* (Vilna, 1931); S. W. Baron, 'The Journal and the Conference of Jewish Social Studies', in *Emancipation and Counter-Emancipation: Selected Essays from Jewish Social Studies*, ed. A. G. Duker and M. Ben-Horin (New York, 1974), pp. 1–11; and *ibid.*, 'Introduction: Reflections on the Achievements and Prospects of Jewish Social Studies', *JSS*, vol. 41 (1979), pp. 1–8; J. Shatzky, 'Finf un tsvantsig yor YIVO', *Shatzky-Bukh*, ed. E. Lifschutz (New York and Buenos Aires, 1958), pp. 303–17.

9 On Schechter as a public figure, see his *Seminary Addresses and Other Papers* (Cincinnati, 1915, repr. 1959); N. Bentwich, *Solomon Schechter: A Biography* (New York, 1938); *EJ*, s.v.

10 B. R. Shargel, *The Practical Dreamer* (New York, 1985); B. Cohen, *Israel Friedlander: A Bibliography of His Writings* (New York, 1936); (Joint Distribution Committee), *Memorial Meeting Israel Friedlaender—Bernard Cantor September 9, 1920* (New York, 1920).

11 E. Ginzberg, *Keeper of the Law: Louis Ginzberg* (Philadelphia, 1966); S. Goldman, 'Portrait of a Teacher'; B. Cohen, 'Bibliography of the Writings of Prof. Louis Ginzberg', both in *Louis Ginzberg Jubilee Volume* (New York, 1945), pp. 1–47; *PAAJR*, vol. 23 (1954), pp. xliv–liii.

12 L. Ginzberg, *Geonica*, 2 vols (New York, 1909), vol. 1: *The Geonim and Their Halakic Writings*.

13 In his *On Jewish Law and Lore* (Philadelphia, 1955), pp. 77–124.

14 *EJ*, s.v.; E. S. Rosenthal, 'Ha-Moreh', *PAAJR*, vol. 31 (1963), (Hebrew section): pp. 1–71; S. Friedman, 'Kavim li-Demuto ha-Mada'it shel Prof. Shaul Lieberman z.l.', *World Union of Jewish Studies Newsletter*, no. 23 (Winter, 1984), pp. 23–37; A. Marx, 'Dr Lieberman's Contribution to Jewish Scholarship', *Proceedings*, Rabbinical Assembly of America (1949), pp. 259–71; Israel Academy of Sciences and Humanities, *Le-Zikhro shel Shaul Lieberman* (Jerusalem, 1984).

15 *EJ*, s.v.; R. Kohut, 'Professor Alexander Marx' and S. Goldman, 'The Man of the Book', both in *Alexander Marx Jubilee Volume* (New York, 1950), pp. xi–xxiii, 1–34; *PAAJR*, vol. 23 (1954), pp. xxxi–xliii.

16 Dropsie College Alumni Association, *Max L. Margolis: Scholar and Teacher* (Philadelphia, 1952), includes bibliography; *EJ*, s.v.

17 S. Schechter, *Documents of Jewish Sectaries*, 2 vols (Cambridge, 1910; repr. in one vol., New York, 1970), vol. 1; *Fragments of a Zadokite Work*; L. Ginzberg, *An Unknown Jewish Sect* (New York, 1976), reviews the discussions before 1911, pp. 304–37, and that of Büchler at length, pp. 338–408.

18 *Texts and Studies in Jewish History and Literature*, 2 vols (Cincinnati, 1931; repr. 1972;); *The Jews in Egypt and in Palestine under the Fatimid Caliphs* (2 vols, Oxford, 1920; repr. 1969; repr. in one vol., New York, 1970, with Preface and Reader's Guide by S. D, Goitein); *The Collected Articles*, 3 vols (Gedera, Israel, 1971); R. Mahler, 'Yaakov Mann un zayn lebensverk', *Historiker un Vegvayzer* (Tel Aviv, 1967), pp. 196–208, including bibliography; G. D. Cohen, 'The Reconstruction of Geonic History', introduction to reprint of Mann, *Texts and Studies*, op. cit.

19 *Rabbinic Essays* (Cincinnati, 1951; repr. New York, 1973), pp. 23–87; includes bibliography, pp. 3–20, and 'An Appreciation' by S. B. Freehof, pp. xiii–xvi, *PAAJR*, vol. 12 (1942); pp. xxiii–xxv; *EJ*, s.v.

20 *Students, Scholars and Saints* (Philadelphia, 1928; repr. 1943, 1961), pp. 88–109

21 e.g. *The Political and the Jewish Leaders of the Jewish Community of Sepphoris in the Second and Third Centuries* (London, 1909); *Das Synedrion in Jerusalem* (Vienna, 1902); *The Economic Conditions of Judaea after the Destruction of the Second Temple* (London, 1912); article in his *Studies in Jewish History* (London, 1956), which includes his bibliography and a tribute by I. Epstein (pp. xiii–xxii); *EJ*, s.v.

22 *EJ*, s.v.; *Jewish Studies in Memory of Israel Abrahams* (New York, 1927), pp. v–lvi (including faulty bibliography, improved by S. Levy in *MJHSE*, vol. 3 [1937], pp. 41–6); *AJYB*, vol. 28, pp. 219–34; H. Loewe, *Israel Abrahams* (London, 1944).

23 *EJ*, s.v.; *PAAJR*, vol. 45 (1978), pp. xlv–xlvii; S. B. Hoenig, *Solomon Zeitlin: The Scholar Laureate: An Annotated Bibliography* (New York, 1971); *ibid.*, introduced to Zeitlin's *The Rise and Fall of the Judean State*, vol. 3 (Philadelphia, 1978), pp. ix–xix.

24 *EJ*, s.v.; see 'The Pharisees: Their Origin and Philosophy', *Harvard Theological Review*, vol. 22 (1929), pp. 185–261. Finkelstein later retracted much of his argument; see 3rd rev. edn (1962), esp., pp. lix–lxiii.

25 Mainly in his *Greek in Jewish Palestine* (New York, 1942) and *Hellenism in Jewish Palestine* (New York, 1950).

26 *PAAJR*, vol. 50 (1983), pp. xv–xviii; his views are set forth in *Der Gott der Makkabäer* (Berlin, 1937), translated as *The God of the Maccabees* (Leiden, 1978); *From Ezra to the Last of the Maccabees* (New York, 1962); *Four Strange Books of the Bible* (New York, 1967); and in his articles, *Studies in Jewish and Christian History*, 3 vols to date (Leiden, 1976–84).

27 See the reviews of earlier volumes listed in *Jewish Symbols . . .*, vol. 13 (Princeton, 1968), pp. 229–30. His views are set forth in *The Jurisprudence of the Jewish Courts in Egypt* (New Haven, 1929); *By Light, Light: The Mystical Gospel of Hellenistic Judaism* (New Haven, 1935); *The Politics of Philo Judaeus* (New Haven, 1938); *An Introduction to Philo Judaeus* (New Haven, 1940). See also *Religions in Antiquity: Essays in Memory of Erwin Ramsdell Goodenough* (Leiden, 1968), pp. 1–20.

28 *EJ*, s.v.; *Christianity, Judaism and Other Greco-Roman Cults*, 4 vols, (Leiden, 1975), vol. 1, pp. ix–x; vol. 4, pp. 190–200 for bibliography.

29 Besides his *Life of Yohanan ben Zakkai* (2nd edn, Leiden, 1970), Neusner undertook large-scale critical study and translation of talmudic literature, which has had controversial aspects. A negative evaluation is S. Lieberman, 'A Tragedy or a

Comedy?', *Journal of the American Oriental Society*, vol. 104, no. 2 (April–June, 1984), pp. 315–21.

30 *EJ*, s.v.; *TJHSE*, vol. 27 (1982), pp. xiii–xv.

31 *EJ*, s.v.

32 *EJ*, s.v. (He was editor-in-chief of this great project). *TJHSE*, vol. 23 (1971), pp. 102–7; I. (Mrs Cecil) Roth, *Historian Without Tears: Cecil Roth* (New York, 1982); bibliography by O. K. Rabinowicz in *Remember the Days: Essays on Anglo-Jewish History presented to Cecil Roth*, ed. J. M. Shaftesley (London, 1966), pp. 351–87, supplemented and corrected by R. Singerman in *TJHSE*, vol. 25 (1977), pp. 243–51; L. P. Gartner, 'Cecil Roth, Historian of Anglo-Jewry', in D. Noy and I. Ben-Ami (eds), *Studies in the Cultural Life of the Jews in England (Hebrew University of Jerusalem, Folklore Research Center Studies*, vol. 5 (Jerusalem, 1975), pp. 69–86; S. W. Baron, *AHR*, vol. 76, no. 2 (April 1971), pp. 591–2; C. Raphael in *Commentary* (Sept. 1970), pp. 75ff.; A. Neppi, in *Rassegna Mensile di Israel* (1971), pp. 3–18, 99–115.

33 *EJ*, s.v.; e.g. *The Jews in Medieval Germany: A Study of Their Legal and Social Status* (Chicago, 1949); *Jewry-Law in Medieval Germany: Laws and Court Decisions Concerning Jews* (New York, 1949).

34 *EJ*, s.v.; *Landmarks and Goals* (Philadelphia, 1953); introduction by S. Zeitlin to *Studies and Essays in Honor of Abraham A. Neuman* (Leiden, 1962), pp. vii–xiii; *The Seventy-Fifth Anniversary Volume of the Jewish Quarterly Review* (Philadelphia, 1967), pp. 30–4.

35 *EJ*, s.v.; *Joshua Starr Memorial Volume* (New York, 1953), 'Joshua Starr' (Abraham G. Duker), pp. 1–7; bibliography, pp. 9–15.

36 *EJ*, s.v.; Central Conference of American Rabbis, *Yearbook*, vol. 70 (1961), pp. 180–1.

37 *EJ*, s.v.; his works periodically contain autobiographical asides, e.g. S. D. Goitein (ed.), *Religion in a Religious Age* (New York, 1974), pp. 3–4, 141–6; R. Attal, *A Bibliography of the Writings of Shelomo Dov Goitein* (Jerusalem, 1973); introduction to *Studies in Judaism and Islam presented to Shelomo Dov Goitein* (Jerusalem, 1981).

38 *EJ*, s.v.; *Rav Saadia Gaon's Translation of the Torah: Exegesis, Halakha, and Polemics* (Hebrew) (New York, 1959); 'New Sections of the Book of Commandments of R. Hafez ben Yasliah and Some Clarifications of the Problems of His Time', *PAAJR*, vol. 29 (1960–1), Hebrew section, , pp. 1–68; 'R. Saadia Gaon's Role in the Dispute over "the morrow of the Sabbath"', *PAAJR*, vol. 20 (1951), Hebrew section, pp. 1–26. On Fischel, *EJ*, s.v.; *PAAJR*, vol. 41–2 (1973–4), pp. xxv–xxvii.

39 *Karayimer* (New York, 1947); cf. A. S. Halkin, *JSS*, vol. 11 (1949), pp. 79–82; S. W. Baron, *Social and Religious History*, vol. 5 (Philadelphia, 1957), pp. 393–4, n. 14. See the re-evaluation by Z. Ankori in Gal-Ed, vol. 10 (1987), pp. 11–40.

40 *EJ*, s.v.; e.g. *Samau'al al-Maghribi, Silencing the Jews*, *PAAJR*, vol. 22 (1964); *Ibn Kammūna's Examination of the Three Faiths* (Berkeley and Los Angeles, 1971); 'Levanda's Jubilee, 1885', *PAAJR*, vol. 42 (1976), pp. 167–82.

41 *The Jews of Medieval Norwich* (London, 1966) and *The Jews of Perpignan in the Thirteenth Century* (New York, 1959); see the introduction on how the latter book came to be written by a non-Jewish mediaevalist.

42 e.g. R. L. Chazan, *Medieval Jewry in Northern France: A Political and Social History* (Baltimore, 1973); 'The Bray Incident of 1192: Realpolitik and Folk Slander', *PAAJR*, vol. 27 (1969), pp. 1–18; (ed.), *Church, State and Jew in the Middle Ages* (New York, 1980). N. Golb, *Toldot ha-Yehudim ba-Ir Ruan Bi-yemey ha-Beynayim* (Tel Aviv, 1976), but cf. B. Blumenkranz, *Art et Archéologie des Juifs en France médiévale* (Toulouse, 1980), pp. 277–303.

43 *PAAJR*, vol. 44 (1977), pp. xxi–xxii; *Mekharim ve-Mekorot*, 2 vols (Jerusalem, 1970); D. Berger, *The Jewish-Christian Debate in the High Middle Ages: A Critical Edition of the Nizzahon Vetus* (Philadelphia, 1979).

44 *David Kimhi: The Man and the Commentaries* (Cambridge, Mass., 1975); *The Polemical Writings of Profiat Duran* (Hebrew) (Jerusalem, 1981).

45 I. G. Marcus, *Piety and Society: The Jewish Pietists of Medieval Germany* (Leiden, 1981); K. R. Stow, *Catholic Thought and Papal Jewry Policy, 1555–1593* (New York, 1976); J. Cohen, *The Friars and the Jews* (Ithaca, 1982).

46 e.g. I. A. Agus, *Rabbi Meir of Rothenberg* (2 vols, Philadelphia, 1947; repr. in one volume, New York, 1970); I. Epstein, *The Responsa of R. Solomon b. Adreth of Barcelona (1235–1310) as a Source of the History of Spain* (London, 1925); ibid., *The Responsa of R. Simon b. Zemach Duran as a Source of the History of the Jews in North Africa* (London, 1930); (both repr. in one volume), I. M. Goldman, *The Life and Times of Rabbi David Ibn Abi Zimra* (New York, 1970); A. M. Hershman, *Rabbi Isaac ben Sheshet Perfet and His Times* (New York, 1943); M. S. Goodblatt, *Jewish Life in Turkey in the XVIth Century as Reflected in the Legal Writings of Samuel De Medina* (New York, 1952).

47 'Problemen fun Yidisher historisher forshung' and 'Problemen fun Yidisher historio-grafie', in *Shatzky-Bukh*, ed. E. Lifschutz (New York and Buenos Aires, 1958), pp. 227–48; bibliog. from 1940, pp. 327–76; the earlier years are covered in *Yorbukh fun Amopteyl*, vol. 2, ed. L. Lehrer and Y. Mark, pp. 255–328 (by M. Unger and M. Kosover). See S. W. Baron in *YIVO Bleter*, vol. 40 (1956), pp. 234–7; I. Howe, *World of Our Fathers* (New York, 1976), pp. 513–15; L. S. Dawidowicz, *The Golden Tradition: Jewish Life and Thought in Eastern Europe* (Boston, 1967), pp. 263–9; compare Shatzky's views of historiography in Israel in *Zion*, vol. 21 (1956), pp. 103–4 with those in *Shatzky-Bukh*, pp. 126–7. Note the caveats in Philip Friedman's review in *JSS*, vol. 13, no. 4 (Oct. 1951), pp. 359–62.

48 *EJ*, s.v.; the work is *Der Kamf tsvishn Haskoleh un Khsides in Galitsie* (New York, 1943), translated into Hebrew and enlarged as *Ha-Hasidut ve-ha-Haskalah* (Merhavia, 1961); an English version has lately appeared, *Hasidism and the Jewish Enlightenment* (Philadelphia, 1986).

49 *AJYB*, vol. 83 (1983), p. 363.

50 *EJ*, s.v.; *PAAJR*, vol. 29 (1960–1), pp. 1–7; P. Friedman, *Roads to Extinction: Essays on the Holocaust* (New York, 1980), pp. 1–8.

51 *EJ*, s.v.; 'The Polish Emigré Socialists on the Jewish Problem', *JSS*, vol. 14, no. 4 (Oct. 1952), pp. 317–42; 'The Polish Democratic Society and the Jewish Problem, 1832–1846', *JSS*, vol. 19, nos 3–4 (July–Oct. 1957), pp. 99–112; 'The Tarniks', *Joshua Starr Memorial Volume* (New York, 1953), pp. 191–201; 'The Polish Political Emigrés and the Jews in 1848', *PAAJR*, vol. 24 (1955), pp. 69–102.

52 *EJ*, s.v.; *The Jewish Community in Russia, 1772–1844* (New York, 1943).

53 *EJ*, s.v.; *The Jews of Poland . . . from 1100 to 1800* (Philadelphia, 1973); *Texts and Studies in the Communal History of Polish Jewry,PAAJR*, vol. 19 (1950).

54 Introduction by J. Frankel to Kahan's *Studies in Jewish Social and Economic History* (Chicago, 1986) and J. Metzer, 'Arcadius Kahan, Profile of a Scholar', in N. Gross (ed.), *Ha-Yehudim ba-Kalkala* (Jerusalem, 1985), pp. ix–xxvi (English), 411–23 (Hebrew).

55 *AJYB*, vol. 68 (1967), pp. 523–4; Central Conference of American Rabbis, *Yearbook*, vol. 76 (1966), p. 136; *The Economic Activities of the Jews of Amsterdam in the Seventeenth and Eighteenth Centuries* (Williamsport, Pennsylvania., 1937); S. W. Baron, 'Modern Capitalism and Jewish Fate' (1942), *HJH*, pp. 43–64; M. A. Meyer, 'Where Does the Modern Period of Jewish History Begin?', *Judaism*, vol. 24, no. 3 (summer, 1975), pp. 329–38.

56 e.g. 'Ghetto and Emancipation', *Menorah Journal*, vol. 14 (1928), pp. 515–26, repr. in *The Menorah Treasury* ed. L. W. Schwarz (Philadelphia, 1964); 'Nationalism and Intolerance', *Menorah Journal*, vol. 16 (June 1929), pp. 405–15; vol. 17 (Nov. 1929), pp. 148–58; 'The Impact of the Revolution of 1848 on Jewish Emancipation', *JSS*,

vol. 11, no. 3 (July 1949), pp. 195–248, repr. in *Emancipation and Counter-Emancipation*, ed. A. G. Duker and M. Ben-Horin (New York, 1974); 'Aspects of the Jewish Communal Crisis in 1948', *JSS*, vol. 14, no. 2 (April 1952), pp. 99–144; 'Church and State Debates in the Jewish Community in 1848', in *Mordecai M. Kaplan Jubilee Volume* (New York, 1953), pp. 49–72; 'The Revolution of 1848 and Jewish Scholarship', *PAAJR*, vol. 18 (1949), pp. 1–66; vol. 21 (1951), pp. 1–100; 'New Approaches to Jewish Emancipation', *Diogenes*, no. 29 (Spring, 1960), pp. 56–81; 'Changing Patterns of Antisemitism', *JSS*, vol. 38, no. 1 (Winter, 1976), pp. 1–38.

57 e.g. 'The Italian and Berlin *Haskalah*, *PAAJR*, vol. 29 (1960–1), pp. 17–54; 'The Treatment of the Jewish Religion in the Literature of the Berlin *Haskalah*', *PAAJR*, vol. 24 (1955), pp. 39–68; 'Moses Mendelssohn (1729–1786)', *Jewish Quarterly Review*, vol. 52 (1961), pp. 69–93, 175–86; 'National and Anti-National Trends in the Berlin *Haskalah*', *JSS*, vol. 21, no. 3 (July 1959), pp. 165–92.

58 A recent translation is *The Circle of the Baal Shem Tov: Studies in Hasidism* (trans. S. H. Dresner) (Chicago, 1985); also *Kotsk: In Gerangl far Emesdikayt*, 2 vols (Tel Aviv, 1973).

59 *Seeker of Unity* (London, 1966); *Hasidic Prayer* (London, 1972) among other works on the subject.

60 *Studies in Braslav Hasidism* (Hebrew) (Jerusalem, 1974); *Studies in Eastern European Jewish Mysticism* (edited posthumously by D. Goldstein) (Oxford, 1985).

61 e.g. P. Gay, *Party of Humanity* (London, 1964), pp. 97–108; A. M. Wilson, *Diderot* (New York, 1972), pp. 236–7; F. E. Manuel, 'Israel in the Christian Enlightenment', *The Changing of the Gods* (Hanover, New Hampshire, 1983), pp. 105–34.

62 See text *infra* for citations as well as the 'Bio-bibliographical Sketch' by A. G. Duker, pp. vi–xiv in Z. Szajkowski, *Jewish Education in France, 1789–1939* (New York, 1980); *PAAJR*, vol. 47 (1981), pp. xxxvii–xliv; *Zion* (Hebrew), vol. 43 (1978), pp. 367–9.

63 Review by I. Barzilay, *JSS*, vol. 36, nos 3–4 (July–Oct. 1974), pp. 330–5; bibliography in *Studies in Jewish Religions and Intellectual History Presented to Alexander Altmann*, ed. S. Stein and R. Loewe (Tuscaloosa, 1979), pp. 1–12, and in *Mystics, Philosphers and Politicians: Essays in Jewish Intellectual History in Honor of Alexander Altmann*, ed. D Swetschinski and J. Reinharz (Durham, North Carolina, 1982), pp. 343–54, as well as 'Alexander Altmann: A Portrait' by D. Swetschinski in *ibid.*, pp. 1–14.

64 *HJH*, pp. 109–345; 'American Jewish History: Problems and Methods' (1950), in his *Steeled by Adversity: Essays and Addresses on American Jewish Life*, ed. J. M. Baron (Philadelphia, 1971), pp. 26–74, 575–91; 'The Jewish Factor in Medieval Civilization' (1942), in his *Ancient and Medieval Jewish History* (New Brunswick, New Jersey, 1972), pp. 239–67, 502–17.

65 See also his *Zakhor: Jewish History and Jewish Memory* (Seattle, 1982); *The Lisbon Massacre of 1506 and the Royal Image in the "Shevet Yehuda"* (Cincinnati, 1976); 'Clio and the Jews: Reflections on Jewish Historiography in the Sixteenth Century', *American Academy for Jewish Research Jubilee Volume*, 2 vols, *PAAJR*, vols 46–7 (1979–80), pp. 607–38; 'Professing Jews in Post-Expulsion Spain and Portugal', *Salo Wittmayer Baron Jubilee Volume*, 3 vols (Jerusalem, 1974), vol. 2, pp. 1023–58.

66 e.g., Josephus Flavius, Works, *Antiquities*, Books V–VIII (ed. and trans. R. Marcus and H. St J. Thackeray); Books IX–XI (ed. and trans. R. Marcus); Books XII–XIV (ed. and trans. R. Marcus); Books XV–XVII (ed. and trans. R. Marcus, completed by A. Wikgren); Books XVIII–XX (ed. and trans. L. H. Feldman) (Loeb Classical Library, Cambridge, Mass., 1934–65), all containing valuable historical appendices; S. J. D. Cohen, *Josephus in Galilee and Rome* (Leiden, 1979); on A. A. Neuman, see n. 34 above and his 'Abraham Zacuto Historiographer', *Harry Austryn Wolfson Jubilee Volume*, 3 vols (Jerusalem 1965), vol. 2, pp. 597–630; on Sonne, *PAAJR*, vol. 29 (1960–1), pp. 9–15, *JSS*, vol. 22 (1961), pp. 130–2, and *Sefunot*, vol. 5 (1961), pp. 11–16 and bibliography pp. 17–25, and his edition *Mi-Pavlo ha-Revi'i ad Pius*

ha-Hamishi (Jerusalem, 1954); M. A. Cohen (ed. and trans.), *Samuel Usque, Consolation for the Tribulations of Israel* (Philadelphia, 1964); M. A. Shulvass, *Hayei ha-Yehudim be-Italia be-Tekufat ha-Renesans* (New York, 1955); H. Graetz, *The Structure of Jewish History and Other Essays*, ed. and trans. I. Schorsch (New York, 1975); on Marcus, Feldman, Neuman, Shulvass, see *EJ*, s.v.

67 *EJ*, s.v.; American Jewish Archives.

68 The emergence of the historiography of the Holocaust is virtually a subject in itself. Philip Friedman was the first to publish serious research (see note 50 above), and a conference on 'Problems of Research in the Study of the Jewish Catastrophe, 1939–1945' held by the Conference on Jewish Relations in co-operation with YIVO in April 1949 was probably the first public discussion of the field. See *JSS*, vol. 12, no. 1 (Jan. 1950), pp. 13–94, esp. p. 14 (S. W. Baron) and 79–83 (A. G. Duker). I clearly recall many, including strongly committed Jews, who resisted research and teaching of the subject. In no sense did they deny that there had been a Jewish Catastrophe, as it was called until the late 1950s, but theirs was the inhibition of loathing and revulsion. It was also felt that intensive research and exposure might hinder the mental rehabilitation of the survivor.

69 *History of the Jews of Cleveland* (Cleveland, 1978); 'Immigration and the Formation of American Jewry 1840–1925', *Journal of World History*, vol. 11, nos 1–2 (1968), pp. 297–312; 'Roumania, America and World Jewry: Consul Peixotto in Bucharest, 1870–1876', *American Jewish Historical Quarterly*, vol. 68, no. 1 (Sept. 1968); 'Urban History and the Pattern of Provincial Jewish Settlement in Victorian England', *Jewish Journal of Sociology*, vol. 18, no. 1 (June 1981), pp. 37–55; 'Anglo-Jewry and the Jewish International Traffic in Prostitution, 1885–1914', *AJS REVIEW*, vols 7–8 (1982–3), pp. 129–78.

70 J. J. Appel, 'Hansen's Third-Generation "Law" and the Origins of the American Jewish Historical Society', *JSS*, vol. 23, no. 1 (Jan. 1961), pp. 3–20.

71 Items listed in R. P. Lehmann, *Anglo-Jewish Bibliography 1937–1970* (London, 1973), pp. 116, 118. The opening pages of each volume of the *TJHSE* (27 vols to date; 1893 ff.) recount the Society's current affairs. See also L. P. Gartner, 'A Quarter-Century of Anglo-Jewish Historiography', *JSS*, vol. 48, no. 2 (Spring, 1986), pp. 105–26.

72 J. R. Marcus, *The Colonial American Jew 1492–1776*, 3 vols (Detroit, 1970); B. W. Korn, 'In Appreciation' and S. F. Chyet, 'Jacob Rader Marcus—A Biographical Sketch', in *Essays in American Jewish History: To Commemorate the Tenth Anniversary of the Founding of the American Jewish Archives . . .* (Cincinnati, 1958), pp. xiii–xvii, 1–22; *A Bicentennial Festschrift for Jacob Rader Marcus*, ed. B. W. Korn (Waltham, Mass., and New York, 1976), pp. vii–xi, 1–3; *The Writings of Jacob Rader Marcus: A Bibliographic Record*, ed. H. C. Zafren and A. J. Peck (Cincinnati, 1978).

73 Examples of two modes in communal history: L. P. Gartner, *Cleveland* (note 69 above); W. Toll, *The Making of an Ethnic Middle Class: Portland Jewry over Four Generations* (Albany, 1982); S. Hertzberg, *Strangers within the Gate City: The Jews of Atlanta 1845–1915* (Philadelphia, 1978); B. Williams, *The Making of Manchester Jewry 1740–1875* (Manchester, 1976). For bibliography and state-of-the-art discussion, see Baron, 'American Jewish History' (note 64 above); M. Rischin, *An Inventory of American Jewish History* (Cambridge, 1954); O. Handlin, 'A Twenty Year Retrospect of American Jewish History', *American Jewish Historical Quarterly*, vol. 65, no. 4 (June 1976), pp. 293–310; J. R. Marcus, *Studies in American Jewish History* (Cincinnati, 1969), pp. 3–22, 31–43; J. S. Gurock, *American Jewish History: A Bibliographical Guide* (New York, 1983).

74 *Tradition and Crisis* (New York, 1961); *Exclusiveness and Tolerance* (New York, 1961); *Jews and Freemasons in Europe, 1723–1939* (Cambridge, Mass., 1970); *From Prejudice to Destruction—Antisemitism, 1700–1933* (Cambridge, Mass., 1980) among others.

4

PERCEPTIONS OF JEWS IN
THE WIDER SOCIETY

The Romans and the Maccabees

Arnaldo Momigliano

I

As is well known, the geographical word *Kittim* in Hebrew originally indicated the city of Kition on Cyprus or the whole island of Cyprus. The prophet Jeremiah (2:10) seems to extend Kittim, or rather 'the islands of Kittim', to indicate the distant West. In the Book of Daniel 11:30 Kittim undoubtedly indicates the Romans with reference to their intervention in Egypt which prevented the occupation of that country by Antiochus IV of Syria in 168 BCE. This is, as far as I know, the first mention of the Romans in a Hebrew or, even more generically, in a Jewish text. The text itself, the Book of Daniel, as the pagan philosopher Porphyry already knew in the late third century CE, is the book of the Old Testament we can date most securely, at least in its final form: it was written under Antiochus IV, and more precisely between those events of 168 BCE and the death of the King towards the end of 164 BCE. Daniel does not yet know the real circumstances of the death of Antiochus IV and ventures in 11:45 a prophecy on his end which in the event was not to be fulfilled. He wrote before the news of the death of Antiochus reached Jerusalem. Because 168 BCE is both the date of the battle of Pydna, which made the Romans the undisputed masters of the Mediterranean world for at least five centuries, and the date at which the Jews of Jerusalem rebelled against Antiochus, who had plundered the Temple of Jerusalem the year before, it is one of the few important historical dates Jews have in common with other nations. Generally speaking, Jewish history goes its own way even in the matter of dates. More specifically, 168 BCE is the only important date the Jews have in common with the Romans.

Let us consider some of the implications of this simple fact. Antiochus IV was no fool, and he knew Rome from the inside. He was a son of Antiochus III whom the Romans had defeated, humiliated and deprived of a part of his kingdom. As one of the hostages whom his father had to send to Rome in 189 or 188 BCE after his defeat, he was kept in Rome for about ten years. It would be surprising if Antiochus

231

had not learned to converse in Latin: it was the custom of aristocratic Romans to open their houses to foreign princes or aristocratic hostages. Later he thanked the Roman aristocrats for their hospitality. In about 178 BCE he was released and spent some time in Athens (as we now know from an inscription, *Hesperia* 51, 1982, p. 61). In 175 BCE he was ready to become King of Syria in succession to his elder brother Seleucus IV, who had been assassinated. He kept quiet for about five years—or rather worked to build up his reputation, through gifts to Greek cities and sanctuaries for the cult of the gods, as Polybius duly remarked (26.1.10). About the year 170 BCE Syria and Egypt entered into one of those periodic wars between themselves to which they were accustomed. They had no fear that the Romans would seriously object: since 171 BCE, Rome had been engaged in a new war with Macedonia which was then ruled by Perseus. Egypt and Syria were free to fight each other as much as they could and liked. In 169 Antiochus appeared to be the winner. But he miscalculated both the endurance of his enemies in Egypt and the foreseeable length of the Macedonian war in which the Romans were involved. He attempted to overrun the whole of Egypt, that is, he went beyond the ordinary limits of the conflicts between Seleucids and Ptolemies, which usually concerned territorial claims at the borders. As it happened, the Egyptian resistance increased; Antiochus did not succeed in conquering Egypt in 169 and had to mobilize greater forces for operations by land and sea in 168. This time he was more successful and headed for Alexandria. But he was too late.

On 22 June 168 the Roman army commanded by L. Aemilius Paulus smashed the Macedonians on the field of Pydna in about one hour of fighting and put an end to the Macedonian Kingdom. A few weeks later the Roman legate C. Popilius Laenas, supported by a fleet, reached Antiochus on the outskirts of Alexandria and ordered him out of Egypt. The scene is described by Livy 45.12 and cannot be improved upon. Popilius the Roman traced a circle round the spot where Antiochus the King was standing and told him not to cross the circle before he had signified acceptance of the Roman ultimatum. Such was the way Rome could treat kings after the battle of Pydna. Egypt, or at least the dynasty of the Ptolemies, was saved by Rome from Antiochus.

The Ptolemies of Egypt had ruled Judaea until 198 with considerable understanding of their Jewish subjects, many of whom found employment in the Ptolemaic army. In 168 the Ptolemies still had followers in Palestine. It is therefore not by chance that one of the first, if not the very first, to register the Roman intervention in Egypt was the compiler of the present Book of Daniel. In the form of prophecy he says: 'For ships of Kittim [that is, of Rome] shall come against him [that is, Antiochus], and he shall be afraid and withdraw and shall turn back and be enraged and take action against the holy covenant. He shall turn back and give heed to those who forsake the holy covenant' (11:30). In this contorted sentence, which was meant to be taken as a prophecy, but was a short summary of what had just happened, the compiler of the Book of Daniel caught the essential connection between the invasion of Egypt by Antiochus, the intervention of the Romans and the events in Judaea in the year 168.

We know of course of the main events in Judaea during those years chiefly from the First and the Second Books of Maccabees. Ferment in Judaea had started a few years before 168, and Antiochus IV had been behind it. He had *de facto* appointed two High Priests in succession to suit his tastes and needs. First Jason, then Menelaos, who ousted Jason, had agreed to increase the tribute they owed to Syria. Jason had also agreed to a moderate Hellenization of the Jewish style of life in Jerusalem. He had introduced into the city a Greek gymnasium which would provide the opportunity for young Jews to behave, or misbehave, like young Greeks. The Hellenization was made even more formal by the introduction of some sort of legal distinction within the population of Jerusalem. A group of citizens was recognized as 'Antiochenes'. The fact is stated in II Maccabees (ch. 4), but the legal implications are obscure to us. It is the hypothesis of Jonathan Goldstein, the author of the most elaborate recent commentary on the Books of Maccabees in the Anchor Bible, that Antiochus IV had been persuaded by his experience in Rome to introduce into the Kingdom of Syria an equivalent of Roman citizenship under the name of Antiochene citizenship. This hypothesis is very attractive, but, I am afraid, without sufficient foundation. The structure of the Roman State was too different. Antiochus IV, as I have said, was anxious to be a champion of Greek religion and institutions and had found limited support among some upper-class Jews, even those of the priestly condition. But in those years Antiochus' prevailing need was for money for his war with Egypt. In 169, before marching into Egypt, he plundered the Temple of Jerusalem and took away treasures. Temples of the Near East, before and after Antiochus IV, were used to being plundered by kings in need of funds. Later pagan writers added religious details to this particular plunder. According to Diodorus 34.1 Antiochus found in the Temple a statue of Moses riding a donkey—one of the versions of the story that the Jews worshipped a donkey.

In the following year, in 168, when Antiochus had to vacate Egypt in haste, the Jews of Jerusalem were among those who rebelled against him. This is not surprising. More surprisingly, the leader of the rebellion was the ex-High Priest Jason who had been an ally of

Antiochus a few years earlier in the introduction of the gymnasium. Incidentally, the date for this rebellion (168 BCE) is made certain by II Maccabees 5:1–5, which puts it at the time of the second expedition of Antiochus against Egypt. The Syrian answer to the Jewish rebellion was to occupy Jerusalem with royal troops. Looting and the sale of women and children as slaves followed. The walls of Jerusalem were razed; a fortress was built for the Syrian garrison and for those Jews who had remained faithful to Antiochus. The latter included the High Priest Menelaos.

A year later, in 167, according to I Maccabees 1:44ff., Jewish sacrifices, circumcision, Sabbath and festivals were prohibited by Antiochus' decree, and copies of the Torah were burned. Later in December of the same year what Daniel called the 'abomination of desolation' was introduced. Jews were compelled to offer pagan sacrifices. The Jewish Temple was now turned into a temple of Zeus Olympios, just as the Samaritan sanctuary of Mount Gerizim was turned into the temple of another variety of Zeus, Zeus Xenios. The difference, however, was that the Samaritans had apparently asked for the conversion of their temple (II Macc. 6:1ff. compared with Josephus, *Antiquities* 12, 257ff.).

It does not matter very much whether the new cult of Zeus Olympios which replaced the cult of Yahweh was meant to be pure Greek or Cananaean or syncretistic. The Jewish answer was given by Mattathias, a minor priest resident at Modin (east of Lydda) who, according to I Macc. 2:22ff., proclaimed in public: 'We will not obey the command of this king . . . Follow me . . . every one who is zealous for the Torah.' Judas Maccabaeus, the son of Mattathias, became the leader of the rebels, supported by his brothers, two of whom, Jonathan and Simon, were to be his successors. Less than three years later, in March 164, Antiochus IV had to acknowledge defeat and put an end to the persecution of the Jewish cult. On the twenty-fifth day of Kislev (about 15 December) 164 the daily sacrifice was offered again to Yahweh in the Temple in the traditional way. And Jews are still celebrating in the Hanukkah festival the rededication of the Temple on that day.

We are simply unable to say what passed through the mind of Antiochus IV when he embarked on a religious persecution which was unheard-of in the world of Greeks and Romans. Prohibition of foreign cults was well-known to them but prohibition of native cults was as yet unknown, though the Romans later interfered with provincial cults such as Druidic practices in Gaul and Britain. Forced conversion, which was what was demanded of the Jews in 167, did not make sense in classical paganism. Nor is the matter helped by a strange, isolated paragraph in I Macc. 1:41–3, according to which the decision of Antiochus IV about the Jews was part of a more general invitation to all the subjects of his Kingdom to become 'one people' and to abandon their own customs. To others besides Jews and Samaritans, what could such an invitation mean? But if we cannot understand Antiochus IV, we cannot separate the persecution of the Jews from his humiliation in Egypt. In its turn the rebellion of the Jews in 168 cannot be separated from the intervention of the Romans in Egypt. The Jews, or at least many of the Jews of Palestine, rejoiced at the Roman intervention against Antiochus in Egypt and immediately rebelled against him and the Syrians. So much is evident from the facts themselves. The Maccabaean rebellion is understandable only within the context of the humiliation of Antiochus by the Romans. The connection of the Roman victory at Pydna with the insurrection by Judas Maccabaeus and his followers is self-evident.

We are therefore entitled to go further and to ask ourselves whether in 168 the anti-Syrian Jews had already established contacts with the Romans or at least meant to establish contacts in the near future. We know of course that the First Book of Maccabees solemnly and pointedly presents Judas Maccabaeus seeking the alliance with the Romans only in 161 BCE, when he had (or appeared to have) established his power through his own military success. According to I Maccabees, the year 161 was memorable for the Jewish discovery of the Romans. Indeed there is no question (and we shall return to this point) that for the author of I Maccabees (at whatever moment he wrote), Rome is still a vaguely mythical, idealized, nation about which he knows very little. The author of I Maccabees was under the impression that there was only one consul a year in Rome and that the Senate met there every day. On the other hand the Romans act from afar with uncanny effectiveness: 'Those whom they wish to help and to make kings, they make kings, and those whom they wish, they depose; and they have been greatly exalted.' The picture we get from I Maccabees is of an idealized Judas Maccabaeus approaching an idealized Roman nation at the right moment, 161 BCE.

Something more prosaic is, however, suggested by II Maccabees, which, though informed about the alliance of Judas in 161, has a strange and undoubtedly authentic document indicating that Romans and Jews were already collaborating three years earlier, in 164, when Antiochus IV was still alive and the traditional cult of Yahweh had not yet been re-established in the Temple of Jerusalem.

The Second Book of Maccabees ch. 11 collects four documents belonging to the dealings between Jews and Syrians before and immediately after the death of Antiochus IV in 164. The strangest of these four texts is a letter from two Roman ambassadors to the people of the Jews in 164, before the death of Antiochus IV. From this letter, which we have no serious reason to consider forged by either Jews, Syrians or Romans, it is apparent that the two Roman legates acted as mediators, on behalf of the Jews, between them and the Syrian government. The operative words are: 'As for the concessions granted to you by Lysias the kinsman of the king, we endorse them. As regards the points he decided to refer to the king, send someone immediately after you have considered them, so that we may present our views as befits your interests, for we are now on our way to Antioch' (trans. J. A. Goldstein). This letter indicates that four years after 168 BCE the Jews already had friendly relations with the Romans and were interested in being protected by them. There is no sign that the letter represents the first exchange between Romans and Jews. The impression it gives is that diplomatic relations had existed before. We are entitled to wonder whether Kittim-Rome was not in contact with Judaea in 168, or even before 168. What is surprising is that I Maccabees does not seem to know anything about the Roman mediation between the Jews and Antiochus IV in 164. The First Book of Maccabees evidently presupposes that the relations between the Romans and the Jews started only in 161 and that the initiative had come from Judas Maccabaeus. We cannot of course say whether this omission was due to ignorance or to design. The result was in any case that the relationship between Jews and Romans appeared in a different light. It had not started in a moment of dire depression; it was the merit of victorious Judas Maccabaeus; and it reflected his bold intiative. The Second Book of Maccabees, which no longer deals with the events of 161–160, gives at least a hint that the first contacts between Romans and Jews belong in 164 BCE or earlier. This had an element of paradox. The two ambassadors despatched to Rome by Judas Maccabaeus in 161 were called Eupolemus and Jason. The names are identical with the names of two Jewish historians in Greek, Eupolemus the historian of the Jewish kings and Jason the author of the history of the Jewish rebellion of which II Maccabees is a summary. Judas Maccabaeus seems to have chosen for the embassy two learned historians who knew their history and their Greek. If so, we have to conclude that when one of these ambassadors, Jason, came to write his history he inserted into it a document which he could not ignore, the text of the letter of the two Roman ambassadors in 164 BCE. If, as seems very probable, Jason the ambassador was Jason the historian, he must have known that the Maccabaean resistance to Antiochus was encouraged by the Romans, if not at the very beginning, certainly within two or three years. The information given by II Maccabees about the early relations between the Jews and the Romans—information which contradicts the account in I Maccabees—seems to come from one of the two Jewish ambassadors who went to Rome on behalf of Judas Maccabaeus. What could be more reliable?

II

To realize what all this implied from the Roman point of view, we must turn to apparently unrelated aspects of the religious situation in Rome.

Cybelis or Cybele was an Oriental goddess who became known to the Greeks approximately from the seventh century BCE. Her name is obviously identical with the goddess Kubala of Carchemish who in the second millennium BCE was also worshipped in the Assyrian trade post of Canis in Cappadocia and was known in Ugarit. Cybele was adopted by the Phrygians with a central cult in the city of Pessinus. From Phrygia the cult probably passed to Lydia (Sardis) and to the Hellenic cities of Asia Minor and Europe. In the Hellenistic period Ilium (the new Troy) and Pergamum were centres of her cult. Relations between the temple-state of Pessinus and the King of Pergamum are documented in the second century BCE. At least in the Hellenistic period and in Greek places the cult of Cybele had mystic, initiatory, elements.

Cybele is often represented standing or sitting between two lions (or two leopards). She is also represented with a lion on her lap or accompanied by two musicians. She was often associated with mountains and caves and was supposed to protect from illness, and generally to help, mothers and children. Oracles and divination were connected with her. A variety of Mother Goddess, she was not easily distinguishable, especially in Greek places, from analogous goddesses such as Rhea and Demeter. One of her epithets was 'Great Mother', and as *Magna Mater* she was officially received in Rome about 204 BCE. One of the disturbing features of this Great Mother was that in many places, but even there not necessarily at all periods, her cult was combined with that of Attis. According to a prestigious version of the myth collected by Ovid in his *Fasti* IV (223 ff.), Attis had been loved by Cybele and had been unfaithful to her. In an access of insanity he castrated himself and died. The resurrection of Attis is explicitly stated by Firmicus Maternus, *De Errore Profanarum Religionum* 3, in the fourth century CE: it is, however, doubtful whether resurrection played a part in the actual cult. In places (but not necessarily in all places) where Cybele and Attis were associated in the cult, devotees known as *galli* castrated themselves in a frenzy and fulfilled special, but subordinate, functions in the cult.

They contributed much to the dancing, the healing and the divining. Some of the *galli* lived as itinerant beggars.

This was the cult of the Magna Mater which was imported from Pessinus in Phrygia to Rome in 204 BCE, apparently with the mediation of the King of Pergamum. The decision was taken by the Roman government at a time of religious agitations and consequent pronouncements from the Sibylline books. It was approved by Apollo's oracle at Delphi and connected with the Trojan origins of Rome. Members of the most prominent *gentes* (such as the Cornelii, the Valerii and the Claudii) patronized the transfer. Magna Mater was given a temple on the Palatine—an exceptional honour for a foreign cult. The temple was dedicated in 191 BCE. An annual festival called *Megalesia* was instituted which included theatrical performances (4–10 April). Banquets, which amounted to aristocratic dinner parties, were connected with the festival. Cicero in *De Senectute* 13.45 presents the severe Cato, who had been a quaestor precisely in 204, as taking part in these aristocratic entertainments. From Rome and Italy the cult spread to the provinces. In so far as it became connected with games and theatrical performances, it favoured Hellenization, rather than Orientalization.

But we must again ask our question: Did the aristocratic groups which supported the new cult know what they were doing? And if they knew, what were they up to?

The cult implied the reception of a black stone, a meteorite, as the chief object of worship (though there was also a female cult-image). It had orgiastic features and encouraged mendicity. It involved, as I said, the association of the cult of Cybele with that of Attis, though the earliest sources (including Ovid in the *Fasti*) are reticent on this point. A great quantity of images of Attis was found by Italian archaeologists in the precincts of the temple on the Palatine and dated to the second and first centuries BCE (cf. P. Romanelli, *Monumenti Antichi dell'Accad. dei Lincei* 46, 1963, 202–330). What counts for more, castrated *galli* soon appear as followers of Cybele in Rome. In the organization of the cult they seem to have been subordinated to a priest and priestess who originally came from Phrygia, but later must have been chosen in Rome. The share of Attis in the cult certainly increased with time and seems to have contributed in the imperial age to giving the whole cult a more mystic form with promises of salvation for the initiated. The ceremony of the *taurobolium*, a sort of baptism with the blood of an ox, came to be associated with this cult at least from the second century CE.

Opposition to the cult was certainly quick to develop because according to a not very clear passage of Dionysius of Halicarnassus, *Roman Antiquites* 2.19.5, which refers to the situation in the first century BCE, the Roman Senate prohibited the participation of Roman citizens in certain ceremonies of the cult of Cybele. We also happen to know from Plutarch, *Life of Marius* 17.5, that when at the time of the war of Marius against the Cimbri a priest of the Magna Mater came all the way from Phrygia to bring an oracle favourable to the Romans, he was not well-received. We also have fragments of a satire against the cult by Varro, a contemporary of Caesar and the greatest authority on Roman religion. The mere fact that Greek always remained the official language of the cult indicates the limits of its assimilation to Roman religion.

Yet Roman citizens act as priests of Cybele during the Empire, and a Roman citizen, as *archigallus*, appears to control the cult in Rome. Fraternities and corporations, such as the *dendrophori*, helping in the ceremonies of this cult became influential clubs in the cities. The share of Attis in the cult was perhaps officially recognized for the first time by the conservative Emperor Claudius I in the first century CE. In the fourth century the cult of Cybele was conspicuously displayed by that part of the Roman aristocracy which had not been converted to Christianity. As late as the fifth century the philosopher Proclus wrote a book, now lost, on Cybele. Anyone who can make complete sense of this story will have understood better than I do the intellectual contacts of the Romans with the East via Greece.

III

We may turn to another bizarre story which is more restricted in time and less ambiguous, at least as far as the Roman ruling class is concerned. The affair of the Bacchanalia in 186 BCE is the best example of the crude reaction of the Roman ruling class to new religious ceremonies. It was not even a question of a new cult. Livy, in Book XXXIX, 8ff., devoted as much space to it as he usually gave to the most important political and military events. Stylistically these are splendid pages. An inscription (*Corpus Inscriptionum Latinarum* I.2.581) substantially confirms Livy's account at least in its legal aspects. What Livy tells us is that in about 186 BCE a new wave of the cult of Dionysos-Bacchus reached Rome and appeared quite different from the cult of Bacchus or Liber (to use the Latin equivalent which everybody knew). Through information received from an unfortunate woman, previously a slave, one of the consuls of 186 BCE discovered that these new fashionable Bacchic rites were spreading in Rome and more generally in Italy. The fact that persons of both sexes were holding ceremonies in secret created the worst suspicions in the minds of the consul and his advisers: sexual immorality, frauds, even murders were attributed to the worshippers, God knows on what evidence. Men who with fanatical tossings of their bodies were uttering prophecies, matrons in the dress of Bacchantes, with dishevelled hair and carrying blazing torches—this was quite enough to warrant the conclusion that the State was in danger and to give rise to a persecution which spread throughout Italy. If we are to believe Livy, 'more were killed than were thrown into prison. The cult of Bacchus was reduced to minimal proportions in Italy'. Here we have, at a distance of about fifteen years from the introduction of the Magna Mater with her cohort of self-castrating *galli*, the appearance of a new, more mystic, variety of an old cult; and that is sufficient to produce a savage reaction. Was that reaction an implicit confession that the assimilation of the Magna Mater had been a bad idea and that the mistake should not be repeated?

Again, I do not know. But we can say something about the origins of this new wave of Dionysiac religious emotions, and we can at the same time observe that in another Mediterranean country the reaction of the authorities had been just the reverse of that of the Roman authorities. The new Bacchic mysteries impressed Egypt perhaps twenty or twenty-five years before these Roman events, during the reign of Ptolemy IV Philopator, that is, between 222 and 204 BCE. As the Jews were involved, negatively so to speak, the main evidence is in the so-called Third Book of Maccabees.

But there is documentary confirmation in a papyrus containing some regulations about the cult of Dionysos enacted by Ptolemy Philopator (this is the so-called Schubart papyrus published in *Berl. Griech. Urk.* VI., 1211 = S.B. 7266). And there is further evidence of Ptolemy's devotion to Dionysos, for example the fragments by Satyrus on the demes of Alexandria. We shall have to return to the Third Book of Maccabees in more detail later on, for reasons which will become apparent. For the moment it is enough to recall that according to this book the Jews of Egypt were asked to join the mysteries of Dionysos in exchange for Alexandrian citizenship. Few Jews were prepared to comply with the King's request. Most Jews refused and were persecuted. To make them recognizable as obstinate Jews, their bodies were branded with Dionysiac symbols. What seems certain is that Ptolemy both encouraged Bacchic associations and tried to control them. What was encouraged by a king in Egypt was furiously opposed in Rome a few decades later.

The matter could be left at that if there were not some signs that in Rome and elsewhere the cult of Dionysos was associated or perhaps identified with the cult of Yahweh, notwithstanding the fact that, at least according to the Third Book of Maccabees, the Jews of Egypt had been the victims of a persecution in the name of Dionysos. Tacitus,

Histories V.5 (the excursus on the Jews), is acquainted with this identification of Yahweh with Dionysos or Liber, and Plutarch has a discussion of this identification in *Table Talk* (*Quaestiones Conviviales*) IV.6. The strangest indication of this tendency to identify the Jews as worshippers of some kind of Bacchus is to be found in a Roman coin of 55 BCE. A description and an illustration of the coin can be found in M. H. Crawford, *Roman Republican Coinage*, 1974, I, pp. 454f. (no.431); II, pl. LII, 7. The coin was struck under the name of the *aedilis curulis* A. Plautius of 55 BCE. The coin, a denarius, refers on the obverse to the festival of the Magna Mater for which A. Plautius, as *aedilis curulis*, was responsible. The reverse type shows a camel and a kneeling human figure with an olive branch in his hand, a scene best interpreted as the surrender of an Oriental ruler to the Romans. As we are in the years of the Roman occupation of Syria by Pompey and the end of the Seleucid state, there is no dearth of Oriental petty rulers to whom the scene could refer. What is surprising, however, is the inscription which is meant to clarify the scene: *Bacchius Iudaeus*.

I shall spare readers the heated discussions about these two words. We happen to know from Flavius Josephus (*Ant.* 14.39) that one of the petty rulers beheaded by Pompey in 63 in his mopping-up operations was a Dionysius of Tripolis in Lebanon. Josephus does not say that he was a Jew, but he may have been, with his name translated into Bacchus for the benefit of the Romans. Everything is possible. What we really have to explain, however, is why a Roman coin struck to celebrate the festival of the Magna Mater in Rome in 55 BCE indulged on the reverse in this display of a surrendering Bacchius Iudaeus. Any contemporary giving a thought to it would have taken the allusion to be to a follower of Bacchus of the Jewish variety who surrendered to the Romans while the Magna Mater was duly worshipped by the same Romans. Of course, it is not superfluous to ask whether any ordinary Roman ever looked at the symbols on his coins; but the men who struck the coins must have had some ideas in their heads. We are left to wonder whether some association between the cult of Dionysos and the cult of the Jewish God was current in Rome and, if so, when this association was first created. True enough, the years between 63 and 55 BCE had meant a momentous change for the worse in the relations between Romans and Jews. After the reduction of Syria to a Roman province, the Jews had become useless to the Romans. Aristobulus II, the Jewish High Priest, was brought to Rome as a prisoner by Pompey to adorn his triumph over Judaea. He was still a prisoner in Rome in 49, when he was liberated by Caesar and assassinated by Pompey's followers. However, there are signs that trouble and misconceptions about Judaism and the Jews began much earlier in Rome, even in the years in which the Romans were still taking the Jews seriously as allies in their relations with Syria. Let us go back to two episodes, one of which seems to belong in the year 142 BCE and the other, more famous, in 139.

Whatever may have been the treaty between Jews and Romans which Judas Maccabaeus arranged in 161 BCE, his death in 160 apparently produced an interrruption of diplomatic relations between Rome and the Jews. Only in 143 BCE did Jonathan Maccabaeus send an embassy to Rome, as I Maccabees says (12:1), to renew 'ties of friendship and alliance' with the Romans. Not much later Jonathan was captured and slain by the Syrians. His brother and successor Simon had to turn again to the Romans for support. Our evidence is a circular letter by a Roman consul called only by his first name, Lucius, to the kings of Egypt, Syria, Parthia and Cappadocia as well as to Greek cities like Sparta. I Maccabees 15:15ff., which reports the letter, seems to place it at about 139 BCE. In fact neither of the Roman consuls of 139 BCE was called Lucius, but a Lucius Caecilius Metellus was consul in 142 BCE. This letter by consul Lucius to Oriental kings and Greek cities not only fulfils the purpose of telling them that the Romans count the Jews among their friends and allies, but requests the recipients of the letter to deliver to Simon, the ruler of Judaea, any traitor who may have escaped from Judaea to their territories. In other words, in about 142 BCE the Romans were helping Simon and his Jews to obtain extradition of any of their enemies who had taken refuge in foreign countries.

So far so good. But according to a famous and controversial passage of the Roman compiler Valerius Maximus of the first century CE, in the year 139 BCE the *praetor peregrinus* Cn. Cornelius Scipio Hispalus, who was responsible for relations between Romans and foreigners in Rome, ordered Chaldeans and Jews out of Rome within ten days (Val. Max. 1.3.2.). The Chaldeans were accused, as we might expect, of cheating the Romans by fallacious interpretations of the stars: they were the specialists in astrology. The Jews were accused in their turn of corrupting the customs of the Romans by the introduction of a cult which is described as that of Jupiter Sabazius. I must add that the text is not preserved in the original, but in two different versions of the summary of Valerius Maximus made by Julius Paris in the fourth century CE and in a third version to be found in another summary of Valerius by Nepotianus of the fifth century CE. Anyone who wants to read an account of the textual situation of this passage of Valerius Maximus may turn to a paper by E. M. Lane in *Journ. Rom. St.* 69, 1979, 34–8, though I would not recommend the conclusions drawn by Professor Lane. Like the majority of scholars, I take it that Valerius Maximus wrote: '*Iudaeos qui Sabazi Iovis cultu Romanos inficere mores conati erant repetere domos suas coegit.*' The meaning, I repeat, is that the

Jews who tried to spread the cult of Jupiter Sabazius in Rome were compelled to leave the city.

Sabazius was a mystery god of Phrygian origin who was already well known in Athens in the fifth century BCE, as Aristophanes shows. He was often identified with Dionysos or Bacchus, but in the Hellenistic period we find him occasionally identified with Zeus or Jupiter, for instance in an inscription from Pergamum which belongs in 135 BCE and implies that this identification has been in existence for some time (W. H. Dittenberger, *Orientis Graeci Inscriptiones Selectae*, no. 331). It is not surprising, therefore, that our text of Valerius Maximus should speak of the spreading of the cult of Jupiter Sabazius in Rome in 139 BCE, four years before the same cult turns up at Pergamum which in those years had close relations with Rome. What is more surprising is that Jews should be accused of spreading the cult of Jupiter Sabazius. The Jews worshipped Yahweh Sabaoth, Yahweh the god of hosts, not Jupiter Sabazius.

It is just possible that Valerius Maximus or his source simply confused the Jewish worshippers of Yahweh with the worshippers of Jupiter or Zeus Sabazius, and that the edict of the *praetor peregrinus* had originally nothing to do with the Jews. But I should not like to believe that either Valerius Maximus or his source added the word Iudaeos, 'Jews', to a praetorian edict which did not contain it. It is better to start from the assumption that Valerius Maximus is a reliable witness. What we have still to consider are the implications of this identification or confusion of the Jews in Rome—or of certain Jews in Rome—with the worshippers of Jupiter Sabazius.

There are two possible alternative explanations of the statement by Valerius Maximus if we take it at its face value. One interpretation is that some or many Jews in Rome had mixed up their ancestral cult of Yahweh Sabaoth with the cult of Jupiter Sabazius and were making propaganda for this mixture. One might add that the name of Sabbath, the weekly festival for which the Jews were famous, may have added to the confusion. Clubs of *Sabbatistai*, evidently pagans who celebrated the Jewish Sabbath, are known in various places of Asia Minor (M. P. Nilsson, *Geschichte der griechischen Religion*, vol. 2, 2nd edn 1961, p. 666). On this hypothesis syncretistic Jews attracted the attention of the *praetor peregrinus* and probably involved in their own condemnation the Jews who knew nothing of Jupiter Sabazius, yet had to share the expulsion from Rome. It would indeed be difficult to expect that a Roman magistrate, acting in Rome in the way we know Roman magistrates to have acted towards foreigners, would try to separate good Jews who were satisfied with Yahweh Sabaoth from bad Jews who mixed up Yahweh Sabaoth with Jupiter Sabazius. But another interpretation has at least to be taken into account. We have seen that some time before, perhaps in 142 BCE, the Romans were helping the Jews of Palestine to obtain extradition of their enemies. It is not inconceivable that Simon, as a High Priest in Judaea, was in favour of the expulsion from Rome of bad Jews who confused Yahweh Sabaoth with Jupiter Sabazius and made propaganda for this confusion. In this interpretation, the expulsion of the bad Jews from Rome might be taken as complementary to the extradition of the bad Jews from other countries. Both measures might have been requested by Simon and agreed to by the Romans.

I do not want to go further in this historical novel. We do not know what exactly happened in Rome in 139 BCE except that Chaldeans and Jews were expelled. But everything that happened in Rome in connection with the so-called Oriental cults between the introduction of the cult of Magna Mater in 204 BCE and the reaction of 139 BCE to the cult of Jupiter Sabazius, passing through the repression of the Bacchanalia in 186 BCE, indicates conflicts of motives and lack of clarity in the Roman ruling class, which was suspicious of novelties from remote territories and alert to the intellectual superiority of Hellenistic culture. To round off this panorama, we may take into consideration two rather improbable texts. One is the Third Book of Maccabees which we have already used, but which, examined in itself, shows a strange self-assertion of the Egyptian Jews in the late second and early first centuries BCE. This self-assertion, while confirming the solidarity of the Jews of Egypt with the Jews of Palestine, explicitly emphasizes the loyalty of the Egyptian Jews to the Ptolemaic regime of Egypt, provided that their position remains safe in Egyptian society. The other text, which comes from anti-Roman Persians, is Hystaspes' prophecy, a text which for centuries symbolized Persian, and therefore Parthian, opposition to Rome. It reminds us that from the beginning of the first century BCE, and even more after the absorption of Syria, the Romans had to reckon with Parthia and its inheritance of Persian political and religious ambitions. By associating these two texts we are also reminding ourselves that Jews, especially at the end of the first century BCE and in the first century CE, were ready to see in the Parthians a desirable alternative to Roman rule. We cannot separate, at least for that period, the Parthians from the Jews; and therefore we must expect the Romans to put together Jews and Parthians in their emotional reactions to the Eastern world. The really obscure point is that the Jews were the allies of the Romans, but something troubled the Romans about Jewish religion.

English Charity and Jewish Qualms:
The Rescue of the Ashkenazi Community
of Seventeenth-Century Jerusalem

David S. Katz

THE notion that 'charity shall cover the multitude of sins' has never
been part of the Jewish tradition. On the contrary, ever since the days
of the Golden Calf the evil effects of living off others have been plainly
seen, even if they have not always been a sufficient deterrent to
accepting alms uncritically. Both the moral and practical dilemmas
involved in *tseddakah* (charity) are instructively illustrated by the
reaction of the Jews of Jerusalem to the efforts of English and Dutch
Christians to save the Ashkenazi community there from financial ruin
and physical destruction during the middle years of the seventeenth
century. At the centre of the row was Rabbi Jacob Hagiz, the leading
scholarly figure of his day in Jerusalem, who was called upon to rule on
whether Jews could in good faith accept charity from Christians, even
those who hoped thereby to bring about their conversion. By the time
Rabbi Hagiz made his decision he was well qualified to speak on the
question, for he was among those who sent Sabbatai Sevi to Cairo in
1663 to raise money on behalf of his own Sephardi community seven
years after the European Christians had sent their own charitable
offering to the Ashkenazim. 'He left a *shaliah* (messenger) and returned
a *mashiah* (messiah),' went the joke in Jerusalem, for it was during this
journey to Egypt that Sabbatai Sevi became convinced of his divine
mission. So the entire question of extra-communal charity was a painful
one indeed by the time that Rabbi Hagiz was forced to make a
definitive statement on the issue.

I

The desperate plight of the Ashkenazi Jews of Jerusalem in the later
1650s was in some sense of their own making. For very many years
they had obsessively guarded their own isolation among the Jews of

that city, and indeed were the only *edah* that was organized as a separate congregation and kept separate institutions. Although they did agree to be represented before the Muslims by the Sephardi *parnassim* and patronized Sephardi ritual slaughterhouses, the Ashkenazim insisted on managing their own financial affairs: they sent their own *shelichim* abroad and ruled that all the money collected by this means would be used for Ashkenazi needs alone. Certainly by the end of the sixteenth century they had their own synagogue for Ashkenazim only, in a Jewish community at Jerusalem that at this time probably did not exceed five hundred souls.[1]

Charitable contributions from abroad, meanwhile, came to occupy a position of ever-increasing importance as the debts owed by the Jewish community as a whole to the Muslim authorities increased. The Jews of Jerusalem were regarded as a single entity by the Muslims, but in any case the total burden of debt skyrocketed, especially during the 1590s. Even more worrying, in accordance with Muslim law, the heads of the Jewish community were forced to contract the loans in their own names, with all the attendant dangers. Apart from charity received from the Jews of Constantinople and elsewhere, in Jerusalem there was no choice but to take on even larger loans from other Muslims in order to pay that which was owed to the authorities. As a result of this necessity to take out many small loans from different people to cover the increasing debt owed to the *cadi*, the amount borrowed needed to be even higher. The fact that the loans had been contracted in the first place to make payments to the local rulers was not legally relevant when the time came to compensate the numerous small creditors. By 1597 these obligataions simply could not be met, and for three successive years the creditors would appeal to the *cadi*, who in turn imprisoned the leaders of the Jewish community until a partial settlement was reached. The distribution of the debt within the Jewish community was by no means the occasion for harmonious agreement, and cases of outright fraud and deception among Jews are recorded, itself an indication of the scale of the problem. In such a difficult situation, charitable aid from abroad became even more critical.[2]

The Muslims made no distinction between Sephardi and Ashkenazi in levying the financial burdens, but not so the Jews. The Ashkenazi system of independent charity worked well for a number of years, thanks to the Jewish communities of Eastern Europe whose members sent about 30,000 Reichsdollars annually, which at least sufficed to pay taxes and ensure minimal support. The Chmielnicki massacres, the Cossack revolt, and the Swedish invasions of 1655 put an end to this comfortable arrangement. According to one contemporary report, since that time they have been in great extremity of want; insomuch, that in the year one thousand six hundred fifty five, four hundred of their widdows were famished to death, and the taxes laid upon them by the Turks, being rigorously exacted, they were haled into prison, their Synagogues were shut up, their Rabbi's and Elders beaten and cruelly used.[3]

The debts to the Muslims grew to 15,000 Reichsdollars, and would have continued indefinitely were it not for the intervention of the Sanjak Bey (District Governor), who proposed to 'buy' the debts by means of supplying various goods to their creditors. In return, the Jews agreed to pay him 7000 Reichsdollars within two years without interest, on the understanding that failure to do so would incur the penalty of slavery. Some money was immediately exchanged to settle existing obligations.[4]

By 1655, then, the Ashkenazi Jews of Jeruslam 'were brought', according to another account, 'into great extremity, not only of Famine and nakednesse . . . but also by the imprisonment and scourgings of their Elders and Rabbyes, by their Creditors'.[5] The Ashkenazim decided to send two of their men to Europe to enlist the support of their more fortunate brethren. One of these was Rabbi Nathan Shapira, 'a man of great learning, and skill in their *Cabala*, and of a very pious, holy and humble disposition'.[6] No further information whatsoever exists concerning the second ambassador; Rabbi Nathan Shapira, however, was one of the most important emissaries of the Jews of Palestine during the seventeenth century.[7] He first journeyed to Italy, and there published in 1655 a book entitled *Tuv ha-Aretz* (The Goodness of the [Holy] Land), with the aim of relating to mankind the holiness of Palestine according to the *kabbalah*.[8] From Italy, Rabbi Nathan travelled to Hamburg, where it was noted in the community records that 'he showed us letters in which was described the great distress in Jerusalem as a result of the lack of financial support from Poland, and it was decided to pay him in Venice one hundred Reichsdollars'.[9]

It appears that Rabbi Nathan Shapira's next stop was Amsterdam, where he turned to the famous Rabbi Menasseh ben Israel for help in rescuing the Ashkenazi Jews of Jerusalem. Certainly Menasseh knew of their plight by December 1655, for in the course of his discussions with Oliver Cromwell about the readmission of the Jews to England, he showed him letters from Jerusalem to 'other Jews in *Germany*, and *Holland, &c:* sent thither by the hand of *R. Nathan Stephira* their Messenger'. Menasseh's letters told of the 'very *great streighs*' of the Jews in Poland, Lithuania and Prussia due to the Swedish wars, as a result of which the 'yearly Alms to the poor Jewes (of the *Germane* Synagogue) at *Jerusalem* hath ceased; and of 700 Widows, and poor Jews there, about four hundred have been famished, as a Letter from *Jerusalem* to their friends relates'.[10]

Rabbi Nathan Shapira was probably also the original source of the accounts of the Eastern European Jews which appeared in the London press during the Whitehall Conference, called by Oliver Cromwell in December 1655 to discuss the question of Jewish readmission. In one number it was reported that the Jews of Poland had presented a petition to the Emperor for protection, as they had 'been soundly pillaged, and many massacred in *Poland*'.[11] In a later issue it was reported that many Jews had come to Hamburg, having been 'ruinated and plundred of all their Goods in Poland'.[12] At the same time, a news-sheet announced the impending visit to Vienna of the 'Patriarch or Generall of the Jewes' from Jerusalem connected with the appearance of an 'unknown starr very bright going from the East towards the North'.[13]

Menasseh ben Israel's mission to England understandably generated a great deal of interest in Jews and Jewish affairs among those who had not turned their attention to this subject before.[14] For those Englishmen who had already been intrigued by the Jews and the divine role which had been ordained for them, the arrival of Menasseh helped to focus their interest on the topics that the rabbi emphasized in the course of his discussions, including the plight of the Ashkenazi Jews of Jerusalem. Chief among these men was Henry Jessey (1601–63), one of the founders of the Baptist movement, who had been in correspondence with Menasseh since at least 1649.[15] Menasseh held Jessey to be a 'worthy Christian Minister', and Jessey repaid the compliment by publishing a sympathetic narrative of the Whitehall Conference.[16] Jessey would throughout his life hold fast to his millenarian vision of the divine plan, and would emphasize the part that the Jews had to play in it. Menasseh's version of R. Nathan Shapira's account of the suffering of the Jerusalem Ashkenazim gave Jessey and his fellow philo-Semites the opportunity to put their support for the Children of Israel into practice.

From Menasseh ben Israel's point of view, the Whitehall Conference ended in failure, because he was unable to extract from Cromwell any written permission which might allow the Jews to resettle legally in England. In practice, the English authorities agreed to turn a blind eye to the reality of a Jewish presence in London, and nascent Anglo-Jewry in turn behaved as if official residence was permitted, acquiring a burial ground and expanding their little synagogue in Creechurch Lane. Henry Jessey and the other Englishmen who had promoted the Jewish cause at the end of the previous year saw their political mission in England as ended, and turned their attention to other matters, including the sufferings of Jews in Jerusalem. Among those who were similarly drawn to this task were John Dury and Samuel Hartlib, those Puritan projectors who saw themselves as members of an Invisible College of mankind's benefactors.[17]

According to the information that they had received from R. Nathan Shapira via Menasseh ben Israel, those who suffered were 'the onely then *Germane Jews* at *Jerusalem*' for the Congregation of *Portugal Jews* were relieved by the Alms of their Rich Brethren in *Portugal*'. They were not aware of the fact, and perhaps would not have been concerned, that the Ashkenazi Jews of Jerusalem had themselves continuously insisted on a separation of charitable enterprises between themselves and the rest of the Jews in the town. According to Jessey's seventeenth-century biographer Edward Whiston, these Englishmen knew that the sum which Shapira had managed to collect on his travels only served to pay the interest on the Jewish debts, and that 'they had still perished, if the bowels of Christians in *Holland*, had not compassionated their State'. The Dutch Gentiles collected money among themselves in the latter part of 1655, 'and by Letters did earnestly press Mr. H.[enry] J.[essey] to further a Collection in England'.[18] Chief among these 'Christian friends' with whom Rabbi Nathan Shapira 'became accidentally acquainted', and who put him in touch with Henry Jessey, was Peter Serrarius of Amsterdam, that elusive mystical figure who himself wrote to John Dury in England reporting on Rabbi Shapira's activities and religious views.[19]

Jessey's biographer explains that he was unwilling to abuse the demonstrated goodwill of his Dutch associates until he had investigated the method by which the charity would be distributed. Jessey had the commissions of the Jerusalem elders checked with Jewish leaders in Germany and the Netherlands, who testified that they knew the hands which signed those documents, as well as the sterling characters of those men, and added that they themselves had contributed on the basis of the same information. The money itself would be transported and guaranteed by two merchants from Frankfurt who demanded a letter from the congregation in Jerusalem to the Dutch Christians, 'both in way of Receipt and Gratitude'. Jessey was sent the original Hebrew commissions, and these arrangements removed all doubts from his mind.[20] Three hundred pounds had been collected in London and dispatched to Jerusalem in 1656, and a bill of receipt and a letter of thanks returned to Jessey. Some money was also sent to Poland to help the distressed Jews there as well.[21] Jessey's aims were clearly conversionist: along with the money was sent a short proselytizing letter from the London ministers to the Jews of Jerusalem.[22] Jessey and John Dury sent a personal appeal of their own.[23]

Furthermore, as an even more personal follow-up to his efforts on behalf of Palestinian and East European Jewry during this period, Jessey had the opportunity to send along to Hartlib and Dury a Jewish refugee who 'fled fro ye persecution of Jews in Poland and that seemes more convinced y^t Jesus is the Messias, then any, y^t professeth to be a Jew, & not a Christian in Religion'. The Jew, named Meyer Isaac, 'being directed unto me by some' had extreme difficulty in conversing with Jessey as they had no language in common, but managed to convey to him that his main objection to Christianity was that 'he thinks Christians beleev their are 3 Gods & Jews confess but one'. Jessey told Hartlib and Dury that he 'should be glad if any may further him to imployment, that he may have food and raiment, & not be discouraged amongst us. But y^t he may be helped spiritually & temporally'. Jessey also reminded them that compassion to the Polish Jews would not be forgotten by the Lord on the Day of Account.[24]

In a purely financial sense, then, Rabbi Nathan's mission was a resounding success. Sent to Europe by the Ashkenazi elders of Jerusalem, he returned with the funds which were so critical to ensure the continuing existence of the community. Soon after his arrival in the Holy Land, however, certain disturbing reports began to filter in which suggested that he might have exceeded his brief. He had, after all, been sent to Europe to seek the assistance of Jews, not Christians. Rabbi Nathan argued that he had met with a flat refusal from the Spanish and Portuguese Jews of Amsterdam, who pointed out that they were the essential source of charity for the Sephardi Jews of Jerusalem, Hebron, and Safed, and could not commit themselves to the Ashkenazi community as well. They may have also heard of the Ashkenazi unwillingness during the years of plenty to share what charity they had garnered from Eastern Europe with any community in Jerusalem but their own. This defence was deemed unsatisfactory, and according to one contemporary report, 'yet nevertheless, having heard, that the Christians had assisted *Rabbi Nathan* and his Companion with a Contribution, and suspecting that they had made their application to crave their assistance from the Christians, they were intending to have disgraced him in their Synagogues'.[25]

Worse than that, rumours were beginning to circulate that Rabbi Nathan may have done an injustice to the Jews of the Holy Land in a more fundamental way. For it was 'apparent by some passages of the converse of some of our friends with their chief *Rabbi Nathan Saphira*, that the sense which their more understanding Rabbi's have of the *Messiah*, is not so far distant from the Principles of Christianity as we ordinarily have imagined'. Indeed, Rabbi Nathan consistently gave the impression to the Christians he spoke with in Holland, 'that the frame of their Spirits, at this time is made more susceptible of the Truth of the Gospel, then at any time heretofore'. This was the secret of his success among the ardent Protestants of Amsterdam and London, and the hopes which he raised among them for the conversion of the Jews in their day opened simultaneously their hearts and their purses.[26]

Among the Dutch Protestants who were most impressed with the apparent Christian inclination of Rabbi Nathan was Peter Serrarius, one of the most important conduits of millenarian intelligence in Europe during this period.[27] Serrarius was also a close associate of Henry Jessey, who heard of the sufferings of the Palestinian Jews from Menasseh ben Israel, and the Dutch translator of Jessey's book about the *Glory and Salvation of Iehudah and Israel*.[28] He wrote several letters to Sarah Wight, Jessey's divinely-inspired protégée who delivered biblical soliloquies in a trance.[29] Serrarius also wrote to Henry Jessey after the Restoration concerning millenarian matters.[30] Once the contact was made between Rabbi Nathan Shapira and Peter Serrarius, it was inevitable that Henry Jessey should have heard about it, and that he should have informed his associates John Dury and Samuel Hartlib and the entire circle of the Invisible College who had been waiting at least since the early 1640s for signs of the conversion of the Jews.

Serrarius wrote to John Dury in April 1657 recounting the discussions that he had had with Rabbi Nathan which led him to expect the imminent conversion of the Jews. He explained that he had already seen signs of Christian feeling from Rabbi Nathan, but these were made more manifest when the Jew came unexpectedly to one of their prayer meetings where some portion of Scripture was read and discussed. In the rabbi's honour it was decided to read that day Christ's Sermon on the Mount. The Christians read the Dutch and gave Rabbi Nathan the Hebrew translation by Sebastian Münster, asking him what he thought of this centrepiece of the Christian tradition. Rabbi Nathan replied

> that therein the ground and fountain of all Wisdom was contained, and that whosoever should keep those Commandments would be more just then he, or his people, and he took notice of some things which he thought were taken out of the most pure and antient Rabbins.

Serrarius recalled that this declaration moved them all to tears, and they offered up prayers for the Jews and for themselves, 'that God would blot out our sins and theirs, and remember his Mercy'. Rabbi Nathan on his part showed how these 'things seemed very much to move him, and he made no doubt to affirm openly, that if there were but ten men at Jerusalem, who should thus with one heart pray for the coming of the Messiah, that without all doubt he would suddenly come'. Serrarius told Dury that Rabbi Nathan would eat with them and take part in their prayer meetings with the easy familiarity of the regular visitor.[31]

By the time the account of Rabbi Nathan's inclination to Christianity reached England, it had already been somewhat amplified. In Serrarius's original letter, the rabbi is shown reproving a Jew who balked at the very name of Christ, saying, 'Do not say so, Let come whoever will come, our prayers and wishes are to this effect simply, That God would be pleased to reveal him.'[32] According to Edward Whiston, what actually happened was that '*Rabbi Nathan* himself, the *Jews* Elder and Messenger consented with divers other *Jews* to be present at a religious meeting of Christians, and hearing with what fervour and affection they prayed, said they were certainly holy men, and such as they expected their Nation should be at the coming of *Messiah*, who would come quickly had they such a spirit of prayer.' These Jews thought so well of Christian devotions and 'seeing our love to them, and hope for them would often say, *If Jesus be the Messiah, Oh that he would come! Let him come, Let him come, whoever he be!*' Whiston concluded that many of these Jews 'seemed not far from the Kingdom of God', and noted that if this pleasant path of persuasion had been followed at the Jewish council reputedly held near Buda in 1650 to discuss the question of the messiah, the results could have been similarly dramatic.[33]

In fairness to Rabbi Nathan, he did take pains to bring in the central subject of the poor Ashkenazi Jews of Jerusalem on every possible occasion. When asked how it felt to be a despised Jew, whose life was in danger as he travelled across Europe, Nathan replied that it was nothing compared with 'the calamities and extream Straits of the poor at *Jerusalem*'. The interpretation Serrarius made of his remarks was after all not the concern of Rabbi Nathan. 'What do you think?' Serrarius asked Dury. 'Is it to be believed that Christ is far distant from a soul thus constituted?' Rabbi Nathan's discussion, even about Christ, remained within the boundaries of the Jewish tradition—just. Was it his fault that Serrarius was so encouraged about the conversion of the Jews? 'For my own part,' Serrarius informed Dury, 'I confess I think I see Christ in his Spirit; and I cannot but love him, and those that are like him, of which he saith many are at *Jerusalem*: for I esteem them the true brethren of him, that is, our *Christ*.' Rabbi Nathan had achieved his goal: Serrarius, and through him Jessey, Dury and Hartlib, were convinced that Nathan was the harbinger and the representative of a community of Jews in Jerusalem who were one small step away from accepting the pure Christianity of Protestantism and thereby bringing about the Second Coming of the Messiah.[34]

Rabbi Nathan had therefore in a sense received the money under false pretences. The Ashkenazi Jews of Jerusalem were undoubtedly in a desperate state, but they had no intention of accepting Jesus as the messiah either before or after the charity was received. Dury had the impression 'that there is no inconsistancy, but rather a Consonancy with the Promise, that Jesus shall be revealed to them as *Joseph* was once to his Brethren'. Rabbi Nathan's words showed him 'that the Lord doth prepare a way for them to be converted unto Christianity,' and the crowning proof of this was

> Namely, that some of those afflicted Jews at *Jerusalem* begin now to confess, That their Forefathers did wickedly in putting *Jesus* of *Nazareth* to death, and that he was a just man, and the Spirit of the Messiah was in him, and that for putting him and others to death, they ought to repent, seeing they cannot attribute this great wrath which is gone forth against them to any other cause so remarkable as to this sin.

Dury was also informed that in order to move things along, a new Hebrew translation of the New Testament was being edited in the Holy Land from the text by Münster which was thought to be 'far different from the Hebrew phrase, which is used in Scripture'. The plan was to bring the improved text back from Palestine to Amsterdam to be printed: 'and if once they begin to read the new Testament; as a true History in their own Hebrew Dialect,' Dury believed, 'there can be no greater preparation for their conversion then this will be'. Dury did not say who was editing the new version of the Gospels in Jerusalem, but he noted that it was being done 'by some of their own Rabbi's'.[35]

It is surely a debatable point to what extent Rabbi Nathan should be held responsible for Dury's interpretation of his words. But Dury's summary of the evangelical implication of the Palestinian rabbi's testimony is not entirely inconsistent with the report transmitted by Serrarius, who spoke with the Jew himself on many occasions. In Rabbi Nathan's defence, it was said 'that the supply came not by any application of the Rabbi to the Christians; but by the free offering of the Christians to help him without his craving of it'. The anger at Rabbi Nathan's behaviour seems to have died down with the acceptance of this argument, that 'the Rabbi only received what was freely offered'. Nevertheless, at least in England it was understood by Hartlib, Dury and Jessey that the very fact that the Jews of Jerusalem were willing to take help from Gentiles only demonstrated the 'greatness of their straits'.[36]

Rabbi Nathan Shapira's later career seems not to have been unduly harmed by this flirtation with the conversionist Protestants of England and Holland. In 1657 he signed a letter of introduction given to two rabbis who were sent as emissaries of the Ashkenazi community in

Jerusalem to Italy, to try to continue the fund-raising enterprise that he had begun. More importantly, at the end of 1657, soon after his return to Jerusalem, he himself was sent once again to Italy, and there received from Jerusalem a copy of the famous letter by Rabbi Baruch Gad which purported to contain a message from the Lost Ten Tribes, and was used with great effect by Palestinian emissaries to Europe during this period.[37] Shapira may have been the 'Jew from Cracovia' who convinced Serrarius that 'the redemption of Israel is drawing near'. Serrarius wrote of this to Hartlib, who passed the intelligence on to his erstwhile correspondent John Worthington in February 1662.[38] Of Rabbi Nathan's private life in Jerusalem all we know is that on the basis of the permission of a hundred rabbis he took a second wife and lived with the two women in the courtyard of the Sephardi synagogue in the city. He wrote several important halakhic works and died in Italy in 1666.[39]

II

By rights, this should have been the end of the entire affair. The Ashkenazi Jews of Jerusalem had suffered a terrible blow, but thanks to the charity received from Hartlib, Dury and Jessey, and the equivocal support for the Christian messiah given by Rabbi Nathan Shapira, they were able to ride out the crisis. The Ashkenazi population of Jerusalem declined drastically, and was probably at a low point when the money was finally received, but throughout the seventeenth century they jealously guarded their right to their own private rabbi who at the very least is known to have recorded their divorce settlements (*get*). The crippling debts continued to be a problem, but some funds did once again begin to come in from Central and Eastern Europe and helped ease the situation. Interestingly, despite having felt the effects of isolation from the other Jewish communities in the city, the Ashkenazim continued to refuse to participate in the general charity fund, and even declined to provide funds for Ashkenazi *yeshivah* students enrolled in the general *yeshivah* and who received some help there from the Sephardim.[40]

Yet at some point within the next fifteen years, and certainly before 1674, the entire sordid problem of the Anglo-Dutch charity appeal was reopened. Someone after the event laid the issue before Rabbi Jacob Hagiz for a definitive ruling on the morality of having accepted money from Hartlib, Dury and Jessey for the payment of Jewish debts in Jerusalem. Rabbi Jacob Hagiz (1620-74) had come to Jerusalem in 1658 and soon established himself as the foremost scholar in the city. He immediately founded a new *yeshivah* with funds supplied by two rich merchant brothers from Livorno, Jacob and Israel Vega, and called the academy after one of them, Beth Ya'akov. The *hesger* ('cloister') of Jacob Hagiz soon became one of the most important talmudic centres in the city, and most of the legal and moral problems of the community were decided there. Rabbi Jacob would habitually consider these issues throughout the week, and his decisions would have legally binding authority after a final sitting on the Sabbath. On one of these Saturday sittings, Rabbi Jacob Hagiz delivered his ruling about the ethical issues involved in accepting charity from John Dury, Henry Jessey and Samuel Hartlib.[41]

The reply of Rabbi Hagiz is such a marvellous piece of casuistry that it is worth quoting in full:

Question: Since in Ingliterra are to be found Gentiles who do not worship images but worship God albeit impurely; and since there are those who offer to send charity to the poor of Palestine, it is doubted whether it is permitted to take [alms] from them in order to redeem pressing Jewish debts owed to [other] Gentiles. Is there any danger here? If it is claimed that it is forbidden to take [alms] from Gentiles, it may be that because of sins in the days that forcible conversion was decreed in that country [in 1290], many were among those who were defiled and taken as a baby to the Gentiles and made apostates of those Christians, so perhaps these [almsgivers] are of the seed of Israel.

Answer: This was [already] asked in correct fashion, when it was suggested that if there is a danger in the matter, how could it be that it was written afterwards that if it is claimed that it is forbidden and if there is a danger it is [indeed] because there is no idolatry here: why is it forbidden to receive [alms] in the first place? And as for the matter if there is a danger to redeem Gentile debts . . . the claim is that there was a forcible conversion, so it should be said that it is Jews who are giving [the charity]. All this depends on whether these same *marranos* [converted] either in order to save their lives, or who did not leave on account of their wealth. Then the reverse is true for this is even worse, because we can receive [charity] from the Gentile but not from a convert, and therefore there is no place for this [argument]. In conclusion, if [the money] has already been transferred, received, and turned over to the said Gentile creditors, there is no cause whatsoever for anxiety.[42]

The occasion and the timing of this *responsum* is not known, but surely it is curious that such a settled issue should have surfaced yet again without provocation. The letter of Jessey and Dury to the Ashkenazi Jews of Jerusalem was dated 22 April 1659 and must certainly have been received by the end of the year.[43] Why should the entire question of charity from abroad and community *shelichim* have arrested the attention of Rabbi Hagiz yet again? The answer may lie with the students of his *yeshivah*, among whom were such men of promise as Joseph Almosnino, later rabbi of Belgrade, and Rabbi Moses ibn Habib of Jerusalem. But his prize pupil was Abraham Nathan ben Elisha Hayyim Ashkenazi, soon to achieve historical immortality under the name of Nathan of Gaza, who would play both John the Baptist and Saint Paul to Sabbatai Sevi, the notorious Jewish false messiah whose movement shook the Jewish world as no event did since the Expulsion from Spain.[44]

Nathan of Gaza was born in Jerusalem about 1643 or 1644, and was himself the son of an active emissary of the Jerusalem Jews, who visited Poland, Germany, Italy and Morocco on their behalf, always carrying with him kabbalistic works from the Holy Land which by this means could be disseminated abroad. R. Jacob Hagiz's son Moses, later his father's successor at the academy and a violent opponent of the Sabbatians, admitted nevertheless that Nathan was one of his father's most gifted pupils. When in 1663 a wealthy Jew living in Gaza asked Jacob to suggest a suitable marriage for his daughter, the rabbi sent Nathan, his best student, who would thereby find the material support for his studies. So Nathan left Jerusalem, having spent most of his life before then in the company of Rabbi Jacob Hagiz at the *yeshivah*.[45]

Sabbatai Sevi lived in Jerusalem from the late summer of 1662 until he left for Egypt at the end of 1663. No evidence survives to prove that he met Nathan during this first period in the city, but the suggestion is not unreasonable, given Sabbatai Sevi's eccentric notoriety and the size of the Jewish population, and of the Old City itself. Yet he could not have been entirely unreliable, for in 1663 it was Sabbatai Sevi who was sent as the emissary of the Jews of Jerusalem to Egypt to try to raise the funds which were being demanded in the latest extortionist persecution of the Turkish overlords. This time the demands of the Muslim authorities were so great that a number of Jewish elders were forced to flee the city, to Ramle or Safed, to avoid detention in lieu of payment. Sabbatai left Jerusalem, and travelled via Hebron to Cairo, where he arrived early in 1664 and stayed for nearly two years. Most importantly, on his way to Egypt he passed through Gaza and met Nathan, who in February or March 1665 had a vision of Sabbatai Sevi as the long-awaited messiah. Nathan of Gaza laboured for several months to convince the mystic rabbi of his true identity, and finally, on 31 May 1665, Sabbatai Sevi declared himself to be the messiah after all.[46]

'He left a *shaliah* and returned a *mashiah*': despite his equivocal success as a messiah, as an emissary he did manage to fulfil the expectations which had been placed upon him. According to a letter sent from Sabbatai's home town of Smyrna to Holland, the messiah did manage to collect about four thousand *Löwenthaler*, a sum equivalent at that time to about one thousand gold ducats. Once the Sabbatian storm had broken, however, even this achievement was insufficient to shield him from the wrath of the unconvinced. Soon after his arrival in Jerusalem in grand and mystic style in June 1665, reports circulated that he had kept some of the money he had collected in Egypt, while others said that the rabbis of the city were incensed that he had distributed the four thousand thalers himself among the poor and widows, without paying the shares due to the elders and the local institutions. At any rate, when Sabbatai was denounced to the Turkish *cadi*, the two charges against him were 'that he wanted to rule, and that he had embezzled some of the money of his mission'.[47]

One of the main problems, of course, was that the rabbis of Jerusalem were well-acquainted with Sabbatai Sevi, and knew him as the pious but undoubtedly bizarre character who was prone to go on lonely pilgrimages to the tombs of the local holy men or to cloister himself at home with the works of the kabbalists. They had always hoped that the messiah when he came would be rather a different sort of person. The rabbis of Jerusalem accordingly took steps to have Sabbatai Sevi excommunicated and expelled from the city. As the leading halakhic authority in Jerusalem, Rabbi Jacob Hagiz was one of the initiators of the procedure. Moses Hagiz wrote that 'I heard my grandfather, the celebrated R. Moses Galante of blessed memory, quoting a remark which my father of blessed memory [R. Jacob Hagiz] used to make in jest: "Behold a messiah who is afraid of my ban of excommunication."' Rabbi Moses Galante was also a leading talmudic figure in Sabbatai's Jerusalem, and his daughter had married Jacob Hagiz. For some time he seems to have been an active follower of the false messiah, and at any rate had certainly known the man since his first arrival in Jerusalem. So his recollection of Rabbi Jacob Hagiz's jest should be taken seriously, including its implication that he had been one of the instigators of the excommunication. In any case, he was certainly among those who took a leading part in the proceedings, and who had won a great victory in the excommunication and expulsion of their sometime emissary from the boundaries of Jerusalem, setting Sabbatai Sevi on those wanderings which would end with his death in Albania as a convert to Islam.[48]

The troubled relationship between Rabbi Hagiz and his now notorious emissary became known eventually to Serrarius, who communicated this information to his friends in England. He had more news of Sabbatai Sevi, he wrote to his anonymous correspondent at the end of 1665, who was 'unknown by face, yet owned by Grace, and by the blessed memory of our dear Friend Mr. Jessee, whom I might have wished to communicate what now I shall communicate to you'. According to Serrarius, the rabbis of Jerusalem sent three of their number to Gaza to test Nathan 'to try and understand if he were a prophet or no'. One of these men was said to be 'Rabbi Gagas, once his Preceptor', certainly a garbled reference to Jacob Hagiz. According to the story, Nathan took Hagiz and the others to the tomb of the prophet Zacharias where they encountered an old man who 'appeared unto them with a Bason full of water in his hand'. Nathan bade them wash themselves and thereby cast away their sins: 'Whereupon the old man answered, They are forgiven, and so he vanished.' Serrarius noted that 'the Jews conclude, the old man was the Prophet Zacharias himself'. Hagiz and the others, 'having heard this Nathan, and seen the Signs that shewed that he was truly a prophet, made penitence in sackcloth and ashes, for having ever opposed him'.[49]

Interestingly, the legend itself is based on fact. Nathan was indeed tested by scholars from Jerusalem, but not by Rabbi Jacob Hagiz. The original figure in the story was Rabbi Israel Benjamin the Second, whom Nathan of Gaza told that his soul was that of the man who had murdered the prophet Zachariah in the Temple of Jerusalem. Within a very short time, however, the legend was transferred to the name of Rabbi Jacob Hagiz, who indeed had disbelieved Nathan and persecuted Sabbatai Sevi and therefore was in need of absolution. 'The story of R. Israel Benjamin, based, most probably, on an actual or visionary experience of some kind,' Gershom Scholem suggested, 'marks the transition to the realm of imaginative legend' which soon dominated the mental climate in Palestine.[50]

Sabbatai Sevi soon left Rabbi Jacob Hagiz's purview and abandoned Palestine as his movement created waves of ever-increasing intensity. When the entire issue of charity and emissaries from questionable sources was brought up yet again, it could not help but be connected with the intervening crisis over the False Messiah. For Sabbatai Sevi had been, depending on one's perspective, the most successful or the least successful of all the emissaries sent by the impoverished Jews of Jerusalem. He too brought back a considerable sum of money which was urgently needed to pay the debts owed to non-Jews. But undoubtedly Rabbi Jacob Hagiz must have had cause to reflect that it would have been better for the Jews if he had not been sent to Cairo at all.

III

For the Ashkenazi Jews of Jerusalem, the efforts of Hartlib, Dury and Jessey to keep them alive only served to stave off temporarily their ultimate decline and dispersion. Their debts continued to press upon them, only occasionally eased by periodic donations from Central and Eastern Europe. By the beginning of the eighteenth century, some efforts were being made to regularize an impossible situation. Between 1711 and 1714 the Ashkenazim conducted negotiations with the Muslim authorities for the payment of their debts, and although they arrived at a compromise, the agreement was never put into practice because of a lack of interest among the Ashkenazi communities abroad. Finally in 1720 the Muslim creditors burned the Ashkenazi synagogue of Jerusalem to the ground and imprisoned some of the elders. The remaining Ashkenazim in the city, those who did not flee to other Jewish centres in Palestine, were forced to disguise themselves as Sephardim in order to survive. The Muslims in turn accused the Sephardim of thereby helping their brethren to avoid the payment of their debts, for if they were denied the use of Sephardi facilities the remaining Ashkenazim would surely find some way to meet their obligations. In any case, in 1735 there were said to be only seventy Ashkenazim in Jerusalem, and although three years later the number is said to have grown to about one hundred Yiddish-speaking Jews, the Ashkenazi community of Jerusalem had been all but destroyed.[51]

One of the most tantalizing elements to emerge from this affair is the link between those English philo-Semites, Hartlib, Dury and Jessey with so many of the central figures in the messianic movement of Sabbatai Sevi. We have already seen how close Henry Jessey was to Peter Serrarius, the conduit for much of the information about Sabbatai Sevi that reached Europe from the Middle East. Rabbi Jacob Hagiz, teacher of Nathan of Gaza and excommunicator of Sabbatai Sevi, knew only too well of Jessey's work and the efforts of his Puritan companions. Henry Jessey at least knew of Raphael Supino, who with Serrarius would be an important source of Sabbatian news. Several of the pamphlets published in London reporting the progress of Sabbatai Sevi in Palestine contain letters written by Supino from Leghorn, a chief entrepôt of Jewish intelligence. Raphael Supino was certainly in contact with Benjamin Levy, a leader of the Jewish community in London, to whom he reported on the subject of Sabbatai Sevi. Indeed, when Jacob Sasportas, the former *hakham* of the London Jews, launched his courageous attack on the new heresy sweeping across Jewish Europe, he focused on Raphael Supino, and denounced the transgressions of the messiah as reported from Leghorn. Surprisingly, even after Sabbatai Sevi converted to Islam and his entire movement collapsed, Supino continued to maintain a centre of devotion at his house at Leghorn.[52]

Henry Jessey was in contact with Raphael Supino as early as 1655, long before Sabbatai Sevi came to Jerusalem, during the campaign for the readmission of the Jews to England. According to Jessey, it was then that a number of Jews who lived in Roman Catholic countries 'entreated *Rabbi Manasses* to be their Agent, to entreat this favour for their coming to *England*, to live and Trade here'. Raphael Haim Supino was one of these men, who came to London at about the same time as Menasseh, in order to settle a case coming up in the Admiralty court concerning some merchandise of his which had been captured on a French ship. The envoy of the grand duke of Tuscany in London, Francesco Salvetti, was sure that Supino had something to do with Menasseh's mission, but could not put his finger on anything definite. In any case, Supino made no secret of his Jewish religion, and even offered to dispute with Salvetti's chaplain on religious issues. So Raphael Supino must have been somewhat of a well-known figure, even in a city like Cromwellian London, riddled with sects and religious groups of the most outlandish beliefs and habits.[53]

Raphael Supino's connection with England may have begun as early as 1652, if he is the Jew of Leghorn, 'one that could speak a little English, a very grave proper man', who discussed the coming of the messiah with some English seamen from the frigate *Phoenix* when they visited the Jewish synagogue there in that year. Henry Jessey may also have had Supino in mind when he reported that

> Merchants had come from beyond seas to *London*, and hoped they might have enjoyed as much priviledge here, in respect of Trading, and of their Worshipping the God of *Abraham*, *Isaac*, and *Jacob*, here, in Synagogues, publickly, as they enjoy in *Holland*, and did enjoy in *Poland*, *Prussia*, and other places. But after the conference and Debate at *VVhite-Hall* was ended, they heard by some, that the greater part of the Ministers were against this: therefore they removed hence again to beyond the Seas, with much grief of heart, that they were thus disappointed of their hopes.[54]

Henry Jessey died three years before Sabbatai Sevi declared himself to be the messiah. But we have already seen how he had been in close contact with John Dury and Samuel Hartlib throughout these years, especially over Jewish matters, and undoubtedly all three men were equally privy to information received from Serrarius, Supino, and Rabbi Jacob Hagiz in Jerusalem after 1658. Dury and Jessey seem to have been especially close. When Dury, serving Cromwell and the cause of religious unity in Germany, discovered that stories had been spread about him by Matthew Cresset, the Baptist clergyman, he did not hesitate to write a long, heartfelt letter to his friend Jessey in the summer of 1655 craving his help in resolving this sensitive matter.[55]

The late Professor Scholem was adamant in his belief that there was no causal connection between the millenarian movement of seventeenth-century Christian Europe and the messianic adventures of Sabbatai Sevi. While admitting that people like Peter Serrarius and Jan Amos Comenius did establish contact with Jewish scholars, Scholem noted that their influence was slight since only 'a small minority of the Jewish people lived at the time in Protestant countries where chiliasm can be said to have been a significant factor in public affairs'. Certainly it is true that in England, the 'handful of marrano Jews in London can hardly be considered a significant historical factor'. Professor Scholem concluded that the millenarian 'computations had no influence whatever on the Sabbatian outbreak of 1665; the synchronism is accidental'.[56]

Scholem's main argument was that 'Sabbatai Sevi needed no Christians to be impressed with the probability of 1666 being a messianic year.' He was refuting the argument put forward by Graetz and others 'that Sabbatai's father, Mordecai Sevi, had heard from the English merchants, whose agent he was, all sorts of rumours about the impending restoration of Israel to their land in the apocalyptic year of redemption 1666. Mordecai Sevi would report these rumours at home and create in his house a messianic atmosphere whose origin was ultimately non-Jewish.' Scholem disposes of this suggestion with the following postulation:

> There is not a shred of evidence to show that Mordecai Sevi's employers were millenarians, and we may positively assert that they could not have mentioned 1666 as a messianic year. The propaganda for this date made its appearance in Dutch and English literature in the fifties only, that is, after Sabbatai had left Smyrna. There had, of course, been a few medieval writers who had interpreted the 'number of the beast', 666, in Revelation 13:18 as a prophecy of the coming of Antichrist in the year 1666, but these isolated views were not widely known. Shortly before 1666, some Protestant chiliasts remembered the date and began to propagate the view that the 'fifth kingdom' would begin in that year.

So the appearance of the movement of Jewish messianism in the year of the expected Christian redemption was in Scholem's eyes a mere coincidence, of the sort that does occasionally occur in history.[57]

While Scholem did demonstrate that the roots of the Sabbatian movement in the Jewish tradition were massively substantial, it is simply untrue that English millenarianism was a philosophy that suddenly revived from mediaeval stagnation in the 1650s. While the abolition of effective press censorship during the Interregnum does create a certain optical illusion of a sudden effusion of millenarian writings, many of these works were written much earlier and were widely known in Protestant Europe. The three most influential millenarian thinkers for Englishmen were Thomas Brightman (1562–1607), Joseph Mede (1586–1668) and Johann Heinrich Alsted (1558–1638). Brightman was therefore already dead when Mede was only twenty-one, and throughout the early seventeenth century one finds a continuous chain of millenarian tradition.[58] This in large measure explains the general approval of eschatological views in England during the period of the Civil War. The historian of the Fifth Monarchy movement has even estimated that up to seventy per cent of the prolific writers publishing in England during this period expressed millenarian views.[59] It may be that it was 'accidental', as Professor Scholem insisted, that both Christians and Jews should have seen these years as the era of Redemption. But it would be a striking coincidence indeed.

In any case, it is not necessary here to weigh the possible paternity claims of English merchants in Smyrna against those of Isaac Luria and the kabbalists. What is most important about the mutual involvement of Henry Jessey, Rabbi Jacob Hagiz, Peter Serrarius, Raphael Supino, John Dury, Samuel Hartlib and others who were like-minded in Jewish matters is that it helps to explain the rapid acceptance of the Sabbatian movement in Europe, and the rather extraordinary interest taken by Christians in many quarters in the progress of Sabbatai Sevi. There was little that was conspiratorial about their search for first-hand knowledge about Nathan of Gaza and his messiah, but it grew out of their common Christianizing impulse which sought to convert the Jews to a purer form of Christianity as a preparation for the End of Days.

'If any be inquisitive to know the success of these large Alms,' Whiston adds in his biography of Jessey, 'whether they were brought to judge more charitably of Christians; we assure them that it much melted many of them, and indeed it hath been an incontroulable Experiment, that this kind of dealing did ever more winne over the hearts of this kind of people in the primitive Church, then all the force and arguments (since used) by moderne Christians could effect to perswade them.'[60] Whiston certainly overestimated the missionary effect of the charity which had been sent to the Ashkenazim of Jerusalem. But undoubtedly the money collected helped to stave off the final decline of the Ashkenazi community, under the combined pressure of debts and persecution.

Notes

1 A. Cohen, *Jewish Life Under Islam: Jerusalem in the Sixteenth Century* (Cambridge, Mass., 1984), pp. 52–3 notes that a court judgement of 1612 shows the existence of a separate spokesman for the Ashkenazim recognized by the *cadi*. See generally M. Rozen, *The Jewish Community of Jerusalem in the Seventeenth Century* (Hebrew) (Tel Aviv, 1984), pp. 91, 99–100; M. Benyahu, 'Towards the History of Academies in Seventeenth-Century Jerusalem: the work of Rabbi Jacob Hagiz and his son Moses on their behalf' (Hebrew), *Heb. Union Coll. Ann.*, vol. 21 (1948), pp. 1–28 (Hebrew sect.).
2 Cohen (note 1 above), pp. 63–71: Cohen's book is largely based on the archives of the Muslim courts.
3 [John Dury?], *An Information Concerning The Present State Of The Jewish Nation in Europe and Judea* (London, 1658), pp. 4–5. This pamphlet appears in the 1945 edition of Wing under the name of John Dury (Wing D2863). In the 1972 edition it was removed from the canon of Dury's writings and the entry cancelled. But on a copy of the work in the Bodleian Library, Oxford (Vet. A 3e. 838) purchased in 1928 is the following notation, written in a seventeenth-century hand: 'aut. Jo. Duraeo'. Portions of this important pamphlet were published in *Misc. Jew. Hist. Soc. Eng.*, vol. 2 (1935), pp. 99–104. The editor claimed that he reproduced 'everything of historical interest in the little work'; in fact it is a bowdlerized text that omits the pro-Christian sentiments expressed therein by Rabbi Nathan Shapira. The censored text is published in D. S. Katz, 'Anonymous Advocates of the Readmission of the Jews to England', *Michael*, vol. 10 (1986), pp. 117–42. Unfortunately, the defective text was the one translated into Hebrew for M. Ish-Shalom, *Christian Travels in the Holy Land* (Hebrew) (Tel Aviv, 1965), pp. 354–8, which was the version used in Rozen (note 1 above).
4 [Dury?] (note 3 above), p. 9
5 E.[dward] W.[histon], *The Life and Death of Mr. Henry Jessey* (np, 1671), pp. 69–70: R. Nathan is referred to here as 'Nathan Levita'.
6 [Dury?] (note 3 above), p. 5
7 The name of the second emissary is not given here, nor in the writings of R. Nathan Shapira himself, nor in A. Ya'ari, *Emissaries from Palestine* (Hebrew) (Jerusalem, 1951), where more information on Nathan Shapira appears,, pp. 277–81. The role of Nathan Shapira during this period is admirably illustrated in R. H. Popkin, 'The Visit of Rabbi Shapira to Amsterdam in 1657', in *Proceedings of the Second Intl. Symposium on the History of the Jews in the Netherlands*, ed. J. Michman (Leiden, 1985), pp. 185–205.
8 Nathan Shapira, *Tuv ha-Aretz* (Hebrew) (Venice, 1655); Ya'ari (note 7 above), p. 278.
9 *ibid.*
10 [Henry Jessey], *A Narrative of the Late Proceeds at White-Hall Concerning the Jews* (London, 1656), pp. 3–4.
11 *Publick Intelligencer*, 11 (10–17 December 1655), p. 169
12 *Mercurius Politicus*, 289 (20–27 December 1655), p. [5841]
13 *ibid.*, 228 (13–20 December 1655), p. 5831.
14 Generally, see D. S. Katz, *Philo-Semitism and the Readmission of the Jews to England, 1603–1655* (Oxford, 1982).
15 See D. S. Katz, 'Menasseh ben Israel's Christian Connection in England: Henry Jessey and the Jews', in *Menasseh ben Israel and his World*, eds R. H. Popkin, M. Edel, & J. Kaplan (Leiden, forthcoming); id., 'Henry Jessey and Conservative Millenarianism in Seventeenth-Century England and Holland', in *Proceedings of the Fourth Intl. Symposium on the History of the Jews in the Netherlands*, ed. J. Michman (Leiden, forthcoming). On Jessey generally, see esp. B. R. White, 'Henry Jessey: A Pastor in Politics', *Bap. Qly.*, ns, vol. 25 (1973–4), pp. 98–110; id., 'Henry Jessey in the Great

Rebellion', in *Reformation, Conformity, and Dissent: Essays in honour of Geoffrey Nuttall*, ed. R. Buick Knox (London, 1977), pp. 132–53; and the references to Jessey in M. Tolmie, *The Triumph of the Saints: The Separate Churches of London 1616–1649* (Cambridge, 1977); and C. Burrage, *The Early English Dissenters* (Cambridge, 1912).

16 [Jessey] (note 10 above), *passim*

17 See D. S. Katz, 'English Redemption and Jewish Readmission in 1656', *Jnl. Jew. Stud.,*, vol. 34 (1983), pp. 73–91.

18 W[histon] (note 5 above), pp. 69–70. Thomas Crosby, *The History of the English Baptists*, vol. 2 (London, 1737–40), i. 316–18 says that the Dutch Christians sent 500 Reichsdollars.

19 [Dury?] (note 3 above), p. 5

20 W[histon] (note 5 above), pp. 70–8

21 *ibid.* The letter of thanks has since disappeared: it was 'an Authentique Copie, written by the said *R. Samuel* [Ben Seth], and signed by all the Elders of the High-Dutch [i.e. Ashkenazi] Synagogue at *Jerusalem*, 1657, *April.* 22.', and described in [Dury?] (note 3 above), sigs. D–D2verso; pp. 5–6. The Hebrew commissions have also not been found. The same source (*ibid.*, p. 5) notes that the Jerusalem Jews received about £1,313 5s. from 'the Christians in *Holland*': 'With this money they went away; and it availed them only to discharge the Interests of their capital debts, and to make some presents to their great ones, that further time might be granted unto them, and the three hundred ninety Ducats relieved some of their private wants.'

22 This letter is printed in W[histon] (note 5 above), pp. 72–4.

23 Henry Jessey and John Dury 'To the Dispersed of *Judah* in *Jerusalem* of the *German* Synagogue', London, 22 April 1659: printed in *ibid.*, pp. 75–7 and repr. in Katz (note 3 above), p. 142. Both the letter of the Jews and this letter from Jessey and Dury are dated 22 April: this may be the result of confusion in the sources or a conscious attempt to recall the day two years later. It seems from a postscript to this letter that the money was sent in stages: first £40, then £172 enclosed with the letter, and the balance paid later.

24 Jessey to Hartlib and Dury, nd: Sheffield Univ. Lib., Hartlib Papers 15/8/15recto; Jessey to [same?], 19 Jan. 1657–8 [?]: Hartlib Papers 15/8/14recto.

25 [Dury?] (note 3 above), p. 6

26 *ibid.*, p. 11

27 Peter Serrarius remains a shadowy and often misidentified figure: see J. Van Den Berg, 'Quaker and Chiliast: the "contrary thoughts" of William Ames and Petrus Serrarius', in *Reformation*, ed. Knox, pp. 180–98. Serrarius is the subject of a doctoral thesis by Ernestine van der Wall of Leiden University.

28 Henry Jesse, *De Heerlickheydt en Heyl van Jehuda en Israel* (Amsterdam, 1653), which according to the title page was 'in 't Neerlandts vertaelt Door P.S.' Although the book seems to have existed in English, Hebrew and Dutch, only now has any copy been uncovered, by Dr Van der Wall in the library at Wolfenbüttel (916. 2 Th. [3]). J.C. Wolf, *Bibliotheca Hebraea* (Hamburg & Leipzig, 1715–33), iv. 901, knew only the Dutch version. N. Sokolow, *History of Zionism 1600–1918* (London, 1919), pp. 214–15, refers to a catalogue of the library of Mr Leon V. Saraval of Trieste published in 1853 in which the book is included as item 619 with the following notation: 'Jesse Henry de Heerlichkeydt en Heyl van Jehuda en Israel (en langue flamande, traduit de l'anglais.) Amst. 1653 in 8º . . . très rare'. Sokolow notes that in 1853 the Saraval library was purchased for the Breslau Seminary. Most of these books were destroyed during the Second World War, and Dr Jozef Długosz, director of the Biblioteka Uniwersytecka in Wrocław (Breslau), Poland, writes (28 October 1983) that they do not have the book. See also C. W. Schoneveld, *Intertraffic of the Mind* (Leiden, 1983), who includes a checklist of nearly 650 books translated from English into Dutch in the seventeenth

century, but does not cite Jessey's work. Cf. Crosby (note 18 above), i. 318–19; vol. 2, pp. 318–19; W[histon] (note 5 above), pp. 80–1.

29 Henry Jessey, *The Exceeding Riches of Grace Advanced* (7th edn, London, 1658), p. H: Jessey promises to print the letters in a new second part to the book which does not seem to have ever appeared. The reference to Serrarius does not appear in the 1st (1647), 3rd (1648) or 6th (1652) editions of the book. For more on Sarah Wight, see Katz, 'Henry Jessey' (note 15 above).

30 Printed in White Kennett, *A Register and Chronicle*, vol. 1 (London, 1728), pp. 137–9. The writer of the 'Two Letters from *Amsterdam* to Mr. *Jessey* and to Mr. *John Durie*, one dated *May 7*, the other *May 20, 1660'* is not mentioned by Kennett, but it is certainly Serrarius. The source of the letter is given as 'Ex MSS. penes J. Worthington, Cantabr. Coll. D. p. Socium, *1688'*. The letter is also referred to in the margin of Thomas Thorowgood, *Jews in America* (London, 1660), p. 66, as 'Letter of P. Serrarius to Mr. John Dury and Mr. H. J., May 4, 1660'. Thorowgood's book is about the millenarian implications of the discovery of a tribe of Israelite Indians in South America, and Menasseh ben Israel's part in promoting it.

31 Peter Serrarius to J[ohn] D[ury], April 1657: printed in [Dury?] (note 3 above), pp. 11–16, and repr. Katz, 'Anonymous Advocates' (note 3 above), pp. 139–42.

32 *ibid.*, p. 140; and [Dury?] (note 3 above), p. 11

33 W[histon] (note 5 above), pp. 77–8. For more on this 'Jewish Council', no doubt a fairy-tale version of the sessions of the Council of Four Lands, see Katz (note 14 above), pp. 105–6. The story was known as early as 18 June 1652, when Moses Wall sent Samuel Hartlib a copy of the 'Narrative of the Jews Councill near Buda': Sheffield Univ., Hartlib Papers, 34/4/1recto: I am indebted to Professor R. H. Popkin for pointing me to this reference, and for his suggestion that Paul Isaiah, the professional Jewish convert, was the original source for this story.

34 [Dury?] (note 3 above), pp. 15–16

35 *ibid.*, pp. 17–18

36 *ibid.*, p. 6

37 Ya'ari (note 7 above), p. 280. For more on the letter of Baruch Gad, see Katz (note 14 above), pp. 141–2. Curiously, the letter appears as well in I. B. Singer, *Satan in Goray*, ch. 1.

38 Hartlib to Worthington, 14 February 1661–2: *The Diary and Correspondence of Dr. John Worthington*, ed. J. Crossley & R. C. Christie (Chetham Soc., xiii, xxxvi, cxi, 1847–86), vol. 2, part I, pp. 107–10. Worthington remained unconvinced: W. to H., 24 February 1661–2: *ibid.*, pp. 111–12.

39 Ya'ari (note 7 above), pp. 280–1. Cf. Nathan Shapira, *Sefer Matzath Shmurim* (Venice, 1660); id., *Ma'amar Yayin Ha-M'shumar* (Venice, 1660).

40 Rozen (note 1 above), pp. 101–2

41 Benyahu (note 1 above), pp. 1–13; Rozen (note 1 above), pp. 148–50, 200–1, 215–16

42 Jacob Hagiz, *Halakhot Ktanot* [Responsa] (Hebrew and Aramaic) (Jerusalem, 1981), p. 53 on (1st edn, Venice, 1704). The expulsion of the Jews from England in 1290 did not include forcible conversion, but the more recent examples of Iberian exile must have been on everyone's mind.

43 See above, note 23

44 G. Scholem, *Sabbatai Sevi* (Princeton, 1973), pp. 199–201.

45 *ibid.*, pp. 199–202

46 *ibid.*, pp. 180–1, 186–7, 191, 199, 215, 220

47 G. Scholem, 'Notes from Italy on the Sabbatian Movement in 1666' (Hebrew), *Zion*, vol. 10 (1945), p. 63; id., *Sabbatai Sevi*, pp. 198–241.

48 *ibid.*, pp. 201, 241–51

49 P. Secarius [Peter Serrarius], *Gods Love to his People Israel* (London, 1666): extremely

rare: copy at University College, London: repr. *Zion*, vol. 17 (1952), p. 170.

50 Scholem (note 44 above), pp. 263–5

51 A. Shohat, 'The Jews of Jerusalem in the Eighteenth Century' (Hebrew), *Cathedra*, vol. 13 (1979), pp. 3–45; id., 'The Jews in Jerusalem in the Eighteenth Century' (Hebrew), *Zion*, vol. 1 (1936), pp. 377–410; A. Cohen, *Palestine in the 18th Century: Patterns of Government and Administration* (Jerusalem, 1973); M. Benyahu, 'The Ashkenazi Community in Jerusalem, 1687–1747' (Hebrew), *Sefunot*, vol. 2 (1948), pp. 128–89.

52 Jacob Sasportas, *Sefer Tsitsit Nobel Tsvi*, ed. I. Tishbi (Jerusalem, 1954), p. 82. See also C. Roth, 'New Light on the Resettlement', *Trans. Jew. Hist. Soc. Eng.*, vol. 11 (1928), pp. 125–6. Supino died about 1691.

53 [Jessey] (note 10 above), pp. 3–4. Salvetti's letters are preserved in the State Archives of Florence, but copies exist in Brit. Lib., Add. MS. 27,962. Transcripts from the Florence MSS., with a partial translation from the Italian, are repr. in Roth (note 52 above), pp. 112–42. See here esp. Salvetti to Senator Bali Gondi, 7/17 December 1655, *ibid.*, pp. 128, 137–8, and *Cal. S. P. Ven.*, *1655–6*, p. 160n.; and Chaissy (Salvetti's chaplain) to Ferdinand II, Grand Duke of Tuscany, 23 December 1655, repr. Roth, op cit., p. 137.

54 [Jessey] (note 10 above), p. 11

55 Dury to Jessey, 24 August 1655: Sheffield Univ., Hartlib Papers 4/3/103recto.

56 Scholem (note 44 above), pp. 101–2, 152–4, 283–4

57 *ibid.* Research into the intensive activity of millenarian Quaker missionaries in Smyrna and other Jewish centres in the east may yet provide a personal link with the employers of Mordecai Sevi.

58 See generally, B. S. Capp, *The Fifth Monarchy Men* (London, 1972); M. Verete, 'The Restoration of the Jews in English Protestant Thought, 1790–1840', *Mid. East. Stud.*, vol. 8 (1972), pp. 3–50; p. Christianson, *Reformers and Babylon* (Toronto, 1978); K. R. Firth, *The Apocalyptic Tradition in Reformation Britain* (Oxford, 1979); and other works cited in Katz (note 14 above), ch. 3.

59 Capp (note 58 above), p. 38

60 W[histon] (note 5 above), pp. 77–8

Gregorio Leti (1631–1701) and the Dutch Sephardi Elite at the Close of the Seventeenth Century

Jonathan I. Israel

It is remarkable that Gregorio Leti's pages on the Amsterdam Sephardi élite of the 1680s and 1690s are never mentioned, much less analysed, by scholars of Dutch Jewish history. Leti's extensive discussion of this select group undoubtedly constitutes a major source of information on the subject, providing detail and opening up perspectives which, in some cases, are wholly new. The reason for the undeserved neglect of Leti as an observer of the Dutch Jewish scene, one can only presume, is that the relevant sections of text have simply escaped attention, buried as they are in unlikely places in his prolific output, none of his many volumes bearing titles which suggest that they are likely to yield material of Jewish interest.

Leti, the illegitimate son of a Milanese nobleman, was a literary adventurer who led a colourful and most unconventional life. After leaving his native Italy filled with fury against petty despots and the Catholic clergy, he settled and married at Geneva and became a Calvinist. However, in 1679, after a public investigation of his writings, and in particular his historical commentary on the role of the 'true Reformed faith' and alleged adoption of the maxims of Machiavelli, he was expelled from Geneva as an undesirable influence on public morality.[1] After this, the pivotal experience of his life, he migrated to Paris and then London. But despite his growing reputation as a writer of fashionable works on the political history of Italy, Spain, France and other countries, he failed to find much favour in either capital, largely on account of his anti-Catholicism. In 1683, on leaving England, he decided to try his fortune in Amsterdam and, finding it much to his taste, there he stayed for the remaining eighteen years of his life. He was an early example of a professional writer who lived by his pen and it is this which explains the profuseness as well as the often hack nature of his writings. Although on arriving in Holland he knew no Dutch, such were his international reputation and his connections that he rapidly moved to the forefront of the Dutch literary *monde* of the day.[2] The Amsterdam city council appointed him city historiographer, in October 1685, at a yearly salary of four hundred guilders. His duties included the giving of regular seminars on historical topics in French to the sons of Amsterdam's regent oligarchy. His appointment was confirmed in 1689 and his salary increased to first five then six hundred guilders. Among the more obviously political literary ventures of these years was the monumental heroic poem that he wrote and published on the subject of William III's passage into England and successful bid for the English throne.

The works which Leti wrote during his Dutch period, though often facile, repetitious and filled with tiresome flattery, do also have a serious side which, still today, deserves a measure of attention. He was always a forthright, eloquent champion of religious and intellectual freedom and a frequently scathing critic of Lutheran and (Swiss) Calvinist as well as Catholic bigotry.[3] Moreover, he went further than probably any other seventeenth-century writer in elevating the Dutch Republic to the status of a political ideal, comparing the United Provinces favourably not only with Europe's monarchies and petty principalities but also with the (in his view) despotic republics of Venice, Genoa and Geneva.[4] What he cherished most about the Dutch Republic was the unique combination to be found there of a high, indeed unparalleled, level of political, religious and intellectual freedom—and not least the great freedom enjoyed by foreigners such as himself[5]—with order, security and good government.[6] What Leti says about the Jews has to be placed in this wider context and linked perhaps especially with his defence of the unprecedented freedom enjoyed by Dutch women.[7] It is difficult for us today, in our more liberal age, to grasp fully that the prevailing image of the Dutch Republic among Europe's educated classes in the late seventeenth century was not always a flattering one and that there was frequently an undercurrent of contempt fed especially by feelings of distaste for the exceptional position of women and Jews in that country.[8] It took a somewhat unconventional intellect, such as that of this flamboyant Milanese token Calvinist, expressly to champion freedom of women and Jews in print.

The substance of Leti's defence of freedom of women in Holland was his contention that its effects were largely beneficial and did not lead to unrestrained licentiousness in society. Again and again Leti returns to the theme that Dutch women enjoyed an altogether exceptional degree of freedom, and in every respect, but that despite this they were not in any way more forward sexually than French or Italian women. In fact, quite the contrary. In a number of passages Leti lavishly praises the modesty of Dutch women, remarking for instance on the fact that in contrast to France, Dutch women of all classes scrupulously kept neck, shoulders and bosom covered up, however taken they might be with French fashions in other respects.[9] Leti is also at pains to defend Amsterdam against the widely-held notion that harlotry and prostitution were allowed to flourish there to excess.[10] Leti compares what he considers the relatively small number of thirty *bordelli* found in Amsterdam with the much larger concentrations of houses of ill-repute encountered in Rome and Venice. 'For every one of these bordelli to be seen in Amsterdam,' he insists, 'there are for sure ten in so-called "holy" Rome and more than twenty in Venice.' He went so far as to assert that the Venetian regime deliberately encouraged sexual licentiousness as an instrument of state, to deflect the attention of the populace from political matters. Nor did he consider the number of brothels the only relevant factor. In Italy, asserts Leti, one is far more likely to meet seductive, brazen and promiscuous behaviour in public places than in Holland.

Leti's principal reason for broaching the subject of Dutch Jewry is that he (once again) wishes to show that one of Europe's chief prejudices against the Dutch Republic—that it allows Jews too much freedom—is unwarranted. But Leti was certainly no defender of Judaism as such. Like so many figures of the early Enlightenment, he boldly asserts the right of Jews to a place in society, and their potential worth to the state and general culture, while totally dismissing the rites and culture of the Jews themselves. We meet this attitude in his book on England, where he describes the Bevis Marks Synagogue in London. Services in Bevis Marks, claims Leti, are unsightly, unpleasant to the ear, and characterized by '*gesti ridicolosissimi*'.[11] And later, in his *Teatro Belgico*, he is scarcely any more flattering about the proceedings in the great Portuguese Synagogue at Amsterdam:

> concorrono giornalmente, e sopra tutto il sabbato, la matina, e il dopo pranso nell'hora degli esecizii Giudaici, numero grande di Christiani, che vengono per vedere, e la sinagoga, e le ceremonie de' Giudei, che per dire il vero son di poca edificatione, gridano, cantano salmi con voci senza tuono, e senza concerto, con i soliti veli sul cappello, ma no veggo gran differenza della maniera con la quale negotiano nella Borsa, e quella con la quale si tengono nella sinagoga; ma piacesse a Iddio che i Christiani potessero in cio rimproverarli, senza esser rimproverati.[12]

Nor, in contrast to so many seventeenth-century writers, does Leti place much emphasis on the economic activities of the Jews. He does believe that tolerating at least some categories of Jews brings economic benefits and has no doubt that where Spain, for instance, ruined herself by expelling her 'Jews, Marranos and Moors' such states as Venice,

Tuscany and Hamburg, as well as the Dutch Republic, had enriched themselves by encouraging Jewish immigration.[13] But he also recognizes the prevalence of poverty among the German Jews and tends to dismiss them as being of little value to society. One point he does stress is that allowing the Jews more freedom, and better terms of residence, does not, as many people fear, lead to a huge, uncontrollable influx of impoverished Ashkenazi Jews.[14] To illustrate this point he provides some most interesting statistics which, though accurate enough as far as the Sephardi community is concerned, wildly underestimate the size of the German–Jewish community in the Dutch state. He tells us that in Amsterdam there are 450 Portuguese Jewish families without counting a number of destitute families.[15] Since in all his works Leti habitually multiplies numbers of families by six to reach his estimates of total numbers of souls, this implies a total of just over three thousand, which is precisely the figure modern historians generally postulate for Amsterdam Sephardi Jewry at this time. Leti's estimate for Rotterdam Jewry, which he puts at eighty families,[16] can probably also be accepted as reasonably accurate though there is little other evidence with which to compare it. But then, in a wild underestimate of the number of Ashkenazim in Amsterdam, he tells us '*in quanto al numero de Giudei tedeschi non arrivano a cento famiglie che vuol dire, sei cento persone in circa*'.[17] Elsewhere in the *Teatro Belgico*, Leti states that the total number of Jews in the United Provinces amounted to no more than 1400 families, yielding a grand total of 8400 Jews, which, as far as we can tell, was only about half the real figure.[18]

But Leti's central point in his discussion of Dutch Jewry is that the Republic, by granting Jews citizenship and public honours, if not access to public office or economic equality with non-Jews, thereby assigning the Jews a higher status than they enjoyed anywhere else in Europe, derived only benefit. They demonstrated a loyalty and political good faith which reinforced the Dutch state, and were an asset culturally also. His discussion of Dutch Jewry thus focuses mainly on the life-style and attitudes of a group almost without parallel in Europe—Amsterdam's Jewish quasi-aristocratic élite, cultivated and wealthy, who live in what Leti styles *palazzi e case nobilissime* who have performed political and financial services for the state and in other ways contributed to the prosperity and well-being of Amsterdam. Leti is aware, as everyone living in Amsterdam was, of the great contrast in life-style and attitudes as between the Sephardi and Ashkenazi communities and shows no interest at all in the latter. It is the Portuguese Jews that interest him and then only their élite. He agrees that the Sephardi community as a whole is impressive. '*La sinagoga de' Portoghesi,*' he wrote, '*sembra un seggio di Nobili, gente ben fatta, quasi tutta civile, ben vestita, ricca e che fa gran figura.*'[19] But when he goes into detail he confines his attention to a handful of leading figures, those who had indisputably performed services for the state, for literature and for general culture.[20]

Essentially, then, Leti concentrates on the Sephardi elite because they fitted his arguments better than any other Jewish group, and best lived up to the political and cultural criteria of his distinctive brand of early Enlightenment republican idealism. But there is also the issue of his personal relations with the group in question. Leti, as a recent southern European immigrant with (at least at the outset) an inadequate knowledge of Dutch, spent much of his time with other members of Amsterdam's flourishing immigrant communities, especially Italians and French Huguenots but on occasion, it would seem, also Portuguese Jews. Clearly he visited and enjoyed hospitality at several of their houses and cultivated the acquaintance of at least several of those whom he describes. He may have obtained some financial benefit from his relations with them. Certainly he shows that the Sephardi élite now formed an integral part of the patronage network which supported Amsterdam's increasingly cosmopolitan community of men of letters at the close of the century. With one of the leading figures whom he describes, Baron Manuel de Belmonte, Resident, or as Leti calls him 'Agent-General', of the Spanish crown in the United Provinces, we know that he came in contact at the very outset of his sojourn in Amsterdam. This was whilst he was finalizing his manuscript of *Il ceremoniale historico* for publication when word got out that there was a great deal in it about the European powers, especially France and Spain, and that the first volume was dedicated to Louis XIV.[21] At the instigation of the Spanish ambassador in The Hague, Belmonte was sent to see Leti and offered him a large sum of money for the deletion of passages derogatory of Spain. Leti afterwards proudly claimed to have refused both the money and any deletions, asserting that his unwavering goal was historical truth.

The Amsterdam Jewish personality to whom Leti devotes most space is Jeronimo Nunes da Costa (Moses Curiel) (1620–97) who had had the title of 'Agent of the Crown of Portugal in the United Provinces' since May 1645.[22] Jeronimo Nunes da Costa, Leti explains, had performed many important services on behalf of Portugal, and during the long periods in which there had been no resident Portuguese ambassador at The Hague had in effect functioned as Portugal's minister in the Dutch Republic. Leti recalls in the *Raguagli historici*, first published in 1698, a year after Jeronimo's death, and then reissued in 1700, that the Portuguese Council of State, in Lisbon, was so satisfied with his services that no sooner did word reach Portugal of his death than patents were dispatched appointing his eldest surviving son,

Alexandre Nunes da Costa,[23] to the same post and with the same honours and privileges as his father had enjoyed 'e con lettere obligantissime'.[24] But having acknowledged Jeronimo's services on behalf of Portugal, Leti at once goes on to say that this pre-eminent Sephardi personage had also performed many notable services for the Dutch state. He was regarded as a citizen of such merit, Leti tells us, that in recognition '*del suo instancabile zelo verso la republica*' he had been presented with '*una bellissima catena d'oro, e misteriosissima medaglia*' and with the much-prized privilege of exemption from taxation such as was enjoyed by scarcely ten other men in the whole of the Dutch Republic, apart from fully accredited ambassadors.[25] Among other details he gives, and which indicate some familiarity with the Da Costa household, Leti reports the exact date of Jeronimo's death, 16 January 1697, and says that Alexandre continued to preside over the family firm, together with his youngest brother Alvaro, but that out of veneration for their departed father, the brothers continued to trade under the name 'Geronimo Nunes da Costa e figli'.[26]

Another Sephardi personage to whom Leti devotes detailed attention is Baron Manuel de Belmonte, who had been first Agent, then Agent-General, and finally Resident of Spain in the United Provinces.[27] Once again, Leti points out that during the sometimes politically crucial periods when there had been no Spanish ambassador in The Hague, Belmonte had in practice served as Spain's representative to the States General. Belmonte had indeed done much on behalf of Spain, but what Leti is even more anxious to point out is that he had also actively assisted and served the interests of the Dutch state. So highly had his activity been appreciated by the States General that he too had been granted tax exemption. Leti adds that Belmonte was always full of the latest European news, which we can well believe; we know that he regularly corresponded with Spanish diplomats in other European countries as well as with ministers at The Hague, Brussels and Madrid. A third figure whom Leti mentions as having played a significant political role was Baron Francisco Lopes Suasso. He tells us that this personality was held in high esteem by the States General and all Dutch ministers as well as by the diplomatic confraternity at The Hague, where he normally lived, and by the Dutch Stadholder, William III, king of England. In particular, Leti alludes to Lopes Suasso's major role in buttressing the finances of the Spanish régime in Brussels and the payments to the Spanish army of Flanders during the 1690s, remarking that during the 'last war' (i.e. the Nine Years War 1689–97) Lopes Suasso had performed '*rilevanti serviggi alla causa commune de' collegati*', that is on behalf of the coalition of European powers allied against Louis XIV's France.[28]

Awareness of their merits and public services, Leti maintains, was the reason that Amsterdam's Jewish élite had come to be not just accepted, but sought after, in the most select circles. Jeronimo Nunes da Costa, he assures us, was esteemed and visited by everyone. Besides a host of lesser dignitaries and noblemen who had visited his famous town house in Amsterdam, and supped at his table, Leti records that the Electress Sophia of Hanover (the mother of the future George I of England) had lodged for some time in his house, as, on one occasion, had the French ambassador, the marquis de Croissy, the 'other Colbert'.[29] And Jeronimo's deceased wife, Ribca Abaz, whose family, as Leti remarks, had been ennobled by the Holy Roman Emperor in the early seventeenth century, had reputedly been just as accomplished and assured in entertaining noble ladies, and welcoming them to her home, as had Jeronimo in receiving noblemen and diplomats.[30] Leti also says that after Jeronimo's death, his sons Alexandre and Alvaro succeeded in maintaining the high social standing which their parents had achieved, and in this he was certainly right. Both Alexandre and, after his death, Alvaro, who was Agent of the crown of Portugal in the United Provinces from 1712 until his death in 1737, are known to have had frequent dealings with an assortment of aristocratic diplomats, most notably Luis da Cunha and the conde de Tarouca who were among the most outstanding Portuguese statesmen of the eighteenth century. These personages spent a good deal of time in the United Provinces especially during the 1712–13 European peace congress at Utrecht. Alexandre and Alvaro were, of course, assisting their diplomatic work and, among other things, arranged their accommodation at Utrecht.[31] But it does seem that they also formed a genuine friendship with these men. The Portuguese Protestant writer Francisco Xavier de Oliveira, who knew Alvaro Nunes da Costa in Amsterdam in the 1730s records that Alvaro

> étoit sans cesse visité de toute la noblesse du pais, et de presque tous les ministres étrangers qui passoient à Amsterdam pour se rendre à la Haye. Deux grands ministres du Portugal, le Comte de Tarouca, et Dom Luis da Cunha, avoient pour lui la plus parfaite considération.[32]

Moreover, it is likely that Luis da Cunha's well-attested philo-Semitic attitude, and hostility to the Portuguese Inquisition, began with, or was at least fomented by, his encounter with the Nunes da Costa at Amsterdam.[33] If so, this would figure as a key instance of the Amsterdam Sephardi élite's success in elevating the standing and improving the image of western Jewry in the eyes of educated non-Jews through their assiduous cultivating of the travelling aristocratic and diplomatic *monde* of their time.

But as Leti emphasizes, the Nunes da Costa, if among the most successful, were by no means alone in finding acceptance in the most select circles. Several other figures were no less notable in this respect. Don Isaac Senior Teixeira, for example, who arrived in Amsterdam from Hamburg in 1698, at the age of fifty, is described by Leti as an immensely cultivated gentleman who had not only performed numerous public services on behalf of the republic of Hamburg but also whilst living there had been constantly visited by distinguished personages. He tells that Queen Christina had lodged in his house on many occasions after her abdication of the Swedish throne and that the Elector and Electress of Brandenburg had lodged with him in 1682.[34] According to Leti, Baron Lopes Suasso was likewise greatly esteemed by '*rappresentanti publici e nobiltà straniera*' and since it is well known that he had many dealings with the Stadholder-king William III, there is no reason to question this.[35] And as for Baron Belmonte, Leti reveals the highly significant, though by no means surprising, fact that Spain's ambassadors to the Dutch Republic, when on visits to Amsterdam from The Hague, where the embassy was, were accustomed to lodge at his house.[36] Possibly part of the explanation as to why Baron Belmonte chose to reside at some distance from the Jewish quarter of Amsterdam, while Jeronimo Nunes da Costa and other Sephardi leaders resided within it or at its edge, was his need to prevent embarrassment to his aristocratic Spanish guests, envoys of the crown which in 1492 had expelled the ancestors of Holland's Sephardi community from Spain.

Besides their activity in support of the Dutch state and its allies, and their success in finding acceptance in high society, what most impressed Leti about Amsterdam's Sephardi élite was its seigneurial life-style and its zeal for literature—especially for men of letters such as himself. This is a theme which recurs in several of his descriptions of leading Amsterdam Sephardi personages and opens up a new dimension to our perceptions of this group whom historians are accustomed to think of as patrons of Jewish, or at any rate of Sephardi literature, but not as patrons of non-Jewish literatures. Jeronimo Nunes da Costa, according to Leti, not only won the affection and esteem of all who knew him but was always zealous to '*proteggere, accarezzare e beneficiare letterati*'.[37] Likewise, Leti assures us, that highly cultivated gentleman Don Diogo Teixeira de Mattos, eldest son of Isaac Teixeira, enthusiastically emulated his father '*nel favorire e accarezzare i letterati*'.[38] Oddly enough, Leti does not mention Baron Belmonte in this connection, though other evidence suggests that Don Manuel was the most serious of all the Amsterdam Sephardi patricians in the sphere of literary patronage. It was Baron Belmonte who set up late seventeenth-century Amsterdam Sephardi Jewry's two literary salons, the Academia de los Sitibundos

(1676) and the Academia de los Floridos (1685), modelled on the Spanish literary fraternities of the day, and it was to Baron Belmonte that Isabel Correa dedicated her monumental Spanish rendering of Guarini's *Il Pastor Fido*.[39]

But when Leti asserts that the Amsterdam Sephardi élite zealously associated with, and cultivated, men of letters what exactly is he telling us? In the case of Sephardi writers, on both religious and secular topics, it is clear enough that the Dutch Sephardi patriciate assisted financially, especially towards the costs of publication; and that they, in turn, were rewarded for their outlay by being festooned with flowery dedications. But in the case of non-Jewish writers there are no known instances of this type. What Leti seems principally to have in mind is the liberal hospitality regularly showered on Amsterdam's resident colony of foreign writers by the Sephardi patricians. It seems clear enough that Leti himself was a frequent guest. Jeronimo Nunes da Costa, he tells us, was fond of nothing more than of extending hospitality to foreign visitors and was used to '*ricevere con nobilissimo accoglio gli stranieri in sua casa*'. Similarly, Baron Lopes Suasso, though he normally resided near the government buildings at the centre of The Hague, was accustomed to offer '*speso tavola ad amici e stranieri*'.[40] In his account of the German Empire, published a decade before Isaac Teixeira's move from Hamburg to Amsterdam,[41] Leti remarks that Hamburg was known everywhere as being one of the chief centres of hospitality and culture in Central Europe, but that no one in Hamburg had a greater reputation for hospitality among travellers of quality than Don Isaac:

> Et in questo genere il signor Resident Teixeira fa grande honore alla città, poiche so sforza più d'ogni altro ad honorare e accarezzare gli stranieri, e a trattar con molta prudenza e amorevolezza con cittadini, di modo che la sua casa splendidissima in ogni cosa, sembra un Teatro, e un Albergo della gentilezza.[42]

But if we now go on to ask why foreign literati were regularly included among the dinner guests of the Sephardi patriciate, we see at once that the function of the non-Jewish men of letters in the life-style of the Sephardi élite must have been very different from that of the Sephardi authors whom they patronized. By assisting the publication of works, religious and secular, by Portuguese Jewish writers, the Amsterdam Sephardi patriciate were consciously striving to enhance their standing and prestige within their own community and the Jewish world at large.[43] For the same reasons, there were sometimes sermons and prayer-gatherings in their homes. Thus, during Passover 1690, Jeronimo Nunes da Costa invited the pick of the Amsterdam Sephardi community, together with three or four rabbis, to his home for a study session. One of those present, Rabbi Samuel da Silva de Miranda, delivered a sermon which was subsequently published, no doubt at Jeronimo's expense, and dedicated to him.[44] In 1683, Joseph Penso de La Vega, one of the most active members of the Amsterdam Sephardi literary coterie, published a flowery panegyric on the 'Divine Law of Moses' which he dedicated to the 'merit and zeal' of Jeronimo Nunes da Costa under his synagogue name, Moseh Curiel.[45] In some cases, the works patronized by the Dutch Sephardi élite, though written by Sephardi authors, were essentially intended to boost their standing in the non-Jewish Spanish- and Portuguese-speaking world. This was the case, for example, with Manoel de Leon's *Triumpho Lusitano* (1688), a eulogy of King Pedro II of Portugal on the occasion of his second marriage, paid for by and dedicated to Jeronimo Nunes da Costa, which Jeronimo specially had published in Catholic Brussels so as to facilitate its sale in Portugal and the Portuguese colonies.[46] This publication, essentially a piece of political propaganda, bore an engraved title-page, representing the arms and insignia of Portugal, of remarkable beauty. Another such general work was Abraham da Fonseca's *Orthographia Castellana* (1663), a treatise on Spanish orthography published at Amsterdam and again dedicated to Jeronimo Nunes da Costa.[47] In the same way, the Amsterdam Sephardi élite gained added lustre from the inflated baroque poetic eulogies which flowed from the ready pen of Daniel Levi de Barrios.

But the reasons for cultivating non-Sephardi writers were different. A man such as Leti could be of no service to building up the image of the Amsterdam Sephardi élite either in the Hispanic world or the European Jewish Diaspora. But where such non-Jewish literati who, being resident in Holland, were generally either Protestant or nominally so, could be of great service was in acting as a cultural bridge between the Sephardi patriciate, on the one hand, and the aristocratic milieu of courtiers and diplomats with which they aspired to rub shoulders, on the other. For Amsterdam's Portuguese Jewish patricians needed more than mere titles, splendid houses, liveried servants and richly laden tables to attract princes, ambassadors and noblemen, and their wives, to their doors. Also indispensable was the capacity to provide the right sort of conversation. Thus culture, and especially the refined talk of fashionable literati, became a zealously sought-after commodity among Amsterdam's quasi-aristocratic Sephardi patricians.

Leti abundantly attests to the Sephardi patricians' interest in cultivating elegant conversation. He tells us that Don Isaac Senior Teixeira *'parla molte lingue con gran franchezza e tra le altre cose ama molto la compagnia de' letterati che accoglie in sua casa con grand' affetto'*.[48] His son,

Don Diogo (Abraham Senior) Teixeira de Mattos, according to Leti, was an even more polished conversationalist:

> Don Diogo può veramente dirsi huomo *ad utrumque paratus*, perche parla di tutto, discorre di tutto, e intende a perfettione quel tanto che conviene nella società civile ad un galanthuomo, essendosi spesso esercitato nella lettura di differenti opere de' più celebrati scrittori, essendo in oltre la gentilezza istessa.[49]

Similarly Baron Lopes Suasso, asserts Leti, whatever his riches in money, was even richer '*in suoi tesori dell'animo, con li quali rende sempre più accreditata la sua nattione*'.[50] And as for Jeronimo Nunes da Costa, none could match him '*nella destra condotta, e accorta prudenze di sapersi maneggiare con tutti*'.

The houses of the Sephardi patriciate of Amsterdam and The Hague, then, were more than just luxurious residences; they also served as the forum for a highly intricate and richly cosmopolitan cultural ritual. The magnificence of at any rate the three-best known Amsterdam Jewish patrician houses—those of the Nunes da Costa, Belmonte and De Pinto—has often been remarked upon. But it is questionable whether the extent to which they functioned as show-cases for both Sephardi and general culture has been fully grasped. It is evident that they were among the major tourist attractions of Amsterdam. Together with their accessories—coaches, barges and liveried servants—they were intended to impress noblemen as well as Jewry and the public at large. Leti describes Baron Belmonte's residence as a '*casa nobilissima*', equipped with a '*carrozza bellissima con le armi di Spagna*'. On the famous Romeyn de Hooghe engraving of the house, we see these arms also over the front entrance and carved on the back of Belmonte's imposing barge. Still more impressive, according to Leti, was the home of Jeronimo Nunes da Costa

> la più commoda, esplendida casa della città almeno tiene un giardino che non ve n'e alcuno altro che l'ugagli; e foura la gran porta della sua casa si vede l'arma di Portogallo; in oltre un carrozzino per suo uso, e una bellissima barca, con l'arma ancora di Portogallo, e è certo che fa nobil figura, e nella sua casa sembra esservi una corte, per il gran concorse de' stranieri . . . [51]

Thus, according to Leti, Jeronimo's garden, of which we snatch just a glimpse on Romeyn de Hooghe's famous engraving, through the open front entrance, and which we know from other sources was exceptionally large for an Amsterdam town house,[52] was arguably the most outstanding in the city. At any rate, it was a particularly fine garden. From this and other evidence, we see that the Nunes da Costa were among the chief propagators of an enthusiasm for fine gardens which arose among the Dutch Sephardi élite at this time.[53] From a letter of Alvaro Nunes da Costa to a Portuguese minister, written in 1712, we learn that a specialist gardener was employed at the house and that the family had a decided interest in new and rare varieties of plants, examples of at least some of which they shipped to Lisbon, intent on delighting the Portuguese court with the spectacle of varieties previously unknown in Portugal.[54] The effort which went in to cultivating fine gardens, we may conclude, was yet another means of seizing the attention of visiting envoys and aristocrats.

But the principal attraction contained in the houses of the Amsterdam Portuguese Jewish patriciate were the precious objects, rarities and exotic items stored in cabinets and display cases within. If the cultivation of elegant conversation about literary topics was one method of forging a path into fashionable society, another (and among the merchant élites of Venice, Antwerp and Amsterdam the traditional) method, was to amass noted collections of antiquities and remarkable objects of fineness, rarity and beauty guaranteed to arrest the eye of eminent visitors. These collections did not necessarily exclude Judaica. In this period, the Dutch Sephardi élite were striving to raise the standing of Jewish culture in the eyes of non-Jewish society, as well as to convert themselves into the embodiment of all that was finest in general culture. Among the items on display in the Nunes da Costa household, for example, was a mediaeval illuminated Hebrew Bible of exceptional beauty which Jeronimo's father, Duarte Nunes da Costa, had purchased from a Spanish Jew from North Africa whilst in Pisa in 1618, and which was regarded as the oldest and most venerable possessed by Dutch Jewry.[55] Nor were the Sephardi patricians in the least inhibited about displaying the various patents of nobility they had received from the kings of Spain and Portugal and letters of appointment from various other princes. But the chief categories of objects on display were the exotica and rarities, especially fine jewels. Paintings and other works of art were included also, but appear to have received less emphasis in these Sephardi homes. When the De Pinto house was pillaged during the riots in Amsterdam in 1696 one of the display cases dragged out into the street contained medallions and old coins.[56]

Jewish wealth in Amsterdam was thus on display, presented to the public, in ways that were to be met with nowhere else in Europe. But much care was taken by the Sephardi patricians to project only what was deemed the right image. No Jewish beggars were allowed to congregate around their doors. Indeed, both the Sephardi and Ashkenazi leadership in Amsterdam were greatly concerned to keep the Jewish destitute as far as possible off the streets. Both communities operated a comprehensive system of community welfare, the net effect of which, as far as an outsider such as Leti was concerned, was to keep the Jewish poor virtually out of sight. But what one did see congregating around the doors of the Sephardi patricians were crowds of Christian beggars whom the former took good care to ply with coins. The Sephardi Jewish community, explains Leti, '*si sogliono raccogliere e spendere dieci mila scudi per anno d'elemosine, e pero tra di loro non vi vedono poveri andar per le porte se non fossero Christiani a quali sogliono dare alcuni bene spesso*'.[57] But while all the Sephardi patricians acted thus, Baron Belmonte stood out in this respect. Belmonte, says Leti,

> si fa conoscere grande amico de' poveri onde hà ristretto di molto gli atti di cortesia, di gratitudine, e di civilità, per esser più generoso verso gli stessi mendici, de' quali se ne vedono spesso in gran copia innanzi la porta della sua casa. Alcuni l'accusano di fare egli questo per ostenttatione, per vanità, ma comunque sia i poveri ne profittano.[58]

Exactly how this strategy influenced popular perceptions of the Amsterdam Sephardi élite is hard to say. Certainly there was in Amsterdam relatively little of the overt popular hostility to the Sephardi patricians which surged up so strongly in the late 1690s at Hamburg, precipitating the flight of the Teixeira to Holland. The leading Sephardi figures felt sufficiently secure to parade their wealth and pretensions in an unprecedentedly public manner, and it is clear that theirs were household names known to practically everyone who lived in the city. Still, there is no reason to suppose that they were looked on with affection by the masses and it is noteworthy that their houses were among the relatively small number of Amsterdam patrician residences—the Christian houses in the group belonging to persons who were particularly unpopular with the mob—which were attacked during the so-called *Aansprekersoproer* (undertakers' riot) of 1696. The De Pinto house, whose owners were then away at The Hague, was the only Jewish residence actually plundered. The mob invaded the house, smashing the porcelein '*dat daer in grote menigte was en zeer costelijck, in stucken*' and carried off jewels, coins and other 'rarities'. But before this the crowd had 'seriously threatened' the residence of the 'Palsgraaf Belmonte' as he was generally known in the city, withdrawing leaving the building intact only because the baron had barricaded himself in so strongly.[59] The same happened at the house of Jeronimo Nunes da Costa, who

> hadde zijn huijs van binnen meede wel bezorgt, de deuren met dwarsboomen 's cruisweegs toegemaakt en verscheijde gewapende in elcke kamer die aan de straat en op de tuijn uijtzien.[60]

The crowd withdrew after being warned from one of the windows that they would be fired on if they came closer.

But whatever the undercurrents of popular resentment against the Jews, Leti was confident that the new finesse, discretion and exemplary conduct of Amsterdam's Sephardi élite were the right tools by which the Jews could win the esteem and affection of all. It was the ancient pride and arrogance of the Jewish people which in the past had brought down so many calamities on their heads.

Leti's central conclusion, then, from his observations on Dutch Jewry, was that the Republic which had taken them in and given them unprecedented freedom was now reaping its just reward. The Jews in Holland had been transformed into valuable citizens capable of rendering significant services both to the state and to culture. As for Jewish religion and tradition, these had no value whatever in Leti's eyes. This was the characteristic stance of the European Enlightenment towards the Jews. Leti's vision extended to the possibility that one day society might accept the Jews as equals and that then, finally, the Jews would show themselves, in their capacity for political service and general culture, to be fully the equals of others:

> nella società civile gli Huomini son tutti uguali, di nodo che basta una buona condotta per acquistar gran merito. E come *apud Deum non est ecceptio personarum*, lo stesso deve seguire della società civile, ond'e che in Holanda si da indifferentemente la cittadinanza.[61]

Notes

1 L. Fassò, *Avventurieri della penna del seicento. Gregorio Leti, Gerolamo Arconati Lamberti, Tomaso Tomasi, Bernardo Guasconi* (Florence, 1923), pp. 71, 88, 100.

2 *ibid.*, pp. 219–20

3 A. Cameroni, *Uno scrittore avventuriero del secolo XVII. Gregorio Leti. Appunti critici* (Milan, 1893), pp. 162–4.

4 See G. Leti, *Raguagli historici e politici o vero compendio delle virtù heroiche sopra la fedeltà de'suditi, e amore verso la patria*, 2 vols (Amsterdam, 1700), vol. 1, raguaglio iii, pp. 262–5 *et seq.*

5 'Ma a proposito di forastieri', averred Leti, 'diro che questi hanno grandissima libertà, poiche entrano e escono a loro piacere, senza esser tropo ricercati ne esaminati come se fa in Italia, o in Francia, o . . . in Germania': G. Leti, *Teatro Belgico, o vero ritratti historici, chronologici, politici, e geografici, della sette Provincie Unite*, 2 vols (Amsterdam, 1690), vol. 2, p. 406.

6 See, e.g., Leti, (note 4 above), vol. 1, raguaglio iii, pp. 408–10.

7 See, e.g., G. Leti, *Il ceremoniale historico e politico, opera utilissima a tutti gli Ambasciatori, e Ministri publici*, 6 vols (Amsterdam, 1685), vol. 5, p. 734.

8 *ibid.* This is perhaps especially so of German opinion; see Julia Bientjes, *Holland und die Holländer im Urteil deutscher Reisender, 1400–1800* (Groningen, 1967), pp. 91–4, 223–4; the writer Heinrich Benthem contemptuously noted of Holland, in 1698, 'Denn hier

krehet die Henne und der Hahn muss nur keckeln', *ibid.*, p. 223.

9 Leti (note 5 above), vol. 2, pp. 28–9

10 Leti (note 4 above), vol. 1, raguaglio iii, p. 269; in another passage, written a few years after the notorious booklet *Le Putanisme d'Amsterdam* (1681) lent further currency to Amsterdam's reputation as a den of sexual promiscuity, Leti noted that the combination of unparalleled religious toleration and alleged licentiousness generated *'un certo horrore'* abroad, Leti (note 7 above), vol. 5, p. 734; Bientjes (note 8 above), pp. 175–6.

11 G. Leti, *Del teatro Brittanico o vero historia dello stato, antico e presente*, ... *della Grande Brettagna*, 2 vols (London, 1683), vol. 1, pp. 251–2, 549–50.

12 Leti (note 5 above), vol. 2, p. 337.

13 Leti (note 7 above), vol. 5, pp. 731–2.

14 *ibid.*, p. 724; Leti (note 5 above), vol. 2, p. 132; in his account of the court of Brandenburg, of 1687, Leti describes Berlin Jewry as being small in number: 'e di poca figura, se non fosse il signor Joost Libman d'ottimi portamenti, che gode il privileggio d'esser Gioielliere de queste serenissimi Altezze, e che in fatti serve con puntualità, e confedeltà, virtù che l'hanno accreditato appresso la persona di S.A.E. che con somma humanità lo vede di buon' occhio, e come spesso si fa veder nella corte, viene da tutti i corteggiani ben visto, più di quello che permette quell'uso ordinario de'Christiani verso i Giudei; perche in fatti dico e buona persona e honorevole,' G. Leti, *Ritratti historici, politici, chronologici e genealogici della Casa Serenissima, e elettorale di Brandenburgo*, 2 vols (Amsterdam, 1687), vol. 1, p. 334.

15 Leti (note 5 above), vol. 2, p. 336.

16 *ibid.*, p. 132; the provision of seating in Rotterdam's new synagogue, built in 1725, suggests that the Ashkenazi community then numbered around 100 families; see C. Reijnders, *Van 'Joodsche Natiën' tot joodse Nederlanders* (Amsterdam, 1970), p. 154.

17 Leti (note 5 above), vol. 2, p. 336; earlier Leti had estimated the total number of Sephardi and Ashkenazi families in Amsterdam at 570, or around 3420 souls in all, adding that in any case 'certo e che non arrivano a quatro mila'; Leti (note 7 above), vol. 5, p. 725.

18 Leti (note 5 above), vol. 2, p. 132; with regard to Anglo-Jewry, Leti gives two different statistics, asserting in one place that there were 300 Jewish families in England in the early 1680s and in another 200; see Leti (note 11 above), vol. 1, pp. 251, 549.

19 Leti (note 7 above), vol. 5, p. 728.

20 Besides those whom he discusses in detail, Leti lists the Amsterdam Jewish élite, or at least the menfolk, as follows: il Barone Antonio Lopez Suasso, David Emmanuel de Pinto, Giacob Perera, Giacomo del Prado, Giacomo de Pinto, Giacomo Aboaf Ozorio, Francisco Emanuel Dias Jorge, Moise Pereira, Henrique Mendes de Silva, Abramo del Soto, Emanuele de Pinto, Giosepe e Abramo Felix, Giacomo e David Bueno de Meschita, Abramo Telles, Antonio Alvarez (Machado), Simone e Luigi Rodrigues de Soze, Emanuel de Vega, il provveditore di Mascado, Emanuel Goma de Silva, e altrui; Leti (note 7 above), vol. 5, p. 725. The Giacomo del Prado mentioned here is the same as the Isaac de Prado who was a *parnas* that year as was Isaac (Manuel?) de Pinto and Isaac (Henrique) Mendes da Silva; Abraham Telles was *parnas* in 1681 as was Jacob de Pinto in 1682 and Jacob Bueno de Mesquita in 1683; regarding the wealth of the community, Leti says 'molte sono quelle Famiglie che godono gran richezze, e ne sono due, o tre che non hanno meno d'un milione di facoltà ciascuna; più di sei di mezo milione al meno, in somma tra queste 450 famiglie si fa il conto che vi siano più di venti milioni di facoltà, la maggior parte in gemme in contanti, in buone lettere'; Leti, (note 5 above), vol. 2, p. 336.

21 Fassò, (note 1 above), p. 230.

22 Quite a lot has now been written about this personality, see D. Swetschinski, 'An Amsterdam Jewish Merchant–Diplomat: Jeronimo Nunes da Costa alias Moseh Curiel (1620–1697), Agent of the King of Portugal', in L. Dasberg and J. N. Cohen (eds), *Neveh Ya'akov. Jubilee volume presented to Dr Jaap Meijer on the occasion of his seventieth birthday* (Assen, 1982) pp. 3–30; and J. I. Israel, 'The Diplomatic Career of Jeronimo Nunes da Costa: an Episode in Dutch–Portuguese Relations of the Seventeenth Century', *Bijdragen en Mededelingen betreffende de Geschiedenis der Nederlanden*, vol. 98 (1983), pp. 167–90; *id.*, 'An Amsterdam Jewish Merchant of the Golden Age: Jeronimo Nunes da Costa (1620–1697), Agent of Portugal in the Dutch Republic', *Studia Rosenthaliana*, vol. 18 (1984), pp. 21–40. Jeronimo was ennobled as a 'cavalheiro fidalgo da casa real' by John IV of Portugal in 1646.

23 Alexandre Nunes da Costa (Selomoh Curiel) (1655–1712) was much less active in his capacity as 'Agent of Portugal' (1697–1712) than his father had been, being mainly employed to send miscellaneous items of various kinds needed by the king and his ministers in Portugal; however, the Portuguese ambassador, Sousa Pacheco, during his temporary absence from the United Provinces in 1698 did name Alexandre as his chargé d'affaires, asking the States General to 'respondere, pendante ejus absentia memorialibus ab Alexandro Nunio a Costa, Regis Domini sui Amstelodami Agent praesentandis'; see Algemeen Rijksarchief, The Hague (ARH), Archive of the States General 7104. Francisco de Sousa Pacheco to SG, The Hague, 11 February 1698; Alexandre was elected *parnas* of the Amsterdam Sephardi community in 1700 but refused the honour and was not subsequently elected, see Gemeente Archief, Amsterdam, Archive of the Portuguese Jewish Community no. 1323. 'Registro dos parnasim'.

24 This detail suggests that Leti had actually been shown the patents; Leti (note 4 above), vol. 2, raguaglio i, p. 123; Alexandre seems also to have inherited his father's position as one of the two permanent deputies of the Amsterdam Sephardi community to the non-Jewish authorities—together with Baron Belmonte; it was in this capacity—and not as I. S. Emmanuel states as a *parnas*—that he went to see the West India Company directors in January 1702, together with Belmonte, to convey Curaçao Jewry's protest at the attempts of the governor of Curaçao to make them send their slaves to work on the island's fortifications on the Sabbath; Belmonte was then a *parnas* of the community but Alexandre was not, see ARH Archive of the West India Company 357 fo.15.res. 17 January 1702 and I. S. and S. A. Emmanuel, *History of the Jews of the Netherlands Antilles*, 2 vols (Cincinatti, 1970), vol. 1, p. 100.

25 On the presentation of the gold chain and Jeronimo's tax exemption, see Israel, 'Diplomatic Career' (note 7 above), vol. 5, pp. 182–3, 186–7; Leti (note 7 above), vol. 5, p. 728; id. (note 4 above), vol. 2, raguaglio i, p. 128.

26 Jeronimo Nunes da Costa had four married sons, the eldest of whom, Duarte Nunes da Costa (Aaron Curiel) (1650–95)—to whom Joseph Penso de la Vega dedicated his *Confusion de Confusiones*, in 1688—died two years before his father; a third son, Francisco Nunes da Costa (Jacob Curiel) (1660–1703), died only five years after his father, so that of the four only the youngest, Alvaro Nunes da Costa (Nathan Curiel) (1666–1737) lived beyond 1712. Given that Alvaro was born in 1666 and that his father was an enthusiastic supporter of Sabbatai Sevi in 1665–6, it may be that Alvaro was given his Jewish name, Nathan, in honour of Nathan of Gaza. (I am indebted to Edgar Samuel, Director of the Jewish Museum, for the dates of birth and death of Jeronimo's sons.)

27 Leti (note 7 above), vol. 5, p. 728.

28 On Lopes Suasso's role in the financing of the Spanish army of Flanders during the 1690s, see J. I. Israel, *European Jewry in the Age of Mercantilism, 1550–1750* (Oxford, 1985), p. 134.

29 Actually both the elector, Ernest Augustus, and the Electress lodged at Jeronimo's house
   when they visited Amsterdam in 1679. Whilst there, the Elector fell ill and had to be
   attended by Jeronimo's physician who was none other than the famous Isaac Orobio de
   Castro; see E. Bodemann (ed.), *Briefwechseln der Herzogin Sophie von Hannover mit ihrem
   Bruder dem Kurfürsten Karl Ludwig von der Pfalz* (Leipzig, 1885), p. 369.

30 Leti (note 7 above), vol. 5, p. 728; Ribca Abaz (1634–86) was a daughter of the Dias
   Jorge family which (whilst still ostensibly Catholic New Christians) had been
   ennobled by the Emperor Rudolph II under patents of 1610 and 1614; see Heinrich
   Schnee, *Die Hoffinanz und der moderne Staat*, 6 vols (Berlin, 1953–4), vol. 4, p. 315.

31 Gemeente Archief, Amsterdam, Notarial Archive 7958 ii, p. 88, a deed of 25 April
   1712 by which Alexandre pledged 13,000 guilders as surety for payment for the hire,
   for Dom Luis da Cunha, of a large house in Utrecht belonging to the Utrecht
   nobleman, the heer van Deijl.

32 F. Xavier de Oliveira, *Discours Pathétique au sujet des calamités présentes arrivées en
   Portugal* (London, 1756), p. 41.

33 See the *Instrucões inéditas de D. Luis da Cunha a Marco António de Azevedo Coutinho*
   (Coimbra, 1929), pp. 75–6, 87, 95–7.

34 Leti (note 7 above), vol. 5, pp. 557–8; id. (note 4 above), vol. 2, raguaglio i, pp. 126–7;
   H. Kellenbenz, 'Königin Christine und ihre Beziehungen zu Hamburg', in *Queen
   Christina of Sweden. Documents and Studies* (Stockholm, 1966), pp. 188–9.

35 Leti (note 4 above), vol. 2, raguaglio i, pp. 127–8

36 Leti (note 5 above), vol. 2, p. 406

37 Leti (note 4 above), vol. 2, raguaglio i, p. 124

38 *ibid.*, i, p. 127

39 Isabel Correa dedicated her poem on 15 November 1693, in Antwerp, to 'Don
   Manuel de Belmonte, Baron de Belmonte, Conde Palatino y Regente de su Magestad
   Catholica', see I. Correa, *El Pastor Fido, Poëma de Baptista Guarino* (Antwerp, 1694);
   see also D. M. Swetchinski, 'The Portuguese Jews of seventeenth-century Amsterdam: Cultural continuity and Adaptation', in F. Malino and P. C. Albert (eds.), *Essays
   in Modern Jewish History: A Tribute to Ben Halpern* (New York, 1982), p. 71–3.

40 'D'ordinario stantia con la sua famiglia nell'Haga, con carozza a sei, servitù, e livrea
   decente . . .'; Leti (note 4 above), vol. 2, raguagli i, p. 127. The Lopes Suasso
   residence on the Nieuwe Voorhout was regarded in the early eighteenth century as
   one of the finest houses in The Hague; see M. Henriquez Pimentel, *Geschiedkundige
   aanteekeningen betreffende de Portugeesche Israelieten in Den Haag en hunne synagogen* (The
   Hague, 1876), p. 35.

41 Another detail for which we must thank Leti is that he tells us, in the *Raguagli historici*,
   that Teixeira's move from Hamburg to Amsterdam took place in September 1698; in
   his notes on Teixeira, Henriques de Castro observes that the move must have taken
   place only shortly before Teixeira's election as *parnas* of the Amsterdam community
   in 1699. Such a speedy elevation to the highest communal honour so soon after arrival
   in Holland would seem to have been unprecedented; Leti (note 4 above), vol. 2,
   raguaglio i, p. 126; D. Henriques de Castro, *Keur van grafsteenen op de Nederl. Portug.
   Israel. begraafplaats te Oudekerk aan den Amstel*, 2 vols (Leiden, 1883) vol. 1, p. 106.

42 G. Leti, *Ritratti historici* (note 14 above), vol. 2, p. 378; in this connection, Teixeira's
   role as host, as well as manager of the income and business agent of Queen Christina
   of Sweden, takes on an added dimension. For Christina regarded herself as the
   standard-bearer of culture, and especially of French and Italian refinement, amid what
   she considered to be the cultural wastes of Germany and Scandinavia, so that both her
   initial choice of and subsequent unbroken adherence to Teixeira, indicate that she
   must have regarded him as not just a reliable business manager but as in some sense an
   embodiment of refined culture in the Hamburg context.

43 The most important such secular work was, of course, Joseph de la Vega's treatise *Confusion de Confusiones*, on the workings of the Amsterdam stock exchange which was published in 1688 and dedicated to Jeronimo's then eldest son, Duarte Nunes da Costa.

44 A. Neves, *Bibliografia Luso-judaica* (Coimbra, 1913). p. 22.

45 J. Penso de la Vega, *La rosa panegirico sacro en encomio de la Divina Ley de Mosseh* (Amsterdam, 1683).

46 M. de Leon, *Triumpho Lusitano. Applausos festivos* (Brussels, 1688); see also M. Kayserling, *Biblioteca Española-Portugueza-Judaica* (Strasbourg, 1890), p. 57.

47 Kayserling (note 46 above), p. 46.

48 Leti (note 7 above), vol. 5, p. 558; in his book on Germany, Leti describes Don Isaac as a 'signore cortese, e civile, e inclinato con molta generosa gentilezza a far servitio ad ogni uno, onde comunemente viene amato da tutti'; id., *Ritratti historici*(note 14 above), p. 375.

49 Leti (note 4 above), vol. 2, raguaglio i, p. 127.

50 *ibid.*

51 Leti (note 11 above), vol. 2, p. 406; the arms of Portugal were still in place above the front entrance several decades later, for Oliveira records that on arriving in Amsterdam from Lisbon in 1734 'à la vue de l'Ecu des Armes de Portugal arboré sur le grand porteil de la maison de cet Agent, j'en fus d'abord un peu desconcerté'; Oliveira (note 32 above), p. 40.

52 J. S. da Silva Rosa, 'Een drietal prenten van joodsche patriciërshuizen te Amsterdam uit het einde der 17e eeuw', *De Vrijdagavond*, vol. 5, no. 3 (20 April 1928), pp. 42–3.

53 The garden of David de Pinto at his country residence, Tulpenburg, was described by a visitor in 1736 as 'le plus beau jardin de toute la Hollande', M. H. Gans, *Memorboek* (Baarn, 1971), p. 114.

54 Biblioteca Pública de Evora, Cod. cxx/2–4, p. 10. Alvaro Nunes da Costa to Conde Unhão, Amsterdam, 18 October 1712.

55 Duarte himself noted on the inside of the cover that he had bought it for its beauty and rarity with a view to passing it on to his heirs. *Catalogue de vente da la succession de feu N. D. Henriques de Castro* (Amsterdam, 1899), pp. 44–5.

56 See J. Craffurd 'Een generaal en kort verhaal vande schrickelycke beroerte binnen Amsterdam voorgevallen en begonnen op den 30 Januarij des s'avonds, ende volcomen t'ondergebragt ende gestilt op den 6de Februarij 1696', in R. M. Dekker, *Oproeren in Holland gezien door tijdgenoten* (Assen, 1979), p. 74.

57 Leti (note 7 above), vol. 5, p. 726.

58 Leti (note 4 above), vol. 2, raguaglio i, p. 128; this imparts a new relevance to Levi de Barrios' descriptive couplet about Belmonte : 'Residente leal del Rey hispano/ piadoso al pobre, atento al cortesano'; D. Levi de Barrios, *Estrella de Jacob* (Amsterdam, 1686), p. 65.

59 Craffurd (note 56 above), p. 73.

60 *ibid.*

61 Leti (note 4 above), vol. 2, raguaglio i, p. 128.

A Historiographical Oversight: The Austrian Consul-General and the Damascus Blood Libel (with the Laurin-Rothschild Correspondence, 1840)

Jonathan Frankel

THE story of the Damascus Blood Libel of 1840 has been told and retold. A detailed and most dramatic account takes up one entire chapter in Heinrich Graetz's multi-volume *History of the Jews*;[1] and the version of the events brilliantly presented there has imposed itself on the many general summaries of the case which have followed since.[2] The main episodes in the affair have thus become well known.[3]

On 5 February 1840, Father Thomas (a monk from Sardinia) and his servant disappeared suddenly in Damascus. Leading members of the Jewish community were arrested as suspects and accused of ritual murder. The French consul, Count de Rattymenton, played an exceptionally vigorous role in pursuing the prosecution of the case on the grounds that France had the duty by treaty to protect the Roman Catholic clergy in the Ottoman Empire.

Prolonged torture led to confessions, and the execution of the accused would have followed had it not been for outside intervention. Reports from the East (most importantly from the Austrian consul in Damascus, G. G. Merlato) alerted public opinion in Europe. The Board of Deputies in London and the Consistoire Central in Paris appealed to their respective governments. Thiers, the French premier (or Minister-President) refused to help. But Lord Palmerston, the British Foreign Secretary (as well as Metternich, the Austrian Chancellor), did intervene with Mehemet Ali, the viceroy of Egypt whose rule then extended to Syria. The lives of the surviving prisoners—four had died under torture—were spared.

In the summer, a Jewish mission led by Moses Montefiore and Adolphe Crémieux went to Egypt amidst a blaze of publicity and eventually obtained from Mehemet Ali the release of the Damascus Jews still in prison. Montefiore then proceeded to Constantinople, where the sultan issued a solemn declaration (a firman) denouncing the belief that Jews commit ritual murder. Montefiore and Crémieux returned to Europe and received a triumphant reception from the Jewish communities through which they passed on their way home.

However, various aspects of the case remain relatively neglected in the historiographical tradition. Among other things, the reader will find very little information there about the role played by the Austrian consul-general in Alexandria, Anton Laurin. When he is mentioned at all, it is either as subordinate to Vienna, dutifully carrying out official policy ('acting on the instructions of Metternich', as Graetz put it),[4] or as Merlato's immediate superior, transmitting the reports from Damascus to Mehemet Ali and to Europe. (A recent historical account mentions him as being 'prompted by Merlato'.)[5] In reality Laurin's part was central at almost every stage of the affair—and of vital importance in the crucial months of March, April and May 1840. He acted more persistently and more effectively than anybody else at that time—when the lives of the prisoners were hanging on a thread—not only to save the Jews of Damascus but also to set in motion a major campaign on their behalf in Europe. At no stage did he hesitate; at no stage did he wait. In this, he proved to be a unique figure among the diplomatic representatives of the European powers in the Middle East.

The extraordinary role played by Laurin in the Damascus case was apparently first noted by the geographer and historian Dr Avraham Yaakov Brawer, writing in 1937. Brawer commented on the fact that Laurin had been largely neglected in accounts of the case and concluded that, 'This man deserves a special place in the annals of the Jewish people, in the front rank of the "righteous gentiles"' (*hasidei umot ha-olam*).[6] Brawer's article, while of the greatest historical value, was published in a little-known volume and does not appear to have made the impact that it deserves. It is the purpose of this present article to reinforce and supplement the case made by Brawer.

Factors of different kinds—some technical, some perceptual, some ideological—combined to exclude Laurin from the centre of the drama as it was described and shaped by Graetz. Thus, it must be noted, first that the diplomatic documents relevant to the case and known to the public were not only few in number until well after the First World War, but also provided a distorted view of the actual events. Before documents, or even summarized reports of diplomatic activity, reached the press in 1840 they had passed through a complex series of filters. One of the side-effects of this selection process was to obscure the extent to which Laurin's behaviour during the early weeks and months of the crisis had been truly *sui generis*.

Letters located in the Foreign Office archives in Vienna and published by N. M. Gelber in 1927[7] reveal just how it came about that a few Austrian diplomatic documents were published in 1840 while most were not. In April 1840, Laurin sent copies of a large number of internal diplomatic reports, written in part by Merlato in Damascus and in part by himself, to James Rothschild in Paris. In turn, Rothschild decided that he could take the risk of passing on the reports from the lower official for publication without further delay, but that he could not do so with the letters of the consul-general in Alexandria. On 7 May he therefore wrote to his brother Salomon in Vienna, requesting him to ask Metternich for permission to make Laurin's letters public. As will be explained below, Metternich must have dismissed this request out of hand. Thus, the dispatches sent from Merlato in Damascus to Laurin starting with his report of 23 March 1840—and first published by Adolphe Crémieux in the French press on 7 May[8]—became one of the few primary sources of information on the case for the contemporary public and later for generations of historians. Laurin remained in the shadows.

Beyond this episode, though, a deliberate attempt was made by those involved in presenting the Jewish case to veil the more unpalatable facts bearing on the behaviour of many of the diplomats in the Middle East. The truth is that during the first month of the case, Rattymenton, in his ruthless determination to find the Jews guilty of ritual murder, enjoyed the open and enthusiastic support in Damascus of both the English and the Austrian consuls, N. W. Werry and G. G. Merlato himself. Werry's commitment to Rattymenton remained unshaken for a very long time and on 22 May he could still write privately to John Bidwell, a high official in the Foreign Office, that the 'conduct of the French consul here was honourable and virtuous'.[9] However, nobody in the Foreign Office or in the Anglo-Jewish leadership believed that any good purpose would be served by dwelling on the extent to which Werry had encouraged and supported Rattymenton. The account of events in Damascus written by the eye-witness, G. M. Pieritz, and published in book form by David Salomons in 1840, refers only in one paragraph to Werry's belief in the ritual murder charge.[10]

Merlato's early support of Rattymenton was even more underplayed. His dispatches in February and early March which argued for the guilt of the Jews were in all probability never passed on, nor even reported, to outsiders by Laurin. And Pieritz's report again skips quickly over this aspect of the case, stating quite misleadingly that until the arrest of an important Austrian subject, Isaac Picciotto, Merlato had 'stood entirely aloof and knew nothing but what report brought him'.[11]

It fell to Rattymenton himself to try to publicize the extent of

Merlato's initial involvement in the case; but the documentation that he released did not reach Europe until July, when it was published in such journals as the French right-wing Catholic paper, *La Quotidienne*, and little noted.[12]

Subsequently, historians have either passsed over Merlato's first reaction to the case very quickly or ignored it altogether. Albert Hyamson, in his important article of 1951 on the subject, stated that 'in the whole sordid affair Merlato stands out as the Christian gentleman in the best sense, one who put his humanity and his human feeling, his sense of right and devotion to it above all other considerations'.[13] So effectively has Merlato's initial co-operation with Rattymenton been obscured that a leading historian could recently note bluntly that 'there is no foundation for Brawer's claim that Merlato initially was inclined to believe in the truth of the blood libel and that it was Laurin who persuaded him of its groundlessness'.[14]

If Merlato's consistency and initiative have thus been exaggerated as the result of largely random factors, the role of Metternich was distorted, in addition, by the Eurocentric bias built in to the historiographical tradition. The Damascus affair, as presented by Graetz and the other classic accounts, was made up essentially of the criminal case at Damascus; the calls for help raised there and elsewhere in the Orient; and the intervention from the West. As the diplomatic dispatches remained hidden in the archives for some ninety years, it was easy to overestimate the extent to which events were directed from the European capitals; and to assume that the senior diplomats assigned to the court of Mehemet Ali at Alexandria were essentially carrying out official policy.

In reality circumstances permitted enormous initiatives to the consuls on the spot. In an age without telephones; when telegraph and railways were still in their very infancy; when steamships only reached Egypt at weekly intervals, the autonomy of the man on the spot was potentially vast. A letter from Alexandria to London would normally take slightly more than three weeks; from Damascus the diplomatic mail was slower still. And we find Werry in his letter to Bidwell of 22 June complaining bitterly that he had to 'lose a month' before he could make his views known at home—as there was 'no prompt conveyance between Beirut and Alexandria', he had to make do with 'the steamer via Falmouth'.[15] The correspondence from Alexandria to Vienna, which went via Trieste, should have been much quicker, but in practice was not. What this meant, in short, was that the diplomatic representatives in Damascus were effectively insulated from their superiors in Alexandria by some two weeks, while the latter had a leeway of at least one and a half months—often much more—in their dealings with their respective foreign ministries. In this particular case, the Austrian consul-general made ample use of the space thus allowed him to act boldly, often without guidance or authorization from above.

Yet another and still more fundamental reason for the neglect of Laurin in the standard version of the Damascus affair is the fact that the role of Austria *per se*, while certainly acknowledged, was always described very briefly. Here, again, the availability of the relevant raw material largely dictated the shape of the finished historiographical product. The Damascus case brought with it a vast amount of public comment, newspaper articles, letters to the editor, memorandums, books, notes, meetings (complete with published minutes) and parliamentary debate—above all in England but also in France and many other countries in western and central Europe as well as in the United States. In contrast, the Austrian government permitted only a very limited account of the affair to be published in its domains, and even that consisted for the most part of general reports, carefully selected from the foreign press and unrelated to specifically Austrian initiatives.[16] Until Gelber and Brawer published much of the relevant material in the Austrian archives it would have required a systematic effort to find the evidence (scattered here and there in the western press) of the central role played throughout by the representatives of the Austrian government. But, in reality, of course, the historians had every reason to underestimate this aspect of the case.

After all, the Damascus affair presented the Jewish historians with a number of unpalatable facts. For liberals, profoundly committed to the struggle for emancipation, it was no easy matter to witness, still more to explain, *inter alia*, the eruption of anti-Jewish sentiment set off throughout Europe by the affair; or the high degree of backing given to the accusations by the government of Orléanist France under Thiers, a renowed historian and left-of-centre parliamentarian; or yet again, the dependence of the Jewish cause on the Hapsburg regime, which—through the so-called 'Metternich system' and in collaboration with Tsarist Russia—not only consituted the bulwark of every reactionary regime in Europe, but also maintained a vast web of highly discriminatory measures against its own Jewish population. (Jews were then still denied rights of residence in Vienna, for example.)

Contemporaries, summing up the history of the Damascus case at the time or in retrospect, followed a number of different paths when faced by these phenomena, which were so hard to reconcile with the emancipationist world-view. An immediate and spontaneous reaction is to be found in Lipman Hirsch Löwenstein's introduction to his book *Damascia*, a collection of materials related to the case, over 400 pages long and first published in the year 1840 itself. Löwenstein directed attention primarily towards the French government, denouncing Thiers in the bitterest terms and at length. How could the French premier defend the man who had 'thrown over every judicial procedure, torturing innocent and decent people'—and this, 'half a century after the declaration of the Rights of Man . . . thirty years after the Code Napoléon, and ten years . . . after the July Revolution?'[17] In order to highlight the betrayal of France's declared values, he contrasted the stance adopted by Thiers with the admirable behaviour of Austria—but he did so only in passing.[18] He was, after all, appealing to the conscience of liberal Europe.

Löwenstein's *cri de cœur* raised by implication many awkward questions which he did not attempt to answer. Others preferred to describe the case in simpler terms. For David Salomons, Leopold Zunz and J. M. Jost, what had happened in 1840 was essentially a clash between the superstition prevailing in the orient (as well as in large stretches of Eastern Europe) and Western enlightenment. 'On the cultured soil of Europe,' as Zunz put it, 'there is no more room for the defamatory hunting down of the Jews.'[19] 'As the mind becomes enlightened by education,' wrote Salomons, 'so do those prejudices disappear which could only have existed amidst the gross darkness of ignorance.'[20] And for his part, Jost noted that 'the European regimes took up the issue with a noble love of humanity'.[21] In this scheme of things, the behaviour of Thiers emerged as a response to pressures exerted by the French diplomats in the East, an incomprehensible but marginal aberration; while the role of Austria merged into that of the European states in general. Indeed, Salomons chose to describe the English consul-general, Colonel Hodges, as the prime champion at Alexandria of the Jewish cause—calling in 'the representatives of Russia, Prussia and Austria'[22] to back up his own efforts.

It fell to Graetz, of course, to give the narrative a firm, architectonic shape. For him, the Damascus case was no transient episode within the chaotic flux of the contingent, but rather a central act in the unfolding drama of Jewish history. In it could be glimpsed the mystery of Jewish destiny, the work of the providential hand, the 'cunning of Reason' not fully understood but manifestly revealed. In his *History of the Jews*, the events of 1840 clearly follow the pattern of the Purim story (a response which had been very widespread among Jews immediately following the denouement of the case).[23] His description dwells at length on Rattymenton and the martyrdom of the Damascus Jews; on the great protest campaign launched by the Jewish communities in Western Europe; on the intervention by the British government; and on the triumph of the rescue mission. Within this framework he could clearly leave only limited space for the French government and Thiers, for

Austria and Metternich and still less, of course, for Laurin and the Rothschilds—although, truly great historian that he was, he left none of them out. The case, he concluded:

> was insignificant at the beginning but of vast importance in its results . . . [It] showed what a wondrous force it is that holds the members of the Jewish people [*Judenheit*] together in indissoluble union.[24]

How Laurin responded initially to the Damascus affair emerges clearly from his letters written in late March 1840 (and first published by N. M. Gelber in his article of 1927).

Merlato had reported to him on the case, it turns out, in a dispatch of 1 March, where he stated his conviction that the Jews of Damascus were indeed guilty of 'human sacrifice' in accord with their 'religious rites'.[25] On 6 March, Isaac Picciotto, a prominent Austrian *protégé*, was apprehended and added to the list of those accused of the murders. But, as Merlato explained in a further dispatch to Laurin, this development did not in the first instance lead him to change his mind.[26]

Writing on 27 March to Baron Bartolomaus von Stürmer (the Austrian ambassador to the Porte who was officially entitled an Internuntius), Laurin interpreted the facts in a totally different way. No credence, he argued, could possibly be given to confessions extorted from the accused after they had each been been subjected to 'five thousand blows from a truncheon'. As for Merlato,

> he probably does not know how often the Jews have been accused of human sacrifice and been found innocent. [He] definitely believes in this crime and has Picciotto and some other Austrian Jews under strict supervision.[27]

Rattymenton would later claim that Merlato had changed sides only after receiving 'instructions from Mr Laurin, the Austrian Consul General'.[28] And from what is known of the timing, this could very well have been the case. In another letter (this time from 31 March), Laurin wrote that the accusations were probably the result of

> those criminal libels which have often been imputed to the Jews but never judicially proved. I therefore did not omit to urge on the consul all necessary caution and to instruct him to treat the two Austrian Jews who had been involved therein with the greatest consideration.[29]

Merlato's famous dispatch exonerating the Jews and exposing Rattymenton's methods of interrogation was (as already mentioned) completed on 23 March. In all probability, he had already had the opporunity by then to study Laurin's initial reactions to the case.

In contrast, it was too early for Laurin to have received guidance from Vienna. The first diplomatic reports from the Middle East to Europe describing the events in Damascus were almost certainly those sent by Rattymenton on 29 February and by the French consul-general in Alexandria, H. Cochelet, to Paris on 5 March.[30] Metternich sent a dispatch about the case to the Austrian consulate in Alexandria on 10 April—but its contents demonstrate that he had then still not heard directly from Laurin.[31]

Reports on the Damascus affair did not begin to appear in major European newspapers until 17 March;[32] while the first attempt made by Jews in Europe to intervene through governmental channels was almost certainly that of Hirsch Lehren (the prominent philanthropist of Amsterdam and director of the Pekidim ve-Amarkalim organization), who addressed a letter to the Dutch Foreign Ministry on 18 March.[33] (Lehren was presumably writing in response to the private reports sent to him from Beirut on 20 and 26 February.)[34] This appeal does not seem to have evoked any initiative from the Dutch government.[35] Finally, it is perhaps worth noting that Lord Palmerston did not write to Colonel Hodges on the subject until 5 May; while the latter made no mention of the Damascus affair in his dispatches to London until 18 June.[36]

In the meantime, Laurin acted with extraordinary energy to halt, and if possible reverse, the juggernaut threatening to overwhelm the Jews in Damascus (and indeed throughout the Middle East). His warnings to Merlato proved to be only one aspect of a much broader campaign. Thus, armed with Merlato's early dispatches—and so in possession of detailed information about the case—he obtained a series of audiences with Mehemet Ali. He there, before all else, urged on the viceroy that an immediate stop had to be put to the torture being applied in Damascus. As early as 28 March he obtained an appropriate order from Mehemet Ali which was sent to the governor of Damascus. But he was rightly dubious about how effective it would prove to be, and he did not rest on his laurels.[37]

'Early today,' he reported to von Stürmer on 31 March,

> I spent much time arguing with Mehemet Ali about the case and learned from him himself that two of the accused had died as the result of torture. If a Jew lets himself be tortured to death he must have a sense of his own innocence.[38]

His relationship with Mehemet Ali which was usually marked by a measure of geniality and trust, now became extremely tense, and Hodges reported that 'the Pasha's deportment towards Mr Laurin in an interview . . . on the 4th inst. [April] was both insulting and degrading'.[39]

In order to reinforce the immediate pressure on Mehemet Ali, Laurin took further initiatives. He co-operated, for example, with the leaders of the Jewish community in Alexandria in drawing up a petition to the viceroy. It referred to letters from Damascus shown to them by Laurin—not from Jews but from Christians (presumably from Merlato)—and demanded not mercy but 'strict justice'. 'The question,' it declared boldly, 'concerns an ancient religion which people are seeking to destroy.'[40] This letter was published in many west European papers in mid-May, where the boldness, foolhardiness even, of the Egyptian Jews was widely commented upon.[41] From a number of references in the Laurin–Rothschild correspondence,* it emerges that this was by no means the only example of contact and co-operation between the Austrian consul-general and the local Jewish community.

Again, it can be safely assumed that it was at the urging of Laurin that Hodges also spoke to Mehemet Ali on the issue—'already in April', as he would later put it to Palmerston.[42] By 6 April, Laurin could report that he had 'spoken to the pasha and the behaviour now to be adopted in the procedure of the case will be of the kind which I have advised him to be of the best. Much has thus been achieved'.[43] A new and much more strongly worded order was issued by Mehemet Ali and sent off to Damascus on 10 April.[44] In his letter to Salomon Rothschild a month later (and reproduced below),† he was able to state that the use of torture had by then been checked 'following on three decrees of the viceroy's which I procured and delivered to our consul in Damascus'. Beyond that, he had, as he then wrote, also obtained a formal order on the night of 3–4 May, guaranteeing the 'personal safety' of the Jewish community in Damascus as a whole and had sent it to Syria by the fastest available means of transport.

Among the many steps which Laurin took in the early stages of the case, probably the most remarkable was his decision (already mentioned) to send a batch of the relevant diplomatic documents on 31 March to James Rothschild. It is true that the latter was not only a citizen of Austria (and held an Austrian title of nobility), but was also the Austrian consul-general in Paris. But it was universally understood that this was a largely honorific position and that diplomatic communications should be sent not to Rothschild but directly to the ambassador. Laurin, however, was determined to leave no stone unturned.

He urged Rothschild to make every effort to ensure that 'the French government issue a strong order . . . seriously rebuking the consul in

* See Letters VI and VIII.
† See Letter II.

Damascus'.[45] He also (as he hinted in another letter of a few days later) expected him to have the true facts published:

> I am convinced that the press will raise a cry of horror at the indescribable crimes to which the unfortunate victims have been subjected in order to extract confessions which have no foundation in reality—and this in a country where Mehemet Ali is spreading civilization and where the Hati Sherif of Gulhani is being publicized.[46]

Laurin may well have expected that Rothschild would only issue summaries of the documents rather than, as he did, have Merlato's reports published verbatim, in major newspapers throughout Western Europe. For his part, though, Rothschild felt that in face of the adamant refusal of Thiers to disassociate himself from Rattymenton's conduct 'there remains for us no choice but to turn for help to a factor which here is omnipotent—the press'.[47]

In response, Metternich twice issued angry and biting rebukes to Laurin. He had already made known his support for the cause of the Damascus Jews in his letter of 10 April (describing the accusations as 'absurd'),[48] but at the end of May he deplored the fact that

> Your Excellency has permitted himself to enter into direct correspondence with the House of Rothschild in Paris. The disputes between the Austrian and French consuls in Damascus are matters for the Imperial Cabinet and not for the consulate in Paris. By sharing with the latter Mr Merlato's reports to you . . . you made the texts . . . known to the public newsheets which are not the authorities which have to deal with the case.[49]

And in a subsequent letter he returned to this same subject, referring to the

> rash publicity which the French von Rothschilds out of exaggerated enthusiasm for their co-religionists have given to the official reports . . . received from Your Excellency. . . . In the present . . . atmosphere between Christians and Jews in Syria it is perceived as though the latter are supported by Austria while France speaks for the former. Another result, likewise without real grounds, is the current misunderstanding between the two regimes and their press which are now quarrelling.[50]

(In his apologetic reply Laurin claimed that he had been totally surprised by the publication of the documents but, none the less, explained that

> in order to forestall still greater misfortunes I had felt obliged to pursue the matter with somebody who as a co-religionist, would be personally interested . . . Mr Rothschild's démarches were so effective that they brought the minister [Thiers] to issue an order immediately that

somebody on the spot should . . . examine Mr Rattymenton's conduct. In this way a great deal has been achieved.)[51]

Once he felt that he had obtained his first object—saving the lives of the remaining prisoners and securing the safety of the Jewish community in Damascus—Laurin turned his attention to what he saw as the basic long-term issue. It was essential, he argued, to have the disappearance of Father Thomas and his servant thoroughly investigated by an objective commission of enquiry and to arrange for a new trial, preferably in Alexandria. Mehemet Ali's initial response was favourable. (He was, after all, very much aware of the fact that without Metternich's still uncertain consent, Palmerston had no chance of constructing a grand coalition—England, Russia, Prussia and Austria—and of dispossessing him, Mehemet Ali, of Syria by armed force.)[52] Laurin, thereupon, drew up a formal proposal requesting a full review of the case; arranged to have it signed by nine of the fourteen European consuls (among them, the Russian and the Prussian) and submitted it to Mehemet Ali on 9 May.[53] Cochelet, of course, refused to sign as did the Greek, Neapolitan, Belgian and Dutch consuls.

A key component of this plan was that prominent lawyers, with the right to gather all possible evidence, should be brought in from Europe to provide a fully professional defence for the accused, and to represent their clients in an open and impartial trial. Even before Laurin had had a chance to draft the memorandum he hastened to write urgent letters to the Rothschilds in Paris, Vienna and Naples to explain what now had to be done:* 'If you could get hold of someone experienced in the law,' he wrote to Salomon on 5 May, 'seize upon him and send him hither and we shall see to accrediting him properly both with our consul in Damascus and with the governor-general.' It was presumably no coincidence that shortly after the receipt of these letters in Europe, Adophe Crémieux, one of the most able court lawyers in France, decided to go to the Middle East to act on behalf of the Damascus Jews. A letter sent from the Consistoire Central in Paris (of which Crémieux was vice-president) to Moses Montefiore announced this decision on 9 June.[54]

The documents published by Gelber in 1927 made it clear that Laurin had co-operated closely with the Rothschilds at crucial moments during the crisis of 1840, but the extent of this collaboration has hitherto remained unknown. The discovery of a large file of contemporary material on the Damascus blood libel in the archives of N. M. Rothschild and Sons in London has brought to light much new

---

* See Letter II (cf. no. III).

evidence about the case in general, and about the Laurin–Rothschild relationship in particular. The entire correspondence of 1840 between the Austrian consul-general and the Rothschild brothers found in the file—seventeen letters in all, some originals, some copies—is reproduced below.

It turns out that Laurin was on terms of personal friendship with Carl Meyer Rothschild, who had established the branch of the family bank in Naples and lived in that city. Laurin and he were in correspondence long before the Damascus affair erupted. One letter, for example, refers to Laurin's role in channelling financial aid from the Rothschilds to the victims of the Druse attack on the Jewish community of Safed in 1838.* Among other things—as the exchange of letters makes clear—the consul-general sought out rare coins, jewellery and other collectors' items on behalf of Carl and various other family members (including particularly Mayer, the oldest son, then twenty years of age).[55] For his part, the Neapolitan Rothschild made sure that Laurin was kept well supplied with good wines and with various foods, no doubt otherwise hard to find in Egypt. He was clearly looking forward to having the chance to entertain Laurin again, as he had done in the past.†

That Laurin was personally acquainted with Salomon, head of the house of Rothschild in Vienna, is also clear; but their relationship was, it seems, rather more distant. It has to be remembered that Salomon was much older than Carl; more formal; and a close personal adviser to Metternich, the effective head of state and Laurin's direct superior. As for the exchange of letters with James in Paris, it was strictly formal and suggests that the two men had probably never met.

From the moment that he became fully familiar with the facts of the Damascus case, Laurin not only kept the Rothschilds very well informed but also, to a large extent, guided their actions.[56] His first letter to James (as already mentioned) went out on 31 March. He clearly took personal pride in the fact that the Rothschild family and the Jewish people had at least one person in the orient well placed to defend their interests. In his letter to Carl of 5 May,‡ when the worst was already behind him and he was planning a retrial, he noted with obvious satisfaction that 'I am writing to you today . . . first of all to be able to say that on one and the same day I wrote to all the brothers Rothschild . . . about the Jewish trial in Damascus.' The correspondence reproduced below makes it abundantly clear, moreover, that he

---

* See Letter III (cf. no. IV).
† See Letter IV (cf. no. VII)
‡ Letter III

did not regard it as his primary goal simply to extricate Picciotto and the few other Austrian citizens from the trap: he saw in them an instrument delivered into his hands to save all the accused.

By the time that Crémieux and Montefiore reached Alexandria in August, Laurin no longer had so exclusive a part to play. Colonel Hodges had by then received a number of dispatches, phrased with Palmerston's inimitable directness, ordering him to act vigorously on behalf of the Damascus Jews.[57] And he did everything he could to help Montefiore, a distinguished British citizen, in his contacts with Mehemet Ali. But, of course, Laurin's advice was always made readily available to the leaders of the mission.[58] On returning to Europe at the end of the year, Montefiore frequently made it clear that he was anxiously awaiting the relevant news contained in Laurin's letters to Carl Rothschild (who was, it will be recalled, Montefiore's close relative by marriage). In a letter from Leghorn on 17 January 1841, for example, Montefiore thanked Carl for 'the copy of Mr Laurin's letter which is very interesting' and asked him to forward 'the papers there referred to'.[59]

On the basis of the evidence at the moment available to the author, it is not possible to decide conclusively what prompted Laurin to act as he did. It is possible that the Rothschilds were his bankers and that there were financial considerations involved; or that he valued the connection with a firm linked by so many ties to Prince von Metternich, Chancellor of the Hapsburg Empire. It is at least as possible, though, that he was acting simply or primarily in accord with the dictates of conscience and friendship. The letters reproduced here tend, if anything, to reinforce this last hypothesis.

CONCLUSION

In his chapter on the Damascus Blood Libel, Heinrich Graetz concluded, rightly it would seem, that the policies adopted towards the case by Thiers and the French government were largely dictated by their consular officials in Syria and Egypt, and this view has been generally absorbed into Jewish historiography. That the Austrian officials on the spot—particulary Anton Laurin—played a parallel role in organizing the defence of the Jews was, however, not recognized at all until A. S. Brawer called for a revision of the standard account some fifty years ago.

That so key a role was played by officials of the Hapsburg regime serves to underline the essential untidiness of a story which Graetz envisioned as clearly structured, unfolding in accord with an inner and providential logic. At the most crucial stages of the case, the Jewish cause was defended most effectively by the representative of a conservative—indeed a reactionary—power identified with what were loosely called 'Holy Alliance' policies and concomitantly possessed of a whole complex of discriminatory legislation directed against the Jews. And yet, however uncomfortable this fact may have been for many to accept, it was, in reality, by no means paradoxical.

Laurin had good reason to assume that his defence of the Jewish community in Damascus would win the backing of Metternich. It was not only that among the accused were a few men enjoying the rights of Austrian protection. More important, the Austrian regime valued its many links with Jewish bankers and merchants and believed that they had a valuable contribution to make to the country's economic development and foreign trade.[60] By demanding the indictment of Isaac Picciotto, nephew of the Austrian consul-general at Aleppo, Rattymenton entered into a head-on collision with this policy.[61] Again, Laurin could anticipate that his own initial reaction to the affair would certainly receive the strong backing of Salomon Rothschild in Vienna, who, in turn, would plead the case with Metternich.

The rules of the game in this essentially traditional system were, after all, well enough known. Salomon Rothschild was still very much in the situation of the eighteenth-century *Hof-Jude*. He often petitioned for the abolition of the discriminatory laws in the Austrian empire, but knew in advance that only the most superficial changes would be made. But in the Damascus affair, where not the governmental system, but rather patronage and favour were involved, there was no reason why intervention, *shtadlanut*, should not evoke a sympathetic response.

However, Laurin also realized that any intervention by the Austrian government, in such a case, would probably be cautious, limited and based on a jealous regard for much broader and more complex foreign policy interests. From the first moment, therefore, he took the decision to cross the boundaries of the traditional political system. By supplying James Rothschild with the diplomatic documents needed to sustain a press campaign—and, later, by calling for the despatch of prominent lawyers from Europe—he knowingly called in the new methods of political action to redress the balance of the old. In so doing he infuriated Metternich, who could not reconcile himself to the independent status attained by the Rothschild Bank in the constitutional states of the West.[62]

In this episode, then, were mirrored the increasing complexity of the Jewish situation in the mid-nineteenth century world and the multi-levelled response which that situation evoked. Laurin and the Rothschilds—no less than Rattymenton and Thiers—chose to fight with an assortment of weapons, some highly traditional, others quintessentially modern.

DOCUMENTS

The following letters are located in File RAL RFamAD/2 at the Archive of N. M. Rothschild and Sons, London, and have been translated for this article from the German. Names are given in a uniform spelling here, even though, in the original, the same name often appears in many variants. The very elaborate forms of address customary in the German usage of the time have in many cases not been translated literally. Where it proved impossible to decipher the original text (hand-written in Gothic script), omissions are marked [. . .]; and cases of doubt are also indicated, [?]. Editorial notes are marked by an asterisk or other sign. The letters here have been numbered afresh; in the Archive, the numbering follows a different order: no. I here is III there and so on.

Letter I [To Naples]

Alexandria, 16 April 1840

My esteemed Baron,

What is happening in Naples at present? Today the steam frigate *Gorgon* and the corvette *Daphne* sailed off to join Stopford's squadron which is supposed to be staging a military demonstration against Naples.* Here everything's warlike, but *quiet*. Mehemet Ali and Kosrew Pasha† are quarrelling properly and slandering each other hard. The decisions of the Powers will however be accepted, let them be what they will. Mehemet Ali seems tired of resisting and sees that England is becoming more and more unfriendly every day.

With regard to the case of the Damascus Jews, I have seen to it that the hearing will be humanely conducted and that there will no longer be any use of torture.

I express my best thanks for the Rhine wine so kindly promised me.

In haste,

Your most humble

A. Laurin

The French consul in Damascus, who has put himself at the head of the persecution of the Jews in Damascus, is the comte de Rattymenton who was hunted out of Sicily. The Marquis Nunziante can give you information on this subject.

The Russian government similarly helped him on his way out of Tiflis, where he was the consul until recently.

---

* In April 1840, the British navy placed a partial blockade on Naples as the result of an international dispute over sulphur-mining rights.

† Kosrew Pasha was the grand vizier in the government of the sultan at Constantinople.

Letter II [To Vienna]

Alexandria, 5 May 1840

Right Honourable Baron
Most esteemed Friend!

Your letter of 10 April reached me yesterday. With regard to the Damascus trial, right from its beginning I have strained every nerve to put a stop to the atrocities that were practised against those professing the Mosaic faith and tackled the viceroy of Egypt to take measures against them. Your Honour will also perhaps soon hear that a check has been put on this use of terror following on three decrees of the viceroy's which I procured one after the other and delivered to our consul in Damascus. The personal safety of the rest of the Jews is also being seen to. For on the night of the 3rd to 4th of this month I received a formal *bugruldi* from the viceroy and immediately, at the same time, despatched it express to Damascus. After this nothing remains to be done except to see to it that all these orders of the viceroy are carried out properly. I have already received a report that the first of these *bugruldi* had an excellent effect on the victims and prevented any further atrocities; so I hope that the others will likewise not fail to have the desired result.

One thing still remains, and this is of the greatest importance, namely, to clear the Jews of the crimes falsely imputed to them—that, of course, by means of the discovery of the real murderers of the Capuchin and his servant. Only then will the Jews living in the holy places of Hebron, Safed, Tiberias and Jerusalem be safeguarded from persecution.

Accordingly, I have worked out a plan to examine this case in a detailed manner and to request the assistance of the pasha for this purpose. The plan is as follows: one or more experts in criminal proceedings should be sent to Damascus to inquire into the state of affairs there on the spot and to prepare a detailed report both on this and on the perpetrator of the murder. This report would then be shown to a tribunal called together to pass judgement. This tribunal should not take place in Damascus nor comprise persons who have already expressed their opinion and called for the imposition of the death penalty on the accused. I have discussed this with the viceroy and I am pleased to tell you that he adopted my view entirely and charged me to present him with my notes, on which he could frame his formal decision.

Besides this, I also put it to him that it would advance matters if at least one of my colleagues could sign this as well. This addendum he also accepted, and tonight I shall busy myself with drafting a collective note for this purpose to be communicated to my friends and submitted to His Highness for its final wording. I shall then no longer stand alone in this affair and have to fight in isolation against the wild outcry of the fanatics.

I shall draw up a report on the matter for His Highness the Prince Metternich, who has written to me very pressingly about it. I do not know, however, whether this report can be ready in time for the departure of the steamship, since I shall only receive the enclosures that are to go with it later. At all events you can discuss it with His Highness. You will perhaps already have heard via Paris through your brother that I have approached our embassy at the

French court through your brother in this matter. I hope to receive a satisfactory reply from there before long.

From what I have said so far, Your Excellency will have gathered that it was not in vain that you urged me to actively undertake the cause of your innocent co-religionists sore afflicted for years; although I would have acted no differently even if I had not been asked.

I close with the assurance that I shall neglect nothing to advance this affair towards a satisfactory ending, and have the honour to be most respectfully

Your humble servant,

A. Laurin

PS *5 May 1840*

If you could get hold of someone experienced in the law who would be in a position to advance this enquiry, seize upon him and send him hither and we shall see to accrediting him properly both with our consul in Damascus and with the governor-general of the country.

While the unfortunate Lagnado was being tortured, the French consul sought out his house and insulted his young wife, daughter to Salomon Mayr of Kronstatd [*sic*], and asked her to sing erotic songs, kiss him, and give him the blood of Padre Tommaso that her husband had hidden; otherwise he [her husband] would die by torture. Doesn't this remind you of Eulogius Schneider of notorious memory?

Letter III [To Naples]

Alexandria, 6 May 1840

My esteemed Baron!

I am writing to you today for two reasons—first of all to be able to state that on one and the same day I wrote to all the brothers Rothschild, of course about the Jewish trial in Damascus; and secondly to report to you that this abominable business has been halted and torture at interrogations brought to a stop. The affair is going to be investigated on the spot by people who will be sent us here from Europe, people experienced in criminal proceedings, and judgement will be pronounced here.

I read that things are bad in Naples. God willing, the weak will assert their right against the Powers.

Everything here is just as it was. Mehemet Ali will have been given a hint that if he can manage to mobilize 150,000 men, France will actively support him against an attack on the part of the sultan's allies. He is therefore arming powerfully so that soon he will be able to show that he is worthy of this help.

The plague is loosening its grip and I hope that very soon we shall be able to go out into the open.

Offering my best respects to your amiable family I sign myself

Your most humble servant,

A. Laurin

Is it really true that the king did not receive either the Count Lebzeltern★ or the Marquis Goser [?], although they had presented theselves at His Majesty's at the appointed time?

I found the receipts for the 500 fl. which you had me distribute to the poor of Safed a year and a half ago among the papers of the late Lapu and I shall send them to you right away.

AL

Letter IV [To Naples]

Alexandria, 25 May 1840

Your Excellency,

I received your esteemed letter of the 2 of this month yesterday and I am pleased to learn that you are very well and looking forward to the arrival of your family. I beg you to be kind enough to present them with my most courteous respects.

As soon as I find something for Mayer Carl, to whom I present especial respects, I shall make it my concern to be of service to him. Good buys become rarer every day, however, particularly coins, which the Arabs prefer to melt down rather than bring for sale. Cut stones are more frequently found, but the work is only mediocre. As for silver, I have only come across a lady's toilet set (Indian work), gilded inside but richly enamelled outside, and the little box itself of ivory, although it is in very poor condition and not complete. If I can get it for you at about 20 per cent higher than engraved work [?], I shall buy it for you anyway and I hope it will give Your Excellency pleasure on account of its attractive appearance and the rare quality of the work.

With regard to the trial of the Jews in Damascus, Your Excellency will have read of the pros and cons in the newspapers. The latest about it is that the Pasha has granted permission for it to be reviewed *by European lawyers whom the friends of the accused choose* and *for it to be brought to a conclusion* here. Send us hither two good lawyers. The French have already sent an official of the Fr. consulate-general here [to Damascus]; only he will be more intent on clearing his Rattymenton than on getting to the bottom of the affair—this official is moreover an extremely narrow person. Apropos, this Rattymenton was vice-consul in Palermo in 1830 and he had some unpleasantness there with the police, who pressed for his recall; he had the same fate in Tiflis as well.

The 2 Austrians, viz. Picciotto and Salomon Mayr, businessmen, can be considered as good as *acquitted*; only I am deliberately leaving them still *in causa* in order to influence the trial of the others, whom they want entrapped. Would you, dear sir, believe that there are people who think the pasha right and me *wrong* and who are spreading rumours that I accepted a sum of money in order to defend these unfortunate and deserted people.

This is the second lot of rich spoils I've bagged this year! The first was to do with an Austrian dealer in jewels, who was accused of having sold false diamonds and so, of course, arrested and sentenced to be hanged. Jewels worth

---

★ The Count Lebzeltern was Austrian ambassador in Naples to the court of the Kingdom of the Two Sicilies.

from 3 to 4 million piastres were confiscated. I proved that the man was innocent and the jewels were genuine. The man was freed and got back his jewels. Since then however the cadi remains ill-disposed towards the Austrian consul. That's Egyptian justice! and civilization. How many such grievous injustices have been committed without anyone's ever mentioning them. Mehemet Ali will not bring the Safed affair, which has cost so many people their property and their lives,* to a conclusion; yet the robbers and the receivers etc. are known.

That's enough of atrocities. My cordial thanks for the 25 bottles of Rhine wine—I shall drink them up to the health of you and your very worthy family. The sulphur affair should soon be adjudicated and settled, but at what an enormous sacrifice of money!—So how much? From the beginning I prophesied a *deplorable* end for the contract [...]

The plague is still going on here. Fortunately the arsenal and the two fleets were put into quarantine in time, thereby forestalling a heavy death rate. I keep very well thanks to my family; I am heartily tired of this sadly prolonged stay here, and I have decided to ask for my recall just as soon as the present quarrels are ended.

I must ask your forgiveness for my bothering you over the commission for Count Lebzeltern, but there is no other way of sending something—except via Malta through Bell & Co. Prince Metternich has sided with the Damascus Jews in chivalrous fashion. S. M. [Rothschild] also wrote me a moving letter on this matter. I was very happy to answer him right away that I had taken action before your letters arrived. J. M. Rothschild also did his bit in the end and I shall now be supported by 4 to 5 of my colleagues, no longer isolated and a *bête noire*.

In money matters, everything is in status quo. Herewith all the best, and write me whether Lebzeltern had a share in the sulphur affair and whether he has kept face.

Yours very faithfully,
A. Laurin

Letter V [To Naples]

Alexandria, 16 June 1840

Highly esteemed Baron!

I received your very esteemed letter of the 2 of this month the day before yesterday. I am much gladdened by the flattering acknowledgement you have been good enough to make of my endeavours which it was only my duty to undertake. Regardless of the complications, I hope that the affair will come to a satisfactory end. I am writing to Paris about having Crémieux, the lawyer, sent here.

Please present my respects to your amiable family. My best thanks for the macaroni della Costa. I am awaiting it impatiently, and when enjoying it I shall recall the friends living in noisy Naples. Likewise I thank you for the news.

* In 1838.

Here the news is interesting this time and will bring in a lot of money to you and yours. *Inshallah!* Mehemet Ali explained to me yesterday when he got back from Cairo, that he wants to send his first adjutant, Samy Bey, to Constantinople today to congratulate the sultan on the birth of his daughter and learn from His Highness whether he would prefer that his (Mehemet Ali's) son, Said Bey, or his admiral, Mutus [?] Pasha, should *bring back the fleet that has been sequestered here until now to Constantinople.**

Mehemet Ali has in fact been induced to take these steps by the rebellious spirit of these guests and by the unrest in Syria, thus facilitating the negotiations now pending; but he himself says that it is the sultan's deposition of Kosrew Pasha which has induced him to do this. At the same time he has sent a present of 50,000 thaler for the sultan's household, as a gift for the newborn sultana. Now we shall see whether Mehemet Ali will be permitted to make a direct settlement with the sultan concerning his claim or whether the London Conference† will go on intervening. Nine frigates of the sultan and 2 Egyptian ships of the line will be readied for sailing to carry troops to Syria where there are signs of a general uprising and great agitation.

Yours most humble servant,

A. Laurin

Letter VI [To Alexandria]

Naples, 25 June 1840

Highly esteemed Sir!

Highly esteemed Consul-General!

Since my latest letter, to my very special joy and surprise, I have received Your Excellency's estimable letter of the 26 of last month [May], for which receive my very best thanks—as well as for the manifold exertions with which Your Honour has burdened himself in this connection. I can only express heartfelt regret that the present moment is so unfavourable for the purchase of antiques including the special coins—I should, Your Excellency, very much have liked to have seen several gaps filled [in the collection]. What attracts me most is the little box of Indian workmanship you described in detail, which promises the most pleasant surprise for me and will be most cordially received by my wife as one more memento of your very friendly sentiments.

Now I turn to the matter of my unfortunate co-religionists so inhumanly treated in Damascus: what great thanks I owe Your Excellency for the truly dedicated way in which you have immersed yourself in this Jewish tragedy. However much I would like to express my most deeply felt gratitude to you, it is truly impossible for me to describe how deep a fellow-feeling the situation must evoke from everyone and most particularly from my family. May your esteemed influence and the endeavours of us all succeed in really unveiling the

---

* During the war of 1839, betwen the forces of Mehemet Ali and those of the Sultan, a large part of the Turkish fleet defected to the Egyptian side.

† The diplomatic consultations betwen England, Russia, Prussia and Austria centred on London from December 1839 and culminated in the treaty of July 1840.

whole truth and proving to an incredulous, misled world with what oriental barbarity the life, tranquillity and conscience of so many people is being sacrificed as the result of incomplete and dishonest charges.

In recent times two detailed reports have reached me from the Jewish congregation in Constantinople about the events; and in June I received a copy of an important letter date 26 ult. [May] from Messrs Wollheim, Valensen and Loria* to my brother, the contents of which cannot but cause me the greatest grief. Although earlier I acted entirely of my own accord and felt myself bound only by a most compelling sense of obligation, now that this appeal has come from there, I have again adopted appropriate measures and may allow myself to hope that we can look forward to a successful outcome. So, Your Excellency, it only remains that these gentlemen themselves, to whom I shall myself write as well, should feel reassured. Many thousand of thanks for the information given me; you offer me such manifold proofs of the highest feelings of appreciation and goodwill that I only wish I could prove my unbounded gratitude.

With respect to the sulphur affair there is nothing new to hand so far, but now one can look forward to a speedy and peaceable outcome of the matter. The person in question—from the little I know about him—is in no way implicated in this question and as in other cases could properly only have acted on behalf of his superiors.

I am sorry to hear that the plague is still continuing to wreak havoc and it is still more saddening for me to learn that Your Excellency is really intending to resign immediately on account of your most upsetting stay. However hard this intention of yours must be for all those who have learned for so many years to regard Your Excellency as a father and protector, I find it easy to understand. The only eventual compensation for me would be the wonderful prospect of being able to greet you again here: I could then assure Your Excellency of my true respect far better than I can now.

My wife and children charge me to offer Your Excellency their heartfelt and sincere gratitude for the kind mementoes received from you; they are, thank God, enjoying the well being you wished them.

The new French ambassador, the Duke of Montebello, seems to want to get on well with us here. He has taken the Palais Acton and intends to be anything but idle in his social relations. From Prussia we have Count Bernstorff here as chargé d'affaires, who with his amiable young wife provides a pretty addition to the social amenities. Now everything is happening in Castellamare, Sorrento or Capodimonte; I have moved to the latter place in order to be able to devote myself in the cool evening hours to the beauties of nature and the greenery.

A part of the English squadron is still in our bay, and nothing certain has yet transpired about its departure.

Pardon the length of this letter, Your Excellency, and together with my

---

* i.e., from leading members of the Jewish community in Alexandria—the letter (a copy of which is in the Rothschild archive) suggests making maximum use of the fact that, in times past, the papacy itself had condemned the notion of the Jewish practice of human sacrifice.

insufficiently renewed expressions of thanks will you kindly receive the reiterated assurance of my ever-increasing esteem and unbounded respect,

Your most faithful servant
[Carl Meyer von Rothschild]

Letter VII [To Naples]

Alexandria, 17 July 1840

Right Honourable Baron!

I received your esteemed letter of the 5th of this month on the 14; the macaroni came on the 15; and your letter is already in Syria. The macaroni was adjudged excellent and I thank you sincerely for sending it.

The Damascus affair is going well, although France [?] is doing eveything to influence the pasha against a review by European criminal lawyers. On this account, the day before yesterday I negotiated with Mehemet on the special instructions of Prince von Metternich. He [Mehemet] is making a mistake which if properly exploited must give the affair a most favourable turn. Prosecutors, witnesses and judges will be compromised in the process.

I am glad about Sir Moses Montefiore and Crémieux. At the moment, I am doing all I can to improve the lot of those imprisoned. Some of them have already been released and are absolutely hysterical.

The opponents are trying to represent Merlato and me as suborners. I have been considering challenging the Danish consul, Dumreicher, who must have misled the governor [. . .] in this matter, to substantiate this libel.

Our news is that the Ottoman navy would be well received in Constantinople, but direct negotiations may not take place. Perier* has arrived here to congratulate the pasha on his brainwave of sending back the Sultan's navy.

The uprising in the Lebanon is as good as suppressed. The Egyptian bulletin has the details about it. The heat is very great, the Nile is rising well. Mehemet Ali is really very shaken; but as a fatalist he is in no hurry at all over anything.

We hear that the London Conference will be able to bring about a peaceful solution of the standing questions of the orient before long.

Goodbye—and think of your old A. Laurin gone on a trip

to Pompei, Castello . . .

Letter VIII [To Naples]

Alexandria, 25 July 1840

Highly esteemed Baron!

I received your very worthy letter of the 15 on the 23 of this month, that is on the 8th day *a dato* and answered per address Bell & Co.

I am impatiently awaiting Sir M. Montefiore and Crémieux. The French first wanted to quash the Damascus affair; then to complicate it; and finally to turn it into a common murder. Nothing succeeded. Those in prison are now much weakened and little hope remains for their complete recovery.

---

* A special emissary sent by the French government to co-ordinate policy with Mehemet Ali.

The local congregation has sent Mr Issak Loria to Damascus. Our consul there presented him to Sherif Pasha.* From the description of his audience given by Mr Loria it emerges that Sherif Pasha denied putting anyone to the torture or accusing anybody of blood sacrifice! It was just a common murder—in fact a private revenge. Thus speaks the governor of Syria, just like Mehemet Ali.

Meanwhile people have been found who are ready to testify for the Jews. Shortly the affair will be brought to the desired conclusion.

The pasha assures us that the uprising in Syria has been settled. Private letters affirm the contrary. At all events the whole to-do will soon come to an end, since the sheikhs are united among themselves and some of them have already secretly made their peace with the pasha.

Meanwhile 4 to 6 ships of the line have been readied in order to keep watch over the English stationed in the port of Beirut. Mehemet Ali believes that they [the English] are encouraging the insurrection. The fleet is to be sent back to the sultan and only the date is still in doubt. The Porte, it is true, has formally rejected direct negotiations, though these are supported by France. The old pasha won't like this at all.

[received] Naples Aug. 15

Of the silver toilet set I have at present bought only the bowl and the goblet. These two pieces weigh over 900 drachmen, and like all the rest are strongly gilded, both inside and out. I would rather have taken the pot, cups and little bottles, but they didn't want to part with them except as a complete set. If you like the piece just described (which I shall have sent at the first opportunity via Malta per Bell & Co.) then I shall send you the rest, weighing 3766 drachmen. This has been paid for, 191 Fara, [?] as shown on the attached receipt, and in fact what is billed for is only the value of the silver and the gold.

Conveying my best regard to your amiable family, I have the honour to remain

your most humble servant

A. Laurin

Letter IX [To Naples]

Alexandria, 5 August 1840

Honourable Baron!

Sir Moses Montefiore has passed on to me your most esteemed letter of 25 July. He and his wife are both well although she seems to have suffered a good deal on the journey.

We shall now occupy ourselves seriously with the Damascus case. Thiers is urging the pasha not to allow the review on which we shall insist. If we fail in this, Thiers will at least let the case against the two Austrian accused, Picciotto and Levi, be carried on according to common German–Austrian criminal laws. It will be possible without great difficulty to apply the result made of this whole procedure to all the others. Sir Moses has just gone to see the pasha. This first audience will certainly not decide anything. This evening I shall have a

* Sherif Pasha was Mehemet Ali's governor of the Damascus region.

meeting with Mehemet Ali and speak about the case as ordered by the prince. I hope to get my plan through. Rattymenton is a dangerous character and Desmeloize* a sufficiently limited young gentleman. We shall, God willing, cope with the two of them. With M. Crémieux we shall see eye to eye very soon. More and more definite facts about this soon.

Mehemet Ali is refusing to send back the sultan's fleet on the pretext that, as he sees it, the sultan's hands are tied and he cannot receive it. He threatens to attack Dyar-Bekir and shut the sultan up in Constantinople. The man seems to be counting on an insurrection in the European Turkish provinces. Under these circumstances we here are awaiting the decisions of the London Conference. It must remain to be seen whether Mehemet Ali will submit to them or not. I think he will bend to the Cross once he sees it is really meant. Herewith I have the honour to be

> your most humble servant
> Laurin

PS Your former merchant's clerk, Kilby, who is in business in Aleppo and Damascus, is intervening in the trial of the wretched Jews, but he hasn't done any harm so far.

Letter X [To Naples]

Alexandria, 26 Aug 1840

Honoured Baron!

I received your most esteemed letter of the 15 of this month early the day before yesterday together with its most peaceful news.

Although France proposes to wash its hands of Mehemet Ali, the latter will not give up all the same. He has actually declared that he is ready to run the risk of war. Early today was the end of the first ten days,† and on his affirming his rejection, Rifaat-Bey‡ informed him in the presence of the 4 consuls-general that the pashalik of Acre devolves upon the sultan. In another ten days this will be the case with Egypt, if he does not give in.

In the meantime the communications with the Syrians are suspended. We have 3 ships of the line, 9 frigates and a couple of English steam-warships here, blocking the exit from the harbour. I hope all this answers Your Excellency. Under no circumstances will this obstinate man cause as big a war as he thinks.

Sir Moses will have written to you regarding the Damascus affair.

> I close in haste
> your most humble servant, A. Laurin

---

* The vice-consul at the French consulate in Alexandria who, in May, was assigned the task by Thiers of investigating Rattymenton's conduct during the trial of the Jews. (See also Letter IV).

† The Treaty of London (concluded on 15 July by England, Russia, Austria and Turkey) permitted Mehemet Ali two ten-day periods of grace starting from mid-August. Increasingly severe measures were threatened if he persisted in refusing the terms offered.

‡ The Turkish emissary sent to Alexandria to deliver the treaty.

Letter XI [To Alexandria]

Naples, 5 September 1840

Honourable Sir!

Highly esteemed Consul-General!

Since my most recent letter *a dato* of [?] August, I was happy to receive the kind letter that Your Excellency had the goodness to address to me on the 5 of the past month. A thousand thanks for the news imparted in it. We must hope for the best as to the successful outcome of the affair in question and wish that the present incidents and disputes will not affect it detrimentally. It is only to be regretted that the journey of Sir Moses Montefiore came precisely at such an unfortunate moment, possibly making the endeavours of that worthy friend of mankind more difficult. Your Honour would oblige me very much if you would kindly find an opportunity to commend me to him and his wife. I am completely lacking in news. My wife and children are most obliged to you and thank you for the mementoes received and present their best wishes.

I shall be uncommonly grateful to Your Excellency if you would be good enough to keep me constantly informed of the news which is of such interest from the scene of action; I should like to keep up my side of things, but everything here is so quiet and inactive. I count entirely therefore on Your Excellency's well-known and oft-proved indulgence towards me. I only request that the letters I receive from you be sent most kindly directed to Messrs James Bell & Co. in Malta, who are already charged to forward them, and not in the envelope formerly used.

Please forgive the length of today's letter and receive the renewed presentation of my great respect and ever-growing esteem.

your very humble servant

[Carl Meyer von Rothschild]

Letter XII [To Naples]

Alexandria, 17 September 1840

Honoured Baron!

Sir Moses Montefiore leaves for Syra today without knowing whether he will be betaking himself to Constantinople or to England.

I have been holding the silver bowl for the English steamer, which leaves per Malta on the 26. Your Excellency will receive the same through the intermediary of Bell & Co.

I abstain from writing about the Jewish affair, as I know that Sir Moses has given you exact information about all its dark aspects.

What still remains to be done will appear all the easier after the settlement at today's interview, as the sultan has already fixed the dates when everything falls due. Mehemet Ali has not yet entirely recovered. His affairs are going badly and getting steadily worse from day to day here just as in Syria.

A week ago the English in Beirut put 3 to 4 thousand Albanians ashore, but they can only maintain themselves there for 4 weeks. The uprising has broken out again and Ibrahim will have to evacuate Aleppo and Damascus. Here everything is quiet: Mehemet Ali does not seem to be giving any further thought to the conquest of Asia Minor. His plans have shrunk to a purely defensive attitude. I hope that everything will proceed without further ado.

With many compliments to your amiable family. I am your most humble servant,

A. Laurin

Letter XIII [To Naples]

Pera, near Constantinople
17 November 1840

Honourable Baron!

Mr [. . .] has just now handed me your esteemed letter of the 14 of last month. You will no doubt have received my letter of exactly the same date from Beirut, which I sent you via Malta. It contains some assessments [?] for Prince Metternich. Please let me know how much you paid for the packet for postage, so that I can record the amount of the debt.

I am sorry to say that I have not met Sir Moses and Lady Montefiore here. In the Sea of Marmora, I did meet the steamer on which they had journeyed to Syra. We have made a big step forward—we have discovered material for the Damascus trial which will put a different, stronger face on the matter and put the friends of justice in a position to clear it up and bring it to a satisfactory ending.

Affairs in Syria are developing for the best. Whether or not France will start a war must remain in question. We hope everything will be over by early next year.

The Egyptians have abandoned the Taunus Pass, considered invincible, as well as the course of the Orontes, and are now limited to unfortified garrison towns or bivouacs. Over 60,000 peasants are in the open waiting for them.

The sultan received me at once; and spoke very kindly and awarded me his Order in diamonds. We have Lord and Lady Ponsonby here; [. . .] [there is] a glorious autumn. The nature [?] is particularly beautiful.

My best compliments to your amiable wife and children.

I remain most respectfully
your most humble servant
A. Laurin

Letter XIV [To Naples?]

Pera, 26 November 1840

Honourable Baron!

I took the liberty of sending you a packet of dispatches for Prince Metternich with the request to forward it. The *Cyclops* took this packet to Malta, to Bell & Co. I presumed it had already reached you on 31 October. Now that I have not had any notification of this from Your Honour by the steamship that arrived here on 24 of this month, I am somewhat worried. Do write to let me know what happened to it.

310

His Excellency Montefiore and Crémieux* will be arriving here very soon. At this hour Damascus is already being evacuated, as Ibrahim had an order from his father to withdraw to Egypt at once.

Whether the insurgents will make his withdrawal easy or whether he will be harassed on the retreat by way of Kuneitra and Gaza remains to be seen. At all events he will not be able to bring back the artillery.

We received news yesterday from Alexandria that Mehemet Ali has broken with the French and thrown himself into the arms of the 4 Powers; he is said to be willing to send a mission hither in order to present his submission in return for his *hereditary* possession of Egypt being left as it was.

Who knows whether his proposals will be acceptable?

I am very busy; otherwise I would write to you at greater length. Your nephew [George] Samuel is at Terassia and last week he saw his house go up in smoke.

The sultan celebrated the festival of Beiram *early* today, between the hours of 6 and 8, with much pomp.

Presenting my best compliments to your amiable family I have the honour to be

Your Honourable
most humble servant
A. Laurin

Letter XV [To Constantinople]

Paris, 5 December 1840

Most deeply respected Mr von Laurin!

Allow me to thank you once more from the bottom of my heart for the wonderful sympathy which you, as a friend of mankind, have had the goodness to demonstrate constantly regarding the fate of our unfortunate co-religionists, and be convinced, dear friend, that I shall never forget the heartfelt efforts you have made to have justice restored. Above all, mankind will now fortunately have to record that in that hell a man like you appeared whose noble mind and warm feelings managed to put a stop to the most shameful atrocities; and—not resting content with that—intervened with courage and caution in order to gain for the unfortunate victims the priceless solace of being freed from their deep trouble and sufferings as quickly as possible. In a lifetime one is to be envied for having been in this situation. And, just as I know how to value this to its full extent, you too can easily guess how deeply moved I have been and how warm my feelings are for you, whom we have to thank for all this. Nor am I able to express to you in words how great our joy is at having fortunately reached the desired goal; Heaven be thanked that the efforts made by you, and by others too, succeeded in accomplishing this so fully.

I have since heard that you will shortly be returning to Germany and I am uncommonly glad that you will thereby be brought closer to us and I hope that

---

* Crémieux, in fact, returned directly to Europe from Egypt. Montefiore had arrived in Constantinople on 5 October, when Laurin was with the Austrian fleet off the Lebanese coast.

it will be possible for you to extend your journey further to the west and pay us a short visit here; I shall count myself lucky therewith to have the opportunity to express to you the sentiments I feel in view of the benevolent actions which you, as a friend of mankind, took on behalf of our unfortunate co-religionists in that sad affair.

In pleasant anticipation, I remain

James von Rothschild

My wife joins me in the above wish and I confidently hope that you will afford us the pleasure of having you with us.

Letter XVI [To Naples]

Pera, 17 December 1840

Honourable Baron!

I hope that, God willing, this letter finds you and your amiable family in good health. I also wish its members a happy New Year. The present year, is, God be thanked, with symptoms of contradictory significance, going to its grave.

Mehemet Ali has now formally submitted to the Porte and it will now be the affair of the Alliance to reconcile him with his sultan and rehabilitate him as pasha of Egypt. In the documents of submission that arrived here yesterday Mehemet Ali speaks of the hereditary status Napier promised him, but Napier's convention* has been set aside and the Porte has been given the right to compound with its vassals.

So there will still be a few little 'disgusti' but no more serious collisions. Besides, all the Powers really want peace, and what everyone wants is easily achieved.

What is happening to Ibrahim Pasha's army is what was prophesied in the report that went through your hands. This army is now put at hardly 20,000 men, and as soon as it reached Damascus it broke down into a mass of the sick and beggars seeking sunshine to warm themselves in and a piece of bread so as to live.

They wanted to evacuate Damascus on 1 December and reach the Jordan at the Cantar el [. . .] bridge by way of Mezareib (the pilgrim road) leading to Mecca. By this route, however, namely Om el Keis, Ibrahim will meet the insurgents, who will do him serious harm. People here are generally either of the opinion that Ibrahim will capitulate or else believe that he will all the same manage to get to El Arish with a few of his people.

In Egypt likewise everything is ripe for an uprising.

The Porte would prefer to break with Mehemet Ali once and for all and destroy him. It is still fairly uncertain whether it will carry this out. The French usually warm things up in July—before then you need not be afraid of them. France will also be ashamed of having got itself so entangled for the sake of Mehemet Ali.

---

* Commodore Charles Napier, acting as emissary for Admiral Stopford, signed an agreement with Mehemet Ali on 27 November. It proved to be not binding.

Please recommend me to Sir Moses Montefiore and be good enough to let him know that according to news reaching here today Damascus was evacuated on the 8th of this month and is occupied by the sultan's forces.

Your most humble servant
A. Laurin

Letter XVII [To Naples]

Constantinople, 26 December 1840

Right Honourable Baron!

My best thanks for the kind congratulations regarding the sultan's decoration awarded me.

With regard to the defamatory epitaph over the remains of Padre Tommaso, I undertake to have it removed at once. It is possible that I shall be sent to Damascus on other matters just as soon as the Egyptian question is cleared up. Meanwhile however I am instructing our Consul Merlato to insist on it with the guardian of the monastery there.

The documents newly received in connection with the trial are the following:

1stly—Hearings of the accused and the witnesses concerning the murder of Padre Tommaso (Arabic and French)

2ndly—Ditto concerning the murder of the servant (likewise Arabic and French)

3rdly—A list of all the Jews arrested, tortured and killed, in connection with the murders of the two aforesaid. And

4thly—A specification of the types of torture practised on them. This highly important document Sherif Pasha wanted to suppress; only the alertness of a Jew succeeded in preventing this. It will be of very great interest to preserve the original (Arabic) copy *most carefully*. Although the translation leaves a lot to be desired, all the same it will make it possible for some competent Neapolitan lawyer to show how atrocious and illegal were the proceedings of the Egyptians [?] who conducted the trial and how grievous were the three judicial murders committed on this occasion.

Whether Advocate Crémieux did *everything* that might have advanced the cause I do not know, but a very probable contention is that as a Frenchman he felt himself closely involved when the investigation was insisted on into the conduct of the French consul; also he preferred that England and not France should pressure Mehemet Ali into giving in. It was politics colliding with co-religionhood, and the former appears to have been stronger than the latter.

Dr Crémieux, as I have seen in the papers, was in Vienna and will by now be in Paris.

I have already written you that Suleiman the barber, the main accuser of the Jews, has declared to the bench that he and also the nine Jews who were denounced by him for the murder of the P[adre] T[ommaso] were absolutely innocent, that he know nothing about it, and that his testimony was given under fear of torture. At this time I am waiting for a document of the court. David Arari's servant (Murad el-Fatal) is also ready to declare that he lent himself as an accuser and accomplice only because of intimidation, on the one hand, and the offer of being rewarded with protection, on the other.

He will also make this declaration to the cadi of Damascus and I shall provide you with both documents as soon as they reach me.

Another circumstance claiming my entire attention is the rumour that is being whispered in Damascus that a young Druse killed the Father with the help of the servant; and the servant is said to have escaped to the Druse mountains, where he is now staying quietly.

Rabbi Abulafia is here; before his official visit to Damascus I shall do what is necessary to get to the bottom of this rumour, which is growing increasingly strong. God only give us peace, I shall take care of the rest, with the backing of our friends. I have forwarded the roll of papers with the trial documents to your correspondent in Malta, James Bell and Co. They were originally meant to be forwarded to Sir Moses Montefiore in London by the intermediary of Lord Ponsonby's courier. May I request that the letters attached be handed on with my kind respects. The expenses for the copies amount to: for the French 100 pages at 6 piastres = 600; for the Arabic 38 pages but at 10 = 380; that is, together 980 piastres or 98 fl. which you should kindly settle with Sir Moses and draw on S. M. von Rothschild.

As for politics, things look fine. Mehemet Ali has surrendered to the Porte and the Porte has accepted his submission. The day after tomorrow the Turkish admiral, Said Pasha [. . .] and Muslum Bey will set out for Alexandria to take over the fleet.

Candia⋆ submitted to the sultan on the 17th of this month. Therewith Ali is stripped of everything with which he was able to threaten the peace of Europe—with the exception of the French, however, who still espouse his cause.

I enclose for you Mehemet Ali's submission, from which you will be able to gather that everything can be seen as over. On 13 December, Ibrahim's army was still in Damascus. At this moment he is already encircled by the insurgents and he will surrender sooner than escape. He is suffering from a terrible lack of provisions.

My best wishes for your happiness in the New Year. Please pass on the enclosure to Lebzeltern and tell him the news, which I heard after sealing this letter, but without saying that you had it from me.

The silver goblet purchased in Alexandria is still there. It could not be sent on because of the blockade. Now I shall write about it.

I remain with true respect

Your honourable servant

A. Laurin

⋆ Crete.

Notes

I am extremely grateful to Esther Ramon and Dafne Allon who undertook, respectively, the most difficult work of transcribing the letters and producing the original draft of the translation. I also wish to thank Yvonne Moss, who discovered the Damascus file at the Rothschild Archive, Daniel J. Cohen, Simone Mace (the present Rothschild archivist) and Paul Jacoby for their painstaking help in deciphering some of the most illegible passages in the letters; and Judith Friedgut for her very skilled work in typing the manuscript.

1 H. Graetz, *Geschichte der Juden von den ältesten Zeiten bis auf die Gegenwart*, vol. 11 (Leipzig, 1900), pp. 464–500. (In English: *History of the Jews*, vol. 5, Philadelphia, 1956, pp. 632–66.)

2 See, e.g., M. Philippson, *Neueste Geschichte des jüdischen Volkes*, vol. 2 (Leipzig, 1910), pp. 300–9; S. M. Dubnov, *Noveishaia istoriia evreiskogo naroda*, vol. 2 (Riga, 1938), pp. 234–43. (In English: *History of the Jews*, vol. 5, New York, 1973, pp. 244–52.)

3 For some more specialized studies not referred to elsewhere in this article, see J. Meisl, 'Beitrage zur Damaskus-Affäre (1840)', in *Festschrift zu Dubnows siebzigstem Geburtstag* (Berlin, 1930), pp. 226–36; J. Gerber, 'The Damascus Blood Libel—Jewish Perceptions and Responses', *Proceedings of the Eighth World Congress of Jewish Studies: Division B* (Jerusalem, 1982), pp. 105–10; T. Parfitt, '"The Year of the Pride of Israel": Montefiore and the Damascus Blood Libel of 1840', in S. and V. D. Lipman, *The Century of Moses Montefiore* (Oxford, 1985), pp. 131–48.

4 Graetz (note 1 above), pp. 477–8

5 U. R. Q. Henriques, 'Who Killed Father Thomas?', in V. D. Lipman (ed.), *Sir Moses Montefiore: A Symposium* (Oxford, 1982), p. 63.

6 A. Y. Brawer, 'Homer hadash le-yediat alilat damesek', in *Sefer ha-yovel le-profesor Shmuel Krois [Krauss]* (Jerusalem, 1937), p. 277.

7 N. M. Gelber, *Österreich und die Damaskusaffaire im Jahre 1840: Nach bisher unveröffentlichten Akten (Sonderabdruck aus dem Jahrbuch der Jüdisch-Literarischen Gesellschaft* (Frankfurt a. Main, 1927).

8 e.g., 'Affaire des Juife de Damas', *Journal des Débats*, 7 May 1840.

9 Public Record Office (London): FO 78/410, 22 May 1840. On the role of Werry, see also A. M. Hyamson, 'The Damascus Affair—1840', *Transactions of the Jewish Historical Society*, vol. 16 (1945–51), pp. 45–71.

10 G. M. Pieritz, 'Narrative of the Cruel Treatment of the Damascus Jews', in D. Salomons, *An Account of the Recent Persecution of the Jews at Damascus* (London, 1840), p. 46.

11 *ibid.*, p. 39

12 'Nouvelle phase de la question d'Orient', *La Quotidienne*, no. 209 (27 July 1840)

13 Hyamson (note 9 above), p. 50

14 M. Eliav, *Be-hasut mamlekhet ostriyah 1849–1917* (Jerusalem, 1986), p. 9, n. 28.

15 FO 78/410

16 The *Österreichischer Beobachter* reported on the Damascus affair from time to time during 1840 and was by implication sympathetic to the Jewish cause from mid-April, but it appears to have revealed nothing about the official actions of the Austrian government and diplomats in the case.

17 L. H. Löwenstein, *Damascia: Die Judenverfolgung zu Damaskus und ihre Wirkungen auf die öffentliche Meinung* (Rödelheim, 1840), p. vii

18 *ibid.*, p. viii

19 '*Damaskus: ein Wort zur Abwehr', von Dr. L. Zunz, nebst einem Verzeichniss der Schriften des Verfassers, mit Anmerkungen (in zweiter Ausgabe) heraugeben von M. Steinschneider* (Berlin, 1859), p. viii (first published in the Leipzig *Allgemeine Zeitung*,

Jonathan Frankel

no. 133, 1840).

20 Salomons (note 10 above), p. 59
21 J. M. Jost, *Neuere Geschichte der Juden von 1815 bis 1845*, vol. 2 (Berlin, 1846), p. 353
22 Salomons (note 10 above), p. 55
23 On the contemporary reaction to the Damascus case as a repetition of the Purim story, see J. I. Helfand, 'A "Megillah" for the Damascus Affair', in L. Landman (ed.), *Rabbi Joseph H. Lookstein Memorial Volume* (New York, 1980), pp. 175–83.
24 Graetz (note 1 above), p. 464
25 See Laurin to von Stürmer (27 March 1840) and to James Rothschild (31 March 1840) in Gelber (note 7 above), pp. 12, 13–14.
26 *ibid.*, p. 12
27 *ibid.*
28 *La Quotidienne*, no. 209 (27 July 1840)
29 Laurin to James Rothschild, in Gelber (note 7 above), p. 15
30 Cochelet to the Duc de Dalmatie, Ministre des Affaires Étrangères, in E. Driault (ed.), *L'Égypte et l'Europe: la Crise de 1839–1841*, vol. 2 (Cairo, 1930), p. 169. (The dispatch from Damascus has not been published but is referred to, for example, by Brawer, note 6 above, p. 271.)
31 Metternich to Laurin in Gelber (note 7 above), pp. 17–18
32 e.g., the *Journal des Débats* carried a news item about the Damascus affair on 17 March based on a report from Beirut dated 21 February and published initially in the *Sémaphore* of Marseille.
33 See p. J. W. Steenwijk, 'De Damascus-Affaire (1840) en haar Weerklang in Nederland', *Studia Rosenthaliana*, vol. 20, no. 1 (1986), p. 70.
34 For the letters to Lehren from E. Kilbee and Pierre Laurella respectively, see Löwenstein (note 17 above), pp. 44–5.
35 Steenwijk (note 33 above), pp. 70–3
36 FO 78/403 no. 9 and FO 78/405 no. 54 (also referred to in Hyamson, note 9 above, pp. 53, 56).
37 Laurin to Metternich, 5 May 1840, in Brawer (note 6 above), p. 288
38 Gelber (note 7 above), p. 14
39 FO 78/404, no. 36. In mid-April Laurin mentioned in a letter to James Rothschild that 'I try to keep Mehemet Ali in a good mood' (Gelber, note 7 above, p. 19).
40 'Affaire de Damas', *Journal des Débats* (31 May 1840). (The paper's correspondent in Alexandria noted that Mehemet Ali 'is not accustomed to hearing such language'.)
41 'The Jews in Damascus: Private Correspondence', *The Times* (18 May 1840), p. 5. (Commenting on the appeal of the Jewish community to Mehemet Ali, the correspondent in France wrote there that: 'Than this no document published for a length of time has attracted more notice, nor secured more sympathy in Paris.')
42 FO 78/404, no 54
43 Laurin to Metternich, in Gelber (note 7 above), p. 17
44 Laurin to Metternich, 5 May 1840, in Brawer (note 6 above), p. 288
45 Laurin to James Rothschild, 31 March 1840, in Gelber (note 7 above), p. 15
46 *ibid.*, 5 April 1840, p. 17
47 James to Salomon Rothschild, 7 May 1840, *ibid.*, p. 25
48 Metternich to Laurin, *ibid.*, p. 18
49 *ibid.*, 27 May 1840, p. 28
50 *ibid.*, no date [July 1840], pp. 45–6
51 Laurin to Metternich, 16 June 1840, *ibid.*, p. 37.
52 On the Middle East crisis of 1840 and the five-power London accord of 15 July 1840, see, e.g., C. Webster, *The Foreign Policy of Palmerston 1830–1841*, 2 vols (London, 1969); K. Bourne, *Palmerston: The Early Years 1784–1841* (London, 1982).

53 FO 78/405, no. 54, 18 June 1840 (enclosure)

54 Consistoire Central/CC/M/Affaires étrangères/Correspondance générale, 1840. (The letter of 9 June specifically suggested that Montefiore consider joining Crémieux in order to represent 'our English brethren worthily'.)

55 The Damascus file in the Rothschild archive (London) contains two letters from Laurin to Carl Rothschild dated 6 and 23 December 1839, which clearly suggests that the two men corresponded regularly about Middle East politics; the purchase of rare coins and other collectors' items; and similar matters of mutual interest (File RAL RFamAD/2, Documents 1–2).

56 On the role of the Rothschild family in the Damascus case, see, e.g., E. C. Corti, *The Reign of the House of Rothschild 1830–1871* (New York, 1928), pp. 204–7; A. Mulstein, *James de Rothschild* (Paris, 1981), pp. 135–57.

57 e.g., FO 78/403, no. 9 (5 May 1840) and no. 11 (30 May 1840) (both quoted in Hyamson, note 9 above, pp. 53–4).

58 See, e.g., *Diaries of Sir Moses and Lady Montefiore*, ed. L. Loewe, vol. 1 (London, 1983), pp. 224, 227, 228, 243, 247, 248; and *The Damascus Affair: Diary of Dr Louis Loewe July–November 1840* (Ramsgate, 1940), pp. 17, 21, 30, 32.

59 The Archive of N. M. Rothschild and Sons, London: File RAL RFamAD2/ Document no. 28.

60 See, e.g., Brawer (note 6 above), pp. 263–6; Eliav (note 14 above), pp. 6–10.

61 Much light is thrown on the role of Jews in the Austrian consular service by the correspondence between Metternich and the Austrian ambassador to Rome, R. Lützow, in May and June 1840 (in Brawer, not 6 above, pp. 293–7).

62 On tensions between Metternich and the Rothschilds, see Corti (note 56 above), pp. 117–18, 145, 157–60.

Did the Russian Jacobins (Blanquists)[1]
Have a Special Attitude Towards the Jews?

Moshe Mishkinsky

THE Russian revolutionary movement's attitude to the Jews can be traced back as far as the first quarter of the nineteenth century, to the time of the Decembrists. Several stages can be identified in its development over this period, but it is clear that a turning-point was reached at the time and as a result of the first great waves of anti-Jewish pogroms between 1881 and 1884.[2] By the nature of things, that stormy period, which ushered in a cycle of progressively worse pogroms over the next forty years, has become the main focus of scholars' attention and has in great measure distracted attention from what went before. Thus, few attempts have been made to review the developments that preceded it, in the period from the end of the 1860s to the events sparked off by the assassination of Tsar Alexander II by the Narodnaia Volia ('People's Will'), of which the pogroms were a focal point.[3] Study of this period, which has entered the record as the years of *narodnichestvo* (populism, or revolutionary populism),[4] reveals the existence of a continuous line, albeit replete with internal contradictions, changes of direction and even reversals in the various ideological, programmatical, organizational and personal aspects. Such continuity lends coherence to the methodical investigation of the Jewish topic, too.

In this context, several questions are to be considered here. First, how did the revolutionary movement in the period prior to the pogroms relate to the Jewish contemporary and historical experience? Second, how and to what extent did such attitudes influence the stands adopted by the different factions within the revolutionary movement to the pogroms and to a wider set of problems, especially those to do with the relations between the Jews and their environment? Specifically, what was the attitude of the Jacobin faction which was then making its mark on the Russian revolutionary movement? Even those who hold that this group, relatively small even at its height (1875–81), was 'very far from the mainstream' of the revolutionary movement nevertheless recognize that its ideological and tactical influence was far in excess of its size.[5] This influence manifested itself primarily through Narodnaia Volia and is often discerned even in Lenin. The growing interest in recent decades in the central personality of that group, P. N. Tkachev (1844–96), both in the West and in the Soviet Union, has also played its part in that assessment.[6] Even so, we find that the attitude of the Jacobins and their journal *Nabat* to the Jews is still a total *tabula rasa*, particularly with regard to the years from 1875 to 1881.[7] Accordingly, this is the area on which this essay focuses.

The crises of the beginning of the 1880s, the traumatic turns of events and the rapidity of developments, the pressures and unrest that accompanied them, the great expectations and the disappointments that they generated—all these gave special character and significance to the positions that the revolutionary movements adopted on the Jews. A brief sketch of the most outstanding aspects of this subject—all that is possible within the scope of this article—may provide a perspective that will help us to ask the right questions and adopt a suitable analytical approach for the study before us.

First, the contrast between the speed with which the pogroms spread and the fact that their development was entirely unforeseen by the revolutionary movement of the 1870s indicates that the latter had failed to understand the importance of the 'Jewish question' in the wider context of Russia's social and political problems. Such discussion as there was on the issue was perfunctory and not particularly deep, the differences revealed reflecting to a great extent the general splits within the movement—for example, between the clearly anti-Jewish Mikhail Bakunin (1814–76) and Petr Lavrov (1823–1900). Towards the end of the 1870s, in fact, despite the continuous increase in Judaeophobia (the Russian counterpart of German and European anti-Semitism), discussion of the Jewish issue was virtually absent from the pages of the revolutionary journals, including those of the two new revolutionary organizations founded in 1879, Narodnaia Volia and Cherny Peredel ('The Black Repartition'). The only place in which it received relatively wide coverage was in periodicals of the Ukrainian Socialists.[8] But even if there was no public discussion of the matter after 1876–7, attitudes were most certainly crystallizing beneath the surface: all that was needed was the appropriate situation to bring them out.

With the outbreak of the pogroms the cards were reshuffled. Assessments no longer followed the orgnizational dividing line in the revolutionary camp, nor was there any clear-cut connection between those same assessments and the various basic stands on programme and tactics. The different approaches to the Jews that were current in the populist (Narodniki) movement in the 1870s can be discerned from the alternative interpretations given to the concept of 'the people' (*narod*, in effect a synonym for 'the peasantry'), and the place attributed to the people in the process leading to social revolution and in the moulding of the future socialist society. This also explains the one-sided approach to the Jews, who of course lacked a real agricultural class and therefore could not be regarded as part of 'the people' in the sense noted above. The cardinal question of the relationship between the intelligentsia and the people was largely influenced by a tendency to idealize 'the people' in all its manifestations: 'the ideals of the people', 'the interests of the people', the 'elemental force of the people', 'the will of the people', 'the views of the people', and so on. Against this background, the increasing social differentiation within Jewish society was ignored and attention was focused instead on the economic relations between the Jews and 'the people', which were simplistically reduced to a stereotyped generalization of 'Jewish exploitation' of the village. In this model, Jews were also seen as the *grande bourgeoisie* who had effected the development of capitalism, a distorted, one-sided view which influenced even some of the Jewish populists (*narodniki*) and populist sympathizers.[9]

However, there was also an anti-Judaeophobic trend in the revolutionary camp that did not exclude the Jewish plebeian strata, and especially the growing Jewish proletariat, from 'the people' as a whole, was sensitive to the Jews as a discriminated against and oppressed minority, and was aware of the religious–national overtones in the hostility to the Jews even when it was clothed in egalitarian–social arguments; most important, it was open to the idea of spreading special socialist–revolutionary propaganda among the Jews in their own languages. Thus, the most important revolutionary periodical of the 1870s, *Vpered* (Forward), edited by P. Lavrov and V. Smirnov (1840–1900), also provided a platform for reports and articles by A. S. Liberman (1843–80), the pioneer of international Jewish socialism. Liberman had developed a broad perspective on the Jewish reality that reflected accurately its internal social contradictions as well as the oppression and suffering imposed by the Russian regime, and accordingly he saw the Jewish proletariat as having an autonomous political and social role. Despite all the differences in mentality, in culture, in background and in orientation, the editors of *Vpered* generally lent their support to his various initiatives aimed at encouraging the collective participation of Jews in the movement of the revolution and socialism.[10]

After the outbreak of the riots against the Jews, some expressions of protest were to be found in the organs of Cherny Peredel, though at base they remained faithful to the populist tradition of supporting 'people's rebellions'. On the other hand, various trends within the Narodnaia Volia favoured a pro-pogrom stance, but the line was ultimately determined by those who had abandoned their emphasis on a populist allegiance to the people in favour of support for a political-terrorist struggle to overthrow the existing political regime and even seize power.

The existence of these two different attitudes side by side within the radical camp indicates the autonomous nature of the Jewish problem— that is, that attitudes to the Jews were not automatically determined by general ideological–political positions. Of particular significance is the fact that in a key matter like the attitude to 'the people', there were notable similarities between the populist camp and the Slavophiles, who were generally regarded as being at the other end of the revolutionary spectrum and generally anti-Jewish.[11] As to the *narodniki* (and here the term is used to include the Narodnaia Volia as well), not only did they hold different views with regard to the objectives and means of the revolutionary struggle: but they were clearly also influenced by a residue of traditional superstitions about the Jews. These seem to have been rekindled by the burning issues of the day and clouded the assessment of short-term perspectives and tactics after March 1881. These points must be borne in mind in our investigation of the attitudes of the Russian Jacobins.

The emergence of Russian Jacobinism as an ideological trend is generally assumed to date from the publication in 1862 of the manifesto *Molodaia Rossiia* ('Young Russia') by P. G. Zaichnevski (1842–96). I have found no evidence that he or his circle concerned themselves in any way with the Jewish issue, so the discussion here will focus on his successor, Petr Tkachev, and on the periodical *Nabat* (Alarm Bell), which appeared, with some gaps, from 1875 to 1881, mostly under Tkachev's editorial direction. Tkachev's main partners in *Nabat* were two revolutionaries of Polish origin, K. Turski (1847–1926)[12] and K. Janitski, who like him had been in contact at the end of the 1860s with S. Nechaev (1842–82) and Narodnaia Rasprava (The People's Retribution), the small group he headed. Nechaev's name is writ large in the history of the revolutionary movement as the principal exponent, in theory and in practice, of a tactical approach that ignored all moral considerations and saw the end as justifying the means. This approach was reflected more than once in the 1870s in the way in which some of the revolutionary organizations and their members as individuals reacted towards the Jews, but I have found no evidence whatsoever that it had any influence on Nechaev's own attitude to the Jews, or that any such attitude was transmitted from him to Tkachev and his colleagues.[13] The latter were the most fanatical proponents of revolutionary action, but their commitment to action was effectively confined to literary expression in their writings, to which we must now turn.

Tkachev was one of the youngest of the figures whose name and work is identified with a specific trend in the history of radical revolutionary thought in Russia in the 1860s and 1870s.[14] He began his writing (mostly in the officially permitted press) and his underground political activity in Russia as well as abroad relatively early, in the early 1860s, continuing until his health failed in the early 1880s. Tremendously erudite, he wrote on a wide range of subjects—philosophy, sociology, literature and the economy. This point is worthy of note, for in the context of the breadth of his knowledge, intellectual awareness and intimate involvement in current affairs, his merely incidental treatment of a problem such as the situation of the Jews, which had received fairly broad expression in the press and literature, is significant. The reasons for this are difficult to trace, since much of Tkachev's writing is not easily accessible; this problem affects the study of his work as a whole, but it hinders more particularly the study of his attitude to the Jews, given that he wrote so little on this issue.[15]

A biographical analogy may be useful here: two of the outstanding individuals in the history of the Russian revolutionary movement, Alexander Herzen (1812–70) and Mikhail Bakunin, grew up far from a Jewish environment and had little direct, personal acquaintance with the Jews. Accordingly, any experiences with Jews at a young and impressionable age would have been etched in their subconscious to influence them afterwards—whether to negative effect, as in the case of Bakunin, or more positively, as with Herzen.[16] It is clearly impossible to assess accurately the relative weight of the memory of any experiences or impressions in the programmatic and tactical stands that they eventually arrived at, but it would seem reasonable to assume that such experiences could have permanently affected their mental attitude to the Jews, or alternatively that they might have been temporarily forgotten, only to resurface in special situations. In Tkachev's case we are relieved of such considerations;[17] he spent his early years on his father's estate, which lay outside the Jewish Pale of Settlement, and went to secondary school in St Petersburg. There is no evidence of contacts with a specifically Jewish environment until he went abroad in the early 1870s. It would therefore seem justified to consider Tkachev's attitude on the Jewish question within the overall frame of reference of the social and political views he championed by virtue of his general attachment to the Russian revolutionary movement and his particular position within it.

The year 1868 appears to be a milestone in Tkachev's writing on socio-political subjects. He now expressed for the first time those basic positions to which he would, in general, continue to adhere in the future—even if on some aspects he became more extreme in the light of the experiences of the revolutionary movement in the first half of the 1870s.[18] Tkachev's distinctive route begins from the key point of the *narodnichestvo*, i.e., from the question of the place of 'the people' in the Russian historical process and of the interrelationship between 'the people' and the revolutionary intelligentsia.[19] From the beginning, Tkachev came out against what he called one of the most dangerous illusions—'the idealization of the uncultured masses' by the 'cultured masses'.[20] In his view, this idealization took two apparently contradictory forms. One trend held that the 'uncultured masses' were so vulgar, ignorant and lacking in awareness of their situation that it was premature to summon them to action; one must wait patiently for the profound change in them that would enable them to liberate themselves from their circumstances and satisfy their needs. This approach, which appeared to evaluate the masses 'realistically', in fact embodied an idealization of the conditions in which the 'uncultured masses' lived because it assumed that these conditions would be a breeding ground for the changes within the masses that would give them a common language with the 'cultured masses' and enable them to arrive at common action. The second approach, apparently incompatible with the first, similarly ascribed to the common masses ideal qualities that in reality they lacked. It perceived them as superior to the 'cultured masses', containing within them the seeds of everything that is worthy of emulation. It is not the masses who must learn from their cultured neighbours; on the contrary—it is the cultured who must draw inspiration from their simple brethren. It would be wrong to impose on them any ideals that were not intrinsic to their class or to push them to a course of action not of their own choosing. Tkachev did not hold with this 'naïve image' of 'the people' and the glorification of its 'spirit' or 'genius'. He concluded that both the exaggerated belief in the power of the people to better themselves and the tendency to attribute lofty characteristics to them were delusory. Furthermore, he contended that both these trends engendered an apathetic approach to the masses—an unwillingness to intervene in and an attitude of optimistic nonchalance to their suffering and distress.

Tkachev differed on this point from both Bakunin and Lavrov, the ideological fathers of the two main streams in the revolutionary movement in the mid-1870s. He rejected the assumption common to them both 'the people' (the peasantry) would be the prime motivating factor in the revolution. He likewise rejected the anti-state stand of anarchism and held that the precondition for a socialist social revolution was a political revolution, the outcome of a political conspiracy—an idea that was strange to the great majority of revolutionaries in Russia until towards the end of the 1870s. He rejected Bakunin's belief in the spontaneous rebelliousness of the people and the conviction that the limited uprisings of the present were the vanguard of the great uprising to come—the longed-for social revolution. On the other hand, he utterly rejected Lavrov's assumption that it would be possible to convert the people to revolutionary ardour through propaganda disseminated by an intelligentsia trained to this role.

Tkachev's view was that the people were ready for revolution, but only the demonstration of force from the outside would make them shake off their fears and their feeling of powerlessness in the face of oppression and suffuse them with a sense of strength and drive to action. In his view, the main catalyst of the revolution would be the non-aristocratic intelligentsia (*raznochintsy*), whose opposition to the regime would come partly from economic interests. He then refined this concept further: the wheels of the revolution would in fact be turned by only a small section of the intelligentsia, working as an organized force. The revolution would thus be led by a small, centralized and hierarchical core under the direction of an authoritative and vigorous leadership implementing a well-conceived plan. A fighting organization of this type, dedicated to what Tkachev called 'disruption and terrorization of the regime' would undermine and demoralize tsarist rule, which he perceived as lacking a real class basis. The revolutionary core who would come to power in the political revolt would then be able to motivate the people, now primed for revolt, and set in motion the true process of social revolution.[21]

For Tkachev, the time factor was decisive: he therefore called for immediate revolution, and he was certain of its chances of success. He feared that, if the plan to seize power was not implemented in time, the development of capitalism in Russia would strengthen the bourgeoisie and could frustrate the possibility of a socialist revolution. On the other hand, the strong, centralist government of a revolutionary minority would pave the way to subsequent and gradual reforms in the social sphere—abandonment of the historical traditions of private property and barter, a change in the system of relations within the family, and the re-education of the people.[22]

In all Tkachev's discussion of the question of 'the people', we find no attempt to deal with Jewish matters; his thoughts on the subject can only be gleaned from occasional passing references. On this basis it emerges that his opposition to the idealization of 'the people' might have served him as a barrier against the notion, prevalent in populist circles and occasionally put into practice, of resorting to traditional, popular anti-Jewish sentiments as an expression of the 'popular view' which might be used to stir the masses to revolutionary action. Tkachev's analysis of the rapid growth of capitalism in both village and town led him to identify a process of socio-economic differentiation among the peasants and the emergence of a kulak class within it. He did not hold with the definition of Jews *per se* as an exploitative class merely on the basis of the economic relationships between Jewish tenants, traders and middlemen on the one hand and the peasants on the other. Furthermore, when mentioning famous Jewish capitalists, Tkachev refrained from the usual propagandist and literary tendency to link their economic role, their social role, or any of their actions with the fact of their being Jewish.[23]

The distinction between economic function and ethno-religious allegiance, and not only with respect to Jews, was not always so rigorously maintained in *Nabat*. In one of the first issues,[24] there was a report entitled 'From Byelorussia', at the centre of which was an incident that the writer claimed was 'one of thousands' known to him. It opened with a review of the worrying state of the peasants and hired labourers created by the emancipation of the serfs: although freed from the bonds of serfdom they had not received land, and had in consequence been forced to leave the villages and become enmeshed in the wheels of the developing capitalist system, in the areas of finance, industry, transport, forestry, trade and credit. At the same time the report also stressed the strengthening of ties between the owners of property of various kinds and the authorities at regional and local level. In characterizing the different elements of the population, the writer did not stop at defining their socio-economic functions. He repeatedly applied stereotyped national characteristics to the Germans, and particularly to the Jews, but not to the Polish land-owners ('The pan, the kulak, the entrepreneurs and the Jews among them . . . '). While it was true that there were moneylenders, merchants and labour contractors who were Jewish, not all Jews belonged to these categories. The characterization may have been true as far as it went, but it was only part of the story; yet the editors claimed that they never interfered with the text of the articles they received—and indeed they left the stigmatic term *Zhid*.[25] *Nabat* never employed editorial powers to counter the stereotyped presentation of the Jews in the Judaeophobic press as being among the privileged, with a broader view of the Jewish socio-economic situation. It thus offered, in fact, a one-sided picture of Jewish society. A comparison with *Vpered* is illuminating here. *Vpered* also had no compunctions about publishing the Judaeophobic expressions often used by correspondents, generally in the context of the economic functions of the Jews,[26] yet some time before the publication of the aforementioned article in *Nabat*, *Vpered* had published a series of articles over about five months dealing with the same region, Lithuania–Byelorussia, and primarily with its Jewish population. This series was much more balanced. it covered such topics as the poverty of the popular-plebeian classes within Jewish society, the existence of exploited Jewish workers (alongside others), instances of struggle and organization to improve their working conditions, and the contrasts within Jewish society; it also presented examples of oppression and discrimination against the Jews on the part of the authorities.[27]

Adopting a socio-economic perspective on the Jews that ignored the internal differentiation among them also created a collective identity for the Jews as belonging to the privileged classes and therefore worthy only of rejection and hostility. Tkachev, as we have seen, refrained from adopting this approach. But the nature of the collective identity of the Jews at a time of modernization, when their distinctive historical traditional religious identity had to be redefined to reflect changing conditions, emerged as an open question. In outlining their paths of action, the revolutionaries frequently stressed the multinational, multiethnic and multilingual reality of the state. In some cases the context was negative—for example, the hatred and mistrust it engendered—in others, positive: accommodation to the specific reality of each element in the population as a way of finding a receptive ear among as wide an audience as possible. Finally, there was the question of the relations between the socialist revolutionary groups of different nationalities. In the light of all this, the place of the national problem in Tkachev's thought and *Nabat* in general must also be considered: the nature and place of nationalities in the historical process; likely trends in their future development; ways in which national oppression can be eliminated, and how they should be incorporated in social and revolutionary actions so as to change the regime; and the practical and organizational implications that the particular multinational reality of Eastern Europe held for revolutionary activity.

However, neither Tkachev nor *Nabat* paid much attention to the national question, and in *Nabat*'s platform the subject is not even mentioned. The historiography of the Jacobin trend virtually ignores the topic, and more or less the same is true of monographs dealing with Tkachev.[28] Both Tkachev and *Nabat* displayed particular sympathy (perhaps tinged to some degree with idealism) to the Poles and their tradition of insurrection, to the many secret organizations that they established, and to the Polish socialist trend that emerged in the 1870s. It would seem that the fact that Tkachev's colleagues on the editorial board were Polish was also not without its influence, or the memory of the most recent revolt (1863) with the participation of radical democrats (the 'reds'). An article in *Nabat* vigorously opposing the views of the Ukrainian socialist M. Dragomanov (1841–95) on the Poles began: 'The Poles, our big brothers in matters of revolution . . . '.[29]

As early as the end of the 1860s, Tkachev concluded from a review of the history of western Europe that the basis for differentiating between individual nationalities was gradually weakening as progress continued to blur socio-cultural distinctions towards total disappearance.[30] He criticized all introverted nationalist explanations of the unfolding of history in Russia and of the Russian people, and also objected to the russification policy of the regime in Polish lands.[31] In a critique of a pamphlet by Bakunin (*Statism and Anarchy*) that was to prove very influential in the revolutionary movement of the 1870s, Tkachev condemned the practice of stereotyping entire nationalities, for good or bad. He summarized his hard line on this subject in a rhetorical statement to the effect that

> such sweeping generalizations abstract at random a single element from the lives of a people and make it a distinguishing characteristic; they reduce all the varied attributes and tendencies to a single uniform formula, laconically labelling entire nations 'frivolous', 'solid-fundamental', 'dissolute', 'philanthropic', 'a nation of anarchists', 'a nation of statists', and so on: all such generalizations are fantasies belonging to the realm of pure poetry and rhetoric . . . nothing more than metaphor.[32]

This statement was made in the context of Bakunin's differentiation between the Germans[33] and the Slavic and Romance peoples (particularly the Spaniards and the Italians).[34] In his refutation Tkachev did not cite the Jews, although clearly they could have served as an outstanding example of how the distortions that are inherent in deep-rooted generalizations are magnified as they are passed from generation to generation. It would have been fairly natural had he done so, particularly as he was discussing psycho-socio-ethnic phenomena in a broad European context. The existence of the Jewish Diaspora was well known, and the fact that the same stereotyped motifs appeared almost universally both in the old hatred of Israel and in modern anti-Semitism could not have been unknown to Tkachev, since their consequences were hardly confined to poetry and rhetoric. Moreover, in the same essay at which Tkachev's trenchant criticism was directed, Bakunin had drawn a connection between the Germans and the Jews, presenting the further entrenchment of the centralist capitalist German state as the victory of 'The *Zhid* kingdom, the bankocracy'.[35] Tkachev would not have been wrong if he had extended his explanation for what he calls Bakunin's hatred of the Germans—which Tkachev attributed to Slavophile influences[36]—to account for the hostility towards the Jews. But for some reason he refrained from doing so.

Some two and a half years passed before Tkachev dealt with the issue again. This time he objected most explicitly to negative generalizations with regard to the Jews. The pretext for such generalizations was accusations levelled against big businessmen, Jewish names prominent among them, of acts of speculation and fraud in supplying the army during the Russo-Turkish war.[37] This affair was used to foment anti-Jewish sentiment, particularly by the main spokesman of the anti-Jewish press of the time, A. Suvorin, the editor of *Novoe Vremia* (New Times).[38] Tkachev commented ironically that the paper was not in fact concerned with the issue but was 'exploiting the lives of soldiers' in order to make generalizations about the Jews 'as extortioners and the scum of humanity', even though pure-bred Russians were also involved in the affair.[39] This statement touches on two subjects: it is an explicit rejection of the identification of Jews as a whole with certain large plutocrats, but at a deeper level it is also a rejection of the tendency to use images—particularly literary images—to protect the idea that even if all financial giants are wicked sinners, the Jews among them are even worse. This last tendency was common in the works of the satirist M. Saltykov-Shchedrin before the pogroms, and these were the object of Tkachev's critical article.[40]

However, Tkachev's objections to the generalized condemnation of the Jews, in this case inspired by an extremely Judaeophobic article[41] by Suvorin, apparently remained an isolated incident, even though it would have been natural for him to broaden the canvas, in the same article, or subsequently, and to call for a clearer stand on the question. Meanwhile, Judaeophobic sentiment was becoming more pronounced; new depths were reached in 1879 with the blood libel in Kutaisi, which emphasized only too clearly the power of the most ancient of religious–ethnic stereotypes. *Nabat* took a different line, for example, over the expression of anti-Polish sentiment when, not long before, it published 'the attacks on the past and present of the entire Polish people, without the smallest recognition that this people, as all other peoples, includes elements of all types, and the bad elements here are fewer than anywhere else'.[42] Tkachev's ability and willingness to appreciate the complexities of the Jewish experience and his rejection of stereotyping can however be put to the test in the context of the pogroms at the beginning of the 1880s.

In 1878, Tkachev for the first time gave a more generalized theoretical exposition of his stand on the question of 'the revolution and the principle of nationality'.[43] The target of his polemic here was the Ukrainian socialists or Ukrainophile-socialists,[44] with whom his ideological differences were constantly intensifying, but in fact the subject was also of relevance to other ethnic groups, including the Jews whom, once again, he fails to mention. Instead he reiterates the argument he had raised several years previously with regard to the historical process of cosmopolitization, the constant weakening of the national factor as a result of bourgeois modernization. According to Tkachev, this result of the process of modernization should have been welcomed by socialists, much as they rejected the process from other points of view.

On what basis does Tkachev reach this conclusion? The first component is statehood: however multinational and multiethnic (tribal) a state may be, there will always be a class of people in it among whom national or ethnic attributes have become almost completely blurred. The bureaucracy, for example, is just such a class, subjugating its own ideals, view and interests to those of the state.

The second component is the intelligentsia, their national character diluted by science and education. Members of this stratum may come from different nationalities and states and yet be closer to each other than to people of the same nationality who are not of the intelligentsia. The attempts of the Ukrainophiles to increase the national distinctiveness of the intelligentsia of their people are useless, in this view, because they contradict the basic laws of human nature, the basic demands of progress as regards the psyche and the intellect. Progress requires an end to man's subjugation to his subconscious feelings, his habits, his traditional notions and inherited inclinations that together constitute national uniqueness.

A third factor is the development of industrial production, which moulds a proletarian type whose needs and interests are common to all members of his class while reducing not only national but also individual differences.

To these factors must be added the process of urbanization, which works in the same direction. All these factors taken together prepare the ground for the realization of the socialist ideals of fraternity and equality. Tkachev's central conclusion is that there is an unresolvable clash between the 'principle of nationhood' and the 'principle of socialism'. Clearly, the profoundly centralist Tkachev opposed the federative–autonomist programmes of Dragomanov and his Ukrainian colleagues. But what of the actual, practical side of the problem—the tactical–organizational side, the question of the means for implementing the revolution and attaining socialism? Tkachev is ready to acknowledge in principle that consideration must be given to the special conditions of any given society, but he makes no real effort to deal with a number of related questions. Both in the domestic arena and abroad, the Ukrainian socialists demanded recognition of Ukrainian nationhood[45] and that the question of the the national, cultural and linguistic oppression of the various peoples within Russia be addressed. They had their own version of 'the obligation owed to the people' by the educated (a central motivating factor in the spiritual world of the Russian Narodniki), according to which the Ukrainian socialists must work within their own people and not be swallowed up in the wider Russian revolutionary movement. This also underlay their demand for a separate organizational framework for Ukrainian socialists, while postulating federative ties among the socialist organizations of the different peoples. The principles embodied in this approach to the minority peoples were extended by the Ukrainian socialists at the end of the 1870s towards the Jews as well.[46]

In the article in question, Tkachev listed, for the purposes of the argument, different peoples and national groups within Russia; but he omitted to include the Jews.[47] Some two years before, *Nabat* had published reports from Vilna on the imprisonment of members of the socialist revolutionary circles, almost all of them Jews, immediately after Liberman had fled the country.[48] A chance statement of Liberman, in a letter to Smirnov which hints at the position that Tkachev was eventually to adopt against him, permits no definite conclusions except that Liberman personally, and the *Vpered* group generally, apparently had some information about certain of Tkachev's opinions on the matter of nationalities and more particularly on the way of socialist action among the different nationalities, relating especially to Liberman's work in the area of Jewish socialism in close collaboration with the Russian socialist camp.[49] At the same time *Nabat* published news items and more comprehensive articles about Jews, as well as obituaries of various revolutionaries in a way that left no doubt as to their Jewish origin; this detail was simply stated in a matter-of-fact way without any comment.[50] From the annals of the revolutionary movement in Russia we know that the participation of individual Jews in the various factions of the movement was to trigger comments—positive and negative, from both right and left—on the fact that the Jews as a group had provided many of the activists of the revolution. As we shall see, towards the end of its days *Nabat* would also use this in putting forward pro-Jewish arguments.

We now come to the concluding chapter in *Nabat*'s history, a short but eventful period in the spring and summer of 1881, of special significance for our present discussion but virtually ignored in the literature.[51] The issue of *Nabat* that appeared in autumn 1877 spoke out against trying to settle old historical accounts between different peoples:[52] ' . . . how out of place to single out one national group for censure, while in barbaric times all people had slaughtered each other indiscriminately; how out of place, for example, to condemn the Malo-Russians and the Veliko-Russians for having slaughtered [and] oppressed the Jews . . . '.[53] Even leaving aside the validity of the optimistic assumption that the slaughter of Jews was a thing of the past,[54] it is difficult to understand how the author could have considered the oppression of the Jews as being a thing of the past in the fact of the reality in Russia: it seems that this is another instance of wilfully ignoring the evidence. However, with the assassination of the tsar and the pogroms that came in its wake, reality could no longer be ignored. No issue of *Nabat* since the beginning of 1875 had ever dealt with the question of the Jews to the extent that it was dealt with in the first issue that appeared with the renewal of publication three months after the assassination of Alexander II.[55] The leader article, written by Tkachev,[56] summarized the new situation. It is hardly surprising that his assessment was replete with superlatives, as Tkachev had more than once in the past seriously exaggerated the strength of the revolutionary organizations and movements in Russia[57] and declared as early as 1879 that 'The revolution has begun.'[58] No wonder that now he was full of rebellious impatience and optimistic hopes for rapid progress towards the final victory of the revolution. The reality unfolding, in the writer's opinion, confirmed all the hopes and assumptions of the revolutionary party.[59] In particular it confirmed *Nabat*'s earlier prophecy that terrorization of the regime would disorganize and undermine it while encouraging the growth of resentment and unrest in all strata of the population, sounding a muffled note of protest in each one that would lead all to open, armed rebellions: in short—a general crisis, the ideal circumstance for overwhelming the tsarist autocracy and advancing along the route to the victory of the socialist revolution. And indeed, Tkachev continued, the depressed and impoverished classes, having suffered exploitation over hundreds of years while patiently waiting for revenge, had now entered into open battle with their exploiters. Tkachev does not support this opinion with facts,[60] merely making indirect reference to the pogroms[61] (which moreover he could hardly claim to have foreseen).

Tkachev leaves no doubt that in his opinion the pogroms were one of the most outstanding consequences of the events of 1 March. They were nothing less than a popular uprising against the exploiters and hangmen[62] of the people, a portent of the emerging social revolution. While some revolutionaries may have opposed the pogroms but preferred not to come out openly against them because revolutionaries must not take a stand against the insurgent people, not so Tkachev. To him pogroms were an integral part of the popular uprising. He therefore rejected explanations of the pogroms as based on religious superstition, simple ignorance, or the notion that revolution simply had to start somewhere.[63] Tkachev's explanation, in his words, was 'simple': 'In the minds of the people the concept "Zhid" is linked inseparably with the image of the "sucker of the people's blood", the merciless usurer and the kulak-exploiter.' Even if Tkachev assumed, and with justification, that the pogroms were not the result of 'theoretical considerations', he could most certainly not claim to be free of them himself in this respect, even from a more sober perspective on reality. Had he not strongly opposed in the not too distant past—and from practical considerations in the interests of the revolutionary struggle—such blind agreement to the opinions and images of the people? The popular image of the 'Zhid',[64] as Tkachev described it, was in reality a generalization about all the Jews; even in practice the pogroms were directed at the Jews *per se*, and most of the victims were poor, not rich Jews. He conveniently forgot his previous explicit objections to Suvorin's negative generalizations concerning the Jews. In the heat of the pogrom, in Kiev in April, a spokesman of another revolutionary organization, the Ukrainian Paulo Ivanov (Ivaniv) had understood this better than Tkachev.[65] This pogrom shattered the image of the pogroms as progressive populism for another reason, too. Many of its perpetrators were drawn not from the ranks of the common people but from social elements whose hatred for the Jews derived from competitive interests.[66] In the event, Tkachev's prognosis proved as wrong as his diagnosis had been. the 'popular uprising against the *Zhids*' heralded not the rolls of thunder that would accompany the popular Day of Judgement but a prolonged counter-revolutionary reaction of which Judaeophobia was generally a key component.

In fairness, one must also mention one element of restraint in Tkachev's reaction to the pogroms. Unlike other revolutionaries (in Narodnaia Volia, for example), he did not call specifically for the continuation of the pogroms, even though he did call in a general way for a concentration of effort on the continuation of revolutionary activity by all means. The small degree of inconsistency he showed here is not to his discredit.[67]

Tkachev was not alone in his stand in *Nabat*. Reports in the same issue reiterated the thesis[68] that the 'anti-Jewish movement' was proof that the spirit of freedom had penetrated the people, who were now 'hitting out at the authorities, hitting quickly—meaning that it is possible to hit . . . and the people have arisen against the Jew, whom they perceive as the embodiment of the exploiter, the leech, their sworn enemy'.[69] The author does not explicitly object to this 'conception of the Jew', just as Tkachev did not object to the images of the *Zhid*. He also finds support in the fact that the tsar had been quoted as having told a deputation of Jewish notables in May that the movement against the Jews was not religious but revolutionary.[70] This incident, which had sent shock-waves through the public and the press, was incorporated at approximately the same time in an anti-pogrom proclamation issued by another revolutionary organization (Cherny Peredel) in St. Petersburg that defined the pogroms as being an expression of the stirrings of national hostility and a consequence of the impounding of the Jews in the Pale of Settlement. It put the responsibility for them on 'the government and the extortioners'. At the same time, however, the *Nabat* columnist deviates from Tkachev's simplistic picture of the pogroms as purely a popular uprising against extortioners. According to him, the government had also played its part in the pogroms, in that it had wanted to contain the popular wave of resentment within the limits of a 'rebellion against the *Zhid*' but had failed to do so. As evidence he presented a few isolated examples of peasants rioting against estate owners and administrators and not against Jewish innkeepers. At the same time he admits that the army was quick to defend Russian and other traders but was slow to intervene in cases of attacks on Jewish persons or property. This description belies the picture of anti-Jewish action as a pure, popular revolt. To complicate matters further, the concluding section of the issue offered another explanation that was brief but completely and significantly different.[71] It too referred to the Jewish delegation to the tsar, but this time the tsar was quoted as having said that the popular movement against the Jews was really stirred up by 'the anarchists' (the revolutionaries), who were not averse to fanning religious impulses. On this the journal reports, without any qualification, a leaflet issued by the executive committee (that is, the highest body) of Narodnaia Volia claiming that it was not the aim of the revolutionaries to fan such impulses in their struggle for the freedom of the people; the revolutionaries see no purpose in anti-Jewish incitement, particularly as the Jewish people had contributed many brave and faithful fighters to the struggle against the Russian autocracy.

As yet there is no evidence that such a leaflet was ever issued by Narodnaia Volia. However, two things must be stated with regard to *Nabat* itself: it presented the pogroms in the broader context of the relations between nationalities; and by stressing the Jews' participation in the revolutionary struggle it countered to some extent the stereotype of the Jewish exploiter, while pointing out, albeit in a general way, the Jewish revolutionaries' collective and objective links to the Jewish people.[72] This would seem to be paving the way for some second thoughts, in the context of the interests of the revolutionary movement itself, lest the pogroms strengthened the regressive elements more than they contributed to revolutionary change.

The next issue stated with greater restraint that the anti-Jewish movement had lost its original impetus, but that the popular unrest and signs of revolt had not let up and were taking on an increasingly revolutionary form.[73] This optimism did not last long. However, the temporary cessation of the pogroms may account for their disappearance from the pages of *Nabat*.[74] The hopes for a movement of rebellion were also not fulfilled, and it was no coincidence that Tkachev and Turski once again accorded pride of place in the struggle to overthrow the tsarist regime to continuous revolutionary terror of a political character.[75]

As we have seen, two distinct periods can be identified in Tkachev's attitude to Jewish matters. In the 1870s, Tkachev and *Nabat* were in no way part of the Judaeophobic trend among the Narodniki. Here and there it is possible to find expressions of reservation about the stereotyping of the Jews as exploiters. At the same time, it is clear that Tkachev preferred to ignore the problem of the Jews in the political and social system of Russia. This manifested itself in the stand that he later took on the pogroms. However, in one way or another *Nabat* also gave expression to another approach to the pogroms, an approach which, on the basis of the available sources, is difficult to link with any one individual. This duality further testifies to the fact that not only in the 1870s but also during the pogroms in the early 1880s there were two distinct, if not always clear-cut, views within the revolutionary movement with regard to the Jews. While the answer to the question that appears in the title of this essay is negative, this does not excuse us the duty of placing the Jacobins' attitude to the Jews within the wider context of the relations between the Jews and the Russian revolutionary movement in the nineteenth century.

Notes

1 Some scholars draw a distinction between the Jacobins and the Blanquists, others use the terms interchangeably. It seems to me unnecessary to enter into this issue here and I have used the term Jacobin throughout. Tkachev accepted it, and the people associated with *Nabat* applied it to themselves: see, e.g., *Nabat* (1878), p. 81. See on this, V. Varlamou, 'Bakunin and the Russian Jacobins and Blanquists', in Cyril E. Black (ed.), *Rewriting Russian History* (New York, 1963), pp. 302–3, nn. 30, 31. On the periodical generally, see also note 7 below.

2 See S. M. Berk, *Year of Crisis, Year of Hope, Russian Jewry and the Pogroms of 1881–1882* (London, 1985); J. Frankel, *Prophecy and Politics* (Cambridge, 1981), s.v. pogroms.

3 M. Mishkinsky, 'On the Attitude of the Russian Revolutionary Movement to the Jews in the 1870s' (Hebrew), *He'avar*, vol. 9 (1962), pp. 38–66; vol. 10 (1963), pp. 212–13. Some of my general conclusions there, notably the call for a differential treatment of the position, serve as a basis for the analysis here, although without specific references to that article. Other works providing partial coverage of the topic are cited in subsequent notes.

4 The literature offers a broad spectrum of opinions on the applicability of the term *narodnichestvo* to different trends and organizations in the 1870s, and particularly with regard to the Jacobins. In the present context it would seem sufficient to mention the relative prominence of 'the people' in the pronouncements of the leaders of this trend in comparison to the others.

5 B. Nikolaevsky, 'In Commemoration of the last "Jacobin" of the Seventies (Gaspar-Mikhail Turski)' (Russian), *Katorga i ssylka*, vol. 23, no. 2 (1926), pp. 211–12; F. Venturi, *Roots of Revolution* (London, 1964), ch. 16, pp. 389–428.

6 See B. M. Shakhmatov's interesting monograph on Tkachev as philosopher and sociologist, particularly in the 1860s but also in the 1870s: *P. N. Tkachev, Sketches towards his Creative Portrait* (Russian) (Moscow, 1981), pt. 1, pp. 35–7; B. Sapir, *Vpered: 1873–1877* (Dordrecht, 1970), vol. 1, pp. 301–9. Sapir accepts (though not without reservations) Nikolaevsky's opinion that at the end of 1873 and the beginning of 1874, Tkachev had still not become an outright Jacobin.

7 *Nabat* first appeared in Geneva in November 1875 with the subtitle 'journal of the Russian revolutionaries'. The next issue, announcing itself as 'no. 1', followed in December 1875. It thereafter continued to be published monthly, though frequently several issues were published together. In 1878 it came out as a large, unnumbered pamphlet. In 1879 it was published in London. In 1880 it did not appear at all (see also note 55 below).

8 Various lines have been drawn from the Ukrainian socialist movement to the Russian socialist–revolutionary movement, but the former was not an integral part of the latter and had its own path of development.

9 One can see this from the biography of the playwright J. Gordin, for example, before he left for the United States, and even more clearly from that of Chaim Zhitlovsky, the renowned Jewish socialist.

10 B. Sapir, 'Liberman et le socialisme russe', *International Review for Social History*, vol. 3 (1938), pp. 25–87; M. Mishkinsky, 'The Historical Image of A. S. Liberman and his writings in *Vpered*', id. (ed.), *A. S. Liberman: Reports and Articles in Vpered, 1875–1876* (Hebrew) (Tel Aviv, 1977).

11 S. Ettinger, *Anti-Semitism in Modern Times* (Hebrew) (Tel Aviv, 1978), pp. 128–33, 149–52.

12 His first name appears as both Gaspar or Kaspar (see, e.g., note 5 above), so the intitial may be either G or K.

13 Contrary to what Frankel appears to imply in *Prophecy and Polities* (note 2 above), p. 101, with regard to the influence of the 'end justifies the means' approach on the attitude of the revolutionaries at the time of the pogroms, in reality it was adopted by many in the *narodnik* camp who had no connection with Nechaev or Tkachev; it therefore seems unjustified to accord the latter a particular influence on the evaluation of the pogroms without concrete proof.

14 For a biographical chronology up to the end of the 1870s, see Shakhmatov (note 6), pp. 40–3.

15 Six volumes of his selected works (to 1880) were published in the USSR in the 1930s; a promised seventh volume did not appear. They were edited by the greatest of the Soviet Tkachev scholars, B. P. Kozmin, and appeared as *P. N. Tkachev: Selected Writings* (Russian) (Moscow, 1932–7). Some of Tkachev's writings remain in manuscript form and a great part are scattered through many official periodicals which are virtually inaccessible. The problem of access is further exacerbated by the fact that he wrote under tens of different pseudonyms, not all of which are known.

16 On Bakunin, see Y. Steklov, *Mikhail Aleksandrovich Bakunin: His Life and Activity* (Russian) (Moscow–Leningrad, 1927), vol. 3, pp. 346–7. The reference to Herzen relates to his encounter with the martyrology of Jewish cantonist children as he

recorded it many years later; see *Memoirs: My Past and Thoughts* (London, 1924), vol. 1, pp. 270–2. Additional examples from the lives of other revolutionaries, e.g. M. Shebalin and Y. Lukashevich, can also be cited.

17 It has been contended that Bakunin's hostility to the Jews was due in part to his rivalry with Marx and N. Utin, head of the Russian Section in the First International. As far as I am aware, no similar claim has been made in connection with Tkachev.

18 The brief summary of his views presented here is derived in large part from his article 'Shattered Illusions' (note 15 above), vol. 1, pp. 324–69; the pamphlet against Lavrov, *The Tasks of the Revolutionary Propaganda in Russia* (1874), and his articles in *Nabat*: 'Summations' (1875); 'Revolution and State' (1876); 'People and Revolution' (1876) are to be found in vol. 3.

19 There are various interpretations of Tkachev's assessment of the role of 'the people' in the revolution; see B. Kozmin's critique of A. Theodorovich, op, cit., Introduction, vol. 1, pp. 48–9.

20 Tkachev uses the terms *tsivilizovannaia* ('civilized') and *netsivilizovannaia Tolpa* ('uncivilized throng'), in *ibid.*, vol. 1, pp. 325–9.

21 The arguments against Tkachev by Lavrov and others on the question of the dangers inherent in unchecked rule, even when exercised by revolutionaries, and in dictatorship *per se*, which by definition tends to corrupt even the best of people involved in it, and Tkachev's response on these points are beyond the scope of this article but can be followed in *ibid.*, vol. 3, pp. 246–51; cf. esp. editor's n. 84, p. 466.

22 *ibid.*, p. 256

23 See, e.g., *ibid.*, vol. 4, s.v. A. Varshavsky, A. Gurevich, S. Poliakov.

24 *Nabat*, no. 4 (March 1876), pp. 8–9

25 See, e.g., *Nabat* (1878), p. 61.

26 The leading scholar of the history of the journal, B. Sapir, has actually listed 15 expressions of this type in 1875 and 1876; see Sapir (note 6 above), vol. 1, pp. 376–7, n. 66.

27 The 7-part series 'From Bialystok' was published anonymously in *Vpered*, nos 18–20 (1875) and 23–5 (1876). The author was A. S. Liberman. For a Hebrew version of the articles, see Liberman (note 10 above), pp. 97–146; *Vpered*, nos. 38–40 and 42 (1876) carried an article entitled 'From Byelorussia' by the Polish socialist Jan Hlasko, which defined all the peoples in the area except the Byelorussians as exploiters. A more detailed comparison of the three works would probably be most illuminating.

28 A. L. Weeks, *The First Bolshevik: A Political Biography of Peter Tkachev* (New York and London, 1968), pp. 97–9, devotes a two-page section to the subject most of which is taken up with quotations from Tkachev's article (see note 43 below). Isolated sentences are to be found in D. Hardy, *Petr Tkachev: The Critic as Jacobin* (Washington, DC, 1977).

29 The unsigned article appeared in *Nabat*, nos 3–6 (1877), pp. 30–1. It will be cited again below.

30 In a review article (1868) of a book by the legal scholar and liberal A. D. Gradovsky on the history of local self-rule in Russia; see Tkachev (note 15 above), vol. 5, pp. 426–38.

31 The objection is only hinted at, apparently from fear of the censor. See *ibid.*, 487–8, editor's nn. 99, 102.

32 'Anarchy of Thought', in *ibid.*, vol. 3, p. 307 (published in *Nabat*, 1876).

33 Bakunin considered them 'statists from birth': 'the state clearly suppresses in them the instinct of freedom'. The key characteristics of the Germans are 'an inherited obedience and an ambition to political domination'. According to Tkachev, Bakunin inherited his uncompromising hatred of the Germans from the Russian Slavophiles (*ibid.*).

34 The latter are anarchists from birth, uncompromising enemies of the state and centralization (*ibid.*).

35 M. Bakunin, 'Statism and Anarchy' (Russian), *Selected Works*, vol. 1 (Petrograd, 1922), p. 55.

36 See note 33 above.

37 See note 23 above.

38 'Harmless Satire' (Russian), *Delo*, vol. 1 (1878); Tkachev (note 15 above), vol. 4, pp. 156–79.

39 *ibid.*, p. 164.

40 In a sort of personal reckoning made only after the pogroms, Saltykov-Shchedrin gave further consideration to the destructive influence of the negative stereotyping of the Jews in literature and publicist writings. On the Jews in the works of Shchedrin, see D. Zaslavsky, 'The Jews in Russian Literature' (Russian), *Yevreiskaia Letopis*, vol. 1 (Petrograd, 1923), pp. 74–7; J. Kunitz, *Russian Literature and the Jew* (New York, 1929); Ettinger (note 11 above), s.v. Saltykov-Shchedrin.

41 Tkachev (note 15 above), vol. 4, editor's n. 80

42 See note 29 above

43 The title of a review article that appeared in *Nabat* in 1878 on *Notes by a Socialist of Southern Russia* (Russian) by D.N. Ovsianiko-Kulikovsky, who was later to gain fame for his research in linguistics and literature. The article deals with a number of controversial topics, but the subject we are concerned with here is that of the national question.

44 The term 'Ukrainophiles' was applied to all those who called for recognition of Ukrainian nationhood. Tkachev opted for it because he rejected the socialism of Dragomanov and his colleagues. An editorial in *Nabat*, no. 10 (1876), p. 16, offered to support the Ukrainophiles on condition that they made a public announcement of their commitment to a socialism undiluted by nationalist principles. It appears that in Tkachev's opinion they were unworthy of such support.

45 The idea of pan-Ukrainian nationalism was controversial even among the Ukrainians themselves, and of course far more so among non-Ukrainians. Tkachev echoes this controversy in his terminology: he has little use for the term 'Ukrainians', preferring instead 'Malo-Russians' or 'Ruthenians'.

46 A few years previously their opinions had been extremely Judaeophobic, and they had given short shrift to the writings of A. S. Liberman in *Vpered*. See M. Mishkinsky, 'The Attitudes of Ukrainian Socialists to Jewish Problems in the 1870s', P. J. Potichnyj and H. Aster (eds), *Ukrainian-Jewish Relations in Historical Perspective* (Edmonton, 1988), pp. 57–68.

47 At least associatively he was likely to remember the Jews of his time when he used a metaphor from the New Testament to represent the cosmopolitan future awaiting mankind: 'Neither Jew nor Greek' (Gal. 3:28).

48 Two reports from Vilna were published in *Nabat*, no. 6 (May 1876), pp. 10–11, one of them definitely written by a Jew, but they reveal nothing more than what was published in *Vpered*. Liberman (note 10 above), pp. 77–9, discusses the arrests themselves and the repercussions within the Jewish community.

49 The Liberman–Smirnov letter of 23 Nov. 1876; see K. Marmor, *The Letters of Aron Liberman* (Yiddish) (New York, 1951), p. 80. Following a difference of opinion with Smirnov, Liberman wrote: 'Perhaps Petr Nikitich [Tkachev] could reject my claim to be a *Russian* socialist.' Liberman went on to state that he saw himself as a Russian socialist not by virtue of nationalism but by virtue of his attachment to the land. The acerbity of Tkachev's relations with Lavrov and the *Vpered* circle apparently also played its part, and Liberman's word were perhaps designed to settle an account with Smirnov, whom he otherwise admired.

338

50 See, e.g., the detailed obituary of Betty Kaminskaia (*Nabat*, 1878, pp. 124–41). A well-known Jewish revolutionary who 'went to the people' and worked in a factory, she committed suicide.

51 cf. note 56 below.

52 These words were directed principally at Dragomanov's accusations against the old Poland.

53 See note 29 above.

54 In fact, despite the experience of isolated pogroms in Russia at intervals throughout the nineteenth century, and the pogrom of 1871 in Odessa (a town that had undergone several similar experiences in the past), which was even mentioned in Liberman's first article in *Vpered* (see Liberman, note 10 above, p. 64), no one foresaw the wave of pogroms that was to break out a few years later.

55 After a long gap (see note 7 above), four issues (out of the entire 18 issues run) came out in 1881 before publication ceased completely. They carried a new subtitle emphasizing the new agitational slant: 'a revolutionary newspaper'. Correspondents and writers were now directed to addresses in Paris, Geneva and London. Another innovation was the listing of the names of the editorial board—N. Graeczko, P. Tkachev (by his initials only—P. T.-A.), and G. Turski. Contrary to previous practice, contributions by members of the editorial board generally bore the author's name, though Tkachev signed himself 'Gracus'. Cf. Hardy (note 28 above), p. 60, on the difference between Tkachev and Turski from 1879 on, which has been cited by Kozmin and others too (see note 74 below). Turksi's influence increased considerably.

56 'The Execution of the Tyrant', *Nabat*, no. 1 (20 June 1881), pp. 1–2. For some reason, Tkachev scholars ignore his articles in *Nabat* in 1881. See Venturi (note 5 above); also Weeks and Hardy (note 28 above). Soviet historiography likewise ignores it; thus Shakhmatov (note 6 above), pp. 75–7, mentions Tkachev and *Nabat* in 1881 but skips over the pogroms—even though in the first issue, at least, they had occupied a relatively significant place; and A. Yarmolinsky, *Road to Revolution* (New York, 1971), p. 297, devotes only one sentence to *Nabat*'s stand and does not identify the author of the article. Cf. C. S. Ingerflorn, 'Idéologie révolutionaire et mentalité antisémite: les socialistes russes face aux pogroms de 1881–1883', *Annales Economies Sociétés Civilisations*, vol. 37, no. 3 (1982), p. 441.

57 See, e.g., Tkachev (note 15 above), vol. 3, pp. 480, nn. 169, 171.

58 *Nabat*, nos 3–5 (1879), p. 4.

59 Although the Narodnaia Volia initiated this eventful development, the article does not mention it at all.

60 This is not to say that there were no instances of revolt and rioting, but the pogroms overshadowed them.

61 See Appendix below.

62 The word 'hangmen' in the context of Jews here is undoubtedly part of the regular revolutionary hyperbole which was not alien to Tkachev (albeit not only to him).

63 Had Tkachev contented himself with the last of these explanations, i.e., that the people started with the Jews because they had to start somewhere, it would at least have been consistent with his utilitarian approach to revolutionary activity and not necessarily derived from an anti-Jewish stand.

64 Tkachev uses the derogatory term *Zhid* in most cases in quotation marks or italics, which could mean that he was drawing a distinction between the people's image of the Jews and his own image of them. However, this explanation is more than counterbalanced by his tendency to stereotype the Jews as usurers and exploiters and to see the pogroms as an expression of popular social rebellion.

65 See M. Mishkinsky, 'The Attitude of the Southern Russian Workers' Union towards the Jews, 1880–1881', *Harvard Ukrainian Studies*, vol. 6, no. 2 (1982), pp. 205–13.

66 See Y. Slutzky, 'The Geography of the Pogroms of 1881' (Hebrew), *He'avar*, vol. 9 (1962), pp. 16–25.

67 G. Romanenko, the author of Narodnaia Volia's pro-pogrom statement that appeared some two and a half months later, and of an article in the same spirit in *Narodnaia Volia*, no. 6 (Autumn 1881), was more consistent: 'You began to rebel against the Jews—well done!' we read in the statement. Romanenko and Tkachev were very close at the end of 1879, but I have found no evidence that this friendship had any real influence in this instance.

68 With very slight differences in wording that we will not go into here. More significant differences are discussed later in the text.

69 *Nabat*, no. 1 (1881), pp. 3–4. The reports were apparently edited together and are signed 'A.'

70 See M. Mishkinsky, 'An Appeal of a Russian Revolutionary Organization against the Pogroms of 1881' (Hebrew), *Mekharim be-Toldot Am Yisrael va-Erets Israel*, vol. 4 (Haifa, 1978), pp. 253–67; the article also contains a comprehensive discussion of the Jewish delegation to the tsar and its repercussions (pp. 255–8). Another study by the present author, 'Cherny Peredel and the pogroms of 1881', is forthcoming.

71 Medley, *Nabat*, no. 1 (1881), p. 8, unsigned.

72 This particular issue of *Nabat* is full of items connected with the story of the Jewish revolutionary Hessia Helfman, who had been involved in the preparations for the attempt on the tsar's life. She was pregnant when she was arrested, and the attitude of the authorities to her during her imprisonment aroused considerable reaction both in Russia and abroad. At the same time, her name also served as an excuse for spreading the word that the Jews were guilty of the death of the tsar. The next edition of *Nabat* also contained several items on Helfman.

73 *Nabat*, no. 2 (1881), p. 4, in a piece entitled 'From a Review of the Domestic Front', based on reports and signed by one of the editors, Graeczko.

74 In *Nabat*, no. 3 (1 September 1881), factual mention of the pogroms is limited to a quotation from another paper at the beginning of an article by Tkachev. He did not contribute to the next (and last) issue (15 September).

75 The historiographic literature points out that there had been differences between Tkachev and Turski on the attitude to terror several years earlier, but this is of no relevance here.

APPENDIX: TKACHEV ON THE POGROMS: NABAT, NO. 1 (1881)[1]

To my knowledge, this is Tkachev's longest and most signficant statement on the Jews, and it is presented here in full.

The exploited slave, who for hundreds of years had allowed others to rob, pillage and subject him to torture by starvation without being punished, who for hundreds of years had patiently allowed his own flesh and blood to be sucked dry by the leech-exploiter that had attached itself to his body, now engaged in open struggle with him and summoned him to his Day of Judgement . . .[2]

In vain do the terrified hangmen of the people, the suckers of their blood, try to console themselves with the naïve fantasy that 'the people' are *rebelling*[3] against 'the *Zhids*' out of sheer stupidity, ignorance, religious intolerance, or because of the secret incitement of scheming *kramolniki*,[4] i.e. us, the revolutionaries. No, the people regard the *faith* of the *Zhids* with absolute equanimity. It is deliberate self-deception to imagine that a popular, consolidated, and violent movement occurring everywhere like 'The Movement Against the Jews', which has spread throughout the whole of southern Russia could arise because of the incitement and death sentences of several *kramolniki*.[5] No, the people 'arose against the *Zhid*' without any external incitement, and not on the basis of any theoretical considerations but simply because in their minds the notion of *Zhid* was inseparably connected with the image of the 'sucker of the people's blood', with the merciless usurer, with the kulak-exploiter. They started by attacking the *Zhid* and not the *priest*[6] only because the *Zhid* exploiter was closer and less well defended,[7] and also because they had to start with someone.

We shall find that the popular uprising against the *Zhids* is nothing but an uprising against the exploiters and executioners of the people. One senses within it all the signs of the awakening *Social Revolution*, hears in it the rumblings of the thunderclouds auguring the great and merciless *Court of the People*.

1 See note 56 to the text above and associated textual comments
2 Ellipses in the original
3 Here and below, all emphases are in the original.
4 *Kramolniki* (from *kramola*): term used for the revolutionaries by their opponents.
5 Apparently a reference to the execution of five of the Narodnaia Volia, including three of its most prominent figures: S. Perovskaya, N. Kibalchyk, and A. Zhelyabov.
6 It is not clear why the author chose the Russian Orthodox priest and not the Russian–Ukrainian 'kulak-extortioner'. Was he not aware of their existence or that they were very close to 'the people'?
7 Tkachev reveals here that he was not unaware that the Jews as a group were not well protected by the security forces, and that their hostile environment was aware of this and exploited it. This circumstance was indeed an important factor in the spread of the pogroms. Even though he reveals something of his knowledge, Tkachev does not attempt to elaborate on the subject.

5

LINGUISTIC TRANSMUTATIONS

A Mediaeval Latin-German Magical Text
in Hebrew Characters*

Raphael Loewe

I must hope that I have not taken the gilt off the gingerbread if, as a tribute to my friend and colleague Chimen Abramsky, I offer the study of a curious document which I have already brought to his notice; indeed, I have profited from some preliminary discussion of it with him. I was myself apprised of its existence by Dr Egon Harmuth of Vienna, who was kind enough to send me a photocopy of one of the folios concerned a year or two ago.

We are concerned with the versos of two folios in a western manuscript, allegedly dateable to 1402, deposited in the Austrian Nationalbibliothek,[1] pressmark Vind. Pal. 5278 (*olim* Ambras 228); it consists of paper, comprising 203 folios, of which ff. 1–173 contain the text of Konrad Kyeser's *Bellifortis*[2]—perhaps the most important military work of the mediaeval period. The manuscript, which was previously in Schloss Amras, near Innsbruck, belonged to Maximilian I.[3] The matter that interests us is found on the verso sides of ff. 162 and 163, both of which are integral to the MS, the rectos carrying part of the text of the *Bellifortis* and the versos having been left blank by the scribe. Of these two, f. 162v. contains a diagram and altogether seven lines in Hebrew characters and six in Latin characters (see fig. 1); f. 163v. (see fig. 2) contains three diagrams (of which the right-hand diagram only is reproduced here) and thirty-seven lines in Hebrew characters and a few words in Latin characters. No single word is Hebrew, the majority being transliterated Latin, and the remainder transliterated German (not Judaeo-German: see below, p. 361). Although the two disparate texts constitute but a curiosity, they are of considerable importance in regard to linguistic history. Of Judaeo-Latin—that is to say, Latin as used by Jews in late antiquity as a vernacular, and (conceivably) written by them in Hebrew characters—we have (as far as I am aware) no written testimony other than odd

† An abbreviated version of this paper was read at the Conference of the European Association for Jewish studies in July 1987.

words embedded in mediaeval Hebrew MSS; although D. S. Blond-
heim reconstructed significant elements in its vocabulary, by collating
the early forms of the (Christianized) Latin Bible with the various
Judaeo-Romance languages that have left a literary deposit and/or
survived as a living vernacular into modern times.[4] Latin quotations in
Hebrew sources, taken from the literature or the forensic terminology
etc. of the Christian environment of mediaeval Jewry, are extremely
rare. The celebrated references of Samuel ben Me'ir to the Vulgate
imply his ability to read it, but do not actually adduce quotations in
Latin.[5] In regard to the German portions of our text, it will be shown
below (p. 360) that they are not to be classified as Judaeo-German,
despite their being written in Hebrew characters; and since the text is a
fifteenth-century one, it affords a valuable object of comparison with
relatively early Yiddish. (The parameters are from around 1402–5, the
date proposed by western palaeographers for MS Vind. 5278, and the
death of Maximilian I in 1519; it may be supposed that he did not
acquire it on his deathbed, and 1459—the year in which he was
born—falling midway between these limits, may serve as a conservative
surmise for the date of the insertions that concern us.

Before we consider the contents of the two texts, it is appropriate to ex-
mine the script itself from several angles, namely (i) palaeography
and (ii) transliterational techniques for (a) Latin and (b) German.

The Hebrew writing, although far from elegant, is that of a
practised hand; it is a style of Ashkenazic rabbinic character used for
writing Yiddish as well as Hebrew. Typical in this respect is the
formation of the *gimel*: an upright shaft, straight or slightly concave,
with the short 'foot' set about half-way up it sometimes horizontally,
giving the approximate effect of rotating the vowel-sign *qamaṣ* though
90 degrees.[6] See for example f. 163v., l. 6, last word, דְגֹמטרֹום, and l.
13, last word, לֶגֶר (*legere*). *Zayin* has been so rigidly 'squared up' that it
resembles a majuscule Roman T, e.g. l. 2, 4th word, זוּפֶר. In l. 22, 3rd
word, נֶזזעל, the double *zayin* has been joined at the top, resulting in
the form of a majuscule Greek Π. The letters *ḥeth, kaph, shin, taw* are not
represented, being superfluous to the writer's transcriptional scheme
(see below, p. 348). Of the four letters other than *kaph* which, in
Judaeo-German as in Hebrew itself, have differentiated final forms, the
final *mem* is sometimes used, e.g. l. 9, second word, וֻנַם (*unam*), but it is
frequently displaced in the final position by the medial form, e.g. l. 4,
1st word, עאדָמ (*eadem*). The medial *nun* invariably usurps the place of
the final form, e.g. l. 2, last word, רוּטלנ (*ruteln*). Final *pe* occurs in l.
10, 4th word (-*kop*); there are no other instances for comparison. For
ṣade in the final position the medial form is written, see l. 23, last word,

מלטצ (*malṭṣ* = *malz*); cf. l. 36, 2nd and antepenultimate words, צו (= *zu: zayin* represents initial *s*, see below).

The transliteration of the Latin is careful, apart from occasional slips such as *scrirbe* for *scribe* (l. 2)—indeed, it is so painstaking that one is tempted to describe it as diplomatic. Thus *eciam*, l. 16, with *qoph* for *c*; *accipe*, ll. 19, 22, with double *qoph* for *cc*, and *mittas* (l. 13) spelled with double *ṭeth* (contrast conventional Yiddish מיטל = *mittel*). Some of the equivalents that the writer has selected have been conditioned by his own dialect of German. *s* in initial or medial position is represented by *zayin*: l. 2, *super*, l. 21, *sine*, l. 17, *missas*, where *samekh* (as regularly in this MS) corresponds to a final *s*. The resolution of *x* into *gimel* + *zayin* rather than *qoph* + *samekh* (l. 6, *dextrum*) likewise points to an emphatically guttural articulation of the writer's vernacular which, when correlated with the dialect reflected by his vocabulary, points towards a southern domicile (see below, p. 360).

There are, however, two features of the transliterational scheme which are, as far as I am aware, unique, and therefore of particular interest. Since Hebrew *pe* expresses both *p* and *f* in Yiddish as well as in Hebrew, the ambivalence can only be eliminated by use of a diacritical sign—the *dagesh* in Hebrew for *p*, the superior *rafe* line for *f* in Yiddish which, in Hebrew, came to be generally abandoned, since one diacritical sign is sufficient. The scribe of our MS does not resort to diacritics, and at the first point on f. 163v. where an *f* is required in his text (l. 3, *fug<ia>s*) he uses the same undifferentiated *pe* that he had employed in l. 2 in *super*. After l. 3 he introduces a character of his own designing for *f*—ꝗ, or sometimes ɣ—faintly reminiscent of a Roman F reversed. He had, indeed, already used it on f. 162v., e.g. l. 1, 2nd and 3rd words, *conficiendum fundamentum*, f. 163v., l. 9, 1st word, *fac*. The same device is used by him in writing German; l. 30, *pfefer* has both the joined and the unjoined form of the symbol.

The other *unicum* concerns an aspect of the scribe's method of indicating vocalization. Of the Tiberian vowel-signs *qamaṣ* is used occasionally for long *a*, e.g. in *portare* (f. 163v., l. 6), *pathaḥ* in *magnas* (מאגנס) (l. 11), *seghol* for short *e*, e.g. l. 11, penultimate word, *stare*, and sometimes *ṣere*, e.g. l. 12, 4th word, *quere*, without apparent distinction of quantity. *Ḥireq* appears, being written either as the usual dot, very faintly, e.g. l. 5 (*omnia animalia*) (unless these supposed dots are but marks on the paper), or by an oblique line descending right to left, as in l. 21, penultimate word, *sine*. These vowel-signs are, however, used sporadically, vowel-indication being either omitted or achieved by an extension of the *mater lectionis* device conventional in Hebrew from the Bible onwards. *Waw* is thus used, either normally, e.g. l. 9, 4th word, *cum*, or—yet another solecism—as a subscript for long *o* (l. 1, *amore*, l. 2,

3rd word, *nomen*, l. 3, 3rd word *robore* (first *o*), or, with a point inserted, for *u*, e.g. l. 14, 5th word, *posterum*. For the most part, however, the *waw* as vowel-indicator is inserted in the normal way, e.g. l. 2, 4th word, *super*. *Yodh* is sometimes lowered, though hardly subscript, e.g. l. 2, scri[r]be, *nomen*. The most astonishing feature, however, of the whole scheme is the extension of the *mater lectionis* convention to represent initial vowels, which in Hebrew have all to be 'carried' by *'aleph*—the innovation obviously imitating Latin orthography. *'Aleph* itself is restricted to initial (and medial) *a*, e.g. l. 1, *amore*, l. 11, penultimate word, *stare*. *Yodh* represents an initial *i*, e.g. l. 14, 4th word, *in*, l. 12, 5th word, *inuenies*, and *waw* initial *o* or *u*, e.g. l. 5, 1st two words, *ut omnia*. (The use of *'ayin* for *e* is, of course, familiar to readers of Judaeo-German. It is found here, e.g. l. 14, 1st word, *nouem*, l. 21, penultimate word, *sine*, but it is also employed for initial *e*, e.g. l. 3, 4th word, *et*, l. 15, last word, *est*.) This system is of course used in Arabic to indicate the *ḥamza*; but we may, I think, safely assume that our scribe will not have been aware of this.

The overall effect, combined with the rejection of the final form of *nun* and frequently also that of *mem* (see above, p. 346), is so bizarre that even a fluent reader of Hebrew or Yiddish even if he had some slight knowledge of Latin—and, no doubt, a better knowledge of German—would probably find the text unintelligible unless he took pains to decipher it. It will be suggested below (p. 362) that this consideration may well have been integral to the purpose of the scribe.

What has been said regarding the transcription scheme for Latin holds good for the German portions also, but a few additional points are to be noted. The endeavour to achieve a quasi-diplomatic transcription is emphasized by the following contrast. As noted above (p. 347) Latin *x* had to be resolved in *gimel* + *zayin* (*gz*). The combination which in German is written *st* is realized now (and presumably was similarly pronounced in mediaeval times) as *sht*; and to express the first element in this Hebrew has available its *shin*. Our text happens to include an instance of the *st* combination of f. 163v., l. 31, 3rd word, *gestossen*: and one would have anticipated that the transliteration would have called *shin* in aid. But its use is rejected, and what we find is גשטוזזען (*gezṭozzen*)—in order, it would seem, to have the two letters *s* and *t* individually represented. Similar nicety presumably accounts for the avoidance of *kaph*, either medial or final, to express the German *ch* (medial or final). Since, however, the scribe had determined on *qoph* to represent Latin *c* (see above, p. 347), consistency bade him represent the German *ch* by the combination *qoph* + *he* despite the incongruity of such a conjunction of Hebrew characters. Thus he writes דורקה *durch* (l. 31, 5th word), איקהן *aich<e>n* (l. 2, penultimate word), and נאקהטס *nachts* (l. 37, last word). (See further below, p. 360).

The same principle was adopted, but not consistently carried through, in order to represent diphthongs. (In the case of the only diphthong that occurs in the Latin portion, f. 163v., l. 2, 2nd word, *hæc*, by error for *hoc*, the vowel has been reduced to a simple *e* and is represented by a *seghol*.) The vowel that modern German orthography represents as *ei* is transcribed in the MS by 'aleph yodh (compare the modern Yiddish convention אײ): e.g. l. 19, penultimate word, *ain* (also ll. 28–32), last word, *tail*, and l. 2, penultimate word, *aichn*. But in regard to the representation of German *au* it is a different story. The first word in l. 3, אראוז, stands for *araus*, *au* here being resolved into 'aleph + *waw* analogously to the 'aleph + *yodh* combination for *ai/ei* already noted. Thereafter, however, a simple *waw* (without internal point) does duty, e.g. l. 10, 3rd word, לוב (*laub*). One cannot assume that in the scribe's specifically Hebrew experience the *waw* (i.e. ו) was realized as the equivalent of modern German *au* (English *ow* as in *cow*), since he also uses *waw* (ו), both in Latin and in German, to represent *ō*: ll. 1, 2, *nomen, robore* (first *waw*); l. 17, 5th word, *illo*; l. 29, 2nd word, *lot*, ll. 35–6, *ungesotten* (for *ŏ*). It seems therefore to follow that in the scribe's German experience the shift *au* > *ō* had occurred, and that the tension between his own pronunciation and the orthographic convention *au* was strong enough to dismiss the endeavour to achieve diplomatic accuracy—an attempt which had succeeded in the case of *ai/ei* because of the absence of any marked tension. *ö* is represented by 'ayin in l. 20, last word, על (*öl*).

We may now turn to the contents of ff. 162v. and 163v. respectively, the texts of which, although in the same hand, deal with heterogeneous matters.

On f. 162v. there is a diagram, much more crudely executed than the illustrations in the body of the *Bellifortis*, of a military machine designed for flinging 'boiling oil' over the enemy. Above and below that diagram a text has been carefully inserted; the portion above consists of five lines in Hebrew characters followed by six in Latin characters, it being clear from the spacing that the 'Hebrew' was written first. Beneath the diagram are two lines of 'Hebrew', their separation from the foregoing being due to their constituting an independent paragraph. The language is Latin throughout. The upper texts concern the preparation of the basic mixture for offensive use of the machine; that below with the cleaning of the container after use.

I here transcribe the text into square Hebrew characters and set beside it a retranscription into Latin.

(1) nota adconficiendum fundamentum recipe נְטָא אֲדקׄ‎ֽ‎ גy‎קׄ‎עעַנְדום y‎ נְדֶמֶנְטׇם רֶקפֿ (1)

oleum arboris ~~oleu~~ pine quod est וּלׄם אֲרבֿרס וׄלֽ‎ פֶֿן קׄ‎ דֿ עזׄט

liquidum admodum uernisi cui לְקׄויד‎ֽ‎ ‎ֽ‎ ם אֲדַמְדֶם וְרֽ‎נׄי קׄוי

(2) admisces ocr et cretam bene אֲדַמֶזקֶס וׄקׄר עׄט קׄרֶטֶם בֶֿנׄע (2)

contritam ita quod ex illo קׄ‎ֽ‎ ‎גׄטׄרֶטֶם יׄטׇא קׄוׄד עׄגֿ יׄלׄלוׄ

conmixto fiat pulmentum קׄ‎ֽ‎ ‎ נְמֹיזׄטׄוׄ y‎אׄט פֿולְמֶנְטׇם

proporcionitum non (3) nimis פֿדֽ‎ ‎ פׄורְקׄוׄנְטֽ‎ ‎ ם נֻנ (3) נֶמׇס

densum nec rarum quod pulmentum דְנׄוֹם נֶק רׄר‎ֽ‎ ‎ ם קׄ‎ֽ‎ וׄד פֿולְמֶנְטׇם

calefactum inponatur module et uide קׇאׄלy‎קׄטׄוׄם יׄנְפֿנׄ‎ֽ‎ ‎ ר מׇדֿל עׄט וׄדִי

predictum confectam sit adeo פֿרֶֽ‎ דֿקׄטׄ‎ֽ‎ ‎ ם קׄ‎ֽ‎ ‎ גׄקׄטֶם זׄט אׄדֿוּ

(4) densum quod nod (*sic*) possit דְנֽ‎ ‎ ם קֻוׄד נׄוׄד פֿוֹחֻזׄט (4)

temperare cum eodem oleo ita טֶמְפֿרָאֵר קֻוֹם עׄוֹדֶם וׄלֽ‎ וׄ יׄט

quod oleum nod (*sic*) sit subtile קׄוֹד וְלׄוׄם נׄוׄד זׄט זׄובׄטׄלׄׄע

uel molle tunc (5) admisce וְל מוׄלׄל טֻונׄק (5) אֲדֿמֶזׄקׄע

uernisium permixto oleo line וְרׄנׄיזֻּום פֶֿרמׄגֿזׄטׄוׄ וׄלׄוׄ לָנׄי

uel alterius promaiore parte וׄעֿל אֲלׄטֶֿרׄוׄס פֿרֽׄ‎ ‎ מׇׄאׄיׄוֹר פֿארׄטׄע

The six lines in Latin characters that follow are much more difficult to decipher than those in Hebrew, even in the original MS and with the assistance of western palaeographers.[7] In the following transcription, what appears to me doubtful is shown in *italic* script; symbols the significance of which I cannot interpret are indicated by ? or ?—?

(1) Ad fundamentum la*ne* ℞ cretam tritam et au*gur de uno ?—?* de aliquo et *oleo* firnisio ex illis faciat (2) unum temperamentum aliqui*d* spissum Et *? s----* (*cancelled*) placet add*atur* modicum de spongzei ut (3) eo c*i*tius *slete* fiat It*em pinus* augur conburet et dolla noua ut faci*at* calore*m(?)* fusti*(?)* (4) et postea tercatur*(?)* in mo*n*datio

(5) Item ad fundam*entum* auri ℞ bittumen non nimium f*ule(?)* augur gluest? *(?)* (6) tatum ex *hiis* fiat temperamentum

After the problematics of the foregoing one turns with some relief to the remaining two lines of Hebrew script:

(1) adpurgandum modulam fac liccinium אֲדֿפֿורׇגֶֿנׄדֽ‎ ‎ ם מֿ‎ֽ‎ דֿלֶם y‎קׄ לְקׄנׄיּום (1)

accutum cui admisce smigma quo אֲקׄוּטׄוׄם קׄוׄי אׄדֿמֶזׄקׄע זׄמַגׄמַׄ קׄוׄׄ

permixto calefac adignem fortiter פֶֿרמַגֿזׄטׄוׄ קׇאׄלׄy‎קׄ אֲדֶֿגֶֿם y‎ֶעׄרׄטׄיׄטֶֿר

(2) quo calefacto accipe setistrum קׄוׄׄ קׇאׄלy‎קׄטׄוׄ אֲקׄקׄיׄפֿ זֶעׄטׄיזׄטׄרׄום (2)

et in tinge ad aquam eandem et עׄט יׄנ טׄיׄנׄגׄׄע אֲדֿ אֲקׄוׄאׄם שׇׄאׄנׄדֶֿם עׄט

purga modulam פֿורׄגֿאׄ מֿודֿולׄאׄם

Here follows a translation. In view of the uncertainty of my transcription of the lines written in Latin characters I do not attempt an

English rendering of them: but it is clear from the reference to *uernisio,
temperamentum* etc. that they deal with similar subject-matter without
being straight transcription of the foregoing written in Hebrew
characters.

(1) Observe that for making the basic ingredient you must take oil of pine,
which is runny, like sandmak-gum. With this (2) you must so mix ochre and
well-crushed chalk that a pulp of the appropriate viscosity is produced, neither
(3) too thick nor too thin. When the pulp has been heated, it is to be placed in
the *modula*: and watch that the aforesaid mixture is (4) thick enough for it not to
be possible to thin it down with the same oil, in order that the oil (i.e. that oil
which has already been mixed into the pulp) may be neither fine nor soft.
Thereafter (5) mix in sandmak-varnish, oil of flax or some other oil having first
been mingled with it in a larger proportion.

The two lines beneath the diagram may be rendered thus:

(1) In order to cleanse the *modula*, make some lint, on which mix up some
detergent. Once it has been mixed, warm it fiercely by the fire. (2) When it has
been heated, take a bristle-brush, dip the same [detergent] into water, and
cleanse the *modula*.

The following points of explication etc. may be noted:

1   *fundamentum* i.e. the basis of the mixture for heating.
      After *arboris, oleu* has been cancelled.
      uernisi, i.e. sandmak-gum (< *veronix*,[8] whence also English
      varnish, German *firnis*).
2   *pulmentum* in classical Latin was a general term for a condiment
      eaten with bread. Recorded semantic extension in mediaeval
      Latin[9] is slight, and Romance derivatives[10] are restricted to the
      same field. Its use in the present context, to mean something like
      paste, gruel, i.e. *pulp*, seems to presuppose a hitherto unrecorded
      application for which military irony furnishes analogues in all
      periods; cf. the name given during the Second World War to a
      large bomb containing numerous smaller ones, "Molotov bread-
      basket".[11]
      proporcionitum. *-itum* appears to be the correct reading, although
      -atum would be expected.[12] But possibly the heavy dot which I
      have read as a *ḥireq* (contast that in *arboris*, l. 1) ought to be
      recognized as a *qamaṣ*.
3   *module* (cf. l. 6, *modulam*). In all instances the transcription
      indicates a Latin feminine ending (cf. the lower text, l. 1, *-am* by
      pathaḥ mem, l. 2, final word, by *'aleph mem*): but apart from an
      isolated *modo/ula* = *cork-oak*[13] a feminine noun seems to be

unattested. From the context it is clear that *modula* here refers to the container, as illustrated in the diagram. The masculine *modulus* seems not to lose the sense of *measure, pattern* in its various applications. In view of the viscosity of the mixture here described, perhaps the container was considered as a "mould"— the sort of food-receptacle in which *pulmentum* might be shaped; and the feminine termination might have been prompted by German *mulde* (fem.).

confectam. The vowel-sign, though faint, appears to be the scribe's oblique *pathah*—a slip, in place of his subscript *waw* as in the immediately foregoing *predictum.*

4   *nod* (*bis*) must be an error for *non*; Grimm[14] record the forms *nût* (*md.*) and *nid* for *nicht.*

l. 5   *uernisium*, see l. 1.

l. 1 (*infra*) *liccinium* is the correct reading; contrast the (thickened) *nun yodh* with the *teth* in the following *ac[c]utum.* I can suggest no reason for the doubling of *c* in this or the foregoing *licinium*,[15] which means linen that has been ravelled, scraped, and thus sharpened to make it into lint. Quarg,[16] who in his summary renders *mit einem spitz zusammengedrehten Tuch*, has misunderstood.

smigma. The third letter may have been first erroneously written as ʿ*ayin*, or as a *gimel* the down-stroke of which was excessively prolonged; a correctly formed *gimel* was therefore written above. *smigma, smegma* (< σμῆγμα) = soap, detergent.

l. 2   *setistrum* must, from the context, mean some kind of scouring-instrument or (less likely) reagent. *Saeta* means *bristle*, and although *saetistrum* is otherwise unattested it may be confidently rendered *stiff brush*, on the analogy of other Latin words ending in -*strum* that indicate instruments, etc. (e.g. *canistrum, basket; capistrum, halter; falcastrum, bill-hook*).[17]

intinge ad aquam eandem presumably cannot mean 'dip [it] into the same water', since water has not been previously mentioned. My translation, 'dip the same [detergent] into water' assumes that *eandem* qualifies *smigma*, wrongly taken by the scribe (or by his source) to be a Latin feminine noun instead of a Greek neuter loan-word.

We may discount the possibility that this fragment of military technology is the scribe's own composition, but his source still awaits identification.[18] I have failed to find anything *ad rem* in Guido da Vigevana's *Texaurus*[19] (1335), or the *Liber Secretorum* (1313) of Manutus Torsellus,[20] or the thirteenth-century *De Regimine Principum* of Aegidius Romanus.[21]

We may now consider f. 163v. On the left there are three parallel diagrams of a strapped hook for attachment to a military belt, for use in order to ease the strain in drawing a crossbow[22]—a type of weapon with which the *Bellifortis* does not concern itself. The space on the right was subsequently[23] used by the scribe to insert a text in Hebrew characters, the language being mainly Latin interspersed with German, but going over to German entirely from l. 22 on. The contents bear no relation at all to the adjoining diagrams, being of a thaumaturgical nature; and although the *Bellifortis* itself does include magical material, what we have here finds no parallel in it. On the middle strap (not reproduced), level with l. 31 of the text, he has written אמור וין i.e. *amor w[e]in*—no doubt in reference to what he details in ll. 22–37 of the text (cf. l. 34, penultimate word, ווין).

Here follows the transcription of the text alongside its retranscription into Latin characters.

דֶ אֹמֶר (1)

(1) de amore

זקרירבֶ הֶק נֶמין זוּפֶר וַנאמ איקהנ רוּטלנ (2)

(2) scribe hec nomen super unam aichen ruteln

אראוּח פוּגז רֶבוּרי עט קוֹאֶנד, וַנאמ טאַנגז קוּמ (3)

(3) araus fugs robore et quando unam tangis cum

עאדֶמ וֶרגא אדקוּטירי יללא אמאַבית טע (4)

(4) eadem uirga ad qutiri illa amabit te

וט ומנֶא אנֶמלֶא טע γוּנַאַנט (5)

(5) ut omnia animalia te fugiant

טוּנק טו דֶבֶּס טֶקוּם פוּרטָרֶ דֶ לוּפו וקוֹלוּם דֶמטרום (6)

(6) tunc tu debes tecum portare de lupo oculum dextrum

עט זעקוּרֶ אמבוּלָבס אינֶמיקיס טוּיס (7)

(7) et secure ambulabis inimicis tuis

דֶ אֹמֶר (8)

(8) de amore

γאֹק וַנַם וּלַלַם קוּם פַּרוּיס פוראמינבוס עט (9)

(9) fac unam ollam cum paruis foraminibus et

ינפוּנֶ ונום לוב γר,זקף עט ינַרȝון וּללאַם אד (10)

(10) inpone unum lob froskop et inra|one ollam ad

מאַגֶנַס ווּרמקאַס עט מיטטֶס עאַם זטאַרֶ אד 14 (11)

(11) magnas formicas et mittas eam stare ad 14

דעס פֹזֹט הוֹק קוֹעֶרֶ עט ין ווינִיעס וּנום וֹס (12)

(12) dies post hoc quere et in uenies unum os

אדמוּדום וניוּס רֶקה זוּפֶּר יללו מיטטאַס לֶגֶר (13)

(13) admodum unius rech super illo mittas legere

נוֹועמ מזזַס עט ין פֹחזטעֶרֶם קוֹעם טו טאַנגֶס (14)

(14) nouem missas et in posterium quem tu tangis

(15) קום יללו וחֶ יללא אמאבט טע אליוד וס עזט

(15) cum illo osse illa amabit te aliud os est

(16) אדמודֶם נאויס עט זְפֶר יללו עקיאם מיטטאס

(16) admodum nauis et super illo eciam mittas

(17) לֶגערֶ נוועם מיזזאס עט קואם קום יללו וחֶ דֶ

(17) legere nouem missas et quam cum illo osse de

(18) טע טרודס יללא ודט טע

(18) te trudis illa odit te

(19) אקקיפע דואס פארטעס לינדין בול אין טאיל

(19) accipe duas partes linden bol ain tail

(20) זקה וועבעל ונד טועס ין אין אמפעל וול על

(20) sach webel und tues in ain ampel vol öl

(21) טונק הומינעס אפפארֶנט זַע קאפיטיבוס

(21) tunc homines apparent sine capitibus

(22) אקקפֶ זֶטטעראן נֶזזעל זומא לאגען פֿעֿעֿער

(22) accipe zetteran nessel suma lagen pfefer

(23) מוחטבערט על ונד ווַאקהטעל זקה מאלטצ

(23) mostbert el und wachtel sach maltz

(24) דאס אללעס בלין מאקהענ צו אינער זאלב בֶרטרֶם

(24) das alles blin machen zu ainer salb bertrum

(25) הורט וקה דאר צו עט פונע אד || דגטומ

(25) hort uach dar zu et pone ad || digitum

(26) אדפוטענקאם אקקיפע | היערז ברונזט | בֶבֶר

(26) adpotenciam accipe | hiers brunst | biber

(27) גאל ונד זעטטיער אן נעזזעל זומא בֶרטרום

(27) gal und zettier an nessel suma bertrum

(28) באר אס בֶרנא זטיערזהוב דַס יעטליקהס אין

(28) bar es berna stiershob das jetliches ain

(29) האלב לוט ונד אין האלב לוט וויזזען ינבֶר ונד אין

(29) halb lot und ain halb lot wissen inber und ain

(30) קוינטלין לאנגען פֿעֿעֿער דאס אללעס ונדֶר אין

(30) quintlin langen pfefer das alles under ain

(31) אנדֶר בלין געזטוחזען ונד דורקה אין זיב גע

(31) ander blin gestossen und durch ain sib ge-

(32) זקה לאגען ונד אין | > האלב לוט בוררים דאס

(32) sach lagen und ain > | halb lot borris das

(33) געזוטטענ מיט מאלמעזער ונד עס דורקה אין

(33) gesotten mit malmeser und es durch ain

(34) ענע טוקה קעזיגען ונד דֶס זעלבען ווין גֶנו

(34) -ene tuch kesigen und des selben win geno-

(35) מען ונד דיע וור גענאנטען זטוב דאר ונגעזוט

(35) men und die war genanten stob dar ungesot-

(36) טען צו אינער לאטווער ונד |\ דאר צו אין הונג

(36) ten zu ainer latwer und |\ dar zu ain honig

(37) ונד דאס געעזזען מורגעס ונד נאקהטס

(37) und das geessen morges und nachts

354

To the left of the innermost diagram, and commencing level with l. 24, there are seven lines in Latin script, each containing a single word, the text reading as follows: *satter, nessel, pfeff, mostbert el* (divided over two lines thus; cf. spelling in Hebrew, l. 23), *Almalz(?), bertrum.*

The following translation is in some places tentative, although the text is in general clear enough. For annotation, see below.

(1) Concerning love.
(2) Write this name on an oaken wand:
(3) 'Be off! flee from oak!' and when thou touchest a woman with
(4) that same staff to calm [her](?), she will love thee.

(5) That all animals may shun thee.
(6) So thou must carry with thee the right eye of a wolf,
(7) and thou shalt walk in safety from thine enemies.

(8) Concerning love.
(9) Make a pot with little holes in it, and
(10) place in it a tree-frog's head, and put the pot in the way of
(11) large ants. And thou shouldst permit it to stand there for fourteen
(12) days. Thereafter examine, and thou wilt find a bone
(13) in the shape of a roe-deer, over which thou shouldst have [someone] read
(14) nine masses; and thereafter whatever woman thou touchest
(15) with that bone will love thee. There is another bone,
(16) in the shape of a ship, and over that, too, shouldst thou have [someone]
(17) read nine masses, and whatever woman with that bone
(18) thou dost push away from thee, she hateth thee.

(19) Take two parts of lime-follicles, one part
(20) of a kind of weevil, and put it into an ampulla full of oil;
(21) Then men appear without their heads.

(22) Take the fibrous part that is on nettle together with long pepper,
(23) mossbeard, and a quail, a quantity of malt.
(24) Make it all smooth (?) into an ointment of pellitory,
(25) listen to it attentively, and place [some] on the second finger.

(26) For potency, take one (?) jay that is on heat, one (?) beaver- (27) gall (*for* gal *doubtless read* geil, *i.e. testicle*), fibre that is on nettle, a quantity of pellitory (28) in a pure state (?); have burned (?) the second stomach of a bull; of each of these one (29) half loth, also a half loth of white ginger, and a (30) touch of long pepper. Let all [of these] be (31) together pounded finely (?), and through a sieve [. . .]ed: (32) a kind of tub (?), and a half loth of borage, that (33) [to be ?] boiled with malmsey; and through a (34) [. . .] cloth strain it as if making cheese; and let the liquor of the same be ta- (35) ken, and the items that have been listed sift over it, unboi- (36) led, into a paste-like confection, and add thereto some honey. (37) And it is to be eaten [every] morning and night.

l. 2 *scrirbe*. In view of the generally careful character of the transcription (see above, p. 347), the erroneous insertion of *r* in scri[r]*be* is surprising.

hec, by error for *hoc*. cf. l. 14, *quem*, where *quam* is clearly intended.

nomen here clearly means *spell* or *charm*. *Nomina* (fem. sing.) in this sense is cited by Du Cange from sixteenth-century sources only.[24]

aichen. Grimm, *Deutsches Wörterbuch*, cite the form *eichîn* as ahd. and mhd.

ruteln. Grimm list the diminutive *rütlein* from 1595. If what the writer intended is *rutlen*, one might have expected some vowel-indication, cf. l. 19, לינדין *linden*. The diminutive suggests that the Latin original read *virgula*, as against *virga* in l. 4.

l. 3 *araus*. Grimm cite *eraus* (s.v. *heraus*, 1, l. 11).

fugs. For *pe* exceptionally (in this document) representing *f*, see above, p. 347. In view of the correct form *fugiant* in l. 5, *fugs* should be expanded as *fug<ia>s*, and not *fuges* from the transitive *fugare*. But one might have expected the insertion of 'aleph.

robore. *Oak* is the primary meaning of *robur* in classical Latin, and is still given lexicographical priority by Du Cange. Niermeyer,[25] however, omits this meaning altogether, despite giving the oak-connection priority for the adjective *roboreus* and including *roboretum* (*oak-wood*). K. E. Georges[26] renders *eiche* first by *quercus* and secondly by *robur* (*steineiche*).

l. 4 *ad qutiri* could be read as a single word. The context appears to desiderate a part of the body (?the *pudenda*) in the accusative, or just possibly a gerund. My translation *to calm* [*her*] is a counsel of despair, presuming that *ad quietare* was intended.

l. 10 *lob froskop*, i.e. *laubfroschkopf*, the head of a tree-frog (*Rana virens, R. arborea*). Grimm, s.v., cite an ahd. form *laupfrosc*. For *kopf* with simple *p* Grimm[27] cite a Silesian primer (*lesebuch*) that rhymes *kop* and *top* (i.e. *taub*).

intrapone is doubtless intended, but not only is *t* unrepresented, but in place of the putative *pe* there is an upright stroke—suggesting that the scribe began to write his own symbol for *f* (see p. 347), realized his error, and left the letter uncompleted.

l. 11 *mittas*. *Mittere* for *permittere* is noted by Du Cange from the correspondence of Paul I (757–67) with Pipin III.

l. 12 Before *os* a letter has been deleted.

l. 13 *rech*, for modern *reh* (English *roe*). Grimm, who cite the form *rêch* from ahd. and mhd., point out that it survived into early nhd.

l. 14 *quem*, error for *quam*, cf. *illa*, l. 15; correctly, l. 17. For a similar confusion of gender in a (demonstrative) pronoun, see l. 2.

l. 18 *odit*, error for *oderit*.

l. 19 *linden bol*. The *beth*, although longer than normal for this scribe (cf. l. 3, *amabit*, l. 21, *capitibus*), seems to be correctly read; cf. the second *beth* in *ambulabis*, l. 7, *bertrum*, l. 24. Presumably the word is *bolle, blossom, follicle*. Grimm[28] cite a form *boll* from the translation of Columella by Michael Herr (16th cent.).

l. 20 *sach*. Grimm[29] note this abbreviation of *sache* as already in *mhd.* They list[30] the meaning *kind (art, weise)* as being found in German at an early stage of the language only, citing from a poem of Jesaias Rompler von Loewenhalt (Strasbourg, 1647), *recht unverschuldten sach*. *Sach* in this sense occurs again, l. 32.

webel, i.e. *wib[b]el, wiebel*, English *weevil*. Grimm cite our form from glosses to (?by) Martin(?) Di[e]fenbach, 1661–1709.

tu es. Place (i.e. = *setzen, stellen*, etc.) is the basic meaning of the verb *thun*.[31]

ampul, mod. German *ampel*; Grimm cite *ahd. ampullâ*, but not this apocopated form.

l. 21 *apparent*. For the present tense cf. *odit*, l. 18.

l. 22 *zetter*. Grimm, s.v. *zatter* (cf. *satter* in Latin script on this folio, see above, p. 355; *fibrous, with separated threads*, etc.) 2) identify our form as from Swabia and Alsace. *Zette* means a drooping branch, from which hang down berries, etc.[32]

suma, i.e. *summa*, in the sense[33] of *quantity*. Grimm point out that Latin *summa* entered German as a loan-word in the high Middle Ages only, and that it at first retained its Latin form. It is found again, l. 27. The writer's omission to represent the doubled *m* invites explanation. In the context *suma* means *together with*.

lagen. *la<n>gen* may be assumed, in the light of l. 30, *langen pfefer*. By "long" pepper is meant the fruit-spike of *Piper officinarum* and *P. longum*, gathered unripe and dried off.[34]

l. 23 *mostbert el*. Grimm, s.v. *Moos*, cite no form in -*st*; there would appear to be confusion with *most (juice, must)*. Grimm also list *Moosbart*, but not the diminutive form. *Moosbart* = *beard-moss, beard lichen (Usnea barbata)*. Hegi (see note 32) indexes no botanical name *Moosbart[el]*.

wachtel, quail, as coming after a list of botanical terms, seems surprising without a prefixed indefinite article.

sach, see l. 20.

maltz, mod. *malz*.

l. 24 *blin*, occurs again, l. 31, where the context requires either an adverb or its equivalent; here also an adverb would be most appropriate, but an infinitive dependent upon *machen* is not impossible (e.g. *blühen?*). I am not able to identify *blin*. A form of *blähen* = *inflate* seems implausible (Grimm list *blan* as an adjective, = *geschwollen*).

salb, modern and *mhd. salbe.*

bertum, i.e. *berchtram, bertram* (< *pyrethrum*), *Anthemis pyrethrum*,[35] pellitory.

l. 25 *hort*. The plural form must be a slip for the imperative singular (cf. *wach*). The scribe's vocalization scheme scarcely takes account of vowel-shift (but note l. 20 עֵל, = *öl*); however, Grimm[36] point out that forms with the unmodified vowel (*horen*) are attested in md. and Oberdeutsch. *Hort wach* presumably directs attention to sounds of effervescence. It is not clear what is the purpose of the prescription contained in ll. 22–5, but presumably it has some aphrodisiac connection. The spacing of the MS makes it clear that a new item begins in l. 26.

l. 26 *hiers brunst. hier* (הִיעֵר) must surely represent modern German *häher* (*mhd. hëher*), *jay, brunst* = *heat*, here in the sexual sense.[37] The meaning is clear enough, but the grammatical inversion is curious, in view of the availability of the adjective *brunstig*. Hegi (see note 32) does not list *hähersbrunst*, and the bird itself is doubtless meant.

biber gal. Presumably what is here intended is *bibergeil*,[38] i.e. *castoreum*, beaver's testicle. Neither for the adjective nor for the noun *geil* do Grimm cite any form with *a* other than the Anglo-Saxon *gâl*, and I assume confusion with *gal[le], gall*. Since the concoction is to be swallowed (see l. 37), surely gall may be excluded, despite the fact that the mixture also contains honey (l. 36). For *Pimpinella, saxifrage*, there are various German names formed with *biber-*, including *bibernalle*;[39] but it seems probable that *castoreum* is here intended literally.

l. 27 *zettier an nessel, suma*, see l. 22. *bertrum*, see l. 24.

l. 28 I have taken *bar* as an adjective referring to *bertrum*, "unadulterated pyrethrum". This is not very convincing, but?

berna. bernen for *brennen* is Niederdeutsch; but how can a form terminating in *a* (presumably *ã*) be an infinitive?

stiershob. Haube, *head-covering*, includes amongst its applied meanings the *reticulum*,[40] i.e. the second stomach of ruminants (cf. the English terms *bonnet*, *king's-hood*).[41] In view of the statement of quantity that follows, this meaning seems more likely than that of *foreskin* (n.b., not *penis*) that is also listed by Grimm under *Haube*.[42] *Stiershaub* is not indexed as a botanical name by Hegi.

jetliches, i.e. each: *ietlich* (= *jeder*) mhd. *ietelîch*.[43]

l. 29 *lot*. *Loth* = *piece of lead*, whence also *weight*. Grimm record[44] the mhd. spelling *lot*. In the sense of a specific weight *loth* sometimes indicates an ounce, but more frequently $\frac{1}{2}$ oz.

wissen. Grimm cite[45] mediaeval forms *wissen*, etc.

inber, as a form of *ingwer*, is cited by Grimm from Lorenz Diefenbach's MS lexicon of 1470.[46]

l. 30 *quintlin*, like *quintin*, means $\frac{1}{4}$ loth, i.e. $\frac{1}{8}$ oz. Grimm record the forms *quintlin*, *quintlîn* from the fifteenth century.

langen pfefer, see l. 22.

l. 31 *blin*, see l. 24.

gestossen. For *stoszen* with reference to spices, etc., see Grimm.[47]

ge-, uncompleted at the beginning of the next line, proves that the scribe was copying from a written source in which he seems to have skipped one or more lines by oversight. One may plausibly restore *getrieben* or *gerieben*.

l. 32 *sach*, see l. 20.

lagen = *lagel*, *lägel* (< *lagena*), *keg, small barrel*. Presumably the foregoing lacuna included directions to place what had been passed through a sieve into a miniature barrel, e.g. [*und das gemenge einschenken in ein*] *sach lagen*.

After *und ain* follows a symbol which may indicate $\frac{1}{2}$.

borris (*burris*?), i.e. *Borago officinalis*, German *borwetch*. Hegi[48] records *burres* as a form of the name.

l. 33 *gesotten* (*sieden*), see Grimm.[49]

malmeser, i.e. *malvasier*, amongst the forms of which Grimm list, from Diefenbach,[50] *malmasier*, cf. English *malmsey* (< [Napoli di] Malvasia, in the Peloponnese).

l. 34 *-ene* at the beginning of the line implies another lacuna, the word at the end of which probably meant something like *clean*.

kesigen. Grimm, who include the adjective *käsig, käsicht*, do not list any corresponding verb. The reading is clear, and the form (cf. *reinigen*) may be accepted.

win. Grimm do not (as far as I can see) note any extended use of the term *wein* comparable to the specialized meaning of *wine* in English pharmaceutical usage,[51] but the reading וויר is clear enough.

l. 35 *und die war genanten*. In spite of the solecism in grammar, the meaning *and the afore-mentioned* [*ingredients*] coheres with the sense of the passage.

stob (perhaps better *stub*) seems to be the imperative of *staüben*, in a transitive sense.[52]

l. 36 *latwer*. *Latwerge* (< *elect(u)arium*, whence also English *electuary*) is the term used for the blending of *materia medica* into a semi-solid state of sluggish fluidity. Grimm notes two *mhd.* forms without *g* (*latware, latweri*). It is worth recording that within living memory the term was used in south-eastern Europe by some Jews as a description of *ḥaroseth*.[53]

The symbol following *und* i; possibly an apothecary's sign meaning *adde* or *mitte*.

hon[*i*]*g*. Grimm note[54] a form *hung* from Josua Maaler's (= Pictorius) German-Latin dictionary, Zürich, 1561.

l. 37 *morge* < *n* > *s* may be corrected with confidence.

geessen. For forms of the past participle of *essen* see Grimm,[55] according to whom examples in *ahd.* are not forthcoming; *mhd.* furnishes *gëzzen*.

How are we to classify the form of German used by this scribe? The transliteration indicates a hardening of sibilants (*zayin* for *s*, e.g. l. 27, *zuma*, l. 29, *wizzen*), dentals in certain positions, e.g. l. 30, *under*, and gutturals (e.g. *gs* for Latin *x*, rather than *ks*, l. 6, *degstrum*), and immediately awakens echoes of Bavaria and its environs; and Germanist colleagues[56] confirm that the form of language points to the south—indeed, I am told that a form like *ein honig* ("some honey", cf. l. 36) might still be heard in Austria today. At the same time, it is to be observed that there is not a single feature in any of the word-forms in these two texts that is specific to Judaeo-German. True, the use of the Hebrew letter *'ayin* to represent *e* is generally regarded as a hallmark of Yiddish; and since the scribe's fluency in writing Hebrew characters implies an Ashkenazic Jewish education, we are to suppose that Yiddish was indeed his mother-tongue. But—to ignore here the Latin component—his transliteration-scheme would have rendered the German at least as puzzling for a mediaeval Jewish reader familiar with Yiddish as it was, to begin with, for myself; *und* and *in* introduced by *waw* and *yodh* respectively (see above, p. 348) would not have been recognized without long pondering.

As it happens, there is available an excellent source with which to compare our material in the Judaeo-German *Dukus Horant* preserved from the Cairo *Genizah*.[57] The MS bears a colophon dating it at 1383, whereas the mean date (see above, p. 346) for our MS is 1459 although it is probably somewhat older than that; in other words, something like half a century separates the two. We may contrast ונד l. 37 etc., with the specifically Yiddish און of *Dukus Horant*[58] (henceforth *DH*). For initial *o*, e.g. Latin *osse*, l. 34 (there is no German instance forthcoming), cf. *DH, oben*[59] (אובן). With יי for *in*, contrast *DH*[60] אין. For the combination *qoph he* for *ch* as in *durch*, l. 33, *DH* uses *kaph*, e.g. דורך.[61] Instead of the scribe's invented symbol for *f* (see above, p. 347), e.g. l.

30, *pfefer, DH* uses *pe* with a diacritically superimposed *v*, e.g. פֿערט = [*p*]*ferd*.[62] Clearly, our text cannot be categorized as Judaeo-German: it is properly to be considered as a distinctly non-Jewish form of Middle High German as this would have sounded to a Jew in southern Germany or Austria somewhat after 1400. So far from diminishing its value for the history of Yiddish, this circumstance probably enhances it.

In regard to the contents of the text on f. 163v., it is probable that its thaumaturgical and similar prescriptions are commonplace, and that, since the scribe was clearly following one or more written sources (see *infra*), a more extensive search than I have been able to conduct might reveal them. There appears to be no point of contact with the magical content of the *Bellifortis* itself, although the latter, like our document (l. 10), does refer to use of a tree-frog—but for quite other purposes.[63] There are two items, however, parallels to which I have succeeded in running to earth—not exact parallels, to be sure, but close enough to reflect a common source. The direction (ll. 6–7) that a wolf's right eye may be carried as a talisman against one's enemies, or more specifically (l. 5) animals, corresponds to the *Liber Aggregationibus* of Albertus Magnus,[64] where it is stated that a wolf's right eye bound to one's right-hand sleeve will prevent both men and dogs from occasioning hurt. And the *De Mirabilibus Mundi*, falsely attributed to Albert, contains instructions[65] how to make men appear headless that may be set alongside those conveyed in ll. 19–21 of our MS.

These thaumaturgical directives and quack aphrodisiacs will inspire the modern reader—according to his individual temperament—with amusement, amazement at the writer's gullibility, or impatience: and he will scarcely entertain any proposition that the sort of people who copied them out found them effective or partially so. (One can, for instance, imagine that an ampulla filled with oil [ll. 20–1], if used as a lens, might so distort an image that human figures might seem to be headless.) What is of interest to note is the way in which such credulousness can accompany an enviable accuracy in observation, and of this also our text offers an instructive example. It refers (ll. 10f.) to two bones that will be all that is left after ants have had a fortnight in which to dispose of the head of a tree-frog; one of them (l. 13) *admodum unius rech, like a deer*, and the other (l. 16) *admodum nauis*. The diagram (fig. 3) of the skeleton of a tree-frog[66] shows how apposite such a comparison is. The upper portion of the skull (shown below) may be said to resemble the head of a young fawn—it is admittedly somewhat full in the face, but, because of the two protrusions that can be visualized as the incipient sprouting of antlers, it is at once recognizable. And one needs little imagination in order to be able to see the lower portion (shown above) as the cross-section of a vessel of deep draught, such as a mediaeval trading ship.

It remains to consider why it was that this unknown scribe transliterated these two texts into Hebrew characters. Let us begin with what we can deduce as to his *Sitz im Leben*. His facility in writing a rabbinic hand shows unmistakably that he had received at least an elementary Jewish education: his is not the writing of a laboriously self-taught Christian Hebraist in the normal sense of that term. He was a person who took thaumaturgical matters seriously—we cannot suppose that the whole thing was but an elaborate joke. The state of modern scholarship regarding Jewish concerns in late antiquity, and the evidence of the *Genizah*, make it clear enough that belief in magic was not so peripheral to the Jewish community that it can be dismissed as insignificant;[67] but I do not think that one who is prepared to entertain the inclusion amongst his magical practices the ninefold recitation of the Mass, as our scribe does (see ll. 14, 17), considers himself to be—or rather, any longer considers himself to be—a Jew, even though in the view of his Gentile compeers he may very well have ranked as one. In other words, we are here dealing either with a convert to Christianity, or with someone who has in effect, even if not formally, apostatized from Judaism. If he was capable of reading a technical treatise in Latin on military technology he was probably capable of writing Latin or German in the western alphabet, even if his penmanship was not up to much; and it is at least possible that the Latin writing on f. 162v. and the few words of German in Latin characters on f. 163v. come from his own hand.

If that picture is soundly drawn, why, we may ask, did he put himself to the trouble of transcribing his material, so ingeniously and laboriously, into Hebrew characters? Whilst I think I can suggest the answer in regard to f. 163v., the same motive would have no relevance in regard to the directions on f. 162v. for working an engine for use of boiling oil as an offensive weapon; and I therefore tentatively conclude that that piece, inscribed around the relevant diagram, was undertaken both by way of practice for the real object and also to camouflage it. The object, in my opinion, was the invention of a convenient cipher in which the thaumaturgical contents of f. 163v. might be concealed from casual view or prying eyes. If the writer was a member of some religious order, he could in this way evade the interest of his superior, who would—or at any rate should—have disapproved of his concerning himself with love-philtres and his own virility. If he were a secular priest or a layman (and this seems more likely, since not many monastic libraries are likely to have contained a copy of the *Bellifortis*), he could similarly rely on his cover to guard his secret from any likely rival.

Even though we can no longer draw a *cordon sanitaire* around the integrity of Judaism that would keep magic out, no one will claim that this document has anything significant to tell us regarding those values and concepts that are generally agreed to give Judaism a claim on humane attention. Its publication, on the other hand, will doubtless be hailed by those whose nihilistic approach leads them to be dismissive of any attempt at defining Judaism even in negative terms, and to insist that anything done by any Jew is *ipso facto* authentically Jewish. For myself, I would regard it as important not for its contents but for its intellectual implications; in that it lends some substance to the supposition that this scribe's capacity to use Latin texts may have been shared by others in mediaeval German Jewry, who preferred to direct their attention to what the culture of the west could contribute to the realm of the mind and spirit.

Notes

* It was only when research embodied in this article had been virtually completed that I learned from G. Quarg's introduction to the facsimile edition (1967) of the Göttingen codex of Kyeser's *Bellifortis* (see note 2 below), pp. xlivf., that the item here treated had been described by Dr E. Roth, who was there stated to contemplate publishing it in German in *Biblos* and in Hebrew in *Yeda' 'Am*. Having failed to trace any such publication I communicated with Dr Roth, now of Luxemburg, who drew my attention to his having referred to it again, briefly, in Ilse Staff (ed.), *Bildung und Konfessionalität* (Kritische Beiträge zur Bildungstheorie, No. 2, Frankfurt a. Main, 1967), p. 106, n. 193, a reproduction of f. 162v. of the MS being there included (p. 108). In his letter to me Dr Roth conveyed an implicit acquiescence in my proceeding to publish a study of the document myself.

1. For the catalogue description of MS Palatina 5278, see note 3 below.

2. For Kyeser (1366–1405 or later) see F. Klemm in H. Körner (ed.), *Neue deutsche Biographie*, vol. 13 (1982), pp. 355–6, and, more fully, H.-P. Hils in Christine Stöllinger-Löser (ed.), *Die deutsche Literatur des Mittelalters Verfasserlexicon*, vol. 5 (1985), cols. 477–84. Kyeser, who was apparently educated for a medical career, composed his *Bellifortis* as an exile in 1402–4; an enlarged, profusely illustrated copy of the work, on parchment (MS Göttingen, Universitätsbibliothek cod. phil. 63) was prepared in 1405. The work includes much astrological, alchemical and other magical material. From the middle of the fifteenth century copies and vernacular versions, derived from the original, less elaborate edition became widely diffused, and the work was frequently quoted. According to Hils (col. 481) our codex (see note 3 below) is closely related to and probably not much later than the fuller text contained in the Göttingen parchment codex; see the facsimile edition of that codex, ed. Götz Quarg (1967), introduction, pp. xxvf.

3. The catalogue (*Tabulae Codicum manu scriptorum praeter Graecos et Orientales in Bibliotheca Palatina Vindobonensi Asservatorum*, vol. 4, 1870, p. 85) describes it as follows: '5278 [Philos. 143] ch. XV, 203f. c. figuris calamo exaratis et col. Tractatus

de arte bellica hexametris compositus. Incip. "Capitulum primum martis qui cedit ad ymum ..." Exp. "Sic et unde fluens de qua complebis quesitum". Multae et latinae et germanicae notulae pro parte cryptographicae a variis adscriptae sunt.' See now also Quarg's introduction (note 2 above), pp. xxvif., xxx. Theodore Gottlieb, *Die ambraser Handschriften Büchersammlung Kaiser Maximilians I* (Leipzig, 1900), p. 81, lists MS Ambras 228; for the Hapsburg subordinate library at Am[b]ras, just east of Innsbruck, see briefly R. J. W. Evans, *The making of the Hapsburg Monarchy 1550–1700* (Oxford, 1979), p. 314, n. 8. A. Z. Schwarz, *Die hebräischer Handschriften der Nationalbibliothek in Wien*, understandably does not refer to the item which we are considering.

4. *Les parlers judéo-romans et le Vetus Latina* (Paris, 1925).

5. Gen. 49: 10, Ex. 20: 13; see D. Rosin, *R. Samuel b. Mëir als Schriftenerklärer* (1880), p. 61.

6. cf. the script in a Worms MS (Stadtarchiv 217) dated 1377; S. A. Birnbaum, *The Hebrew Scripts* (1957), no. 356, col. 305f., cf. also no. 349, cols. 303f. Professor Abramsky has pointed out to me that the Yiddish *Yosippon* printed in Zürich, 1546 (reproduced in the *Jewish Encyclopedia*, vol. 7, p. 263) has a similarly squared *gimel*; since, however, its 'foot' is correctly positioned, the proportions are quite different from those of the *gimel* of our scribe.

7. I am grateful to Dr Mazzal, of the Nationalbibliothek in Vienna, for examining the MS with me.

8. W. Meyer-Lübke, *Romanisches Etymologisches Wörterbuch* (3rd edn., 1935), no. 9236; cf. R. E. Latham, *Revised Medieval Latin Word-List* (1965), s.v. *vernica, vernicium*, etc.

9. Du Cange, s.v.

10. Meyer-Lübke, no. 6832.

11. *Oxford English Dictionary*, Supplement 1 (1972), p. 351; 2 (1976), p. 1003.

12. Du Cange, s.v.

13. Du Cange, s.v., citing an edict (643 CE) of the Lombard king Rothari; J. F. Niermeyer, *Mediae Latinitatis lexicon minus*, s.v. *modola*.

14. s.v. *nicht*, col. 690, 1), a), 691, l. 5.

15. Meyer-Lübke, no. 5018.

16. (note 2 above), vol. 2, pp. xlivf.

17. O. Gradenwitz, *Laterculi vocum latinarum a fronte et a tergo* (1904), p. 341.

18. For military pyrotechnics from antiquity onwards see A. R. Hall in C. Singer *et al.*, *A History of Technology*, vol. 2 (1956), pp. 374f., 379; G. Sarton, *Introduction to the History of Science*, vol. 3, pt. 2 (1948), pp. 155of., lists and briefly describes 14th–15th-century treatises on (or including) military technology.

19. The *Texaurus* contains a chapter *de rebus bellicis*. For translation see A. Rupert Hall, 'Guido's *Texaurus*, 1335', in *On pre-modern technology and science; A volume of studies in honor of Lynn White, jr.* (Malibu, 1976), pp. 6–52.

20. = Marino Sanudo il Vecchio, *Liber secretorum fidelium crucis* (ed. Hanover, 1611; facsimile ed. Jerusalem, 1972); see book II, iv, chap. 8, pp. 59f. and end, p. 60, *de diversis armorum generibus*. Translation by A. Stewart, Palestine Pilgrims Trust Society, London, 12, 1897.

21. = Columnus, Colonna (*c*.1285), *de Regimine Principum* (Rome, 1607), book III, iii, chap. 21, p. 615, where stores requisite for defensive warfare are discussed: these include sulphur, pitch, oil, and large quantities of powdered chalk (*calcem puluerizatam*), but this is for scattering dry in order to blind an attacking force. Most

important, although post-dating Kyeser, is the *Feuerwerksbuch* (*c*.1422, printed 1529) ascribed to Abraham of Memmingen; this I have not perused.

22.   See R. Payne-Gallwey, *The Crossbow* (London, 1903, repr. 1958), pp. 31, 73; reproduced in R. Loewe, 'Jewish Evidence for the History of the Crossbow', in B.G. Dahan (ed.), *Les Juifs au regard de l'histoire, Mélanges en l'honneur de Bernhard Blumenkranz* (Paris, 1985), pp. 96–7, figs. 5, 6.

23.   In the reproduction (fig. 2) it appears that the left end of ll. 32 and 33 are covered by the diagram and that one or more letters have thus been obscured. Inspection of the original, which is polychromatic, makes it clear that this is an illusion due to monochrome reproduction.

24.   Synod Limana: *Item si quae persona utantur amuletis, vulgo Nominas, et in eis recondendo scripturas verborum vel nominum incognitorum, etc.* Have we perhaps here a distant echo of Hebrew *shemoth*?

25.   See note 13 above, p. 921.

26.   *Ausführliches deutsch-lateinisches Handwörterbuch* (7th edn., 1882), vol. 1, col. 959.

27.   s.v., II *A* 1 *c β* (col. 1749).

28.   vol. 2, col. 232, l. 8.

29.   vol. 8, col. 1592, l. 7 from foot.

30.   col. 1600, 8).

31.   Grimm, s.v., col. 435, I, 1).

32.   G. Hegi, *Illustrierte Flora von Mittel-Europa*, vol. 1, p. 292, *infra*, records *Zettergräs* as a Swiss variant for *Zittergras* (*quaking-grass, Briza media L.*), but his index of German names (vol. 7, pp. 468f.) lists no *Zetter-* or *Zitter(an) Nessel* as a specific plant-name.

33.   Grimm, s.v. *Summe*, col. 1069, 2) a); see also the introductory remarks, col. 1065.

34.   *Enc. Britannica* (14th edn., 1929), vol. 17, p. 497.

35.   *Index Kewensis*, I, i (1893), p. 145; Hegi (note 32 above), vol. 6, ii, pp. 673f.

36.   s.v., vol. 1806, I, 1), l. 18.

37.   Grimm, s.v., col. 438, 8).

38.   Grimm, s.v., and s.v. *Geil*, col. 2589, 3).

39.   Hegi (note 32 above), vol. 5, ii, p. 1199; vol. 7, p. 387.

40.   Grimm, s.v., col. 585, 8).

41.   *Oxford English Dictionary*, s.v. *Reticulum*.

42.   col. 565, 5).

43.   Grimm, s.v., col. 2043; cf. 2184 (*itslich*), 2315 (*jetzlich*).

44.   col. 1205, 5), a), b).

45.   e.g. col. 1182, c), l. 10.

46.   See Grimm, vol. 2, col. ix.

47.   col. 506, 6), d), *a*).

48.   Note 32 above, vol. 5, iii, p. 2230.

49.   col. 869, *l*).

50.   See note 46 above.

51.   *Oxford English Dictionary*, s.v., p. 169, col. 1, 3.

52.   Grimm, s.v., col. 1101, 4.

53.   Information from Dr T. Barta, of the Department of Civil and Municipal Engineering at University College London, who grew up in Romania; *ḥaroseth*, used on the night of Passover, is of the consistency of jam—according to the

predominant practice somewhat stiff, although according to some jurists it ought to be runny.

54. s.v., l. 8.
55. s.v., col. 1160.
56. I am grateful in particular to Mr A. Stillmark of the Department of German at University College London for advice in connection with this text.
57. MS Cambridge, T.-S. K. 22. Edited by P. F. Ganz *et al.* (1964). For the date (5413 = 1383 CE), see Ganz, pp. 4, 7.
58. See e.g. f. 23 recto (which Ganz reproduces), p. 140.
59. f. 29v., p. 166, l. 410.
60. f. 26r., p. 152, l. 234.
61. f. 23r., p. 140, l. 92.
62. f. 22r., p. 136, l. 53.
63. MS Göttingen (see note 2 above), f. 93b: 'Cum uis accendere lampadem et uidere quod sit omne nigrum astantis et in eius manu uirga ita ut fugiant homines edis ex eo: Accipe ranam uiridem et decolla eam super pannos exsequiarum uirides . . .'
64. Printed post-1480: there is a copy in the library of University College London, pressmark SRA 4b, but none apparently in the British Library. See f. 12r., col. ii, *infra*: 'si quis oculum dextrum lupi ligauerit in manica dextra: homines neque canes ei nocere poterunt.' Cf. R. Best and F. Brightman, *The Book of Secrets of Albertus Magnus* (1973), book 3, end, p. 61.
65. Noted by L. Thorndyke, *History of Magic*, vol. 2 (1923), p. 736; edn. Amsterdam, 1648, pp. 202f.: 'Ut homines videantur sine capitibus, accipe spolium serpentis, & auripigmentum, & picem Graecam, . . . & facias cereum, & omnis qui illuminabitur eo, videbitur sine capite.'
66. From G. A. Boulenger, *The Tailless Batrachians of Europe*, vol. 2 (Ray Society, 75, 1898), p. 256.
67. A revealing measure of the distance separating the academic axioms of students of Jewish scholarship in the age of Graetz from those acknowledged in the age of Scholem is afforded by the following comparison. The article on *magic* in the *Jewish Encyclopedia* of 1906 runs to less than four columns, ending with cross-references to other headings such as *Abracadabra*. In the *Encyclopaedia Judaica* of 1971 the article *magic* covers over thirteen columns, nearly a whole column being occupied by its bibliography.

MS Vienna 5278 f. 162v.

MS Vienna 5278 f. 163v.

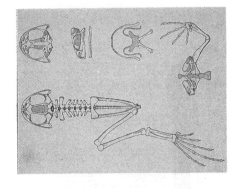

Pierre Leroux and the Book of Job

Anita Haimon-Weitzman

PIERRE Leroux (1797–1871) is renowned as a pioneer of humanitarian socialism. What is less commonly known is that he studied Hebrew to produce his own translation of the Book of Job, where he found confirmation of his socialist doctrines.

Leroux was a follower of Saint-Simon until 1831, when he left the movement because of its preoccupation with capital and industry. He wrote widely on religion and socialism. One of his best-known writings is *Egalité* (1839), an article from the *Encyclopédie Nouvelle*, devoted to history, religion and science, which he edited together with Jean Reynaud. Other works are *De l'Humanité* (1840) and *Malthus* (1845–6), a bitter attack on capitalism and the *esprit juif*. Leroux equated socialism with messianism, and looked forward to salvation in this world rather than the next.

Among the many who promulgated Leroux's ideas were Louis Blanc[1] and George Sand, who incorporated them in many of her novels, which, in the words of Berdyaev, 'played a decisive role in the development of the emotional life of Russia'.[2] The three figures whom Dostoevsky describes as the moving force of humanity are George Sand, Pierre Leroux and Cabet. The religious socialist Weitling acknowledges his debt to Leroux.[3] Again many parallels with Leroux's writings testify to his influence on Moses Hess, who dedicated a copy of his *Jugement dernier du vieux monde social* in 1851 to the 'citoyen Pierre Leroux'.[4] Leroux's influence on socialist thought in Europe has been fully documented by Viard.[5] He is also known as an opponent of the eclectic philosophy of Victor Cousin, who elevated intellect above emotion. For Leroux, man has three indispensable components— knowledge (*connaissance*), emotion (*sentiment*) and sensation. In 1848 and 1849, Leroux was elected to the Constituent and Legislative Assemblies, but in 1851 he was exiled, together with many other socialist politicians, to Jersey.

It was in Jersey, around 1860, that Leroux conceived the translation of Job. He worked in a theological library of some 4000 volumes, bequeathed by one Revd Falle, in St Helier.[6] The translation was first intended to form part of *La Grève de Samarez*, a long poetic meditation also written during his exile in Jersey and recently re-edited with copious notes by J. P. Lacassagne. In the event, however, Leroux's Job was published separately in France in 1866, through the generosity of the Freemasons of Grasse, a fellowship to which Leroux himself belonged.

The book of Job has fascinated many socialists, such as Proudhon,[7] Bernard-Lazare[8] and Simone Weil.[9] One possible reason is its international interest; every character comes from a different land. Furthermore the problem of undeserved suffering, together with the sufferer's restoration in ch. 42, appealed to Leroux (p. 222 *et passim*) as to other socialists, for whom Job represented the downtrodden proletariat. Again like other socialists, Leroux considered Job a favourite book of the Essenes (p. 218), whose way of life as described in Josephus and Philo marked them as models of socialism. For Leroux, however, the book of Job held yet another lesson: the resurrection and perfectibility of mankind.

Leroux had decided to devote his last years to the biblical prophets. He held Job to be the work of Isaiah, and claimed the support of a rabbinic tradition. However, the existence of such a tradition is very doubtful.[10] More probably, Leroux thought of Isaiah because the main doctrines that he found in Job—resurrection, messianism and the call for social justice—feature prominently in Isaiah.

The biblical Book of Job tells how Job suffered; how his three friends declared that all suffering must be deserved; how Job protests his innocence; and how the Lord finally appears, declaring that his will must be accepted without question. Leroux's Job is not simply a translation. The biblical drama is enacted, as it were, on the stage, with added directions, while Leroux, together with another character, comment at a distance, their function not unlike that of the chorus in a Greek drama. This dramatic expansion of a biblical book creates a form that is unusual if not unique.

The biblical portions covered in the five acts, each of which has its own title, may be tabulated as follows:

I	3:3–13:22	The human complaint
II	13:23–21:6	Man pleads his cause before God
III	21:7–28:28	The earth abandoned to sinners
IV	29:1–31:37	[Job's] final words
V	38:1–42:6	The perfectibility [of mankind]

The structure of Acts I–III is more regular than that of the underlying biblical text. The latter shows three rounds of speeches. In the first, Job makes the first speech, and the three friends follow, with Job replying to each; the second round is similar, except that there is no initial speech by Job; in the third round, too, Job is not the first speaker, and moreover one of his friends (Bildad) speaks only five verses while another (Zophar) does not speak at all. Leroux, by contrast, gives the second and third acts exactly the same structure as the first. To allow Job to start Act II, he ends the preceding act in the middle of what is in the Bible an undivided speech by Job, leaving the remainder to begin the new act. By the same device he makes Job commence Act III. To allow all three friends adequate speeches in this act, he transfers 27:11–23 and 28 from Job to Zophar. The suggestion as regards ch. 27 goes back to Benjamin Kennicott (1718–83), and Leroux's proposal to add ch. 28 is not unreasonable, since its theme—the unfathomable wisdom of God—better suits Zophar's case (see ch. 11) than Job's. The same suggestion was later made by Graetz,[11] who seems unaware of Leroux's work, even though he was in correspondence with Moses Hess. At the same time Leroux transfers 22:3–11 from Eliphaz to Bildad, inserting in its place 25:2–6 (which thus passes from Bildad to Eliphaz), and places ch. 24 after ch. 21. Leroux also shared the widespread view that Elihu's speeches (chs. 32–7) were to be rejected as interpolations. His authority for all this recasting is the tradition (in the pseudepigraphic *Ascension of Isaiah*) that the prophet was sawn asunder. Leroux, who identified Isaiah with Job, interpreted this to mean that the book had become disfigured, and that his amendments had restored its original form.

The translation is in clear and idiomatic French. Examples of particularly sensitive rendering are:

10:11 Hebrew: *u-ba-'aṣamot we-gidim teśokekeni*
Leroux: *et tu m'a composé un lacis d'os et de nerfs*

21:23 Hebrew: *zeh yamut be-'eṣem tummo*
Leroux: *l'un meurt dans la perfection de son embonpoint*

To produce a translation that reads well, in spite of the difficulties of the Hebrew original, Leroux often stretches the meanings of words further than today's philologists could justify. At 5:5, for example, the Hebrew states that the hungry will eat the harvest of the wicked, and continues with the obscure lines:

we-'el miṣ-ṣinnim yiqqaḥehu we-ša'ap ṣammim ḥelam

The difficult *ṣinnim* is sometimes connected with *ṣinnah* 'shield' or *zayin* 'weapon', whence the Vulgate's *armatus*. On that basis Leroux writes that the harvest will be so well devoured that the wicked 'will need no *pitchfork* to take it'; he considered 'pitchfork' a valid development from 'weaponry'. Again in the second line, he interprets *ṣammim* as *ṣeme'im*, 'thirsty' (so Vulgate *sitientes*), but further shifts to 'drunkard' (*quelque ivrogne boira sa subsistence*).

Sometimes, again, Leroux alters the meaning entirely, to heighten the effect or to improve the consistency of sense within a verse. At 4:16, for example, Eliphaz describes an apparition whose form he could not discern. He continues *temunah le-neged 'enay*; but Leroux, rather than given *temunah* its straightforward meaning 'image', translates 'a *veil* before my eyes'. Similarly, at 5:10 the *ḥuṣot*, 'open spaces' over which God sends water become 'mountains'.[12]

Leroux once treats a name with equal freedom. He rejects Renan's proposal to locate Job in Edom, and instead infers from the mention at 1:17 of Chaldaeans (who elsewhere are synonymous with Babylonians) that we should instead look eastwards, towards Syria and Iraq. His argument is imperilled, however, by the reference to raiders from Sheba, i.e. Sabaeans from Arabia, in 1:15. He therefore regards the Hebrew name (*Šeba*) as a mere variant of *Ṣobah*, the name of a portion of Syria (p. 254). This involves exchanging two Hebrew sibilants that are in fact wholly different.

Leroux is no less free in his treatment of grammar than of vocabulary. At 5:7, where the Hebrew says that man is born (*yulad*) for sorrow, Leroux instead writes that man himself creates (which in Hebrew would be *yolid*) sorrow. This yields a fine contrast with the preceding verse, which stated where sorrow did *not* come from, and the emendation has become fairly common.[13]

Some of his treatments, it must be admitted, look very improbable. At 3:8 he makes Job call for his day of birth to be dreaded by 'those who are disturbed by any light when they set out to strike the crocodile in the darkness'. Leroux was thinking (p. 271) of the constant warfare between two neighbouring Egyptian towns mentioned by Juvenal (*Satires, 15.33*), each of which abhorred the creatures venerated by the other; in the vicinity of people who venerated the crocodile, one could not kill a crocodile without cover of darkness, and would dread any light at that moment. Quite apart from the fact that 'strike' cannot be obtained from the Hebrew (*'orer*), and 'darkness' has to be supplied from the next verse, the meaning is indeed curious. In 3:22, again, he sees a description of the moment of death: 'For the hour of my last sigh will come; it comes; it has come; the death-rattle (*hoquets*) begins, it flows on.' In fact, however, the crucial word 'last' does not occur in the Hebrew, the verb 'come' occurs only once, while *ša'agah*, the word translated *hoquets*, usually denotes a lion's roar and here denotes loud cries.

All in all, philology is not for Leroux the ultimate arbiter. It was more important for the translator to know the language into which he was translating than the language of his source (p. 231). He had always admired a certain cardinal who had employed Jews to turn up passages in rabbinic sources but never felt bound by their translations. 'Le sens, c'est mon affaire,' the cardinal affirmed; ' ne sutor ultra crepidam.'

This laxity regarding the sense of a word fits with his view that there are families of Hebrew words which each go back to a single root of broad meaning, often common to the European languages also. He thus traces Hebrew gag, 'roof', gew, 'back', geled, 'skin', go'el, 'protector', and Latin glacies to a root comprising the single letter g meaning 'envelopment' (p. 342). He similarly connects Hebrew bor, 'purity', with Latin purus (p. 293), or Hebrew geber, 'man', with Latin vir (p. 324). The above transliterations are those of a modern philologist; Leroux himself writes gali for Hebrew go'ali 'my redeemer' (p. 338), as he follows the system of the eighteenth-century Christian scholar Masclef, who ignored the massoretic punctuation and did not pronounce the guttural letters.[14] In this way he analyses kimerire yom (3:5), which he reads 'Chamarid-ioum', as a compound of ham, 'hot' (even though k and h are different consonants), ri 'flow' and yom 'day'. This yields the meaning 'feux faisant effluve et surgissant au jour', i.e. a volcano. (Here he seems to confuse two Hebrew letters of similar appearance [r, d], but his independent treatment of three passages discussed below shows that he was a serious Hebraist.) In his preface to the fables of P. Lachambeaudie[15] he develops these philological theories. For example, German essen and Latin esse are equated; to exist is to consume. Leroux similarly derived Greek hama, 'together', and Latin amare from a primitive root AUM, meaning 'union', which he thought also underlay Hebrew 'amen. In the same spirit, he makes equations between the Hebrew Bible and classical mythology, identifying hošek we-salmawet (Job 3:5) with Hades, and 'ananah and 'opel (3:5–6) with Erebus. All these comparisons with other languages and literatures are in keeping with Leroux's doctrine of the unity of mankind.

There are three so-called messianic passages where Leroux defends his version in detail with reference to the Hebrew (pp. 322–52). The first passage is 16:19–22. Verse 21 longs, according to Leroux, for the time when 'the Universal man might debate with God, just as an individual man with a friend', though in fact the words 'universal' and 'individual' do not appear in the Hebrew; and v. 22 declares that in due time Job would depart and not return. Leroux sees here the unity of mankind, with every individual rooted in the 'universal man', whom he identifies with Christ, and at the same time with Job; he is the 'witness in heaven' (v. 19); and v. 22 is thus a prophecy of Christ's first coming.

The second passage is ch. 17, where Job declares that he has been made an example for mankind (v. 6) to strengthen man's faith (v. 9). His thoughts have advanced beyond earthly life (v. 11). (Leroux does not try to justify this last rendering, which in fact cannot be wrung from the Hebrew *zimmotay nittequ moraše lebabi*.) Here we have the hope of 'resurrection of man in a humanity that has been perfected' (p. 329). This does not mean the physical resurrection of individuals, but rather the regeneration of mankind in an improved (no doubt a socialist) society.

Inevitably, the third passage is 19:2–29. Jerome had already found a reference to resurrection in 25b–26: *et in novissimo die de terra surrecturus sum,* (26) *et rursum circumdabor pelle mea, et in carne mea videbo Deum meum.* Leroux however denied Jerome's doctrine of physical resurrection (p. 343). In v. 26 he takes the speaker to be mankind, whose resurrection again means the improvement of society. He translates the verse: 'After they (i.e. God in his three qualities of Power, Love and Intelligence) have embodied this (i.e. the ideal) in my skin, then I shall see God from my flesh (i.e. when I am resurrected).' Leroux later defines 'the ideal' as what exists in the mind before it exists in reality, but here it seems to mean the concept of a just society.

Resurrection, which Leroux calls the principal lesson of Job, seems to have more than one meaning. It applied, first of all, to great messages which might be taught by a succession of men in different ages. In this sense, ancient Egyptian scientists were resurrected both in Moses and in the Greek philosophers Pythagoras and Plato. This recalls his idea that the same primeval root (*hiéroglyphe sonore*) reappears in different languages, whatever geographical distance separates them. Secondly, it indicated the improvement of society, as in Leroux's exegesis of Job 17. Only in a letter written towards the end of his life[16] does he consider the resurrection of an individual, when he comforts a friend who has lost his wife: '*Vous l'avez perdue, vous la retrouverez.*'

The comments by Leroux and other additional characters occupy more than twice as much space as the biblical text. In the prologue he introduces 'la Morte', a lady who had given him a Bible. Leroux's prologue to the drama begins by telling how she appeared to him after her death when he had been unable to sleep, and bade him read the book of Job. When he awoke next morning he found his Bible open at that very spot, and he proceeded to read it, ever feeling that she was present. He records their reactions. On 2:9, for example, he admires the Satanic finesse of taking Job's wealth and children but leaving him with his wife. When Job's three friends arrive, to advance the false doctrine that Job's sufferings must have been deserved, Leroux explains to 'la Morte' why there are exactly three. Each, he says, illustrates the error that arises from stressing just one of the three indivisible components of man—knowledge, emotion and sensation. Eliphaz is the theologian, rich in knowledge; Bildad is the emotional priest; while Zophar is the scribe, more interested in facts than in ideas. It is Leroux who in fact utters (to 'la Morte') the opening words of the first act: 'What will these theologians say to this man, who is man in general, overwhelmed with grief?' He murmurs sympathy for Job, but has nothing but abuse for the friends; he considers them hypocrites, who do not believe the doctrine of earthly retribution that they preach (p. 224). Eliphaz represents the 'infâme sacerdoce' (p. 35), and to Bildad he cries: 'you are the one who will burn Jean Huss and Joan of Arc, you will grill Servet. That's all you're good for—stoking pyres.' As the drama progresses, the asides of Leroux and 'la Morte' become ever more frequent, until the biblical drama is almost lost from sight. In the last act, which has as many as forty scenes, he adds and argues with further characters—a crowd of 'positivist' phantoms, and the atheistic socialist Proudhon. The phantoms represent the philosophy of Auguste Comte, which was dominant in Leroux's day; confining itself to observable phenomena, it was not concerned with theological questions. Proudhon had once been Leroux's friend, but his socialism had become totalitarian, breeding racism, sexism and hatred of religious believers. In Leroux's portrayal, Proudhon appropriates for himself God's title 'I am that I am,' and understands it to mean that his human existence confers upon him the right to dominate others. In reply, Leroux declares that his opponents, like Zophar, have relied exclusively on what can be observed through sensation, and have ignored emotion, which is an essential component of man.

In an epilogue, he feels dissatisfied with the outcome of the debate. He asks whether the redeemer to whom Job looked forward had actually come. 'La Morte' replies that the redeemer was none other than Jesus, but Leroux could only sigh that man was not yet redeemed. After he had read the last verses of Job, he was even more dejected; if Job was a fiction, how real was the redeemer himself? The door of his room opened, and a man entered. Leroux recognized him as Jesus, who like Job had suffered oppression and demanded God's explanation. Leroux heard in a thunderclap a celestial voice proclaiming: 'The Christians have killed him, the socialists will share him.' In other words, socialism was now the true messianism.

In considering what motivated Leroux to undertake this translation, one must take into account his extensive citations and trenchant criticisms of the French translation by Renan.[17] Upon the sufferings that Satan had inflicted on Job, said Leroux, Renan had heaped yet more (p. 236). He charges Renan with falsification, when in fact Renan departed from literalness for the sake of idiom (e.g., in adding *encore* in his translation of 16:19: *car j'ai encore un témoin dans le ciel*). One reason for this hostility may be that Renan's version was the most recent and prestigious, with which Leroux's work had to compete. What particularly angered Leroux, however, were the racist doctrines which Renan expressed both in his work on Job and elsewhere. In his preface Renan remarked that the author 'like all Semites has no conception of the beauties of composition which result from a severe discipline of the mind.' The Semites were characterized by 'the complete absence of the scientific instinct' and were 'condemned never to go beyond the barren and grandiose simplicity of monotheism'. Projecting his racism on to the biblical authors, Renan took Job 30:3–8 to refer to 'the inferior races to which was hardly accorded the name of man'. These races, according to Renan, are excluded from the table of nations in Genesis 10 'because the Hebrews regarded them rather as animals than as men.' In his *Histoire*[18] he declares that the Semitic race, compared to the Indo-European, represented an inferior combination of human nature, bereft of any mythology, epic poetry, science, philosophy, plastic arts or civic life. Leroux rejects Renan's racist ideas, and affirms his own belief in the unity of mankind. He scorned Renan as the would-be successor to Cousin (p. 387), who, according to one of his followers, taught that the vanquished always deserve their fate.[19] This doctrine is of course that of Job's friends, which, on any showing, the book of Job sets out to refute; and in that light we can understand why Leroux argues so vehemently that Renan had missed the whole point of the book. And although Leroux could not match Renan's philological knowledge, he had a surer intuition of the evil to which Renan's racial doctrines could lead.

Notes

1 J. J. L. Blanc, *Révolution française. Histoire de dix ans* (Paris, 1841–4)

2 N. A. Berdiaeff, *Dialectique existentielle du divin et de l'humain* (1947), p. 55

3 W. Weitling, *Das Evangelium eines armen Sünders* (Munich, 1894)

4 A. Haimon, *Deux penseurs socialistes révolutionnaires: Pierre Leroux et Bernard-Lazare* (Doctoral dissertation, Aix-Marseille, 1979), p. 21

5 See J. Viard, *Pierre Leroux et les socialistes européens* (Le Paradou, 1983)

6 P. Leroux, *Job. Drame en cinq actes* (Paris, 1866), p. 434

7 P.-J. Proudhon, *Lettres au citoyen Rolland . . . présentées avec une introduction et des notes par Jacques Bompard* (Paris, 1946)

8 Bernard-Lazare, *Le Fumier de Job. Fragments inédits* (Paris, 1926)

9 S. Weil, *La connaissance surnaturelle* (Paris, 1950)

10 The main discussion in the Babylonian Talmud as to when Job lived (*Baba Batra* 15) offers a range of dates between the times of Jacob and Ahasuerus, but says nothing of

the age of Isaiah. The only reference to Isaiah in the discussion may be paraphrased thus:

> Rabbi Johanan said: Job's generation was steeped in lewdness, as it is said: 'Behold you have all *gazed* (*hazitem*), so why do you speak emptily?' (Job 27:12). Now 'gaze' indicates lewdness, for it is written (Song of Songs 7:1): 'Return, O Shullamite girl, and let us *gaze* (*we-nehezeh*, from the same root) upon you'. But it is objected that 'gaze' might instead indicate prophecy, as it is written (Isaiah 1:1): 'The vision (*hazon*, from the same root) of Isaiah'! This objection, however, falls; had 'gaze' in Job indicated prophecy, the verse would not have ended: 'why do you speak emptily?'

It is just possible that Leroux's connection of Job with Isaiah depends on some faint recollection of this passage.

11 H. Graetz, 'Die Integrität der Kapitel 27 und 28 in Hiob', *Monatsschrift für Geschichte und Wissenschaft des Judentums*, vol. 21 (1872), pp. 241–50

12 At 5:24b, where the Hebrew reads *u-paqadta naweka we-lo' teheta'*, Leroux's translation shows a parallel with the exegesis of Rabbi Joshua ben Levi (third century CE), preserved in TB *Yebamot* 62b. The phrase is normally translated: 'when you visit your home, you will find nothing missing.' Leroux and Rabbi Joshua, however, agree in interpreting *naweka* as 'your wife' (rather than 'your home') and *teheta'* in its usual sense 'sin' rather than 'find missing'. Leroux's respect for rabbinic tradition (p. ii) raises the possibility that he might have followed Rabbi Joshua. The conclusions that Leroux and Rabbi Joshua draw from the verse, however, are diametrically opposed. Rabbi Joshua explained that a man was a sinner if he did not 'visit' his wife, at least in certain situations, e.g. before setting out on a journey. By contrast, Leroux translates: 'when you visit your wife you will not sin', and his immediate comment (*Malthus lui-même, en ce cas, ne me refuserait pas sa permission*) shows that he considered sinful the very act that Rabbi Joshua prescribed as a man's duty. He does not therefore seem dependant on Rabbi Joshua's exegesis. One might perhaps suppose that he at least knew the common rabbinic interpretation of 'house' as 'wife' (e.g. Mishnah *Yoma* 1:1). The opposite, however, is suggested by the absence of any such reference in Leroux's defence of his translation of this verse against that by Renan (p. 282), who has the normal translation ('abode' . . . 'find missing'); had Leroux known of rabbinic support, he would have cited it. Most probably, therefore, this is yet another of Leroux's free translations.

13 See, e.g. S. R. Driver and G. B. Gray, *A Critical and Exegetical Commentary on the Book of Job* (Edinburgh, 1921); they do not, however, cite Leroux.

14 For Masclef's system and its influence, see M. Hadas-Lebel, 'Les études hébraïques en France au XVIIIe siècle et la création de la première chaire d'écriture sainte en Sorbonne', *Revue des Etudes Juives*, vol. 143 (1985), pp. 93–126.

15 P. Lachambeaudie, *Fables* (Paris, 1851)

16 P. Leroux to H. Darier, 19 September 1866; see Haimon (note 4 above), p. 187.

17 E. Renan, *Le livre de Job* (Paris, 1860)

18 id., *Histoire générale et Système comparé des langues sémitiques* (Paris, 1855)

19 See Viard (note 5 above), p. 59.

'Prinzessin Sabbat' by H. Heine in a Yiddish Translation by H. N. Bialik.

Chone Shmeruk

THE well-known poem 'Prinzessin Sabbat' by Heinrich Heine opens the cycle 'Hebräische Melodien' (after Byron's 'Hebrew Melodies'), which forms the third part of Heine's *Romanzero*, first published in 1851. This part of the *Romanzero* is considered as both 'the result and the expression of Heine's re-awakening interest in the Jewish tradition'.[1]

In the poem 'Prinzessin Sabbat', as in the two other works included in 'Hebräische Melodien', 'Jehuda ben Halevy' and 'Disputation', contradictory and ambivalent elements find expression which are characteristic of Heine's sentiments and opinions with regard to the various manifestations of Judaism. In 'Prinzessin Sabbat' the traditional Jew is presented as he might seem to a modern outsider.[2] The poem fuses 'caricature, realistically observed detail, allegory and symbolism into a complex whole; to show how the poetic and the prosaic [. . .] exist together [. . .].'[3] Revulsion expressed by mockery and emotional attachment based on sympathetic appreciation are here interwoven in the attempt to create an equilibrium between the detested weekday existence of the Jew and the admirable solemnity of the Sabbath which embraces him week after week. Yet irony, even sarcasm, are not absent even from the descriptions of the Jewish Sabbath.

Bialik's initiative in translating Heine's poem, or at least his willingness to undertake this work, can be interpreted as demonstrating his identification with the poem and the contradictory elements of which it is constituted, even though a certain measure of reservation about the original can be detected in his translation.[4] At the same time, one has to recognize in the Yiddish translation an indication of the great popularity enjoyed by the 'Prinzessin Sabbat' among those Eastern European Jews who, in the course of the modernization process, had come to relate ambivalently to their own Jewish experience. The poem represented their identification with the complexities of this experience.

The first translation of Heine's poem into Russian was published in the first Jewish periodical in the Russian language—*Razsvet* (no. 18, 23

379

September 1860). This weekly was published in Odessa and edited by Osip (Joseph) Rabinovich who was one of the first Jewish writers in the Russian language. But more instructive than the publication of this translation, as well as several other Russian translations of Heine's poems,[5] were the direct and indirect echoes of the poem in Jewish literature in various languages throughout Eastern Europe. It is almost certain that the first reaction of this kind appeared in a Russian novel entitled *Kaleidoscope* by the same Osip Rabinovich. Like the first Russian translation of the poem, the book was first published in 1860. In this novel the themes of Heine's poem are transplanted into a contemporaneous Eastern European Jewish environment in the region of Odessa, through the description of the Sabbath in a Jewish inn.[6] The brusque change from the profane to the sacred is presented here in direct reference to a legend 'which has been adapted into a poem by a well known German poet', without mentioning Heine explicitly.

We have no proof that Bialik was acquainted with the novel by Rabinovich, but there can be no doubt that he knew well the works of Shalom Jacob Abramowitsch (Mendele Moykher Sforim). From the 1860s on Mendele's Yiddish as well as his Hebrew writings contain both direct and indirect references to Heine's poem. They occur, for example, in the 1868 version of the Hebrew novel *Fathers and Sons*:

> You my afflicted people are an enigma to the Gentiles who knew you not! You are all riddles to them with your sadness of heart as you labour throughout the six days of Creation, and as you rejoice on the Sabbath and festivals, which you call a delight and which you honour by refraining from your daily tasks and not speaking of them! You puzzle them with your filthy clothes, your weekday rags, and with your splendid garments, silk and fineries on festivals! You puzzle them with the way you earn your livelihood, with your scant and inferior food on weekdays, and your pleasant bread—meat, fish and delicacies, with nuts and sweetmeats on the Sabbath, the day of delights! You puzzle them with the neglect of your homes [the loathsomeness] and the dirt which prevails in them during the working days, and with the purity of your dwellings and the pleasantness of your laid tables on the festivals and Sabbaths; [the kindling of your lights, the laying of your beds, your sons like olive saplings around your table, your wife sits by your side like a matron dressed in splendour with the scarf of purity on her head.] You are both slave and King! You are poor and rich! Your are naked and robed in splendour! You are starving and feasting! You are loathsome and beautiful, like the black tents of the desert dwellers or the tapestries of Solomon!
>
> You, my people, bewilder the nations who knew you not [. . .] On weekdays the Jew is a maggot, not a man, a caterpillar in its chrysalis, but on every Sabbath eve the caterpillar breaks out and *the worm of Jacob* is

suddenly transformed and turns into a man with a new soul and new feelings; he acquires a noble spirit. Then he sings to his bride, his beloved Sabbath, the hymn 'Come, bridegroom', and the dark spirit is passed and gone—this is his power unto his God'.[7]

The parallel with Heine's poem is quite obvious, even though the poet and his poem are not mentioned at all, and of the magic transformation only a faint echo remains in the reference to 'the worm of Jacob' which 'is suddenly transformed and turns into a man'. Lachover has pointed out that Bialik may have derived the same echoes of Heine's poem from *Di kliatshe* (*The Nag*) and *Dos vintshfingerl* (*In the Valley of Tears*), Mendele's later works in which the references to Heine's poem are more explicit. *Di kliatshe* is based on the idea of the Jewish prince's reincarnation as an animal, in this case a horse.[8] More directly—although again, without mentioning Heine's name—the same transformation occurs in Mendele's description of the Sabbath in the home of Shmulik the rag-and-bone man of *Dos vintshfingerl*. In a famous chapter of this book he contrasts the dog on weekdays with the prince on Sabbath days. Here the 'Princess Sabbath' in Yiddish and 'Sabbath the queen' in Hebrew are explicitly mentioned.[9] Above all, we have to remember that the Hebrew versions of *Fathers and Sons, The Nag* and *In the Valley of Tears* were all included in the three-volume edition of Mendele's collected works, which was produced by the 'Jubilee Committee' and published in Odessa between the years 1909 and 1912. Bialik was actively involved in the preparation of this edition and even wrote his famous article 'Mendele and the three volumes' as a preface to Volume 3. Moreover, Volume 3 also contained the story entitled 'For the Sabbath Day' where, towards the end, Mendele highlights the same contrasting features of traditional Jewish existence.[10]

What is common to Mendele's treatment of this subject and all the other literary echoes of Heine's poem is the transposition of the hero into an Eastern European reality, with the unequivocally positive evaluation of his Sabbath experience. This approach is marked by the evident inclination to pathos.

It appears, then, that Mendele was providing Bialik with reminders and echoes of Heine's poem and its subject-matter over a considerable number of years. Even if we consider as immediately relevant only the final compilation of all these reminders and echoes—the three-volume Hebrew edition of Mendele's works which had been prepared for publication shortly before Bialik's translation of Heine's poem into Yiddish—there is no doubt, as is evident in a number of expressions which occur in this translation, that Bialik had direct access to at least some of the earlier Yiddish versions of Mendele's works.

Heine's works were translated into Hebrew and Yiddish relatively late.[11] We know of no Yiddish translation of the poem before Bialik's. But two translations of 'Prinzessin Sabbat' into Hebrew had appeared earlier. One, by Solomon Mandelkern, was published in 1890, and the other in 1901 by Asaf Feferman.[12] The absence of a Yiddish translation may have prompted Bialik to respond to an invitation to translate the poem.

Bialik's is neither an exact nor an adequate translation, attempting to create in the language of translation exact equivalents of the language of the original; it is fairly free, following the conventional standards of poetic translation which prevailed during the nineteenth century. Bialik's Yiddish version is close in character to the Hebrew translations of the poem, where both alterations and cuts can be detected of which some occur in Bialik's translation as well. In any case, one can discern in Bialik's Yiddish translation an intentional toning down or even elimination of all the elements of caricature and mockery which characterize the German original. The same tendency had been displayed earlier by the Hebrew translators of the poem, especially Feferman. Lachover has already observed that Bialik left out certain sections of the poem.[13] In the German original there are 38 strophes of four trochaic, unrhymed lines, a total of 152 lines; 30 strophes, similar in construction, make up 120 lines in Bialik's translation. This discrepancy is highlighted by the fact that most of the strophes which are present in the translation are parallel in content with the original strophes. A similar abridgement occurred earlier in both Hebrew translations of the poem: Mandelkern's translation contains 34 strophes, Feferman's 39. Even though he occasionally widens the scope of one strophe in the original to two strophes in the translation, Feferman clearly skips over at least some of the same subject-matter which is later omitted by Bialik.

Heine devotes twelve lines to the figure of the cantor at the Sabbath eve service in the synagogue.[14] The cantor is vain and affected in his clothes and gestures:

> [...] *Schmuckes Männchen, das sein schwarzes*
> *Mäntelchen kokett geachselt.*
> *Um die weisse Hand zu zeigen,*
> *Haspelt er am Halse* [...]   (51–4)

In Mandelkern's Hebrew version we find nearly all the components of this original section. Its purpose is to emphasize the hollow vanity of the cantor, who is eager to impress with both his clothes and his good looks. To be sure, Mandelkern translates 'and with his prayer-shawl on his shoulder he endeavours to look handsome' and also 'to show his snow white hand he fidgets at his neck.' He makes changes only within the limits of accepted usage, and so instead of 'the little black coat' of Heine we find 'his prayer-shawl on his shoulder' with the word 'prayer-shawl' stressed in the translation, most likely in order to draw attention to the translator's emendation. Feferman retains the 'black coat' but leaves out the dandyism of the original, and he also omits the cantor's gestures.

In Bialik's translation the entire section is compressed into only one strophe[15] which sums up the cantor's appearance in a distinctly positive vein:

שטייט און וואַרט . . . אָט קומט דער חזן
אײַנגעהילט אין ווײַסן טלית
רופֿט ער אויס דעם זיסן רוף:
"לכה דודי לקראת כלה!"

Instead of the black coat 'a white prayer-shawl' makes its appearance, perhaps following Mandelkern's rendering of this line. The cantor's dandyish manners are left out altogether, perhaps following Feferman, and clearly in order to avoid disrespect towards the cantor. As D. Sadan has pointed out,[16] this is an elimination of 'the Jewish Reform Movement (Temple, Cantor)' and an effective transposition of the synagogue to an East European Jewish setting.

A further example will demonstrate with greater cogency the likelihood that Bialik was dependent on the two Hebrew translations, and at the same time bring to the fore the tendentiousness of his translation. Heine dedicated lines 97–127, seven strophes of the poem, to the Sabbath dish *tsholent* (*schalet*). His words of esteem for the dish are mingled with hyperbolical irony. Mandelkern reduces this section to two strophes, but he includes in them the comparison of the *schalet* to 'ambrosia, the delicacy of the Greek gods' and, as in Heine's original, the ambrosia compares unfavourably with the *tsholent* . . . Feferman dedicates eight strophes to the *tsholent* theme, but even here he omits a few points such as the reference to Schiller in line 103 of Heine, which Mandelkern similarly leaves out. In Bialik's translation of this section only three strophes remain:

איך וועל דיך דערפֿאַר באַלוינען
מיט אַ מאכל—טעם גן-עדן.
טשאָלנט הייסט ער—אָט דעם מאכל
האָט אונדז גאָט אַליין געגעבן

אַ מתנה פֿון זײַן נאָמען
מיט דעם שבת פֿון באַרג סיני
דורך די דונערן און בליצן—
טשאָלנט זאָלסטו מיר הײַנט עסן . . .

אָפּגעגעסן סעודת-שבת,
זיצט דער פּרינץ און שײַנט פֿון תּענוג.
מיט פֿאַרקלערטע אויגן קוקט ער,
רעדט עפּעס מיט זיך און שמייכלט:

Only a splash of Heine's irony has remained here. Like his predecessors, Bialik leaves out the reference to Schiller, but he omits also the comparison with the ambrosia of the Greek gods. Once again, however, a direct link to the Hebrew translations is uncertain. Bialik could have decided independently to leave out names and subject-matter which would not have been comprehensible to the ordinary Yiddish reader without further explanations. Sadan has already remarked that 'as a result of this twofold omission, Heine's work has been left deficient, for what remains is all glorification, while the element of irony is totally lacking. This is an organic element in Heine's poetry which Bialik, himself under Heine's influence, employs quite liberally in his own poems.'[17] At the same time, it must be stressed that in this Yiddish translation of Heine's poem, Bialik was adhering to what had become an established practice among Jewish writers in Eastern Europe, from Osip Rabinovich to Mendele, and to a certain extent also to the Hebrew translators of the same poem. All had read Heine selectively, consciously ignoring some or all of the scorn and mockery of the original. To this tendentious practice belongs also the transposition of the scenery from a West European to an East European setting, in the cases of both Rabinovich and Mendele. The same transposition is even more striking in Bialik's translation of the poem into the language of the Jews of Eastern Europe.

In spite of all probable links with the Hebrew translations which were available to him, there can be no doubt that in his Yiddish translation of the 'Prinzessin Sabbat', Bialik relied on Heine's German original. This is borne out by a number of German expressions which were taken over from the original into the translation, even in those instances where Yiddish could have provided perfectly adequate equivalents. Bialik translates the word *Hirt* (l. 132) as *pastekh*, shepherd (l. 103), but he leaves *Herdenglöckchen* as *herden-gleklekh* (ll. 129 in the German and 101 in the translation) even though the word *stade*, herd, would have been more appropriate in the Yiddish text. However, cases such as these are few[18] and they do not affect the quality of the translation.

The popular Jewish character of Bialik's translation is determined from the beginning of the poem, where Heine cites a tale from the *Arabiens Märchenbuch* ('Book of Arabian fairy tales'), as well as the story of a prince who had been turned into a hairy monster. Bialik substitutes these legendary sources with *Alte Bovo mayse* (l. 1), a phrase whose original source is the Italian chivalric romance *Buovo d'Antona* which, thanks to the translation and adaptation by Elijah Levita Bakhur at the beginning of the sixteenth century, became immensely popular among Yiddish readers until the nineteenth century, first as *Bovo D'Antona* and eventually as *Bove bukh* or *Bove mayse*. This is also the origin of the expression *bobe mayse*, whose literary origin has been obscured through the reading of the hero's name Bovo or Bove as *bobe*—grandmother in Yiddish.[19] The spelling *Bovo* occurs consistently since the first edition of Bialik's translation of the poem, and points to the fact that Bialik was well aware of the source of the expression and exploited its double meaning. In line with the Judaization of the original story, instead of the hairy monster of the German version, we find in Bialik's translation the *volkulak*, a werewolf (ll. 5, 12), which is known through the Hasidic hagiographical tradition as preserved in *Shivkhei ha-Besht*, a creature whose source is to be found in Slavonic folklore. This was also recognized by Lachover[20] and it is no accident that the *volkulak* occurs in Mendele's *Di kliatshe* as well.[21]

Indeed, the very first strophes of Bialik's translation determine its intended popular character. The tales of Bovo and the *volkulak* place the text in a completely different tradition from the one to which Heine's poem belongs. References to Schiller, to Greek gods and their ambrosia become superfluous and even out of place in a translation whose character is determined from the start by memories of Bovo and the *volkulak*. In tune with this approach, Bialik leaves out also the *Minnesinger*, troubadour (l. 67), the title which Heine had given to the author of 'Come, bridegroom'.[22]

The popular quality of Bialik's translation is articulated through expressions and idioms such as *beynashmoshes*, twilight (l. 86), and *di reynikeyt*, scroll of the Torah (l. 44), as well as *tam ganeydn*, luscious heavenly taste (l. 86) with reference to the *tsholent*, that takes the place of the ironic comparison with the pagan ambrosia. Most revealing is Bialik's utilization of the Yiddish translation of the Bible (*taytsh*) where Heine's text leads him in the Jew's dreams (ll. 97–100) to the biblical landscape of Jordan and Beyt-El:

הער איך נישט דעם ירדן רוישן?
איז דאָס נישט אַ קלאַנג פֿון קװאַלן
אין דעם פֿאַלמענטאָל פֿון בית-אל,
װוּ סע "הוירען" די קעמעלען?

From the first publication of the Yiddish poem in 1913, the word *hoyern* appears here, which is unusual in common Yiddish speech and is used only in *taytsh*, meaning 'to crouch'.[23] Bialik must have sensed the oddity of the word in spoken Yiddish, and from the edition of 1922 he enclosed it in inverted commas.

The cuts which intentionally change the character of the poem, the leanings on Yiddish conventions and traditions, the popular and idiomatic language, all these together have turned what is commonly referred to as Bialik's translation of Heine's poem into a conscious, calculated and tendentious adaptation. This adaptation is in tune with the prevailing attitude to Heine's poem in the Jewish literature of various Eastern European languages. Yiddish, the language of Bialik's translation, opened up additional and new possibilities, yet at the same time it prevented Bialik from reproducing directly certain parts of the original which were alien to the potential readers of the poem in Yiddish.

At the same time, it appears that Bialik's most immediate motivation for preparing this translation–adaptation of the 'Prinzessin Sabbat' was not his consciousness of the translation tradition and possible literary echoes of the poem in Eastern Europe, as discussed above. His adaptation appeared in an anthology entitled *Lekoved shabes un yontev*. The contents of the anthology suggest that it was published in Odessa before Passover 1907. It served as one of the means by which the Jews were protesting against the law making Sunday the compulsory rest-day throughout Russia. The Jews feared that the law would have an adverse effect on Jewish traders and artisans who observed the Sabbath on Saturday. Either they would be forced to close their businesses on both Saturdays and Sundays or, it was feared, such an economic sanction would prompt Jews to desecrate the Sabbath by opening their businesses.

The law was promulgated on 15 November 1906, together with another law restricting the number of daily working hours of all employees. Both laws were regarded as a step calculated to generate support for the government among the labouring masses in Russia, in anticipation of the imminent elections to the Duma.[24]

It seems that only at the beginning of 1907 were the Jews of Russia alerted to this threat. They embarked on a campaign against the law of compulsory Sunday rest: articles directed against it appeared in the Jewish press, the Jewish public was called to protest meetings and intense political agitation in the Duma was initiated.[25] The Central Zionist Bureau in Poland published a special proclamation on 'The Question of Sabbath Rest', and it invited all Polish Jews to sign a protest petition.[26]

The anthology in which Bialik's adaptation of Heine's famous poem appeared must be seen, therefore, as one of the expressions of protest against this law. On page 3 of *Lekoved shabes un yontev* was printed the statement that this was only the first collection of its type, and that the second would include 'protocols of all the meetings and sessions of the Sabbath Committee [in Odessa] as well as several articles'. It has not been possible to establish whether or not the second collection ever appeared. But even the first, which we do possess, indicates clearly by its contents that the aim and purpose of the booklet was to protest against the compulsory rest-day which interfered with Jewish tradition and all those who observed it. In addition to Bialik's adaptation of Heine's poem, it included a poem by B. Shafir entitled 'Pessah', and the first instalment of a story by Yona Rosenfeld, *Der farshterter shabes* ('The broken Sabbath'), with the next instalment promised in the forthcoming second issue. The main point of the collection was expressed in indignant and outspoken articles against the law, written by Y. H. R. (Y. H. Rawnitzki), Chaim Tchernowitz, Moses Leib Lilienblum and E. L. Lewinsky. Some of these articles refer to Heine's poem explicitly or allude to it. The following are Lilienblum's explicit remarks:

> Our ancient sages have said that on the Sabbath all Jews acquire an additional soul (a new soul, in addition to the one which dwells within the body permanently). It is true that young Jewish rebels have begun to make light of the words of our sages, and it is not difficult to find in Odessa a Jew who knows nothing of this new soul; but such a soul truly inhabits the body of any Jew who knows the flavour of the Sabbath. Even the poet *Heine*, famous throughout the world and a freethinker, sensed this with his whole being. Otherwise he would not have been able to write his famous poem, the 'Prinzessin Sabbat'.[27]

The publication of the Yiddish adaptation of Heine's poem in this collection points clearly to Bialik's motivation. It is immaterial whether he undertook the task of translation at his own initiative or in response to an invitation by the editors of the volume, one of whom must have been his close friend Y. H. Rawnitzki, who launched the collection with an article entitled 'Kheyrus' ('Liberty'). In this context, Bialik's adaptation acquires the significance of a national-political act, which highlights also the programmatic nature of his adaptation as a response to a topical issue. This explains the peculiarities of the adaptation beyond the influence of literary convention and the earlier references to the poem in the literature of Eastern European Jewry.

Notes

1 H. Heine, *Sämtliche Schriften*, ed. Klaus Briegleb, 12 vols. (Frankfurt a. Main–Berlin–Vienna, 1981), vol. 12 (commentary on vol. 11), p. 58.

2 S. S. Prawer, *Heine's Jewish Comedy* (Oxford, 1983), p. 555: 'it is a portrait from the outside, an unassimilated Jew partially seen by a Europeanized observer.'

3 *ibid.*, p. 561

4 Bialik's abridged (see below) Yiddish translation of Heine's poem, 'Die Prinzessin Sabbat (Heine)' was first published in the collection *Lekoved shabes un yontev* (Odessa, 1907), pp. 2–3. The booklet was produced in the printing press of H. N. Bialik and S. Borishkin, and it contains eight pages altogether. The poem is followed by the statement in Yiddish: 'Translated by B... ' Bialik included it in the 'Translations' section of his own collections of Yiddish poetry starting with the first: H. N. Bialik, *Poezye (Lider un poemen)*, Ferlag *"Progress"* (Warsaw, 1913), pp. 49–55. Since then, the translation has appeared, with minor alterations only, in all the subsequent editions of Bialik's Yiddish poems published both during his lifetime and after his death. Concerning Bialik's response to the invitation to translate the poem, see below. I am grateful to Mr Nathan Cohen for locating the earliest publication of this translation, and for his valuable help in other bibliographical searches connected with it.

5 Генрих Гейне, *Библиография русских переводов и критической литературы на русском языке* (Moscow, 1958), стр. 457.

6 «Калейдоскоп», *Сочинения О. А. Рабиновича*, vol. II (Odessa, 1888), pp. 93–5. The novel was first published in 1860 in the Russian periodical *Русское слово*.

7 From the final version in Hebrew of *Fathers and Sons*, ha-Avot ve-ha-Banim, kol kitvei Mendele Mokher Sefarim (1958), p. 46; the text in brackets appeared only in the 1868 version, pp. 123–4.

8 P. Lachover, *Bialik, Hayyav vi-Yetsirotav*, vol. 2, (Tel Aviv, 1944), pp. 722–3

9 In the second chapter of Book 3, the final version in Hebrew and in Yiddish. The text was first published in Yiddish in 1888, in the first volume of *Di yidishe folks bibliyotek*, edited by Sholem Aleykhem, pp. 56–60 according to the special pagination at the end of the volume. The Hebrew version was first published in *ha-Shiloah*, vol. 4 (1897), pp. 300–3.

10 The story was first published in *ha-Shiloah*, vol. 24 (1911), pp. 192–5. On Bialik's involvement with the publication of Mendele's writings in Yiddish and in Hebrew, see *The Correspondence between S. J. Abramowitsch, H. N. Bialik and Y. H. Rawnitzki, 1905–1908* (Hebrew), edited with Introduction and Commentary by Chone Shmeruk (Jerusalem, 1976).

11 M. J. Zweig, 'Heine ba-Sifrut ha-Ivrit', *Orlogin*, vol. 11 (1955), pp. 179–95; J. Raphael, 'Heinrich Heine in der jiddisch-literarischen Welt', *Heine Jahrbuch* (1970), pp. 140–7

12 On these translations, see Zweig (note 11 above).

13 Lachover (note 8 above), p. 722

14 See the text in Heine (note 1 above), vol. 11: *Schriften 1851–1855*, pp. 125–9.

15 The text is quoted here from the version I have prepared for the critical edition of Bialik's poems, edited by Dan Miron, which is currently being published by the Katz Research Institute for Hebrew Literature, Tel Aviv University, Dvir Publishing House, vol. 3, forthcoming.

16 D. Sadan, *Sugiyat Yidish be-Masekhet Bialik*, (ed.) D. Mashbits (Jerusalem, 1965), p. 18

17 *ibid.*

18 See also *hoheit*—line 129 of the original, line 101 of the translation.

19 On this, see C. Shmeruk, *Yiddish Literature: Aspects of its History* (Hebrew) (Tel Aviv, 1978), pp. 92–104.

20 Lachover (note 8 above), p. 723

21 p.47 of the Jubilee edition of his works in Yiddish, and the parallels in all earlier versions. In the Hebrew version Mendele omitted the *volkulak* altogether.

22 In Heine's original (l. 68), erroneously, Judah Halevi. Bialik has *Velt-barimter zinger*—the world-famous poet—without mentioning his name.

23 S. Noble, *Khumesh-Taytch. The Traditional Language of the Yiddish Pentateuch Translation* (Yiddish) (New York, 1943), no. 168, p. 60

24 A summary of this law, its significance and ramifications is to be found in *Еврейская энциклопедия*, vol. 14, pp. 597–9; cf. notes 25–6 below. I have not been able to find a comprehensive treatment of this issue.

25 An examination of the central organ of Russian Jewry, *Der fraynd*, published in St Petersburg, has suggested that the first item on the rest-day law appeared in issue no. 21, dated 26 January (8 February) 1907. Only in issue no. 37 of 14 (27) February did the paper carry the article entitled 'Zuntik ru' (Sabbath Rest) which was signed by 'a soykher' ('a trader'), and in issue no. 52 dated 5 (18) March 1907, the programmatic article 'Dos gezets fun Zuntik ru' ('The Law of Sunday Rest') appeared unsigned, reporting the details of the affair up to that date.

26 The proclamation by the Central Zionist Bureau in Poland was printed in the Zionist weekly *Dos yidishe folk* which was published in Vilna. It appeared in issue no. 8 dated 28 February 1907, and was accompanied by a list of Warsaw addresses at which it was possible to sign the petition against the law. The petition itself was published in the same weekly, in issue no. 15 dated 26 April 1907: 'Petitsye vegn shabes-ru' ('A petition against the Sabbath Rest'). The text was preceded by the statement that the Central Zionist Bureau in the state of Poland had presented the petition to the chairman of the committee for freedom of conscience in the Duma, together with 16,287 signatures of Jewish traders and trade employees in Poland.

27 M. Lilienblum, '*Shabes ru*', *Lekoved shabes un yontev*, p. 7. Heine's name is stressed in the original.

6

HASIDISM

Between *Yesh* and *Ayin*: the Doctrine of the Zaddik in the Works of Jacob Isaac, the Seer of Lublin

Rachel Elior

POLISH Hasidism has not, so far, had the benefit of exhaustive research from the social-historical, the theological or even from the bio-bibliographical point of view. As a result, this school of Hasidism has not yet been fully understood. First steps were taken by Dubnow, Aescoly, Mahler and Rabinowicz,[1] but none went so far as to produce a study in depth of the beginnings of Polish Hasidism and its development as reflected in the teachings of its leaders.

In the generation of the disciples of the Maggid of Mezhirech, Hasidism split into separate schools. Each of these was to emphasize different aspects of Hasidic doctrine and of the way of life incumbent on its adherents, while also generating different patterns of inter-relationship between the mystical heritage of Hasidism and its social manifestations. The schools, centred in different geographical regions, were characterized by the religious inspiration peculiar to their leaders and by the extent to which it could be adapted to the cultural and social circumstances typical of each region. Thus we can discern, at the end of the 1770s and throughout the 1780s, the emergence of various Hasidic centres, each taking on a character of its own, all over Eastern Europe.

Hasidism in Poland is generally reckoned to have begun with the activities of R. Samuel Shmelke Horowitz and R. Elimelech of Lyzhansk. R. Samuel Shmelke (1726–78), a disciple of the Maggid of Mezhirech, taught in Sieniawa, in the district of Lwów in Galicia, from the beginning of the 1760s to the first third of the 1770s. R. Elimelech settled in Lyzhansk, in Galicia, in the early 1770s and set up a Hasidic 'court' there which functioned until his death in 1787. It appears, however, that the emergence of Polish Hasidism as a widespread phenomenon is in great measure due to the work of the disciple of both these men, R. Jacob Isaac Halevi Horowitz, 'the Seer of Lublin'.[2]

R. Jacob Isaac personifies the stage at which new norms were being established for practical application in the religious renaissance which

Hasidism brought with it. He stands at the head of Polish Hasidism at the juncture when it is taking on a distinct character. For this reason, a study of R. Jacob Isaac can shed some light on this new phase in which Hasidism broadens the scope of its appeal, develops new patterns of leadership and crystallizes a theory which gives expression to this novel orientation.

R. Jacob Isaac has been the subject of several biographies based almost entirely on Hasidic tales.[3] These works are marked by their uncritical approach, presenting events out of chronological sequence and failing to distinguish sufficiently between, on the one hand, the issues which emerge from his books and the state of mind in which they were composed and, on the other, the conventions of late Hasidic hagiography. The figure of the Seer served as an important source of inspiration for many Hasidic tales; but these are concerned mainly with the last period of his life, in the nineteenth century. We have no direct evidence relating to this period either from the Seer himself or from his circle of associates. The depiction of this period in this literature thus falls into the realm of hagiography more than that of history.

The present study deals with the period in which R. Jacob Isaac began to exercise leadership, when he had not yet become widely known by virtue of his charismatic qualities and messianic reputation, and when his name was not yet associated with celebrated Hasidic controversies. Yet his principal works, *Zot Zikaron* and *Zikaron Zot*, were written during this inaugural period of his leadership, as we shall see below. These works reveal his inner doubts and his reflections on the nature of his mission, assessing the Hasidic teaching as a source of spiritual inspiration and as a new mode of religious life. Our premise is that his books are a faithful reflection of the author's outlook on the social setting in which he lived and on the place of Hasidic thought in his period and region. They form a religious document charged with the ideological tension which marked the emergence of Hasidism in Poland. An analysis of the subjects which are central to the Seer's works would highlight the change of direction which was taking place in the Hasidic movement at the time: breaking out of the domain of the chosen few and becoming accessible to wider circles. This change necessitated a reconsideration of the mystical values and social assumptions of Hasidism, as well as their consolidation round the figure of the Zaddik in his relationship to the community.

The present paper attempts to throw light on some of the theoretical constituents of the Seer's teaching and the circumstances which influenced its development. This would enable us to assess the importance of theological factors in shaping the Hasidic response to the problems which confronted the movement during the 1780s. We shall begin with a short biographical sketch and proceed to consider the principal aspects of the Seer's teaching.

BIOGRAPHY

R. Jacob Isaac Halevi Horowitz, known as the Seer of Lublin, was born in 1745,[4] in the small town of Lukow, near Tarnograd in the province of Lublin.[5] His father, R. Abraham Eliezer Halevi, who was known as the *iluy* (prodigy) of Szczebrzeszyn, was a scion of the Horowitz-Halevi family, a distinguished family of rabbis descended from the Shelah (R. Isaiah ben Abraham Halevi Horowitz).[6] He was rabbi of Josipow in Poland until his death in 1769.

R. Jacob Isaac grew up in Tarnograd in the home of his grandfather, R. Jacob Koppel of Lukow, a well-known scholar in his day.[7] He acquired his grounding in Torah in the *yeshivah* of R. Moses Zevi Hirsch Maisels, rabbi of Zulkowa.[8] From there he moved to the *yeshivah* in Sieniawa, Galicia, of R. Samuel Shmelke Horowitz, a pupil of the Maggid of Mezhirech and the first disseminator of Hasidism in Poland.[9] During the years when he was studying in Sieniawa, that township was a centre for the propagation of Hasidism, where scholars who later became famous as leaders of Hasidic communities had gathered round the figure of Samuel Shmelke.[10] R. Jacob Isaac quotes extensively from the teachings of R. Samuel Shmelke in his works and repeatedly refers to him with admiration and respect as his distinguished teacher.[11]

His years in Sieniawa were to shape R. Jacob Isaac's relationship to his Hasidic heritage, and to prepare him for his subsequent association with the Maggid of Mezhirech. Hasidic tradition numbers him among the disciples of R. Dov Baer of Mezhirech, but we have no precise details concerning his stay in the court of the Maggid.[12] He calls R. Dov Baer 'the Maggid of Rovno' and relies greatly on his teachings in his own formulation of the doctrine of the Zaddik, as will be demonstrated below.

After the death of the Maggid of Mezhirech in 1772, R. Jacob Isaac spent some time as a disciple of R. Samuel Shmelke Horowitz, who served as head of the rabbinical court in Nikolsburg, Moravia, from 1772, and R. Levi Isaac of Berdichev during his period of residence in Zelechow. With the death of R. Samuel Shmelke in 1778, R. Elimelech of Lyzhansk, a disciple of the Maggid of Mezhirech, became his mentor. R. Elimelech was the spokesman of Hasidism in Galicia who fashioned the patterns of Zaddikism as a social institution. He stood at the centre of the controversy with the Opponents of Hasidism in Brody and Krakow until his death in 1787.[13]

During the years R. Jacob Isaac spent in Lyzhansk, his conception of the role of the Zaddik as leader took definite shape. These years also served to crystallize his views on the ways of imparting the Hasidic heritage to wider circles, and it seems that in Lyzhansk, under the influence of his teacher, he turned his personal spiritual path into an ideological platform for a broadly based movement.[14] During this time, in the light of R. Elimelech's teaching on the nature of the Zaddik, he developed an inner consciousness of leadership as his destined role. This became an obligation, imposed by a sense of mission, to act in the interests of the community, and it was accompanied by the willingness to fight to achieve his way.[15]

From his books it emerges that the Seer was in close contact with several Zaddikim of the circle of the Maggid's disciples, and that he frequented the houses of R. Levi Isaac of Berdichev, the Maggid of Zolochev, R. Zusya of Hanipoli and others.[16] R. Elimelech withdrew from public office in his old age and, with his blessing, R. Jacob Isaac undertook the leadership of a Hasidic community in Lancut, in the district of Lwów in Galicia. In the books of the disciples of R. Elimelech, and in the works of the Seer's disciples, we have allusions to the special nature of this period of the Seer's leadership during the lifetime of his teacher. R. Shlomo ha–Cohen of Radomsk recorded the tradition which was current in the circle of the Seer's disciples in regard to the commencement of his leadership and its relation to the retirement of R. Elimelech from office:

> *One sometimes encounters a Zaddik whose holiness burns so fiercely within him that he cannot endure the society of a person who has committed minor transgressions and has not corrected them as he should, and as is known concerning our late master and teacher, the man of God R. Elimelech . . . in his old age his holiness was so very great that it was not possible for him to speak with those who sheltered in his shadow, the Torah seething as it did within him.*[17]

R. Elimelech was in his late sixties at the time, and his withdrawal from the leadership cannot easily be explained on the grounds of old age. It is not impossible that the words 'in his old age his holiness was so very great' conceal an additional reason to which the text is alluding discreetly. Be that as it may, according to Hasidic tradition, R. Elimelech was no longer able, in the evening of his days, to meet the twin demands of personal purification and self-abnegation, on the one hand and, on the other, sensitivity to the ordinary ways of life and the ability to respond to the needs of the Hasidic community. He preferred to retire from communal leadership and to entrust the day-to-day contact with his followers as well as the responsibility for public needs to his disciple, R. Jacob Isaac.[18]

The Seer's disciple, R. Kalonymos Kalman of Krakow, author of *Maor va-Shemesh*, alluded to this situation in his discussion of the anointing of Elisha in the lifetime of Elijah:

> Because of the great degree of sanctity and purity which Elijah had attained, his thoughts were beyond the reach of his contemporaries and it was impossible for them to receive from him instructions for their daily life. For this reason, when Elijah was offering his excuses to the Lord, blessed be His name—'I have been very zealous for the Lord . . . ' etc., the Holy One, blessed be He, replied to him: 'That is because their intelligence is insufficient to grasp your great luminosity and holiness; therefore anoint Elisha as prophet in your stead, for he is of lesser stature than you and they will be able to comprehend him and learn ways of life from him according to the measure of their understanding.'[19]

The stress on the disciple's inferiority to his master, and on the master's spiritual stature which transcends the intellect but is expressed as 'purification', 'luminosity' and 'holiness' as against the more prosaic character of the disciple, betrays the tension generated by the problem of succession, and by the conflict between pneumatic experience on the one hand and the demand for leadership in daily life on the other.

There is no doubt that the tension between the two poles of the Zaddik's existence is to be read between the lines: on the one hand, self-purification, holiness and seclusion; on the other, the contact with worldly affairs necessitated by the requirements of communal leadership. Moreover, the traditions cited above, and others like them, make it quite clear that the leadership of the Seer during his master's lifetime and in his place required some explanation and justification in the opinion of his disciples.

Hasidic traditions testify to the tension arising from the bestowal of authority on R. Jacob Isaac by his teacher, R. Elimelech, during the lifetime of the latter.[20] It appears that the tension sprang from the broadening of the scope of the Seer's leadership beyond what R. Elimelech had intended for him, and from the problems inherent in the transfer of charismatic leadership, as we shall consider below.

In regard to the years of his leadership in Lancut and Lyzhansk during the 1780s and 1790s, we have hostile evidence in the literature of the *Mitnaggedim*,[21] testifying to the extent of his influence and his charismatic image. Dubnow asserted that 'on his life in Lancut we have only the evidence of his opponents',[22] but he was mistaken, as were R. Jacob Isaac's other biographers, for the Seer's principal two works, *Zot Zikaron* and *Zikaron Zot*[23] were written during his years in Lancut, and afford first-class testimony on an important, early stage of the crystallization of the Hasidic community in Galicia.

It is clear that both works were written during this period. This certainty arises from the examination of quotations from other works which occur in *Zot Zikaron* and *Zikaron Zot*. R. Jacob Isaac frequently quotes his teachers and other associates, appending to their names the conventional blessings for the living or for the dead. He clearly wrote the greater part of his works after the death of his teacher R. Shmelke in 1778, since R. Shmelke is mentioned many times with the blessing for the dead. However, both R. Elimelech (1714–86) and the Maggid of Zolochev (d. 1786) were still alive at the time of writing and are often mentioned with the blessing for the living.[24] The books, therefore, were written after 1778 and before 1786, or between the end of the 1770s and the mid-1780s. One can be even more precise: the time within which his second work, *Zot Zikaron*, must have been written can be limited to the beginning of the 1780s onwards, for he mentions things which he saw 'in the holy book *Toledot Ya'akov Yosef*' by R. Jacob Joseph of Polonnoye, a book which was printed in 1780. The failure of the Seer's biographers to take into account this evidence regarding the period in which he wrote the bulk of his works has led to faulty assessments of various incidents in his life and to the application of erroneous inferences from later to earlier developments. It accounts also for the discrepancy between his portrayal in the hagiographical tradition, which deals with the last period of his life, in Lublin in the nineteenth century, and his image as it emerges from his own works, which were written at the beginning of his career.

The greater part of *Zot Zikaron* and *Zikaron Zot* was written, then, in the 1780s, when R. Jacob Isaac began to lead a community of the followers of R. Elimelech. These are the years in which Hasidism spread in Galicia and Poland and crystallized as a movement, establishing its own spiritual and organizational frameworks.[25]

This coincidence of the first years of his leadership with the spread of Hasidism in Galicia and Congress Poland lent an unusual perspective to his efforts to delineate the ideological characteristics and the unique social role of Hasidism, at a time when the movement was contending with the tension between the mystical élitism of its beginnings and the new requirements inevitably resulting from the broadening of its social base and the communal mission it had undertaken.[26]

R. Jacob Isaac's works are principally homilies on the weekly Torah readings which had been delivered before his followers on the Sabbaths; these are accompanied by autobiographical passages, guidance intended for himself,[27] notes on forgetfulness and memory[28] and 'new insights' or 'matters which have come to mind'. Unlike many other Hasidic books, written and edited by disciples and compilers, these books were written by the author himself soon after the oral delivery of his sermons. Seeing that one of them was printed without any textual or editorial amendment,[29] and the other without textual amendations but arranged according to the order of the weekly Pentateuchal portions,[30] they largely reflect the original manner of writing and the range of the problems facing the author at the time. One must of course allow for a certain disparity between the oral sermon and the text as written and printed, but in this case the disparity would be smaller than with other books of Hasidic homilies, because the sermons were written down by the speaker himself very shortly after he spoke them. It is reasonable to assume, therefore, that the written works are an authentic expression of the author's outlook and his response to challenging problems close to the time when they arose.[31]

The time at which these sermons and teachings were committed to writing is of the utmost importance. The works reflect the Seer's first steps on the road of leadership. Subsequently, in the course of his years as leader, he achieved great prestige and a central position in the Hasidic world on the strength of his exceptional spiritual powers and his style of leadership: during his residence in Lublin his name became associated with the Lublin–Przysucha controversy and the messianic struggle, with a mass following and with miracle-working; the books of his disciples testify to the powerful impression he made, and Hasidic legend, too, heaped praises on him. The only period of his life on which his own writings afford us an insight into his personal point of view is the initial period of his leadership in the 1780s, a period in which his charismatic status, his authority and influence had not yet been firmly established.

R. Jacob Isaac was the leader of Hasidism in Galicia and Poland for thirty years (1785–1815), but when he first assumed this position there were no fixed patterns for the leadership and consolidation of a Hasidic community, and no agreement on the scope of the Zaddik's operations, either in theory or in practice. This emerges clearly from polemical evidence preserved in various Hasidic traditions.[32] The need for clarification and definition was apparent.

R. Jacob Isaac's two works faithfully reflect the subjects which were of central concern to him in this period. Substantial sections of his homilies deal with the figure of the Zaddik and his role, while at the same time clarifying the relationship between the mystical heritage and the social aspect of Hasidism. The inner doubts arising from the definition of his role as communal leader leave their mark on all his writings. His works are characterized by a consciousness of changing leadership patterns, the extension of responsibility, and the change in the relationship between the mystical and social elements. The sermons are not arranged with the purpose of presenting a systematic formulation of speculative-theological teachings. They set out to clarify pragmatically the relationship between the spiritual objectives as taught by the Maggid of Mezhirech, the social objectives inspired by R. Elimelech of Lyzhansk, and the religious norms and conventions of the time. These in turn are considered within the framework of new leadership patterns, at a time when the need had arisen, on the one hand to define the special spiritual character of Hasidism and, on the other, to establish a religio-social framework for the life of the growing Hasidic community.

THE DOCTRINE OF THE ZADDIK:
PERSONAL, PROPAGANDIST AND POLEMICAL ASPECTS

The Seer's explanations of the doctrine of the Zaddik are not presented as a speculative construct but are drawn up against the concrete background of the crystallization of Zaddikism as an institution. They attempt to clarify, as a practical matter, the place of the Zaddik in relation to the needs of the Hasidic community.[33] In this he was clearly influenced by his teachers, the Maggid of Mezhirech, R. Samuel Shmelke of Nikolsburg and R. Elimelech of Lyzhansk. All three had laid down clear criteria governing the responsibility towards a community which falls upon its spiritual élite. They also established the ideal of a leader who works simultaneously on the metaphysical and the earthly planes, his spiritual authority imposing on him the duty to act in the interests of all Israel. Indirectly, the teachings of R. Jacob Joseph of Polonnoye also may have influenced the Seer's views on the position of the Zaddik in Hasidism. As we have seen, R. Jacob Joseph's book, *Toledot Ya'akov Yoseph*, was available to him and offered an extensive treatment of this subject.[34]

It is not our intention in what follows to examine the historical evolution of the ideas which make up the doctrine of the Zaddik or to subject them to critical analysis. We propose, rather, to focus on the problematics of the doctrine of the Zaddik in the Seer's teachings, and to throw light on some of its inherent values.

It is in the teaching of the Maggid of Mezhirech and in the circles of his disciples that a change takes place in the way the Zaddik is perceived. From being regarded as an individual privately realizing a religious ideal, he comes to be thought of as one who must accomplish both an ideal of holy life and a mission on behalf of the public.[35] R. Elimelech of Lyzhansk, Jacob Isaac's teacher, was of course the exponent *par excellence* of the doctrine which attributed to the Zaddik, earthly being though he is, the power to 'impose decrees' and exert supernatural influence on both the upper and the lower worlds. This was the doctrine which assigned to the Zaddik the task of 'drawing down' the divine 'flow' by virtue of his function as a mediator between heavenly and earthly existence. It was R. Elimelech who prescribed it as the duty of the Zaddik to secure, through his own service of Heaven, the satisfaction of the earthly needs of his followers, by means of a power which the Zaddik derived from his unique merit as a mystic, giving him special access to the worlds above. R. Elimelech subjected this theory to the test of practical application during the years of his own leadership.[36] R. Jacob Isaac accepted these basic premises, but although the teaching of the author of No'am Elimelech undoubtedly influenced his outlook, he himself had to grapple with the problem of the values of Hasidic leadership when he began to lead a community of his own and to apply the theory of the Zaddik in practice. This led him to reassess the place, purpose and conditions of Zaddikism, while expanding his range of spiritual concerns beyond the confines of R. Elimelech's thought. His reassessment reflects, first and foremost, the continuous transformation of the concept of the Zaddik from a theological principle rooted in Kabbalistic thought, inspiring the private spiritual lives of individual ascetics and mystics, into a concept which operated in the public-social domain and could be subjected to the test of practical application. The Zaddik was no longer conceived simply as an individual realizing a sublime religious ideal: he became the bearer of responsibility for religious leadership defined as both mystical and social. The complexity of this notion must be appreciated in full.

R. Jacob Isaac's conceptual innovations and the principles he laid down as a programme for Hasidic leadership reflect his deliberations on various aspects of mystical thought against a background of lively awareness of social considerations and great sensitivity to public needs. Here there appears clearly, in all its strength, the tension inherent in the mode of life of the Zaddik who, on the one hand, is sustained by spiritual and mystical forces which are the source of his authority and, on the other, is obliged to accept a mission on behalf of the community, and is confronted with the need to pass the test of public exposure. In other words, the concepts defining the mode of life of a Zaddik, while they had to reflect his inner consciousness of charisma, his spiritual authority and inspiration from on high, had also to apply to his role as a communal leader representing, so to speak, the personal embodiment of an idea.

Three issues were topical in the Hasidic world of R. Jacob Isaac's time and form the central core of his works:

1 The search for a definition of the nature of the Zaddik in his ideal as

well as in his earthly aspects, and the clarification of the changing relationship between the mystical and social elements of his role.

2 The search for a definition of the mutual relationship between Zaddik and community, establishing a link between the Hasidic ethos and the emerging doctrine of the Zaddik, together with an analysis of the sources of the Zaddik's authority and an examination of his response to the challenge of new responsibilities—the obligation owed by the élite to the community.

3 The clarification of the complex relationship between normative patterns of conduct and mystical-spiritual forces arising in the life of the Hasidic community at a time of religious revival.

In addition to the personal dimension of the struggle to shape a new pattern of leadership and to express the Zaddik's conception of his role, two other aspects of R. Jacob Isaac's teaching must be considered, which marked his appeal to the community. These were, first, the ideology of Zaddikism as organizational propaganda directed at circles of potential recruits into the Hasidic movement and, secondly, that ideology as a polemical posture confronting the conventional patterns of leadership. These two aspects are interconnected, since both aspire to shape a religio-social alternative to the existing order of society.

The elements of propagandism and an organizational ideology are both present in the Seer's exposition of the doctrine of the Zaddik; undoubtedly the doctrine helped to establish, and then mould, the social organization of Hasidism at that time. The dissemination of the teachings of Hasidism and the widening of the circles to which it directed its appeal were rooted in the conception which bound together leader and led in a direct and intimate bond.

An explicit expression such as 'for the Zaddikim who cleave to the Lord draw down a flow of holiness and awe to those who are at one with them' (*Zot Zikaron*, p. 36) testifies to a conscious effort to create a community in which the dependence of the individual on his unity with the Zaddik is the decisive value. The line of argument pursued is a tendentious one: it aims to demonstrate convincingly the importance and necessity of leadership by the Zaddik. It clarifies the spiritual and material significance of the ties between him and the community, and thus establishes new patterns of affiliation, responsibility and leadership.

Express statements as to the benefit to be derived from the affiliation with the Zaddik and the significance of the relationship of dependence and union occur repeatedly:

'Through his attachment to the Zaddik he will have delight in His light, blessed be He, which reaches the Zaddik and from him is drawn down to those who cleave to him' (*Zot Zikaron*, p. 140).

'Hold fast to a rebbe, who is called a father, and he will help you in every matter in which you have need, for he is attached to Him through the truth, which is God, and He will bless you' (*Diverey Emet*, p. 46).

'And if a man loves the Zaddikim greatly he benefits in regard to the service of the Lord in several respects in which he has difficulty if he is by himself but which, through his association with the Zaddikim, become easy for him because he attains *devekut* through their goodwill' (*Zot Zikaron*, p. 17).

'For even though everyone fulfils His commandments and occupies himself with Torah studies, it is not possible for each one acting individually to raise them sufficiently high, but rather one must compound one's study and actions with those of the Zaddikim, who serve with fear and love' (*Zot Zikaron*, p. 187).

'And anyone who is at unity with the Zaddikim will himself enter into eternal life because he is bound up with them' (*Zot Zikaron*, p. 35).

We have here a new emphasis on the difficulty inherent in the execution of both divine and worldly tasks, and on the need for help which recalls to the individual his dependence on his relationship with the Zaddik. This prepares the ground for a new basis on which to build the relationship and from which to draw the authority conferred on the Zaddik. The ideas are drawn in no small measure from the oral teachings of R. Elimelech of Lyzhansk and the written teachings of R. Jacob Joseph of Polonnoye. It appears, however, that R. Jacob Isaac regarded their views as not generally known, and deserving to be emphasized and propagated. He made them a basis for his own appeal to the public and his outlook on spiritual and social affairs.

The explicit statements that, through their affiliation with the Zaddik, people will benefit from 'drawing down the flow of divine bounty', that help is assured to them in all areas of material need, and that they will gain spiritual advantages also, are indications of the author's loss of confidence in man's ability to fulfil his duty of serving God by his own unaided efforts. At the same time, these statements suggest the renunciation of human responsibility for the material domain within the conventional framework of social-religious life. This amounts to the effective transfer of responsibility for both spiritual and worldly affairs from the ordinary individual to the Zaddik; and it sets the relationship between them on the basis of intimate links of 'guardianship': 'love', 'adherence', 'unity' and 'connection', as symbolized by the relationship of mother and child, nurse and nursling, shepherd and flock and so on. These premises which underlie the ideology of the Zaddik are stated in terms of 'the flow of divine bounty', 'life, children and sustenance', 'blessing', 'drawing down', 'raising' or 'binding up', and the like, all of which, in some measure, give expression to the casting of man's burden exclusively on the Zaddik who acts as mediator between man and God; for the possibility of man's casting his burden directly on God is rejected here. These concepts were a powerful influence on the emerging consciousness of spiritual and social ties of partnership and empathy, and in establishing patterns of loyalty and responsibility between the Zaddik and his community.[37]

The ability to invest man's specific needs with a wider significance, and to place his material and spiritual existence within the comprehensive framework of his relationship with the Zaddik was an important element in the endeavour to establish the doctrine of the Zaddik and spread the message of Hasidism. In his opening remarks R. Jacob Isaac states that the basic relationship of Zaddik and community is founded on the premise that the Zaddik and those who have affiliated themselves to him are joined together in a state of metaphysical unity and in the mutual commitment which derives from it. The Zaddik, who is compounded of all the souls of Israel and who identifies himself at the profoundest level with the essential quality of his congregants' existence, feels empowered to act on their behalf by the consciousness of the common destiny he shares with them and the mutual accountability of Zaddik and community, as well as by his sense of mission and responsibility towards them:

> As is known, he is [made up of] our souls; the Zaddik of the generation is our soul, for he is compounded of many of the house of Israel, as Moses was compounded of six hundred thousand; for this reason the Zaddikim love Israel greatly and sacrifice their lives for them, loving them as they love their own souls, for they (the Zaddikim) are compounded of them and they (Israel) are part of them (*Zot Zikaron*, pp. 11–12).

Joseph Weiss has already observed the decisive place occupied in the beginnings of Hasidism by the assertion that the bond between the Zaddik and his community was a matter of 'unity and integration', that is to say, of the spiritual affinity between them, founded on a metaphysical base;[38] but only with the development of Hasidism as a movement was this principle extended to apply to all aspects of life.

R. Jacob Isaac emphasizes the depth of this affinity and the principle of identification by comparing his followers to 'branches from the root of his soul'.[39] He identifies the expression of this unity in the deep love between the Zaddik and his close associates, as well as in the selfless devotion which characterizes the Zaddik's approach to his mission.

The emotional values on which the affinity between the Zaddik and his followers is founded are drawn from Kabbalistic metaphysical thought, but even without tracing their origin in the Lurianic doctrine of the sparks, there is no doubt that the sense of a shared destiny and the intimate bond between Zaddik and community exercised a decisive influence on the crystallization of the Hasidic community and the entire range of its expectations. It would seem that while the Kabbalah had provided the conceptual underpinning for the essentially social process of forging novel relationships and affinities, the force which triggered off this process was derived from a comprehensive world-view formulated in the doctrine of Zaddikism specifically in the material domain. The endeavour to forge a relationship of dependence, founded on the metaphysical unity between the Zaddik and his followers and his empathy with their earthly experience, resulted in a growing sense of brotherhood and communal responsibility. This was the inward-facing aspect of Zaddikism; alongside it we find its outward-facing polemical aspect, which emerged from a sense of dissatisfaction with the existing leadership and was formulated as a protest against its spiritual and social attitudes:

> '. . . that the congregation of the Lord be not like sheep which have no shepherd', for there are some who have gone forth for no other purpose than to pasture themselves,[40] that is to say, there are leaders whose desire is to gain honour and wealth and it is not their purpose to seek the good of the people. That is why Scripture says, 'that the congregation . . . which have no shepherd', and not 'them' (the people) (*Zot Zikaron*, p. 28).[41]

Seen through Hasidic eyes, this leadership is pictured as adopting an attitude of élitist isolation, as turning its back on the plight of the people and shrugging off its material and spiritual responsibility towards 'the men of the[ir] generation', a responsibility which is considered an obligation largely because of the world-view discussed above, which denies man's ability to face his spiritual and earthly tasks unaided, or even to do so by casting his burden directly upon God.

Against the extreme polarization between 'the leaders of the generation' and 'the men of the generation' as it is depicted in Hasidic polemics, the Zaddik's leadership offers a deep empathy, responsibility and commitment by the élite towards the community, coupled with great sensitivity to the spiritual and material plight of the common people:

> And thus all the leaders must study the needs of their generation in order to pray for them . . . that is why they are called *parnasim* (providers of sustenance, leaders) . . . And in connection with this Scripture says (Is. 49:23), 'And kings'—which is to be interpreted as 'our rabbis'—'shall be thy nursing fathers' . . . This means that they should consider your well-being and your physical health like a nurse (*Zot Zikaron*, p. 74).

These and similar passages present the relationship between the infant and his nurse as a model for the ties between the Zaddik and his community, a relationship of dependence and helplessness on the one hand, responsibility and loving care on the other. But the analogy may also conceal a hint of the intention to take over power and areas of concern which had traditionally been entrusted to the *Kehillah* organization,[42] in order to form an alternative to the traditional leadership. Altogether, it appears that religious and social powers which had traditionally been distributed among various communal institutions and authorities were gradually transferred, in Hasidic propaganda, to the area of responsibility of the Zaddik.[43] R. Jacob Isaac, writing at a time when Hasidism, through struggle and controversy, was becoming a real force in Eastern European Jewry, protested against the self-segregation of the scholarly élite and the obtuseness of the rabbinic leadership; he supplied a theological basis for the social obligations laid upon the Hasidic leader, while at the same time clarifying the similarities and differences between the two conceptions of leadership.[44]

These controversial views naturally excited no little criticism in the ranks of the existing leadership, as emerges clearly from the literature of the *Mitnaggedim*. Zaddikism, and the realization in practice of the Hasidic style of worship, roused both rabbinic circles and *Maskilim* to public denunciation and humiliating, scornful responses.[45] And indeed, R. Jacob Isaac's teaching displays a keen awareness of the criticism levelled against the Hasidic leadership, and of the attempts to discredit the modes of worship which were emerging under its inspiration. He does not, however, attempt to refute his critics, but holds that the viewpoint of 'the quarrellers, the mockers and those who put to shame' should not be taken into account, because in his opinion the values of Zaddikism are not susceptible to criticism by society and should not be judged by traditional norms. This is because their authority derives from the inner mystical truth possessed by the Zaddik and from his consciousness of mission, while on the part of his followers this authority is validated by the very fact of the social response to the Zaddik's mission, expressed in the formation of Hasidic communities built on a new basis:

> For when a man desires to serve the Lord, blessed be He, in truth, he must first beware of being concerned if people quarrel with him and mock him and seek to put him to shame, for that is the way to begin with, and afterwards if a man does not allow his to affect him, people join him, as it is said (Prov. 16:7), 'When a man's ways please the Lord, He makes even his enemies to be at peace with him' (*Zot Zikaron*, p. 76).

The response from society validates the religious path of the Zaddik and confirms the truth of his service of Heaven;[46] he does not, therefore, need to reply directly to the arguments of his opponents but prefers to clarify in principle the nature of charismatic leadership and the measure of commitment to the demands of public office which is required of the élite.

To sum up, in the writings of R. Jacob Isaac the doctrine of the Zaddik in relation to society was informed by factors operating on three levels:

on the personal level, the Zaddik's inner consciousness of spiritual authority presented him with the challenge of forming a community united by its response to his charisma. He had to subject the ideals of Zaddikism to the test of practical application under conditions actually encountered in the daily experience of leading a Hasidic group.

on the level of organization and propaganda, the crystallization of the doctrine of the Zaddik became central to the process of establishing Hasidism and determining its distinct character at the time when the movement was spreading throughout Eastern Europe.

on the polemical level, the responsibilities of the Zaddik were so formulated, and his relationship with his followers so defined, as to amount to a protest against the values of rabbinic leadership and its social attitudes, while at the same time presenting an alternative to these traditional values.

In addition to the external circumstances which determined the nature of the Zaddik's relations with society, four internal factors appear to have marked out his unique spiritual constitution according to R. Jacob Isaac:

1 charisma anchored in spiritual authority which derives its strength from the consciousness of direct contact with God.

2 the dialectic tension between the divine 'nothing' and the auspicious flow of divine 'bounty' on which the existence of the Zaddik is founded, a tension reflected in his self-annulment and humility on the one hand and his ecstatic exaltation and *devekut* (attachment to, communion with, God) on the other.

3 a call to operate simultaneously on the metaphysical and earthly planes, or to maintain contact with the divine 'nothing' (*ayin*) and the material 'being' (*yesh*), which requires conflicting states of consciousness.

4 the explicit imposition of responsibility for the material prosperity of the community, which implies the rehabilitation of materiality and its restoration to the realm of religious thought, while linking this process with the dialectics of the Zaddik's existence.

Each of these four interconnected factors will be separately considered in order to clarify the distinctive nature of each one and to assess their relative importance in shaping R. Jacob Isaac's concept of Zaddikism.

CHARISMA

The Zaddik's leadership is founded on the recognition of charismatic authority—the gift of divine inspiration graciously bestowed by God.[47] This recognition is expressed unambiguously in R. Jacob Isaac's opening pages: 'that the Creator, blessed be He, empowers the Zaddik to act' (*Zikaron Zot*, p. 25). The assertion is explained from various angles throughout R. Jacob Isaac's works—'for the Zaddik's soul must . . . be purified . . . in order that he should be prepared for the inspiration of His holiness, blessed be He, upon him and within him' (*ibid.*, p. 73).

The direct contact with God which occurs during ecstatic exaltation endows its subject with supernatural authority and a charismatic quality together with the sense of mediating between the upper and the lower worlds, and a powerful consciousness of mission:[48] 'the Zaddik is above the masses, *and in his root the divine bounty flows in spiritual form*, and the light of His holiness, blessed be He, reaches him' (*ibid.*, p. 2); 'for the Zaddik must . . . draw down divine bounty to the world . . . and in this respect the Zaddikim are called *malakhim* (messengers, angels) in the sense of performing a mission, for the Zaddik executes His mission, blessed be He, to do good to His creatures' (*ibid.*, p. 139); 'and he must also ask for mercy upon Israel, and in regard to this he is called '*angel-like*' and 'His emissary', blessed be He, to draw down good to Israel . . . and he has divine inspiration which is given to him so as to know what is necessary and when it is necessary and how to act . . . and he effects *Yihudim* ('unifications' of distinct aspects within the Divinity and its Creation) like burning fire' (*Zot Zikaron*, p. 206).

The charismatic quality of the Zaddik as it is understood by him and others is to be found in his relation to God and his decisive influence on essential aspects of human existence by virtue of this connection. The power of this charisma to establish, create, maintain, guide and alter vital areas in the life of man bestows on the person who is favoured with it a supernatural status setting him apart from ordinary mortals, as well as an awe-inspiring authority drawing its strength from a transcendental source.[49] The greater weight given to charismatic authority in Hasidism can be recognized both in the Zaddik's own awareness of his role as a medium of divine forces and in his deep conviction that he is acting under the inspiration of God and is revealing information imparted to him by divine revelation.

Naturally enough the Zaddik does not elaborate on the exact nature of this inspiration, but he does allude to it and invoke it as the source of his authority, for in his view there is concealed in the Zaddik a power which points beyond his own being to his Creator, and in every action of his there is, as it were, the power of a symbol to throw light on what lies beyond it. At the beginning of his address to his followers R. Jacob Isaac indicates that the source of his authority is in the flow which he draws down from Heaven and which is quite distinct from conventional human knowledge: 'Hearken to [that which is] from Him and incline your ears to me, for I do not wish to say what I know but what has been imparted to me from the Lord, blessed be He, for you' (*Zot Zikaron*, p. 6). The charisma is drawn from personal revelation and the express connection with a wondrous and supernatural power. Indeed, it can clearly be seen that the spiritual authority in the name of which he addresses his audience is based on transcendental inspiration, an inspiration which invests his authority with an aura of mystical certainty.[50] The authority discovered within himself through illumination from on high is conditioned internally while being justified externally. Internally, the recognition of the profound lowliness of human existence, and the sense of its abnegation in the face of divine plenitude, condition the flow of divine forces to the Zaddik. Externally, the consciousness of his mission to his community and all Israel is the justification for the illumination from Heaven which he has received. As to the internal requirement of humility: 'It must be firmly established in your heart that it is not by your righteous acts that you have achieved this but by the grace of God, who helps those who come to purify themselves and is near to all who call upon Him, for you must thoroughly grasp your lowliness' (*Zot Zikaron*, p. 25). Set beside this is the external justification: the Zaddik is favoured with help from on high for the benefit of the 'world'—the community—on behalf of which he is executing his mission. Through this help he is concerned both in the discovery of spiritual levels of existence and in drawing down material bounty: 'And Jacob journeyed from strength to strength and so achieved spiritual vision . . . which means a higher level at which he is privileged with vision not only in regard to his own affairs but also to the needs of the world' (*Zikaron Zot*, p. 27). 'People must associate themselves with the Zaddikim of every generation, for they do not ascribe merit to themselves and the Lord is with them and also they have explored their own humility and they are helped from on high, particularly for the needs of the world' (*ibid.*, p. 34).

The external expression of the gift of charisma is bound up with the tension between the esoteric and the exoteric. Careful consideration is required as to the extent to which it may be disclosed and as to the danger of revealing the meaning of the most exalted insights and their possible repercussions. R. Jacob Isaac points this out many times in his 'guidelines': '. . . and to be very careful not to disclose any matter which is not known to everybody' 'and to beware of disclosing anything in the nature of prophecy, and if it is necessary to do so, to do it with great wisdom with the help of God, blessed be He' (*Diverey Emet*, Guidelines [*Hanhagot*], p. 8).[51] The great caution thus demanded in regard to the disclosure of spiritual insights is clearly indicated as the lesson to be learned from a specific historical incident which is invoked by R. Jacob Isaac and quoted in his name by his disciple R. Zvi Hirsch of Zhidachov:

> I heard this from my teacher, of blessed memory [the Seer], who said of those disciples, in reference to what occurred when a certain sect embarked on that notorious sacrilege in the days of the author of the *TuZ* (R. David ben Samuel Ha-Levi: *TuZ = Turey Zahav*). It occurred, he said, because they wanted to attain the divine insight of Elijah, the gift of prophecy and the holy spirit, by means of the manipulation of divine names, but they did not subdue their natures or control their material desires, nor were they free from guilt, nor did they take heed to themselves, but they pursued wonders which lay beyond their grasp and meditated [the mysteries of] divine unification . . . without purifying their material existence; and they depicted the forms of the supreme beings under the celestial chariot. In consequence of this they were overcome by lecherous forms and thoughts (from which Heaven preserve us), and that which we know of occurred, Heaven save us. Such were the words of my teacher. He also said, in the name of the Baal Shem Tov, whose soul rests in the storehouse on high, that those foolish people had learned this skill without the ability to tremble for fear of Heaven. They therefore gave corporeal form [to the celestial beings] and thus they stepped out of bounds.[52]

The 'sacrilege in the days of the *TuZ*' is of course an allusion to the Sabbatean movement, on the failure of which the Seer was expressing his opinion. From the bitter lesson of the attempt to attain divine inspiration without the restraints of esotericism, self-purification and fear of Heaven, he inferred the vital need for extreme caution in the pursuit of spiritual insight, since such a pursuit opened up the danger of false interpretation and 'materialization', and could lead to sectarian heresy. Esotericism, caution, submission, humility and self-purification were restraints which must be accepted by anyone contemplating the disclosure of spiritual insights to the public. The Seer outlined both external and internal criteria for testing the authenticity of such disclosures.

The charismatic dimension of the Zaddik and his role as divine agent, rooted in spiritual authority and in the certainty of his connection with the worlds above, is demonstrated by the constant flow of words of Torah which emanate 'from on high',[53] and by a capacity for supernatural action which manifests itself in supertemporal knowledge and the ability to perform 'miracles and wonders'.

Both aspects of the Zaddik are conditioned by his inner acceptance of the uncompromising demands of life in the presence of God and by his capacity for self-abnegation. He sees himself as worthless and devoid of substance in face of the plenitude of God: '. . . and it is of the first importance that man's sense of shame before the Creator, blessed be He, should never leave him; for He is before us and behind us and fills all the earth; there is no place where He is not; He observes our thoughts and the secrets of the heart, and we must always bear this in mind, at all events, and feel shame before Him' (*Zot Zikaron*, p. 4).[54] A clear-cut expression of the same attitude, in the first person, is found in his 'guidelines': 'I am resolved to be very lowly in my own eyes, at all events' (*Diverey Emet*, p. 8).

The transmission of new words of Torah from Heaven is the first criterion by which to judge the validity of any claim to charismatic authority and the certainty which is based on transcendental inspiration. This is emphasized in R. Jacob Isaac's earliest writings: 'Behold, I am about to commit to writing those new insights which the Lord, blessed be He, has helped me to acquire and communicate in the sessions of companions (*haverim*) hearkening to my voice, my voice being [directed] towards Him . . .' (*Zot Zikaron*, p. 4).[55] The disclosure to others of new interpretations of the Torah imparted from Heaven is a source of 'great vitality' (*hiyyut gadol*) and 'ardour' (*hitlahavut*), or a sort of ecstatic illumination which brings about an emotional change in the speaker; this, in turn, radiates upon his audience: '"Creatures of fire speak"—this means that one should not speak except through the vital force of the Torah and ardour for love and fear of the Creator, blessed be He, who is called *shalhevetyah* (flame of the Lord: S. of S. 8:6) . . . which means that one should not speak until visited by the great vitality (*ha-hiyyut ha-gadol*) and ardour, which is the creatures (*hayyot*) of fire speaking with power' (*Zot Zikaron*, p. 18).

Power, fire, ardour, *ha-hiyyut ha-gadol*, flame and love—all these expressions convey some idea of the strength of the emotional experience involved in this illumination, and of the ecstatic change it brings about in the person who is its subject. It made a strong impression on those who witnessed it, and may be regarded as having created a unique pattern of affiliation with the Zaddik: 'and everyone who receives [instruction] from him, and listens to his teaching and his prayer, has within him light from the Zaddik's soul, as we know' (*Zot Zikaron*, p. 76).

The shared experience of the Zaddik's ecstatic piety and its strong effect on his audience is again alluded to by the Seer: 'that the Torah should be received with fear and awe and trembling—this must apply at least to the reading of the Torah in public and to public sermons' (*Zot Zikaron*, p. 18). This shared experience became, in itself, a source of religious authority, for the sense of direct contact with the sphere of the divine during the Zaddik's religious exaltation in the presence of the congregation conferred on him supernatural status and authority.[56]

The second criterion of charismatic authority is concerned with the earthly aspect of this illumination and its relation to the general good: it is the ability to influence the upper worlds and to perform miracles. R. Jacob Isaac gives twofold expression to his views on this sensitive issue, mixing the objective with the subjective and the description of reality on the ideal plane with his sense of being a Zaddik performing wonders on the earthly plane: 'The tabernacle of testimony—this means that His tabernacle should also be over us in this way, to perform miracles and wonders for the good of Israel, and this is a testimony that the divine presence, which answers whenever we call, dwells in our midst' (*Zikaron Zot*, p. 73); '. . . and they (the Zaddikim) are also called angels of the Lord of hosts because thereby they perform miracles and wonders, for the Lord is with them' (*ibid.*, p. 139). The charismatic leader acquires his authority by proving his ability to perform miracles, and recognition of this ability by his followers is a crucial test of his charisma. This recognition is unreservedly assured him when a sign or proof of a miraculous nature is given.[57] But it is in the nature of the charismatic power that it must constantly be proved, which is why the Seer repeats several times in his prayers a request which he puts in these terms: 'And we ask . . . for example, that He may give help to the helpers of those who come to be purified, and also to the Zaddikim of every generation to perform miracles and wonders and the like, in order that the house of Israel may draw near to the Creator, blessed be He' (*Zot Zikaron*, p. 192).[58]

The mystical experience and the possession of charisma must prove themselves by activity within society, according to R. Jacob Isaac, since the internal dialogue between the individual and his God cannot legitimate them or give them suitable expression.

The ability to influence the upper worlds is bound up with the good of Israel as both a condition and an aim: 'But he should know that every response to him by the Lord, blessed be He, even in the form of miracles and wonders, is granted by God's grace for the good of Israel . . . therefore to anyone who knows this it is possible to reveal the secrets of the Torah and He will perform miracles and wonders through him for the good of Israel' (*Zot Zikaron*, p. 5). The test of the authenticity of ecstatic and spiritual experiences is in social activity and its public manifestation. For this reason, the Zaddik's activity in the upper worlds is not theurgic, as in Kabbalistic tradition, but it takes on an earthly character, with the function of helping the whole community of Israel. This help, which is defined as responsibility for 'children, life and sustenance', consists of the manipulation of magical power in the material world and the ability to influence the will of the Creator. Indeed, the ability to effect supernatural change in the material world plays a central part in the Seer's doctrine, for he regards the social sphere as the appropriate arena for the display of the Zaddik's spiritual power.[59]

The focus, then, has shifted from the upper worlds to earthly existence. The mission of the Zaddik to his community is based on the premise that the community needs an emissary who will cause divine bounty to flow down for them from on high and who will represent its earthly interests before Heaven. The following quotation illustrates how strongly R. Jacob Isaac was imbued with the sense of mission—on the one hand imposed by God and conditioned by a consciousness of personal lowliness, and on the other derived from mystical experience and the religious authority thus acquired: '"And this is the sign that it is I who have sent you" (Exodus 3:12): the straightforward meaning is as follows: "this" refers to my request that you, rather than any others of Israel, should undertake a mission. To this you say, "Who am I?" and are humble; "this", then, "is the sign that it is I who have sent you", for you go in perfect truth' (*Zot Zikaron*, p. 195).[60]

The emphasis on the relationship between the gift of charisma and the mission on behalf of the public which it imposes recurs throughout the Seer's teaching: a person who is granted help from on high receives this privilege for the benefit of the world. The idea of mediation between Heaven and earth by chosen individuals is fraught with far-reaching dialectical possibilities, as will be shown below. However, its main point is that those to whom the favour of Heaven has been granted and who are called upon to carry out a charismatic mission must acknowledge their special quality and act upon it, since the measure of the truth and significance of their mystical experience is the execution of the mission on behalf of the community. The mystical experience in itself, and a life of spiritual purity and seclusion, do not fulfil the requirements of the doctrine. R. Jacob Isaac saw himself as carrying a heavy burden of responsibility through his spiritual inspiration and insight; he was a leader by virtue of his ties with higher worlds, which enabled him to draw down benefits from those worlds.

It was this premise which guided him in his disclosures of Torah and in the spiritual leadership of his community, just as much as it underpinned his claim of exclusive responsibility for the material affairs of 'children, life and sustenance': 'For in every generation there are Zaddikim who set right and correct their ways before the Lord and cause the many to be righteous . . . for they have attained the holy spirit, because they have walked in the path of truth' (*Diverey Emet*, p. 42). The interconnection between the Zaddik's attainment of the holy spirit on the one hand, and his duty to the public on the other is a complex one: cause and effect, and the precise channels of mutual influence between these two poles of the Zaddik's existence, are not clearly distinguished, but there is no doubt that such a connection exists in the view of R. Jacob Isaac. He sees the authority to exercise leadership as drawn from mystical insight and the spiritual inspiration as tied to concern for the public good. A similarly complex link exists between the new social realities of Hasidism and the mystical values which underlie them. The identification of this link is complicated by the fact that the social-historical data to which we have allusions in the texts come to our notice through the subjective medium of the Zaddik's consciousness, but there seems no reason to doubt the central position of the consciousness of charisma in determining the pattern of relationships within Hasidic society at the end of the eighteenth century.[61]

AYIN AND *YESH* IN ZADDIKISM

R. Jacob Isaac bases the theology of Zaddikism on the dialectical Kabbalistic concepts of *ayin* and *yesh* and their ethical and mystical metamorphosis in Hasidism—*ayin* ('nothing') corresponding to 'submission', 'humility' and 'self-abnegation', while *yesh* ('being', 'existence') corresponds to 'expansiveness', 'bounty' and 'drawing down'. Both the internal and the external aspects of reality are to be explained, as he sees it, in the light of these concepts. The absorption of this double set of values into the inner consciousness of the Zaddik in his relationship to God and the world is a central theme of the Seer's writings.

In Kabbalistic thought, *ayin* and *yesh*, or the divine and the material, the two ontological opposites of human consciousness, are transformed into two modes of divine existence which complement and condition each other. In Hasidic thought they become ambivalent opposites which condition each other at both levels of meaning.[62] *Ayin* in its divine sense is the source of all *being*, but it is also, in its human application, the embodiment of nothingness, complete nullity or non-being.[63] *Yesh* in its divine sense signifies the essence of all being; in its earthly meaning it relates to corporeal, material existence.[64] These two opposites are described in the Lurianic system as *haatsalah* and *tsimtsum* (emanation and contraction) or *hitpashtut* and *histalkut* (spreading out and withdrawal).[65] The emanation, the spreading out and the flow of bounty reflect the transformation of *ayin* into *yesh*, or the drawing down of divine 'being' from on high to the world below, while contraction and withdrawal signify the transformation of *yesh* into *ayin* or the divine dynamic of a return from worlds below to worlds on high.[66]

In parallel with the two dynamic modes of divine existence, *hitpashtut* and *histalkut*, the Zaddik's existence embodies two opposites on which his religious experience is founded. The first is *devekut*—communion with God, exaltation and the 'drawing down' of divine bounty—which are parallel to the emanation and flow of the divine 'being' or the transformation of *ayin* into *yesh*; the second is self-abnegation (*bitul*), submission and humility, corresponding to divine withdrawal and contraction, or the transformation of *yesh* into *ayin*.

Just as, in the Lurianic dialectic, there is no flow or emanation in the absence of contraction and withdrawal, so, in the dialectic of the Zaddik, there is no unification, exaltation, or communion with God, nor any drawing down of divine bounty from the upper to the lower worlds, in the absence of *bitul ha-yesh* (annihilation of material existence), acknowledgement of lowliness, and awareness of the insubstantial nature of human existence.[67] To fulfil the basic conditions of Zaddikism as a reflection of the two opposite modes of divine existence, the Zaddik must be conscious of these two extremes within him: he is 'the lowliest of men, and the worst', but at the same time he is the man who can operate in higher worlds, 'who can work miracles and wonders': 'for a man who is humble . . . can perform miracles and wonders for the good of Israel' (*Zot Zikaron*, p. 2). The relationship known to Jewish tradition between man's self-abasement and his spiritual elevation and proximity to God[68] changes in the perception of the Seer into the contradiction inherent in the nature of one who realizes in his own person both the *ayin* and the *yesh*. The Zaddik who reduces his material self to 'a desert', 'no man's property' (*hefker*) and 'a trampled doorstep', is the same person who is elevated to the level of bestowing bounty and doing good 'in righteousness and loving kindness' (*Zot Zikaron*, p. 80) in his capacity as a person connected with the divine *yesh*: 'If he makes himself like a desert, withdraws from materiality and does not think of corporeal pleasure . . . it is given to him to draw down bounty of every kind' (*ibid.*, p. 111). It is, indeed, man's transformation of himself into *ayin* which determines his unification with the divine *ayin* and the Zaddik's transformation of this *ayin* into *yesh*, as will be demonstrated below.[69]

Indifference to the values of this world, recognition that man is of little worth and the consciousness that he is as nothing compared to the fullness of God are among the basic values of the Hasidic ethos.[70] Their purpose is to wrest man away from his material existence in order to establish in his consciousness a change which prepares the way for the attainment of *devekut*. This emerges clearly from the words of the Maggid of Mezhirech: 'And man must separate himself from all materiality to such an extent that he ascends through all the worlds and becomes one with the Holy One, blessed be He, until he is annulled from existence; and then he may be called Man.'[71]

In the doctrine of the Zaddik a new purpose is added to the well-known mystical aim of separation from materiality and unification with God. It is the drawing down of divine bounty to earthly existence; that is to say, the ways previously mapped out by which the boundaries of the material world could be breached and mystical experience attained by the individual now became a means of achieving a twofold purpose, directed on the one hand to the ascent to *devekut*—from *yesh* to *ayin*—and, on the other, to the drawing down of bounty to earth—from *ayin* to *yesh*. Moreover, the drawing down of bounty by the Zaddik became a touchstone of his spiritual transformation, which had previously been a goal in its own right: 'Whoever makes himself as nought (*ayin*) can come and draw down [good] from there (i.e. from the *ayin*) as was said by the rabbi, the Maggid of Rovno, on the Talmudic statement '*eyn mazal le-Yisrael*' (Israel is not under the influence of any planet [*mazal*]), 'one who makes himself as nought can draw down *mazal* (interpreted as meaning 'the divine flow')[72] for Israel; and so, too, one who gives up himself and his body and submits himself to the Lord and accepts the yoke of the Torah as if surrendering possession of himself to the Lord, blessed be He, can similarly draw down benefit from that world where there are no rights of possession. It goes without saying that for him, material sustenance flows down freely from there' (*Zot Zikaron*, p. 127).[73] In these and similar statements the emphasis is more on drawing down the flow of material bounty than on self-annihilation, i.e. not so much on the mystical goal as on the transmission of the bounty which follows from it.

It is precisely the denial of material existence, the indifference to worldly values on the part of the Zaddik who is at home in the upper worlds, who regards himself as nought and who experiences the lower, material world as a sojourner and stranger since 'he dwells chiefly in the world above', that enables him to draw down divine bounty from *ayin* to *yesh*:

Let man remember the truth that the chief place of his existence is not here . . . and the expression 'Who shall sojourn' (Ps. 15:1) means he shall regard himself as a sojourner 'in Your tent' . . . 'and who shall dwell in Your holy mountain'—that is the world to come (i.e. the reference is to one whose chief place of existence is not here but in the world to come)—he dwells chiefly in Your holy mountain . . . such a person draws down to the world the bounty of children, life and sustenance . . . but, for this, the quality of *ayin* is necessary, as I heard from the man of God, R. Baer of Rovno, on the expression *eyn mazal le-Yisrael*: he who regards himself as nought can draw down benefits which are dependent on *mazal* (interpreted as meaning 'divine flow')—'children, life and sustenance'(*Zikaron Zot*, p. 9).

The Kabbalistic concept of *ayin* here takes on an ambivalent character, both divine and earthly. In its divine sense *ayin* is 'the divine *yesh*', the *eyn-sof* (infinite) and plenitude, the source of re-creation and emanation, while in its earthly sense it is nothingness, the negation of *yesh*. The Zaddik must absorb the earthly meaning into his inner consciousness in order to achieve the divine quality, for only through the negation of his earthly existence and the obliteration of his individual self can he unite with the divine *ayin* and turn that *ayin* into earthly *yesh*.[74]

Above all the Zaddik must be submissive and recognize his deficiency, whether because of His majesty, blessed be He, or because he knows his true worth . . . for he who knows the truth can truly cleave to God who is truth. Furthermore, his disposition is humble as if he had offered all the sacrifices [ordained by Scripture], and thus he is stirred into action and raises the matter . . . for, through his humility, he stirs the world of *ayin* to sustain the world by way of making *yesh* from *ayin*, just as at the beginning *yesh* came out of *ayin* (*Diverey Emet*, p. 16).

The Zaddik who has annulled his own existence so as to become *ayin* in the earthly sense and who, in divesting himself of corporality, has achieved the transformation of *ani* (I, the self) into a[y]in (nought), becomes a receptacle for the mystical *ayin*, that is to say, for the emanation of divine vitality which flows through him to the world at large. In this way he completes a cycle of change: the material *yesh* becomes the divine *ayin*, which in turn becomes a material *yesh*.[75] That the material *ayin* and the divine *ayin* are conditioned on one another and interrelated is expressly stated throughout the Seer's writings: 'for "*eyn mazal le-Yisrael*"—this expression means that he who regards himself as *ayin* can draw down the divine flow (*mazal*) of "children, life and sustenance" . . . for he can draw down all manner of emanation of *yesh* from *ayin* because of his lowliness in his own eyes' (*Zot Zikaron*, p. 198); 'he who becomes . . . submissive and as low as *ayin*, he will be able

417

to draw down as we have stated above' (*Zikaron Zot*, p. 9).

By regarding himself as nought and turning his being into a receptacle, the Zaddik causes the divine *ayin* to dwell in him;[76] it is the transformation of the earthly *yesh* into *ayin* in the consciousness of the Zaddik which makes possible the transformation of the divine *ayin* into the earthly *yesh* in the shape of the material bounty which he draws down.

To sum up, the dialectical change brought about by the doctrine of the Zaddik may be characterized as follows: it was a departure from the view of *devekut* and unification with the divine *ayin* as ends in themselves—the direct outcome of self-abnegation and indifference towards material existence, towards a *devekut* which has the aim of drawing down material plenty and providing leadership for the world. This shift of mystical endeavour from the metaphysical to the earthly sphere is also a shift of emphasis from the single purpose of fusion with God (transformation of *ani* into *a[y]in*) to the complexity of simultaneous identification with the *ayin* and the *yesh*.

The world of the Zaddik is not founded on an ideal existence in which all is harmonious unity but on an imperfect existence, subject to conflicting forces and struggling between the two poles of *ayin* and *yesh*: 'Contemplate the majesty of God in the worlds on high which are called the heavens above so that you may ascend ever higher in attachment (*devekut*) to the Creator, blessed be He, and on the earth beneath consider the lowliness of your physical existence, so that you may be the lowliest of creatures in your own eyes' (*Zot Zikaron*, p. 67).

It may be that this change in the dialectical view of the Zaddik is grounded in the internal symmetry of the doctrine of the Zaddik, which places the mystical yearning to grasp hidden realities side by side with the demand to plumb to the full the meaning of human reality; it puts the mystical connection with the divine *ayin* alongside the intimate connection with the earthly community. As one studies the teachings of R. Jacob Isaac, it sometimes seems that against the increased importance given to spiritual authority—which is founded on a close relationship to the divine *ayin*, as well as on the assumption that the Zaddik can ascend to worlds on high—he is required also to strengthen his image as a man and to identify with the human *ayin*, along with sin, repentance, submission and lowlinesss. This acts as a counterweight to his claim of charismatic status which magnifies his godly image. Humility, lowliness and self-abnegation are the Zaddik's states of consciousness whenever he is not experiencing *devekut*: 'Humility must be rooted in his heart, except when he is filled with *devekut*, when it is certainly good to be in a state of *hitpashtut* (expansion) so that he should not consider his lowliness' (*Zikaron Zot*, p. 79). And indeed, a deep awareness of lowliness as the state of human existence is the most important ethical teaching that the Zaddik is required to observe, and the guideline which recurs most in the Seer's works.[77] Humility and lowliness are the external expression of the stages in the transformation of the *ani*—the 'I'—into the *a[y]in* which is nothingness, nullity. The Zaddik, by absorbing these attributes into his inner being and by giving expression to them in public, earns the conferment of divine inspiration and the consequent right to exercise leadership. Moreover, these qualities are established as the basis of the affiliation and empathy between the Zaddik and the community:

> And what kind of man shall he be? Shall he be a man of eloquence, important and a master over the community? Let him be precisely one 'who shall go out before them' (Num. 27:17); the text means, let him be lowly in his own eyes and regard himself as a greater sinner than all of them.[78] This is the meaning of the expression 'go out'; it relates to when he considers his lowliness and his sins. The term 'going out' is used for this, because one must always cleave to the Creator, blessed be He, to the love and fear of Him and to His Torah, but consideration of one's lowliness is called going out because, while holiness is described as lying within the domain of the individual, its opposite lies without in the public domain. When a man considers his sins, when he confesses and regrets them while they occupy his mind, he is devoutly engrossed (*davuk*) at that time in lowliness and in the going out (i.e. the departure) of his sins, and he himself is worse than all of them. That is what is meant by 'who shall go out before them', for when the leader of the people repents, all those who love him and all his followers cleave to him and they are attached to him in his thoughts; his conduct arouses them to behave similarly, which is to say, he shall go out before them and they [shall go] after him' (*Zot Zikaron*, p. 27).

The recognition of his lowliness as a basis for the empathy between the Zaddik and his community is one of the fundamental principles of R. Jacob Isaac's doctrine of the Zaddik. As we have seen, there is reason to suppose that it constitutes a counterweight to the powerful influence of charismatic authority. Therefore the Zaddik should always emphasize the obligation to recognize one's lowliness, while he should present charismatic inspiration and ecstatic transformation—*hitlahavut*, burning enthusiasm—as a boon from God and a miracle not due to any merit other than the exhaustive exploration and acknowledgement of his own worthlessness.

> 'Make a fiery serpent' (Num. 21:8)—that is *hitlahavut*, and it means that henceforward it must be firmly established in your heart that it is not through your righteous acts that you have attained this but through the grace of God who helps those who come to purify themselves and is near

to all who call upon Him, for you must thoroughly grasp your lowliness
. . . And this is why Scripture continues 'and set it'—that is, the fiery
serpent, which is *hitlahavut*—'on a pole' (=*nes*) since it is a miracle
(=*nes*) from the Creator that it should be so in your heart, and in this
matter you will act so that others also may benefit by learning from you
to conduct themselves in this way, for otherwise they will despair, saying
'You are the Zaddik and *hitlahavut* may be all very well for you, but it is
not so for us', because they are aware of their own shortcomings. That is
why Scripture says: if you set the matter on a *nes* [i.e. if you ascribe it to a
miracle] and you accept that you have not merited this by reason of your
character but, on the contrary, that it would not have been possible for
you to achieve this by yourself, but only by means of a miracle (*Zot
Zikaron*, pp. 25–6). For the Zaddik must draw down abundance to the
world and if he is of lowly disposition and submissive he draws it in
proportion to his own level of lowliness, both for the lowly and for the
great (*Zikaron Zot*, p. 54).[79]

The Seer repeatedly stresses man's passive position in regard to the
privilege of receiving God's grace and drawing near to the divine *ayin*,
as against the active obligation to be mindful of the human *ayin*, the
nullity of man and the lowliness of human existence. His view of the
relationship between the Zaddik and his followers is instructive. It
appears to be based on a certain transformation of the idea of 'the
descent of the Zaddik' which marked the early stages of Hasidic
thought.[80] In the works of R. Jacob Joseph of Polonnoye 'the descent
of the Zaddik' to the level of 'the ordinary man' is, of course, the basis
of the empathy between the Zaddik and the common people, whereas
in the form in which this idea appears in the Seer's teaching, it is his
self-reproach, the 'consciousness of his own lowliness' or 'the descent
into himself' that is advanced as the means of establishing the bond
between the Zaddik and his followers. It does not seem too far-fetched
to regard this as an elaboration of the idea of the 'descent of the Zaddik'
but on a different footing, that of partnership and empathy. The
interest in the doctrine of evil has been replaced by the social interest.

BETWEEN THE UPPER WORLDS AND
EARTHLY EXISTENCE

The pattern of leadership set up by the Hasidic movment was that of a
'man of the spirit' possessed of pneumatic authority who is called upon
to deal with metaphysical and earthly matters at one and the same time.
In the metaphysical domain the Zaddik strives to raise himself to such
levels of holiness and *devekut* that through his merit God's spirit will be
brought to dwell within him; in the earthly domain he works, by
virtue of the holy spirit with which he has been endowed, to strengthen

the presence of God in the world and to draw down divine bounty.

His efforts in the metaphysical domain take the form of a mystical, individual endeavour, to cut himself off from his earthly attachments and strive upwards to worlds above. This is expressed, for example, in the following: 'He who detaches himself is a tower soaring in the air, which means divested of corporality' (*Zot Zikaron*, p. 11). His connection with the earthly plane, on the other hand, is reflected in his assumption of responsibility for the material and social well-being of the community, with the purpose of bringing the divine presence to dwell among them—whence the formula 'to work miracles and wonders for the good of Israel' and 'to draw down abundance to the world'.

This twofold requirement is presented unambiguously as the essence of the Zaddik's leadership:

> For the Zaddik must see to two things: one, that his soul is purified and cleansed of sin and of every evil thought and so, too, he must be ready for the holiness of the Lord, blessed be He, to come to rest on him and within him; and secondly, and even more importantly, he must bring about the fulfilment of the will of God and see that God's holiness, blessed be He, is strengthened in the world, and bring about the salvation of Israel and work miracles and wonders (*Zikaron Zot*, p. 73).

S. Ettinger, in his study of the Hasidic leadership, has already drawn attention to the fundamental change which the Hasidic concept of leadership represented: '. . . instead of the ideal personality of the pre-Hasidic generation, the remote self-mortifying mystic, Hasidism idealized the mystic who leads the people and lives among them.'[81]

And indeed this change occurs in Polish Hasidism too: the mystic who has cut himself off from the community, who hopes 'for His holiness to come to rest on him', and who immerses himself in godly abstraction, gives place to another religious ideal, that of a man who relates positively to the world and society and who must radiate his own spirituality to the whole community. This idea is marked by the aspiration to 'draw down the divine presence to dwell among us', as well as upon the Zaddik, and to draw down abundance for all Israel. It is in this way that the Zaddik is seen by R. Jacob Isaac: he must combine mystical asceticism with involvement in earthly matters.

The dual requirement had wide repercussions in society. But while there is no doubt that the image of the reclusive Zaddik no longer answered what was felt to be the need, and that a clear preference had emerged for a leader who could combine the two roles described by R. Jacob Isaac, the deeper reason for the double requirement has not, hitherto, been adequately explained. It appears that the underlying reason for the tension between separation from and concern with material things is to be found in the tension between transcendence and immanence, or the two aspects of the Godhead with which the Zaddik stands in relationship and which he both absorbs and expresses.

The whole of R. Jacob Isaac's doctrine of the Zaddik bears the stamp of the tension between the shedding of corporality, in order to achieve the ascetic separation from his environment which is a precondition for attaining a state of holiness, and the responsibility for material things which requires close contact with earthly existence. This is reflected in the imagery the Seer chooses. The Zaddik's longing is expressed, for example, in '"Our soul is escaped like a bird" (Ps. 124:7)—this means shedding corporality as mentioned above, flying in the air and having no concern for this world' (*Zot Zikaron*, p. 11). But he returns from this flight of the spirit, for 'the Zaddik must always seek mercy for Israel and also for everything in the world which bears on material existence, because it pleases the Creator, blessed be He, that it should be so' (*Zot Zikaron*, p. 24). The return from mystical exaltation in order to devote attention to earthly matters is a fundamental obligation: 'for a personal duty is laid upon the Zaddikim of the generation always to draw down abundant good, great acts of loving-kindness, [and] greatness for Israel so that every good thing should be theirs' (*ibid.*, p. 24).

Moreover, while he yearns to be 'one whose chief abode is not here' but 'in the world to come' or 'in Your holy mountain' (*Zikaron Zot*, p. 9), and compares himself to 'a tower soaring in the air, as one who departs from earthliness and corporality' (*Zot Zikaron*, p. 11), he returns from his abstract existence in order to 'draw down to the world the bounty of children, life and sustenance' (*Zikaron Zot*, p. 9) and to be active 'in the midst of the congregation' (*Zot Zikaron*, p. 191). These two essentially contradictory elements of the Zaddik's existence require a split of his consciousness between the opposite poles of the spiritual and the material.[82] His response to this split conforms to the regular pattern of the mystical dialectic of *yesh* and *ayin* and inspires the social character of the Zaddik's leadership: the Zaddik must reflect both the transformation of the earthly *yesh* to the divine *ayin*—by seclusion, asceticism and *devekut*—and the transformation of the divine *ayin* to the earthly *yesh*, by drawing down benefits from heaven to earth and by the acceptance of the obligation to attend to earthly needs such as are expressed in 'children, life and sustenance'. R. Elimelech of Lyzhansk, R. Jacob Isaac's teacher, made this dual requirement a *sine qua non*, expressed in this form: 'The Zaddik must be both solitary and together with all Israel' (*Noam Elimelech*, p. 73b); and the Seer extended it to the metaphysical and social planes: '. . . for the Zaddik's chief abode is above, in his attachment (*devekut*) to Him, blessed be He, but he must also consider the needs of the public, to lessen the severity of judgements and similarly to seek mercy for Israel' (*Zikaron Zot*, p. 19). 'For the Zaddik must act in two ways, firstly for His sake, blessed be He . . . which should be [done] with fervour (*hitlahavut ha-lev*), and secondly he must seek mercy for Israel, and for this reason he is called 'angel-like' and 'His emissary', blessed be He, to draw down good for Israel' (*Zot Zikaron*, p. 206). 'For the Zaddik must serve the Holy One, blessed be He, in two ways: one, to cleave to Him, blessed be He . . . and also to draw down abundance for the world' (*Zikaron Zot*, p. 139).

This tension between the elevation to *ayin* and drawing down to *yesh* sets up the Zaddik as a dialectical figure, reflecting the inner struggles of a man who is required to respond to the diametrical opposites of holiness and earthliness, and to embody spiritual longing and material involvement at one and the same time. The tension is derived from the relationship between the Zaddik and the two aspects of the Godhead. The Zaddik is called upon to effect a union of opposites in himself, reflecting, as he does, both divine transcendence which leaves the world behind and is stripped of materiality, and divine immanence which bestows abundance on the world, endows it with its vitality and is present in it. The Zaddik, who is at home both in the upper worlds and in this world below, in spite of the two quite different frames of mind which this requires—the shedding of materiality as against concern with material affairs—embodies the ambivalence of *yesh* and *ayin* in their heavenly and earthly manifestations. In other words, he embodies both transcendence and immanence in relation to material existence.

It is the same divine dialectic of 'withdrawal' from the world and 'expansion' into it which is absorbed into the inner being of the Zaddik in the form of 'exaltation' and 'lowliness' that marks his contact with the world. The tension between the dual aspects of the Godhead, transcendence and immanence, *tsimtsum* and *shefa* (contraction and abundance), creates an image of the Zaddik who yearns for exaltation to worlds on high, but at the same time longs to be the means of bestowing abundance from God on earthly existence.

It appears that the doctrine of the Zaddik in the minds of those who formulated it was founded on the premise that the Zaddik was not simply a person complete in himself but that there were forces concealed within him which pointed beyond his personality to their divine origin, to an other-worldly existence which was symbolized by his actions and reflected in them. The Seer describes the complex relationship between the Zaddik and God from various homiletical points of view: '"and what are the cities"—these are the Zaddikim—

"in which he dwells" (Num. 13:19)—that is to say, the Creator, who dwells within them' (Zot Zikaron, p. 12). R. Jacob Isaac is saying, in effect, that many qualities traditionally ascribed to God are transferred to the Zaddik.[83] Every action of the Zaddik is in some measure an expression of divine power and a reflection of life on the divine level: '"Ye are men" (adam atem) (Ezek. 34:31)—this means I am likened (edameh) to the Supreme Being, for the Zaddik compares the Creator, blessed be He, to himself: in the same way as the Creator, blessed be He, decrees and performs, so, too, does the Zaddik decree and the Holy One, blessed be He, perform and he can also annul the decrees of the Creator, blessed be He' (Zikaron Zot, p. 38). 'The Zaddik can also act (in) the camp of God . . . and so he is called rakia [firmament, or one of the seven heavens], a title indicating importance, because he is important in all the worlds and whatever he decrees, the Lord, blessed be He, performs, for the Creator, blessed be He, empowers the Zaddik to act' (Zikaron Zot, p. 25). The significant departure from midrashic tradition and its Kabbalistic interpretations of the figure of the Zaddik[84] is to be found in the intensification of the dialectical connection to the upper worlds while at the same time testing it on the earthly plane. The Zaddik's actions imitate the divine dynamic of withdrawal from below upwards (conversion of yesh to ayin), and of conferment of abundance from above downwards (conversion of ayin to yesh); in relation to Heaven he 'raises up worlds', 'performs unifications', 'gives great pleasure to the Creator', 'brings about unification between the world below and the worlds above' and 'raises up female waters' (mayim nukvin),[85] while in relation to the material world he 'brings down abundance', 'draws down to the world the bounty of children, life and sustenance', 'desires to do acts of true kindness' and 'draw down an abundance of holiness to the world from above'.[86] Notably, in all the statements relating to the mystical aspects of his actions, Kabbalistic-theurgic terminology is prominent, with the Zaddik 'unifying', 'attaching' (medabek), 'raising up', and 'joining together worlds above'; in regard to his relationship to earthly existence, however, the Zaddik is presented as a 'saviour', a 'bestower of abundance', and one who 'sustains and feeds',[87] with verbs and adjectives which are generally reserved for the loving-kindness of God towards His creatures.

The activity connected with earthly existence—the emanation, drawing down and conferment of abundance—is, as it were, an embodiment and intensification of the work of God, an imitation of Creation in bringing yesh out of ayin and an expression of divine immanence.[88] On the other hand, the Seer's picture of the activity connected with heavenly existence is based on the Kabbalistic-theurgic tradition of the restoration of *yesh* to *ayin* and on a transcendental perspective: 'for it is the desire of the Holy One, blessed be He, to do good to his creatures; so, too, it should be the desire of the Zaddikim that there should be deeds of kindness and good done for Israel' (*Zot Zikaron*, p. 11). 'And it is simply the case that he who has the attributes of the Creator desires to do acts of true kindness like the Creator, blessed be He, who desires to do good without any reward whatsoever' (*Zikaron Zot*, p. 78).

The Seer interprets the drawing down of bounty as the transformation of the divine *ayin* to *yesh*: 'For he can draw down to him the bounty of *yesh* from *ayin*; moreover, the interpretation of this is that he is the divine flow (*mazal*) on which depend (the blessings of) children, life and sustenance' (*Zikaron Zot*, p. 34). One cannot ignore the clear aim of forming the figure of the Zaddik in the image of God; equally, it should not be forgotten that mystical exaltation in the teachings of the Seer draws strength from earthly needs. The Zaddik can reinforce his empathy with earthly needs through the mystical power of his contact with worlds on high; he is able to found his leadership of the community on mystical authority by establishing the essential unity between the metaphysical and the earthly orders.

MATERIAL ZADDIKISM

The doctrine of 'material Zaddikism' is founded on an intimate relationship between the spiritual bonds between the Zaddik and the community and the material help he brings them. This relationship in turn is based on the subtle appreciation of people's expectations concerning existential needs, and on the Zaddik's ability to invest his empathy with them on the earthly level with a mystical power derived from his connection with the upper worlds. The doctrine offers a religious response to expectations which arise directly out of man's material existence. The Zaddik is made responsible for all the material wants of the community, from prosperity and wealth to 'children, life and sustenance'.[89] The burden of responsibility laid upon him accords completely with the charismatic source of his authority, for the claim to charismatic authority itself implies that Heaven has made him guardian of his followers and given him responsibility for their welfare.

There are two aspects to the doctrine of material Zaddikism. The first reflects the responsibility which a charismatic leader must bear towards the members of his congregation and is clearly aimed at establishing the vital need for his tutelage. This aspect is founded on a conception of the Zaddik as the law governing the distribution of the divine 'flow' which secures the existence of all beings. The second is based on a new evaluation of materiality in both the religious and the social contexts.

The basic premise which is advanced is that in the dynamic relationship between God and the world which is defined by the Kabbalistic concept of *shefa* (divine flow, bounty or abundance)[90] there is a spiritual dimension and a material one. This spiritual and material flow, connected in Kabbalistic symbolism with the *sefirah* named *Yesod* (foundation), is drawn to earth by the Zaddik, who is perceived as the earthly hypostasis of that *sefirah*,[91] and the flow develops from the potential to the actual through the Zaddik's service of Heaven:

> The Zaddik draws down *shefa* from the latent acts of kindness (*hasadim*) of the Holy One, blessed be He, for He 'keeps mercy' [in] (*notser hesed*—Ex. 34:7) . . . and the Zaddik draws out the letters of the word *notser* from the potential to the actual state so as to bring to the world [the blessing of] children, life and sustenance . . . for this reason the Zaddik is called *tsofenat pa'neah* (applied to Joseph in Gen 41:45; traditionally, 'decipherer of hidden things'); whereas the acts of kindness were concealed and latent, he deciphers them so as to draw them out into the open for the needs of the world (*Zikaron Zot*, p. 32). The Zaddik must draw down abundance for the world; like the Zaddik Joseph, he is the provider of nourishment . . . and what was actual in the generations of old is now in a potential state, for they are like souls to us, and what is actual for the soul is potential for the body; therefore the Zaddik must now draw down abundance for the world (*Zot Zikaron*, p. 190).

The emanation of the *eyn-sof* (infinite) concealed in God's loving-kindness becomes a flow of bounty which is channelled by the Zaddik to meet material and spiritual needs:

> . . . for the man who is a Zaddik must draw down all kinds of emanation, both for the soul—His holiness, blessed be He, and penitent thoughts, fear and love of Heaven and a wholesome intellect—and also the material concerns of 'children, life and sustenance', for the soul and for the body (*Zikaron Zot*, pp. 118–19).

Linking those things of which human existence is constituted—children, life and sustenance—with the mystical–charismatic element contained within the divine bounty, and the providential function of the Zaddik, brought about a profound change in the realm of religious responsibility. Material affairs were not now regarded as falling in a separate and independent area, but as being within the range of the divine flow and within the realm of religious commitment; the Zaddik's responsibility for them was validated and endowed with significance by his ties with worlds above:

> for the Holy One, blessed be He, gives the Zaddik power to draw down

[benefits] from the divine flow (*mazal*) which governs children, life and sustenance . . .[92] And as for the Zaddik who acts thus, the Holy One, blessed be He, is with him, because he cleaves (*davuk*) to God, blessed be He, through cleaving to His attributes and also in order to increase his power to draw down the bounty of the Lord from Him and he has the power to do His will, blessed be He, to bestow bounty (*Zikaron Zot*, pp. 138–9). For the Zaddik is called Joseph (Yosef—etymologically linked to YSF meaning 'to add') because it is his constant desire to add to the fulfilment of the needs of Israel[93] and to the loving-kindness of God all day long (*ibid.*, p. 31).

As we have said, the material aspects of human existence are withdrawn from the independent control of man and become dependent on the drawing down of the divine *shefa* by the Zaddik. The material *shefa* (bounty or abundance) is conceived of as the spiritual *shefa* (divine emanation or flow) made concrete, and therefore the responsibility for both the material and spiritual dimensions of human existence—for all the needs of both soul and body—is laid on the Zaddik:

> Now as for the world below, we who are at present in this lowly world desperately require their benevolence, both materially and spiritually . . . This is not the case in the worlds above, [which are concerned] only with spiritual matters . . . that which he (= the Zaddik or, possibly, He = God) bestows on us to satisfy our needs comes down from Him, blessed be He, through all the worlds until it reaches us and its spirituality assumes material form here . . . for it is a personal duty laid upon the Zaddikim of the generation always to draw down benevolent emanations and great acts of kindness [and] greatness for Israel so that all good things should be theirs (*Zot Zikaron*, pp. 203–4).

This removal of all aspects of daily existence from the field of human action and their transfer from the responsibility of the individual to the mystical sphere, where they are under the control of the Zaddik, merits our attention. The Zaddik causes the divine flow to emanate from the upper worlds and translates it into the satisfaction of human needs. This belief (which gave rise to trenchant criticism in contemporary circles of *Maskilim* in Galicia)[94] was very influential in changing the character of the Hasidic community, and the part it played in this process needs to be assessed.

The quality of the Zaddik's leadership was now estimated by reference to this criterion of his ties to the upper worlds and his ability to draw down Heavenly bounty, since without his responsibility, as guardian for the totality of human existence, his mission would lose most of its meaning.

The precise time at which the doctrine of material Zaddikism crystallized in the Hasidic movement has not been established conclusively. The view of scholars is that this is a phenomenon of the 'third' generation of Hasidism, whereas the proponents of the doctrine attribute its origin to the teaching of the Maggid of Mezhirech in the 'second' generation. Joseph Weiss stated unequivocally: 'In the doctrine of the Zaddik of the first two generations there is no theory relating to the activity of the Zaddik in extending material help to his followers; the theory that the Zaddik brings salvation in regard to children, life and sustenance belongs to the third generation of the Hasidic movement.'[95] Rivka Schatz, in her study of the doctrine of the Zaddik, remarked: 'While early Hasidism knows of the charismatic power of the Zaddik only in the spiritual realm, in the teaching of R. Elimelech the Zaddik is often presented as responsible towards the community not only for matters in the spiritual sphere but also for those in the material sphere; it is in the power of the Zaddik to confer blessings on his followers in regard to children, life and sustenance.'[96]

Contrary to these views, R. Jacob Isaac ascribes this doctrine to the Maggid of Mezhirech and attributes to him the formulation of the dialectical principle on which it is founded: 'But, for this, the quality of *ayin* is necessary, as I heard from the rabbi, the man of God R. Baer of Rovno, on the expression *eyn mazal le-Yisrael*, he who regards himself as nought (*ayin*) can draw down benefits which are dependent on the "divine flow" (*mazal*) which governs "children, life and sustenance" (*Zikaron Zot*, p. 9). There is therefore no doubt that R. Jacob Isaac saw the spiritual inspiration for the doctrine of material Zaddikism as having originated with the Maggid; but we need to examine this attribution as a systematic and fully developed teaching of the Maggid in the light of the opposition to it by some of his other disciples. We must also consider the influence of the teachings of R. Jacob Joseph of Polonnoye in this connection.

Essentially, the Zaddik's ability to bring down the flow of divine bounty to this world is founded on the well-defined dialectic pattern to which his life conforms, and which expresses itself as a union of opposites partaking of both *ayin* and *yesh*—'nothing' and 'existence'—as has been explained above. The Zaddik who can transform himself into material *ayin* in order to cleave to the divine *ayin* is the self-same person who can draw down the flow of the divine *yesh* to us on earth. That is to say, his ability to bestow material bounty is dependent on his charismatic and mystical character; it is a necessary corollary of his claim to metaphysical ties and serves to test the validity of that claim. It is his elevation to superior worlds and the cleaving (*devekut*) of his soul to its divine origin (this being the principal aim of his mystical endeavour) which generate the flow from the springs of Heavenly bounty and draw it down through all the levels of existence. This process is picturesquely described by the Seer (in imagery largely borrowed from the Scriptures):

> The Zaddikim who cleave to the Lord, blessed be He, who exalt and elevate themselves to cleave to the Lord, blessed be He, will forthwith drip sweet wine; as soon as they raise themselves up they will be accepted, and through them will come the pleasantness of the glory of the Most High, which is sweeter than honey and the honeycomb; and the treader of grapes (who shall overtake) the sower of seed is the Zaddik, who draws down the flow of *devekut* and His light, blessed be He, to give light to the world (*Zikaron Zot*, p. 107).

The concept of *shefa* has its origin in the world of the Kabbalah, where it relates to the dynamic of the *sefirot* in the upper worlds, whereas in its Hasidic meaning it expresses the continuity of the divine 'vitality', a creative force which flows through the agency of the Zaddik, between the upper and the lower worlds. It is this continuity which brings about the transfer of the *shefa* to the area of responsibility of the Zaddik as leader, and which turns it into the basis of the bond between the mystical and material planes.

Shefa in the Hasidic sense is the concept which determines the relations of partnership between the Zaddik and the community; it is the provision for the orderly maintenance of the world, in accordance with divine law, which is embodied in the Zaddik, or the dynamic in accordance with which the needs of all created beings are satisfied through his agency. 'The Zaddik is exalted above the mass of the people and through his root the *shefa* passes in spiritual form and the light of His holiness reaches him' (*Zikaron Zot*, p. 2). This assertion of the Zaddik's charismatic superiority necessarily implies an assumption of guardianship over material existence in general and over his followers in particular. The responsibility for the satisfaction of material needs is rooted in the dynamic of the *shefa*, while the materiality which is drawn from the *shefa* becomes the arena for the forging of a religious connection between Zaddik and community. The Zaddik's leadership is assessed by his ability to bestow *shefa* (in the sense of bounty from Heaven), by his concentration on the needs of daily life and by the explicit definition of his position as guardian responsible for the full scope of human existence, on the strength of his ties with upper worlds: '[The Zaddik] draws down *shefa* through all the worlds, whatever is necessary for the things implicit in these three: children, life and sustenance, which are the root of all material *shefa* . . . and because materiality is indispensable' (*Zikaron Zot*, p. 83).

The ideal view of the interconnection of God, the Zaddik and mankind which is involved in the drawing down of the divine flow is contrasted with the view of materiality in the absence of that flow. This is seen as a condition of abject poverty, deprivation and disunion. In Hasidic thought these material values lose their exclusive existential meaning as soon as they become a measure of the Zaddik's ability to confer Heavenly bounty and a precondition for drawing near to God. Bounty from Heaven is unequivocally declared to be an essential condition for the approach to God, and it is therefore the Zaddik's task to devote his attention to caring for the material prosperity of his community by drawing down the divine flow in its material form, and not to make these things conditional on any spiritual elevation on the part of the community: 'The Zaddik's first aim should not be that the world should repent and thereby secure the satisfaction of their material needs as a matter of course, but rather he should first see to it that he draws down their needs from above' (*Zikaron Zot*, p. 71): because 'people to whom good is done enter the private domain [i.e. holiness, see above] and so cleave to the Creator, blessed be He' (*ibid.*, p. 16).

The manner in which R. Jacob Isaac expressed himself indicates that he was propounding new ideas which were not widely shared, still less taken for granted, and that he felt the need to justify and explain them. Indeed, his words are to be understood as a polemic against the opinions of R. Menahem Mendel of Vitebsk and R. Shneur Zalman of Lyadi. Against these two leaders, he was defending his claims that the Zaddik's metaphysical ties empowered him to extend material aid to mankind and take responsibility for material prosperity while releasing its beneficiaries from having to fulfil any spiritual demands, whether in private or public matters.[97] He replaced the traditional pattern of responsibility for spiritual leadership by an all-embracing responsibility for matters both spiritual and material, with the emphasis actually on materiality, but placing the drawing down of material bounty in its spiritual context. He expatiated on the special nature of the leadership that he proposed as a contrast to the traditional patterns, and pointedly criticized the forces of conventional Hasidism:

> For there are two kinds of Zaddik; every Zaddik must draw down bounty from heaven but there are exalted Zaddikim and there are Zaddikim whose degree of exaltation is not so great. And although Joseph, too, certainly provided spiritual sustenance, it is written (Gen. 47:12) '*va-yekhalkel*'—'and he provided [his father and brothers] with everything', because one who draws down the means of sustenance from above creates unity in all the worlds, for the divine bounty passes through all of them, and Joseph drew down both spirituality and materiality; therefore it is written 'and he provided . . . with everything'—*va-yekhalkel*—for he acted in both ways in the totality of

worlds, but the result of his action was principally revealed in materiality (*Zikaron Zot*, p. 61).

The tension and controversy within the Hasidic community in regard to the areas of the Zaddik's concern and the extent of his responsibility for the satisfaction of spiritual and material needs found incisive expression in a later tradition handed down by the Seer's disciples:

'Go now, see whether it is well . . . with the flock' (Gen. 37:14). For we have found great and good Zaddikim who all their lives had no other aim than to increase His glory, blessed be His name, and gave no thought to securing the well-being of this world by bestowing abundance on their generation; but that is not as it should be, for the Zaddik must also consider the livelihood of Israel in this world below so that they lack no good thing; let him look to the welfare of his brethren—[they are] the flock in this world.[98]

The polemical thread which runs through these words is to be understood as a criticism of accepted norms both inside and outside the Hasidic camp. It is repeatedly expressed in the following unequivocal demand: 'All the leaders of the generation must consider the needs of their generation and pray for them, and that is why they are called *parnasim* ("sustainers", leaders)' (*Zot Zikaron*, p. 74). There is no doubt that in expressing this responsibility for the material welfare of the community, and linking it to demands of a spiritual nature, the Seer was setting up new norms of leadership and challenging the accepted ones.[99] This change in the dialectic of Hasidic thought and in the response to contemporary social conditions marks the turning-point which occurred in the third generation of Hasidism, when it developed from a cluster of élitist groups into a broadly-based social movement.

The significant feature of the change in the definition of the Zaddik's area of responsibility is the altered relation to materiality. In the teaching of the Seer the world of action and material existence is at the centre of religious thought, for the materiality which separates man from God becomes the plane on which empathy is established between man and the Zaddik. An appreciable part of his deliberations, as we have shown above, is devoted to the theologization of material leadership and to clarification of the relationship between the source of the divine emanation, the material needs of mankind and the leadership of the Zaddik. There is an allusion to this in the following statement: 'If people are shown kindness and good is done to them they enter the private domain and thereby cleave to the Creator, blessed be He' (*Zikaron Zot*, p. 16). It is this aspect of the doctrine of the Zaddik which underlies the formation of the new socio-religious movement which coalesced round the leadership of the Zaddik, and there is no doubt that it played a decisive part in determining the character of Hasidism in Galicia and Poland during the period in question. It appears, however, that from R. Jacob Isaac's point of view, the social change was only an expression of a theology which proposed to reassess both materiality and spirituality.

The Seer's attitude to man's existential needs represents a significant departure from the attitude towards material existence adopted in the Hasidism of the Maggid of Mezhirech: the restoration of materiality to the centre of the relationship between religion and society, and the assignment of religious importance to material prosperity, amounted to a reinterpretation of the spiritual tendency developed by the school of the Maggid, if not an outright opposition to it.[100] The élitist spirituality of the Maggid's doctrine in its original form was unsuited to the social and spiritual conditions with which the Hasidic leadership had to deal in the third generation: it needed the modification which it received in the Seer's reinterpretation, an interpretation which was better adapted to meet the needs of the community in his time and place.

The essential teachings of Hasidism required that the Hasidic ethos should be based on indifference to material existence and the abandonment of material wants so far as man could achieve that, for the aim was the removal of the arena of religious effort to upper worlds where the 'I' (*ani*) becomes 'nothing' (*a[y]in*), where materiality is 'cast off' and material existence is 'annulled'.[101]

Scholars disagree over the question of whether these spiritualistic notions could really generate a widespread social ethos or whether they were intended from the outset for the circles of the élite,[102] but there is no doubt that they occupied a central position in the system of thought of the Maggid, with which R. Elimelech and R. Jacob Isaac had been imbued. Their express formulation in the literature of the 'guidelines' (*hanhagot*) does not testify to an appeal to a limited circle of the élite, but at most to a delineation of a guiding principle, worded as an ideal to be followed in practice as far as possible. To all appearances, however, it was the broadening of the scope of the appeal together with confinement of spiritual responsibility to the Zaddik, which led to the fundamental change in regard to material values.

Rivka Schatz has clarified the significance of the spiritualistic attitude and its essential position in Hasidic thought:

> In the Hasidic teaching of the first generations of the movement there is already present, as an accepted fact, the tension between the two poles of human existence—those of the spirit and of man's material fabric: its theoretical significance is to be understood as a constant tipping of the

scale towards Existence (*yeshut*), and there is only one Existence, which is that of God—all other existence of which we have knowledge is devoid of essential meaning. Anyone who attributes essential meaning to the world cuts it off from the metaphysical source of its nourishment. This position determines the negative attitudes to the world as being devoid of ontological meaning.[103]

The school of the Maggid had set out to break off the yoke of materiality, and defined its alienation from it in categorical terms as 'equanimity' (*hishtavut*), 'annihilation of material existence', 'casting off corporality', and 'worship through corporality', the essence of which consists in emptying corporality of its material content and exposing the divine element which gives it life.[104] On the other hand, Polish Hasidism saw the demands made by this spiritualistic approach as falling exclusively on the Zaddik in his relationship with the upper worlds, while in regard to this world below the Polish doctrine called for a new view of materiality which would restore its religious significance; it rejected outright the call for worship in corporality as incapable of being addressed to the masses.

The effort to spiritualize materiality, and the accompanying alienation from worldly life and earthly needs, were rejected out of hand as a basis for a widespread social ethos, while their opposites—positive regard for material bounty and legitimation of the urge to satisfy material needs—became a basis for empathy between the community and the Zaddik. This new division of responsibilities—the Zaddik taking upon himself spiritual effort and guardianship in material affairs, the community affirming material existence and undertaking a close association with the Zaddik—reflected a fundamental change in Hasidic thought which accompanied a change in the social basis of the movement. The radical spiritual obligation and indifference to material existence were required of the Zaddik alone and were even justified as essential for the drawing down of the material bounty from the upper worlds to the earthly level of existence. The 'bestowal of the divine emanation in material form' takes its place alongside 'the shedding of corporality', and the Zaddik is called upon to personify this dialectic. The change in the position of materiality in religious worship and in the allocation of reponsibilities is noteworthy: the material bounty which is drawn down by the Zaddik for the community stems from the shedding of materiality by the individual; that is to say, while abundance is conferred on the community as a whole, the spiritual effort involved in the shedding of materiality and the negation of corporeal existence is the responsibility of the Zaddik alone. Whereas (as we know from the literature of the 'guidelines') the Hasidic ethos in its previous stage cast a considerable measure of responsibility for both worldly and heavenly matters on every individual in the Hasidic community, the situation was reversed in Polish Hasidism. The more important the Zaddik became in Hasidic life, the more the ordinary individual's responsibilities were withdrawn from him and transferred to the charismatic guardianship of the Zaddik. It may have been the Zaddik's inner certainty of his supernatural powers which caused him to release the members of his community from any spiritual effort and to take over from them the responsibility for all earthly matters connected with their daily life; what is certain is that the new social order of the Hasidic community took shape round a leadership which diverted religious tension towards the Zaddik instead of towards God, and responsibility for daily life to the Zaddik instead of the individual.[105] The two opposing concepts, 'casting off corporality' and 'corporeal love', together express the tension between spiritual commitment and the relation to earthly existence, but now this tension was exclusively the province of the Zaddik, who invigorated the new attitude to earthly existence in the name of charismatic authority. The categorical statements 'materiality is indispensable' (*Zikaron Zot*, p. 83) and 'but the essence is revealed in materiality' (*ibid.*, p. 61), which recur in various forms throughout the Seer's writings form an explicit challenge to the radical spiritualistic orientation of the school of the Maggid, while at the same time they redefine the field of responsibility of spiritual leadership:

> For Abram is called ardour and great *devekut* through casting off corporality, and his name is to be interpreted as *av ram*, lofty father on a supreme level of spirituality . . . but the Holy One, blessed be He, desired that *love should be spread in corporality* also, so that he should love the Creator, blessed be He . . . which means that he desires to do His will and loves Him as a son loves his father, and not only by casting off corporality but in that (earthly) world (*Zikaron Zot*, p. 17).

The spiritual obligation is no longer limited to leading a life 'stripped of corporality' in the presence of God: there is now an express requirement to attach significance to material existence and recognize its religious value, such as is expressed in 'spreading out love in corporality also'.

The tension between spiritual longings and the legitimation of materiality takes on a complex character, for the requirement to 'cast off corporality' is at the heart of Hasidic spiritual endeavour as formulated in the school of the Maggid, whereas the requirement to have regard to materiality in the form of love and abundance, subsistence and livelihood is diametrically opposed to it. But here the former attitude applies to the Zaddik alone, as a duty, while the latter is the justification for his service of Heaven and his leadership, and it complements his spiritual side with its charismatic manifestation. The natural longings of the mystic distance him from material existence on his way to upper worlds, but in the doctrine of R. Jacob Isaac he returns to the level of material existence at the command of God, who requires of him that he respond to material life and take it into account in religious worship:

> 'Go from thy country' etc. (Gen. 11:21) this means that you are to go away, in your thoughts, from your corporality, i.e. it is to be your wish and your desire not to lead a corporeal existence. 'And from thy kindred'—that you should not wish to occupy yourself with procreation and cohabitation . . . 'and from thy father's house'—that you should not think at all of relationship and kinship. . . 'to the land that I will show thee'—this means, even though it was your wish to go and refrain from corporality, for, on the contrary, you should understand that *it is His will that you should occupy yourself with corporality also*, as it is said (Eccles. 7:18), '. . . take hold of *this*, and from *this* withdraw not thy hand', and 'this' is 'to the land that I will show thee' (*Zot Zikaron*, p. 126).

R. Jacob Isaac depicts the Zaddik, casting off corporality and departing from earthliness on his way to God, as displaying ardour, *devekut*, devotion, love of God and ecstatic fire. But God leads the Zaddik back to his community—'to the land that I will show you' for the sake of the love of man, and for this he requires the quite different qualities of an earthly perspective, sound reason, responsibility, care and concern for the material needs of those who are around him. The Seer's response to the spiritualist teaching of the Maggid and his circle is an attempt to place the heavenly and earthly levels of existence on an equal footing in Hasidism.

Having discussed above the importance of the Kabbalistic dialectic of 'expansion' and 'withdrawal' in shaping this complex attitude to the two poles of existence, and having argued that 'casting off corporality' referred solely to the experience of the Zaddik, while the conferment of material bounty related to the needs of the community, who were freed from the responsibility for spiritual matters, we must also note the change in the meaning attached to prosperity and poverty in the spiritual life of man as it is to be seen in the writings of the Seer. This is a new and instructive development.[106]

The altered attitude to materiality, and its inclusion within the realm of religious thought as the responsibility of the Zaddik, stemmed from the transfer of attention to the relation between the material position of man and the limits of his spiritual commitment, as well as from recognition of the altered character of the community with which the

Hasidic leadership and Hasidic thought had to contend. Here we have one of the expressions of the transition from an élitist spiritual phenomenon—which devotes its attention to *ayin* ('nothing', the negation of existence) and sees everything in mystical perspective—to a broadly based popular movement forcing religious thought to address itself to *yesh* ('existence') and materiality.

The relation between the material prosperity of the individual and his spiritual satisfaction, which together condition the service of God, are extensively discussed in R. Jacob Isaac's teaching. He begins his consideration of the connection between poverty and wealth with a flat condemnation of the former and an equally decisive approval of the latter, in their religious context:

> The main concern is to serve Him, blessed be He, and to study his Torah, but 'if there is no flour, there is no Torah' (*Avot* 3, 18), and we also learn that ' . . . poverty makes a man disregard [his own sense and] the sense of his Creator'.[107] It is, therefore, an excellent thing to have sustenance in plenty and even wealth, so as to serve Him, blessed be He, out of satisfaction of the heart (*Zot Zikaron*, p. 136; and cf. *Diverey Emet*, p. 76).

The early Hasidic leaders' doctrine of indifference to material existence, together with the asceticism propounded in the ethical literature of the time, give way to a new conception of the place of earthly prosperity in relation to the demands of religion. Poverty, too, acquires a new significance as reflecting on the spiritual position of man. Poverty and want are accounted an impediment of the first importance to man's ability to draw near to God, and therefore their opposites, wealth and abundance—which are entrusted to the hands of the Zaddik—become a prime condition for the service of God, which itself falls within the responsibility of the Zaddik: 'For the Zaddik draws Israel near to their Father in Heaven and also sees to it that if any of them are prevented from doing His will, blessed be He, as it should be done, because of lack of necessities as, for example, through poverty (Heaven forbid), which "makes a man disregard the sense of his Creator", he draws down their needs for them' (*Zikaron Zot*, p. 40).

These references to poverty and want indicate that we have before us a society in a state of material distress and spiritual crisis, and indeed historical research into the period points distinctly to conditions of particular hardship in the region.[108] There is no doubt that R. Jacob Isaac is expressing ideas which arise from actual conditions. The alertness to the state of society displayed in the doctrine of the Zaddik—which takes responsibility for material existence and offers to draw down Heavenly bounty without spiritual preconditions—is a response to an actual socio-religious challenge to act within a Jewish community whose social fabric has been fractured and whose spiritual constitution has been weakened by hardship. Until then, moralistic rebuke and spiritual demands—the preaching of repentance, calls for the correction of faults—had been the order of the day. Lacking a sense of empathy with the plight of the community and appreciation of its seriousness, these demands could not stand up to the test of contemporary conditions.[109]

Traditional religious attitudes to material needs called for resignation, equanimity, frugality and acceptance of poverty; material well-being was regarded as conditional on repentance and spiritual improvement. As against this, the doctrine of material Zaddikism offered keen alertness to existential needs and a sympathetic understanding of the seriousness of poverty, together with tutelage which imposed no conditions on its wards but bestowed loving-kindness, plenty and assistance through the power of its charismatic ties to upper worlds:

> For there is a kind of Zaddik who always reproves the world in order that they should be moved to repent, and there is another kind who does not behave thus[110] but always earnestly desires that Israel should have nothing but good . . . and the latter is preferable because by his drawing down bounty for man, whose soul is well aware of the root of that bounty and by what means it has come to him, there will in any event be a bond between him and the Zaddik, and this way holiness and fear of Heaven will be his (*Zikaron Zot*, p. 153). Let not the first aim of the Zaddik be that the world should repent and thereby be granted their material needs in any event, but rather, before that, let him see to it that he draws down their needs (*Zikaron Zot*, p. 71).

This original evaluation of the relationship between the spiritual and the material, and the psychological subtlety of the approach which places the Zaddik in the position of guardian over the existential well-being of man, stand out against the background of the ethical literature of 'rebuke' of the period, which sharply condemns subservience to earthly needs, from the standpoint of an acutely ascetic ethos combined with extreme spiritual demands.[111]

R. Jacob Isaac was alive to the great importance of the expectations connected with everyday needs and was well aware that response to those needs could foster a profound socio-religious relationship between the Zaddik and his followers. At first sight the consciousness of unity in Hasidic society might be thought to be realized more in empathy on the material plane and in everyday life than on the spiritual plane, but in the Zaddik's mind empathy in regard to material matters was a gateway to the spiritual goal: acknowledgement of material needs was only a first step towards the intended achievement of spiritual targets, but spiritual endeavours which turned away from material existence were worthless. The definite relationship between material response and spiritual rapprochement, or between the assumption of material responsibility and the crystallization of Hasidic society, receives a lengthy exposition in the writings of the Seer. He sets up the ideal of a Zaddik who clears a path for his community through the pitfalls of earthly existence, and of a community crystallizing round the Zaddik's charismatic inspiration, which is revealed in earthly abundance and in his guardianship leading to a close spiritual affinity.

> The Zaddik is called Pharaoh (following the spelling *peraoh* = 'he let [the people] loose', 'laid them open'—Ex. 32:25) because he reveals the glory of Heaven by his prayer, visibly performing miracles—that is the meaning of '*parua hu*', i.e. 'he is uncovered' (*ibid.*; the versions have 'broken loose', 'out of control'). And the Zaddik makes the world mend its ways and brings it near to Him, blessed be He . . . and 'He did not lead them' (Ex. 13:17) in strict justice . . . but how did he (Moses) lead them? Through the land of the Philistines (*Pelishtim*), meaning a way was broken open (*mefulash*, taken to be etymologically linked to *Pelishtim*—Philistines) for them through earthliness so that all good things should be theirs, 'for it was near' by this route—to be good before the Lord, blessed be He (*Zikaron Zot*, p. 50).

The loving kindness, bounty, aid and livelihood which are bestowed through the Zaddik transform earthly existence by opening it up so that God can be perceived through it. Their antitheses, on the other hand—'strict judgement', punishment, rebuke and asceticism, or estrangement from, and condemnation of, materiality—are completely rejected by the Seer in the social circumstances in which he operates.

The religious significance of material prosperity and the challenge to the ethos of asceticism are set out in his statements on the sacrifices. He explains the sacrifices in terms of the drawing near of Israel to their Father in Heaven by means of the abundance bestowed by the Zaddik, who acts out of the sense of mission implicit in his recognition that material prosperity is spiritually important:

> 'When any man from among you brings an offering' etc. (Lev. 1:2): the verse teaches us that if we desire that Israel should be brought to repentance, the [Zaddik's] aim should be no other than to bestow all their needs upon them. Thus they will, in any event, be good . . . And also, by this means they will come to know the loving-kindness of God and recognize his kindnesses and wonders, and will make their hearts burn for the Creator, blessed be He . . . And for this reason we say 'If any man brings an offering from among you', i.e. in case he wishes actually to offer up (or bring near) one of you to God, I counsel him by what means he is permitted to offer them (bring them near) to the Lord: '[by

means] of the cattle', for he may draw down for them material things and things of an animal nature[!]. That is a general statement in regard to material things; after that [the Zaddik] specifies in detail items from the general bounty [bestowed on man]. This bounty includes all things to do with 'children, life and sustenance', on which depend other gifts that are necessary and good for us (*Zikaron Zot*, p. 75).

The Seer's words represent a bold alteration of the relation between the end and the means, and a wise recognition of the place of material things in man's life as a whole. In these respects, and in his appreciation of the connection between empathy on the material level and spiritual rapprochement, he clearly departs from traditional thought-patterns, which show a preference of extreme spiritual and ethical demands while ignoring existential requirements. The external response to material needs is nurtured by the inner spiritual intent, for the special gift of drawing down Heavenly bounty with which the Zaddik is favoured is conferred on him for the purpose of helping to remove the earthly obstacles on the road to the realization of the religious ideal.

The drawing down of material bounty, or the obligation to attain this end, brings about rapprochement, close association, holiness and spiritual exaltation, and therefore the Zaddik, who prays for this bounty, justifies his prayer by the connection between poverty and want, 'which make man disregard the sense of his Maker', and their antithesis 'abundance', which draws man near to his God.[112] The obligation of the Zaddik to do everything in his power to overcome poverty is tirelessly stressed in short epigrams as well as complex homilies: 'For if there is no flour there is no Torah, therefore it is necessary to draw down sustenance in plenty' (*Zikaron Zot*, p. 39); 'And also to make the world rich so that there should be no poverty which makes man disregard the sense of the Holy One, blessed be He' (*Zikaron Zot*, p. 139); 'But this also is necessary and brings advantage, giving pleasure to Him, blessed be He: wealth in order to serve Him, blessed be He, out of satisfaction of the heart: thus also wealth is for the service of the Creator' (*Zot Zikaron*, p. 136); 'A livelihood is indispensable . . . If a man draws down abundance and a good livelihood to the world, the service of Heaven comes in any event, for if there is no flour there is no Torah' (*Zot Zikaron*, p. 136; *Diverey Emet*, p. 46).

This optimism about the relationship between material prosperity and spiritual exaltation is sober enough and is based on actual experience, as can be seen from the Seer's witty observation on the attractiveness of Heavenly bounty: 'And because the Zaddikim have an abundance of good, those people who desire to share in the good things of this world are envious and draw near to God, blessed be He, so that through doing so for extraneous reasons they come to do it for its own sake' (*Zot Zikaron*, p. 73). But as against the material interest which appears to be 'earthly', there is always, on the part of the Zaddik, a spiritual intention behind the material action: 'If a person integrated his materiality and earthliness into one, so that his whole intention in material action is solely for the sake of Heaven, it will follow that they all ascend to one place' (*Zot Zikaron*, p. 89).

The declared obligation of the Zaddik to satisfy earthly needs in order to overcome earthly impediments to the fulfilment of the religious ideal implies a complete withdrawal of man's responsibility for his actions. He is even prevented from casting his burden of responsibility upon God. Instead, he must rely for everything connected with both his material and spiritual existence on the bounty entrusted to the Zaddik. An examination of the nature of the relationship between the Zaddik and his followers would be outside the scope of the present study, which is concerned with the basic claims of the Zaddik as seen from his point of view. We are in no doubt, however, that by the conferment of religious significance on deprivation and abundance, by making man's spiritual potential dependent on his material position, and by the very conception of poverty as a cause of disintegration and separation between man and God, the foundation is laid for a new social ethos. This description of the Zaddik's function, 'To be a mighty man in the land, to overcome earthliness . . . but because of the lack of the necessaries of life the term *perud*—disintegration—applies to them, for they are in less than a state of unity and complete *devekut* . . . the work of the Zaddik, may he be blessed, draws down blessing for them, whereby they become fully united' (*Zikaron Zot*, p. 40), sets out clearly the religious significance of removing the material stumbling-blocks on the road to fulfilment of the ideals of drawing near to God and *devekut*. Nothing is now excluded from the range of the Zaddik's responsibilities and nothing remains within the scope of the individual or of direct ties between the individual and God. The new patterns of thought are reflected in a leadership exercising an all-embracing tutelary control and attending to spiritual and material needs on both the ideological and practical levels.

The Seer's doctrine of the Zaddik, which expresses novel spiritual and social attitudes, raises the question whether this turning point in the understanding of Zaddikism was a response to the demands of the public, an *ex post facto* formulation of attitudes which had already begun to crystallize in the region, or whether we have before us a delineation of new directions of thought, setting unconventional norms of a bold and original kind, to which the public was responding in large numbers, turning Hasidism into a broadly-based popular movement.

It is probable that we have here a mutual relationship between social conditions which set new spiritual and material challenges and, on the other hand, spiritualistic currents of thought which generated a comprehensive ideology of the connection between *yesh* and *ayin*, applicable to both spiritual and material leadership. The novel ideas of the Seer, and the new patterns of leadership he developed, were his attempt to grapple with spiritual and social processes which reflected the changing character of the Hasidic community; but they were also an expression of the ideological regeneration which accompanied the emergence of leadership patterns suited to new social circumstances.

It is not impossible that the rapid spread of Hasidism, and the broadening of its orbit of influence in Galicia and Poland during the Seer's leadership, were closely connected with this mutual relationship, so clearly reflected in his teaching.

From R. Jacob Isaac's point of view, the changing perception of the scope of leadership in the Hasidic community was rooted in mystical thought and its inherent values. The relation between the mystical and social dimensions was, therefore, not solely the product of changing external conditions and a response to social circumstances but a development of mystical dialectics. It occurred when mystical thought extended the area of its interest from heavenly opposites to the opposition between heavenly and earthly existence, as it did when it established the immanent continuity between the divine *ayin* and its earthly manifestations. It then demanded a response to this continuity in developing a new religious idea of activity in both the metaphysical and the earthly spheres.

The relation between religious ideas and the emergence of a social ethos is instructively illustrated in the doctrine of material Zaddikism, which conferred a spiritual dimension on elements of ordinary life while transferring responsibility for it to the Zaddik. This change reflected sensitivity to the complex relation between man's earthly existence and the limits of his spiritual capacity. It not only altered the scope of religious leadership in Hasidism but it reshaped the expectations of the community, formed new patterns of communal activity, and created the new social ethos of the movement.

Notes

My thanks go to my friends and colleagues Professor Imanuel Etkes, Dr Ada Rapoport-Albert, Dr Israel Bartal, Dr Avraham Shapira and Professor Yehuda Liebes, who took the trouble to read my manuscript and made helpful and instructive suggestions.

1 S. Dubnow, *History of Hasidism* (Hebrew) (Tel Aviv, 1967), pp. 175–204, 215–17, 326–7; A. Z. Aescoly, 'Ha-Hasidut be Polin', in I. Halpern (ed.), *Beyt Yisrael be Polin*, vol. 2 (Jerusalem, 1953), pp. 86–141; R. Mahler, *Hasidism and the Jewish Enlightenment* (Philadelphia, 1985), ch. 9, 'The Schools of Hasidism in Poland', pp. 245–314; H. M. Rabinowicz, *Ha-Yehudi ha-kadosh mi-Pshiskha* (Tel Aviv, 1960). Dubnow noted (op. cit., p. 380) that he had before him a manuscript entitled 'On the History of Hasidism in Poland from 1790 to 1840—recollections and traditions recorded in 1891 by Jacob Shapira of Mezhirech' (Hebrew). According to the catalogue of the Hebrew University and National Library in Jerusalem, A. H. Rubinstein wrote a doctoral dissertation on 'The beginnings of Hasidism in Central Poland' (Hebrew) in 1957, but this work is not to be found in that or any other library known to me, and I have not been able to consult it.

2 Cf. the traditions quoted by I. Berger in *Zekhut Yisrael, Eser Orot* (Warsaw, 1925), p. 90, par. 26, and by M. M. Walden in *Nifleot ha-Rabi* (Warsaw, 1911), p. 10b. H. Liberman noted this fact in the following statement: 'In 1785 . . . Hasidism in Poland was still in its infancy; the only *Admor* (Hasidic *rebbe*) in Poland and Galicia was R. Elimelech of Lyzhansk in Eastern Galicia . . . who had only a few followers in Poland . . . it was only thanks to his disciple R. Jacob Isaac Horowitz "the Seer" of Lublin that Hasidism struck root in Poland. The rest of the hasidic dynasties in Poland and Galicia were almost all founded by the disciples of the *Rebbe* of Lublin'. (*Ohel Rahel*, vol. 3, New York, 1981, p. 58). G. Scholem, 'The Polemic against Hasidism and its Leaders in *Nezed ha-Dema*' (Hebrew), *Zion*, vol. 20, pp. 73–81), asserts that the picture presented in *Nezed ha-Dema*, a work published in Dyhernfurth in 1773, relates to Galician Hasidism at the beginning of the 1770s (p. 81), but this does not accord with the fact that at that time the only *Admor* in Galicia was R. Elimelech.

3 See the hagiographic anthologies of M. M. Walden, *Nifleot ha-Rabi* (Bilgoraj, 1911); id., *Ohel ha-Rabi*, which comprises three books, *Or ha-Torah, Or ha-Hokhmah* and *Or ha-Niflaot* (Bene Berak, 1965); I. Berger (note 2 above), pp. 83–111 and dozens of collections of Hasidic tales throughout which are scattered various stories about him. Many of these traditions were collected in J. J. Kornblitt, *Aspaklaryah ha-Meirah* (Jerusalem, 1977). Cf. the tales relating to the Seer in M. Buber, *Tales of the Hasidim* (New York, 1972), vol. 1, *The Early Masters*, pp. 300–18, and the list of Hasidic works from which these tales were drawn at the end of the Hebrew version of the same work, *Or ha-Ganuz* (Jerusalem, 1977), pp. 482–3. Two biographies of the 'Seer', based on Hasidic tales, are, A. Bromberg, *Ha-Hozeh mi-Lublin* (Jerusalem, 1962: cf. his *Mi-Gedoley Ha-Hasidut*, Bk. 1, Jerusalem, 1959), and I. Alfasi, *Ha-Hozeh mi-Lublin* (Jerusalem, 1969). The Lublin period in the Seer's life features in M. Buber's historical novel *Gog and Magog* (Hebrew) (Tel Aviv, 1955), which is based on traditions drawn from Hasidic tales.

4 (All the quotations from R. Jacob Isaac Horowitz's works are taken from the collected edition of his three books *Zot Zikaron, Zikaron Zot* and *Diverey Emet*, published in Munkacs in 1942, and reissued in facsimile in Jerusalem in 1973. On the first editions of the Seer's works, see note 23 below.) See *Zikaron Zot*, p. 162, 'Toledot R. Jacob Isaac'. Another tradition which holds that he was born in 1747 is recorded in *Shulhan Tahor*, Pt. 2 (Tel Aviv, 1965), in the section 'Shoshelet ha-Kodesh', where this

date is given on the basis of a tradition of the Zhidachov dynasty.

5 See M. M. Walden, *Nifleot ha-Rabi* (Piotrkow, 1913), p. 44, s. 80; p. 71, s. 184.

6 On the Seer's descent from the family of the Shelah, see J. L. Shapira, *Mishpahot Atikot be-Yisrael* (Tel Aviv, 1982), p. 196; Alfasi (note 3 above), p. 10, n. 4, and cf. *Zikaron Zot*, p. 162, s. 3.

7 See the *responsa* of Isaac Harif (head of the rabbinical court in Uleynov), *Peney Yizhak* (Jaroslav, 1905), near the end of the foreword by the author's grandson, and cf. *Zikaron Zot*, s. 4. See also N. Ortner, *Devar Hen* (Tel Aviv, 1963), pp. 165–73.

8 Moses Zevi Hirsch Maisels was rabbi of Zulkowa from 1754 to 1801.

9 See Samuel Shmelke of Nikolsburg, *Diverey Shmuel* (Jerusalem, 1974), on the weekly portion Noah, p. 5. R. Samuel Shmelke was rabbi of Sieniawa *c.*1756–66. See also *Pinkas Ha-Kehillot*, on Poland, Pt. 3 (Jerusalem, 1984), s.v. 'Sieniawa'; and cf. A. S. B. Michelsohn, *Shemen ha-Tov* (Piotrkow, 1902), foreword.

10 See Dubnow (note 1 above), pp. 80–1; Michelsohn (note 9 above) loc. cit.; J. Kamelhaar, *Dor Deah* (Bilgoraj, 1933), pp. 133–7. R. Samuel Shmelke taught first in Rychwal and later moved to Sieniawa. Among the students in his *yeshivah* were Menahem Mendel of Rymanow, Israel of Koznitz and Moses Leib of Sasov.

11 See, e.g., *Zikaron Zot*, p. 72: 'True words which I heard in the name of the great rabbi, the glory of the Exile, of blessed memory, the head of the rabbinical court in the province of Nikolsburg'; see also p. 73; *Zot Zikaron*, pp. 18, 173; *Diverey Emet*, p. 18. And cf. Berger (note 2 above), pp. 87–8.

12 See *Zikaron Zot*, p. 164, s. 6. Cf. Meshullam Phoebus of Zbarazh, *Sefat Emet* (Lwów, 1879), on the weekly portion *Vayyeshev*. Hasidic tales expatiate on the period the Seer spent with the Maggid. See Walden, *Nifleot ha-Rabi* (note 3 above), p. 50, s. 102; id. *Ohel Rabi* (note 3 above), Pt. 3, *Or ha-Niflaot* p. 23; Berger (note 2 above), p. 89 ss. 24–5; and cf. A. Walden, *Shem ha-Gedolim he-Hadash* (Warsaw, 1864), p. 30b. Dubnow was in error in questioning whether R. Jacob Isaac was a disciple of R. Dov Baer of Mezhirech, for the Seer includes in his works many direct quotations from the words of the Maggid, using dozens of times such formulae as these: 'As I heard from my teacher, the Maggid of Rovno' or 'for I heard from my master the rabbi, the Maggid of Rovno, Rabbi Baer, of blessed memory' (*Diverey Emet*, p. 32); 'I heard this from the mouth of the holy man, the rabbi of Rovno' (*ibid.* p. 103), etc. It appears that he was with the Maggid in Rovno in the late 1760s or early 1770s (note his approbation of Solomon of Lutsk's *Divrat Shelomo*, Jerusalem, 1972). However, the sources available to us show that he did not regard his period with the Maggid as a sufficient source of authority to act as a leader, and he spent further time as the disciple of R. Shmelke and R. Elimelech. When he first undertook leadership he based his authority on charismatic inspiration alongside the authority conferred on him by R. Elimelech.

13 On R. Elimelech of Lyzhansk see G. Nigal (ed.), *Noam Elimelech le-Elimelech mi-Lyzhansk*, vol. 1 (Jerusalem, 1978), pp. 9–18; M. Wilensky, *Hasidim u-Mitnaggedim* (Jerusalem, 1970), vol. 2, p. 370 (the index entry referring to him).

14 On R. Elimelech of Lyzhansk's own spiritual path and on his disciples' understanding of his legacy, see the letter of R. Zachariah Mendel of Jaroslaw in *Sefer Iggeret ha-Kodesh* (see G. Nigal, note 13 above, vol. 2, pp. 603–8).

15 See *Zikaron Zot*, p. 164, s. 10, and cf. his enlightening remarks on pp. 147–9, which are in the nature of a personal confession affording an insight into his character. It is very doubtful if they were originally intended for publication. See note 23 below, and cf. the publisher's foreword to *Zot Zikaron* (Lemberg, 1861, not included in most of the other editions), which testifies that this passage was not originally written for publication.

16 See his references to these personalities, *Zikaron Zot*, pp. 47, 60, 90, 99, 113, 129; *Zot*

Zikaron, pp. 16, 51, 77, 117, 118, 163. Cf. his signature to the letter quoted by D. Z. Hillmann in *Iggerot Baal ha-Tanya u-Bheney Doro* (Jerusalem, 1953), no. 108, p. 187, and the references to his teachers there.

17 Solomon Ha-Cohen of Radomsk, *Tiferet Shelomo* (Piotrkow, 1890), on Deuteronomy, weekly portion 'Vayyelech', p. 141.

18 Cf. S. Ettinger, 'The Hasidic Movement—Reality and Ideals', in *Social Life and Social Values of the Jewish People, Journal of World History*, vol. 11, nos. 1–2 (1968), pp. 263–4; Rabinowicz (note 1 above), p. 110.

19 *Ma'or va-Shemesh* (Lemberg/Breslau[?], 1842), weekly portion Phinehas, p. 182, where there is a wide-ranging discussion of this question.

20 See A. S. B. Michelsohn, *Ohel Elimelech* (Przemysl, 1847), p. 165. Cf. Walden (note 3 above), *Or ha-Niflaot*, p. 11, s.24; Buber (note 3 above), vol. 2, *Later Masters*, 'Introduction', pp. 10–12; I. Tishby and Y. Dan, 'Torat ha-Hasidut ve-Sifrutah', *Hebrew Encyclopedia*, vol. 17, s.v. 'Hasidut', reprinted in A. Rubinstein (ed.), Studies in Hasidism (Hebrew) (Jerusalem, 1977), p. 781.

21 See Dubnow (note 1 above), pp. 216–17, and cf. the sources he mentions (*Zemir Arizim* [1798], pp. 4, 9, 10, 11) and the remarks of Wilensky (note 13 above), pp. 195, 207–9, 212. See also I. Loebel, *Sefer ha-Vikkuah* (Warsaw, 1798), p. 18a (Wilensky, op. cit. pp. 314–15) and J. Perl, *Megalleh Temirin* (Vienna, 1819), end of letter 1 and end of letter 104.

22 Dubnow (note 1 above), p. 216.

23 We possess three works by R. Jacob Isaac: *Zot Zikaron* (Lemberg, 1851); *Zikaron Zot* (Warsaw, 1869); and *Diverey Emet* (Zholkva, 1808) (probably printed in 1830–1). See A. Toyber, *Mehkarim Bibliographiyim* (Jerusalem, 1932), p. 95; A. Rubinstein, 'Sifrey ha-Hozeh mi-Lublin', *Kiryat Sefer*, vol. 37 (1962), pp. 123–6. *Zot Zikaron* was written first. It is unedited and was printed by the publisher from the MS just as he found it, with the author's notes for his own use and his recollections and guidelines, which he had not prepared for publication. They contain repetitions, slips of the pen, annotations and remarks such as 'I do not remember any more, nor did I understand it' (p. 18); 'and for the rest, I have forgotten how I interpreted it' (p. 140). The publisher's foreword to the edition of 1851 alludes to the fact that the book was not originally prepared for publication but existed as a collection of memorandums intended only for the writer's eyes:

Before I conclude, I will set before you here the reason why this book is entitled *Zot Zikaron*, which was the name chosen by the author himself, may the memory of this righteous and holy man be a blessing to us. For in his great humility, this righteous man did not seek to make himself a great name in the land by writing a book in order to spread it among the people of Israel, and therefore he did not write down his new insights in sequence, according to the order of the weekly readings of the Torah, but his whole desire was to record all his new insights into the Torah so as to preserve them in his keeping. And his holy custom was to write down every week the words of Torah which had issued from his holy lips on the previous Sabbath; and sometimes he set down first all the scriptural verses and rabbinic sayings which had been the cornerstones of his discourse so that he should not forget any of them while writing, and then he recorded his new insights concerning them. That is why the name he gave to this 'good solder' (Is. 41:7) was *Zot Zikaron* ('This as a memorial': Ex. 17:14), for he said 'This will serve as a memorial, to be with me', so that it should never be forgotten by him.

The publication of *Zikaron Zot*, R. Jacob Isaac's second work, was undertaken in Warsaw in 1869 by the Seer's grandson, David ben Meshullam Zusha Halevi Horowitz. The MS he used had been in the possession of his father, the Seer's son. He says in his foreword: 'I should point out that in a number of places the writing of his holy hand in this holy book is very strange. And in his holy words there are noticeable defects of style, because in his great fervour while writing he paid no attention at all to language, but only to the holy subject-matter. Nevertheless, I was afraid to interfere by correcting his holy words.' This book, like the previous one, was not originally structured round the sequence of the weekly Torah portions, since it was not prepared for the press by the author. However, David ben Meshullam Zusha, while stating that he had not corrected the text, testified that he had rearranged it: 'But this addition I took it upon myself to make, and I took great trouble with it, arranging the holy book according to the order of the weekly Torah readings.' Observations by the author such as, 'The brackets which occur from time to time indicate ideas which occurred to me at the time of writing, but not on the holy Sabbath [on which the original teaching was delivered orally], and I have made a separate section of them' (p. 66) prove that the text was indeed not revised or corrected for publication, and therefore we have in these two books first-class evidence of the state of mind of the author, unaffected by any later revision or editing.

Diverey Emet, the third of the Seer's books to be written, was seen into print by his grandson Isaac Jacob Koppel, the son of Abraham, the Seer's son, in the 1830s, although the title-page gives the year of publication as 1808. The latter date has long been proved false by Toyber (note 23 above, p. 95). This book, which was printed first, was in fact the last of the three to be written; its original name, indicating the sequence of writing, was *Hiddush ha-Shelishi* ('The Third New Insight'), as we learn from Isaac Jacob Koppel's foreword and the beginning of the book itself. The name *Diverey Emet* was given to it by R. Isaac Jacob Koppel, as he states in the foreword. The book was written, in part, after the death of R. Elimelech of Lyzhansk in 1786–7, as emerges from R. Jacob Isaac's remarks on p. 99, and it contains many parallels to his two earlier works. It is terse in style, referring back to earlier treatments of the same subjects in the two other works.

Rubinstein argued (Kiryat Sefer, vol. 37, p. 125) that in the Lemberg edition of 1851, *Zot Zikaron* ended at p. 42a (p. 127 in the Munkacs edition of 1942) and that from there on the homilies were copied from the previously printed *Diverey Emet*, but this conclusion does not follow at all, for it is most probable that the MS from which *Zot Zikaron* was printed comprised that work and *Hiddush ha-Shelishi* as one continuous text. The fact is that in *Zot Zikaron* the homilies are presented out of sequence, while in *Diverey Emet* they are arranged according to the order of the weekly Torah readings. We can accept as reliable the testimony of the redactor: 'and therefore he did not write his new insights in sequence, according to the order of weekly readings of the Torah', and there is no reason to suspect that the publisher copied from *Diverey Emet* but distorted the sequence, as suggested by Rubinstein. We should rather assume that there were several copies in the hands of the Seer's grandsons. (On the existence of manuscripts of the Seer's works and of copies made in his lifetime see Rabinowicz, note 1 above, p. 46, n. 92.) The references to his teachers in *Zot Zikaron* and *Zikaron Zot* indicate that parts of the books were written in parallel at various times; this may apply also to some of the homilies in *Diverey Emet*. Cf. note 24 below.

24 See e.g. *Zot Zikaron*, p. 173: 'In the name of the rabbi of Nikolsburg, my teacher and master, of blessed memory.' Contrast with this 'I heard this from the rabbi, the Maggid of Zolochev, may he be preserved in life' (*ibid.*, p. 118); 'I also heard this from my teacher, may he be preserved in life' (*ibid.*, p. 77); 'I heard from my master, may he be preserved in life' (*Zikaron Zot*, pp. 47, 60, 113; *Zot Zikaron*, p. 118). Quotations in the name of 'my master' or 'my teacher' refer to R. Elimelech, as emerges from *Zikaron Zot*, p. 99: 'As I heard by way of parable from my master, who said in the

name of his brother R. Zusha'; 'and I heard it said in the name of my master R. Melech, may he be preserved in life' (*Zikaron Zot*, p. 7). R. Jacob Isaac, writing during the lifetime of his master and in close proximity to his place of residence, did not mention him by name out of respect. R. Elimelech is mentioned together with the blessing for the living in *Zikaron Zot*, p. 113; only from p. 155 of *Zot Zikaron* onwards, and from p. 99 of *Diverey Emet*, is he mentioned with the blessing for the dead. It should be pointed out that the Seer's works were written before R. Elimelech's book was published in 1788. On differing opinions as to whether R. Elimelech died in 1786 or 1787 see B. Landau, *Ha-Rav R. Elimelech mi-Lyzhansk* (Jerusalem, 1963), pp. 291–3.

25 Cf. Dubnow (note 1 above), pp. 175–204, 215–17, 326–7, and see Aescoly (note 1 above), pp. 92–7. On the special position of Galicia during these years, and the social and economic milieu in which R. Jacob Isaac was active, see A. J. Brawer, *Studies in Galician Jewry* (Hebrew) (Jerusalem, 1956), pp. 162–7, 141–53, and p. R. Magocsi, *Galicia, a Historical Survey and Bibliographical Guide* (Toronto, 1983), pp. 92–115.

26 On the connection between the ethical and mystical values of Hasidic leadership, the influence of those values on the spread of Hasidism, and the involvement of the leadership in the problems of daily life and the needs of the community see Ch. Shmeruk, 'Ha-Hasidut ve-Iskey ha-Hakhirut', *Zion*, vol. 35 (1970), pp. 182–192.

27 See *Zikaron Zot*, pp. 145, 147–52 for autobiographical references, and *ibid.*, p. 148, for guidelines intended for his own use. Cf. also the publisher's foreword: 'and near the end of the book there are about four leaves containing his holy guidelines, which include some very wonderful things.'

28 *Ibid.*, pp. 40, 56, 125, 132, 146, 151–2; *Zot Zikaron* pp. 18, 68, 108, 130, 136, 140, 137: 'And now I do not remember [these things] properly; I am therefore writing headings only, and those are not very exact'; 'Alas for those who forget now, when they come to write.' Cf. also the conclusion of the foreword to *Diverey Emet*.

29 The fact that *Zot Zikaron* was unedited is made very clear by the author's notes which remained in the text as printed: 'I have forgotten what I said in regard to this' (*Zot Zikaron*, p. 62); 'I cannot remember properly what I said' (*ibid.*, p. 63); 'And I have forgotten and no longer remember, nor do I understand [it]' (*ibid.*, p. 18); 'to be looked up in the *Zohar*—I do not now know the place' (*ibid.*, p. 69) and so on. See also note 23 above.

30 See note 23 above. The Seer's grandson, who saw the book into print, made no deletions or alterations and pointed out in his foreword that it had not been revised or corrected but preserved the original text of the author's MS, and that its peculiarities of style and language were due to the circumstances in which it was written and to its ecstatic inspiration. The division according to the weekly Torah readings was, however, the work of the grandson; see note 23 above.

31 See the most interesting foreword to *Diverey Emet* by the Seer's grandson, R. Isaac Jacob Koppel ben Abraham Halevi Horowitz, on the circumstances in which the book was written, its esoteric dimensions and its ecstatic origin, and on the Seer's attempts to reconstruct the inspirational sermon and commit it to writing.

32 Cf. R. Shneur Zalman of Lyadi, *Tanya, Iggeret ha-Kodesh*, letter no. 22, p. 134; and see *Iggerot Kodesh*, ed. D. B. Levin (New York, 1980), pp. 55–6; R. Elior, 'Vikuah Minsk', *Jerusalem Studies in Jewish Thought*, vol. 1, no. 4 (1982), pp. 180–93: I. Etkes, 'Darko shel R. Shneur Zalman mi-Lyadi ke-Manhig shel Hasidim', *Zion*, vol. 50 (1985), pp. 323–7, 329–30.

33 On the Hasidic doctrine of the Zaddik see G. Scholem, 'Ha-Zaddik', in *Pirkey Yesod be-Havanat ha-Kabbalah u-Semaleha* (Jerusalem, 1976), pp. 213–58; on the special quality of the Hasidic Zaddik, *ibid.* pp. 241–58; id., *Major Trends in Jewish Mysticism*, (New York, 1976), pp. 337–8, 342–7; id., 'Mysticism and Society', *Diogenes*, vol. 58

(1967), pp. 1–24; S. Dresner, *The Zaddik*, (New York, 1960), pp. 113–222; B. Z. Dinur, 'Reshitah shel ha-Hasidut' in *Be-Mifneh ha-Dorot* (Jerusalem, 1955), pp. 221–5; M. Buber, *Be-Phardes ha-Hasidut* (Tel Aviv, 1945), pp. 67–78; J. Weiss, 'Reshit Zemihatah shel ha-Derekh ha-Hasidit', *Zion*, vol. 16 (1951), pp. 69–88, reprinted in Rubinstein (note 20 above), pp. 145–64); id., *Mehkarim be-Hasidut Braslav* (Jerusalem, 1974), pp. 99–107; Tishby and Dan (note 20 above), 'Torat ha-zaddik', pp. 779–84; Ettinger (note 18 above), pp. 251–66; A. Rapoport-Albert, 'God and the Zaddik as the two Focal Points of Hasidic Worship', *History of Religion*, vol. 18 (Chicago, 1979), pp. 296–325; A. Green, 'The Zaddik as Axis Mundi in Later Judaism', *Journal of the American Academy of Religion*, vol. 45 (1977), pp. 327–47.

34 See Rapoport (note 33 above), pp. 319–20; Weiss, *Mehkarim* (note 33 above), pp. 104–7.

35 See Scholem (note 33 above), *Major Trends*, p. 342, and 'Ha-Zaddik', p. 247; and id., 'Sheloshah Tipusim shel Yir'at Shamayim Yehudit', in *Devarim be-Go* (Tel Aviv, 1975), pp. 547–56; Dinur (note 33 above), p. 224; Ettinger (note 18 above), pp. 256–60.

36 On R. Elimelech of Lyzhansk's doctrine of the Zaddik, see R. Schatz, 'Le-Mahuto shel ha-Zaddik ba-Hasidut', *Molad*, vol. 18 (1960), pp. 365–78; G. Nigal, *Mishnat ha-Hasidut be-khitvey R. Elimelech mi-Lyzhansk u-Bheyt Midrasho* (doctoral dissertation, Jerusalem, 1972); id. (note 13 above), introduction. On the manner of his leadership see the testimony of both his son and his disciple, *Sefer Iggeret ha-Kodesh* (note 14 above), pp. 591–608. Elimelech's doctrine of the Zaddik differs appreciably from that of R. Jacob Isaac, even though the latter was decisively influenced by it. This, however, is beyond the scope of the present paper; I hope to deal with this topic elsewhere.

37 On the denial to mankind of direct contact with God, on the transfer of *devekut* from God to the Zaddik, and its socio-religious background, see Rapoport (note 33 above), pp. 305–6, 313, 318–22.

38 J. Weiss, 'Reshit Zemihatah' (note 33 above), p. 73.

39 According to a tradition quoted by his disciple Kalonymos Kalman Epstein, the author of *Ma'or va-Shemesh*, 'therefore every Zaddik has men who travel to him to attach themselves to him, and they are branches from the root of his soul' (note 19 above, weekly portion 'Hukkat', p. 171).

40 For a description of the state of society at that time, and of the failure of the leadership, which accords with this and similar criticisms, see R. Mahler, *Le-Toledot ha-Yehudim be-Polin* (Merhavia, 1946), pp. 357–72, 395–415; Dinur (note 33 above), pp. 95–110, 121–31; Y. Heilpern, *Yehudim ve-Yahadut be-Mizrah Europa* (Jerusalem, 1968), pp. 30–3; J. Katz, *Tradition and Crisis* (New York, 1971), pp. 225–30; but cf. note 98 below for the preferability of the Hebrew edition of this work; Brawer (note 25 above), pp. 141–53.

41 Cf. *Zot Zikaron*, p. 191: 'The Zaddik who has *devekut* [while he operates] within the community and without, while dealing with worldly affairs, can serve Him, blessed be He, which is not the case with the one who occupies himself solely with the Torah; while such a person is so occupied, he is in a state of devekut, but when he is not occupied with the Torah, he does not serve Him, blessed be He.' For a sharp criticism of those who study Torah but not for its own sake, and who ignore the needs of their people, see *Zot Zikaron*, p. 95. And cf. *Ma'or va-Shemesh*, where the author quotes the views of the Seer on 'those who study Torah who have not abandoned their evil ways' in a commentary on the verse 'What right have you to recite my statutes?' (Ps. 50:16: *Ma'or va-Shemesh* (note 19 above) on the weekly reading 'Mishpatim', p. 90d, on 'Devarim', p. 194a.

42 See Katz (note 40 above), pp. 79–90.

43 See S. Ettinger in *A History of the Jewish People*, ed. H. H. Ben-Sasson (London, 1976), Pt. 4, 'The Modern Period', pp. 774–6, and cf., for a practical example of this, Shmeruk (note 26 above), pp. 182–92.

44 On the character of the Hasidic as opposed to the rabbinic leadership see G. Scholem, *Major Trends* (note 33 above), pp. 333–4, 344–5, and cf. Ettinger (note 18 above), p. 261; Katz (note 40 above), pp. 225–30; see the important observation of Brawer on the connection between the abolition of the political rights and rights of jurisdiction of the *Kehillah* in Galicia and the spread of Hasidism there: Brawer (note 25 above), p. 182. And see C. Abramsky, 'The Crisis of Authority within European Jewry in the 18th Century', *Studies in Jewish Religious and Intellectual History, Presented to Alexander Altmann* (Tuscaloosa, 1979), pp. 13–28.

45 See note 21 above, and cf. this with the arguments and counter-arguments in regard to the contempt shown for the Zaddikim to which R. Jacob Isaac refers in *Zikaron Zot*, p. 96; *Zot Zikaron*, pp. 13, 36, 50, 71, 162, 171, 187.

46 Cf. the view of R. Elimelech: 'And this will be the sign for him: if people become his followers—then he is a Zaddik' (*Noam Elimelech*, ed. Nigal, note 13 above on 'Bo' 37c); 'If he is a Zaddik he has men who draw near to him and live with him in perfect love' (*ibid.*).

47 On the definition of charisma in its religious context see M. Weber, *Theory of Social and Economic Organizations* (London, 1964), pp. 328, 358–73, 380–92. Cf. the Hebrew Weber reader: S. N. Eisenstadt (ed.), *M. Weber—Al ha-Charisma u-Bheniyat ha-Mosadot* (Jerusalem, 1980), pp. 29–30. See also E. Shils, 'Charisma, Order and Status', *American Sociological Review*, vol. 30 (1965), pp. 199–213; S. Sharot, 'Hasidism and the Routinization of Charisma', in *Messianism, Mysticism and Magic* (Chapel Hill, 1982), pp. 155–88. On the view of the Hasidic leadership as a charismatic leadership see Scholem, *Major Trends* (note 33 above), pp. 334, 344, 347; id., 'Demuto ha-Historit shel R. Israel Baal Shem Tov', *Devarim be-Go* (Tel Aviv, 1975), pp. 295, 307–12; Buber (note 33 above), p. 105; Katz (note 40 above), pp. 269, 274. On the importance of the Sabbatian heritage in shaping pneumatic leadership, see note 33 above, Scholem, 'Ha-Zaddik', pp. 244–5, and Weiss, 'Reshit Zemihatah', pp. 69–88.

48 On the view of his teacher, R. Elimelech, as to the mission of the Zaddik, cf. *Noam Elimelech* (note 13 above), on 'Shelah Lekha': 'The Zaddikim always care for the community of Israel and pray for them constantly'; and on 'Pekudey': 'The Zaddik, who represents the quality of the male [who pours out the flow, rather than the female who receives it], pays no regard to his own benefit but his whole purpose is to confer an abundance of good on all Israel.' On mediation between upper and lower worlds, see Tishby and Dan (note 20 above), pp. 781–2.

49 His outstanding disciple R. Kalonymos Kalman of Krakow, the author of *Ma'or va-Shemesh*, throws light on the way the close associates of the Seer conceived his relationship with the upper worlds: 'This is the end of every man, that his soul should be stripped of its materiality; let him see to it without delay while he is yet alive . . . to attain this condition, namely to divest himself of the materiality of this world, so that there should remain with him nothing but spirituality, and then he will be in communion with upper worlds. And this is well known of great Zaddikim, and I myself have seen it, that when they enter into communion with upper worlds and are stripped of the robes of corporality, the Divine Presence rests upon them and speaks from their throat, and their mouth utters prophecies and declares what is to come, and afterwards those Zaddikim do not themselves know what they have been saying, for they are in communion with upper worlds and the Divine Presence speaks from their throat' (note 39 above, on 'Va-yiggash', p. 50a). For further testimony by his disciples and associates on the revelation of his spiritual powers and his charismatic leadership, see Zevi Elimelech of Dynow, *Agra de-Pirka* (Lemberg, 1858), s.25 and id., *Agra*

de-kallah (Przemysl, 1868), on 'Pekudey', p. 31; Isaac Judah Jehiel Safrin of Komarno, *Megillat Setarim*, ed. Ben Menahem (Jerusalem, 1944), pp. 8, 11. See also Berger (note 2 above), pp. 84, 92; *Eser Kedushot* (Warsaw, 1925), pp. 89–90 s. 22; and cf. Aaron Marcus, *Ha-Hasidut* (Tel Aviv, 1980), p. 114; Kornblitt (note 3 above), pp. 9–16.

50 R. Jacob Isaac is an outstanding example of a Zaddik who attributed his authority to his metaphysical merit and his ties with upper worlds and not to the instruction of his teachers or his connection with the chain of Hasidic tradition. Cf. Etkes (note 32 above), pp. 344–5. Etkes rightly points to the importance of the link with the Maggid as a source of authority for Hasidic leadership, but his generalization of this pattern, which is valid for some of the Maggid's disciples, cannot be applied to all of them. Further research is needed into the relative importance of charismatic inspiration as against the kabbalistic-Hasidic tradition in establishing the authority of the Zaddik in Hasidism.

51 On the problems connected with the claim to be favoured with the revelation of the Holy Spirit, cf. the evidence of a contemporary of the Seer who lived in the same region, R. Zachariah Mendel of Jaroslaw, a disciple of R. Elimelech (note 14 above).

52 Zevi Hirsch of Zhidachov, *Sur me-Ra va-Aseh Tov* (Lublin, 1912), p. 55. The expression 'In the days of the *TuZ*' relates to the occasion when R. David Halevi, author of the Turey Zahav, sent envoys from Lemberg to Sabbatai Zevi in Gallipoli. See G. Scholem, 'Ha-Tenuah ha-Shabbeta'it be-Polin', in *Studies and Texts Concerning the History of Sabbatianism and its Metamorphoses* (Hebrew) (Jerusalem, 1974), pp. 73–4. R. Zevi calls the Seer 'my teacher': see *Sur me-Ra*, pp. 17–18, and the additions of Zevi Elimelech of Dynow, *ibid.* p. 21.

53 On speaking words of Torah under divine inspiration, cf. Berger (note 2 above), p. 93, s. 36. And cf. the foreword to *Diverey Emet* by the Seer's grandson (note 31 above): 'For we and our contemporaries know of the great force and power of the holiness and asceticism and fervour of my honoured lord, my grandfather the rabbi, the author of this book (may his memory be for a blessing), and especially while he was speaking these words of Torah with reverence and love and trembling and quaking, for flaming brands issued from his mouth.' Cf. also *Ma'or va-Shemesh* (note 19 above) on 'Va-Ethanan', p. 201d, and on 'Mishpatim', p. 91b.

54 Cf. his 'guidelines' at the beginning of *Diverey Emet*, esp. nos. 1–5, 14, 40, 50, 52, 77, 82. See also his 'guidelines' at the beginning of *Zot Zikaron*, pp. 3–4, and cf. the traditions reported in Kornblitt (note 3 above), pp. 45–50. On variant forms of his guidelines and their printed editions see Z. Gries, 'Sifrut ha-Hanhagah ha-Hasidit', *Zion*, vol. 46 (1981), p. 281.

55 There is a clear allusion here to Joseph Karo's *Maggid*, referred to as 'the voice of my beloved'. Cf. R. J. Z. Werblowsky, *Joseph Karo, Lawyer and Mystic* (Philadelphia, 1977), pp. 9–23, 148–68.

56 Hasidic tradition has preserved many testimonies to the powerful influence exerted by the Seer's public displays of transcendental inspiration and to the excitement and emotion it generated in those around him. See the sources quoted in notes 3 and 49 above. And see R. Jacob Isaac on the ecstatic nature of the 'burning fire', *Zot Zikaron* pp. 124–6. In his *Gog and Magog* (note 3 above), Martin Buber, basing himself on these traditions, was able to convey in brilliant literary form the power of the religious experience undergone by the members of the Seer's court. It is interesting to compare this to the Habad tradition in regard to the strength of the emotional influence exerted by the Hasidic utterances of R. Shneur Zalman: 'His manner of delivering Hasidic teachings was most frightening and all those present were smitten with terror and repented wholeheartedly there and then, eager to serve the Lord in the most awesome way.' H. M. Hielman, *Beyt Rabi*, (Berdichev, 1902), Bk. 1, p. 31, note 2.

57 Cf. *Zikaron Zot*, pp. 9, 47, 50, 58, 73, 121; *Zot Zikaron*, pp. 181, 142; *Diverey Emet*,

pp. 106–7. On his supernatural powers of vision, which earned him the name of 'the Seer', see Samuel of Sieniawa, *Ramatayim Zofim* (Warsaw, 1881), p. 247, s. 106, and the indirect reference by R. Jacob Isaac, *Zot Zikaron*, p. 89. Cf. Weber, *Theory* (note 47 above), pp. 359–60. As to the impact of the Seer's wonder-working powers on the circle of R. Elimelech's disciples, see the letter of Zachariah Mendel of Jaroslaw (note 14 above).

58 Cf. the foreword by Dov Baer of Linits to *Shivhey ha-Besht* (*In Praise of the Baal Shem Tov*) as to the role of 'miracles and wonders' and tales of miracles in attracting a popular following, and the significance of wonder-working in any assessment of the Zaddik. See also *Zikaron Zot*, p. 3, and cf. *Diverey Emet* pp. 106–7. Cf. also Solomon of Lutsk (note 12 above), on 'be-Shalah', p. 79, concerning the significance of miracles in Hasidic circles.

59 See also *Diverey Emet*, pp. 106–9.

60 On the nature of the charismatic mission, cf. Weber (note 47 above), 'Charisma', pp. 29–30, and *Theory*, pp. 358 ff. See Scholem, 'Ha-Zaddik' (note 33 above), p. 247.

61 On the tension between charismatic authority and the established leadership, and on the gap between them in terms of values and patterns of leadership, see Weber, *Theory* (note 47 above), pp. 361–3, 386–92, and the introduction to that work by T. Parsons, pp. 64–6.

62 On the dialectical aspects of the concepts of *yesh* and *ayin*, see R. Elior, *Torat ha-Elohut ba-Dor ha-Sheni shel Hasidut Habad* (Jerusalem, 1982), pp. 48–50, 125–33; id., 'Iyyunim be-Mahashevet Habad', *Daat*, vol. 16 (1986), pp. 145–54. On the opposing principles which condition existence according to Hasidic thought, see *Maggid Devarav le-Yaakov*, ed. R. Schatz-Uffenheimer (Jerusalem, 1976), pp. 91, 134, 170, 210; Tishby and Dan (note 20 above), pp. 773–5.

63 On the mystical and ethical aspects of the *ayin* see Scholem, 'Ha-Zaddik' (note 33 above), pp. 252–3, and *Maggid Devarav le-Yaakov* (note 62 above), pp. 12, 74, 109, 134; on *ayin* as the source of *yesh*, see ibid., pp. 19–20, 24, 91. See also Tishby and Dan (note 20 above), p. 808.

64 Cf. Elior (note 62 above), pp. 43–51.

65 See *Ets Hayyim* (Warsaw, 1891), pp. 25, 56–7, and Scholem, *Major Trends* (note 33 above), pp. 261–3.

66 On *histalkut* and *hitpashtut* (withdrawal and expansion) in their Hasidic meaning see *Maggid Devarav le-Yaakov* (note 62 above), pp. 210, 289–90, and the index entries for those headings; see also Tishby and Dan (note 20 above), p. 773.

67 See Scholem *Major Trends* (note 33 above); for the dialectic of Zaddikism, cf. *Noam Elimelech* (note 13 above) on 'Bo': 'The Zaddik must work in the same way as in the creation of the worlds, first destroying, then rebuilding'; 'And in order to commence, the most important thing is that you should be able to attain the ultimate root, which is humility, so that you bear in mind your lowliness, for you are dust' ('Lekh Lekha', p. 5a, and cf. ibid., on 'Hayyey Sarah', p. 10b).

68 See *Babylonian Talmud*, *Sotah* 21b: Rabbi Johanan said: 'The words of Torah are preserved only by him who makes himself as if he did not exist, as it is said "And wisdom is found from *ayin*"' (a play on the two meanings of *ayin*: Job 28:12, '*ve-ha-hokhmah me-ayin timaze*' literally meaning 'And wisdom, where shall it be found?'). Cf. *Babylonian Talmud*, *Erubin* 54a: 'The Torah is preserved only by one who makes himself like a wilderness.'

69 On the Zaddik in the domain of the *ayin*, see Scholem, 'Ha-Zaddik' (note 33 above), pp. 252–3. On the consciousness of lowliness and exaltation in R. Elimelech, cf. Nigal (note 13 above), introduction, p. 32. On the quietistic significance of man's turning himself into *ayin*, cf. R. Schatz, *Ha-Hasidut ke-Mystikah* (Jerusalem, 1968), pp. 21–31, and id. (note 36 above), pp. 369–70. Cf. A. Green, 'Hasidism—Discovery and

Retreat', in p. Berger (ed.), *The Other Side of God* (New York, 1981), pp. 104–30. See also the statement by R. Meir Apta of Stobnitsa, a disciple of the Seer: 'I heard from my honoured *Admor*, my teacher R. Jacob Isaac, may the memory of that Zaddik be for life in the world to come, who said this in the name of the great rabbi [Levi Isaac] of Berdichev, may the memory of that Zaddik be for life in the world to come: man must stir up in himself the quality of *ayin* and be lowly in his own eyes and continue increasingly in this way, more and more every day; by increasing in his service of the Lord, he will come to know the greatness of the creator and his own lowliness and renew the quality of *ayin* in himself' (*Or la-Shamayim* (Lewów, 1850), on Beshallah).

70 See *Zava'at ha-Ribash* (Kehot Publication Society, New York, 1975), ss.2, 5, 10, 53, summed up in s.53 with the epigram: '"let him make himself like one who does not exist" . . . the meaning is that he should consider himself as if he were not in this world. And cf. *Maggid Devarav le-Yaakov* (note 62 above), pp. 186, 325; Buber (note 33 above), p. 112; G. Scholem, 'Devekut, or Communion with God', in *The Messianic Idea in Judaism* (London, 1971), pp. 213–14; Schatz (note 69 above), pp. 15, 27–9.

71 *Maggid Devarav le-Yaakov* (note 62 above), pp. 38–9. On man's view of himself as inhabiting the upper world and having shaken off the values of this world, see *Zava'at ha-Ribash* (note 70 above), ss.6, 53, 62, 84.

72 The Hasidic interpretation of the talmudic saying 'Children, life and sustenance are a matter dependent not on merit but on planetary influence (*mazzala*)' (*Mo'ed Katan* 28, 1) is based on the kabbalistic understanding of the word *mazzala* as derived from the noun *nezilah*, 'flow', i.e. what is described here is the flow of the *shefa*, the divine flow of bounty which is the source of 'children, life and sustenance'. Cf. also *Noam Elimelech* (note 13 above) on '*Toledot*', p. 12c and d.

73 On the views of the Maggid, see *Maggid Devarav le-Yaakov* (note 62 above), p. 351, index entries for *ayin*, *mahazik azmo le-ayin* ('holds himself to be nought') and *mahashiv et azmo le-ayin* ('considers himself as nought'). On the dialectical relationship between *ayin* and material bounty, cf. I. Tishby, *Mishnat ha-Zohar* (Jerusalem, 1957, 1961), Pt. 2, pp. 253–4.

74 On the mystical meaning of conversion to *ayin*, cf. William James, *The Varieties of Religious Experience* (New York, 1929), pp. 379, 408–10; and cf. Schatz (note 69 above), pp. 24–31.

75 In the doctrine of the Maggid the Zaddik turns *yesh* into *ayin* by way of reversing the action of God, who brings forth *yesh* from *ayin*, whereas in the Seer's doctrine the Zaddik turns *yesh* into *ayin* but also turns *ayin* into *yesh*. See the enlightening remarks of R. Elimelech, *Noam Elimelech* (note 13 above) on '*Terumah*', p. 48a. On the central position of this concept in Hasidic thought, cf. Elior, 'Iyyunim be-Mahashevet Habad' (note 62 above), pp. 143–72.

76 See Scholem, 'Ha-Zaddik' (note 33 above), pp. 252–3.

77 R. Jacob Isaac's views on humility and lowliness were greatly influenced by his teacher, R. Elimelech, who stressed this requirement repeatedly: 'for in order to reach the root it is principally necessary for man to be very humble, and lowly in his own eyes, and [bear in mind] "how little he is to be accounted"' (Is. 2:22) (note 13 above), on 'Hayyey Sarah', p. 10b). 'Lowliness and humility' in the Seer's doctrine are his new formulation of the quality of *ayin* as described by the Maggid of Mezhirech. Cf. also R. Shneur Zalman's statements on the centrality of lowliness in the Hasidic tradition, *Iggerot Kodesh* (note 32 above), p. 183; 'Hanhagot Yesharot' ('honest guidelines') at the end of *Teshuot Hen*, by R. Gedaliah of Linits (Jerusalem, 1965); Dresner (note 33 above), pp. 142–7; Dinur (note 33 above), p. 210. And see Kornblitt (note 3 above), pp. 46–50. See also *Zikaron Zot*, p. 79, and cf. the unequivocal view of R. Elimelech on 'the Zaddikim who regard themselves as more worthless and lowly than all other men', *Noam Elimelech* (note 13 above), pp. 50d–51a.

78 Cf. the Seer's 'Guidelines', in which he again stresses this consciousness of being 'a worse sinner than all other men'. And see Schatz (note 36 above), pp. 376–7. Cf. also the letter of Zachariah Mendel of Jaroslaw (note 14 above): 'They [the Zaddikim] always make known their disgrace and put themselves to shame in public', and similar statements.

79 For the concept of humility and lowliness as a basis for empathy, cf. Samuel of Sieniawa (note 57 above), ch. 24, s.22. And see Schatz (note 36 above), p. 370. Cf. a tradition quoted by the Seer's disciple, Itamar of Konskowola: 'I heard this from the holy mouth of the *Admor*, the rabbi of Lublin, may his soul rest in Paradise: heartbroken and with extreme humility, he condemned himself, "Alas for the generation which has me as its leader".' *Mishmeret Itamar* (Warsaw, 1869), on 'Ki tisa'.

80 On 'the descent of the Zaddik' see Weiss, 'Reshit Zemihatah' (note 33 above), pp. 69–88, and M. Piekarz, *Bi-Yemey Zemihat ha-Hasidut* (Jerusalem, 1978), pp. 280–304; Nigal (note 13 above), introduction, pp. 63–4; Tishby and Dan (note 20 above), pp. 779–81.

81 Ettinger (note 18 above), p. 255.

82 On the tension between devotion to communal needs and his own spiritual exaltation cf. R. Shneur Zalman of Lyadi, *Iggerot Kodesh* (note 32 above), letter no. 24 'venil'eti linso' ('I am weary of bearing'), and cf. Scholem, *Major Trends* (note 33 above), p. 343. On R. Elimelech's viewpoint on this subject see Nigal (note 13 above), pp. 33–7. For a literary expression of the powerful tension between the two poles of the Zaddik's existence see the tales about the Seer 'flying', falling and being thrust into the 'abyss' in the anthologies mentioned in note 3 above.

83 On this question, which is central to the doctrine of the Zaddik, see Rapoport (note 33 above), pp. 305–6, 313, 318–22. And see the Seer's own words on the relationship between the Zaddik and God: 'And those who love Him have dominion over all his works, and they have power to draw down all kinds of bounty and to nullify all decrees' (*Zikaron Zot*, p. 3).

84 See Scholem, 'Ha-Zaddik' (note 33 above), pp. 213–36.

85 *Zikaron Zot*, pp. 78, 32.

86 See *Zot Zikaron*, pp. 8, 54, 203–4; *Zikaron Zot*, pp. 13, 19, 39, 104.

87 'And this is the meaning of "he that has no light" [Is. 50:10], let him trust in the name of the Lord and lean upon his God, for it is He who saves and bestows bounty by the hand of the Zaddik, for such is his pleasure, blessed be He' (*Zikaron Zot*, p. 34).

88 'We draw Him down to this world so that His presence should be among us', *Noam Elimelech* (note 13 above), on 'Korah', p. 79d. 'Attain the state of *ayin*, for *Hokhmah me-ayin timaze* (see note 68 above) and thereby there will be brought about a renewal of everything which requires the bringing forth of *yesh* from *ayin*, like the Creation' (*Zot Zikaron*, p. 141).

89 On the responsibility of the Zaddik for the material state of society cf. Dresner (note 33 above), pp. 148–73; Ettinger (note 18 above), p. 232; Tishby and Dan (note 33 above), pp. 780–2. On the social framework of the relations between Zaddik and community, see Scholem, 'Ha-Zaddik' (note 33 above), pp. 251–2; Schatz note 36 above), pp. 373–4.

90 On *shefa* in its kabbalistic sense, see Scholem, 'Ha-Zaddik' (note 33 above), pp. 228–31, 249; Tishby (note 73 above), Pt. 1, pp. 265ff. On its Hasidic sense see Nigal (note 13 above), introduction, pp. 24–40, and cf. A. Gottlieb, *Studies in the Literature of the Kabbalah* (Hebrew) (Tel Aviv, 1976), pp. 29–37.

91 On the Zaddik as a hypostasis of the kabbalistic *sefirat Yesod*, see Scholem, 'Ha-Zaddik' (note 33 above), pp. 218, 228, 249.

92 Cf. note 72 above.

93 On Joseph the 'Zaddik' the *sefirat Yesod*, the channel through which the *shefa* flows,

cf. Isaiah Horowitz, *Sheney Luhot ha-Berit*, (Amsterdam, 1748), p. 299b.

94 M. Levin, *Erekhey Hevrah ve-Khalkalah ba-Ideologyah shel Tekufat ha-Haskalah* (Jerusalem, 1976), should be consulted for evidence on the world-view underlying this approach—which caused intense irritation to *Maskilim* in Galicia—and on the explicit accusations of the *Maskilim* in regard to the spiritualization of materiality and its severance from the domain of rationality, which, they said, drew the Hasidic community into passivity and anarchy.

95 Weiss (note 33 above), 'Reshit Zemihatah', p. 70; *Mehkarim be-Hasidut Braslav*, p. 102.

96 Schatz (note 36 above), p. 373; see also p. 371.

97 Cf. the criticisms by R. Menahem Mendel of Vitebsk and by R. Shneur Zalman of Lyadi (who began to lead the Hasidim of White Russia in the 1780s, at about the same time as the beginning of R. Jacob Isaac's leadership in Galicia) and their negative attitude to material Zaddikism: *Peri ha-Arez* (Zhitomir, 1849), p. 38b; *Tanya, Iggeret ha-Kodesh*, letter no. 22, p. 134. And see Hillmann (note 16 above), p. 56; Elior (note 32 above), pp. 189–93; Etkes (note 32 above), pp. 323–7, 329–30. Etkes has reservations as to whether R. Shneur Zalman's viewpoint should be defined as a rejection of material Zaddikism, but he does not take into account his fundamental theological standpoint, which denies the validity of the charismatic relationship in regard to worldly affairs.

98 Solomon ha-Cohen of Radomsk (note 17 above) on 'Vayyeshev' pp. 65–6. For a characterization of the two kinds of Zaddikim, see *Noam Elimelech* (note 13 above), on 'Shemot', p. 30b, and 'Shelah lekha', p. 72b. Cf. R. Jacob Isaac's own words: 'For there are degrees of elevation at which a man concerns himself to correct his soul and attach it to its root, but that is not the highest degree, for there is a degree higher than that—at which he concerns himself for the good of Israel . . . a man over the congregation [from Num. 27:16] to declare His praise, one who has not sought to advance his own affairs but only the needs of the community' (*Zot Zikaron*, p. 77). And see Katz (note 40 above), Hebrew version, *Masoret u-Mashber* (Jerusalem, 1958), p. 158, on the importance of the concepts of 'the needs of the community' and 'the good of Israel'. (The English version, which is abridged, omits the relevant paragraph.)

99 Later on, of course, some members of the Hasidic camp sharply criticized the socio-religious system that had been developed in the Hasidism of Lublin and the place of materiality in that system. R. Jacob Isaac of Pshiskha and his followers protested at the position occupied by earthliness and material Zaddikism in Lublin. They broke away from the world and denied its religious value, demanding the restoration of the spiritualistic tendencies of the movement to their former pre-eminence. From a study of the arguments of the Pshiskha school it is possible, by inferring opposites, to characterize the Seer's form of Hasidism. However, as the controversy arose at a later time, it is not dealt with in the present study. For the time being, see Rabinowicz (note 1 above).

100 For the rejection by the school of the Maggid of the principle of prayer for material aid, cf. Schatz (note 69 above), pp. 80–2, 87–95; Etkes (note 32 above), p. 330, and *Iggerot Kodesh* (note 32 above), pp. 57–8.

101 See R. Schatz, 'Adam nokhah Elohim ve-Olam be-Mishant Buber al ha-Hasidut', *Molad*, nos. 149–50 (1960), pp. 596–609. Cf. note 70 above.

102 See Scholem, 'Devekut' (note 70 above), pp. 208, 212; Weiss, 'Reshit Zemihatah' (note 33 above), p. 63; Rapoport (note 33 above), pp. 305–6, 309; Etkes (note 32 above), p. 322.

103 Schatz (note 101 above), p. 597.

104 Scholem 'Perusho shel Martin Buber la-Hasidut', *Devarim be-Go* (note 35 above),

pp. 372–8. Schatz (note 101 above), pp. 596–601; for an examination of the central place of these concepts in Hasidic thought, see *Zava'at ha-Ribash* (note 70 above) and the index to *Maggid Devarav le-Yaakov* (note 62 above).

105 For an analysis of the socio-religious cause of a parallel separation of responsibilities which required, of the Zaddik, devotion (*devekut*) to God and, of his Hasidim, devotion to the Zaddik, see Rapoport (note 33 above), p. 320; Tishby and Dan (note 33 above), p. 801.

106 On the place of poverty and wealth in Hasidic thought, cf. Dinur (note 33 above), pp. 155–7, and Piekarz (note 80 above), index entries for '*osher*' and '*ashirut*' ('riches, wealth'). For R. Jacob Isaac's viewpoint as described in the traditions of his disciples see Berger (note 2 above), p. 105, s. 113. And see the Seer's enlightening remarks in *Diverey Emet* on 'Be-haalotekha', pp. 96–9.

107 Poverty '*ma'avirah et ha-adam al da'to ve-al daat kono*' (*Erubin* 41b. Jastrow translates: 'makes a man disregard his own sense (of right) and the sense of his Maker', but other dictionaries translate the verbal phrase as 'confuses'. On the significance of this evaluation of poverty, specifically in Galicia, see Jacob Goldberg, *Converted Jews in the Polish Commonwealth* (Hebrew) (Jerusalem, 1985), p. 35.

108 See Mahler (note 40 above), p. 430, for a description of the situation at that time: 'In the second half of the eighteenth century the economic plight of the Jewish masses in Poland reached its lowest level; their great poverty was the result of the political situation and also of the first changes in the legal position of the Jews connected with the Reform.' See also *ibid.*, p. 440. Several students of Poland have argued recently that the economic position of Polish Jewry in the eighteenth century was not critical, contrary to the opinion of Dubnow and Mahler. But it appears that this is not valid for Galicia, where conditions of hardship prevailed. For a detailed documentation of this assertion in regard to the Jewish community in the period under review, see the sources quoted in Magocsi (note 25 above), pp. 92–115, 235–6. Cf. E. Ringelblum, *Die Poylishe Yidn in Oyfshtand fun Kosciuszko 1794* (Warsaw, 1937). On exceptionally severe economic conditions in Galicia in the 1780s—in R. Jacob Isaac's time and in his area—following the prohibition of the arenda, see Brawer (note 25 above), pp. 151–3, 162–7, 190–1. Brawer analyses the economic and political data and concludes that the Jews of Galicia in 1785 were left destitute, describing their condition as 'calamitous' (p. 165). He identifies as harshest the years 1785–9, coinciding with the beginning of the Seer's leadership. On poverty in Galicia see *ibid.*, p. 185. See also Dinur (note 33 above), pp. 125–31, and the essays by M. Balaban and I. Schiper in Halpern (note 1 above), vol. 1, which summarize their detailed studies, reviewed by Magocsi in his bibliography (note 25 above). Against the background of such hardship it is reasonable to assume that the doctrine of material Zaddikism was not divorced from the actual circumstances of those who propounded it; it was no mere abstract theory, but an expression of the effort to contend with social realities and a bold attempt to offer remedy to both physical and spiritual distress.

109 On the negative attitude of R. Jacob Isaac to rebukes which ignore actual conditions, see the very end of *Zikaron Zot* and Berger (note 2 above), p. 107, s. 125, quoting traditions handed down orally by his disciple Jacob Zevi Jolish, author of *Melo ha-Ro'im*. See also Weiss, 'Reshit Zemihatah' (note 33 above), pp. 58–60, 71–2.

110 Cf. the attitude of R. Elimelech of Lyzhansk, who emphasized the importance of preaching rebuke, and see Nigal (note 13 above), introduction, pp. 19, 61–3. On the relationship between the preacher who rebukes and the Zaddik, see Weiss, 'Reshit Zemihata' (note 33 above), pp. 58–60, 71–2, and Scholem, 'Ha-Zaddik' (note 33 above), p. 242.

111 Cf. Piekarz (note 80 above), pp. 96–170, and in particular p. 160. On the extreme ascetic orientation of R. Elimelech, and his outright hostility to materiality, see the

beginning of *Noam Elimelech* (note 13 above), in the 'guidelines' and in the 'small Zettel'. It is interesting to examine the dialectical relationship between estranging oneself from materiality, on the one hand, and the doctrine of material Zaddikism, on the other—both of which are combined in the Seer's teaching. For testimony to the asceticism of R. Elimelech, see Moses of Koznitz, *Be'er Moshe* (Josefov, 1883), on 'Va-ethanan' and 'Mase'ey'.

112 Compare this with the opposite view, current in the Hasidic camp, which holds that the correction of faults will, of itself, solve the problems of earning a living (see Etkes (note 32 above, p. 325) or which tends to ignore material needs and to cast man's burden upon God. See *Zava'at ha-Ribash* (note 70 above) opening paragraphs.

Self-sacrifice of the Zaddik in the Teachings of R. Dov Ber, the *Mitteler Rebbe*

Naftali Loewenthal

IN his article 'The Crisis of Authority within European Jewry in the Eighteenth Century',[1] Professor Abramsky makes it clear that one of the key elements in the dynamic of Jewish history in that epoch was the question of the nature of leadership. In that age of controversy, incipient fragmentation and crisis, new forms of authority, of social structure and of hero emerged.

The traditional bearers of power and influence in Eastern Europe had been the official rabbis, preachers, talmudic–cum–kabbalistic scholars, magnates and, using the term in its widest sense, the *shtadlanim*. Combinations of these figures made up the official communal structure which set the pattern of life for most Jews. They also, in varying degrees, provided role models for men of original spirit and set standards of endeavour for the ordinary members of the community.

During the eighteenth century two very different new sources of authority evolved: on the one hand the *Haskalah* movement, and on the other Hasidism. While the sources of both can be discerned in the past,[2] and in the contemporary balance of communal power, it is probably not surprising that both challenged and were challenged by the existing structures of Jewish leadership. Both new movements survived these challenges and it is noteworthy that when they became cognizant of each other, as rival forces in the Jewish community, bitter hostility ensued.

Like all movements of whatever kind, both produced men of fame and of influence, leader figures.[3] In the case of Hasidism, this aspect of the movement became especially and exceptionally significant.

Hasidism provided not only ideals and direction, it also created a unique form of leadership, in which several powerful streams of traditional Jewish imagery were combined. The Hasidic Zaddik manifested for his followers the qualities of prophecy and of kingship, of esoteric wisdom and of knowledge of the hearts of men. These aspects have to varying degrees been described and discussed by previous writers.[4] The present paper introduces a further dimension of the Zaddik—self-sacrifice, an aspect seen particularly clearly in the writings of a Hasidic leader of the fourth generation of the movement: Rabbi Dov Ber of Lubavitch, known as the *Mitteler Rebbe* (1773–1827).[5] Drawing on a deep fount of Jewish tradition reaching back to remote antiquity, R. Dov Ber describes the Zaddik as a paradigm of *mesirat nefesh*, self-sacrifice and martyrdom.[6] Our aim in the following pages is to define and clarify this aspect of R. Dov Ber's teachings. In order to do this, we must first consider the concept of the Zaddik as taught by R. Dov Ber's father, R. Shneur Zalman of Lyadi (d. 1813), founder of the Habad school of Hasidism.[7]

THE HABAD CONCEPT OF THE ZADDIK

How did R. Shneur Zalman's views on the Zaddik compare with those of his contemporaries?

In the teachings of his mentor, the Maggid of Mezhirech (d. 1772), the key to the concept of the Zaddik is the theme of self-nullification, *bitul*. The idea is found in the fragmented scraps we possess of the teachings of the Baal Shem Tov: *ani*, 'Self', is to be changed into *a[y]in*, 'Nought'.[8] In the thought of the Maggid the concept of *bitul* becomes paramount. Through it the individual ascends beyond the limitation implicit in existence. He reaches beyond the *Shevirah*, the Lurianic 'Breaking of the Vessels', the source of the grossness of the material world and of all evil.[9] Through *bitul* the individual attains a state of consciousness 'above time . . . where all is equal: life and death, the sea and dry land'.[10] He is transformed into a man of exceptional power and responsibility in both upper and lower worlds. Characteristic of Hasidism, as distinct from earlier Kabbalism, is the way this power is exercised in society.

In the teachings of the second and third generations of Hasidism, a clearly defined theory of the interrelation between the Zaddik and the world around him was expounded. The relationship concerns material existence, encompassing and transforming everyday activities such as eating; it also concerns people. The mystical link between the Zaddik and the Jewish people, and especially his bond with and inner effect on his followers and those who turn to him, is described by several writers, most notably R. Jacob Joseph of Polonnoye (d. *c.* 1784) and R. Elimelech of Lyzhansk (d. 1786).[11]

In the case of R. Shneur Zalman of Lyadi, sparse reference is found to this aspect of Hasidic thought. The Zaddik is described, but only rarely is there mention of his effect on his followers. Instead, the emphasis in R. Shneur Zalman's teachings is on the attempt to develop in his followers their own potential for spiritual consciousness. He does this not by inviting them to become Zaddikim (which seems to be the import of the recorded teachings of the Maggid),[12] but by communicating to them methods of reaching *bitul* through contemplation, prayer and the normative processes of Jewish religious life: Torah study and the performance of the *mitzvot*.[13] This emphasis on the spiritual possibility of the Hasidic follower was a point of controversy in the third generation of Hasidism. R. Avraham of Kalisk (d. 1810), who became the main opponent of the Habad path, claimed that all that needed to be demanded of the members of the Hasidic fraternity was 'faith in the Zaddik' and basic ethical values.[14]

R. Shneur Zalman's focus on transforming the inner life of the Hasid has given some writers the impression that the concept of the Zaddik is muted in early Habad Hasidism.[15] In fact he and his followers believed fully in the mystical structure linking the Zaddik with the Jewish world in general and with his followers in particular.

We see this from R. Shneur Zalman's own rules for the organization of his fraternity, and also from his theoretical teachings. The rules, called *Takkanot Liozna*[16] and dating from the 1790s, indicate large numbers of followers flocking to R. Shneur Zalman. A letter by him dated 1791–2 mentions forty or fifty visitors every week, and sometimes two hundred. A special free communal kitchen was established to feed the visitors.[17] The Liozna rules ensure that order is maintained, and that new followers are given precedence in having private audience (*Yehidut*) with the Hasidic leader, so that he can impart to each of them a path in Divine Service. It is noteworthy that Avigdor of Pinsk, the enemy of Hasidism who laid the accusations against R. Shneur Zalman which led to the latter's second arrest in 1800, included reference to this first *Yehidut* in his petition to the Tsar. While his account was distorted, it is likely there was truth in the significance he attributed to this event and the bond he described between the Hasidic following and R. Shneur Zalman. The soul of the latter, he said, 'includes all the souls that cleave to him'.[18]

On the theoretical level, the beginning of R. Shneur Zalman's basic tract, *Sefer shel Benonim* (the first section of *Likkutei Amarim* or *Tanya*), portrays a vast anthropomorphic union of all Jewish souls. Those of the Zaddikim, both of the past and of one's own time, play a key role in drawing a Divine flow into this corporate being, and hence, states R. Shneur Zalman, citing a talmudic text, attachment to the Zaddik is of prime importance in the religious life of the individual.[19] He elaborates further on the significance of the Zaddik–Hasid relationship in a letter written to members of the fraternity after the death of R. Menahem Mendel of Vitebsk in 1788. This emphasizes the importance of *hitkasherut* (bonding) and love between Hasid and Zaddik.[20] In R. Shneur Zalman's discourses we also find occasional references to the way the Zaddik, by means of his exalted 'Unifications' in Divine Service, heals the souls of those who are of his 'root'.[21] He imparts 'understanding of the Divine' and arouses the depths of the heart of those in his generation.[22] R. Shneur Zalman also explains the nature of a 'General' soul, i.e. that of the Zaddik, who includes in himself many other souls and therefore 'feels' the souls of others, 'even the lowest in level'.[23] In R. Shneur Zalman's early, brief teachings, which have recently been collected and published,[24] we find themes such as the 'descent' of the Zaddik to the people[25] or, through thoughts of sin, to *Gehinom* to raise the evil-doers.[26] Here too we find emphasis on the need of the Hasid to cleave to the Zaddikim 'for they are above the world and through their mind can raise everything to its root'[27] and also to give charity to them so as to elevate and purify one's own religious emotions.[28] Further elaboration on the significance of giving material support to the Zaddik is found in a letter by R. Aaron Halevi Horowitz (d. 1828), a major Hasid who later became leader in his own right of a section of the *Habad* following. His letter, probably from the early 1800s, addresses the fraternity in an appeal for funds for R. Shneur Zalman. This support is described as 'an intermediary' which enables the individual to draw life-force from the soul of the Zaddik.[29] Such funding was institutionalized under the name *maamad* (support) and is so referred to in a letter by R. Dov Ber shortly after the death of his father R. Shneur Zalman.[30]

These references in early Habad sources to the role of the Zaddik in society are few and far between. None the less, it is clear that in Habad the underlying structure linking Zaddik and Hasid was conceived in rather similar terms to those taught by R. Jacob Joseph and R. Elimelech of Lyzhansk. The overt emphasis, however, was on the Hasid himself gaining a higher level of religious service and of 'understanding of the Divine'. Hence R. Shneur Zalman's well-known letter which in effect condemns the basing of a relationship with the Zaddik on the need for material blessing.[31] The central theme in Habad was and remains the Hasidic teachings imparted by the Zaddik. These, studied by the Hasid and used as an aid in contemplation and life, enable him to attain his own level of inner transformation and self-transcendence.

A further dimension of this relationship is that the Zaddik himself acts as an example for the Hasid to revere and, as far as possible, to emulate, in his quest for the spiritual in life. The key values embodied by the Zaddik in Habad are, on the one hand, esoteric *bitul*, self-abnegation which, in its upper reaches, is inimitable; on the other, the somewhat more accessible value of *mesirat nefesh*, self-sacrifice.

AN ACTIVIST CONCEPT OF THE ZADDIK

The careful depiction in *Tanya*, particularly in its first ten chapters, of the spiritual self-transformation achieved by the Zaddik is in fact a detailed elaboration of the Maggidic theme of *bitul*. As a background, the Lurianic cosmology and taxonomy of the soul is employed.[32] The normal self of the individual, with its desires and passions, is termed the Animal Soul or Vital Soul. In addition, a Divine force, called the Divine Soul, nestles within the person but is concealed by his everyday self.[33] For most people the struggle of life is to control this self; the one who achieves constant control is the *benoni*, the 'Intermediate Man', a figure with clearly described pneumatic qualities.[34] The Zaddik goes immeasurably further: he achieves not mere control, but *transformation* of his everyday self, the Animal Soul. That aspect of the self which makes it opaque to the Divine dissolves away, and the Animal Soul is transformed into a pure expression of the Divine force and will which transcend self and all existence. R. Shneur Zalman employs the term *bitul* for this dissolution of the opacity ('dirty garments') of the self, explaining that there are different levels of *bitul* and that only the 'perfect Zaddik' achieves total nullification of the opacity within.[35]

We can perceive, standing behind the reasoned description in the pages of the *Tanya*, the brief epigram of the Baal Shem Tov mentioned earlier concerning the *ani* (Self) which must be transformed into the *a[y]in* (Nought) of the Divine.

There are, however, two very distinct ways of understanding the effect of Hasidic self-transformation: passive or active. The teachings of the Maggid on the theme of *bitul* can be interpreted as tending towards quietism.[36] R. Shneur Zalman makes quite clear that the 'perfect Zaddik' does not simply indulge in delight in *unio mystica*. He partakes of this individual union with the Divine for the sake of a yet more exalted purpose: to achieve the Divine self-expression in the lower world which is the purpose of Creation.

> [The 'perfect Zaddikim'] are called 'exalted' because their service . . . is for an extremely exalted purpose, exalted to the highest level, and not just to cleave to the Divine alone, to quench the thirst of their souls thirsting for the Divine . . . but instead it is in order to . . . unify the Holy One and His *Shekhinah* in the lower world . . . [which means] to draw down the flow of Divine holiness from above to below, to be enclothed in the lower world.[37]

This implies energetic activity, perhaps employing spiritual instruments, as we see in the case of the Baal Shem Tov[38] and also in the teachings of the Maggid concerning the elevation of evil. The tenor of *Tanya*, however, is to direct the individual towards active, *practical* encounter with the world, and the image of the Zaddik imparted is likewise of one who deals with the world face to face, the practical commandments of the Torah being the vehicle for this activity. For the most part it is through them that ultimate *bitul* is achieved. They transcend, too, the intriguing 'spiritual ego', which itself takes form as a subtle concealment of the Divine. Beyond the barrier of all selfhood lie the practical commandments of Judaism, in which 'there is no concealment of the Countenance at all.'[39] R. Shneur Zalman laid great stress on the significance of the commandment of charity,[40] and personally put his ideas into practice in his energetic collection of funds for the Hasidic leaders in the Holy Land, and also later for the villagers dispossessed by the implementation of the 1804 Statute Concerning the Jews.[41]

It was in connection with this latter endeavour that R. Shneur Zalman met R. Barukh of Medziboz, grandson of the Baal Shem Tov, in 1810. In this encounter, the practical activity of the leader of Habad was criticized. According to R. Shneur Zalman's letter describing the meeting, R. Barukh asked him 'Why do you need to do all this? Couldn't you "sweeten the harsh forces"[42] by passing your hand over your forehead and face?' R. Shneur Zalman countered by citing the practical efforts of Jacob, who sent a material gift to appease Esau. 'I said to him, surely Jacob the Patriarch knew how to "sweeten the harsh forces", and none the less said "I will appease him with a present"' (Gen. 32:20). In an aside to his followers reading the letter, R. Shneur Zalman comments 'The truth is you need the [spiritual] "sweetening of the harsh forces" and also the gift sent to Esau'—a valuable statement on the Habad view of the relationship between spirit and matter in the activity of the Zaddik. The account of R. Barukh's attack continues: 'Then he asked me: "Is it dignified for you to travel around these distant towns?" I answered: "Am I greater than R. Pinhas ben Yair who spent all his life travelling [collecting for] the redemption of captives?"'[43] Asked again 'Why did you come to my territory?', R. Shneur Zalman answered: 'I could not bear the pain and suffering of the villagers who have been driven from their homes into the towns and are lying in the streets dying of hunger.' These words gained only a scornful reply.[44]

R. Shneur Zalman's personal example, together with the teachings in *Tanya*, present an activist concept of the Zaddik. His inner *bitul* and transcendence of self might not be imitable by the Hasid, but the effect of that *bitul* in the daily world—dedication to Torah, its practical directives and its values—could be taken as an example to be followed.

In the second generation of Habad another element comes to the fore in the self-depiction of the Hasidic leader: *mesirat nefesh*, self-sacrifice. In the teachings of R. Dov Ber, this concept is used to express the exalted attainment of the Zaddik, leading to some rather esoteric pathways. However, there is also a universal dimension to the concept of *mesirat nefesh*. This made it particularly suitable in providing a perspective on a a mystic leader so that he could clearly by seen by the men and women of the Hasidic fraternity as an inspiring example in the struggle for spirituality in daily life.

THE CONCEPT OF SELF-SACRIFICE

The powerful theme of *mesirat nefesh* for *Kiddush ha-Shem* (self-sacrifice for the Sanctification of the Divine Name) has a long and important history in early and mediaeval Jewish thought.[45] Apart from straightforward martyrology, which eulogizes the martyr in his or her historical context, the ideal of self-sacrifice was also 'spiritualized' so as to have direct bearing on the daily life of the contemporary individual.[46] This is found particularly in kabbalistic literature, but also in halakhic texts. Thus R. Yoel Sirkis (d. 1640) included in his commentary on R. Jacob ben Asher's *Arbaah Turim* the idea that when saying the *Shema*, one should take on the readiness to die for *Kiddush ha-Shem*.[47] A comparable idea is found in the Hasidic *hanhagot* (rules of conduct) literature 150 years later.[48] R. Elimelech of Lyzhansk declares that at any free moment one should picture a great fire burning and imagine throwing oneself into it for the sake of the Sanctification of the Divine Name.[49] Similar ideas should be maintained in one's mind during prayer and while eating and enjoying physical pleasures.[50] Clearly this is a translation of the esoteric theme of *devekut* into the more concrete concept of self-sacrifice so as to make it accessible to the Hasid. Another disciple of the Maggid who employs the theme of self-sacrifice is R. Menahem Mendel of Vitebsk, the associate and teacher of R. Shneur Zalman. In his teachings, the concept of self-sacrifice for *Kiddush ha-Shem* becomes a means to express the Hasidic-mystical ideal on a level of great intensity:

> To sum up the matter: a person should be like someone *who is not*, with utter abandon of his body and soul, to be eradicated for Sanctification of His Blessed Name, from this world and from the World to Come, in whatever way it might be; and wherever he is he yearns and is concerned with nothing but the Divine . . . Even from Hell he turns to the Divine, for what does he care for himself? Whether . . . he was not born, or being born, is wiped out like an animal . . . he is already completely annihilated, because of his gazing at the greatness of the Creator.[51]

Although it appears relatively infrequently in their teachings, these quotations indicate that the theme of self-sacrifice had a place in the thought of the disciples of the Maggid.[52] The historical reality of dying for *Kiddush ha-Shem* was close at hand.[53] Indeed, the famous letter of the Baal Shem Tov describing a spiritual ascent of the soul includes both a vision and also a factual account of a number of people sacrificing their lives in this way.[54] The powerful concept of *mesirat nefesh*, already utilized to some extent by his colleagues for transmitting the Hasidic ethos, was given an important role by R. Shneur Zalman and became even more prominent in the teachings of his son R. Dov Ber.

An important cornerstone of the system of thought expounded by the *Tanya* is the idea that every Jew has within him or her the propensity for self-sacrificial martyrdom. Taken as a self-evident fact of history, this propensity is cited as an indication of the existence of the Divine Spark within the Jewish soul: when faced with a clear choice ('baptism or death') this Divine force gives the individual the power of self-sacrifice even if hitherto he has conducted himself as 'the lowest of the low'.[55] In addition, R. Shneur Zalman makes this theme the basis of a number of contemplative strategies in order to gain self-mastery: for example, the individual thinks of the readiness for martyrdom he and all other Jews possess, and thereby summons the force to restrain his passion for something forbidden or to inspire himself to devotion to positive goals such as Torah study or prayer.[56]

The idea that every Jew has the inner power to give up his or her life for Judaism is likewise emphasized by R. Dov Ber, in the second generation of Habad. It is referred to several times in his *Kuntres ha-Hitpaalut*,[57] a tract giving a subtle classification of different stages of enthusiasm, inspiration, ecstasy or utter *bitul* in prayer.[58] The highest level, a state of self-abandon to the Divine in which 'there is nothing left of him at all'[59] and all consciousness of self is lost, is described as being very rare.[60] It is noteworthy that this exalted state, which is openly apparent as a positive force only in the case of 'perfect Zaddikim', is compared with the moment of death for *Kiddush ha-Shem*.[61] This brief association of the concept of the Zaddik with the powerful theme of self-sacrifice in what is probably R. Dov Ber's earliest tract, received amplification in his later work 'Gate of Repentance and Prayer', *Shaar ha-Teshuvah ve-ha-Tefilah*.[62] Here the concept of self-sacrifice in general is brought to the fore and the *mesirat nefesh* of the Zaddik is clearly defined.

An interesting aspect of this work is that it provides a kabbalistic perspective on the historical phenomenon of *Kiddush ha-Shem*.[63] R. Dov Ber focuses on the period from 1096—the time of the incidents of mass martyrdom in the Rhine consequent on the People's Crusade—to 1573, the death of R. Isaac Luria. During these 500 years, he states, there were many incidents of *Kiddush ha-Shem*. He refers to Solomon ibn Verga's martyrological chronicle *Shevet Yehudah*, and mentions specifically 1096 and the Spanish Expulsion of 1492. (Elsewhere R. Dov Ber refers to the Chmielnicki massacres of 1648-9).[64] The kabbalistic background to this intensive period of Jewish self-sacrifice lies in the concept of transmigration of souls and the theme of *Tikkun*, 'Repair'. The Jews who died for *Kiddush ha-Shem* in that 500-year epoch were incarnations of souls of people who had lived in the time of the First Temple, when they had served idols. Their *Tikkun* and 'ascent' were effected through their return to the world and subsequent death for *Kiddush ha-Shem*.[65] The Jewish philosophy of that epoch, declares R. Dov Ber, was itself a partial atonement for idolatry, for the philosopher 'will only believe the investigation of his intellect and will mock all idolatry and loathe it'. However, complete *Tikkun* was achieved by the philosopher himself going beyond reason and sacrificing his life with *mesirat nefesh* for *Kiddush ha-Shem*, with simple faith transcending all intellect.[66]

The idea that the incidents of death for *Kiddush ha-Shem* were in atonement for past sins of the Jewish people is found in *Emek ha-Melekh* by R. Naftali Bacharach, a work which seems to have had some influence on Habad.[67] The significant point, within the framework of our present study, is that R. Dov Ber had a conception of *Kiddush ha-Shem* as a historical phenomenon and that, as such, it had a definite place in his view of Jewish history as a whole. This underlines the significance of the concept of the *mesirat nefesh* of the Zaddik in his teachings.

NEFILAT APAYYIM

To help us understand R. Dov Ber's ideas, let us first consider their background in kabbalistic thought. In the *Zohar* and later kabbalistic writings the link is made between *Kiddush ha-Shem* and *Nefilat Apayyim*, the *Tahanun* supplicatory prayer recited after the *Amidah* on non-festive days. Tishby has discussed the different ways in which this theme is expressed in the *Zohar*; the common denominator is that the act of *Nefilat Apayyim* (in which, in normal synagogal practice, the head is bowed and the face is hidden),[68] is interpreted as 'symbolic death'.[69]

This theme is found also in the teachings of R. Moshe Cordovero, who states concerning one's attitude during *Nefilat Apayyim* that: 'he should consider himself dead for the Sanctification of His great Name, and that he is giving over his soul in that unity'.[70] This idea has prominence in R. Haim Vital's discussion of *Nefilat Apayyim* in *Shaar ha-Kavanot*, and becomes part of a scheme of analysis of 'actual' and 'potential' *Kiddush ha-Shem*. 'Actual' *Kiddush ha-Shem* means literally dying, 'like the Ten Martyrs', while 'potential' *Kiddush ha-Shem* takes place in prayer. In prayer, states R. Haim Vital, there are two kinds of *mesirat nefesh*: one in the recital of the *Shema*, the other in *Nefilat Apayyim*.[71] The general significance of the latter prayer is that then the soul, after its total inclusion with the *Shekhinah* during the *Amidah*, throws itself down from *Atsilut* 'like a man throwing himself from a roof down to the ground' in order to raise up the 'sparks' from the *kelipah*.[72] This is compared to the descent of the Zaddikim after their death to *Gehinom* ('the domain of the *kelipot*') in order to rescue the evildoers from there.[73] In the same way the person in prayer

> gives himself over to death, and has the intention that his soul should descend to the realm of death . . . in order to extract from there, with the power of his prayer, the 'sparks' [lit. 'siftings'] which are there.[74]

These 'siftings' are identified as 'the souls who have fallen there'.[75] R. Haim Vital emphasizes that the one who undertakes this should be a Zaddik, otherwise not only will he fail to raise up any souls, but he might remain there himself.[76] This *mesirat nefesh* causes an exalted Unification above, and also is of great benefit to his own soul which thereby 'renews itself and is totally perfected'.[77] Further, one who has committed the grievous sin of profanation of the Divine Name (*Hilul ha-Shem*), for which the Sages say there is no atonement until death,[78] can achieve such atonement 'by giving over his soul to death during *Nefilat Apayyim*'.[79]

It is to be noted that a number of these ideas are central to Hasidism, in which they are translated into social terms. Central of course is the role of the Zaddik.[80] With this background we are able to approach R. Dov Ber's schematization of *mesirat nefesh*, through which the nature of the Zaddik is communicated to his followers.

PERMANENT DEVEKUT

In the *Seder Tefilot* published by R. Dov Ber, comprising mainly discourses of his father arranged as a commentary on the liturgy, we find *Nefilat Apayyim* characterized as the expression of total *bitul*.[81] This idea is developed in the later *Shaar ha-Teshuvah ve-ha-Tefilah*.

Here R. Dov Ber distinguishes between the *bitul* of the *Amidah* and that of *Nefilat Apayyim*. In that of the *Amidah* the person is in a state of abnegation, yet he has not achieved union with the Essence (*mahut ve-atsmut*). In the 'second *bitul*' of *Nefilat Apayyim*, the person achieves a higher level of *bitul* and no longer has a separate existence of his own. The first level is described as a passive state, which is compared to that of a villager who is stunned on seeing the glory of the king. He is confused and unable to stand; he is completely abnegated. He has not actually grasped anything of the greatness of the king, however. To achieve this there must be the 'second *bitul*' which, at least cerebrally, is an active state in which the villager 'returns to his reason in order to grasp the essence of the exaltation and greatness of the wealth, glory and splendour of Majesty in all its details'. Through this he achieves total union.[82]

Another way in which R. Dov Ber distinguishes between these two varieties of *bitul* (or *devekut*) concerns the question of permanence. The ideal of achieving a permanent state of union with the Divine is an important issue in Habad.[83] R. Shneur Zalman makes clear in *Tanya* that permanence of *devekut* is one of the differences distinguishing the Zaddik from the *benoni*. Although the 'intermediate man' can attain ecstatic states of enthusiasm during prayer, after the prayer has ended the inspired mood ebbs away and the person again 'desires the pleasures of this world'[84] and must return to his more usual stance of self-control. Rather severely, R. Shneur Zalman states that an intermittent mood of inspiration 'is not termed true service at all, since it disappears after prayer, and it is written "the lip of truth stands for ever, but the tongue of falsehood is only for a moment"' (Prov. 12:19).[85] Subsequently R. Shneur Zalman does accord a certain level of 'truth' to the service of the *benoni*, since at least he is able in a constant way to summon up the state of pneumatic inspiration whenever he immerses himself in prayer.[86] Nonetheless, the direction is clear: the attainment of the Zaddik is of an order entirely different from that of the inspired enthusiast, even the one who has achieved total self-mastery, the *benoni*.

This distinction is enlarged on by R. Dov Ber in the context of the *bitul* of the *Amidah*, which is impermanent, and, far higher, the constant *devekut* achieved through the *mesirat nefesh* of *Nefilat Apayyim*.

The utter *bitul* of the *Amidah*, despite its impermanence, is itself described in exalted terms by R. Dov Ber. The individual in such a state 'becomes a true vessel for the Divine *ayin* at that moment'.

However, not only is this impermanent, leaving only an 'afterglow' (*reshimu*) of Divine radiance after the prayer; even during this state of *bitul*, the person does not attain total 'absorption' in the Divine. Spiritually he remains 'a created thing', separate from the Divine even if temporarily abnegated before the Infinite and a vessel to its radiance.[87]

By contrast, through the higher state which R. Dov Ber terms 'the *mesirat nefesh* which is in *Nefilat Apayyim*', the person attains *devekut* and 'absorption' in the Divine to such an extent that he is no longer termed a 'vessel' and loses the quality of separate existence. Together with the concept of total *unio mystica* goes the theme of the permanence of this state. *Devekut*, says R. Dov Ber, is called that because like glue (*devek*) it joins two things into a permanent bond in which they are one. Through *mesirat nefesh* of *Nefilat Apayyim* the person attains a unity and bond with the Divine which 'lasts continually and eternally, without ever being loosened for any reason in the world'.[88] This is not the passive, quietistic state of the motionless *Amidah* prayer. *Nefilat Apayyim* represents active involvement with the practical world.

> . . . even if he occupies himself with business, deeply preoccupied and involving all his energy, with very close relationship to the external forces [of the *kelipah*], they do not separate him at all, not even a hairsbreadth, because of his utter cleaving to the Divine . . . 'Even though he walks here and there'—in the realms of [*Kelipat*] *Nogah*— 'My Divine Visage remains with you'; truly, with utter cleaving . . . This is the superiority of *Nefilat Apayyim* above the Eighteen Benedictions and the *Shema*. Concerning this it says 'and to Him shall you cleave' (Deut. 13:5)—literally to Him.[89]

Thus, in the state of *mesirat nefesh* of *Nefilat Apayyim*, according to R. Dov Ber, the ideal of permanent *devekut* is achieved, even in the profane realms of daily life lived in an intensely active way. This is a state of *devekut*, of *mesirat nefesh*, consistent not only with the performance of essential human functions but also with intense involvement in worldly affairs.

As an example of this descent into worldly activities R. Dov Ber refers to 'Joseph, who carried out his work of writing accounts and was a chariot to *Atsilut* itself, and was not separated at all [from the Divine] even when he was totally involved in writing'.[90]

This presents a further stage in the concept of the Zaddik. In the case of R. Shneur Zalman we encountered the example of the mystical R. Pinhas ben Yair, actively involved in raising money for the redemption of captives. R. Dov Ber gives us here the picture of the biblical Joseph, a 'chariot' (i.e. total expression)[91] of the Divine realm of *Atsilut* yet simultaneously controlling the distribution of grain during the years of the famine. This leads to a remarkable typology of *mesirat nefesh*, through which the Habad ideal of the Zaddik is yet further defined.

A TYPOLOGY OF MESIRAT NEFESH

In *Kuntres ha-Hitpaalut*, R. Dov Ber presents us with a typology of *hitpaalut*, ecstatic feeling in prayer. In a somewhat similar way we find in *Shaar ha-Teshuvah ve-ha-Tefilah* a typology of *mesirat nefesh*, culminating in the most exalted level, the *mesirat nefesh* of *Nefilat Apayyim* which is higher than the 'death of a kiss' of Moses and is described in near-messianic terms. The central purpose of this typology is, we feel, the communication of the stature of the Zaddik. (The same may, indeed, be so in the case of *Kuntres ha-Hitpaalut*). This purpose is emphasized by the fact that the *hiner bet* (trance-like state)[92] of the Baal Shem Tov is presented as an example of the most exalted form of *mesirat nefesh*. *Shivhei ha-Besht*, in the introduction to which the state of *hiner bet* is described, was published in Kopyst in 1815 by the Habad printer R. Yisrael Jaffe,[93] obviously with the agreement of, if not direct instruction from, R. Dov Ber. The reference to this state in *Shaar ha-Teshuvah ve-ha-Tefilah*, published in 1817, was therefore addressed to an audience which was familiar with the concept as the attribute of the exalted Zaddik, the Baal Shem Tov. Further, as we will see below, R. Dov Ber himself was described by a contemporary as undergoing similar states. To some extent we can therefore interpret R. Dov Ber's typology of *mesirat nefesh* as an attempt at self-communication.[94]

The typology is based on the distinction between 'potential' and 'actual' *mesirat nefesh* which, as we have seen, is found in the writings of R. Haim Vital. R. Dov Ber develops this further. In potential *mesirat nefesh* he describes two levels. The first is one of *hitpaalut*, intense emotion or ecstasy, which is expressed particularly by the Divine Soul. In this state the Natural Soul too yearns to leave the physical sheath of the body. Nonetheless, this is only the first level of potential *mesirat nefesh*, for

> It might be that if at that very moment they were demanding of him that he apostatize, or similar, and they said to him 'a sword to [your] throat at once!', it is possible he would fall into uncertainty and give in.[95]

The second level is a deeper ecstasy:

> However there can be a second level in potential *mesirat nefesh*, namely that he has achieved such a strong and deep ecstasy of the Natural Soul to leave the materiality of the body, that he is really ready actually to be killed for *Kiddush ha-Shem* if they would demand this of him at that moment.[96]

This is still only potential, states R. Dov Ber, for although it might be true at the time when he felt it, if the demand for *Kiddush ha-Shem* were made at another time, the strength of his resolve might evaporate.[97] Both levels are aspects of what Katz terms 'spiritualized' *mesirat nefesh*, i.e. preparedness for death in a situation which is but in the imagination, taking place on an internal level during prayer.[98] R. Dov Ber now turns his attention to 'actual' *mesirat nefesh*. This too has different levels. The first of these is found in a situation when the person has made the final step in giving himself up to death, even though he has not yet actually been killed. R. Dov Ber cites the example of

Hananiah, Mishael and Azaria (Shadrach, Meshach and Abednego) who declared: 'Our G-d can save us . . . and if not, you should know, O King, that we will not serve your god, and we will not bow to the golden idol you have set up' (Dan. 3:17–18). This is considered actual fulfilment of the commandment of *Kiddush ha-Shem*, for as far as they were concerned they had given themselves over to death. Whether or not the decree is carried out is not up to them.

> This is a genuine resolve of the soul for actual *mesirat nefesh*, and this is really as if they had actually sacrificed their lives; if the decree had been cancelled and they had not been thrown into the furnace, through this firm resolve they would [nonetheless] actually have fulfilled the commandment of *Kiddush ha-Shem*, since only the practical action was lacking. As far as they were concerned there was no hindrance.[99]

A further level of actual *mesirat nefesh* is expressed in a case where not only has the soul been prepared for death but also the body itself. An example of this is the case of Isaac; although the final action was not carried out, this is none the less a fulfilment of the commandment of *Kiddush ha-Shem*:

> . . . their bodies are actually prepared, such as by their hands and feet being bound with cords, and being put on top of the woodpile as in the *Akedah* of Isaac. This is like actual *mesirat nefesh*; even though they were taken down immediately they fulfilled the commandment of *Kiddush ha-Shem* with this practical preparation of their bodies, as in the *Akedah* of Isaac when only the final action was lacking.[100]

It has long been noted that *Akedah* imagery has a significant role in the mediaeval *Kiddush ha-Shem* literature.[101] R. Dov Ber employs this theme in different ways. Here we find the concept of the fulfilment of the ideal of *Kiddush ha-Shem* together with the continuation of life. For R. Dov Ber it is not the act of dying for *Kiddush ha-Shem* that is of highest significance, but the life which continues with the quality of *mesirat nefesh*. This life is the life of the Zaddik, yet it also embodies an ideal not beyond the comprehension of the Hasid.

In order to establish and communicate this ideal, R. Dov Ber continues his typology, delineating an ever more 'actual' expression of *Kiddush ha-Shem*. The highest form of this, as in the case of the Ten Martyrs, is when the body 'is actually burnt and slaughtered'. It is this highest stage which has a direct parallel in life—the *mesirat nefesh* of *Nefilat Apayyim*, the *mesirat nefesh* of the Zaddik.

Thus, emphasizing the need for actuality, R. Dov Ber stresses that the case in which the body was bound on the woodpile yet not actually slaughtered, was not the *mesirat nefesh* for which Rabbi Akiva yearned: 'the main thing' was lacking.

Rabbi Akiva, however, who used to yearn [for martyrdom] and would say 'when will I be able to carry it out'[102]—his desire was specifically to carry it out in actuality, which is the burning or slaughter of the body in actual fact, and not just the preparation of the body alone. This is the plain sense of his saying 'carry it out'. The preparation without actually being killed, that he remains alive in his body, means that his body has not actually been sacrificed for *Kiddush ha-Shem*, and the fact that the act of slaughter is lacking is a lack of the main thing.[103]

Elaborating on this R. Dov Ber cites the *Zohar* and *Ets Hayyim*, which depict the greatness of the attainment of the Ten Martyrs; this attainment is specifically because they were actually killed, states R. Dov Ber, 'for the sacrifice of the body is more exalted than the sacrifice of the soul.'[104]

Based on this conclusion he divides the subject of *mesirat nefesh* into two categories: the sacrifice of the soul (*Mesirat ha-Nefesh*) and the sacrifice of the body (*Mesirat ha-Guf*). Each has a potential and an actual state. The potential sacrifice of the soul is the yearning for the Divine experienced during the *Shema*; the actuality of the sacrifice of the soul is the 'death by a kiss'[105] of Moses and Aaron, whose souls expired through their intense yearning for the pure Unity of the Divine. The potential sacrifice of the body is, as depicted above, when the person is absolutely prepared to be killed—'his judgement is concluded, and he is going out to be killed and they throw him down'—but he is not killed because the decree is annulled. The actual sacrifice of the body is when he is actually burnt and slaughtered; 'the sacrifice of the body together with the soul'. Only through this can the purely spiritual *mesirat nefesh* of the soul alone be verified

> When he is actually burnt and slaughtered, this is the real sacrifice of the body together with the soul. Only then is the sacrifice of the soul itself verified, despite its actualization through the expiring of the soul from yearning.[106]

This statement might well be interpreted as expressing an anti-quietist position. R. Dov Ber constructs an image which embodies the quietist ideal; the sacrifice of the soul in prayer, culminating in dissolution—the 'death by a kiss'; yet this in itself requires 'verification', through the sacrifice of the body. Behind this, one discerns the shadow of the controversy with R. Aaron,[107] the pneumatic spiritualist who perhaps was seen as representing the sacrifice of the soul alone, while R. Dov Ber claims as his attainment and teaching the sacrifice of the body as well: not in death, but in life.[108] The bridge connecting the case of burning and slaughter with continued life in this world is the *mesirat nefesh* of *Nefilat Apayyim*, and the trancelike states of the Baal Shem Tov.

NEFILAT APAYYIM AND HINER BET

Having described the exaltation of actual death for *Kiddush ha-Shem*—the gruesome death, 'with iron combs' for which R. Akiva yearned—R. Dov Ber makes the striking statement that 'This is the real significance of *Nefilat Apayyim* . . . for it says in the *Zohar* concerning *Nefilat Apayyim* that it should seem to him as if he really has departed from this world.'[109] In R. Dov Ber's typology, mystical *Nefilat Apayyim* is thus equated with actual death for *Kiddush ha-Shem*. He asks how *Nefilat Apayyim* can be the equivalent of 'real *mesirat nefesh* in actual fact with slaughter and burning'; perhaps the statement in the *Zohar* implies only a state of readiness for *mesirat nefesh* in the imagination of the person, not at all the actual fact of death. He answers that, on the contrary, what is meant is that the person does not simply imagine himself ready for *mesirat nefesh*, but actually enters a state which is the equivalent of death; only a small spark of life remains in him. Returning to the *Akedah* image, now in another mode, R. Dov Ber compares this to the situation of Isaac lying bound on the woodpile. All life has fled from him owing to 'dread of death'; the spark of life which remains is only so that he should be able to revive when taken down. This state is contrasted with more conventional ecstasy in which the person yearns for 'expiry' in the radiance of the Divine. In this more conventional state 'one cannot say that he has really died, nor that it is as if he has died.' By contrast:

> But when there falls on him actual dread of death, as in the *Akedah* of Isaac and similar, when he was bound, lying on the wood, and his soul really fled[110] and was not within him at all, just a residual spark of life so that he could revive when taken down . . . it is as if he had really died, and there remains in him only a residual spark of life. This is not imagination, with the power of imagination alone, but it is genuine.[111]

Here the *Akedah* is a symbol not merely of practical preparation for self-sacrifice, but of the mystical equivalent of death itself. It is the paradigm of *Nefilat Apayyim*. R. Dov Ber does not leave this ideal as pertaining only to the Patriarchs in the remote past.[112] Thus, expanding on this state of 'actualized' *mesirat nefesh*, he writes:

> He is not actually thought to be dead, but slumbering in a deep sleep, as is told of the greatest Zaddikim of the generation, like the Baal Shem Tov . . . that when he had an ascent of the soul he was stripped of all the physicality of the material life of his body . . .[113]

This is compared to the sleep of Adam in which one of his ribs was taken; for in this state 'he feels no pain.'[114] R. Dov Ber describes this state as more exalted than that of the prophets at the moment of prophesying, for in their case the body has not expired but has merely become insensible. This underlines the extent to which R. Dov Ber equated the trancelike state of the Baal Shem Tov with actual death, and also gives some indication of the place he ascribes to it in the scale of religious attainment.

HINER BET OF THE BAAL SHEM TOV AND OF R. DOV BER

In the Baal Shem Tov's famous letter recounting to his brother-in-law R. Gershom of Kuty his spiritual ascent on the night of Rosh Hashana, there is no indication as to how at that moment he appeared to others. However, in *Shivhei ha-Besht* we find an account of an 'ascent' of the Baal Shem Tov during the *Neilah* prayer on the Day of Atonement. This includes a physical description. The Baal Shem Tov 'leaned backwards till his head came near his legs . . . and his eyes were bulging and with his voice he was making sounds like a slaughtered ox. He was like that for about two hours.'[115] Even though the passage concludes with an account by the Baal Shem Tov of his journey through upper realms during his trance, the description of the frightening physical appearance of this state seems beyond the conventions of hagiography. It is striking that the importance of this trancelike state is emphasized by the original redactor[116] of *Shivhei ha-Besht*:

> In previous times it sometimes happened that they would lie comatose, which is called *hiner bet*, and when they got up they would tell of the wondrous things they had seen in the upper world.[117]

As mentioned above, *Shivhei ha-Besht* was published by the Habad Hasidim, followers of R. Dov Ber.[118] A contemporary figure named Yakov Cadaner[119] gives an eye-witness description of R. Dov Ber himself undergoing a trancelike state, in which he stood 'like a stick, without any movement or feeling' for several hours. Descriptions of this kind are very rare in Jewish mystical literature, and it merits quotation at length. The event described took place in the village of Krislave, where R. Dov Ber and a group of Hasidim including Cadaner were staying while on a journey. On the second evening there R. Dov Ber delivered a discourse which greatly impressed his hearers. 'Even the exceptional, famous, original Hasidim said they had never heard anything like that from him, nor from his father . . .' The Hasidim went to eat their evening meal.

> Soon after the meal the serving man came to me very excitedly and said to me: 'If you want to look at the face of the *Rebbe*, this is a good time.' I said to him, 'I do not want to, for I know he greatly objects to such things because of his reticent nature.' The serving man promised that 'at

the moment he will not notice you at all.' I decided it would be right to have a look, and went with the serving man. He opened the door of his room and I saw the *Rebbe* standing in the middle of the room without any movement. His face was glowing as with flames, and his eyes were open. I said to myself he could certainly see me, and I was afraid of his anger so I jumped backwards. The serving man took hold of my coat and said loudly: 'Do not be afraid at all, for now he cannot see and cannot hear for he is in upper worlds, even though you see his body in this world.' I said, 'How do *you* know such things? You are just an ordinary person.' He said, 'It is not my idea, but from experience. For several times I have seen him like this.' After that I gazed at his face and I too realized that then he could not see nor hear, even though his eyes were open; he had no sensation from any physical senses at all. I stood at the entrance of the room gazing very intently at his face: perhaps I would detect some animation in it. Simply his eyes were open and his face glowed like a Seraph. I stood like that from the tenth hour till the third hour. The servants were coming and going in the room and the *Rebbe* was standing like a stick, without any movement or feeling. At the end of the third hour the serving man said to my cart-driver, 'Lay the table, for it is time he ate a little, for he has not eaten all day.' He did this, laid the table and took the ewer in his hand and stood in front of him so that he should wash his hands. He stood some time by the *Rebbe* and understood that he could not see him at all, although his eyes were open. The serving man said to him, 'Why do you not wake up the *Rebbe* so he should wash his hands. He has not eaten warm food all day.' He said, 'I am afraid to touch him.' The serving man said, 'If so, whatever happens to me I have to wake him up.' The serving man went and took hold of the sleeve of his coat and said, 'I am asking the *Rebbe* to wash his hands.' He did not answer him at all, but walked from the middle of the room to the wall and stood there as before.[120]

At this point Cadaner was no longer able to see R. Dov Ber's face, so he retired to his room. Later the serving man told him that after another hour of immobility R. Dov Ber had suddenly come out of his trance and sat down at the table where he ate normally 'with great joy'.

According to Cadaner's account of what the serving man later told him, R. Dov Ber then revealed to this faithful attendant that during his Hasidic discourse earlier in the evening he had had a spiritual visitation from the souls of his late father R. Shneur Zalman, the Maggid and the Baal Shem Tov. After the discourse the sense of contact with R. Shneur Zalman continued. Then, R. Dov Ber told the serving man: 'The fact that I stood a long time in the middle of the room was because I was repeating the discourse again before my father, and he revealed to me wonderful secrets concerning it.'[121]

There is no doubt that Cadaner was a Hasidic raconteur and loved a good story, as his book *Sipurim Noraim* attests. Unlike most of the stories in this work, however, his accounts of R. Dov Ber are based on what he claims to be events he saw himself. It is quite plausible that Cadaner should be among the entourage of Hasidim accompanying R. Dov Ber on a journey. Further, it seems unlikely that an account of this kind should be completely fabricated. The trance state in itself embodies no obvious miracle. Indeed, it might well not be considered very meaningful to the ordinary reader. These points lead us to feel that R. Dov Ber himself indeed underwent such states and his reference to them in the context of the *mesirat nefesh* of *Nefilat Apayyim* is to some extent an example of the self-communication which is sometimes a characteristic of Hasidic leadership. The very fact that *Shivhei ha-Besht* was published by R. Dov Ber's followers might have a bearing on this, especially in the light of the struggle with R. Aaron for leadership of Habad. For implicit in R. Dov Ber's teaching concerning the *hiner bet* of the Zaddikim is the idea that the most exalted attainments of the enthusiast—such as those we associate with R. Aaron—do not compare with the step beyond life within life of the Baal Shem Tov and—by implication—of R. Dov Ber himself. The comatose state of *hiner bet* is the bridge, so to speak, between death for *Kiddush ha-Shem* and continued life in this world. This is the attainment of the ultimate Zaddik; his silent self-abnegation in *Nefilat Apayyim* is an expression of total, permanent *devekut*, with messianic overtones, which, like actual death for *Kiddush ha-Shem* is described as being more exalted than all other spiritual attainment.[122]

R. Dov Ber concludes his typology of *mesirat nefesh* with the depiction of the way *mesirat nefesh* of *Nefilat Apayyim* raises the Lurianic sparks from even the lowest level of existence. This is the achievement of the true Zaddik by virtue of his very being, whether he is in a pneumatic trance, or active in the world. For him the veil of physicality no longer has the power to conceal.[123]

THE REALITY OF THE SELF-SACRIFICE OF THE ZADDIK

The presentation of the Zaddik in terms of the ultimate expression of *mesirat nefesh* is repeated in another discourse in R. Dov Ber's *Shaar ha-Teshuvah ve-ha-Tefilah*.[124] This enlarges on the verse 'He redeemed in peace my soul' (Ps. 55:19), a scriptural quotation which had special meaning for R. Dov Ber's followers. At the height of the conflict with the *Mitnaggedim*, R. Shneur Zalman's release in 1798 on 19 Kislev from his first arrest had been at the moment when he was reading this verse. He made this fact known in letters to R. Levi Yitzhak of Berdichev and R. Barukh of Medziboz.[125] For the Habad followers this verse therefore represented self-sacrifice in practical reality—the plight of R.

Shneur Zalman in prison, under threat of death, for the cause of Hasidism. In the discourse on this verse R. Dov Ber describes different levels of spiritualized *mesirat nefesh* which in effect are different stages of self-abnegation, described in terms of the struggle between the Divine Soul and the Animal Soul, as in *Tanya*. The level of total *mesirat nefesh*, i.e. total self-abnegation, is an expression of the esoteric fifth and highest aspect of the Divine soul, termed *Yehidah*.[126] This is found in every Jew, and can never be defiled.[127] In the ordinary person the power of *Yehidah* is seen but rarely; by contrast, the Zaddik serves the Divine from this ultimate aspect of his being. On the one hand this leads to depiction of the realization of total *devekut*,[128] similar to that discussed above. On the other it leads to a discussion of suffering. In this actualized form of self-sacrifice there is again a typology, leading towards a further definition of the Zaddik.

R. Dov Ber employs the image of close friendship. The intense love of the faithful friend 'is only recognized in a time of trouble, when he really sacrifices himself' for the sake of the beloved. The faithful friend 'does not care about his possessions, nor his life. He goes into danger and accepts physical suffering to the last extreme.'[129]

The typology introduced by R. Dov Ber concerns the extent to which the 'friend' feels this physical suffering. On one level he does feel it, yet accepts it because of his love for his friend. On a higher level, his love is so intense that the feeling of pain is muted. On yet a higher level, due to his total bonding (*hitkashrut*) to the soul of his friend, he does not feel the pain at all.[130]

It is clear that the final stage is a description of the relationship of the Zaddik to the Divine. For R. Dov Ber's hearers, this is a statement about R. Shneur Zalman, the previous *Rebbe*, who suffered in prison because of his role as Hasidic leader. However, R. Dov Ber assures his followers, for him this was not felt as suffering, due to his total bond with the Divine. As expressed by the verse from Psalms, his soul was redeemed 'in peace'.

This leads to the formulation of an unusual distinction among those who actually die for *Kiddush ha-Shem*. Some feel the suffering; but no pain is felt by those who are on the highest level of Zaddik, who attain the ultimate level of *mesirat nefesh*. The exemplars of this are the Ten Martyrs, such as Rabbi Akiva. Even while the Romans were tearing his flesh with iron combs 'he did not feel the pain at all' because of his total self-abnegation.[131] R. Dov Ber states that the fact that the Ten Martyrs did not feel pain distinguished them from other righteous men who died for *Kiddush ha-Shem*. The Ten Martyrs attained a higher spiritual achievement, expressed physically by their redemption 'in peace', without pain. Why did they have to enter the situation of suffering at all? 'Because of the root of the connection of the *kelipah* to the realm of holiness.'[132] In other words, because of the dialectic of the nature of evil, the Zaddik sometimes enters a situation of apparent suffering. However, his bond (*hitkashrut*) to the Divine is so great, and his *bitul* is so total, that this experience is 'in peace'.

R. Dov Ber emphasizes that the quality *Yehidah* which expresses this total bond, exists in every Jew. However its open radiance is in the leadership of the Jewish people throughout the generations.

> The general radiance of *yehidah* (which includes all Jewish souls . . .) shines in the outstanding individuals (*yehidei segulah*) who are in each generation, who are called leaders, each having a 'general' quality in relation to the individual Jews. Hence this exalted level of utter *mesirat nefesh* is only found in the leaders, such as the Ten Martyrs.[133]

Due to the link of the concept of *bitul*, the basis of this total level of self-sacrifice, with the *Sefirah Hokhmah* (Wisdom), the leader who attains this level of *mesirat nefesh* is also distinguished by his wisdom. Hence it is this kind of leader, such as the 'thirty-six Zaddikim in every generation, who see the face of the *Shekhinah* every day' who is able to give guidance and function as 'the eyes of the community'.[134]

In this discourse the nature of the leadership of the Zaddik as conceived by R. Dov Ber has been yet further defined. His utter *bitul* is a total level of *mesirat nefesh* which here is not only an inner, spiritual movement but also relates to grappling in practical fact with the harshness of reality. The Zaddik retains his exalted stature, even when arrested or exposed to other suffering. Inwardly his struggle relates to his task to transform the source of evil, the point at which the impure realm draws life from the realm of holiness; outwardly the dedicated self-sacrifice of a Jewish leader is seen.

The depiction of the Zaddik as a model of actual self-sacrifice for Judaism continues in a later work by R. Dov Ber, *Shaarei Orah*.[135] This book was published in 1822, when the relationship between the Tsar and the Jewish community was rapidly deteriorating,[136] and functions to a considerable extent as a call to the Jewish community to express self-sacrifice for Judaism—not, it was hoped, to die, but to be firm in their dedication to the Jewish religion in the face of harsh treatment from the government. Tsar Alexander I, in his later years, influenced by the English missionary Lewis Way, was filled with zeal to convert the Jews to Christianity, and *Shaarei Orah* contains powerful statements about the glory of the Jew who has *mesirat nefesh* for Judaism and refuses to convert. While the bulk of the book is about the self-sacrifice of the Hasid, or the ordinary Jew,[137] the introduction makes clear that the Jewish leader, the 'Prince of Torah', is the ultimate paradigm of the theme of self-sacrifice. The two sections of *Shaarei Orah* (one on Hanukkah, the other on Purim) extol two subtly different kinds of *mesirat nefesh*. The introduction states that both are combined in the leaders who disseminate Torah to the Jewish people.[138] In their power of self-sacrifice, these leaders are compared to the Ten Martyrs of Roman times. The image of the Zaddik as the one who is capable of self-sacrifice in his struggle to preserve Judaism, as well as on an esoteric metaphysical plane, is thus complete.

From R. Dov Ber's time to the present, the conception of the Zaddik in terms of self-sacrifice has remained a constant feature of Habad.[139] The *mesirat nefesh* of the Zaddik can be interpreted literally, as supreme effort in the face of opposition or danger; it also has a mystical dimension culminating in trancelike states which reach beyond the confines of the ordinary world. At the same time the theme of *mesirat nefesh* of *Nefilat Apayyim* includes the energetic activism of R. Shneur Zalman's depiction of the Zaddik, with heavy emphasis on the point that this activism is an expression of the highest and most permanent level of *devekut*.

The power of this mode of depiction of the Zaddik in terms of *mesirat nefesh* (rather than solely in terms of *bitul* and *devekut*) lies in the possibility it affords of presenting the Zaddik as an example to be emulated. Every moment of the life of the Zaddik is seen as virtual *mesirat nefesh* for *Kiddush ha-Shem*, whether his adversaries have the concrete form of Russian officials or that of the spiritual *kelipot* embodied in the everyday world. Seen from this perspective, the concept of the Zaddik is able to act as a role model in the lives of ordinary people. Their own struggle might be in prayer, and in finding spirituality in daily life. Or it might lie in facing persecution of Judaism and of Jews. Complementary to R. Dov Ber's teachings of the self-sacrifice of the Zaddik, are those which describe that of the Hasid, and present it as the ultimate in spiritual attainment. In the writings of the *Mitteler Rebbe*, through the ancient ideal of *mesirat nefesh*, the otherwise quite different paths of Hasidic leader and Hasidic follower are joined.

Notes

This article is based on a section of my doctoral thesis *The Concept of Mesirat Nefesh ('Self-Sacrifice') in the Teachings of R. Dov Ber of Lubavitch (1773–1827)* (University of London, 1981). Professor Chimen Abramsky was the supervisor of this thesis, as well as having been a generous teacher and adviser during my undergraduate studies of Jewish History at University College London.

1 In *Studies in Jewish Religious and Intellectual History*, ed. S. Stein and R. Loewe (Alabama, 1979), pp. 13–28.

2 Concerning the sources of the *Haskalah*, see J. Katz, *Tradition and Crisis: Jewish Society at the End of the Middle Ages* (New York, 1961); id., *Out of the Ghetto* (Cambridge, Mass., 1973); A. Shohet, *Im Hilufei Tekufot* (Jerusalem, 1961). As for Hasidism, discussion of the origin of this movement in relation to the social and intellectual milieu in which it emerged is to be found in J. G. Weiss, 'Reshit Tsemihatah shel ha-Derekh ha-Hasidit', *Zion*, vol. 16 (1951), collected in A. Rubinstein, *Perakim be-Toledot ha-Hasidut* (Jerusalem, 1978); a critique of the latter: S. Ettinger, 'Ha-Hanhagah ha-Hasidit be-Itsuvah', *Dat va-Hevrah be-Toledot Yisrael u-ve-Toledot he-Amim* (Jerusalem, 1965) (English version: 'The Hasidic Movement—Reality and Ideals', *Journal of World History*, vol. 11, 1968, pp. 251–66); M. Piekarz, *Bi-Yemei Tsemihat ha-Hasidut* (Jerusalem, 1978). See also G. Scholem, *Major Trends in Jewish Mysticism* (New York, 1961), p. 325ff.; B. Dinur, 'Reshitah shel ha-Hasidut vi-Yesodoteha ha-Sotsialim ve-ha-Meshihiyim', in *Be-Mifneh ha-Dorot* (Jerusalem, 1955), and the introduction to S. Dubnow's *Toledot ha-Hasidut* (Tel Aviv, 1944). A recent critique of the latter's explanation for the rise of Hasidism is to be found in an unpublished doctoral thesis, R. Foxbruner, 'Habad: the Ethical thought of R. Shneur Zalman of Lyadi' (Harvard University, 1984), pp. 2–12.

3 In the *Haskalah* the outstanding example of such a figure was, of course, Moses Mendelssohn. See A. Altmann, *Moses Mendelssohn, A Biographical Study* (Alabama and London, 1973).

4 See H. Dresner, *The Zaddik* (London–New York–Toronto, 1960); G. Scholem, 'Demuto ha-Historit shel R. Yisrael Baal Shem Tov', *Molad*, nos. 144–5 (1960); R. Schatz, 'Le-Mahuto shel ha-Zaddik ba-Hasidut', op. cit.; G. Nigal, *Manhig ve-Edah* (Jerusalem, 1962); id., introduction to *No'am Elimelech* (Jerusalem, 1978); S. Ettinger (note 2 above); A. Rapoport-Albert, 'God and the Zaddik, etc.', *History of Religion*, vol. 18 (Chicago 1979); I. Etkes, 'Reshitah shel ha-Hasidut ki-Tenuah: ha-Shalav ha-Rishon' (forthcoming). Piekarz (note 2 above) has pointed out the extent to which the concept of the Zaddik is found in the kabbalistic and homiletical literature which preceded Hasidism (*passim*, particularly pp. 280–8, 300–2). The following single example in which R. Haim Vital speaks of his teacher R. Isaac Luria, will suffice here: 'My teacher discerned the source of each individual Jew in the Torah. He would teach each person the interpretations of Torah which related to his soul. Sometimes he would reveal the interpretation of one verse, sometimes of other verses. According to the need of the moment . . . he would teach that person the interpretation of the verse that was then revealed . . .' R. Haim Vital, *Shaar Ruah ha-Kodesh* (Tel Aviv, 1963), pp. 108–9. This passage describes the relationship between a teacher and his disciples in the intense atmosphere of an intimate mystic circle. The Hasidic Zaddik, by contrast, was in many ways the same teacher but now active in a far broader range of society.

5 Concerning R. Dov Ber see L. Jacobs's translation of his *Tract on Ecstasy* (London, 1963); R. Elior, *The Theory of Divinity of Hasidut Habad, Second Generation* (Hebrew) (Jerusalem, 1982); 'Kuntres ha-Hitpaalut le-R. Dov Ber Schneerson', *Kiryat Sefer*, vol.

54 (1979); 'Ha-Mahloket al Moreshet Habad', *Tarbiz*, vol. 49 (1980). R. Dov Ber succeeded to leadership of Habad in 1813 after the death of his father, and settled in the town of Lubavitch. He was opposed by R. Aaron Halevi Horowitz (d. 1828), who became a rival Hasidic leader in Staroselye. R. Dov Ber is unusual among early Hasidic leaders in his concern for publishing. Immediately after the Napoleonic war, despite the devastation of the area, he ensured the publication of his father's *Shulhan Arukh* (Kopyst and Shklov, 1814), and a collection of R. Shneur Zalman's letters, *Iggeret ha-Kodesh* (Shklov, 1814). He then edited and published his own transcripts of his father's teachings: *Seder Tefilot mi-Kol ha-Shanah . . . im Perush ha-Milot* and *Biurei ha-Zohar* (both Kopyst, 1816). Subsequently about eight volumes of R. Dov Ber's teachings were printed during his lifetime, most of them by a printer in Kopyst who was one of his followers. Other tracts and discourses were published posthumously. His best-knwn works are: *Kuntres ha-Hitpaalut* (Königsberg, 1831?), a discussion of ecstasy in prayer which circulated in manuscript long before its posthumous publication; *Pokeah Ivrim*, a tract in Yiddish (?, 1817); *Shaar ha-Teshuvah ve-ha-Tefilah I–II* (Shklov, 1817–18); *Derekh Hayyim* (Kopyst, 1819); *Ner Mitzvah ve-Torah Or*, which includes a manual on contemplation (Kopyst, 1820); *Ateret Rosh* (Kopyst, 1821); *Imrei Binah* (Kopyst, 1821); *Shaarei Orah* (Kopyst, 1822); *Al Totsar et Moav* (Kfar Habad, 1976), a long discourse delivered in the presence of R. Akiva Eger in 1825; *Torat Hayyim* (Kopyst, 1826); *Bad Kodesh*, a long epistle addressed to the Governor of Vitebsk (Warsaw, 1871). Publication of R. Dov Ber's writings still continues in a series entitled *Maamarei Admur ha-Emtsai* (Brooklyn, 1985–6). Two volumes of his halakhic teachings have also been published: *Piskei Dinim . . . Yoreh Deah* (Brooklyn 1958), *Piskei Dinim . . . Even ha-Ezer* (Brooklyn, 1977).

6 Much scholarly attention has been devoted to this theme; see note 45 below.

7 For the bibliography of Habad see A. M. Haberman, 'Shaarei Habad', in *Alei Ayin* (Jerusalem, 1948–52); Y. Mondshein, *Torat Habad,*. vols. 1–2 (Kfar Habad, 1982–4). The history and thought of Habad are discussed in M. Teitelbaum, *Ha-Rav mi-Lyadi u-Mifleget Habad* (Warsaw, 1910–13); R. Schatz, 'Anti-spiritualizm ba-Hasidut', *Molad*, nos. 171–2 (1962); L. Jacobs, *Tract on Ecstasy* (London, 1963); id. *Seeker of Unity* (London, 1966); N. Mindel, *Rabbi Schneur Zalman* (New York, 1969); id. *The Philosophy of Chabad* (New York, 1974); *Sefer hakan—Kovets Maamarim al . . . R. Shneur Zalman mi-Lyadi* (Jerusalem, 1969); M. Hallamish, 'Mishnato ha-Iyunit shel R. Shneur Zalman mi-Lyadi', doctoral thesis (Hebrew University, Jerusalem, 1976); id., 'Al Mahadurot ha-Sefer "Torah Or"', *Alei Sefer*, vol. 5 (1978); id., 'Torat ha-Tsedakah be-Mishnato shel R. Shneur Zalman mi-Lyadi', *Daat*, no. 1 (1978); id., 'Yahasei Zaddik ve-Edah be-Mishnat R. Shneur Zalman mi-Lyadi', *Hevra ve-Historiya* (Jerusalem, 1980); id., 'Alim Rishonim mi-Perush ha-Tanya', *Daat*, no. 13 (1984); id., *Netiv la-Tanya* (Tel Aviv, 1987); Y. Jacobson, 'Torat ha-Beriah shel R. Shneur Zalman mi-Lyadi', *Eshel Beer Sheva* (1976); R. Elior (note 5 above) and 'Vikuah Minsk', *Mehkerei Yerushalayim be-Mahashevet Yisrael* no. 4 (1982), 'La-Dialektika shel Shelemut ve-Giluy' *Daat*, no. 9 (1982); 'Mekomo shel ha-Adam ba-Avodat ha-Shem ha-Habadit', *Daat*, no. 12 (1984); 'Iyyunim be-Mahashevet Habad', *Daat*, no. 16 (1986); T. Ross, 'Shnei Perushim le-Torat ha-Tsimtsum: R. Hayyim mi-Volozhyn ve-R. Shneur Zalman mi-Lyadi', *Mehkerei Yerushalayim be-Mahashevet Yisrael*, no. 2 (1982); Foxbruner (note 2 above); I. Etkes, 'Aliyato shel R. Shneur Zalman mi-Lyadi le-Emdat Manhigut', *Tarbiz*, vol. 54 (1985); id., 'Darko shel R. Shneur Zalman mi-Lyadi ke-Manhig shel Hasidim', *Jubilee Vol. of Zion*, vol. 50 (1986); Loewenthal, 'Early Hasidic Teachings—Esoteric Mysticism, or a medium of Communal Leadership?' *Journal of Jewish Studies*, vol. 37 (1986); id., 'The Apotheosis of Action in Early Habad', *Daat*, no. 18 (1986–7). Letters concerning early Habad are collected in D. Z. Hillmann, *Iggrot Baal ha-Tanya u-Bheney*

Doro (Jerusalem, 1953) and S. B. Levin, *Iggerot Kodesh me-et Admur ha-Zaken, Admur ha-Emtsai, Admur ha-Tsemah Tsedek* (Brooklyn, 1984). See also E. Kupfer in *Tarbiz*, vol. 47 (1978). An account of the first three generations of Habad written by a follower of the Kopyst line is H. H. Hielman's *Beit Rebbe* (Berdichev, 1902). See also the exposition of Habad thought by Tishby and Dan in 'Torat ha-Hasidut ve-Sifrutah', *Hebrew Encyclopedia*, vol. 17, collected in A. Rubinstein, *Perakim be-Torat ha-Hasidut u-ve-Toledoteha* (Jerusalem, 1978).

8 *Toledot Yaakov Yosef* (Koretz, 1780), fols. 20a, 29b. Cf. G. Scholem, *The Messianic Idea in Judaism* (London, 1971), p. 214.

9 *Maggid Devarav le-Yaakov*, ed. R. Schatz (Jerusalem, 1976), p. 74, sec. 51.

10 *ibid.*, p. 186, sec. 110. Scholem considers the concepts of *bitul* and *unio mystica* through *devekut* to be primarily of Hasidic origin, relating particularly to the Maggid and his immediate disciples (note 8 above, pp. 214, 222–7). Tishby, by contrast, discerns parallel ideas in earlier kabbalistic texts, such as Azriel of Gerona's commentary on the *aggadot* (13th cent.) and R. Eliyahu di Vidas' *Reshit Hokhmah*, a work known to have been studied in eighteenth-century Eastern Europe. See I. Tishby, *Mishnat ha-Zohar*, vol. 2 (Jerusalem, 1961), p. 289, n. 69.

11 See Dresner, Schatz and Nigal (note 4 above).

12 The question of to whom the early Hasidic teachings on *bitul* and *devekut* were addressed has received contrasting answers. Scholem suggested that they were addressed to everyone (note 8 above, pp. 203–27). The contrary view — that they were directly relevant only to a small élite of incipient leaders — has been expressed by Rapoport-Albert (note 4 above), pp. 296–317, and Loewenthal, 'Early Hasidic Teachings' (note 7 above), p. 64. See also G. Nigal, 'Al Mekorot ha-Devekut be-Sifrut Reshit ha-Hasidut', in *Kiryat Sefer*, vol. 46 (1970–1), p. 343.

13 See Loewenthal, 'The Apotheosis of Action' (note 7 above) on R. Shneur Zalman's teachings on the role of the practical *mitzvot* in the quest for *bitul*.

14 Concerning R. Avraham of Kalisk, see J. G. Weiss, 'R. Avraham Kalisker's concept of communion', *Journal of Jewish Studies*, vol. 6 (1955); Z. Gries, 'mi-Mitos la-Etos, Kavim li-Demuto shel R. Avraham mi-Kalisk', *Umah ve-Toledoteha* (Jerusalem, 1984). The controversy began with R. Shneur Zalman's publication of *Tanya*, which makes a strong demand on the individual to strive for an elevated level of spiritual attainment. R. Avraham feared this would be too much for the ordinary person: 'too much oil in the lamp will extinguish the flame' (Hillmann, note 7 above, p. 105). Various aspects of the controversy have been discussed by A. J. Braver, in *Kiryat Sefer*, vol. 1 (1924); Elior 'Vikuah Minsk' (note 7 above), p. 193ff; I. Etkes, in *Tarbiz*, vol. 54 (1985).

15 'In Habad thought, the basic concept of the Zaddik was pushed to a corner,' (Tishby and Dan, note 7 above, col. 783). Schatz maintains a more extreme view (note 7 above), p. 521–2. Many of the points raised in that article have been answered by Moshe Hallamish in his doctoral thesis (note 2 above), p. 253ff. He discusses R. Shneur Zalman's concept of the Zaddik on pp. 352–63, and in his 'Yahasei Zaddik' (note 7 above). See also Elior, 'Vikuah Minsk' (note 7 above), p. 193, and Gries (note 14 above), p. 119, n. 10. In addition see the works by Etkes in note 7 above, and Foxbruner (note 2 above), pp. 149, 195, 217, 267–8.

16 See note 7 above, Hillmann, pp. 58–69; Levin, pp. 75–9, 103–5; Mindel, *Rabbi Schneur Zalman*, pp. 109–18.

17 Levin, op. cit., p. 47.

18 M. Wilensky, *Hasidim u-Mitnaggedim*, vol. 1 (Jerusalem, 1970), p. 276

19 *Tanya* I, ch. 2, fol. 7a, explaining T. B. *Ketubot* 111b: 'He who cleaves to a scholar is considered as if he cleaved to the *Shekhinah*.'

20 *Tanya* IV, sec. 27, fol. 145b–147b. R. Menahem Mendel, who travelled to the Holy

Land in 1777, was an older colleague and teacher of Rabbi Shneur Zalman. On the relationship between them see Etkes, 'Aliyato shel R. Shneur Zalman' (note 7 above).

21 *Maamarei Admur ha-Zaken (MAHZ)* 5568 (Brooklyn, 1972), p. 26. For this and the following points I am indebted to Foxbruner's collection of sources on Zaddikism in Habad (note 2 above), pp. 195, 217, 267–8. 'Unifications' are a mystical joining of soul to soul, the importance of which is emphasized in the Lurianic Kabbalah. See *Shaarei Kedushah*, III:6; *Shaar Ruah ha-Kodesh* (Tel Aviv, 1963), pp. 74–6, 108–9, 111; *Shaar ha-Yihudim* (Koretz, 1783), fol. 1a, 4c–5b.

22 *MAHZ Ethalekh Liozna* (Brooklyn 1957), p. 36.

23 *MAHZ 5569* (Brooklyn 1981), p. 102.

24 *Maamarei Admur ha-Zaken ha-Ketsarim* (Brooklyn, 1981), ed. S. B. Levin with notes, an informative article on the development of R. Shneur Zalman's teachings and a chronological list of known discourses from the earliest years to 1801.

25 *ibid.*, p. 58

26 *ibid.*, p. 130. See R. Schatz, 'Perusho shel ha-Besht le-Mizmor 107', *Tarbiz*, vol. 42 (1972–3). (Scholem disputes the attribution of the text discussed in this article to the Baal Shem Tov and considers it was written by R. Mendel of Bar. See note 8 above, p. 189. See also Foxbruner, note 2 above, p. 98.)

27 *MAHZ ha-Ketsarim*, p. 314

28 *ibid.*, p. 535. Concerning these aspects of Zaddikism in Habad, see Foxbruner (note 2 above), p. 295, no. 108.

29 Y. Mondshein (ed.), *Likkutei Reshimot u-Maasiyot* (Kfar Habad, 1969), p. 43

30 Levin (note 7 above), p. 235

31 *ibid.*, pp. 53–9. Part of this letter is printed in *Tanya* IV, sec. 22, fol. 134a. Similar ideas are expressed by R. Menahem Mendel of Vitebsk and R. Avraham of Kalisk in Y. Barnai, *Iggerot Hasidim me-Erets Israel* (Jerusalem, 1980), pp. 153–5, 234–8. Cf. Gries (note 14 above), p. 119, n. 10, and Etkes, 'Darko shel R. Shneur Zalman' (note 7 above), p. 331.

32 Elsewhere R. Shneur Zalman openly declares that he employs the Lurianic teachings in order to explain the ideas of the founders of Hasidism. See *Tanya* IV, sec. 25, fol. 141b.

33 *Ets Hayyim*, Portal 48, ch. 2, states that 'the Jew has a soul . . . of holiness.' Portal 50, ch. 2, describes the Animal Soul, which is from *kelipat nogah*, a spiritual concealment of the Divine. On this dualism in the make-up of the individual in the Lurianic writings, see I. Tishby, *Torat ha-Ra ve-ha-Kelipot be-Kabalat ha-Ari* (Jerusalem, 1960), pp. 105–8. The theme of the Divine Soul is found in the writings of Judah Halevi, cf. *Kuzari* I: 27, 95, 103. It is also expounded in the thought of R. Judah Loeb, the Maharal. See his *Tiferet Yisrael*, end of ch. 1 and ch. 7, and A. P. Kleinberger, *The Educational Theory of the Maharal of Prague* (Hebrew) (Jerusalem, 1962), p. 40, n. 58. See also L. Jacobs 'The Doctrine of the "Divine Spark" in Man in Jewish Sources', in *Studies in Rationalism, Judaism and Universalism in Memory of Leon Roth* (London, 1966). R. Shneur Zalman makes clear that in normal consciousness the Divine Soul is concealed by the Animal or Vital Soul. The Vital Soul is the everyday 'self' of anyone who is not a Zaddik. See *Tanya* I, ch. 29, Fol. 36a.

34 See the description of the pneumatic inner change within the *benoni* during prayer, in *Tanya* I, ch. 12, fol. 16b.

35 See *Tanya* I, ch. 10, fol. 15a. Schatz regards the rarity of the 'perfect Zaddik' in R. Shneur Zalman's system as concealed anti-Zaddikism, 'for it is impossible to claim that all those called Zaddikim in his generation had reached the level described here' (note 7 above, p. 521). Our view is that R. Shneur Zalman was indeed critical of the self-deception possible among those seeking the higher rungs of the spiritual ladder. Part of the effect of his *Likkutei Amarim* was to disenchant the person who thought he

was a Zaddik (cf. *Tanya* I, fols. 34a, 35a). Nonetheless, the contemporary existence of the Zaddik, his exalted spiritual stature and his ability to lift the world (and, in particular, the Hasid) towards the Divine is an integral aspect of R. Shneur Zalman's thought.

36 Schatz presents the Maggid and a number of his disciples as the source of a quietistic episode in the history of Hasidism. Later, she states, in the third and fourth generations, the tension of quietism decreased *Ha-Hasidut ke-Mistikah* (Jerusalem, 1980, p. 22). By contrast, Scholem emphasizes the active nature of Maggidic self-annihilation, and states that through the total union with the Divine described in the Maggidic texts, 'man . . . has, in truth, only then started to be man, and it is only logical that only then will he be called upon to fulfil his destiny in the society of men' (note 8 above, p. 227).

37 *Tanya* I, ch. 10, fol. 15b.

38 See Etkes (note 4 above).

39 'The soul of a man, even if he is a perfect Zaddik . . . is none the less not completely and utterly . . . annulled and absorbed in the Divine radiance . . . Rather he is a separate entity, fearing the Divine and loving Him. This is not the case with the commandments . . . which are the inwardness of the Divine Will, and there is no concealment of the Countenance at all' (*Tanya* I, ch. 35, fol. 44b). In relation to the Essence, to which contact is granted through the commandments of the Torah, the Divine Soul itself has a concealing quality and must be transcended. Cf. Loewenthal, 'The Apotheosis of Action' (note 7 above). It should be noted that there is also a quietistic aspect of R. Shneur Zalman's depiction of the Zaddik, although his allusions to this are very rare. See Hallamish, 'Mishnato ha-Iyunit' (note 7 above), pp. 254–5; the reference in *Tanya* I, ch. 40, fol. 55b–56a to 'love without service which has the quality of the World to Come'; and *Tanya* V, fol. 154a, which quotes the *Zohar* II, 244b to the effect that through 'gazing' alone, i.e. an internal contemplative movement, the same effect can be achieved as through the practical commandments. This, states R. Shneur Zalman, is an example of the *mesirat nefesh* of *Nefilat Apayyim* (see below). However a few pages later, referring to this theme, he insists that nonetheless the practical commandments are also essential (*Tanya* V, fol. 157a–b).

Another instance of a quietistic depiction of the Zaddik is an intriguing but obscure discourse which speaks of two types of Zaddik; one is involved with the practical world, the other is predominantly concerned with *Yihudim* and spiritual ascents. See *Likkutei Torah, Shemini*, fol. 18a. There is an oral tradition in Habad that *Likkutei Amarim*, termed the 'Book of the Intermediate Man', only describes the Zaddik in terms that are suitable for the 'Intermediate Man', i.e. the non-Zaddik. According to this tradition, R. Shneur Zalman wrote another book, 'Book of Zaddikim', which was lost in the fire of 1810 that destroyed many of his writings (including a considerable portion of his *Shulhan Arukh*). Concerning this fire see the introduction to the *Shulhan Arukh* and *Iggerot Kodesh*, p. 225. See also Mondshein (note 7 above), vol. 2, p. 28, and his article in *Biteon Habad*, vol. 32 (1971), p. 18. Mondshein quotes a tradition that in the fire of 1810 there was burned 'a volume of Hasidic teachings in manuscript bound on both edges' which bore a warning forbidding anyone to study it.

40 He states that this commandment is so important in the eyes of the sages that it is simply termed *mitzva* in the Palestinian Talmud; it is the most important of the practical commandments, for a person puts all the energy of his Vital Soul into earning a living, and when he gives of this money to charity 'his whole Vital Soul rises to the Divine' (*Tanya* I, ch. 37, fol. 48b). Further, most of R. Shneur Zalman's letters collected (presumably by his son R. Dov Ber) in the fourth part of *Tanya* concern charity. R. Shneur Zalman also recommends charity as the manner of

repentance most suitable for the generation (rather than undertaking self-imposed fasts) and states that the talmudic limitation of donating no more than one-fifth of one's wealth to charity (T. B. *Kethubot* 50a) does not apply to charity given for this reason (*Tanya* III, ch. 3, fol. 93a).

41 Other aspects of R. Shneur Zalman's reaction to this statute are discussed in Loewenthal, 'Early Hasidic Teachings' (note 7 above), pp. 67–74.

42 A kabbalistic phrase meaning 'transform evil to good'.

43 T. B. *Hullin* 7a. R. Pinhas is presented in the *aggadah* as a man with mystic power (cf. T. J. *Demai* 1:3).

44 Levin (note 7 above), p. 141–2. Part of the letter is printed in *Beit Rebbe*, p. 86. Concerning R. Shneur Zalman's meeting with R. Barukh and other aspects of the dispute between them, see Y. Mondshein's article in *Biteon Habad*, vol. 32 (1971), pp. 14–16. This suggests that R. Barukh was critical of R. Shneur Zalman's path of broad communication of Hasidic teachings.

45 The concept of self-sacrifice for Judaism is found in Daniel, chs. 1, 3 and 6 and II Maccabees 6. The term *Kiddush ha-Shem* is first found in *Sifra* to Lev. 22:32. The Talmud and later Codes provide halakhic guidance as to when the person should give up his life rather than transgress. In normal times martyrdom is declared to be obligatory when the alternative is the transgression of laws prohibiting idolatry, immorality or murder. However, in a time of religious persecution, or in public, it is obligatory when the transgression of other laws or even mere customs is involved. Cf. T. B. *Sanh.* 74a–b, Maimonides, *Yad, Hil. Yesodei HaTorah*, ch. 5, *Shulhan Arukh, Yoreh De'ah*, sec. 157. It is noteworthy that a full halakhic treatise on *Kiddush ha-Shem* was compiled by R. Eliyahu Yosef Rivlin (d. 1865), a follower of the *Mitteler Rebbe*: *Oholei Yosef* (Jerusalem, 1868), pt. I. The theme of *mesirat nefesh* for *Kiddush ha-Shem* is emphasized in Talmud and Midrash (for the actual term *mesirat nefesh* see T. B. *Ber.* 20a and *Tanhuma, Lekh Lekha* 2) and the tenth-century work *Yosipon*, which eulogizes instances of Jewish martyrdom in the Hellenistic period, and the later communal self-sacrifice at Massada. This phenomenon recurred in the communities of the Rhineland during the People's Crusade of 1096, and the theme of *Kiddush ha-Shem* was given an exalted position in *Sefer Hasidim*. A long catalogue of incidents of *Kiddush ha-Shem* is found in Solomon ibn Verga's *Shevet Yehudah*. There is a considerable literature on this topic. A brief list is as follows: H. G. Friedman, 'Kiddush Hashem and Hillul Hashem', *HUCA* (1904); I. Baer's introduction to Haberman's edition of *Sefer Gezerot Ashkenaz ve-Tsorfat* (Jerusalem, 1946); id., 'Sefer Yosipon ha-Ivri', in *Sefer Dinaburg* (Jerusalem, 1949); id., 'Gezerot TaTNU', *Sefer Asaf* (1953); id., 'Am Yisrael, ha-Kenesia ha-Notzrit ve-ha-Kesarut ha-Romit', *Zion*, vol. 21 (1956): the last three reprinted in his collected essays, *Studies in the History of the Jewish People* (Hebrew) (Jerusalem, 1985), vol. 2, pp. 101–27, 147–61, vol. 1, pp. 254–302; S. Spiegel, 'Mipitgemei ha-Akedah, etc.' in *Kaplan Jubilee Vol.* (1953); id., *The Last Trial* (New York, 1979); J. Katz, 'Beyn TaTNU le-TaH-TaT', *I. F. Baer Jubilee Vol.* (Jerusalem, 1960), and *Exclusiveness and Tolerance* (New York, 1962), pp. 82–92; A. Shohet, 'Kiddush ha-Shem ba-Hagutam shel Megoreshei Sefarad u-Mekubelei Tsfat', in *Holy War and Martyrology* (Hebrew) (Jerusalem, 1968); Y. Dan, 'Baayat Kiddush ha-Shem be-Toratah ha-Iyunit shel Tenuat Hasidut Ashkenaz', op, cit.; H. H. Ben-Sasson, *Perakim be-Toledot ha-Yehudim* (Tel Aviv, 1969), pp. 172–84; G. J. Weiss, 'Kiddush ha-Shem u-Mitat Korban', *Mehkarim be-Hasidut Braslav* (Jerusalem, 1974).

46 The concept of the 'spiritualization' of the theme of *Kiddush ha-Shem* was defined by Katz: see 'Beyn TaTNU le-TaH-TaT' (note 45 above).

47 'When one recites the *Shema* one should have the intention to accept on oneself the yoke of the Kingdom of Heaven, to be killed for *Kiddush ha-Shem* ... This is what is

meant by "with all your soul" (Deut. 6:5)—even if He takes your soul (*Sifre* and *Rashi* loc. cit.; T. B. *Ber.* 54a, 61b) . . . With this *kavanah* one will recite it with fear and trembling (*Bayit Hadash* to *Tur Orah Hayyim*, sec. 61). This is emphatically expressed in Azkiri's *Sefer Haredim* (Zolkiew, 1804), fol. 20b ('Positive commands concerning the heart', I:14ff).

48 Concerning the *hanhagot* (rules of conduct) literature and its significance in the history of Hasidism, see Z. Gries 'Sifrut ha-Hanhagot ha-Hasidit', *Zion*, vol. 46 (1981) and 'Hagdarat ha-Hanhagah ke-Sug Sifruti be-Sifrut ha-Musar ha-Ivrit', *Kiryat Sefer*, vol. 56 (1981).

49 *Noam Elimelech*, '*Tsetel katan*', sec. 1.

50 *ibid.*, secs. 2–3.

51 *Pri ha-Arets* (Jerusalem, 1974), p.76 (sect. Kedoshim). See Schatz (note 36 above), p.30.

52 See Schatz, 'Contemplative Prayer in Hasidism', in *Studies in Mysticism and Religion presented to Gershom G. Scholem* (Jerusalem, 1967), p.226, and note 36 above, p.110. *Maggid Devarav le-Yaakov* (Jerusalem, 1976) refers to prayer with self-sacrifice, sect. 152, 209.

53 In eighteenth-century Poland the blood libel was the cause of a considerable number of cases of Jewish martyrdom. A book on this theme by an apostate Jew named Serafinovitch was published in 1716, 1758 and 1760. There were trials and executions of Jews in Sandomir (1698–1710); Posen (1736); Zaslav (1747). In the latter case a group of Jews celebrating a circumcision were arrested and tortured. One or two of them agreed to convert to Christianity; none the less all were killed in a barbaric way. This trial was followed by a series of ritual murder accusations, occurring almost annually for the next fifteen years. Particularly notable are the cases of Dunaigrod (1748); Zhytomir (1753), in which eleven Jews were flayed alive while another thirteen saved themselves from death by accepting baptism; Yampol (1756); Stupnitza (1759); and Voislavitza, near Lublin (1760). In this last incident the rabbi of the community killed himself, and four others accused in the blood libel were sentenced to be quartered. They were induced to let themselves be baptized, and their sentence was therefore made more lenient: they were beheaded. As a result of Jewish endeavours, in 1763 the new Pope Clement XIII made an official denial of the blood libel, but martyrdoms continued, particularly as a result of Haidamack persecution. The worst massacre was in Uman in 1768, where three thousand Jews were killed in the synagogue after the Polish governor of the city of Mladanovich betrayed them, following a pattern familiar from the massacres associated with the People's Crusade in 1096. See Dubnow, *History of the Jews of Russia and Poland*, vol. 1 (Philadelphia, 1916), pp.172–86. According to R. Nathan of Nemirov, his *Rebbe*, R. Nahman of Braslav, wished to be buried in Uman because of the martyrs who had died there for *Kiddush ha-Shem* (*Hayyei MoHaRaN*), fol. 39a.

54 The letter mentions the vision of Jews who were killed and some who became apostates and were still put to death. The Baal Shem Tov, in his visionary experience, asks Samael about the Divine justice of the incident. (See the text of that letter at the end of R. Jacob Joseph of Polonnoye's *Ben Porat Yosef* [Koretz, 1781], and the variant text printed by D. Frankel in *Mikhtavim me-ha-Besht* [Lvov, 1923], pp. 1–5. Another version was published by Y. Mondshein in *Migdal Oz* [Kfar Habad, 1980], pp. 119–26. A series of discussions on the text of the letter, by A. Rubinstein and S. Bauminger, is published in *Sinai*, vols. 67–8, 71–3. Each of the three versions of the letter gives a different answer from Samael.) The letter continues (in the version printed in 1781 and also in that of Frankel; only briefly in that of Mondshein) with an account of the actual events in the Zaslav blood libel of 1747 and mentions two other contemporary instances of Jews dying for *Kiddush ha-Shem*. In these the Jews did not

convert (since in Zaslav also those who had converted were killed). Instead 'All gave up their lives for *Kiddush ha-Shem* and sanctified the Name of Heaven and withstood the test. By this merit will come our Messiah . . . ' (see Dubnow, *Toledot ha-Hasidut*, p. 61, note 2). A further reference to *mesirat nefesh*, pointed out to me by Chimen Abramsky, in the first printed text of this letter is that the Baal Shem Tov employs the phrase 'masarti mamash nafshi' (I really surrendered my soul), to describe his spiritual activity during the ascent of his soul, in which, he says, there was great danger. This important text by the founder of Hasidism thus refers both to the classical *Kiddush ha-ha-Shem* martyrology and also to the 'spiritualized' form of the theme of *mesirat nefesh*.

55 *Tanya* I, ch. 18, fol. 24a: 'And therefore even the lowest of the low and sinners give up their lives for *Kiddush ha-Shem*, generally, and suffer severe torture rather than deny the One G-d, even if they are coarse and ignorant, without knowledge of the greatness of the Divine. And even that little they do know they do not think about at all; for they do not give up their lives because of knowledge and contemplation of the Divine. Rather, without any knowledge, nor contemplation, just as if it were absolutely impossible to deny the One G-d, without any reason or explanation at all. This is because the One G-d illuminates and gives life to the entire soul . . . ' The significance of this idea in Habad Hasidism was noticed by Tishby and Dan (note 7), col. 814.

The idea of the propensity of even the lowest Jew to give up his life for *Kiddush ha-Shem* occurs in the writings of R. Jacob Joseph of Polonnoye, but without amplification: 'I heard a saying that a woman from the holy community of Medziboz said in Russian: "We made a good choice in G-d, but also G-d made a good choice in the Jews. For Faivush is a low person, yet he Sanctifies the Blessed Name"' (*Toledot Yaakov Yosef*, Koretz, fol. 43a). Tradition records that R. Shneur Zalman's grandson, the *Tsemah Tsedek*, was asked about the fact that Gentiles too sacrifice their lives for their faith. If this is so, how can the propensity for *Kiddush ha-Shem* be proof of the presence of the 'hidden love' of the Divine Spark within the Jew? He answered that among the Gentiles only the pious give up their lives, whereas among the Jews even 'the lowest of the low' are ready to do so (J. Korf, *Likutei Biurim be-Sefer ha-Tanya*, vol. 1 [New York, 1974], p. 139).

56 See *Tanya* I, ch. 25, fol. 31a–32b.

57 This work, probably the earliest tract by R. Dov Ber, was read by his followers in manuscript during his lifetime. It was first published in Königsberg, perhaps in 1831 (see Elior in *Kiryat Sefer*, note 5 above). We will refer to the Warsaw, 1868, edition entitled *Likkutei Biurim*. This includes a commentary by R. Hillel of Poritch (d. 1864). The text of *Kuntres ha-Hitpaalut* has been translated and annotated by L. Jacobs, with the title *Tract on Ecstasy* (London, 1963).

58 Cf. *Likkutei Biurim*, 49a, 51a–b, 56a.

59 *ibid.*, 55b.

60 *ibid.*, 56a. 'Since this [level] is hardly found at all among most people, it would be superfluous to expound on it further.'

61 *ibid.* ' . . . and also at the moment of *Kiddush ha-Shem* this power radiates.' However, in this case it radiates 'bi-vehinat histalkut;, i.e. as a form of removal from the world. The same is so also of 'the true *baal teshuvah*', like R. Eliezer b. Dordaya, whose soul expired in his repentant weeping (*ibid.*, cf. T. B. *Av. Zar.*, 17a). The *mesirat nefesh* of the Zaddik, by contrast, is a force expressed positively within the world.

62 This was published in two parts in Shklov, 1817 and 1818. They were later reprinted together, with the title *Shaarei Teshuvah* (Zhitomir, 1864). A third section of this work is entitled *Derekh Hayyim* (Kopyst, 1819).

63 *Shaarei Teshuvah* (Brooklyn 1983, reprint of Zhitomir, 1864), sec. I, p. 9 (originally misprinted p. 5).

64 *Derekh Hayyim* (Brooklyn 1955), p. 23.

65 R. Dov Ber states that the epoch of intensive *Kiddush ha-Shem* was brought to a close because of the stature of R. Isaac Luria 'who had the quality of Tikkun' (*loc. cit.*, note 63 above). Elsewhere he mentions the phenomenon of *Kiddush ha-Shem* during the later Chmielnicki massacres (note 64 above).

66 This rather positive attitude to mediaeval Jewish philosophy is noteworthy; it contrasts with the negative attitude which G. Nigal (note 12 above), p. 344, states permeated the early generations of Hasidism through the commentary of R. Yosef Yabetz to *Pirkei Avot*. (An outstanding example is R. Nahman of Braslav, although in his case this is not a simple question at all: see Weiss, note 45 above, pp. 109–49). According to R. Dov Ber's explanation, *mesirat nefesh* achieves *Tikkun* for idolatry because, like idolatry (*Keter* of the *Kelipah*), it is beyond Reason.

67 See *Emek ha-Melekh* (Amsterdam, 1648, reprinted Bene Berak, 1973), *Shaar Olam ha-Tohu*, ch. 66, fol. 37a–b, which speaks of the deaths of the Ten Martyrs of Mishnaic times as having been necessary because, as a result of the idolatry of the epoch of the First Temple, 'the world began to totter'. At the same time, they were atoning for the act of the brothers who sold Joseph. (This idea is found in the Martyrology in the Yom Kippur liturgy.) Further, later souls deriving from them 'sacrifice their lives for *Kiddush ha-Shem* in every generation.'

68 Cf. *Shulhan Arukh, Orah Hayyim*, sec. 131, paras. 1–2.

69 See Tishby (note 10 above), vol. 2, pp. 275–6. Thus: 'There are six commandments expressed in prayer . . . the sixth: to sacrifice one's soul to Him . . . A fitting time to sacrifice one's soul to Him . . . is when carrying out *Nefilat Apayyim*, saying "To you, G-d, I lift up my soul" (Ps. 25:1). One should have the intention to sacrifice one's soul to Him with full determination' (*Zohar* II, 202b). Cf. also *ibid.*, 200b. Similar ideas are expressed by R. Abraham ben Eliezer Halevi, living at the time of the Expulsion, in his *Megilat Amrafel*; see G. Scholem, 'Perakim mi-Toledot Sifrut ha-Kabbalah', *Kiryat Sefer*, vol. 7 (1930–1), p. 154. See also A. Shohet (note 45 above), p. 143 and Elior *Theory of Divinity* (note 5 above), pp. 276–8.

70 Quoted by Shohet, op. cit., p. 143, from *Tefilah le-Moshe* (Premiszlan, 1892), 107a. Shohet makes the point that in this, as in a number of passages from R. Hayyim Vital, *Nefilat Apayyim* is described as an act directly manifesting (spiritualized) *Kiddush ha-Shem*, rather than a mere affirmation of one's readiness for self- sacrifice.

71 *Shaar ha-Kavanot*, vol. 1 (Tel Aviv, 1962), pp. 310–11.

72 *ibid.*, p. 303.

73 *ibid.* Cf. Tishby, *Torat ha-Ra ve-ha-Kelipah be-Kabalat ha-Ari* (Jerusalem, 1960), pp. 128–30.

74 Note 71 above, p. 304.

75 *ibid.*, p. 303.

76 *ibid.*, p. 305. The 'perfect Zaddik', through *Nefilat Apayyim*, can raise the souls of others. One who has a lesser level of attainment cannot raise others but is able himself to leave *Gehinom*. Some on a lower level are unable to leave. This last eventuality explains sudden transformations for the bad, such as that of Yohanan the High Priest who, after eighty years of priesthood, suddenly became a Sadducee. On account of such danger R. Haim Vital writes: 'Therefore I am warning you stringently that the person who undertakes *Nefilat Apayyim* in this way should be a perfect Zaddik, or at least should have *kavanah* in that prayer from beginning to end' (*ibid.*, pp. 304–5).

77 *ibid.*, p. 304.

78 Cf. T. B. *Yoma* 86a.

79 *Shaar ha-Kavanot*, vol. 1, p. 310.

80 See Weiss (note 2 above), pp. 69, 74–5. See also Schatz (note 26 above), pp. 154–84, which explores the concept of the descent of the Zaddik to *Gehinom* as found in

Hasidism; on p. 174 she discusses the relationship of these ideas to the Lurianic teachings concerning *Nefilat Apayyim*. Cf. the Maggidic passage in *Maggid Devarav le-Yaakov*, ed. R. Schatz-Uffenheimer (Jerusalem, 1976), sec. 147, which speaks of the dangers of *Nefilat Apayyim*. The theme of *Nefilat Apayyim* as a descent into the *kelipot* is briefly referred to by R. Shneur Zalman in the name of R. Avraham, the son of the Maggid. See *Torah Or*, 6a.

81 *Seder Tefilot mi-Kol ha-Shana . . . im Perush ha-Milot* (Brooklyn, 1971), fol. 92d.

82 *Shaarei Teshuvah* I, p. 87. This passage expresses R. Dov Ber's position in contrast to that of his contemporary rival R. Aaron Halevi of Staroselye. R. Dov Ber maintained that detailed intellecual contemplation was the path to the highest level of *bitul*. His *Kuntres ha-Hitpaalut* emphasizes this point. This cerebral ecstasy was rejected by R. Aaron, who instead advised his followers to seek heartfelt emotional enthusiasm. Concerning R. Aaron, see L. Jacobs, *Seeker of Unity—the Life and Works of Aaron of Starosselje* (London, 1966) and Elior, *Theory of Divinity* (note 5 above).

83 Gershom Scholem, in his article on *devekut* in Hasidism took it for granted that this was an intermittent state. He explained the Hasidic concepts 'descent' (*yeridah*) and 'smallness' (*katnut*) as forms of temporary cessation from *devekut*, citing teachings of the Baal Shem Tov and R. Jacob Joseph of Polonnoy (note 8 above, pp. 218–22). Rivka Schatz has shown that in the teachings of R. Elimelech of Lyzhansk, while *devekut* is seen as generally intermittent, there is also an ideal of permanent *devekut*, which is the achievement of a higher level of Zaddik, or which will be realized in the messianic age (note 4 above, pp. 368–9). To R. Elimelech, contact with the physical world is itself a disturbance of *devekut* which the teaching of the Lurianic 'sparks' present in food and other necessities of physical life does not completely mitigate. See *Noam Elimelech* (New York, 1956), *Vayigash* 25c: ' . . . it is permitted to have benefit from this world, that is, from physical things such as eating and drinking . . . in order that the Zaddikim should . . . extract the holy sparks from them. But for this, the Zaddik would not be permitted to interrupt and be separated, even for a moment, from holiness and *devekut*, to turn to physical things. Only in order to bring [the sparks] into holiness is he permitted to descend a little bit and slightly to interrupt his *devekut* . . . ' In Braslav teaching there is strong emphasis on the concept of *katnut*. However, as is made clear in A. Rapoport-Albert's '"Katnut", "peshitut", ve–"Eyni Yode'a" shel R. Nahman mi-Braslav', *Studies in Jewish Religious and Intellectual History presented to Alexander Altmann* (Alabama, 1979), p. 21: 'the descent to the bottom of the ladder is not just the path which prepares the Zaddik for his rise . . . but is itself the ascent to the most exalted level.' In other words, in Braslav thought the Zaddik is in a state of permanent spiritual exaltation whatever he is doing and whatever the area of his struggle. In the teachings of the Maggid we also find the term *katnut* employed not as an implication of any lowering of the level of the Zaddik but rather as an expression of his transforming existence around him to express its Divine quality (cf. Tishby and Dan, note 7 above, p. 292). We also find a clear statement from the Maggid to the effect that *devekut*, if it is real at all, is permanent: '"One who makes his *tefilah* (lit. phylactery) circular—it is dangerous and it is not a *mitzvah*" (T. B.*Meg.*, 24b). "His *tefilah*"—this means, his cleaving to the Holy One; "circular"—this means sometimes he is cleaving to the Holy One and sometimes he is not, like a wheel which revolves; "it is not a *mitzvah*"—"mitzvah" meaning connection, as the Aramaic word *tzavta*—presumably he is not connected to the Holy One' (*Maggid Devarav le-Yaakov* [Jerusalem, 1976], sec. 3). Indeed it is likely that, despite Scholem, in the teachings of the Baal Shem Tov too the concept of *katnut* is nothing but an opportunity to 'sweeten the harsh forces at their root'. (Cf. *Toledot Yaakov Yosef* [Koretz, 1780], 146c). J. G. Weiss, in his account of the way the approach to *devekut* in the thought of the Baal Shem Tov went further than in that of R. Nahman of

Kossov, similarly indicates that this is a state which is not diminished by social or material involvements with the world and shows that there are several ways in which this teaching of 'unification' and 'raising' of the world is expressed, one of them being in terms of the Lurianic sparks (note 2 above, pp. 60–9). Thus Weiss quotes from *Zofnat Pane'ah*, 60a: 'For I heard from my teacher that there are "unifications" in speech; whether in speech of Torah and prayer, or in speech with one's fellow in the market. One can "connect" him and raise him up, each one according to his level: some through sacred speech and some through profane speech; for it has in it the twenty-two letters [of the sacred Alef Bet] . . . ' (*ibid.*, p. 64). It is noteworthy that Weiss considered the concept of the 'descent' of the Zaddik only peripheral to the teachings of the Baal Shem Tov (*ibid.*, p. 88). Perhaps the concept of the intermittence of *devekut* is to be traced specifically to R. Yaakov Yosef—because his works are addressed not primarily to pneumatics of the highest rank, but to the generality of the scholarly class, Hasidim rather than Zaddikim.

84 *Tanya* I, ch. 12, fol. 16b
85 *ibid.*, ch. 13, fol. 19a
86 *ibid.*
87 *Shaarei Teshuvah*, Pt. I, pp. 88–9
88 *ibid.*, p. 90
89 *ibid.* The quotation is from *Zohar* II, 114a.
90 *Shaarei Teshuvah*, loc. cit. It is interesting to note that while *Nefilat Apayyim* is hardly mentioned in the teachings of R. Shneur Zalman, it is discussed extensively by both his son R. Dov Ber and his leading disciple R. Aaron Halevi Horowitz of Staroselye. This indicates the presence of an 'oral teaching' imparted by R. Shneur Zalman which only took written form in the next generation. Concerning R. Aaron's treatment of the theme of *Nefilat Apayyim*, see Elior, *Theory of Divinity* (note 5 above), pp. 273–81. As in the teachings of R. Dov Ber, in those of R. Aaron the *mesirat nefesh* of *Nefilat Apayyim* concerns entry into the daily world (cf. his *Shaarei Avodah*, *Petah ha-Teshuvah*, ch. 12, fol. 18b). However the emphasis in R. Aaron's treatment of this subject is on giving counsel to the reader on achieving a true negation of the world and its desires even while having to come in contact with it. He stresses the mental movement of 'giving oneself over to death', in a manner comparable to R. Elimelech of Lyzhansk's employment of the theme of *mesirat nefesh*, mentioned above. Thus R. Aaron speaks of 'the extinction and total burning away of "being" (*yesh*) which has the quality of *Nefilat Apayyim*, that he delivers himself to death. This means, that he really does not want to continue existing . . . ' Through this, promises R. Aaron, the person attains an inspired sense of closeness to the Divine 'the whole day long' and is able to join the otherwise contrary qualities of being and non-being (*Avodat Halevi*, Tetzaveh, fol. 47c). In another passage he states that the fact that after prayer one has to be involved with earning a living could be disastrous spiritually ('one could fall completely, Heaven forfend'), and therefore one says *Nefilat Apayyim*. The effect of this is to impart a 'coldness' to one's worldly activities, as if one's possessions were not really one's own (*Avodat Halevi*, Vayehi, fol. 71b). Through the concept of *Nefilat Apayyim*, R. Aaron found a suitable medium to transmit in meaningful terms the ascetic, kabbalistic world-view to his followers, imparting also the acosmistic yearning which is the cornerstone of his system. By contrast R. Dov Ber, through employment of this theme, sought to communicate a concept of unity with the Divine which lay far beyond even the most exceptional of his followers, and is clearly the province of the rare Zaddik alone.
91 Cf. *Tanya* I, ch. 34, fol. 43a: 'It is known that "the Patriarchs were the Chariot" (*Ber. Rab.*, ch. 47 on Gen. 17:22) that all their lives, perpetually, they never ceased even for a moment from binding their minds and souls to the Master of the Worlds in the

above mentioned state of *bitul*.' See also *Tanya* I, ch. 23, fol. 28b.

92 *Hiner bet*, also *hiner plet* or *himmel plet*. See Horodecky (ed.), *Shivhei ha-Besht* (4th edn, Tel Aviv, 1975), p. 185, n. 1.

93 He is noted as a follower of R. Dov Ber by Hielman in *Beit Rebbe*, p. 149. Concerning *Shivhei ha-Besht* see Dubnow (note 2 above), pp. 382; 411–16; J. G. Weiss, 'A circle of Pneumatics in Pre-Hasidism', *JJS*, vol. 8 (1957), p. 207, n. 21; Y. Mondshein, *Shivhei ha-Besht* (Jerusalem, 1982), pp. 5–75, and the bibliography pp. 69–70. A second edition of *Shivhei ha-Besht* was printed in Berdichev in 1815. In the same year a Yiddish version was printed in Ostraho. English translation by Dan Ben-Amos and Jerome R. Mintz, *In Praise of the Baal Shem Tov* (Bloomington, 1970).

94 At the same time it relates to the conflict with R. Aaron (see below).

95 *Shaarei Teshuvah*, Pt. I, p. 91

96 *ibid.*

97 *ibid.*

98 See Katz, 'Beyn TaTNU le-TaH–TaT' (note 45 above), p. 324ff. See also A. Shohet (note 45 above), pp. 143–4.

99 *Shaarei Teshuvah*, loc. cit. Compare *Sefer Hasidim* (Jerusalem, 1970), sec. 222: 'Many Jews were killed during the persecution and many decided to be killed but were saved. A Jew whose name was R. Shabtai saw in a dream a person who had been killed . . . he said "all those who decided in their hearts to be killed for *Kiddush ha-Shem*, their portion is with us in the Garden of Eden".' Cf. I. Baer, 'Ha-Megamah ha-Datit-Hevratit shel Sefer Hasidim', *Zion*, vol. 3 (1937), p. 14ff. (*Studies in the History* . . ., vol. 2, p. 188ff.)

100 *Shaarei Teshuvah*, loc. cit.

101 This image occurs in the talmudic account of 'the woman and her seven sons' (T. B. *Gittin*, 57b), and in the Fourth Book of Hasmoneans, ch. 8. (Cf. *Encyclopaedia Judaica*, vol. 2 [Berlin, 1928], pp. 5–6.) For discussion of *Akedah* imagery in the mediaeval chronicles and *piyyutim* see L. Zunz, 'Die Synagogale Poesie des Mittelalters' (Berlin, 1855), pp. 136–40; Spiegel (note 45 above); Baer, 'Gezerot TaTNU' (note 45 above), p. 136ff. and n. 46.

102 T. B. *Berakhot*, 61b.

103 *Shaarei Teshuvah*, loc. cit.

104 *ibid.*

105 T. B. *Moed Katan*, 28a.

106 *Shaarei Teshuvah*, pt. I, pp. 92–3.

107 Concerning this controversy see Jacobs, *Tract on Ecstasy* (note 7 above), pp. 11–12, 41–49 and *Seeker of Unity*, pp. 12–14; Elior, 'Ha-mahloket al Moreshet Habad' (note 5 above) and *Theory of Divinity*, pp. 5–15 and *passim*. Elior characterizes the approach of R. Aaron as 'theocentric', contrasting with that of R. Dov Ber which was 'anthropocentric'. One could add, translating this into the terminology of Habad thought, that R. Aaron sought above all the acosmistic contemplative perspective termed 'the Upper Unity', in which no world, only the Divine, is perceived; R. Dov Ber, by contrast, emphasized the perspective termed 'the Lower Unity', in which the world, as world, is seen (at least potentially) as a full expression of the Divine.

108 Rivka Schatz makes the point that Hasidism exhibits both quietist and activist aspects, and that this paradox is the key to its unique nature (note 36 above, pp. 14–19). On the one hand there is the demand to be involved in the world, whether the world of the practical *mitzvot*, or the wider realms of physical and social life and involvement which are their outer framework; on the other there is the emphasis on contemplation, *bitul*, self-abnegation in the Infinite Divine. She emphasizes the significance of the concept of 'service with materiality', which is based on the teaching of the Lurianic 'sparks', in providing a bridge between these two

490

aspects (*ibid.*, p. 16). Weiss, too, deals with this question, but makes it clear that the teaching of *devekut* in the midst of practical action is not expressed solely in terms of the Divine Sparks (note 2 above, p. 65). It seems that the *mesirat nefesh* of *Nefilat Apayyim* also has the quality of such a bridge, connecting *bitul* with involvement in the practical world. In fact, the basis of both this kind of *mesirat nefesh* and the 'service with materiality' is the same concept of raising of the Divine Sparks, for in the kabbalistic sources this is the underlying significance of *Nefilat Apayyim*. R. Dov Ber too speaks of *Nefilat Apayyim* in terms of the raising of the 'sparks'. Thus in the discourse under discussion in *Shaar ha-Teshuvah ve-ha-Tefilah* he asks why the word *tidbakun* in the phrase 'To him shall ye cleave' (Deut. 13:5) ends in a long (final) *nun*; his answer is that 'the long *nun* indicates spreading downwards ... to the lowest level. . . . This is through *Nefilat Apayyim*, when the Divine Radiance descends far below, even into the coarseness of *nogah*, to sift out the sparks and raise them, that they should cleave above, to the highest level' (*Shaarei Teshuvah* Pt. I, p. 94). R. Dov Ber goes on to explain that the body of the person who has achieved this state of *mesirat nefesh* of *Nefilat Apayyim* is no longer a concealment of the Divine. This is a state of being with messianic connotations: '. . . for the materiality of his body does not conceal, in *Nefilat Apayyim*, for it too rises; of this it says "and to Him you shall cleave" (*tidbakun*) with a *nun* extending below, so that everything can rise, as it will be in the Time to Come, when evil will be completely eradicated.' For one in such a state, action is possible together with the highest *devekut*, the physical world no longer conceals or contradicts the Divine. This is the special connotation of *Nefilat Apayyim*, and it is by virtue of this that it is distinguished from other varieties of *devekut*. Thus through the esoteric concept of the *mesirat nefesh* of *Nefilat Apayyim*, R. Dov Ber arrives at an activist delineation of the Zaddik which complements that found in the teachings of R. Shneur Zalman. Discussion of the relationship of *mesirat nefesh* and activism cannot end without reference to the historical background of this concept and the fact that there too we find an emphasis on practical action. Jacob Katz has commented that in 1096 and subsequently the Jewish martyrs did not passively allow themselves to be killed, their minds in distant contemplation of radiant unity. On the contrary, they first 'employed every worldly means of saving themselves' including political machinations and physical battle. (*Exclusiveness and Tolerance*, note 45 above, pp. 86–7.) Only when these means failed did they give themselves over to death for *Kiddush ha-Shem*. There has even been an attempt to distinguish Jewish martyrdom from its Christian counterpart by the presence of this form of activism (*ibid.*, p. 87, n. 6). An echo of the activist aspect of historical *mesirat nefesh* is preserved in its mystical 'spiritualized' delineation in the teachings of R. Dov Ber.

109 *Shaarei Teshuvah*, Pt. I, p. 92. See *Zohar* III, 120b–121a.

110 This idea is found in the Midrash: 'When the sword reached his neck, the soul of Isaac left him. When the voice came forth . . . "do not stretch out your hand against the lad", his soul returned to his body. [Abraham] released him and Isaac stood up: he knew that thus would the dead be revived and he said "Blessed are You ... Who revives the dead"' (*Yalkut Shimoni*, *Vayera* ch. 22, sec. 101).

111 *Shaarei Teshuvah*, loc. cit.

112 One of the points of conflict between R. Aaron and R. Dov Ber concerned whether anyone in their own generation could achieve the most exalted heights of spiritual attainment. Near the beginning of his polemical attack on R. Dov Ber in small print in the introduction to *Shaarei Avodah* (Shklov, 1821), R. Aaron states that true abnegation of self was only achieved by Moses and the giants of the past. This is a shaft aimed at the claim implicit in R. Dov Ber's teachings that contemporary figures might reach the highest level.

113 *Shaarei Teshuvah*, loc. cit.

114 See note 131, below.

115 *Shivhei ha-Besht*, Mintz edn. (Tel Aviv, 1961), p. 63; Horodecky edn. (Tel Aviv, 1975), p. 106.

116 He is identified as Dov Ber of Lintz, the son-in-law of Alexander Shohet who for eight years had been the scribe of the Baal Shem Tov (cf. Dubnow, note 2 above p. 413).

117 *Shivhei ha-Besht*, Horodecky edn., p. 35. (This is the text for the most part as published in the Kopyst, 1815, edition, albeit arranged by Horodecky in a different order. Compare with Mintz, p. 23.)

118 R. Shneur Zalman himself had a role in editing at least part of this work—a fact which itself is informative about his concept of the Baal Shem Tov. R. Menahem Mendel of Vitebsk, the colleague and teacher of R. Shneur Zalman, also had an exalted view of the power of the Baal Shem Tov. See Israel Jaffe's preface to *Shivhei ha-Besht*, Horodecky edn., p. 33, and R. Menahem Mendel's *Pri ha-Arets* (Jerusalem, 1974), p. 8.

119 After R. Shneur Zalman died, Yakov Cadaner apparently initially followed R. Aaron of Staroselye but later became a prominent follower of R. Dov Ber. He outlived the latter and followed his successor R. Menahem Mendel, the *Tsemah Tsedek*. He is the author of *Sipurim Noraim* (Lemberg, 1875) and had a hand in the editing or writing of *Matsref ha-Avodah* (Königsberg, 1851) and *Vikuha Rabah* (Tchernovitz, 1864). Cf. Y. Mondshein, 'Vikuha Rabah u-Matsref he-Avodah', *Alei Sefer*, vol. 5 (1978), p. 169. A commentary on *Tanya* is also attributed to him. Cf. Hielman (note 7 above), p. 213.

120 Y. Cadaner, *Sipurim Noraim* (Jerusalem, 1957), pp. 34–5

121 *ibid.*, p. 35

122 Reports of visitations from departed souls, who transmit Torah teachings from a higher world, remain a feature of the Habad leadership, extending to the present day. See Rabbi M. M. Schneerson, *Ha-Yom Yom* (Brooklyn, 1981), pp. 43, 122–3, 186; *Sefer ha-Maamarim 5709* (Kfar Habad, 1976), pp. 92–7; *Likkutei Sihot*, vol. 2, p. 496; Mondshein, *Migdal Oz* (note 54 above), pp. 471–82. In the case of the present Lubavitcher Rebbe, in 1955 a remarkable incident took place in the presence of about 400 followers. An eyewitness account by the Lubavitch emissary to England, R. Nahman Sudak, describes a Hasidic gathering at the close of the Shavuot festival. The gathering began before sunset. The *Rebbe* would normally recite Grace after Meals, signifying the end of the gathering, before midnight. On this occasion he made the assembled gathering sing Hasidic melodies for more than two hours. During this time he sank deep into himself, his eyes becoming glazed. At certain moments, however, he would suddenly lift himself from his seat, as if greeting someone. Around 2.45 a.m. the *Rebbe* delivered a brief speech about the way R. Shneur Zalman would say 'Greeting!' (*barukh ha-ba*) to the soul of the Baal Shem Tov at the Hasidic gathering on Shavuot (the *yahrzeit* of the Baal Shem Tov). The *Rebbe* then in effect greeted each of the Habad leaders in turn, from the Previous Rebbe back to R. Shneur Zalman, and then the Maggid and the Baal Shem Tov. He also mentioned Elijah and Ahiyah the Shilonite (the heavenly teacher of the Baal Shem Tov). He stated openly that all were present and said 'anyone who can see them should say *barukh ha-ba!*' The *Rebbe* then began the *Shir ha-Maalot* Psalm which introduces Grace. Then, in an extraordinary way, the *Rebbe* invited everyone present to say '*le-hayyim*' to the Previous Rebbe, Rabbi Joseph Isaac, who had passed away five years earlier. Everyone said '*le-hayyim*'. The event is remembered as a mystical experience in which all who were present took part. A brief record of the incident is found in *Sefer ha-Sihot* (unedited transcript) 5755 (1955), p. 142.

123 See above, no. 108

124 *Shaarei Teshuvah*, Pt. I, pp. 97–112

125 Levin (note 7 above), pp. 98–9.

126 See G. Scholem, *Kabbalah* (Jerusalem, 1974), pp. 157–8. For R. Shneur Zalman's use of this term in his discourses see Hallamish, 'Mishnato ha-Iyunit' (note 7 above), pp. 181–4.

127 'During the Ten Days of Penitence, even the lowest of the low who has transgressed the whole Torah is moved in full repentance to weep . . . This is because of the aspect *Yehidah* within him, which has not been defiled with the impurity of his sins . . . ' (*Shaarei Teshuvah*, Pt. I, p. 108).

128 'When a man serves the Divine with the aspect *Yehidah*, which is the Essence, then there is no battle; this means, even after the prayer, when he walks all day in the market, in the valley of the shadow of death, [he] does not fear evil at all . . . This is the meaning of the level of "stripping off materiality" of the perfect Zaddikim, and this is also the basis of the concept of *hishtavut* (equanimity) . . . A man such as this is really in the image of G-d, for he has a Divine quality . . . ' (*ibid.*, pp. 108–9).

129 *ibid.*, p. 109

130 *ibid.*, pp. 109–10

131 *ibid.*, p. 111. Possibly this relates to the tradition found in martyrological literature that the martyr feels no pain. Cf. I Baer, 'Gezerot TaTNU' (note 45 above), p. 139, n. 57; for the appearance of this idea in the Spanish kabbalistic tradition, see G. Scholem, 'Perakim mi-Toledot Sifrut ha-Kabbalah', *Kiryat Sefer*, vol. 7 (1930–1), p. 153; Shohet (note 45 above), p. 134. See also D. Tamar, 'Perakim le-Toledot Hakhmei Eretz Yisrael ve-Italia u-le-Toledot Sifrutam', *Kiryat Sefer*, vol. 33 (1958), pp. 376–7.

132 *Shaarei Teshuvah*, loc. cit.

133 *ibid.*, p. 112

134 *ibid.* The concepts 'Wisdom' and 'sight' (*reiyah dehokhmah*) are linked in kabbalistic thought.

135 There is a Habad tradition that this work, printed in Kopyst, is distinguished among R. Dov Ber's writings by virtue of the breadth of its intended audience. We thus find, in the name of R. Shmuel (1834–82), the fourth-generation leader and grandson of R. Dov Ber: 'The books *Shaar ha-Yihud* and *Shaarei Orah* are general, and written for all the Hasidim; for *Shaar ha-Yihud* is the table of contents to the teachings of Hasidism, and *Shaarei Orah* is the Alef-Bet of the teachings of Hasidism.' (Rabbi Joseph I. Schneerson, *Kuntres Limud ha-Hasidut* [New York, 1956], p. 30). This is in distinction to R. Dov Ber's other works, which according to this tradition were compiled for particular 'types' of Hasid; for some the emphasis was intellect, for others it was ethical striving.

136 See S. Dubnow, *History of the Jews*, vol. 5 (New Jersey, 1973), pp. 142–51. In 1817 the 'Society of Israelite-Christians' was set up, to persuade Jews to convert. In 1820 a vast tract of land was set aside in Ekaterinoslav for the hoped-for converts. These did not materialize. Further, the government was alarmed to learn in 1817 of the existence of a large group of Judaizers, called 'Subbotniks', who claimed they wished to return to the teachings of the Old Testament. Legislation against the Jews began in 1819, with the banning of *Krestenzie* lease contracts; this was followed in 1820 by a piece of mediaeval-style legislation in which Jews were forbidden to employ Christian domestics—lest they convert them to their faith (this was clearly a reaction to the 'Subbotnik' phenomenon). The government now resumed the realization of its old intention to expel the Jews from the villages, which had been expressed in the Statute Concerning the Jews of 1804: the operation of this had been halted shortly before the Napoleonic war. A crop failure in 1821 led to renewed urges from the noblemen that the Jews be deported from the villages. In April 1823 a decree was passed banning Jews from holding leases and from dwelling in villages in the regions of Moghilev and

Vitebsk—the Habad area. Long before 1823 news of this impending decree was no doubt conveyed to Jewish leaders by the Jewish deputies, headed by Zundel Zonnenberg, who functioned as 'Delegation of the Jewish People', residing in St Petersburg and maintained by the Jewish communities between 1818 and 1825. Indeed, the deputies were accused of divulging information on impending government plans to the Jewish leaders (*ibid.*, pp. 144–5). When the 1823 edict was passed, there was impassioned reaction by the Jewish community at large. The Hasidic leader R. Yehoshua Heshel of Apt called for three days of public fasting, 'the saying of the whole book of Psalms in all the synagogues', the saying of Psalms with children, and the giving of charity. See I. Halpern, 'R. Yehoshua Heshel me-Apto u-Gezerot ha-Malkhut be-Sof Yamav shel Aleksander ha-Rishon', *Tarbiz*, vol. 27 (1957–8), pp. 372–9, reprinted in his *Eastern European Jewry* (Hebrew) (Jerusalem, 1968), pp. 348–54.

137 In the introduction the distinction is made between 'spiritualized' *mesirat nefesh*, expressed in prayer, and the more concrete *mesirat nefesh* 'which everyone has for *Kiddush ha-Shem* in actual fact, which is only for Torah and *mitzvot*, that when they are forcing him to change his religion . . . he gives himself up actually to be killed. And this is like nature in every one, to give up his life for *Kiddush ha-Shem*, even in the worthless ones . . . as is known that the Jews have withstood trials for three thousand years . . . ' (*Shaarei Orah*, Brooklyn 1956, p. 3).

138 One form of *mesirat nefesh* stems from the essence of the Divine which reveals the Torah; the other from the essence of the Jewish soul which receives it. These are expressed in Purim and Hanukkah respectively and relate to the kabbalistic concepts of 'white radiance' and 'dark radiance' (cf. *Zohar* I, 51b). The author states that it is because of these two kinds of radiance that he is calling the book 'Gates of Radiance' (*Shaarei Orah*, p. 5).

It is in terms of the distinction between the two kinds of *mesirat nefesh* that R. Dov Ber expresses the nature of the Ten Martyrs. Their level of *mesirat nefesh* was higher than that expressed either by Purim or by Hanukkah, for they included in themselves *both* aspects. Their nature is that of 'Princes of Torah', who disseminate Torah to the Jewish people. Because of this they have both the *mesirat nefesh* of the revelation of Torah, as well as that of receiving it. 'And far more than this was the *mesirat nefesh* of the Ten Martyrs who gave up their lives for the Torah itself . . . which is because of the bond of the essence of the souls of the Jews with the Upper Torah. And they were the "Princes of Torah", disseminating Torah to the Jewish people. In this there is involved some of the power of the essence of the Divine. They include both kinds of *mesirat nefesh*' (*ibid.*).

139 An outstanding example is the figure of Rabbi Joseph I. Schneersohn (1880–1950), who in 1927 himself suffered harsh imprisonment by the Communists for his dissemination of Judaism. His writings are filled with exhortations to his followers and other Jews to act with *mesirat nefesh* for the same cause.

On Women in Hasidism, S. A. Horodecky and The Maid of Ludmir Tradition

Ada Rapoport-Albert

'THE Jewish woman was given complete equality in the emotional, mystical, religious life of Beshtian Hasidism.' This statement was made in 1923 by S. A. Horodecky in his book *Ha-Hasidut ve-ha-Hasidim*, where he devoted a short chapter to 'The Jewish Woman in Hasidism'.[1] It was Horodecky who first singled out the position of women in Hasidism as an area of sufficient novelty and interest to merit particular discussion, and his view of the matter, now more than sixty years old, has been remarkably durable. In one form or another, acknowledged or unacknowledged, Horodecky's findings as well as his analysis lie behind virtually every subsequent treatment of the subject in the popular, belletristic and semi-scholarly literature about Hasidism, as well as in the now growing library of works, of limited scholarly merit but considerable apologetic thrust, about the position of women in Judaism generally.[2] Notably, the scholarly literature on the history of Hasidism has generally ignored the subject, implicitly dismissing it as marginal or at any rate insufficiently documented to permit serious consideration.

Horodecky highlighted the equality he perceived between men and women in Hasidism by contrasting it with the exclusion of women from active participation in the intellectual and devotional life of what he called 'official Judaism' or 'rabbinism'.[3] Deploying here the categories from which he was later to construct a framework for the interpretation of Jewish civilization as a whole, the categories of 'intellectual' versus 'emotional' Judaism,[4] he identified 'rabbinism' as 'intellectual' while portraying the distinct mystical–messianic elements of the tradition, from which he believed Hasidism to have evolved, as primarily 'emotional'. Since he shared as a matter of course the common assumption that intellectuality was by nature a male quality while the female temperament was innately emotional,[5] he was able to portray 'rabbinism' as inherently, and so also effectively, the exclusive domain of men, while conceiving of mystical-messianism, and ultimately Hasidism, as inherently, and so historically, more accessible to women:

495

Emotional religion which transcends all rules and regulations, emotional Judaism which knows no limitations or differentiation, accommodated the Jewish woman and allowed her much scope for direct involvement. [In] messianism . . . that popular movement which arose to liberate . . . pure faith and religious emotion from the yoke of innumerable laws and regulations . . . we see the Jewish woman taking part with the full ardour of her emotions. She played an especially important role in the messianic movement of Sabbatai Zevi, which produced women leaders of immense influence. With the rise of Kabbalism, as it gradually descended from its esoteric heights to affect directly the spiritual lives of all the people, it also affected the life of the Jewish woman. The Lurianic Kabbalah in particular had a great impact on the Jews of Poland in the sixteenth and seventeenth centuries, and the Polish-Jewish woman was emotionally receptive to it in full.[6]

Horodecky does not supply any evidence to support these far-reaching claims, and it is difficult to imagine what concrete instances he may have had in mind. In fact the total absence of women from the Jewish mystical tradition as it has come down to us contrasts sharply with the relative prominence of women in the comparable traditions of both Christian and Islamic mysticism.[7] Women did take part in such phenomena as mass prophecy inspired by Sabbatianism in its earlier phases,[8] but they were not central to it and could hardly be conceived as 'leaders of immense influence'. Nor does this description fit any of Sabbatai Zevi's wives, who appear to have played no significant role in the development of the movement.[9] Jacob Frank's daughter Eva does perhaps fit the bill a little better,[10] but it would be absurd for Horodecky to anchor his claims in this grotesque aberration of Jewish mystical messianism. As for the receptivity of women to the Lurianic Kabbalah in particular, or its special impact on their lives, there seems to be no evidence for it whatsoever.

It is only when he comes to his main subject of concern, the position of women in the Hasidic movement, that Horodecky is able to focus his argument more precisely. He identifies three areas in which the equality between men and women in Hasidism is manifest:

1. Hasidism improved the position of women in the community and altogether strengthened Jewish family life by uniting husband and wife through their joint allegiance to the Zaddik, an affiliation which acted as an equalizing force between the sexes.
2. Hasidism threw open the gates of scholarship to women by producing, in addition to works in Hebrew which were accessible only to educated men, a large body of literature for women in the vernacular Yiddish. As a result, the largest obstacle on the way to women's spiritual and intellectual equality with men was removed.

3. Given the right circumstances, Hasidism enabled some women to rise even to the ranks of the Zaddikim, the predominantly male leaders of the movement. 'If the woman was worthy, nothing could stand in her way.'[11]

Every one of these claims may be qualified, countered or quite plainly reversed. They appear to have been inspired by Horodecky's Zionist feminism, combined with his evaluation of Hasidism as anticipating, and so capable of providing, an authentically Jewish model for the rebirth of the Jewish nation on its land, cleansed of all the Diaspora maladies of 'rabbinism'.[12]

Considering his arguments in order, the following observations seem pertinent.

1. Far from improving the condition of women within Hasidic family life, reinforced, as alleged, by the equality of husband and wife before the Zaddik, Hasidism can be seen as effecting precisely the opposite: *Mitnaggedim* and *Maskilim* alike accused Hasidism, with considerable justification, of undermining the institution of Jewish marriage and aggravating the condition of women by drawing young married men—the main recruits to the movement in its formative years[13]—away from their wives and children for periods ranging from several weeks to several months and more. They abandoned the women to fend for themselves materially[14] and, even more crucially, absented themselves at precisely those points in the Jewish calendar—the Sabbath and Festivals, the most popular times of assembly at the 'court' of the Hasidic leader[15]—at which the presence of the husband and father was essential for proper ritual celebration at home.[16] In fact, as an emotionally charged and exclusively male fraternity, grouped around the figure of the Zaddik as father,[17] speaking of 'love' as the mutual relationship between the Zaddik and his followers as well as among the members of the fraternity themselves,[18] celebrating the highest moments of communal activity at a 'table', during a 'meal', on the occasions traditionally set aside for domestic worship and festivity, Hasidism provided an effective alternative to traditional family life. It did not, of course, renounce marriage formally or on a permanent basis, but it allowed its followers some room for periodic liberation from marital and family ties, for the sake of the higher pursuit of spiritual invigoration.[19] In the early generations the Hasidic movement offered young men the opportunity for an emotionally intense affiliation with a new, women-free spiritual family, an affiliation which entailed in some cases a partial or even complete break with the non-Hasidic or anti-Hasidic biological families of the recruits.[20] This separation diminished in time, as the initial affiliation with Hasidism ceased to be a voluntary act by individual males and became more commonly

inherited, encompassing whole families which were now associated with one Hasidic group or another by established family tradition.

Whether or not at this stage the position of Hasidic women was significantly different from that of their non-Hasidic counterparts is extremely difficult to assess. The general impression, however, is that the women continued, on the whole, to be excluded from the life of the Hasidic 'court'. They did not usually accompany their husbands on their visits to the *rebbe*, although they could, at least in some 'courts', gain direct access to him in their own right, to be advised and blessed by him as were the male followers; but they did not attend the all-important sessions at his 'table', where he delivered his teachings to the exclusively male following.[21] It is difficult to estimate to what extent this degree of access, and its impact on the women's sense of active personal involvement with Hasidism, differed from the access a non-Hasidic woman would have had to a local rabbinic authority, and her sense of involvement and identification with the values of what Horodecky calls 'rabbinism'.

2. Hasidism did produce a considerable body of literature in Yiddish, but this was by no means created especially for women, nor did it represent an attempt to make universally accessible in Yiddish all that had been previously restricted to the Hebrew-reading male élite.

The translation of Hasidic works from Hebrew into Yiddish[22] began relatively late, with the publication of the Yiddish version of *Shivkhey ha-Besht* in 1815.[23] This appeared in several editions and versions a few months after the first Hebrew edition of the book was published. Significantly, *Shivkhey ha-Besht*, as well as being the first Hasidic work to become available in Yiddish, was also the first Hasidic work which may be classified as belonging to the hagiographical genre, a genre which was never invested with the full legitimacy of the earlier, speculative–homiletical literature of Hasidism.[24] Moreover, subsequent to this initial publication in both Hebrew and Yiddish, the development of Hasidic hagiography was arrested—possibly because of its uncertain status—for at least another fifty years, to be renewed and to achieve popularity, if not full sanction, only in the second half of the nineteenth century.[25] The hagiographical collections which proliferated from this point on, whether they were written in Hebrew or in Yiddish or both, were not directed primarily at women, although women may well have formed a significant proportion of their readership.

The point is that Hasidism did not possess, at least not until relatively recently and for extraneous reasons, any ideology of women's education as such.[26] What it did possess was an internally controversial but nevertheless pervasive ideology of the dissemination of the teachings of Hasidism as widely as possible, at such different levels of communication and varying degrees of exposure to its more radical esoteric aspects as were considered appropriate for different classes of recruits into the movement.[27] However much it was promoted from the start as a meritorious activity of the highest degree of holiness,[28] the telling, the hearing and ultimately the reading of tales in praise of the saintly leaders of Hasidism in Hebrew, and even more so in Yiddish, served as the lowest point of access into the Hasidic orbit.[29] The tales captured the imagination even of ordinary, uneducated Jews, a class within which women had traditionally formed a sub-category.[30] It was only in this incidental capacity that women became a target audience for the hagiographical literature of Hasidism. While it is doubtful (although it cannot be ruled out) that they constituted a significant element of the reading public of the *Shivkhey ha-Besht* when it was first published at the beginning of the nineteenth century, by the 1860s and 1870s, when the second wave of Hasidic hagiography was beginning to flood the book market, it is much more likely that they did. By this time, as we have seen, the Hasidic movement had become an affiliation into which one was born, within which one married and which one passed on to one's offspring both male and female. Whole families, including the women, became identified by their inherited association with particular Hasidic groups. Although the women were no more directly involved in the devotional life of their community than they had been in the early days of the movement,[31] their Hasidic identity was firmly established and would have fed on the hagiographical literature that was available to them.

However, alongside this popular literature in the vernacular, Hasidism continued to produce also, and ascribed the highest value to, a speculative mystical and ethical literature of its own, which was published conservatively in Hebrew only, following the publication tradition of comparable works of this genre long before and outside Hasidism. These works consisted largely of transcripts and recensions of the sermons and discourses delivered orally, to an exclusively male audience, by the exclusively male leaders of the movement. Once in print—always in Hebrew—they remained virtually inaccessible to the women. Moreover, it was with this genre, and in Hebrew, rather than with the hagiographical genre and in Yiddish, that Hasidism had first launched itself in print in the 1780s and 1790s. In the three and a half decades between 1780 and 1815, from the publication of the first homiletical Hasidic book in Hebrew to that of the first hagiographical work in Yiddish, at least thirty Hasidic books of the former type were published in Hebrew, and they formed an important element of the campaign for the wider dissemination of Hasidism during the crucial stage of its expansion beyond the regions of its provenance.[32] It was during this period also that the internal Hasidic controversy began about the degree to which it was appropriate to publicize the traditionally esoteric, Kabbalistic aspects of Hasidism in print.[33] Significantly, though not surprisingly, throughout this debate, no mention was ever made of women as a distinct class to be initiated into, or, conversely, to be excluded from, any particular level of instruction. Women might be implicitly classified together with 'the ignorant', but they were not explicitly addressed in the literature of Hasidism.[34]

3. Horodecky's final and most dramatic claim is that under the conditions of equality between men and women in Hasidism, certain women could attain even the position of Zaddik, performing the same functions and exerting the same authority as their male colleagues. He begins his account of this by describing a number of mothers, sisters and daughters (though, interestingly, not wives) of the most famous leaders of Hasidism[35] as 'endowed with divine inspiration', 'famous in the world of Hasidism for . . . knowledge of rabbinic legends and tales of the lives of the Zaddikim', 'influential', 'charitable' or 'sought after by many of the Hasidim . . . for a blessing'. Horodecky does not supply any sources for these epithets. Some of them can be traced back to well-known and early Hasidic works[36] while others must be based on later oral traditions whose authenticity is difficult to establish. Nevertheless, the fact that these women enjoyed considerable prestige and reputation in Hasidic circles need not be questioned, however late or fragmentary the traditions which portray them in this light. After all, traditional Judaism, going as far back as the classical rabbinic sources, had always acknowledged the possibility that some of the glamour and authority generated by its most distinguished leaders in the realms of piety, humility, and even scholarly and halakhic acumen, would reflect on the women most intimately associated with them, who were indeed well placed to acquire many such accomplishments through their proximity to these eminent men.[37] It is not surprising, therefore, that Hasidism, a movement which almost uniquely in the history of Judaism, had placed at the very centre of its theology and social organization the charismatic personality of the leader, should exploit this tradition to the full, and allow the aura of perfect scholarly, moral and spiritual attributes, combined with supernatural powers surrounding the figure of the Zaddik, to percolate to some of his female relations.

Horodecky's account of these women is confined to reports of their personal virtues and informal influence in the Hasidic world, which was facilitated by their proximity to the distinguished males to whom they were related. He interprets these reports, however, as suggesting that the women in question were considered to be fully-fledged 'female Zaddikim', and even cites one tradition whereby the brothers of

Hannah Hayah of Chernobyl, all Zaddikim in their own right and heirs to their famous father R. Mordecai of Chernobyl, had said 'that she was a Zaddik just like them',[38] but he supplies no details to illustrate any formal, institutional aspects of her leadership or the leadership of any of the women he mentions in this connection. Such information is provided in abundance by subsequent authors in Yiddish, Hebrew and more recently also in English. All are inspired by Horodecky, but are more systematically, and perhaps more apologetically, concerned to produce a full record of the role of women in the history of Judaism, where Hasidism invariably features as an exceptionally dignified chapter. Here we find descriptions of various daughters, mothers and sisters (again, rarely wives) of the famous Zaddikim, including all those originally mentioned by Horodecky but also others,[39] operating as leaders of Hasidic communities in their own right—regularly receiving *kvitlekh* and *pidyonot*, delivering Hasidic and ethical teachings to a mixed male and female following (although the mechanics of this are not always clear) at their formal, public 'tables', distributing *shirayyim*, performing miracles, consulted as equals by their male colleagues and often adopting rigorous standards of personal piety, displayed by the unusual practices for women of wearing *tsitsit*, as well as *talit* and *gartel* during prayer, and fasting on Mondays and Thursdays.[40] In some cases they are said to have engaged also in learned literary work, and to have produced original Hasidic writings.[41]

Most of this is reported without references to written documentation, and it appears in popular histories, belletristic works, personal memoirs and newspaper articles published since the 1930s, but mostly after the Second World War and increasingly (although without any substantial additions to the information contained in the initial reports) in the past two decades or so, since the challenge of modern feminism has made women leaders in historical Judaism something more than a mere curiosity. Some of the female Zaddikim described in this literature are located in the distant past of the beginnings of Hasidism in the eighteenth century, but most are nineteenth-century figures and one or two appear to have lived to a very old age, well into the twentieth century, within the lifetimes and living memories of their popular biographers.[42] The lack of earlier, internal Hasidic evidence for the institutional leadership of these women, coupled with the abrupt disruption, with the Second World War, of the Eastern European Hasidic world in which they are said to have operated, has made it virtually impossible to authenticate these late traditions. Nevertheless, as is generally the case with literary adaptations of oral traditions, allowing for a certain measure of exaggeration and romantic idealization, one must assume that they contain an element of truth. The important historical question, however, is not so much whether or not these prominent women existed, which is probable, but rather whether or not the phenomenon of independent female leaders was integrated into the ideology and organization of Hasidism and considered to be fully legitimate.

The answer to this question is unequivocally negative. Hasidism did not evolve an ideology of female leadership, any more than it improved the position of women within the family or set out to educate them in Yiddish.

Significantly, it was not the legitimate, internal literature of Hasidism, not even the popular hagiographical works of the nineteenth and early twentieth centuries, that promoted these female Zaddikim as authentic leaders. To the best of my knowledge, we do not possess a single volume of the 'praises' of any one of these women,[43] nor any collection of their teachings in Hasidism, Kabbalah or ethics. If such writings exist, they have not been published and remain totally inaccessible. All the reports celebrating the activities of female Zaddikim in Hasidism have emanated from the periphery of the Hasidic world. They have been assembled by writers and scholars who at best, like Horodecky, were born into the heart of a Hasidic environment before the two World Wars, and would have had good access to its living traditions, but who stepped out of this environment in later life, and became exposed to a variety of modern ideologies through whose perspectives they now evaluated the experiences of their youth.[44] While the factual core of the traditions which they report need not be questioned and may be essentially correct, if not in all its details, the interpretation which they impose on it cannot be taken at face value.

No example can better illustrate this point than the case of Hannah Rachel, 'the Maid of Ludmir'. Her story, in brief, is as follows: The only daughter of Monesh Verbermacher, a well-to-do and educated Jew, she was apparently born in or around 1815, in the Volhynian town of (Vladimir) Ludmir. From an early age she attracted attention by her beauty and unusual mental abilities: she studied the Bible in the original and learned to write Hebrew, progressing to the study of talmudic Aggadah, Midrash and halakhic works. She distinguished herself also by her extraordinary piety, praying with ecstasy three times a day, like a man. As soon as she came of age she was betrothed to a young man from her native city whom she had known and loved since childhood. However, once the engagement was announced, she was forced by custom to stop all contact with her groom until the wedding. This distressed the Maid and she gradually withdrew from society. During this period her mother died, and she began to isolate herself completely.

She would spend whole days alone in her room, going out only to visit her mother's grave. On one of these visits in the cemetery she fell into unconsciousness, followed by a prolonged and mysterious illness from which she eventually recovered, endowed, as she said, 'with a new and elevated soul'. She broke off her engagement and declared that she would not marry because she had 'transcended the world of the flesh'. From that time on she adopted the full rigour of male ritual observance, and absorbed herself in study and prayer. When her father died, she used her considerable inheritance to build a new *Beyt Midrash* in Ludmir, where she lived in complete seclusion. She soon acquired a reputation for saintliness and miracle-working and became known as 'the holy Maid of Ludmir'. Men and women from the neighbouring localities, among them scholars and rabbis, began to flock to what became her 'court'. She would not allow anyone into her room, but would address her teachings and blessings from behind the closed door to the many followers gathered in the adjacent room every Saturday, at the third Sabbath meal. While her popular following grew, the response of the famous male Zaddikim of the region was negative. Some said that an 'evil' or 'unclean' spirit was speaking through her. Pressure was put on the Maid to abandon the practice of Zaddikism and resume her rightful female role in marriage. R. Mordecai of Chernobyl, the most eminent Zaddik brought into the case, is reported as saying: 'We do not know which famous Zaddik's soul has transmigrated into this woman, but it is hard for the soul of a Zaddik to find peace in the body of a woman.'[45] Through his intervention she finally agreed to marry,[46] but the marriage was never consummated and soon ended in divorce. She married again, but divorced once more, remaining a 'maid' to the end of her life. Her marriages, however unsuccessful, did have the desired effect of putting an end to her career as a Zaddik, and her following declined sharply. She spent her last years in the Holy Land where she died in obscurity in old age.

This biographical sketch is based on what appears to be the earliest written report of the Maid of Ludmir—a short article in Russian published by S. A. Horodecky in 1909.[47] All subsequent accounts, including Horodecky's own adaptation of the material in his Hebrew book of 1923,[48] are derived from this original version.[49] Horodecky informs his readers in a note[50] that his account is based on 'the reports of old women from Volhynia who remembered the Maid of Ludmir personally'. This suggests that no written accounts of the Maid were available to him. M. Klaczko, responding to Horodecky's article in a note published two years later,[51] adds a further detail to the story: apparently the Maid not only received supplicants in her house but also travelled to the neighbouring towns and villages where she preached in the synagogues. In addition, 'it is quite certain that she once travelled to Staro-Konstantinow [Constantin *Yashan*] (quite far from Vladimir-Ludmir) where the local women gathered and she delivered a religious sermon to them. Old women in Staro-Konstantinow still talk about this visit.' This report confirms the nature of the evidence: the author, like Horodecky, is drawing on what he had heard from old women who claimed to have witnessed the events themselves. Interestingly, this report of the Maid conflicts with her reclusive image as it emerges from Horodecky's tradition, as well as suggesting, in contrast to Horodecky, that her leadership was directed primarily toward a female, not a male, following. Another detail is supplied by a later source in Horodecky's name, although it is not present in Horodecky's own accounts of the Maid's life: during her final years in the Holy Land, she was apparently involved, together with an old Kabbalist, in a private and abortive attempt to bring about the Advent of the Messiah.[52]

Some of the subsequent versions of the story are richer in detail but clearly further removed from the oral sources, or else quite plainly construed as works of fiction—fanciful adaptations of the material contained in these first reports.[53] Common to all is the evaluation of the story as the most conclusive evidence for the 'equal opportunities' aspect of Hasidism, which opened up to women the fullest scope for publicly acknowledged intellectual and spiritual leadership. The fact that the Maid of Ludmir was not related by family ties to any of the male Zaddikim of her time, observed by Horodecky and taken up by others, is used to highlight the revolutionary novelty of the phenomenon, since the reports relating to her practice of Zaddikism cannot easily be dismissed as belonging to the more traditional category of the associative authority which could always be derived by some women from their distinguished male relatives.[54]

While Horodecky's account of the Maid in his 1923 Hebrew book contains no additional information to that which was available to him in 1909, his interpretation of the material had altered somewhat in the intervening years. The tone of the earlier version is restrained and cautious:

> In Hasidism a modest, passive role is attached to a woman. From time to time she may approach a Zaddik, pour out her soul before him and receive counsel and a blessing from him. Very rarely in the history of Hasidism do we encounter active female characters who have influence on their surroundings. Among these holy women who came close to the level of Zaddik is the enigmatic personality . . . immortalized in popular tradition under the name of 'the Maid of Ludmir'.[55]

By 1923, Horodecky had come to regard the same material as

representing a radical change in the position of women, to which he referred as 'complete equality' with men in every aspect of the Hasidic way of life.[56] Those few 'active female characters' who in 1909 had been portrayed cautiously as 'coming close to the level of Zaddik', were being celebrated by 1923 as 'veritable Zaddikim', of whom the most remarkable and clear-cut example was the Maid of Ludmir—'one woman from amongst the masses [that is, rather than from the household of an established Hasidic leader] who had merited and risen to the rank of a famous "Zaddik"'.[57] This shift in Horodecky's perception may be accounted for in part by the fact that at the time when he was writing the later, Hebrew version of the story, he had been living in Western Europe for some fifteen years, having left his native Ukraine in 1907 under the impact of the pogroms in the earlier years of the decade. By contrast, the first, Russian version in *Evreiskaia Starina* had been written while he was still freshly steeped in the atmosphere of the traditions which he set out to record.[58] One must take into account also Horodecky's exposure to Western society and culture during those years of university education and intellectual work in Zurich, Berne and particularly Berlin, where German feminism, including Jewish feminism under the leadership of Bertha Pappenheim, was well in evidence.[59] All this, together with his growing involvement in the Zionist movement, during the period when the Second and Third *aliyot* were experimenting with the foundations of a revolutionary society in the Holy Land, where the women were to play, in theory if not always in practice, an equal part alongside the men,[60] may have combined to heighten Horodecky's sensitivity to the issue of the equality of women. He now thought it to have been anticipated in an indigenously Jewish form by the emergence of women leaders in Hasidism.[61]

There is little doubt, however, that the tradition that reached Horodecky is, in itself, untinted by his later, extraneously inspired outlook, authentic enough. His general credibility in this area is good: the Maid is said by some to have died in 1892 or 1895,[62] a date which fits reasonably well with Horodecky's own tradition of her birth in 1815. She was thought to have been still alive, therefore, when Horodecky himself was born in 1871. Moreover, the decisive intervention of R. Mordecai of Chernobyl in the course of events relating to the Maid (and he is the only Zaddik who is mentioned by name in this connection) puts the story within the orbit of the Chernobyl dynasty, from which Horodecky was descended and with whose traditions he was intimately acquainted.[63] It is rather his interpretation of the tradition that needs to be examined critically.

Horodecky presents the Hasidic career of the Maid of Ludmir as a success story. It is his strongest evidence for the presence of egalitarian elements in Hasidism, which he perceives as liberating women from their traditional disabilities under 'rabbinism'. In fact, the story reads much more convincingly as the record of a failure. Certainly it echoes a certain aspiration or yearning, which may well have been profound and could have found expression in reality for a while, at a grassroots level, in a Christian environment which was not, after all, unfamiliar with 'holy maidens' and female saints. Nevertheless, it constitutes the perfect exception which confirms the rule whereby no woman could legitimately claim the full powers of spiritual leadership in Hasidism, any more than she could establish the legitimacy of such a claim at any previous stage in the development of Jewish mysticism.

The story of the Maid is the story of a deviant, whose ultimate failure serves precisely to reinforce the boundaries which she attempts to cross, not to undermine them. It may suggest that deviance was 'in the air', and that a society which produces such a story senses that those boundaries are frail and in need of reinforcement; but it certainly does not reflect the programmatic eradication of boundaries which is implied in Horodecky's interpretation and that of all those who follow him.

The first of these boundaries is confronted by the Maid while she is still acting out her role as a woman. She is engaged to a man she knows and loves, but she cannot accept the traditional constraint of the total separation between the bride and groom before marriage.[64] The vulnerability of this particular boundary in the region and during the period in which the story arises is well attested. By the second half of the nineteenth century, Eastern European *Maskilim* were voicing their criticism of traditional marriage customs, while observing also the growing reluctance of young girls to comply with the parental discipline of totally unromantic, conventionally arranged marriages.[65] This criticism must have resounded within the traditional world under attack. The incidence of young girls who left home rather than enter such a marriage, to gain a secular education and join radical political circles in the final decades of the Tsarist regime in Russia was small, but not unheard of.[66] The story of the Maid may present an implicit warning against this danger, by making her rejection of pre-marital convention trigger off further and more serious deviation.

The Maid responds to the constraints of the traditional norm in male–female relations by altogether denying her female role. Her sexual identity had been unstable from the start; her desire and aptitude for learning, as well as her ardour in prayer, were more fitting for a boy than for a girl. These childhood aberrations, however, could be tolerated and would more than likely have been curtailed by normal marital responsibilities. But the Maid does not outgrow them; instead she crosses the sexual boundary in a spectacular way by embracing celibacy and claiming that, equipped with 'a new and elevated soul', she has 'transcended the world of the flesh'.[67]

Renunciation, and in particular the celibate life, was the path which led a large number of Christian and, to a certain extent, also some Muslim women to the publicly acknowledged and fully legitimate realization of their spiritual aspirations. Celibate asceticism, which strove to enhance spiritual existence by means of diminishing or transcending physicality, provided the means also of transcending physical, and especially sexual differentiation. It thus secured a place for women, stripped of their worldly sexuality, alongside the men in the ranks of the saints and mystics of both Christianity and Islam. It is to be noted that virtually all the great female mystics of the Christian tradition were virgins. And even when, in the late Middle Ages, the ideal of virginity was spiritualized to some extent, so that married women and widows could be counted among the saints, this was only achieved through their ultimate renunciation of all worldly ties, and the strict observance of celibacy, from which moment alone they saw themselves and were recognized as being free to join the mystical path.[68] Similarly, the Sufi tradition, despite the early and explicit denunciation of celibacy in orthodox Islam,[69] displayed ascetic tendencies from its earliest beginnings, and included among its most celebrated saints a number of women who had embraced the celibate life to transcend the limitations of their sex.[70] By contrast, rabbinic tradition unequivocally denied any access to this path to women. Its attitude to asceticism in general had always been ambivalent, but in certain circumstances, especially within spiritually or mystically orientated élitist circles, the practices of ritual and penitential asceticism, which could include prolonged periods of sexual abstinence, were accorded full legitimacy and even sanctity for men, albeit within the conflicting constraints of the world-affirming halakhah.[71] In women, on the other hand, such conduct was considered as inherently false, hypocritical or self-deluding.[72]

The Maid's adoption of the ascetic, celibate life was a declaration of her spiritual-mystical and, probably, also her scholarly orientation, an orientation which had often been marked by the strict ascetic piety of the men who chose it.[73] This was particularly so since the emergence of the Lurianic Kabbalah, whose strong ascetic inclination was popularized through a cluster of ethical works promoting ascetic ideals.[74] These exerted a powerful, if problematic, influence on the Hasidic ideals of mystical piety to which the Maid was trying to conform.[75] Had this tradition bestowed any legitimacy on the ascetic piety of women, the Maid might have found an outlet for it even within marriage, as did the men who managed to achieve it without altogether renouncing their halakhically prescribed obligations towards worldly existence. But in the lack of any legitimacy for this type of piety in women, and since no model was available in Judaism for an asexual spirituality oblivious of sexual boundaries,[76] the Maid was forced to renounce her identity as a woman, only to embrace a false identity as a man, emulating the standard discipline of ritual observance, and so also the rigour of ascetic piety traditionally confined to males. As a 'false male' she could only be regarded an aberration of nature and a social deviation. In traditional terms she was understood as having acquired the soul of a man, albeit a Zaddik (but probably a 'fallen' Zaddik who had committed a serious transgression, most likely a sexual one, and who was being punished by transmigrating into her female body).[77] It is not surprising that the device to which R. Mordecai of Chernobyl is said to have resorted in attempting to rectify the situation was to force the Maid back into her female role by contracting a marriage. This was perfectly effective: from the moment that she resumed her natural role and social function, however reluctantly or inadequately, her claim to special spiritual powers was invalidated and her Hasidic following abandoned her.[78] Her chastity, which survived two unconsummated marriages, was no longer 'holy' and became her private affair. Her final dispatch to the Holy Land, whether factual or not, amounted to her relegation to a safely remote corner of the nineteenth-century Hasidic world—the method by which the movement is known to have disposed of some of its other embarrassments.[79]

This analysis of the story of the Maid exposes as false the claim for which it has so often been cited as proof, that the Hasidic movement pioneered the equality of men and women in Judaism. Far from promoting such a novel ideal, Hasidism embraced unquestioningly all the conceptions of women produced by classical rabbinic Judaism, as well as the Kabbalistic association of women with the demonic,[80] and the concomitant representation by women of negative, material sexuality. This ought to be avoided by all men at all costs, or, at best, to be stripped of its corporeal exterior and 'raised' to the spiritual origin of all things by a small minority of spiritual giants from among the founding fathers of Hasidism.[81]

It is noteworthy that the relatively recent interest in the position of women in Hasidism, displayed by the Habad movement since the leadership of its previous *Rebbe*, the Admor Joseph Isaac Schneersohn, should have taken the form of a heightened concern for the education of women in halakhic matters relating primarily to their roles as women, and appealing to them as guardians of the Jewish identity of the younger generation.[82] The Admor's direct appeal to women was inspired by the threat of modern secularism and assimilation, first in inter-war Russia and Poland and eventually in the USA. With considerable insight, he identified in women a resource which had hardly been tapped before. He enlisted their energies in a campaign, not for the dissemination of Hasidic doctrine specifically but for the very preservation of traditional, halakhic Judaism as such. This direction, which has opened up much scope for positive action and full participation by women, is authentic and legitimate by traditional yardsticks—however we value them—inasmuch as it is based on stressing, rather than obliterating the difference between men and women in Judaism.[83]

Notes

The present paper arises from work carried out during 1984–5 at Harvard Divinity School, where I spent a most stimulating and enjoyable year as Visiting Lecturer and Research Associate to the Women in Religion programme. I would like to use this opportunity to thank all my friends and colleagues there and at the Center for the Study of World Religions, not only for their generous hospitality but above all for wearing down my initial resistance to thinking in sexual categories, and pointing me in the direction of a new field of investigation which has proved most rewarding.

I would like to thank also Rabbi Ben-Zion Gold of Harvard Hillel who kindly brought to my attention relevant Yiddish materials, and a number of colleagues and friends who offered valuable suggestions and comments: Professors Chimen Abramsky, Raphael Loewe and Eli Yassif, Rabbi Dr Louis Jacobs and Drs Ella Almagor, Zeev Gries, Naftali Lowenthal and Steve Zipperstein. Help offered by others on specific points is acknowledged in the notes. The responsibility for such mistakes and misconceptions as still remain is, of course, entirely mine.

1 S. A. Horodecky, *Ha-Hasidut ve-ha-Hasidim* (2nd edn, Tel Aviv, 1943), vol. 4, p. 68; cf. the abridged one-volume edition in English, *Leaders of Hasidism* (London, 1928), the chapter entitled 'The Maid of Ludmir', p. 113.

2 See for example, D. L. Mekler, *Fun Rebbins hoyf (fun Chernobyl biz Talne)* (New York, 1931), vol. 1, pp. 209–45; J. S. Minkin, *The Romance of Hassidism* (1st edn 1935) (3rd edn, Los Angeles, 1971), pp. 345–7; M. Feinkind, *Froyen Rabbonim un barimte perzenlekhkeiten in Poylen* (Warsaw, 1937), pp. 21–69; M. Biber, 'Ha-Almah mi-Ludmir', in *Reshumot* (Tel Aviv, 1946), pp. 69–76; Y. Twersky, *Ha-Betulah mi-Ludmir* (Jerusalem [1950]); S. Ashkenazi, *Ha-Ishah be-Aspaklaryat ha-Yahadut* (Tel Aviv, 1953), vol. 1, pp. 55–60; M. S. Geshuri, *Ha-Niggun ve-ha-Rikkud ba-Hasidut*, vol. 3 (Tel Aviv, 1959), pp. 366–70; E. Taubenhaus, *Bi-Netiv ha-Yakhid* (Haifa, 1959), pp. 37–41 (I am grateful to Mr Ezra Kahn, the Librarian of Jews' College London, for drawing my attention to this work); H. Rabinowicz, *A Guide to Hassidism* (New York and London, 1960), pp. 102–13; N. Shemen, *Batsiung tsu der froy* (Buenos Aires, 1969), vol. 2, pp. 328–38; H. Rabinowicz, *The World of Hassidism* (London, 1970), pp. 202–10; Y. Alfasi, *Ha-Hasidut* (Tel Aviv, 1974), p. 242; S. Henry and E. Taitz, *Written Out of History* (Fresh Meadows, New York, 1983), pp. 175–83; M. M. Brayer, *The Jewish Woman in Rabbinic Literature*, vol. 2, *A Psychohistorical Perspective* (Hoboken, New Jersey 1986), pp. 37–48. The above list is more representative than exhaustive.

3 Horodecky (note 1 above), pp. 67–8.

4 See his *Yahadut ha-Sekhel ve-Yahadut ha-Regesh* ('The Judaism of Intellect and the Judaism of Emotion'), 2 vols. (Tel Aviv, 1947).

5 For the presumed universality of this perception, and a feminist critique of it, see M. Zimbalist Rosaldo, 'Woman, Culture, and Society: a Theoretical Overview', in M. Zimbalist Rosaldo and L. Lamphere (eds.), *Woman, Culture, and Society* (Stanford, 1974), pp. 29–30; N. Chodorow, 'Family Structure and Feminine Personality', op. cit., pp. 43–66; A. Oakley, *Sex, Gender and Society* (1st edn 1972) (rev. edn, Aldershot, 1985), ch. 2, 'Sex and personality', pp. 49–78, and ch. 3, 'Sex and intellect', pp. 79–98. See also J. N. Burstyn, *Victorian Education and the Ideal of Womanhood* (New Brunswick, New Jersey, 1984), pp. 37, 86–7, and ch. 4, 'Woman's Intellectual Capacity', pp. 70–83.

6 Horodecky (note 1 above), pp. 67–8.

7 See G. G. Scholem, *Major Trends in Jewish Mysticism* (New York, 1961), pp. 37–8.

8 See G. G. Scholem, *Sabbatai Sevi* (Princeton, 1973), pp. 254, 418–23.

9 *ibid.*, pp. 124, 191–7, 799, 850–1, 885, 887–9.

10 See G. G. Scholem, *Kabbalah* (Jerusalem, 1974), pp. 302–8.

11 Horodecky (note 1 above), p. 69.

12 See *ibid.*, the chapter entitled 'Ha-Hasidut kemo she-Hi' ('Hasidism as it is'), sect. 4, pp. 128–9: 'Let us admit the truth: official, legalistic Judaism is obsolete . . . This type of Judaism never agreed with the true spirit of the nation. Only through external factors—the Exile and all its ramifications—was it able to dominate the Jewish world . . . The question arises: how can this Judaism be reformed on the basis of the true foundations of Judaism [This is an implicit rejection of the Reform movement which Horodecky considered to be based on extraneous foundations.] . . . This question is particularly pertinent now, when there is hope that in time, many Jews will settle in Eretz Israel and lead a normal, independent life . . . What should be done there, in Eretz Israel, to this Diaspora Judaism? . . . The time has come for the 'other' Judaism—the Judaism of emotion, of mysticism, of ecstasy . . . This type of Judaism does not need to be created; it does not need to be discovered in books and manuscripts. It is alive and well now, among thousands of Jews; it is Hasidism . . . The immense spiritual force which is contained in Hasidism will reveal itself in full once the movement has stripped off its Diaspora guise . . . in Eretz Israel . . . Through Hasidism . . . it should be possible to renew . . . the type of communal life which existed first among the Essenes and last among the Hasidim. *Through Hasidism it should be possible to put right the great wrong which legalistic Judaism had committed against the Jewish woman . . . whom Hasidism has granted equal religious rights for the first time in Judaism*' [my emphasis]. Horodecky's view of Hasidism as capable of reforming Judaism from within, in preparation for the realization of the Zionist vision, is not dissimilar to Buber's. See for example, M. Buber, *Be-Phardes ha-Hasidut* (Tel Aviv, 1945), p. 132; cf. G. G. Scholem, 'Martin Buber's Interpretation of Hasidism', in *The Messianic Idea in Judaism* (London, 1971), p. 229. Cf. above, p. 505.

13 See S. Dubnow, *Toledot ha-Hasidut* (Tel Aviv, 1960), pp. 365, 369; J. Katz, *Masoret u-Mashber* (Jerusalem, 1963), p. 282, n. 18 (the English version of this work, *Tradition and Crisis*, New York, 1971, p. 243, excludes the relevant note). For an interesting observation that young men in similar circumstances constituted the majority of recruits not only to Hasidism but also to the Haskalah and Musar movements, and for similar reasons, see D. Biale, 'Eros and Enlightenment: Love Against Marriage in the East European Jewish Enlightenment', in *Polin*, vol. 1 (1986), pp. 49–67, especially pp. 50–3, 57. Cf. below, note 15.

14 This in itself was not quite as serious as it may sound, since the women in any case often carried this burden alone or within their parental households, enabling their husbands to devote as much time as possible to their studies. The custom is amply documented, but see for example, J. Katz, 'Nisu'in ve-Khayey Ishut be-Motsa'ey Yemey ha-Beynayyim', *Zion*, vol. 10 (1944), pp. 33, 43. Eastern European *Maskilim*

were particularly critical of this aspect of traditional life, and they advocated the retreat of women from the market-place to the home, after the model of the nineteenth-century ideal bourgeois marriage. See for example, A. B. Gottlober, *Zikhronot u-Masa'ot* (Jerusalem, 1976), vol. 1, p. 86; cf. Biale (note 13 above), p. 60.

15 See Dubnow (note 13 above), pp. 353, 361–5. R. Nahman of Braslav restricted the weekly Saturday visits to his 'court', allowing only a small number of close disciples to come each week. However, he made obligatory on all his followers the three annual pilgrimages to Braslav on Rosh ha-Shanah, Shabbat Hanukkah and Shavuot, of which the first was the most important. In addition he used to visit, on three Saturdays a year, the three communities in which the largest numbers of his followers were concentrated, and all would travel to see him there. See *Hayey Moharan* Pt 1, 'Mekom Yeshivato u-Nesi'otav', sect. 24. R. Shneur Zalman of Lyadi permitted all his followers to come to his 'court' four times a year, for Simkhat Torah, Shabbat Hanukkah, Purim and Shabbat 'Shuvah'. The Saturdays preceding each new moon were also established as times of assembly, but R. Shneur Zalman continuously restricted attendance on these occasions to particular types of recruits, to cope with the growing numbers of his followers, and he prohibited all visits on some of these Saturdays. See *Takkanot Liozna* and the letters relating to them, in D. Z. Hillmann, *Iggerot Baal ha-Tanya u-Bheney Doro* (Jerusalem, 1953), pp. 58–69. Cf. I. Etkes, 'Darko shel R. Shneur Zalman mi-Lyadi ke-Manhig shel Hasidim', *Zion*, vol. 50 (1985), pp. 334–8.

16 For these complaints, see '*Herem Vilna*' (the ban issued against the Hasidim in Vilna in 1781) in M. Wilensky, *Hasidim u-Mitnaggedim* (Jerusalem, 1970), vol. 1, p. 103; vol. 2, p. 151 (this is R. David of Makov's version of the ban); David of Makov, *Shever Poshe'im*, *ibid.*, pp. 107, 159–60, 173; Israel Loebel, *Sefer Vikku'akh*, *ibid.*, p. 315; Solomon Maimon, *The Autobiography of Solomon Maimon* (London, 1954), p. 168; Joseph Perl, *Uiber das Wesen der Secte Chassidim*, ed. A. Rubinstein (Jerusalem, 1977), p. 125. There is probable confirmation for this from within the Hasidic literature. In a *sikhah* of R. Nahman of Braslav, recorded by R. Nathan Sternharz, R. Nahman laments this situation and ascribes it to the activities of Satan: 'I was told this by a certain man who was talking to him (to R. Nahman), of blessed memory, about the situation of [our] young men. It is very common for the relations between them and their wives to deteriorate. They separate for a while, and sometimes this results in the complete breakup of the marriage, Heaven forbid. He said that this was due to the activities of Satan who is particularly concerned to spoil the domestic harmony of [our] young men, so that they would fall into his trap by means of this [namely, that through their separation from their wives and the concomitant cessation of their properly conducted conjugal relations, which results in sexual frustration and increased appetite, they would be driven to erotic fantasies and possibly illicit sex. A. R-A]. Satan lies in wait for them, to catch them in their youth, by means of spoiling their domestic harmony, Heaven forbid, which he brings about by his cunning . . . And he spoke of this matter at length' (*Sikhot Haran* [with *Shivkhey Haran*], Lemberg, 1901, sect. 261, p. 77a). Interestingly, this is followed by an injunction 'to prize and honour one's wife . . . for the women suffer greatly . . .' (*ibid.*, sect. 262). While reflecting a rare concern for the condition of the women, this nevertheless confirms its gravity.

17 See for example, Elimelech of Lyzhansk, *No'am Elimelech*, ed. G. Nigal (Jerusalem, 1978), vol. 2, p. 469; Jacob Isaac, the Seer of Lublin, *Zot Zikkaron* (in *Sefarim ha-Kedoshim mi-Kol Talmidey ha-Besht ha-Kadosh*, vol. 2, Brooklyn, 1981), p. 66 (on the verse 'Even by the God of thy father', Genesis 49:25); *Divrey Emet* (*ibid.*), p. 25 (on the same verse); cf. the description of a Hasidic gathering in E. Z. Hacohen Zweifel, *Shalom al Yisrael*, Pt 3, 'Hashkafah le-Tovah', ed. A. Rubinstein (Jerusalem, 1972),

vol. 2, p. 31. Zweifel claims in the same passage that 'the Hasidim love and honour their wives, and they spend more money to adorn and beautify them than do the Mitnaggedim.' But this is in tune with the generally apologetic tone of the book, and is not reliable. A little further on (p. 32) Zweifel confirms, however, that the prolonged stay at the 'court' of the Zaddik offered the Hasid temporary relief from his domestic troubles in liberating him from his obligations to his wife and children. It should be pointed out that alongside the analogy between the father and the Zaddik as head of an alternative 'family', Hasidic sources also compare the Zaddik to a son in quite a different relation to God as father. See for example the index entry for father-son parables (*mishley av*) in *Maggid Devarav le-Ya'akov*, ed. R. Schatz-Uffenheimer (Jerusalem, 1976), p. 372.

18 See J. G. Weiss, 'Abraham Kalisker's Concept of Communion with God and Man', *Journal of Jewish Studies*, vol. 6 (1955), pp. 87–99 (now included in id., *Studies in Eastern European Jewish Mysticism*, ed. D. Goldstein, Oxford, 1985, pp. 155–69); Z. Gries, 'Mi-Mythos le-Ethos—Kavim li-Demuto shel R. Avraham mi-Kalisk', in *Umah ve-Toledoteyha* (Jerusalem, 1984), vol. 2, pp. 117–43. Cf. Y. Liebes, 'Ha-Mashi'akh shel ha-Zohar', in *Ha-Ra'ayon ha-Meshikhi be-Israel* (Jerusalem, 1982), pp. 160–5.

19 The pattern of periodic departures from home, which could turn into prolonged stays affording young married men little contact with their wives and families, was by no means unique to Hasidism, although it was only Hasidism that offered these young men an alternative and coherent focus for their social and emotional lives. This pattern was already prevalent among the students of the mediaeval Ashkenazi *yeshivot*, for whom the pursuit of scholarship away from their native towns was considered meritorious enough to legitimate the neglect of their sexual obligations to their wives as these were prescribed by the *halakhah*. For the middle of the nineteenth century, see, for example, E. Deinard, *Zikhronot Bat Ami* (St Louis, 1920), Pt 1, pp. 38–9, where he describes the *perushim* (abstinents) of the *yeshivah* at Eisiskes (Eishishok) in Lithuania: 'To a certain extent, the *yeshivah* of Eisiskes enjoyed a higher status than the *yeshivah* of Volozhin. Eisiskes was not a place for young boys. Only fully grown men or married men were accepted there. They were called '*perushim*', and most of them had obtained '*semikhah*' (rabbinic ordination) before arriving at Eisiskes. Anyone entering the *beyt midrash* of the 'abstinents' would be awestruck. He would see before him some 100 young men, all standing . . . each at a small table called a '*stender*', with a volume of Gemara open in front of him . . . For twenty hours a day, and in some cases even longer, these men would stand on their feet without sitting down to rest for a moment . . . They are oblivious of the world . . . totally absorbed in another world which is all spirit . . . Such . . . extraordinary enthusiasm is displayed by young men in their early years of marriage. They reject all the pleasures of life before they have had a chance to enjoy them. Their young, beloved wives stay at their parents' homes and take pride in their husbands, who exist on dry morsels of bread, sleeping on hard wooden benches at their place of study. They make no distinction between Sabbath and Festivals and ordinary weekdays [that is, they do not visit their wives even on Sabbath and Festivals]. So they live at the *yeshivah* for several years without a break, without breathing the fresh air of the world. Many of them do not even find time to remember their families by as much as a letter.' A different pattern of 'wanderings', or 'exile' for its own sake rather than to a particular, if distant, centre of scholarship, became prevalent in Eastern European scholarly circles in the nineteenth century, and served as an ascetic discipline, designed to concentrate the scholar's mental faculties on his studies and to eliminate all worldly distractions. See on this I. Etkes, 'Mishpakhah ve-Limud Torah be-Khuggey ha-Lomedim be-Lita ba-Me'ah ha-19', *Zion*, vol. 51 (1986), pp. 96–7; id., *R. Israel Salanter ve-Reshitah shel*

Tenu'at ha-Musar (Jerusalem, 1982), pp. 28–31, 69–70. The most celebrated model for the sacrifice of domestic and marital comforts for the sake of Torah was, of course, R. Akiva (*Nedarim* 50a), and an extreme manifestation of the ideal of *perishut* for the sake of scholarship can be found in the historically obscure but ethically unequivocal mediaeval document entitled *Khukkey ha-Torah* (see S. Assaf, *Mekorot le-Toledot ha-Khinukh be-Yisra'el*, vol. 1, Tel Aviv, 1925, pp. 6–16), which promotes not abstinence within marriage during periods of study, however long, but something approaching an ideal of virginity, until well into manhood, for boys dedicated by their parents to intense study at 'the houses of the abstinents'. It is my impression that the tradition of renouncing all worldly pleasures, including conjugal relations, at least intermittently and within the halakhic constraints of the obligation to marry and procreate (which could be disposed of either early or late in life while leaving much scope for ascetic deprivation in between) was continuous, if not universal, in both scholarly and mystical circles, right up to and including Hasidism. I have dealt with this in a lecture entitled 'Asceticism and Mysticism in the Jewish Tradition' which was delivered at the second Scholem Memorial Conference in Jerusalem in February 1986, which I hope to publish elsewhere. For the position in early rabbinic literature, see, now, S. D. Fraade, 'Ascetical Aspects of Ancient Judaism', in A. Green (ed.), *Jewish Spirituality from the Bible through the Middle Ages* (London, 1986), pp. 253–88, with which I am in full agreement.

20 See Katz (note 13 above), p. 282 (243 of the English version). See also, Nathan Sternharz, *Yemey Moharnat* (Bney Brak, 1956), pp. 11–13.

21 There are numerous reports by *Mitnaggedim* concerning the presence of women in the 'courts' to seek a blessing from the *Rebbe*. They often suggest all manner of licentious conduct between these women and the *Rebbe* himself or the male Hasidim present. See, for example, David of Makov, in Wilensky (note 16 above), vol. 2, pp. 66, 105, 137; Dubnow (note 13 above), p. 366. Dubnow is right in observing that these reports could well have been inspired by a distorted understanding of the early Hasidic doctrine of the 'raising of wayward thoughts' (which the *Mitnaggedim* denounced vehemently), more than by any direct experience of Hasidic practice in this respect. Notably, the reports which refer to the presence of women in the 'courts' conflict, in the writings of the same authors, with the common complaint against the Hasidim who flock to the 'courts' while abandoning their wives at home. Cf. Wilensky's comment in Wilensky, op. cit., p. 46. In addition, there are references to women visiting the Zaddikim in their 'courts' throughout the Hasidic hagiographical literature of the nineteenth century. See, for example, M. Buber, *Tales of the Hasidim* (New York, 1972), vol. 2, *Later Masters*, pp. 111, 141, 204, 210, 293. By contrast, the *Takkanot Liozna* of R. Shneur Zalman of Lyadi (see note 15 above), which divide the Hasidim into various distinct categories in order to regulate their visits to the 'court', make no mentionn of women at all. Nor does one hear of women among the Hasidim who visited R. Nahman of Braslav. There may well have been regional differences between the different 'courts' in this respect, as well as differences in the personal styles of leadership of various Zaddikim. Both R. Nahman of Braslav and R. Shneur Zalman of Lyadi disapproved of the more vulgar displays of miracle-working Zaddikism, and may well have excluded women from their 'courts' on the grounds that this was all that the women might have expected of them, barred as they were from hearing their Hasidic *torah*. An interesting insight into the questionable desirability of women at the 'courts' is supplied by Isaac ben Loeb Landau in his *Zikkaron Tov*—a collection of stories about the life of his venerated Hasidic master, the Admor Isaac (ben Mordecai) of Nezkhis—essentially a miracle-working Zaddik whose modest collection of homilies, *Toledot Yitskhak*, was published by the same Isaac Landau shortly after the Admor's death in 1868: *Zikkaron Tov* (Piotrkow, 1892)

(now reprinted in vol. 3 of the series *Sefarim ha-Kedoshim mi-Talmidey ha-Besht . . .*, note 17 above. I am grateful to Professor G. Nigal for drawing my attention to this book, although in connection with another matter: cf. note 43 below). In Pt 2, p. 27b (54), sect. 30 we read: 'Towards the end of his life he did not allow women to enter his house unless they were accompanied by their husbands. [If they came unaccompanied they could enter] only for the purpose of paying him his *pidyon* money; otherwise he would speak to them through the window. He explained this by saying that he did not wish the women to frequent his 'court', since he could not bear the burden of dealing with the large crowds that were always coming to see him. However, it was his manner to offer simple explanations for actions which he had taken for sublime reasons known only to himself.' Although the phrasing is a little ambiguous, it seems that the 'large crowds' of visitors to which the author refers are not crowds of women specifically but rather the Hasidic following of R. Isaac of Nezkhis as a whole. When these crowds became too large, the simplest method of pruning them was to discourage the women from coming. However, the author's speculation that R. Isaac's 'simple' explanation concealed a more sublime and esoteric reason reflects his sense that, at its face value, the Admor's explanation was not fully satisfactory. This suggests in the first instance that the policy of deliberately discouraging women from attending the 'court' may have been unusual enough in this particular environment to require some further explanation, but it may allude also to the sexual, and therefore esoteric, direction of the Admor's sublime intention, a direction which would be pointed quite naturally by any address to women as a category.

In trying to assess the extent to which women were received in the 'courts' it is interesting to note the evidence of Sarah Schnierer, the founder of the Beyt Ya'akov network of Orthodox schools for girls. She came from a Polish Hasidic family—precisely the region from which many of the Hasidic tales relating to woment who visited the 'courts' have emanated. She describes the situation in her youth, at the turn of the last century, as one in which, especially during the High Holidays, 'fathers and sons travel and those who can afford it make this journey several times a year. Thus they are drawn to Ger, to Belz, to Alexander, to Bobo[v] . . . And we stay at home, the wives, the daughters with the little ones. We have an empty Yomtov . . . ' (Judith Grunfeld-Rosenbaum, an early collaborator of Sarah Schnierer, reminiscing about her friend's impressions, in J. Grunfeld-Rosenbaum, 'Sara Schenierer—The Story of a Great Movement', in Leo Jung (ed.) *Jewish Leaders*, New York, 1953, pp. 410–11). It seems that if the women visited these *Rebbes*, they did not do so at the times of the regular assemblies of the Hasidim at the 'courts', on Sabbaths and Festivals. This impression is corroborated by the memoirs of E. Shmueli regarding the same region during the inter-war period. He describes the men taking leave of their wives and small children who stay at home while they, accompanied by their older sons, travel to the 'courts' at the fixed times of assembly. See E. Shmueli, *Ba-Dor ha-Yehudi ha-Akharon be-Polin* (Tel Aviv, 1986), p. 15, pp. 9–110 *passim*. Cf. also S. Elberg, *Warsaw shel Ma'la* (Bney Brak, 1969), p. 64. The book contains reminiscences about pre-war Warsaw. The author stresses the importance of leaving the home and the family behind when visiting the *Rebbe*, and suggests that the Hasidim preferred to travel a long distance away rather than visit a local *Rebbe*, precisely because this took them away from their wives and children who stayed behind.

22 In fact this was a re-translation from the Yiddish in which the material was first narrated, only to be translated into Hebrew for publication. See, Kh. Shmeruk, *Sifrut Yiddish: Perakim le-Toledoteyha* (Tel Aviv, 1978), pp. 213, 218.

23 See *ibid.*, p. 217.

24 See *ibid.*, pp. 205ff.

25 See J. Dan, *Ha-Sippur ha-Hasidi* (Jerusalem, 1975), pp. 189–95; Shmeruk (note 22 above), p. 211; G. Nigal, *Ha-Sipporet ha-Hasidit* (Jerusalem, 1981), pp. 70–80. For a contemporary Hasidic ambivalence about the printing of such tales, see, J. R. Minz, *Legends of the Hasidim* (Chicago and London, 1968), pp. 5–6.

26 See below, pp. 523–5 and notes 82–3.

27 This is the subject of a book in progress entitled *Communicating the Infinite* by Dr Naftali Loewenthal. The book focuses on the Habad movement, but surveys the position both before and outside it. For the time being, see his preliminary comments in 'The Apotheosis of Action in Early Habad', *Daat*, no. 18 (1987), pp. vi–viii. Cf. Etkes (note 15 above), pp. 341–2. For the distinction between the communication of Hasidism by means of the '*torah*' and prayer of the Zaddik to one class of people, and by means of his common talk or tales and parables to another, see, M. Piekarz, *Hasidut Braslav* (Jerusalem, 1972), pp. 87–106. For a clear distinction between Hasidic '*torah*' as a higher level of teaching, accessible to a select minority of disciples, and '*musar*' as a lower level, in which the same '*torah*' may be clothed in order to make it accessible to all, see Nathan Sternharz, *Hayey Moharan*, Pt I, 'Nesi'ato le-Eretz Israel', sect. 19.

28 See *In Praise of the Baal Shem Tov*, ed. D. Ben Amos and J. Minz (Bloomington–London, 1972), 'The Printer's Preface', p. 1. Cf. G. G. Scholem, 'The Neutralisation of the Messianic Element in Early Hasidism' in *The Messianic Idea in Judaism* (note 12 above), pp. 198–9 for the Sabbatian origin of this notion.

29 See Shmeruk (note 22 above), pp. 206–7.

30 See L. Jacobs, *Encyclopedia Judaica*, vol. 16, p. 627, s.v. 'Woman'.

31 See note 21 above.

32 See Dubnow (note 13 above), pp. 138ff.

33 For this controversy, triggered off by the publication of R. Shneur Zalman of Lyadi's *Tanya* in 1796, see Dubnow, op. cit., pp. 335–8; H. M. Heilman, *Beyt Rabbi* [Berdichev 1903], pp. 81–90; A. J. Braver, 'Al ha-Makhloket she-Beyn RSHZ ve-R. Avraham mi-Kalisk', *Kiryat Sefer*, vol. 1 (1924–5), pp. 142–50, 226–38; E. Kupfer, 'Te'udot Khadashot bi-Devar ha-Makhloket beyn ha-RSHZ mi-Lyadi u-bheyn R. Avraham ha-Kohen mi-Kalisk ve-R. Baruch mi-Medzibezh', *Tarbiz*, vol. 47 (1978), pp. 230–7; R. Elior, 'Vikku'akh Minsk' in *Mekhkerey Yerushalayim be-Makhshevet Yisrael*, vol. 4 (1982), pp. 194–5; Etkes (note 15 above), pp. 343–4; Gries (note 18 above), pp. 127–32.

34 One possible exception should be mentioned, although it seems marginal in this context. This is the short Yiddish book entitled *Poke'akh Ivrim* by R. Shneur Zalman of Lyadi's son Dov Ber, the second leader of Habad (see, on this book, H. Liberman, *Ohel Rachel*, New York, 1984, vol. 3, pp. 646–9; Shmeruk note 22 above, pp. 199–200). Published in Yiddish in the second decade of the nineteenth century, the book offers advice on ethical matters and calls for repentance. The introduction addresses it to ordinary people who cannot read the many books on this subject which are available to the better educated Hebrew readers (see *Poke'akh Ivrim*, Brooklyn, 1955, p. 35). Although no mention of women as part of the anticipated readership is made in the introduction itself, women may well be addressed directly in ch. 17, p. 42: 'Similarly, the women who sit in between the shops should take great care not to indulge in conversation with the young men [who had been warned never to look at the women in the shops in the immediately preceding passage], because this is very harmful to the health of children, Heaven forbid.' This suggests that a female readership could have been assumed by the author. However, the book clearly belongs to the ethical genre and, but for the identity of its Hasidic author, displays no distinctly Hasidic characteristics at all. *Musar* books in Yiddish had traditionally attracted a mixed male and female readership (see Ch. Shmeruk, *Sifrut Yiddish be-Polin*, Jerusalem, 1981, pp. 43 ff.). I am grateful to Dr Naftali Loewenthal for drawing my attention to this passage.

35 These are: Edel, the daughter of the Baal Shem Tov; her daughter Feige, who was the sister of both R. Baruch of Medzibezh and R. Ephrayim of Sudlykow and the mother of R. Nahman of Braslav; Rachel, the daughter of R. Joshua Heschel of Opt; and Hannah Hayah, the daughter of R. Mordecai of Chernobyl. See Horodecky (note 1 above) p. 69.

36 For the status of Edel as a female Zaddik, Horodecky alludes to the tradition whereby the Baal Shem Tov had derived her soul, and so also her name, from the Torah, by constructing it out of the initial letters of the verse in Deuteronomy 33:2—'A fiery Law unto them' (Esh Dat Lamo). This tradition appears in the *In Praise of the Baal Shem Tov* (note 28 above), p. 137 (p. 102 of the Hebrew *Shivkhey ha-Besht*, ed. B. Minz). It concludes a story in which Edel appears in a rather more negative light: the Baal Shem Tov was engaged in an ecstatic exposition of a point to one of his disciples. 'His face burned like a torch.' Suddenly Edel entered the room and summoned her father to dinner. The Baal Shem Tov's state of trance ended abruptly. He reproached Edel for interrupting him and explained that both Elijah the Prophet and his own personal teacher, Ahijah the Prophet of Shiloh, had been present in the room but were driven away at the sound of Edel's voice, which had confused him. Far from displaying visionary capacities of her own, Edel by her very presence, which is robustly corporeal on two scores—her female nature and the food which she delivers— interferes with her father's spiritual endeavours and puts an end to his vision. In fact, this portrayal of Edel is sufficiently negative to raise suspicions with regard to the authenticity of the discrepant concluding 'praise'. It could well have been added to the original story by a later hand, more programmatically committed to the idealization not only of the Besht, but also of all those associated with him (but cf. G. Nigal, 'Nashim be-Sefer Shivkhey ha-Besht', *Molad*, vol. 31 [no. 241], 1974, p. 143 for a totally different reading of this story). The Yiddish version of *In Praise of the Baal Shem Tov* sheds no light on the matter, since this story does not appear in it at all (see A. Yaari, 'Shetey Mahadurot Yesod shel Shivkhey ha-Besht', *Kiryat Sefer*, vol. 39, 1963–4, pp. 557–8). For another tradition in the same book, in which Edel appears as a typical woman by conventional standards, devoid of any spiritual ambition or Zaddik-like qualities but rather excluded from the ecstatic male fraternity of her father and his disciples, and seeking, like any ordinary woman, a 'blessing' from one of them in order to ensure that she would conceive a male child, see *In Praise of the Baal Shem Tov* (note 28 above), pp. 223–4 (p. 144 of the Hebrew edition). Cf. also *Sefer Sippurey Kedoshim*, ed. G. Nigal (Jerusalem, 1976), p. 41. S. Ashkenazi (note 2 above) adds to the account of Edel which he derives from Horodecky the following information: 'The Besht considered her as one of his disciples. With his permission, she gave out magical remedies to the sick. In a letter she wrote to R. Shalom of Prohobyst (dated Monday [the week in which the Pentateuchal portion of] '*Bereshit*' [is read, in the year] 5547 [1787]), she reported on her father's conduct in study and worship' (op. cit., p. 55). In a note on the same page, Ashkenazi directs the reader to his source for this—the book *Butsina di-Nehora ha-Shalem* 'by R. Baruch [of Medzibezh]'—Edel's son. A book entitled *Butsina di-Nehora* indeed contains traditions which are ascribed to R. Baruch of Medzibezh, and has been published many times since 1880. However, its relation to R. Baruch is problematic and probably false (see A. Schischa Halevi, 'Al ha-Sefer Butsina di-Nehora', *Aley Sefer*, no. 8 (1980), pp. 155–7). The book *Butsina di-Nehora ha-Shalem* is even more problematic in that it contains numerous additions from extraneous sources, put together by its modern editor-author, Reuben Margaliot. It was first published by Margaliot through his bookselling business in Lemberg, and printed in Bilgogaj, in or around 1930. The edition is undated. The date was suggested to me by Mr A. Schischa, on the basis of the fact that in 1931 Margaliot published, and printed in Zamosc, the first part of *Butsina di-Nehora*

ha-Shalem as a separate pamphlet entitled *Mekor Baruch*, from the matrices of the first edition of the complete work. On *Mekor Baruch* see Schischa in *Aley Sefer* (as above), p. 157. I am grateful to Mr Schischa for his help in clarifying this point. The material portraying Edel as a disciple of the Besht, the author or letters and magical remedies, appears in *Butsina di-Nehora ha-Shalem*, Pt 1—*Mekor Baruch*, pp. 5–7. It contains three letters from the Besht to his daughter and one letter by her to R. Shalom of Prohobyst, incorporated by R. Margaliot into his own sketch of R. Baruch's life. These letters are drawn from the notorious Kherson *genizah* of Hasidic forgeries, and were copied by Margaliot from H. E. Bikhowsky, *Ginzey Nistarot* (Jerusalem, 1924), Pt 1, *Or Yisra'el*, p. 9, letter 31; p. 10, letter 32; p. 16, letter 53; Pt 2, *Or Ne'erav*, pp. 14–15, letter 33 (on the Kherson *genizah* see Y. Raphael, 'Genizat Kherson', *Sinai*, no. 81, 1977, pp. 129–50). The most extensive collection of the Kherson letters appeared in the Habad periodical *Ha-Tamim*, published in Warsaw between 1935 and 1938, and it was endorsed as authentic by the then leader of Habad, the Admor J. I. Schneersohn, against the growing conviction of most scholars of Hasidism that the letters were all recent forgeries. For additional letters 'by' or 'to' Edel, see *Ha-Tamim* (photographic edition in two volumes, Kfar Habad, 1975), vol. 2, p. 444, letter 111; pp. 449–50, letter 143; p. 452, letter 154; p. 454, letter 163. Needless to say, all these letters are turn-of-the-century fabrications and can tell us nothing about Edel's role and status in the Hasidic movement of her own time. Nevertheless, it is interesting to note that the forger, whose identity is not known but who clearly belonged to or was intimately familiar with the Hasidic world of the end of the nineteenth century and the beginning of the twentieth, did not attempt to 'promote' Edel to the rank of a fully-fledged Zaddik, but simply manufactured more information about her in line with the traditions contained in *Shivkhey ha-Besht* and stressed her close relationship with her father. The Kherson letters lend themselves to a 'feminist' interpretation no more and no less than do the authentic traditions about women in Hasidism. For an authentic model of female piety in *Shivkhey ha-Besht*, which is unequivocal in its endorsement of traditional female virtues such as charity, humility, empathy and compassion, and totally innocent of any desire to 'liberate' women or to acknowledge their capacity for charismatic leadership, see the traditions on Rivaleh the Pious in *In Praise of the Baal Shem Tov* (note 28 above), pp. 120–2 (pp. 94–5 of the Hebrew edition). Dr Zeev Gries has suggested to me in a private communication that the Rivaleh tradition in *Shivkhey ha-Besht* must be taken not at its face value but as an ironic denunciation of *excessive* piety, a quality which the classical rabbinic sources deplore, especially in women (cf. note 72 below). This interpretation of the story seems to me possible but by no means certain, since various groups at various times in Jewish history did produce extreme norms of piety which would have been frowned on, to say the least, by those among the Sages who advocated a more sober balance between worldly pleasures and spiritual concerns, but which were nevertheless accepted as fully legitimate in their own context. Hasidism sprang from within an environment where such extreme norms of piety prevailed, and its reaction to or against them was by no means unequivocal (cf. note 75 below). Rivaleh's extreme piety as it is portrayed in the *Shivkhey ha-Besht* could well have been valued positively, especially since, with the possible exception of her apparent idealization of poverty, it was free from the inclination toward ascetic mortification and sexual abstinence which characterized Kabbalistic piety and which would have been utterly unacceptable in a woman (cf. note 19 above and notes 72–4 below with the corresponding discussion in the main body of the text). Be that as it may, what is relevant at this point is the stress in *Shivkhey ha-Besht* on Rivaleh's traditional female virtues, however extreme, and the total absence of any pneumatic or charismatic powers among her qualities.

Horodecky's account of Edel's daughter, Feige, is drawn from Sternharz (note 27 above), 'Mekom Yeshivato u-Nesi'otav', sect. 11. This confirms that Feige was indeed considered to be endowed with prophetic insight, and was able to 'see' the Besht at the wedding of her grandaughter, R. Nahman of Braslav's daughter. But there is no indication whatsoever, in this passage or anywhere else in the Braslav literature, that Feige's visionary powers had made her a Zaddik in her own right.

37 See the considerable amount of material on this, assembled uncritically but nevertheless a useful indication of the scope and continuity of this phenomenon, in Ashkenazi (note 2 above), vol. 1, pp. 115–36.

38 Horodecky (note 1 above), p. 69.

39 See note 2 above. The women are: Malkah of Trisk, daughter of R. Avraham of Trisk and granddaughter of R. Mordecai of Chernobyl; Pereleh, daughter of the Maggid of Kozienice; Hayah, mother of R. Yitskhak Meir of Ger; Mirosh, daughter of R. Elimelech of Lyzhansk; Frieda, daughter of R. Shneur Zalman of Lyadi; Eidel, daughter of R. Shalom Roke'akh of Belz; Hayah Moskowitz, daughter of R. Meir of Premyslyany; Sareleh, mother of Joshua Heschel of Olkusz and wife of Hayim Shmuel of Chenciny (who was the grandson and heir of the 'Good Jew of Neustadt'); Hannah-Brakhah, her daughter, who was the wife of R. Elimelech of Grodzinsk; Nekhamah, daughter of R. Hayim of Zanz; and Sarah-Shlomtse, daughter of R. Menakhem Mendel of Zhidachov. Sareleh of Chenciny and her daughter Hannah-Brakhah appear to be among the very few wives rather than mothers, daughters or sisters of the Zaddikim, who are said to have commanded a following in their own right. In the case of Sareleh, however, this appears to have begun only after her husband's death, when her son Joshua Heschel succeeded his father. See, on her, Feinkind, pp. 56–61; Ashkenazi, pp. 57–8; Shemen, pp. 328–9 (all in note 2 above), and cf. note 78 below.

40 See Feinkind, Ashkenazi, Geshuri, Shemen, Alfasi and Brayer (note 2 above).

41 Regarding the literary and scholarly activities of Frieda, the daughter of R. Shneur Zalman of Lyadi, see note 2 above, Ashkenazi, pp. 55–6; Shemen, p. 328. This can be anchored in an authentic Habad tradition, whereby R. Shneur Zalman used to teach Hasidism to Frieda, and she would allow her brother, R. Dov Ber (who later succeeded R. Shneur Zalman) to hide in the room to listen, occasionally prompting his sister to ask their father for further clarifications. See Heilman (note 33 above), p. 114. A letter addressed to R. Dov Ber, which explains in Hasidic and Kabbalistic terms the reasons why the time is not ripe for the disclosure of the date of the messianic Advent, has been ascribed to Frieda and published several times. See, for example, M. Teitelbaum, *Ha-Rav mi-Lyadi u-Mifleget Habad* (Jerusalem, 1970; 1st edn, Warsaw, 1914), vol. 1, p. 265; *Iyyun Tefilah* (Lódź, 1926), pp. 38–9; Hillmann (note 15 above), pp. 235–7 (in two distinct versions). Notably, however, Heilman expresses doubts about her authorship of this letter (op. cit., p. 114), and Hillmann is unsure of her authorship at least of the second version of the letter. The two versions were published again recently by J. Mondshein in *Kerem Habad* I (Kfar Habad, 1986), pp. 100–1. He ascribes both to R. Aaron ha-Levi of Staroselye. Ashkenazi (note 2 above), p. 56, states that 'after her death, manuscripts of her Hasidic teachings were found, written to her brother, the Admor David [*sic*], of blessed memory.' This must be a muddled reference to the same letter, and the addressee was R. Dov Ber. R. Shneur Zalman had no son by the name of David.

42 One such example is the account of Sareleh of Chenciny by M. Feinkind (note 2 above), pp. 56–61. The chapter devoted to her ends with precise information concerning her death, at the age of 99, in February 1937—'Friday night, 15 Adar 5697, at 12 o'clock'. This must have been added by Feinkind's children who published the book posthumously in 1937, their father having died in June 1935. See on him,

Lexikon fun der nayer Yiddisher literatur (New York, 1965–81), vol. 7, pp. 357–8.

43 Professor G. Nigal, who has examined most of the available Hasidic hagiographical collections, was kind enough to confirm that he has not come across any references to female Zaddikim in this literature. He did, however, point out one possible allusion to the Maid of Ludmir (on her, see below) in *Zikkaron Tov* (note 21 above). This is a reference to 'a pious woman (*ishah kesheyrah*) in the city of Ludmir who was able to foretell the future' (Pt 2, p. 15a [29], sect. 4). It appears in the middle of a rather obscure story featuring R. Isaac of Nezkhis (son of R. Mordecai of Nezkhis, d. 1868; see *ibid.*, p. 20a, sect. 38), whose own prophetic insight corroborated the woman's prediction of the imminent death of a certain man. I am grateful to Professor Nigal for drawing my attention to this reference.

44 For Horodecky, see above, p. 497 and note 12; cf. above, p. 505. In one form or another, all the authors listed in note 2 can be said to have undergone a similar process of acculturation, although not necessarily in the same direction as did Horodecky.

45 See above, p. 508.

46 The abridged English version of Horodecky's book, *Leaders of Hasidism* (see note 1 above), is at odds with the Hebrew original in suggesting that the Maid 'became the wife of the celebrated Tsaddik. Rabbi Mordecai of Czernobyl, who prevailed upon her'. There is no trace of evidence for this, and it must be a mistake in translation by Horodecky's wife Maria.

47 S. A. G. (S. A. Horodecky), 'The Maiden of Ludmir' ('Die Ludmirer Moid'), *Evreiskaia Starina*, Year 1, vol. 2 (1909), pp. 219–22. I am grateful to Dr S. Redlich who helped me locate the article, and to Dr M. Pinson who translated it for me.

48 See note 1 above. Another adaptation of the same material appeared in one of his later works, *Oley Zion* (Tel Aviv, 1947), pp. 172–5. This contains a few minor additions, including the promotion of Rivaleh the Pious (see note 36 above) to the ranks of the female Zaddikim (p. 172).

49 See note 2 above.

50 Note 47 above, p. 219.

51 M. Klaczko, 'Some more about the "Maiden of Ludmir"', *Evreiskaia Starina*, Year 3, vol. 4 (1911), pp. 389–93.

52 See Biber (note 2 above), p. 75, n. 7. Further details about the activities of the Maid during her old age in Jerusalem and Safed are supplied by Taubenhaus (note 2 above) in a short chapter entitled 'Ba-Khatsar Beytah shel Ishah Zaddik' (At the Court of a Female Zaddik) (pp. 37–41) and in a note on p. 372. The book is based on written materials collected by the author as well as on his personal reminiscences about his father, R. Meir Taubenhaus who was one of the most outstanding figures in the 'old Yishuv' of Jerusalem and who later settled in Safed and pioneered the 'productiviza-tion' of Jewish life in that city. Drawing on his father's personal notes and diary, and on his own recollections, the author reports that as a young man R Meir Taubenhaus (who was born in 1865) knew the Maid of Ludmir in Jerusalem, where she conducted herself 'as a Polish Rebbe' and had a considerable following. R. Meir was so intrigued by her that he made a study of her career, and during one of his many journeys to Eastern Europe (probably in the 1880s), he visited Ludmir and made extensive enquiries about her. However, Ephraim Taubenhaus' account of the Maid's early history in Poland adds practically nothing to Horodecky's version and could well be dependent on it. He does not appear to be quoting it from his father's notes, as he does elsewhere in the book.

53 See especially Mekler and Twersky (note 2 above).

54 The only other woman Zaddik portrayed as belonging to this category is Yente the Prophetess who is said to have lived at the time of the Baal Shem Tov, in the middle decades of the eighteenth century. She was the daughter of a simple Galician Jew, and

her husband, Yoseph Spravedliver, was a follower of the Besht. She once accompanied him on a visit to the Besht, and was so impressed by the Baal Shem Tov's ascetic piety that she decided to adopt it on her return home. She abstained from conjugal relations, took frequent ritual baths, fasted and prayed intensely, wearing a prayer shawl like a man. When her husband went to the Besht to complain about his wife's irregular conduct, the Besht endorsed it fully, proclaiming Yente a prophetess. Once this became known, Hasidim began to flock to her, seeking blessings and cures, which she apparently effected while refusing to accept *pidyon* money for her services, as customary amongst the male Zaddikim (see Feinkind, pp. 20–5; Ashkenazi, pp. 55–6, and all the subsequent derivative accounts, note 2 above). The story seems somewhat anachronistic and is almost certainly apocryphal. It is extremely vague in terms of time and place, and although the Baal Shem Tov did have a few early disciples from Galicia (see Dubnow, note 13 above, pp. 101–4), Galicia did not become a part of the Hasidic world until after the death of the Maggid of Mezhirech in the 1770s. However, the story bears a few strikingly significant parallels to the Maid of Ludmir tradition. These include not only Yente's common background and lack of any connection to the household of a Zaddik, but also her adoption of celibate asceticism. For the significance of this, see above, pp. 507–8.

55 Horodecky (note 47 above), p. 219.
56 See above, p. 495.
57 Horodecky (note 1 above), p. 69.
58 See S. A. Horodecky, *Pirkey Zikhronot* (Tel Aviv, 1957), p. 72.
59 See M. Kaplan, *The Jewish Feminist Movement in Germany: The Campaigns of the Judischer Frauenbund, 1904–38* (Westport, 1979).
60 See N. Rein, *Daughters of Israel* (Harmondsworth, 1980), pp. 25–43; D. Bernstein, *Ishah be-Eretz Israel—ha-She'ifah le-Shivyon bi-Tekufat ha-Yishuv* (Tel Aviv, 1987), pp. 16–69.
61 Cf. above, p. 497 and note 12.
62 See Shemen (note 2 above), pp. 330, 338 (n. 5a).
63 For Horodecky's Hasidic '*yikhus*', see Horodecky (note 58 above), p. 11.
64 See above, p. 502.
65 See for example, Gottlober (note 14 above), pp. 85–108, especially p. 98. This section of the autobiography appears, on the basis of internal evidence, to have been written in 1859 (see the editor's note on the same page). For *Haskalah* autobiography in general, see S. Vilnai (Werses), 'Darkhey ha-Autobiographia bi-Tekufat ha-Haskalah', *Gilyonot* no. 17 (1948), pp. 175–83; A. Mintz, 'Guenzburg, Lilienblum, and the Shape of Haskalah Autobiography', *Association of Jewish Studies Review*, vol. 4 (1979), pp. 71–110. For an analysis specifically of the *Maskilim's* critique of traditional marriage, see Biale (note 13 above), pp. 49–67, especially pp. 55, 61.
66 See S. Dubnow, *History of the Jews in Russia and Poland* (Philadelphia, 1918), vol. 2, pp. 243–4; L. Greenberg, *The Jews in Russia* (New Haven, 1944), ch. 11, 'Jews in Revolutionary Movements', pp. 146–59, especially pp. 151, 154; S. W. Baron, *The Russian Jew Under Tsars and Soviets* (New York–London, 1964), p. 167; R. Stites, *The Women's Liberation Movement in Russia* (Princeton, 1978), pp. 85, 133, 135–6, 150, 169, 270, 274–6; Barbara Alpern Engel, *Mothers and Daughters—Women of the Intelligentsia in Nineteenth-Century Russia* (Cambridge, 1983), p. 159.
67 See above, p. 503.
68 On the connection between mysticism and celibacy in a number of religious traditions, see *Mistique et continence*, in the series Etudes Carmélitaines (Bruges, 1952). For the virtual universality of celibacy among the Christian saints and mystics, especially the women, see, P. Brown, 'The Notion of Virginity in the Early Church', in B. McGinn, J. Meyndorff and J. Leclercq (eds.), *Christian Spirituality—Origins to the*

Twelfth Century (London, 1986), pp. 427–43; D. Weinstein and R. M. Bell, *Saints and Society* (Chicago and London, 1982), ch. 3, 'Chastity', pp. 73–99; Sh. Shahar, *The Fourth Order* (Hebrew), ch. 4, pp. 57–65; E. Underhill, *Mysticism* (London, 1960), ch. 3, 'The Purification of the Self', pp. 198–231. For an indication of the sheer scope of the phenomenon of women mystics in the Christian tradition, see *ibid.*, Appendix A, 'Historical Sketch of European Mysticism from the Beginning of the Christian Era to the Death of Blake', pp. 453–73. For the late mediaeval spiritualization of virginity, but still within the confines of chastity, either by mutual consent within marriage or by the adoption of celibacy in later life, see C. Atkinson, '"Precious Balsam in a Fragile Glass": The Ideology of Virginity in the Later Middle Ages', *Journal of Family History* (Summer 1983), pp. 131–43.

69   See Koran, Sura 57:27; *Encyclopaedia of Religion and Ethics* (New York and Edinburgh, 1910), vol. 2, pp. 99–105.

70   See M. Smith, *Rabi'a the Mystic and her Fellow-Saints in Islam* (Cambridge, 1928), especially ch. 13, pp. 165–75; A. Schimmel, *Mystical Dimensions of Islam* (Chapel Hill, 1975), Appendix 2, 'The Feminine Element in Sufism', pp. 426–35; S. Trimingham, *The Sufi Orders in Islam* (Oxford, 1971), pp. 18, 114, 176, 232.

71   See note 19 above.

72   See the condemnation of the 'female ascetic' in the Mishnah, Gemara and Tosafot on *Sotah* 20aff., and cf. *T. Yerushalmi, Sotah* 3, 4. Cf. also S. Lieberman, *Texts and Studies* (New York, 1974), pp. 33, 35ff., 39–40. See also the Maharal's comment on the same passage in *Sotah*, in Judah Loew ben Bezalel of Prague, *Perushey Maharal mi-Prague . . . le-Agadot ha-Shas* (Jerusalem, 1968), p. 52.

73   See note 19 above.

74   See R. J. Z. Werblowsky, *Joseph Karo Lawyer and Mystic* (Oxford, 1962), ch. 4, 'Spiritual Life in Sixteenth-Century Safed: Mystical and Magical Contemplation', pp. 38–83, 133–8, 149–51, 161–8; M. Pachter, 'The Concept of Devekut in the Homiletical Ethical Writings of 16th Century Safed', in I. Twersky (ed.), *Studies in Medieval Jewish History and Literature*, vol. 2 (Cambridge, Mass., and London, 1984), pp. 171–230, especially pp. 179, 186–7, 190–1, 195–7; J. Dan, *Jewish Mysticism and Jewish Ethics* (Seattle and London, 1986), ch. 4, 'Mystical ethics in Sixteenth Century Safed', pp. 76–103, especially pp. 82–7.

75   Although Hasidism enjoys a popular image of robust this-worldliness, its orientation toward the material world and corporeal pleasures is complex, and by no means as unequivocally anti-ascetic as may be suggested by some of its most famous denunciations of self-mortification and its rejection of pessimism (*atsvut*) with regard to the moral frailty of human nature. For examples of Hasidic anti-asceticism see *Tsava'at ha-Rivash*, ed. J. I. Schochet (Brooklyn, 1975), pp. 14–16, sect. 44–7; p. 18, sect. 56. As against this posture, however, see in the same work, pp. 2–3, sect. 5–7; pp. 12–13, sect. 43a. The common assumption in Hasidic scholarship is that Hasidism reacted against, and differentiated itself consciously from, the powerful ascetic tendencies of the Kabbalistic schools from which the movement arose in the middle of the eighteenth century. The ideal of *devekut*—'mystical communion with God'— which was promoted by Hasidism to the top of its scale of values, is considered to be fundamentally non-ascetic, and is said to have ousted the ascetic ideal in a process of direct progression from one posture to the other, a process which often manifested itself in the individual biographies of the early founders of Hasidism (see, for example, *In Praise of the Baal Shem Tov*, note 28 above, p. 156, sect. 133—p. 112 of Hebrew edition—with regard to R. Nahman of Horodenka's spiritual development; cf. Dubnow, note 13 above, pp. 78–80 with regard to the Maggid of Mezhirech; A. J. Heschel, *The Circle of the Baal Shem Tov*, Chicago and London 1985, pp. 11–12 with regard to R. Pinkhas of Korets). In fact, asceticism and sexual abstinence were not uncommon

practices in Hasidism. As ideals of piety and saintliness, they co-existed with rather than making way for the more 'optimistic' approach to the problems of materiality and evil, an approach which has become so prominently associated with the Baal Shem Tov and his followers. For a discussion of this, primarily in the writings of R. Elimelech of Lyzhansk, see R. Schatz Uffenheimer, 'Le-Mahuto shel ha-Zaddik ba-Hasidut', *Molad*, nos. 144–150 (1960), pp. 369–70; G. Nigal, the introduction to his edition of *No'am Elimelech* (note 17 above), vol. 1, pp. 69ff. For the ascetic mortifications of R. Nahman of Braslav, see the discussion in A. Green, *Tormented Master* (Alabama, 1979), index s.v. 'asceticism'. For the co-existence of the ascetic ideal and the ideal of 'joy' in the Kabbalistic ethical literature before Hasidism, see A. Shohet, 'Al ha-Simkhah ba-Hasidut', *Zion*, vol. 16 (1951), pp. 30–43. I intend to deal with this more extensively elsewhere.

76 See M. Idel, 'Métaphores et pratiques sexuelles dans la cabale', in C. Mopsik (ed.), *Lettre sur la sainteté* (Paris, 1986), pp. 353–5, although I disagree with his view of the concomitant Kabbalistic evaluation of sexuality and marriage in the human sphere as unequivocally positive. See note 75 above.

77 See, for example, R. Hayim Vital, *Sha'ar ha-Gilgulim* (Tel Aviv, 1963), *hakdamah* 9, p. 33. For the notion of transmigration of souls in the Kabbalah generally, see G. G. Scholem, *Pirkey Yesod ba-Havanat ha-Kabbalah u-Semaleyhah* (Jerusalem, 1976), pp. 308–57; id., *Kabbalah* (Jerusalem, 1974), pp. 344–50. The view that sinful men appear as women at their second incarnation can already be found in Plato, *Timaeus* (Loeb Classical Library, New York, 1929), p. 91.

78 The fact that most of the other women described as Hasidic leaders in their own right were not the wives of Zaddikim but rather their widows, mothers, sisters or daughters (cf. above, pp. 500–1 and note 39) may belong in this context. If her relationship to the Zaddik is marital, namely sexual, the woman's powers, however great, are unequivocally confined wtihin the boundary of her female role, and they are more likely to be perceived as being complementary rather than analogous to her husband's powers. Interestingly, marriage features as a solution to the problem of a spiritually ambitious woman in a story associated with the Gaon of Vilna. The story is reminiscent of the Maid of Ludmir Tradition: 'A certain maiden performed miracles, spoke of high and mighty things and studied *Zohar* as well as other esoteric matters. The Gaon R. Elijah, of blessed memory, said: "When she marries, the spirit would depart from her", and this is just what happened' (Asher Kohen, *Keter Rosh [Orkhot Khayim]*, Jerusalem, n. d., p. 29). The Gaon of Vilna, a supreme representative of what Horodecky labels 'legalistic' or 'intellectual' Judaism (see note 4 above, vol. 2, 'Ha-Gaon mi-Vilna', pp. 346–86, especially pp. 364–5), and R. Mordecai of Chernobyl, a central spokesman for that 'other' Judaism of Horodecky's scheme, are portrayed as responding to the aberration of mystical spirituality in women in precisely the same way, despite the gulf between the Hasidic and the Mitnagdic perspectives in other respects. Altogether, this gulf was not as wide as might be suggested by the initial level of hostility between the two camps. Both shared a wide range of common sensibilities which were fundamental to traditional, halakhic Judaism. Cf. Z. Gries, 'Sifrut ha-Hanhagot ha-Hasidit', *Zion*, vol. 46 (1981), pp. 228–36.

79 This is where the family of R. Shneur Zalman of Lyadi's son, Mosheh, were sent after his apparent conversion to Christianity. See Heilman (note 33 above), pp. 113–14. For his apostasy, see S. Katz, 'Iggerot Maskilim bi-Genutam shel Hasidim', *Moznayim*, no. 10 (1940), pp. 266–70, and all the bibliographical references cited there. Cf. R. Elior, 'Ha-Makhloket al Moreshet Habad', *Tarbiz*, vol. 49 (1979–80), pp. 167–8. For a rather muddled but relatively early reference to the affair, see L. Rosenthal's supplement, *Yode'a Sefer*, to M. Roest, *L. Rosenthal'schen Bibliotek*, vol. 2 (Amster-

dam, 1875), p. 164, no. 866 (the entry for *Likkutey Amarim* [*Tanya*]). I am grateful to Professor C. Abramsky for drawing my attention to this last reference.

80 See I. Tishby, *Mishnat ha-Zohar*, vol. 1 (Jerusalem, 1957), pp. 221–31; Scholem (note 77 above), pp. 300–3; id. (note 7 above), pp. 37–8. Scholem offers the kabbalistic association between the feminine sphere and the demonic as the reason for the exclusion of women from the Jewish mystical tradition (*ibid.*). My own impression is that this association in the writings of the kabbalists was not novel but constituted a direct continuation of classical rabbinic and philosphical conceptions of women as more inclined to sorcery and witchcraft, more susceptible to ritual impurity, exhibiting a more intense and untamed sexuality and altogether representing the material-physical element of creation rather than the element of form or spirit. This was a perception of women which was common to Judaism, Christianity and Islam, and yet it did not prevent the active participation of women in either of the other two mystical traditions as it did, according to Scholem, in the case of Jewish mysticism. The total absence of women from the kabbalistic tradition (and all other varieties of Jewish mysticism and esotericism) cannot, therefore, be explained by what is, after all, a symptom rather than the cause of the condition. I hope to deal with this in detail elsewhere.

81 Instances of this abound throughout the literature of Hasidism. See for example, *Tsava'at ha-Rivash* (note 75 above), pp. 30–1, sect. 90, and the parallels in the collections of teachings by the Maggid of Mezhirech cited there in the notes; *Maggid Devarav le-Ya'akov* (Jerusalem, 1971), the section 'Likkutim Khadashim', p. 142b (from *Or ha-Me'ir* by R. Ze'ev Wolf of Zhitomir); *No'am Elimelech* (note 17 above), vol. 1, p. 280; N. Sternharz, *Likkutey Halakhot, Yoreh De'ah*, vol. 1 (Jerusalem, 1950), 'Hilekhot Gilu'akh', *halakhah* 4, sect. 15–16, p. 476; 'Hilekhot Niddah', *halakhah* 2, sect. 7, p. 494; vol. 2 (Jerusalem, 1953), 'Hilekhot Reshit ha-Gez', *halakhah* 5, sect. 4, p. 538; 'Kelalim Nora'im . . . Dov Ber mi-Mezhirech', in Hayim Haykel of Amdur, *Hayim va-Hesed* (Jerusalem, 1970), p. 158. On worship 'through corporality' and the 'raising of wayward thoughts' as élitist ideals, see. I. Tishby and J. Dan, 'Torat ha-Hasidut ve-Sifrutah', in *Ha-Encyclopedia ha-Ivrit*, vol. 17, pp. 788–9 (included in A. Rubinstein, ed., *Perakim be-Torat ha-Hasidut vu-bhe-Toledtoeyhah*, Jerusalem, 1978, pp. 274–5); Piekarz (note 27 above), pp. 95–7; A. Rapoport-Albert, 'God and the Zaddik as the Two Focal Points of Hasidic Worship', *History of Religion*, vol. 18 (Chicago, 1979), pp. 301ff.

82 His father, the Admor Shalom Dovber had already identified the crucially important part played by women in determining the degree of Jewish religious commitment of the younger generation. He wrote in 1902: 'Satan dances first among the women, to cast into them the filth of secularism. They then run their households in the spirit of secularism, take into their hands the guidance and education of their children, prevail upon their husband with their own frivolous notions, and send their sons to the [secular] teachers who corrupt them rather than to traditional, religious teachers' (*Iggerot Kodesh . . . Shalom Dovber*, Brooklyn, 1982, vol. 1, p. 274). In terms which echo traditional rabbinic and kabbalistic notions of women's frivolity, and especially their sexual susceptibility to the influence of Satan (cf. note 79 above), he blames them for starting the fashion for modern, secular education as well as for lowering the standards of religious observance generally (see p. 279). This evaluation of the responsibility of women for initiating the process of estrangement from tradition in many households is not without historical foundation. Lacking in any formal traditional education themselves, but increasingly encouraged, unlike the boys, to acquire some secular accomplishments and skills in early life, women were more inclined and able to expose their children to secular European culture. This, after all, was the basis for the ideology of the Beyt Ya'akov movement for the Orthodox

Jewish education of women, which began some fifteen years after the Admor Shalom Dovber had written the letter quoted above. (For the Beyt Ya'akov movement, see note 21 above. See also D. Weissman, 'Bais Yaakov: A Historical Model for Jewish Feminists', in E. Koltun, ed., *The Jewish Woman*, New York, 1976, pp. 139–48). The Admor Shalom Dovber's endeavours to arrest the tide of secularism and assimilation were confined, however, to educational activities by and for men. It was his son and successor, R. Joseph Isaac Schneersohn, who drew the logical conclusion from his father's diagnosis of the malaise and prescribed a more directly effective remedy, harnessing women to positive action for the preservation of traditional Judaism. During his visit in the USA in 1929–30, where he was particularly struck by the complete estrangement of the younger generation of Russian Jews from all aspects of religious observance (see for example his letter from Baltimore, *Iggerot Kodesh . . . Joseph Isaac*, vol. 2, Brooklyn, 1982, pp. 225–7), he set up what became eventually a whole network of 'Women's Associations for the Purity of the Family', spreading information in Hebrew, Yiddish and English about the laws of ritual purity, encouraging women to teach others how to observe these laws meticulously, as well as providing the facilities for this (see *ibid.*, editor's introduction, pp. 20–2, and pp. 224, 252). When he returned from America and settled for three years in Riga, he visited his followers in Lithuania and founded similar women's associations there, of which the first was in the town of Roskiskis (see *ibid.*, p. 332). He repeatedly invited women to take the initiative in founding these associations (see for example, *ibid.*, vol. 4, Brooklyn, 1983, pp. 12–13). In the same letter from Otwock, written in 1936 to the Habad community in the Holy Land, he wrote: 'It is the duty of the wives and daughters of the Hasidim, may they live, to stand in the forefront of any enterprise for the strengthening of religion and Judaism in general, and in particular with regard to the purity of the family. This is an area which they must take entirely upon themselves, in order to establish the foundations of the purity of the daughters of Israel. Naturally, the men, the communities in general and all their institutions must help them in whatever they require, but the entire area of family purity is the responsibility of the women. It is up to them to establish and sustain it in such a way that one woman alert another, the other yet another woman and all the women should in turn alert their husbands, sons and daughters . . . ' (p. 13). The same letter makes it quite clear that while he was not displeased with the initiation of women to a certain level of the the teachings of Hasidism as such, so long as this was carefully supervised by their fathers or husbands, he was primarily interested in their contribution to the campaign for the reinforcement of orthodox Jewish practice in general, and specifically in those areas where their influence as women could be most direct. Notably, this type of direct appeal to women, to maintain 'the purity of the family' against the current of relaxation of strict orthodox practice and secularization was not unique to Habad. During the same period similar initiatives directed at women were being taken by orthodox and *Aggudat Yisra'el* circles generally. In the winter of 1930, for example, R. Israel Me-ir ha-Kohen, the *Hafets Hayim*, delivered a sermon on this subject to an exclusively female audience in the Great Synagogue of Vilna, from which all the men had been barred for the occasion (although apparently some men gathered in the women's gallery). This was an unprecedented event, as the *Hafets Hayim* himself observed in his sermon (see on this, M. M. Yoshor, *He-Hafets Hayim, Hayav u-Pho'olo*), vol. 2, Tel Aviv, 1959, pp. 506–12. After his installation in the USA in 1940, the Admor Joseph Isaac Schneersohn founded various other women's organizations, and his son-in-law and successor, R. Menachem Mendel Schneerson, continues in the same direction. He has founded the Lubavitch Women's Organization, and generated a vast literature for women as well as numerous frameworks for women's activism all over the world (for a sample of these see note 83 below).

83 Habad publications for and by women invariably feature the traditional areas of Jewish female responsibility: the three [time-bound] commandments which apply specifically to women, modesty, maternal responsibilities and the creation of a proper Jewish atmosphere in the home. Aggressively appealing to women outside the Orthodox sector of Judaism, who have inevitably become exposed to the modern feminist critique of 'patriarchy' in both its religious and secular manifestations, they are quite ingenious in appropriating feminist concens and terminology, and exploiting precisely those areas of overlap between the female separatism of some of the more extreme feminists and the traditional separation of the sexes as practised in the strictest possible way within Habad. A discussion of the periodical abstinence from conjugal relations arising from the ritual impurity of women during and after menstruation—a feature of Orthodox Judaism which has been particularly offensive to modern Jewish feministsOcan thus be entitled '"Space" For Myself' (see Yehudis Groner, in Raizel Schnall Friedfertig and Freyda Shapiro, eds., *The Modern Jewish Woman—A Unique Perspective*, Brooklyn, 1981, pp. 59–60); and the traditional women's festival of Rosh Khodesh (New Moon) is re-invigorated in much the same way as this has been done by some Jewish feminist groups attempting to create a new 'spirituality' for women outside the conventional Orthodox framework (see R. Menachem Mendel Schneerson—the present leader of Habad—*Letters by the Lubavitcher Rebbe . . . to N'shei uBnos Chabad 1956–1980*, Brooklyn, 1981, pp. 31–2 of the English text, 28–9 of the Yiddish). In addition to these works, see, for example, the Lubavitch Foundation of Great Britain, *A Woman of Valour—An Anthology for the Thinking Jewess* (London, 1976); Lubavitch Women's Organization, *Aura—A reader on Jewish Womanhood* (New YHork, 1984); id., *The Gift* (on the Sabbath, which has a particular relation to women) (New York, 1985); M. M. Schneerson, *Equal Rights* (a pamphlet which contains an adaptation and translation into English of 'an address given bythe Lubavitcher Rebbe Shlita on the sixth of Tishrei 5745, the 20th Yartzeit of Rebbetzin Chana, the Rebbe's mother'), published and distributed in late 1984. There are numerous additional books, pamphlets and journals for women in the same vein.

7

JEWISH SOCIALISM

Rosa Luxemburg, Leo Jogiches and the Jewish Labour Movement, 1893–1903

Robert S. Wistrich

THE purpose of this article is to re-examine a neglected aspect of Rosa Luxemburg's intellectual and political legacy, namely the attitude which she and Leo Jogiches, her closest associate in the SDKPiL (Social Democracy of the Kingdom of Poland and Lithuania), adopted towards the Jewish national problem in Eastern Europe. We shall seek in particular to elucidate the evolution of their positions towards the emerging Jewish labour movement in the decade between 1893 and 1903, undoubtedly the crucial period in crystallizing the reciprocal relations between the SDKPiL, the PPS and the Bund. The complex triangular relationship between these three workers' parties in Eastern Europe has an intrinsic importance in the history of Polish socialism before 1914, as well as an indirect bearing on the development of Russian Social Democracy. At the same time, the growing differences between Luxemburg's SDKPiL and the Bund were typical of the rift between the assimilated Jewish Marxist intelligentsia (which dominated the leadership of the SDKPiL) and the Jewish masses in Eastern Europe, who had preserved many of their national characteristics.[1]

Rosa Luxemburg (1871–1919), born in Zamość in Russian Poland (the birthplace of the famous Yiddish poet Y. L. Peretz), was the daughter of assimilated Jewish middle-class parents. There is no evidence that any of her immediate family took an active interest in Jewish affairs, and Polish rather than Yiddish was the language of the Luxemburg household. Her father, Eliasz, a timber merchant with a definite sympathy for Polish national-revolutionary aspirations, moved with the family to Warsaw when Rosa Luxemburg was three years old. Here she was able to enter an exclusive High School for Girls, reserved for the children of Tsarist officers and officials, to which few Poles, let alone Jews, were admitted. Rosa's mother (*née* Line Löwenstein) was a cultivated woman with a passion for classic Polish and German literature, which she inculcated in her daughter, and also a more traditional reverence for the Bible. It is highly possible that her mother's love of the Bible derived from the fact that she was the daughter as well as the sister of rabbis.[2] The Löwenstein family tree reveals indeed an impressive line of rabbinical ancestors, including the talmudic commentator and eighteenth-century *maskil*, Rabbi Yaakov Yehoshua Falk.[3]

Rosa Luxemburg, like Karl Marx, never made any public or private references to her rabbinical ancestry and it appears to have escaped the attention of her various biographers. However, she did mention in one of her prison letters that her mother regarded Schiller and the Bible as 'the supreme sources of wisdom' and fervently believed that King Solomon 'understood the language of birds'. With all the adolescent superiority of a clever fourteen-year-old girl, trained in the natural sciences, Rosa Luxemburg attributed this belief to her mother's 'simplicity', but, as she later pointed out with touching self-irony, she too had learnt to 'understand the language of birds and beasts' during her wartime incarceration in a German prison.[4]

Rosa Luxemburg became involved in the Polish socialist movement, Proletariat, while still at high school in Warsaw. This led to her surveillance by the Tsarist police and her subsequent flight from Poland to Zurich in 1889. It was here in 1893 that she founded, together with Julian Marchlewski, Adolf Warski and Leo Jogiches, the SDKP (Social Democracy of the Kingdom of Poland).[5] With the exception of Marchlewski, who came from a patrician background, the nucleus of the SDKP leadership (Warski, Jogiches and Luxemburg) were all from assimilated Jewish families.[6] There was nothing particularly suprising in this, for the Jewish urban intelligentsia, along with members of the ruined nobility and petty gentry, formed the élite of the Polish socialist leadership by the 1890s. In the ranks of the nationalistic Polish Socialist Party (PPS), founded in Paris in 1892, Jews like Stanisław Mendelsohn, Feliks Perl, Herman Diamand and Herman Lieberman were also to play a very prominent role.

The SDKP had originally set itself up as a breakaway splinter-group which opposed the main platform of the PPS, the restoration of Polish independence as a prerequisite for achieving the social emancipation of the Polish working class. The PPS from the outset asserted its all-Polish character and worked for the unification of the socialist movements in Russian, Prussian and Austrian Poland. It aimed to harness the emotional patriotism of the Polish masses for its programme of national self-determination and the establishment of an independent, democratic Polish republic. The SDKP, on the other hand, as its name implied,[7] restricted its activities to Russian Poland and stigmatized the aim of Polish independence as a Utopian and reactionary goal. At most it favoured territorial cultural-national autonomy for Poland in the framework of a democratic all-Russian constitution.

In her doctoral dissertation, published under the title *Die industrielle Entwicklung Polens* (1898), Rosa Luxemburg had buttressed her opposition to Polish independence with economic arguments, suggesting that the Kingdom of Poland was dependent on Russian markets and that its 'organic incorporation' into the Russian State was in the interests of the Polish working class. The Luxemburg group (like the first socialist mass party in Poland organized by Ludwik Waryński in the 1880s) emphasized the need for common action with the Russian revolutionaries and asserted the primacy of international social revolution over national interests. It was in this context that the SDKP first sought to define its attitude to the emerging Jewish labour movement in the Tsarist Empire. The origins of this movement were in Vilna,[8] although subsequently, under the aegis of the Bund, it was able to spread its influence to the Ukraine and Russian Poland, especially Warsaw and Łódź. Like the older Polish workers' movement, which to a certain degree influenced its development, the specifically Jewish labour movement had emerged as a result of growing industrialization in the Russian Empire, the impact of Marxist ideology, and the gradual secularization of Jewish life.[9] It also had certain specific features which resulted from its isolation in the Pale of Settlement and the peculiar demographic and socio-economic characteristics of the Jewish population in the Russian Empire.

In Vilna, the cradle of Jewish socialism, the mass of oppressed Jewish workers and craftsmen did not speak Russian or Polish. In the late 1880s an attempt had been made to overcome the gulf between Jewish and non-Jewish workers by the establishment of socialist circles (*kruzhki*) in which the workers were taught Russian literature, economics and natural sciences. The aim was to produce cadres for the Russian revolutionary movement, but the 'circles' failed to achieve a mass impact comparable to that of the Polish workers' movement in the region. Leo Jogiches (1867–1919), himself a 'Russified' Jew from Vilna and the son of wealthy parents, had been involved in the activities of the 'circles' before his exile to Switzerland.[10] His links with the Jewish labour leaders in Vilna continued after his forced expulsion from Tsarist Poland. Co-founder of the SDKP and Rosa Luxemburg's closest comrade, Jogiches followed the emerging Jewish workers' movement in the 1890s with careful attention and some sympathy.

In 1893 he published as a brochure the *Four Speeches of Jewish Workers* made in Russian and Yiddish at a May Day rally in Vilna. The brochure appeared in Geneva with an introduction by Boris Kritchevsky. It was almost certainly edited by Rosa Luxemburg.[11] Both Leo Jogiches and Luxemburg, whose ideas are virtually impossible to separate at this time, clearly regarded the speeches as an important manifestation of Jewish working-class solidarity with the ideals of the international socialist movement. It is therefore worth looking in some detail at the article which Jogiches wrote in January 1894 for *Sprawa Robotnicza* (the organ of the SDKP edited by Rosa Luxemburg) about the Vilna speeches.[12] 'In moving words, full of feeling and in the picturesque form characteristic of the Yiddish language, the poor, persecuted Jewish proletarians paint their working-class situation and express their aims and aspirations.' Approvingly, Jogiches then quotes a Jewish worker denouncing the common yoke of capital which oppresses his brethren as much as the proletarians of other nationalities. There was no question, Jogiches pointed out, but that Russian Jewry was subjected to particular oppression by the Tsarist despotism. 'Jews are the most deprived of rights and the most enslaved of all the subjects of the Tsar.' 'Laws exist,' he added, 'which do not permit the Jews entry to a whole range of occupations, which limit their numbers in schools, forbid them to acquire property, etc. We shall not discuss that; although the laws themselves merit condemnation, they do not touch the Jewish proletariat much. But the greatest onus of persecution falls as usual on the backs of the poor working people.'[13]

It was 'the poor, defenceless Jewish proletarian' not the wealthy Jews (who could bribe officials to ensure their protection) who received the worst blows. Moreover, the Tsarist autocracy since the pogroms of 1881 had unscrupulously used the Jews as a scapegoat for the discontent of other subject nationalities. The most recent example had been the anti-Jewish pogrom organized by the Tsarist police in Łódź as a pretext for bloodily repressing the strikes and demonstrations by Polish workers.[14] The SDKP in its paper *Sprawa Robotnicza* had praised the Polish workers of Łódź for refusing to become the accomplices of the Tsarist autocracy by participating in the pogrom.

> You have shown the whole world that for you a Jew or a German does not exist, that you know your enemies well, the capitalists of all faiths and nationalities—that a Jew like Poznanski or a German like Scheibler are your deadly enemies, but that the poor Jewish tinker or German textile worker are your comrades in misery and oppression.[15]

In a report from Warsaw (July/August 1893) the SDKP organ again noted that

> at a time when violent anti-Semitism is raging in bourgeois intellectual circles, the workers are once more demonstrating as they did last May in Łódź, by courageous actions, that they understand the meaning of class solidarity with the Jewish proletariat and that no prejudices of racial hatred exist for them.[16]

It is important to bear this background in mind, for it helps to explain Leo Jogiches' emphasis on the readiness of the Jewish workers in Vilna to rise above the special anti-Jewish persecution to which they were subjected. Rosa Luxemburg, Jogiches and Warski understood that Jewish workers could scarcely become convinced of their common class interests with the Polish and Russian proletariat unless they had complete confidence in the ability of the latter to resist anti-Semitism. This preoccupation becomes clear in Jogiches' commentary on the Vilna speeches, and it also explains the opposition of the SDKP to Zionism.

> The yoke which they perpetually bear as Jews could conceal from them the yoke which they suffer as workers. In a word, they could fall into a trap and perceive their chief enemies as foreign nationalities rather than the capitalist class and the Tsarist regime.

This might occur the more easily since a 'patriotic' movement had arisen among Russian Jews during the past decade under the influence of the Hovevei Zion circles, which were particularly active in Vilna. Jogiches referred in some detail to the polemics of the Jewish workers against this 'Palestinian' movement, as it was then called.

> The ancestors of Jewry, say the leaders of the Palestinian movement, once lived in Palestine and had their own independent State. In order to free ourselves from the persecution of the Russian government and society, we should build up our own independent Jewish State—let us go out to Palestine, let us buy land and arrange things to suit ourselves.[17]

The 'Palestinophiles' had told the Jewish workers that only in their own country could they become masters of their own fate and live in freedom and material contentment. If the Jewish workers had been won over to this programme, Jogiches observed, then

> the Jewish proletariat would dissociate itself from all the Polish and Russian workers. Instead of the class standpoint, it would adopt a nationalistic one and following Jewish patriotism arrive at hatred for other nationalities. The Jewish worker would hate his brothers—the Polish and Russian workers— he would feel solidarity with every Jew, even if he were a capitalist, his enemy and exploiter.[18]

It is evident from this chain of reasoning that Jogiches and the SDKP leaders considered any form of Jewish ethnic solidarity as inimical to international proletarian brotherhood. This was their fundamental objection to Zionism, even before it had been given a precise political formulation by Theodor Herzl. Jogiches noted with satisfaction that the Vilna workers did not appear to have been seduced by the nationalist programme of the 'Palestinophiles'. With approval he quoted the argument of the Vilna speakers that they would encounter in Palestine the same social system based on exploitation as in the Russian Pale, and that socialism could only be built by proletarian struggle against both Russian and Jewish capitalists.

> And so our comrades understand that the rebuilding of their own State will not destroy capitalism, that the working people will continue to be the exploited and persecuted class, that freedom to use their own language will neither feed nor clothe them. As for political freedom, which is indispensable for the improvement of the workers' welfare and for the struggle against capitalism, the Jewish comrades also understand clearly that this, not the rebuilding of a utopian Jewish State, is their goal.[19]

Political freedom could only be achieved according to the Luxemburgist view (and this was also the line later adopted by the Jewish Bund) through a common struggle by all the nationalities of the Russian Empire against Tsarist autocracy. The fact that Jewish workers in Vilna, 'notwithstanding all the national persecution and despite the patriotic agitation', had none the less been able to adopt a consistent class standpoint was therefore a matter of considerable importance to Jogiches, Luxemburg and the SDKP. It was concrete evidence, Jogiches remarked, of 'how fertile the soil in the Russian State has become for socialistic agitation, and this fills us with confidence as regards its further development in the workers' movement'. Even if the 'Palestinophile' movement which 'recruits its few adherents chiefly among the petty bourgeoisie and a certain part of the intelligentsia' became a movement of 'social-patriotic' flavour, Jogiches and Luxemburg were sure that 'our comrades will certainly give a sharp retort'. The class solidarity of the international proletariat 'will be the answer of our Jewish comrades if the Jewish patriots would want to combine the socialist movement among their co-religionists with national aspirations'.[20] On this common platform of opposition to Jewish nationalism the SDKP welcomed the Vilna workers as 'new comrades' to the 'international family of the proletariat' and to the struggle against Tsarist absolutism.

Leo Jogiches, Rosa Luxemburg and the future leaders of the Bund (established in 1897) shared a common belief in the need for united mass action by the Russian, Polish and Jewish proletariat. This attitude contrasted sharply with that of the PPS, which jealously guarded its independence from the Russian Social Democracy and regarded the non-Russian nationalities as its closest allies. At a time when Jogiches was welcoming Jewish workers as 'new comrades' of the Polish and Russian proletariat, Josef Pilsudski, the leader of the PPS, was seeking to win them away from 'Russian' influence. Pilsudski, in his appeal to

Jewish social democrats in 1893, depicted anti-Semitism as a product of alien Russian domination and recalled the historic friendship between Poles and Jews. At the same time (and this complaint was constantly echoed in PPS literature before 1914) he reproached Jewish socialists for their indifference to Polish independence and their use of the Russian language.[21]

The PPS was opposed from the outset to the creation of a specifically Jewish organization to protect the interests of the Jewish proletariat. It made considerable efforts to win over Jewish workers in the 1890s by sponsoring propagandist literature in Yiddish, founding a Jewish section in its own party and even published Jewish newspapers (especially in Austrian-ruled Galicia). But the PPS insisted on the outright assimilation of Jewish workers to the Polish culture and their support for the Polish national cause. The cosmopolitan SDKPiL rejected any form of Polish chauvinism, although it too favoured linguistic and cultural assimilation as part of its Marxist internationalism. However, the SDKP, unlike the PPS, did not regard the emergence of the Jewish Bund in 1897 as a serious threat to its own position within the general workers' movement on Polish soil. The numerically large Jewish proletariat, including factory workers and weavers in Łódź and Warsaw as well as craftsmen and pedlars, constituted an important social stratum in Russian Poland and Lithuania. This fact was well known to the PPS, which now found itself competing with the Bund as well as SDKPiL for their support. It was particularly angered by the Russian orientation which the Bund shared with the SDKPiL (in 1898 the Bund had become a constituent member of the all-Russian Social Democratic Party, which it helped bring into existence). Significantly, at its Fourth Congress the PPS attacked the policy of the Bund as lacking solidarity 'with the Polish and Lithuanian proletariat in the struggle for liberation from the Russian yoke'.[22] This was not an accusation that either Rosa Luxemburg or Leo Jogiches would have levelled at the Bund, although like the PPS they sharply disapproved of its 'separatist' tendencies as contributing to divisions in the international proletarian movement.

The Bund, for its part, responded at its Third Congress in 1899 by refusing support for an independent Poland and accused the PPS of seeking to 'weaken its independence and undermine its existence'.[23] The *Yidishe Arbeter* even published at this time an article by Rosa Luxemburg against the PPS, though it was fully aware that she was critical of its own separatism.[24] Still more significant, the Bund at its Fourth Congress envisaged a federal link with the SDKPiL, something that would have been inconceivable with the PPS. John Mill, one of the leaders of the Bund who enjoyed close contacts with Leo Jogiches and

Rosa Luxemburg, summarized in his memoirs the reasons for the Bund's negative attitude to the PPS:

> We, who looked upon the common struggle of all socialist and revolutionary organizations against Tsarism as the most important task . . . could not accept the distrust of the Russian socialists by the PPS, its unfounded doubts concerning the possibility of revolution in Russia, its chauvinist language.[25]

The Bund, like Rosa Luxemburg, Jogiches and the leaders of the SDKPiL, believed that the liberation of the Jewish masses would come not through Polish independence but as a result of the victory of socialist revolution in both Russia and Poland. This was the primary reason why both the Bund and the SDKPiL sought a federal link with the Russian Social Democratic Party to achieve these ends.

The SDKPiL was critical of the way in which the PPS treated the 'Jewish question', especially at its Sixth Congress in 1902. A month later, an editorial in the leading theoretical review of the SDKPiL, *Przegląd Socjaldemokratyczny*, expressed a sympathetic attitude to the Bund. It argued that this 'fraternal organization' was a valuable ally in the struggle to awaken the class consciousness of Jewish workers and defended a common cause. Through the class struggle waged by the Bund, the Jewish proletariat was becoming more aware of its common interests with the Polish proletariat. In that sense the Bund was performing an indispensable integrative function and the fact that 'this assimilation must express itself in Yiddish changes nothing'.[26] The editorial observed: 'Without the Bund the Polish proletariat would not have such a valuable partner in the struggle as it now possesses in the Jewish proletariat.' At the same time the SDKPiL, while recognizing the Bund as an 'independent fraternal organization' and the 'sole class organization of the proletariat', did not share its viewpoint on certain issues. This included the crucial question of whether the Russian Empire should be transformed into a federation of nationalities—a position which led to the rift between the Bund and the Bolshevik faction of the Russian Social Democratic Party led by Lenin. There was also a significant difference between the position of the SDKPiL and the Bund on the Jewish national problem. An indication of this difference had already appeared in Leo Jogiches' comments on the Vilna speeches (1893), made at a time when the national programme of the Jewish labour movement had not yet crystallized. Jogiches omitted any mention of the fact that the Vilna speakers had also claimed that they were fighting for their nation as well as mankind.[27] The Vilna speeches had included certain references to the history of the Jews as constituting a history of glorious martyrdom, and emphasized that there was no shame in belonging to the Jewish race. By the late 1890s the national component in the Jewish workers' movement was slowly beginning to emerge. Julius Martov, the future leader of Russian Menshevism, in a famous speech in May 1895 that has often been seen as the founding charter of Bundism, even described the national 'indifference' of the Jewish masses as a hindrance to the awakening of their class consciousness.[28] Martov urged the need to stamp a definite 'Jewish' character on the movement and to create a specifically Jewish socialist organization. The Jewish proletariat had a national as well as a social role in the struggle for obtaining equal rights for Russian Jewry. It could no more rely on the Russian and Polish proletariat than it could on the Jewish bourgeoisie to secure the national rights of the Jewish masses.

By 1901, at its Fourth Congress, the Bund had recognized that the concept of 'nationality' applied to the Jews of the Russian Empire and protested against the 'oppression of the Jewish nation', although it hesitated to define a clear national programme, for fear that this might dilute the class consciousness of Jewish workers. By 1903 the Bund had even incorporated the demand for Jewish cultural-national autonomy into its programme. Though hesitant and often torn between particularism and a more universalist socialist stance, the Bund after 1900 felt obliged to revise its negative position on Jewish nationality in the face of Zionist rivalry from within and Polish and Russian socialist pressures for assimilation from without. This development inevitably brought it on to a collision course with the radically assimilationist Jewish Marxist intelligentsia in the Russian and Polish revolutionary movements.[29]

The SDKPiL (like the German, Austrian and Russian Social Democrats) appreciated the services of the Bund in so far as it opposed traditional Judaism, Hebrew culture and above all Zionism. It was even sympathetic to the Bund in so far as it was subjected to PPS attackers for its alleged role as an agent of 'Russification'. It consistently praised the contribution of the Bund to fostering class consciousness among Jewish workers. But it could not abide the Bund's increasing cultivation of Yiddish culture, its desire to maintain Jewish ethnic identity and a separate organization—above all its championing of Jewish proletarian nationalism in the name of socialist ideals.

The SDKPiL wished on the contrary to make Polish Jewry less separatist in its way of life, to bring about a gradual assimilation of Jewish workers to the Polish proletariat. This programme clearly entailed the abandonment of Jewish customs and national festivals and the adoption of the Polish language and culture. On the issue of assimilation the Luxemburgists differed from the PPS in that they advocated an internationalist rather than a national form of integration—an approach more consistent with the Marxist premise that, under socialism, all forms of national differentiation (which was a by-product of capitalist class antagonisms) would eventually disappear. In this respect, the positions held by Luxemburg, Jogiches or Warski were close enough to the orthodox German and Russian Marxists. Significantly, in 1903, when the SDKPiL was seeking a rapprochement with the RSDRP (Russian Social Democratic Workers' Party), it began to indict the Bund for its 'separatism', though its polemics were less strident in tone. The Bund was duly criticized for failing to see that the closest unity of the proletariat of all nationalities in the Russian Empire must be the priority goal.

Although Rosa Luxemburg disagreed with Lenin's ultra-centralist, monolithic concept of party organization, and negotiations for a merger with RSDRP broke down over Bolshevik insistence on the principle of national self-determination,[30] the SDKPiL began to criticize 'Bundist nationalism' in terms not dissimilar from Lenin's. It had never been willing to recognize the Jews as a separate national group, although the issue had not come to a head before 1903. Rosa Luxemburg would certainly have agreed with Lenin's assessment in February 1903 that the autonomy provided under the rules establishing the Russian Social Democratic Party in 1898 gave the Jewish working class all it needed:

> propaganda and agitation in Yiddish, its own literature and congresses, the right to advance separate demands, to supplement a single general Social-Democratic programme and to satisfy local needs and requirements arising out of the special feature of Jewish life. In everything else there must be complete fusion with the Russian proletariat, in the interests of the struggle waged by the entire proletariat of Russia.[31]

Rosa Luxemburg certainly agreed with Lenin's condemnation of the Bund for seeking the 'complete separation and demarcation of the Jewish and non-Jewish proletariat of Russia', a policy which the Polish Social Democrats also considered would ultimately lead to division and dismemberment of the working-class movement. As Lenin, Martov and Trotsky argued at the 1903 Congress of the RSDRP, the Bund's separatism implied a suspicion that the Social-Democratic convictions of the Russian party were not completely sincere and consistent. There was, however, an inconsistency in the fact that Rosa Luxemburg and the SDKPiL went along with these Russian criticisms and were prepared to advocate the Bund's complete subordination to the centralized control of the Russian party. For one of the chief reasons that the SDKPiL itself refused to merge with the RSDRP was that its Polish-Jewish élite disliked the hierarchical structure and rigid discipline which Lenin sought to impose upon the all-Russian party.[32] This paradox can perhaps be explained by the fact that Rosa Luxemburg, one of the sternest critics of Lenin's bureaucratic ultra-centralism in organizational matters, was even more centralist than the Bolshevik leader with regard to the national problem.

But in the Polish context the organizational issue which lay at the heart of Lenin's increasingly violent polemics against the Bund was far less acute. Moreover, the attitude of the SDKPiL was modified by its remorseless antagonism to the PPS chauvinism in respect of which the Bund was still a potential ally.[33] Thus Rosa Luxemburg could afford to adopt a position of benevolent neutrality vis-à-vis the Jewish labour movement when it accused the PPS of inflaming anti-Semitism among Polish workers. The PPS resented the influx of Lithuanian Jews, 'Litvaks', into the Kingdom of Poland and the extension of the Bund's influence among Jewish craftsmen, apprentices and workers in Warsaw and Łódź. It continued to consider the Bund as an agent of 'Russification' and even accused it of being a tool of the Jewish bourgeoisie and of the Tsar. Rosa Luxemburg sympathized with the Bund's indignation at these charges,[34] the more so as similar accusations had been flung by PPS leaders against her own party. In reviewing a Bund pamphlet against the PPS in April 1903, she pointed out that the Bund's defensive nationalism was simply the reverse side of the aggressive chauvinism espoused by the PPS. She warned that it was in the nature of every nationalism, whether bourgeois or socialist, to adopt an exclusivist or hegemonic attitude to minorities in its midst.

Rosa Luxemburg was none the less critical of the Bund's self-assertiveness as a specifically Jewish organization which claimed to defend the national rights of Jewish workers as well as their class interests. She could not accept that the cultural and linguistic peculiarities of the Jewish proletariat or its special 'national psychology' justified the separatist approach of the Bund. In particular, she opposed the Bund's position that there was a need to defend the national rights of Russian Jewry if it was to achieve full civic equality. The achievement of civil rights was an issue affecting the Russian and Polish proletariat no less than the Jewish workers, and it was therefore an integral part of the programme of the RSDRP and the SDKPiL. Hence with the abolition of the Pale of Settlement and the establishment of a democratic Russian republic, the raison d'être of an organization like the Bund would disappear.[35] Its only real justification in the present situation was in the sphere of local agitation and propaganda among the Jewish masses in the Yiddish language, an area in which the Bund had, according to Rosa Luxemburg, achieved 'excellent results'.

Rosa Luxemburg's standpoint was echoed by her close associate Adolf Warski (a future leader of the Polish Communist Party) in a letter written in June 1903 to Karl Kautsky, then the leading theoretician of the German Social Democrats. In this previously unpublished letter, Warski urgently requested Kautsky to write an article for the SDKPiL theoretical organ, *Przegląd Socjaldemokratyczny* (Social Democratic Review) on anti-Semitism and the tasks of Social Democracy, 'in the wake of the recent dreadful massacre in Kishinev'.[36] The SDKPiL feared that the latest pogroms instigated by the Tsarist autocracy might divert the Polish and Russian workers away from the revolutionary movement and incite them against the Jewish population. Russian anti-Semitism had caused an influx of 'Litvaks' into Russian Poland and thereby aroused nationalistic feelings against the alien immigrants. 'The issue has even greater significance for Polish social democracy because the bulk of the Jewish population lives in Russian Poland and Lithuania, as a result of laws which forbid them to settle in other parts of Russia.'[37] The Kishinev pogroms, Warski pointed out, also had the effect of reinforcing the separatist tendencies among Jewish workers and especially the national programme of the Bund.

> The 'Bund' has, for example, created a superior organization, thereby bringing much enlightenment and still more revolutionary enthusiasm to the Jewish working class, by means of Yiddish (*Jargon*) and its knowledge of Jewish life in general. But at the same time, ever more nationalistically inclined, the 'Bund' increasingly demonstrated the tendency towards separate party organization and the separatist removal of the Jewish working masses from the working class as a whole in the Empire and its provinces.[38]

The SDKPiL leaders were obviously concerned about the impact of this trend on the united proletarian front against Tsarism. 'Now we fear that the recent pogroms will drive the Bund further in the same separatist direction, thanks to its theoretical confusion, though it is more than ever necessary to bind the Jewish working masses firmly to the Russian and Polish [proletariat].' Warski informed Karl Kautsky that the SDKPiL had issued a proclamation to the Polish workers after the Kishinev massacre, denouncing Tsarist anti-Semitism and calling on them 'to defend the Jewish population'. But this appeal was made more difficult by the Bund's insistence that it alone could defend the national interests of Jewish workers.

> Recently we have got to the point (as have our Russian comrades) that in every town we have two party organizations—Polish (or Russian) and national-Jewish—which can only complicate the tasks of social democracy with respect to anti-Semitism. Quite apart from the question of whether the Jews are really a nation and have a national future in Russia—as the Bund asserts—the problem of party organizations and the relation of the Jewish

workers to the working class as a whole—must be solved according to common interests—and not according to burning national interests.[39]

Kautsky responded to the appeals of Warski and Rosa Luxemburg by writing his important article 'The Kishinev massacre and the Jewish Question', which he published in the *Neue Zeit* (the leading German Marxist journal) in 1903.[40] It was also published in *Przegląd Socjaldemo-kratyczny* and in Lenin's *Iskra* and became the classic statement of the Marxist assimilationist position on the Jewish problem before 1914. Kautsky's immense prestige as the guardian of German Marxist orthodoxy assured his views an immediate influence. Although he did not mention the Bund in the course of the article (his polemic was primarily directed against the Tsarist autocracy and the diversionary role of Zionism), the implications of his line of argument could be turned against it. Both the Russian and Polish Social Democrats interpreted Kautsky's article as clear disapproval of any separatist tendencies in the Jewish community and in favour of a united proletarian front against Tsarism. In a letter to Kautsky, Rosa Luxemburg reported with satisfaction that Warski was 'highly delighted' with his Kishinev article.[41]

This was scarcely suprising considering Kautsky's main thesis: that the segregation of the Jewish masses in the ghetto was the cause of Russian anti-Semitism. As long as the Russian (and Polish) Jews retained their 'alien' national characteristics they would remain the easiest and most natural scapegoats of the Tsarist regime. The only solution to this condition lay in the most rapid assimilation of the Jewish masses with the neighbouring peoples through participation in the common revolutionary struggle. Anything that retarded the fusion of Jewish and non-Jewish workers in the socialist movement was to be condemned—a viewpoint that could be turned (as it was by Lenin, Trotsky and Stalin) against the Bund as much as the Zionists.

Although Rosa Luxemburg never drew the crude parallel between Bundism and Zionism as twin forms of 'Jewish separatism', made by Plekhanov, Trotsky and Lenin, she undoubtedy shared the central Marxist premise that assimilation was the only 'progressive' solution to the Jewish national problem in Eastern Europe. In her view and that of the SDKPiL, any concessions to nationalism could only delay the advent of socialism and retard the class struggle. Anti-Semitism was not a specifically 'Jewish problem', necessitating a special struggle, but one of a whole range of social problems created by capitalist society and the manoeuvres of the counter-revolution.[42] As she put it in a polemic against the so-called 'progressive' Polish intelligentsia in Warsaw, written in 1910:

... for the followers of Marx, as for the working class, *the Jewish question as such does not exist*, just as the 'Negro question' or the 'Yellow Peril' does not exist. From the standpoint of the working class, the Jewish question ... is a question of *racial hatred as a symptom* of social *reaction*, which to a certain extent is an indivisible part of all societies based on class antagonism.[43]

In other words, the radical transformation of the capitalist system through socialist revolution would automatically solve the 'Jewish question', a position to which the Bund theoretically also adhered, though its practical policy was more ambiguous.

Where Rosa Luxemburg continued to differ from the Bund was over its growing insistence on regarding the Jews as a distinct national entity with a right to full cultural autonomy. In this respect her position was not substantially different from that of Kautsky, Otto Bauer or Lenin although, for reasons which we have already suggested (notably her intransigent opposition to the PPS), it was less forcefully expressed. Referring in 1910 to an SDKPiL polemic against the Bundist theoretician Bronisław Grosser, Rosa Luxemburg made it clear that she considered the long-term prospects for an independent Jewish culture in Poland to be hopeless:

The separateness of the Jewish nationality is based in Russia and Poland on the socially backward petty-bourgeois small-scale production, on petty commerce, life in small towns and close links with the religious element. As a consequence, the separate Jewish consciousness which is supposed to be the basis of extra-territorial Jewish autonomy displays itself not through a separate bourgeois metropolitan culture—but through small-town lack of culture. All the efforts to develop a Jewish culture through the initiative of a number of Yiddish publicists and translators are futile.

For Rosa Luxemburg and most of the Jewish Marxist intelligentsia from Russia and Poland the only culture worth fighting for was not that of the bourgeois past or present but the 'proletarian' internationalist culture of the socialist millennium. As she put it in a famous letter of 1917 to Mathilde Wurm, there was no special corner in her heart for the sufferings of the ghetto. In her eyes the Bund, whatever its merits in heightening the class consciousness of Jewish workers, was guilty, like the Zionists, of seeking to perpetuate this ghetto, and hence its objectives had to be resolutely opposed.

Notes

1 On this theme see R. S. Wistrich, *Revolutionary Jews from Marx to Trotsky* (London and New York, 1976), and the massive study by J. Frankel, *Prophecy and Politics. Socialism, Nationalism and the Russian Jews 1862–1917* (Cambridge, 1981).

2 See A. Bick (Shauli), *Me-rosh tsurim. Metaknei hevra al taharat ha-kodesh shalshelet ha-yihusin shel avot ha-sotsialism* (Jerusalem, 1972), pp. 76–90 for Rosa Luxemburg's family tree and rabbinical ancestry on her mother's side.

3 *ibid.* For some interesting observations on Luxemburg's Jewishness see H. Arendt, 'Rosa Luxemburg 1871–1919' in *Men in Dark Times* (London, 1973), pp. 39–61.

4 Bick (note 2 above)

5 In December 1899, the SDKP (the self-styled vanguard of a virtually non-existent mass movement) was strengthened by the adhesion of the Union of Polish Workers in Lithuania founded by Stanisław Trusiewicz (Zalewski). Henceforth it became known as the SDKPiL (Social Democracy of the Kingdom of Poland and Lithuania). Zalewski's influence was considerable and eventually drew the rank and file of the party away from the more dogmatic Luxemburgist position on the national problem. See also O. B. Schmidt (ed.), *Socjaldemokracja Królestwa Polskiego i Litwy: materiały i dokumenty 1893–1904* (Moscow, 1934), vol. 1, pp. 177–88, 195 ff.

6 Both Warski and Marchlewski had previously been active in the Union of Polish Workers which became defunct in 1892–3. See Schmidt (note 5 above), pp. vi–vii.

7 M. K. Dziewanowski, *The Communist Party of Poland* (Cambridge, Mass., 1959), p. 23. 'The very name was, to a certain extent, a political platform.'

8 On the geographic and ethnic factors influencing the predominantly Lithuanian character of the Bund in its early history, see M. Mishkinsky, 'Regional Factors in the Formation of the Jewish Labour Movement in Czarist Russia', *YIVO Annual of Jewish Social Science*, vol. 14 (1969), pp. 27–52.

9 There is an extensive literature on the early Jewish labour movement in Russia. Among the more important works are A. L. Patkin, *The Origins of the Russian-Jewish Labour Movement* (London and Melbourne, 1947); M. Mishkinsky, 'Yesodot leumiim be-hitpathutah shel tnuat ha-poalim ha-yehudim be-rusia' (unpublished Ph.D. thesis, Hebrew University, 1965); B. K. Johnpoll, *The Politics of Futility. The Jewish Workers Bund of Poland 1917–1943* (New York, 1967); E. Mendelsohn, *Class Struggle in the Pale: The Formative Years of the Jewish Workers Movement in Tsarist Russia* (Cambridge, 1970); H. J. Tobias, *The Jewish Bund in Russia* (Stanford, 1978); Frankel, (note 1 above).

10 Mendelsohn (note 9 above), pp. 35, 40

11 *Pervoe maia, 1892. Chetyre rechi evreiskikh rabochikh* (Geneva, 1893), re-edited with parallel texts in Russian and Hebrew under the title *Arba'at ha-neumim shel poalim yehudim* (Jerusalem, 1967), introduction by M. Mishkinsky. I would like to thank Professor C. Abramsky for first drawing my attention to this re-edition.

12 See L. Jogichesa-Tsyszki, 'Nowi towarzysze', in H. Buczek and F. Tych (eds.), *Socjaldemokracja Królestwa Polskiego i Litwy. Materiały i Dokumenty*, vol. 1

1893–1903, (Warsaw, 1957), vol. 1, pp. 146–52. These passages from the Polish original, which I have translated, have not previously appeared in English.

13 *ibid*. p. 148

14 *ibid*. See also O. B. Schmidt (note 5 above), vol. 1, pp. 12–14.

15 *ibid*. p. 157. From a report entitled 'Święto I Maja 1892 Roku w Łodzi', *Sprawa Robotnicza* no. 38 (1894).

16 *ibid*. p. 44. From 'Korespondencje z kraju' (Warsaw), *Sprawa Robotnicza*, no. 16 (July/August 1893).

17 *ibid*. p. 149

18 *ibid*.

19 *ibid*. p. 150

20 *ibid*. p. 152

21 See *Przedświt* (May 1893), where Piłsudski appealed to the 'Jewish socialist comrades in the stolen Polish provinces', by which he meant the region that once belonged to the Grand Duchy of Lithuania.

22 *Robotnik*, nos. 5–6 (1894)

23 J. Bunzl, *Klassenkampf in der Diaspora. Zur Geschichte der judischen Arbeiterbewegung* (Vienna, 1975), p. 92.

24 *Yidishe Arbeter*, no. 8 (December 1899). The article, originally entitled 'Der Sozialismus in Polen', first appeared in the *Sozialistische Monatshefte* (December 1897). Its appearance in a Bund newspaper did not of course signify that Rosa Luxemburg's views on Polish independence were officially supported by the Bund leadership.

25 J. Mill, *Pioner un boyer* (New York, 1946), vol.1, pp. 116ff.

26 'W Kwestii żydowskiej', in *Socjaldemokracja Królewstwa Polskiego i Litwy: materiały i dokumenty*, vol. 2 (Warsaw, 1961), pp. 85–90. Taken from *Przegląd Socjaldemokratyczny*, no. 3 (July 1902), pp. 21–5.

27 The same omission was made by I. Ignatieff (pseudonym of Alexander Israel Helphand-Parvus) in his article on the Vilna speeches, 'Russisch-jüdische Arbeiter über die Judengrage', *Die neue Zeit*, vol. 1 (1892–93), pp. 176ff.

28 On Martov's role in the early history of the Bund, see his *Povorotnyi punkt v historii evreiskogo rabochego dvizhenia* (Geneva, 1900), especially pp. 17–19. Also I. Getzler, *Martov. A Political Biography* (Cambridge, 1967) and Wistrich (note 1 above), ch. 9.

29 See J. S. Hertz, 'The Bund's Nationality Program and Its Critics in the Russian, Polish and Austrian Socialist Movements', *YIVO Annual of Social Science*, vol. 14 (1969), pp. 53–6.

30 The differences between the SDKPiL and the Bolsheviks over the question of national self-determination persisted even after the October Revolution. See Peter Nettl, *Rosa Luxemburg* (London, 1966), vol.2, pp. 699–700, 796–7, 851–9.

31 V. I. Lenin, 'Does the Jewish Proletariat Need An "Independent Political Party"?', *Iskra*, no. 34, 15 February 1903.

32 R. Luxemburg, 'Organisationsfragen der russischen Sozialdemokratie', *Die neue Zeit* (1903–4), vol. 2, pp. 484–92, 529–35.

33 On the Bund's attitude towards Polish independence, see M. G. Rafes, *Ocherki po istorii Bunda* (Moscow, 1923), p. 45; N. A. Bukhbinder, *Istoriya evreiskogo rabochego dvizhenia v Rossii* (Leningrad, 1925), p. 87. During the 1905 Revolution in Russia, the SDKPiL and the Bund did in fact collaborate

closely and theoretical disputes were temporarily forgotten. In sharp contrast to the PPS, both parties stressed more than ever the need for unity with the Russian social democracy.

34 See Rosa Luxemburg's review of the Bund pamphlet, *Polska Partia Socjalistyczna o żydowskim ruchu robotniczym* (London, 1903) which appeared under the heading 'Krytyka i bibliografia' in *Przegląd Socjaldemokratyczny* (April 1903), no. 4, pp. 159–63.

35 *ibid.*

36 Adolf Wars(zaws)ki to Karl Kautsky, 20 May 1903 (unpublished letter in the Kautsky Nachlass D XXIII, International Institute of Social History, Amsterdam).

37 *ibid.*

38 *ibid.*

39 *ibid.*

40 K. Kautsky 'Das Massaker von Mischineff und die Judenfrage, *Die neue Zeit*, vol. 2 (1903), pp. 303–9. For a detailed discussion of Kautsky's views on the Jewish national problem and their influence, see R. S. Wistrich, *Socialism and the Jews. The Dilemmas of Assimilation in Germany and Austria 1880–1914* (London, 1982).

41 R. Luxemburg, *Briefe an Karl und Luise Kautsky* (Berlin, 1923), to Karl Kautsky, 6 June 1903.

42 R. Luxemburg, 'Diskusja', *Młot*, no. 14 (5 November 1910), pp. 5–7. *Młot* (The Hammer) was the organ of the SDKPiL in Warsaw for which Rosa Luxemburg wrote four unsigned articles during October–November 1910 sharply attacking the 'progressive' anti-Semitism of Andrzej Niemojewski and the free-thinking Polish intelligentsia.

43 *ibid.*

The Bund in Polish Political Life, 1935–1939

Antony Polonsky

The Jewish worker worries too little about himself and too much about others. Look at the Jewish labour press of the past few years. Note how much space is devoted to foreign news, alien news with which we have no direct contact and which we cannot influence, and how little is devoted to Jewish news in general and the Jewish workers' life in particular. At Jewish labour rallies, called for specific purposes, discussion veers to all sorts of foreign issues and away from the point under discussion. Jewish workers live much more each day with the problems of Germany, Russia, England and America than with the immediate issues which we must solve.

Jakub Hertz, *Sotsialistishe Bleter* (June 1931)

The death of Marshal Józef Piłsudski in May 1935 brought to an end an era in Polish politics. Piłsudski had played little part in the running of the state in the last years of his rule. Worn out by the stresses of his life, and increasingly wracked by the pain of liver and stomach cancer with which he was affected, he became a remote figure who only rarely attended cabinet meetings and who gave only the vaguest directives as to government policy. But his mere presence as the 'Grandfather' (*Dziadek*) to whom his inner circle of acquaintances, linked with him in conspiratorial work from before and during the First World War, owed unquestioning allegiance, furnished a degree of stability. His charismatic presence provided a unifying force around which the disparate and often mutually incompatible elements which had made up his administration in his last years could coalesce. With his death, the unresolved questions of Polish political life—how to revitalize the Polish economy devastated by the slump, what foreign policy should be pursued in an increasingly threatening environment, and how should the government, gravely weakened by the Marshal's death, acquire a measure of political support—all came to the surface. The government was riven with divisions over whether to continue the *détente* in Polish–German relations which had been initiated with the Polish–German Non-aggression Agreement signed in January 1934. Similarly it was split between those who believed that the government's

547

unpopularity and isolation should be overcome by a return to liberal democratic norms, severely undermined by Piłsudski's clash with Parliament, and those who believed that some specifically Polish variant of the right-radical nostrums increasingly in vogue in Europe should be adopted.[1]

These developments had very significant consequences for the position of Poland's nearly three and a half million Jews. Even before Piłsudski's death, the relative security the Jews had enjoyed in the early years of his rule had begun to erode. The economic crisis had been particularly acute in Poland, already a poor country, and had led to a decline between 1929 and 1933 of nearly 25 per cent in the country's national income; the slump radicalized political life and led to an increase in anti-Semitism. The fall in the price of agricultural products had been particularly sharp and had also undermined the position of Jewish traders, particularly once the government failed to extend a moratorium on farmers' debts to those of merchants. At the same time, the success and speed with which the German National Socialists had politically disenfranchised and dispossessed one of the wealthiest and most assimilated Jewish communities in Europe acted as a great stimulus to anti-Semites elsewhere, not least in Poland. The many violent anti-Jewish incidents which followed the Nazi takeover in Germany were widely reported in the Polish press, and even led to some efforts at emulation. Piłsudski himself had always regarded anti-Semitism as a crude political tool of his most irreconcilable opponents, the National Democrats led by Roman Dmowski. Thus, when in August 1929 the National Democrats had attempted to make use of an alleged Jewish profanation of a Corpus Christi procession in Lwów to initiate a campaign of anti-Jewish disturbances, his government had acted firmly and swiftly to restore order and stop attacks on the Jews.[2] Similarly, the Ministry of Higher Education had set itself firmly against any attempt by nationalist students and academic staff to introduce segregated seating for Jewish students and to restrict the number of Jews admitted to university (although in practice a *numerus clausus* operated widely, though unofficially).[3] The government had also acted quickly in the early 1930s to ban the fascist offshoots of the National Democrats, the Camp for a Greater Poland and the National Radical Camp. There was thus a widespread perception in Jewish circles that the Piłsudski government constituted an important barrier to the advance of anti-Semitic views in Poland. This awareness coexisted with mounting resentment at the failure of the authorities to take sufficiently seriously the disastrous impact of the great depression on large sections of the Jewish community, as well as unease at the implications of the government's flirtation with Nazi Germany after the Non-aggression Agreement of January 1934.

The situation changed drastically after the death of Piłsudski. The relatively liberal government of Manan Zyndram-Kościałkowski collapsed in less than a year in the face of serious labour unrest and the largely non-ideological 'Non-Party Bloc for Co-operation with the Government' (Bezpartyjny Blok dla wspólpracy z Rządem—BBWR) set up by the Marshal was also soon dissolved, a victim of the increasingly bitter power struggle among his heirs. The dominant figure in the new government of General Felicjan Sławoj-Składkowski, set up in May 1936, was Piłsudski's successor as Commander of the Armed Forces, General Edward Rydz-Śmigły. Rydz-Śmigły had few clearly defined views, but inclined towards a traditional right-wing attitude to Polish politics. He and his closest advisers, notably Colonel Adam Koc, favoured co-operation with the National Democrats, hoping in this way to acquire greater support for the government and bridge the rift which they regarded as largely anachronistic between the followers of Dmowski and of Piłsudski. As a consquence, when a new pro-government political organization, the Camp of National Unity (Obóz Zjednoczenia Narodowego—OZON), was established in February 1937, the principles it espoused bore many resemblances to those traditionally upheld by the National Democrats. It stressed the importance of the Catholic Church, underlined the leading role of the army in the state, and attacked Communism as 'alien to the Polish spirit'. It was also prepared to make concessions to anti-Semitism. When asked whether Jews could be members of the Camp of National Unity, Koc's deputy, Colonel Jan Kowalewski, replied that he accepted that there were some Jews who had sincerely adopted Polish nationality. He continued:

Nevertheless, Christian principles, which are the basis of Colonel Koc's declaration, will be the decisive factor in the choice of members. In exceptional cases, Polishness must be established not only by the fact of accepting this nationality, but by the sacrifice of blood voluntarily spilt, or by other services rendered to the Fatherland in the course of a whole life which bear witness to the fact that a person truly belongs to the Polish nation. We have in Poland Jews who have fought for the independence of the country and who, by virtue of this, are organized in the Association of Jews who have fought for Polish Indepedence. We respect this page of their life, which proves that they are good citizens, just as we respect the attachment, which they do not hide, to their Jewish nationality. It is obvious that they cannot belong to the Camp of National Unity. All the more so, Jews who do not have a past of this type cannot be given privileges by the mere action of professing Polish nationality.[4]

The government came increasingly to argue that only the emigration of a large proportion of the country's Jewish population could resolve the issue. Foreign Minister Jósef Beck claimed repeatedly that three million of the country's three and a half million Jews should leave Poland. The government now permitted the establishment of special 'ghetto benches' for Jewish students at universities and lent encouragement to the burgeoning movement to boycott Jewish shops and stalls. the OZON programme had indeed proclaimed that 'it is understandable that the country should possess the instinct compelling it to defend its culture, and it is natural that Polish society should seek economic self-sufficiency.'[5] As early as July 1936, faced with the increasing violence of the boycotters, Sławoj-Składkowski had told parliament: 'My government considers that nobody in Poland should be injured. An honest host does not allow anybody to be harmed in his house. An economic struggle. That's different (*Owszem*).'[6]

For many on the fascist and near-fascist right, even these actions were too moderate. The universities were scenes of frequent anti-Jewish violence; force was also frequently used to implement the boycott of Jewish trade, leading to brutal confrontations and deaths, as in Przytyk, Mińsk Mazowiecki and many other towns.[7] Commenting on the government's attempts to facilitate Jewish emigration, the main National Democratic newspaper *Warszawski Dziennik Narodowy* commented on 20 November 1938 that it was not enough to show the Jews the door; one should push them through by means of a 'surgical operation (*sic*) which will deprive them legally of the means to live in Poland'.

These developments had important implications for the strategies of the various Jewish political groups in Poland. Jewish politics in the Diaspora in the modern period have essentially taken the form of establishing and maintaining alliances with sympathetic groups in the larger society. The years after 1935 saw the bankruptcy of most existing Jewish alliances. Growing anti-Semitism further weakened the influence of the assimilationists, who had already been reduced to a fringe group in Jewish circles after the First World War. It became increasingly difficult to uphold the optimistic assimilationist view that education and the passage of time would make possible Polish–Jewish coexistence.[8] As early as 19 April 1932, the assimilationist journal *Zjednoczenie* wrote plaintively:

> At this moment, when such strong clashes have erupted [against Jews at the universities], our task is even greater, for we must show that we shall not collapse, that we shall survive in our viewpoint despite the great difficulties and continue to follow the road which we consider proper.

We have to build the bridge on which people of the same land and different faiths can be brought together.

It was despair at the unrealizable character of this idea that led the prominent Polish-Jewish writer Benedykt Hertz, previously sympathetic to the assimilationist position, to comment in 1937 in his *Żydowska Krew* (Jewish Blood) 'Assimilation. Today this movement is generally considered ineffectual, bankrupt and in some measure rightly so.'[9]

Zionist groupings also saw their position undermined. In the 1920s, Zionist politics in Poland had been racked by a bitter dispute between the Galician group, headed by Leon Reich, and that in the Congress Kingdom led by Yitzchak Grünbaum. The difference between them related not to questions connected with Palestine, but to the correct political strategy to be pursued in Poland.[10] Grünbaum, coming from an area where ethnic antagonisms had become quite pronounced, stressed the need for a vigorous and uncompromising defence of Jewish national rights, especially as they had been guaranteed by the constitution and the National Minorities Treaty. The Jews, in his view, would only find a reasonable place for themselves when Poland had been transformed from a national state into a state of national minorities, in which the various ethnic groups enjoyed a wide measure of autonomy. This view of the Polish situation lay behind Grünbaum's advocacy of a united front of the minorities, Jews, Germans, Ukrainians and Byelorussians, which led to the establishment of the National Minorities Bloc in the elections of November 1922. During the 1920s this strategy did not prove very effective: it was clear that it needlessly antagonized the Poles, and that the Jews' objectives were quite different from those of the other minorities. The Jews wanted only the implementation of rights they were guaranteed, the German were openly revisionist, while the Slavic Minorities wanted at least territorial autonomy and, at the most, secession. By the 1930s, the liberal illusions of the Versailles era were almost entirely dead. In 1934 the Poles repudiated the National Minorities Treaty, while from 1933 on the majority of the Germans showed themselves sympathetic to National Socialism. Neither the Byelorussians nor the Ukrainians showed any real desire to make common cause with the Jews.

Reich, coming from Galicia where ethnic tensions were much less acute, rejected Grünbaum's maximalism and favoured a direct approach to the Polish authorities. This resulted in the agreement of May 1925 with Premier Władysław Grabski, which soon collapsed amidst a welter of accusations and counter-accusations of bad faith by the parties involved. Yet after the May coup, Reich (who died in 1929) and his associates, who dominated the Jewish Parliamentary Club, still hoped to establish lines of communication with the government. They were generally satisfied with government behaviour in the twenties and, although uneasy about the impact of the depression, still regarded the government as far better than the alternatives, whether of the right or the left. After 1935, and in particular after the creation of OZON, these hopes were clearly without foundation. It is true that the government was able to find some common ground with Zionist groups, above all the Revisionists because of their support for Jewish aspirations in Palestine. Yet the hope of large-scale emigration to the Middle East was effectively destroyed by British policy; this made the Zionists appear not only ineffective, but naïve and toadying in their attempts to win support for a government policy whose real aim was to end the Jewish presence in Poland.

The Orthodox were even more seriously affected by developments after 1935. The main Orthodox political organization, Agudas Yisrael, in accordance with its understanding of the talmudic principle *Dina de Malkhuta Dina* (The Law of the State is Law) had quickly established friendly relations with the Piłsudski regime after May 1926.[11] It had been rewarded by a decree in 1927 extending and re-organizing the Jewish communal organizations (*Kehillot*) which were now granted wide powers in religious matters, including the maintenance of rabbis, synagogues, *mikvot*, religious education and Kosher slaughtering. Some welfare for poor members of the community was also to be provided. The Aguda, in return, supported the government in the elections of March 1928 and November 1930. In 1928 one of its leaders, Eliasz Kirszbraun, was even elected on the government (BBWR) list. The Aguda continued to regard the government as sympathetic in the early 1930s, and in these circumstances it came as a particularly cruel blow when in April 1936 the government introduced a law effectively banning ritual slaughter. This move was justified on hygienic and humanitarian grounds, but it was clear to all that its main objectives were to make life difficult for Jews and to damage the Jewish slaughterers who also sold meat to Christians.[12]

These developments—the increasingly critical situation of the Jewish minority and the bankruptcy of the previously dominant political orientations within the Jewish community—created a new set of opportunities for a group which between 1920 and 1935 had played only a marginal role in both Polish and Jewish politics, the General Jewish Workers' Alliance, or Bund.[13] The political isolation of the Bund in its first fifteen years was largely self-imposed. Throughout this period it had adopted a resolutely anti-religious and anti-Zionist attitude which had isolated it from most of Jewish opinion. Its actions on the 'Jewish street' were often deliberately provocative, and the party constantly played down its Jewish character, stressing instead its broader concerns. At its 1924 convention, for instance, one of its leaders had asserted: 'We are above all a revolutionary socialist party and only secondarily Jewish socialists.'[14]

The Bund's hostility to Zionism was certainly deep-rooted, and it was to be a consistent feature of the party's ideology throughout the inter-war period. Its basis had been clearly articulated by the Bund's leader Vladimir Medem in July 1920. He had declared:

> We are asked why we are opposed to Zionism. The answer is simple: because we are socialists. And not merely socialistically inclined or socialists in name only, but active socialists. And between Zionist activity and Socialist activity there is a fundamental and profound chasm . . . Across that chasm there is no bridge . . . A national home in Palestine would not end the Jewish exile . . . The Jewish exile would exist as before. All that would change would be the belief of Jewry in its future—the hope of the Jews in exile—the struggle for a better life would be snuffed out.[15]

This hope was, of course, the socialist millennium. Throughout the inter-war period the Bund held firmly to the view that anti-Semitism was essentially a secondary phenomenon which would disappear with the destruction of capitalism and the establishment of socialism. Viktor Alter, writing in 1937, bluntly told the Jews in Poland that they could expect 'no end to persecution unless there is a simultaneous freeing of the Polish masses from social oppression . . . Your liberation can only be a by-product of the universal freeing of oppressed people'.[16] The party was thus determined to ally itself with other socialist groups, regardless of nationality, and regarded any co-operation with those Jewish groups which it stigmatized as 'clerical' or 'nationalist' as unthinkable.

Yet the left-wing character of the Bund militated against its close co-operation with the Polish Socialist Party (Polska Partia Socjalist-yczna—PPS), the main socialist grouping in Poland. The Bund, still obsessed with the political struggles of the Russian Empire, in which it had been close to the Mensheviks and had clashed bitterly with the PPS, continued to see that party as a grouping too strongly wedded to the goal of regaining Polish independence, and insufficiently revolutionary or socialist. Its attitude to the PPS was well summed up in a programmatic statement in 1928: 'The working class of each nationality needs its own organization, but not its own party. In a land composed of several nationalities there should be only one Socialist party, with as many autonomous organizations within it as there are nationalities in the state.' The Bund was not by its own wish a separate party. The fact was that conditions in Poland were not yet ripe for the political unification of the workers. 'The party of the Polish proletariat is not yet ready to break the bounds of nationalism to become a state party rather than a national-Polish party; to become instead of Polish Socialist Party, the Socialist Party of Poland.'[17]

The Bund firmly retained its belief in the socialist revoltuion, although by the mid-1920s it had lost some of its illusions about communism. Its political stance was closest to that of the Austrian Social Democrats, and like that party it tried to establish a position for itself between the Second and Third Internationals. Along with the Austrians, a similar position was adopted by the Swiss Social Democrats, a section of the French Socialists, the German Independent Solcial Democrat Party, the Russian Mensheviks and Socialist Revolutionaries and the British ILP. In February 1921 in Vienna they established their own international grouping, sometimes referred to as the $2\frac{1}{2}$ International. It had little political impact. By 1923 the Independent Social Democrats had rejoined the SPD in Germany, and hopes for a European revolution had faded. As a result the Second and $2\frac{1}{2}$ International reunited in Hamburg, to form what was now called the Labour and Socialist International. The Bund, together with the Norwegian Labour Party and some other smaller groupings, refused to join the united International and created their own Bureau of Revolutionary Socialist Parties headed by the left-wing German Socialist Georg Lebedour.

In Poland the Bund's intransigent leftism brought it few political dividends. It impeded co-operation with other political groups and kept the Bund vote small. In the 1922 elections it polled about 87,000 votes, a figure which fell to 80,000 in 1928 and 71,000 in 1930, when the party stood together with the German Socialist Party of Labour. The 1930 figure should be compared with 185,000 for the Jewish National Bloc in Galicia, 247,000 for the Bloc to defend Jewish National Rights, and 150,000 for the General Jewish National and Economic Bloc.[18] In the years 1929 and 1930 the Bund resolutely refused to support the Centre-Left alliance of six parties including the PPS which was formed, vainly as it turned out, to use parliamentary means to overthrow the Piłsudski dictatorship. The failure of the Centre-Left alliance was indeed explained by the Bundist paper *Naye Folkstsaytung* as a consequence of the inclusion within it of non-socialist parties which were 'nationalist' and 'reactionary'. Hence it was impossible to mobilize the workers against the regime and they were left 'apathetic and disappointed'. They 'could not become enthusiastic about the democracy proclaimed by parties which ignored the rights of the workers'.[19]

In the early 1930s, the Bund began gradually to modify its political stance. The first stage in this process was the final collapse of the Bureau of Revolutionary Socialist Parties. In 1927 the Norwegians had seceded to join the Second International, to be joined in 1930 by the Bund. This had followed long and bitter debates at the Fourth Conference of the Bund (March 1929) and at a special conference held in Łódź in 1930. On that occasion the decision was taken to affiliate to the Labour and Socialist International. This decision resulted in the institutionalization of two factions in the party, the majority led by Henryk Ehrlich and Viktor Alter and the Leftist minority led by Jozef Chmurner. The resolution itself gives a characteristic picture of the Bund's view of the world. It affirmed:

> The Comintern is ideologically bankrupt and plays a deleterious role in the labour movement; the International Socialist Bureau has failed after seven years to become a centre for revolutionary Socialist parties, while the Socialist International has grown because of the increasing desire of non-communist socialist parties for unity. The Labour and Socialist International now includes within its ranks all the orientations in the socialist movement apart from the Communists and allows them all to coexist within its ranks.[20]

The decision to join the Second International was welcomed by the PPS as removing an important barrier to co-operation between the two parties. At the Łódź conference, Zygmunt Zaremba, one of the leaders of the PPS, had issued a strong appeal for co-operation.

> The Jewish and Polish workers have not only points of contact but also points which divide them. The prejudices which divide the workers of different nationalities still wield a powerful influence over us . . . Yet if, despite this, Polish and Jewish workers are drawing closer together, it is because there exists on one side the Bund and on the other side the PPS . . . both of which are building a bridge between the proletariats of the two nationalities. If there are differences between us we should not lose our tempers: let us instead try to understand each other and seek ways to end our differences. And because there is developing a better understanding of our different viewpoints we are becoming—year by year—closer to each other.[21]

Some obstacles to co-operation remained. Even when acceding to the Second International, the Bundist leadership made it quite clear that it would not abandon its basic ideological position. Explaining the decision in *Naye Folkstsaytung* on 6 June 1930, Henryk Ehrlich wrote:

> The Łódź convention had to solve a problem: How could our party reconcile its ideological world-view with an institutional involvement with the international socialist workers movement?

It is the task now of the Jewish working class to create an appropriate place for its party, the Bund, in the ranks of the Second International. We have no illusions about this body . . . We are aware of all its mistakes.

The early 1930s were difficult years for both the PPS and the Bund. The PPS's strategy of using parliamentary means to overthrow the Piłsudski regime had failed and this contributed to a fall in party morale and diminution of support. There was also some disillusionment with the party's allies in the Centre-Left bloc. In the early 1930s both the Christian Democrats and the National Workers Party tended to distance themselves from the PPS. The three peasant parties united in March 1931 to form a single party, the Stronnictwo Ludowe (SL). Though there were those in its ranks who advocated close links with the PPS, there were also others, of whom the most significant was Poland's leading peasant leader Wincenty Witos, who favoured common action with Endecja, the main right-wing and anti-Semitic party. In these circumstances the PPS tended to become more radical and more willing to co-operate with groups like the Bund.[22]

The Bund also had seen its influence decline in the early 1930s. Membership of the party had fallen from about 7600 in 1919 to 7000 in 1935. The fall in members was most marked in small towns, since more than 6700 of the Bund's members in 1935 were in the twelve largest Polish towns. While the number of Bundist branches had in fact grown slightly, from 200 to 213, there were still 300 smaller towns with individual members but no branches. Bundist representation on local councils also declined between 1928 and 1934, from 187 to 90.[23] Relations between the two socialist parties remained somewhat tense, with the PPS's continued commitment to reformism clashing with the Bund's persistent conviction that only revolutionary action could topple the Piłsudski regime. The differences between the two parties were sharply highlighted in 1931, when the Second International attempted to mediate and bring them closer together. On that occasion, Henryk Ehrlich asserted bluntly that only a struggle for revolutionary proletarian democracy could lead to unity between the different socialist groups. This provoked Mieczysław Niedziałowski of the PPS to retort that it was easy for the Bund to spout revolutionary phrases. Unlike the PPS, which had assumed real political obligations, the Bund had never taken any responsibility for the fate of Poland.[24]

The establishment in 1932 of a short-lived Bundist daily *Pismo Codzienne* also acted as an irritant in inter-party relations. The paper was closed by the authorities after barely two weeks (on the spurious grounds that its printing press did not comply with government safety legislation), but it was soon succeeded by a weekly, *Nowe Pismo*, which repeated the Bundist criticism of PPS 'reformism', much to the irritation of the Polish party. The newspaper's frequent attacks on the PPS led Niedziałowski to claim that they raised doubts about the Bund's claim that it genuinely sought an improvement in mutual relations.[25]

Political developments were, however, pushing both in this direction. In 1933, for instance, the parties ran joint lists in local elections in both Tarnów and Kraków and did relatively well, a sign that the political tide was beginning to turn. In Tarnów the socialist list won 17 of 40 seats and in Kraków, where socialist influences were much weaker, 13 of 72.[26] Both parties were deeply shocked by Hitler's rise to power and his suppression of German working-class political organizations. The Bund asserted that this had not only been the result of the 'adventurist policy' of the communists, but that it also constituted 'a defeat of the reformist policy of hanging on to formal democracy and legality'. The SPD's coalition with non-socialists strengthened the very forces it had been formed to defeat. By creating the illusion of democracy, the SPD had caused paralysis in the ranks of the working class and rendered itself impotent to resist Hitler.[27] Even more significant in changing the mood of the two parties was the brief civil war in Austria in February 1934, which led to the destruction of the Austrian Social Democrats, a party with close links with both the Bund and the PPS.

Another factor increasing the co-operation of the two parties was the fact that the illusions of the Bund about communism were now finally all but shattered. The adoption by the Comintern in 1928 of a radical leftist line, which saw the social democrats, stigmatized as 'social fascists', as the main obstacle to a revolutionary polarization of society, had led to a series of bitter ideological attacks, above all on the more left-wing social democratic groups such as the Bund. 'In a period of feverish preparations for war against the Soviet union,' wrote the Communist Party of Poland's (KPP) journal *Czerwony Sztandar* in April 1931, 'the Bund assists—organizationally and politically—in preparing that war.' The attacks were not only verbal. Physical assaults on Bundist activists within the trade union movement and on Bundist offices multiplied. At least fifty such incidents were recorded in 1932; in one, a young Bundist member of the Jewish Bakers Union, Abraham Neuerman, was murdered.

These attacks, which were condemned by the Bund as 'helping the Fascist reaction', contributed, along with developments within the Soviet Union, to a reassessment by the Bund of Communism as a political philosophy. In June 1931, for example, Maurycy Orzech wrote brutally that 'there is no socialism in the Soviet Union. There only terror rules.'[28] In the same vein Ehrlich asserted:

> The tragedy of communism as an international movement lies in its emptiness and lack of positive values. The entire philosophy of communism is limited to two things:
> (1) Apologetics for the Soviet Union,
> (2) hatred for all non-communist movements. The communists have no other positive principles.[29]

In his pamphlet *The Essence of Bundism* (*Der Iker fun Bundism*), published in 1934, he strongly assailed the lack of freedom under communism. 'That regime without freedom, that garrison state which the Communist Party would set up, is alien to our way of life . . . We reject the communists' goal of crushing the will of the working class by establishing a dictatorship of the Politburo.'[30]

The first Five-Year Plan and the sufferings which the policy of forced industrialization entailed also provoked bitter criticism. In April 1931 an anonymous writer in *Unzer Tsayt* observed: 'The way of the Five-Year Plan is not the way to socialism, [it is] rather a false path to dictatorship.'[31] According to another Bundist theoretician, M. Kligsberg, the abolition of private property and the development of heavy industry could not on their own achieve socialism—this required the collective control of industry for the good of the whole of society. The aim of the Five-Year Plan was rather 'a terroristic dictatorship of industry against the interests of the masses'. If the Five-Year Plan was, in fact, a step towards socialism, he concluded, it would raise serious questions as to the ideology's value; capitalism had achieved industrialization at far less cost in human suffering.[32]

The Bundist leaders were also gravely shocked by the wave of show trials and executions which began in the Soviet Union in 1934 and which affected many (Zinoviev, for example) with whom they might have clashed in the past, but whom they knew well and respected. 'That which has occurred since 1 December' wrote Ehrlich at the end of 1934, 'and which is still going on in the Soviet Union in relation to the murder [of Kirov], no socialist conscience can excuse.'[33] Viktor Adler went still further. Either the verdicts in the trials were just, in which case the leaders of the revolution had been unworthy traitors from its inception, or they were not, in which case an appalling crime had been perpetrated against the revolution and those who had carried it out. 'The shots have not only hit those condemned,' he concluded, 'they have severely wounded the revolution itself.'[34] He drew drastic conclusions from this. By 1938, in his *Człowiek w społeczeństwie* (Man in Society), he was strongly critical of the 'totalitarian' drive of Communism:

We must revise the old theory that communism and socialism, growing from the same root—and even the same branch, are divided only on matters of tactics and the methods of struggle, [and that they] should unite in a joint stand in fighting for the society of tomorrow.

So it was once: now it is different. Even the ends have changed. If socialism has remained true to the concepts of a society of tomorrow, based on freedom, communism has gone further and further away from it, until it has reached the present Stalinist anti-libertarian totalitarianism.[36]

Given these views, attempts to achieve common action between the Communist Party of Poland and the Bund proved extremely difficult. The KPP was also very shocked by Hitler's rise to power and shortly afterwards, in March 1933, suggested a united front against fascism to the Bund and the other socialist parties in Poland. The Bund executive laid down two conditions: the communists should end their campaign of violence against the Bund and negotiations would be best conducted in secret. These negotiations did in fact begin, but they were soon broken off in the face of renewed violence between Bundists and communists in which one man was killed and another seriously wounded. A similar fate attended attempts to mount a joint campaign in June 1934 to save the life of Ernst Thaelmann, the German communist leader who had been sentenced to death for his alleged role in the Reichstag fire. After the Seventh Conference in 1935, the Comintern adopted a policy of a broad popular front of all anti-fascist forces in those countries threatened by fascist and, above all, Nazi aggression. This was a concept which the Bund had long rejected, as it had opposed the Centre-Left alliance, since it felt that any co-operation with bourgeois groups was likely to damage the workers' movement. The basic position of the Bund on this question was clearly articulated in a mimeographed bulletin, 'Popular Front or Proletarian Front', which was distributed by the party central committee to local party officials. It read;

Just as the previous theory of a united front from below, the tactic of warfare against the socialists, was harmful to the working class, so too is the new tactic of the popular front. To limit the struggle against fascism to general democratic issues such as the defence of democracy or the defence of the republic [is a delusion] . . . Democracy alone is not enough.

The fascists made use of democracy to propagate their ideas. Hitler came to power legally under the democratic Weimar constitution.

Under such conditions (where democracy can aid a fascist seizure of power) the working-class struggle is not for general democracy but . . . favours the sharpest repression of fascist organizations . . .[36]

Paradoxically, the PPS was much more sympathetic to the idea of a Popular Front. In June 1935 the KPP and PPS agreed on a 'pact of non-aggression' involving a mutual cessation of attacks in the party press and at public meetings and joint campaigns against Beck's foreign policy and the concentration camp established by the government at Bereza Kartuska. By May 1936, relations between the two parties had deteriorated, however, and in November of that year the PPS finally renounced the pact, partly out of disagreement with the Communists' policy of exploiting a major wave of labour unrest in the spring of 1936 to provoke an all-out clash with the government.[37] Certainly the death of Piłsudski had given a considerable fillip to opposition activity both on the left and on the right. The PPS became much more active and found new common ground with the Bund in the belief of both parties that the real danger was not from the government, but rather that some of its members would make common cause with the also resurgent right-wing forces to create some sort of fascist-style regime in Poland. It is true that, in a somewhat plaintive echo from the past, the annual report of the Bund's Central Committee in December 1935 affirmed:

> The reformist behaviour of the PPS, its opposition to the Bund, make it impossible to unite with the party of the Polish proletariat against the nationalist and Zionist tendencies . . . as was the case many years ago in Russia.[38]

In practice, however, the two parties were now much more closely aligned and co-operated in organizing the fairly successful bycott of the national elections called by the government in September 1935. This alliance was of great value to the Bund. At a time when the other main Jewish groupings saw their political strategies collapsing in ruins, it could claim that in had allies in Polish society who had a real chance of achieving power. Bundist confidence grew, and the party became much more active and self-assured in its belief that it could 'conquer the Jewish street'.

One sign of the Bund's new activism was its response to the intensification of organized attempts to boycott Jewish shops and stalls which followed Piłsudski's death and which frequently led to violence. One of the most serious incidents occurred on 9 March 1936 in the small town of Przytyk, near Radom, when a clash between fascists intent on implementing the boycott and a Jewish self-defence group resulted in three deaths (two Jews and a Pole). The Bund responded by calling for a half-day protest strike. Its intentions were to fight:

> (1) Against the anti-Semitism of the Endeks and the Sanacja, against the continuing pogrom agitation and physical extermination of the Jewish population.

(2) Against Jewish nationalist and clerical reaction.

(3) Against the boycott of Jewish workers, against the elimination of Jews from all positions in the economy, against the policy of starving the Jewish masses.

(4) Against the persecution of Yiddish schools and the culture of the Jewish masses; against attempts to create a Jewish ghetto and all forms of national persecution.

(5) Against reaction, fascism and capitalism.

(6) For full equality for the Jewish population at all levels of economic, political and social life in Poland.

(7) Work, bread and freedom for all nationalities in Poland.

(8) For international proletarian solidarity.

(9) For effective self-defence by the Jewish population against all attempts at pogroms.

(10) For a workers' and peasants' government, for socialism.[39]

The strike was a great success, although there was some criticism of the Bund, for instance in *Moment* on 16 March, for not involving non-socialist Jewish organizations. It was widely supported in the Jewish areas of Warsaw, Białystok, Wilno, Kraków, Lwów, Łódź and several other towns, while a number of PPS-controlled unions also came out in solidarity, particularly in Warsaw, Łódź, Białystok, Będzin and Lublin.

According to *Haynt* on 17 March:

In all businesses where Jewish workers and staff are employed, the strike was a complete success. All Jewish businesses—almost without exception—were closed.

In the municipal slaughterhouse, no Jewish workers appeared nor did any Christian workers who are under the influence of the PPS. A meeting of Jewish and non-Jewish workers there heard fiery speeches.

Varshever Radio, a popular Jewish newspaper, commented: 'Sabbath of Sabbaths! That is the only way to describe today's loud silence, the protest by the Jewish population against Przytyk and against uncontrolled anti-Semitism generally.'

The strike was followed by an attempt to arrange a 'socialist conference on anti-Semitism', involving the Bund and PPS but excluding non-socialist Jewish parties. This was, however, banned by the government. In May of the following year, the unwillingness of the Bund to work with Jewish organizations was again made clear when it refused to participate in a two-hour protest strike against anti-Jewish violence in Białystok on the grounds that, since it had been called by Zionists and other 'bourgeois elements', it was nationalist and therefore reactionary. Instead, it issued a joint statement together with the PPS and the German Socialist Party of Labour.

The Bund was also prepared to take up other Jewish issues. It protested strongly against the banning in April 1936 of Jewish ritual methods of slaughering animals, and in 1936 reversed a decision it had made in 1930 not to participate in *Kehillot* elections. When the first elections were organized in Poland, the Bund decided to participate. It aimed to transform the *Kehillot* from religious into secular bodies which could administer Jewish autonomous life. The failure to achieve this goal, and the clear limitation of the functions of the *Kehillot* by the decree of 1927 (confirmed in the circular of 1930), led the Bund to decide in April 1929 to boycott further elections. This stance was justified by Shmuel Zygelboym on the grounds that these bodies were purely religious and attracted little attention from the Jewish public. 'Is is worth expending the energy,' he asked 'which participation in the *Kehillot* demands of us?'[40] By 1931 the Bund had withdrawn from all *Kehillot*. Thus when new elections were scheduled for the Warsaw *Kehilla* for 6 September 1936, it was not surprising that the Bund Executive Council, meeting on 7 July, decided again not to participate. This time, however, the electoral boycott aroused strong opposition among the party rank and file, which led to the decision's being reversed.

In an interview with *Nasz Przegląd* on 31 July, Viktor Alter explained the change. While two opinions had always existed in the Bund on the tactical question of whether to participate in *Kehilla* elections, there had never been an ideological bar to this. Hence, on this occasion, the majority decided to participate so that they could continue the fight against the reactionaries and conservatives. The Bund's decision to participate transformed the elections, which now became essentially a struggle over who controlled the 'Jewish street'. Although forty-four parties stood in all, it was essentially a contest between the Bund, the orthodox Aguda, and the Zionists, who put up a single National bloc made up of the two principal Zionist factions, *Al Ha-Mishmar* (A) and *Et Livnot* (B), as well as the Union of Jewish Merchants. The turnout was relatively low (many members of the Jewish intelligentsia, for example, regarded the *Kehilla* as a religious body of little interest), and only 40,475 of a possible 94,300 votes were cast, about 45 per cent. None the less, the results were a great success for the Bund, which won 15 of the 50 seats, as against 10 for the Aguda, 9 for the National bloc (Zionists), 3 for Mizrahi, 2 for Poalei Zion Right, 1 for Poalei Zion Left and 1 for the Folkists. The *Kehilla* executive was now made up of 5 Bundists, 5 Agudaniks, 3 bloc Zionists, 2 members of Mizrahi and one member of Poalei Right.[41]

The Bund's victory was widely commented on. *Chwila* wrote on

8 September that the low poll resulted from the political apathy of the Jewish intelligentsia. The Bund owed its growth in support to intensive propaganda, good organization and the radicalization of the Jewish votes. *Haynt* (8 September) commented on the weak showing of the National bloc and its failure to mobilize Zionist support. What the election showed, it claimed, was that neither the Zionists nor the Aguda could any longer speak on behalf of the 'Jewish masses'. A similar point of view was expressed by the Aguda paper *Yidishe Togblat* (8 September). It observed that 'one has now to recognize that there are three forces in conflict on the Jewish street, and that many Jews have been seduced by the Bund's false propaganda.' The Bund, it charged bitterly, had not changed its politics—it wished to uproot traditional and religious values and extend its poisonous influence. For its part, the *Folkstsaytung* saw the party's success as part of a process. In May 1935 it had succeeded in inducing a significant proportion of the Jewish electorate to boycott the parliamentary elections, as had also been advocated by the PPS and other Polish opposition parties. Its growth in support was the result of a real revolution in the 'Jewish street', although it was also a reaction to the ineffectual and feeble way the Aguda and Zionists had previously run the Warsaw *Kehilla*.[42]

It proved very difficult to induce the various parties on the *Kehilla* to work together, in spite of a strong appeal from the General Zionist, Moshe Kleinbaum. He called for all groups on the council to co-operate in order to prevent government interference, on the grounds that the *Kehilla* was not performing its proper functions. His appeal went unheeded and indeed the first meeting, on 21 September, of the *Kehilla* was adjourned by the government, on the grounds that a political discussion had taken place, which was not on the agenda and which went beyond its sphere of competence. No agreement between the parties proved possible even on the question of choosing a *Kehilla* president, and on 8 January 1937, the authorities dissolved the executive, governing the *Kehilla* directly through the Ministry of Religious Cults and Public Education.[43]

After its relative success in Warsaw, the Bund was determined to participate in other *Kehilla* elections. It was more successful in larger than in smaller towns. In Wilno the Zionists won 9 seats, the Bund 5; in Lublin the Aguda won 8, the Bund 8 and the Zionist bloc 3; in Piotrków the Bund won 6, the Aguda 2 and the Zionists 3. Altogether in 1936, elections took place in 97 towns in Poland (excluding Warsaw). The results are set out in Table I. They show the difficulty for the Bund in repeating the Warsaw success in small towns, where Orthodox and Zionist influence was still strong.

TABLE I

Results of Kehilla *elections in 97 Polish towns in 1936 (excluding Warsaw)*

	% of seats
Aguda	21
General Zionists	17
Non-party Orthodox	15.5
Other non-party	9.5
Householders	9.4
Bund	8.8
Mizrahi	6.2
Poalei Zion Right	5.5
Revisionists	2.7
Poalei Zion Left	1.8
Merchants	1.0
Folkists	1.0

Another sign of the new interest of the Bund in Jewish matters was its taking up of the question of the growing anti-Semitism within Polish universities. The Bund responded strongly to the wave of disturbances at the beginning of the academic year of 1935–6, which aimed at the introduction of restrictions on the number of Jewish students and the creation of 'ghetto' benches. After violent riots at the Polytechnic of Lwów, the college's authorities gave in for the first time and instructed Jewish students temporarily to use separate seats. This was widely opposed not only by Jews, but by many leading academics. In the PPS paper *Robotnik*, on 15 December 1935, Professor Zygmunt Szymanowski attacked the professors of the Lwów Polytechnic for not opposing the 'mediaeval custom' of the ghetto benches.

The agitation revived with greater force at the beginning of the academic years 1936–7, with riots in Warsaw, Lwów and Wilno. They became the focus for further co-operation between the Bund and the PPS, with members of both organizations fighting side by side against nationalist students. On 26 November the Bund and the Jewish Trade Unions organized a one-day work stoppage in protest against the situation in the universities, which was also supported by many shopkeepers and artisans as well as some Polish workers. On 10 December 1936 *Robotnik*, explaining its attitude, claimed that the agitation against the Jews in the universities threatened the independence of Poland, since the real aim was to introduce Nazi-style legislation in the country. Paradoxically, the Bund's stand was less forthright. On 11 December, *Naye Folkstsaytung* wrote that, although it might seem that the demand for 'ghetto benches' concerned only a small portion of the Jewish community, it was of the greatest significance in the wide struggle against anti-Semitism. The aim of such regulations was to break the spirit of the Polish-Jewish community and prepare the way for the introduction of Nuremburg-style legislation. 'As a result the Jewish public must not abandon the students. Jewish workers are obliged to join this struggle, as is proletarian Polish society.'

The increasing strength of the Bund and its closer, though still uneasy, relations with the PPS were both clearly in evidence in the elections to the City Council of Łódź which took place on 27 September 1936.[44] Łódź, a major textile centre with a population of over 600,000, had nearly 200,000 Jewish inhabitants and many Germans. It was a town with a strong working-class tradition, but also one with deep ethnic antagonisms. In 1934, after six years of socialist rule, the right-wing National Democrats had succeeded in taking control of the municipality. They had soon clashed with the government and the premature dissolution of the council was the reason for the elections.

On this occasion, the PPS decided that, for tactical reasons, it should not run on a common list with the Bund, as it had done in 1934, as this would enable the right to call it a Jewish party. Furthermore, the PPS was eager to enlist Communist support, but felt it would be best if the Communists supported the Bund list. These elaborate manoeuvres caused some irritation, which was compounded when, less than two weeks before the election, the PPS leadership in Łódź decided that it wished to stand as the sole Socialist list, and attempted unsuccessfully to persuade the Bund to withdraw.

In the end, the tactics of the PPS proved successful, and the socialist parties won a resounding victory in the elections. The PPS received 34 seats (of 72), the Bund 6, the Nationalists 27, the Aguda 3 and the Zionists 2. One of the reasons for the PPS's success was that while many poorer Jews voted for the Bund, many middle-class Jews, to the irritation of the Endeks, voted PPS in order to oust the Endejca.

The result of the election was both a relief and a shock to the established Jewish parties. In *Haynt*, on 29 September, Moshe Kleinbaum (Sneh) argued that the Bund had done well because of its 'uncompromising and clear' stance, and that other Jewish groups should seek common ground with the PPS, though remaining independent. The Bund saw the election as a triumph and a clear sign of the 'ideological bankruptcy' of the middle class. Jewish groups, who had only with great difficulty disengaged themselves from supporting the government party (the BBWR), it claimed, were only half-hearted in their allegiance to the socialists.[45]

The new city government proved even less durable than its Endek predecessor. The socialist majority put forward Nobert Barlicki as its candidate for mayor. He was unacceptable to the central government and his candidature was not approved by it, as was required by law. In response, the majority refused to vote in a budget, forcing the government to rule Łódź through the centrally-appointed mayor who had replaced the Endek administration. The government responded by dissolving the City Council on 1 April and ruling the city directly.

TABLE 2

Results of city council elections in Łódź in 1935 and 1936

	Seats in 1934	Seats in 1936	Vote in 1936
PPS	7[1]	34[3]	94,995
Bund		6[4]	23,685
National Party (Endecja)	39	27	77,831[5]
Orthodox (Aguda)	10[2]	3	14,935
Zionists	4	2	10,599
Pro-government (ZZZ)	10		
Nazis			
Poalei Zion Left	1		

1 Together with Bund representatives and German Socialists
2 Together with Folkists
3 Together with German Socialists
4 Together with Poalei Zion Left
5 Down from 98,000 in 1934

There was one issue on which the Bund and the Aguda agreed. Large sections of Jewish opinion, in addition to the Zionists, were coming to see emigration, and not only to Palestine, as the only means of alleviating the worsening situation of Jews in Poland. On this question all the other Jewish parties were resolutely opposed by both the Bund and the Aguda.

On 2 August 1936, for instance, Yitzchak Grünbaum called a press conference at which he stated that Jewish organizations should co-operate with the Polish authorities in facilitating emigration. The development of a desire among Poles to establish independent businesses, and the support given to this by the government, would, he claimed, deprive many Jews of their livelihood and emigration was the only solution[46] This statement was widely criticized in Jewish circles, by the Aguda, *Chwila* and *Nasz Przegląd*, but most strongly by the Bund. *Naye Folkstsaytung* on 4 August reminded its readers that in 1927 Grünbaum had talked in the USA of 'one million surplus Jews' in Poland. This was the type of argument, the paper continued, 'which incites anti-Semitism', since it seems to imply 'that the Jews are responsible for the social problems under which they suffer'.

There was some justification for the Bundist position, but the total refusal to consider emigration as a possibility was somewhat short-sighted. The fact is that the exodus of Jews to Western Europe and America had not only provided many of them with opportunities for a better life, but had also brought many benefits to those who had remained in the *Heym*. Paradoxically, the PPS was much more sympathetic to emigration. In 1936 a member of the party, Jan Borski, published a pamphlet, *Sprawa Żydowska a Socjalizm* (The Jewish Question and Socialism), which was, in a sense, intended to challenge the Bund's rigid opposition to emigration.[47] Borski argued that Jewish emigration had long been a feature of East European life. It was a 'natural phenomenon, a necessity', given the poverty of the area, and should not be seen as a byproduct of anti-Semitism. Rather it was the result of the separate national existence of the Jewish group in the region.

Another, rather less attractive side of the Bund was reflected in its opposition to the attempts in 1937 and 1938, in the face of the worsening political climate, to establish a representative Congress of Polish Jews which would speak for the whole Jewish community.[48] It is true that the Aguda opposed the Congress and favoured an unelected body, chosen by representatives of the different parties. Significant divisions also existed among the Zionist groups, and the project was further undermined by the belief, particularly in the influential American Jewish Committee, that it was the brainchild of Nahum Goldmann of the World Jewish Congress. In addition, the authorities were hostile to the idea. Yet these difficulties could probably all have been overcome had the Bund not been resolutely opposed to co-operation with orthodox or Zionist groupings.

The Congress was first proposed in mid-1937 by Moshe Kleinbaum (formerly Yitzchak Grünbaum's political secretary), and in the second half of that year it was subjected to a stream of virulent attacks in *Naye Folkstsaytung*. The Congress, claimed the Bundist paper on 30 October, would merely serve as a stage to publicize Zionism and divert the Jewish masses from their real problems. It held no interest for the Bund. Paradoxically, the stance of the Communist Party was less hostile. If the Congress was democratic and representative of the Jews in Poland, wrote *Czerwony Sztandar*, it would be a useful way of strengthening

567

the anti-fascist front. The main issue, the paper argued, was not who organized the conference but what it did. By the end of the year the communists had cooled somewhat to the idea, seeing it as effectively a Zionist front, but they blamed this development on the failure of the Bund to participate.

Bundist attacks continued in 1938. According to Viktor Adler in *Naye Folkstsaytung* on 7 January 1938, in an article characteristically entitled 'The Zionist Jewish Congress', the proposed meeting would be a conference of the Jewish 'right'—nothing more than a demonstration in favour of Jewish emigration. A similar position was upheld by the Bundist-controlled unions, which argued that they could not participate since at their Sixth Congress they had resolved that 'No one must co-operate with reactionary or clerical elements, even if the issue is anti-Semitism.'

By the summer of 1938 it was clear that the whole idea of a unified representative body was dead. The Bund highlighted its satisfaction by calling a congress of Jewish workers to protest against anti-Semitism. Describing the aim of this meeting on 23 August 1938, *Naye Folkstsaytung* stated that the goal of the Bund was to protect Jews by struggling against reaction and anti-Semitism and for a democratic Poland, which so many Jews saw as their homeland. It opposed any plan for evacuation or emigration. These, proclaimed the paper proudly, 'are the main principles of the common workers' fight in Poland'.

A telling critique of the Bund's political inflexibility was formulated by the doyen of Jewish historians Shimon Dubnow, Henryk Ehrlich's father-in-law, in an open letter 'To a Bundist colleague. On the isolationism of the Bund', which *Naye Folkstsaytung* printed on 29 July 1938. In this letter, Dubnow criticized Bundist policy, which he described as 'withdrawing from *Klal Yisrael*'. He was not a Zionist, he stated, and had often criticized the mistakes of the Zionists. Yet he felt obliged to express astonishment at the hostility of the Bund to Zionism at a time of such critical danger for the Jewish people. The Zionists had achieved great things in Eretz Israel. 'The majority of the Jewish people is impressed by these achievements and is Zionist. The error of the Bund is that it does not see itself as part of the Jewish people, but of the Jewish proletariat. The Bund will only ensure its future if it abandons its separation and works together with all democratic and progressive forces within the Jewish people.'

This reproach certainly stung and provoked a reply from Ehrlich on 31 July under the heading 'Is Zionism a democratic and progressive force?' The Bund, he asserted, was the largest political force in Jewish Poland and not merely a temporary phenomenon.

The Bund is an organic part of the Jewish people and represents its true interests. It is concerned for all Jews in Poland and not only for the workers. Yet the concept of *Klal Yisrael* cannot involve co-operation with reactionaries, with the Aguda or with the Revisionists. Zionism has become an ally of anti-Semitism. The worsening situation of the Jews throughout the world is exploited by the Zionists. The Zionists regard themselves as second-class citizens in Poland. Their aim is to be first-class citizens in Palestine and make the Arabs second-class citizens. The Bund, therefore, cannot see the Zionists as partners in the struggle against the reactionary forces in Poland.

Yet for all the Bund's bold talk of the unity of working people regardless of nationality, relations with the PPS, though considerably closer than before 1935, were not without their tensions. In 1936 the PPS resolved to hold its May Day processions together with the parties of the national minorities, including the Bund. In the event, the government forbade the Bund to march alongside the PPS in Warsaw, and it had to organize a separate parade. Elsewhere the two parties marched together. In 1937, however, relations continued to be problematic. The preparations for demonstrations on 1 May were accompanied by severe repression on the part of the government and an unwillingness on the part of some of the PPS rank and file to march with the Bund. Some of the PPS leaders also felt that separate parades might be desirable so as not to 'frighten off' potential support, above all from the Peasant Party, whose attitudes towards the Jews were not always friendly. At the beginning of April the PPS Executive Committee issued a directive calling for processions 'together with the parties of the national minorities where possible'. This was interpreted by members of local party organizations as a green light to arrange May Day parades without the Bund; this occurred in Lublin and Kielce. When the authorities in most areas prohibited common parades, the decision was greeted with relief by several local PPS leaders. According to the governor of Łódź, 'The government's decision was highly convenient to the PPS leadership.'[49]

The situation was not much better in 1938. The first of May coincided with a heightened period of international tension, with attempts by the government Camp of National Unity to strengthen its position in the State and with an intensified anti-Jewish campaign by the Endecja and its Fascist offshoots. On 7 April the PPS executive committee issued a directive on the conduct of May Day which a Ministry of the Interior Report described as 'an astute compromise between the two currents of opinion developing in the party. One of these, the leftist, aims at giving 1 May processions a broad all-socialist democratic character and calls for common action with socialist groups, above all those of the Jews; the other, rightist, wishes to cut itself off quite decidedly from the Jews, accenting the Polish character of the PPS.'[50] The resolution, in fact, held that wherever common parades were arranged, all socialist organizations would be admitted 'provided they can take responsibility for the discipline of their followers'. In the event it was decided to hold a parade without Jews in Kielce, Kraków, Lublin and Piotrków. In Łódź and Warsaw the authorities insisted on separate parades.

It would be misleading to overstress the conflicts between the PPS and the Bund. It is true that, for tactical reasons, the PPS was unwilling to ally itself too closely to a Jewish party and that its growing links with the Peasant Party caused some concern within the Bund. But by and large there was now much greater willingness on both sides to co-operate and a much greater understanding of each other's point of view. One example of this was the decision of the two parties in May 1937 to found jointly a Polish-language newspaper in Łódź, *Dzennik Ludowy*. The two parties also co-operated closely in the local government elections of late 1938 and early 1939, called by the government in an attempt to improve the political climate by allowing a freer expression of opinion. They took place without much administrative pressure, and for that very reason they were regarded by all parties as a crucial test of their support. For the opposition they were even more important, because, as was widely repeated in the press, it was after a defeat of his party in local government elections in 1931 that the King of Spain had allowed the introduction of a democratic political system.

In the event, the elections proved somewhat inconclusive and failed to provide clear victors, at least in the context of Polish politics, with each of the main Polish groupings taking a minority share of the vote. If we look at the results in towns with not more than 25,000 inhabitants, for instance (Table 4), we see the pro-government OZON taking 29 per cent of the votes, the PPS 26.8 per cent and the National Party 18.8 per cent. In the 'Jewish street' the result was considerably more clear-cut. The Bund went into the elections in alliance with the PPS, though for tactical reasons each party put up a separate list. The reason for this strategy was explained in a characteristically tortuous way by Viktor Alter: 'The PPS,' he wrote in *Naye Folkstsaytung* on 16 December,

> wanted to uphold the purely Polish character of its list on the grounds that this would make it easier to fight Polish nationalism; therefore it was necessary for the Jewish workers to go to the polls independently. To argue that the Jewish workers forgo candidates would indicate an attitude of capitulation on our part. If we allowed the main role in the

battle for Jewish masses' rights to be taken by the Polish socialists this would show that we suffer from a dependency complex.

The results were certainly a triumph for the Bund. In towns with more than 25,000 inhabitants it won 9.5 per cent of the total vote as against about 13 per cent for all other Jewish parties. Even in smaller towns (using the table for the 1600 towns in which the PPS put up candidates, Table 3) it obtained 3.57 per cent of the seats as against 12.75 per cent for all other Jewish lists. Many of these were very small towns where Bundist influence was minimal. The showings in the bigger towns demonstrate the real sources of Bundist strength. In Warsaw the party received nearly 62 per cent of votes cast for Jewish parties, as against 19 per cent for the Zionists, 16.7 per cent for the Aguda and 2.6 per cent for the Poalei Zion Left. In Łódź, it won 57.4 per cent of the votes cast for Jewish parties as against 20.4 per cent for the Aguda and 22.2 per cent for the Democratic Zionist bloc. In Wilno, of 17 Jewish councillors, 10 represented the Bund, 5 the Zionist bloc and 2 Poalei Zion Right. In Grodno, nine of 11 councillors were Bundists, in Białystok 10 of 15, in Radom 9 of 11, in Lublin 10 of 15 and in Zamość 5 of 6. Only in Galicia, where the Bund had never been strong, did traditional political loyalties hold fast. In Kraków, of 13 Jewish councillors, 9 were Zionist, 2 Bundist and 2 represented other Jewish groups, while in Lwów, all 16 Jewish councillors were elected on the Zionist bloc list.

In recent years, large claims have been made for the Bund in the period 1935–9. According to Bernard Johnpoll, political developments in the 1930s 'handed the Bund the leadership of Polish Jewry. Because the Bund was an *ecclesia militanta* (sic), it was able to defy the threats from within and without and to lead the Jewish people during a period of despair.'[52] These views have been widely echoed. Majer Bogdanski, a former Bundist activist in Łódź, wrote in the *Jewish Chronicle* on 31 October 1986, 'Because the Bund led—yes, led—the struggle of life and death for the whole Jewish population in Poland, the population put its complete trust in it.'

In this article, I have tried to determine how accurately these views represent the true situation. It is certainly the case that, in the local government elections of 1938 and 1939, a very significant proportion of the Jewish population of Poland cast its vote for the Bund. The nature of these elections makes it difficult to assess just how large Bundist support was. I have given the electoral results for the towns (Warsaw, Łódź, Lwów, Wilno, Kraków and Lublin) which had a population of more than 40,000 Jews. In them lived about one-third of the urban Jews in Poland (77 per cent of the Jews in Poland lived in towns, the remainder in villages and in the country). In these same elections, it has been calculated that in towns with a Jewish population of 10–40,000 (18 per cent of all urban Jews), the Bund received about 40 per cent of Jewish votes, while in those 26 towns with less than 10,000 Jews in which elections were held (6.5 per cent of the Jewish urban population), the Zionists won 45 per cent of the vote, the Bund 20 per cent and other parties (mainly the Aguda) 35 per cent. According to one estimate of the Jewish votes cast in these elections, 38 per cent went to the Bund, 36 per cent to the Zionists, 23 per cent to middle-class groups (in many cases the Aguda) and others (mainly Poalei Zion) 3 per cent.[53] What does emerge is the increase in Bundist support, the decline of the Aguda vote and the persistence of a different voting pattern in Galicia. One can also assume that the remaining small-town and rural Jews would have voted for the Zionists and Aguda rather than the Bund. What is also clear is that the three-fold division of Jewish political life retained its hold, and that Bundist claims to a political monopoly, or even a majority of Jewish support, are greatly overplayed. It should also be pointed out that Jewish political life in Poland, partly as a consequence of the perilous situation of the Jews, was subject to violent swings of mood. The Bundist upswing was partly the result of Jewish hopes that the Bund could intercede on their behalf with a victorious Polish Socialist Party. Had the socialists not been able to take power (perhaps in co-operation with the Peasant Party), or had they failed to fulfil the hopes the Jews placed in them, these attitudes could very quickly have changed.

The Bund had thus not been entrusted with 'the leadership of Polish Jewry'. Given this fact, while accepting the important role the Bund, like all socialist parties, played in providing cultural and educational facilities for its members, and recognizing its growing political maturity, an assessment of the party's political stance in the last years before the war must be negative: Johnpoll's account of the Bund's history is justly entitled *The Politics of Futility*. The Bund had improved its relations with the PPS, although the co-operation of the two parties was often fraught with conflict. Yet its intransigent opposition to any common action with other Jewish groups, whether to provide an executive for the Warsaw *Kehilla* or to create an umbrella organization to defend the interests of Polish Jewry, was both arrogant and shortsighted. The emergence of such an organization, as was established in Romania, might not have done much to aid Jews in Poland. Yet the deep political divisions in the community, perpetuated and intensified by the Bund, could only weaken it in an increasingly critical situation. Thus one cannot but agree with Dubnow that, by its rigid pursuit of its own political and ideological goals, the Bund had in fact withdrawn from *Klal Yisrael*, seeing itself as a part, not of the Jewish people, but of the Jewish proletariat.

Results of local government elections in late 1938–early 1939

TABLE 3

Results of local government elections in
the 160 towns contested by the PPS in 1938 and 1939

Political Groupings	Seats	Percentage of total seats
PPS	1078	27.33
National Party	671	17.01
OZON	864	21.90
OZON in alliance with other groups (NP & Christian Democrats)	468	11.86
Peasant Party	26	0.06
Party of Labour	55	1.39
Christian Democracy	6	—
National Radical Camp	6	—
PPS—former revolutionary faction	2	
Non-party	56	1.41
Bund	141	3.57
Other Jewish lists	503	12.75
Ukrainians	30	0.76
Germans	26	0.06
Czechs	2	—
Others	55	1.39

3944

TABLE 4

Votes in local government elections in towns with more than 25,000 inhabitants

Political groupings	Percentage
PPS	26.8
OZON	29.0
National Party	18.8
Bund	9.5
Party of Labour	1.6
National Radicals	1.2
Others (mainly Jewish)	13.1

100.00

TABLE 5

Result of elections in Warsaw 18 December 1938

	Percentage of votes given to Jewish parties	Seats
OZON		40
National Party		8
Bund	61.7	17
PPS		27
ONR		5
Left Democratic		1
Zionist group Al ha-Mishmar and Poalei Zion Right	19.0	
State and Economic Bloc (Aguda and Merchants' group)	16.7	2
Poalei Zion Left	2.6	0

TABLE 6

Result of Election in Łódź 18 December 1938

	Percentage of votes given to Jewish parties	Seats
		84
		—
PPS		33
National Party		18
OZON		11
Bund	57.4	11
Aguda	20.4	3
Democratic Zionist Bloc	22.2	3
German Parties		5

TABLE 7

Result of election in Kraków, 18 December 1938

	Seats
	72
	—
OZON	23
PPS	24
National Party	12
Zionists	9
Bund	2
Other Jewish Parties	2

TABLE 8

Result of election in Wilno in 1939

OZON	19
PPS	9
National Party	26
Bund	10
Zionists	5
Poalei Zion right	2

TABLE 9

Results of election in Lwów in 1939

OZON	23
PPS	9
National Party	22
Zionist Bloc	16

Antony Polonsky

Notes

1 On these developments, see T. Jedruszczak, *Piłsudczycy bez Piłsudskiego* (Warsaw, 1963); H. and T. Jedruszczak, *Ostatnie lata II Rzeczypospolitej* (Warsw, 1970); E. D. Wynot Jr., *Polish Politics in Transition: The Camp of National Unity and the Struggle for Power 1935–1939* (Athens, Georgia, 1974).
2 See A. Polonsky, 'A failed pogrom: The Corpus Christi riots in Lwów in June 1929', to be published in the proceedings of the Conference on Polish Jewry in the Interwar Period held in April 1986 at Brandeis University.
3 On the whole question of anti-Jewish activities in the universities, see S. Rudnicki, 'From "numerus clausus" to "numerus nullus"', *POLIN: A Journal of Polish-Jewish Studies*, vol. 2 (Oxford, 1987).
4 *Gazeta Polska*, 22 April 1937
5 *ibid.*, 22 February 1937
6 *Sprawozdanie Stenograficzne Semu Rzeczypospolitej*, vol. 7, 4 June 1936.
7 On the incident in Przytyk, see J. Rothenburg, 'The Przytyk pogrom', *Soviet Jewish Affairs*, vol. 16, no. 2 (1986), pp. 29–46.
8 On the assimilationists, see Heller, 'Poles of Jewish Background—The Càse of Assimilation without Integration in Interwar Poland', in J. A. Fishman (ed.), *Studies on Polish Jewry, 1919–39* (New York, 1974), pp. 242–76; C. Heller, *On the Edge of Destruction* (New York, 1977), pp. 183–209; J. Lichten, 'Notes on the assimilation and acculturation of Jews in Poland', in C. Abramsky et al. (ed.) *The Jews in Poland* (Oxford, 1986).
9 B. Hertz, *Żydowska Krew* (Warsaw, 1936), p. 6.
10 On these questions, see E. Mendelsohn *Zionism in Poland: The Formative Years, 1915–1926* (New Haven and London, 1982); Y. Grünbaum, *Milhamot Yehudey Polania, 1913–40* (JerusalemTel Aviv, 1941)–; P. Korzec, 'Das Abkommen zwischen der Regierung Grabskis und der jüdischen Parlaments—vertretung,' in *Jahrbücher für Geschichte Osteuropas*, vol. 20, no. 3 (1972), pp. 331–66.
11 On the Aguda, see E. Mendelsohn, 'The Politics of Agudas Israel in Inter-War Poland', *Soviet Jewish Affairs*, vol. 2 (1972), pp. 47–60; G. Bacon, 'The Aguda in Inter-war Poland', to be published in the proceedings of the Conference on Polish Jewry in the Interwar Period held in April 1986 at Brandeis University.
12 The issue of *Shekhita* has given rise to a vast literature which is well reviewed by Emanuel Meltzer in his *Maavak medini be-malkodet; Yehudey Polin 1935–39* (Tel Aviv, 1982), pp. 97–110.
13 There is quite a large literature on the Bund, but it is mostly of an apologetic character. See, for instance, the following Yiddish-language works: J. Hertz (ed.), *Doyres Bundistn* (New York, 1956); J. Hertz et al. (ed.), *Di geshikhte fun Bund*, 4 vols. (New York 1960–72). The last volume is devoted to the Bund in inter-war Poland. The atmosphere of the movement is well captured in J. Hertz (ed.), *Der Bund in Bilder* (New York, 1958).
14 'Der 11ter Tsuzamenfor fun Algemayner Idishn Bund fun Poyln', *Arbeter Luakh*, vol. 6 (1925), p. 234.
15 Quoted in B. K. Johnpoll, *The Politics of Futility: The General Jewish Workers Bund in Poland, 1917–1942* (Ithaca and New York, 1967), p. 182.
16 V. Alter, *Tsu der Idn in Poyln* (Warsaw, 1937), reprinted in *Henryk Ehrlich un Viktor Alter Gedenkbukh* (Buenos Aires, 1943), p. 402.
17 *Unzer Tsayt*, vol. 2 (May 1928).
18 For the results of these elections, see 'Statistique des élections à la Diète et au Sénat effectuées le 5 et le 12 Novembre [1922]', *Statystyka polska*, vol. 8 (1926); Rzepecki, T. and Rzepecki, W., *Sejm i Senat 1928–33* (Poznań, 1928); *Statystyka Polski* series C, no.

4, *Statystyka wyborów do Sejm i Senatu z dnia 18 i 23 listopada 1930 roku'*.

19 6 August 1934

20 Quoted in Johnpoll (note 15 above), p. 187

21 *ibid.*, pp. 186–7

22 On these developments, see J. Żarnowski, *Polska Partia Socjalistyczna w latach 1939–39* (Warsaw, 1965), pp. 19–30.

23 Johnpoll (note 15 above), p. 171

26 *ibid.*

27 H. Ehrlich, *The Struggle for Revolutionary Socialism* (New York, 1934)

28 *Sotsialistishe Bleter*, vol. 1 (June 1931), pp. 24–5

29 *Unzer Tsayt*, vol. 6 (February 1932), p. 4

30 *Der Iker Fun Bundizm* (Warsaw, 1934), p. 13

31 *Unser Tsayt*, vol. 5 (April 1931), p. 3

32 *Sotsialistishe Bleter*, vol. 1 (June 1931), p. 49

33 *Henryk Ehrlich un Viktor Adler Gedenkbukh* (note 16 above), p. 265

34 *ibid.*, pp. 369–70

35 Quoted in *ibid.*, pp. 49–20.

36 Quoted in Johnpoll (note 15 above), p. 178.

37 On this, see Żarnowski (note 22 above), pp. 30–138; J. Kowalski, *Komunistyczna Partia Polski 1935–1938* (Warsaw 1975).

38 Quoted in Johnpoll (note 15 above), p. 172.

39 *Naye Folkstsaytung*, 14 March 1936

40 Quoted in Johnpoll (note 15 above), p. 181.

41 The statistics on *Kehilla* and local government elections in the latter part of this article are put together on the basis of reports in the contemporary press, as well as the material in Johnpoll (note 15 above), Meltzer (note 12 above), and J. Marcus, *Social and Political History of the Jews in Poland 1919–39* (Berlin, 1983).

42 *Naye Folkstsaytung*, 9, 13 September 1936

43 See R. Sakowska, 'Z dziejów gminy żydowskiej w Warszawie 1918–1939', in *Warszawa II Rzeczypospolitej* (Warsaw, 1972), vol. 4, pp. 243–71.

44 On the Łódź elections, see Żarnowski (note 22 above), pp. , pp. 147–54; P. Korzec '"Czerwona" Łódźka Rada Miejska w latach 1936–37', *Studia i Materiały do dziejow Lodz i okregu łódźkiego* (Łódź, 1962), pp. 207–54; Meltzer (note 12 above), pp. 123 7.

45 Meltzer (note 12 above), p. 126

46 *ibid.*, p. 147

47 J. K. Borski, *Sprawa Żydowska a Socjalizm: Polemika z Bundem* (Warsaw, 1936).

48 On this question see Meltzer (note 12 above), pp. 260 73; Marcus (note 41 above), pp. 372–5; Z. Szajkowski, 'Western Jewish Aid and Intercession for Polish Jewry 1919–39', in *Studies on Polish Jewry* (note 8 above), pp. 201–10.

49 Quoted in Żarnowski (note 22 above), p. 245

50 *ibid.*, p. 310

51 On these elections, see *ibid.*, pp. 328–34; Meltzer (note 12 above), pp. 274–89; Marcus (note 41 above), pp. 382–86.

52 Johnpoll (note 15 above), p. 195

53 Marcus (note 41 above), p. 468

8

PALESTINE AND THE JEWISH NATIONAL MOVEMENT

The Establishment of the Jewish Settlement in Eretz Israel and the Gaster Papers

Ran Aaronsohn and Yehoshua Ben Arieh

INTRODUCTION

THE First *Aliyah* (1882–1904) and the establishment of the Jewish settlement in Eretz Israel which commenced at that time are largely identified with Baron Edmond de Rothschild.

Undoubtedly, Baron Rothschild was extremely important during the greater part of the First *Aliyah* period: his employees, called regularly the 'Administration', left their mark on most of the settlement activities of the period. However, before the Baron became active in the Zionist settlement of Eretz Israel, there had been a short but significant independent first stage.

During this first stage thousands of Jews, the vanguard of subsequent Zionist *aliyot*, had arrived in the country. They established many of the most important *moshavot* without any help whatsoever from the Baron. The year 1882 saw the establishment of Rishon Lezion, Rosh Pina, Zikhron Yaakov and the resettled Petach Tikvah (first founded in 1878 by settlers from the old *yishuv* in Jerusalem). Nahalat Reuven (which later became the *moshava* Nes Tsiona) was founded in 1883; Yesod Hamaalah and Gedera in 1884.[1]

These *moshavot*, as well as others such as Rehovot or Hadera, which were established without the Baron's help during the 1890s, were founded as a result of the private initiative and resources of the Hovevei Zion societies in Eastern Europe. The very first settlers were drawn from the membership of these societies. The difficult situation in Eretz Israel, then an undeveloped part of the Ottoman Empire, posed grave problems for the original settlers—problems so severe that the continued existence of the settlements was in question. At that point, Baron Rothschild stepped in and provided the settlements with funds, capital investment and administrative staff. He managed the settlements for an extended period (until 1900 directly, afterwards to a lesser extent).[2]

In much of the historiography of the period, the first phase in the settlement of the *moshavot* is mentioned only in passing; historical accounts often begin with the Baron's involvement. Occasionally the first phase is entirely ignored; the literature sometimes states that the Baron himself founded the first *moshavot*. In fact, not only were many of them planned, organized and founded without any connection with Rothschild, but even in the short period between establishment and patronage by the Baron, they managed to develop, function vigorously and make a significant impact on the landscape.

The present study, along with the documents appended to it, is meant to present several key phenomena which occurred during the first period of the existence of the *moshavot*. It focuses on the Hovevei Zion society of Romania and the establishment of Zikhron Yaakov by this society as a specific example of the general phenomenon. The paper offers an analysis of the establishment of Zikhron Yaakov as this process is described in some of the original documents.

HOVEVEI ZION IN ROMANIA AND THE BEGINNING OF THE ZIKHRON YAAKOV SETTLEMENT

The Zikhron Yaakov settlement was founded in October 1882 on the slopes of Mount Carmel by immigrants from Romania and was placed under Baron Rothschild's patronage a year later, in October 1883. In fact the foundation of the settlement should be dated back to January 1882, when it was first conceived. At that time a general organization of nearly all the Hovevei Zion societies in Romania was set up in the city of Focsani.

The organization was established at a meeting of more than one hundred representatives of thirty-three Hovevei Zion societies throughout Romania. Its official name was 'The Central Committee for Encouraging Jewish Immigration from Romania', but it was also known as 'The Central Committee in Galatz', since it was located in the town of Galatz (Galati). The officers of the committee were Isak Lobel (chairman) and Josef Abalas (vice-chairman), but its principal activists were Dr Karl Lippe and Sam Pineles.[3]

The 'Central Committee in Galatz' functioned as a settlement organization. It bought the land (which was registered in the name of the chairman of the committee) and organized and funded the journey, as well as settling the new immigrants. In addition, the committee continued to manage the *moshava* in its formative years: the settlers in Zikhron Yaakov received guidelines for communal life from the committee in Romania rather than making their own collective decisions. The settlement was managed by an administration which was appointed by the committee, and the settlers had very little influence on the decisions which were to shape their lives in their new home.[4]

The importance of the Central Committee in Galatz, we feel, extends beyond its particular role in the history of the settlement of Zikhron Yaakov. It was the first country-wide organization of the Hovevei Zion movement anywhere. (Hovevei Zion in Russia were not to form such an organization for almost another two years.) In 1882 it founded two of the first three *moshavot* of the First *Aliyah* (if we include Rosh Pina, established by Romanian Jews, which it helped found indirectly and continued to support). In addition, some of the Galatz Committee leaders were active on the world Jewish scene over an extended period. These included Lippe, Pineles and Moses Gaster, who, fifteen years later, were among the founders of the World Zionist Organization.

MOSES GASTER AND THE GASTER ARCHIVE

The story of the establishment of Zikhron Yaakov (at that time still called 'Zamarin') is generally known from a number of secondary sources, especially the important book by Samsonov.[5] A recent article, partially based on primary sources, deals with the first stage in the settlement's development. It covers the two-year period which began with the establishment of the Central Committee in Galatz and ended with the transfer of administrative responsibility for the *moshava* to Baron Rothschild, an event which symbolized the end of Zikhron Yaakov's first phase.[6] Nevertheless, some important points remain unclear: when the Zamarin property was first offered for sale, who decided to purchase the land and how the decision was made; what was the size of the property purchased; how much it cost, etc.

All these gaps in our knowledge of the earliest history of the *moshava* are due primarily to the limited number of primary sources available: the original documents which dealt with the establishment of Zikhron Yaakov have been lost; there are relatively few known documents which refer to the correspondence of the Central Committee in Galatz, and none of its protocols have survived. The documents which exist, located for the most part in the Central Zionist Archives in Jerusalem,[7] are complemented by the material available in the Gaster Archive at the library of University College London, where it is located in the Mocatta library.

Rabbi Doctor Moses Gaster (1856–1939) was a renowned scholar and Jewish leader. He was a linguist, a researcher into Judaic studies as well as Romanian literature and folklore, and a Zionist activist. He spent his first thirty years in Romania and Germany and lived in England for the rest of his life.[8]

Gaster was educated at the University of Bucharest, the city of his birth. He received his doctorate from the University of Leipzig and was ordained at the Rabbinical Seminary of Breslau. Upon completion of his studies, he returned to Bucharest and lectured at the university there. He was also appointed a member of the Romanian Royal Academy. At the same time he was active in Jewish organizations: first in the Alliance Israelite and then, from 1882, in the Hovevei Zion organization, where he served as a member of the Central Committee in Galatz representing Bucharest.

Towards the end of 1885, Gaster was expelled from Romania because of his Jewish national involvement and settled in England, where he continued his academic as well as his Jewish activities. He conducted academic research and lectured at the University of Oxford. He also continued to function as a rabbi, serving as both the *hakham* of the Sephardic community and the director of the Montefiore Rabbinical Seminary at Ramsgate. He was an active Zionist, and his name could typically be found among the founders or directors of every major Jewish organization supporting settlement in Eretz Israel. Thus he was involved with the Nodedim (wanderers) group (which later became the Maccabees), with the committee of the Agudat Ahim (fraternal society) at the end of the 1880s, and with the English Hovevei Zion society in the 1890s. He represented England at the first Zionist Congresses, eventually holding the position of vice-president, and in 1907 became head of the Zionist Federation of England.

The Gaster archives in the library of University College London contain Gaster's extensive correspondence, including correspondence from his Romanian period. During this period he served as a member of the Central Committee of the Hovevei Zion movement in Romania between 1882 and 1885. The Central Committee in Galatz would send to Gaster, who was based in Bucharest, detailed reports on the state of the settlement in Eretz Israel. These reports often contained telegrams and other important documents (either originals or copies). Gaster also received the notices distributed among the various local Hovevei Zion committees throughout Romania. Thus, even though the archives of the Central Committee are not extant, it is possible to reconstruct much of the missing information concerning the activities of this committee during the first stage of the Jewish settlement in Eretz Israel. We have reproduced four documents from the Gaster papers in order to illustrate the process of the establishment of Zikhron Yaakov.[9]

THE ESTABLISHMENT OF ZIKHRON YAAKOV

According to selected documents in the Gaster archives, it appears that the process of founding the *moshava* began earlier than is commonly assumed: the first group of immigrants sent by the Central Committee arrived in Eretz Israel as early as August 1882. They immediately received an offer to sell them the Zamarin property, which was located on the slopes of Mount Carmel to the south of Haifa. In the correspondence with the Central Committee, the property was described (see Document 1) as being much more suited for settlement than it later proved to be.[10]

Two of the immigrants inspected the property and one of the activists of the small Jewish community in Haifa mediated between the buyers and the seller. The property was purchased hastily because of pressure the source of which is not known (perhaps it was a strategem on the seller's part) in disregard of the regulations of the Central Committee. The transaction itself was executed by an authorized representative of the Central Committee located in Beirut who was apparently involved in the Romanian settlement at Gauni—Rosh Pina (Document 2 below).

The negotiations lasted approximately six weeks and were completed early in October 1882. The purchase was concluded on the basis of erroneous information and, apparently, without examination of alternative proposals. The agreement involved the payment of 4600 francs in exchange for property reported to cover an area of 6500 *dunams* (see Document 3; generally one *dunam* equals 1000 square metres; old [Turkish] *dunam* = 'Dulam' = 919 sq. metres). Afterwards it turned out that the actual area of the property was a good deal smaller.

At first the immigrant families lived in Haifa, which they used as their home base. The men moved to the Zamarin hill in December 1882. They began to work optimistically, functioning as a commune without dividing the land into private plots. The settlers at Zamarin were primarily involved in building the infrastructure (mainly preparing the stony land for cultivation), ploughing the land or sowing. They made use of European tools and methods: wagons, hoes and horse-drawn ploughs. They sowed wheat and planned to sow potatoes and plant a vegetable garden. It is also clear from the existing documents that the residents of Zamarin maintained a religious life-style and that they were astonished by the pleasant weather. Although internal social difficulties became apparent, they waited optimistically for the property to be subdivided into plots, and for the construction of private houses. They dreamed of expanding the limits of the *moshava* and even envisaged the establishment of a port near their settlement (see Document 4 below).[11]

SUMMARY

The Gaster papers contain a rich source of primary information, some of it unique, on the establishment of Zikhron Yaakov during the years 1882–3. A small sample of the documents concerning the settlement of Zikhron Yaakov which are available in the Gaster collection is appended to this article. These documents contain many precise details. They serve to illustrate the first stage of the establishment of Jewish settlements in Eretz Israel, a stage which was characterized by the initiative and independent resources of the Hovevei Zion societies and the settlers themselves, before the involvement of Baron Rothschild. This material has shed light on an important but little-known period in the history of the modern Jewish settlement in Eretz Israel.

Appendix

DOCUMENT I   [Gaster Archive, 30/11]

Telegram from Beirut (copy)[12]

There is no hope from Gauni.[13]
We were with the French seller[14] on Mt Carmel, near the sea, four hours by wagon.[15]
3000 *dolem* land suitable for cultivation, 3000 *dolem* forest.
Fruit trees,[16] eighteen dwelling units,[17] water.[18]
A good place for 75 families.
Price 40,000 francs. Please send power of attorney [to withdraw] the francs.
Negotiations must be expedited. Time is short; otherwise [the transaction] will be lost.

Engener, Klister, Rapaport[19]

DOCUMENT 2 [Gaster Archive, 30/11]

Letter from the Central Committee in Galatz to Gaster (Romanian)

Galatz
29 August 1882
– Number 1310 –

The Central Committee
For Promoting Immigration
of Jews from Romania
— Galatz —

To Mr Gaster, Member of the Supervisory Committee of
Immigration from Romania, Bucharest

Dear Sir,

We have just received a telegram from Beirut,[20] whose contents we would like to share with you. It reads as follows: An advantageous proposal of a property offered for sale.[21] This proposal will enable us to eliminate risks for the immigrants who have already left here and who are unable to settle in the village of Gauni which was purchased by the people of Moinesti.[22] The property in Gauni is not at all suitable as a *moshava*, but in order to be of assistance, we have agreed in principle to allow Messrs Levi Frank and Associates of Beirut (who are known by the Committee to be very respectable and honest)[23] to deal with this problem.

Since our constitution advises us to purchase land only by means of a special committee chosen by a general meeting (Paragraph 73),[24] a procedure which would be impossible to follow because of the urgency of the matter, and in order not to hinder the transaction, the Central Committee requests that the regional committee declare its agreement to this departure from the [constitutional] procedure, as well as its agreement to the purchase of the land by Messrs Levi Frank and Associates. In addition to the decision made by each [local] committee on how to deal with this problem, [we may be able] to come to a collective agreement. Replies must be received immediately so as to allow enough time for instructing Messrs Levi Frank and Associates clearly.

We permit ourselves to recommend to you a complete ban on publicity—spreading rumours and especially reports in the press which would be disadvantageous. We hope that you will agree with our thoughts on the matter.[25]

We await your reply,
Sincerely yours

Vice-President   Secretary
Josef Abalas   Sam Pineles[26]

DOCUMENT 3

**Telegram from the Central Committee in Galatz
to Gaster (German)**

4 October [1882],[27] Galatz
Zamarin with another five *fedan*[28]
Purchased for 46,000 francs.[29]
      Abalas, Pineles

DOCUMENT 4   [Gaster Archive, 12/3]

Letter from a Settler at Zamarin (Yiddish)

A Letter by Letter Copy[30]
Zamarin, 4 January 1883

To my friend the honoured rabbi and leader, our teacher and master Reb Pinhas Vallach, may his light shine.

Please be informed that we, thank God, are healthy and I hope to hear the same from you.

With great joy I put pen to paper in order to describe the *moshava* of Zamarin to you, as I have not seen you since the trip to Galatz.

Know that we are living in Haifa, together with all the immigrants and their families. Lodging is not very expensive. We do not have to purchase wood since it is warm here. All of us male immigrants travel to Zamarin to work. We have been working there for the past three weeks and, with God's help, our work is already bearing fruit which we can see with our own eyes. The wheat which we have sown has sprouted nicely everywhere and has grown to the height of a finger.

What shall I tell you, my esteemed Reb Pinhas? As you approach the *moshava* you see in front of you a frightening mountain, but as you go up the mountain it is a pleasure to see the wonderful fields found above. The air is clean and very healthy; it could not be any healthier or cleaner. Drinking water is very expensive [but] much better than in Haifa. There are a good many trees, a lot of building stones, there are even trees for working, thank God. I'll give you a small example: last week our blacksmith needed a heavy wooden block to place under a coach. We went down into the valley and cut a thick block of wood. Eight people tried to bring it up [to the *moshava* on the mountain] but couldn't manage. Fourteen of us had to go in order to haul up the wooden block. You can imagine, then, that there are trees for working.

There are also a good many carob trees with a lot of carobs from last year still on them, because there was no one to gather the fruit. There are also a lot of fig trees. We have not yet seen olive trees, although the agent from Berlad says that there are also olive trees.[31] We work the entire week and the only time to see the whole *moshava* is on the Sabbath: I have been here for three weeks already and I haven't seen more than a quarter of the colony.

Now I'd like to describe our work. Believe me, it is a pleasure to see us on the Sabbath, when we gather together to pray in a *minyan* [quorum] and observe the Sabbath as commanded by God. On Sunday mornings everyone wakes up early, finishes praying, takes food, and goes to the field with a plough or a hoe on his back. It's pleasant to see how the ploughmen walk with the horses, seeing that we don't yet have any oxen. Many people plough with their hoes, including me—about fifteen to twenty people plough with hoes; and believe me, not one of us has ever walked with a hoe before in his life. I certainly haven't. You should see, my dear Reb Pinhas, how we stand with hoes in our hand and work, thank God, industriously: one works with the hoe, another with the plough; some clear rocks from the fields and other carry them away.

588

I'll explain to you about the rocks which have to be cleared. The fields have a lot of large rocks, which the lazy Arabs never removed. We want our field, however, to be clean and pretty; and the rocks also damage the plough. We made things for carrying, each carried by two men. We gather the large rocks into a big heap, and everyone carries them gladly. At the moment, we are all working together, in a fashion called a 'commune'. Every immigrant gathers rocks diligently, because he wants the part of the field which will eventually be his to be free of rocks. So everyone is pleased to work on any part of the field.

Everything is near the sea, and the air everywhere is good. When we get up to go to the field early in the morning it is somewhat chilly, but later, after a few hours, you have to take off your jacket. It becomes so hot that it is uncomfortable to wear a shirt. And the air, the trees, and the grass! A few days ago, rain fell and the wheat sprouted; our hearts are filled with great happiness.

We also ploughed a large field for planting potatoes. Next week we will plant a vegetable garden at Tantura. Tantura is a piece of land five *fedan* big which is located near the sea. In time, a port may be established there, as in Haifa. If God, may His name be blessed, will help and the Central Committee will purchase other plots of land in the area, then we will be the happiest of men.

My esteemed friend, Reb Pinhas, I would write more but I am very tired because of the work. I will write more another time. Believe me, if I had to write everything, I would have to fill three [more] pages. [But] we come back from the fields tired, we eat and go right to sleep because we have to wake up early every morning in order to go to work. Our work is very sweet, like sugar.

We hope, may God be blessed, that shortly we will not have to worry any longer and that every adult will receive five *falshes* of land.[32] Every immigrant will build a house for himself and plant a garden near the house, like the Germans in Haifa.[33] God willing, everything will work out.

Reb Pinhas, it is possible that some people wrote bad letters (I know about this very well) because there are some immigrants who are not happy with the settlement. They are not cut out for colonization. Each of them wants to be a president, like R . . . and others, too; I can't write about all of them.[34] The people who are sending bad reports are themselves bad. They don't want to work, they made a mistake in thinking that they would find in Zamarin trees which grow baked *hallah* [Sabbath loaves] and fried geese. It's a pity; because of this, they aren't happy with anything. But first we have to work, to plough and sow. Later, with the help of God, and when our own wheat is harvested—it will be possible to eat bread and *hallah* as well. But first we have to work, not first talk and do nothing! In order to be a farmer, one has to farm, not be a Jewish loafer. These are people who don't want to work, but we hope, may God be blessed, that everything will turn out all right. We are waiting for Mr Abalas to arrive this week.[35] There is nothing else new. I wish you lots of happiness and health. Your best friend,

Written by Meir Hirsch Heifler[36]

Notes

The present study is based on MA and PhD theses submitted to the Hebrew University by R. Aaronsohn, under the supervision of Y. Ben Arieh: 'The Establishment and the Beginnings of Zikhron Yaakov and Rishon Lezion as Agricultural Settlements' (Hebrew), (MA thesis, Jerusalem, 1979); and 'The Jewish Colonies at their Inception and the Contribution of Baron Rothschild to their Development' (Hebrew) (PhD thesis, Jerusalem, 1985). The authors would like to thank Mrs Trude Levi, Hebrew Librarian and Archivist of the Gaster Papers at University College, London, for her help in connection with this paper.

1 Ekron (Mazkeret Batya), founded in 1883 and settled in 1884, was the first and only *moshava* during that period which was established by Baron Rothschild.

2 R. Aaronsohn, 'Building the Land: Stages in First *Aliyah* Colonization (1882–1904)' *Cathedra*, vol. 3 (1983), pp. 236–79.

3 I. Klausner, *Hibbat Zion in Romania* (Hebrew) (Jerusalem, 1958), pp. 77–86; M. Schaerf, *The Torch Was Lit in Romania—Shmuel Pineles and Early Zionism in Romania* (Hebrew) (Jerusalem, 1986), pp. 33–67; C. Jancu, *Les Juifs en Roumanie 1866–1919* (Aix-en-Provence, 1978).

4 Klausner (note 3 above), pp. 86–8, 129–37, etc.; Aaronsohn, 'The Establishment', *passim*. See Document 4 below for the subdivision of the land and the acquisition of new land by the Central Committee.

5 A. Samsonov, *Zikhron Yaakov: Its History* (Hebrew) (Tel Aviv, 1943?).

6 R. Aaronsohn, 'Zikhron Yaakov, 1883–1884: Vision versus Reality', (Hebrew) *Geographical Horizons*, vol. 20 (1987), pp. 19–50.

7 These documents are found in the collection of the Hovevei Zion society of Romania, Central Zionist Archives A133, and the collected papers of Sam Pineles, CZA A144.

8 The biographical details presented here were drawn from the following sources: B. Schindler, *Gaster Centenary Publication* (London, 1958); *Encyclopedia Judaica*, vol. 7 (1971), pp. 332–4; A. Oren, *Hibbat Zion in Great Britain* (Hebrew) (Jerusalem, 1974).

9 In translating the Hebrew documents, we have attempted to be as true as possible to the original language, which was simple and flowing. At the same time, all the documents were written in everyday language which often contained mistakes and foreign phrases, making translation difficult. We relied, therefore, on the expert advice of Mr and Mrs Kalman Kaftori (Yiddish), Mrs Gerty Rubinstein (Romanian) and Mr Zvi Filhart (German), whom we would like to thank.

10 Cf. Klausner (note 3 above), pp. 129ff.; Samsonov (note 5 above), pp. 57ff. See also notes 15–18 below.

11 These details, based on the documents appended to this article, are corroborated by several sources. A port was never built near Zamarin, but the area of the *moshava* was widely extended by Baron Rothschild. In addition, the Baron's administrators built permanent housing units with his funding (beginning in 1885). However, temporary housing had been built at the Zamarin site even earlier: several settler families moved from Haifa to Zamarin in the course of 1883. For further information on the temporary housing and the improvements made to the infrastructure of the settlement (i.e. paving roads and improvement of water supplies), as well as other activities which took place before the Baron's involvement, see Klausner (note 3 above), pp. 134–7, and Aaronsohn (note 6 above), pp. 29–37.

12 The copy of the telegram is undated. Since it was attached to a letter dated 29 August 1882 (Document 2 below), it would seem that the telegram arrived in Romania on that day. According to the operational procedures of the telegraph system at the time, it can be assumed that the telegram was sent from Haifa on one of the three days which preceded its arrival, i.e. between 27 and 29 August 1882.

13 Some of the land of this Arab village in the upper Galilee was bought by the representatives of the Society for Jewish Settlement in Eretz Israel in Moinesti, Romania. They called their future colony Gei Oni (later Rosh Pina).

14 This refers to an *effendi* (aristocrat), probably of Christian Arab origin, by the name of Frances Germain who lived in Haifa and was a French citizen. Historical accounts of the period often claim that Germain served as the French vice-consul in Haifa, but this is not borne out by the details of the correspondence between the French foreign ministry and its agents in Eretz Israel.

15 The Zamarin property is located more than thirty kilometres south of Haifa. Under the conditions of the time, the journey usually took eight hours by wagon, rather than four.

16 All accounts indicate that the only 'fruit trees' on the property were a few scattered fig and carob trees. For other data concerning the extent of the property and its cost, see below, note 29.

17 This refers to the houses occupied by the Arab tenant farmers of Zamarin. According to other sources, the property contained about twelve mud huts and two other stone houses.

18 The property of Zamarin included three small springs yielding a meagre flow of muddy water. For detailed reports and maps, see C. R. Conder and R. E. Kichener, *The Survey of Western Palestine, P.E.F.—Memoirs*, vol. 2 (London, 1882), pp. 1–35; *P.E.F.—Maps* (London, 1880), sheets 7–8.

19 The three signatories on the telegram, like all the other settlers, lived at that time in Haifa. Shmuel Engener (Ingner or Ingener) was a Jewish watchmaker who mediated between the immigrants and Germain. He had emigrated to Eretz Israel from Romania in the 1860s and had first settled in Tiberias then moved in the 1870s to Haifa. Mordechai Klister of Galatz, one of the leaders of the settlers, made a first exploratory trip to the Zamarin property as a representative of the immigrants (together with Moshe Kornfeld of Berlad) and warmly recommended purchasing the property. Nahman Rapaport of Galatz was one of the more respected and prosperous of the settlers. He died in Haifa in 1885, shortly before the stone houses of the *moshava* were built and before the first families of settlers had moved to the property.

20 Document 1 above. The telegram was originally sent from Haifa (see note 12 above). Document 2 indicates, however, that the telegram was apparently sent via Beirut by Emil Levi Frank (note 23 below).

21 See notes 15–18 above for more information on the claimed advantages of the property's location near Haifa, its size, value, water supplies and existing vegetation.

22 See note 13 above.

23 Emil Levi Frank, a Jew born in Alsace who had spent twenty years of his life in Beirut, acted as a British shipping agent in the ports of Syria. He had served as vice-consul of Germany, Austria and the United States in Alexandria and was one of the heads of the Alliance Israelite branch in Beirut (Gaster Papers, 25/12, his letter dated 2 February 1883).

24 This appears to be a reference to the regulations passed by the Central Committee in Galatz in February 1882, which comprised 149 paragraphs. However, Paragraph 73 of the regulations in Yiddish (according to the copy in Klausner, note 3 above, p. 335) does not deal with the purchase of land.

25 The immigration of Jews to Eretz Israel from Romania was widely covered by the press at the time. Newspaper publicity produced an immediate and negative effect: members of local societies who wanted to be sent to Eretz Israel increased their pressure on the Central Committee. These members were for the most part poor and unskilled (and therefore unsuitable for settlement according to the regulations). The authors of the letter appear to have been concerned that this might happen.

26 Josef Abalas was a wealthy merchant from Galatz; Sam Pineles, also a merchant from Galatz, was active in the local branch of the Alliance Israëlite and in the Zion bureau (Bnai Brith) of his city. Isak Löbel, president of the committee, could not have been active at that point because of the illness from which he died in February 1883 (for information on Löbel's death, see Pineles' letter dated 18 February 1883, Gaster Papers, 19/12).

27 The date of the telegram is not clear. In our opinion it should be read as 4 October, but 10 October is an alternative reading. The year is not mentioned, but 1882 is certain.

28 A *fedan*, a traditional Arab measure, is the area which a pair of oxen is capable of ploughing in one season, in other words about one hundred *dunam*. This refers to the area of about five hundred *dunam* which belonged to Germain in the Arab village of Tantura on the Mediterranean shore, five kilometres from Zamarin.

29 At first, 40,000 francs were mentioned, for the 6000 *dunam* of the Zamarin property alone (see Document 1 above). The additional 6000 francs were for the purchase of the five hundred *dunam* of Tantura. In fact the final price was higher. According to one source, the property cost a total of 50,000 francs, including 4000 francs for registering ownership of the land (letter dated 5 December 1882, CZA J41/69). A second source indicates that the final price was 52,000 francs including 5000 francs for registration (Samsonov, note 5 above, p. 58).

30 An abridged version of this letter appeared in the Hebrew newspaper *Ha-Magid*, vol. 8 (21 February 1883) (and was reproduced in Samsonov, note 5 above, pp. 65–66). More recently, a further abridged version appeared in Schaerf (note 3 above), pp. 57–8.

31 This refers to one of the two representatives who went to examine the property when it was offered for sale (see note 19 above).

32 *Falsh*: a measure of area, nearly twenty *dunam*. A stretch of land of almost one hundred *dunam* was to be surveyed and subdivided among each of the 69 settlers in Zikhron Yaakov at the end of the first year of the colony.

33 The German colony, established near Haifa by the Templars of Württemberg in 1869, was the most modern housing development in the north of Palestine at that time.

34 It is possible that this refers to bitterness about the method of managing the *moshava*, which expressed itself in the 'rebellion' against the 'local administrators' of the colony, Brasseur and Brill (see note 35 below), which broke out in February 1883. A second 'rebellion' against the whole method of managing the *moshava* and against the Central Committee in Galatz broke out in May 1883. See Friedenstein, 'The Cry of Samaria' (Hebrew) *Ha-Melitz*, vol. 27, no. 70 (17 August 1883).

35 As far as we know, Josef Abalas, the vice-president of the Central Committee in Galatz, never visited Eretz Israel. However, the agent representing the Central Committee, Emil Levi Frank, visited the colony at the beginning of 1883. In addition, Frank's agent Brasseur, and an agricultural adviser sent from Romania, Shlomo Brill, lived with the settlers on a permanent basis. Even though they are not mentioned in this document, they were the actual managers of the *moshava*.

36 Meir Hirsch Heifler of Galatz arrived in Eretz Israel on 24 November 1882, with the second group sent by the Central Committee from Romania.

First buildings of Zamarin (Zikhron Yaakov), 1885

COMITETUL CENTRAL
pentru inlesnire
Emigrârei Israeliților
DIN
ROMANIA.

Formal title of the Romanian 'Central Committee' (letter, 1883).

Rabbi Moses Gaster.

Reflections on the Growth of the Jewish National Home, 1880–1948*

Jehuda Reinharz

I

THE right of Jewish immigrants to determine the patterns of Israel's future existence has a strong ideological grounding in Zionist principles. Israel exists, according to its own proclamation, in order 'to solve the problem of Jewish homelessness by opening the gates to all Jews and lifting the Jewish people to equality in the family of nations'[1]—that is, to provide a rational solution for the problem of Jews in exile and to allow the Jews of the dispersion, in returning to the homeland, to become masters of their own national destiny. This surely means that the new immigrants are no less entitled to advocate their own patterns of living as appropriate for the whole of Israeli society, or for part of it, than were their predecessors, who established the social institutions with which Israel began in 1948.

Zionist immigrants since the 1880s had developed those institutions in deliberate opposition to the patterns of living of the older, traditionalistic, economically dependent Jewish settlement that preceded them in Palestine. Accordingly, they proudly called themselves the 'New *Yishuv*' in contradistinction to the older community, whom they named the 'Old *Yishuv*'. Moreover, each 'generation' of Zionist settlers—or, to use the more common expression, each 'wave of immigration' (*Aliya*)—felt obliged, to the extent that it was imbued with the Zionist spirit of autonomy, to mould the emerging institutions of the New *Yishuv* in its own image.[2] Other *Aliyot*, not marked by a clear Zionist enthusiasm, nevertheless altered the patterns of living in Jewish Palestine simply because they arrived in such large numbers that by persisting in social habits brought over from the Diaspora, which were new to the country, they produced new institutions.

The innovations thus introduced, whether out of Zionist enthusiasm

* The following discussion is based on a larger study tentatively entitled 'The Emergence of the Jewish State' by Ben Halpern and Jehuda Reinharz.

or simple inertia, far from becoming universal, provoked principled opposition among some of the earlier settlers, in the New as well as the Old *Yishuv*, or simply failed to gain the participation of others. Thus the social structure of Israel in 1948 was composed of a loose aggregation of organized groupings, reflecting, on the one hand, ideological principles and, on the other hand, common origins in a particular Diaspora region or in a particular Jewish or Zionist generation with its specific historical experience; and with each grouping bent on pursuing its separate course apart from the rest, or even on setting a course unilaterally which it expected or insisted that all the rest must follow.

The major cleavage dividing Israeli society, inherited from history by the Jewish state, is this division between the Old and the New *Yishuv*.[3] The new idea that precipitated this division was the perception, which became dominant among Western European Jews from the end of the eighteenth century, that the immemorial affliction of the Jews in their dispersion should not be borne piously as a divine decree, but treated as a social problem to be nationally overcome. Such attitudes had only an indirect effect on the Palestine Jewish community until late in the nineteenth century.[4] Not until the rise of Zionism among Eastern European Jews in the 1880s was immigration to Palestine conceived as a rational programme for the solution of the Jewish Problem. The new immigrants, inspired by this new perception from the very outset, stressed the radical difference of their enterprise from the aims with which traditionalist Jews had been coming to settle in Palestine for centuries past.

The source of their *élan* was an emotional enthusiasm for what they called 'auto-emancipation': their desire and will to be masters of their own national destiny. Its most elemental, original manifestation was not any positive goal at all, but rather a powerful revulsion against the subjection of the Jews in its manifold aspects: economic, cultural and social, as well as political. Hence not only the State of Israel itself, but the other institutions with which Israel began, grew out of a reaction against specific conditions of the modern Jewish Diaspora—The Exile—which the Zionists hoped to eliminate in building the Jewish National Home.

The crucial experience that first set off the Zionist revolt was, to be sure, the experience of a particular generation in a particular region: specifically, the disillusionment of Eastern European intellectuals with civic emancipation and social progressivism as solutions of the Jewish Problem following the Russian pogroms of the 1880s. However, the revulsion which Eastern European Jews felt, and which was reinforced by the experiences of succeeding generations of Zionists, there and in other Jewish communities, illuminated for them the most general conditions that they believed made Jewish life abnormal everywhere in the Diaspora: the political homelessness, economic dependency, cultural inadequacy and social disintegration of the Exile. To free themselves from all these conditions by an effort of national revival was the aim these men and women pursued as pioneer immigrants to Palestine, as well as in all the social, economic, cultural and political institutions they established there.

To the Zionist, as to many other modernist critics, the traditional Jewish community, in spite of its 'tribal' cohesion and unparalleled religious solidarity through centuries, seemed, for example, to lack a firm social consensus that could serve as a basis for dealing with critical modern problems. The traditional firmness and unity of the Jews, according to such critics, depended on the ghetto or other forms of mediaeval isolation from the Gentile world. The values and institutions upon which it was based—the uniformity of religious practice, the loose but comprehensive world-wide communal organization, the universal, intensive education in the Jewish tradition—seemed suitable only for adjustment to the problems of ghetto life. Once the ghetto was broken, Jewish solidarity based on these foundations could no longer be sustained. Accordingly, nineteenth-century Jews emerging from the 'ghetto' were considered by modernist critics of all kinds as a disorganized throng of individualists, unable to subordinate their egotistical motives to the common interest—however the latter might be defined.

The advocates of general enlightenment and civic emancipation of the Jews as the solution of the modern Jewish problem often felt, moreover, that certain traditional elements of Jewish solidarity that survived the ghetto were handicaps in adjusting to a more modern situation. They held that, apart from such common Jewish religious values as remained after Judaism developed Reform and Orthodox sects, other values and institutions specific to the Jews and common to all Jews were of dubious efficacy. Most should be replaced by new values and institutional bonds specific to the secular state in which each group of Jews lived and common to all its citizens. Jewish languages and folk customs should, for example, give way to the national languages and customs of modern Europe. The independent discipline of the Jewish community should be abandoned as far as necessary for its proper subordination to the state. In this way the modernist reformers hoped to supply the social consensus needed to unite Jews with their Gentile fellow-citizens in the common body politic.

For Zionists, on the other hand, the modern Jewish situation demanded a new social consensus that should unite nineteenth-century Jews throughout the world. That consensus, they held, could no longer be religious alone but must be national, for it had to unite not only diverse religious groupings within Judaism, but also believing and unbelieving Jews. In addition, it had to organize the Jews not for the pious, passive acceptance of oppression but for the rebellious, active struggle for liberation.

Zionists found the source of such a consensus—just as had the traditionalists—in the Hebrew language (or in another Jewish language, Yiddish), and they, too, sought to establish it as the solid foundation of a system of intensive, general Jewish education. But for Zionists, unlike the traditionalists, the Hebrew language and Jewish education became instruments by which the Jews could unite to master their own fate and determine their own destiny, not instruments of self-discipline and submission to divine decrees. The revival of the national language and culture desired—and, indeed, achieved—by some Zionists was thus an expression of the same myths of self-liberation and self-determination that found a direct expression in the creation of the sovereign state of Israel.

Attempts to solve the Jewish Problem nationally, whether through the principles of emancipation or of auto-emancipation, were not necessarily rejected in every aspect by traditionalists, even though they regarded the Exile as a fate decreed by God, not by social and political circumstance, and expected to be redeemed from it by the Messiah, not by any human agency. The Old *Yishuv* in Palestine did not reject *in toto* the specific projects for educational reform, linguistic revival or communal organization proposed by the modernists. Before the years of Zionist immigration, Western Jewish philanthropists were already offering aid to the community in Palestine by setting up modern schools, which taught not only the three R's and European languages in addition to the traditional curriculum, but where girls as well as boys were educated and vocational training was given in a variety of trades, including agriculture.[5]

The Old *Yishuv* was not united in its reaction to these projects. The Sephardim were ready to accept new Zionist educational facilities as they had the modern schools founded by British, French, Austrian and German Jews. They welcomed the revival of spoken Hebrew, all the more as the Zionists adopted the Sephardic pronunciation. They also participated in the general community organization initiated by Zionists toward the end of the First World War and officially established and recognized under the British Mandate. But while the Sephardim developed no ideological opposition to the cultural and social institutions of the New *Yishuv*, as did some of the traditionalist Ashkenazim, they remained divided from the newer European immigrants by a sharp segregation. Far fewer of their children went to the modern schools than did the children of the New *Yishuv*. Intermarriage between Sephardim and the new immigrants remained relatively low. The economic and social position of the Sephardim, in time, became distinctly inferior to that of the new European immigrants. And in all these respects, what was true of the settled Sephardic community was true in an even greater degree for most of the immigrants from other oriental Jewish communities who came to Palestine simultaneously with the settlers of the New *Yishuv*.

As against the Old *Yishuv*, whether Sephardic or Ashkenazic, and the oriental communities that became amalgamated with it, those who constituted the New *Yishuv*—that is, most (though not all) of the European immigrants after 1880—not only actively adhered to the principles of the new Zionist social and cultural institutions, but participated fully in them. Nevertheless, there were significant differences in regard to cultural issues within the New *Yishuv* too. A major issue which continued to divide the Zionists, both ideologically and in terms of institutional organization, was education. On other matters referred to, the 'language question' and issues of communal and political organization, the differences that arose—between Yiddishists and Hebraists, between those socialist Zionists who worked with the World Zionist Organization and those who would not—were fairly well decided by 1948. Hebrew, not Yiddish, was the established language of the New *Yishuv*. Only a small fringe of communist and ultra-left socialist Zionists continued to oppose participation in the Zionist Organization and its several affiliated organs. There was even an odd arrangement for a general communal organization of Palestine Jewry in which major ideological concessions were made by both the secular and socialist and the religious Zionists. Orthodox Jews recognized the right of women to vote and hold office, while agnostic nationalists upheld a Chief Rabbinate made up of a Sephardic and an Ashkenazic Chief Rabbi, presiding over a religious court system authorized to judge cases of personal status arising between all members of the community. But differences over education led to the branching off not only of a religious Zionist but of a socialist Zionist school system (divided into several ideological sub-systems), in addition to the general Zionist school system, all supported by the World Zionist Organization and the Palestine Jewish community and sponsored under very loose supervision by the community.

II

The social and economic situation of the Jews in the Diaspora also provoked the Zionist rebellion. The long years of isolation from the body politic and social communion of the countries where Jews lived in exile produced a very restricted range of occupations and economic functions among them. In Eastern European countries, legal disabilities and social oppression continued well into the twentieth century to deny Jews a wider range of economic opportunities. The rapidly increasing population suffered under a mounting burden of poverty from which there seemed no prospect of escape. Emigration to a freer and more generous environment in Western Europe or overseas was an expedient that could commend itself to any kind of Jew, no matter what his ideological position—traditionalist or modernist, Zionist or anti-Zionist.

But only the modernists, and not Jews of a traditional cast of mind, were inclined to see in the 'abnormal' occupational distribution, economic functions and social composition of the Jews, particularly in Eastern Europe, something for which the Jews themselves deserved, in some part, to be reproached. Proponents of European enlightenment and civic emancipation as the solution of the Jewish Problem held that there were certain obligations which the Jews must accept in order to smooth the adjustment to a free, secular, industrial society. Among their demands was a reform of the occupational distribution and economic functions of the Jews, converting them from middlemen to primary producers and breaking up their concentration in a narrow range of ghetto trades. In order to achieve this goal, the reformers felt, it was necessary not only to remove barriers that had been erected by Christian society, but also to overcome the mental habits and the institutional values that had arisen among Jews, attaching them to a 'parasitic' economic position. It was usually assumed, however, that with civic emancipation and general enlightenment, the necessary social and economic reforms of the traditional position would follow naturally and in due course. It may be added that Jewish emigration to Western countries was regarded as a radical short-cut towards achieving all these goals.

Much the same attitude, but with a characteristic difference, prevailed among the Zionists. They, too, considered the 'abnormal' social position and 'parasitic' economic functions of the Jews (mainly, but not only, in Eastern Europe) as both a misfortune brought about by external, Christian pressures and, at the same time, a national disgrace. The traditional Jewish community was to be blamed, they argued, for accepting the humiliating and dishonourable position into which it had, indeed, been forced, but to which it had inwardly adjusted. Not only would it be a great national benefit to abolish the 'abnormalities' and the 'parasitism' of the Jewish social and economic position, it was also a paramount obligation of national honour to do so. Thus the Zionists made the self-liberation of the Jews from their social and economic 'abnormalities' a far more direct and urgent demand upon the Jewish community than did the anti-Zionist modernists. The Zionists wished, moreover, to transfer masses of Jews not to America but to Zion—in other words, to a backward country of very limited apparent resources. It was essential for their main purpose, therefore, to retrain Jews in a wide range of altogether new occupations, and to impose upon them, as a national necessity, social functions they had not performed for centuries during the Jewish dispersion. Thus the fundamental Zionist drive towards 'auto-emancipation' expressed itself not only directly in the campaign for political sovereignty but also, indirectly, in all aspects of 'practical' Zionism.

III

Successive generations of immigrants to Palestine are usually described according to the different manner and degree in which they shared and displayed the fundamental Zionist social and economic ethos. Each in turn is credited with some major significant contribution to the developing institutional structure of the New *Yishuv* in Palestine. The final product, as it existed upon the creation of Israel as an independent state in 1948, is pictured as a kind of stratified deposit of the successive historical epochs designated the First (1882–1903), Second (1904–14), Third (1919–23), Fourth (1924–31) and Fifth *Aliyot* (1932–8), together with the refugee immigration, both legal and illegal, of the period during which Britain ruled Palestine in accordance with its White Paper of 1939.

Of these, the First *Aliya* is said to have laid the foundations of Israel's private, plantation agriculture, the Second to have produced the Jewish farm labourer and the prototype of Israel's communal labour settlements and its mixed farming. The Third *Aliya* is credited with continuing the socialist labour traditions of the Second in a more organized fashion, signalled above all by the creation of Israel's labour federation, the Histadrut.

The Fourth *Aliya* is generally described as a relapse from the Zionist and socialist enthusiasm of the two preceding *Aliyot*. The immigrants of this period, it is said, were the first to have been brought to Palestine not by their Zionist ideals but by external compulsions: the US Immigration Act of 1922 shut the doors of the main receiving country against Jews shortly before the anti-Jewish economic policies of the Grabski government in Poland produced a new large wave of Jewish emigration. Palestine from 1924 to 1926 accordingly received immigrants at a rate, relative to the established Jewish settlement, not matched again until the first years of the State of Israel. Many of the immigrants were small businessmen who were able to bring with them capital to invest (hence the Fourth *Aliya* is spoken of as 'middle class'). The consequence was a rapid cycle of inflationary real estate development, followed by the collapse of the boom, with considerable unemployment among labourers. During the last years of the Fourth *Aliya*, from 1924 to 1931, however, the plantation economy of Palestine first developed a considerable export capacity in citrus fruits and a certain advance was made in industrialization.

The Fifth *Aliya* is usually described in similar terms to the Fourth, of which it represented a much larger version produced by much more drastic conditions. Here, too, not Zionist enthusiasm but the apocalyptic oppression of the Hitler regime, together with the closed doors of other countries from 1932 to 1935, produced an unprecedently large refugee immigration to Palestine, reaching a peak of some 60,000 in 1935.[6] The expansion of the entire Jewish economy in Palestine, and especially the development of a considerable variety of modern industrial enterprises, was the characteristic contribution to the developing institutional structure of the New *Yishuv* achieved by the skills and capital brought in by the Fifth *Aliya*. The slow refugee immigration from 1939 to 1948 fitted in to more or less the same framework, for the industrialization of Palestine received a powerful impetus through the exceptional marketing conditions of the war period.

The historical descriptions conventionally attached to the above periods do not, of course, apply universally or exclusively to the immigrants of the respective periods. They are no more than conventional labels to indicate the particular contribution each immigrant generation made to the institutions of Israel. While the New *Yishuv* is dated from the 1880s, when the concerted effort to colonize Palestine in line with Jewish nationalist aims began, the ensuing years brought a continuing stream of immigrants of the same type as the established Old *Yishuv*, who became a part of that segregated community that was the historic achievement of their time. The creation of an independent Jewish farmer-worker class in Palestine was the characteristic achievement of the Second and Third *Aliyot*. But intellectuals of the First *Aliya* were imbued with similar aims; and far more of the Second *Aliya* immigrants joined the Old *Yishuv* or became private planters or urban middlemen, like many settlers of the First *Aliya*, than joined the new communal settlements or remained workers. The significance of this periodization cannot be denied, however, for in fact each of the generations generally distinguished did leave its mark on the development institutions upon which Israel arose.

The social and economic innovations of each period produced repercussions in the older, established population, who in part adapted to the new opportunities and new ways that were introduced and in part developed a more specific ideological opposition to them. All elements in the settled Jewish community, including the most rigid conservatives of the Old *Yishuv*, were so affected. On the other hand, after 1880 the older settlers to a greater or lesser degree succeeded in controlling the reception of new immigrants. The institutions and values they had established in Palestine were accepted by many—if not most—newcomers as subject to modifications that might be introduced to meet the special demands of each *Aliya*. So, too, the new immigrants pouring in in unprecedented numbers after 1948 necessarily viewed the shifting structure of Israeli institutions, in the first encounter, as a fixed framework to which they must adjust.

IV

To outsiders, as well as to newcomers, perhaps the most striking feature of Israel's social and economic structure in 1948 was the extraordinary way in which political parties were involved at every turn. Through the ideological bonds of parties, successive generations were not only welded together on political issues for common action, but joined in common party schools, common party agricultural settlements and residential quarters, common party labour unions, common athletic organizations, all of which were financed at least in part by common party funds. Differences of country of origin and time of arrival were more or less bridged by party membership. On the other hand, a community whose life was so comprehensively regulated by partisan organizations was obviously divided in an unprecedented manner, overriding in many respects the bonds that in other countries unite immigrant sub-communities.

The prototype of the New *Yishuv* was to be found in the labour groups, beginning with the Second and Third *Aliyot* and growing at a rapid rate with each generation of immigrants. Their ruling passion was a determination to be autonomous and yet to be workers. They began in rebellion against the subordination of the earlier settlers to the paternalistic administration established by Baron Edmond de Rothschild over the colonies of the First *Aliya*. The new immigrants after the First World War had been trained and organized in the Diaspora to continue in the footsteps of the Second *Aliya*, but they intended to exceed their predecessors in the sweep and boldness of their conceptions.

Two labour parties during the Second *Aliya*, Poalei Zion and Hapoel Hazair, acting separately and often in opposition or in duplication, had created a wide range of social services and communal experiments, combining socialist with Zionist ideals, to help young Jewish immigrants become co-operatively self-employed workers and farmers in Palestine. The Third *Aliya* sought not only to expand these sporadic experiments into broad, systematically planned activities, but to create a single workers' organization that would eliminate the rivalry between the two labour parties. The Histadrut, organized in 1920 under pressure from Third *Aliya* immigrants, achieved this purpose. It also succeeded through the following periods of immigration in organizing a continually increasing proportion of the Jewish workers and of the whole Jewish population. Its influence spread to every stratum of the *Yishuv*, both New and Old, and its functions—including medical, educational, vocational, financial and technical, as well as purely trade union and traditional co-operative services—touched almost every aspect of community life. The Histadrut became a regulatory institution operating on a scale approaching that of a modern state, or at least its welfare and development ministries.

To pursue this trend to its logical conclusion was, indeed, the purpose of the socialist Zionists who founded and led the Histadrut. Their movement began with the feeling that their predecessors of the First *Aliya* had made a false start, that the institutions of the Jewish national home should be built upon the foundations that they, as autonomous worker-settlers, were establishing, and that it should be guided by their socialist Zionist principles. Not all the immigrants of later generations had the same ideals, although the labour Zionists were successful in obtaining by themselves a considerable proportion of the immigration certificates allocated for labourers for the recruits they had organized and trained in the Diaspora. But it continued to be the purpose of the Histadrut to bring into its fold a continually larger segment of the Jewish population, including those not trained in socialist Zionist principles abroad. Their ultimate aim was to convert the entire people into a body of autonomous workers, so that the whole society, and not only its labouring class, would be organized in accordance with Histadrut principles. The ever-expanding coverage of Histadrut functions seemed to be steadily advancing the movement toward this goal. With the influx of so large an immigration largely without means and essential skills after 1948, the Histadrut faced its greatest opportunity as well as its greatest test.

Even though their underlying purpose was to unify the entire people under the rule of socialist Zionist principles, and even though they advanced a long way towards that goal through the Histadrut, the institutions the labour groups set up still retained a partisan character and provoked a partisan reaction among their principled adversary. One important form of this reaction, however, was the adoption of socialist Zionist innovations by the opponents of socialist Zionism.

The bitterest opposition to the Histadrut arose not on economic, social or cultural, but on political issues. For the labour groups were organized in the Histadrut not only as a welfare and development agency of governmental scope but as a political caucus in all questions of internal and external relations with which the World Zionist Organization concerned itself. The coalition of Zionist labour parties that organized the Histadrut also dominated the World Zionist Organization from 1929 on, in close partnership with Chaim Weizmann and those 'middle-class' Zionist groups that backed him. The Revisionist Zionists, beginning in the 1920s with passionate opposition to Weizmann's external policy of co-operating with the British administration on the existing formulation and interpretation of the Palestine Mandate, came to oppose the Histadrut, Weizmann's political partner, on the whole range of internal Zionist policies. They sought, accordingly, to provide their members with medical services similar to those enjoyed by members of the Histadrut. They organized the workers among their members into a parallel trade union organization with the aim of breaking the power of the Histadrut. Their parallel youth and athletic organizations, taking paramilitary form, and later the communal groups they organized for settlement on the threatened borders of the *Yishuv*, were intended to take over the same general functions of national defence and to achieve the same kind of political avant-garde position as the Histadrut's youth groups, the labour-led Haganah, and the chain of socialist agricultural settlements.

Both the political opponents of the labour Zionist coalition and its opponents on religious and cultural issues remained outside the framework of the Histadrut. Thus they offered new immigrants a partisan institutional alternative, concerned with both social welfare and economic development, within which absorption into the New *Yishuv* could take place.

The major concerns of the partisans of Orthodoxy involved questions of culture and education and of religious observance. Ideally they wished to make all Jews conform to traditional principles; and like the labour Zionists, they considered the institutions they set up as prototypical and believed that they should, and ultimately perhaps would, serve to unite the whole people. However, they were less successful in obtaining the submission of the population at large to rabbinical regulation than were the labour groups in extending the coverage of Histadrut services. The Ashkenazic Orthodoxy of the Old

Yishuv cultivated its own way of life in isolation, shunning all contact with the newcomers except for like-minded groups among the new immigrants. The major effect of the new era upon these traditionalists was that they were no longer focused around the Halukka, the organization that distributed alms to the pious in the Holy Land. Their political antagonism to the New *Yishuv*, expressed through a partisan political organization, *Agudat Israel*, now bound them together in a new union.

The Sephardim—and the increasing number of 'oriental' Jewish communities—were isolated from the institutions of the New *Yishuv* not by ideology but—as they often felt—by discrimination. To be sure of full social participation, all partisan groupings in the New *Yishuv* made a certain effort to enlist them in their ranks. The Revisionists achieved some success through their political and paramilitary organizations, and the Histadrut reached the Sephardim to a rather greater extent through its welfare agencies. But a sense of exclusion was more marked than a feeling of belonging to the New *Yishuv* in the quarters inhabited by these communities.

The only Orthodox groupings that were fully included within the New *Yishuv* were the Religious Zionists. They, too, felt in principle that rabbinical law should rule the entire community in all fields of activity. In this aim they had only minor success. The limited jurisdiction of the Chief Rabbinate in matters of personal status was applied to all enrolled members of the Jewish community, pious and unobservant alike. But this was won at the cost of counter-concessions in the matter of women's suffrage that were enough to make the anti-Zionist Orthodoxy of the Old *Yishuv* place a ban on the institutions of the Jewish community, including the Chief Rabbinate; and it gave these ultra-traditionalists a polemical weapon used unsparingly in their agitation against their rival, the Orthodox Zionist organization Mizrahi. Within the Zionist organization, the Mizrahi party was able to obtain a certain deference to tradition in general public functions, so that its participation in such activities became possible. But the Zionist schools remained secular and the private activities of groups sponsored and aided by the Zionist organization were not subjected to any traditional or rabbinical discipline. For their part, the Zionist Orthodox organizations segregated themselves not only in a separate school system, but in separate residential quarters and settlements where they could make the traditional spirit prevail in the fullest degree.

As part of the segregation of Orthodoxy, separate welfare and economic development agencies paralleling those of the Histadrut were developed by the religious parties, especially their labour wings, somewhat in the same way as the Revisionists had done. However, separation did not in this case mean antagonism as surely as it did in the case of the Revisionists. The members of the Orthodox labour organizations, Hapoel Hamizrahi and Poalei Agudat Israel, were served by the Histadrut medical organization, Kupat Holim, and the trade unions of these two organizations benefited by a close relationship with the Histadrut in the settling of wages and working conditions for employees. Nevertheless, a new immigrant seeking housing, settlement on the soil and employment found two religious labour organizations as well as the Histadrut available to help him.

Thus the aim of the Histadrut leadership to create an autonomous welfare and development agency on socialist Zionist lines, uniting all the Jews or even all the Jewish workers who came to Palestine, fell far short of complete success. The Revisionist workers, the religious Zionist workers, and the religious anti-Zionist workers all had their separate labour organizations, parallel and opposed to the Histadrut. Furthermore, the fringe of Israeli society not involved in any of the labour organizations, despite all the services they offered, included not only large groups of employers and other 'middle-class' elements, but also unorganized casual labourers of all sorts recruited mainly from the oriental communities.

Such was the measure of the failure of the Histadrut to extend its principle of unity to all of Israel. But even internally there were divisions of critical importance that ran counter to the Histadrut's impulse towards a unified discipline. Originating in a merger of two rival labour organizations, the Histadrut ended by spawning a number of internal cleavages, through which important functions were withdrawn from effective central control and left to the competition of rival parties.

The major divisions were between the various types of rural labour settlements within the Histadrut framework. Even in the narrower category of collectivist settlements comprised by the Histadrut there were sharp divisions between three distinct communal federations. In the critical decades before the Second World War, when the growth of the Jewish national home under the Mandate was most severely challenged and the problem of Jewish refugees reached its most acute stage, the communal federations were the most active and reliable agency for absorbing untrained, penniless Jewish immigrants. It was they who were best able to provide the leadership needed to organize the prospective immigrants abroad, give them initial training for a new life in Palestine, convey them out of Europe and into the Jewish national home, whether legally or by running the British blockade; and it was they who could most easily accommodate the hapless fugitives upon arrival. There arose, however, a sharp rivalry among the three communal federations within the Histadrut, and between them jointly and the extra-Histadrut parties (which were also represented in this competition mainly by their labour affiliates and especially their youth organizations, often led by delegates from communal settlements). Each party strove to organize a greater membership among potential young immigrants abroad, and they competed for the immigration certificates granted by the Mandate government to the Jewish Agency for the admission of workers within the legal quota.

Competition for new recruits among the new immigrants between the Histadrut and its rivals was part of a broader ideological, partisan conflict. The same competition among the three Histadrut communals developed into full-scale party rivalry. Three (secular) socialist Zionist parties emerged: the dominant Mapai party, based on a broad constituency of all the various kinds of Jewish workers in Palestine, together with considerable non-proletarian support; a left-wing party based on the federation of Hashomer Hazair communes and some urban supporters who had traditionally been radical opponents of Mapai; and a new party, based on the largest federation of communal settlements, Ha-Kibbutz Ha-Meuhad, which split from Mapai over a variety of domestic and foreign policy issues.

In terms of their broadest social and economic aims, all three of the major Histadrut parties upheld the same socialist and Zionist principles. The idealization of labour on the soil and settlement on the exposed frontiers of the *Yishuv* was also characteristic of the Orthodox labour parties and even of the labour wing of the Histadrut's bitterest political foes, the Revisionists. None the less, a new immigrant, sharing the same ideals, found numerous organizations available to absorb him or her, each with its own apparatus of welfare and development agencies ready to grant aid and advice supplementary to the general provisions directly supplied by the Jewish Agency.

Which of these rivals the immigrant turned to, or was recruited by, was by no means a matter of indifference. In spite of the common aims and principles, there were crucial differences among them. The relative success of the recruiting efforts of each party would do much to determine the shape of Israel's institutional structure after 1948. If the parties previously dominant gained the adherence of the majority of the immigrants, the established institutions would be maintained— although even in that case, these would have to make far-reaching readjustments to absorb so large a mass of immigrants, especially if they differed very greatly from the type that had built the existing institutions. If, on the other hand, the parties previously in the minority—even those which shared many of the labour ideals of the dominant group—were able to establish themselves among a major part of the newcomers, the existing structure would undergo significant revisions. It was also possible that the new immigrants would in very large proportions escape organization into an institutional structure derived from the New *Yishuv*, as had the Sephardic and oriental communities in varying degrees. If so, the huge numbers of newcomers would ensure an impact far more extensive than the marginal non-participation of oriental Jews before 1948. Finally, those middle-class groups who were opposed in principle to the labour-oriented welfare and development policies of the New *Yishuv*—in political terms, the majority wing of the Palestine 'General Zionist' party—might find enough support among the new immigrants so that they, in combination with other 'class' opponents of the Histadrut, could reverse the trend of the Jewish national home toward an advanced type of mixed economy, strongly socialist in form.

Such were the possibilities that, at first sight, seemed to face the new Israeli society, as it opened its doors to mass immigration of Jews in 1948. What actually happened involved previously unanticipated possibilities of institutional development whose full evolution has yet to run its course.

Notes

1 The Proclamation of Independence of the State of Israel, 14 May 1948, in *Israel in the Middle East*, I. Rabinovich and J. Reinharz (eds) (New York, 1984), p. 14.
2 See R. Elboim-Dror, *Ha-hinukh ha-ivri be-Erets Israel 1854–1914* (Jerusalem, 1986), chs. 3–4.
3 See I. Bartal, 'Yishuv yashan ve-yishuv hadash—ha dimui ve-ha-metsiut', *Cathedra*, vol. 2 (1977), pp. 3–19, and Y. Ben-Arieh and I. Bartal (eds), *Ha-historyah shel Erets Israel*, vol. 8 (Jerusalem, 1983), pp. 194–257.
4 See B. Halpern, *The Idea of the Jewish State* (Cambridge, 1961, 2nd rev. edn), pp. 95–124.
5 *ibid.*, pp. 95ff.
6 On population and immigration figures, see D. Gurevich, A. Gertz and R. Bachi, *Ha-aliyah, ha-yishuv ve-ha-tnuah ha-tivit shel ha-ukhlusiyah be-Eretz Israel* (Jerusalem, 1949).

Patterns of Communal Conflict in Palestine*

Bernard Wasserstein

THE purpose of this paper is to suggest that a characteristic, recurring pattern of communal violence can be detected in Palestine in the modern period—a pattern which bears striking resemblances to that of communal disturbances in other places and periods. The focus is on the Palestine riots of the mandatory period (especially those of 1920, 1921 and 1929), with some glances back to the final decades of Ottoman rule. The discussion is divided into six parts. First, what is the *calendar* of communal rioting? Secondly, is there a characteristic *prelude* to these riots? Thirdly, what is the *geography* of communal violence? Fourthly, *who* are the rioters? Fifthly, what is the role of the *authorities* in relation to these disturbances? Sixthly and finally, what may such an examination suggest as to the *character and significance* of the riots?

1 THE CALENDAR OF COMMUNAL RIOT

The calendar of communal violence in Palestine was closely bound up with the calendar of religious festivity. Certain feast days were traditional occasions of riot. The conjunction of feast days of different communities living close together was a particularly common occasion of riot. Sometimes secular anniversaries or commemorations acquired a quasi-religious garb which was red rag to the bull of communal riot. Further, the creation or revival of competitive festivities was traditionally associated with communal disorder.[1]

On 4 April 1920 serious communal riots between Muslims and Jews broke out in Jerusalem. It was the (western) Christian Easter, the Jewish Passover, and the Muslim pilgrim festival of *Nebi Musa*. The latter was an annual pilgrimage to the supposed tomb of Moses in the Judaean desert between Jerusalem and Jericho, which attracted participants from all over Palestine. The pilgrimage was not fixed by the Muslim calendar, but by the Christian calendar in Easter week, so that (as the Mufti of Jerusalem put it in 1920) 'the Muslims at that time should have a feast as those of other communities'.[2] This was the traditional season of communal strife in Jerusalem. In 1847, for example, the British consul in Jerusalem, James Finn, reported:

> A Greek pilgrim boy, in a retired street, had thrown a stone at a poor little Jew boy, and strange to say, the latter had the courage to retaliate by throwing one in return which unfortunately hit its mark, and a bleeding ankle was the consequence. It being the season of the year when Jerusalem is always thronged with pilgrims, a tumult soon arose, and the direst vengeance was denounced against all Jews indiscriminately, for having stabbed (as they said) an innocent Christian child with a knife, in order to get his blood, for mixing in their Passover biscuits.[3]

At the same season in 1852, Finn noticed

> serious alarm lest a collision should occur between the crowds of Greek pilgrims assembled for Easter—sturdy, well-armed fellows, some of whom had been Russian soldiers, and the Moslem pilgrims to Nebi-Moosa, who poured into the city in unusual numbers from the Nabloos district. The Nabloosians are noted for their brutality and fanaticism.[4]

In 1914 an English Jewess observing the festivities in Jerusalem reports the torture and murder of a Christian by Turkish soldiers at the *Nebi Musa* pilgrimage.[5] Ronald Storrs, who was military governor of Jerusalem at the time of the 1920 riots, noted that the Easter season 'when, if only for three days, the death of strife becomes the victory of peace . . . in the Holy Land, and most of all in the Holy City, had meant for generations the sharpening of daggers and the trebling of garrisons.'[6]

On 1 May 1921 bloody communal disturbances broke out in Jaffa between Muslims and Jews. The date was the Greek Orthodox Easter. It was also the date of quasi-religious festivities by sections of the Jewish community celebrating the socialist May Day. Indeed, the fighting in Jaffa began with a clash between rival processions of socialists and communists, later developing into a communal riot. Meanwhile at nearby Ramleh 25,000 Muslim pilgrims were gathering for their annual festival at the tomb of *Nebi Saleh*. This concourse provided the occasion for the spread of the riots from Jaffa to Jewish villages inland.[7]

On 23 August 1929 Muslim–Jewish riots broke out again in Jerusalem. The riots began after the Friday morning services in the mosque of al-Aqsa. In this case too the cycle of violence began on a holy day of two religions. The previous Saturday, 17 August, the Jewish Sabbath, was also the date of the Muslim celebration of the birthday of the Prophet. An Arab–Jewish disturbance in the Bukharan quarter of Jerusalem resulted in the death of one Jew and injuries to Arabs and Jews. From this beginning tension increased until the explosion on the following Friday.[8]

Other religious or quasi-religious festivities provided similar, if less bloody, cues for communal disturbances. The celebration by the Zionists of the anniversary of the Balfour Declaration on 2 November often produced Arab protests and communal violence—for example, in 1918 and 1921. More recent communal disturbances have often followed a similar pattern. For example, the Jewish–Muslim clashes in Hebron in 1976 took place on the Jewish Day of Atonement, Yom Kippur, a date which since the outbreak of the Yom Kippur war in 1973 has acquired special political significance in the eyes of many Muslim Arabs.

2 THE PRELUDE TO COMMUNAL RIOT

The calendar of communal violence was not a secret. Police, government, communal leaders were all generally aware of the traditional seasons of danger and made appropriate dispositions. The expectation of riot was consequently often a major element in the prelude to trouble. But communal riots were rarely the consequence of self-fulfilling prophecy alone. Neil Smelser stresses among the preconditions for riot a period of intensified rumour and provocation of crowds by symbols.[9] Music, particularly loud, raucous music, as if designed with the express intention of provoking the opposing group, was a recurring element in the prelude to communal riot. Above all, processions, marches, parades past places of worship or residential districts of opposed groups tended to provide the immediate occasions of riot.

In 1856 Muslim anti-Christian riots at Nablus were preceded by the symbolic pealing of a bell in the Protestant missionary chapel in the town on the orders of the Anglican bishop in Jerusalem. The British consul in Jerusalem described this bell as 'an instrument of peril to the public peace for such a town as Nablus'.[10] Jewish riots directed against Christian missionaries in Jerusalem in the mid- and late nineteenth century were often precipitated by symbolic outrages against graves. For example, the British consul W. T. Young reported to the Earl of Aberdeen on 31 March 1843 that a Jewish commotion against missionaries and Jewish converts to Christianity had followed the spreading of rumours that converts 'have been to the Jews' cemetery and desecrated the Tombs, by displacing some, and inscribing crosses and their names as Believers in Christianity on others, to the great annoyance of the Jewish community'.[11] Jewish anti-missionary riots, sparked off by such incidents, have been a recurring feature of communal relations in Jerusalem until the present day.

The prelude to the major Muslim–Jewish riots of the 1920s falls into the familiar pattern. The *Nebi Musa* riots of April 1920 were preceded by a period of intense, threatening rumour. On 1 January 1920 a Zionist intelligence report noted a speech said to have been delivered in a mosque at Ramleh by a Muslim sheikh who declared: 'The days of revenge are nearing . . . Get rid of the Jews who want to rob your country and violate your wives.'[12] This was succeeded by a spate of similar reports which seriously alarmed the Jews. A report by a Zionist agent in Jerusalem on 16 March 1920 stated: 'There is a great movement felt for "Neby Moussa" . . . The Extremists are sure that a great revolution could be brought forth on this occasion.'[13] Rumours among the Arab population of troubles in Egypt appear to have contributed to the excitement.[14] As the date of the outbreak of the riots approached, the rumours of impending violence assumed an increasingly specific character.[15] The rumours stimulated Jewish military preparations for defence of the community in the event of an outbreak.[16] As the official British commission of inquiry into the riots concluded, 'It seems to have been evident to everybody that a storm was beating up and might burst at any moment.'[17]

In the riots in Jaffa and the coastal plain of Palestine in May 1921, rumour played a major part in the spread of the violence. For example, the attack on the Jewish settlement of Haderah on 6 May appears to have been stimulated by widespread rumours that the Jews had destroyed a neighbouring Arab town, and that Jews in Haderah were holding prisoner a large number of Arab labourers.[18]

In the prelude to the riots which erupted in Jerusalem in 1929, general rumours among the Arab population that the Jews were planning to seize the Muslim holy places on the Haram al-Sharif (Temple Mount) were given wide currency by the Arabic press and played a major part in the heightening of communal tension.[19] Jewish anxieties were increased by the publication of specific threatening rumours in the Hebrew press. The issues of the Hebrew daily newspapers, *Davar* and *Ha-Aretz*, dated 22 and 23 August reported rumours that disturbances were scheduled for Friday 23 August. Village Arabs were said to be flocking into Jerusalem, angered by reports that the Jews were planning to attack the mosques on the Friday. Crowds were said to be gathering in the vicinity of the mosques armed with bludgeons.[20] After the morning prayers in the mosque of al-Aqsa on the Friday, the riots duly began. The spread of the violence beyond Jerusalem to towns such as Hebron and Safed was hastened by exaggerated rumours as to the extent and nature of the violence in Jerusalem.

Processions and provocative music were major elements in the prelude to communal riot in Palestine in the 1920s. The immediate occasion of the outbreak in Jerusalem in April 1920 was the arrival of the *Nebi Musa* procession of pilgrims at the Jaffa Gate of the old city. In accordance with Turkish custom, the British military authorities had provided gun salutes and a regimental band which marched with the pilgrims. The question of the participation of the government band was a matter of issue in 1920: on orders from London it had originally been decided to refuse permission for the band to participate; but, upon the urgent representation of the military governor of Jerusalem, Colonel Storrs, the prohibition was rescinded and the band played, to the satisfaction of the pilgrims and the chagrin of the Jews.[21] The 1921 riots seem to have been sparked off by a clash between rival Jewish socialist and communist processions celebrating May Day. The 1929 riots were preceded by rival processions and demonstrations by Zionists and Arab nationalists focused on the Western ('Wailing') Wall holy place. On 15 August 1929 a procession of Jewish youths had marched to the wall and sung the Jewish national anthem, 'Hatikvah'. The following day a large Muslim demonstration had convened at the same spot. During the months preceding the riot particular offence had been taken by Jews at the revival by the Muslims of the old and noisy custom of banging drums and cymbals during Muslim prayers; the Jews complained that these percussive accompaniments to songs and chants appeared to be deliberately timed and positioned so as to drown the words of Jewish services taking place in the wall passage immediately below the Muslim holy compound.[22]

Symbolic violence and affronts which helped to exacerbate communal feelings were also signs of impending violence, especially when magnified (perhaps on occasion invented) by rumour. For example, in 1920 it was the rumour that a Jew had spat contemptuously at one of the banners being carried by the *Nebi Musa* pilgrims that was said to have sparked off the violence.[23] In 1929 the tearing by Arabs of prayer books, and the burning of supplicatory notes left by pious Jews in the crevices between the stones of the Western Wall, were regarded by Jews as outrages. As in the case of communal riots in India, animal provocation accompanied human: in 1929 there were Jewish complaints that Muslims were driving mules through the narrow passage adjacent to the wall, and encouraging them to drop excrement near Jews performing their devotions.[24]

3 THE GEOGRAPHY OF COMMUNAL RIOT

Appropriately, the characteristic location of riots between adherents of different religions or sects was the holy place—church, mosque, synagogue or shrine, or their precincts. In particular, places whose holiness was a matter of competitive dispute between different religions or sects tended to be riot 'black spots'. If the primary focus of religious riot was often the holy place or holy city, its tendency was to spread rapidly to neighbouring areas of mixed population, and thence often further afield.

Jerusalem, with its large concentration of holy places and mixed population of three religions and a multiplicity of sects, was a natural focus of communal disturbance. But it is the greatest, not the only, holy city of Palestine. Bethlehem, and in particular the Church of the Nativity, was a traditional location of unedifying disputes, often degenerating into physical violence, between adherents of different Christian sects. For example, Storrs noted shortly after his appointment as military governor of Jerusalem in December 1917:

> The Greeks and Armenians, whose respective Epiphany and Christmas fall on the same day, came to blows in the Grotto of the Nativity at Bethlehem, and had to be parted by the special guard (chosen from experts at these disgraceful brawls) that I had posted there.[25]

Hebron, holy to both Jews and Muslims, was the scene of occasional bloodshed in the nineteenth century, of a terrible massacre of Jews in 1929, and of renewed communal strife centred on rivalry over holy places from 1976 to the present.

The geography of the riots in Palestine in the 1920s provides striking examples of the contagious spread of crowd violence. In 1921 the bloodshed swept from Jaffa and the Muslim pilgrim shrine of *Nebi Saleh* near Ramleh, northwards and southwards through the Jewish townships of the coastal plain, but not to the hill country of the north and east. In 1929 the reverse was the case. From the initial outburst in Jerusalem, the disturbances spread south to Hebron and north to Safed (also a city holy to the Jews), encompassing other Jewish settlements on the way. In 1929, however, the coastal plain was relatively quiet. The 1920 riots did not spread beyond Jerusalem at all. The reason is perhaps that on that occasion the British army managed to seal off the area of rioting from the outset, inside the walls of the old city of Jerusalem; unauthorized access or egress was forbidden for four days. Lack of troop strength prevented any such hermetic enclosure in 1929. In 1921 no such attempt could have been contemplated by the authorities: neither the sprawling urban mess of Jaffa nor the open countryside around Ramleh afforded scope for such action; instead, the authorities tried to head off marauding crowds by means of aerial bombardment.[26]

4 WHO ARE THE RIOTERS?

The works of George Rudé and others on the composition of revolutionary crowds have taught us the importance of not treating the crowd merely as an anonymous lump of humanity and have warned us of the limitations of taking at face value statistical conclusions derived from inherently biased sources such as police or court records. In Palestine, as elsewhere, the repressive authorities are the main chroniclers of disorder. Rather than attempting to deduce any quantitative conclusions from these flawed data, the less ambitious approach used here is to isolate certain characteristic faces in the communal crowd.

In his pioneering study *The Crowd*, Gustave Le Bon divided crowds into two types: homogeneous and heterogeneous.[27] The former included crowds defined primarily by sect, caste or class. In the case of religious riots we are generally confronted by homogeneous crowds defined primarily by sect. This may seem an obvious conclusion: it is not. For it applies not only to those riots which occur in societies where two religious groups live together (such as anti-Jewish riots in mediaeval England, or anti-Protestant riots in sixteenth-century France), but also to riots which take place in societies where *more than two* groups live in close proximity. Third parties to religious conflict are rarely found to join in the violence.[28]

Palestine affords an excellent illustration of these general points. For here, in spite of the proximity of three major religious communities and a myriad of minor splinters, riots have traditionally been two-sided confrontations, one Christian sect versus another, Muslims versus Jews, Jews versus Christian missionaries, and so on. Occasionally in the nineteenth century there were Muslim attacks against both Jews and Christians, but such a triangular pattern is exceptional. In the case of the Arab–Jewish riots of the mandatory period, Christian involvement was slight. Indeed, we may more properly call these riots Muslim–Jewish rather than Arab–Jewish, since Christians in general remained ostentatiously neutral—to the extent of displaying large crosses on the outsides of their houses.[29] This is the more noteworthy in that the Muslims made great efforts in the 1920s to draw Christian Arabs into a joint political movement on a nationalist basis.[30]

Let us now try to identify some characteristic faces in the rioting communal crowd. In Palestine there appear to be at least three: young males, strangers from out of town, and policemen.

Children and youths seem to have been prominent particularly in the early stages of riots in Palestine. In 1918 the military governor of Jerusalem reported that a riot had narrowly been prevented when 'two or three ragamuffins of the lowest class, one a Muslim and one a Christian' (such references to Christian participation, however, are exceptional) had seized a processional banner from a Jew, and started beating it about its bearer.[31] Among those arrested by the police as a result of the riots in Jaffa in May 1921 were reported to be two children aged six and eight; both were Jews accused of Bolshevism.[32] A government report on a near-riot in Jerusalem in March 1923 stated:

> The procession was headed by a crowd of small boys of the riff-raff (not the schoolboy or Boy Scout type), led by an Effendi who appeared to be giving them the time for the songs they were singing. When the vanguard had got just beyond the Governorate Gate, preceded by the Commandant of Police and some of his officers, they began to sing
>
> > Filastin biladna
> > Al-Yahud kilabna
> > [Palestine is our country
> > The Jews are our dogs]
>
> Mr Quigley [Police Commandant] twice ordered them to desist, and at his second warning was struck by one of them with a large stone on the hand, while his orderly received a stone in the face. He thereupon ordered the Police to turn back the crowd. This they did . . . Truncheons were freely used.[33]

An Arab nationalist version of the same incident stated:

> The Commandant of Police instructed his mounted men to attack the first line of the crowd, which consisted of a number of boys of nearly [*sic*] ten years of age, and began to strike at them with clubs in a rough way. . . . It is regrettable to state that some of the Boy Scouts were also beaten while they were attending to the injured.[34]

The two accounts agree at least on the extreme youth of the demonstrators. However, the role of children appears in general to have been greater in the initial stages of Palestinian riots than in later serious bloodshed.

After children and young men, a characteristic face in the communal crowd is that of the stranger from out of town. In Palestine peasants from the surrounding countryside appear to have played a major role in urban communal violence, particularly in Jerusalem. This may be explained in large measure by the coincidence of riots with major pilgrim festivals. James Finn's anxieties regarding the propensity to violence of pilgrims to the *Nebi Musa* festivities have already been cited. In the riots of 1920 and 1921 pilgrims to *Nebi Musa* and *Nebi Saleh* were outstanding among the rioters. Similarly in 1929 villagers from surrounding districts were prominent in attacks on Jews in Jerusalem.

Thirdly, we find police and soldiers among the most bloodthirsty of communal rioters. In Jerusalem in 1920, Arab policemen participated in the attacks on Jews to such an extent that the entire force had to be withdrawn, disarmed and confined to barracks. The men were reported to be 'inclined to be mutinous on receipt of these orders'.[35] Meanwhile in Jaffa, although there was no serious outbreak of bloodshed, tension was running high and there were minor affrays between Jewish soldiers (members of the so-called 'Jewish Legion' in the British army) and Arab policemen and civilians.[36]

Policemen played a major role in the riots of 1921 in Jaffa and the surrounding district. In one of the most bloody incidents, the attack by a crowd of Arabs on a Zionist hostel for new immigrants in Jaffa, Arab policemen firing rifles led the attackers. A senior Arab police officer, Hanna Effendi Bordcosh, a Christian, who witnessed the incident, was severely censured by the British commission of inquiry into the riots for merely going home to lunch. Mounted Arab policemen were in the thick of the attack a few days later on the Jewish colony of Haderah. The British chief of police was reproved by the commission for having 'left Arab policemen in control of an Arab mob . . . They were being swept along with the crowd, clinging to it, but quite unable to control it.'[37] Jewish soldiers from the nearby military camp at Sarafand rushed to Jaffa to join in the defence of the Jewish quarters. They remained there under arms until ordered to disband and disarm by a senior British officer.[38]

In 1929 Arab policemen were once again leading figures among the rioters. A British police constable in Hebron during the massacre of Jews there describes one such incident:

> On hearing screams in a room I went up a sort of tunnel passage and saw an Arab in the act of cutting off a child's head with a sword. He had already hit him and was having another cut, but on seeing me he tried to aim the stroke at me but missed. He was practically on the muzzle of my rifle. I shot him low in the groin. Behind him was a Jewish woman smothered in blood, with a man I recognised as a police constable named Issa Sherif from Jaffa in mufti. He was standing over the woman with a dagger in his hand. He saw me and bolted into a room close by, and tried to shut me out, shouting (in Arabic), 'Your Honour, I am a policeman.'. . . I got into the room and shot him.[39]

5 THE ROLE OF THE AUTHORITIES

The frequent presence among the rioters of low-level authority-figures such as policemen and soldiers immediately leads to a consideration of the role of the authorities in these disturbances. In communal riots in Palestine the ability of the relevant authority (whether Turkish, British or Israeli) to mobilize its forces effectively was often limited by the questionable impartiality of policemen and soldiers in riots involving their own co-religionists.

Almost as important as the actual attitude of the authorities, particularly in the early stages of riots, are popular beliefs concerning the governing power. Often the crowd seems to see itself as acting in some sense on behalf of the authorities in order to root an evil element out of society. The belief in the indulgent wink of government, whether or not based on reality, can be a stimulus to riot. On other occasions the crowd sees itself as acting in the stead of the authorities where the latter are constrained by weakness or malign forces from acting resolutely against an enemy group. Conversely, the belief on the part of the victim group in communal riots that the government has winked at or helped to engineer communal aggression, may stimulate the organization of self-defence measures by the victim group, measures which may raise communal tension further, and increase antagonism between the victim group and the authorities.[40]

In Palestine, as elsewhere, rioting communal crowds have traditionally seen themselves as acting either with the support of the government, or (in cases where the authorities are felt to have been remiss) in place of the government. In the mid-1830s there were Muslim anti-Christian and anti-Jewish riots in various parts of Palestine in the course of a general revolt against the authority of the Egyptian ruler, Ibrahim Pasha, son of Muhammad Ali. A major element in these disturbances was resentment by Muslims of the grant by the new government of rights of equal status to Christian and Jewish communities. Muslim susceptibilities were further upset by the use of mosques as barracks for Egyptian troops, the carrying of crosses by Christians in processions, the granting of permission to build or repair churches and synagogues. The primary grievances of the rebels appear to have been as much economic and social (objections to conscription, to taxes, to administrative reforms) as religious. But the riots against Jews and Christians were not merely anti-government; the rioters were also acting, in a sense, on behalf of the legitimate government of the Muslim state; the riots represented efforts by the Muslim majority to reaffirm, in place of the apparently remiss government of the Egyptian usurper, their traditional status of superiority. Ma'oz notes the complaint of Muslims: 'O my brother, the state has become a Christians' state, the Islamic state has ended.'[41]

If Muslims required the ideological encouragement derived from the idea that they were defending the traditional Muslim state in order to embark on communal riot, Jews, as a small and depressed community in Palestine in the nineteenth century, would rarely dare to engage in riot unless they were confident of tangible government backing. Moreover such Jewish riots were never directed against Muslims (for attacks on Muslims could hardly be expected to gain the support of a Muslim government), and appear to have been restricted to Jerusalem where the Jews were the largest community by the middle of the century. In 1846 there were Jewish riots in Jerusalem directed against the hospital of the London Society for Promoting Christianity Amongst the Jews. The British consul in Jerusalem reported to Lord Aberdeen:

> The butcher who kills the meat for the hospital, a French subject, has been mobbed and severely beaten, and the hospital has been daily surrounded by a number of Jews sent by the Rabbies to prevent patients and even servants access to it . . . Without wishing to interfere in the least with the motives [sic] of the Rabbies for preventing Jews from frequenting the hospital, I think they are using unlawful means to prevent free access to the house of a British subject. His Excellency, the Pasha, however, answers my application for protection against these outrages by an accusation against the Protestant clergy residing at Jerusalem; accusing them from information obtained from the Rabbies of unworthy attempts to convert the Jewish Raias; an accusation entirely without foundation.[42]

In a later dispatch the consul complained that the Pasha 'has made himself a party with the Rabbies against the British residents here'.[43] But the Pasha, in a letter to the consul, rejected such criticism, insisting that it was his duty to uphold the Jews' freedom of worship, and that the activities of the missionaries were being conducted 'd'une manière peu digne, d'après les dires de ces Rabbins, mes protégés'.[44] The final words may be seen as a sly dig at the consul, since one of the traditional functions of the British consulate in Jerusalem (based on an instruction dispatched by Palmerston in 1841) was the protection of Jews.

The Jerusalem riots of 1920 led to Jewish accusations of government complicity in what they insisted on terming the 'pogrom'. Izhak Ben-Zvi wrote:

> We have lived to be eye-witnesses to an actual pogrom in Jerusalem, a pogrom the like of which we did not have during hundreds of years of Turkish rule . . . Worst of all is the attitude of the local authorities to the whole matter. All our doubts have become certainties. The English administration knew of all the preparations for the slaughter, and not only did not try to prevent it but even did everything in its power to encourage the thieves and murderers, and on the other hand used every means to impede the Jewish self-defence and arrest its members. Now it is trying to suppress any publication of the disturbances, even mention of the word 'pogrom' in a telegram.[45]

In an interview with the *Manchester Guardian*, shortly after the riots, the Zionist leader Chaim Weizmann similarly insisted that they could 'only be characterized as organized pogroms'.[46] The Jews were supported in this view by the strongly pro-Zionist chief political officer of the

military government, Colonel Richard Meinertzhagen, who accused
his colleagues in the administration of having directly encouraged Arab
leaders to organize violent disturbances in order to impress the British
government with the strength of popular feeling in Palestine against
Zionism. In his diary Meinertzhagen noted: 'On the day of the rioting
the following notice was displayed all over Jerusalem: "The Government is with us, Allenby is with us, kill the Jews; there is no punishment
for killing Jews."'[47]

Whatever the truth of Meinertzhagen's allegations, there seems
little doubt of a widespread popular belief among Arabs in Jerusalem, immediately before the riots, that the government looked
favourably on the Arab cause. The Arab nationalist newspaper *Suria
al-Janubiyyah*, on 26 February 1920, described an interview between
the governor of Jerusalem and one of the nationalist leaders regarding a nationalist demonstration to be held two days later. The
newspaper remarked:

> You see, o people, that the government has not forbidden peaceful
> demonstrations on condition that we will be orderly in all our actions,
> and for this we should thank the government because it has proved that
> it does not want to block the path of our development, our renaissance,
> and our unity, and our efforts to make our words heard in the outside
> world. We are very hopeful that it will transmit our complaints to the
> higher authorities and add to our complaints what it itself sees and feels
> of our national feelings, and that it will add action to words in this
> matter, famous as it is for justice and good government.[48]

The fact that senior officials of the government were known to be
sympathetic to the claim of the Emir Faisal's Damascus regime to
extend its authority over Palestine seems further to have encouraged
popular belief on the eve of the riots that 'the government is with us'.[49]

In the riots of 1929 the Muslims seem to have been stimulated less by
the belief that they were acting with the support of the government
than by the feeling that they were acting in place of the government in
order to assert their rights at the holy places, rights which, as they saw
it, the government openly admitted, but was too pusillanimous to
vindicate. In a public proclamation (apparently designed for use as a
wall poster) issued immediately before the outbreak of the violence in
August 1929, the Association for the Protection of the Aqsa Mosque
and the Islamic Holy Places in Jerusalem declared:

> In the matter of the *Buraq* [the Western Wall] . . . the right of the
> Muslims is quite clear, in their possession of every part of its grounds, its
> walls, its skies, and its ends. The London government could not but
> admit this Muslim right unequivocally in its White Paper which the

Colonial Secretary published about ten months ago. Unfortunately, until this day it has not been implemented.[50]

In all riots in mandatory Palestine the capacity of the government to contain communal violence was limited by the fact that the majority of the police were Muslims or Jews. The Palestine Defence Scheme in 1920 stated: 'In the case of universal internal trouble, the 3000 police must be reckoned with as a potential hostile factor.'[51] The behaviour of Arab policemen in the disturbances of the 1920s, as we have seen, certainly lent substance to this reckoning. The government was, however, anxious not to rely only on Jewish forces in communal conflicts, fearing that this might further provoke Arabs. Hence the disarming of Jewish soldiers in 1921 in Jaffa. In 1929 the government had at its disposal only 292 British policemen in the whole of Palestine.[52] The armed forces other than the police were almost non-existent. As soon as the riots broke out, therefore, the government hastily enrolled as special constables a party of fifty theology students from Oxford who happened to be on a pilgrimage to Jerusalem. A further seventy government officials were enrolled, and these included a number of English Jews in government service. The cry immediately went up that the government was arming the Jews. On government insistence, the Mufti of Jerusalem and other Muslim leaders issued a statement declaring the rumour false: nevertheless it persisted. The acting high commissioner, H. C. Luke, reluctantly decided to demobilize the Anglo-Jewish special constables, although his decision aroused considerable Jewish indignation. Luke described the decision as 'very unpleasant, distasteful' and 'one of the most painful and difficult decisions, if not the most painful and difficult, I have ever had to take in my service'.[53] Luke's uneasiness may be readily understood, since he himself was rumoured (correctly) to be of what was termed 'Hebraic blood'.[54] Such actions by the government had the perhaps inevitable effect of stimulating the creation by the Jews of their own underground military force, the Haganah, which first saw action in the riots of the 1920s.

6 CHARACTER AND SIGNIFICANCE OF THE RIOTS

Three tentative conclusions suggest themselves. First, one is struck, in the case of the crowd in Palestine as elsewhere, by its overwhelming traditionalism.[55] This was accentuated by the fact that the ostensible issue of dispute was so often conflict over rights in holy places. In such disputes, in Palestine tradition, lay the beginning and the end of the debate. It was by tradition that rights accrued in all matters relating to holy places. Hence the elaborate efforts of the Jewish Agency in 1929 to prove to the Shaw Commission that the Jews had traditionally brought screens and chairs to the Western Wall in the Ottoman period. Such proof, if accepted, would of itself have strengthened immeasurably their claim to be allowed to continue these practices under the British. Conversely the Muslim crowd was concerned, above all, to vindicate the tradition of Jerusalem as the site of the first *Qibla* (the direction in which Muslims turn to pray, now that of Mecca), and the place of Muhammad's miraculous ascent to the seventh heaven after his night-time flight from Mecca on the winged steed al-Buraq. The Jewish tradition that the *Shekhinah*, or spirit of God, hovered especially around the last few standing stones of the Temple was of no less importance. Traditionalism often magnified or distorted existing tradition in order to suit current political needs. The ascription to Jerusalem of the passage in the Koran describing Muhammad's ascent is dubious, and probably dates only from the Caliphate of 'Abd al-Malik bin Marwan (685–87), who, being engaged in conflict with a rival caliph installed at Mecca, 'avait grand besoin d'un texte sacré qui affirmât la supériorité du sanctuaire de Jérusalem', as one historian has put it.[56] Little had, in fact, been heard before the 1920s of the particular holiness to Muslims of the Western Wall area; yet the sanctity in Islamic tradition of the 'stable of Buraq' became an article of faith when the Jews began to assert new 'traditional' rights there.

Secondly, behind this exaggerated traditionalism may be detected on the one hand attempts to redefine the balance of communal power and status, on the other reaction against such redefinition.[57] In the 1830s and 1850s, Muslim riots against Christians and Jews expressed defiance of attempts by the Egyptian and Ottoman governments of Palestine to redefine the status of these traditionally second-class citizens. In nineteenth-century Palestine the Jews were traditionally the most despised element in the population, not fit to walk on the same pavement or wear the same clothes as the Muslims. Unlike Jewish communities in other parts of the Ottoman Empire, the Jews of Palestine had no notable class to protect them. They were known to subsist primarily on charitable doles from abroad. Suddenly, in the early twentieth century their status and power were transformed. The country was conquered by a Christian power with the avowed object of establishing a Jewish National Home. Large-scale Jewish immigration and land purchase began. The Jews began to establish their own institutions of communal self-government with the recognition of the authorities. The numerical balance of the population began to change. In 1920 a Jewish high commissioner was appointed as head of the government of Palestine. Riots represented an attempt to restore the communal 'balance' of Ottoman times.

Thirdly, the concept of riot as a form of political bargaining may well be applicable here. Just as the food riot was a form of bargaining in early nineteenth-century England, perhaps the only 'means by which normally inarticulate sections of the population served notice of grievances to the authorities',[58] so it may be suggested that the communal riot in Palestine in the 1920s was a form of political bargaining designed to counter the Zionist attempt to redefine the traditional Jewish position in Palestine. That the government of Palestine tended to regard the riots much in this light is apparent from the official response to the troubles, especially in 1921 and 1929. In 1921 the civil secretary, Wyndham Deedes, hurried down from Jerusalem to the *Nebi Saleh* pilgrimage shrine shortly after the outbreak in Jaffa and secured an agreement with the leading notables among the pilgrims whereby they would prevent further outbreaks; they were given to understand that Jewish immigration would be temporarily halted; no public announcement, however, was made to this effect. The riots continued; on 14 May the town crier in Ramleh announced that immigration had been suspended; the riots stopped. In 1921 the riots did not spread to Jerusalem; in effect, this can be seen as the result of a bargain between the high commissioner and the former nationalist politician Haj Amin al-Husseini, whereby the latter was appointed Mufti of Jerusalem in return for his assurances (given to Sir Herbert Samuel on 11 April, three weeks before the riots in the rest of Palestine) 'that the influence of his family and himself would be devoted to maintaining tranquillity in Jerusalem, and he felt sure that no disturbances need be feared this year.'[59]

Seen in this perspective, communal riots may be regarded as a traditional form of political mobilization utilized for new purposes. The political enemy might be Zionism; but the immediate victims of attack in the riots of April 1920 in Jerusalem and August 1929 in Hebron were non-Zionist Orthodox Jews resident in the ancient Jewish quarters of these holy cities. The riots of the 1920s conformed to the traditional character of religious riot; they were preceded by the characteristic pattern of rumour, music and processions; they spread according to the customary geographical pattern; the participants were familiar faces in the communal crowd; the role (both perceived and actual) of the authorities was unchanged, even though the rulers were now British rather than Turks. A broad comparative survey lies beyond the scope of this paper, but those acquainted with patterns of communal and sectarian violence between Protestants and Catholics in early modern Europe and in modern Ireland, or between Hindus and Muslims in modern India, may find that these features ring some familiar bells.[60]

Notes

1 Cf. R. C. Cobb, *The Police and the People: French Popular Protest 1789–1820* (Oxford, 1970), p. 20: 'The calendar of violence and riot [is] almost as fixed as that of the saints. To the general eighteenth-century pattern of May to September, Sundays and Mondays, feast days, hot days, the Revolution adds the anniversaries of revolutionary *journées*, or of counter-revolutionary atrocities.'

2 Evidence of Muhammad Kamil al-Husseini, Mufti of Jerusalem, to the Commission of Inquiry into the Jerusalem riots, *Palestine Weekly*, 25 June 1920

3 J. Finn, *Stirring Times* (London, 1878), vol. I, p. 107

4 *ibid.*, p. 203

5 H. Bentwich, *If I Forget Thee: Some Chapters of Autobiography 1912–1920* (London, 1973), p. 20

6 R. Storrs, *Orientations* (London, 1943), p. 304

7 *Palestine. Disturbances in May 1921. Reports of the Commission of Inquiry with Correspondence Relating Thereto* (Haycraft Commission), Cmd. 1540 (London, 1921), p. 41

8 *Palestine. Commission on the Disturbances of August 1929: Minutes of Evidence* (Shaw Commission), Colonial no. 48 (London, 1930), 3 vols

9 N. J. Smelser, *Theory of Collective Behaviour* (London, 1962), p. 247

10 A. L. Tibawi, *British Interests in Palestine 1800–1901* (London, 1961), p. 116

11 A. M. Hyamson, *The British Consulate in Jerusalem in Relation to the Jews of Palestine, 1838–1914* (London, 1939), vol. I, p. 61

12 Report dated 1 January 1920, no. 117, Central Zionist Archives, Jerusalem, (CZA), L4/276 III

13 Report dated 16 March 1920, Jerusalem, CZA L4/276 Ia

14 Zionist intelligence report, 20 March 1920, Jaffa, CZA Z4/3886 I

15 Report to Zionist Commission by Alex Aaronsohn, 28 March 1920, CZA L4/276 IIb; Dr Sonne to L. J. Stein, Jerusalem, 30 March 1920, CZA Z4/16084/55

16 'Extract from a private letter from a reliable source', Jerusalem, 30 March 1920, CZA L3/27; Note by Colonel Storrs, 31 March 1920, CZA Z4/16078/66

17 Report of Commission of Inquiry into 1920 Jerusalem riots (Palin Commission), Port Said, 1 July 1920, Public Record Office (PRO) FO 371/5121/83 & ff.

18 Haycraft Commission (note 7 above), pp. 7–11

19 *Al-Jami'a al-Arabiyya*, 11 February and 15 August 1929; *Al-Yarmuk*, 18 January 1929

20 *Davar* and *Ha-Aretz*, 22 and 23 August 1929

21 Storrs (note 6 above), pp. 329–30

22 Shaw Commission *Minutes* (note 8 above), *passim.*

23 Palin Commission (note 17 above), pp. 83ff.; Frances Newton, *Fifty Years in Palestine* (London, 1948), p. 133

24 Shaw Commission *Minutes* (note 8 above), *passim.*

25 Storrs (note 6 above), p. 304

26 Haycraft Commission (note 7 above), pp. 7–10

27 G. Le Bon, *The Crowd: A Study of the Popular Mind* (London, 1947), pp. 155ff.

28 Cf. the 1915 riots in Ceylon which consisted almost entirely of affrays between Buddhists and Muslims; members of other communities, Tamils, 'Burghers' (of Portuguese origin) and Sinhalese Christians, largely stood aloof. See C. S. Backton, 'The Action Phase of the 1915 Ceylon Riots', *Journal of Asian Studies*, vol. 29 (1969–70), no. 2, pp. 235–54

29 Shaw Commission (note 8 above), vol. I, p. 42

30 Y. Porath, *The Emergence of the Palestinian Arab National Movement 1918–1929* (London, 1974), esp. pp. 293–303.

31 Storrs to Occupied Enemy Territory Administration Headquarters, 4 November 1918, PRO FO 371/3385/424

32 H. B. Samuel, 'The Palestine Government', *Fortnightly Review*, August 1921, p. 272

33 Storrs to Chief Secretary, Government of Palestine, 16 March 1923, Israel State Archives (ISA) 2/169

34 Omar Bittar, acting president of Executive Committee of Fifth Palestine Arab Congress, to high commissioner for Palestine, 15 March 1923, *ibid.*

35 Palin Commission (note 17 above), pp. 181ff.; Meinertzhagen to Foreign Office, 13 April 1920, PRO FO 371/5117/126.

36 Note of telephone conversation between military governor of Jaffa and G. S. R. I., 3rd Division, Ber Salem, 9 April 1920, Tolkowsky Papers, CZA A/248/1/6

37 Haycraft Commission (note 7 above), pp. 14, 26

38 *ibid.*; report by Colonel Byron, 14 May 1921, PRO CO 733/13/99

39 Report by Constable R. Cafferata on events at Hebron, 24 August 1929, Shaw Commission (note 8 above), vol. 2, p. 983

40 In communal riots in India in 1906 one witness reported: 'Priestly mullahs went through the country preaching the revival of Islam, and proclaiming that the British Government was on the Mohammedan side, that the law courts had been specially suspended for six months, and no penalty would be enacted for violence done to Hindus or for the loot of Hindu shops, or for the abduction of Hindu widows.' Ram Gopal, *Indian Muslims: A Political History, 1858–1947* (Bombay, 1959), pp. 93–5.

41 Moshe Ma'oz, *Ottoman Reform in Syria and Palestine, 1840–1861* (Oxford, 1968), p. 18. See also A. J. Rustum, *The Royal Archives of Egypt and the Disturbances in Palestine, 1834* (Beirut, 1938).

42 H. Newbolt to Lord Aberdeen, 5 March 1846, in Hyamson (note 11 above), vol. 1, p. 86

43 H. Newbolt to Sir Stratford Canning, 25 March 1846; *ibid.*, p. 87

44 Mehemed Pasha to Newbolt, 4 March 1846; *ibid.*, p. 90

45 Article in *Kuntres*, April 1920, printed in I. Ben-Zvi, *The Hebrew Battalions* (Jerusalem, 1969), p. 242

46 *Manchester Guardian*, 26 April 1920

47 R. Meinertzhagen, *Middle East Diary 1917–1956* (London, 1959), p. 82, entry dated 26 April 1920

48 *Suria al-Janubiyya*, 26 February 1920. I am grateful to Mr Musa Budeiri for showing me a rare copy of this newspaper which is in his possession.

49 See Porath (note 30 above), p. 99

50 'Statement Concerning Recent Incidents at the *Buraq*', CZA S25/2948

51 Quoted in Palin Commission (note 17 above)

52 'Establishment of the Palestine Police, 1929', report by A. Saunders, ISA 65/01940

53 Shaw Commission (note 8 above), vol. 1, pp. 273, 314

54 Colonial Office minutes, PRO CO 733/60/117ff.

55 Cf. 'What *is* the distinctive feature of the "pre-industrial" crowd is, I believe, its attachment to the traditional ways (or the believed traditional ways) of the old village community or urban craft—and its violent reaction to the sort of changes promoted in the name of "progress" by governments, capitalists, corn-merchants, speculative landlords or city authorities. So we find the constant and continuous presentation of demands for the "restoration" of "lost" rights, such as the "just wage", and the "just price."' George Rudé, 'The "Pre-Industrial" Crowd', in *Paris and London in the Eighteenth Century: Studies in Popular Protest* (London, 1970), pp. 22–3

56 M. Gaudefroy-Demombynes, *Mahomet* (Paris, 1969), p. 93

57 Cf. 'Violence is more likely to occur when the minority group is not content to accept the assignment of low rank from the so-called majority group, and when it attempts a

redefinition of the situation which will bring about assimilation or at least equal status without assimilation. This means that a redistribution of power and of opportunities is to be effected. This struggle will bring forth the opposition of the superordinate group.' H. Otto Dahlke, 'Race and Minority Riots—A Study in the Typology of Violence', *Social Forces*, vol. 30, no. 4 (1951–2), pp. 419–25

58 J. Stevenson, Introduction to Stevenson and R. Quinault (eds.), *Popular Protest and Public Order* (London, 1974), p. 26

59 Note by Sir Herbert Samuel, 11 April 1921, ISA 2/245

60 See e.g. N. Zemon Davis, 'The Rites of Violence', in *Society and Culture in Early Modern France* (Stanford, 1975), pp. 152–87; S. E. Baker, 'Orange and Green Belfast, 1832–1912', in H. J. Dyos and M. Wolff, *The Victorian City: Images and Realities* (London, 1973), vol. 2, pp. 789–814; K. W. Jones, 'Communalism in the Punjab: The Arya Samaj Contribution', *Journal of Asian Studies*, vol. 28, no. 1 (1968–9), pp. 39–54

The Dynamics of Zionist Leftist Trends

Anita Shapira

THE relationship of the Zionist-Socialist movement in Palestine to the October Revolution, and thereafter to Soviet Russia, contains all the ingredients of a romance of unrequited love: burning passion, tempestuous hatred, attraction and repulsion, disillusionment and despair and falling in love all over again. On the face of it, the reader might assert, there is nothing remarkable about that; for the magnetic force which 'the world of the Revolution' exerted on workers' movements and intelligentsias all over the world between the two world wars, and even as late as the mid-1950s, was equivalent to a mighty force of nature which swept away national and class loyalties. The Palestine labour movement, small in size, created only one ripple in the ocean of enthusiasm and identification with the Bolshevik revolution which inundated the Left throughout the world. Furthermore, if we concentrate our attention on the influence of the October Revolution on the non-Zionist Jewish workers' movement, the phenomenon of intoxicated love becomes even more clearly apparent. What is it, then, that distinguishes the Palestine Zionist labour movement in its blighted love affair with Soviet Russia?

There were, indeed, distinguishing traits in the relationship of the Zionist Left to the USSR. By far the greater part of the Palestine labour movement had its origin in the Pale of Settlement, and it burgeoned and developed in the early twentieth century in a Russia tossed by the storms of revolution. Affection for Mother Russia, the loved and hated land of their birth, was an integral part of the consciousness of its members. Their relationship was not only to a physical homeland but also to a spiritual one. Most of them knew Russian and this was generally the only foreign language which they did know, their bridge to the wide world. They felt a deep admiration for Russian culture, and especially for nineteenth-century Russian literature. For them, it was Literature; even if, in the course of time, they got to know the treasures of western culture, they continued, in their hearts, to identify themselves directly with that literature. Its similes, its style, the problematics of the human predicament which characterize it, the patterns of thought and behaviour of its heroes—all these were absorbed into their inner consciousness, and became part of the collective personality of the members of the early *aliyot*, especially of the Second and the Third *Aliya*.

Together with Russian literature they brought with them the political culture of the Russian revolutionary movement. From the days of the Bilu movement onwards, the Narodniks and their successors the social revolutionaries were an object of admiration and a model for imitation. The Russian literature of political and social protest served as a base for a philosophy of life which proclaimed as its principles the duty of self-fulfilment and the obligation of the individual to work for the betterment of the world; it crystallized an ethos for the revolutionary which blended the asceticism of the hermit who dedicates himself as a sacrifice, the cruelty of the pioneer who demands the impossible of himself and feels entitled to demand it of others, and the pathos and naïveté of a man who believes he can bring about the Kingdom of Heaven on earth (in the words of the *Kaddish*) 'speedily and at a near time'. These ingredients were an integral part of the ethos of the Palestine labour movement. When the October Revolution took place, there drained towards it all the feelings of love and personal identification which the Pioneers felt towards both the physical and the spiritual Russia. In Palestine there was no workers' movement with a deep and well-rooted local tradition such as, in other countries, could act as a restraint on identification with 'the world of the Revolution'. The relationship to revolutionary Russia was to a large extent a substitute for that tradition. The events in the Soviet Union were perceived as something intimate, an inseparable part of 'our' existence, something which belonged to 'us', for better or worse.

Moreover, in the struggle between the forces of light and darkness in the world, the Zionist workers had no doubt on which side of the barricades they stood. They saw themselves as active partners in the struggle for justice, equality, and the exaltation of man and society. Even if they did not identify themselves in all respects with Soviet Russia, they saw her as giving practical realization to the best of their desires and dreams. An integral part of their Russian tradition was the revolutionary impulse. They did not see themselves as belonging to that camp which was derogatorily defined as 'reformist'. The image they had of themselves was of revolutionaries who were not content with a pious hope of setting the world to rights, but worked day by day and hour by hour to achieve it.[1] True, this self-image did not earn the approval of those appointed to oversee the revolutionary orthodoxy of the movement—the leaders of the Comintern. And if we adopt the narrow Marxist definition of 'revolutionary', it is true that they were not revolutionaries. But for our purpose that makes no difference. This self-image, together with a strong desire to change the face of existence, constituted a creative force and a motive for action which were the distinguishing marks of the workers' movement. And so, naturally, they lifted their eyes to the great land which, as they understood it, was doing on a large scale what they were doing on a small scale: in both places a new society was being built, but in Russia it was necessary first to pull down the old, whereas in Palestine they had to build from the ground up. And just as Russia had taken a giant and historic leap forward—Lenin, after all, had not waited for the processes of history to mature, but had created a new starting-point through the force of the revolutionary impulse—so, too, the socialist society would be built in Palestine—forthwith.

The love and admiration felt by the Palestine Zionist Left for the land of the Revolution was unrequited from the start. As early as April 1920 the Comintern declared Zionism to be a movement unfit to be granted membership.[2] This was a grievous blow, but the Left quickly recovered from it: their relationship to the land of the Revolution answered spiritual desires too deep for a repulse from her to wipe them out at a stroke. An opinion developed that the opposition between Zionism and Communism did not spring from a true opposition of interests but from a misunderstanding. This misunderstanding had its origin in the hatred felt for them by their traitorous brothers the men of the Yevsektsiya, who bequeathed to the Communist movement the enmity of the Bund for Zionism and Hebrew. When socialist Zionism was presented to Soviet Russia in its true colours, it would become clear that the opposition to it was founded on a misapprehension. This dream served as a torch to light the path of the Palestine labour movement from the beginning of the 1920s to the middle of the 1950s. The hope that the day would come when Soviet Russia would take them to her heart, just as they were, was shared—at different times—by men like Ben-Gurion, Eliezer Livneh, Yizhak Tabenkin and others.[3] It was an example of a pattern of thought peculiar to this movement, its main characteristic being the conduct of a stormy internal debate, drawing up rule upon rule on a subject affecting an external factor without regard to the actual position of the body under discussion. A similar debate was carried on, of course, in relation to the Arab question. The element of an intellectual exercise divorced from reality is prominent in both cases.

Side by side with their admiration and enthusiasm for what was being done in the Soviet Union, there was concern about the competition of a rival ideal. Socialist Zionism prided itself on being a synthesis of Zionism and socialism. The balance between the two components of this *Weltanschauung* marked the relative position of every individual and movement over the broad and diffuse spectrum of socialist Zionism. Potential loss by erosion to the 'world of tomorrow' was built into the ideology: where was the borderline between admiration of Soviet Russia as a natural part of the socialist component of this view of the world, and admiration which distorted orders of preference and subordinated the Zionist element in the equation to the socialist one? The primacy of Zionism was accepted as axiomatic by all the social bodies which belonged to what was known as 'Labour Palestine' i.e. the various kibbutz movements and the Labour-affiliated youth movements. But the danger of losing this primacy accompanied them like a shadow. At a time when it appeared that the flower of Jewish youth in Europe was being swept up in the wave of Communism and being lost to the Jewish national movement, the leaders of the small workers' movement in Palestine watched with mounting anxiety individuals and groups being swept away from their camp leftwards. This phenomenon, even if not of appreciable dimensions, with losses amounting to no more than a few thousand, was not regarded by the leadership as a marginal matter, but as arising from the very nature of the movement, an inherent danger. 'This phenomenon', wrote Berl Katznelson, 'threatens each one of us, even the child born in our midst.'[4] The departure from the Socialist-Zionist domain to that of Communism was never viewed as a change of ideology—a legitimate act in a democratic society—but as a 'deviation', a notion fraught with emotions and moral judgement, which embodies a recognition of affinity and a sense of betrayal. The preference for the rival ideal was interpreted as an attack on the delicate synthesis between Zionism and socialism and a challenge to its validity. Hence the fear and hostility, the anger and the sense of danger. No such feelings ever accompanied the departure of people towards the right: that was not a 'deviation' but a desertion. It did not imperil the image of the world that they had created; nor did it represent the choice of an alternative, for the primacy of Zionism remained unaffected. By contrast, the move to the left undermined an entire world, even though the ideological distance traversed by the renegade was less than that covered by one who turned to the right.

The phenomenon of erosion towards the left and out of the Zionist-Socialist consensus was the constant companion of Labour Palestine. Mostly it occurred on the individual level, without hitting the headlines: after all, the great majority of the members of the Palestine Communist Party had been convinced Zionists when they came to the country: otherwise, in the words of Plekhanov, they would not have risked getting seasick. Only in Palestine did they change their opinions and come under the influence of the leftist 'heresy'. But so long as this was a phenomenon which only affected individuals who had come to the ideological or personal parting of the ways, it did not attract attention. Even when the trend to the left affected limited groups within a body of society, and that body succeeded in coping with them by internal measures, arresting the process by its own efforts, public interest was not aroused. That is what happened, for example, in two cases of a shift towards the left within ha-Shomer ha-Zair at the beginning of the 1930s—one in Binyamina, led by Yaakov (Kuba) Riftin, and the second in Nes-Ziona, under the leadership of Mordechai Ornstein (Oren). These two episodes ended in the leaders' confessing their sins, accepting the judgement passed by the movement and falling into line. It is true that in both cases an appreciable number of individuals fell away. But so long as the framework of the movement was not shaken, the struggle remained an internal matter. The situation was different when the organizational foundations were also impaired. Two episodes of this kind occurred in the history of Labour Palestine: the shift to the left in Gedud ha-Avodah (1924-7) and in Mapam (1949-54). In the present study I shall seek to examine the characteristic features of the leftward shift in these two cases, and to outline the similarities and differences between them.

There are essential differences between the leftward inclinations of members of Gedud ha-Avodah in the 1920s and those of Mapam members in the early 1950s; some of these differences relate to the situation in the world and in Palestine at the time, and others to the human element. The shift to the left in Gedud ha-Avodah occurred at a time when the Soviet regime was still in its transitional stages. The rule of Stalin had not yet been firmly established. The manifestations of tyranny and corruption, to the extent that they had become known beyond the borders of Soviet Russia, could still be explained as arising from the necessities of a great revolution struggling against enemies without and the sabotage of reactionaries within. The great hope that a new society was being built 'there' was an accepted convention in the circles of the Left and among liberal intellectuals. In Palestine it was shared by men as remote from socialism and youthful enthusiasm as Arthur Ruppin: 'Were I not won over by Zionism,' he wrote in his diary on 31 December 1921, 'I would not envisage any goal in life for myself superior to that of taking part in the formation of a new peace-seeking regime in Russia.'[5] After the disappointments with the democratic regimes, following the First World War and the subsequent structural crises, belief in the land of the great Revolution became an integral part of the faith of those who were striving to set the world to rights. The leftward shift of some members of the Gedud was part of a contemporaneous world-wide phenomenon.

By contrast, the move to the Left in Mapam came after the disillusionment with the Soviet Union which followed the show trials and the purges at the end of the 1930s and the Molotov-Ribbentrop agreement. Moreover, revolutionary Russia was no longer the underdog in the battles of world politics. The resilience of the regime and its ability to cope with its greatest crisis had been proved in the Second World War. The USSR emerged from the war as one of the two superpowers. She spread her influence over Eastern and Central Europe. The period under consideration—1949–54—was characterized by the development and intensification of the Cold War on the one hand, and, on the other, the emergence of the first of the splits in the camp of the Comintern—the appearance of Tito as an independent leader, which broke the monolithic character of the Communist bloc. True, the authority of the USSR as a great power continued to increase, but her attraction for progressive circles in the world was on the decline. The phenomenon of groups and prominent persons in the free world being drawn to the light rising in the east was extremely rare by this time. Whereas the move to the left in the Gedud had taken place against the background of a general tendency in this direction, that which occurred in Mapam ran contrary to the prevailing trend in countries which were not under the domination of the USSR.

Within Palestine, too, the background to the two occurrences was completely different: the episode of the shift to the left in the Gedud had as its background the development of the gravest crisis that the Zionist movement had ever known. From the end of the Fourth *Aliyah* (1924–6) onwards, an economic depression led to the suspension of building, mass unemployment (a third of the workforce in Tel Aviv was out of work), the cessation of *aliyah* and large-scale emigration (in 1927, emigration—*yeridah*—was nearly twice as great as *aliyah*); all this when the Jewish population in the country had not yet reached 100,000. The collapse of Solel Boneh (the construction co-operative) in 1927 symbolized the helplessness of the workers' movement and the Zionist Organization. Zionist resources dwindled and settlement by means of national capital and on national land came to a halt. The economic crisis quickly became a crisis of confidence in Zionism. Doubt as to the credibility of the Zionist experiment and its ability to survive and develop was felt by many, some with anxiety, others with malicious pleasure.

By contrast, the shift to the left in Mapam developed within a young, dynamic State, looking forward confidently to a future of great achievement. Before people had had time to recover from what was regarded as the miracle of the establishment of the State of Israel, there came the news of the victories of the War of Independence to prove that the new-born nation was very much alive and kicking. The first years of independence were occupied in the work of absorbing mass immigration, in a mighty upsurge of production and construction in all branches of the economy, in expansion to the point of bursting out of the old restraining frameworks and creating new ones. It was a period when self-confidence was high and the dominant feeling was that great events were taking place. Truly, if in 1927 Zionism seemed like a story of failure, in 1949 it was a success story.

The nucleus of the Trumpeldor Gedud ha-Avodah, which was founded in the summer of 1920, consisted of members of He-Halutz, the pioneer organization established by Trumpeldor in the Crimea, who were to follow him to Palestine. By the time they arrived, Trumpeldor was already dead, and they regarded themselves as his executors. They were young people who had reached adulthood in the Russia of the First World War, the Revolution and the Civil War. To them Russia was first and foremost their native land—tangible, flesh and blood. Their spiritual world was interwoven with its landscapes, its images, its dreams, and the type of person it bred. It was not a country beyond the hills of darkness, but a native land which they knew and loved, and for which they had feelings of nostalgia. Their families had lived there for generations, and the link between them had not been broken. Many of them spoke and read Russian, whereas their knowledge of Hebrew was laboriously acquired only after their arrival in Palestine. The fact that Brenner taught Hebrew in the Gedud camp at Migdal was not a coincidence. They read avidly the newspapers and books which came 'from there': how good it was to read a language which came naturally to one! Many of them had experienced the terrors of the Civil War and had witnessed the atrocities committed by the White Russians against the Jews and the rescue of the Jews by the Red Army. They identified themselves closely with the Revolution, and although they saw themselves as having a pre-eminently Zionist role, they coupled with it the hope of a Hebrew Revolution: 'the building up of the land by a general commune of the workers of Palestine'.

The Russia of real life, however, scarcely existed for the young people who were caught up in the shift to the left in Mapam thirty years later. Among the adult leadership there were some who had come from Russia and whose relationship to that country had in it something of the intimacy felt by people for the place of their birth (this type, though, was more common among the members of Ahdut ha-Avodah[6] than in Ha-Shomer ha-Zair). But beyond this small leadership group, those who were moving to the left and being swept away by admiration for the USSR at the beginning of the 1950s had, for the most part, either been born in Palestine or received their education there. Their Russia was the Russia of literature, of novels, an ideal. Most of them could not read Russian. Their picture of the world, and of the particular place of Soviet Russia in it, was not the result of actual experience but of education and indoctrination. During and after the Second World War many books were translated from Russian into Hebrew. The literature of the war years, from *Rainbow in the Cloud* to *Panfilov's Men* and *The One-legged Pilot*, created a heart-warming image of Russia as a land of the ordinary people, mobilizing forces from the depths of the nation's soul to defend the land of their birth. The jargon, the slogans, the simplicity of conduct and the self-sacrifice, all seemed almost a part of the reality of life in Palestine: the struggle there against the British was perceived as parallel to the people's war, and more particularly the guerrilla struggle in the USSR against the Nazis. The anti-bourgeois patterns of conduct described in Russian literature were perceived by those who had been trained in the Palmah and the youth movements as reflecting their own aspirations. The leftist ideology grew out of a spiritual bedrock composed of songs, stories and noble thoughts. The image of Russia that they formed did not so much reflect the real Russia as the dreams and hopes of the youngsters of Labour Palestine. The question of why the youth of Palestine felt the need of this image of Soviet Russia will be considered in another paper. For our present purpose it suffices to establish the fact that the attitude to Russia in the 1940s and 1950s, unlike that in the 1920s, was based more on an imaginary Russia than on Russia as she actually was.

Apart from these basic differences between the two historic episodes—differences which hinged on the time of their occurrence—there are many similarities and parallels between them.

In both cases it was a development within a socio-political body which had been in the centre of Zionist activity and which was forced into opposition to the Zionist-Socialist establishment. The result was a process in which opposition to the establishment and the shift to the left fostered each other. The leftward shift was the result of the oppositional stance; concomitantly, it served as a catalyst to it, strengthened and encouraged it, and turned differences of policy into differences of principle.

The oppositional attitude in Gedud ha-Avodah began with the first rift in its midst. In 1923 the two settlements established by the Gedud—Ein Harod and Tel Yosef—split up, and Ein Harod left Gedud ha-Avodah. The schism, which originated in disputes within the Gedud between veterans of the Second *Aliyah* and the younger members of the

Third *Aliyah* over the way in which the Gedud should be managed, led to a quarrel between the Gedud and the Histadrut. There had, indeed, been tensions between the two even before that, for the Gedud was distinguished by a strong leadership, a highly centralized organization and a marked preference for independent action. But it was the split between Ein Harod and Tel Yosef, in which the Histadrut, under the leadership of Ben-Gurion, adopted a one-sided stance against the Gedud, that turned the latent opposition into active estrangement. The conscious posture of opposition of the Gedud began from then. The body which was nearest to them from the political point of view—Ahdut ha-Avodah—no longer came into consideration as a focus for their sympathies, for the leadership of the Histadrut was also the leadership of Ahdut ha-Avodah. Very soon a tendency arose in the Gedud to search for a distinctive political content of their own. At first the discussion revolved round the question of whether the Gedud really needed a distinctive political character, but the tendency to support politicization soon gained the upper hand, and they went on to debate what should be the content of the distinctive political programme which they were now committed to formulating. It was natural that politicization should lead towards the left: that was the spirit of the time, in which the Bolshevik Revolution served as a source of inspiration and legitimacy. To a radical body like the Gedud it went without saying that their distinctive character would be thrown into relief by an ideology to the left of that accepted by the 'establishment' of the Labour movement.

A parallel development was to occur in the history of Mapam. There was, indeed, a basic link with the Soviet Union in the constituent parts of Mapam, which was formed in January 1948 from 'Ha-Tnuah le-Ahdut ha-Avodah' (The Movement for the Unity of Labour) and the Left Poalei Zion party, together with the Socialist League, an organization which represented Ha-Shomer ha-Zair and its associates in urban areas. Sympathy for the USSR during the Second World War was felt by a wide range of groups in Palestine, among them some outside Labour circles. The altered Soviet attitude to Zionism that was expressed in the well-known speech by Gromyko to the United Nations, and subsequently in the support of the Soviet Union for the establishment of the State of Israel, strengthened the feeling that there was, indeed, no real conflict of interests between 'the world of tomorrow' and Zionism. To this were added the USSR's immediate recognition of the State, the supply of Czech armaments, which stood the fighters in the War of Independence in good stead, and the permission given to large numbers of Jews in East European countries under Soviet hegemony (though not to the Jews of Soviet Russia itself) to emigrate to Israel. All these things seemed to indicate that the USSR was at a turning point in its attitude to the Jewish people and the Zionist movement, that is to say that it was intending to recognize the Jewish people as a nation, and the Zionist movement as its national liberation movement. This hope became a basic tenet of Mapam.

However, the origins of the process of the shift to the left are more specifically to be found in the policy of opposition into which Mapam was pushed. A party which, before the establishment of the State and during the War of Independence, had been at the centre of Zionist activity, found itself thrust by Ben-Gurion to a marginal position. In the newly founded State, Ha-Kibbutz ha-Meuhad and Ha-Shomer ha-Zair no longer played the central parts they had in the 'State in the making' stage. Their importance in the security forces, in government institutions and even in settlement projects diminshed steadily. Bitterness towards Ben-Gurion and his policy was coupled to a fervent hope that it would be within the power of Mapam to replace Mapai as the central party of the workers. This hope rested on electoral successes which had made Mapam the second largest party in the State.[7]

In spite of the bitterness and anger over the way in which Ben-Gurion had dismissed Israel Galili from his position as civil supervisor of the Haganah, unceremoniously disbanded the Palmah[8] and ousted its commanders from the army, Mapam remained in the government until 1949. To leave the government went against the grain of this activist party, and the decision was taken with the utmost reluctance and many qualms. But once they had left it was hard for them to return: the dynamic of 'oppositionism' had begun to act. Three times in two and a half years the question of Mapam's joining a coalition came up for discussion—in the winter of 1949, the winter of 1949–50 and the autumn of 1951. The negotiations on the first occasion, after the first elections to the Knesset (January 1949), reflected Ben-Gurion's efforts to rob Mapam of its legitimacy and humiliate it. The negotiations were conducted discourteously, in a harsh atmosphere, a firm decision having been taken by Ben-Gurion to exclude Mapam from the government. The internal discussion in Mapam reflected its bitterness over the expulsion of its men from the army and the humiliation inflicted on it by Ben-Gurion in the negotiations; the great majority of the party council voted against joining the government on the terms offered.[9] Even so, the decision was not easy, especially for the members of Ahdut ha-Avodah, who felt it as the essence of their existence to be actively involved in national affairs. The consolation offered them by Hazan, that Ha-Shomer ha-Zair had spent twenty years in opposition but had not lost any of its constructionism, afforded them no comfort.

The next discussion took place between November 1949 and March 1950. This time Mapai conducted the negotiations calmly and respectably, indicating a sincere readiness to parley. But the months which had passed since it went into the political wilderness had brought about a change of heart in Mapam. This was understood by Ben-Aharon, who said that if Mapai had shown the same readiness to make concessions at the beginning of 1949, 'I have no doubt at all that the council would not have decided nine months ago against joining the government.' Now Riftin declared: 'We must prepare to spend a lengthy period in opposition. We must not grow tired after eight months in opposition.'[10] What, nine months before, had been the result of manoeuvring by Ben-Gurion, now became a sacred principle for some members of the Mapam leadership. It is true that participation had not been presented by Ha-Shomer ha-Zair as a question of principle but as a question of conditions suitable for participation, and Yaari and Galili differed over those conditions, the one as representing the views of Ha-Shomer ha-Zair—the hard line—and the other as representing those of Le-Ahdut ha-Avodah, who wanted to join the government.[11] But within Ha-Shomer ha-Zair a debate was already going on as to whether they should not entirely oppose any entry into the government. A view began to take shape supported by Riftin, Eliezer Peri and Aharon Cohen, that joining the government would put an end to the position of Mapam as a radical, leftist party. Riftin, as was his manner, did not mince his words: 'Our task is to go on crystallizing our revolutionary status. Our participation in the government would be a brake on this process.'[12] Between the lines the question could be seen emerging whether co-operation with the 'reformist' Mapai was a fit and desirable object, and Meir Yaari thought it necessary to warn against this trend: 'As soon as we lose the ability to co-operate with another Zionist element—Mapai—the process [the leftist orientation] will take control over us.'[13] Objection in principle, too, was voiced against entry into the government: 'both because of the effect this would have in Cominform countries and because the footsteps of the Revolution are beating in their heads'.[14] The feeling that remaining outside the government was a catalyst for radicalization was common to both those who sought to re-enter the government and those who wanted to stay in opposition.

The discussion at this stage took the form of a drama in three acts: debate in the council of Mapam, debate at a meeting of the executive committee of Ha-Kibbutz ha-Arzi, and renewed debate in the council of Mapam in Petah Tikvah (5–6 March 1950). In this last debate the members of Ha-Shomer ha-Zair adopted a tactical position, arguing that the minimum conditions acceptable to Mapam for entry into the government had not been met. This position concealed the differences of opinion on the subject within Ha-Shomer ha-Zair, which obliged Yaari, against his better judgement, to resign himself to the view of the leftist faction, and to oppose entry. Since there were also some members of Le-Ahdut ha-Avodah who held that Mapam's minimum conditions had not been fulfilled, the Petah Tikvah council meeting decided against joining the government, but this time by a smaller majority than before.[15] The decision stipulated participation in the government with the fulfilment of specified conditions. But in the branches of the party other winds were already blowing, and opinion there favoured non-participation in the government on grounds of principle.[16]

In August 1951 a new round of talks on joining the government was begun with Mapai. This time the situation was clear: at the end of January 1951 the various divisions of Mapam had published their manifestos for the elections at the party conference which was to be held in Haifa (30 May–6 June 1951). A new section made its appearance, Ha-Hazit le-Likkud ha-Miflagah (The Front for the Unification of the Party), which broke the historic line of separation between Ha-Shomer ha-Zair and Le-Ahdut ha-Avodah. Members of Le-Ahdut ha-Avodah, led by Moshe Sneh, joined forces with the leadership of Ha-Shomer ha-Zair and entered into a political pact marked by the shift to the left. In the elections for the conference the Unification Front won 60 per cent of the votes, as against 36 per cent obtained by Le-Ahdut ha-Avodah (the rest of the votes went to the Left Poalei Zion party under Moshe Erem).[17] Mapam became more and more identified with a leftist direction. In their internal discussions the frustration of the members of Le-Ahdut ha-Avodah stood out, and this time a note of urgency was added to it. Tabenkin warned that 'a party that merely criticizes and does no constructive work corrupts the individual member'.[18] But the Unification Front presented a unanimous stand: Mapai must accept the decisions taken by the second Mapam conference in Haifa, namely to set up a coalition headed by a workers' front on the basis of an agreed programme of action. This included a series of conditions connected with economic and social policy, aimed at the radicalization of the Histadrut, the national ownership of the means of production and a policy giving absolute preference to wage earners. Another series of conditions related to foreign policy, the main points being the 'genuine neutrality' of the state, preservation of her independence, no bases to be made available to foreign powers (meaning the United States) and no involvement in the system of Western alliances.[19] Opinions on whether or not the 'Haifa conditions' had been accepted depended on previous positions: while Israel Galili summed up the negotiations with Mapai as successful, Israel

Barzilai's conclusions were negative. The executive of the Unification Front had discussed the matter and decided that the negotiations with Mapai should be assessed as having ended in failure. Yaari and Hazan were not of that opinion but, as Hazan said, 'The vote in the executive of the Front was, in effect, a vote of no confidence in me and in Meir (Yaari)'[20] on this subject. In the joint discussions with Le-Ahdut ha-Avodah, all the members of the Unification Front clung to the decisions of the Haifa conference as if to the horns of the altar, turning the party platform into a *sine qua non* for entry into the government. As there was no prospect of getting Mapai to accept the platform, the possibility of Mapam's entering the government became a theoretical one. At the beginning of September 1951 the council of Mapam called for the negotiations to be broken off.[21] The possibility that Mapam might join the government was laid to rest for a number of years.

Within two years the departure from the government forced upon Mapam by Ben-Gurion acquired an ideological rationale. Their stay in the political wilderness developed into a fundamental attitude of opposition which shunned any involvement in the reformist rule of Mapai. The prolonged spell in opposition of bodies which had been brought up on practical activity was accompanied by the search for an outlet for these men's thirst for action and their quest to give meaning to their lives. Devotion to the USSR provided an answer to the frustration of young men who had suddenly found themselves without a goal. Thus the attitude of opposition as a matter of principle was both an expression of the shift to the left and a spur to it.

The search for an alternative involvement in the national sphere of activity is linked to two further characteristics of the shift to the left: one of the phenomena peculiar to that process in Israel was that the leftward shift of any group always affected the agricultural settlements, i.e. the kibbutz movement, precisely those who were regarded as the very nucleus of the Zionist avant garde. The fathers of the labour movement, who were conscious of the danger of the leftward tendency, saw active settlement, physical contact with soil and scenery, and the concrete challenge of pioneering, as the barrier against the winds of heresy. That, among other reasons, was why they were so shocked at the case of the Gedud, and why the leaders of Ha-Shomer ha-Zair were so alarmed when the influence of the Left on the young kibbutzim became apparent. The process was accompanied on both occasions by contact between members of kibbutzim and urban workers: the Gedud had urban groups and, through the members of these, links were established between the members of the Gedud and radical groups of workers in the towns. Mapam had been built from the start on an alliance between workers' agricultural settlements and urban workers. But the direct contact between young kibbutzim and the 'Young Division' in the towns and a radical urban branch like the one in Tel Aviv was an expression of the process of radicalization, marked by a decline in the importance of agricultural settlement in the eyes of kibbutz members. This alliance of town and country is even more prominent in the establishment of the Unification Front at the beginning of 1951. The Front was founded on an alliance between Ha-Kibbutz ha-Arzi–Ha-Shomer ha-Zair and former town members in Le-Ahdut ha-Avodah and the Socialist League. The diminished importance of agricultural settlement in the eyes of its members is connected with two central issues which were inextricably linked: the attitude to the implementation of Zionism and to the 'short-cut'. What is the watershed in the leftward process, i.e. at what point does a Zionist left orientation become a non-Zionist 'deviation'? It appears that so long as a group accords primacy to Zionist build-up, we are dealing with a Zionist Left. When, however, the actual work of building up the country is no longer considered of prime importance, and confidence in its practicability is undermined, a 'deviant' leftward shift has taken place, with unforeseeable consequences. In both cases, whether the principle of building up the country was devalued or upheld, it was connected in the experience of the left with the attitude to the 'short-cut'.

Gedud ha-Avodah emblazoned on its banner the device 'building up the country by way of establishing a general commune'. In doing so it gave expression to the belief which was current in the workers' movement in Palestine that there it would be possible to omit the capitalist stage in the historical development foreseen by Marx and build a socialist society from the start. Some thirty years later Meir Yaari was to remark: 'All the workers in the country . . . went about at that time believing that the nation would volunteer its support and produce the means, while the workers would provide the hands, the skill, the devotion and the vision. And thus the whole country would be built up on foundations of equality, justice and co-operation.'[22] Lenin's 'short-cut' in the October Revolution furnished the proof that the thing was feasible. At that stage the Zionist component in the ideology of the Gedud was dominant. The building up of the country was perceived as the task of the Gedud, and as the way in which socialism, too, would be achieved here and now. This faith was undermined in the crisis of the Third *Aliyah*, and especially with the arrival of the Fourth *Aliyah*. National capital and pioneering immigrants, expected to join forces in building a socialist society, had failed to materialize. The Fourth *Aliyah* was characterized by immigrants of a new kind, with a bourgeois mentality and some private capital. It became clear that Palestine would not avoid capitalism.

The question now arose: what role was assigned to the Gedud in a society condemned to undergo class war and revolution? What meaning was there now to living in a commune? An argument developed in the Gedud concerning the role of the commune under the new conditions. Some members resigned themselves to the limited role of the commune in the framework of a capitalist society, and viewed it only as a cell—a prototype of the future society. Others, however, were not content with this passive role. They wanted to turn the Gedud into an avant garde, an active revolutionary cell, committed to the struggle for changing the regime. Those with this aim very soon came to the conclusion that they must see to the party's economic independence and avoid burdening it with tasks involving losses. An avant garde which sought to overthrow the foundations of existing society could not expect its losses to be covered by the national institutions. Indeed, by its very nature it was prevented from appealing to them for help.[23] Thus, one after another, constructive paths of action were closed to the Gedud. The more these were closed, the greater grew the scepticism as to the importance of the building up of the country by the Gedud. The commune with a limited function seemed meaningless: 'There is no point in eating together and running a communal kitchen.'[24] The emphasis was shifted from constructive action, which was now perceived as both unimportant and impracticable, to political activity, under the slogan of class war. At that time—the time of the crisis of the Fourth *Aliyah*—the essence of the new tendency was expressed in the demand put forward by Levi Kantor to the leaders of the Histadrut—'at a time of unemployment and hunger, to put aside concern for the whole of Israel and Zionism, and to demand forcefully work and bread for the hungry'.[25] From this it was but a short step to outright despair about the future of the commune in Palestine, especially in the face of the Zionist crisis and the interruption of agricultural settlement at that time. The idea of building a commune in a land where the regime looked kindly on communes and where their existence fitted in with the general aims of that regime—to wit, the USSR—grew naturally in this group, a group which was action-oriented but whose attempts to take action were being thwarted.

Whereas, in the case of the Gedud, it was disappointment in regard to the short-cut that started a process ending in despair of building up the country, in the case of the Mapam left it was precisely the hope of a short-cut that led in the same direction.

Ha-Kibbutz ha-Arzi–ha-Shomer ha-Zair was founded in 1927 in the shadow of the disaster which befell Gedud ha-Avodah. In 1926 the Gedud split into 'Left' and 'Right', and in 1927–8 some of its members—about 60 in all, under the leadership of Elkind—left

Palestine for Soviet Russia. It was alarm at the various attempts to 'hasten the Redemption' and at demands for the establishment of the Kingdom of Heaven on earth here and now which was behind Meir Yaari's famous 'doctrine of stages', a doctrine which from then on constituted the basic ideological and educational framework of Ha-Shomer ha-Zair. This doctrine, the ultimate aim of which was the establishment of a bi-national socialist society in Eretz Israel and its environs, distinguished between the first stage in the realization of its programme—the Zionist stage—and the second—the socialist stage. In the first stage their members were expected to occupy themselves in building like the best of *halutzim* (pioneers), to work for *aliyah* and agricultural settlement, and, for this purpose, to avail themselves of the financial allocations of the Zionist Organization. It followed as a matter of course that they meant to take part in the management of the Zionist Organization. Only when the process of 'territorial concentration' (as defined by Borochov) of the Jewish masses in their homeland was complete, and the national home of the Jewish people safely established, only then would the rules of the game be changed, and Ha-Shomer ha-Zair be harnessed to fight, without restraint, the class war for the advancement of the Revolution. In this way, their members were enabled to feel a deep spiritual affinity to the forces of revolution in the world, and at the same time to co-operate with the other Zionist parties in the work of implementing Zionism. Thus Ha-Shomer ha-Zair rejected all short-cuts, and although the exaltation of the revolution was constantly on their lips, in fact the revolutionary urge in them was less prominent than in Ha-Kibbutz ha-Meuhad, which inherited the impatience typical of Gedud ha-Avodah.

However, from 1949 onwards the tendency to 'hasten the Redemption' revealed itself in Ha-Shomer ha-Zair too. The policy of the USSR towards the establishment of the State of Israel and during the first years of the state's existence gave rise to the hope that 'the barrier between us and the world of the Revolution'—a euphemism which meant the USSR's opposition to Zionism and to the rights of the Jewish people as a nation—was about to be removed. Coupled with this great hope was a particular view of the international situation. The intensification of the Cold War was interpreted by devotees of the USSR in Israel as indicating that a new world war was on the way, and that it would end with the Red Army spreading its wings over the Middle East. For at least two years (1949–51) the Left in Mapam saw this as a real possibility.

This analysis of the situation by supporters of the Left in Ha-Shomer ha-Zair mixed emotion with cold calculation, ideology with apparent pragmatism, the desirable with the attainable. If ever there was a situation to which the expression 'rejoice with trembling' (Ps. 2:11) could suitably be applied, this was it.

In the autumn of 1949 a red star rose in the skies of China—the Communists took complete control of that enormous country. The Soviet momentum seemed unstoppable.[26] At the same time tension grew between East and West with the outbreak of the Korean war. The United States began organizing the series of alliances which had the purpose of halting the Soviets. The Marshall Plan was seen by Mapam as an American plot to exercise control over Europe by economic means. That, too, was how they saw the American loan to the State of Israel, which Mapam voted against in the Knesset.[27] This was a period of public hysteria, pro- and anti-Soviet, in which everything was said in high moral tones, in an almost eschatological atmosphere. The air was full of prophecies of the impending war of Gog and Magog. An integral part of these prophecies was the belief (for some, the hope) that the Red Army would very soon appear on the northern border of the State of Israel. And the question how to prepare for that day and how to greet the Red Army suddenly became the subject of concrete discussions, both among the rank and file of the movement and at the top level, on the plane of policy and leadership.

Among the rank and file, this atmosphere found expression in ways that could be described as odd: there were young couples, members of kibbutzim in the south of the country, who sought to move to one of the border settlements in the north in order to be among the first to greet the Soviet tanks.[28] A member of one of the kibbutzim in the north chose explicitly to work on a tractor because in his opinion that was the appropriate equipment with which to meet the Red Army.[29] The ceremony in which the delegates at the Haifa conference rose to their feet and took the oath traditional to the Communist parties of the world—'We will never lift up our hands against the Soviet Union'[30]—was connected in Israel with the expected day of meeting. More serious were the deliberations of the leaders of the Left. Aharon Cohen raised the question as early as the autumn of 1949: 'The world is taking giant strides towards its socialist emancipation ... Communism and the forces of progress are conquering countries and continents— Red China, Vietnam, etc., etc. If we do not join now, others will celebrate at the feast.' And he added: 'We must think and think with all seriousness what will happen when they arrive here.' (Interjection by A. K. [Abba Kovner?]: 'Better not to think.')[31] The feeling that time was pressing and that it was necessary to make haste to enter into discussion with the world power that was going to conquer the region also underlay the outlook of Moshe Sneh. It appears that Sneh's opinion at that time, like that of the members of the Left in Mapam, was clearly formulated in the words of Sheike Weinberg: 'All the Powers are conducting their affairs on the assumption that the war will break out within two years. There is a feeling that there is no time ... The conclusion is—in full loyalty to Zionism, we must be an integral part of the world of the Revolution. There is no contradiction between the two. On this depends the fate of Zionism in the future.'[32] He was supported by Aharon Cohen: 'The fate of Zionism depends on Mapam from now on. The victory march of Socialism is advancing with giant strides and Zionism is not being realized in a vacuum.'[33]

The aspiration and hope for the coming of the Red Army was only a step away—a mere difference of nuance—from the idea that its coming was inevitable and that they must not miss the bus because to do so would be fatal. Those who spoke of the need to prepare for that day also longed for it to come, and awaited it with the exaltation of spirit of people who yearn to take part in the march of progress and history.

How should one prepare for the appearance of the Red Army in the Middle East? The hope of those who tended to the left in Mapam was that Mapam would be able to achieve the recognition of the Soviet Union and, with it, that of the Cominform, as the Communist Party of Israel in place of Maki (the Israeli Communist party). True, such recognition would require a radical change in the policy of the Soviets towards the Jewish nation and Zionism. That policy had first found expression in Lenin's description of the Jews as not being a nation; it was continued by Stalin's definition of the distinguishing marks of a nation (territory, economy, language and a common history) and by the exclusion of the Jews from those who fell within these definitions; it was canonized by the Second Congress of the Comintern in 1920, which anathematized Zionism, declaring it to be reactionary, Utopian and serving imperialism. Since then the USSR had not gone back on this definition. The leftists in Mapam believed that a change in this attitude was not only possible but even imminent. Moreover, the removal of the barrier between the Zionists and the world of the Revolution depended first and foremost on the behaviour of the State of Israel. In the judgement of Sneh, Riftin and their colleagues, the policy followed by the Israeli government under Ben-Gurion was doing nothing to bring nearer the day for which they hoped. Therefore Mapam must take it upon itself to break the barrier, with the object of presenting a Zionist-Communist alternative to the government of Israel. Mapam would do this by restricting the differences between itself and the world at whose door it was knocking to the sole question of its relationship to Zionism and the Jewish people, or, better, to Zionism alone. For this purpose Mapam must be purged of ideological and organizational dross and become a Leninist party.[34] What was meant by becoming a Leninist party? Did it mean scrapping the divisions within Mapam and setting up an internationalist (Jewish–Arab), centralizing, monolithic party on the model of the Bolshevik party, or were they thinking of a party submitting to the authority of the Cominform? This point was never completely clarified. What was clear, however, was that such a decision would mean splitting up Mapam, because Le-Ahdut ha-Avodah would not agree to give up the divisional structure of the party and would not reconcile itself to the admission of Arab members. Therefore, anyone who sought to set up a Leninist party was consciously striving for a split in the party and the secession of its right wing.[35] Then it would become a territorialist, internationalist party, divided from the Soviet Union only by Zionism. A split over an ostensibly organizational matter would presumably recall the famous split between the Mensheviks and the Bolsheviks in 1903 over a similar issue.

The question of integration into the world of the Revolution had thus been transformed from an article of faith, a vision of the distant future, into a concrete and immediate aim with political significance for their own time. This had fatal consequences for the 'doctrine of stages', that solid ideological rock against which previous waves of movement to the left had shattered. For if the Red Army was at the door and integration into the world of the Revolution was no longer merely an ideal but a real possibility, this meant that the Zionist stage of the doctrine of stages had ended—or was about to end—and the Socialist stage had begun. This conviction carried immediate repercussions on the various links between the Left and the bourgeois parties, especially the one they labelled a 'reformist' party—Mapai. Co-operation between all the Zionist parties in the building up of Palestine had followed naturally from the doctrine of stages. But if, now, the aim of the greatest urgency and importance was integration into the world of the Revolution, the ideological basis for continuing 'Zionist co-operation' was demolished.[36] When the objections to the doctrine of stages first became known, Yaari was called upon to defend it (1949):

> The period of pioneering and building up the Land is not yet over! We have not yet reached the stage when everything is ready for [our] entry [to the communist world]. We are not standing on the threshold ... At the present stage we cannot integrate! When did we forget this—overnight, as it were? ... R. [Riftin] said to me: 'You talk like Ben-Gurion, "first the ingathering of the exiles, then Socialism"'. I have never said 'first', but 'through'. Through the ingathering of the exiles.[37]

Some time later (1951), Yaari entered into a discussion with David Hanegbi, one of the younger element who were impatient to join the world of the Revolution. Yaari directed the main thrust of his argument towards demonstrating that the acceptance of Mapam in particular and Zionism in general by the world of the Revolution was not a practical question at that time. He castigated the attempt at integration 'with watch in hand' as unrealistic, and demanded that they 'make history without hysteria' (*historiyah bli histeriyah*).[38] A few months afterwards he declared at a meeting of the executive committee of Ha-Kibbutz ha-Arzi–ha-Shomer ha-Zair: 'I was an enemy of Trotsky from the outset, for I was a pioneer and we knew that we needed time and needed to make history without hysteria.'[39]

But once the process began, it developed a dynamic of its own. The conclusion that it was pointless, or even discreditable, to co-operate with Zionist elements (and Mapai in particular) went naturally with the effort to integrate with the world of tomorrow. Besides, the constructive role of Ha-Shomer ha-Zair seemed less important to those members who were moving towards the left: if the Red Army were about to arrive, what was the value of pioneering activity in the Land compared with the importance of political dialogue with them? 'There are members who are shifting the centre of gravity from the imperative of pioneering to accelerating the consolidation of the party,' observed Shlomo Rosen, 'because they appraise the situation as leading towards a catastrophe [a world war].'[40]

The three elements of their belief—that the war of Gog and Magog was about to break out, that the 'fall of the barrier' was now a real possibility, and that Mapai, as a reformist party, 'were, are and will be traitors' (to quote the words of members of the Left) and, on the other hand, that everything being done in Israel was dwarfed in importance by the approach of the great and terrible day when the forces of Revolution would appear in the Middle East—all these things led naturally to the conclusion that the days of co-operation with Zionism were over. This attitude allied itself readily with the point of view which favoured opposition as a matter of principle, and each fostered the other.[41] The inference drawn, much as in the case of the Gedud, was that the time had come for 'a pause in Zionist activity'. The view that an intermission was needed in the process of building up the Land stemmed from the fact that an interruption of 'Zionist co-operation' was bound to be followed by an interruption in the flow of money from world Jewry—money from the western world. The 'pause in Zionist activity' would also be a natural consequence of the boycott of Mapam—including Ha-Kibbutz ha-Arzi—by the Zionist Organization and its sources of assistance which would result from the cessation of

'Zionist co-operation'. It meant being cut off from the world pioneering movement, from sources of manpower and from the allocations of the national funds. This would have far-reaching effects on the development of Ha-Kibbutz ha-Arzi. The 'pause' appears in statements by the men of the Left as an inevitable consequence of the dynamic of Mapam's development into a revolutionary party, which would lead to antagonism towards it; but they also declared it to be a desirable process that would cut the umbilical cord linking Mapam to an enterprise which had lost its importance, and their connection with which involved more than a suspicion of straying from the straight and narrow path.

The utterances of the men of the Left in Ha-Kibbutz ha-Arzi on the question of the 'pause in Zionist activity' remained veiled in obscurity and ambiguity, softened by the implication that a change in the character of the Zionist Organization was required as a condition of co-operation with it.[42] Moshe Sneh, too, was careful not to speak about this in public, but he revealed what he thought about it to Meir Yaari as early as 1950. So far as is known, he did not use the expression 'pause in Zionist activity' which was used by the opponents of this aim, but according to Meir Yaari he put forward the idea that it was best to leave Ben-Gurion to dirty himself with American dollars; until the popular-democratic regime was established, Mapam for its part would be content to carry on the oppositional and anti-imperialist struggle.[43] He also appeared in kibbutzim where he sermonized in the same vein. In private conversations, too, Sneh did not refrain from expressing his opinion that the time had come to leave the Zionist coalition—meaning the Zionist Organization.[44] As early as the beginning of 1951, members of Le-Ahdut ha-Avodah were displaying intense alarm and revulsion at Sneh's views. They felt that he belittled the value of constructive work, and that he regarded pioneering and agricultural settlement as secondary matters in face of the expected victory of the Red Army.[45] This tendency of Sneh's was expressed at the time of the Prague trial in his demand, supported by Riftin and his friends on the Left, that they leave the Zionist Actions Committee which was accused at the trial of spying on behalf of imperialism.

The degree of importance attached to the debate on the 'pause in Zionist activity' can be gauged from the references, scattered here and there through the minutes of the executive committee of Ha-Kibbutz ha-Arzi to the possibility that Mapam might be forced to go underground. This possibility was presented by men of the Left like Sheike Weinberg or Riftin as a necessary consequence of the process of development of Mapam into a consistent revolutionary opposition, which would entail repressive measures on the part of the Ben-Gurion government. On the other hand, the men of the right in Ha-Shomer ha-Zair took the view that the prospect of becoming an underground movement was more than Ha-Kibbutz ha-Arzi could endure, not only because of their bonds with the state and the sense of duty towards it, but also because they were a kibbutz movement. The possibility also played a part in the reasons they advanced against splitting up Mapam. One of the arguments put forward by Meir Yaari, who was opposed to a split, was that it would identify Mapam as a leftist party and lead to its repression by Ben-Gurion to such an extent that it would be forced underground. There was no organized debate on the subject of going underground, but there is no doubt that it was discussed behind closed doors and was considered as a conseqence of 'the pause in Zionist activity'.[46]

One of the by-products of the shift to the left was the intensification of the ideological debate and the cleaning-up of all residues originating in Zionist compromises. The Zionist-Socialist synthesis was not cast in one solid block. Neither the teaching of Syrkin nor the more sophisticated theories of Borochov stand up to the critique of pure reason. The leaders of the Palestine labour movement, even the greatest of them like Brenner and Berl Katznelson, did not profess to be systematic thinkers. An outstanding example of 'creative inconsistency' is to be found in Yizhak Tabenkin, who borrowed from Kropotkin, Marx and Borochov, and produced something original of his own. The fragments of ideas and terminology taken from the Marxist school sufficed to give the Zionist labour movement an appearance of belonging to that world of which it felt itself intuitively to be a part—the world of the poor and the oppressed, to whom salvation would come with the coming of the day of the kingdom of justice—Socialism—on earth. People who were in any event convinced that their movement was travelling the right road were not so strict as to demand that its ideology should have great intellectual depth. Those eclectic ideas, mutually contradictory as they sometimes were, served as the fertile and productive myths from which men drew strength of mind and the blessing of faith. But as soon as faith in any component of Socialist Zionism was shaken, it was easy to attack the ideology. For this reason one of the characteristics of the shift to the left was the emergence of the demand to deepen its ideological base.

One of the first signs of the shift to the left in the Gedud was the establishment of the 'Seminary for Social Science'. Lukacher, a well-known Communist, justified the need for it to be set up by a slogan borrowed from the archives of the Bolshevik Party: 'Without theory there is no practice.' The seminary was intended to be 'the pillar of fire which will light the difficult way of the Gedud member in his work to create a constructive Communist Eretz Israel'.[47] But concern with the Marxist dialogue soon revealed the 'scientific' weaknesses of socialist constructionism: in less than a year they were already writing in *Me-Hayyeinu*, the journal of the Gedud, about 'the myth of constructive Communism'.[48] The confrontation between Marxist theory and the Zionist-Socialist synthesis revealed that all constructionism within the framework of a capitalist society was to be rejected as serving the interests of the existing regime. Therefore the commune—the proud creation of constructionism—was a creation 'at once Utopian and reactionary'.[49] In place of the Palestinocentrism which was characteristic of the ideology of the Gedud, there now appeared an internationalist tendency. On the 1 May 1925 festivities this was given expression in an editorial in *Me-Hayyeinu*: 'We must remember that we are an inseparable part of the world movement of the workers which is fighting for emancipation, that our movement is but one drop in the great revolutionary ocean.'[50] This tendency was even more manifest in a speech by D. Horowitz, the ideologue of the Left in the Gedud. He reviewed the heroic struggle of the workers all over the world, and summed up as follows: 'We must realize that the blood spilt in all the capitals of Europe binds us together ... that we cannot survive as an island on our own, that we are but one point on the great battlefront.'[51] In the whole speech not a word was heard on the subject of Zionism or the Jewish nation and its unique character. The transformation of Palestine into a link at the far end of the chain of progress at once robbed it of its importance. It was surely no coincidence that Elkind said on the same occasion: 'The first question which is presented to us by this day of reckoning is that of our association with and direct participation in the work of the social revolution,'[52] and everything else was secondary to that. It was not that they had rejected Zionism and the building up of the Land, but these ideals were no longer deemed to be their concern. This tendency was also prominent in the courses in social science which were arranged at the beginning of 1926 for members of the Gedud. The subjects of discussion encompassed Marxist theory, political economy, history of the trade union movement, the crisis in the coal industry in England, and the world political situation. Two subjects which may or may not have had a connection with events in Palestine were 'In the Co-operative Movement' and 'The Workers' Movement and the [our?] youth'.[53]

Ideological purism soon led to a hankering for the patterns of organization of Bolshevik parties. This did not progress beyond the theoretical stage, but it was not without significance. The demand for 'an organized central revolutionary force'[54] was accompanied by contempt for democracy, which was now presented as the opposite of the revolutionary way: 'The right to enjoyment and to live life as human beings is one of those primitive and fundamental rights of the proletariat which may be attained by force. What value has a decision of the majority taken under the rule of the oppressive class ...'[55] A demand for selectivity also made its appearance: it was clear that not everyone who had been suitable for membership of the 'old' Gedud would be suitable, from the point of view of his outlook and political maturity, for the avant garde which was to be established. Some would have to go.[56]

These features recurred in more pronounced form in the Mapam of the end of the 1940s and the beginning of the 1950s. Marxism had been an accepted part of education within Ha-Shomer ha-Zair since the founding of Ha-Kibbutz ha-Arzi in 1927. But the syllabus was a varied one. The youthful writings of Marx earned the same attention as later works. Their study was combined with instruction in the teachings of Borochov and chapters in the history of Zionism and the Jewish people. When the leftward shift began, Riftin came forward with a demand to base education in the ideological study groups in the kibbutzim on the *Short Course on the History of the Communist Party*, with the aim of checking 'the Social-Democratic deviation in the study of Marxism' which manifested itself in the fact that the pupils did not get as far as drawing practical conclusions from Marxism. The addition of Leninism and, with it, the Bolshevik system as a vital constituent of the educational programme was to be at the expense of the peculiarly national constituents, which would be limited to 'Hebrew and other important things'.[57] In the council of Ha-Kibbutz ha-Arzi at Ein ha-Mifratz in October 1952, where Riftin and Hazan debated this issue, young kibbutz members came out in unequivocal support of Riftin: 'The arguments in regard to "the specific problems" [i.e. Jewishness] are baseless,' was the view of one of them, and he added: 'and I know of an ideological study group which is being successfully run by an important member of the executive committee on the lines we have been discussing,' the allusion being to the group run by Riftin at Ein Shemer.[58] In young kibbutzim the *Short Course* became the focus of intellectual discussion in the study groups.[59]

A further stage in the process of ideological 'purification' concerned the teaching of Borochov. Borochov had always been considered a bridge between Marxism and Zionism. It is therefore not surprising that one of the ways in which the shift to the left expressed itself was the objection of the Left (especially Riftin and Eliezer Peri) to the teaching of Borochov. The argument went on for about two years, and reached its height when Sneh had already left Mapam. When Meir

Yaari tried to sum up the traumatic experience undergone by his kibbutz, he devoted a considerable amount of space to the theoretical discussion of the synthesis between Zionism and Marxism-Leninism.[60] The discussions of the Eighth Council of Ha-Kibbutz ha-Arzi in Givat Havivah in April 1954 turned on an apparently academic subject: was there a synthesis between Marxism and Zionism in accordance with the theory of Borochov, as Yaari held; or was it the case, as claimed by Riftin and Peri, that Marxism-Leninism was a self-contained doctrine, and the Zionist aspect added by Borochov was no more than a realization of that doctrine in the special circumstances of the Jewish people? It was a repetition in different terms of the discussion on the centrality of the *Short Course* in the educational programme as against the emphasis on national elements. 'Our Leftists are fanatical in their belief that Marxism-Leninism is complete, all-inclusive in both theory and practice, whereas Zionism is "merely" supplementary to it, a quite secondary matter.'[61] The question of the primacy of Zionism recurred, as in the episode of the Gedud: 'Who was the first in the workers' movement to raise objection to Borochov and the synthesis?' asked Yizhak Ronkin at the same council, and gave the answer: 'It was Elkind of Gedud ha-Avodah. He put forward all those arguments about parallelism and so on.'[62]

The demand for a fresh examination of the significance of Socialist Zionism was a natural concomitant of the process of deepening the Marxist ideological base of the movement. In 'Communism and Us', an article which had important repercussions, Riftin declared that the socialist component of 'Socialist Zionism' necessitated 'fighting for the victory of Socialism in practice, in the Land of Israel, the Near East, and throughout the world'.[63] He demanded the strengthening of the internationalism of the movement, on the basis that 'in a small country there is no possibility of fighting an effective battle for Socialism without a powerful bond with the fighters for Socialism in other countries.'[64] In his view, true militant Socialism existed only in the Communist world, which was the headquarters of world Revolution, and therefore a genuinely internationalist policy must involve readiness to accept the discipline of that headquarters: 'Such people [people who truly wish for the revolution] are not afraid even of "the loss of their independence" in relation to the world of the Revolution [for] the question is one of choice between dependence on the capitalistic world (which means slavery) and dependence on the world of progress (which means true independence).'[65] The decisive step would be the conversion of Mapam into a revolutionary party. Reconciliation to the Zionist content of Mapam on the part of the USSR would follow readily in the wake of its Bolshvization. Mapam must become a party which toed the line of Marxism-Leninism in ideology and organization, and this required strict discipline, complete centralization, and a well-organized cadre. This process would, of course, require a weeding out among members of the party: 'The revolutionary party *must* periodically cleanse its ranks, without sparing ordinary members or their leaders, if that is essential in order to carry out the revolutionary task.'[66] Just as in the case of the Gedud, the demand to adopt Bolshevik patterns of organization was accompanied by a demand to give up democracy as the ruling principle of party life. Reading between the lines, one could detect the assumption that such a party must be prepared to go underground, which constituted both a reason and a justification for their release from the rules of the democratic game.[67]

Side by side with their criticism of Borochov, members of the Left showed a tendency to use the terminology of the school of Borochov in those cases in which its intention was to replace clearly nationalistic concepts—such as Zionism—by 'objective' concepts like 'territorial concentration'. Riftin adopted this course, and so, too, did Mordecai Oren, Israel Barzilai and others, especially when appearing at international forums in which representatives of the world of the Revolution took part. Very soon the members of a young kibbutz like Harel were also making use of this concept, this time not for external consumption but in an internal document. Not that they had shaken off Zionism, but the change in terminology was of importance to them in defining the focus of their activity. When they laid it down that, from the workers' point of view, 'the kibbutz is the most highly perfected mode of life which has arisen under the regime of capitalism',[68] they were implying that really this mode of life was limited to the pre-revolutionary period, that it had no specific contribution to make towards changing the face of society, and that in any event it was well understood that it was not 'a pioneering cell of the new society'[69] as they had previously held. Young members accused veterans of seeing the kibbutz as the be-all and end-all, a goal in itself, instead of turning it into a militant cell fighting for the Revolution.[70] Sneh, in his lectures, talked in the same spirit: the importance of communal settlement lay in the fact that the ground used for it was nationalized, and after the Revolution there would be no need for collectivization. At the same time, it was one of the manifestations of social democracy, which prevented the polarization of classes; thus, while the illiterate peasant in China was fighting for the realization of Socialism, 'the farmer of Degania does not participate in the implementation of the socialist regime in his country.'[71]

Thus, in the case of Mapam as in that of the Gedud, the leftward move was accompanied by a decline in the value placed on the commune as a mode of life, and a shifting of the centre of gravity from the commune to what was called 'the class war', i.e. trade union and political activity among urban workers. As a rule, the greater the importance the Left attached to the coming revolution, the less it valued the agricultural settlement in general and the kibbutz in particular.

Both in the case of the Gedud and in that of the Left in Mapam, the attitude of suspected deviationists to the Communist Party and its members served as a touchstone for the sincerity of their professed Zionism.

The attitude of the Palestine labour movement to the Palestine Communist Party—the PCP—from 1924 on was one of total ostracism. The Communists rejected the primacy of Zionism as a solution to the problem of the Jewish people, and were regarded as heretics. Until 1924 the PCP or 'the Workers' Fraction', as the branch of the party attached to the Histadrut was called, was an accepted party in the Histadrut. The Afula incident, in which the PCP published announcements calling on Arab *fellahin* to oppose Jewish settlement, served as grounds for its expulsion (by resolution of the council of the Histadrut in April 1924), accompanied by exclusion from the labour exchange.[72] The ban applied to all aspects of life and society: the *Yishuv* leadership did not protest against the expulsion from Palestine of Communists who were outlawed by the Mandatory authorities—this in spite of the prevailing sentiment that every Jew who set foot upon the shores of the Land had the unassailable right to live there. Inhabitants of co-operative settlements like Kiryat Hayyim prevented communists from settling in them. They were regarded as 'the enemy within'. Only in the 1940s was the ban on them somewhat moderated, not, however, because of any new-found tolerance but because of political considerations on which it would be beyond the scope of this paper to elaborate.

Gedud ha-Avodah accepted in principle the standpoint of the workers' movement in regard to the PCP—excommunication and boycott. It is true that when, in 1924, Ben-Gurion took the course of removing the members of the PCP from the Histadrut by administrative action through the workers' councils, the Gedud abstained on grounds of principle, which were no different from those on which Ha-Poel ha-Zair withheld its support from this arbitrary act. To the end of its existence the Gedud had no direct organizational connection with the PCP. There were attempts to form direct links with 'the world of the Revolution': in 1926, Mendel Elkind and Israel Shohat went to the USSR in the hope of obtaining some sort of pro-Zionist declaration, but without success. As part of the growing internationalist tendency, members of the Left in the Gedud participated in the clubs of the unification movement, a front organization of the Communists, set up at that time all over the world under the slogan of reunification of the workers' movement which had split into the Second and Third Internationals. Concurrently, Elkind and his colleagues accepted the boycott of the Communists as a basic tenet. Thus, the emigration plan of Elkind and his followers to the USSR was settled directly between him and the Soviet authorities; the members of the PCP did no more than help with the technical details of the journey, and the two sides remained estranged from one another to the last.

The problem in the Gedud was not their relations with the PCP as a party but with those members of the Gedud who were Communists. Ever since the Gedud was formed, it had had members with Communist views, but these views had not been regarded as necessarily at variance with Zionist activity. However, with the growing polarization between Left and Right in the Gedud and, in parallel with this, the exclusion of the Communists from the workers' movement from 1924 onwards, things changed. The question whether the members of the 'Fraction' (i.e. the Communist trade union branch) should retain membership of the Gedud became a central bone of contention between the Left and the Right. In September 1924 the council of the Gedud passed a resolution in favour of holding a referendum on whether the Communists should remain members of the Gedud or not. The referendum was never completed. Attempts by the Right and the Centre in the Gedud to secure the expulsion of notable members of the 'Fraction' like Lukacher, who was even accused of besmirching Zionism and being guilty of acts of provocation, were frustrated by the Left. It was only on the eve of the split in the Gedud (November 1926) that a decision was taken to carry out a referendum of members on the question of the continued membership of the 'Fraction' in the Gedud. Even at this late stage the forces were almost evenly balanced, 238 voting for expulsion and 209 against.[73]

The failure to expel the members of the 'Fraction' from the Gedud aroused great wrath in the ranks of the 'Right' and 'Centre' and undermined the credibility of the party's leaders, who were mostly associated with the Left. The close relations between the Zionist and the non-Zionist Left blurred the borderline between the two and accentuated the feeling of the Right that the Left was drifting towards an anti-Zionist deviation. The demarcation between Zionist and non-Zionist Leftism became a cardinal question for those who were not of the Left. On the other hand, in the eyes of those actually involved in the shift leftward, the problem was seen as part of the power struggle between Left and Right for control of the Gedud. The removal of members of the 'Fraction' from the Gedud would have undermined its control by the Left and transferred power to the Right in alliance with the Centre. This change would not have been merely organizational but also significant in deciding the direction to be followed in the ideological development of the Gedud: whether it was to be an active avant garde with political potentialities as demanded by the Left, or only a prototype of the society of the future, with no greater ambitions, as demanded by the Right. For this reason, what was seen by the Right as a test of Zionist credibility was perceived by the Left as a sophisticated attempt to alter a political line.

Since the decisive element in the life of a kibbutz is usually its internal social dynamic, the question of mutual credibility quickly developed into one of the very ability of the Left and Right to continue to live together. The destruction of internal trust led to the destruction of the Gedud.

The process by which the problem of what attitude to adopt to the Communists in the Gedud was transformed from a question of the Zionist credibility of the Left into a central element in the struggle for control between Left and Right, and thence into a factor which destroyed the fabric of life in the Gedud. The process did not entail the adoption of the Communist outlook by the Left, but it was undoubtedly instrumental in the isolation of the Left and in its members being identified with the Communists.

The question of Mapam's attitude to the Communist Party, far from demonstrating the similarity between the two leftward shifts, throws into relief the difference between them. In principle and in practice the attitude of Mapam to Maki, the Communist Party of Israel, was *a priori* a negative one. In this it was a faithful heir of Ha-Shomer ha-Zair and Ha-Kibbutz ha-Meuhad, which had both, during the period of the *Yishuv* (the Mandate period), taken part in the general ban against the Communists. After all, Mapam hoped that when the longed-for day arrived on which the 'tragic misunderstanding' between the world of the Revolution and Zionism would disappear, the USSR would transfer its recognition from Maki to Mapam as the country's legitimate Communist Party. Mapam therefore sought direct channels of communication with the USSR (in continuation of the contacts which had been fostered during the Second World War). Even in the heady days which followed the establishment of the State of Israel, when Maki accepted the verdict of Moscow and made its peace with the state, the attitude to Maki continued to be suspicious and hostile. In 1949, in Kibbutz Zikim (Ha-Shomer ha-Zair), a group undergoing training, called Zikey Peladah, were found to have fallen under the influence of Communism and were forced to leave the kibbutz.[74] Fear of Communist agitation in the agricultural settlements of Ha-Shomer ha-Zair was very real, as a consequence of the so-called 'rectification of the line' leftist trend at the beginning of the 1930s in all the kibbutzim of Ha-Shomer ha-Zair, a trend which had lost the movement valuable reserves of manpower.

At the same time, in parallel with the adoption of the policy of 'opposition on principle' and the rejection of co-operation with Mapai, voices began to be heard favouring co-operation with Maki. In spite of all their reservations, it remained true that Maki was the representative of the Cominform in Israel, and the Soviets, even when they showed friendship and sympathy towards Mapam, did not distance themselves from Maki; on the contrary, they declared their support for it.[75] The question of co-operation with Maki became a focus of controversy in Mapam, and in Ha-Shomer ha-Zair too, from the end of 1951. As early as 30 April 1950, Riftin, in his article 'Communism and Us', had urged in dialectical terms that no progressive action should be rejected because Maki supported it. In other words, they should automatically co-operate with Maki in matters on which their points of view were similar. He also declared that Mapam would oppose any McCarthy-style persecution of Maki. These two points represented a departure from what had up to then been the accepted attitude in Mapam. However, the subject did not immediately give rise to any real discussion. The turning-point came when the 'Front for the Unification of the Party' was set up at the beginning of 1951. This event marked the growing leftward shift: Riftin had demanded the abolition of the divisions within Mapam in preparation for the creation of a Leninist party, and that was the declared aim of the Unification Front. Very soon a left wing was formed within the Front, headed by Sneh and Riftin (we shall refer to this below). The emergence of the Front was not attended by any immediate acceleration of co-operation with Maki. The agenda for the Haifa conference and the actual resolutions of the conference made co-operation with that party conditional on the cessation of its anti-Zionist activity, the alteration of its outlook on the Jewish national question and its recognition of the principle of the territorial concentration of the Jewish nation in Israel, and also on its abandoning clandestine activity inside Mapam and its organizations. Until these conditions were fulfilled, they ruled, co-operation would be restricted to general and international organizational frameworks, such as the peace movement, the League for Friendship with the Soviet Union, and 'the world democratic organizations', i.e. front organizations established on the initiative of the Soviets, in which Communist parties took part together with non-Communist parties. Mapam also dissociated itself from 'the anti-Communist campaign', that is to say, from McCarthyism in its various forms. But at the same time it warned Maki against subversive agitation inside Mapam.[76]

However, a short time after the conference a new note began to make itself heard within the Unification Front. The idea of a joint front with Maki on the various subjects on which the two parties were in confrontation with the Ben-Gurion government began to crop up with increasing frequency. The Front became a framework for a growing radicalization, through the cross-fertilization between Sneh and the Left in Ha-Kibbutz ha-Arzi under Riftin, to the point where it was hard to determine by whom any particular idea had first been put forward. We do not have the minutes of the discussions of the Unification Front and, indeed, it is doubtful if any minutes were taken. At any rate we have the testimony of Riftin that Sneh, at meetings of the executive of the Front, more than once put forward a proposal for a broad popular front together with Maki, and although his proposal was not accepted, neither did his colleagues reproach him for making it.[77] The new attitude fitted with the decision in autumn 1951 not to enter the government. The debate now turned on the question, with whom to co-operate—Mapai or Maki. The formula 'Mapai were, are and will be traitors' served as a basis for a new definition which classed Mapai as 'the enemy' whereas Maki was mildly termed an 'opponent'. 'As regards Maki,' declared Aharon Cohen, 'we have no quarrel with them over the path they are pursuing, only over the tactics ... we are in the same world as they are, whereas in the case of Mapai we are in two different worlds.' And he added, in support of Maki, 'We must co-operate more with them while continuing an ideological struggle against them.'[78] Riftin interpreted the Haifa Conference resolutions as saying that Mapai was turning its back on its labour base, while the criticism of Maki contained in those resolutions was, in his view, less fundamental. He repeatedly argued that opposition to Maki should be restricted to the sphere of Zionism and to that alone. In other words, in all matters not connected with Zionism it was both permissible and desirable to co-operate.[79] Among such matters were the fight against the agreement on German reparations and against alliances with the West, the trade union struggle, etc. The executive committee of Ha-Kibbutz ha-Arzi–ha-Shomer ha-Zair was divided, but the Left was strong enough to prevent an outright decision against co-operation with Maki.[80]

The Left tried to pass resolutions extending the scope of co-operation with Maki in the senior institutions of Mapam. The discussions of the central and political committee of Mapam in 1952 reveal constant tension on this topic between the Le-Ahdut ha-Avodah division and the Left in the Unification Front. Meir Yaari's partners in

Le-Ahdut ha-Avodah were much relieved when he announced that he rejected the extension of co-operation with Maki and set a limit to it.[81]

The clearest open demonstration of support for the joint front with Maki came from Sneh when he established the Left division in Mapam in January 1953, following the decision of the centre of the party in regard to the Prague trial. The platform of the Left division called for the establishment of a broad popular front with Maki which would operate not only in regard to the League for Soviet Friendship, the peace movement and 'the world democratic organizations', but also in regard to 'all those national and class matters on which this co-operation is essential'—meaning the fight against the Ben-Gurion government and its policy.[82] The disbandment of the 'Unification Front' division in the wake of the Prague episode did not put an end to these tendencies. For a long time after Sneh had left Mapam, Riftin continued to contest the boycott of Maki by Yaari and his colleagues. 'It is not easy to explain to the Communist world why we cannot establish a united front with Maki,' he argued, 'and therefore we must strive at least to broaden the framework of co-operation with that party.'[83]

The effort to fit into the world of the Revolution, of which Mapam had been declared by the Haifa Conference to be an inseparable part,[84] was bound up in the Left with a strategy of reducing to the minimum the differences between the Soviet Union and the Zionist Left. This was, in effect, restricted to the subject of Zionism and the Jewish people—and on that subject there was a tendency on the part of Riftin and his colleagues of the Left to gloss over the difference of opinion. The rapprochement with Maki developed out of the same tendency to give prominence to the points which Mapam and the world of the Revolution had in common and to blur the points of contrast. Nothing like this had occurred in Gedud ha-Avodah. It throws into relief one of the essential differences between the leftward shift in the Gedud and that in Mapam: in the Gedud the shift was a result of processes internal to the group, which were influenced by its social and economic situation; the Gedud did not seek to achieve any concrete political aims but was merely an expression of deeply-felt yearnings and ideological development. The tactical pros and cons of co-operation with the PCP did not enter at all into the considerations of the Left in the Gedud. By contrast, the Left in Mapam were led by strong political instincts and characterized by an acute sense of immediacy. Because they felt the need to reach an understanding—and at once—with the Soviet Union, they did apply tactical and political considerations. The practicality of co-operation with Maki was therefore a key question for them, just as, on the other hand, they were considering the possibility of breaking away from the Zionist leadership.

By contrast, there was an affinity between the dynamic of the development of the Gedud, which came about as a consequence of the episode of the Communists, and the dynamic of the development of Mapam, which resulted from what, in the course of time, would come to be called 'the Sneh group'. As will be recalled, the problem of the relations between the Left and the Communists in the Gedud was the factor which destroyed mutual trust and which rent the fabric of social life within the Gedud. A somewhat similar process occurred in Mapam as a whole, and in Ha-Kibbutz ha-Arzi–ha-Shomer ha-Zair in particular.

When the Unification Front was established at the beginning of 1951, it seemed that in this way Ha-Kibbutz ha-Arzi could gain control over Mapam and get rid of the right of veto which the Le-Ahdut ha-Avodah division had been granted on the establishment of Mapam. Meir Yaari and Yaakov Hazan, the 'historic leadership' of Ha-Shomer ha-Zair, associated themselves unreservedly with the move to create the Front. But it was not long before they realized the dangers involved: a powerful political alliance was formed inside the Unification Front between the Left in Ha-Kibbutz ha-Arzi (led by Yaakov Riftin, Eliezer Peri, Aharon Cohen, Avraham Lipsker, Feiga Ilanit, Sheike Weinberg, Heikah Grossman, Simha Flapan, Yehuda Kaspi and others) and the seceders from the Le-Ahdut ha-Avodah division, headed by Moshe Sneh. The views of Hazan had always been to the right of those of Yaari, and it was accepted in Ha-Shomer ha-Zair that consensus meant being no further left than Yaari and no further right than Hazan. Even though Yaari was not far removed from the Left in admiration of the Soviet Union, his assessment of the immediate prospects for 'breaking down the barrier' was different. The outbreak of a new world war, which was seen by the members of the Left as 'inevitable', was regarded by him as 'possible'. He was extremely wary of anything that might disturb the 'doctrine of stages', and even though he co-operated with the Left, he lent an attentive ear to other voices in his camp. His heart would appear to have been with the Left, but his intellect and his balanced judgement as leader of a movement obliged him to adopt a different line. Within the Unification Front a coalition of the Left was formed under the leadership of Riftin and Sneh. Yaari and Hazan found themselves overruled on topics of fundamental importance such as the decision not to join the government (1951). The Left continued to grow in strength. Its influence in the 'young section' of Mapam was predominant. The Tel Aviv branch, under Yehuda Kaspi, was controlled by the Left. A number of young kibbutzim showed signs of Moshe Sneh's influence; Sneh, sparing no effort, gave many lectures in the kibbutzim and was very much in demand among them. Very soon the 'historic leadership' of Ha-Kibbutz ha-Arzi felt that control of their own home ground was slipping from their grasp.

In order to prevent any further occurrence in which they would find themselves in a minority in the executive of the Unification Front, they sought to restore to the executive committee of Ha-Kibbutz ha-Arzi the authority for collective decisions on political matters which had been transferred from it to the executive of the Front when the Front was established. In discussions on this subject it became evident that, in fact, three factions had developed in Ha-Kibbutz ha-Arzi: the Left, the Right and the so-called Centrists—Yaari and Hazan.[85] Whereas the older kibbutzim (such as Mishmar ha-Emek) were in a ferment of opposition to the leftward shift, the strength of the Left in the executive committee of Ha-Kibbutz ha-Arzi was enough, at that stage, to prevent the acceptance of the proposals put forward by Yaari and Hazan. Those proposals were summed up in the demand that in cases where the historical leadership found it necessary to appeal to the executive committee of Ha-Kibbutz ha-Arzi against a decision adopted by the 'Front', the decisions of the executive committee should bind its members. The proposals were hedged about with conditions and restrictions, and even then the disputants were unable to arrive at an agreed proposal in accordance with the traditional practice of Ha-Shomer ha-Zair in the past. The Left threw down a challenge to the 'historic leadership', contested its entitlement to lead, categorized it as out of date and misreading the spirit of the age.[86] 'The present hour requires boldness on the part of the leadership,' declared Eliezer Peri. 'And the leadership has no boldness of decision.'[87] This sense of confidence and the momentum of victory characterized the performance of the leaders of the Left in the debate: again and again Riftin repeated 'There is no harm in Meir being in the minority for once.' He described the debate on the restoration of primacy from the Unification Front to Ha-Kibbutz ha-Arzi as 'a victory of the Right in Mapam', and accused Hazan and Yaari of 'inviting' 'rebellion' in the older kibbutzim against the leftward shift.[88] The line taken by the members of the Left in the debates was aggressive. They were trying to push the movement into splitting up Mapam in the hope that, in the smaller party, the 'selection' prophesied by Riftin in his article would occur, and the Bolshevik party would emerge. For precisely the same reason, Yaari and Hazan fought with all their might against splitting the party, for the prospect of remaining 'in captivity' to the Left was not one they found reassuring. Nor, on the other hand, did they dare bring about a rift in the Unification Front; firstly because the Front gave them hegemony in Mapam, with Sneh and his comrades fulfilling in Mapam a role parallel to that of the Communists in the Gedud; and secondly because of fear of what might happen in Ha-Shomer ha-Zair in the event of a rift. Gradually the danger lying in wait for Ha-Kibbutz ha-Arzi–ha-Shomer ha-Zair was laid bare. It was the time of the split in Ha-Kibbutz ha-Meuhad. The moral drawn from that episode was that a kibbutz movement anxious to avoid schisms must shun ideological divisons which lead to the emergence of factions in its midst. And what had been happening in Ha-Kibbutz ha-Arzi–ha-Shomer ha-Zair from the beginning of 1952 was not essentially different from the emergence of factions. It seemed that part of Ha-Kibbutz ha-Arzi preferred an alliance with external forces—Sneh and his comrades—to internal solidarity. And thus the question of the shift to the left was transformed from a political and ideological question into one of the very existence of Ha-Shomer ha-Zair as a united group. Just as in the Gedud, so, too, in Ha-Shomer ha-Zair, the leftward shift and the controversy which followed it threw into relief the vulnerability of the social system of the kibbutz. Questions which, outside the kibbutz, remained theoretical were translated in that closely-knit society into essential existential ones, and could endanger the fabric of communal life there. In the end, the question whether it was possible to go on living together became crucial. In the Gedud, it led to a split; in Ha-Shomer ha-Zair, to an explosion which brought about the denunciation of the foreign element—Sneh—and his removal from Mapam.

The explosion was centred on the Prague trial, but it should be seen as the culmination of a more protracted process. Events in Prague served only as a mirror in which were reflected all the earlier arguments and tensions. In the first stage of this crisis (November–December 1952) they served as a dividing line between those for whom the trial represented the moment of truth from the Zionist and Jewish points of view and those who saw in it the moment of truth from the point of view of their integration into the world of the Revolution. When it became known that Oren had been imprisoned in Prague and that the indictment in the trials of Slansky and Oren included grave accusations against Zionism and the State of Israel; when, too, news was received of the publication in the Prague newspaper *Rude Pravo* of an article stressing the Jewish origin of the eleven accused, Mapam was shaken to its foundations. Everyone was shocked, but not all in the same way: two different attitudes could be distinguished in the way this historic moment was assessed. One of these saw in the Prague trial a serious change in the relationship of the Communist world to Zionism, the State of Israel and the Jewish people—a change against which a stand must be made; the other regarded the response to the trial as a test of the sincerity of their identification with the world of the Revolution. The argument centred on the question of whether or not to mention, if only in guarded terms, the manifestations of anti-Semitism in the trial and in the press. Certainly the innocence of guilt of Mordecai Oren was another question of great importance. But above all, the case was seen as putting Zionism on trial—calling into question its legitimacy as a liberation movement—and as a gross assault on the Jewish nation and its right of self-determination. As against this, Sneh, Riftin and their colleagues considered that the scope of the dispute between them and the world of the Revolution should not be enlarged at that time beyond the point that had always been a matter of disagreement, namely Zionism. Anti-Semitism, they argued, had always been condemned by the Communists, and therefore to accuse them of it now would constitute both absurdity and error. Any reservation, however cautious, which they expressed in regard to Socialist justice, and especially any allusion to anti-Semitism, would be interpreted as an attack on the world of the Revolution: 'This world of which we are an inseparable part is no kindergarten. It is very demanding,' urged Riftin.[89]

This was the first stage, in which fundamental positions were taken up and camps established. But very soon the organizational-political stratum was also exposed. When controversy broke out over the Prague trial, the executive of the Unification Front was divided on the attitude which Mapam should adopt. Up to that point, Yaari and Hazan had loyally co-operated with Riftin and Sneh, and had not aired their internal disagreements in public.[90] In vain had the members of Le-Ahdut ha-Avodah attacked Sneh and Riftin with the accusation that they were leading the party towards the path of the Cominform. Until Prague the Unification Front had been able to speak with one voice in the political committee of Mapam and had given full backing to Sneh. In the first debate on the Prague question in the executive of the Front, a motion was formulated by Meir Yaari and approved by the executive. It did not mention anti-Semitism, although it did repel the attack on Zionism. Yaari's effort to appease the Left by the terms of his motion was clear. When it was brought before the political committee of Mapam, a motion by Israel Galili—a prominent member of Le-Ahdut ha-Avodah—was presented in opposition to it. Galili's motion not only mentioned, delicately to be sure, the expressions of anti-Semitism in the Prague trial, but also emphasized the participation of Mapam in the Zionist Executive and their solidarity with it, and put forward a demand for immigration from all countries and all regimes—an allusion to the USSR.[91] The demands of Le-Ahdut ha-Avodah, though not explicitly stated to be so, were understood as an ultimatum. Negotiations were begun in the political committee and in the executive of the Unification Front. This took several days, at the end of which Hazan and Yaari ranged themselves behind a compromise between Galili's motion and Yaari's first version, the main point of the compromise being the acceptance of the first two components of Galili's motion and their insertion in Yaari's original motion. The Unification Front split over this compromise. The request by Yaari and Hazan to be allowed to reach a compromise with Le-Ahdut ha-Avodah in order to prevent a split in Mapam was vigorously rejected by the Left, who described the Le-Ahdut ha-Avodah motion as Titoist. The Left's sense of power was still as strong as ever. 'I make bold to say,' retorted Hazan, 'that this motion is nearer to my point of view than is Kuba's [Riftin].'[92] This was the moment of truth: the 'historic leadership' of Ha-Shomer ha-Zair was forced to choose between an alliance with Sneh and his comrades and one with Le-Ahdut ha-Avodah. And they did not hesitate: 'If the choice is between Sneh and Ha-Kibbutz ha-Meuhad, I will choose Ha-Kibbutz ha-Meuhad,' declared Yaari.[93] This decision reflected the growing alarm of the leadership of Ha-Kibbutz ha-Arzi at the erosion of Zionist loyalties in the young kibbutzim, as well as Yaari's disquiet and his lack of confidence in Sneh. 'We must work with people with whom we can reach profound agreement,' said Yaari,[94] expressing, in this way, his doubts as to the depth of his understanding with Sneh. This was also the end of Yaari's attempts to appease the Left in Ha-Shomer ha-Zair; the head-on collision with them became inevitable.

The manner in which Riftin and Peri, Aharon Cohen and other members of the Left in Ha-Kibbutz ha-Arzi rallied to the defence of Sneh and his men against the onslaught of Le-Ahdut ha-Avodah in alliance with the historic leadership of Ha-Shomer ha-Zair is more than a little reminiscent of the manner in which the Left in the Gedud rallied to the defence of the Fraction. Kuba Riftin and his comrades saw Mapam's decision on the Prague trial as the first indication of a drastic change in Mapam's political course in a direction which, for them, was intolerable. To them it represented the choice of a political alliance with the Right in preference to one with the Left, in deviation from the political line which had been agreed as the guideline for Mapam. Aharon Cohen described the change by saying that the party had fallen captive to Le-Ahdut ha-Avodah.[95] Riftin expressed similar ideas: 'There are indications of Centrism in our party,' he complained, these being 'acquiescence in regard to Rightist fractions and making war against the Left.'[96] When Sneh announced the establishment of the Left division in the Unification Front, Hazan prophesied 'It will be a smoke-screen division that will lead to Maki,' and he explained the secession of Sneh from the Unification Front as due to Sneh's wish to separate himself from his comrades in Mapam in anticipation of the verdict in the Prague trial which would convict Oren (and, by implication, Mapam).[97] Riftin and his colleagues, on the other hand, saw Sneh as a victim of the Rightist deviation of the party.[98]

Even six months later, when Sneh's route towards Maki had already been mapped out, Peri and Riftin continued to blame Yaari and Hazan for having made Sneh leave Mapam in the wake of his establishment of the Left division in the party. Peri and Riftin saw this as an arbitrary act.[99] The two continued to defend zealously the standpoint represented by Sneh during his membership of Mapam. The legitimacy of Sneh's views conferred legitimacy on their own views as well. Those views, which virtually achieved canonization at the Haifa Conference (1951), were found in 1953 to be leading to what was described as 'the liquidation of Zionism'. The anti-Sneh move, in fact, represented a revision of the views held by the majority in the party during the previous two years, and the turning of their backs on the lines of policy which had stemmed from those views. The essence of the policy reversal consisted in the abandonment of the belief that there was a real prospect of breaking down the barrier between Zionism and the world of the Revolution, and that it was within the power of Mapam, by forming a revolutionary party, to hasten and assist this process. The rightward shift from this consensus within Mapam turned those who were loyal to the old line into 'deviationists'.

The phenomenon of the 'migration' of the consensus appeared both in the case of the "Gedud" and in the case of Mapam. There could be no absolute answer to the question of what was a legitimate viewpoint, remaining within the bounds of the consensus, and what was a deviation—a view which departed from the accepted political norms. The answer was relative: what had been acceptable yesterday became a deviation today. The efforts of the Gedud towards establishing 'a general commune of the workers of Eretz Israel' had at first been acceptable to broad sections of the Palestine Labour movement, and especially to the first Ahdut ha-Avodah party. Its belief in the 'short-cut' had also been part of the accepted conventions in the circles of the Histadrut at the beginning of the 1920s. The rift between these ideas and what was regarded as normative came about with the collapse of faith in the 'short-cut' during the years of the fourth *Aliyah* and subsequently. Ahdut ha-Avodah drew a political conclusion from that collapse and turned its attention to the 'class war', setting its sights on control of the Zionist Organization as a means of securing the resources needed for the development of the country. That decision plunged it into the midst of Zionist activity. The conclusion drawn by the Left from the ruined hope of the 'short-cut' was that of forswearing Zionist activity. And so, overnight, the Left became deviationists in the eyes of those who, the day before, had been their ideological partners. In this case the consensus moved to the right, while the Gedud turned leftwards. The movements were not very great, but they were enough to remove the Left in the Gedud from the Zionist consensus.

Events in the case of Mapam took a parallel course. The ambition to reach an understanding with the Soviet Union and to gain its support had been an accepted policy of the executive of the Jewish Agency since 22 June 1941. In 1948, when Mapam came into existence, enthusiasm over the support of the Soviet Union for the establishment of the State of Israel was shared by everybody. Neutrality between the power blocs was the official policy of the Israeli government. Thus the viewpoint of Mapam (which was working harder than anyone to achieve the recognition of Zionism by the USSR and showing even greater enthusiasm than others for manifestations of Soviet support) was not outside the Zionist consensus. But from 1949 onwards, with the intensification of the Cold War and the outbreak of the Korean war, Ben-Gurion made it clear that the place of Israel was in the Western camp. The national consensus shifted from a so-called 'neutral' attitude to one of support for the Western bloc. To this, of course, was added the change in the policy of the Soviet Union, which, in the course of 1952, became one of clear hostility to Israel. This took place concurrently with the shift to the left by Mapam. And again, the distance which developed between the two attitudes, which had up to then been so close together, became the source of the rift which ended in 'deviation'.

A similar process occurred inside Mapam itself. For more than two years the Unification Front had been moving to the left. Yaari and Hazan, in spite of all their reservations, co-operated with this process, and gave it their blessing—inside the movement, and even more so outside it. The viewpoints of Sneh and Riftin were accepted as those of the Front, and the reflex action of closing ranks against attacks from without operated to protect them against Le-Ahdut ha-Avodah, and most certainly against Mapai. The Prague trial led to a change in the orientation of Yaari and Hazan: the world of the Revolution had hidden its face from Mapam. And what had been accepted the day before as the standpoint of the movement turned overnight into 'deviation'.

The question of 'deviation' as against 'consensus' is linked with another problem: how did those who were going over to the Left see themselves, and how were they seen by those who stood on the sidelines? Most of the participants in the process, whether in the case of the Gedud or that of Mapam, did not realize that they were being drawn into positions which led logically to non-Zionism. They regarded their Zionism as a basic and obvious fact needing neither proof nor reinforcement. As they understood it, they were being persecuted not for anti-Zionism but 'for the crime of loyalty to the world of Revolution'.[100] Their defence against accusations of anti-Zionist 'deviation' took the form of attacks on the bona fides of their accusers, who from the start, they said, had been out to harm the Gedud, or the Left in Mapam.

Awareness of the leftist nature of the process and the consequences to which it was leading came much earlier to outside observers than it did to those involved in it. The feeling of the leaders of (the first) Ahdut ha-Avodah that a dangerous move towards the left was occurring in the Gedud developed fairly early on. So did the accusations of Mapam by Mapai, and especially by 'Yariv's grandfather'—a pseudonym used by Ben-Gurion in a series of famous polemical articles against Mapam—in regard to the path Mapam was pursuing. To outsiders it is always easier to discern ideological and political identification marks. On the other hand it seems safe to assume that the 'attack from without' contributed not a little to the strengthening of the internal solidarity of the group in following the line for which they had been attacked. In this connection, therefore, we can speak of a prophecy which, in some measure, was self-fulfilling.

One of the by-products of the shift to the left was the emergence of a secret faction within the social group. Such an occurrence scarcely needs explanation: people of similar opinions came together in a more or less solid political alliance, with the aim of propagating their doctrine, gaining more allies and increasing their power and influence. There can be no doubt as to the destructive effect of such a development on the fabric of kibbutz life: in a society intended to be based on mutual trust and complete openness, any alliance between some of the members which excludes others will destroy trust and break the solidarity of the group.

In the summer of 1926 it was discovered that there was a strong secret organization established on a permanent basis inside the Gedud. The leaders of the Left did, indeed, continue to be the leaders of the Gedud, but for the purpose of contact with allies outside (with a view to appearing in a separate list for the elections to the Third Conference of the Histadrut in 1927), they had formed another organization—a faction within the Gedud.[101] The discovery of this secret organization —and in a kibbutz it is hard to hide secret contacts—quickly led to the formation of a parallel organization of the Right. The appearance of organized factions marked the final stage of the break-up of the Gedud as a social body. The factions hastened the destruction of mutual trust, which had already been shaken by the controversy over the continued membership of the Communists in the Gedud, and by the ideological disputes. The social dynamic led inevitably to the splitting up of the Gedud.

In Ha-Shomer ha-Zair the process was similar to begin with, but finished differently. As early as the beginning of 1952, Yaari and Hazan began complaining of the factionalism which was becoming evident in Ha-Kibbutz ha-Arzi and was endangering 'ideological collectivism', that mainstay of the unity and wholeness of Ha-Shomer ha-Zair. At that stage the complaints were based on differences of opinion among the leadership, i.e. between them and Sneh and Riftin and their associates. The Left leaders presented to their young followers the picture of a leadership split into Right, Left and Centre. Yaari and Hazan were not, at that stage, hinting at the existence of a permanent organization of the Left in Ha-Kibbutz ha-Arzi. But the fear that such an organization would make its appearance was already in the air. Even in the first debates following the Prague trial (December 1952) no accusation of factionalism was voiced. True, Hazan was already demanding of Riftin that he subject himself to 'self-criticism', but the Left, too, continued their aggressive stance. Yaari was striving with all his might to secure the passage of the Yaari–Galili motion in the executive committee of Ha-Kibbutz ha-Arzi. Against him, the men of the Left were pressing the splitting-up of Mapam against the background of the trial, and Riftin was accusing the leadership of conducting a campaign of disinformation in the kibbutzim.[102] The struggle between the Left and the 'historic leadership' went indeed in favour of the leadership, but it was a knife-edge decision.[103]

However, in less than a month the situation had changed: a defensive note was heard in the arguments of the members of the Left, and even when an appearance of aggressiveness was maintained (as in the case of Riftin, for example) it was on the basis that attack is the best form of defence. In parallel with this, the charge of having formed a faction was levelled against the Left. In the council of Mapam, on 26 December 1952, there was a dramatic vote on the compromise Yaari–Galili motion in regard to the Prague trial. In that vote, the discipline of the Unification Front was broken (the composition of its executive having been altered in the meantime by the co-option of five adherents to the Yaari–Hazan line).[104] Forty-nine members of the Front, including members of Ha-Shomer ha-Zair, voted against the resolution while another eighteen abstained.[105] The break in internal discipline was interpreted by most members as a concerted action planned by an organized faction. This interpretation was reinforced by reports from kibbutzim of clandestine subversion and incitement against the decision of the council of Mapam, as well as by evidence of stands coordinated between the leaders of the Left in Ha-Kibbutz ha-Arzi—Riftin and Peri—and kibbutz members, and by information that members of the Left had been distributing printed literature in the kibbutzim.[106] In vain did Avraham Lipsker (one of the abstainers in the crucial vote) plead that 'no one in Ha-Kibbutz ha-Arzi has any intention of establishing a faction'.[107] Sanctions followed quickly: Riftin was removed from his post as political secretary of Mapam; Peri gave up his editorial position with *Al ha-Mishmar*; Simha Flapan ceased to be organizing secretary of Ha-Kibbutz ha-Arzi, and Yehuda Kaspi was forced to retire from the office of secretary of the Tel Aviv branch of Mapam.[108]

The demand that people accused of deviation should do public penance was natural in this politico-social system. The part of chief prosecutor was played by Hazan, who declared: 'Justice here is not tempered with mercy.' He demanded of those who had voted against the Yaari-Galili motion, or who had abstained, that they make a public retraction; and he added: 'and here I will make the gravest statement of all. If the comrades do not retract, I shall begin to think that they are acting in accordance with a premeditated plan ... and that would begin a completely new reckoning.'[109]

The leadership were haunted by the fear of a hidden faction operated by its own central control and constituting a source of Leftist indoctrination in the kibbutzim, and especially in the young ones, whose bonds with the movement, their kibbutz and the landscape did not yet constitute a counterweight to the attraction of the world of the Revolution. This anxiety was by no means groundless. It transpired that the Left had a hold in a fairly long list of kibbutzim: Harel, Amir, Safiyah, Gaaton, Dangur, Zikim, and especially Karmiyah, Shoval, Ein Shemer, Mesillot, and Nahshon, in Ha-Kibbutz ha-Arzi; Yiron, Yad Hannah, Mashabei Sadeh, and Kisufim, in Ha-Kibbutz ha-Meuhad. An appreciable proportion of the groups undergoing training which went Left were disciples of Riftin or were subject to the direct influence of Sneh.[110] The nightmarish thought that Sneh would succeed in establishing a base for himself in the kibbutzim and detaching a number of them from their parent movements weighed heavily on the leaders of the kibbutz movement. In one case—Yad Hannah—this fear was actually realized. For this reason the leadership of Ha-Shomer ha-Zair decided to hold a 'referendum' in the kibbutzim which would force the members to sign a declaration binding them to accept the decisions of the party in relation to the Prague trial, to accept the authority of the movement, and, above all, to reject any factional activity, whether within the framework of any individual kibbutz, within Ha-Kibbutz ha-Arzi movement as a whole, or within the Unification Front.[111] A similar referendum was conducted in Ha-Kibbutz ha-Meuhad, too, requiring a declaration of loyalty to the decisions of the council of Shefayim, which, like its parallel in Ha-Shomer ha-Zair, had passed a resolution criticizing the Prague trial (5–7 December 1952).[112] The referendum in Ha-Kibbutz ha-Arzi took place in January–February 1953, and when it was over, Yaari and Hazan were able to breathe more freely: until then they had had no indication of the extent of the 'deviation'. The referendum disclosed that the nucleus of opposition was fairly small and certainly amounted to no more than a trivial percentage of the total membership of the movement.[113]

Nevertheless, there was continued alarm at the clandestine subversion by the 'hidden faction'. Outside, Sneh was conducting propaganda encouraging members of Mapam, and especially kibbutz members, to join him, and news reached the heads of Ha-Kibbutz ha-Arzi that an underground movement of Sneh supporters had been established in the kibbutzim.[114] It was hinted in the newspapers of Sneh's 'Left' division that the 'Riftinists' in Ha-Kibbutz ha-Arzi had decided to remain in the party and to set up an underground movement from within, instead of openly joining Sneh.[115] The appearance of Riftin and Peri at the executive committee meeting of Ha-Kibbutz ha-Arzi—both of them, and particularly Riftin, having refused to accept the verdict of the movement and do penance—led Yaari to pronounce that 'Kuba has become an advocate of Sneh in our midst'.[116] At the same time Sneh's men, the pupils of Riftin, bitterly attacked their former teacher because, as they said, he had chosen to 'enter the Trappist monastery' and silently accept 'the verdict of the movement', and because, although he had not recoiled from the ideology he preached, he had failed to draw from it the necessary organizational conclusions.[117]

The adherents of the Left, of course, vigorously denied the existence of a faction, claiming that they merely took a different ideological standpoint, as they were entitled to do. But the evidence from the scene of the action was against them: 'In visits [to the kibbutzim] I became convinced that there is factional activity, country-wide consultation, transmission of information, instructions, etc.'[118] The appearances of the Leftists at meetings of the executive committee of Ha-Kibbutz ha-Arzi and its councils likewise betrayed hints of preconcerted action: the unanimity of the votes and abstentions by the Leftists was not a matter of coincidence. Abba Kovner challenged Haykah Grossman, who, like her comrades, had remained silent in the face of the accusations that they were responsible for young members going over to the Left: 'There is only one set of circumstances in which anyone could face such charges and not answer. Only if someone else is telling him to act in that way.'[119]

It seems that there were good grounds for the assertion by the Ha-Shomer ha-Zair leadership that there was an organized faction in the kibbutzim. The dynamic of development led in that direction. It was not necessarily a 'Snehist', anti-Zionist underground movement. More likely, it was a grouping of leftists who remained Zionists, inside Ha-Shomer ha-Zair. Presumably, certain links remained between the leaders of this faction and Sneh. That does not mean to say that every youngster who went over to the Left was a member of the faction or was even aware of its existence. Nor was it a question of an 'underground movement' in any subversive sense. But the need to close ranks and organize in face of the dramatic change which had occurred in the situation of the Left—virtually from one day to the next—was self-evident. Since the struggle they were conducting had the dual purpose of capturing, on the one hand, the souls of loyal supporters and, on the other, the positions of power in the movement, it needed a centre to co-ordinate it and guide and direct its course. The leadership of the Left existed, and continued to lead. At the same time, it may be assumed with considerable confidence that Sneh did not cease his attempts to exert influence in the kibbutzim, from which he drew the most in number, and the best in quality, of his recruits.

The remedies which the leadership of Ha-Kibbutz ha-Arzi employed against the danger of clandestine subversion from within—and in this Hazan stood out from the rest—were borrowed from the school of Riftin. Hazan again used the analogy of a revolutionary party: in a Bolshevist party the minority must unhesitatingly accept the judgement of the majority, because it expressed the will of the movement. Talk of 'subjective conscience' was out of place for peole who supported the principle of a revolutionary party: 'in a revolutionary movement the minority deviates and the majority is right.'[120] The notion that people educated in Ha-Shomer ha-Zair 'could not beg for pardon on bended knees [as Peri argued] is romanticism intolerable in a Bolshevist party'.[121] In addition to the removal of the members of the Left from all positions of influence in Ha-Kibbutz ha-Arzi and in the kibbutzim, the first referendum was followed up with a second, this time selective, in those kibbutzim and directed to those people whose attitude in the first referendum had revealed cracks in their loyalty. This time they were required to declare outright their opposition to Sneh and to all factionalism in Ha-Kibbutz ha-Arzi. Anyone who could not meet these demands— whether because of objection in principle to 'inquisitions' or because of identification with the Left—was disqualified from teaching, acting as an instructor, or any other educational activity.[122] Those who refused to repent of their pro-Sneh attitude were forced to leave the kibbutzim. Some 210 members of Ha-Kibbutz ha-Arzi chose to leave rather than do penance.

The situation was now transformed: those who had previously argued in favour of hastening the establishment of a revolutionary party now urged the opinion that Bolshevism had never been accepted in Ha-Shomer ha-Zair, and that a distinction must be drawn between relations within a party—in which 'Bolshevism' was desirable—and relations within a kibbutz—in which it was unacceptable.[123] To this Hazan repeatedly replied that if the minority—i.e. the Left—had been the majority, it would have made the same demand of them.[124]

It was a struggle for control and for the determination of a political course, and it was carried on with a feeling that the future of Ha-Kibbutz ha-Arzi was at stake: 'We are working night and day. It is no exaggeration to say that at no other time in our lives have we worked under such stress,' wrote Hazan.[125]

The methods adopted by Hazan and Yaari were not regarded as objectionable by the leaders of the Left except when they were used against them. The two sides in the contest accepted the fundamental tenets of Bolshevism as axiomatic, and both belonged to the same intellectual world. Nevertheless, as one studies the documents, doubt creeps in from time to time whether those who supported Bolshevist principles had really absorbed them or whether those principles served them rather as slogans indicating loyalty to a particular camp, without drawing any binding conclusions. The feeling that we are concerned here with 'Jewish bandits', i.e. comparatively harmless miscreants, and not with hardened Bolsheviks, never leaves the reader.

The analogy between the episode of the Gedud and that of Sneh and his followers was constantly present to the minds of those involved in this drama. When Yaari settled accounts with Riftin in the council of Ha-Kibbutz ha-Arzi–ha-Shomer ha-Zair (2–5 April 1954), he drew a parallel with events long past.

I remember again and again a man of the Third *Aliyah* in Ha-Shomer ha-Zair, one of the leaders of the Leftists at that time, who went over from us to Gedud ha-Avodah and carried on his well-known activity within that organization. That man was pleasant in manner, like Kuba, and at least as talented. Within the Gedud he set himself at the head of a sort of 'Yad Hannah' on a national scale ... He was a catalyst par excellence. He brought his followers into a state of confusion and some of them left the country, whereas he remained, like the *Sneh* [the burning bush, Ex. 3:2] which was not consumed ... There are people living among us who are continuing the function of that catalyst of Leftist liquidation from the days of the Third *Aliyah*. They, too, are bringing whole generations of innocent followers into confusion, while they themselves remain intact like that *Sneh* which is not consumed.'[126]

There is, indeed, a resemblance between David Horowitz—to whom Yaari was referring—and Kuba Riftin, two partners in the process of the shift to the Left, who did not go the whole way. Horowitz was instrumental in drawing M. Elkind to his 'liquidatory' conclusion. But when Elkind presented him with his plan of emigration to Russia, he vehemently rejected it. Kuba Riftin was no different from Sneh in his opinions, and it may be that on some points he even preceded Sneh in his move to the left. But Sneh's move took him outside the Zionist camp, whereas Riftin stopped on the threshold. Riftin did not retract his opinions even after Sneh's desertion. But he never took the decisive step of leaving the movement and his kibbutz. He halted on the brink.

With all their resemblances, there were several essential differences between the episode of the Gedud and that of Sneh. While it was the leadership of the Gedud which led the move to the left, that was not the case in Ha-Shomer ha-Zair in particular and in Mapam in general. True, Sneh left the party and went his way, but except for him, there was not one top-ranking leader who pursued the leftward move to its conclusion. Apart from Yad Hannah, not one kibbutz chose to leave its movement. The centrifugal processes which had operated in the Gedud did not recur this time. The attraction of the kibbutz home, which had become firmly established since the days of the Gedud, was stronger than the allure of the world of the Revolution. Those who were hit by the leftward shift were principally people who were not yet integrated into kibbutz life—members of young kibbutzim, groups undergoing training (*hakhsharot*), and *hakhsharot* from abroad. The 'Young section' in the towns was also hit. But the hard core of the veteran kibbutzim was very little affected.

We may regard the departure of Sneh and his comrades from the Zionist camp, and their subsequent entry into the anti-Zionist Communist Party of Israel, as a phenomenon essentially parallel to the emigration of Elkind and his comrades to the Soviet Union (bearing in mind that, at the beginning of the 1950, the idea of going to the Soviet Union did not come into consideration for those who had 'gone Left', not only because the USSR was not their country of origin and therefore they saw no reason to 'return' there, but also because the USSR did not encourage such migration and expected its adherents to fight for their beliefs wherever they lived). We can then compare the scale of what took place in the case of the Gedud and in that of Mapam. It appears that the proportion of the total membership of the Gedud who left with Elkind was much higher than the proportion of the membership of Ha-Kibbutz ha-Arzi and Ha-Kibbutz ha-Meuhad who accompanied Sneh. Out of some 400 members of the Gedud, of whom about 200 were members of the Left, about 60 went to the Soviet

Union, i.e. 15 per cent of the total, or about a third of the members of the Left. As against this, only a few hundred members left the kibbutzim of Ha-Shomer ha-Zair and Ha-Kibbutz ha-Meuhad in consequence of the Sneh episode, and, in total, less than 1000 people went with Sneh. The percentage of people in the workers' settlements who were 'swept away' did not exceed low single figures. This fact was undoubtedly connected with the uncompromising stand taken by the leadership of the two kibbutz movements against the shift to the left.

The break-up of Gedud ha-Avodah was part of an acute crisis in Zionism and gave expression to that crisis. The departure of Elkind and his companions to the world of the Revolution took place at a time of deep despair: despair of Zionism, of building up the Land, of building a commune in a non-communist country. Those concerned despaired of realizing the dreams of their youth, and even of the possibility of making their living in Palestine. The Sneh episode, on the other hand, took place in a young state alive with activity. The feeling which characterized the spirit of the time was one of a mighty upswing, of unprecedented achievements and of self-confidence. It was, indeed, the great optimism of the time which underlay the whole shift to the left. The road of Riftin and Sneh to the world of the Revolution was lit by the shining hope of realizing the long-cherished dream of integrating the national ideal, now victorious, with the Communist ideal which, too, had triumphed in the Second World War and was at its peak. To that hope was joined their assessment of the world situation, of the relations between the powers, and of the future of humanity as a whole and the Jewish state in particular. Cold calculation was coupled with overwhelming enthusiasm, and thus was born a movement founded on misunderstanding—misunderstanding of the aims of the USSR in the region in general, and its attitude to Zionism in particular; misunderstanding of the international situation; misunderstanding of the nature of the Soviet regime. At different levels these three misunderstandings were common to the leadership of the Left and the general body of their adherents. Certainly the lower the age of the members and the less their experience of history, the higher the level of misunderstanding, especially as regards the nature of the regime in the Soviet Union. However, the leaders, too, were not far behind their followers in their misreading of the political and ideological map. In contrast to the Gedud members, for whom Russia had a very real existence, for the Sneh group it was first and foremost an abstract ideal that ideology had sketched in their imagination and which bore only a marginal relationship to reality.

The subject of the Gedud did not cease to exercise the Palestine labour movement. In 1940 (22 years after the emigration of the group to Russia) the affair was 'a matter which pains me now no less than it did, which, for me, has never been consigned to the past, the fate not of a handful of people but of us all, a vision which, for me, is still unexplained'.[127] The despair and disillusionment which accompanied their departure, and the personal tragedy of these emigrants from the Land (some lost their lives in the purges of the 1930s, and most of the others in the Holocaust) lent a dimension of deep drama to the disaster which befell the Gedud, and turned it into a subject which continued to pre-occupy the movement. Feelings of guilt were not wanting; nor were accusations, either that the leadership of Ahdut ha-Avodah should never have allowed matters to reach the stage they did in the Gedud; or that the root cause of the failure of the Gedud was the iron-fisted policy adopted towards it by the leadership of the Histadrut, which pushed it into the role of an opposition. Sorrow and pain at the loss of pioneers, as well as the apprehension that the phenomenon might be repeated, were the feelings which predominated in the labour movement in regard to the Gedud.

The case of the Sneh group was different. Here there was no question of a group in despair; the community that they chose to leave was not on the verge of ruin. The ideological and political decisions they took were indeed connected with a change in their mode of life, with economic hardship, and a sense of estrangement from society. But these were conscious decisions, taken of their own free will and from choice, and, after all, they did not pay for them with their lives. For this reason the sense of collective guilt which accompanied the episode of the Gedud was absent in the case of the Sneh group. There was a feeling of anger and a sense of betrayal, there was alarm over the erosion of Zionist faith, but no feelings of guilt or expressions of remorse. In Mapai—and in Mapam too—there was even relief that a borderline had been established. The riddle of Sneh and his political path was a fascinating subject for conversation and debate, and some people expressed regret over the loss of an important leader who had left the beaten track, but that was all. It was felt that Sneh had chosen his course for reasons of his own, and that therefore the Sneh episode said more about the man and his sympathizers than about the Israeli workers' movement.

The disaster of the Gedud was seen as a disaster of the labour movement as a whole, as a proof of the shaky nature of the Zionist-Socialist synthesis, and a warning that it could not be reliably protected from a crisis of faith even by creative pioneering. The Sneh episode, in the final analysis, was perceived as a marginal occurrence in the Israeli labour movement, limited in scope and effects, a passing phase of political intoxication. It was a sort of finale, the last scene in the drama of the unrequited love of the Zionist Left for the Soviet Union and the world of the Revolution. The shift to the left in the Palestine workers' movement was a phenomenon characteristic of a particular period, and disappeared together with it. The utter hostility displayed towards the State of Israel by the USSR from the time of the Prague trial onwards, and the unequivocal identification of the Soviets with the cause of the enemies who were threatening to destroy it, made it more and more difficult for those who believed in 'breaking down the barrier' between Zionism and the world of the Revolution to persevere in their belief. At the same time, the lustre of the 'Redeeming Revolution' was dimmed as the injustices of the Communist regime were revealed. Even loyal adherents were forced to recognize the truth after Khrushchev's speech at the Twentieth Congress of the Communist Party. The special status of the Soviet Union as leader of the world Revolution slowly diminished as it was challenged by national Communist leaders who wished to open up their own route to the fulfilment of Communism. The growth of national Communism led to the decline of internationalism as a powerful intellectual force and as a focus for political organization. 'In every era progressive man has had two homelands: one in which he lives and the other the spiritual homeland of progress. Once this other homeland was Paris, today it is Moscow.'[128] This statement by Yaakov Hazan has ceased to reflect reality. The magnet which for many decades exercised a powerful attraction on those who sought to set the world aright had lost much of its force.

Such general phenomena were accompanied by parallel factors in Israel, which have made the shift to the left, as a politico-social phenomenon, no longer a subject for topical discussion. Enthusiasm for setting the world to rights has largely evaporated in the *Yishuv* in general and the workers' settlements in particular. The revolutionary urge which underlay the attraction to the USSR and the sense of identification with her has slowly petered out. Members of the kibbutzim have turned their faces inwards to their own homes, and the great questions of building a new society and the Elevation of Man which troubled their parents no longer disturb their rest. Ideology, which occupied so central a position in the lives of young Israelis until the middle of the 1950s, has given place to questions of construction, economics, farming and other such matters. The intellectual daring, ever striving to reach out to the horizon, which characterized the previous generation, has been replaced by pragmatism accompanied by conformity. The power of the collective as a factor moulding and guiding the individual has drastically declined, with the opening up of Israeli society to the individualistic cultural influences of the West.

677

Tolerance and apathy, those two Janus-faces of the same phenomenon, have gone hand in hand with that process. Decisions in the realm of ideas, therefore, to the extent that there have been any, have been confined in their scope to the individual, and have carried no wider social or political significance.

It would seem that the disappearance of the 'leftward shift' as a historical phenomenon in Israel reflects the subsidence of the revolutionary wave in the whole world, concurrently with its local ripples. Have men really ceased to believe that it is possible and necessary to change society, or is what we are now witnessing only a temporary phase?

Notes

Abbreviations

Efal	Ha-Kibbutz ha-Meuhda Archives, Efal
GH	Givat Havivah Archives
LA	Makhon Labon, Labour Archives
KA–SZ	Ha-Kibbutz ha-Arzi–ha Shomer ha-Zair

1 See, e.g. B. Katznelson, reply to debate, Fifth Convention of the Histadrut, April 1942, LA.
2 See, e.g., N. Syrkin, 'Ha-Internazional ha-Shelishi ve-ha-Zionut', *Kunteres*, 17 Heshvan 5681 (1920).
3 As regards Ben-Gurion, for example, see Ben-Gurion to Syrkin from London, 2 December 1920, *Iggerot Ben-Gurion* (Tel Aviv, 1972), vol. 2, p. 47; see also Ben-Gurion to the executive committee of the Histadrut from Moscow, 24 September 1923, op. cit.
4 Letter from B. Katznelson to D. Sherira, 13 Heshvan 5701 (1940), LA 104 IV, Katznelson file no. 5.
5 A. Ruppin, *Pirkei Hayyai* (Tel Aviv, 1968), vol. 3, p. 29 .
6 Throughout the present paper the term Ahdut ha-Avodah refers to the party known by that name during the 1920s. The term Le-Ahdut ha-Avodah is short for Ha-Tnuah le-Ahdut ha-Avodah, which seceded from Mapai in 1944 and became one of the constituent elements of Mapam.
7 In the first election to the Knesset, 25 January 1949, Mapai won 46 seats and Mapam 19, out of a total of 120.
8 See A. Shapira, *Mi-Piturei ha-Rama ad Peruk ha-Palmah* (Tel Aviv, 1985).
9 150 against, 33 in favour; Second Council of Mapam, 2 March 1949, Efal, sect. 13, container 3, file 2.
10 Third Council of Mapam, 25–28 November 1949, *ibid.*
11 *ibid.*, 28 November 1949
12 Meeting of the executive committee of Ha-Kibbutz ha-Arzi in Maabarot (undated, apparently November 1949), GH 5.10.5 (15).
13 *ibid.*
14 Yaari, *ibid.*

15 155 voted against joining the government (motion by Yaari and Lievshitz), 17 in favour of continuing negotiations with the object of agreeing terms (motion by Galili), and another 16 in favour of motions by Ziesling and Benny Maharshak which were variations of the preceding motions. Fourth Council of Mapam, Petah Tikvah, 5–6 March 1950, Efal.

16 Executive committee of KA–SZ, 17 September 1949, GH 5.10.5. (15).

17 See debate in the Le-Ahdut ha-Avodah section of Mapam on the eve of the Haifa conference, LA 104 IV, David Lievshitz Archives.

18 Political committee of Mapam, 17 and 19 August 1951, Efal.

19 Platform of the United Workers' Party (Mifleget ha-Poalim ha-Meuhedet = Mapam), Haifa 30 May–6 June 1951; pamphlet published by Merkaz Mapam (Mapam Centre).

20 Meeting of the executive committee of Ha-Kibbutz ha-Arzi, Merhavyah, 23 March 1952, GH 5.10.15 (15). This fact is repeatedly mentioned in the committee's discussions during 1952, and also in the general council of KA–SZ at Givat Havivah, 2–5 April 1954; GH 5.20.7 (2a).

21 Political committe of Mapam, 19 September 1951, Efal.

22 Opening speech by M. Yaari, Silver Jubilee council of KA–SZ, Ein ha-Mifratz, 3 October 1952, GH 5.20.6 (2).

23 See, e.g., M. Elkind, 'Kivunenu ha-Klali', Me-Hayyeinu, 1 Sivan 5685 (1925); Emanual, 'Revizia', ibid.; 'Ehad be-Mai' (from a speech by David Horowitz), ibid.

24 B. Hyman, 'Likrat ha-Moatza', ibid.

25 L. Kantor, ibid., p. 51.

26 Yaari was later to assert that Riftin had begun his efforts to 'hasten the Redemption' immediately after the victory of the Communists in China. Executive committee of KA–SZ, Sarid, 1 January 1953, GH 5.10.5 (15).

27 The vote on the loan took place on 10 January 1951. Proceedings of the Knesset, vol. 8, p. 752.

28 Attested to by B. Eshel.

29 Minutes of debate in the Le-Ahdut ha-Avodah section of Mapam on the eve of the Haifa conference (May 1951); LA 104 IV, David Lievshitz Archives.

30 Attested to by I. Galili.

31 Executive committee of KA–SZ, Shaar ha-Amakim, 17 September 1949; GH 5.10.5 (15).

32 ibid., Givat Havivah, 24 September 1950; GH 5.10.5 (15)

33 ibid.

34 See, e.g., Y. Riftin, 'Anu ve-ha-Komunizm' [Communism and Us], Al ha-Mishmar, 30 April 1950; debates of the executive committee of KA–SZ (note 32 above); also the Yaari–Yizhaki platform for the Haifa conference, 1951 (pamphlet).

35 Indeed, this was one of the points on which the discussion turned at the session of the executive committee of Ha-Kibbutz ha-Arzi at Givat Havivah in September-October 1950; GH 5.10.5 (15).

36 In Hazan's words: 'For a number of comrades—Kuba, Aharontchik—Zionism is turning into a sort of spontaneous force, self-perpetuating and self-fulfilling—while we concern ourselves with the problems of our revolutionary socialist standpoint'; executive committee of KA–SZ (note 32 above).

37 See note 31 above; GH 5.10.5 (13).

38 M. Yaari, commenting on one flight of fancy beyond time and space, Geneva, 13 December 1951; GH 95.2.2 (1b).

39 Executive committee of KA–SZ, Maabarot, 29 March 1952; GH 1.10.5 (15)

40 ibid., Givat Havivah, 22 October 1950; GH 5.10.5 (15)

41 Hazan, addressing himself to these matters at a meeting of the executive committee

of Ha-Kibbutz ha-Arzi in Kfar Menahem, 17 October 1949, said: 'If you decide that Mapai is a typical social-democratic party and we are a typical revolutionary party, far-reaching consequences follow'; GH 5.10.5 (15).

42 Riftin, for example, said: 'There is no one among us who favours leaving the Zionist Organization. But there are comrades who are of the opinion that fundamental changes have occurred in the Zionist Organization which may perhaps necessitate different tactics.' Executive committee of KA–SZ, Merhavyah, 23 March 1952; GH 5.10.5 (15). At the time of the Prague trial, Yaari reported: 'Some kibbutzim are already talking of breaking off Zionist co-operation in consequence of the Prague trial.' Executive committee of KA–SZ, Ein ha-Horesh, 2 December 1952; GH 5.10.5 (15).

43 M. Yaari, *Kibbutz Galuyot be-Aspaklaryah shel Yamenu* (Merhavyah, 1954), p. 80.

44 See the remarks of Bar-Nir, executive committee of KA–SZ, Merhavyah (note 42 above). At the time of the Prague trial, Yona Golan said, after a conversation with Sneh: 'He said, in effect, that the time had come for a pause in Zionist activity (*pausa Zionit*).' Executive committee of KA–SZ (note 26 above).

45 See discussion in Le-Ahdut ha-Avodah section of Mapam on the eve of the Haifa conference (May 1951); LA 104 IV, David Lievshitz Archives. Yaari, too (see note 43 above), reveals that Sneh also expressed his opinion to his comrades in Le-Ahdut ha-Avodah.

46 On this subject, see the meetings of the executive committee of KA–SZ, Givat Havivah, 24 September 1950, Merhavyah, 23–24 March 1952, Maabarot, 28–29 March 1952; GH 5.10.5 (15).

47 *Me-Hayyeinu*, 14 Tishri 5685 (1924)

48 Y. Richter, 'Agadat ha-Komunizm ha-Konstruktivi', *Me-Hayyeinu*, 13 Heshvan 5686 (1925)

49 D. Horovitz, 'Ha-Perud ba-Gedud ve-Emdat ha-Vaad ha-Poel shel ha-Histadrut', *Me-Hayyeinu*, Left, 11 February 1927; see also Emanuel (Bar-Hayyim), 'Aharei Hamesh Shanim', *Me-Hayyeinu*, 20 Elul 5686 (1925).

50 *Me-Hayyeinu*, no. 61, 9 Iyyar 5686 (1925)

51 *ibid.*

52 *ibid.*

53 *ibid.*, 18 Kislev 5686 (1925)

54 D. Horowitz, 'Yesodot Mifalenu', *Me-Hayyeinu*, 20 Elul 5685 (1925)

55 id. (note 23 above)

56 M. Haskel, 'Ha-Tokhen ha-Maamadi shel ha-Gedud', *Me-Hayyeinu*, 10 Nisan 5686 (1926)

57 Y. Riftin, council of KA–SZ (note 22 above)

58 G. Amir, *ibid.*

59 The attitude adopted by Riftin to the whole affair did not go beyond a limited expression of regret: perhaps, he said, he should not have spoken to young comrades as if they were adults. Letter to Peri, 27 July 1953 GH 95.2.1 (4h); see also the pamphlets of 'Harel', *Ba-Mishlat*.

60 Yaari (note 43 above)

61 M. Yaari, Eighth General Council of KA–SZ (note 20 above)

62 *ibid.*

63 Riftin (note 34 above)

64 *ibid.*

65 *ibid.*

66 *ibid.*

67 'Our party, like every revolutionary party, must be capable of acting under all conditions, whether it is permitted to act or forbidden', *ibid.*

68 Statement by the spokesman for Harel, council of KA–SZ (note 22 above).

69 Y. Hazan, *ibid.*

70 G. Amir (Lehavot Havivah), *ibid.*

71 M. Sneh, *Ha-Matsav ha-Medini ba-Misrah ha-Tikhon* (undated, apparently 1950). This material was kindly placed at my disposal by Bracha Eshel, who is editing a volume of Sneh's letters dealing with the period in question.

72 See, e.g., S. Tevet, *Kinat David* (Tel Aviv, 1980), vol. 2, pp. 273–9; see also B. Katznelson to A. Schwadron, 19 January 1934, *Iggerot Bert Katznelson* (Tel Aviv, 1984), vol. 6, p. 215.

73 See A. Shapira, 'Ha-Smol bi-Gedud ha-Avodah ve-ha-PKP', *Ha-Zionut*, vol. 2 (Tel Aviv, 1971), pp. 148–68.

74 '*To be precise*', a statement by the executive committee of KA–SZ, 24 June 1949; GH 5.4 (8).

75 Meir Yaari reported having had a meeting while abroad with a sympathetic Soviet functionary, who said: 'Maki are the legitimate representatives of our policy in your country, although we think the future lies with both you and them.' To members of the executive committee of KA–SZ, Geneva, 13 December 1951; GH 95.2.2 (1B).

76 Resolutions of the conference of Mapam, Haifa 30 May–4 June 1951 (pamphlet, undated)

77 Letter from Riftin and E. Peri to Yaari, 27 July 1953; GH 95.2.1 (4H)

78 Executive committee of KA–SZ, Maabarot, 4 January 1953; GH 5.10.5 (15)

79 *ibid.*, Merhavyah, 23 March 1952; GH 5.10.5 (15)

80 *ibid.* (note 39 above)

81 See meeting of the political committee of Mapam, 17 September 1952, Efal.

82 Manifesto by the Left division in Mapam, 17 January 1953 (pamphlet)

83 See note 77 above.

84 Mapam platform, adopted at the second Haifa conference, 30 May–6 June 1951, Merkaz Mapam publication, p. 12

85 See debates of the executive committee of KA–SZ, Merhavyah (note 79 above), Maabarot, 28 March 1952 (note 39 above); and the council of KA–SZ (note 22 above).

86 See, especially, meeting of the executive committee of KA–SZ (note 39 above).

87 *ibid.* (note 79 above)

88 *ibid.*, 24 March 1952

89 Meeting of the executive committee of KA–SZ, Ein ha-Horesh, 2 December 1952, GH 5.10.5 (15); resolutions of the council of Mapam in regard to the Prague trial, *Ha-Shavua ba-Kibbutz ha-Arzi*, 1 January 1953.

90 Hazan later wrote to Riftin: 'You know that it was only because of the divisional structure of the party that, in our external relations, we defended Sneh. Internally a hard struggle was going on, and you always placed yourself unreservedly at his side. Not once did you deny the conclusive fact that there were, so to speak, two fronts in existence: on one side Yaari–Hazan and, on the other, Sneh–Riftin. Even before the council at Ein ha-Mifraz you found it possible to come to Meir [Yaari] and propose setting up a leadership of the movement composed of Meir, Hazan, Sneh and Riftin. In other words, parity between two different tendencies' (16 April 1953); GH 95.2.1 (4g).

91 Minutes of meetings of the political committee of Mapam, 23 and 30 November, 2 and 3 December 1952 (the minutes between that date and 11 February 1953 are missing), Efal.

92 Meeting of the executive committee of KA–SZ (note 89 above)

93 *ibid.*

94 *ibid.*

95 Executive committee of KA–SZ (note 78 above)
96 *ibid.* (closed session, apparently in Mishmar ha-Emek), 15 January 1953; GH 5.10.6 (1)
97 *ibid.*
98 *ibid.*
99 See note 77 above.
100 *La-Smol ba-Kibbutz*, information sheet no. 2, published by the Left division; LA 104 IV, Idelberg Archives, file no. 57.
101 A. Lipa, 'Le-Rokhel ve-Iserzon', Z. Iserzon, 'Teshuvah le-Lipa', *Me-Hayyeinu*, 11 Tishri 5687 (1926); L. Koyfman, 'Likrat Moetset ha-Gedud', *ibid.*, 26 Tishri 5687.
102 Meeting of the executive committee of KA–SZ (note 89 above)
103 At the council in Givat Havivah (note 20 above), Yaari called to mind the fact that the Left were almost in the majority at the time of the Prague trial.
104 Executive committee of KA–SZ (note 26 above), 31 December 1952. See also letter on the subject from members of the Left to Yaari, Tel Aviv, 18 January 1953. GH 95.2.1 (4d)
105 *Al ha-Mishmar*, 26 December 1952
106 Executive committee of KA–SZ (note 26 above), 31 December 1952 and 1 January 1953: statements by Hazan and H. Shur of Shoval; and further testimony of Shur, 30 January 1953, GH 5.10.5 (16).
107 *ibid.*
108 Executive committee of KA–SZ (note 78 above)
109 *ibid.*
110 See letter from Hazan to Riftin (note 90 above).
111 *Ha-Shavua ba-Kibbutz ha-Arzi*, Merhavyah, 8 January 1953; GH 5.10.5 (16)
112 See *El mul ha-Din*, Debates in the Council of Ha-Kibbutz ha-Meuhad following the Prague trial, Shefayim, 5–7 December 1952, published by Ba-Kibbutz.
113 907 members returned a negative answer to the first section of the referendum, whereas in the other sections about 600 answered in the negative or did not answer. Executive committee of Ha-Kibbutz ha-Arzi, Mishmar ha-Emek, 15 February 1953; GH 5.10.6 (1).
114 Two meetings of the executive committee of KA–SZ (see note 113 above).
115 See, e.g., *Ba-Smol ba-Kibbutz*, news-sheet published by the Left division (note 100 above).
116 Executive committee of KA–SZ (note 114 above), 15 March 1953
117 See note 100 above; see also *Skirat ha-Itonut* (Press Survey), published by KA–SZ, Merhavyah, 5 April 1953.
118 Hazan, in the executive committee of KA–SZ (note 116 above).
119 General council of KA–SZ (note 20 above)
120 Hazan, executive committee of KA–SZ (note 78 above)
121 *ibid.*
122 Circular from the executive of the Ha-Shomer ha-Zair (resolutions of the executive committee, note 113 above), private collection.
123 Said by Peri, meeting of the executive committee of KA–SZ, Daliyah, 12–13 December 1953, private collection.
124 Executive committee of KA–SZ, Maabarot (note 78 above), Mishmar ha-Emek (note 113 above) (closed session), Daliyah (note 123 above).
125 Hazan to Riftin (note 90 above)
126 Eighth Council of KA–SZ (note 20 above)
127 See note 4 above.
128 Y. Hazan, council of KA–SZ (note 22 above)

Diplomacy in the Jewish Interest*

David Vital

A JEWISH diplomat—if one has in mind a person or functionary analogous to an English diplomat, a French, or American, or Russian or Japanese diplomat—implies a Jewish diplomacy. That in turn, if one excludes mere intercession by one well-placed element or member of Jewry on behalf of another, less well-placed, implies a Jewish interest: a Jewish *collective* interest; some would say, a Jewish national interest. But combine the terms and speak of Jewish national diplomacy, or diplomacy in the Jewish interest, and two things are immediately clear: that there has been nothing remotely like it since the onset of the Exile until very recent times; and that even today it is by no means clear what it could or should signify, or even whether, in a strict sense, there can be such a function at all. Even in our own times, let alone fifty or a hundred years ago, the question whether there is in any material, which is to say social, economic and political-organizational sense, a Jewish collectivity is open. There may be strong views on the subject. There may be myths. There may be intentions. There may even be dreams. But the reality of Jewish life remains complex and protean. Jewry has no formal boundaries and its informal boundaries are subject to constant movement, change and debate. There is no person, group or institution competent to represent it in its entirety, let alone capable of doing so, because, of course, there is no central authority governing it. But more: there is no agreement about what constitutes the Jewish national interest, or what could constitute it, or how it might be determined, or even what might serve as the major elements and points of reference upon which such a determination would be based. Nor indeed could this exercise be satisfactorily performed and agreement achieved—for who would constitute the forum which would pronounce upon it?—without doing violence to the central facts of Jewish life. And these, today, having regard to the present context are four in number.

---

* An early version of this article was circulated privately under the auspices of the Nahum Goldmann Chair in Diplomacy, Tel-Aviv University, 1983.

Firstly, Jews, however we may wish to define them, live under two sharply divided and distinct regimes: some live under a Jewish government which purports to be pursuing Jewish national purposes; others live under governments which may or may not include individual Jews, but certainly do not, indeed may not, pursue any but the purposes of the nations they rule and claim to represent. Since governments, the Jewish government among them, have powers of compulsion, and since, in addition, the great majority of Jews in Israel bear loyalty to their government, while the great majority of Jews elsewhere bear loyalty to other governments, to compulsion—at least as a potentiality—there is added obligation, to say nothing of sentiment, everywhere.

Secondly, Jews in all parts are profoundly divided among themselves on the matter of Judaism itself, its content, its validity, its interpretation, and its contemporary relevance. The fundamental division is, of course, between believers and freethinkers. The subsidiary, but hardly less important, division is between those for whom the Jewish past is cardinal both for its intrinsic value and as a guide to the contemporary perplexed and those for whom there is much in the past that deserves to be rejected in principle and, so far as it survives in our times, to be shaken off in practice.

Thirdly, the Jews are subject to cultural differences and divisions which go beyond (but may to some extent help explain) the different regimes to which they are subject and their differences on the matter of Judaism itself. Using the term in a very loose, but, I think, useful sense, Jewry is partly European, at least at one or two removes, and partly non-European. 'Europe', for present purposes, may be said to include North America and the Antipodes. Whether it includes America south of the Rio Grande I am not competent to say; but certainly it does not, except to a limited and diminishing degree, include Israel.

Fourthly, the Jews are divided ideologically on the great and immensely difficult issue which in some sense underlies the subject of this essay. I have in mind the conversion of the Jews—the re-conversion, one might say—into a political people. The engine of this process of reconversion has been the Zionist movement; and the process itself has been intensified and accelerated by that much more powerful motor force, the sovereign Israel. More powerful because the circumstances of Israel, its conflict with the Arab states, its further involvement in the East–West conflict, its striking series of military victories and political defeats, its decades-long location at the centre of one of the great international whirlpools of our times into which Jews everywhere have all been sucked, and the fear, the love, the hatred, the admiration and the dislike it evokes variously and sometimes simultaneously—all these have tended to involve the Jews outside Israel, and beyond its formal jurisdiction, in its affairs: in spirit and in fact, for good and for ill. The government of Israel therefore appears to stand to world Jewry in a relationship to which none of the accepted and conventional political categories are applicable, for which there are no true precedents, and which evokes joy, dismay, comfort and dread—again variously and sometimes simultaneously—as the case may be: too weak and indeterminate a relationship for some, too strong and binding a relationship for others.

So it appears. Is it so in fact? Is the so-called 'centrality' of Israel a true fact of Jewish life, as opposed to being a principle which some hold, while others with, if anything, greater vehemence deny? On the face of it, the evidence is abundant. Academic investigators speak of a 'Jewish civil religion', at the very foundation of which lies regard (to use no stronger term) for Israel. Successive crises in the Middle East have irritated and frightened non-Israelis as often as they have heartened them. Still, the passion of the response in either case may be taken as the measure of the degree to which the eyes of world Jewry are now consistently upon Israel, a Mecca to which, if Jews do not all make pilgrimage, they do tend to make a form—admittedly, a very mild form—of obeisance. Reform Judaism, once strident in its objection to Zionism and to the notion of Jewish political autonomy, is now, by and large, sympathetic. A 'task force' organized some years ago by that supremely cautious and respectable institution, the American Jewish Committee, to consider the 'interaction' between Israel and the American Jewish community went so far as to resolve *inter alia* that 'the State of Israel has a crucial role in the future of the Jewish people' and that 'the Israeli and American Jewish communities share an agenda of common concern that requires reciprocal and mutual determination.'[1] It could hardly have gone further without undermining its own moral position and social authority in the United States—or, at all events, without a change of heart so radical as to entail a complete reversal of position and a discrediting of all it had traditionally stood for. Jews who dislike most or all of what the present government of Israel stands for, Jews who were never happy about the establishment of an independent state in the first place, and even Jews who, to this day, are firm in their public protestation of exclusive loyalty to the countries of their domicile—all these and other categories and classes in that amorphous social entity we term world Jewry, all these, with only marginal exceptions, feel bound to declare an attachment of some kind, at least in principle. Qualitatively, the exceptions (chiefly in the ultra-orthodox and the ultra-left or universalist wings of Jewry) are of interest and importance. Statistically, they verge on the insignificant. So far as the majority are concerned, the louder and more public the criticism of the government of Israel and all its works, the warmer, generally speaking, are the terms in which the bond with the people of Israel is evoked.

Why this should be so is an important and interesting question; but it is not one to which I propose to address myself in this article. This is partly because of the complexity of the question, because, plainly, there is no single or simple answer to it, which is to say no answer such as can be discussed in such limited compass as the present one. Partly, it is because I believe it is too early in time, too soon historically, to arrive at a clear view of the matter. Too much, in a word, is still in flux. But chiefly, it is because what should, to my mind, be of immediate and urgent concern is the issue which arises as a consequence of the new post-1948 circumstances. These circumstances are that, on the one hand, Jewry is subject to unprecedented divisions of the kind to which I have already alluded; and, on the other hand, it now has within it, as one of its principal components, a political force and authority which has assumed (or should one say, presumes to) something approaching overall leadership, a leadership to which no other force or body can conceivably, or does in fact, lay claim.

The fundamental issue that arises may, I believe, be defined thus. It has two parts or two faces. It is, in the first place, the question to what extent, and in what sense, policy made by the government of Israel is in fact and in principle policy for Jewry as a whole. In the second place, it is what the further consequences of this new state of affairs might be for the various classes and communities of Jews, in Israel itself and outside it, but chiefly in Israel. I must add the caveat 'chiefly in Israel' because the concerns and outlook of the Jews of the Diaspora cannot be those of the Jews in Israel except indirectly and somewhat unnaturally and by a special effort of empathy. It is with their society and polity here that the Jews of Israel are directly (and properly) concerned; and there is no doubt that it is their very particular circumstances that largely shape their outlook on this as on other matters. Therein lies the problem.

The central fact of Jewish public life today, some forty years after 1948, is that what is done, what is intended, and equally what is said by the relevant authorities in Israel all impinge not only on the lives and fortunes of its citizens, but directly and indirectly, in one degree or another, on the lives and fortunes and expectations of the members of other Jewish communities. Such is the case, by and large, no matter how remote they may be from us in space, in culture, in material circumstances, in concerns, and, indeed, in terms of their own specific interests as they themselves understand them. It follows that the policies—I have external and defence policies in mind in the first place, but also public policy in the sphere of personal status—pursued by a government of Israel, whatever its complexion, tend strongly to be regarded as policies of, at all events for, the Jewish people as a whole; and that there are not unreasonable grounds for so regarding it. It is certainly the case that many in this country and outside it, Jews and non-Jews, friends and enemies, would so argue. The policies of Israel may be policies for all Jewry only very imperfectly—as would accord with the imperfect, ill-defined, uncertain nature of the ties and mutual obligations that obtain between Israel and the Jewish Diaspora. There may be a thousand exceptions to what is, anyway, less a rule than a blanket characterization. But the entanglement of Jewry in all its variety of condition, belief and desire in the affairs of Israel—which is to say, in the Zionist enterprise in its contemporary stage—is now beyond dispute and, probably, beyond unscrambling. And the upshot has been that Jewry has taken on an increasingly national aspect: 'national' in a sense that accords increasingly with what is commonly accepted and expected of nations, which is to say, a political sense. The causes are complex. They derive, in part, from the enormous injury to body and spirit suffered by the Jews in this century. In part, the phenomenon represents the triumph of Zionism: indeed, it was precisely to this that the most acute critics of Zionism had always objected and this was the development they had always feared. When, in October 1917, the President of the Anglo-Jewish Association, C. G. Montefiore, was asked by the British government for his views on the draft of what later became the Balfour Declaration, he replied:

> I deprecate the expression 'a national home'. For it assumes that the Jewish race constitutes a 'nation', or might profitably become a nation, both of which propositions I deny. The phrase 'a national home for the Jewish race' appears to assume and imply that the Jews generally constitute a nationality. Such an implication is extremely prejudicial to Jewish interests, as it is intensely obnoxious to an enormous number of Jews. There can be no objection to Jews who *want* to form themselves into a nationality going to Palestine and forming themselves into a nationality in that country, but it must be effected without any prejudice to the character and position of the Jews as nationals of other countries. [2]

But how does Israel, as a sovereign state among other sovereign states, affect the lives and fortunes of non-Israeli Jews in practice?

Broadly, there are three ways in which Israeli diplomacy—using the term 'diplomacy' in its looser sense: namely the management of a country's foreign relations—impinges on the Jewish Dispersion. The first, most obviously and directly, is as a function of the ever wider sweep of the Arab–Israel conflict: international terrorism and counter-terror, economic sanctions and pressure, and, in a general way, the ever-greater felt need of all those who are nominally on the sidelines to take a public position on the issue—Jews, Christians, Muslims, the political left, the political right, anti-Semites, philo-Semites, intellectuals, men and women in the street; political leaders of nations with a real stake in the outcome, as well as those which are geographically and psychologically remote from the eastern Mediterranean; and of course the men and women of the mass media. Who, today, can stand aside? Who wishes to be silent when he and she can plunge into the fray at little or no cost to themselves, and often to their advantage? Who, preferring to be silent, does not in some measure regret it? The precise degree to which the deeds of Israel, and of those who act in its name, have served to create this atmosphere and continue to affect it is open to question. What cannot be denied is that the floodlights of world opinion are fully upon us and that whatever we do, as opposed, perhaps, to whatever is done to us, is liable to instant broadcast and magnification; and that the effect on Jews outside this country has been severe. It may be that the process by which all Jewry is in one way or another entangled in our affairs is not yet at its height; but it is clearly under way and has been gathering force for some years. Of all this the events of the latter half of 1982 consequent upon the war in Lebanon provide ample demonstration.

The second way in which the diplomacy of Israel impinges heavily on the Jewish world as a whole pertains to the realm of belief, principle, and view of self. This is the realm of the intangible, the realm of dignity, and, if one may use so old-fashioned a term (which many may think ridiculous), honour. By the same token, it is the realm of obligation. There is much to be said about it, far too much for more than a hint of the immensity of the problem to be touched upon here and now. But nor may it be neglected or merely referred to in passing, the more so as there is one great issue, entirely appropriate for mention on the present occasion, which encapsulates, and continues to encapsulate, both the specific question of national dignity and posture and the general topic of national diplomacy. The great issue I have in mind is that of the demand for, and acceptance of, reparations from Germany in the immediate aftermath of the destruction by Germany of European Jewry—the major part of the Jewish Diaspora as it was then constituted.

I do not propose to address myself directly to the question whether it was legitimate to make that demand, still less why those concerned at the time, namely the government of Israel and a group of Jewish leaders representing the principal non-Israeli Jewish institutions, resolved to make it. That is a chapter in the history of the Jews that remains to be properly written, part of the larger, vastly more complex, vastly more painful history of the Jewish people during the Second World War and in its immediate aftermath. When that is done it may be explained to us how it came about that the leaders and institutions concerned to press and negotiate the matter of the reparations were, for all intents and purposes, identical with those functioning *before* the war; how it was, in other words, after all that had happened to the Jews, that there was in Jewry no subsequent change of a *political* order, no great sweeping away of the old guard, no radical re-thinking of the basis of Jewish life in the Diaspora, and that, with one, salient exception it was *continuity* that marked the Jews once more in all their public and collective affairs. Even that great exception, the establishment of Israel, owed more to the internal dynamic of the Anglo-Arab-Jewish conflict in Palestine than to any other set of factors, not excluding the events of 1939–45. At all events, it is instructive and, perhaps, characteristic that the first approach to Allied Powers in the matter of German reparations (in 1945) was made by the Jewish Agency; and that it was followed up, as if in the normal course of events, by the new State of Israel five and a half years later.

The precise wording of Weizmann's note of 1945 to the four Allied Powers is of great interest. For the question that evidently arose in the minds of those who drafted it was that of their own *locus standi* in the matter. It was a major question in its own right; it was the first question they would expect to have put to them by those to whom they were applying. Who were they, these claimants? Whom did they represent? What grounds were there, what grounds could there be, for treating with them in a context which by all accepted criteria pertained exclusively to the familiar *personae* and protagonists of international law, international relations and diplomacy, namely the recognized, sovereign states? The answer given by Weizmann and his colleagues to the anticipated question was clear-cut. On 'the problems of requiring Germany and her satellites in the measure of the practicable, to make good the losses they have inflicted', they stated, 'the Jewish Agency for Palestine, as the representative of the Jewish people, desires to draw attention to that aspect of the problem which affects the Jewish people and in particular to their relation to Palestine.'[3] Thus, explicitly: 'the Jewish Agency, as the representative of the Jewish people'. No formulation could be clearer. And therefore, perhaps, it was doomed from the first to be ignored by the Powers and to be dropped before long both by the Agency and by its successor, the government of Israel. Neither the Jewish Agency, nor the State of Israel, nor any one of the twenty institutions ranging from *Agudat Israel* to the World Jewish Congress and from the American Jewish Committee to the Alliance Israélite Universelle that constituted the Claims Conference, were ever referred to again, even by themselves, as representatives of 'the Jewish people'. Israel's *locus standi* was said to rest on the part it played in the absorption and rehabilitation of the survivors of Germany's war against the Jews;[4] and it was for that very specific reason that Israel was entitled to economic support. It may be added, that the formal resolutions adopted by the Conference on Jewish Material Claims against Germany are notable for beginning with the qualifying statement that 'This Conference was called together for the *sole* purpose of considering Jewish material claims against Germany.'[5] (My emphasis.)

The final agreements signed at Luxemburg say no more and were drafted in the same spirit. This issue of representation was left open, unsettled and unstated. And yet: who would deny that, in some sense, over and above the 'material claims' presented and the material reparations agreed upon, a form of peace was concluded at Luxemburg between Jews and Germans? To be sure, it was no ordinary peace. It had been no ordinary conflict. The protagonists were not symmetrical, either in their conflict or in its resolution. On the German side there was a conventionally and democratically constituted governmental body. On the Jewish side, the people on whose behalf and, it might be argued, in whose name this peace was concluded had not been consulted and could not be consulted; and those who spoke for them were possessed of very unusual, not to say imperfect credentials. It may be argued that there was here an arrogation of authority, the more extraordinary for no such authority being entirely plausible or possible even in theory. Yet the moral consequences for all of Jewry at the time, as well, no doubt, as for later generations, have been, and will remain, profound.

Could things have been otherwise? Surely all action on behalf of Jewry as a whole entails some such arrogation of authority? Are we to deny Weizmann, Ben-Gurion, Sharett and Goldmann what we have retroactively condoned in Herzl? Or would Herzl and his contemporaries have acted differently in this particular case? Clear answers to such questions as these have never been forthcoming. It is not too much to say that they have never been properly and publicly debated.

The third way in which the management of the foreign relations of Israel impinges on the lives and fortunes of Jews who are neither residents nor citizens of the country is in every sense of the term *political*. It has a great deal to do with Israel's slender resources, political and others, and the effort which successive governments have pursued to enlarge and enhance them. At its mildest it is the welcome extended to pro-Israel circles in other countries which offer spontaneous help and encouragement. At its strongest, and at its most controversial, it is the deliberate, if necessarily cautious, recruitment and encouragement of such circles and the attempt to guide them into effective and profitable channels. Such circles, leaders of opinion, churches, societies and so forth, need not be Jewish; and often are not. Insofar as they are not, they differ in no way from such friends and resources as any one nation may seek legitimately to have within the body politic of another. But where they are Jewish, in whole or in part, matters are otherwise; so too when the grounds for support by non-Jews are, at least ostensibly, reducible to likely Jewish sympathy or pressure and a desire to accommodate it. The power and influence of such pro-Israel lobbies vary from place to place and from time to time. The demonic, power-hungry qualities ascribed to them by Arab politicians openly and by a surprisingly large number of western diplomats and journalists more or less privately have no basis in fact. But it would be absurd to say that they are devoid of power and influence altogether. What does seem clear is that such influence as they can bring to bear tends to be effective and, so to speak, measurable only at the margin. That is to say, it is effective, if at all, where the considerations governing the view of the foreign government in question, considerations which derive from other sources, are more or less balanced. Where policy is firmly set, where minds are made up, where the 'national interest' is beyond debate, and where a particular consideration or factor is clearly dominant—there no pro-Israel lobby, no matter how constituted, can ever swing things in a contrary direction. Nor, if the policy happens to be favourable to Israel, will the role of the lobby be found to have been significant, let alone crucial, in its formulation and adoption. The history of Israel's relations with the European powers great and small provides ample illustration of this rule. But so does the history of relations with the United States—from the cruel American decision to impose an arms embargo when Israel, upon its creation, was fighting for its life down to this very day. In other words, the degree of influence a pro-Israel lobby may exert is, before all else, and in the final analysis, a function of the general structure of politics—but foreign politics, rather than domestic—of the country in question. Thus, when all is said and done, even in the United States.

United States policy in the Middle East, as elsewhere, has long been informed by two distinct and contradictory modes of thought—and action. One has its expression in the classic and necessary tendency in diplomacy as such, in all times and places, to deal with problems as and when they arise. This is the tendency to pragmatism coupled with the tendency to concentrate on matters which pertain to the short term. The other mode has its expression in a type of political thought which is in many ways distinctively American, namely to think large rather than small and, above all, in terms of the solution of problems. This follows from the desire (again, distinctively American) to establish a better world order, to seek to ensure that human affairs be based on surer foundations than those that have obtained until now, that men be freed finally from the endemic pain, violence and misery to which they are subject. Thus it was from Woodrow Wilson to Jimmy Carter; but also, at a deeper level, throughout American history.

There is a great deal more to be said about both modes of diplomatic and strategic thinking. The forward-looking one is, to some extent, fuelled by impatience and dissatisfaction with the short-term attitude. There is something in American behaviour in the international political arena which suggests a wish to have done with the messy world to the east, west and south of the United States and, when it has finally been tidied up, return home to peaceful, agreeable middle America, there to deal at long last with the vastly more satisfying, private matters that are central to the deepest of American concerns. And there is in the perfectly genuine American longing to improve the world in its entirety a unique mixture of idealism, moralism, belief in the uses of social engineering, self-confidence, schematic thinking, and crudeness, not to say brutality. It is all this together, of course, that makes American foreign policy, most of the time, qualitatively different from the foreign policy of other great powers: more attractive, less consistent, and, to the professionals of diplomacy, immensely disturbing. It is this, too, which has led to the makers of American foreign policy being, it seems, eternally torn between the dictates of these two distinct tendencies, the two modes of thinking on the matters which confront them, the short-term, pragmatic and the long-term, idealistic. And it has been Israel's extraordinary good fortune to occupy a place at the very point at which these two lines of thought have tended to intersect.

Speaking very generally, what is peculiar to the diplomacy and strategy of the United States at least since the end of the First World War, but much more clearly since the Second, is that in many regions, if not all, its purposes have been two-fold and mutually contradictory. The United States is the status quo power *par excellence*. It wishes to preserve and protect, to hold together, to secure and to stabilize. In this sense, its overall approach is defensive. But equally, it is, by conviction, an anti-status quo power. It wishes to improve and to induce change. It has been very ready to foster some forces, often the weaker, at the expense of others, the stronger, to accelerate some processes (decolonization, for example), to inhibit others, and generally to encourage movement and to choose—and all this in the interests of an improved international order and with large, dramatic goals in mind. It has followed, inevitably, that its approach to Israel has been (and will no doubt long remain) variable and ambivalent. On the one hand, the prospect of an independent Jewish state almost two generations ago was judged an undesirable one at the time, if only because it was bound to upset the then status quo and because, once proclaimed and set up, it would constitute a factor which would plainly inhibit a swift return to the status quo ante. On the other hand, once established, a faltering Israel soon came to be seen as equally undesirable because of the still greater damage that its eventual collapse and failure would assuredly inflict on the new Middle Eastern status quo, however fragile, unstable and uncomfortable it might now be. Israel and the effects of its creation could not be easily undone. A defeated and destroyed Israel would throw the entire region into deeper turmoil still.

But Israel is not only an object of policy; it is a subject as well. How was and is the United States to respond to Israel's own initiatives, to its independently generated policy? Israel has pursued different policies at different times. It has veered from an effort to uphold the Middle Eastern status quo to an equally great effort to overthrow it. But it may be argued, I think, that in the very long term, it has been a prime mover for change within the area and that such change, in important respects, has been useful to the United States. Thus it has done something to confront the United States with the profound dilemma that follows naturally from the contradiction between, on the one hand, America's pragmatic dislike of change and disturbance (doubled and redoubled when the source of the disturbance is Israel) and, on the other hand, the welcome it is inclined to offer, on other grounds, to any serious opportunity to re-shuffle the political cards and deal itself and everyone else new hands.

The United States has not been able to resolve this dilemma; and Israel's diplomats have confronted the Americans (at least in theory; whether they have ever done so in practice and in so many words I have no way of knowing) with an excruciating demand for clarity. What do the Americans wish for ultimately? A strong Israel or a weak one? An active Israel or a passive one?

It is plain that a firm move by the United States towards either target means substantial disturbance to the present, delicate, regional status quo. At the same time abstention from movement and from choice for the sake of total stability, means an end to any conceivable progress towards the solution of the fundamental problems that the region is beset with. The American dilemma can be put in starker terms yet. The problems and ills of the region may really be beyond solution, in which case a truly American-style diplomacy is out of the question anyway. But if so pessimistic an outlook is rejected and solutions are to be advanced and improvements are to be encouraged after all, then, in practice, success is likely to be directly proportionate to the clarity and lack of ambiguity with which policy towards Israel is defined and pursued, namely the degree to which it is either unambiguously destructive of Israel or unambiguously supportive. But this is precisely the decision successive American administrations have found it extremely difficult to make—not so much because of such influence as the pro-Israel lobby has been able to exert, but because of the inherent contradiction between the two approaches which continue to inform thinking in Washington on Middle Eastern, as well as on many other matters. It is not the pro-Israel, or Jewish lobby in Washington that has created this contradiction. It is the contradiction which has made the lobby possible—and, for Israel, necessary. It is for this reason that talk in Washington of 'reappraisal' or 'reassessment' is always worrying in Jerusalem. By the same token, it is the inability of the Americans to resolve their dilemmas that explains why, thus far, no true reappraisal and no entirely clear-cut and firm American policy has ever eventuated.

To what conclusions does this rapid survey of 'Diplomacy in the Jewish Interest' seem to point? I would suggest three.

First, that while the concept of a collective (which is to say, national) Jewish interest is strictly speaking untenable, behaviour indicates that many hold it and some rely upon it in practice.

Second, that in Jewry it is only the Zionist movement, followed by its successor, the State of Israel, which has with ever greater confidence and force asserted—indeed arrogated to itself—the right to define and promote the national Jewish interest. Diplomacy in the Jewish interest such as it is and in practice is therefore exceedingly close to being identical with the diplomacy of Israel. Opposition to this posture by forces outside the Zionist/pro-Israel circle has weakened steadily over the years; other contenders for the capacity to represent the Jewish collective have dropped away. The ability of Israel to fulfil this role may be dubious, but it has no real competitors and few are disposed at present to fight it on this issue.

Third, the structure of international politics, and, notably, the structure of American foreign policy within it, require Israel to make the most of its slender political resources. The encouragement to assume a form of national Jewish leadership and involve non-Israeli Jewish communities in its affairs is overwhelming.

But taken together, there are here the sources of a great, underlying tension in Jewish life. Israel, its needs, its self-view, and the essential logic of its existence are sharply different from the needs, self-view and logic of Jewish life in the Dispersion and, in important respects and in the long run, incompatible with it. This incompatibility (and the tension it produces) follows from the fact that the Jewish community of Israel, as we may call it, is a polity, while Jewish communities elsewhere are not. Political autonomy, sovereignty, statehood, legal and armed authority, in a word: power, have come to only part of Jewry; but that part has been transformed. The questions that now arise are two: whether and, if at all, at what speed and in what way, the political and politicized segment of Jewry will work the transformation—the politicization—of the rest; and what will be the eventual ethos and structure of Diaspora Jewry—indeed, of all Jewry as a whole—if the pull and pressure of Israel upon it are resisted.

Notes

1 *Israel and American Jewish Interaction* (New York, 1978), pp. 10–12
2 Appendix I(8) to Note by the Secretary of the War Cabinet, 17 October 1917, PRO, CAB 21/58
3 Israel, Ministry for Foreign Affairs, *Documents relating to the Agreement between the Government of Israel and the Government of the Federal Republic of Germany* (Jerusalem, 1953), Doc. 1, pp. 10–11
4 Note to the four Occupying Powers, 12 March 1951; *ibid.*, pp. 22–3
5 26 October 1951; *ibid.*, Doc. 15, pp. 46–7

Notes on Contributors

Ran Aaronsohn is a lecturer in Geography at the Hebrew University, Jerusalem. He is the author of a forthcoming publication on the beginning of Jewish colonization in modern Eretz Israel.

Yom Tov Assis is Senior Lecturer in Mediaeval Jewish History at the Hebrew University, Jerusalem. He is the author of *The Jews of Santa Coloma de Queralt*, and of other studies in the history of mediaeval Spanish Jewry.

Yehoshua Ben Arieh is Professor of Geography at the Hebrew University, Jerusalem. He is the author of *The Rediscovery of the Holy Land in the 19th Century*, and *Jerusalem in the 19th Century*, in two volumes.

Risa Domb is Lecturer in Modern Hebrew Literature at Cambridge. She is the author of *The Arab in Hebrew Prose 1911–1948*.

Rachel Elior is a Senior Lecturer in Jewish Thought at the Hebrew University, Jerusalem. She is the author of *The Theory of Divinity of Hasidut Habad*, and many other studies in Jewish mysticism and Hasidism.

Jonathan Frankel is Professor of Russian and Jewish History at the Institute of Contemporary Jewry, the Hebrew University, Jerusalem. He is the author of *Prophecy and Politics: Socialism, Nationalism and the Russian Jews, 1862–1917* and co-editor of the annual *Studies in Contemporary Jewry*.

Lloyd Gartner is Abraham and Edith Spiegel Family Foundation Professor of European Jewish History at Tel-Aviv University. He is the author of many works, including *The Jewish Immigrant in England, 1870–1914*.

Suzanne Kirsch Greenberg is a lecturer and the co-ordinator of the Program in Structured Liberal Education at Stanford University. Her research concentrates on east-European Jewish immigrants in London at the beginning of the twentieth century.

Avraham Grossman is Professor of Jewish History at the Hebrew University, Jerusalem. He is the author of *The Early Sages of Ashkenaz*, *The Early Sages of France* and *The Babylonian Exilarchate in the Gaonic Period*, (in Hebrew).

Eleazar Gutwirth is Lecturer in Hispano–Jewish History and co-ordinator of Mediaeval Studies and of the Jewish History Department at Tel-Aviv

University. He is presently editing a collection of studies on Jews and *judeoconversos* in Christian Spain.

Anita Haimon-Weitzman is Honorary Lecturer in French at University College London. Her research has concentrated on Pierre Leroux and Bernard-Lazare.

Jonathan Israel is Professor of Dutch History and Institutions at University College London. His published works include *The Dutch Republic and the Hispanic World, 1606–1661* and *European Jewry in the Age of Mercantilism 1550–1750*.

David Katz is Associate Professor of History at Tel-Aviv University. He is the author of *Philo-Semitism and the Re-admission of the Jews to England* and *Sabbath and Sectarianism in 17th-Century England*. He is now at work on a history of the Jews of England, 1500–1850.

Raphael Loewe, who succeeded Chimen Abramsky as Goldsmid Professor of Hebrew at University College London, has concerned himself mainly with mediaeval Hebrew poetry and biblical exegesis. He has pubished a Hebrew rendering, in mediaeval style, of Edward Fitzgerald's re-working of *Omar Khayyám (Gilguley merubba'im)* and is the author of a forthcoming book on Solomon Ibn Gabirol.

Naftali Loewenthal is Honorary Research Fellow at the Department of Hebrew and Jewish Studies, University College London. He is active in the Lubavitch movement. He is the author of several articles on the history of Hasidism and mysticism and of a forthcoming book entitled *Communicating the Infinite: The Emergence of the Habad School*.

Moshe Mishkinsky is Emeritus Professor of Jewish History at Tel-Aviv University. He is the former editor of *Gal-Ed: Studies on the History of the Jews in Poland*, the editor of *Makor u-Mekhkar*, and the author of numerous works on the history of the Jewish labour movement.

Arnaldo Momigliano was Professor of Roman History at the University of Turin. From 1951 to 1975 he was Professor of Ancient History at University College London and from 1964 he was also Professor at the Scuola Normale Superiore at Pisa. After his retirement he held Fellowships at All Souls College, Oxford and Peterhouse, Cambridge. He was Distinguished Visiting Professor for life at the University of Chicago. He is the author, among other works, of *The Development of Greek Biography* and *Alien Wisdom: The Limits of Hellenization*. His collected papers are published in eleven volumes of his *Contributi alla storia degli studi classici e del mondo antico*.

Antony Polonsky is Reader in International History at the London School of Economics and Political Science. He is the author of *Politics in Independent*

Poland 1921–39 and *The Great Powers and the Polish Question*. He is co-author of *A History of Modern Poland* and *The Beginnings of Communist Rule in Poland* and editor of *POLIN: A Journal of Polish-Jewish Studies*.

Ada Rapoport-Albert is a lecturer in Jewish History in the department of Hebrew and Jewish Studies, University College London. She is the author of various articles on the history of Hasidism and is presently editing a volume on Jewish historiography for *History and Theory*, and writing a general history of the Hasidic movement as well as a study of Israel Ba'al Shem Tov and early Hasidism.

Jehuda Reinharz is Richard Koret Professor of Modern Jewish History and director of the Tauber Institute for the study of European Jewry at Brandeis University. His two most recent books are *Chaim Weizmann: The Making of a Zionist Leader* and *Hashomer Hazair in Germany, 1928–1939*.

Anita Shapira is Professor of Jewish History at Tel-Aviv University and the author of many works, including a biography of Berl Katznelson and *Futile Struggle: Jewish Labour Controversy*.

Joseph Shatzmiller is a professor in the Department of History, Toronto University. He is the author of *Recherches sur la communauté juive de Manosque au Moyen Age*. He is presently working on a study of Jewish moneylending in mediaeval society.

Chone Shmeruk is Professor of Yiddish Literature and Chairman of the Centre for Research on the History and Culture of Polish Jews at the Hebrew University, Jerusalem. He is the author of many books including *The Esterka Story in Yiddish and Polish Literature*, *Sifrut Yidish: Prakim le-Toldoteya* and *Sifrut Yidish be-Polin*.

Chava Turniansky is Professor of Yiddish and Head of the Department of Yiddish at the Hebrew University, Jerusalem. She is the author of several works including *Sefer Massah U'Merivah by Alexander ben Yizhak Pfaffenhofen, 1627*.

David Vital is Professor of Diplomacy at Tel-Aviv University and Professor of Jewish Civilization at Northwestern University. His publications include studies in international politics and a three-volume political history of the Zionist movement.

Bernard Wasserstein is Professor of History and Chairman of the History Department at Brandeis University. He is the author of *The British in Palestine*, *Britain and the Jews of Europe 1939–1945* and *The Secret Lives of Trebitsch Lincoln*.

Joanna Weinberg is a lecturer in Rabbinics, Leo Baeck College, London and part-time lecturer in Judaism, Department of Cultural and Historical Studies, Goldsmith's College, London University. She is preparing an English translation of the *Me'or 'Enayim* by Azaria de' Rossi which is to be published in the Yale Judaica Series.

Robert Wistrich is Professor of Modern European and Jewish History at the Hebrew University, Jerusalem. He is the author of many books, the most recent of which is *The Jews of Vienna in the Age of Franz Joseph*. He has also edited *The Wiener Library Bulletin*.

Steven Zipperstein is Associate Professor of Modern Jewish History at the University of California. He is the author of *The Jews of Odessa: a Cultural History, 1794–1881*. He is presently writing a biography of Ahad Ha'am and a study of Russian Jewry during the First World War.